Advanced Accounting

Eighth Edition

Joe B. Hoyle
*David Meade White
Distinguished Teaching Fellow*
Robins School of Business
University of Richmond

Thomas F. Schaefer
KPMG Professor of Accounting
Mendoza College of Business
University of Notre Dame

Timothy S. Doupnik
Professor of Accounting
The Darla Moore School of Business
University of South Carolina

 Irwin

Boston   Burr Ridge, IL   Dubuque, IA   Madison, WI   New York   San Francisco   St. Louis
Bangkok   Bogotá   Caracas   Kuala Lumpur   Lisbon   London   Madrid   Mexico City
Milan   Montreal   New Delhi   Santiago   Seoul   Singapore   Sydney   Taipei   Toronto

ADVANCED ACCOUNTING

Published by McGraw-Hill/Irwin, a business unit of The McGraw-Hill Companies, Inc., 1221 Avenue of the Americas, New York, NY, 10020. Copyright © 2007, 2004, 2001, 1998, 1994, 1991, 1987, 1984 by The McGraw-Hill Companies, Inc. All rights reserved. No part of this publication may be reproduced or distributed in any form or by any means, or stored in a database or retrieval system, without the prior written consent of The McGraw-Hill Companies, Inc., including, but not limited to, in any network or other electronic storage or transmission, or broadcast for distance learning.

Some ancillaries, including electronic and print components, may not be available to customers outside the United States.

This book is printed on acid-free paper.

3 4 5 6 7 8 9 0 VNH/VNH 0 9 8 7

ISBN-13:   978-0-07-299188-8
ISBN-10:   0-07-299188-7

Editorial director: *Brent Gordon*
Publisher: *Stewart Mattson*
Executive editor: *Tim Vertovec*
Developmental editor: *Kelly Odom*
Executive marketing manager: *Rhonda Seelinger*
Media producer: *Elizabeth Mavetz*
Project manager: *Gina F. DiMartino*
Senior production supervisor: *Sesha Bolisetty*
Senior designer: *Adam Rooke*
Media project manager: *Matthew Perry*
Senior supplement producer: *Carol Loreth*
Cover design: *Jillian Lindner*
Typeface: *10/12 Times New Roman*
Compositor: *Cenveo*
Printer: *Von Hoffmann Corporation*

Library of Congress Cataloging-in-Publication Data

Hoyle, Joe Ben.
    Advanced accounting / Joe B. Hoyle, Thomas F. Schaefer, Timothy S. Doupnik. — 8th ed.
        p. cm.
    ISBN-13: 978-0-07-299188-8 (alk. paper)
    ISBN-10: 0-07-299188-7 (alk. paper)
    1. Accounting. I. Schaefer, Thomas F. II. Doupnik, Timothy S. III. Title.
HF5635.H863   2007
657'.046—dc22   2005056229

www.mhhe.com

To our families

The real purpose of books is to trap the mind into doing its own thinking.

Christopher Morley

About the Authors

Joe B. Hoyle, *University of Richmond*

Joe B. Hoyle is Associate Professor of Accounting at the Robins School of Business at the University of Richmond, where he teaches Intermediate Accounting I and II and Advanced Accounting. He is currently the David Meade White Distinguished Teaching Fellow. He has been named a Distinguished Educator five times and Professor of the Year on two occasions. He is also author of *Fast Track CPA Examination Review* and coauthor of *The Lakeside Company Case Studies in Auditing.*

Thomas F. Schaefer, *University of Notre Dame*

Thomas F. Schaefer is the KPMG Professor of Accounting at the University of Notre Dame. He has written a number of articles in scholarly journals such as *The Accounting Review, Journal of Accounting Research, Journal of Accounting & Economics, Accounting Horizons,* and others. His primary teaching and research interests are in financial accounting and reporting. Tom is active with the International Association for the Advancement of Collegiate Schools of Business (AACSB) and is a past president of the American Accounting Association's Accounting Program Leadership Group (APLG).

Timothy S. Doupnik, *University of South Carolina*

Timothy S. Doupnik is Professor of Accounting at the University of South Carolina, where his primary teaching and research interest is in international accounting. Tim has published extensively in this area in journals such as the *International Journal of Accounting* and the *Journal of International Business Studies.* He has also written two research monographs on foreign currency translation published by the FASB. Tim is active in the American Accounting Association and completed a term as president of the International Accounting Section in 2000.

Students Solve the Accounting Puzzle

The approach used by Hoyle, Schaefer, and Doupnik allows students to think critically about accounting, just as they will do as they prepare for the CPA exam. Read on to understand how students will succeed as accounting majors and as future CPAs by using *Advanced Accounting, 8e.*

Thinking Critically

With this text, students gain a well-balanced appreciation of the accounting profession. As Hoyle 8e introduces them to the field's many aspects, it often focuses on past and present issues. The text shows the development of financial reporting as a result of a history of considered debate that continues today and into the future.

Readability

The writing style of the seven previous editions has been highly praised. **Students easily comprehend** chapter concepts because of the conversational tone. The authors have made every effort to ensure that the writing style remains engaging, lively, and consistent.

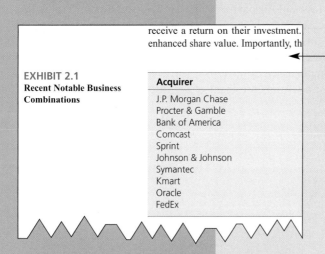

EXHIBIT 2.1
Recent Notable Business Combinations

receive a return on their investment. enhanced share value. Importantly, th

Acquirer
J.P. Morgan Chase
Procter & Gamble
Bank of America
Comcast
Sprint
Johnson & Johnson
Symantec
Kmart
Oracle
FedEx

Real-World Examples

Students better relate what they learn to what they will encounter in the business world after reading these frequent examples. Quotations and articles from *Forbes, The Wall Street Journal, Time,* and *BusinessWeek* are incorporated throughout the text. Data have been pulled from business and government financial statements as well as official pronouncements.

Discussion **Question**

HOW DO WE REPORT THIS?
The Southwestern Corporation oper
hopes of expanding into more profit
a small subsidiary in the nearby cour
some time, the government of tha
equaled $0.20 (or 5 vilseks equaled
new operation; its $90,000 was conv
ern used one-third of this money (15
the possible construction of a plant.

Discussion Questions

This feature **facilitates student understanding** of the underlying accounting principles at work in particular business events. Similar to minicases, these questions help explain the issues at hand in practical terms. Many times, these cases are designed to demonstrate to students why a topic is problematic and worth considering.

CPA Simulations

Hoyle et al.'s new CPA Simulations, powered by Kaplan, are found in Chapters 3, 5, 10, 17, and 18 of the 8th edition. Simulations are set up in the text and completed online at the 8th edition Web site (mhhe.com/hoyle8e). This allows students to practice advanced accounting concepts in a Web-based interface identical to that used in the actual CPA exam. There will be no hesitation or confusion when students sit for the real exam; they will know exactly how to maneuver through the computerized test.

KAPLAN®
CPA Review

Please visit the text Web site mhhe.com/hoyle8e

Situation: Giant Company acquired all of ago for $240,000 more than book value. T inventory (sold within 1 year), and goodw Giant reported sales of $900,000, cost of g No investment income was included in the year, Tiny reported sales of $500,000, c $100,000. Both companies paid dividends rent ratios of above 1 to 1.

Topics to be covered in simulation:

End-of-Chapter Materials

As in previous editions, the homework material remains a strength of the text. The sheer number of questions, problems, and Internet assignments will test and therefore **expand the students' knowledge** of chapter concepts.

Excel Spreadsheet Assignments extend specific problems and are located on the 8th edition Web site at mhhe.com/hoyle8e. An Excel icon appears next to those problems that have corresponding spreadsheet assignments.

"Develop Your Skills" asks questions that address the four skills students will need to master to pass the CPA exam: Research, Analysis, Spreadsheet, and Communication. An icon indicates when these skills are tested.

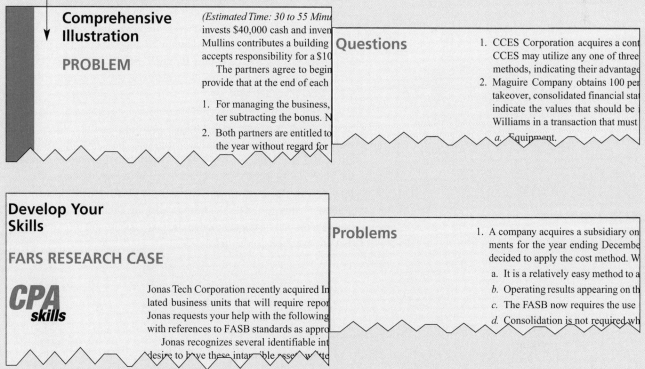

Comprehensive Illustration

PROBLEM

(Estimated Time: 30 to 55 Minu invests $40,000 cash and inven Mullins contributes a building accepts responsibility for a $10 The partners agree to begin provide that at the end of each

1. For managing the business, ter subtracting the bonus. N
2. Both partners are entitled to the year without regard for

Questions

1. CCES Corporation acquires a cont CCES may utilize any one of three methods, indicating their advantage
2. Maguire Company obtains 100 per takeover, consolidated financial stat indicate the values that should be Williams in a transaction that must
   a. Equipment.

Develop Your Skills

FARS RESEARCH CASE

CPA skills

Jonas Tech Corporation recently acquired In lated business units that will require repor Jonas requests your help with the following with references to FASB standards as appro Jonas recognizes several identifiable int desire to have these intangible asse

Problems

1. A company acquires a subsidiary on ments for the year ending Decembe decided to apply the cost method. W
   a. It is a relatively easy method to a
   b. Operating results appearing on th
   c. The FASB now requires the use
   d. Consolidation is not required wh

Supplements

Instructor's Resource CD
ISBN 0072991909
(9780072991901)
includes electronic files
for all of the Instructor
Supplements:

For the Instructor

- **Instructor's Resource and Solutions Manual,** revised by the text authors, includes the solutions to all discussion questions, end-of-chapter questions, and problems. It provides chapter outlines to assist instructors in preparing for class.
- **Test Bank,** revised by Lynn Clements, Florida Southern College, and Tara Shawer, King's College, has been significantly updated in accordance with the new CPA exam and FASB standards. In addition, the number of questions in each chapter has been increased, offering a larger pool of material to choose from when creating a test.
- **EZ Test Computerized Test Bank** can be used to make different versions of the same test, change the answer order, edit and add questions, and conduct online testing. Technical support for this software is available at (800) 331-5094 or visit mhhe.com/eztest.
- **PowerPoint Presentations,** revised by Dan Hubbard, Mary Washington University, deliver a complete set of slides covering many of the key concepts presented in each chapter.
- **Excel Template Problems and Solutions,** revised by Jack Terry of ComSource Associates, Inc., allow students to develop important spreadsheet skills by using Excel templates to solve selected assignments.

For the Student

- **Study Guide/Working Papers** ISBN 0072991917 (9780072991918). Revised by Richard Rand, Tennessee Technological University, this combination of study guide and working papers reinforces the book's key concepts by providing students with chapter outlines, multiple-choice questions, and problems for each chapter in the text. In addition, this paperback contains all forms necessary for completing the end-of-chapter material.
- **Excel Template Problems** (mhhe.com/hoyle8e) are available on the Student Center of the text's Online Learning Center. The software includes innovatively designed templates that may be used with Excel '97 and 2000 to solve many complicated problems found in the book. These problems are identified by a logo in the margin.
- **PowerPoint Presentations** (mhhe.com/hoyle8e) are available on the Student Center of the text's Online Learning Center. These presentations accompany each chapter of the text and contain the same slides that are available to the instructor.

Technology

CPA Simulations

The McGraw-Hill Companies and Kaplan have teamed up to bring students CPA simulations to test their knowledge of the concepts discussed in various chapters, practice critical professional skills necessary for career success, and prepare for the computer-based CPA exam.

Simulations were introduced on the CPA Exam in 2004 when it became a computer-based test (CBT). Kaplan CPA Review provides a broad selection of Web-based simulations that were modeled after the AICPA sim format. Exam candidates need to practice with simulations prior to their exam day to become familiar with the item format, the research database, and the spreadsheet and word processing software used exclusively on the CPA exam (not Excel and Word). Practice with the Kaplan CPA Review simulations will ensure that the candidate is familiar with the functionality of the simulations, including the tabs, icons, screens, and tools used on the exam.

CPA simulations are found in the homework material after the very last cases in Chapters 3, 5, 10, 17, and 18.

Online Learning Center

www.mhhe.com/hoyle8e

For instructors, the book's Web site contains the Instructor's Resource and Solutions Manual, PowerPoint slides, Excel templates and solutions, Interactive Activities, Text and Supplement Updates, and links to professional resources.

The student section of the site features online chapter quizzing activities, including a multiple-choice quiz and a key term flashcard quiz to accompany each chapter of the text. Students are able to download a sample Study Guide chapter in PDF format. PowerPoint presentations and Check Figures are also available to download, and the chapter Excel template exercises also are located here. The authors have listed several CPA-related and other important links relating to text and professional material.

In addition, students and instructors alike will appreciate the OLC's links to many of McGraw-Hill's most popular online technologies, including PageOut and ALEKS.

ALEKS® for Financial Accounting

ALEKS (Assessment and LEarning in Knowledge Spaces) delivers precise, qualitative diagnostic assessments of students' knowledge, guides them in selecting appropriate new study material, and records their progress toward mastery of curricular goals in a robust classroom management system.

ALEKS interacts with the student much as a skilled human tutor would, moving between explanation and practice as needed, correcting and analyzing errors, defining terms, and changing topics on request. By sophisticated modeling of a student's knowledge state for a given subject, ALEKS can focus clearly on what the student is most ready to learn next. When students focus on exactly what they are ready to learn, they build confidence and a learning momentum that fuels success.

Chapter Changes for *Advanced Accounting,* 8th Edition:

Chapter 1

- Additional references to *FIN 46R,* "Consolidation of Variable Interest Entities," have been added.
- Added mention of former equity method investments that are now consolidated in financial statements.

Chapter 2

- Updated real-world examples.
- While maintaining *SFAS 141* coverage, new material has been added on the "Acquisition Method" as proposed in the June 30, 2005, FASB Exposure Draft, *Business Combinations.* The extra coverage includes exposition, examples, and EOC material.

Chapter 3

- Updated real-world examples.
- Added discussion of the new treatment for contingent payments in mergers and acquisitions as proposed by the FASB Exposure Draft, *Business Combinations.*
- New Excel cases and a new goodwill impairment case in EOC material.
- New Kaplan CPA Computerized Simulation.

Chapter 4

- The June 30, 2005, FASB Exposure Drafts, *Business Combinations* and *Consolidated Financial Statements, Including Accounting and Reporting of Noncontrolling Interests in Subsidiaries,* clearly embrace the economic unit concept as applied to the total fair value of an acquired firm at acquisition date. New discussion and examples are provided that address the issues in these new EDs.
- The 8th edition has replaced the "purchased income" treatment for consolidated income statements following mid-year acquisitions. Consistent with current practice and recommendations in *SFAS 141* and the June 30, 2005, Exposure Drafts, the text now shows consolidation of only post-acquisition revenues and expenses.

Chapter 5

- Additional discussion on the treatment of intercompany sales on the noncontrolling interest has been added.
- New Kaplan CPA Computerized Simulation.

Chapter 6

- Updated for the revision of *FIN 46R,* "Consolidation of Variable Interest Entities."
- New Financial Reporting Case in the end-of-chapter material on consolidation of variable interest entities.

Chapter 7

- Updated to reflect proposed effects of June 30, 2005, FASB Exposure Drafts.

Chapter 8

- Replaced old discussion question with new question: How Does a Company Determine if a Foreign Country Is Material?
- Updated annual report excerpts.
- Revised section on Change in Accounting Principle to reflect changes brought about by *SFAS 154,* "Accounting Changes and Error Corrections," issued in May 2005.

Chapter 9

- Added discussion as to why companies might prefer to designate a forward contract used to hedge a foreign currency denominated transaction as a cash flow hedge rather than as a fair value hedge.
- Updated annual report excerpts.

Chapter 10

- Updated anecdotal references to international mergers in introduction to chapter.
- Updated annual report excerpts.
- New Kaplan CPA Computerized Simulation.

as the Accounting Profession Changes

Chapter 11

- Updated excerpts from foreign company annual reports.
- Added two new subsections into the section on the International Accounting Standards Board: "FASB–IASB Convergence" and "Differences between IFRSs and U.S. GAAP."
- Updated discussion of accounting in Germany and Japan.
- Deleted section: "The Handling of Specific Accounting Problems around the World."
- Replaced Comprehensive Illustration at the end of the chapter with a new problem that demonstrates differences between IFRSs and U.S. GAAP in accounting for (a) inventory, (b) fixed assets, (c) research and development costs, and (d) sale-leaseback transactions.
- Added end-of-chapter material to cover the material added to the section on the International Accounting Standards Board.

Chapter 12

- Provided additional explanation of the various SEC divisions, along with updated data concerning SEC operations.
- Identified specific provisions of the Sarbanes-Oxley Act that relate to the creation of the Public Accounting Oversight Board.
- Included additional information concerning EDGAR.

Chapter 13

- Chapter material extensively rewritten for continuity and readability.

Chapter 14

- Updated references from the American Bar Association on the advantages of the partnership form of business and *The Jobs and Growth Tax Relief Reconciliation Act of 2003*.

Chapter 15

- Revised instructions for Analysis Case 1.

Chapter 16

- Chapter material extensively rewritten for continuity and readability.

Chapter 17

- Chapter material extensively rewritten for continuity and readability.
- New Kaplan CPA Computerized Simulation.

Chapter 18

- Chapter material extensively rewritten for continuity and readability.
- New Kaplan CPA Computerized Simulation.

Chapter 19

- Updated changes in federal tax law and tax rates as the changes impact the professional's advice and planning role.
- Provided additional comprehensive problem to reflect change(s) in tax law.

Acknowledgments

We could not produce a textbook of the quality and scope of *Advanced Accounting* without the help of a great number of people. Our sincere thanks to James A. O'Brien, University of Notre Dame, for his contributions to the text and solutions manual. We also extend a special thank you to Lynn Clements of Florida Southern College and Tara Shawer of King's College for revising and adding new material to the Test Bank; Dan Hubbard of Mary Washington University for revising and adding new material to the PowerPoint presentations; Joann Segovia of Minnesota State University–Moorhead for updating and revising the online student quizzes; Jack Terry of ComSource Associates for creating Excel Template Exercises for students to use as they work through select end-of-chapter material; Richard Rand of Tennessee Technological University for revising and adding new material to the Study Guide and Working Papers; Beth Woods of *Accuracy Counts* and Ilene Persoff of Long Island University/CW Post Campus for checking the text and solutions for accuracy; and Lisa Enfinger for checking the test bank and online quizzes for accuracy.

We acknowledge that FASB Exposure Drafts, "Business Combinations—A Replacement of FASB Statement No. 141" and "Consolidated Financial Statements, Including Accounting and Reporting of Noncontrolling Interests in Subsidiaries—A Replacement of ARB No. 51," are copyrighted by the Financial Accounting Standards Board, 401 Merritt 7, P.O. Box 5116, Norwalk, Connecticut 06856-5116, U.S.A. Portions are reprinted with permission. Complete copies of these documents are available from the FASB. GASB Statement No. 34 is copyrighted by the Governmental Accounting Standards Board, 401 Merritt 7, P.O. Box 5116, Norwalk, Connecticut 06856-5116, U.S.A. Portions are reprinted with permission. Complete copies of this document are available from the GASB.

We also want to thank the many people who completed questionnaires and reviewed the manuscript. Our sincerest thanks to them all:

John Bildersee
New York University

Julia Brennan
University of Massachusetts–Boston

Gene Bryson
University of Alabama–Hunstsville

Suzanne M. Busch
California State University–Hayward

Harlow P. Callander
University of St. Thomas

Linda DeBarthe
Graceland University

Kathy Dunning
University of Mobile

Mark Finn
Northwestern University

George Gardner
Bemidji State University

Marianne James
California State University–Los Angeles

Gordon Klein
University of California–Los Angeles

Mark Lawrence
University of North Alabama

David Mautz
North Carolina A&T University

Ilene Persoff
Long Island University/CW Post Campus

Jamie Wang
University of Wisconsin–Parkside

Gloria Worthy
Southwest Tennessee Community College

We also pass along a word of thanks to all the people at McGraw-Hill/Irwin who participated in the creation of this edition. In particular, Gina DiMartino, Project Manager; Sesha Bolisetty, Production Supervisor; Adam Rooke, Designer; Kelly Odom, Developmental Editor; Tim Vertovec, Executive Editor; Elizabeth Mavetz, Media Technology Producer; Daniel Wiencek, Advertising Copywriter; Rhonda Seelinger, Executive Marketing Manager; and Stewart Mattson, Editorial Director, all contributed significantly to the project and we appreciate their efforts.

Brief Contents

About the Authors v

1 The Equity Method of Accounting for Investments 1

2 Consolidation of Financial Information 35

3 Consolidations—Subsequent to the Date of Acquisition 93

4 Consolidated Financial Statements and Outside Ownership 155

5 Consolidated Financial Statements— Intercompany Asset Transactions 211

6 Variable Interest Entities, Intercompany Debt, Consolidated Cash Flows, and Other Issues 258

7 Consolidated Financial Statements— Ownership Patterns and Income Taxes 314

8 Segment and Interim Reporting 364

9 Foreign Currency Transactions and Hedging Foreign Exchange Risk 409

10 Translation of Foreign Currency Financial Statements 469

11 Worldwide Accounting Diversity and International Standards 524

12 Financial Reporting and the Securities and Exchange Commission 566

13 Accounting for Legal Reorganizations and Liquidations 590

14 Partnerships: Formation and Operation 632

15 Partnerships: Termination and Liquidation 670

16 Accounting for State and Local Governments (Part 1) 706

17 Accounting for State and Local Governments (Part 2) 756

18 Accounting and Reporting for Private Not-for-Profit Organizations 814

19 Accounting for Estates and Trusts 853

Index **887**

Contents

About the Authors v

Chapter One
The Equity Method of Accounting for Investments 1

Reporting Investments in Corporate Equity Securities 1
Applying the Equity Method 4
Criteria for Utilizing the Equity Method 4
Accounting for an Investment—The Equity Method 6
Accounting Procedures Used in Applying the Equity Method 8
Reporting a Change to the Equity Method 8
Discussion Question: Does the Equity Method Really Apply Here? 10
Reporting Investee Income from Sources Other Than Continuing Operations 10
Reporting Investee Losses 11
Reporting the Sale of an Equity Investment 12
Excess of Investment Cost over Book Value Acquired 13
The Amortization Process 15
Elimination of Unrealized Gains in Inventory 17
Downstream Sales of Inventory 17
Discussion Question: Is This Really Only Significant Influence? 19
Upstream Sales of Inventory 19
Decision Making and the Equity Method 20
Criticisms of the Equity Method 21
Summary 22

Chapter Two
Consolidation of Financial Information 35

Expansion through Corporate Takeovers 36
Why Do Firms Combine? 36
Procter & Gamble and Gillette 37
Sprint and Nextel 38
Symantec and Veritas 38
The Consolidation Process 39
Business Combinations—Creating a Single Economic Entity 39
Control—An Elusive Quality from ARB 51 to FIN 46R 40
Consolidation of Financial Information 42
Financial Reporting for Business Combinations—SFAS 141 43
The Purchase Method: Change in Ownership 43
Procedures for Consolidating Financial Information 43
SFAS 141*: Purchase Method When Dissolution Takes Place 44*
Related Costs of Business Combinations 48
Purchase Method When Separate Incorporation Is Maintained 49

2005 FASB Proposals on Financial Reporting for Business Combinations 53
The Acquisition Method (Proposed to Replace the Purchase Method) 53
Illustrations of the Acquisition Method 54
Purchase Price Allocations—Additional Issues—SFAS 141 59
Intangibles 59
Purchased In-Process Research and Development 59
The Pooling of Interests Method of Accounting for Business Combinations 62
Continuity of Ownership 62
Pooling of Interests When Dissolution Takes Place 64
Pooling of Interests When Separate Incorporation Is Maintained 66
Pooling of Interests—The Controversy 69
FASB Position 70
Summary 71
Appendix
APB No. 16 **Criteria for a Pooling of Interests 76**

Chapter Three
Consolidations—Subsequent to the Date of Acquisition 93

Consolidation—The Effects Created by the Passage of Time 93
SFAS 142—Goodwill and Intangible Assets 94
Investment Accounting by the Acquiring Company 94
Subsequent Consolidation—Investment Recorded by the Equity Method 96
Acquisition Made during the Current Year 96
Determining Consolidated Totals 98
Consolidation Worksheet 99
Consolidation Subsequent to Year of Acquisition—Equity Method 102
Subsequent Consolidations—Investment Recorded Using Cost or Partial Equity Method 106
Acquisition Made during the Current Year 106
Consolidation Subsequent to Year of Acquisition—Cost and Partial Equity Methods 109
Discussion Question: How Does a Company Really Decide Which Investment Method to Apply? 115
Intangibles Acquired in Business Combinations and Related Amortizations 115
SFAS 142—Goodwill Impairment 116
Testing Goodwill for Impairment 116
Assigning Values to Reporting Units 117

Purchase Price—Contingent Consideration   120
SFAS 141 *Accounting for Contingent Consideration in Business Combinations   120*
Discussion Question: Is This Income?   121
FASB 2005 Exposure Draft Business Combinations—Accounting for Contingent Consideration in Business Combinations   122
Push-Down Accounting   123
External Reporting   123
Internal Reporting   124
Subsequent Consolidations—Pooling of Interests   125
Summary   127

Chapter Four
Consolidated Financial Statements and Outside Ownership   155

Consolidations Involving a Noncontrolling Interest   156
The Economic Unit Concept   157
Discussion Question: How Do We Report This Other Owner?   158
The Proportionate Consolidation Concept   160
The Parent Company Concept   161
Discussion Question: What Decision Should the FASB Make?   163
Valuation Theories—Overview   164
Consolidations Involving a Noncontrolling Interest Subsequent to Acquisition (Parent Company Concept)   166
Effects Created by Alternative Investment Methods   172
Consolidations Involving a Noncontrolling Interest Subsequent to Acquisition (Economic Unit Concept)   173
Step Acquisitions   176
Step Acquisitions—Parent Company Concept   177
Worksheet Consolidation for a Step Acquisition   178
Retrospective Treatment Created by Step Acquisition   179
Step Acquisitions—Economic Unit Concept   180
Revenue and Expense Reporting for Mid-Year Acquisitions   181
Consolidate Only Post-Acquisition Subsidiary Revenue and Expenses   181
Sales of Subsidiary Stock   183
Establishment of Investment Book Value   184
Cost-Flow Assumptions   185
Accounting for Shares That Remain   185
Parent Sales of Subsidiary Stock under the Economic Unit Concept   186
Summary   186

Chapter Five
Consolidated Financial Statements—Intercompany Asset Transactions   211

Intercompany Inventory Transactions   212
The Sales and Purchases Accounts   212
Unrealized Gains—Year of Transfer (Year 1)   213
Discussion Question: Earnings Management   214

Unrealized Gains—Year Following Transfer (Year 2)   215
Unrealized Gains—Effect on Noncontrolling Interest Valuation   217
Intercompany Inventory Transfers Summarized   218
Intercompany Inventory Transfers Illustrated   219
Discussion Question: What Price Should We Charge Ourselves?   225
Effects of Alternative Investment Methods on Consolidation   225
Intercompany Land Transfers   229
Accounting for Land Transactions   229
Eliminating Unrealized Gains—Land Transfers   230
Effect on Noncontrolling Interest Valuation—Land Transfers   231
Intercompany Transfer of Depreciable Assets   231
The Deferral of Unrealized Gains   232
Depreciable Asset Transfers Illustrated   232
Depreciable Intercompany Asset Transfers—Downstream Transfers When the Parent Uses the Equity Method   234
Effect on Noncontrolling Interest Valuation—Depreciable Asset Transfers   235
Summary   235
Appendix
Transfers—Alternative Approaches   240

Chapter Six
Variable Interest Entities, Intercompany Debt, Consolidated Cash Flows, and Other Issues   258

FIN 46R—Consolidation of Variable Interest Entities   258
What Is a VIE?   259
Consolidation of Variable Interest Entities   260
Procedures to Consolidate Variable Interest Entities   264
Other FIN 46R *Disclosure Requirements   266*
Intercompany Debt Transactions   266
Acquisition of Affiliate's Debt from an Outside Party   267
Accounting for Intercompany Debt Transactions—Individual Financial Records   267
Effects on Consolidation Process   269
Assignment of Retirement Gain or Loss   270
Discussion Question: Who Lost This $300,000?   271
Intercompany Debt Transactions—Subsequent to Year of Acquisition   271
Subsidiary Preferred Stock   274
Preferred Stock Viewed as a Debt Instrument   274
Preferred Stock Viewed as an Equity Interest   277
2005 FASB Business Combinations Exposure Draft and Subsidiary Preferred Stock   280
Consolidated Statement of Cash Flows   280
Consolidated Earnings per Share   284
Subsidiary Stock Transactions   287
Changes in Subsidiary Book Value—Stock Transactions   288
Subsidiary Stock Transactions—Illustrated   290
Summary   293

Chapter Seven
Consolidated Financial Statements—Ownership Patterns and Income Taxes   314

Indirect Subsidiary Control   314
  *The Consolidation Process When Indirect Control
  Is Present   315*
  Consolidation Process—Indirect Control   317
Indirect Subsidiary Control—Connecting Affiliation   323
Mutual Ownership   324
  Treasury Stock Approach   325
Discussion Question: Mutual Ownership: What Do Those
Shares Represent?   326
  Conventional Approach   326
  Mutual Ownership Illustrated   327
Income Tax Accounting for a Business Combination   333
  Affiliated Groups   334
  Deferred Income Taxes   334
  Consolidated Tax Returns—Illustration   335
  Assigning Income Tax Expense—Consolidated Return   336
  Filing Separate Tax Returns   337
  *Temporary Differences Generated by Business
  Combinations   341*
  *Business Combinations and Operating Loss
  Carryforwards   342*
Summary   343

Chapter Eight
Segment and Interim Reporting   364

Segment Reporting   365
SFAS 14   365
Usefulness of Segment Information   367
SFAS 131   369
  The Management Approach   369
Determining Reportable Operating Segments   370
  Quantitative Thresholds   370
Testing Procedures—Complete Illustration   371
Other Guidelines   374
Information to Be Disclosed by Operating Segment   375
  Reconciliations to Consolidated Totals   376
Examples of Operating Segment Disclosures   379
Enterprisewide Disclosures   379
  Information about Products and Services   379
  Information about Geographic Areas   379
  Information about Major Customers   381
Discussion Question: How Does a Company Determine if
a Foreign Country Is Material?   383
Interim Reporting   383
  Revenues   384
  Inventory and Cost of Goods Sold   384
  Other Costs and Expenses   385
  Extraordinary Items   386
  Income Taxes   386
  Change in Accounting Principle   387
  Seasonal Items   389

Minimum Disclosures in Interim Reports   389
Segment Information in Interim Reports   390
Summary   391

Chapter Nine
Foreign Currency Transactions and Hedging Foreign Exchange Risk   409

Foreign Exchange Markets   410
  Exchange Rate Mechanisms   410
  Foreign Exchange Rates   410
  Spot and Forward Rates   412
  Option Contracts   412
Foreign Currency Transactions   413
  Accounting Issue   414
  Accounting Alternatives   414
  Balance Sheet Date before Date of Payment   415
Hedging Foreign Exchange Risk   417
Accounting for Derivatives   418
  Fundamental Requirement of Derivatives Accounting   418
  Determining the Fair Value of Derivatives   418
  *Accounting for Changes in the Fair Value of
  Derivatives   419*
Hedge Accounting   419
  Nature of the Hedged Risk   419
  Hedge Effectiveness   420
  Hedge Documentation   420
Hedges of Foreign Currency Denominated Assets and
Liabilities   420
  Cash Flow Hedge   420
  Fair Value Hedge   421
Forward Contract Used to Hedge a Foreign Currency
Denominated Asset   421
  Forward Contract Designated as Cash Flow Hedge   423
  Forward Contract Designated as Fair Value Hedge   425
Discussion Question: Do We Have a Gain or What?   427
  Cash Flow Hedge versus Fair Value Hedge   428
Foreign Currency Option Used to Hedge a Foreign
Currency Denominated Asset   428
  Option Designated as Cash Flow Hedge   429
  Option Designated as Fair Value Hedge   431
  Spot Rate Exceeds Strike Price   432
Hedges of Unrecognized Foreign Currency Firm
Commitments   433
  *Forward Contract Used as Fair Value Hedge of a Firm
  Commitment   434*
  *Option Used as Fair Value Hedge of Firm
  Commitment   436*
Hedge of Forecasted Foreign Currency Denominated
Transaction   438
  *Forward Contract Cash Flow Hedge of a Forecasted
  Transaction   438*
  *Option Designated as a Cash Flow Hedge of a Forecasted
  Transaction   439*
Use of Hedging Instruments   441
  The Euro   442

Foreign Currency Borrowing   442
Foreign Currency Loan   443
Summary   443

Chapter Ten

Translation of Foreign Currency Financial Statements   469

Exchange Rates Used in Translation   470
Discussion Question: How Do We Report This?   471
Translation Adjustments   472
Balance Sheet Exposure   472
Translation Methods   473
Current Rate Method   473
Temporal Method   473
Translation of Retained Earnings   474
Complicating Aspects of the Temporal Method   476
Calculation of Cost of Goods Sold (COGS)   476
Application of the Lower-of-Cost-or-Market Rule   476
Fixed Assets, Depreciation, Accumulated Depreciation   476
Gain or Loss on the Sale of an Asset   477
Disposition of Translation Adjustment   477
U.S. Rules   478
SFAS 52   478
Highly Inflationary Economies   480
The Process Illustrated   481
Translation of Financial Statements—Current Rate Method   483
Translation of the Balance Sheet   484
Translation of the Statement of Cash Flows   485
Remeasurement of Financial Statements—Temporal Method   486
Remeasurement of the Income Statement   486
Remeasurement of the Statement of Cash Flows   489
Nonlocal Currency Balances   489
Comparison of the Results from Applying the Two Different Methods   490
Underlying Valuation Method   490
Underlying Relationships   491
Hedging Balance Sheet Exposure   491
Disclosures Related to Translation   492
Consolidation of a Foreign Subsidiary   494
Translation of Foreign Subsidiary Trial Balance   494
Determination of Balance in Investment Account—Equity Method   495
Consolidation Worksheet   496
Summary   498

Chapter Eleven

Worldwide Accounting Diversity and International Standards   524

Evidence of Accounting Diversity   525
Magnitude of Accounting Diversity   525
Reasons for Accounting Diversity   528
Legal System   528

Taxation   528
Providers of Financing   529
Inflation   529
Political and Economic Ties   529
Correlation of Factors   529
Problems Caused by Diverse Accounting Practices   529
Accounting Clusters   531
A Hypothetical Model of Accounting Diversity   532
International Harmonization of Financial Reporting   533
Arguments for Harmonization   533
Arguments against Harmonization   533
Major Harmonization Efforts   534
European Union   534
International Accounting Standards Committee   535
The IOSCO Agreement   536
International Accounting Standards Board   536
International Financial Reporting Standards (IFRSs)   536
Use of IFRSs   537
FASB–IASB Convergence   540
Short-Term Convergence Project   540
Joint Projects   541
Differences between IFRSs and U.S. GAAP   542
Recognition Differences   542
Measurement Differences   544
Presentation and Disclosure Differences   545
U.S. GAAP Reconciliations   545
The Accounting Profession and Financial Statement Presentation   548
United Kingdom   548
Germany   549
Japan   554
Discussion Question: Which Accounting Method Really Is Appropriate?   557
Summary   557

Chapter Twelve

Financial Reporting and the Securities and Exchange Commission   566

The Work of the Securities and Exchange Commission   566
Purpose of the Federal Securities Laws   568
Full and Fair Disclosure   569
Corporate Accounting Scandals and the Sarbanes-Oxley Act   571
Creation of the Public Company Accounting Oversight Board   572
Registration of Public Accounting Firms   573
The SEC's Authority over Generally Accepted Accounting Principles   574
Filings with the SEC   577
Electronic Data Gathering, Analysis, and Retrieval System (EDGAR)   582
Discussion Question: Is the Disclosure Worth the Cost?   583
Summary   584

Chapter Thirteen

Accounting for Legal Reorganizations and Liquidations   590

Accounting for Legal Reorganizations and
Liquidations   591
  Bankruptcy Reform Act of 1978   592
Discussion Question: What Do We Do Now?   595
  Statement of Financial Affairs   596
Discussion Question: How Much Is That Building Really
Worth?   597
  Statement of Financial Affairs Illustrated   597
Liquidation—Chapter 7 Bankruptcy   600
  Role of the Trustee   601
  Statement of Realization and Liquidation Illustrated   602
Reorganization—Chapter 11 Bankruptcy   604
  The Plan for Reorganization   605
  Acceptance and Confirmation of Reorganization Plan   607
  Financial Reporting during Reorganization   607
  *Financial Reporting for Companies Emerging from
  Reorganization   609*
  Fresh Start Accounting Illustrated   610
Discussion Question: Is This the Real Purpose of the
Bankruptcy Laws?   613
Summary   613

Chapter Fourteen

Partnerships: Formation and Operation   632

Partnerships—Advantages and Disadvantages   633
Alternative Legal Forms   634
  Subchapter S Corporation   635
  Limited Partnership (LPs)   635
  Limited Liability Partnerships (LLPs)   635
  Limited Liability Companies (LLCs)   636
Partnership Accounting—Capital Accounts   636
  Articles of Partnership   636
  Accounting for Capital Contributions   637
Discussion Question: What Kind of Business
Is This?   638
  Additional Capital Contributions and Withdrawals   640
  Allocation of Income   641
Discussion Question: How Will the Profits Be Split?   642
Accounting for Partnership Dissolution   645
  Dissolution—Admission of a New Partner   646
  Dissolution—Withdrawal of a Partner   651
Summary   653

Chapter Fifteen

Partnerships: Termination and Liquidation   670

Termination and Liquidation—Protecting the Interests of
All Parties   671
  Termination and Liquidation Procedures Illustrated   672
  Schedule of Liquidation   674
  Deficit Capital Balance—Contribution by Partner   675
  Deficit Capital Balance—Loss to Remaining Partners   676
  Marshaling of Assets   678
Discussion Question: What Happens if a Partner Becomes
Insolvent?   683
  Preliminary Distribution of Partnership Assets   684
  Predistribution Plan   687
Summary   690

Chapter Sixteen

Accounting for State and Local Governments (Part 1)   706

Introduction to the Accounting for State and Local
Governments   707
  Governmental Accounting—User Needs   708
  Two Sets of Financial Statements   708
  Financial Reporting and Accountability   709
  *Reporting Diverse Governmental Activities—Fund
  Accounting   710*
  Fund Accounting Classifications   711
Overview of State and Local Government Financial
Statements   715
  Government-Wide Financial Statements   715
  Fund-Based Financial Statements   717
Accounting for Governmental Funds   719
  *The Importance of Budgets and the Recording of Budgetary
  Entries   719*
  Encumbrances   721
  *Recognition of Expenditures for Operations and Capital
  Additions   723*
Discussion Question: Is It an Asset or a Liability?   725
  Recognition of Revenues—Overview   726
  *Derived Tax Revenues Such as Income Taxes and Sales
  Taxes   727*
  *Imposed Nonexchange Revenues Such as Property Taxes
  and Fines   728*
  *Government-Mandated Nonexchange Transactions and
  Voluntary Nonexchange Transactions   729*
  Issuance of Bonds   730
  Special Assessments   732
  Interfund Transactions   734
Summary   737

Chapter Seventeen

Accounting for State and Local Governments (Part 2)   756

Capital Leases   757
  Government-Wide Financial Statements   757
  Fund-Based Financial Statements   758
Solid Waste Landfill   760
  Government-Wide Financial Statements   760
  Fund-Based Financial Statements   761
Compensated Absences   761
Works of Art and Historical Treasures   762

Infrastructure Assets and Depreciation 764
Management's Discussion and Analysis 765
The Primary Government and Component Units 767
Primary Government 767
Component Units 768
Discussion Question: Is It Part of the County? 769
Special Purpose Governments 769
Government-Wide and Fund-Based Financial Statements
Illustrated 770
*Statement of Net Assets—Government-Wide Financial
Statements 771*
*Statement of Activities—Government-Wide Financial
Statements 772*
*Balance Sheet—Governmental Funds—Fund-Based
Statements 778*
*Statement of Revenues, Expenditures, and Changes in
Fund Balances—Governmental Funds—Fund-Based
Statements 779*
*Statement of Net Assets—Proprietary Funds—Fund-Based
Statements 779*
*Statement of Revenues, Expenses, and Changes in Fund Net
Assets—Proprietary Funds—Fund-Based Statements 784*
*Statement of Cash Flows—Proprietary Funds—Fund-Based
Statements 784*
Reporting Public Colleges and Universities 785
Summary 794

Chapter Eighteen
Accounting and Reporting for Private Not-for-Profit Organizations 814

Financial Reporting 815
*Financial Statements for Private Not-for-Profit
Organizations 816*
Statement of Financial Position 817
Statement of Activities and Changes in Net Assets 818

Evolution of Standard-Setting Authority 821
The GAAP Hierarchy 825
Accounting for Contributions 827
Discussion Question: Are Two Sets of GAAP Really
Needed for Colleges and Universities? 828
Donations of Works of Art and Historical Treasures 828
Holding Contributions for Others 829
Contributed Services 830
Exchange Transactions 831
Transactions Illustrated 832
Reporting Transactions on Statement of Activities 834
Accounting for Health Care Organizations 834
Accounting for Patient Service Revenues 835
Discussion Question: Is This Really an Asset? 836
Summary 837

Chapter Nineteen
Accounting for Estates and Trusts 853

Accounting for an Estate 853
Administration of the Estate 854
Property Included in the Estate 855
Discovery of Claims against the Decedent 855
Protection for Remaining Family Members 856
Estate Distributions 856
Estate and Inheritance Taxes 858
The Distinction between Income and Principal 862
Recording the Transactions of an Estate 863
Discussion Question: Is This Really an Asset? 866
Charge and Discharge Statement 867
Accounting for a Trust 867
Record-Keeping for a Trust 871
Accounting for the Activities of a Trust 872
Summary 873

Index 887

Chapter **One**

The Equity Method of Accounting for Investments

The first several chapters of this text present the accounting and reporting for investment activities of businesses. The focus is on investments when one firm possesses either significant influence or control over another through ownership of voting shares. When one firm owns enough voting shares to be able to affect the decisions of another, accounting for the investment becomes challenging and often complex. The source of such complexities typically stems from the fact that transactions among the firms affiliated through ownership cannot be considered independent, arm's-length transactions. As in all matters relating to financial reporting, we look to transactions with *outside parties* to provide a basis for accounting valuation. When firms are affiliated through a common set of owners, objectivity in accounting calls for measurements that recognize the relationships among the firms.

REPORTING INVESTMENTS IN CORPORATE EQUITY SECURITIES

In a recent annual report, JB Hunt Transport Services describes the creation of Transplace, Inc. (TPI), an Internet-based global transportation logistics company. JB Hunt contributed all of its logistics segment business and all related intangible assets plus $5 million of cash in exchange for an approximate 27 percent initial interest in TPI, which subsequently has been increased to 37 percent. The company accounts for its interest in TPI utilizing the equity method of accounting and stated, "The financial results of TPI are included on a one-line, nonoperating item included on the Consolidated Statements of Earnings entitled 'equity in earnings of associated companies.'"

Such information is hardly unusual in the business world; corporate as well as individual investors frequently acquire ownership shares of both domestic and foreign businesses. These investments can range from the purchase of a few shares to the acquisition of 100 percent control. Although purchases of corporate equity securities (such as the one made by JB Hunt) are not uncommon, they pose a considerable number of problems for the accountant because a close relationship has been established without the investor gaining actual control. These issues are currently addressed by the **equity method.** This chapter deals with the procedures utilized in accounting for stock investments that fall under the application of this method.

At present, accounting standards recognize three different approaches to the financial reporting of investments in corporate equity securities:

The fair-value method.

The consolidation of financial statements.

The equity method.

These three approaches are not interchangeable; a specific method is required by any given situation. The reporting of a particular investment depends on the degree of influence that the investor (stockholder) has over the investee, a factor typically indicated by the relative size of ownership.[1]

Fair-Value Method

In many instances, an investor possesses only a small percentage of an investee company's outstanding stock, perhaps only a few shares. Because of the limited level of ownership, the investor cannot expect to have a significant impact on the investee's operations or decision making. These shares are bought in anticipation of cash dividends or in appreciation of stock market values. Such investments are recorded at cost and periodically adjusted to fair value according to the Financial Accounting Standards Board (FASB) in its *Statement of Financial Accounting Standards No. 115 (SFAS 115),* "Accounting for Certain Investments in Debt and Equity Securities," May 1993.

Since a full coverage of *SFAS 115* is presented in intermediate accounting textbooks, only the following basic principles are noted here.

- Initial investments in equity securities are recorded at cost and subsequently adjusted to fair value if fair value is readily determinable; otherwise, the investment remains at cost.
- Equity securities held for sale in the short term are classified as *trading securities* and reported at fair value, with unrealized gains and losses included in earnings.
- Equity securities not classified as trading securities are classified as *available-for-sale securities* and reported at fair value, with unrealized gains and losses excluded from earnings and reported in a separate component of shareholders' equity as part of *other comprehensive income.*
- Dividends received are recognized as income for both trading and available-for-sale securities.

These procedures are required for equity security investments when neither significant influence nor control is present. The recognition of unrealized gains and losses for *SFAS 115* investments represents a departure from past procedures that prevented the anticipation of income. As will be shown, the procedures for significant influence investments in equity securities, while somewhat complex, adhere more closely to traditional accrual accounting.

Consolidation of Financial Statements

Although many investments involve only a small percentage of stock, an investor can acquire enough shares to gain actual control over an investee's operation. In financial accounting, such control is recognized whenever a stockholder accumulates more than 50 percent of an organization's outstanding voting stock. At that point, rather than simply influencing the decisions of the investee, the investor clearly can direct the entire decision-making process. A review of the financial statements of America's largest organizations indicates that legal control of one or

---

[1] The relative size of ownership is most often the key factor in assessing one company's degree of influence over another. However, other factors (e.g., contractual relationships between firms) can also provide influence or control over firms regardless of the percentage of shares owned.

more subsidiary companies is an almost universal practice. PepsiCo, Inc., as just one example, holds a majority interest in the voting stock of literally hundreds of corporations.

A level of ownership large enough to enable an investor to control an investee presents an economic situation not adequately addressed by *SFAS 115*. Normally, when a majority of voting stock is held, the investor-investee relationship has become so closely connected that the two corporations are viewed as a single entity for reporting purposes. Hence, an entirely different set of accounting procedures is applicable. According to *Accounting Research Bulletin No. 51 (ARB No. 51),* "Consolidated Financial Statements," August 1959, control generally requires the consolidation of the accounting information produced by the individual companies. Thus, a single set of financial statements is created for external reporting purposes with all assets, liabilities, revenues, and expenses being brought together.[2] The various procedures applied within this consolidation process are examined in subsequent chapters of the textbook.

More recently, FASB *Interpretation No. 46R,* "Consolidation of Variable Interest Entities, an Interpretation of ARB No. 51" (*FIN 46R*; revised December 2003) expands the use of consolidated financial statements to include entities that are financially controlled through special contractual arrangements rather than through voting stock interests. Prior to *FIN 46R,* many firms (e.g., Enron) avoided consolidation of entities in which they owned little or no voting stock but otherwise were controlled through special contracts. These entities were frequently referred to as "special purpose entities (SPEs)" and provided vehicles for some firms to keep large amounts of assets and liabilities off their consolidated financial statements.

Equity Method

Finally, another investment relationship is appropriately accounted for using the equity method. JB Hunt's ownership of 37 percent of the voting stock of TPI is less than enough to control the voting stock. Despite the lack of voting control, however, JB Hunt maintains a large interest in this investee company. Through its ownership, JB Hunt can undoubtedly affect TPI's decisions and operations.

Especially important is the investor's ability to influence the timing of dividend distributions. Because of this influence, the receipt of a dividend from an investee does not qualify as an objective basis for recording income to the investor firm. Because managerial compensation contracts often are based on net income, incentives exist for managers to use whatever discretion they have available in reporting net income. *Thus, to provide an objective basis for reporting investment income, the equity method requires that income be recognized by the investor as it is earned by the investee, not when dividends are received.*

In today's business world, many corporations such as JB Hunt hold significant ownership interests in other companies without having actual control. The Coca-Cola Company alone holds between 20 and 50 percent ownership in dozens of separate corporations. Many other large investments are created through joint ventures in which two or more companies form a new enterprise to carry out a specified operating purpose. For example, Microsoft and NBC formed a joint venture to operate MSNBC, a cable channel and online site to go with NBC's broadcast network. Each partner owns 50 percent of the joint venture.

For each of these investments, the investors do not possess absolute control because they hold less than a majority of the voting stock. Thus, the preparation of consolidated financial statements is inappropriate. However, the large percentage of ownership indicates that each investor possesses some ability to affect the decision-making process of the investee. To reflect this relationship, such investments are accounted for by the equity method as officially established by *Opinion 18,* "The Equity Method of Accounting for Investments in Common Stock," issued by the Accounting Principles Board (APB) in March of 1971, and as amended in 2001 by *SFAS 142,* "Goodwill and Other Intangible Assets."

---

[2] As is discussed in the next chapter, owning a majority of the voting shares of an investee does not always lead to consolidated financial statements.

APPLYING THE EQUITY METHOD

An understanding of the equity method is best gained by initially examining the APB's treatment of two questions:

1. What parameters identify the area of ownership for which the equity method is applicable?
2. How should the investor report this investment and the income generated by it to reflect the relationship between the two companies?

Criteria for Utilizing the Equity Method

In sanctioning the equity method, the APB reasoned that an investor begins to gain the ability to influence the decision-making process of an investee as the level of ownership rises. According to *APB Opinion 18* (para. 17), achieving this "ability to exercise significant influence over operating and financial policies of an investee even though the investor holds 50 percent or less of the voting stock" is the sole criterion for requiring application of the equity method.

Clearly, a term such as *the ability to exercise significant influence* is nebulous and subject to a variety of judgments and interpretations in practice. At what point does the acquisition of one additional share of stock give an owner the ability to exercise significant influence? This decision becomes even more difficult in that only the *ability* to exercise significant influence need be present: The pronouncement does not specify that any actual influence must have ever been applied.

APB Opinion 18 provides guidance to the accountant by listing several conditions that indicate the presence of this degree of influence:

- Investor representation on the board of directors of the investee.
- Investor participation in the policy-making process of the investee.
- Material intercompany transactions.
- Interchange of managerial personnel.
- Technological dependency.
- Extent of ownership by the investor in relation to the size and concentration of other ownership interests in the investee.

No single one of these guides should be used exclusively in assessing the applicability of the equity method. Instead, all are evaluated together to determine the presence or absence of the sole criterion: the ability to exercise significant influence over the investee.

These guidelines alone do not eliminate the leeway available to each investor when deciding whether the use of the equity method is appropriate. To provide a degree of consistency in applying this standard, the APB established a general ownership test: *If an investor holds between 20 and 50 percent of the voting stock of the investee, significant influence is normally assumed and the equity method applied.*

> The Board recognizes that determining the ability of an investor to exercise such influence is not always clear and applying judgment is necessary to assess the status of each investment. In order to achieve a reasonable degree of uniformity in application, the Board concludes that an investment (direct or indirect) of 20 percent or more of the voting stock of an investee should lead to a presumption that in the absence of evidence to the contrary an investor has the ability to exercise significant influence over an investee. Conversely, an investment of less than 20 percent of the voting stock of an investee should lead to a presumption that an investor does not have the ability to exercise significant influence unless such ability can be demonstrated.[3]

At first, the 20 percent rule appears to be an arbitrarily chosen boundary established merely to provide accountants with a consistent method of reporting all investments. However, the essential criterion is still the ability to significantly influence the investee, rather than 20 percent ownership.[4] If the absence of this ability is proven, the equity method should not be applied

---

[3] *APB Opinion 18,* para. 17.

[4] Not everyone agrees with the wisdom of this rule. Two members of the APB, George R. Catlett and Charles T. Horngren, voted for *Opinion 18* but argued in an attached statement that "they do not agree with the arbitrary criterion of 20 percent combined with a variable test of 'significant influence' in paragraph 17, because such an approach is not convincing in concept and will be very difficult to apply in practice."

regardless of the percentage of shares held. Conversely, whenever this ability can be demonstrated, the equity method is appropriate even with less than 20 percent ownership.

As an example, in a recent annual report, International Paper Company disclosed that it accounts for its investment in Scitex Corporation using the equity method despite holding only a 13 percent interest. International Paper cited its ability to exercise significant influence "because the Company is party to a shareowners' agreement with two other entities which together with the Company own just over 39% of Scitex."

Further guidance on the precise applicability of the equity method was provided in May 1981 when the FASB issued its *Interpretation 35,* "Criteria for Applying the Equity Method of Accounting for Investments in Common Stock." This pronouncement dealt specifically with using the equity method for investments in which the owner holds more than 20 percent of the outstanding shares. It is important because companies had tended to apply the equity method to all investments in the 20 to 50 percent range with little regard for the degree of influence actually present.

According to *Interpretation 35* (para. 3), above the 20 percent level of ownership, "the presumption that the investor has the ability to exercise significant influence over the investee's operating and financial policies stands until overcome by predominant evidence to the contrary." However, the pronouncement then went on to offer clarification by listing examples of occurrences that would provide evidence to nullify this presumption. *Interpretation 35* specifically states that the equity method is not appropriate for investments that demonstrate any of the following characteristics regardless of the investor's degree of ownership:

- An agreement exists between investor and investee whereby the investor surrenders significant rights as a shareholder.
- A concentration of ownership operates the investee without regard for the views of the investor.
- The investor attempts but fails to obtain representation on the investee's board of directors.

Although a controlling financial interest usually requires consolidation, conditions can exist so that the equity method is appropriate despite a majority voting interest. As discussed in the FASB's Emerging Issues Task Force (EITF) *Issue 96-16,* in some instances the powers of the majority shareholder can be restricted by approval or veto rights granted to the minority shareholder. If the minority rights are so restrictive as to call into question whether control rests with the majority owner, the equity method is employed for appropriate financial reporting rather than consolidation. As noted in *EITF 96-16,* substantive minority participation rights can affect the hiring, termination, and compensation of management. Other important minority rights can include establishing operating and capital decisions of the investee. In these cases, minority rights can overcome the presumption that an investor with a majority voting interest should consolidate its investee. For example, in its 2004 annual report, SBC Communications stated that "we account for our 60 percent economic investment in Cingular under the equity method of accounting because we share control equally with our 40 percent partner BellSouth."

Finally, FASB *Interpretation No. 46R,* "Consolidation of Variable Interest Entities," expands the definition of a controlling financial interest. *FIN 46R* addresses situations in which financial control exists absent ownership of a majority voting interest. In these situations, control is achieved through contractual and other arrangements called *variable interests.*

For example, one firm may create a separate legal entity in which it holds little or no voting interests but nonetheless controls that entity through governance document provisions and other contracts that specify the distribution of profits and losses and other risks. Such an entity is typically designated as a *variable interest entity.* If the controlling firm is deemed a primary beneficiary of a variable interest entity, consolidation of financial statements is required regardless of the percentage of voting stock held by the primary beneficiary. Many firms (e.g., The Walt Disney Company, Mills Corporation) have recently reclassified former equity method investments as variable interest entities. As primary beneficiaries, they now consolidate these investments.[5]

---

[5] Chapters 2 and 6 provide further discussions of *FIN 46R.*

To summarize, the following table indicates the method of accounting that is typically applicable to various stock investments:

Criterion	Normal Ownership Level	Applicable Accounting Method
Lack of ability to significantly influence	Less than 20%	Fair value (*SFAS 115*) or cost
Presence of ability to significantly influence	20%–50%	Equity method (*APB Opinion 18* and *SFAS 142*)
Control through voting interests	More than 50%	Consolidated financial statements (*ARB No. 51, SFAS 141* and *142*)
Control through variable interests (governance documents, contracts)	Primary beneficiary status (no ownership required)	Consolidated financial statements (*FIN 46R*)

Accounting for an Investment—The Equity Method

Now that the criteria leading to the application of the equity method have been identified, a review of its reporting procedures is appropriate. Knowledge of this accounting process is especially important to users of the investor's financial statements because the equity method affects both the timing of income recognition as well as the carrying value of the investment account.

In applying the equity method, the accounting objective is to report the investor's investment and investment income reflecting the close relationship between the companies. After recording the cost of the acquisition, two equity method entries periodically record the investment's impact:

• The investor's investment account is *increased as the investee earns and reports income.* Also, investment income is recognized by the investor using the accrual method—that is, in the same time period as it is earned by the investee. If an investee reports income of $100,000, a 30 percent owner should immediately increase its own income by $30,000. This earnings accrual reflects the essence of the equity method by emphasizing the connection between the two companies; as the owners' equity of the investee increases through the earnings process, so the investment account also increases. Although the acquisition is initially recorded by the investor at cost, upward adjustments in the asset balance are recorded as soon as the investee makes a profit. A reduction is necessary if a loss is reported.

• The investor's investment account is *decreased whenever a dividend is collected.* Because distribution of cash dividends reduces the book value of the investee company, the investor mirrors this change by recording the receipt as a decrease in the carrying value of the investment rather than as revenue. Once again, a parallel is established between the investment account and the underlying activities of the investee: The reduction in owners' equity of the investee creates a decrease in the investment. Furthermore, because income is recognized immediately by the investor when the investee earns it, double counting would occur if subsequent dividend collections also were recorded by the investor as revenue. Importantly, the collection of a cash dividend is not an appropriate point for income recognition. Because the investor can influence the timing of investee dividend distributions, the receipt of a dividend is not an objective measure of the income generated from the investment.

Application of Equity Method	
Investee Event	**Investor Accounting**
Income is earned.	Proportionate share of income is recognized.
Dividends are distributed.	Dividends received are recorded as a reduction in investment.

EXHIBIT 1.1   **Comparison of Fair-Value Method and Equity Method**

Year	Income of Little Company	Dividends Paid by Little Company	Accounting by Big Company When Influence Is Not Significant (available-for-sale security)			Accounting by Big Company When Influence Is Significant (equity method)	
			Dividend Income	Carrying Value of Investment	Fair-Value Adjustment to Stockholders' Equity	Equity in Investee Income	Carrying Value of Investment
2007	$200,000	$ 50,000	$10,000	$235,000	$ 35,000	$ 40,000*	$230,000†
2008	300,000	100,000	20,000	255,000	55,000	60,000*	270,000†
2009	400,000	200,000	40,000	320,000	120,000	80,000*	310,000†
Total income recognized			$70,000			$180,000	

*Equity in investee income is 20 percent of the current year income reported by Little Company.
†The carrying value of an investment under the equity method is the original cost plus income recognized less dividends received. For 2007, as an example, the $230,000 reported balance is the $200,000 cost plus $40,000 equity income less $10,000 in dividends received.

Application of the equity method causes the investment account on the investor's balance sheet to vary directly with changes in the equity of the investee. As an illustration, assume that an investor acquires a 40 percent interest in a business enterprise. If the investor has the ability to significantly influence the investee, the equity method must be utilized. If the investee subsequently reports net income of $50,000, the investor increases the investment account (and its own net income) by $20,000 in recognition of a 40 percent share of these earnings. Conversely, a $20,000 dividend collected from the investee necessitates a reduction of $8,000 in this same asset account (40 percent of the total payout).

In contrast, the fair-value method reports investments at fair value if readily determinable. Also, income is recognized only on receipt of dividends. Consequently, financial reports can vary depending on whether the equity method or fair-value method is appropriate.

To illustrate, assume that Big Company owns a 20 percent interest in Little Company purchased on January 1, 2007, for $200,000. Little then reports net income of $200,000, $300,000, and $400,000 in the next three years while paying dividends of $50,000, $100,000, and $200,000. The fair values of Big's investment in Little, as determined by market prices, were $235,000, $255,000, and $320,000 at the end of 2007, 2008, and 2009, respectively.

Exhibit 1.1 compares the accounting for Big's investment in Little across the two methods. The fair-value method carries the investment at its market values, presumed to be readily available in this example. Because the investment is classified as an *available-for-sale security,* the excess of fair value over cost is reported as a separate component of stockholders' equity.[6] Income is recognized as dividends are received.

In contrast, under the equity method, Big recognizes income as it is earned by Little. As shown in Exhibit 1.1, Big recognizes $180,000 in income over the three years, and the carrying value of the investment is adjusted upward to $310,000. Dividends received are not an appropriate measure of income because of the assumed significant influence over the investee. Big's ability to influence the decisions of Little applies to the timing of dividend distributions. Therefore, dividends received do not objectively measure Big's income from its investment in Little. However, as Little earns income, under the equity method Big recognizes its share (20 percent) of the income and increases the investment account. The equity method reflects the accrual model: Income is recognized as it is earned, not when cash (dividend) is received.

Exhibit 1.1 shows that the carrying value of the investment fluctuates each year under the equity method. This recording parallels the changes occurring in the net asset figures reported by the investee. If the owner's equity of the investee rises through income, an increase is made

[6] Fluctuations in the market values of *trading securities* are recognized in income in the period in which they occur.

in the investment account; decreases such as losses and dividends cause reductions to be recorded. Thus, the equity method conveys information that describes the relationship created by the investor's ability to significantly influence the investee.

ACCOUNTING PROCEDURES USED IN APPLYING THE EQUITY METHOD

Once guidelines for the application of the equity method have been established, the mechanical process necessary for recording basic transactions is quite straightforward. The investor accrues its percentage of the earnings reported by the investee each period. Dividend declarations reduce the investment balance to reflect the decrease in the investee's book value.

Referring again to the information presented in Exhibit 1.1, Little Company reported a net income of $200,000 during 2007 and paid cash dividends of $50,000. These figures indicate that Little's net assets have increased by $150,000 during the year. Therefore, in its financial records Big Company records the following journal entries to apply the equity method:

Investment in Little Company	40,000	
Equity in Investee Income		40,000
To accrue earnings of a 20 percent owned investee ($200,000 × 20%).		
Cash	10,000	
Investment in Little Company		10,000
To record receipt of cash dividend from Little Company ($50,000 × 20%).		

In the first entry, Big accrues income based on the reported earnings of the investee even though this amount greatly exceeds the cash dividend. The second entry reflects the actual receipt of the dividend and the related reduction in Little's net assets. The $30,000 net increment recorded here in Big's investment account ($40,000 − $10,000) represents 20 percent of the $150,000 increase in Little's book value that occurred during the year.

Although these two entries illustrate the basic reporting process used in applying the equity method, several other issues must be explored for a full understanding of this approach. More specifically, special procedures are required in accounting for each of the following:

1. Reporting a change to the equity method.
2. Reporting investee income from sources other than continuing operations.
3. Reporting investee losses.
4. Reporting the sale of an equity investment.

Reporting a Change to the Equity Method

In many instances, an investor's ability to significantly influence an investee is not achieved through a single stock acquisition. The investor could possess only a minor ownership for some years before purchasing enough additional shares to require conversion to the equity method. Before the investor achieves significant influence, any investment should be reported by the fair-value method. After the investment reaches the point at which the equity method becomes applicable, a technical question arises about the appropriate means of changing from one method to the other.[7]

APB Opinion 18 (para. 19) addresses this concern by stating that "the investment, results of operations (current and prior periods presented), and retained earnings of the investor should be adjusted retroactively." *Thus, all accounts are restated so that the investor's financial statements appear as if the equity method had been applied from the date of the first acquisition.*

---

[7] A switch to the equity method also can be required if the investee purchases a portion of its own shares as treasury stock. This transaction can increase the investor's percentage of outstanding stock.

By mandating retrospective treatment, the APB attempted to ensure comparability from year to year in the financial reporting of the investor company.[8]

To illustrate this restatement procedure, assume that Giant Company acquires a 10 percent ownership in Small Company on January 1, 2007. Officials of Giant do not believe that their company has gained the ability to exert significant influence over Small. The investment is properly recorded through the use of the fair-value method as an available-for-sale security. Subsequently, on January 1, 2009, Giant purchases an additional 30 percent of the outstanding voting stock of Small, thereby achieving the ability to significantly influence the investee's decision making. From 2007 through 2009, Small reports net income, pays cash dividends, and has fair values at January 1 of each year as follows:

Year	Net Income	Cash Dividends	Fair Value at January 1
2007	$ 70,000	$20,000	$800,000
2008	110,000	40,000	840,000
2009	130,000	50,000	930,000

In Giant's 2007 and 2008 financial statements, as originally reported, dividend revenue of $2,000 and $4,000, respectively, would be recognized based on receiving 10 percent of these distributions. The investment account is maintained at fair value since it is readily determinable. Also, the change in the fair value of the investment results in a credit to an unrealized cumulative holding gain of $4,000 in 2007 and an additional credit of $9,000 in 2008 for a cumulative amount of $13,000 reported in Giant's 2008 stockholders' equity section. However, after changing to the equity method on January 1, 2009, Giant must restate these prior years to present the investment as if the equity method had always been applied. Subsequently, in comparative statements showing columns for previous periods, the 2007 statements should indicate equity income of $7,000 with $11,000 being disclosed for 2008 based on a 10 percent accrual of Small's income for each of these years.

The income restatement for these earlier years can be computed as follows:

Year	Equity in Investee Income (10%)	Income Reported from Dividends	Retrospective Adjustment
2007	$ 7,000	$2,000	$ 5,000
2008	11,000	4,000	7,000
Total adjustment to Retained Earnings			$12,000

Giant's reported earnings for 2007 will be increased by $5,000 with a $7,000 increment needed for 2008. To bring about this retrospective change to the equity method, Giant prepares the following journal entry on January 1, 2009:

Investment in Small Company	12,000	
Retained Earnings—Prior Period Adjustment— Equity in Investee Income		12,000
To adjust 2007 and 2008 records so that investment is accounted for using the equity method in a consistent manner.		
Unrealized Holding Gain—Shareholders' Equity	13,000	
Fair Value Adjustment (Available-for-Sale)		13,000

To remove the investor's percentage of the increase in fair value
    (10% × $130,000) from stockholders' equity and the available-for-sale
    portfolio valuation account.		

---

[8] *SFAS 154, Accounting Changes and Error Corrections,* recently introduced the term "retrospective" to describe retroactive applications of accounting principles. *SFAS 154* (p. 3) includes in its definition of *retrospective* the application of a different accounting principle to prior periods as if that principle had always been used.

DOES THE EQUITY METHOD REALLY APPLY HERE?

Abraham, Inc., a New Jersey corporation, operates 57 bakeries throughout the northeastern section of the United States. In the past, its founder, James Abraham, has owned the company's entire outstanding common stock. However, during the early part of this year, the corporation suffered a severe cash flow problem brought on by rapid expansion. To avoid bankruptcy, Abraham sought additional investment capital from a friend, Dennis Bostitch, who owned Highland Laboratories. Subsequently, Highland paid $700,000 cash to Abraham, Inc., to acquire enough newly issued shares of common stock for a one-third ownership interest.

At the end of this year, the accountants for Highland Laboratories are discussing the proper method of reporting this investment. One argues for maintaining the asset at its original cost: "This purchase is no more than a loan to bail out the bakeries. Mr. Abraham will continue to run the organization with little or no attention paid to us. After all, what does anyone in our company know about baking bread? I would not be surprised if these shares are not reacquired by Abraham as soon as the bakery business is profitable again."

One of the other accountants disagrees, stating that the equity method is appropriate. "I realize that our company is not capable of running a bakery. However, the official rules state that we must have only the *ability* to exert significant influence. With one-third of the common stock in our possession, we certainly have that ability. Whether we use it or not, this ability means that we are required to apply the equity method."

How should Highland Laboratories account for its investment in Abraham, Inc.?

The $13,000 adjustment removes the accounts required by *SFAS No. 115* that pertain to the investment prior to obtaining significant influence. Because the investment is no longer part of the available-for-sale portfolio, it is carried under the equity method rather than at fair value. Accordingly, the fair-value adjustment accounts are reduced as part of the reclassification.

Continuing with this example, Giant will make two other journal entries at the end of 2009, but they relate solely to the operations and distributions of that period.

Investment in Small Company	52,000	
Equity in Investee Income		52,000
To accrue 40 percent of the year 2009 income reported by Small Company ($130,000 × 40%).		
Cash	20,000	
Investment in Small Company		20,000
To record receipt of year 2009 cash dividend from Small Company ($50,000 × 40%).		

Reporting Investee Income from Sources Other Than Continuing Operations

Traditionally, certain elements of income are presented separately within a set of financial statements. Examples include extraordinary items (see *APB Opinion 30*, "Reporting the Results of Operations," June 1973) and prior period adjustments (see FASB *SFAS 16*, "Prior Period Adjustments," June 1977). A concern that arises in applying the equity method is whether items appearing separately in the investee's income statement require similar treatment by the investor.

To examine this issue, assume that Large Company owns 40 percent of the voting stock of Tiny Company and accounts for this investment by means of the equity method. In 2007, Tiny reports net income of $200,000, a figure composed of $250,000 in income from continuing operations and a $50,000 extraordinary loss. Large Company accrues earnings of $80,000 based on 40 percent of the $200,000 net figure. However, for proper disclosure, the extraordinary loss incurred by the investee must also be reported separately on the financial statements of the investor. This handling is intended, once again, to mirror the close relationship between the two companies.

Based on the level of ownership, Large recognizes $100,000 as a component of operating income (40 percent of Tiny Company's $250,000 income from continuing operations) along with a $20,000 extraordinary loss (40 percent of $50,000). The overall effect is still an $80,000 net increment in Large's earnings, but this amount has been appropriately allocated between income from continuing operations and extraordinary items.

The journal entry to record Large's equity interest in the income of Tiny would be as follows:

Investment in Tiny Company	80,000	
Extraordinary Loss of Investee	20,000	
Equity in Investee Income		100,000
To accrue operating income and extraordinary loss from equity investment.		

One additional aspect of this accounting should be noted. Even though the investee has already judged this loss as extraordinary, Large does not report its $20,000 share as a separate item unless that figure is considered to be material with respect to the investor's own operations.

Reporting Investee Losses

Although most of the previous illustrations are based on the recording of profits, accounting for losses incurred by the investee is handled in a similar manner. The investor recognizes the appropriate percentage of each loss and reduces the carrying value of the investment account. Even though these procedures are consistent with the concept of the equity method, they fail to take into account all possible loss situations.

Permanent Losses in Value

APB Opinion 18 recognizes that investments can suffer permanent losses in fair value that are not properly reflected through the equity method. Such declines can be caused by the loss of major customers, changes in economic conditions, loss of a significant patent or other legal right, damage to the company's reputation, and the like. Permanent reductions in fair value resulting from such adverse events might not be reported immediately by the investor through the normal equity entries discussed previously. Thus, *APB Opinion 18* (para. 19) established the following guideline:

> A loss in value of an investment which is other than a temporary decline should be recognized the same as a loss in value of other long-term assets. Evidence of a loss in value might include, but would not necessarily be limited to, absence of an ability to recover the carrying amount of the investment or inability of the investee to sustain an earnings capacity which would justify the carrying amount of the investment.

Thus, when a permanent decline in an equity method investment's value occurs, the investor must recognize an impairment loss and reduce the asset to fair value. However, *APB Opinion 18* stresses that this loss must be permanent before such recognition becomes necessary. Under the equity method, a temporary drop in the fair value of an investment is simply ignored.

For example, Cingular Wireless noted the following in its 2004 annual report:

> In accordance with *Accounting Principles Board (APB) Opinion No. 18,* "The Equity Method of Accounting for Investments in Common Stock," the Company reviews its equity method investments for impairment. These reviews are performed to determine whether any decline in the fair value of an investment below its carrying value is deemed to be other than temporary, in which case an impairment charge would be recorded.

Investment Reduced to Zero

Through the recognition of reported losses as well as any permanent drops in fair value, the investment account can eventually be reduced to a zero balance. This condition is most likely to occur if the investee has suffered extreme losses or if the original purchase was made at a low, bargain price. Regardless of the reason, the carrying value of the investment account could conceivably be eliminated in total.

At the point at which an investment account is reduced to zero, the investor should discontinue using the equity method rather than establish a negative balance. The investment retains a zero balance until subsequent investee profits eliminate all unrealized losses. Once the original cost of the investment has been eliminated, no additional losses can accrue to the investor (since the entire cost has been written off) *unless* some further commitment has been made on behalf of the investee.

Noise Cancellation Technologies, Inc., for example, in recent financial statements explains the discontinued use of the equity method when the investment account has been reduced to zero:

> When the Company's share of cumulative losses equals its investment and the Company has no obligation or intention to fund such additional losses, the Company suspends applying the equity method. . . . The Company will not be able to record any equity in income with respect to an entity until its share of future profits is sufficient to recover any cumulative losses that have not previously been recorded.

Reporting the Sale of an Equity Investment

At any time, the investor can choose to sell part or all of its holdings in the investee company. If a sale occurs, the equity method continues to be applied until the transaction date, thus establishing an appropriate carrying value for the investment. The investor then reduces this balance by the percentage of shares being sold.

As an example, assume that Top Company owns 40 percent of the 100,000 outstanding shares of Bottom Company, an investment accounted for by the equity method. Although these 40,000 shares were acquired some years ago for $200,000, application of the equity method has increased the asset balance to $320,000 as of January 1, 2007. On July 1, 2007, Top elects to sell 10,000 of these shares (one-fourth of its investment) for $110,000 in cash, thereby reducing ownership in Bottom from 40 percent to 30 percent. Bottom Company reports income of $70,000 during the first six months of 2007 and distributes cash dividends of $30,000.

Top, as the investor, initially makes the following journal entries on July 1, 2007, to accrue the proper income and establish the correct investment balance:

Investment in Bottom Company	28,000	
Equity in Investee Income		28,000
To accrue equity income for first six months of 2007 ($70,000 × 40%).		
Cash	12,000	
Investment in Bottom Company		12,000
To record receipt of cash dividends from January through June 2007 ($30,000 × 40%).		

These two entries increase the carrying value of Top's investment by $16,000, creating a balance of $336,000 as of July 1, 2007. The sale of one-fourth of these shares can then be recorded as follows:

Cash	110,000	
Investment in Bottom Company		84,000
Gain on Sale of Investment		26,000
To record sale of one-fourth of investment in Bottom Company (¼ × $336,000 = $84,000).		

After the sale is completed, Top continues to apply the equity method to this investment based on 30 percent ownership rather than 40 percent. However, if the sale had been of sufficient magnitude to cause Top to lose its ability to exercise significant influence over Bottom, the equity method ceases to be applicable. For example, if Top Company's holdings were reduced from 40 percent to 15 percent, the equity method might no longer be appropriate after the sale. The shares still being held are reported according to the fair-value method with the remaining book value becoming the new *cost* figure for the investment rather than the amount originally paid.

If an investor is required to change from the equity method to the fair-value method, no retrospective adjustment is made. Although, as previously demonstrated, a change to the equity method mandates a restatement of prior periods, the treatment is not the same when the investor's change is to the fair-value method.

EXCESS OF INVESTMENT COST OVER BOOK VALUE ACQUIRED

After the basic concepts and procedures of the equity method are mastered, more complex accounting issues can be introduced. Surely one of the most common problems encountered in applying the equity method concerns investment costs that exceed the proportionate book value of the investee company.[9]

Unless the investor acquires its ownership at the time of the investee's conception, paying an amount equal to book value is rare. Dell Computer Corporation, as just one example, reported a book value of approximately $2.61 per share on April 1, 2005, but on that date, the company's common stock traded near $38 per share on the NASDAQ Exchange. To obtain Dell Computer shares as well as the stock of many other businesses, payment of a significant premium over book value is required.

A number of possible reasons exist for such a marked difference between the book value of a company and the price of its stock. A company's value at any time is based on a multitude of factors such as company profitability, the introduction of a new product, expected dividend payments, projected operating results, and general economic conditions. Furthermore, stock prices are based, at least partially, on the perceived worth of a company's net assets, amounts that often vary dramatically from underlying book values. Asset and liability accounts shown on a balance sheet tend to measure historical costs rather than current value. In addition, these reported figures are affected by the specific accounting methods adopted by a company. Inventory costing methods such as LIFO and FIFO, for example, obviously lead to different book values as do each of the acceptable depreciation methods.

If an investment is acquired at a price in excess of book value, logical reasons should explain the additional cost incurred by the investor. The source of the excess of cost over book value is important. Income recognition requires matching the income generated from the investment with its cost. Excess costs allocated to fixed assets will likely be expensed over longer periods than costs allocated to inventory. In applying the equity method, the cause of such an excess payment can be divided into two general categories:

1. Specific investee assets and liabilities can have fair values that differ from their present book values. The excess payment can be identified directly with individual accounts such as inventory, equipment, franchise rights, etc.
2. The investor could be willing to pay an extra amount because future benefits are expected to accrue from the investment. Such benefits could be anticipated as the result of factors such as the estimated profitability of the investee or the relationship being established between the two companies. In this case, the additional payment is attributed to an intangible future value generally referred to as *goodwill* rather than to any specific investee asset or liability. For example, in a recent annual report, Ameritech Corporation disclosed that its long-term investment in Tele Danmark, accounted for under the equity method, includes goodwill of approximately $1.4 billion.

As an illustration, assume that Big Company is negotiating the acquisition of 30 percent of the outstanding shares of Little Company. Little's balance sheet reports assets of $500,000 and

---

[9] Although encountered less frequently, investments can be purchased at a cost that is less than the underlying book value of the investee. Accounting for this possibility is explored in later chapters.

liabilities of $300,000 for a net book value of $200,000. After investigation, Big determines that Little's equipment is undervalued in the company's financial records by $60,000. One of its patents is also undervalued, but only by $40,000. By adding these valuation adjustments to Little's book value, Big arrives at an estimated worth for the company's net assets of $300,000. Based on this computation, Big offers $90,000 for a 30 percent share of the investee's outstanding stock.

Book value of Little Company (assets minus liabilities [or stockholders' equity])	$200,000
Undervaluation of equipment	60,000
Undervaluation of patent	40,000
Value of net assets	$300,000
Portion being acquired	30%
Acquisition price	$ 90,000

Although Big's purchase price is in excess of the proportionate share of Little's book value, this additional amount can be attributed to two specific accounts: Equipment and Patents. No part of the extra payment is traceable to any other projected future benefit. Thus, the cost of Big's investment is allocated as follows:

Payment by investor		$90,000
Percentage of book value acquired ($200,000 × 30%)		60,000
Payment in excess of book value		30,000
Excess payment identified with specific assets:		
Equipment ($60,000 undervaluation × 30%)	$18,000	
Patent ($40,000 undervaluation × 30%)	12,000	30,000
Excess payment not identified with specific assets—goodwill		–0–

Of the $30,000 excess payment made by the investor, $18,000 is assigned to the equipment whereas $12,000 is traced to a patent and its undervaluation. No amount of the purchase price is allocated to goodwill.

To take this example one step further, assume that the owners of Little reject Big's proposed $90,000 price. They believe that the value of the company as a going concern is higher than the fair value of its net assets. Because the management of Big believes that valuable synergies will be created through this purchase, the bid price is raised to $125,000 and accepted. This new acquisition price is allocated as follows:

Payment by investor		$125,000
Percentage of book value acquired ($200,000 × 30%)		60,000
Payment in excess of book value		65,000
Excess payment identified with specific assets:		
Equipment ($60,000 undervaluation × 30%)	$18,000	
Patent ($40,000 undervaluation × 30%)	12,000	30,000
Excess payment not identified with specific assets—goodwill		$ 35,000

As seen from this example, *any extra payment that cannot be attributed to a specific asset or liability is assigned to the intangible asset goodwill.* Although the actual purchase price can be computed by a number of different techniques or simply result from negotiations, goodwill is always the excess amount not allocated to identifiable asset or liability accounts.

Under the equity method, the investor enters total cost in a single investment account, regardless of the allocation of any excess purchase price. If all parties accept Big's bid of $125,000, the acquisition is initially recorded at that amount despite the internal assignments made to equipment, patents, and goodwill. The entire $125,000 was paid to acquire this investment, and it is recorded as such.

The Amortization Process

The preceding extra payments were made in connection with specific assets (equipment, patents, and goodwill). Even though the actual dollar amounts are recorded within the investment account, a definite historical cost can be attributed to these assets. With a cost to the investor as well as a specified life, the payment relating to each asset (except goodwill, which will be explained subsequently) should be amortized over an appropriate time period.

Historically, goodwill implicit in equity method investments had been amortized over periods less than or equal to 40 years. However, in June 2001, the FASB approved a major and fundamental change in accounting for goodwill. *SFAS No. 142,* "Goodwill and Other Intangible Assets," states that for fiscal periods beginning December 15, 2001, and after, the useful life for goodwill is considered indefinite. Therefore, no goodwill amortization expense will be allowed in future periods. The change was accounted for prospectively with no retrospective adjustments permitted. Firms continued to amortize existing goodwill for the 2001 fiscal year (prior to the *SFAS 142* effective date) and then discontinued the practice. The unamortized portion of implicit goodwill is carried forward without adjustment until the investment is sold or a permanent decline in value occurs.

In arriving at its decision, the FASB noted that goodwill can maintain its value and can even increase over time. The notion of an indefinite life for goodwill recognizes the argument that amortization of goodwill over an arbitrary period fails to reflect economic reality and therefore does not provide useful information. A primary reason for the presumption of an indefinite life for goodwill relates to the accounting for business combinations (covered in Chapters 2 through 7). The FASB reasoned that goodwill associated with equity method investments should be accounted for in the same manner as goodwill arising from a business combination. One difference, however, is that goodwill arising from a business combination will be subject to annual impairment reviews, whereas goodwill implicit in equity investments will not. Equity method investments will continue to be tested in their entirety for permanent declines in value.

Assume, for illustration purposes, that the equipment has a 10-year remaining life, the patent a 5-year life, and the goodwill an indefinite life. If the straight-line method is used with no salvage value, *the investor's cost* should be amortized initially as follows:[10]

Account	Cost Assigned	Useful Life	Annual Amortization
Equipment	$18,000	10 years	$1,800
Patent	12,000	5 years	2,400
Goodwill	35,000	Indefinite	–0–
Annual expense (for five years until patent cost is completely amortized)			$4,200

In recording this annual expense, Big is reducing a portion of the investment balance in the same way it would amortize the cost of any other asset that had a limited life. Therefore, at the end of the first year, the investor records the following journal entry under the equity method:

Equity in Investee Income	4,200	
Investment in Little Company		4,200
To record amortization of excess payment allocated to equipment and patent.		

---

[10] Unless otherwise stated, all amortization computations are based on the straight-line method with no salvage value.

Because this amortization relates to investee assets, the investor does not establish a specific expense account. Instead, as shown in the previous entry, the expense is recognized through a decrease in the equity income accruing from the investee company.

To illustrate this entire process, assume that Tall Company purchases 20 percent of Short Company for $200,000. Tall can exercise significant influence over the investee; thus, the equity method is appropriately applied. The acquisition is made on January 1, 2007, when Short holds net assets with a book value of $700,000. Tall believes that the investee's building (10-year life) is undervalued within the financial records by $80,000 and equipment with a 5-year life is undervalued by $120,000. Any goodwill established by this purchase is considered to have an indefinite life. During 2007, Short reports a net income of $150,000 and pays a cash dividend at year's end of $60,000.

Tall's three basic journal entries for 2007 pose little problem:

January 1, 2007		
Investment in Short Company	200,000	
Cash		200,000
To record acquisition of 20 percent of the outstanding shares of Short Company.		

December 31, 2007		
Investment in Short Company	30,000	
Equity in Investee Income		30,000
To accrue 20 percent of the 2007 reported earnings of investee ($150,000 × 20%).		
Cash	12,000	
Investment in Short Company		12,000
To record receipt of 2007 cash dividend ($60,000 × 20%).		

An allocation of Tall's $200,000 purchase price must be made to determine whether an additional adjusting entry is necessary to recognize annual amortization associated with the extra payment:

Payment by investor		$200,000
Percentage of 1/1/07 book value ($700,000 × 20%)		140,000
Payment in excess of book value		60,000
Excess payment identified with specific assets:		
Building ($80,000 × 20%)	$16,000	
Equipment ($120,000 × 20%)	24,000	40,000
Excess payment not identified with specific assets—goodwill		$ 20,000

As can be seen, $16,000 of the purchase price is assigned to a building, $24,000 to equipment, with the remaining $20,000 attributed to goodwill. For each asset with a definite useful life, periodic amortization is required.

Asset	Attributed Cost	Useful Life	Annual Amortization
Building	$16,000	10 years	$1,600
Equipment	24,000	5 years	4,800
Goodwill	20,000	Indefinite	–0–
Total for 2007			$6,400

At the end of 2007, Tall must also record the following adjustment in connection with these cost allocations:

Equity in Investee Income	6,400	
Investment in Short Company		6,400
To record 2007 amortization of extra cost of building ($1,600) and equipment ($4,800).		

Although these entries are shown separately here for better explanation, Tall would probably net the income accrual for the year ($30,000) and the amortization ($6,400) to create a single entry increasing the investment and recognizing equity income of $23,600. Thus, the first year return on Tall Company's beginning investment balance (defined as equity earnings/beginning investment balance) is equal to 11.80 percent ($23,600/$200,000).

ELIMINATION OF UNREALIZED GAINS IN INVENTORY[11]

Many equity acquisitions establish ties between companies to facilitate the direct purchase and sale of inventory items. Such intercompany transactions can occur either on a regular basis or only sporadically. For example, The Coca-Cola Company recently disclosed that syrup and concentrate sales of $5.2 billion were made to its 36 percent-owned investee Coca-Cola Enterprises, Inc.

Regardless of their frequency, inventory sales between investor and investee necessitate special accounting procedures to ensure proper timing of revenue recognition. An underlying principle of accounting is that "revenues are not recognized until earned . . . and revenues are considered to have been earned when the entity has substantially accomplished what it must do to be entitled to the benefits represented by the revenues."[12] In the sale of inventory to an unrelated party, recognition of revenue is normally not in question; substantial accomplishment is achieved when the exchange takes place unless special terms are included in the contract.

Unfortunately, the earning process is not so clearly delineated in sales made between related parties. *Because of the relationship between investor and investee, the seller of the goods is said to retain a partial stake in the inventory for as long as it is held by the buyer.* Thus, the earning process is not considered complete at the time of the original sale. For proper accounting, income recognition must be deferred until substantial accomplishment is proven. Consequently, when the investor applies the equity method, reporting of the related profit on intercompany transfers is delayed until the ultimate disposition of the goods by the buyer. When the inventory is eventually consumed within operations or resold to an unrelated party, the original sale is culminated and the gross profit is fully recognized.

In accounting, transactions between related companies are identified as either *downstream* or *upstream. Downstream transfers* refer to the investor's sale of an item to the investee. Conversely, an *upstream sale* describes one that the investee makes to the investor (see Exhibit 1.2). *Although the direction of intercompany sales does not affect reported equity method balances for investments when significant influence exists, it has definite consequences when financial control requires the consolidation of financial statements, as discussed in Chapter 5.* Therefore, these two types of intercompany sales are examined separately even at this introductory stage.

Downstream Sales of Inventory

Assume that Big Company owns a 40 percent share of Little Company and accounts for this investment through the equity method. In 2007, Big sells inventory to Little at a price of $50,000. This figure includes a markup of 30 percent, or $15,000. By the end of 2007, Little

---

[11] Unrealized gains can involve the sale of items other than inventory. The intercompany transfer of depreciable fixed assets and land is discussed in a later chapter.

[12] FASB, *Statement of Financial Accounting Concepts No. 6,* "Recognition and Measurement in Financial Statements of Business Enterprises" (Stamford, Conn.: December 1984), para. 83.

EXHIBIT 1.2

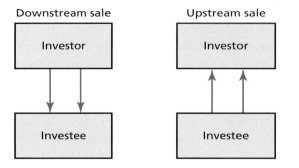

has sold $40,000 of these goods to outside parties while retaining $10,000 in inventory for sale during the subsequent year.

The investor has made downstream sales to the investee. In applying the equity method, recognition of the related profit must be delayed until the buyer disposes of these goods. Although total intercompany transfers amounted to $50,000 in 2007, $40,000 of this merchandise has already been resold to outsiders, thereby justifying the normal reporting of profits. For the $10,000 still in the investee's inventory, the earning process is not finished. In computing equity income, this portion of the intercompany gain must be deferred until the goods are disposed of by Little.

The markup on the original sale was 30 percent of the transfer price; therefore, Big's profit associated with these remaining items is $3,000 ($10,000 × 30%). *However, because only 40 percent of the investee's stock is being held, just $1,200 ($3,000 × 40%) of this gain is unearned.* Big's ownership percentage reflects the intercompany portion of the gain. The total $3,000 gross profit within the ending inventory balance is not the amount deferred. Rather, 40 percent of that gain is viewed as the currently unrealized figure.

Remaining Ending Inventory	Gross Profit Percentage	Gain in Ending Inventory	Investor Ownership Percentage	Unrealized Intercompany Gain
$10,000	30%	$3,000	40%	$1,200

After calculating the appropriate deferral, the investor decreases current equity income by $1,200 to reflect the unearned portion of the intercompany gain. This procedure temporarily removes this portion of the profit from the books of the investor in 2007 until the inventory is disposed of by the investee in 2008. Big accomplishes the actual deferral through the following year-end journal entry:

Deferral of Unrealized Gain

Equity in Investee Income	1,200	
Investment in Little Company		1,200
To defer unrealized gain on sale of inventory to Little Company.		

In the subsequent year, when this inventory is eventually consumed by Little or sold to unrelated parties, the deferral is no longer needed. The earning process is complete and Big should recognize the $1,200. By merely reversing the preceding deferral entry, the accountant succeeds in moving the investor's profit into the appropriate time period. Recognition shifts from the year of transfer to the year in which the earning process is substantially accomplished.

Subsequent Realization of Intercompany Gain

Investment in Little Company	1,200	
Equity in Investee Income		1,200
To recognize income on intercompany sale that has now been earned through sales to outsiders.		

Discussion **Question**

IS THIS REALLY ONLY SIGNIFICANT INFLUENCE?

The Coca-Cola Company accounts for its ownership of Coca-Cola Enterprises (CCE) by use of the equity method as described in this chapter. In 2004, Coca-Cola held approximately 36 percent of the outstanding stock of CCE. According to the financial statements of CCE, the products of The Coca-Cola Company account for approximately 94 percent of total CCE revenues. Moreover, three directors of CCE are executive officers of The Coca-Cola Company. CCE conducts its business primarily under agreements with The Coca-Cola Company. These agreements give the company the exclusive right to market, distribute, and produce beverage products of The Coca-Cola Company in authorized containers in specified territories. These agreements provide The Coca-Cola Company with the ability, in its sole discretion, to establish prices, terms of payment, and other terms and conditions for the purchase of concentrates and syrups from The Coca-Cola Company.

If Coca-Cola acquires approximately 14 percent more of CCE, a majority of the stock will be held so that consolidation becomes a requirement. However, given the size of the present ownership and the dependence that CCE has on Coca-Cola for products and marketing, does Coca-Cola truly have no more than "the ability to exercise significant influence over the operating and financial policies" of CCE? Does the equity method fairly represent the relationship that exists? Or does Coca-Cola actually control CCE despite the level of ownership, and should consolidation be required? Currently, the FASB is reexamining the boundary between the application of the equity method and consolidation. Should the rules be rewritten so that Coca-Cola must consolidate CCE rather than use the equity method? If so, at what level of ownership would the equity method no longer be appropriate?

Upstream Sales of Inventory

Unlike consolidated financial statements (see Chapter 5), the equity method reports upstream sales of inventory in the same manner as downstream sales. Hence, unrealized gains remaining in ending inventory are deferred until the items are used or sold to unrelated parties. To illustrate, assume that Big Company once again owns 40 percent of Little Company. During the current year, Little sells merchandise costing $40,000 to Big for $60,000. At the end of the fiscal period, Big still retains $15,000 of these goods. Little reports net income of $120,000 for the year.

To reflect the basic accrual of the investee's earnings, Big records the following journal entry at the end of this year:

Income Accrual

Investment in Little Company	48,000	
Equity in Investee Income		48,000
To accrue income from 40 percent owned investee ($120,000 × 40%).		

The amount of the gain remaining unrealized at year-end is computed using the markup of $33\frac{1}{3}$ percent of the sales price ($20,000/$60,000):

Remaining Ending Inventory	Gross Profit Percentage	Gain in Ending Inventory	Investor Ownership Percentage	Unrealized Intercompany Gain
$15,000	33⅓%	$5,000	40%	$2,000

Based on this calculation, a second entry is required of the investor at year-end. Once again, a deferral of the unrealized gain created by the intercompany transfer is necessary for proper timing of income recognition. *Under the equity method for investments with significant influence, the direction of the sale between the investor and investee (upstream or downstream) has no effect on the final amounts reported in the financial statements.*

Deferral of Unrealized Gain

Equity in Investee Income	2,000	
Investment in Little Company		2,000
To defer recognition of intercompany unrealized gain until inventory is used or sold to unrelated parties.		

After the adjustment, Big, the investor, reports earnings from this equity investment of $46,000 ($48,000 − $2,000). The income accrual is reduced because a portion of the intercompany gross profit is considered unrealized. When the investor eventually consumes or sells the $15,000 in merchandise, the preceding journal entry is reversed. In this way, the effects of the gain are reported in the proper accounting period when the gain is earned by sales to an outside party.

In an upstream sale, the investor's own inventory account contains the unrealized gain. The previous entry, though, defers recognition of this profit by decreasing Big's investment account rather than the inventory balance. *APB Accounting Interpretation No. 1 of APB Opinion 18,* "Intercompany Profit Eliminations under Equity Method," November 1971, permits the direct reduction of the investor's inventory balance as a means of accounting for this unrealized gain. Although this alternative is acceptable, decreasing the investment remains the traditional approach for deferring unrealized gains, even for upstream sales.

Whether upstream or downstream, the investor's sales and purchases are still reported as if the transactions were conducted with outside parties. Only the unrealized gain is deferred, and that amount is adjusted solely through the equity income account. Furthermore, since the companies are not consolidated, the investee's reported balances are not altered at all to reflect the nature of these sales/purchases. Obviously, readers of the financial statements need to be made aware of the inclusion of these amounts in the income statement. Thus, the FASB issued *Statement No. 57,* "Related Party Disclosures," in March 1982; it required reporting companies to disclose certain information about related-party transactions. These disclosures include the nature of the relationship, a description of the transactions, the dollar amounts of the transactions, and amounts due to or from any related parties at year-end.

Decision Making and the Equity Method

It is important to realize that business decisions, including equity investments, typically involve the assessment of a wide range of consequences. For example, managers frequently are very interested in how financial statements report effects of their decisions. This attention to financial reporting effects of business decisions arises because measurements of financial performance often affect the following:

- The firm's ability to raise capital.
- Managerial compensation.
- The ability to meet debt covenants and future interest rates.
- Managers' reputations.

Managers are also keenly aware that measures of earnings per share can strongly affect investors' perceptions of the underlying value of their firms' publicly traded stock. Consequently, prior to making investment decisions, firms will study and assess the prospective effects of applying the equity method on the income reported in financial statements. Additionally, such analyses of prospective reported income effects can influence firms regarding the degree of influence they wish to have or even on the decision of whether to invest. For example, managers could have a required projected rate of return on an initial investment. In such cases, an analysis of projected income will be made to assist in setting an offer price.

For example, Investmor Co. is examining a potential 25 percent equity investment in Marco that will provide a significant level of influence. Marco projects an annual income of $300,000 for the near future. Marco's book value is $450,000, and it has an unrecorded newly developed technology appraised at $200,000 with an estimated useful life of 10 years.

In considering offer prices for the 25 percent investment in Marco, Investmor projects equity earnings as follows:

Projected income (25% × $300,000). $75,000
Excess patent amortization ([25% × 200,000]/10 years) . . . . (5,000)
      Annual expected equity in Marco earnings $70,000

Investmor's required first year rate of return (before tax) on these types of investments is 20 percent. Therefore, to meet the first year rate of return requirement indicates a maximum price of $350,000 ($70,000/20% = $350,000). If the shares are publicly traded (leaving the firm a "price taker"), such income projections can assist in making a recommendation to wait for share prices to move to make the investment attractive.

Criticisms of the Equity Method

In the past several decades since *APB Opinion 18,* thousands of business firms have accounted for their investments using the equity method. Recently, however, the equity method has come under criticism for the following:

- Emphasizing the 20–50 percent of voting stock in determining significant influence versus control.
- Allowing off-balance sheet financing.
- Potentially biasing performance ratios.

The guidelines for the equity method suggest that a 20–50 percent ownership of voting shares indicates significant influence that falls short of control. But can one firm exert "control" over another firm absent an interest of more than 50 percent? Clearly, if one firm controls another, consolidation is the appropriate financial reporting technique. However, over the years, firms have learned ways to control other firms despite owning less than 50 percent of voting shares. For example, contracts across companies can limit one firm's ability to act without permission of the other. Such contractual control can be seen in debt arrangements, long-term sales and purchase agreements, and agreements concerning board membership. As a result, control is exerted through a variety of contractual arrangements. For financial reporting purposes, however, if ownership is 50 percent or less, a firm can argue that control technically does not exist.

In contrast to consolidated financial reports, when applying the equity method, the investee's assets and liabilities are not combined with the investor's amounts. Instead, the investor's balance sheet reports a single amount for the investment and the income statement reports a single amount for its equity in the earnings of the investee. If consolidated, the assets, liabilities, revenues, and expenses of the investee are combined and reported in the body of the investor's financial statements.

Thus, for those companies wishing to actively manage their reported balance sheet numbers, the equity method provides an effective means. By keeping its ownership of voting shares below 50 percent, a company can technically meet the rules for applying the equity method for its investments and at the same time report investee assets and liabilities "off balance sheet." As a result, relative to consolidation, a firm employing the equity method will report smaller values for assets and liabilities. Consequently, higher rates of return for its assets and sales, as well as lower debt-to-equity ratios, could result. For example, *Accounting Horizons* recently discussed Coca-Cola's application of the equity method as follows:

> Even today, if Coca-Cola consolidates its equity method investments in which it owns more than 40 percent of the outstanding voting stock, Coke's total liabilities increase by almost 300 percent, substantially raising its debt-to-equity ratio from 1.24 to 4.79. Media reports indicate that the debt-rating agencies actually calculate Coke's ratios on a pro forma basis assuming consolidation.[13]

---

[13] A. Hartgraves and G. Benston, "The Evolving Accounting Standards for Special Purpose Entities and Consolidations," *Accounting Horizons,* September 2002.

On the surface, it appears that firms can avoid balance sheet disclosure of debts by maintaining investments at less that 50 percent ownership. However, *APB 18* requires "summarized information as to assets, liabilities, and results of operations of the investees to be presented in the notes or in separate statements, either individually or in groups, as appropriate." Therefore, supplementary information could be available under the equity method that would not be separately identified in consolidation. Nonetheless, some companies have contractual provisions (e.g., debt covenants, managerial compensation agreements) based on ratios in the main body of the financial statements. Meeting the provisions of such contracts could provide managers strong incentives to maintain technical eligibility to use the equity method rather than full consolidation.

Summary

1. The equity method of accounting for an investment reflects the close relationship that could exist between an investor and an investee. More specifically, this approach is applied whenever the owner achieves the ability to apply significant influence to the investee's operating and financial decisions. Significant influence is presumed to exist at the 20 to 50 percent ownership level. However, the accountant must evaluate each situation, regardless of the percentage of ownership, to determine whether this ability is actually present.

2. To mirror the relationship between the companies, the equity method requires the investor to accrue income when earned by the investee. In recording this profit or loss, the investor separately reports items such as extraordinary gains and losses as well as prior period adjustments to highlight their nonrecurring nature. Dividend payments decrease the owners' equity of the investee company; therefore, the investor reduces the investment account when collected.

3. When acquiring capital stock, an investor often pays an amount that exceeds the underlying book value of the investee company. For accounting purposes, such excess payments must be identified with either specific assets and liabilities (such as land or buildings) or allocated to an intangible asset referred to as *goodwill*. The investor then amortizes each assigned cost (except for any amount attributed to land or goodwill) over the expected useful lives of the assets and liabilities. This amortization reduces the amount of equity income being reported.

4. If the investor sells the entire investment or any portion, the equity method is applied consistently until the date of disposal. A gain or loss is computed based on the adjusted book value at that time. Remaining shares are accounted for by means of either the equity method or the fair-value method, depending on the investor's subsequent ability to significantly influence the investee.

5. Inventory (or other assets) can be transferred between investor and investee. Because of the relationship between the two companies, the equity income accrual should be reduced to defer the intercompany portion of any markup included on these transfers until the items are either sold to outsiders or consumed. Thus, the amount of intercompany gain in ending inventory decreases the amount of equity income being recognized in the current period although this effect is subsequently reversed.

Comprehensive Illustration

(*Estimated Time: 30 to 50 Minutes*) Every chapter in this textbook concludes with an illustration designed to assist students in tying together the essential elements of the material presented. After a careful reading of each chapter, attempt to work through the comprehensive problem. Then review the solution that follows the problem, noting the handling of each significant accounting issue.

PROBLEM

Part A

On January 1, 2006, Big Company pays $70,000 for a 10 percent interest in Little Company. On that date, Little has a book value of $600,000, although equipment, which has a five-year life, is undervalued by $100,000 on its books. Little Company's stock is closely held by a few investors and is traded only infrequently. Because fair values are not readily available on a continuing basis, the investment account is appropriately maintained at cost.

On January 1, 2007, Big acquires an additional 30 percent of Little Company for $264,000. This second purchase provides Big the ability to exert significant influence over Little. At the time of this transaction, Little's equipment with a four-year life was undervalued by only $80,000.

During these two years, Little reported the following operational results:

Year	Net Income	Cash Dividends Paid
2006	$210,000	$110,000
2007	250,000	100,000

Additional Information

- Cash dividends are always paid on July 1 of each year.
- Any goodwill is considered to have an indefinite life.

Required:

a. What income did Big originally report for 2006 in connection with this investment?

b. On comparative financial statements for 2006 and 2007, what figures should Big report in connection with this investment?

Part B (This problem is a continuation of Part A)

In 2008, Little Company reports $400,000 in income from continuing operations plus a $60,000 extraordinary gain. The company pays a $120,000 cash dividend. During this fiscal year, Big sells inventory costing $80,000 to Little for $100,000. Little continues to hold 30 percent of this merchandise at the end of 2008. Big maintains 40 percent ownership of Little throughout the period.

Required:

Prepare all necessary journal entries for Big for the year of 2008.

SOLUTION

Part A

a. Big Company accounts for its investment in Little Company at cost during 2006. Since Big held only 10 percent of the outstanding shares, significant influence was apparently not present. Because the stock is not actively traded, fair values are not available and the investment remains at cost. Therefore, the investor records only the $11,000 ($110,000 × 10%) received in dividends as income in the original financial reporting for that year.

b. To make comparative reports consistent, a change to the equity method is recorded retrospectively. Therefore, when the ability to exert significant influence over the operations of Little is established on January 1, 2007, both Big's 2006 and 2007 financial statements must reflect the equity method.

Big first evaluates the initial purchase of Little's stock to determine whether either goodwill or incremental asset values need be reflected within the equity method procedures.

Purchase of 10 Percent of Voting Stock on January 1, 2006

Payment by investor	$70,000
Percentage of book value acquired ($600,000 × 10%)	60,000
Payment in excess of book value	10,000
Excess payment identified with specific assets:	
Equipment ($100,000 × 10%)	10,000
Excess payment not identified with specific assets—goodwill	–0–

As shown here, the $10,000 excess payment was made in recognition of the undervaluation of Little's equipment. This asset had a useful life at that time of five years; thus, the investor records amortization expense of $2,000 each year.

A similar calculation must be carried out for Big's second stock purchase:

Purchase of 30 Percent of Voting Stock on January 1, 2007

Payment by investor	$264,000
Percentage of book value* acquired ($700,000 × 30%)	210,000
Payment in excess of book value	54,000
Excess payment identified with specific assets:	
Equipment ($80,000 × 30%)	24,000
Excess payment not identified with specific assets—goodwill	$ 30,000

*Little's book value on January 1, 2007, is computed by adding the 2006 net income of $210,000 less dividends paid of $110,000 to the previous book value of $600,000.

In this second acquisition, $24,000 of the payment is attributable to the undervalued equipment with $30,000 assigned to goodwill. Because the equipment now has only a four-year remaining life, annual amortization of $6,000 is appropriate ($24,000/4).

After the additional shares are acquired on January 1, 2007, Big's financial records for 2006 must be retrospectively restated as if the equity method had been applied from the date of the initial investment.

Financial Reporting—2006

Equity in Investee Income (income statement)	
Income reported by Little	$210,000
Big's ownership	10%
Accrual for 2006	$ 21,000
Less: Equipment amortization (first purchase)	(2,000)
Equity in investee income—2006	$ 19,000
Investment in Little (balance sheet)	
Cost of first acquisition	$ 70,000
2006 Equity in investee income (above)	19,000
Less: Dividends received ($110,000 × 10%)	(11,000)
Investment in Little—12/31/06	$ 78,000

Financial Reporting—2007

Equity in Investee Income (income statement)	
Income reported by Little	$250,000
Big's ownership	40%
Big's share of Little's reported income	$100,000
Less amortization expense:	
Equipment (first purchase)	(2,000)
Equipment (second purchase)	(6,000)
Equity in investee income—2007	$ 92,000
Investment in Little (balance sheet)	
Book value—12/31/06 (above)	$ 78,000
Cost of 2007 acquisition	264,000
Equity in investee income (above)	92,000
Less: Dividends received ($100,000 × 40%)	(40,000)
Investment in Little—12/31/07	$394,000

Part B

On July 1, 2008, Big receives a $48,000 cash dividend from Little (40% × $120,000). According to the equity method, receipt of this dividend reduces the carrying value of the investment account:

Cash	48,000	
Investment in Little Company		48,000
To record receipt of 2008 dividend from investee.		

Big records no other journal entries in connection with this investment until the end of 2008. At that time, the annual accrual of income as well as the adjustment to record amortization is made (see Part A for computation of expense). The investee's continuing income is reported separately from the extraordinary item.

Investment in Little Company	184,000	
Equity in Investee Income		160,000
Extraordinary Gain of Investee		24,000

To recognize reported income of investee based on a 40 percent
ownership level of $400,000 operating income and $60,000
extraordinary gain.

Equity in Investee Income	8,000	
Investment in Little Company		8,000

To record annual amortization on excess payment made in relation to
equipment ($2,000 from first purchase and $6,000 from second).

Big needs to make only one other equity entry during 2008. Intercompany sales have occurred and a portion of the inventory continues. Therefore, an unrealized gain exists that must Little continues to held be deferred. The markup on the sales price was 20 percent ($20,000/$100,000). Because the investee still possesses $30,000 of this merchandise, the related gain is $6,000 ($30,000 × 20%). However, Big owns only 40 percent of the outstanding stock of Little; thus, the unrealized intercompany gain at year's end is $2,400 ($6,000 × 40%). That amount must be deferred until Little consumes or sells the inventory to unrelated parties in subsequent years.

Equity in Investee Company	2,400	
Investment in Little Company		2,400

To defer unrealized gain on intercompany sale.

Questions

1. A company acquires a rather large investment in another corporation. What criteria determine whether the equity method of accounting should be applied by the investor to this investment?
2. What indicates an investor's ability to significantly influence the decision-making process of an investee?
3. Why does the equity method record dividends received from an investee as a reduction in the investment account, not as dividend income?
4. Jones Company possesses a 25 percent interest in the outstanding voting shares of Sandridge Company. Under what circumstances might Jones decide that the equity method would not be appropriate to account for this investment?
5. Smith, Inc., has maintained an ownership interest in Watts Corporation for a number of years. This investment has been accounted for by means of the equity method. What transactions or events create changes in the Investment in Watts Corporation account being recorded by Smith?
6. Although the equity method is a generally accepted accounting principle (GAAP), recognition of equity income has been criticized. What theoretical problems can be brought up by opponents of the equity method? What managerial incentives exist that could influence a firm's percentage ownership interest in another firm?
7. Because of the acquisition of additional investee shares, an investor can be forced to change from the fair-value method to the equity method. Which procedures are applied to effect this accounting change?
8. Riggins Company accounts for its investment in Bostic Company by means of the equity method. During the past fiscal year, Bostic reported an extraordinary gain on its income statement. How would this extraordinary item affect the financial records of the investor?
9. During the current year, the common stock of the Davis Company suffers a permanent drop in market value. In the past, Davis has made a significant portion of its sales to one customer. This buyer recently announced its decision to make no further purchases from the Davis Company, an action that led to the loss of market value. Hawkins, Inc., owns 35 percent of the outstanding shares of Davis, an investment that is recorded according to the equity method. How would the loss in value affect the financial reporting of this investor?

10. Wilson Company acquired 40 percent of Andrews Company at a bargain price because of losses expected to result from Andrews' failure in marketing several new products. The price paid by Wilson was only $100,000, although Andrews' corresponding book value was much higher. In the first year after acquisition, Andrews lost $300,000. In applying the equity method, how should Wilson account for this loss?

11. In a stock acquisition accounted for by the equity method, a portion of the purchase price often is attributed to goodwill or to specific assets or liabilities. How are these amounts determined at the time of acquisition? How are these amounts accounted for in subsequent periods?

12. Princeton Company holds a 40 percent interest in the outstanding voting stock of Yale Company. On June 19 of the current year, Princeton sells part of this investment. What accounting should Princeton make on June 19? What accounting will Princeton make for the remainder of the current year?

13. What is the difference between downstream and upstream sales? How does this difference impact application of the equity method?

14. How is the unrealized gain on intercompany sales calculated? What effect does an unrealized gain have on the recording of an investment if the equity method is applied?

15. How are intercompany transfers reported in the separate financial statements of an investee if the investor is using the equity method?

Problems

1. When an investor uses the equity method to account for investments in common stock, cash dividends received by the investor from the investee should be recorded as
   a. A deduction from the investor's share of the investee's profits.
   b. Dividend income.
   c. A deduction from the stockholders' equity account, dividends to stockholders.
   d. A deduction from the investment account.
   (AICPA adapted)

2. Which of the following does not an indicate an investor company's ability to significantly influence an investee?
   a. Material intercompany transactions.
   b. The company owns 30 percent of the company but another owner holds the remaining 70 percent.
   c. Interchange of personnel.
   d. Technological dependency.

3. Sisk Company has owned 10 percent of Maust, Inc., for the past several years. This ownership did not allow Sisk to have significant influence over Maust. Recently, Sisk acquired an additional 30 percent of Maust and now has this ability. How will the investor report this change?
   a. A cumulative effect of an accounting change is shown in the current income statement.
   b. No change is recorded; the equity method is used from the date of the new acquisition.
   c. A retroactive adjustment is made to restate all prior years using the equity method.
   d. Sisk has the option of choosing the method to be used to show this change.

4. On January 1, Puckett Company paid $1.6 million for 50,000 shares of Harrison's voting common stock, which represents a 40 percent investment. No allocation to goodwill or other specific account was made. Significant influence over Harrison is achieved by this acquisition. Harrison distributed a dividend of $2 per share during the year and reported net income of $560,000. What is the balance in the Investment in Harrison account found in Puckett's financial records as of December 31?
   a. $1,724,000.
   b. $1,784,000.
   c. $1,844,000.
   d. $1,884,000.

5. In January 2007, Wilkinson, Inc., acquired 20 percent of the outstanding common stock of Bremm, Inc., for $700,000. This investment gave Wilkinson the ability to exercise significant influence over Bremm. Bremm's assets on that date were recorded at $3,900,000 with liabilities of $900,000. Any excess of cost over book value of the investment was attributed to a patent having a remaining useful life of 10 years.

In 2007, Bremm reported net income of $170,000. In 2008, Bremm reported net income of $210,000. Dividends of $70,000 were paid in each of these two years. What is the reported balance of Wilkinson's Investment in Bremm at December 31, 2008?

a. $728,000.

b. $748,000.

c. $756,000.

d. $776,000.

6. Ace purchases 40 percent of Baskett Company on January 1 for $500,000. Although Ace did not use it, this acquisition gave Ace the ability to apply significant influence to Baskett's operating and financing policies. Baskett reports assets on that date of $1,400,000 with liabilities of $500,000. One building with a seven-year life is undervalued on Baskett's books by $140,000. Also, Baskett's book value for its trademark (10-year life) is undervalued by $210,000. During the year, Baskett reports net income of $90,000 while paying dividends of $30,000. What is the Investment in Baskett balance in Ace's financial records as of December 31?

a. $504,000.

b. $507,600.

c. $513,900.

d. $516,000.

7. Goldman Company reports net income of $140,000 each year and pays an annual cash dividend of $50,000. The company holds net assets of $1,200,000 on January 1, 2006. On that date, Wallace purchases 40 percent of the outstanding stock for $600,000, which gives it the ability to significantly influence Goldman. At the purchase date, the excess of Wallace's cost over its proportionate share of Goldman's book value was assigned to goodwill. On December 31, 2008, what is the Investment in Goldman balance in Wallace's financial records?

a. $600,000.

b. $660,000.

c. $690,000.

d. $708,000.

8. Perez, Inc., owns 25 percent of Senior, Inc. During 2007, Perez sold goods with a 40 percent gross profit to Senior. Senior sold all of these goods in 2007. How should Perez report the effect of the intercompany sale on its 2007 income statement?

a. Sales and cost of goods sold should be reduced by the intercompany sales.

b. Sales and cost of goods sold should be reduced by 25 percent of the intercompany sales.

c. Investment income should be reduced by 25 percent of the gross profit on intercompany sales.

d. No adjustment is necessary.

9. Panner, Inc., owns 30 percent of Watkins and applies the equity method. During the current year, Panner buys inventory costing $54,000 and then sells it to Watkins for $90,000. At the end of the year, Watkins still holds only $20,000 of merchandise. What amount of unrealized gain must Panner defer in reporting this investment on the equity method?

a. $2,400.

b. $4,800.

c. $8,000.

d. $10,800.

10. Alex, Inc., buys 40 percent of Steinbart Company on January 1, 2007, for $530,000. The equity method of accounting is to be used. Steinbart's net assets on that date were $1.2 million. Any excess of cost over book value is attributable to a trade name with a 20-year remaining life. Steinbart immediately begins supplying inventory to Alex as follows:

Year	Cost to Steinbart	Transfer Price	Amount Held by Alex at Year-End (at Transfer Price)
2007	$70,000	$100,000	$25,000
2008	96,000	150,000	45,000

Inventory held at the end of one year by Alex is sold at the beginning of the next.

Steinbart reports net income of $80,000 in 2007 and $110,000 in 2008 while paying $30,000 in dividends each year. What is the equity income in Steinbart to be reported by Alex in 2008?

a. $34,050.

b. $38,020.

c. $46,230.

d. $51,450.

11. On January 3, 2007, Haskins Corporation acquired 40 percent of the outstanding common stock of Clem Company for $990,000. This acquisition gave Haskins the ability to exercise significant influence over the investee. The book value of the acquired shares was $790,000. Any excess cost over the underlying book value was assigned to a patent that was undervalued on Clem's balance sheet. This patent has a remaining useful life of 10 years. For the year ended December 31, 2007, Clem reported net income of $260,000 and paid cash dividends of $80,000. At December 31, 2007, what should Haskins report as its investment in Clem?

12. On January 1, 2007, Alison, Inc., paid $60,000 for a 40 percent interest in Holister Corporation. This investee had assets with a book value of $200,000 and liabilities of $75,000. A patent held by Holister having a $5,000 book value was actually worth $20,000. This patent had a six-year remaining life. Any further excess cost associated with this acquisition was attributed to goodwill. During 2007, Holister earned income of $30,000 and paid dividends of $10,000. In 2008, it had income of $50,000 and dividends of $15,000.

Assuming that Alison has the ability to significantly influence Holister's operations, what balance should appear in the Investment in Holister account as of December 31, 2008?

13. On January 1, 2007, Ruark Corporation acquired a 40 percent interest in Batson, Inc., for $210,000. On that date, Batson's balance sheet disclosed net assets of $360,000. During 2007, Batson reported net income of $80,000 and paid cash dividends of $25,000. Ruark sold inventory costing $30,000 to Batson during 2007 for $40,000. Batson used all of this merchandise in its operations during 2007. Make all of Ruark's 2007 journal entries to apply the equity method to this investment.

14. Waters, Inc., acquires 10 percent of Denton Corporation on January 1, 2007, for $210,000 although the book value of Denton on that date was $1,700,000. Denton held land that was undervalued on its accounting records by $100,000. During 2007, Denton earned a net income of $240,000 while paying cash dividends of $90,000. On January 1, 2008, Waters purchased an additional 30 percent of Denton for $600,000. Denton's land is still undervalued on that date, but then by $120,000. Any additional excess cost was attributable to a trademark with a 10-year life for the first purchase and a 9-year life for the second. The initial 10 percent investment had been maintained at cost because fair values were not readily available. The equity method will now be applied. During 2008, Denton reported income of $300,000 and distributed dividends of $110,000. Prepare all of the 2008 journal entries for Waters.

15. Tiberand, Inc., sold $150,000 in inventory to Schilling Company during 2007 for $225,000. Schilling resold $105,000 of this merchandise in 2007 with the remainder to be disposed of during 2008. Assuming that Tiberand owns 25 percent of Schilling and applies the equity method, what journal entry is recorded at the end of 2008 to defer the unrealized gain?

16. Hager holds 30 percent of the outstanding shares of Jenkins and appropriately applies the equity method of accounting. Excess cost amortization (related to a patent) associated with this investment amounts to $9,000 per year. For 2007, Jenkins reports earnings of $80,000 and pays cash dividends of $30,000. During that year, Jenkins acquired inventory for $50,000, which it then sold to Hager for $80,000. At the end of 2007, Hager continues to hold merchandise with a transfer price of $40,000.

a. What Equity in Investee Income should Hager report for 2007?

b. How will the intercompany transfer affect Hager's reporting in 2008?

c. If Hager had sold the inventory to Jenkins, how would the answers to (a) and (b) have changed?

17. On January 1, 2006, Monroe, Inc., purchased 10,000 shares of Brown Company for $250,000, giving Monroe 10 percent ownership of Brown. On January 1, 2007, Monroe purchased an additional 20,000 shares (20 percent) for $590,000. This latest purchase gave Monroe the ability to apply significant influence over Brown. Assume that no goodwill is involved in either acquisition and the original 10 percent investment was categorized as an available-for-sale security.

Brown reports net income and dividends as follows. These amounts are assumed to have occurred evenly throughout these years.

	Net Income	Cash Dividends (paid quarterly)
2006	$350,000	$100,000
2007	480,000	110,000
2008	500,000	120,000

On July 1, 2008, Monroe sells 2,000 shares of this investment for $46 per share, thus reducing its interest from 30 to 28 percent. However, the company retains the ability to significantly influence Brown. What amounts appear in Monroe's 2008 income statement?

18. Collins, Inc., purchases 10 percent of Merton Corporation on January 1, 2007, for $345,000 and classifies the investment as an available-for-sale security. Collins acquires an additional 15 percent of Merton on January 1, 2008, for $580,000. The equity method of accounting has now become appropriate for this investment. No intercompany sales have occurred.

    a. How does Collins initially determine the income to be reported in 2007 in connection with its ownership of Merton?

    b. What factors should have influenced Collins in its decision to apply the equity method in 2008?

    c. What factors could have prevented Collins from adopting the equity method after this second purchase?

    d. What is the objective of the equity method of accounting?

    e. What criticisms have been leveled at the equity method?

    f. In comparative statements for 2007 and 2008, how would Collins determine the income to be reported in 2007 in connection with its ownership of Merton? Why is this accounting appropriate?

    g. How is the allocation of Collins's acquisition payments made?

    h. If Merton pays a cash dividend, what impact does it have on the financial records of Collins under the equity method? Why is this accounting appropriate?

    i. On financial statements for 2008, what amounts are included in Collins's Investment in Merton account? What amounts are included in Collins's Equity in Income of Merton account?

19. Parrot Corporation holds a 42 percent ownership of Sunrise, Inc. The equity method is being applied. No goodwill or other allocation occurred in the purchase of this investment. During 2007, intercompany inventory transfers were made between the two companies. A portion of this merchandise was not resold until 2008. During 2008, additional transfers were made.

    a. What is the difference between upstream transfers and downstream transfers?

    b. How does the direction of an intercompany transfer (upstream versus downstream) affect the application of the equity method?

    c. How is the intercompany unrealized gain computed in applying the equity method?

    d. How should Parrot compute the amount of equity income to be recognized in 2007? What entry is made to record this income?

    e. How should Parrot compute the amount of equity income to be recognized in 2008?

    f. If none of the transferred inventory had remained at the end of 2007, how would these transfers have affected the application of the equity method?

    g. How do these intercompany transfers affect Sunrise's financial reporting?

20. Several years ago, Einstein, Inc., bought 40 percent of the outstanding voting stock of Brooks Company. The equity method is appropriately applied. On August 1 of the current year, Einstein sold a portion of these shares.

    a. How does Einstein compute the book value of this investment on August 1 to determine its gain or loss on the sale?

    b. How should Einstein account for this investment after August 1?

    c. If Einstein retains only a 2 percent interest in Brooks so that virtually no influence is held, what figures appear in the investor's income statement for the current year?

    d. If Einstein retains only a 2 percent interest in Brooks so that virtually no influence is held, does the investor have to retroactively adjust any previously reported figures?

21. Russell owns 30 percent of the outstanding stock of Thacker and has the ability to significantly influence the investee's operations and decision making. On January 1, 2007, the balance in the Investment in Thacker account is $335,000. Amortization associated with this acquisition is $9,000

per year. In 2007, Thacker earns an income of $90,000 and pays cash dividends of $30,000. Previously, in 2006, Thacker had sold inventory costing $24,000 to Russell for $40,000. Russell consumed all but 25 percent of this merchandise during 2006. It used the remainder during the first few weeks of 2007. Additional sales were made to Russell in 2007; inventory costing $28,000 was transferred at a price of $50,000. Of this total, 40 percent was not consumed until 2008.

a. What amount of income would Russell recognize in 2007 from its ownership interest in Thacker?

b. What is the balance in the Investment in Thacker account at the end of 2007?

22. On January 1, 2007, Ace acquires 15 percent of Zach's outstanding common stock for $52,000 and classifies the investment as an available-for-sale security. On January 1, 2008, Ace buys an additional 10 percent of Zach for $43,800. This second purchase gives Ace the ability to influence Zach's decision making significantly.

   During 2007 and 2008, Zach reports the following:

	Income	Dividends	Market Value
2007	$ 80,000	$30,000	$ 60,000
2008	100,000	40,000	117,000

In each purchase, Ace attributes any excess of cost over book value to Zach's franchise agreements that had a remaining life of 10 years at January 1, 2007. As of December 31, 2008, Zach reports a net book value of $390,000.

a. On Ace's December 31, 2008, balance sheet, what amount is reported for the Investment in Zach account?

b. What amount of equity income should Ace report for 2008?

c. Prepare the January 1, 2008, journal entries to retroactively adjust the Investment in Zach account to the equity method.

23. Anderson acquires 10 percent of the outstanding voting shares of Barringer on January 1, 2006, for $92,000 and categorizes the investment as an available-for-sale security. An additional 20 percent of the stock is purchased on January 1, 2007, for $210,000, which gives Anderson the ability to significantly influence Barringer. Barringer has a book value of $800,000 at January 1, 2006, and records net income of $180,000 for that year. Barringer paid dividends of $80,000 during 2006. The book values of Barringer's asset and liability accounts are considered as equal to fair values except for a copyright whose value accounted for Anderson's excess cost in each purchase. The copyright had a remaining life of 16 years at January 1, 2006.

   Barringer reports $210,000 of net income during 2007 and $230,000 in 2008. Dividends of $100,000 are paid in each of these years.

a. On comparative income statements issued in 2008 by Anderson for 2006 and 2007, what amounts of income would be reported in connection with the company's investment in Barringer?

b. If Anderson sells its entire investment in Barringer on January 1, 2009, for $400,000 cash, what is the impact on Anderson's income?

c. Assume that Anderson sells inventory to Barringer during 2007 and 2008 as follows:

Year	Cost to Anderson	Price to Barringer	Year-End Balance (at Transfer Price)
2007	$35,000	$50,000	$20,000 (sold in following year)
2008	33,000	60,000	40,000 (sold in following year)

   What amount of equity income should Anderson recognize for the year 2008?

24. Smith purchases 5 percent of Barker's outstanding stock on October 1, 2006, for $7,475. An additional 10 percent of Barker is acquired for $14,900 on July 1, 2007. Both of these purchases were accounted for as available-for-sale investments. A final 20 percent is purchased on December 31, 2008, for $34,200. With this final acquisition, Smith achieves the ability to significantly influence the decision-making process of Barker.

   Barker has a book value of $100,000 as of January 1, 2006. Information follows concerning the operations of this company for the 2006–08 period. Assume that all income was earned uniformly in each year. Assume that one-fourth of the total annual dividends are paid at the end of each calendar quarter.

Year	Reported Income	Dividends
2006	$20,000	$ 8,000
2007	30,000	16,000
2008	24,000	9,000

On Barker's financial records, the book values of all assets and liabilities are the same as their fair values. Any excess cost from either purchase relates to identifiable intangible assets. For each purchase, the excess cost is amortized over 15 years. Amortization for a portion of a year should be based on months.

a. On comparative income statements issued in 2009 for the years of 2006, 2007, and 2008, what would Smith report as its income derived from this investment in Barker?

b. On a balance sheet as of December 31, 2008, what should Smith report as investment in Barker?

25. Hobson acquires 40 percent of the outstanding voting stock of Stokes Company on January 1, 2007, for $210,000 in cash. The book value of Stokes's net assets on that date was $400,000, although one of the company's buildings, with a $60,000 carrying value, was actually worth $100,000. This building had a 10-year remaining life. Stokes owned a royalty agreement with a 20-year remaining life that was undervalued by $85,000.

Stokes sells inventory to Hobson during 2007 with an original cost of $60,000. Stokes sold this merchandise to Hobson at a price of $90,000. Hobson still holds $15,000 (transfer price) of this amount in inventory as of December 31, 2007. These goods are to be sold to outside parties during 2008.

Stokes reports a loss of $60,000 for 2007, $40,000 from continuing operations, and $20,000 from an extraordinary loss. The company still manages to pay a $10,000 cash dividend during the year.

During 2008, Stokes reports a $40,000 net income and distributes a cash dividend of $12,000. Additional inventory sales of $80,000 are made to Hobson during the period. The original cost of the merchandise was $50,000. All but 30 percent of this inventory has been resold to outside parties by the end of the 2008 fiscal year.

Prepare all journal entries for Hobson for 2007 and 2008 in connection with this investment. Assume that the equity method is applied.

26. Penston Company owns 40 percent (40,000 shares) of Scranton, Inc., which was purchased several years ago for $182,000. Since the date of acquisition, the equity method has been properly applied, and the book value of the investment account as of January 1, 2007, is $248,000. Excess patent cost amortization of $12,000 is still being recognized each year. During 2007, Scranton reports net income of $200,000, $320,000 in operating income earned evenly throughout the year, and a $120,000 extraordinary loss incurred on October 1. No dividends were paid during the year. Penston sells 8,000 shares of Scranton on August 1, 2007, for $94,000 in cash. However, Penston does retain the ability to significantly influence the investee.

During the last quarter of 2006, Penston sold $50,000 in inventory (which it had originally purchased for only $30,000) to Scranton. At the end of that fiscal year, Scranton's inventory retained $9,000 (at sales price) of this merchandise, which was subsequently sold in the first quarter of 2007.

On Penston's financial statements for the year ended December 31, 2007, what income effects would be reported from its ownership in Scranton?

27. On July 1, 2006, Abernethy Company acquires 65,000 of the outstanding shares of the Chapman Company for $13 per share. This acquisition gave Abernethy a 25 percent ownership of Chapman and allowed Abernethy to significantly influence the decisions of the investee.

As of July 1, 2006, the investee had assets with a book value of $2 million and liabilities of $400,000. At the time, Chapman held equipment appraised at $120,000 above book value. Company land was valued at $160,000 above book value. The equipment was considered to have an 8-year life with no salvage value. Remaining excess cost is attributable to a copyright with a 15-year remaining life. Depreciation and amortization are computed using the straight-line method.

Chapman follows a policy of paying 50 cents per share as a cash dividend every April 1 and October 1. Chapman's income, earned evenly throughout each year, was $280,000 in 2006, $360,000 in 2007, and $380,000 in 2008.

In addition, Abernethy sold inventory costing $90,000 to Chapman for $150,000 during 2007. Chapman resold $90,000 of this inventory during 2007 and the remaining $60,000 during 2008.

a. Prepare a schedule computing the equity income to be recognized by Abernethy during each of these years.

b. Compute Abernethy's investment balance as of December 31, 2008.

28. On January 1, 2006, Plano Company acquired 8 percent (16,000 shares) of the outstanding voting shares of the Sumter Company for $192,000, an amount equal to the underlying book and fair value of Sumter. Sumter pays a cash dividend to its stockholders each year of $100,000 on September 15. Sumter reports net income of $300,000 in 2006, $360,000 in 2007, $400,000 in 2008, and $380,000 in 2009. Each income figure can be assumed to have been earned evenly throughout its respective year. In addition, the fair value of these 16,000 shares was indeterminate and therefore the investment account remained at cost.

    On January 1, 2008, Plano purchased an additional 32 percent (64,000 shares) of Sumter for $965,750 in cash. This price represented a $50,550 payment in excess of the book value of Sumter's underlying net assets. Plano was willing to make this extra payment because of a recently developed patent held by Sumter with a 15-year remaining life. All other assets were considered appropriately valued on Sumter's books.

    On July 1, 2009, Plano sold 10 percent (20,000 shares) of the outstanding shares of Sumter for $425,000 in cash. Although this interest was sold, Plano maintained the ability to significantly influence the decision-making process of Sumter. Assume that Plano uses a weighted average costing system.

    Prepare the journal entries for Plano for the years of 2006 through 2009.

29. On January 1, 2007, Lake Company acquired 40 percent of the outstanding voting shares of Slide Company for $600,000. On that date, Slide reports assets and liabilities with book values of $1.8 million and $600,000, respectively. A building owned by Slide had an appraised value of $250,000, although it had a book value of only $100,000. This building had a 12-year remaining life and no salvage value. It was being depreciated on the straight-line method.

    Slide generated net income of $250,000 in 2007 and a loss of $100,000 in 2008. In each of these two years, Slide paid a cash dividend of $60,000 to its stockholders.

    During 2007, Slide sold inventory to Lake that had an original cost of $50,000. Slide sold the merchandise to Lake for $80,000. Of this balance, $60,000 was resold to outsiders during 2007, and the remainder was sold during 2008. In 2008, Slide sold inventory to Lake for $150,000. This inventory had cost only $90,000. Lake resold $100,000 of the inventory during 2008 and the rest during 2009.

    For 2007 and then for 2008, compute the equity income to be reported by Lake for external reporting purposes.

Develop Your Skills

EXCEL CASE 1

On January 1, 2007, Acme Co. is considering purchasing a 40 percent ownership interest in PHC Co., a privately held enterprise, for $700,000. PHC predicts its profit will be $185,000 in 2007, projects a 10 percent annual increase in profits in each of the next four years, and expects to pay a steady annual dividend of $30,000 for the foreseeable future. Because PHC has a patent on its books that is undervalued by $375,000, Acme realizes that it will have an additional amortization expense of $15,000 per year over the next 10 years—the patent's estimated useful life. All of PHC's other assets and liabilities have book values that approximate market values.

Required:

1. Using an Excel spreadsheet, set the following values in cells:
   • Acme's cost of investment in PHC.
   • Percentage acquired.
   • First-year PHC reported income.
   • Projected growth rate in income.
   • PHC annual dividends.
   • Annual excess patent amortization.

2. Referring to the values in (1), prepare the following schedules using columns for the years 2007 through 2011.
   • Acme's equity in PHC earnings with rows showing these:
     • Acme's share of PHC reported income.
     • Amortization expense.
     • Acme's Equity in PHC Earnings.

- Acme's Investment in PHC balance with rows showing the following:
    - Beginning balance.
    - Equity earnings.
    - Dividends.
    - Ending balance.
  - Return on beginning investment balance = Equity earnings/Beginning investment balance in each year.
3. Given the preceding values, compute the average of the projected returns on beginning investment balances for the first five years of Acme's investment in PHC. What is the maximum Acme can pay for PHC if it wishes to earn at least a 10 percent average return on beginning investment balance? (*Hint:* Under Excel's Tools heading, use the Solver or Goal Seek capability to produce a 10 percent average return on beginning investment balance by changing the cell that contains Acme's cost of investment in PHC. Excel's Solver should produce an exact answer while Goal Seek should produce a close approximation. You may need to first add in the Solver capability under Excel's Tools heading.)

EXCEL CASE 2

On January 1, Intergen, Inc., invests $200,000 for a 40 percent interest in Ryan, a new joint venture with two other partners each investing $150,000 for 30 percent interests. Intergen plans to sell all of its production to Ryan, which will resell the inventory to retail outlets. The equity partners agree that Ryan will buy inventory only from Intergen.

During the year, Intergen expects to incur costs of $850,000 to produce goods with a final retail market value of $1,200,000. Ryan projects that, during this year, it will resell three-fourths of these goods for $900,000. It should sell the remainder in the following year.

The equity partners plan a meeting to set the price Intergen will charge Ryan for its production. One partner suggests a transfer price of $1,025,000 but is unsure whether it will result in an equitable return across the equity holders. Importantly, Intergen agrees that its total rate of return (including its own operations and its investment in Ryan) should be equal to that of the other investors' return on their investments in Ryan. All agree that Intergen's value including its investment in Ryan is $1,000,000.

Required:

1. Create an Excel spreadsheet analysis showing the following:
    - Projected income statements for Intergen and Ryan. Formulate the statements to do the following:
        - Link Ryan's cost of goods sold to Intergen's sales (use a starting value of $1,025,000 for Intergen's sales).
        - Link Intergen's equity in Ryan's earnings to Ryan's net income (adjusted for Intergen's gross profit rate × Ryan's ending inventory × 40 percent ownership percentage).
        - Be able to change Intergen's sales and see the effects throughout the income statements of Ryan and Intergen. Note that the cost of goods sold for Intergen is fixed.
    - The rate of return for the two 30 percent equity partners on their investment in Ryan.
    - The total rate of return for Intergen based on its $1,000,000 value.

2. What transfer price will provide an equal rate of return for each of the investors in the first year of operation? (*Hint:* Under Excel's Tools heading, use the Goal Seek or Solver capability to produce a zero difference in rates of return across the equity partners by changing the cell that contains Intergen's sales.)

ANALYSIS CASE

Refer to the Web sites www.cokecce.com and www.coca-cola.com.

Required:

Address the following:

1. How does Coca-Cola account for its investment in Coca-Cola Enterprises (CCE)? What are the accounting implications of the method Coca-Cola uses?
2. What criterion does Coca-Cola use to choose the method of accounting for its investment in CCE?
3. Describe the relationship between Coca-Cola and CCE.

4. Calculate the debt-to-equity ratios in the most recent two years for both Coca-Cola and CCE. Does Coca-Cola have the ability to influence the debt levels of CCE?

5. How are Coca-Cola's financials affected by its relationship with CCE? In general, how would Coca-Cola's financials change if it consolidated CCE?

RESEARCH AND COMMUNICATION CASE

BellCo, your client, is interested in making an investment in the equity shares of CellCo and asks your guidance about financial reporting for equity investments. BellCo has frequent and substantial intercompany transactions with CellCo and hopes to be able to significantly influence CellCo's operating and financing decisions through the ownership of its voting shares. BellCo states that because it does not wish to use the equity method, it intends to make sure it purchases less than 20 percent of the outstanding voting shares of CellCo to comply with the technical provisions of *APB No. 18,* "The Equity Method of Accounting for Investments in Common Stock."

Required:

Prepare a memo to BellCo's management that responds to its request for your guidance. Be sure your memo

- Cites appropriate references from *APB No. 18.*
- Identifies the relevant decision parameters for determining the appropriate accounting for an equity investment.
- Comments on BellCo's plan to avoid the equity method by owning less than a 20 percent voting interest.

RESEARCH CASE

FASB *Statement No. 94* states that consolidation is appropriate when one entity has a controlling financial interest in another entity and that the usual condition for a controlling financial interest is ownership of a majority voting interest. But *FASB 94* also notes that in some circumstances, control does not rest with the majority owner—especially when minority owners are contractually provided with approval or veto rights that can restrict the actions of the majority owner. In these cases, the majority owner employs the equity method rather than consolidation. The FASB's Emerging Issues Task Force (EITF) 96-16 provides guidance on these issues.

Required:

Address the following by searching EITF 96-16.

1. How does EITF 96-16 define protective minority rights?
2. How does EITF 96-16 define substantive participating minority rights?
3. What minority rights overcome the presumption that all majority-owned investees should be consolidated?
4. Zee Company buys 60 percent of the voting stock of Bee Company with the remaining 40 percent minority interest held by the former owners of Bee who negotiated the following minority rights:
   - Any new debt above $1,000,000 must be approved by the 40 percent minority shareholders.
   - Any dividends or other cash distributions to owners in excess of customary historical amounts must be approved by the 40 percent minority shareholders.

According to EITF 96-16, what are the issues in determining whether Zee should consolidate Bee or report its investment in Bee under the equity method?

Chapter Two

Consolidation of Financial Information

Financial statements published and distributed to owners, creditors, and other interested parties appear to report the operations and financial position of a single company. In reality, these statements frequently represent a number of separate organizations tied together through common control (a *business combination*). Whenever financial statements represent more than one corporation, we refer to them as *consolidated financial statements*.

Consolidated financial statements are typical in today's business world. Most major organizations, and many smaller ones, hold control over an array of organizations. For example, from 2000 through 2004, Cisco Systems, Inc., reported 45 business acquisitions that now are consolidated in its financial reports. PepsiCo, Inc., as another example, annually consolidates data from a multitude of companies into a single set of financial statements. By gaining control over these companies (often known as *subsidiaries*)—which include among others Pepsi-Cola Company, Tropicana Products, and Frito-Lay—a single business combination and single reporting entity is formed by PepsiCo (the *parent*).

The consolidation of financial information as exemplified by Cisco Systems and PepsiCo is one of the most complex procedures in all of accounting. To comprehend this process completely, the theoretical logic that underlies the creation of a business combination must be understood. Furthermore, a variety of procedural steps must be mastered to ensure that proper accounting is achieved for this single reporting entity. The following coverage introduces both of these aspects of the consolidation process.

Parent	
	Business combination
Subsidiary	

Financial reporting for business combinations has experienced many changes over the past several years, and standard setters plan further modifications. In 2001 the FASB issued *Statement of Financial Accounting Standards 141*, "Business Combinations," and *SFAS 142,* "Goodwill and Other Intangible Assets." One of the most important changes in these documents is the requirement that all business combinations be accounted for using the purchase method, thus effectively eliminating the pooling of interests method.

In 2005, the FASB proposed two new Exposure Drafts, (1) *Business Combinations* and (2) *Consolidated Financial Statements, Including Accounting and Reporting of Noncontrolling Interests in Subsidiaries*. These Exposure Drafts embrace the fair value concept for all business combinations and represent a departure from the fundamental cost principle embraced by the purchase method.

FASB Interpretation No. 46R (revised December 2003), "Consolidation of Variable Interest Entities," an interpretation of *ARB No. 51 (FIN 46R)*, represents further recent changes in accounting for business combinations. *FIN 46R* addresses the consolidation of an entity whose control is established not through voting interests but through other arrangements such as governance agreements and contracts among the various parties with financial interests in the entity. In this chapter we introduce such entities in our discussion of controlling financial interests. Later, in Chapter 6, we include more comprehensive coverage of *FIN 46R*.

In this chapter, we next discuss expansion through corporate takeovers and an overview of the consolidation process. Then we present the purchase method of accounting for business combinations under *SFAS 141* followed by specific coverage of the proposed new rules in the 2005 FASB Exposure Drafts on business combinations and consolidated financial statements. Finally, coverage of pooling of interests is provided in a separate section.

EXPANSION THROUGH CORPORATE TAKEOVERS

Why Do Firms Combine?

A common economic phenomenon is the combining of two or more businesses into a single entity under common management and owner control. During recent decades, the United States and the rest of the world have experienced an enormous number of corporate mergers and takeovers, transactions in which one company gains control over another. According to *Mergers & Acquisitions* (February 2005), the number of business combinations in 2004 totaled 6,919 with a combined market value of $823.5 billion. As indicated by Exhibit 2.1, the magnitude of recent combinations continues to be large.

As with any other economic activity, business combinations can be part of an overall managerial strategy to maximize shareholder value. Shareholders—the owners of the firm—hire managers to direct resources so that the value of the firm grows over time. In this way, owners receive a return on their investment. Successful firms receive substantial benefits through enhanced share value. Importantly, the managers of successful firms also receive substantial

EXHIBIT 2.1
Recent Notable Business Combinations

Acquirer	Target	Cost (in billions)
J.P. Morgan Chase	Bank One	$58.8
Procter & Gamble	Gillette	57.0
Bank of America	FleetBoston Financial	49.3
Comcast	AT&T Broadband	50.0
Sprint	Nextel	35.2
Boston Scientific	Guidant	27.0
Symantec	Veritas	13.5
Kmart	Sears Roebuck	11.5
Oracle	PeopleSoft	10.3
FedEx	Kinko's	2.4

benefits in salaries, especially if their compensation contracts are partly based on stock market performance of the firm's shares.

If the goal of business activity is to maximize the firm's value, in what ways do business combinations help achieve that goal? Clearly, the business community is moving rapidly toward business combinations as a strategy for growth and competitiveness. Size and scale are obviously becoming critical as firms compete in today's markets. If larger firms can be more efficient in delivering goods and services, they gain a competitive advantage and become more profitable for the owners. Increases in scale can produce larger profits from enhanced sales volume despite smaller (more competitive) profit margins. For example, if a combination can integrate successive stages of production and distribution of products, substantial savings can result in coordinating raw material purchases, manufacturing, and delivery. As an example, Ford Motor Co.'s acquisition of Hertz Rental (one of its largest customers) not only enabled Ford to ensure demand for its cars but also allowed Ford to closely coordinate production with the need for new rental cars. Other cost savings resulting from elimination of duplicate efforts, such as data processing and marketing, can make a single entity more profitable than the separate parent and subsidiary had been in the past.

Although no two business combinations are exactly alike, many share one or more of the following characteristics that potentially enhance profitability:

- Vertical integration of one firm's output and another firm's distribution or further processing.
- Cost savings through elimination of duplicate facilities and staff.
- Quick entry for new and existing products into domestic and foreign markets.
- Economies of scale allowing greater efficiency and negotiating power.
- The ability to access financing at more attractive rates. As firms grow in size, negotiating power with financial institutions can grow also.
- Diversification of business risk.

Business combinations also result because many firms seek the continuous expansion of their organizations, often into diversified areas. Acquiring control over a vast network of different businesses has been a strategy utilized by a number of companies (sometimes known as *conglomerates*) for decades. Entry into new industries is immediately available to the parent without having to construct facilities, develop products, train management, or create market recognition. Many corporations have successfully utilized this strategy to produce huge, highly profitable organizations. Unfortunately, others have discovered that the task of managing a widely diverse group of businesses can prove to be a costly learning experience. Even combinations that purportedly take advantage of operating synergies and cost savings often fail if the integration is not managed carefully.[1]

Overall, the primary motivations for many business combinations can be traced to an increasingly competitive environment. Three recent examples of large business combinations provide interesting examples of some distinct motivations to combine: Procter & Gamble and Gillette, Sprint and Nextel, and Symantec and Veritas. Each is discussed briefly in turn.

Procter & Gamble and Gillette

On January 28, 2005, in its largest acquisition to date, Procter & Gamble (P&G) announced an agreement to purchase 100 percent of Gillette Company in a transaction valued at approximately $57 billion. Under the agreement, P&G will issue 0.975 share of its common stock for each share of Gillette common stock. Both P&G and Gillette manufacture and distribute a wide variety of consumer products including many personal care, home cleaning, and food products. Prior to the deal, Gillette and P&G operated in more than 30 and 80 countries, respectively. P&G has expertise in developing, manufacturing, and distributing leadership brands including 16 brands that produce sales of more than $1 billion each. The Gillette acquisition will add five more brands to this category.[2]

---

[1] Mark Sirower, "What Acquiring Minds Need to Know," *The Wall Street Journal—Manager's Journal*, February 22, 1999.

[2] "P&G Acquires The Gillette Company," *PR Newswire—First Call*, January 28, 2005.

Upon completion of the acquisition, P&G plans to utilize its increased size to accelerate market entry for new and existing products. P&G's international operations include marketing and distribution networks in developing markets such as China, Russia, Mexico, Turkey, and other locations. By utilizing existing marketing and distribution capabilities for Gillette products, P&G anticipates sales growth for many Gillette brands. Expected economies of scale from the combination include the ability to negotiate greater value in advertising from broadcasters and other media companies and from suppliers.[3]

Finally, because both P&G and Gillette are primarily consumer product firms, they share many similar business functions. Cost-saving synergies will be available through reducing duplicate costs and creating other efficiencies. In particular, P&G notes in its press release announcing the combination that it "anticipates enrollment reductions of approximately 6,000 employees, or about four percent of the combined workforce of 140,000. Most of these reductions should come from eliminating management overlaps and consolidation of business support functions."[4]

Sprint and Nextel

Sprint Corporation announced in late 2004 that it had agreed to acquire Nextel Communications, Inc., in a transaction valued at $35 billion. The acquisition was only the latest in a series of combination activities in the wireless communications industry. Many viewed Sprint's purchase of Nextel as a competitive response to recent moves by other large national wireless companies. In the past several years, growth by Verizon Wireless (a joint venture between Verizon and Vodaphone) and Cingular (a joint venture between SBC and BellSouth) had produced customer bases of approximately 47 and 42 million, respectively. Recently Cingular increased its market share by acquiring ATT Wireless. With the Nextel acquisition, Sprint is able to rapidly compete for market share with Verizon Wireless and Cingular by adding 15 million customers for a total base of approximately 35 million.

According to Sprint, the combined Sprint Nextel is expected to deliver operating cost and capital investment synergies with an estimated net present value of more than $12 billion. The expected synergies include these:

- Saving operating expenses by reducing the number of cell sites and switches.
- Reducing capital expenditures by extending Sprint's technology to the combined customer base.
- Optimizing customer care, billing, and IT costs by consolidating operations, infrastructure support costs, and overhead.
- Reducing combined sales and marketing costs.
- Obtaining large-volume discounts for equipment, warehousing facilities and procedures, and product distribution.[5]

Beyond cost synergies, research and development resulting in timely new communication service offerings to the market ultimately will determine success in this highly competitive industry. Through business combinations, wireless communications firms not only assemble large amounts of financial resources for development of new technologies but also position themselves for marketing resulting products to more customers. For example, Sprint Nextel's combined capabilities position it to remain competitive with the largest wireless carriers in the industry with enhanced wireless multimedia, Web browsing, and music and data transmission.[6]

Symantec and Veritas

Also in late 2004, Symantec Corporation agreed to buy Veritas Software Corporation for about $13 billion in stock. Under the terms of the agreement, Veritas will emerge as a wholly owned subsidiary of Symantec. After the combination, Symantec shareholders will own

---

[3] "P&G to Buy Gillette for $57B; Stock Merger Would Link Some of the World's Best-Known Household Brands, Could Spur More Deals," *CNN/Money*, January 28, 2005.

[4] "P&G Acquires The Gillette Company," *PR Newswire—First Call*, January 28, 2005.

[5] Sprint Corporation SEC Registration Statement S-4 Amendment No. 1, April 28, 2005.

[6] "Sprint and Nextel to Combine in Merger of Equals," Sprint press release, December 15, 2004.

approximately 60 percent and former Veritas shareholders will own approximately 40 percent of the combined firm.

Symantec, perhaps best known among consumers for its Norton antivirus products, provides a variety of software, appliances, and services designed to secure and manage information technology resources. Veritas delivers products and services for data protection, storage, and application performance management. The business combination signals Symantec's strategy to converge the information security and storage software markets. According to the press release announcing the acquisition, the combined firm is expected to "deliver information security and availability across all platforms, from the desktop to the data center, from consumers and small businesses to large organizations and service providers."[7]

The combined company is expected to generate about $5 billion in revenues, thus positioning itself against other large software competitors such as Microsoft, SAP, and Oracle. The combination further reflects the fact that growth through acquisitions compared to internal growth allows for the rapid marshaling of resources in the highly competitive and fast-paced software development industry.

THE CONSOLIDATION PROCESS

The consolidation of financial information into a single set of statements becomes necessary whenever a single economic entity is created by the business combination of two or more companies. As stated in *Accounting Research Bulletin No. 51* (abbreviated *ARB 51*), "Consolidated Financial Statements," August 1959 (para. 2): "There is a presumption that consolidated statements are more meaningful than separate statements and that they are usually necessary for a fair presentation when one of the companies in the group directly or indirectly has a controlling financial interest in the other companies."

This sentiment was reiterated nearly 30 years later in *Financial Accounting Standards Board Statement No. 94*, "Consolidation of All Majority-Owned Subsidiaries," October 1987 (para. 30): "Consolidated financial statements became common once it was recognized that boundaries between separate corporate entities must be ignored to report the business carried on by a group of affiliated corporations as the economic and financial whole that it actually is."

Thus, in producing financial statements for external distribution, the reporting entity transcends the boundaries of incorporation to encompass all companies for which control is present. Even though the various companies may retain their legal identities as separate corporations, the resulting information is more meaningful to outside parties when consolidated into a single set of financial statements.

To explain the process of preparing consolidated financial statements for a business combination, we address three questions:

- How is a business combination formed?
- What constitutes a controlling financial interest?
- How is the consolidation process carried out?

Business Combinations—Creating a Single Economic Entity

A business combination refers to any set of conditions in which two or more organizations are joined together through common control. *SFAS 141* defines a business combination as follows:

> A *business combination* occurs when an enterprise acquires net assets that constitute a business or equity interests of one or more other enterprises and obtains control over that enterprise or enterprises.

Business combinations are formed by a wide variety of transactions with various formats. For example, each of the following is identified as a business combination although differing

---

[7]"Software Industry Leaders Symantec and Veritas Software to Merge; Combination Reduces Complexity of Securing and Managing Information," *Business Wire*, December 16, 2004.

widely in legal form. In every case, two or more enterprises are being united into a single economic entity so that consolidated financial statements are required.

1. One company obtains the assets, and often the liabilities, of another company in exchange for cash, other assets, liabilities, stock, or a combination of these. The second organization normally dissolves itself as a legal corporation. Thus, only the acquiring company remains in existence, having absorbed the acquired net assets directly into its own operations. Any business combination in which only one of the original companies continues to exist is referred to in legal terms as a *statutory merger*.

2. One company obtains the capital stock of another in exchange for cash, other assets, liabilities, stock, or a combination of these. After gaining control, the acquiring company can decide to transfer all assets and liabilities to its own financial records with the second company being dissolved as a separate corporation.[8] The business combination is, once again, a statutory merger because only one of the companies maintains legal existence. This statutory merger, however, is achieved by obtaining equity securities rather than by buying the target company's assets. Because stock is purchased, the acquiring company must gain 100 percent control of all shares before legally dissolving the subsidiary.

3. Two or more companies transfer either their assets or their capital stock to a newly formed corporation. Both original companies are dissolved, leaving only the new organization in existence. A business combination effected in this manner is a *statutory consolidation*. The use here of the term *consolidation* should not be confused with the accounting meaning of that same word. In accounting, *consolidation* refers to the mechanical process of bringing together the financial records of two or more organizations to form a single set of statements. A statutory consolidation denotes a specific type of business combination in which two or more existing companies are united under the ownership of a newly created company.

4. One company achieves legal control over another by acquiring a majority of voting stock. *Although control is present, no dissolution takes place; each company remains in existence as an incorporated operation.* The National Broadcasting Company (NBC), as an example, continued to retain its legal status as a corporation after being acquired by General Electric Company. Separate incorporation is frequently preferred to take full advantage of any intangible benefits accruing to the acquired company as a going concern. Better utilization of such factors as licenses, trade names, employee loyalty, and the company's reputation can be possible when the subsidiary maintains its own legal identity.

One important aspect of this final type of business combination should be noted. Because the asset and liability account balances are not physically combined as in statutory mergers and consolidations, each company continues to maintain an independent accounting system. To reflect the combination, the acquiring company enters the takeover transaction into its own records by establishing a single investment asset account. However, the newly acquired subsidiary omits any recording of this event; its stock is simply transferred to the parent from the subsidiary's shareholders. Thus, the financial records of the subsidiary are not directly affected by a takeover.

As can be seen, business combinations are created in many distinct forms. Because the specific format is a critical factor in the subsequent consolidation of financial information, Exhibit 2.2 provides an overview of the various combinations.

Control—An Elusive Quality from *ARB 51* to *FIN 46R*

Control Exercised through Voting Interests

ARB 51, as quoted previously, states that consolidated financial statements are usually necessary when one company has a controlling financial interest over another. However, nowhere in the official accounting pronouncements is a "controlling financial interest" actually defined. Traditionally in the United States, control is considered to exist if one company holds more than 50 percent of another company's voting stock. Thus, control has been tied directly to ownership. Control through ownership of a majority of voting shares continues to define the vast

---

[8] Although the acquired company has been legally dissolved, it frequently continues to operate as a separate division within the surviving company's organization.

EXHIBIT 2.2
Business Combinations

Type of Combination	Action of Acquiring Company	Action of Acquired Company
Statutory merger through asset acquisition.	Acquires assets and often liabilities.	Dissolves and goes out of business.
Statutory merger through capital stock acquisition.	Acquires all stock and then transfers assets and liabilities to its own books.	Dissolves as a separate corporation, often remaining as a division of the acquiring company.
Statutory consolidation through capital stock or asset acquisition.	Newly created to receive assets or capital stock of original companies.	Original companies may dissolve while remaining as separate divisions of newly created company.
Acquisition of more than 50 percent of the voting stock.	Acquires stock that is recorded as an investment; controls decision making of acquired company.	Remains in existence as legal corporation, although now a subsidiary of the acquiring company.
Control through ownership of variable interests (see Chapter 6). Risks and rewards often flow to a sponsoring firm rather than the equity holders.	A sponsoring firm creates an entity—often referred to as an *SPE*—to engage in a specific activity.	Remains in existence as a separate legal entity—often a trust or partnership.

majority of "controlling financial interests." However, in the decades since *ARB 51* was issued, the complexity of business combinations has grown significantly so that control is not always that easy to define.

Control Exercised through Variable Interests

The difficulty in defining control is exemplified in FASB *Interpretation 46R*, "Consolidation of Variable Interest Entities," December 2003 (*FIN 46R*). One popular type of variable interest entities has become widely known as a *special purpose entity* (SPE). SPEs typically take the form of a trust, partnership, joint venture, or corporation. In most cases, a sponsoring firm creates these entities to engage in a limited and well-defined set of business activities. For example, a business may create an SPE to finance the acquisition of a large asset. The SPE purchases the asset using debt and equity financing and then leases the asset back to the sponsoring firm. If their activities are strictly limited and the asset is pledged as collateral, SPEs are often viewed by lenders as less risky than their sponsoring firms. As a result, such arrangements can allow financing at lower interest rates than would otherwise be available to the sponsor.

Control of an SPE, by design, often does not rest with its equity holders. Instead, control is exercised through contractual arrangements with the sponsoring firm who may become the "primary beneficiary" of the entity. These contracts can take the form of leases, participation rights, guarantees, or other residual interests. Through contracting, the primary beneficiary bears a majority of the risks and receives a majority of the rewards of the entity, often without owning any voting shares. Consequently, an exclusive examination of voting interests can fail to identify the firm with the controlling financial interest in an SPE or similar entity.

Throughout the 1990s and early 2000s, SPEs and other variable interest entities became very popular. The increasing use of SPEs was criticized in part because these structures allowed off-balance-sheet financing for the sponsoring firm. Other critics observed that sponsors recorded questionable profits on sales to their SPEs. Many SPEs were often characterized simply as vehicles to hide debt and manipulate earnings. Prior to *FIN 46R*, many sponsoring entities of SPEs did not technically meet the definition of a controlling financial interest and thus did not consolidate their SPEs.

To prevent future financial reporting abuses, *FIN 46R* expands the definition of control beyond simply holding a majority of another entity's voting shares. An entity (e.g., an SPE) whose control rests with a primary beneficiary is referred to as a *variable interest entity*. The following characteristics indicate a controlling financial interest in a variable interest entity:

- The direct or indirect ability to make decisions about the entity's activities.
- The obligation to absorb the expected losses of the entity if they occur.
- The right to receive the expected residual returns of the entity if they occur.

The primary beneficiary bears the risks and receives the rewards of a variable interest entity and is considered to have a controlling financial interest. The fact that the primary beneficiary may own no voting shares whatsoever becomes inconsequential because such shares do not effectively allow the equity holders to exercise control. *FIN 46R* reasons that if a "business enterprise has a controlling financial interest in a variable interest entity, assets, liabilities, and results of the activities of the variable interest entity should be included with those of the business enterprise" (Summary, *FIN 46R*).

In this text, we first examine control relationships established through voting interests. Owning a majority of voting interests continues to be the primary mechanism through which one firm controls another. In Chapter 6, however, we expand our coverage to include the consolidation of firms where control is exercised through variable interests.

Consolidation of Financial Information

Whenever one company gains control over another, a business combination is established. Financial data gathered from the individual companies are then brought together to form a single set of consolidated statements. Although this process can be complicated, the objectives of a consolidation are straightforward. The asset, liability, equity, revenue, and expense accounts of the companies simply are combined. As a part of this process, reciprocal accounts and intercompany transactions must be adjusted or eliminated to ensure that all reported balances truly represent the single entity.

Applicable consolidation procedures vary significantly depending on the legal format employed in creating a business combination. *For a statutory merger or a statutory consolidation, when the acquired company (or companies) is (are) legally dissolved, only one accounting consolidation ever occurs.* On the date of the combination, the surviving company simply records the various account balances from each of the dissolving companies. Because all accounts are brought together permanently in this manner, no further consolidation procedures are necessary. After all of the balances are transferred to the survivor, the financial records of the acquired companies are closed out as part of the dissolution.

Conversely, in a combination when all companies retain incorporation, a different set of consolidation procedures is appropriate. Because the companies preserve their legal identities, each continues to maintain its own independent accounting records. *Thus, no permanent consolidation of the account balances is ever made. Rather, the consolidation process must be carried out anew each time that the reporting entity prepares financial statements for external reporting purposes.*

When separate record-keeping is maintained, the accountant faces a unique problem: The financial information must be brought together periodically without disturbing the accounting systems of the individual companies. Because these consolidations are produced outside the financial records, worksheets traditionally are used to expedite the process. Worksheets are neither part of either company's accounting records nor the resulting financial statements. Instead, they are an efficient structure for organizing and adjusting the information used in the preparation of externally reported consolidated statements.

Consequently, the legal characteristics of a business combination have a significant impact on the approach taken to the consolidation process:

What is to be consolidated?

- If dissolution takes place, all account balances are physically consolidated in the financial records of the surviving company.
- If separate incorporation is maintained, only the financial statement information is consolidated and not the actual records.

When does the consolidation take place?

- If dissolution takes place, a permanent consolidation occurs at the date of the combination.
- If separate incorporation is maintained, the consolidation process is carried out at regular intervals whenever financial statements are to be prepared.

How are the accounting records affected?

- If dissolution takes place, the surviving company's accounts are adjusted to include all balances of the dissolved company. The dissolved company's records are closed out.
- If separate incorporation is maintained, each company continues to retain its own records. Using worksheets facilitates the periodic consolidation process without disturbing the individual accounting systems.

Because of the substantial changes in financial reporting for business combinations proposed by the FASB, we first provide coverage of the *SFAS 141 purchase method* followed by the *acquisition method* recommended in the 2005 FASB Exposure Draft, *Business Combinations*. In illustrating the new concepts and procedures proposed in the Exposure Draft, we use the same examples with minor modifications as noted.

FINANCIAL REPORTING FOR BUSINESS COMBINATIONS—*SFAS 141*

The Purchase Method: Change in Ownership

The fundamental characteristic of any purchase—whether a single asset or a multibillion dollar corporation—is a change in ownership. In any exchange transaction, a basic accounting principle is to record the cost to the new owners. Thus, in a business combination accounted

EXHIBIT 2.3
Business Combination—Purchase

for as a purchase, the acquisition cost to the new owners provides the valuation basis for the net assets acquired. For example, as shown in Exhibit 2.3, MGM Grand, Inc., purchased Mirage Resorts, Inc., for approximately $6.4 billion. This purchase price then served as the basis for valuing Mirage Resorts' assets and liabilities in the preparation of MGM Grand's consolidated financial statements.

When a single asset is purchased, application of the cost principle is straightforward. In a business combination, however, the application of the cost principle is complicated because of the literally hundreds of assets and liabilities that often are acquired. *As a result, the purchase method not only establishes cost as the valuation basis for these items but also allocates the total acquisition cost among the various assets and liabilities received in the bargained exchange.* The cost allocation procedure employed by the purchase method is based on the fair values of the acquired assets and liabilities at the date of acquisition. *Fair value* is the price at which an asset or liability could be exchanged in a current transaction between knowledgeable, unrelated willing parties.[9] Moreover, because income can accrue to owners only after the purchase of an asset (or an entire company), only revenues and expenses generated by these assets and liabilities after the acquisition date are attributed to the business combination.

PROCEDURES FOR CONSOLIDATING FINANCIAL INFORMATION

Legal as well as accounting distinctions divide business combinations into at least four separate categories. To facilitate the introduction of consolidation accounting, we present the various procedures utilized in this process according to the following sequence:

1. Purchase method when dissolution takes place.
2. Purchase method when separate incorporation is maintained.

[9] FASB Exposure Draft, *Fair Value Measurements*, para. 4, June 23, 2004.

As a basis for this coverage, assume that Smallport Company owns computers, telecommunications equipment, and software that allow its customers to implement billing and ordering systems through the Internet/World Wide Web. Although the computers and equipment have a book value of $400,000, they have a current value of $900,000. The software developed by Smallport has only a $100,000 value on its books; the costs of developing the software were primarily expensed as incurred. The observable fair value of the software, however, is $1,600,000. Smallport also has a $200,000 note payable incurred to help finance the software development. Because interest rates are currently low, this liability (incurred at a higher rate of interest) has a present value of $250,000.

BigNet Company owns Internet communications equipment and other business software applications that complement those of Smallport. BigNet wants to expand its operations and plans to acquire Smallport on December 31. The accounts reported by both BigNet and Smallport on that date are listed in Exhibit 2.4. In addition, the estimated fair values of Smallport's assets and liabilities are included.

Smallport's net assets (assets less liabilities) have a book value of $600,000 but a fair value of $2,550,000. Only the assets and liabilities have been appraised here; the capital stock, retained earnings, dividend, revenue, and expense accounts represent historical measurements rather than any type of future values. Although these equity and income accounts can give some indication of the overall worth of the organization, they are not property and thus not transferred in the combination.

SFAS 141: Purchase Method When Dissolution Takes Place

The purchase method employs the cost principle in recording a business combination—the total value assigned to the net assets received equals the total cost of the acquisition. The major accounting challenge, however, is the allocation of that cost among the various assets and liabilities obtained in the acquisition. These allocations depend on the relation between total cost and the fair values of the acquired firm's assets and liabilities. Therefore, we demonstrate the consolidation procedures in this initial section using four examples, each with a different price relative to fair value.

Purchase Price Equals Fair Value of Net Assets

Assume that after negotiations with the owners of Smallport, BigNet agrees to pay $2,550,000 for all of Smallport's assets and liabilities: cash of $550,000 and 20,000 unissued shares of its

EXHIBIT 2.4   **Basic Consolidation Information**

	BigNet Company Book Value December 31	Smallport Company Book Value December 31	Smallport Company Fair Value December 31
Current assets	$1,100,000	$300,000	$ 300,000
Computers and equipment (net)	1,300,000	400,000	900,000
Capitalized software (net)	500,000	100,000	1,600,000
Notes payable	(300,000)	(200,000)	(250,000)
Net assets	**$2,600,000**	**$600,000**	**$2,550,000**
Common stock—$5 par value	$1,600,000		
Common stock—$10 par value		$100,000	
Additional paid-in capital	40,000	20,000	
Retained earnings, 1/1	870,000	370,000	
Dividends paid	(110,000)	(10,000)	
Revenues	1,000,000	500,000	
Expenses	(800,000)	(380,000)	
Owners' equity 12/31	**$2,600,000**	**$600,000**	
Retained earnings, 12/31	960,000*	480,000*	

*Retained earnings balance after closing out revenues, expenses, and dividends paid.

$5 par value common stock that is currently selling for $100 per share. Smallport will then dissolve itself as a legal entity.

As with any acquisition, the price is based on the fair value of the consideration paid.

Cash	$ 550,000
Common stock issued (20,000 shares at a $100 per share fair market value)	2,000,000
Purchase price	$2,550,000

Therefore, BigNet's cost is exactly equal to the $2,550,000 fair value of the individual assets and liabilities acquired.

The purchase method is appropriate for consolidating the financial information of these two companies; all of the essential characteristics are present. A bargained exchange occurred between BigNet, the acquiring company, and the owners of Smallport. This transaction indicates that a $2,550,000 purchase price will form the basis for the consolidated figures in the financial statements of the resulting single economic entity.

At the date of acquisition, the purchase method consolidates all subsidiary asset and liability accounts based on their fair values. The acquired assets and liabilities are recorded as if the parent had simply obtained them by paying fair value. Because the negotiated price here equals this total value, the parent records each of these accounts as though they had been purchased individually. As we subsequently demonstrate, variations from this rule exist if the parent pays less than fair value.

Because Smallport Company will be dissolved, BigNet (the surviving company) directly records a consolidation entry in its financial records. As a purchase, BigNet consolidates Smallport's assets and liabilities at fair value; original book values are ignored. Revenue, expense, dividend, and equity accounts cannot be transferred to a parent and are omitted in recording the business combination as a purchase.

Purchase Method—Parent Pays Fair Value—Subsidiary Dissolved

BigNet Company's Financial Records—December 31		
Current Assets	300,000	
Computers and Equipment	900,000	
Capitalized Software	1,600,000	
Notes Payable		250,000
Cash (paid by BigNet)		550,000
Common Stock (20,000 shares issued by BigNet at $5 par value)		100,000
Additional Paid-In Capital (value of shares issued by BigNet in excess of par value)		1,900,000
To record purchase of net assets of Smallport Company for $2,550,000. Subsidiary accounts are recorded at fair value which total (net) to the same $2,550,000.		

BigNet's financial records now show $2,200,000 in the Computers and Equipment account ($1,300,000 former balance + $900,000 acquired), $2,100,000 in Capitalized Software ($500,000 + $1,600,000), and so forth. These items have been added into BigNet's balances (see Exhibit 2.4) at their fair values. Conversely, BigNet's revenue balance continues to report the company's own $1,000,000 with expenses remaining at $800,000 and dividends of $110,000. *In a purchase, only the subsidiary's revenues, expenses, dividends, and equity transactions that occur subsequent to the takeover affect the business combination.*

Purchase Price Exceeds Fair Value of Net Assets

The negotiated price in this second illustration is assumed to be $3,000,000 in exchange for all of Smallport's assets and liabilities. BigNet's mode of payment will be $1,000,000 in cash plus 20,000 shares of common stock with a market value of $100 per share. The resulting purchase price is $450,000 more than the $2,550,000 fair value of Smallport's net assets. In purchase combinations, such excess payments are not unusual. For example, when

Amazon.com acquired Junglee, a provider of Web-based virtual database technology, substantially the entire $180 million purchase price was allocated to goodwill and other intangibles.

The $2,550,000 fair value of Smallport's net assets certainly can influence any takeover offer. However, any number of other factors can affect BigNet's $3,000,000 acquisition offer, such as Smallport's history of profitability, the company's reputation, the quality of its personnel, or the economic condition of the industry in which it operates. If Smallport, for example, demonstrates the ability to generate especially high profits, BigNet could be willing to pay an extra amount for this company. One additional factor frequently affects an acquisition price: the presence of competitive buyers. If BigNet must outbid other companies to acquire Smallport, the purchase price could simply represent the bidding war.

Whenever the price paid in a purchase exceeds total fair value, all of the subsidiary's assets and liabilities are consolidated at fair value with the additional payment allocated to the intangible asset goodwill. This excess amount could actually reflect the profitability often inherent in a going concern, the creative ability of a research group, market conditions that surrounded the acquisition, or myriad other possible factors. Because the conditions that can influence a purchase price are virtually unlimited, any amount paid in excess of the fair value assigned to identifiable assets (both tangible and intangible) is simply assigned to goodwill.[10]

Returning to BigNet's $3,000,000 purchase, $450,000 of this price is in excess of the fair value of Smallport's net assets. Thus, goodwill of that amount is entered into BigNet's accounting system along with the fair value of each individual account. The journal entry made by BigNet at the date of acquisition follows:

Purchase Method—Parent Pays More Than Fair Value—Subsidiary Dissolved

BigNet Company's Financial Records—December 31		
Current Assets	300,000	
Computers and Equipment	900,000	
Capitalized Software	1,600,000	
Goodwill	450,000	
Notes Payable		250,000
Cash (paid by BigNet)		1,000,000
Common Stock (20,000 shares issued by BigNet at $5 par value)		100,000
Additional Paid-In Capital (value of shares issued by BigNet in excess of par value)		1,900,000
To record purchase of net assets of Smallport Company for $3,000,000. Subsidiary accounts are recorded at fair value with $450,000 excess payment attributed to goodwill.		

Once again, BigNet's financial records now show $2,200,000 in the Computers and Equipment account ($1,300,000 former balance + $900,000 acquired), $2,100,000 in Capitalized Software ($500,000 + $1,600,000), and so forth. As the only change, a Goodwill balance of $450,000 is established to account for the excess purchase price paid by BigNet.

Purchase Price Less Than Fair Value of Net Assets

For this third example, the price paid to Smallport's owners is assumed to be $2,000,000. BigNet conveys no cash and issues 20,000 shares of common stock having a $100 per share fair value. BigNet's total purchase price of $2,000,000 is $550,000 less than the fair value of Smallport's net assets. Strict adherence to the cost principle and allocation of full fair values

---

[10] As discussed in Chapter 3, the assets and liabilities (including goodwill) acquired in a business combination are assigned to identified *reporting units* of the combined entity. A *reporting unit* is simply a level of business in which an acquired asset or liability will be employed. Overall, the objective of the assignment of acquired assets and liabilities to reporting units is to facilitate periodic impairment testing.

to each asset and liability are simply not possible; some reduction must be made. A cost of $2,000,000 cannot be assigned to accounts having a fair value of $2,550,000 without an adjustment. To address this problem, the values otherwise assignable to noncurrent assets acquired should be reduced by a proportionate part of the excess to determine the assigned values.[11] *Therefore, when a purchase price is less than total fair value of the net assets, noncurrent accounts, such as Computers and Equipment and Capitalized Software, are consolidated at reduced balances. All remaining assets and liabilities continue to be recorded at their fair values.*

Because BigNet paid $550,000 less than fair value ($2,000,000 − $2,550,000), the balances of the noncurrent assets being acquired must be decreased by that amount. As indicated in Exhibit 2.4, the two applicable accounts in this example have a total fair value of $2,500,000:

Noncurrent Asset Accounts	Fair Values	
Computers and Equipment	$ 900,000	36%
Capitalized Software	1,600,000	64
Total	$2,500,000	100%

Because of BigNet's payment, these two accounts are reduced in consolidation by a total of $550,000 (from $2,550,000 to $2,000,000). The balance reported for Computers and Equipment is lowered by $198,000 ($550,000 × 36%). The remaining $352,000 ($550,000 × 64%) is assigned as a decrease to the Capitalized Software account. Therefore, for consolidation purposes, BigNet records Smallport's Computers and Equipment at $702,000 ($198,000 less than its $900,000 fair market value). The Capitalized Software account is entered at $1,248,000 ($1,600,000 − $352,000). All other assets and liabilities are consolidated at their fair values.

Purchase Method—Parent Pays Less Than Fair Value—Subsidiary Dissolved

BigNet Company's Financial Records—December 31

Current Assets	300,000	
Computers and Equipment	702,000	
Capitalized Software	1,248,000	
Notes Payable		250,000
Common Stock (20,000 shares issued by BigNet at $5 par value)		100,000
Additional Paid-In Capital (value of shares issued by BigNet in excess of par value)		1,900,000

To record purchase of net assets of Smallport. Total purchase price of $2,000,000 is $550,000 less than fair value of the net assets, an amount assigned to reduce noncurrent assets.

Purchase Price Substantially Less Than Fair Value of Net Assets

In this illustration, the exchange price for Smallport's net assets is assumed to be $40,000 with payment made entirely in cash. Obviously, expending this amount for net assets valued at $2,550,000 is an extreme case that indicates an unusual circumstance such as imminent bankruptcy, large contingent liabilities, or an urgent need by the present owners for immediate liquidation. A company, for example, that has its entire business centered on marketing one patent could see the price of its stock drop to nearly zero if the legality of that patent were seriously threatened.

---

[11] Excluded from the proportionate reduction are financial assets other than equity method investments, assets to be disposed of by sale, deferred tax assets, and prepaid assets relating to pension or other post-retirement benefit plans. According to *SFAS 141*, these assets should be recorded at assessed fair values.

With a purchase price of only $40,000, BigNet must reduce the valuation it assigns to Smallport's assets and liabilities by $2,510,000 for recording the combination. As was indicated in the previous example, this decrease initially is made in recording the noncurrent assets. However, these two assets (computers and equipment and capitalized software) have a total worth of only $2,500,000. Even decreasing their balances to zero will not fully account for the $2,510,000 difference between the purchase price and total fair value. A further reduction of $10,000 must be assigned within the consolidation process.

Whenever a purchase price is less than fair value so that the acquired applicable noncurrent asset balances are eliminated entirely, an additional reduction is needed. According to SFAS 141, *the additional reduction is reported as an extraordinary gain.*[12] All other assets and liabilities are still brought into the combination at fair value. The extraordinary gain results from a bargain purchase but comes into existence only after the applicable noncurrent assets are first decreased to zero. Thus, either the price has to be extremely low or the acquired noncurrent assets must be of a relatively small value.

The FASB decision that an unallocated excess fair value over cost should be reported as an extraordinary gain was not without its critics. Some argued that to record a gain upon a purchase transaction is conceptually unsound. However, the FASB reasoned that the extraordinary gain treatment appropriately highlights the fact that an excess exists and that such occurrences are both infrequent and unusual in nature.

Because the $40,000 price in this illustration is $2,510,000 less than fair value, BigNet's journal entry to record its purchase of Smallport's assets and liabilities would do the following:

1. Recognize no balances for the two noncurrent asset accounts.
2. Allocate the remaining $10,000 reduction to an extraordinary gain.
3. Report all remaining asset and liability accounts at fair value.

Purchase Method—Parent Pays Substantially Less Than Fair Value— Subsidiary Dissolved

BigNet Company's Financial Records—December 31		
Current Assets	300,000	
Computers and Equipment	–0–	
Capitalized Software	–0–	
Notes Payable		250,000
Extraordinary Gain—Excess of Fair Value over Cost of Acquisition		10,000
Cash (paid by BigNet)		40,000
To record acquisition of Smallport's net assets for $40,000, an amount $2,510,000 below fair value.		

Related Costs of Business Combinations

In addition to the purchase prices (cash, common stock, etc.) seen in the preceding examples, an acquiring firm typically incurs additional costs in connection with a business combination. Three categories of these costs exist with three distinct accounting treatments. First, firms usually engage attorneys, accountants, investment bankers, and other professionals to perform services related to the business combination.[13] The purchase method considers such

---

[12] Prior to *SFAS 141*, such additional reductions were reported in a deferred credit account and systematically amortized to income.

[13] Such combination costs can be large. In describing the takeover battle for RJR Nabisco, *Time* magazine estimated that "hundreds of lawyers and investment bankers involved in the bidding stand to earn a total of as much as $1 billion for their expertise." December 5, 1988, "Where's the Limit," p. 66.

EXHIBIT 2.5
Accounting for Additional Costs Frequently Associated with Business Combinations

Direct combination costs (e.g., accounting, legal, investment banking, appraisal fees, etc.).	Include in the purchase price for the acquired firm.
Indirect combination costs (e.g., internal costs such as allocated secretarial or managerial time).	Expense as incurred.
Costs to register and issues securities.	Reduce the value assigned to the fair value of the securities issued (typically a debit to Additional Paid-In Capital).

costs to be directly related to the business combination and includes them in the purchase price of the entity.

A second category of costs associated with a business combination concerns the internal costs incurred by an acquiring firm that it allocates to the acquisition activity. Examples include secretarial and management time. Such indirect combination costs are not considered incremental (whether one time or recurring) and are expensed as incurred.

Finally, costs to register and issue securities in connection with a business combination simply reduce the otherwise determinable fair value of the securities. As in stock issues for any other financing reason, a common accounting treatment is simply to debit Additional Paid-In Capital for these costs. Exhibit 2.5 provides a summary of the three categories of related payments that accompany a business combination and their respective accounting treatments under *SFAS 141*.

As an example, assume that BigNet issues $2,500,000 in common stock in exchange for all of Smallport's assets and liabilities. Additionally, BigNet pays $100,000 in accounting and attorney fees and $20,000 in costs to register and issue securities. The total cost for the acquisition is recorded at $2,600,000, effectively capitalizing the direct acquisition costs as follows:

Current Assets	300,000	
Computers and Equipment	900,000	
Capitalized Software	1,600,000	
Goodwill	50,000	
Notes Payable		250,000
Common Stock (20,000 shares issued by BigNet at $5 par value)		100,000
Additional Paid-In Capital		2,400,000
Cash		100,000
To record Smallport acquisition for $2,600,000 including $100,000 direct combination costs.		
Additional Paid-In Capital	20,000	
Cash		20,000
To record costs to register and issue stock in connection with the Smallport acquisition.		

Summary of the Purchase Method

In a purchase, acquired assets and liabilities are normally consolidated at their fair values. However, the relationship between purchase price and total fair value can necessitate some alterations to this rule. An excess payment, for example, leads to the creation of a Goodwill account. A low purchase price forces a reduction in the recorded balance of applicable noncurrent assets and possibly the recognition of an extraordinary gain. Exhibit 2.6 summarizes the possible allocation scenarios.

Purchase Method When Separate Incorporation Is Maintained

When each company retains separate incorporation in a business combination, many aspects of the consolidation process are identical to those demonstrated in the previous section. Fair

EXHIBIT 2.6
Consolidation Values—
The Purchase Method

Purchase price equals the fair value of the net assets.	Acquired assets and liabilities are assigned their fair values.
Purchase price is more than the fair value of the net assets.	Acquired assets and liabilities are assigned their fair values. The excess payment is attributed to goodwill.
Purchase price is less than the fair value of the net assets.	Current assets, liabilities, financial assets, deferred taxes, assets to be held for sale, and prepaid pension assets are assigned their fair values. The values of other noncurrent assets are reduced proportionally. If necessary, an extraordinary gain is recognized.

value, for example, remains as the basis for initially consolidating the subsidiary's asset and liability accounts.

Several significant differences exist in combinations in which each company remains a legally incorporated entity. Most noticeably, the consolidation of the financial information is only simulated; the acquiring company does not physically record the acquired assets and liabilities. Because dissolution does not occur, each company maintains independent record-keeping. To facilitate the preparation of consolidated financial statements, a worksheet and consolidation entries are employed using data gathered from these separate companies.

A worksheet provides the structure for generating information to be reported by the single economic entity. An integral part of this process is the inclusion of consolidation worksheet entries. *These adjustments and eliminations are entered on the worksheet and represent alterations that would be required if the financial records were to be physically united.* Because no actual union occurs, consolidation entries are never formally recorded in the journals of either company. Instead, they are produced solely for use on the worksheet to assist in deriving consolidated account balances of the two separate companies. The resulting consolidated balances then form the basis for the financial reports of the consolidated entity.

To illustrate using the previous information, assume that BigNet acquires Smallport Company on December 31 by issuing 26,000 shares of $5 par value common stock valued at $100 per share (or $2,600,000 in total). BigNet also pays direct combination costs of $40,000, resulting in a total purchase cost of $2,640,000.

For business reasons, BigNet decides that Smallport should continue as a separate corporation. Therefore, whenever financial statements for the combined entity are prepared, a worksheet is utilized in simulating the consolidation of these two companies. Although the assets and liabilities are not transferred, BigNet must still record the payment made to Smallport's owners. When the subsidiary remains separate, the parent establishes an investment account that initially reflects the purchase price.

Purchase Method—Subsidiary Is Not Dissolved

BigNet Company's Financial Records—December 31		
Investment in Smallport Company (purchase price)	2,640,000	
Cash (paid for direct combination costs)		40,000
Common Stock (26,000 shares issued by BigNet at $5 par value)		130,000
Additional Paid-In Capital (value of shares issued by BigNet in excess of par value)		2,470,000
To record purchase of Smallport Company, which will maintain its separate legal identity.		

EXHIBIT 2.7   Purchase Method—Date of Acquisition

BIGNET COMPANY AND SMALLPORT COMPANY
Consolidation Worksheet
For Period Ending December 31

Accounts	BigNet	Smallport	Consolidation Entries Debits	Consolidation Entries Credits	Consolidated Totals
Income Statement					
Revenues	(1,000,000)				(1,000,000)
Expenses	800,000				800,000
Net income	(200,000)				(200,000)
Statement of Retained Earnings					
Retained earnings, 1/1	(870,000)				(870,000)
Net income (above)	(200,000)				(200,000)
Dividends paid	110,000				110,000
Retained earnings, 12/31	(960,000)				(960,000)
Balance Sheet					
Current assets	1,060,000*	300,000			1,360,000
Investment in Smallport Company	2,640,000*	–0–		(S) 600,000 (A) 2,040,000	–0–
Computers and equipment	1,300,000	400,000	(A) 500,000		2,200,000
Capitalized software	500,000	100,000	(A) 1,500,000		2,100,000
Goodwill	–0–	–0–	(A) 90,000		90,000
Total assets	5,500,000	800,000			5,750,000
Notes payable	(300,000)	(200,000)		(A) 50,000	(550,000)
Common stock	(1,730,000)*	(100,000)	(S) 100,000		(1,730,000)
Additional paid-in capital	(2,510,000)*	(20,000)	(S) 20,000		(2,510,000)
Retained earnings, 12/31 (above)	(960,000)	(480,000)	(S) 480,000		(960,000)
Total liabilities and equities	(5,500,000)	(800,000)			(5,750,000)

Note: Parentheses indicate a credit balance.
*Balances have been adjusted for issuance of stock and payment of consolidation costs.

As demonstrated in Exhibit 2.7, a worksheet can be prepared on the date of acquisition to arrive at consolidated totals for this combination. The entire process consists of seven steps:

Step 1

Whenever a worksheet is constructed, a formal allocation of the purchase price should be made as was done for the equity method in Chapter 1.[14] Thus, the following schedule is appropriate for BigNet's purchase of Smallport:

Purchase Price Allocation Schedule

Purchase price paid by BigNet		$2,640,000
Book value of Smallport (see Exhibit 2.4)		600,000
Excess of cost over book value		$2,040,000
Allocations made to specific accounts based on difference in fair values and book values:		
Computers and Equipment ($900,000 − $400,000)	$ 500,000	
Capitalized Software ($1,600,000 − $100,000)	1,500,000	
Notes Payable ($250,000 − $200,000)	(50,000)	1,950,000
Excess cost not identified with specific accounts—goodwill		$ 90,000

[14] This allocation procedure is helpful but not critical if dissolution occurs. Unless the purchase price is less than total fair value, the asset and liability accounts are simply added directly into the parent's books at their assessed worth with any excess assigned to goodwill.

Note that the preceding schedule initially subtracts Smallport's book value from the purchase price. The resulting $2,040,000 difference represents the total amount needed on the Exhibit 2.7 worksheet to adjust Smallport's net assets from book value to fair value. Next, the schedule shows how this $2,040,000 total is allocated to adjust each individual item to fair value. The purchase price allocation schedule thus effectively serves as a convenient supporting schedule for the Exhibit 2.7 worksheet and is routinely prepared for every consolidation.

No part of the $2,040,000 excess payment is attributed to the current assets because the book value and fair value are identical. The Notes Payable shows a negative allocation; because this debt's present value is more than book value, the company's net assets are actually worth *less.*

Step 2

The first two columns of the worksheet (see Exhibit 2.7) show the financial figures from the separate companies as of the date of acquisition (see Exhibit 2.4). BigNet's accounts have been adjusted for the investment entry recorded earlier. As another preliminary step, Smallport's revenue, expense, and dividend accounts have been closed into its Retained Earnings account. The operations of the subsidiary prior to the December 31 takeover have no direct bearing on the business combination. These activities occurred before Smallport was acquired; thus, the resulting data should not be reported as income earned by the new owners in the consolidated statements.

Step 3

Smallport's stockholders' equity accounts are eliminated through consolidation Entry **S** (**S** is a reference to beginning subsidiary **S**tockholders' equity). These balances (Common Stock, Additional Paid-In Capital, and Retained Earnings) are historical measurements of subsidiary transactions that occurred prior to the combination. By removing these accounts, only Smallport's assets and liabilities remain to be combined with the parent company figures.

Step 4

Also, worksheet Entry **S** removes the $600,000 component of the Investment in Smallport Company account that equates to the book value of the subsidiary's net assets. For external reporting purposes, the combination should report each individual account rather than a single investment balance. In effect, this portion of the Investment in Smallport Company account is deleted and replaced by the specific assets and liabilities that it represents.

Step 5

Entry **A** removes the $2,040,000 excess payment in the Investment in Smallport Company and assigns it to the specific accounts indicated by the purchase price allocation schedule. Consequently, Computers and Equipment is increased by $500,000 to agree with Smallport's fair value; $1,500,000 is attributed to Capitalized Software and $50,000 to Notes Payable. The unexplained excess of $90,000 is recorded as goodwill. This entry is labeled Entry **A** to indicate that it represents the **A**llocations made in connection with the parent's purchase price. It also completes the elimination of the entire Investment in Smallport account.

Step 6

All accounts are extended into the Consolidated Totals column. For accounts such as Current Assets, this process is no more than the addition of Smallport's book value to that of BigNet. However, when applicable, this extension also includes any allocations to establish the fair value of Smallport's asset and liability accounts. Computers and Equipment, as an example, is increased by $500,000. By raising the subsidiary's book value to fair value, the reported balances are the same as in the previous examples when dissolution occurred. The use of a worksheet does not alter the consolidated figures but only the method of deriving those numbers.

Step 7

Consolidated expenses are subtracted from revenues to arrive at a net income of $200,000. Note that because this is a date of acquisition worksheet, no amounts for Smallport's revenues and expenses are included in the Smallport Company column. BigNet has just purchased Smallport and therefore Smallport has not yet earned any income for the owners of BigNet. Consolidated revenues, expenses, and net income are identical to BigNet's balances. In years subsequent to acquisition, of course, Smallport's income accounts will be consolidated with BigNet's.

In general, totals (such as net income and ending retained earnings) are not directly consolidated across on the worksheet. Rather, the components (such as revenues and expenses) are extended across and then combined vertically to derive the appropriate figure. Net income is then carried down on the worksheet to the Statement of Retained Earnings and used (along with beginning retained earnings and dividends paid) to compute this December 31 equity balance. In the same manner, ending Retained Earnings of $960,000 is entered into the balance sheet to arrive at total liabilities and equities of $5,750,000, a number that reconciles with the total of consolidated assets.

The balances in the final column of Exhibit 2.7 are used to prepare consolidated financial statements for the business combination of BigNet Company and Smallport Company. The worksheet entries serve as a catalyst to bring together the two independent sets of financial information. The actual accounting records of both BigNet and Smallport remain unaltered by this consolidation process.

2005 FASB PROPOSALS ON FINANCIAL REPORTING FOR BUSINESS COMBINATIONS

In June 2005, the FASB issued the following two Exposure Drafts of proposed statements that, if approved, will significantly affect financial reporting for business combinations:

- *Business Combinations* (to replace *SFAS 141*).
- *Consolidated Financial Statements, Including Accounting and Reporting of Noncontrolling Interests in Subsidiaries* (to replace *ARB 51*).

With limited exceptions, the provisions of these statements would be applied prospectively. The new statements, if approved, are scheduled to become effective for financial statements issued for fiscal years beginning after December 15, 2006.

The FASB Exposure Drafts propose extensive changes in the way firms report business combinations, both at acquisition date and subsequent to acquisition. Coverage of these changes appears in this chapter and each of the following chapters as appropriate.

The Acquisition Method (Proposed to Replace the Purchase Method)

The FASB Exposure Draft *Business Combinations* proposes the **acquisition method** to account for business combinations instead of the purchase method as required under *SFAS 141*.
Applying the acquisition method involves both

- Measuring the **fair value of the acquired business as a whole.** Business fair value for 100 percent acquisitions is typically determined by the fair value of the consideration transferred in exchange for a business.
- Measuring and recognizing the **fair values of the separately identified assets acquired and liabilities assumed** at the date of combination.

The emphasis of the *Business Combinations* Exposure Draft on fair value as a measurement concept represents a distinct departure from the cost-based provisions of *SFAS 141*. Therefore, prior to examining specific applications of the procedures recommended in the Exposure Draft, we present a brief discussion of the business fair value concepts.

Business Fair Value

According to the FASB Exposure Draft *Business Combinations* (para. 18),

> The business acquired shall be measured at its fair value on the acquisition date. The objective is to estimate a price that knowledgeable, unrelated willing parties could exchange for the entire

equity interest in the business acquired based on circumstances that exist on the acquisition date. The fair value of the business acquired shall be determined based on the fair values of the items of consideration transferred in exchange for the business unless the consideration transferred does not represent the fair value of the business acquired.[15]

The acquisition method thus embraces a fair value concept for reporting business combinations. Furthermore, in most combinations,[16] the valuation basis for the acquired firm is the *business fair value as measured by the fair value of consideration transferred* as opposed to a *cost-based measure.* This distinction recognizes that, in some cases, different elements comprise these two measures.

For example, recall that under *SFAS 141,* direct combination costs (e.g., finders' fees, legal fees for arranging or completing the combination) are considered part of the overall cost and thus are included in the valuation basis for the acquired firm. In contrast, under the acquisition method, these direct combination costs are considered payments for services received, not part of the fair value exchanged for the business. Thus, under the acquisition method, direct combination costs are expensed as incurred.

Another departure from *SFAS 141* involves contingent consideration. Often business acquisition negotiations result in agreements to provide additional payment to former owners if certain future performance measures are met. Under *SFAS 141,* such obligations for contingent consideration are not considered part of the acquisition cost but are recognized as postcombination adjustments to the purchase price when the contingency is finally resolved. Under the acquisition method, contingent consideration obligations are recognized as part of the purchase price, consistent with the fair value concept.

A third departure from the cost principle relates to bargain purchases (i.e., when the net amount of the fair values of the separately identified assets acquired and liabilities exceeds the fair value of the consideration transferred). Under the acquisition method, when a bargain purchase occurs, the consideration transferred is not used as a valuation basis for the business acquired. Instead, the acquirer measures and recognizes the fair values of each of the assets acquired and liabilities assumed at the date of combination, regardless of the consideration transferred in the transaction. As a result, (1) no assets are recorded at amounts below their assessed fair values as is the case with bargain purchases under *SFAS 141* and (2) a gain on bargain purchase is recognized at the acquisition date.

Several implications of adopting a fair value measurement and recognition concept are illustrated next. In a subsequent section, we also discuss accounting for purchased in-process research and development costs under the acquisition method.

Illustrations of the Acquisition Method

Using the same example of BigNet and Smallport (see pages 43–53), we illustrate accounting and reporting under the acquisition method at the date of acquisition. In each case, BigNet acquires 100 percent of Smallport.

Under the acquisition method, the amount recorded for the business combination depends on the relation between the business fair value and the net amount of the fair values of the assets acquired and liabilities assumed. Therefore, the next three examples demonstrate the recording of the business combination, each with different business fair values relative to acquired net asset fair values, assuming that the acquired firm is dissolved. A final example demonstrates the acquisition method for a wholly owned subsidiary that continues its separate legal existence.

Business Fair Value Equals Net Amount of Fair Values of Assets Acquired and Liabilities Assumed

Again assume that after negotiations with the owners of Smallport, BigNet agrees to pay $2,550,000 for all of Smallport's assets and liabilities: cash of $550,000 and 20,000 unissued shares of its $5 par value common stock that is currently selling for $100 per share. Smallport

---

[15] Exceptions include situations in which control is achieved without a transfer of consideration or determination of the fair value of the consideration transferred is less reliable than other measures of the business fair value.

[16] An exception occurs in a bargain purchase when the net amount of the fair values of the assets acquired and liabilities assumed serves as the valuation basis for the acquired firm.

will then dissolve itself as a legal entity. In this case, the consideration transferred represents the fair value of the business acquired.

This $2,550,000 Smallport business fair value will become part of the consolidated balances in the financial statements of the resulting combined economic entity. In this case, Smallport's business fair value is exactly equal to the $2,550,000 collective net fair values of the individual assets and liabilities acquired.

Under the acquisition method, all asset and liability accounts of an acquired business are recorded at their individual fair values at the transaction date as follows:

Acquisition Method: Business Fair Value Equals Net Asset Fair Values, Subsidiary Dissolved

BigNet Company's Financial Records—December 31		
Current Assets	300,000	
Computers and Equipment	900,000	
Capitalized Software	1,600,000	
Notes Payable		250,000
Cash (paid by BigNet)		550,000
Common Stock (20,000 shares issued by BigNet at $5 par value)		100,000
Additional Paid-In Capital		1,900,000
To record acquisition of Smallport Company. Assets acquired and liabilities assumed are recorded at fair value.		

Note that in this case, the purchase method and the acquisition method yield identical financial reporting results. The valuation bases for the transaction are the same because the purchase price and the business fair value equal the acquired firm's net asset fair value.

Business Fair Value Exceeds Net Amount of Fair Values of Assets Acquired and Liabilities Assumed

In this illustration, BigNet agrees to pay $3,000,000 in exchange for all of Smallport's assets and liabilities. The consideration transferred by BigNet is $1,000,000 in cash plus 20,000 shares of common stock with a market value of $100 per share. The Smallport business fair value is evidenced by the $3,000,000 consideration and is $450,000 more than the $2,550,000 total of fair values of Smallport's net assets. When the acquired business fair value exceeds the amount of net fair values of the assets acquired and liabilities assumed, the excess fair value is recognized as goodwill. All of the other acquired assets and liabilities are recorded at their individual fair values as follows:

Acquisition Method: Business Fair Value Exceeds Net Asset Fair Values, Subsidiary Dissolved

BigNet Company's Financial Records—December 31		
Current Assets	300,000	
Computers and Equipment	900,000	
Capitalized Software	1,600,000	
Goodwill	450,000	
Notes Payable		250,000
Cash (paid by BigNet)		1,000,000
Common Stock (20,000 shares issued by BigNet at $5 par value)		100,000
Additional Paid-In Capital		1,900,000
To record acquisition of Smallport Company. Assets acquired and liabilities assumed are recorded at individual fair values with excess fair value attributed to goodwill.		

As in the previous example, the purchase method and the acquisition method yield identical financial reporting results. The valuation bases for the transaction are the same because the business fair value equals the purchase price, which exceeds the acquired entity's net asset fair value.

Bargain Purchase—Consideration Transferred Is Less Than Net Amount of Fair Values of Assets Acquired and Liabilities Assumed

In this third example, consideration of $2,000,000 is transferred to the owners of Smallport in exchange for the business. BigNet conveys no cash and issues 20,000 shares of common stock having a $100 per share fair value.

In accounting for this acquisition, at least two competing fair values are present. First, the $2,000,000 consideration transferred for Smallport represents a negotiated transaction value for the business. Second, the net amount of fair values individually assigned to the assets acquired and liabilities assumed produces a net fair value of $2,550,000. Additionally, based on expected synergies with Smallport, BigNet's management may believe that the fair value of the business as a whole exceeds the net asset fair value. Nonetheless, because the consideration transferred is less than the net asset fair value, a bargain purchase has occurred.

Under the acquisition method, in all cases, identifiable assets acquired and liabilities assumed are recorded at their individual fair values. In a bargain purchase situation, this net asset fair value is effectively used as the acquired business fair value instead of the consideration transferred. The consideration transferred serves as the acquired firm's valuation basis only if the consideration equals or exceeds the net amount of fair values for the assets acquired and liabilities assumed (as in the first two examples). In this case, however, the $2,000,000 consideration paid is less than the $2,550,000 net asset fair value, indicating a bargain purchase. Thus, the $2,550,000 net asset fair value serves as the valuation basis for the combination. A $550,000 *gain on a bargain purchase* results because a value of $2,550,000 is recorded accompanied by a payment of only $2,000,000.

Acquisition Method: Consideration Transferred Is Less Than Net Asset Fair Values, Subsidiary Dissolved

BigNet Company's Financial Records—December 31		
Current Assets	300,000	
Computers and Equipment	900,000	
Capitalized Software	1,600,000	
Notes Payable		250,000
Common Stock (20,000 shares issued by BigNet at $5 par value)		100,000
Additional Paid-In Capital		1,900,000
Gain on Bargain Purchase		550,000
To record acquisition of Smallport Company. Assets acquired and liabilities assumed are each recorded at fair value. Excess net asset fair value is attributed to a gain on bargain purchase.		

A consequence of implementing a fair value concept to acquisition accounting is that an unrealized gain on the bargain purchase is recognized. A criticism of the gain recognition is that the acquirer recognizes profit from a buying activity that occurs prior to traditional accrual measures of earned income (i.e., selling activity). Nonetheless, the FASB proposal requires an exception to the general rule of recording business acquisitions at fair value of the consideration transferred in a bargain purchase.

Summary of the Acquisition Method

Fair values for the assets acquired and liabilities assumed provide the basis for recording a business combination at the date of acquisition. Goodwill is also recorded if the fair value of the consideration transferred exceeds the net asset fair value. If the net asset fair value of the business acquired exceeds the consideration paid, a gain on a bargain purchase is recognized and reported in current income of the combined entity. Exhibit 2.8 summarizes possible allocations under the proposed acquisition method.

The Acquisition Method When Separate Incorporation Is Maintained

This example illustrates the FASB's proposed acquisition method should BigNet decides to maintain Smallport as a separate corporate entity. We employ the same basic scenario as provided in the purchase method example (pages 49–53). Again, assume that BigNet acquires

EXHIBIT 2.8
Consolidation Values—
The Acquisition Method

Business fair value (consideration transferred) equals the fair values of net assets acquired.	Assets acquired and liabilities assumed are recorded at their fair values.
Business fair value (consideration transferred) is greater than the fair values of net assets acquired.	Assets acquired and liabilities assumed are recorded at their fair values. The excess consideration transferred over the net asset fair values is recorded as goodwill.
A bargain purchase transfers consideration less than the fair values of net assets acquired. The total of the individual fair values of the net assets acquired effectively becomes the acquired business fair value.	Assets acquired and liabilities assumed are recorded at their fair values. The excess amount of net asset fair value over the consideration transferred is recorded as a gain on bargain purchase.

Smallport Company on December 31 by issuing 26,000 shares of $5 par value common stock valued at $100 per share (or $2,600,000 in total). Also as in the previous example, direct combination costs of $40,000 are paid to third parties. We then change the example by introducing an element of contingent consideration as part of the acquisition agreement between BigNet and Smallport as follows.

To settle a difference of opinion regarding Smallport's fair value, BigNet promises to pay an additional $83,200 to the former owners if Smallport's earnings exceed $300,000 during the next annual period. BigNet estimates a 25 percent probability that the $83,200 contingent payment will be required. A discount rate of 4 percent (to represent the time value of money) yields an expected present value of $20,000 for the contingent liability ($83,200 × 25% × 0.961538). The fair value approach of the acquisition method views such contingent payments as part of the consideration transferred. According to this view, contingencies have value to those who receive the consideration and represent measurable obligations of the acquirer.[17]

Because Smallport's separate incorporation is maintained, BigNet would prepare the following journal entries on its books to record the business combination.

Acquisition Method—Subsidiary Is Not Dissolved

BigNet Company's Financial Records—December 31		
Investment in Smallport Company (purchase price)	2,620,000	
Contingent Performance Liability		20,000
Common Stock (26,000 shares issued by BigNet at $5 par value)		130,000
Additional Paid-In Capital (value of shares in excess of par value)		2,470,000
Combination Expenses	40,000	
Cash (paid for direct combination costs)		40,000
To record purchase of Smallport Company, which maintains its separate legal identity.		

Similar to the purchase method, the acquisition method requires adjustments to the assets acquired and liabilities assumed based on their individual fair values as follows:

Business fair value (consideration transferred by BigNet)	$2,620,000	
Book value of Smallport (see Exhibit 2.4)	600,000	
Excess of cost over book value		$2,020,000
Allocations made to specific accounts based on difference in fair values and book values:		
Computers and equipment ($900,000 − $400,000)	$ 500,000	
Capitalized software ($1,600,000 − $100,000)	1,500,000	
Notes payable ($250,000 − $200,000)	(50,000)	1,950,000
Excess fair value not identified with specific accounts—goodwill		$ 70,000

[17] Contingent consideration is not unusual in business acquisitions. *Mergers & Acquisitions* reports that in 2004, 154 acquisitions involved contingent payments including combinations by General Electric, SunTrust Banks, Citrix Systems, and others. Contingent consideration is discussed further in Chapter 3.

EXHIBIT 2.9   Acquisition Method—Date of Acquisition

Accounts	BigNet	Smallport	Consolidation Entries Debits	Consolidation Entries Credits	Consolidated Totals
Income Statement					
Revenues	(1,000,000)				(1,000,000)
Expenses	840,000*				840,000
Net income	(160,000)				(160,000)
Statement of Retained Earnings					
Retained earnings, 1/1	(870,000)				(870,000)
Net income (above)	(160,000)*				(160,000)
Dividends paid	110,000				110,000
Retained earnings, 12/31	(920,000)				(920,000)
Balance Sheet					
Current assets	1,060,000*	300,000			1,360,000
Investment in Smallport Company	2,620,000*	–0–		(S) 600,000	–0–
				(A) 2,020,000	
Computers and equipment	1,300,000	400,000	(A) 500,000		2,200,000
Capitalized software	500,000	100,000	(A) 1,500,000		2,100,000
Goodwill	–0–	–0–	(A) 70,000		70,000
Total assets	5,480,000	800,000			5,730,000
Notes payable	(300,000)	(200,000)		(A) 50,000	(550,000)
Contingent performance liability	(20,000)*				(20,000)
Common stock	(1,730,000)*	(100,000)	(S) 100,000		(1,730,000)
Additional paid-in capital	(2,510,000)*	(20,000)	(S) 20,000		(2,510,000)
Retained earnings, 12/31 (above)	(920,000)	(480,000)	(S) 480,000		(920,000)
Total liabilities and equities	(5,480,000)	(800,000)			(5,730,000)

Note: Parentheses indicate a credit balance.
*Balances have been adjusted for consideration transferred and payment of consolidation costs. Also note the follow-through effects to net income and retained earnings from the expensing of the direct acquisition costs.

In addition to the inclusion of the $2,600,000 stock payment, the preceding business fair value differs from the cost concept of *SFAS 141* in two respects. First, the consideration transferred includes $20,000 for the expected present value of the contingent consideration.[18] Second, it excludes direct acquisition costs because such costs are not part of the fair value exchanged for the business.

Like the purchase method, the acquisition method employs a consolidated worksheet to determine the reported values for the combined firm's financial statements. The financial figures from the separate companies as of the date of acquisition (see Exhibit 2.4) are shown in the first two columns of the worksheet (see Exhibit 2.9). BigNet's accounts have been adjusted for the acquisition method investment entry recorded earlier. Note in particular that BigNet's expenses include the $40,000 of direct combination costs and BigNet's liabilities include $20,000 for the contingent performance obligation.

The worksheet consolidation adjustments are similar to those in the purchase method example except that goodwill is $20,000 less ($90,000 − $70,000) because of the combined effect of excluding direct acquisition costs and including the contingent consideration in the initial recording of the investment account. The steps used to determine the consolidated balances mirror those of the *SFAS 141* purchase method. The final balances reflect the difference in accounting for direct acquisition costs and contingent consideration.

[18] Under *SFAS 141*, obligations for contingent consideration are not considered part of the acquisition cost but are recognized and measured as a postcombination adjustment to the purchase price when the contingency is finally resolved.

PURCHASE PRICE ALLOCATIONS—ADDITIONAL ISSUES—*SFAS 141*

Intangibles

An important accounting element of business combinations is the proper allocation of the purchase price to the underlying assets and liabilities acquired. In particular, the advent of the information age brings new challenges for a host of intangible assets that provide value in generating future cash flows. Often, intangible assets comprise the largest proportion of the purchase price of an acquired firm. For example, when AT&T acquired AT&T Broadband (formerly TCI), AT&T allocated approximately $19 billion of the $52 billion purchase price to franchise costs. Franchise costs are an intangible asset representing the value attributed to agreements with local authorities that allow access to homes. In addressing the importance of proper asset recognition, the FASB in *SFAS 141* observes that intangible assets include both current and noncurrent assets (not including financial instruments) that lack physical substance. Further, in determining whether to recognize an intangible asset in a business combination, *SFAS 141* relies on two essential attributes. First, does the intangible asset arise from contractual or other legal rights? Second, is the asset capable of being sold or otherwise separated from the acquired enterprise? As stated in *SFAS 141*,

> An intangible asset shall be recognized as an asset apart from goodwill if it arises from contractual or other legal rights (regardless of whether those rights are transferable or separable from the acquired entity or from other rights and obligations). If an intangible asset does not arise from contractual or other legal rights, it shall be recognized as an asset apart from goodwill only if it is separable, that is, it is capable of being separated or divided from the acquired entity and sold, transferred, licensed, rented, or exchanged (regardless of whether there is an intent to do so). For purposes of this statement, however, an intangible asset that cannot be sold, transferred, licensed, rented, or exchanged individually is considered separable if it can be sold, transferred, licensed, rented, or exchanged with a related contract, asset, or liability. For purposes of this statement, an assembled workforce shall not be recognized as an intangible asset apart from goodwill.[19]

Exhibit 2.10 provides a listing of intangible assets with indications of whether they typically meet the legal/contractual or separability criteria.

The FASB (Exposure Draft, *Business Combinations and Intangible Assets,* para. 271) recognized the inherent difficulties in estimating the separate fair values of many intangibles and stated that

> Difficulties may arise in assigning the acquisition cost to individual intangible assets acquired in a basket purchase such as a business combination. Measuring some of those assets is less difficult than measuring other assets, particularly if they are exchangeable and traded regularly in the marketplace. . . . Nonetheless, even those assets that cannot be measured on that basis may have more cash flow streams directly or indirectly associated with them than can be used as the basis for measuring them. While the resulting measures may lack the precision of other measures, they provide information that is more representationally faithful than would be the case if those assets were simply subsumed into goodwill on the grounds of measurement difficulties.

Undoubtedly, as our knowledge economy continues its rapid growth, asset allocations to items such as those identified in Exhibit 2.10 are expected to be frequent.

Purchased In-Process Research and Development

As discussed in this chapter, the accounting for a purchase business combination begins with the identification of the tangible and intangible assets acquired and liabilities assumed by the acquirer. The fair values of the individual assets and liabilities then provide the basis for purchase price allocations and financial statement valuations.

Recently, many firms—especially those in high-tech industries—have allocated significant portions of the purchase cost of acquired businesses to in-process research and development (IPR&D). A unique characteristic of IPR&D assets is that they must be written off immediately

---

[19] The 2005 FASB Exposure Draft, *Business Combinations,* retains the provision (and related application guidance) of *SFAS 141* that requires that intangible assets that meet the contractual or separability criteria be recognized as assets apart from goodwill.

EXHIBIT 2.10   Illustrative Examples of Intangible Assets That Meet the Criteria for Recognition Separately from Goodwill (*SFAS 141*)

The following are examples of intangible assets that meet the criteria for recognition as an asset apart from goodwill. The following illustrative list is not intended to be all-inclusive; thus, an acquired intangible asset might meet the recognition criteria of this statement but not be included on that list. Assets designated by the symbol (c) are those that would generally be recognized separately from goodwill because they meet the contractual-legal criterion. Assets designated by the symbol (s) do not arise from contractual or other legal rights, but should nonetheless be recognized separately from goodwill because they meet the separability criterion. The determination of whether a specific acquired intangible asset meets the criteria in this statement for recognition apart from goodwill should be based on the facts and circumstances of each individual business combination.*

Marketing-related intangible assets:
1. Trademarks, trade names.c
2. Service marks, collective marks, certification marks.c
3. Trade dress (unique color, shape, or package design).c
4. Newspaper mastheads.c
5. Internet domain names.c
6. Noncompetition agreements.c

Customer-related intangible assets:
1. Customer lists.s
2. Order or production backlog.c
3. Customer contracts and related customer relationships.c
4. Noncontractual customer relationships.s

Artistic-related intangible assets:
1. Plays, operas, and ballets.c
2. Books, magazines, newspapers, and other literary works.c
3. Musical works such as compositions, song lyrics, advertising jingles.c
4. Pictures and photographs.c
5. Video and audiovisual material, including motion pictures, music videos, and television programs.c

Contract-based intangible assets:
1. Licensing, royalty, standstill agreements.c
2. Advertising, construction, management, service, or supply contracts.c
3. Lease agreements.c
4. Construction permits.c
5. Franchise agreements.c
6. Operating and broadcast rights.c
7. Use rights such as landing, drilling, water, air, mineral, timber cutting, and route authorities.c
8. Servicing contracts such as mortgage servicing contracts.c
9. Employment contracts.c

Technology-based intangible assets:
1. Patented technology.c
2. Computer software and mask works.c
3. Unpatented technology.s
4. Databases, including title plants.s
5. Trade secrets, including secret formulas, processes, recipes.c

*The intangible assets designated by the symbol (c) also could meet the separability criterion. However, separability is not a necessary condition for an asset to meet the contractual-legal criterion.

unless those assets have an alternative future use. FASB *Interpretation No. 4*, "Applicability of FASB *Statement No. 2* to Business Combinations Accounted for by the Purchase Method," requires the identification and separation of assets resulting from research and development activities (e.g., core technology) and assets to be used in research and development activities. The latter group of assets is considered to be "in-process research and development" and thus is expensed as part of the business combination. Thus, the criteria to determine whether to expense or capitalize the value assigned to acquired IPR&D are whether (1) the project has reached technological feasibility and (2) alternative future uses exist for these assets if the current project fails. Regardless of the decision to capitalize or expense, fair value estimates of the IPR&D must be made. Important in estimating the fair value of research and development costs are factors such as stage of completion, technological uncertainties, and projected costs to complete the project.

The accounting for the immediate write-off of IPR&D acquired in a business combination is fairly straightforward. The fair value of the IPR&D simply becomes part of the allocated purchase price similar to an unrecorded asset except that the amount is allocated to an expense. For example, assume that ProKey Company acquires 100 percent of the voting stock of SysLock for $900,000. SysLock is a start-up company with $50,000 in equipment (fair value = $110,000) and research and development in process for a computer file locking system (fair value = $790,000). The locking system software is not technologically feasible yet and, if the project is unsuccessful, no alternative use is envisioned. Nonetheless, ProKey is confident that the software locking system will be ready for the market sometime during the next few years. Therefore, ProKey allocates its purchase price of SysLock as follows:

Purchase price (cash)		$900,000
Book value acquired		
Common stock—SysLock	$ 50,000	
Retained earnings—SysLock	–0–	50,000
Excess of cost over book value		$850,000
Write-up equipment (110,000 − 50,000)	60,000	
Write-off IPR&D	790,000	850,000
		–0–

ProKey makes the following entries on its books on acquisition of SysLock:

Investment in SysLock	900,000	
Cash		900,000
To record the purchase of SysLock for $900,000 cash.		

At acquisition, ProKey now has two options to accomplish the write-off of the acquired IPR&D. Under the first option, ProKey can simply leave the Investment in SysLock at $900,000 and rely on subsequent consolidated worksheet adjustments to accomplish the IPR&D allocation to expense.

Alternatively, ProKey can make the following entry on its books:

Research and development expense	790,000	
Investment in SysLock		790,000
To immediately write off to expense the $790,000 allocated to purchased in-process research and development.		

Under this second option, because the IPR&D has been expensed on ProKey's financial records, no other adjustments to IPR&D are required in consolidated worksheets. The Investment in SysLock simply carries forward a $110,000 balance. Whether ProKey chooses to rely on subsequent consolidated worksheet adjustments to accomplish the IPR&D write-off or immediately adjusts its own financial records, the reporting effect is the same. Current year income will be reduced by the $790,000 research and development expense.

Another example of an IPR&D expense is seen in the Yahoo! purchase of Log-Me-On.com. As noted in a Yahoo! 10-Q SEC filing, Log-Me-On's efforts were focused solely on developing an Internet browser technology that at the time was approximately 30 percent complete. This IPR&D was considered not to have reached technological feasibility and had no alternative future use as of the acquisition date. Of the $9.9 million purchase price for Log-Me-On.com, $9.8 million was allocated to IPR&D and immediately expensed.

The immediate expensing of IPR&D, although recently popular (see Exhibit 2.11), can be criticized as resulting in understated assets and distorted financial ratio results for many firms involved in purchase acquisitions. IPR&D in most cases clearly possesses value: One party pays another for the right to future cash flows resulting from the ongoing activity. However,

EXHIBIT 2.11
Notable In-Process Research and Development Write-Offs

WorldCom	$3,300 million
Compaq Computer	3,200 million
DuPont	1,441 million
Cadence Systems Design	339 million*

*Restated to $194 million in response to discussions with SEC.

the relevant FASB pronouncements not only allow immediate expensing but require it when technological feasibility and alternative future uses are not present in a research and development activity. Moreover, many firms prefer the immediate expensing of IPR&D. Although a one-time reduction of reported earnings takes place in the period of an acquisition involving IPR&D, subsequent reported earnings are free from such expenses and result in enhanced measures of return on equity, return on assets, and earnings per share.

The current application of the rules for expensing IPR&D has generated a great deal of controversy drawing the attention of the SEC. The SEC has cited several firms for overstating the allocated portion of IPR&D in business combinations. In a September 9, 1998, letter to the AICPA, Lynn Turner, the chief accountant for the SEC, noted that

> Although there was no change in the relevant accounting literature, IPR&D write-offs increased significantly in the 1990s. More intense merger activity in the technology sector may explain some of the increases, but abuses in the valuation of IPR&D are also suspected. This trend of larger write-offs could undermine public confidence in financial statements and presents significant challenges for the accounting profession.

The FASB is also struggling with the IPR&D controversy. On February 24, 1999, the FASB voted unanimously to revise the accounting rules for purchased IPR&D, calling for its capitalization and subsequent amortization to income. Nonetheless, the revision was short-lived when the FASB later reversed itself, allowing the continued immediate expensing of IPR&D. In *SFAS 141,* "Business Combinations," the FASB reaffirmed the expensing of acquired IPR&D until the matter is addressed comprehensively with all research and development activities, not just those involving business combinations. Then in its 2005 Exposure Draft, *Business Combinations,* the FASB again proposed that "the tangible and intangible assets acquired in a business combination to be used in a particular research and development activity, including those that may have no alternative future use," shall be recognized and measured at fair value at the acquisition date. These capitalized research and development costs would be considered intangible assets with indefinite lives subject to periodic impairment reviews. Given the value placed on research ideas and process development in today's economy, the problem of how to report the uncertain benefits associated with IPR&D will likely receive continued attention from regulators.

THE POOLING OF INTERESTS METHOD OF ACCOUNTING FOR BUSINESS COMBINATIONS

In *SFAS 141,* "Business Combinations," the FASB states that "all business combinations should be accounted for using the purchase method," thereby eliminating the pooling method. However, the application of the purchase method will be applied prospectively, leaving intact long-lasting financial statement effects from past poolings. Because differences between the purchase and pooling methods relate to fundamental issues of asset valuation and income recognition, the financial ratios resulting from past poolings will be affected for years to come. Therefore, to appreciate fully the financial reporting for business combinations, a solid familiarity with the pooling of interests accounting method remains necessary.

Continuity of Ownership

Historically, many transactions did not involve a clean break in ownership. Often, former owners of separate firms would agree to combine for their mutual benefit and continue as owners of a combined firm. It was asserted that the assets and liabilities of the former firms were never really bought or sold; former owners merely exchanged ownership shares to become joint owners of the combined firm.

Combinations characterized by exchange of voting shares and continuation of previous ownership became known as *pooling of interests.* Rather than an exchange transaction with one ownership group replacing another, a pooling of interests was characterized by a continuity of ownership interests before and after the business combination. Prior to its elimination, this method was applied to a significant number of business combinations.

EXHIBIT 2.12
Business Combination—
Pooling of Interests*

*This diagram is intended merely to represent the relationship created by a pooling of interests. The shares delivered by Celeron actually came from its owners who in turn received the 24.7 million shares of Goodyear Tire & Rubber directly from the company.

For example, the Goodyear Tire & Rubber Company exchanged nearly 25 million shares of its common stock for all of the outstanding common stock of Celeron Corporation to create a combination accounted for as a pooling of interests. As noted in Exhibit 2.12, Goodyear actually issued its stock in exchange for the shares held by the owners of Celeron. Consequently, the combined assets of these two companies were controlled by both the Goodyear shareholders and the previous Celeron owners (who now held Goodyear stock).

A pooling of interests was characterized as a continuation of ownership in which neither a parent nor subsidiary could be easily identified. The combination was created by an exchange of voting stock and was not viewed as a bargained transaction with a precise acquisition price. To reflect these qualities, two important steps were required in accounting for a combination created as a pooling of interests:

1. The book values of the assets and liabilities of both companies became the book values reported by the combined entity. Because of the continuity of ownership, no new basis of accountability arose.
2. The revenue and expense accounts were combined retrospectively as well as prospectively. Again, continuity of ownership allowed for the recognition of income accruing to the owners both before and after the combination.

Therefore, in a pooling, reported income is typically higher than under purchase accounting. Under pooling, not only did the firms retrospectively combine incomes but the smaller asset bases also resulted in smaller depreciation and amortization expenses. Because net income reported in financial statements often is used in a variety of contracts, including managerial compensation, managers considered the pooling method an attractive alternative to purchase accounting.

The APB, in *Opinion 16,* allowed both the purchase and pooling of interest methods to account for business combinations. However, the Board placed tight restrictions on the pooling method to prevent managers from engaging in purchase transactions and reporting them as poolings of interest. *Opinion 16* established 12 criteria that had to be present in a business combination to justify adoption of the pooling method. By setting strict guidelines, the Board hoped to ensure that only combinations clearly outside the essence of a purchase would fall under the pooling of interests classification. *Business combinations that failed to meet even 1 of these 12 criteria had to be accounted for by the purchase method.*

These criteria, which are presented in the appendix at the end of this chapter, had two overriding objectives. First, they defined a pooling of interests as a single transaction (or series of transactions occurring over a limited time) in which two independent companies are united solely through the exchange of voting common stock. To ensure the complete fusion of the two organizations, one company had to obtain substantially all (90 percent or more) of the voting stock of the other.

The second general objective of these criteria was to prevent purchase combinations from being disguised as poolings. Past experience had shown the APB that combination transactions were frequently manipulated so that they would qualify for pooling of interests treatment (usually to increase reported earnings). However, subsequent events, often involving cash being paid or received by the parties, revealed the true nature of the combination: One company was purchasing the other in a bargained exchange. The APB designed a number of the 12 criteria to stop this practice.

For example, to be considered a pooling of interests, no agreement could exist to reacquire any of the shares issued in creating the combination. This rule prevented the parties from eventually receiving cash or other assets as part of the transaction. For the same reason, significant assets of the combined companies could not be sold for two years unless duplication existed. These restrictions helped to ensure that only combinations meeting the essence of a pooling were given that treatment—a continuation of the companies and a continuation of the ownership.

Pooling of Interests When Dissolution Takes Place

To demonstrate the formation of a pooling of interests, assume that BigNet Company and Smallport Company decide to join operations on December 31 (see Exhibit 2.4).[20] This combination is created when BigNet issues 23,000 new shares of its common stock, with a $5 par value and a $100 market value per share, to the owners of Smallport in exchange for all of the company's outstanding common shares. Smallport transfers its assets and liabilities to BigNet and dissolves itself as a separate corporation. Stock registration fees of $5,000 are paid by BigNet as well as $3,000 in other costs directly associated with the combination. In creating this business combination, the companies followed all 12 criteria established by *APB Opinion 16* for a pooling of interests (see the appendix at the end of the chapter).

Pooling of Interests Method—Subsidiary Dissolved

BigNet Company's Financial Records—December 31

Current Assets	300,000	
Computers and Equipment	400,000	
Capitalized Software	100,000	
Dividends Paid	10,000	
Expenses	380,000	
Notes Payable		200,000
Revenues		500,000
Common Stock (23,000 shares issued by BigNet at $5 par value)		115,000
Additional Paid-In Capital (to equate contributed capital with $120,000 amount reported by Smallport)		5,000
Retained Earnings, 1/1 (to record amount equal to book value of Smallport)		370,000
Expenses (combination costs)	8,000	
Cash		8,000

To record book value of Smallport's account obtained through a pooling of interests. Direct combination costs are expensed.

As stated earlier, a pooling of interests consolidates all accounts at their historical book values. Therefore, the reported value of each of Smallport's accounts (assets, liabilities, revenues, expenses, and dividends paid) simply can be transferred into BigNet's financial records through a journal entry. To ensure that adequate disclosure is provided, *APB Opinion 16* does require that the details of the separate operations be presented in a note to the consolidated statements.

In contrast to the purchase method, no part of the $8,000 in combination costs is capitalized; the entire amount is recorded here as an expense. According to *APB Opinion 16* (para. 58), "The pooling of interests method records neither the acquiring of assets nor the obtaining of capital. Therefore, costs incurred to effect a combination accounted for by that method and to integrate the continuing operations are expenses of the combined corporation rather than additions to assets or direct reductions of stockholders' equity." To maintain book value, the cost of uniting the organizations is not viewed as a change in either asset or contributed capital accounts; thus, an expense is recorded by the combined entity.

Entering the book values of Smallport's assets, liabilities, revenues, expenses, and dividends into the records of BigNet poses little trouble.[21] Likewise, the $8,000 in direct

[20] We assume the initiation date for the combination occurs on or prior to June 30, 2001—the deadline for pooling accounting as stated in *SFAS 141*, "Business Combinations."

[21] As is discussed in Chapter 3, dividends paid between the related companies after a combination is created are intercompany transfers that have to be eliminated. In a pooling of interests, though, any amounts distributed to previous owners before the combination was created continue to be reported as Dividends Paid.

combination costs is simply assigned directly to expense. However, the recording of the 23,000 shares of stock being issued by BigNet should be noted. According to Exhibit 2.4, Smallport is reporting contributed capital (the Common Stock and Additional Paid-In Capital accounts) of $120,000 and retained earnings of $370,000.[22] Because poolings retain book value, BigNet uses these same figures in recording the issuance of its own stock. In that way, Smallport's equity balances are included within the combined totals.

Regardless of the amounts reported by Smallport, BigNet's Common Stock account must be increased by $115,000 to reflect the $5 par value of these 23,000 shares. To arrive at the $120,000 figure that corresponds with Smallport's total contributed capital, BigNet also records $5,000 as Additional Paid-In Capital. The entry is then completed with a $370,000 credit to Retained Earnings. Smallport's contributed capital total and Retained Earnings both have been added into the business combination at book value.

After recording these accounts, BigNet's financial records show $1,392,000 in Current Assets ($1,100,000 + $300,000 − 8,000), $1,700,000 in Computers and Equipment ($1,300,000 + $400,000), and so on. The Revenues account now holds $1,500,000 ($1,000,000 + $500,000) while expenses are recorded at $1,188,000 ($800,000 + $380,000 + $8,000 in combination costs). *Because book values are retained, the various asset, liability, revenue, expense, and dividend balances are not affected by the number of shares issued by BigNet.* If 2,300 shares or 230,000 shares had been exchanged rather than 23,000, the same consolidated figures still would have been appropriate for these accounts.

By comparing this consolidation to previous illustrations, several areas of distinct contrast can be seen between the purchase method and the pooling of interests method:

	Consolidation	
	SFAS 141 **Purchase Method**	**Pooling of Interests Method**
Assets and liabilities of subsidiary	Recorded at fair value.*	Recorded at book value.
Goodwill	Excess of purchase price over fair value of subsidiary net assets.	Not recognized.
Revenues and expenses of subsidiary	Accrued only after date of acquisition.	Recognized retrospectively.
Shares issued to create business combination	Recorded at fair value if any shares are issued.	Based on book value of subsidiary's contributed capital and retained earnings at beginning of year.
Combination costs	Included as part of purchase price unless incurred in connection with issuance of stock, a cost that reduces paid-in capital.	Expensed immediately.

*If purchase price is less than fair value, noncurrent assets (except for any long-term investments in marketable securities) are recorded at reduced amounts.

When reviewing the recording of a past pooling of interests, one potential variation to the previous entry can be encountered. Although poolings are based on retaining book values, the recording of contributed capital can cause a problem. Because issued shares are always credited for par value, BigNet's common stock had to be recorded as $115,000, although Smallport's balance for this same account was $100,000. As indicated, BigNet increased its additional paid-in capital by $5,000 so that total contributed capital equaled Smallport's $120,000 balance (see Exhibit 2.13).

[22] Although the date of the pooling was December 31, Smallport's Retained Earnings balance as of the first day of the year is recorded by the combination with the company's current revenues, expenses, and dividends being reported separately.

EXHIBIT 2.13 Recording of Shares Issued in a Pooling of Interests

(Exhibit 2.4)	Smallport's Book Values	BigNet Company Issues			
		18,000 Shares	23,000 Shares	26,000 Shares	35,000 Shares
Common stock	$100,000	$ 90,000	$115,000	$130,000	$175,000
Additional paid-in capital	20,000	30,000	5,000	(10,000)	(40,000)*
Total contributed capital	120,000	120,000	120,000	120,000	135,000
Retained earnings	370,000	370,000	370,000	370,000	355,000†

*BigNet's Additional Paid-In Capital account is reduced from $40,000 to zero.
†Because the contributed capital of issued shares is $55,000 greater than that reported by Smallport, BigNet's APIC is first reduced to zero ($40,000 reduction) and the amount recorded for Retained Earnings ($355,000) reflects the remaining $15,000 reduction.

If BigNet had originally issued only 18,000 shares, its Common Stock account would be credited for $90,000 with an accompanying $30,000 added to Additional Paid-In Capital. Once again, the $120,000 total book value of Smallport's contributed capital is replicated by the entry. Conversely, as shown in Exhibit 2.13, if 26,000 shares with a par value of $130,000 were exchanged by BigNet to create this pooling, a $10,000 *reduction* to Additional Paid-In Capital is necessary to arrive at the appropriate $120,000 total. In each case, the book value of Smallport's total contributed capital is retained by the combination.

A slightly different problem arises in recording total contributed capital for a pooling when the number of issued shares is relatively large. Assume, as an example, that 35,000 shares of common stock are exchanged by BigNet to establish this pooling of interests with Smallport. The $175,000 par value of the stock necessitates a $55,000 reduction in BigNet's Additional Paid-In Capital to equal the $120,000 contributed capital reported by Smallport.

However, Exhibit 2.4 indicates that BigNet's Additional Paid-In Capital account holds only a $40,000 balance. Because a negative contributed capital balance is not possible, BigNet's additional paid-in capital is first dropped to zero with the remaining $15,000 decrease being made in Retained Earnings. Exhibit 2.13 shows that only $355,000 in retained earnings (rather than Smallport's $370,000 balance) is recorded by the business combination when 35,000 shares are issued. *Thus, if BigNet's issued shares have a total par value more than Smallport's total contributed capital, a reduction must be made. BigNet initially decreases its own Additional Paid-In Capital account. However, if that amount proves to be insufficient, the Retained Earnings balance also must be reduced.*

Pooling of Interests When Separate Incorporation Is Maintained

The combination of BigNet Company and Smallport Company is presented again to demonstrate a pooling of interests, one in which both companies retain their separate legal identities. For this illustration, the same financial information is used as in the purchase consolidation shown in Exhibit 2.7. As in the purchase situation, BigNet issues 26,000 shares of common stock on December 31 for all of Smallport's outstanding shares. Also, direct combination costs of $40,000 are incurred. Smallport's accounts are not transferred to BigNet's financial records; both companies continue as separate corporations and maintain independent accounting systems. However, the assumption is made here that the combination has met all 12 requirements for a pooling of interests.

BigNet must first record the issuance of 26,000 shares of common stock to create this business combination. Because Smallport is not being dissolved, BigNet establishes an investment balance rather than recording Smallport's individual accounts. Because the combination is a pooling, this figure is based on Smallport's $490,000 book value as of the beginning of the year. Using the January 1 total allows the current revenues, expenses, and dividends to be included as separate items in recording the business combination.

The issued shares are recorded by BigNet at their par value of $130,000. BigNet's Additional Paid-In Capital account is reduced by $10,000 to arrive at total contributed capital of $120,000, the same book value as Smallport's contributed capital. Retained earnings at January 1 also are included in this entry because operating activities are retroactively consolidated in a pooling of interests. The direct combination costs are expensed immediately.

Pooling of Interests Method—Subsidiary Not Dissolved

BigNet's Financial Records—December 31		
Investment in Smallport Company (1/1 book value)	490,000	
Additional Paid-In Capital (to align contributed capital with that of Smallport)	10,000	
Common Stock (26,000 shares at $5 par value)		130,000
Retained Earnings, 1/1 (to record balance equal to book value of Smallport)		370,000
Expenses (direct combination costs)	40,000	
Cash		40,000
To record issuance of 26,000 shares of stock in exchange for all of the outstanding shares of Smallport in a combination accounted for as a pooling of interests. Direct combination costs are properly expensed.		

When the common stock shares are exchanged, the combination is formed, and consolidated financial statements can be prepared using the worksheet in Exhibit 2.14. This pooling of interests is carried out through the following series of steps.

Step 1

Prior to creating this worksheet, BigNet's balances are adjusted to show (1) the effect of its issuance of stock and (2) the direct combination costs. The updated accounts are then entered into the appropriate columns on the worksheet (see Exhibit 2.4 for original book values).

Step 2

The Investment in Smallport Company account is eliminated as part of the basic consolidation Entry **S**. In the same manner as the purchase method, the Investment account is not consolidated; rather, the specific accounts that it represents should be reported by the business combination.

Step 3

Smallport's stockholders' equity balances also are eliminated by this same Entry **S**. In a pooling when a fusion of ownership interests is said to occur, the equity figures for both companies must be included. The initial investment entry has already added these equity balances to BigNet's records prior to consolidating the financial statements. Thus, Smallport's Common Stock, Additional Paid-In Capital, and Retained Earnings must be eliminated on the worksheet to prevent their inclusion in the final figures a second time.

Step 4

For a pooling of interests, the consolidation process is carried out by adding together the book values of each account. For example, BigNet's revenue of $1,000,000 and Smallport's revenue of $500,000 are extended for a consolidated total of $1,500,000. When a consolidation entry affects an account (such as the elimination of Smallport's equity accounts), the impact of that adjustment also must be reflected in this extension process. However, because a purchase price is not determined in a pooling, no goodwill is recognized and no valuation adjustments are made to any asset or liability.

EXHIBIT 2.14 Pooling of Interests—Date of Acquisition

BIGNET COMPANY AND SMALLPORT COMPANY
Consolidation Worksheet
For Period Ending December 31

Accounts	BigNet Company	Smallport Company	Consolidation Entries Debits	Consolidation Entries Credits	Consolidated Totals
Income Statement					
Revenues	(1,000,000)	(500,000)			(1,500,000)
Expenses	840,000	380,000			1,220,000
Net income	(160,000)	(120,000)			(280,000)
Statement of Retained Earnings					
Retained earnings, 1/1	(1,240,000)*	(370,000)	(S) 370,000		(1,240,000)
Net income (above)	(160,000)	(120,000)			(280,000)
Dividends paid	110,000	10,000			120,000
Retained earnings, 12/31	(1,290,000)	(480,000)			(1,400,000)
Balance Sheet					
Current assets	1,060,000*	300,000			1,360,000
Investment in Smallport Company	490,000*	–0–		(S) 490,000	–0–
Computers and equipment	1,300,000	400,000			1,700,000
Capitalized software	500,000	100,000			600,000
Total assets	3,350,000	800,000			3,660,000
Notes payable	(300,000)	(200,000)			(500,000)
Common stock	(1,730,000)*	(100,000)	(S) 100,000		(1,730,000)
Additional paid-in capital	(30,000)*	(20,000)	(S) 20,000		(30,000)
Retained earnings, 12/31 (above)	(1,290,000)	(480,000)			(1,400,000)
Total liabilities and equities	(3,350,000)	(800,000)			(3,660,000)

Note: Parentheses indicate a credit balance.
*Balances have been adjusted for issuance of stock and payment of consolidation costs.

Step 5

For each of the financial statements on the worksheet, a total is calculated. The income statement ends with a net income balance, the statement of retained earnings computes ending Retained Earnings, and the balance sheet arrives at Total Assets as well as Total Liabilities and Equities. As discussed previously, these final figures are not derived by consolidating the respective balances of the separate companies. Instead, the components in each statement are extended and then used to compute the ending balance.

On the income statement demonstrated here, revenues and expenses are added to produce totals of $1,500,000 and $1,220,000, respectively, indicating consolidated net income of $280,000. This figure is moved to the corresponding line within the statement of retained earnings. Each of the other elements constituting this second statement is extended to produce ending retained earnings of $1,400,000. This total is then included within the stockholders' equity section of the consolidated balance sheet, enabling it to properly balance.

Step 6

After all accounts have been consolidated, the final balances on the worksheet are used to prepare financial statements for the business combination of BigNet Company and Smallport Company. Exhibit 2.15 provides a comparison of the figures developed for the purchase

EXHIBIT 2.15

Comparison of Purchase Method and Pooling of Interests Method

General Information: 26,000 shares of BigNet Company (par value of $5 per share but a market value of $100 per share) issued for all outstanding shares of Smallport Company on December 31. Cash of $40,000 paid for direct consolidation costs.

	Purchase Method (Exhibit 2.7)	Pooling of Interests Method (Exhibit 2.14)
Revenues	$(1,000,000)	$(1,500,000)
Expenses	800,000	1,220,000
Net income	$ (200,000)	$ (280,000)
Beginning retained earnings	$ (870,000)	$(1,240,000)
Net income (above)	(200,000)	(280,000)
Dividends paid	110,000	120,000
Ending retained earnings	$ (960,000)	$(1,400,000)
Current assets	$ 1,360,000	$ 1,360,000
Computers and equipment	2,200,000	1,700,000
Capitalized software	2,100,000	600,000
Goodwill	90,000	–0–
Total assets	$ 5,750,000	$ 3,660,000
Notes payable	$ (550,000)	$ (500,000)
Common stock	(1,730,000)	(1,730,000)
Additional paid-in capital	(2,510,000)	(30,000)
Retained earnings (above)	(960,000)	(1,400,000)
Total liabilities and equities	$(5,750,000)	$(3,660,000)
Financial Performance Ratios		
Net income/Total assets	3.48%	7.65%
Net income/Total equity	3.85%	8.86%

Note: Parentheses indicate credit balances.

consolidation shown previously in Exhibit 2.7 and the pooling of interests in Exhibit 2.14. Note the more favorable portrayal of two popular financial performance ratios for pooling versus purchase despite the combination of identical firms.

POOLING OF INTERESTS—THE CONTROVERSY

Over the years, the legitimacy of the pooling of interests method has frequently been questioned. One major theoretical problem associated with the pooling method is that it ignores cost figures indicated by the transaction that created the combination. The number of shares exchanged has no impact on consolidated asset and liability balances. What is normally a significant event for both companies is simply omitted from any accounting consideration. *All book values are retained as if nothing has happened. APB Opinion 16 (para. 39) itself admits*

> The most serious defect attributed to pooling of interests accounting by those who oppose it is that it does not accurately reflect the economic substance of the business combination transaction. They believe that the method ignores the bargaining which results in the combination by accounting only for the amounts previously shown in accounts of the combining companies.

As a further argument against pooling of interests, many accountants believe that only one accounting approach should be applicable for all business combinations. They hold that all combinations are essentially the same. Even though a variety of formats does exist, critics contend that a parent and an acquisition price can be determined in virtually every case.

In addition, conveying freely traded stock is held to be the same as conveying cash. According to this argument, the availability of two radically different accounting methods is simply not warranted. Interestingly, the pooling of interests method has been primarily found in the United States. "Of all the major industrialized countries, only Great Britain allows anything resembling pooling, and its rule makers are modifying the rules to prevent most poolings."[23]

Notably, in a dissent to *APB Opinion 16,* Sidney Davidson, Charles Horngren, and J. S Seidman asserted that

> The real abuse is pooling itself. On that, the only answer is to eliminate pooling. . . . Elimination of pooling will remove the confusion that comes from the coexistence of pooling and purchase accounting. Above all, the elimination of pooling would remove an aberration in historical cost accounting that permits an acquisition to be accounted for on the basis of the seller's cost rather than the buyer's cost of the assets obtained in a bargained exchange.

The pooling of interests method was very popular in the business world largely based on the desirable impact that it usually produced on reported net income. The most obvious effect is the inclusion of the subsidiary's net income as if that company had always been part of the consolidated entity. This retrospective treatment can lead to immediate improvement in the profitability picture being reported.

Another income effect helped to further account for the popularity enjoyed by the pooling of interests method. In a purchase combination, the subsidiary's assets and liabilities are adjusted to fair value with goodwill often recognized. Such allocations are viewed as cost figures of the business combination, costs that have only limited useful lives (except when relating to land). Thus, these amounts (which can be extremely large) required amortization over future accounting periods. The resulting expense, encountered only in the purchase method, served to reduce consolidated net income year after year.

Conversely, a pooling of interests consolidated all accounts at their book values so that no additional amortization expense was ever recognized. Therefore, in most past business combinations, the income reported for each succeeding year was higher using the pooling method than would have been the case if consolidated by the purchase method.[24] To the extent that managerial compensation contracts are based on accounting measures of profitability, a further motivation to employ the pooling of interests method to accounting for a business combination was provided.

Given these reporting advantages, the desire by businesses to create combinations that would qualify as poolings is not surprising. Historically, the accounting profession attempted to define the characteristics of a pooling of interests in such a way as to restrict its use to combinations that were clearly fusions of two independent companies. Over the years, however, the identification of attributes considered to be essential to a pooling of interests proved to be a difficult task.

FASB Position

In an article supporting their unanimous decision to eliminate the pooling of interests method of accounting for business combinations, the FASB cited the following reasons for their action:

- The pooling method provides investors with less information—and less relevant information—than that provided by the purchase method.
- The pooling method ignores the values exchanged in a business combination while the purchase method reflects them.
- Under the pooling method, financial statement readers cannot tell how much was invested in the transaction, nor can they track the subsequent performance of the investment.
- Having two methods of accounting makes it difficult for investors to compare companies when they have used different methods to account for their business combinations.
- Because future cash flows are the same whether the pooling or purchase method is used, the boost in earnings under the pooling method reflects artificial accounting differences rather than real economic differences.

---

[23] Michael Davis, "APB 16: Time to Reconsider," *Journal of Accountancy,* October 1991, p. 99.

[24] For example, see Andrew Fioriti and Thomas Brady, "Anatomy of a Pooling: The AT&T/NCR Merger," *Ohio CPA Journal,* October 1994, p. 20.

- Business combinations are acquisitions and should be accounted for as such, based on the value of what is given up in exchange, regardless of whether it is cash, other assets, debt, or equity shares.[25]

[25] "Why Eliminate the Pooling Method," August 31, *1999 Financial Accounting Series Status Report No. 316* (Financial Accounting Foundation/FASB).

Summary

1. Consolidation of financial information is required for external reporting purposes whenever one organization gains control of another, thus forming a single economic entity. In many combinations, all but one of the companies is dissolved as a separate legal corporation. Therefore, the consolidation process is carried out only at the date of acquisition to bring together all accounts into a single set of financial records. In other combinations, the companies retain their identities as separate enterprises and continue to maintain their own individual accounting systems. For these cases, consolidation is a periodic process necessary whenever financial statements are to be produced. This periodic procedure is frequently accomplished through the use of a worksheet and consolidation entries.

2. Under the *SFAS 141* purchase method for business combinations, the acquisition price is based on the exchange transaction and includes all direct consolidation costs unless expended to issue stock. The assets and liabilities of the acquired company are consolidated based on their fair values at the date of purchase. If the price paid exceeds the total fair value of the net assets, the residual amount is recorded in the consolidated financial statements as goodwill, an intangible asset.

3. Using the purchase method, if the acquisition price is less than total fair value, a reduction in the consolidated balances is necessary. The acquired company's assets and liabilities are recorded at fair value except for noncurrent assets (however, financial assets other than equity method investments, assets to be disposed of by sale, deferred tax assets, and prepaid pension assets still are recorded at fair values). Because of the bargain purchase, these noncurrent assets are consolidated at amounts less than their fair values. The reduction is the difference between the parent's purchase price and the total fair value of the subsidiary's assets and liabilities. This figure is prorated based on the fair values of the various noncurrent assets. An extraordinary gain is reported if the reduction exceeds the total value of the applicable noncurrent assets.

4. *SFAS 141* pays particular attention to the recognition of intangible assets in business combinations. It specifically identifies many categories of intangibles. An intangible asset must be recognized in an acquiring firm's financial statement if the intangible arises from a legal or contractual right (e.g., trademarks, copyrights, artistic materials, royalty agreements). If the intangible asset does not represent a legal or contractual right, the intangible will still be recognized if it is capable of being separated from the firm (e.g., customer lists, noncontractual customer relationships, unpatented technology). Acquired assets identified as in-process research and development will continue to be expensed at the acquisition date if the research has not reached technological feasibility and the assets associated with the research have no alternative future uses.

   In June 2005, the FASB issued the Exposure Draft, *Business Combinations,* which if approved, would substantially alter the financial reporting for acquisitions under *SFAS 141.* The Exposure Draft adopts a fair value perspective for recording business combinations as opposed to the *SFAS 141* cost-based provisions. Business fair value (as indicated by the fair value of consideration transferred) would serve as the valuation basis for recording most acquisitions. Also, the individual assets acquired and liabilities assumed would be recorded at their fair values. Direct combination costs would be expensed as incurred because they are not part of the acquired business fair value. Contingent consideration would be included in the fair value of the consideration transferred. Similar to *SFAS 141,* goodwill would be recorded as the excess of the consideration transferred over the acquired net asset fair value. Unlike *SFAS 141,* when a bargain purchase occurs, individual assets and liabilities acquired continue to be recorded at their fair values and a gain on bargain purchase is recognized.

5. Past policy allowed a business combination to be accounted for as either a purchase or a pooling of interests. To differentiate the applicable use of these methods, 12 criteria were established by the APB. If all 12 were satisfied, the combination was to be viewed as a pooling of interests. Otherwise, the purchase method was appropriate. The two methods were not interchangeable; a specific approach was required based on these criteria. However, the FASB has mandated elimination of the pooling method, thus requiring all combinations to be accounted for as purchases.

6. The pooling of interests method was criticized often because it relied on book values only and, therefore, ignored the exchange transaction that formed the economic entity. Poolings also were questioned because of the retroactive treatment of operating results. Consequently, companies were able to increase reported earnings by pooling with another company rather than by improving operating efficiency.

Comprehensive Illustration

(*Estimated Time: 45 to 65 Minutes*) Following are the account balances of Marston Company and Richmond Company as of December 31. The fair values of Richmond Company's assets and liabilities are also listed.

PROBLEM

	Marston Company Book Value 12/31/06	Richmond Company Book Value 12/31/06	Richmond Company Fair Values 12/31/06
Cash.	$ 600,000	$ 200,000	$ 200,000
Receivables.	900,000	300,000	290,000
Inventory	1,100,000	600,000	820,000
Buildings (net)	3,000,000	800,000	900,000
Equipment (net)	6,000,000	500,000	500,000
In-process research and development	–0–	–0–	100,000
Accounts payable	(400,000)	(200,000)	(200,000)
Notes payable.	(3,400,000)	(1,100,000)	(1,100,000)
Totals	$ 7,800,000	$1,100,000	$ 1,510,000
Common stock—$20 par value . . .	$(2,000,000)		
Common stock—$5 par value		$ (720,000)	
Additional paid-in capital	(900,000)	(100,000)	
Retained earnings, 1/1/06.	(2,300,000)	(130,000)	
Revenues	(6,000,000)	(900,000)	
Expenses	3,400,000	750,000	

Note: Parentheses indicate a credit balance.

Also assume that Marston relies on consolidated worksheet adjustments to reflect appropriate accounting for acquired in-process research and development.

Additional Information (not recorded in the preceding figures)

- On December 31, 2006, Marston issues 50,000 shares of its $20 par value common stock for all of the outstanding shares of Richmond Company.
- In creating this combination, Marston pays $10,000 in stock issuance costs and $20,000 in other direct combination costs.

Required:

a. Assume that Marston's stock has a fair value of $32.00 per share. Using the *SFAS 141* purchase method, prepare the necessary journal entries if Richmond is to dissolve itself as a separate legal entity.

b. Assume that Marston's stock has a fair value of $28.52 per share. Richmond will retain separate legal incorporation and maintain its own accounting systems. Using the *SFAS 141* purchase method, prepare a worksheet to consolidate the accounts of the two companies.

c. Using the acquisition method as described in the 2005 FASB Exposure Draft *Business Combinations,* prepare a worksheet to consolidate the two companies. As in (*b*), Richmond will retain legal incorporation and maintain its own accounting system. Marston's stock has a market value of $28.52.

SOLUTION

a. In a business combination, the accountant should first determine the parent company's acquisition price. Since Marston's stock is valued at $32 per share, the 50,000 issued shares are worth $1,600,000 in total. The $10,000 stock issuance cost is reported as a reduction to Additional Paid-In Capital. The other $20,000 direct combination costs are added to the value of the issued shares to arrive at a purchase price of $1,620,000. This total is compared to the $1,510,000 fair value of Richmond's assets and liabilities (including the value of IPR&D). Since Marston has paid $110,000 more than fair value ($1,620,000 − $1,510,000), that figure is recognized as goodwill.

Because dissolution will occur, Richmond's asset and liability accounts are transferred to Marston and entered at fair value with the excess recorded as goodwill. The payment of the stock issuance costs is journalized separately to avoid confusion.

Marston Company's Financial Records—December 31, 2006

Cash	200,000	
Receivables	290,000	
Inventory	820,000	
Buildings	900,000	
Equipment	500,000	
Research and Development Expense	100,000	
Goodwill	110,000	
Accounts Payable		200,000
Notes Payable		1,100,000
Common Stock (Marston) (par value)		1,000,000
Additional Paid-In Capital (market value in excess of par value)		600,000
Cash (paid for combination costs)		20,000
To record purchase of Richmond Company.		
Additional Paid-In Capital	10,000	
Cash (stock issuance costs)		10,000
To record payment of stock issuance costs.		

b. Under this scenario, because a different value is attributed to the issued shares, a new purchase price must be calculated:

50,000 shares of stock at $28.52 each	$1,426,000
Other direct combination costs	20,000
Purchase price	$1,446,000

Because the subsidiary is maintaining separate incorporation, Marston establishes an investment account to reflect the $1,446,000 purchase price:

Marston's Financial Records—December 31, 2006

Investment in Richmond Company	1,446,000	
Common Stock (Marston) (par value)		1,000,000
Additional Paid-In Capital (market value in excess of par value)		426,000
Cash (paid for combination costs)		20,000
To record purchase of Richmond Company.		
Additional Paid-In Capital	10,000	
Cash (paid for stock issuance costs)		10,000
To record payment of stock issuance costs.		

Separate incorporation is being maintained; thus, a worksheet is developed for consolidation purposes. The parent allocates the purchase price to assets acquired and liabilities assumed based on their fair values:

Purchase price paid by Marston	$1,446,000
Book value of Richmond	1,100,000
Excess of cost over book value	$ 346,000

Allocations are made to specific accounts based on differences in fair values and book values:

Receivables ($290,000 − $300,000)	$(10,000)	
Inventory ($820,000 − $600,000)	220,000	
Buildings ($900,000 − $800,000)	100,000	
In-process research and development	100,000	410,000
Bargain purchase		$ (64,000)

Marston's $1,446,000 purchase price is $64,000 less than the $1,510,000 fair value of Richmond's net assets. A reduction must be assigned to the subsidiary's applicable noncurrent assets (including IPR&D) based on their relative fair values:

	Fair Value	Percentage of Fair Value	Reduction	Allocation of Bargain Purchase to Reduce Individual Assets
Buildings	900,000	60.00%	64,000	38,400
Equipment	500,000	33.33%	64,000	21,333
IPR&D	100,000	6.67%	64,000	4,267
Totals	1,500,000	100.00%		64,000

Thus, within the consolidation worksheet, the subsidiary's buildings are assigned a reduced value of $861,600 ($900,000 − $38,400). The equipment is adjusted to $478,667 ($500,000 − $21,333), and the in-process research and development is expensed at $95,733 ($100,000 − $4,267).

Exhibit 2.16 can now be developed using the following steps to arrive at totals for the consolidated financial statements:

- Marston's balances have been updated on this worksheet to include the effect of both the newly issued shares of stock and the combination costs.

EXHIBIT 2.16   Comprehensive Illustration—Solution—Purchase Method

MARSTON COMPANY AND RICHMOND COMPANY
Consolidation Worksheet
For Period Ending December 31, 2006

Accounts	Marston Company	Richmond Company	Consolidation Entries Debit	Consolidation Entries Credit	Consolidated Totals
Income Statement					
Revenues	(6,000,000)				(6,000,000)
Expenses	3,400,000		(A) 95,733		3,495,733
Net income	(2,600,000)				(2,504,267)
Statement of Retained Earnings					
Retained earnings, 1/1/06	(2,300,000)				(2,300,000)
Net income (above)	(2,600,000)				(2,504,267)
Retained earnings, 12/31/06	(4,900,000)				(4,804,267)
Balance Sheet					
Cash	570,000*	200,000			770,000
Receivables	900,000	300,000		(A) 10,000	1,190,000
Inventory	1,100,000	600,000	(A) 220,000		1,920,000
Investment in Richmond Company	1,446,000*	–0–		(S) 1,100,000	–0–
				(A) 346,000	
Buildings (net)	3,000,000	800,000	(A) 61,600		3,861,600
Equipment (net)	6,000,000	500,000		(A) 21,333	6,478,667
Total assets	13,016,000	2,400,000			14,220,267
Accounts payable	(400,000)	(200,000)			(600,000)
Notes payable	(3,400,000)	(1,100,000)			(4,500,000)
Common stock	(3,000,000)*	(720,000)	(S) 720,000		(3,000,000)
Additional paid-in capital	(1,316,000)*	(100,000)	(S) 100,000		(1,316,000)
Retained earnings, 12/31/06 (above)	(4,900,000)	(280,000)†	(S) 280,000		(4,804,267)
Total liabilities and equities	(13,016,000)	(2,400,000)			(14,220,267)

Note: Parentheses indicate a credit balance.
*Balances have been adjusted for issuance of stock and payment of combination costs.
†Beginning Retained Earnings plus revenues minus expenses.

- Richmond's revenue and expense accounts have been closed out to Retained Earnings since this combination is a purchase.
- Entry **S** on the worksheet eliminates the $1,100,000 book value component of the Investment in Richmond Company account along with the subsidiary's stockholders' equity accounts.
- Entry **A** adjusts all of Richmond's assets and liabilities to fair value based on the allocations determined earlier. However, the values attributed to the Buildings account, the Equipment account, and the Expenses account (for IPR&D) have been reduced by a total of $64,000 to reflect the bargain purchase made.

c. Under the acquisition method, the consideration transferred is first compared to the net amount of the fair values of assets acquired and liabilities assumed.

Fair value of consideration transferred	$1,426,000
Net fair values of assets acquired and liabilities assumed	1,510,000
Excess net asset fair value over consideration transferred	$ 84,000

EXHIBIT 2.17 **Comprehensive Illustration—Solution—Acquisition Method (FASB Exposure Draft)**

MARSTON COMPANY AND RICHMOND COMPANY
Consolidation Worksheet
For Period Ending December 31, 2006

Accounts	Marston Company	Richmond Company	Consolidation Entries Debit	Consolidation Entries Credit	Consolidated Totals
Income Statement					
Revenues	(6,000,000)				(6,000,000)
Expenses	3,420,000*				3,420,000
Gain on bargain purchase	(84,000)*				(84,000)
Net income	(2,664,000)				(2,664,000)
Statement of Retained Earnings					
Retained earnings 1/1/06	(2,300,000)				(2,300,000)
Net income (above)	(2,664,000)				(2,664,000)
Retained earnings, 12/31/06	(4,964,000)				(4,964,000)
Balance Sheet					
Cash	570,000*	200,000			770,000
Receivables	900,000	300,000		(A) 10,000	1,190,000
Inventory	1,100,000	600,000	(A) 220,000		1,920,000
Investment in Richmond Company	1,510,000*	–0–		(S) 1,100,000 (A) 410,000	–0–
Buildings (net)	3,000,000	800,000	(A) 100,000		3,900,000
Equipment (net)	6,000,000	500,000			6,500,000
Capitalized research and development	–0–	–0–	(A) 100,000		100,000
Total assets	13,080,000	2,400,000			14,380,000
Accounts payable	(400,000)	(200,000)			(600,000)
Notes payable	(3,400,000)	(1,100,000)			(4,500,000)
Common stock	(3,000,000)*	(720,000)	(S) 720,000		(3,000,000)
Additional paid-in capital	(1,316,000)*	(100,000)	(S) 100,000		(1,316,000)
Retained earnings, 12/31/06 (above)	(4,964,000)	(280,000)†	(S) 280,000		(4,964,000)
Total liabilities and equities	(13,080,000)	(2,400,000)			(14,380,000)

Note: Parentheses indicate a credit balance.
*Balances have been adjusted for issuance of stock, payment of combination costs, and gain on bargain purchase.
†Beginning retained earnings plus revenues minus expenses.

Because the fair value of the net assets exceeds the consideration transferred, a bargain purchase has occurred. In all combinations, each asset acquired and each liability assumed is recorded at fair value. In a bargain purchase, the amount assigned to this net asset value effectively becomes the business fair value. Therefore, an $84,000 gain on bargain purchase results because a value of $1,510,000 is recorded accompanied by a payment of only $1,426,000. The acquisition method also requires expensing the direct acquisition costs and reducing the value assigned to the stock issue by the costs to register and issue securities. Marston would thus make the following entries on its books:

Investment in Richmond	1,510,000	
Common Stock (Marston, par value)		1,000,000
Additional Paid-In Capital (market value in excess of par)		426,000
Gain on Bargain Purchase		84,000
Combination expenses	20,000	
Additional Paid-In Capital	10,000	
Cash		30,000

Exhibit 2.17 on page 75 shows the worksheet to consolidate the accounts of the parent and subsidiary. The worksheet differs from the solution to part (b) in the following respects:

- Because the acquisition method records all acquired assets and liabilities at fair value, there is no proportionate reduction to Richmond's long-term assets.
- The direct acquisition costs have increased the combined expenses by $20,000.

Appendix

APB No. 16 Criteria for a Pooling of Interests

1. Attributes of combining companies.
   a. Each of the combining companies is autonomous and has not been a subsidiary or division of another corporation within two years before the plan of combination is initiated.
   b. Each of the combining companies is independent of the other combining companies.
2. Characteristics of the combination.
   a. The combination is effected in a single transaction or is completed in accordance with a specific plan within one year after the plan is initiated.
   b. A corporation offers and issues only common stock with rights identical to those of the majority of its outstanding voting common stock in exchange for substantially all of the voting common stock interest of another company at the date the plan of combination is consummated. Substantially all of the voting common stock means 90 percent or more for this condition.
   c. None of the combining companies changes the equity interest of the voting common stock in contemplation of effecting the combination either within two years before the plan of combination is initiated or between the dates the combination is initiated and consummated; changes in contemplation of effecting the combination may include distributions to stockholders and additional issuances, exchanges, and retirements of securities.
   d. Each of the combining companies reacquires shares of voting common stock only for purposes other than business combinations, and no company reacquires more than a normal number of shares between the dates the plan of combination is initiated and consummated.
   e. The ratio of the interest of an individual common stockholder to those of other common stockholders in a combining company remains the same as a result of the exchange of stock to effect the combination.
   f. The voting rights to which the common stock ownership interests in the resulting combined corporation are entitled are exercisable by the stockholders; the stockholders are neither deprived of nor restricted in exercising those rights for a period.
   g. The combination is resolved at the date the plan is consummated and no provisions of the plan relating to the issue of securities or other consideration are pending.

3. Absence of planned transaction.
   a. The combined corporation does not agree directly or indirectly to retire or reacquire all or part of the common stock issued to effect the combination.
   b. The combined corporation does not enter into other financial arrangements for the benefit of the former stockholders of a combining company, such as a guaranty of loans secured by stock issued in the combination, which in effect negates the exchange of equity securities.
   c. The combined corporation does not intend or plan to dispose of a significant part of the assets of the combining companies within two years after the combination other than disposals in the ordinary course of business of the formerly separate companies and to eliminate duplicate facilities or excess capacity.

Questions

1. What is a business combination?
2. Describe the different types of legal arrangements that can take place to create a business combination.
3. What is meant by consolidated financial statements?
4. Within the consolidation process, what is the purpose of a worksheet?
5. Jones Company obtains all of the common stock of Hudson, Inc., by issuing 50,000 shares of its own stock. Under these circumstances, why might the determination of an acquisition price be difficult?
6. What is the accounting basis for consolidating assets and liabilities in a business combination recorded as a purchase? What was the accounting basis for consolidating assets and liabilities in a business combination recorded as a pooling of interests?
7. How are a subsidiary's revenues and expenses consolidated?
8. Morgan Company purchases all of the outstanding shares of Jennings, Inc., for cash. Morgan pays more than the fair value of the company's net assets. How should the payment in excess of fair value be accounted for in the consolidation process?
9. Catron Corporation is having liquidity problems, and as a result, all of its outstanding shares are sold to Lambert, Inc., for cash. Because of Catron's problems, Lambert is able to acquire this stock at less than the fair value of the company's net assets. How is this reduction in price accounted for within the consolidation process?
10. Sloane, Inc., issues 25,000 shares of its own common stock in exchange for all of the outstanding shares of Benjamin Company. Benjamin will remain a separately incorporated operation. How does Sloane record the issuance of these shares in a purchase combination?
11. To obtain all of the stock of Molly, Inc., Harrison Corporation issued its own common stock. Harrison had to pay $98,000 to lawyers, accountants, and a stock brokerage firm in connection with services rendered during the creation of this business combination. In addition, Harrison paid $56,000 in costs associated with the stock issuance. In a purchase combination, how will these two costs be recorded?

Problems

Note: Problems 1 through 26 relate to the purchase method of accounting for business combinations. Problems 27 through 29 relate to the acquisition method. Problems 30 through 37 relate to the pooling of interests method.

Purchase Method

1. Which of the following is the best theoretical justification for consolidated financial statements?
   a. In form the companies are one entity; in substance they are separate.
   b. In form the companies are separate; in substance they are one entity.
   c. In form and substance the companies are one entity.
   d. In form and substance the companies are separate.
   (AICPA)

2. What is a statutory merger?
   a. A merger approved by the Securities and Exchange Commission.
   b. An acquisition involving both the purchase of stock and assets.
   c. A takeover completed within one year of the initial tender offer.
   d. A business combination in which only one company continues to exist as a legal entity.

3. What is the appropriate accounting treatment for the value assigned to in-process research and development acquired in a business combination?

   a. Always expense upon acquisition.

   b. Always capitalize as an asset with future economic benefit.

   c. Expense if there is no alternative use for the assets used in the research and development and technological feasibility has yet to be reached.

   d. Expense until future economic benefits become certain and then capitalize as an asset.

4. Principles for allocating the cost of a business acquisition are provided in *SFAS 141,* "Business Combinations." When the current fair value of the net assets acquired exceeds the total cost of the acquisition, which of the following assets may be assigned an amount less than its fair value?

   a. Deferred tax assets.

   b. Assets to be disposed of by sale.

   c. Prepaid assets related to a pension plan.

   d. Investments accounted for by the equity method.

5. Principles for allocating the cost of a business combination are provided in *SFAS 141,* "Business Combinations." When the fair value of the net assets acquired exceeds the total cost of the investment, the difference should be

   a. Applied pro rata to reduce, but not below zero, the amounts initially assigned to specific non-current assets of the acquired firm.

   b. Treated as negative goodwill to be amortized over the period benefited, not to exceed 40 years.

   c. Treated as goodwill and tested for impairment on an annual basis.

   d. Allocated on a pro rata basis to the assets of the acquired firm.

6. An acquired entity has a long-term operating lease for an office building used for central management. The terms of the lease are very favorable relative to current market rates. However, the lease prohibits subleasing or any other transfer of rights. In its financial statements, the acquiring firm should report the value assigned to the lease contract as

   a. An intangible asset under the contractual-legal criterion.

   b. A part of goodwill.

   c. An intangible asset under the separability criterion.

   d. A building.

7. Williams Company obtains all of the outstanding stock of Jaminson, Inc. In a consolidation prepared immediately after the takeover, at what value will the inventory owned by Jaminson be consolidated?

   a. Jaminson's historical cost.

   b. A percentage of the acquisition cost paid by Williams.

   c. The inventory will be omitted in the consolidation.

   d. At the fair value on the date of the purchase.

8. Under *SFAS 141,* when is an extraordinary gain recognized in consolidating financial information?

   a. When any bargain purchase is created.

   b. In a combination created in the middle of a fiscal year.

   c. In a purchase, when the value of all assets and liabilities cannot be determined.

   d. When the amount of a bargain purchase exceeds the value of the applicable noncurrent assets (other than certain exceptions) held by the acquired company.

9. On June 1, 2007, Cline Co. paid $800,000 cash for all the issued and outstanding common stock of Renn Corp. The carrying values for Renn's assets and liabilities on June 1, 2007, follow:

Cash	$150,000
Accounts receivable	180,000
Capitalized software costs	320,000
Goodwill (net of accumulated amortization of $80,000)	100,000
Liabilities	(130,000)
Net assets	$620,000

On June 1, 2007, Renn's accounts receivable had a fair value of $140,000. Additionally, Renn's in-process research and development was estimated to have a fair value of $200,000. All other items were stated at their fair values. On Cline's June 1, 2007, consolidated balance sheet, how much is reported for goodwill?

a. $320,000.

b. $120,000.

c. $80,000.

d. $20,000.

10. Prior to being united in a business combination, Atkins, Inc., and Waterson Corporation had the following stockholders' equity figures:

	Atkins	Waterson
Common stock ($1 par value)	$180,000	$ 45,000
Additional paid-in capital	90,000	20,000
Retained earnings	300,000	110,000

Atkins issues 51,000 new shares of its common stock valued at $3 per share for all of the outstanding stock of Waterson. Assume that Atkins acquired Waterson through a purchase. Immediately afterward, what are consolidated Additional Paid-In Capital and Retained Earnings, respectively?

a. $104,000 and $300,000.

b. $110,000 and $410,000.

c. $192,000 and $300,000.

d. $212,000 and $410,000.

Problems 11 and 12 are based on the following information: Hampstead, Inc., has only three assets:

	Book Value	Fair Value
Inventory	$110,000	$150,000
Land	700,000	600,000
Buildings	700,000	900,000

Miller Corporation purchases Hampstead by issuing 100,000 shares of its $10 par value common stock.

11. If Miller's stock is worth $20 per share, at what value will the inventory, land, and buildings be consolidated, respectively?

a. $110,000, $600,000, $900,000.

b. $110,000, $700,000, $700,000.

c. $150,000, $600,000, $900,000.

d. $150,000, $700,000, $900,000.

12. If Miller's stock is worth $15 per share, at what value will the inventory, land, and buildings be consolidated, respectively?

a. $110,000, $695,000, $695,000.

b. $150,000, $600,000, $900,000.

c. $150,000, $540,000, $810,000.

d. $136,363, $545,455, $818,182.

Problems 13 through 16 are based on the following information: Allen, Inc., obtains control over Tucker, Inc., on July 1. The book value and fair value of Tucker's accounts on that date (prior to creating the combination) follow, along with the book value of Allen's accounts:

	Allen Book Value	Tucker Book Value	Tucker Fair Value
Revenues	$250,000	$130,000	
Expenses	170,000	80,000	
Retained earnings, 1/1	130,000	150,000	
Cash and receivables	140,000	60,000	$ 60,000
Inventory	190,000	145,000	175,000
Land	230,000	180,000	200,000
Buildings (net)	400,000	200,000	225,000
Equipment (net)	100,000	75,000	75,000
Liabilities	(540,000)	(360,000)	(350,000)
Common stock	(300,000)	(70,000)	
Additional paid-in capital	(10,000)	(30,000)	

13. Assume that Allen issues 10,000 shares of common stock with a $5 par value and a $40 fair value to obtain all of Tucker's outstanding stock. How much goodwill should be recognized?

   a. –0–.

   b. $15,000.

   c. $35,000.

   d. $100,000.

14. For the fiscal year ending December 31, how will consolidated net income of this business combination be determined if Allen acquires all of Tucker's stock in a purchase?

   a. Allen's income for the past year plus Tucker's income for the past six months.

   b. Allen's income for the past year plus Tucker's income for the past year.

   c. Allen's income for the past six months plus Tucker's income for the past six months.

   d. Allen's income for the past six months plus Tucker's income for the past year.

15. Assume that Allen issues preferred stock with a par value of $200,000 and a market value of $335,000 for all shares of Tucker. What will be the balance in the consolidated Inventory, Land, and beginning Retained Earnings accounts?

   a. $365,000, $410,000, and $130,000.

   b. $365,000, $430,000, and $130,000.

   c. $352,500, $417,500, and $280,000.

   d. $335,000, $430,000, and $280,000.

16. Assume that Allen pays a total of $370,000 in cash for all of the shares of Tucker. In addition, Allen pays $30,000 to a group of attorneys for their work in arranging the acquisition. What will be the balance in consolidated goodwill and retained earnings?

   a. 0 and $90,000.

   b. 0 and $280,000.

   c. $15,000 and $280,000.

   d. $15,000 and $130,000.

   (AICPA adapted)

17. Prycal Co. merges with InterBuy, Inc., and acquires several different categories of intangible assets including trademarks, a customer list, copyrights on artistic materials, agreements to receive royalties on leased intellectual property, and unpatented technology.

   a. Describe the criteria put forth in *SFAS No. 141* for determining whether an intangible asset acquired in a business combination should be separately recognized apart from goodwill.

   b. For each of the acquired intangibles listed, identify which recognition criteria (separability and legal/contractual) may or may not apply in recognizing the intangible on the acquiring firm's financial statements.

18. Bakel Corporation has the following December 31 account balances:

Receivables	$ 80,000
Inventory	200,000
Land	600,000
Building	500,000
Liabilities	(400,000)
Common stock	(100,000)
Additional paid-in capital	(100,000)
Retained earnings, 1/1	(700,000)
Revenues	(300,000)
Expenses	220,000

Several of Bakel's accounts have fair values that differ from book value: land—$400,000; building—$600,000; inventory—$280,000; and liabilities—$330,000. Homewood, Inc., obtains all of the outstanding shares of Bakel by issuing 20,000 shares of common stock having a $5 par value but a $55 fair value. Stock issuance costs amount to $10,000.

    a. What is the purchase price in this combination?

    b. What is the book value of Bakel's net assets on the date of the takeover?

    c. How are the stock issuance costs handled?

    d. How does the issuance of these shares affect the stockholders' equity accounts of Homewood, the parent?

    e. What allocations are made of Homewood's purchase price to specific accounts and to goodwill?

    f. If Bakel had in-process research and development assets (with no alternative future uses) valued at $60,000, how would the allocations in part (*e*) change? Where is acquired in-process research and development typically reported on consolidated financial statements?

    g. How do Bakel's revenues and expenses affect consolidated totals? Why?

    h. How do Bakel's common stock and additional paid-in capital balances affect consolidated totals?

    i. In financial statements prepared immediately following the takeover, what impact will this acquisition have on the various consolidated totals?

    j. If Homewood's stock had been worth only $40 per share rather than $55, how would the consolidation of Bakel's assets and liabilities have been affected?

19. Winston has the following account balances as of February 1, 2006:

Inventory	$ 600,000
Land	500,000
Buildings (net) (valued at $1,000,000)	900,000
Common stock ($10 par value)	(800,000)
Retained earnings (1/1/06)	(1,100,000)
Revenues	(600,000)
Expenses	500,000

Arlington pays $1.4 million cash and issues 10,000 shares of its $30 par value common stock (valued at $80 per share) for all of Winston's outstanding stock. Stock issuance costs amount to $30,000. Prior to recording these newly issued shares, Arlington reports a Common Stock account of $900,000 and Additional Paid-In Capital of $500,000. For each of the following accounts, determine what balance would be included in a February 1, 2006, consolidation.

    a. Goodwill.

    b. Expenses.

    c. Retained Earnings, 1/1/06.

    d. Buildings.

20. Use the same information as presented in question (19) but assume that Arlington pays cash of $2.3 million. No stock is issued. An additional $40,000 is paid in direct combination costs. For each of the following accounts, determine what balance would be included in a February 1, 2006, consolidation.

    a. Goodwill.

    b. Expenses.

    c. Retained Earnings, 1/1/06.

    d. Buildings.

21. Use the same information as presented in question (19) but assume that Arlington pays $2,020,000 in cash. An additional $20,000 is paid in direct combination costs. For each of the following accounts, determine what balance will be included in a February 1, 2006, consolidation.

    a. Inventory.

    b. Goodwill.

    c. Expenses.

    d. Buildings.

    e. Land.

22. Following are the financial balances for Parrot Company and Sun Company as of December 31, 2005. Also included are fair values for Sun Company accounts.

	Parrot Company Book Value 12/31/05	Sun Company Book Value 12/31/05	Sun Company Fair Value 12/31/05
Cash	$ 290,000	$ 120,000	$ 120,000
Receivables	220,000	300,000	300,000
Inventory	410,000	210,000	260,000
Land	600,000	130,000	110,000
Buildings (net)	600,000	270,000	330,000
Equipment (net)	220,000	190,000	220,000
Accounts payable	(190,000)	(120,000)	(120,000)
Accrued expenses	(90,000)	(30,000)	(30,000)
Long-term liabilities	(900,000)	(510,000)	(510,000)
Common stock—$20 par value	(660,000)		
Common stock—$5 par value		(210,000)	
Additional paid-in capital	(70,000)	(90,000)	
Retained earnings, 1/1/05	(390,000)	(240,000)	
Revenues	(960,000)	(330,000)	
Expenses	920,000	310,000	

Note: Parentheses indicate a credit balance.

In the following situations, determine the value that would be shown in consolidated financial statements for each of the accounts listed. Each problem should be viewed as an independent occurrence. These transactions all take place on December 31, 2005.

Accounts

Inventory	Revenues
Land	Additional Paid-In Capital
Buildings	Expenses
Goodwill	Retained Earnings, 1/1/05

a. Parrot acquires the outstanding stock of Sun by issuing $760,000 in long-term liabilities.

b. Parrot acquires the outstanding stock of Sun by paying $160,000 in cash and issuing 10,000 shares of its own common stock with a value of $40 per share. Direct combination costs of $20,000 are paid by Parrot as well as $5,000 in stock issuance costs.

23. The financial statements for Willeslye, Inc., and Barrett Company for the six-month period ending June 30, 2006, follow:

	Willeslye	Barrett
Revenues	$ (900,000)	$ (300,000)
Expenses	660,000	200,000
Net income	$ (240,000)	$ (100,000)
Retained earnings, 1/1/06	$ (800,000)	$ (200,000)
Net income	(240,000)	(100,000)
Dividends paid	90,000	–0–
Retained earnings, 6/3/06	$ (950,000)	$ (300,000)
Cash	$ 80,000	$ 110,000
Receivables and inventory	400,000	170,000
Patented technology (net)	900,000	300,000
Equipment (net)	700,000	600,000
Total assets	$ 2,080,000	$ 1,180,000
Liabilities	$ (500,000)	$ (410,000)
Common stock	(360,000)	(200,000)
Additional paid-in capital	(270,000)	(270,000)
Retained earnings	(950,000)	(300,000)
Total liabilities and equities	$(2,080,000)	$(1,180,000)

On June 30, 2006, after these figures were prepared, Willeslye issued $300,000 in debt and 15,000 new shares of its $10 par value stock to the owners of Barrett to purchase all of the outstanding shares of that company. Willeslye shares had a fair value of $40 per share.

Willeslye also paid $30,000 to a broker for arranging the transaction. In addition, Willeslye paid $40,000 in stock issuance costs. Barrett's equipment was actually worth $700,000 but its patented technology was valued at only $280,000.

What are the consolidated balances for the following accounts?

a. Net Income.

b. Retained Earnings, 1/1/06.

c. Patented technology.

d. Goodwill.

e. Liabilities.

f. Common Stock.

g. Additional Paid-In Capital.

24. Merrill acquires 100 percent of the outstanding voting shares of Harriss Company on January 1, 2006. To obtain these shares, Merrill pays $200,000 in cash and issues 10,000 shares of its own $10 par value common stock. On this date, Merrill's stock has a fair value of $18 per share. Merrill also pays $10,000 to a local investment company for arranging the acquisition. Merrill paid an additional $6,000 in stock issuance costs.

The book values for both Merrill and Harriss as of January 1, 2006, follow. The fair value of each of Harriss's accounts is also included. In addition, Harriss holds a fully amortized patent that still retains a $30,000 value.

	Merrill, Inc. Book Value	Harriss Company Book Value	Harriss Company Fair Value
Cash	$300,000	$ 40,000	$ 40,000
Receivables	160,000	90,000	80,000
Inventory	220,000	130,000	130,000
Land	100,000	60,000	60,000
Buildings (net)	400,000	110,000	140,000
Equipment (net)	120,000	50,000	50,000
Accounts payable	(160,000)	(30,000)	(30,000)
Long-term liabilities	(380,000)	(170,000)	(150,000)
Common stock	(400,000)	(40,000)	
Retained earnings	(360,000)	(240,000)	

a. Assume that this combination is a statutory merger so that Harriss's accounts are to be transferred to the records of Merrill with Harriss subsequently being dissolved as a legal corporation. Prepare the journal entries for Merrill to record this merger.

b. Assume that no dissolution is to take place in connection with this combination. Rather, both companies retain their separate legal identities. Prepare a worksheet to consolidate the two companies as of January 1, 2006.

25. On January 1, 2006, Lee Company purchased 100 percent of the outstanding common stock of Grant Company. To acquire these shares, Lee issued $200,000 in long-term liabilities and 20,000 shares of common stock having a par value of $1 per share but a fair value of $10 per share. Lee paid $30,000 to accountants, lawyers, and brokers for assistance in bringing about this purchase. Another $12,000 was paid in connection with stock issuance costs.

Prior to these transactions, the balance sheets for the two companies were as follows:

	Lee Company Book Value	Grant Company Book Value
Cash	$ 60,000	$ 20,000
Receivables	270,000	90,000
Inventory	360,000	140,000
Land	200,000	180,000
Buildings (net)	420,000	220,000
Equipment (net)	160,000	50,000

	Lee Company Book Value	Grant Company Book Value
Accounts payable	(150,000)	(40,000)
Long-term liabilities	(430,000)	(200,000)
Common stock—$1 par value	(110,000)	
Common stock—$20 par value		(120,000)
Additional paid-in capital	(360,000)	–0–
Retained earnings, 1/1/06	(420,000)	(340,000)

Note: Parentheses indicate a credit balance.

In Lee's appraisal of Grant, three accounts were deemed to be undervalued on the subsidiary's books: Inventory by $5,000, Land by $20,000, and Buildings by $30,000.

a. Determine the consolidated balance for each of these accounts.

b. To verify the answers found in part (a), prepare a worksheet to consolidate the balance sheets of these two companies as of January 1, 2006.

26. Pratt Company purchased all of the outstanding shares of Spider, Inc., on December 31, 2005, for $495,000 cash. Although many of Spider's book values approximate fair values, several of its accounts have fair values that differ from book values. In addition, Spider has internally developed assets that remain unrecorded on its books. In deriving a purchase price, Pratt made assessments of Spider's fair and book value differences as follows:

	Book Value	Fair Value
Computer software	$20,000	$70,000
Equipment	40,000	30,000
Client contracts	–0–	100,000
In-process research and development*	–0–	40,000
Notes payable	(60,000)	(65,000)

*Technological feasibility has not yet been achieved. No future alternative uses are available for IPR&D assets employed in these projects.

At December 31, 2005, the following financial information is available for consolidation:

	Pratt	Spider
Revenues	$ (200,000)	
Expenses	125,000	
Net income	(75,000)	
Retained earnings 1/1	(707,000)	
Net income	(75,000)	
Dividends	30,000	
Retained earnings 12/31	$ (752,000)	
Cash	36,000	$ 18,000
Receivables	116,000	52,000
Inventory	140,000	90,000
Investment in Spider (cost)	495,000	–0–
Computer software	210,000	20,000
Buildings (net)	595,000	130,000
Equipment (net)	308,000	40,000
Client contracts	–0–	–0–
Goodwill	–0–	–0–
Total assets	$ 1,900,000	$ 350,000
Accounts payable	(88,000)	(25,000)
Notes payable	(510,000)	(60,000)
Common stock	(380,000)	(100,000)
Additional paid-in capital	(170,000)	(25,000)
Retained earnings	(752,000)	(140,000)
Total liabilities and equities	$(1,900,000)	$(350,000)

Prepare a consolidated balance sheet for Pratt and Spider as of December 31, 2005.

Acquisition Method

27. Allerton Company acquires all the assets and liabilities of Deluxe Company for cash on January 1, 2006, and subsequently formally dissolves Deluxe. At the acquisition date, the following book and fair values were available for the Deluxe Company accounts:

	Book Value	Fair Value
Current assets	$ 60,000	$60,000
Building	90,000	50,000
Land	10,000	20,000
Trademark	–0–	30,000
Goodwill	15,000	?
Liabilities	(40,000)	(40,000)
Common stock	(100,000)	
Retained earnings	(35,000)	

   a. Using the purchase method, prepare Allerton's entry to record its acquisition of Deluxe in its accounting records assuming the following cash exchange amounts:

   (1) $145,000.

   (2) $110,000.

   b. Using the acquisition method, prepare Allerton's entry to record its acquisition of Deluxe in its accounting records assuming the following cash exchange amounts:

   (1) $145,000.

   (2) $110,000.

28. On June 30, 2006, Sampras Company reported the following account balances:

Receivables	80,000	Current liabilities	$ 10,000
Inventory	70,000	Long-term liabilities	50,000
Buildings (net)	75,000	Common stock	90,000
Equipment (net)	25,000	Retained earnings	100,000
Total assets	$250,000	Total liabilities and equities	$250,000

   On June 30, 2006, Pelham paid $300,000 cash for all assets and liabilities of Sampras, which will cease to exist as a separate entity. In connection with the acquisition, Pelham paid $10,000 in direct combination costs. Pelham also agreed to pay $50,000 to the former owners of Sampras contingent on meeting certain revenue goals during 2008. Pelham estimated the present value of its probability adjusted expected payment for the contingency at $15,000.

   In determining its purchase offer, Pelham noted the following pertaining to Sampras:

   - It holds a building with a fair value $40,000 more than its book value.
   - It has developed a customer list appraised at $22,000, although it is not recorded in its financial records.
   - It has research and development activity in process with an appraised fair value of $30,000. However, the project has not yet reached technological feasibility and the assets used in the activity have no alternative future use.
   - Book values for the receivables, inventory, and liabilities approximate fair values.

   Prepare Pelham's accounting entry to record the combination with Sampras using the

   a. Purchase method.

   b. Acquisition method.

29. On December 31, 2006, Pacifica, Inc., acquired 100 percent of the voting stock of Seguros Company. Pacifica will maintain Seguros as a wholly owned subsidiary with its own legal and accounting identity. The consideration transferred to the owner of Seguros included 50,000 newly issued Pacifica common shares ($20 market value, $5 par value) and an agreement to pay an additional $130,000 cash if Seguros meets certain project completion goals by December 31, 2007. Pacifica estimates a 50 percent probability that Seguros will be successful in meeting these goals and uses a 4 percent discount rate to represent the time value of money.

Immediately prior to the acquisition, the following data for both firms were available:

	Pacifica	Seguros Book Values	Seguros Fair Values
Revenues	$(1,200,000)		
Expenses	875,000		
Net income	$ (325,000)		
Retained earnings, 1/1/06	(950,000)		
Net income	(325,000)		
Dividends paid	90,000		
Retained earnings, 12/31/06	$(1,185,000)		
Cash	110,000	$ 85,000	$ 85,000
Receivables and inventory	750,000	190,000	180,000
Property, plant, and equipment	1,400,000	450,000	600,000
Trademarks	300,000	160,000	200,000
Total assets	$ 2,560,000	$ 885,000	
Liabilities	(500,000)	(180,000)	$(180,000)
Common stock	(400,000)	(200,000)	
Additional paid-in capital	(475,000)	(70,000)	
Retained earnings	(1,185,000)	(435,000)	
Total liabilities and equities	$(2,560,000)	$(885,000)	

In addition, Pacifica assessed a research and development project under way at Seguros to have a fair value of $100,000. Pacifica paid legal and accounting fees of $15,000 in connection with the acquisition and $9,000 in stock issue and registration costs.

Using the acquisition method, prepare the following:

a. Pacifica's entries to account for the consideration transferred to the former owners of Seguros, the direct combination costs, and the stock issue and registration costs. (Use a 0.961538 present value factor where applicable.)

b. A postacquisition column of accounts for Pacifica.

c. A worksheet to produce a consolidated balance sheet as of December 31, 2006.

Pooling Method

30. How would equipment obtained in a business combination have been recorded under each of the following methods?

	Pooling of Interests	Purchase
a.	Recorded value	Recorded value
b.	Recorded value	Fair value
c.	Fair value	Fair value
d.	Fair value	Recorded value

(AICPA adapted)

31. Prior to being united in a business combination, Atkins, Inc., and Waterson Corporation had the following stockholders' equity figures:

	Atkins	Waterson
Common stock ($1 par value)	$(180,000)	$ (45,000)
Additional paid-in capital	(90,000)	(20,000)
Retained earnings	(300,000)	(110,000)

Atkins issues 51,000 new shares of its common stock valued at $3 per share for all of the outstanding stock of Waterson. Assume that Atkins and Waterson were joined in a pooling of interests. Immediately afterward, what were the amounts in consolidated Additional Paid-In Capital and Retained Earnings, respectively?

a. $104,000 and $300,000.

b. $104,000 and $410,000.

c. $110,000 and $300,000.

d. $110,000 and $410,000.

32. Flaherty Company entered into a business combination with Steeley Company during 2000. The combination was accounted for as a pooling of interests. Registration fees were incurred in issuing common stock in this combination. Other costs, such as legal and accounting fees, were also paid.

    a. In the business combination accounted for as a pooling of interests, how should the assets and liabilities of the two companies be included within consolidated statements? What was the rationale for accounting for a business combination as a pooling of interests?

    b. In the business combination accounted for as a pooling of interests, how were the registration fees and the other direct costs recorded?

    c. In the business combination accounted for as a pooling of interests, how were the results of the operations for 2000 reported?

    (AICPA adapted)

33. Harcourt Company has the following account balances:

Receivables	$ 90,000
Inventory	500,000
Land	700,000
Buildings	200,000
Liabilities	(800,000)
Common stock	(100,000)
Additional paid-in capital	(90,000)
Retained earnings, 1/1/00	(440,000)
Revenues	(400,000)
Expenses	340,000

    Several of Harcourt's accounts have fair values that differ from book value: land—$900,000; building—$400,000; inventory—$470,000; and liabilities—$840,000. Lee Corporation obtains all of the outstanding shares of Harcourt by issuing 20,000 shares of common stock having a $10 par value but a $62 fair market value. Stock issuance costs amount to $10,000. The transaction is to be accounted for as a pooling of interests. Before recording the issuance of these new shares, Lee has a Common Stock account of $2 million and Additional Paid-In Capital of $1.3 million.

    a. What is the book value of Harcourt's net assets on the date of the takeover?

    b. How are the stock issuance costs handled?

    c. Assume that both companies will retain their identities as separate corporations. What journal entry would Lee record for the issuance of its stock?

    d. How would the answer to part (c) have changed if Lee's stock had a $1 per share par value rather than $10 per share?

    e. How would the answer to part (c) have changed if Lee's stock had a $10 per share par value but Lee issued 30,000 shares rather than 20,000?

    f. How do Harcourt's revenues and expenses affect consolidated totals? Why?

    g. In financial statements prepared immediately following the takeover, what impact would Harcourt's accounts have on the various consolidated totals?

34. On February 1, 2001, Pearl Corporation completed a combination with Stanton Company accounted for as a pooling of interests. At that date, Stanton's account balances were as follows:

	Book Value	Fair Value
Inventory	$ 600,000	650,000
Land	500,000	750,000
Buildings	900,000	1,000,000
Unpatented technology	–0–	1,500,000
Common stock ($10 par value)	(800,000)	
Retained earnings (1/1/01)	(1,100,000)	
Revenues	(600,000)	
Expenses	500,000	

    Pearl issued 30,000 shares of its common stock with a par value of $25 and a fair value of $150 per share to the owners of Stanton for all of their Stanton shares. Upon completion of the combination,

Stanton Company was formally dissolved. Stock issue costs of $35,000 were paid along with $24,000 of other direct combination costs.

a. Prepare Pearl's entry in its accounting records for its February 1, 2001, combination with Stanton.

b. Prepare Pearl's entry to record the Stanton combination assuming the transaction did not qualify for pooling of interests accounting.

c. Explain the alternative impact of pooling versus purchase accounting on performance ratios such as return on assets and earning per share in periods subsequent to the combination.

35. The financial statements for Hope, Inc., and Kaisley Corporation for the year ending December 31, 2000, follow. Kaisley's buildings were undervalued on its financial records by $50,000.

	Hope	Kaisley
Revenues	$ (400,000)	$ (400,000)
Expenses	240,000	240,000
Net income	$ (160,000)	$ (160,000)
Retained earnings, 1/1/00	$ (600,000)	$ (400,000)
Net income	(160,000)	(160,000)
Dividends paid	90,000	90,000
Retained earnings, 12/31/00	$ (670,000)	$ (470,000)
Cash	$ 130,000	$ 100,000
Receivables and inventory	200,000	200,000
Buildings (net)	600,000	300,000
Equipment (net)	600,000	500,000
Total assets	$ 1,530,000	$ 1,100,000
Liabilities	$ (200,000)	$ (200,000)
Common stock	(630,000)	(360,000)
Additional paid-in capital	(30,000)	(70,000)
Retained earnings	(670,000)	(470,000)
Total liabilities and equities	$(1,530,000)	$(1,100,000)

On December 31, 2000, Hope issued 45,000 new shares of its $10 par value stock to the owners of Kaisley in exchange for all of the outstanding shares of that company. Hope's shares had a market value on that date of $30 per share. Hope paid $30,000 to a bank for assisting in the arrangements. Hope also paid $20,000 in stock issuance costs. This combination was accounted for as a pooling of interests. What were the appropriate consolidated balances?

36. Lincoln Company obtained all of the outstanding shares of Swathmore, Inc., on December 31, 2000, in exchange for 7,000 shares of common stock. The combination was accounted for as a pooling of interests. Each of Lincoln's shares had a $10 par value and a $40 market value. Several of Swathmore's accounts had fair values that differed from their book values on that date:

	Book Value	Fair Value
Inventory	$120,000	$100,000
Land	30,000	30,000
Equipment	50,000	60,000
Notes payable	(50,000)	(45,000)

Financial statements for 2000 for the two companies were as follows:

	Lincoln	Swathmore
Revenues	$(990,000)	$(540,000)
Expenses	640,000	330,000
Net income	$(350,000)	$(210,000)
Retained earnings, 1/1/00	$(830,000)	$(110,000)
Net income	(350,000)	(210,000)
Dividends paid	220,000	130,000
Retained earnings, 12/31/00	$(960,000)	$(190,000)

	Lincoln	Swathmore
Cash	$ 60,000	$ 29,000
Receivables	150,000	65,000
Inventory	190,000	120,000
Land	310,000	30,000
Buildings (net)	840,000	60,000
Equipment (net)	320,000	50,000
Totals	$ 1,870,000	$ 354,000
Accounts payable	$ (110,000)	$ (34,000)
Notes payable	(370,000)	(50,000)
Common stock	(400,000)	(50,000)
Additional paid-in capital	(30,000)	(30,000)
Retained earnings	(960,000)	(190,000)
Totals	$(1,870,000)	$(354,000)

a. Determine the consolidated balance for each of these accounts.

b. To verify the answers found in part (*a*), prepare a worksheet to consolidate the financial statements of these two companies.

37. On December 31, 2000, Sherman Company exchanged 17,000 shares of its common stock with a market value of $57 per share for 100 percent of the outstanding shares of Atlanta Company. This transaction was accounted for as a pooling of interests. Prior to the exchange, the trial balances of both companies for the year 2000 were as follows:

	Sherman Company Book Value	Atlanta Company Book Value
Debits		
Cash	$110,000	$ 20,000
Receivables (net)	300,000	290,000
Inventory	440,000	260,000
Land	280,000	80,000
Buildings (net)	270,000	290,000
Equipment (net)	810,000	320,000
Expenses	540,000	210,000
Dividends	30,000	–0–
Credits		
Accounts payable	(120,000)	(60,000)
Long-term liabilities	(960,000)	(330,000)
Common stock—$20 par value	(520,000)	
Common stock—$25 par value		(300,000)
Additional paid-in capital	(110,000)	(100,000)
Retained earnings, 1/1/00	(470,000)	(200,000)
Revenues	(600,000)	(480,000)

Additional information:

- After the preparation of these trial balances, Sherman paid $20,000 in cash for costs incurred relating to this exchange. These expenditures covered the fees charged by lawyers and accountants involved with creating the business combination.

- Atlanta possesses land that has appreciated in value since it was acquired. The book value of this land is estimated to be $60,000 less than fair value.

a. Prepare a worksheet to consolidate the financial information of these two companies for the year ending December 31, 2000.

b. Prepare a worksheet to consolidate the financial information of these two companies for the year ending December 31, 2000, assuming that this combination was actually a purchase.

Develop Your Skills

EXCEL CASE

Alhambra, Inc., is considering acquiring all of the assets of Granada Co. after which Granada would be formally dissolved. Granada has no liabilities. Alhambra estimates the value of Granada's assets as follows:

Accounts receivable	$ 60,000
Equipment	360,000
In-process research and development	180,000

The in-process research and development has not yet reached technological feasibility, but Alhambra is confident that the research will produce a product that will eventually justify the initial value assigned.

In considering the acquisition, Alhambra wishes to assess the sensitivity of the acquired long-term asset valuation to the purchase price.

Required:

Prepare an Excel spreadsheet analysis that automatically recomputes amounts allocated to the acquired accounts receivable, equipment, in-process research and development, and goodwill as the purchase price changes. Assume a purchase price range of $500,000 to $900,000. Calculate the asset allocations for the following purchase prices using the guidance in *SFAS 141*.

1. $500,000.
2. $550,000.
3. $600,000.
4. $900,000.

FARS RESEARCH CASE—*SFAS 141* "BUSINESS COMBINATIONS"

Acello Company has agreed to merge with BlairCo using an exchange of equity interests. The terms of the agreement include the following:

- BlairCo, the larger firm, will issue additional shares of common stock to the owners of Acello in exchange for their shares after which the corporate entity Acello will be formally dissolved. BlairCo will survive as the continuing firm.
- The former owners of Acello will hold 65 percent of the voting shares of the combined firm. The exchange ratios reflected a premium paid by Acello's owners over the market value of BlairCo's stock.
- BlairCo's former chief executive office (CEO) and chief financial officer (CFO) will continue their roles in the combined firm for at least two years.
- The former chairman of the board of directors of Acello will be the initial new chairman of the board of directors of the combined firm. Within two months after the merger, shareholders will elect a new board of directors.

Required:

SFAS 141 requires the identification of the acquiring firm in a business combination. Which of the firms, Acello or BlairCo, should be considered as the acquiring firm?

RESEARCH AND ANALYSIS CASE 1—PEPSICO–QUAKER OATS MERGER

At the Pepsico.com Web site, obtain references to various SEC filings, press releases, and financial statements surrounding PepsiCo's merger with Quaker Oats to address the following items. In particular, the 2001 Quaker S-4/A Filing and SEC Form 8-K should be useful in addressing these questions.

Required:

1. How was the merger between PepsiCo and Quaker Oats structured? Which firm is the survivor? Who holds what stock after the merger?
2. What accounting method was used to account for the merger of PepsiCo and Quaker Oats? What are the reporting implications of the chosen accounting method?
3. What were the approximate amounts for the
   a. Recorded value of the acquisition of the surviving firm's books?
   b. Fair value of the acquisition?
4. What items of value did Quaker Oats bring to the merger that will not be recorded in the acquisition? How will these items affect future reported income for the combined firm?
5. Using the criteria stated in the Summary to *SFAS 141* (first four pages of the document), evaluate the financial reporting for the PepsiCo acquisition of Quaker Oats.

RESEARCH AND ANALYSIS CASE 2

Access the most recent financial statements for one of the following firms:

- Yahoo!.
- Cisco Systems.
- Cadence Designs.
- Pennzoil–Quaker State.
- Apple Computer.
- Amazon.com.
- Wendy's International.

Required:

Write a brief report that describes the firm's merger and acquisition activity for the past several years. Be sure to identify the accounting methods employed, cost allocations for purchase acquisitions, and motivations cited for the merger activities.

RESEARCH AND ANALYSIS CASE 3

Find the annual 10-K reports for any firms involved in recent merger and acquisition activity and identify several of their recent successful takeovers. Then determine the fair value of the target firm two months prior to the takeover announcement.

Required:

Write a brief report that

- Compares the price paid in the acquisition with the previous fair value.
- Discusses possible motivations for any difference.
- Identifies the Web sites used in your search.

RESEARCH AND ANALYSIS CASE 4

Search the Internet for financial reports containing references to purchased in-process research and development. Identify three firms that report purchased in-process research and development expenses in connection with merger and acquisition activities.

Required:

1. Discuss how they determined the proper amount for the write-off of the purchased in-process research and development.
2. Identify the percentage of the purchase price allocated to in-process research and development and other assets.

COMMUNICATION CASE 1

Read the following as well as any other published information concerning the pooling of interests method:

"The Financial Statement Effects of Eliminating the Pooling-of-Interests Method of Acquisition Accounting," *Accounting Horizons,* March 2000.

"Why Eliminate the Pooling Method?" *Financial Accounting Series Status Report No. 316* (Financial Accounting Foundation/FASB), August 31, 1999.

"Special Report: The Battle over Pooling of Interests," *Journal of Accountancy,* November 1999.

"FASB Plan Would Provide False Accounts," *The Wall Street Journal,* January 31, 2000, Manager's Journal, page C1.

"Valuing the New Economy—How New Accounting Standards Will Inhibit Economically Sound Mergers and Hinder the Efficiency and Innovation of U.S. Business," *Merrill Lynch Forum White Paper,* June 1999.

Required:

Write a report discussing whether you agree with the FASB decision to eliminate the pooling of interests method as a generally accepted accounting principle.

COMMUNICATION CASE 2

From the SEC's Web site (www.sec.gov), locate and read a speech given by Lynn Turner, then Chief Accountant at the SEC, on February 10, 1999, entitled "Making Financial Statements Real: Recent Problems in the Accounting for Purchased In-Process Research and Development."

Required:

Write a brief report that discusses the issues surrounding the current accounting treatment for in-process research and development costs. Provide three annual report examples of footnote disclosure and discussion for IPR&D costs related to business combinations.

Chapter **Three**

Consolidations— Subsequent to the Date of Acquisition

Questions to Consider

- How does a parent company account for a subsidiary organization in the years that follow the creation of a business combination?

- What impact does the parent's method of accounting for a subsidiary have on subsequent consolidations?

- Why do intercompany balances exist within the financial records of the separate companies? How are these reciprocals eliminated on a consolidation worksheet?

- Why did the FASB decide that goodwill amortization should not be allowed and that instead goodwill should be periodically tested for impairment? How do firms determine when and whether goodwill is impaired? How are goodwill impairment losses recognized in consolidated financial statements?

- How is amortization of other purchase price allocations recognized within consolidated financial statements?

- If the exact purchase price of a subsidiary is based on a future event, what effect does this contingency have on the consolidation process?

- Should a subsidiary company report on its financial statements the purchase price allocations and later amortization that can result from the purchase price paid by the parent?

In the mid-1980s, the General Electric Co. (GE) acquired the National Broadcasting Company (NBC) as part of its $6.4 billion cash purchase of RCA Corporation. Although this transaction involved well-known companies, it was not unique; mergers and acquisitions have long been common in the business world.

The current financial statements of GE indicate that NBC (now NBC Universal) is still a component of this economic entity. However, NBC Universal continues to be a separately incorporated concern long after its purchase. As discussed in Chapter 2, a parent often chooses to let a subsidiary retain its identity as a legal corporation to better utilize the value inherent in a going concern.

For external reporting purposes, maintenance of incorporation creates an ongoing challenge for the accountant. In each subsequent period, consolidation must be simulated anew through the use of a worksheet and consolidation entries. Thus, for almost 20 years, the financial data for GE and NBC Universal have been brought together periodically to provide figures for the financial statements that represent this business combination.

CONSOLIDATION—THE EFFECTS CREATED BY THE PASSAGE OF TIME

In Chapter 2, consolidation accounting is analyzed at the date that a combination is created. The present chapter carries this process one step further by examining the consolidation procedures that must be followed in subsequent periods whenever separate incorporation of the subsidiary is maintained.[1]

---

[1] Except for recommended changes to accounting for contingent consideration in a business combination, the 2005 FASB Exposure Drafts on consolidated reporting have little or no effect on the issues presented in this chapter.

Despite complexities created by the passage of time, the basic objective of all consolidations remains the same: to combine asset, liability, revenue, expense, and equity accounts of a parent and its subsidiaries. From a mechanical perspective, a worksheet and consolidation entries continue to provide structure for the production of a single set of financial statements for the combined business entity.

The time factor introduces additional complications into the consolidation process. For internal record-keeping purposes, the parent must select and apply an accounting method to monitor the relationship between the two companies. The investment balance recorded by the parent varies over time as a result of the method chosen, as does the income subsequently recognized. These differences affect the periodic consolidation process but not the figures to be reported by the combined entity. Regardless of the amount, the parent's Investment account is eliminated on the worksheet so that the subsidiary's actual assets and liabilities can be consolidated. Likewise, the income figure accrued by the parent is removed each period so that the subsidiary's revenues and expenses can be included when creating an income statement for the combined business entity.

SFAS 142—GOODWILL AND INTANGIBLE ASSETS

In *SFAS 142,* "Goodwill and Other Intangible Assets," July 2001, the FASB approved significant changes in the way income is determined for combined business entities. The most prominent of these changes relates to the treatment of goodwill in periods subsequent to acquisition. For fiscal periods beginning after December 15, 2001, goodwill is no longer amortized systematically over time.[2] Instead, goodwill is now subject to an annual test for impairment. This nonamortization approach is applied to both previously recognized and newly acquired goodwill. Consequently, goodwill that arose from pre-*SFAS 142* combinations is simply carried forward at unamortized cost as of the beginning of annual reporting periods in 2002.

For consolidations of parent and subsidiary companies, goodwill amortization expense no longer appears on the combined income statement. The consolidated balance sheet frequently carries acquisition-related goodwill at its original cost. Only upon the recognition of an impairment loss (or partial sale of a subsidiary) will goodwill decline from one period to the next. In the next several sections of this chapter, the relation of the parent's investment accounting to the adjustments required for consolidation will be presented along with specific procedures for amortizing the cost of a business combination and testing for impairment as appropriate.

INVESTMENT ACCOUNTING BY THE ACQUIRING COMPANY

For external reporting, consolidation of a subsidiary becomes necessary whenever control exists. For internal record-keeping, though, the parent has the choice of three alternatives for monitoring the activities of its subsidiaries: the cost method, the equity method, or the partial equity method. *Because both the resulting investment balance and the related income are eliminated as part of every recurring consolidation, the selection of a particular method does not affect the totals ultimately reported for the combined companies.* However, this decision does lead to distinct procedures subsequently utilized in consolidating the financial information of the separate organizations.

The internal reporting philosophy of the acquiring company often determines the accounting method choice for its subsidiary investment. The *cost method* might be selected because it is easy to apply. The investment balance remains permanently on the parent's balance sheet at original cost. The cost method uses the cash basis for income recognition. Therefore, only the dividends subsequently received from the subsidiary are recognized as income. No other

---

[2] Additionally, goodwill was not amortized for new business combinations occurring subsequent to June 30, 2001.

EXHIBIT 3.1   **Internal Reporting of Investment Accounts by Acquiring Company**

Method	Investment Account	Income Account	Advantages
Equity	Continually adjusted to reflect ownership of acquired company.	Income is accrued as earned; amortization and other adjustments are recognized.	Acquiring company totals give a true representation of consolidation figures.
Cost	Remains at initially recorded cost.	Cash received is recorded as Dividend Income.	Easy to apply; measures cash flows.
Partial equity	Adjusted only for accrued income and dividends received from acquired company.	Income is accrued as earned; no other adjustments are recognized.	Usually gives balances approximating consolidation figures, but is easier to apply than equity method.

adjustments are recorded. Thus, this method requires little effort while providing an accurate measure of the cash flows between the two companies.

In contrast, under the *equity method,* the acquiring company accrues income when earned by the subsidiary. To match acquisition costs against income, amortization expense stemming from the original acquisition is recognized through periodic adjusting entries. Unrealized gains on intercompany transactions are deferred; dividends paid by the subsidiary serve to reduce the investment balance. As discussed in Chapter 1, the equity method is designed to create a parallel between the parent's investment accounts and changes in the underlying equity of the acquired company.[3]

Under the equity method, the parent's accounts reflect the income of the entire combined business entity. Consequently, the equity method often is referred to in accounting as a *single-line consolidation.* The equity method is especially popular in companies where management wants to get a picture of overall profitability by looking at periodic (such as monthly) figures developed by the parent.

A third method available to the acquiring company is a *partial application of the equity method.* Under this approach, the parent recognizes the reported income accruing from the subsidiary. Dividends that are collected reduce the investment balance. However, no other equity adjustments (amortization or deferral of unrealized gains) are recorded. Thus, in many cases, earnings figures on the parent's books approximate consolidated totals but without the effort associated with a full application of the equity method.

Each acquiring company must decide for itself the appropriate approach in recording the operations of its subsidiaries. For example, Alliant Food Service, Inc., applies the equity method. According to Joe Tomczak, vice president and controller of Alliant Food Service, Inc., "We maintain the parent holding company books on an equity basis. This approach provides the best method of providing information for our operational decisions."[4]

In contrast, Reynolds Metals Corporation has chosen to utilize the partial equity method approach. Allen Earehart, director of corporate accounting for Reynolds, states, "We do adjust the carrying value of our investments annually to reflect the earnings of each subsidiary. We want to be able to evaluate the parent company on a stand-alone basis and a regular equity accrual is, therefore, necessary. However, we do separate certain adjustments such as the elimination of intercompany gains and losses and record them solely within the development of consolidated financial statements."[5]

Exhibit 3.1 provides a summary of these three reporting techniques. The method adopted affects only the acquiring company's separate financial records. No changes are created in either the subsidiary's accounts or the consolidated totals.

[3] In Chapter 1, the equity method was introduced in connection with the external reporting of investments in which the owner held the ability to apply significant influence over the investee (usually by possessing 20 to 50 percent of the company's voting stock). Here, the equity method is utilized for the *internal* reporting of the parent for investments in which control is maintained. Although the accounting procedures are identical, the reason for using the equity method is different.

[4] Telephone conversation with Joe Tomczak.

[5] Telephone conversation with Allen Earehart.

Because specific worksheet procedures differ based on the investment method being utilized by the parent, the consolidation process subsequent to the date of combination will be introduced twice. Initially, consolidations in which the acquiring company uses the equity method are reviewed. All procedures are then redeveloped when the investment is recorded by one of the alternative methods.

SUBSEQUENT CONSOLIDATION—INVESTMENT RECORDED BY THE EQUITY METHOD

Acquisition Made during the Current Year

As a basis for this illustration, assume that Parrot Company obtains all of the outstanding common stock of Sun Company on January 1, 2007. Parrot acquires this stock for $800,000 in cash.

The book values as well as the appraised fair values of Sun's accounts are as follows:

	Book Value 1/1/07	Fair Value 1/1/07	Difference
Current assets	$ 320,000	$ 320,000	–0–
Land	200,000	220,000	+ 20,000
Buildings (10-year life)	320,000	450,000	+130,000
Equipment (5-year life)	180,000	150,000	(30,000)
Liabilities	(420,000)	(420,000)	–0–
Net book value	$ 600,000	$ 720,000	$120,000
Common stock—$40 par value	$(200,000)		
Additional paid-in capital	(20,000)		
Retained earnings, 1/1/07	(380,000)		

For this combination, the assumption is being made that any amortization relating to purchase price allocations is calculated using the straight-line method with no estimated salvage value.[6]

A total of $800,000 has been paid by Parrot in this purchase of Sun Company. As shown in Exhibit 3.2, individual allocations are used to adjust Sun's accounts from their book values on January 1, 2004, to fair values. Because the total value of these assets and liabilities was only $720,000, goodwill of $80,000 must be recognized for consolidation purposes.

Each of these allocated amounts (other than the $20,000 attributed to land and the $80,000 for goodwill) represents a cost incurred by Parrot that is associated with an account having a definite life. As discussed in Chapter 1, Parrot must amortize each of these cost figures over

EXHIBIT 3.2

PARROT COMPANY
Allocation of Purchase Price
January 1, 2007

Purchase price by Parrot Company.		$ 800,000
Book value of Sun Company		(600,000)
Excess of cost over book value.		200,000
Allocation to specific accounts based on fair values:		
Land	$ 20,000	
Buildings	130,000	
Equipment (overvalued)	(30,000)	120,000
Excess cost not identified with specific accounts—goodwill		$ 80,000

[6] Unless otherwise stated, all amortization expense computations in this textbook are based on the straight-line method with no salvage value.

EXHIBIT 3.3
**Annual Excess
Amortization**

	PARROT COMPANY		
	Excess Amortization Schedule—Allocation of Purchase Price		
Account	**Allocation**	**Useful Life**	**Annual Excess Amortizations**
Land	$ 20,000	Indefinite	–0–
Buildings	130,000	10 years	$13,000
Equipment	(30,000)	5 years	(6,000)
Goodwill	80,000	Indefinite	–0–
			$ 7,000*

*Total excess amortizations will be $7,000 annually for five years until the equipment allocation is fully removed. At the end of each asset's life, future amortizations will change.

their expected lives. The expense recognition necessitated by this purchase price allocation is calculated in Exhibit 3.3.

One aspect of this amortization schedule warrants further explanation. The fair value of Sun's Equipment account was $30,000 *less* than book value. Therefore, instead of attributing an additional cost to this asset, the $30,000 allocation actually reflects a cost reduction. As such, the amortization shown in Exhibit 3.3 relating to Equipment is not an additional expense but rather an expense reduction.

Having determined the allocation of the purchase price in the previous example as well as the associated amortization, the parent's separate record-keeping for 2007 can be constructed. Assume that Sun earns income of $100,000 during the year and pays a $40,000 cash dividend on August 1, 2007.

In this initial illustration, Parrot has adopted the equity method. Apparently, this company believes that the information derived from using the equity method is useful in its evaluation of Sun.

Application of the Equity Method

	Parrot's Financial Records		
1/1/07	Investment in Sun Company	800,000	
	Cash		800,000
	To record purchase of Sun Company including direct combination costs.		
8/1/07	Cash	40,000	
	Investment in Sun Company		40,000
	To record receipt of cash dividend from subsidiary, an investment that is being accounted for by means of the equity method.		
12/31/07	Investment in Sun Company	100,000	
	Equity in Subsidiary Earnings		100,000
	To accrue income earned by 100 percent owned subsidiary.		
12/31/07	Equity in Subsidiary Earnings	7,000	
	Investment in Sun Company		7,000
	To recognize amortizations on allocations made in purchase of subsidiary (see Exhibit 3.3).		

Parrot's application of the equity method, as shown in this series of entries, causes the Investment in Sun Company account balance to rise from $800,000 to $853,000 ($800,000 − $40,000 + $100,000 − $7,000). During the same period, a $93,000 equity income figure (the $100,000 earnings accrual less the $7,000 excess amortization expenses) is recognized by the parent.

EXHIBIT 3.4
Separate Records—
Equity Method Applied

PARROT COMPANY AND SUN COMPANY
Financial Statements
For Year Ending December 31, 2007

	Parrot Company	Sun Company
Income Statement		
Revenues	$(1,500,000)	$ (400,000)
Cost of goods sold	700,000	250,000
Depreciation expense	200,000	50,000
Equity in subsidiary earnings	(93,000)	–0–
Net income	$ (693,000)	$ (100,000)
Statement of Retained Earnings		
Retained earnings, 1/1/07	$ (840,000)	$ (380,000)
Net income (above)	(693,000)	(100,000)
Dividends paid	120,000	40,000
Retained earnings, 12/31/07	$(1,413,000)	$ (440,000)
Balance Sheet		
Current assets	$ 1,040,000	$ 400,000
Investment in Sun Company (at equity)	853,000	–0–
Land	600,000	200,000
Buildings (net)	370,000	288,000
Equipment (net)	250,000	220,000
Total assets	$ 3,113,000	$ 1,108,000
Liabilities	$ (980,000)	$ (448,000)
Common stock	(600,000)	(200,000)
Additional paid-in capital	(120,000)	(20,000)
Retained earnings, 12/31/07 (above)	(1,413,000)	(440,000)
Total liabilities and equity	$(3,113,000)	$(1,108,000)

Note: Parentheses indicate a credit balance.

    The consolidation procedures for Parrot and Sun one year after the date of acquisition are illustrated next. For this purpose, Exhibit 3.4 presents the separate 2007 financial statements for these two companies. Both investment-related accounts (the $853,000 asset balance and the $93,000 income accrual) have been recorded by Parrot based on applying the equity method.

Determining Consolidated Totals

Before becoming immersed in the mechanical aspects of a consolidation, the objective of this process should be understood. As indicated in Chapter 2, in the preparation of consolidated financial reports, the revenue, expense, asset, and liability accounts of the subsidiary are added to the parent company balances. Within this procedure, several important guidelines must be followed:

- Sun's assets and liabilities are adjusted to reflect the allocations originating from the purchase price.
- Because of the passage of time, the income effects (e.g., amortizations) of these allocations must also be recognized within the consolidation process.
- Any reciprocal or intercompany accounts must be offset. If, for example, one of the companies owes money to the other, the receivable and the payable balances have no connection with an outside party. Both should be eliminated for external reporting purposes. When the companies are viewed as a single entity, the receivable and the payable are intercompany balances to be removed.

A consolidation of the two sets of financial information in Exhibit 3.4 is a relatively uncomplicated task and can even be carried out without the use of a worksheet. Understanding the origin of each reported figure is the first step in gaining a knowledge of this process.

- *Revenues* = $1,900,000. The revenues of the parent and the subsidiary are added together.
- *Cost of goods sold* = $950,000. The cost of goods sold of the parent and subsidiary are added together.
- *Depreciation expense* = $257,000. The depreciation expenses of the parent and subsidiary are added together along with the $13,000 additional building depreciation and the $6,000 reduction in equipment depreciation, as indicated in Exhibit 3.3.
- *Equity in subsidiary earnings* = –0–. The investment income recorded by the parent is eliminated so that the subsidiary's revenues and expenses can be included in the consolidated totals.
- *Net income* = $693,000. Consolidated revenues less consolidated expenses.
- *Retained earnings, 1/1/07* = $840,000. The parent figure only because the subsidiary was not owned prior to that date.
- *Dividends paid* = $120,000. The parent company balance only because the subsidiary's dividends were paid intercompany to the parent, not to an outside party.
- *Retained earnings, 12/31/07* = $1,413,000. Consolidated retained earnings as of the beginning of the year plus consolidated net income less consolidated dividends paid.
- *Current assets* = $1,440,000. The parent's book value plus the subsidiary's book value.
- *Investment in Sun Company* = –0–. The asset recorded by the parent is eliminated so that the subsidiary's assets and liabilities can be included in the consolidated totals.
- *Land* = $820,000. The parent's book value plus the subsidiary's book value plus the $20,000 allocation within the purchase price.
- *Buildings* = $775,000. The parent's book value plus the subsidiary's book value plus the $130,000 allocation within the purchase price less 2007 amortization of $13,000.
- *Equipment* = $446,000. The parent's book value plus the subsidiary's book value less the $30,000 cost reduction allocation plus the 2007 expense reduction of $6,000.
- *Goodwill* = $80,000. The residual allocation shown in Exhibit 3.2. Note that goodwill is not amortized.
- *Total assets* = $3,561,000. A vertical summation of consolidated assets.
- *Liabilities* = $1,428,000. The parent's book value plus the subsidiary's book value.
- *Common stock* = $600,000. The parent's book value since this combination was a purchase.
- *Additional paid-in capital* = $120,000. The parent's book value since this combination was a purchase.
- *Retained earnings, 12/31/07* = $1,413,000. Computed previously.
- *Total liabilities and equities* = $3,561,000. A vertical summation of consolidated liabilities and equities.

Consolidation Worksheet

Although the consolidated figures to be reported can be computed as just shown, accountants normally prefer to use a worksheet. A worksheet provides an organized structure for this process, a benefit that becomes especially important in consolidating complex combinations.

For Parrot and Sun, only five consolidation entries are needed to arrive at the same figures previously derived for this business combination. As discussed in Chapter 2, *worksheet entries are the catalyst for developing totals to be reported by the entity but are not physically recorded in the individual account balances of either company.*

Consolidation Entry S

Common Stock (Sun Company)	200,000	
Additional Paid-In Capital (Sun Company)	20,000	
Retained Earnings, 1/1/07 (Sun Company)	380,000	
Investment in Sun Company		600,000

As shown in Exhibit 3.2, Parrot's $800,000 purchase price reflects two components: (1) a $600,000 amount equal to Sun's book value and (2) a $200,000 figure attributed to the difference, at January 1, 2007, between the book value and fair value of Sun's assets and liabilities (with a residual allocation made to goodwill). Entry **S** removes the $600,000 component of the Investment in Sun Company account so that the *book value* of each subsidiary asset and liability can be included in the consolidated figures. A second worksheet entry (Entry **A**) eliminates the remaining $200,000 portion of the purchase price, allowing the specific allocations to be included along with any goodwill.

Entry **S** also removes Sun's stockholders' equity accounts as of the beginning of the year. Subsidiary equity balances generated prior to the acquisition are not relevant to the business combination and should be deleted. The elimination is made through this entry because the equity accounts and the $600,000 component of the investment account represent reciprocal balances: Both provide a measure of Sun's book value as of January 1, 2007.

Before moving to the next consolidation entry, a clarification point should be made. In actual practice, worksheet entries are usually identified numerically. However, as in the previous chapter, the label "Entry **S**" used in this example refers to the elimination of Sun's beginning Stockholders' Equity. As a reminder of the purpose being served, all worksheet entries are identified in a similar fashion. Thus, throughout this textbook, "Entry **S**" always refers to the removal of the subsidiary's beginning stockholders' equity balances for the year against the book value portion of the investment account.

Consolidation Entry A

Land	20,000	
Buildings	130,000	
Goodwill	80,000	
Equipment		30,000
Investment in Sun Company		200,000

Consolidation entry A removes the $200,000 component of the purchase price, replacing it with the specific allocations from the original purchase price (see Exhibit 3.2). This entry is labeled "Entry **A**" to indicate that it represents the **A**llocations made in connection with the parent's purchase price. The individual assets and liabilities of the consolidated entity now reflect the cost incurred by Parrot in making this purchase. Sun's accounts are adjusted based on the $200,000 paid at the time of acquisition that was in excess of Sun's book value. However, no basis exists for continually revaluing the accounts to newly determined fair values at the date of subsequent consolidations.

Consolidation Entry I

Equity in Subsidiary Earnings	93,000	
Investment in Sun Company		93,000

"Entry **I**" (for **I**ncome) removes the subsidiary income recognized by Parrot during the year so that the underlying revenue and expense accounts of Sun (and the current amortization expense) can be brought into the consolidated totals. The $93,000 figure eliminated here represents the $100,000 income accrual recognized by Parrot, reduced by the $7,000 in excess amortizations. For consolidation purposes, the one-line amount appearing in the parent's records is not appropriate and is removed so that the individual revenues and expenses can be included. The entry originally recorded by the parent is simply reversed on the worksheet to remove its impact.

Consolidation Entry D

Investment in Sun Company	40,000	
Dividends Paid		40,000

The dividends distributed by the subsidiary during 2007 also must be eliminated from the consolidated totals. The entire $40,000 payment was made to the parent so that, from the viewpoint of the consolidated entity, it is simply an intercompany transfer of cash. The distribution did not affect any outside party. Therefore, "Entry **D**" (for **D**ividends) is designed to offset the impact of this transaction by removing the subsidiary's Dividends Paid account. Because the equity method has been applied, receipt of this money by Parrot was recorded originally as a decrease in the Investment in Sun Company account. To eliminate the impact of this reduction, the Investment account is increased.

Consolidation Entry E

Depreciation Expense	7,000	
Equipment	6,000	
Buildings		13,000

This final worksheet entry records the current year's excess amortization expenses relating to Parrot's purchase price. Because the equity method amortization was eliminated within Entry **I**, "Entry **E**" (for **E**xpense) now records the 2007 expense attributed to each of the specific account allocations (see Exhibit 3.3).

Thus, the worksheet entries necessary for consolidation when the parent has applied the equity method are as follows:

Entry S—Eliminates the subsidiary's stockholders' equity accounts as of the beginning of the current year along with the equivalent book value component within the parent's purchase price in the investment account.

Entry A—Recognizes the unamortized allocations as of the beginning of the current year, costs that were associated with the original purchase price.

Entry I—Eliminates the impact of intercompany income accrued by the parent.

Entry D—Eliminates the impact of intercompany dividend payments made by the subsidiary.

Entry E—Recognizes excess amortization expenses for the current period on the allocations from the original purchase price.

Exhibit 3.5 provides a complete presentation of the December 31, 2007, consolidation worksheet developed for Parrot Company and Sun Company. The series of entries just described successfully brings together the separate financial statements of these two organizations. Note that the consolidated totals are the same as those computed previously for this combination.

Note that Parrot separately reports net income of $693,000 as well as ending retained earnings of $1,413,000, figures that are identical to the totals generated for the consolidated entity. However, subsidiary income earned after the date of acquisition is to be *added* to that of the parent. Thus, a question arises in this example as to why the parent company figures alone equal the consolidated balances of both operations.

In reality, Sun's income for this period is contained in both Parrot's reported balances and the consolidated totals. Through the application of the equity method, the 2007 earnings of the subsidiary have already been accrued by Parrot along with the appropriate amortization expense. *The parent's Equity in Subsidiary Earnings account is, therefore, an accurate representation of Sun's effect on consolidated net income.* If the equity method is employed properly, the worksheet process simply replaces this single $93,000 balance with the specific

EXHIBIT 3.5

PARROT COMPANY AND SUN COMPANY

Consolidation: Purchase Method
Investment: Equity Method

Consolidated Worksheet
For Year Ending December 31, 2007

Accounts	Parrot Company	Sun Company	Consolidation Entries Debit	Consolidation Entries Credit	Consolidated Totals
Income Statement					
Revenues	(1,500,000)	(400,000)			(1,900,000)
Cost of goods sold	700,000	250,000			950,000
Depreciation expense	200,000	50,000	(E) 7,000		257,000
Equity in subsidiary earnings	(93,000)	–0–	(I) 93,000		–0–
Net income	(693,000)	(100,000)			(693,000)
Statement of Retained Earnings					
Retained earnings, 1/1/07	(840,000)	(380,000)	(S) 380,000		(840,000)
Net income (above)	(693,000)	(100,000)			(693,000)
Dividends paid	120,000	40,000		(D) 40,000	120,000
Retained earnings, 12/31/07	(1,413,000)	(440,000)			(1,413,000)
Balance Sheet					
Current assets	1,040,000	400,000			1,440,000
Investment in Sun Company	853,000	–0–	(D) 40,000	(S) 600,000	–0–
				(A) 200,000	
				(I) 93,000	
Land	600,000	200,000	(A) 20,000		820,000
Buildings (net)	370,000	288,000	(A) 130,000	(E) 13,000	775,000
Equipment (net)	250,000	220,000	(E) 6,000	(A) 30,000	446,000
Goodwill	–0–	–0–	(A) 80,000		80,000
Total assets	3,113,000	1,108,000			3,561,000
Liabilities	(980,000)	(448,000)			(1,428,000)
Common stock	(600,000)	(200,000)	(S) 200,000		(600,000)
Additional paid-in capital	(120,000)	(20,000)	(S) 20,000		(120,000)
Retained earnings, 12/31/07 (above)	(1,413,000)	(440,000)			(1,413,000)
Total liabilities and equities	(3,113,000)	(1,108,000)			(3,561,000)

Note: Parentheses indicate a credit balance.
Consolidation entries:
  (S) Elimination of Sun's stockholders' equity accounts as of January 1, 2007, and book value portion of purchase price.
  (A) Allocation of Parrot's cost in excess of Sun's book value.
  (I) Elimination of intercompany equity income.
  (D) Elimination of intercompany dividends.
  (E) Recognition of excess amortization expenses on purchase price allocations.

revenue and expense accounts that it represents. *Consequently, when the equity method is employed, the parent's net income and retained earnings mirror consolidated totals.*

Consolidation Subsequent to Year of Acquisition—Equity Method

In many ways, every consolidation of Parrot and Sun prepared after the date of acquisition incorporates the same basic procedures outlined in the previous section. However, the continual financial evolution undergone by the companies prohibits an exact repetition of the consolidation entries demonstrated in Exhibit 3.5.

As a basis for analyzing the procedural changes necessitated by the passage of time, assume that Parrot Company continues to hold its ownership of Sun Company as of December 31, 2010. This date was selected at random; any date subsequent to 2007 would serve equally well to illustrate this process. As an additional factor, assume that Sun now has a $40,000 liability that is payable to Parrot.

For this consolidation, assume that the January 1, 2010, Sun Company's Retained Earnings balance has risen to $600,000. Because that account had a reported total of only $380,000 on January 1, 2007, Sun's book value apparently has increased by $220,000 during the 2007–2009 period. Although knowledge of individual operating figures in the past is not required, Sun's reported totals help to clarify the consolidation procedures.

Year	Sun Company Net Income	Dividends Paid	Increase in Book Value	Ending Retained Earnings
2007	$100,000	$ 40,000	$ 60,000	$440,000
2008	140,000	50,000	90,000	530,000
2009	90,000	20,000	70,000	600,000
	$330,000	$110,000	$220,000	

For 2010, the current year, we assume that Sun reports net income of $160,000 and pays cash dividends of $70,000. Because it applies the equity method, Parrot recognizes earnings of $160,000. Furthermore, as shown in Exhibit 3.3, amortization expense of $7,000 applies to 2010 and must also be recorded by the parent. Consequently, Parrot reports an Equity in Subsidiary Earnings balance for the year of $153,000 ($160,000 − $7,000).

Although this income figure can be reconstructed with little difficulty, the current balance in the Investment in Sun Company account is more complicated. Over the years, the initial $800,000 purchase price has been subjected to adjustments for

1. The annual accrual of Sun's income.
2. The receipt of dividends from Sun.
3. The recognition of annual excess amortization expenses.

However, by analyzing these changes, Exhibit 3.6 can be developed to show the components of the balance in the Investment in Sun Company account as of December 31, 2010.

EXHIBIT 3.6

PARROT COMPANY
Investment in Sun Company Account
As of December 31, 2010
Equity Method Applied

Purchase price		$ 800,000
Entries recorded in prior years:		
Accrual of Sun Company's income		
2007	$100,000	
2008	140,000	
2009	90,000	330,000
Sun Company—Dividends paid		
2007	$ (40,000)	
2008	(50,000)	
2009	(20,000)	(110,000)
Excess amortization expenses		
2007	$ (7,000)	
2008	(7,000)	
2009	(7,000)	(21,000)
Entries recorded in current year—2010:		
Accrual of Sun Company's income	$160,000	
Sun Company—Dividends paid	(70,000)	
Excess amortization expenses	(7,000)	83,000
Investment in Sun Company, 12/31/10		$1,082,000

EXHIBIT 3.7

Consolidation: Purchase Method	**PARROT COMPANY AND SUN COMPANY**				
Investment: Equity Method	**Consolidated Worksheet**				
	For Year Ending December 31, 2010				

Accounts	Parrot Company	Sun Company	Consolidation Entries Debit	Consolidation Entries Credit	Consolidated Totals
Income Statement					
Revenues	(2,100,000)	(600,000)			(2,700,000)
Cost of goods sold	1,000,000	380,000			1,380,000
Depreciation expense	300,000	60,000	(E) 7,000		367,000
Equity in subsidiary earnings	(153,000)	–0–	(I) 153,000		–0–
Net income	(953,000)	(160,000)			(953,000)
Statement of Retained Earnings					
Retained earnings, 1/1/10	(2,044,000)	(600,000)	(S) 600,000		(2,044,000)
Net income (above)	(953,000)	(160,000)			(953,000)
Dividends paid	420,000	70,000		(D) 70,000	420,000
Retained earnings, 12/31/10	(2,577,000)	(690,000)			(2,577,000)
Balance Sheet					
Current assets	1,705,000	500,000		(P) 40,000	2,165,000
Investment in Sun Company	1,082,000	–0–	(D) 70,000	(S) 820,000	–0–
				(A) 179,000	
				(I) 153,000	
Land	600,000	240,000	(A) 20,000		860,000
Buildings (net)	540,000	420,000	(A) 91,000	(E) 13,000	1,038,000
Equipment (net)	420,000	210,000	(E) 6,000	(A) 12,000	624,000
Goodwill	–0–	–0–	(A) 80,000		80,000
Total assets	4,347,000	1,370,000			4,767,000
Liabilities	(1,050,000)	(460,000)	(P) 40,000		(1,470,000)
Common stock	(600,000)	(200,000)	(S) 200,000		(600,000)
Additional paid-in capital	(120,000)	(20,000)	(S) 20,000		(120,000)
Retained earnings, 12/31/10 (above)	(2,577,000)	(690,000)			(2,577,000)
Total liabilities and equities	(4,347,000)	(1,370,000)			(4,767,000)

Note: Parentheses indicate a credit balance.
Consolidation entries:
  (S) Elimination of Sun's stockholders' equity accounts as of January 1, 2010, and book value portion of Investment account.
  (A) Allocation of Parrot's cost in excess of Sun's book value, unamortized values as of January 1, 2010.
  (I)   Elimination of intercompany income.
  (D) Elimination of intercompany dividends.
  (E) Recognition of excess amortization expenses on purchase price allocations.
  (P) Elimination of intercompany receivable/payable balances.

Following the construction of the Investment in Sun Company account, the consolidation worksheet developed in Exhibit 3.7 should be easier to understand. Current figures for both companies appear in the first two columns. The parent's investment balance and equity income accrual as well as Sun's income and stockholders' equity accounts correspond to the information given previously. Worksheet entries (lettered to agree with the previous illustration) are then utilized to consolidate all balances.

Several steps are necessary to arrive at these reported totals. The subsidiary's assets, liabilities, revenues, and expenses are added to those same accounts of the parent. The unamortized portion of the original purchase price allocations are included along with current excess amortization expenses. The investment and equity income balances are both eliminated as are the subsidiary's stockholders' equity accounts. Intercompany dividends are removed with the same treatment required for the debt existing between the two companies.

Consolidation Entry S Once again, this first consolidation entry offsets reciprocal amounts representing the subsidiary's book value as of the beginning of the current year. Sun's January 1, 2010, stockholders' equity accounts are eliminated against the book value portion of the parent's investment account. Here, though, the amount eliminated is $820,000 rather than the $600,000 shown in Exhibit 3.5 for 2007. Both balances have changed during the 2007–2009 period. Sun's operations caused a $220,000 increase in retained earnings. Parrot's application of the equity method created a parallel effect on its Investment in Sun Company account (the income accrual of $330,000 less dividends collected of $110,000).

Although Sun's Retained Earnings balance is removed in this entry, the income this company earned since the date of purchase is still included in the consolidated figures. Parrot accrues these profits annually through application of the equity method. Thus, elimination of the subsidiary's entire Retained Earnings is necessary; a portion was earned prior to the purchase and the remainder has already been recorded by the parent.

Entry **S** removes these balances as of the first day of 2010 rather than at the end of the year. The consolidation process is made a bit simpler by segregating the effect of preceding operations from the transactions of the current year. Thus, *all worksheet entries relate specifically to either the previous years (**S** and **A**) or the current period (**I, D, E,** and **P**).*

Consolidation Entry A In the initial consolidation (2007), cost allocations amounting to $200,000 were entered, but these balances have now undergone three years of amortization. As computed in Exhibit 3.8, expenses for these prior years totaled $21,000, leaving a balance of $179,000. Allocation of this amount to the individual accounts is also determined in Exhibit 3.8 and reflected in worksheet Entry **A.** As with Entry **S,** these balances are calculated as of January 1, 2010, so that the current year expenses can be included separately (in Entry **E**).

Consolidation Entry I As before, this entry eliminates the equity income recorded currently by Parrot ($153,000) in connection with its ownership of Sun. The subsidiary's revenue and expense accounts are left intact so they can be included in the consolidated figures.

Consolidation Entry D This worksheet entry offsets the $70,000 intercompany dividend payment made by Sun to Parrot during the current period.

Consolidation Entry E Excess amortization expenses relating to Parrot's purchase price are individually recorded for 2010.

Before progressing to the final worksheet entry, note the close similarity of these entries with the five incorporated in the 2007 consolidation (Exhibit 3.5). Except for the numerical changes created by the passage of time, the entries are identical.

Consolidation Entry P This last entry (labeled "Entry **P**" because it eliminates an intercompany **P**ayable) introduces a new element to the consolidation process. As noted earlier, intercompany debt transactions do not relate to outside parties. Therefore, Sun's $40,000 payable and Parrot's $40,000 receivable are reciprocals that must be removed on the worksheet because the companies are being reported as a single entity.

In reviewing Exhibit 3.7, note several aspects of the consolidation process:

- The stockholders' equity accounts of the subsidiary are removed.
- The Investment in Sun Company and the Equity in Subsidiary Earnings are both removed.

EXHIBIT 3.8
Excess Amortizations Relating to Individual Accounts as of January 1, 2010

Accounts	Original Allocation	Annual Excess Amortizations			Balance 1/1/10
		2007	2008	2009	
Land	$ 20,000	–0–	–0–	–0–	$ 20,000
Buildings	130,000	$13,000	$13,000	$13,000	91,000
Equipment	(30,000)	(6,000)	(6,000)	(6,000)	(12,000)
Goodwill	80,000	–0–	–0–	–0–	80,000
	$200,000	$ 7,000	$ 7,000	$ 7,000	$179,000
			$21,000		

- The parent's Retained Earnings balance is not adjusted. Since the equity method has been applied, this account should be correct.
- The original allocations created by the purchase price are recognized but only after adjustment for annual excess amortization expenses.
- Intercompany transactions such as dividend payments and the receivable/payable are offset.

SUBSEQUENT CONSOLIDATIONS—INVESTMENT RECORDED USING COST OR PARTIAL EQUITY METHOD

Acquisition Made during the Current Year

As discussed at the beginning of this chapter, the parent company may opt to use the cost method or the partial equity method for internal record-keeping rather than the equity method. Application of either alternative changes the balances recorded by the parent over time and, thus,

EXHIBIT 3.9

PARROT COMPANY AND SUN COMPANY					
Consolidation: Purchase Method	**Consolidated Worksheet**				
Investment: Cost Method	**For Year Ending December 31, 2007**				

Accounts	Parrot Company	Sun Company	Consolidation Entries		Consolidated Totals
			Debit	Credit	
Income Statement					
Revenues	(1,500,000)	(400,000)			(1,900,000)
Cost of goods sold	700,000	250,000			950,000
Depreciation expense	200,000	50,000	(E) 7,000		257,000
Dividend income	(40,000) *	–0–	(I) 40,000 *		–0–
Net income	(640,000)	(100,000)			(693,000)
Statement of Retained Earnings					
Retained earnings, 1/1/07	(840,000)	(380,000)	(S) 380,000		(840,000)
Net income (above)	(640,000)	(100,000)			(693,000)
Dividends paid	120,000	40,000		(I) 40,000 *	120,000
Retained earnings, 12/31/07	(1,360,000)	(440,000)			(1,413,000)
Balance Sheet					
Current assets	1,040,000	400,000			1,440,000
Investment in Sun Company	800,000 *	–0–		(S) 600,000	–0–
				(A) 200,000	
Land	600,000	200,000	(A) 20,000		820,000
Buildings (net)	370,000	288,000	(A) 130,000	(E) 13,000	775,000
Equipment (net)	250,000	220,000	(E) 6,000	(A) 30,000	446,000
Goodwill	–0–	–0–	(A) 80,000		80,000
Total assets	3,060,000	1,108,000			3,561,000
Liabilities	(980,000)	(448,000)			(1,428,000)
Common stock	(600,000)	(200,000)	(S) 200,000		(600,000)
Additional paid-in capital	(120,000)	(20,000)	(S) 20,000		(120,000)
Retained earnings, 12/31/07 (above)	(1,360,000)	(440,000)			(1,413,000)
Total liabilities and equities	(3,060,000)	(1,108,000)			(3,561,000)

Note: Parentheses indicate a credit balance.

*Boxed items highlight differences with consolidation in Exhibit 3.5.

Consolidation entries:

- (S)   Elimination of Sun's stockholders' equity accounts as of January 1, 2007, and book value portion of purchase price.
- (A)   Allocation of Parrot's cost in excess of Sun's book value.
- (I)   Elimination of intercompany dividends recognized by parent as income.
- (D)   Entry is not needed when cost method is applied because Entry I eliminates intercompany dividends.
- (E)   Recognition of excess amortization expenses on purchase price allocations.

the procedures followed in creating consolidations. However, *choosing one of these other approaches does not affect any of the final consolidated figures to be reported.*

When a company utilizes the equity method, it eliminates all reciprocal accounts, assigns unamortized cost allocations to specific accounts, and records amortization expense for the current year. Application of either the cost method or the partial equity method has no effect on this basic process. For this reason, a number of the consolidation entries remain the same regardless of the accounting method being applied by the parent.

In reality, just three of the parent's accounts actually vary because of the method applied:

- The investment account.
- The income recognized from the subsidiary.
- The parent's retained earnings (in periods after the initial year of the combination).

Only the differences found in these balances affect the consolidation process when another method is applied. Thus, any time after the date of purchase, accounting for these three accounts is of special importance.

To illustrate the modifications required by the adoption of an alternative accounting method, the consolidation of Parrot and Sun as of December 31, 2007, is reconstructed. Only one differing factor is introduced: the method by which Parrot accounts for its investment. Exhibit 3.9 presents the 2007 consolidation based on Parrot's use of the cost method. Exhibit 3.10 demonstrates this same process assuming that the partial equity method was applied by the parent. Each entry on these worksheets is labeled to correspond with the 2007 consolidation in which the parent used the equity method (Exhibit 3.5). Furthermore, differences with the equity method (both on the parent company records and with the consolidation entries) are highlighted on each of the worksheets.

Cost Method Applied—2007 Consolidation

Although the cost method theoretically stands in marked contrast to the equity method, just a narrow range of reporting differences actually results. In the year of acquisition, Parrot's income and investment accounts relating to the subsidiary are the only accounts altered.

Under the cost method, income recognition in 2007 is limited to the $40,000 dividend received by the parent; no equity income accrual is made. At the same time, the investment account retains its $800,000 cost. Unlike the equity method, no adjustments are recorded in the parent's investment account in connection with the current year operations, subsidiary dividends, or amortization of any purchase price allocations.

After the composition of these two accounts has been established, worksheet entries can be used to produce the consolidated figures found in Exhibit 3.9 as of December 31, 2007.

Consolidation Entry S As with the previous Entry **S** in Exhibit 3.5, the $600,000 component of the investment account is eliminated against the beginning stockholders' equity account of the subsidiary. Both are equivalent to Sun's net assets at January 1, 2007, and are, therefore, reciprocal balances that must be offset. This entry is not affected by the accounting method in use.

Consolidation Entry A Parrot's $200,000 excess payment is allocated to Sun's assets and liabilities based on the fair values at the date of acquisition. The $80,000 residual is attributed to goodwill. This procedure is identical to the corresponding entry in Exhibit 3.5 in which the equity method was applied.

Consolidation Entry I Under the cost method, the parent records dividend collections as income. Entry **I** removes this Dividend Income account along with Sun's Dividends Paid. From a consolidated perspective, these two $40,000 balances represent an intercompany transfer of cash that had no financial impact outside of the entity. In contrast to the equity method, subsidiary income has not been accrued by Parrot, nor has amortization been recorded; thus, no further income elimination is needed.

Dividend Income	40,000	
Dividends Paid		40,000
To eliminate intercompany income.		

EXHIBIT 3.10

			Consolidation Entries		
PARROT COMPANY AND SUN COMPANY					
Consolidation: Purchase Method	**Consolidated Worksheet**				
Investment: Partial Equity Method	**For Year Ending December 31, 2007**				

Accounts	Parrot Company	Sun Company	Debit	Credit	Consolidated Totals
Income Statement					
Revenues	(1,500,000)	(400,000)			(1,900,000)
Cost of goods sold	700,000	250,000			950,000
Depreciation expense	200,000	50,000	(E) 7,000		257,000
Equity in subsidiary earnings	(100,000) *	–0–	(I) 100,000 *		–0–
Net income	(700,000)	(100,000)			(693,000)
Statement of Retained Earnings					
Retained earnings, 1/1/07	(840,000)	(380,000)	(S) 380,000		(840,000)
Net income (above)	(700,000)	(100,000)			(693,000)
Dividends paid	120,000	40,000		(D) 40,000	120,000
Retained earnings, 12/31/07	(1,420,000)	(440,000)			(1,413,000)
Balance Sheet					
Current assets	1,040,000	400,000			1,440,000
Investment in Sun Company	860,000 *	–0–	(D) 40,000	(S) 600,000	–0–
				(A) 200,000	
				(I) 100,000 *	
Land	600,000	200,000	(A) 20,000		820,000
Buildings (net)	370,000	288,000	(A) 130,000	(E) 13,000	775,000
Equipment (net)	250,000	220,000	(E) 6,000	(A) 30,000	446,000
Goodwill	–0–	–0–	(A) 80,000		80,000
Total assets	3,120,000	1,108,000			3,561,000
Liabilities	(980,000)	(448,000)			(1,428,000)
Common stock	(600,000)	(200,000)	(S) 200,000		(600,000)
Additional paid-in capital	(120,000)	(20,000)	(S) 20,000		(120,000)
Retained earnings, 12/31/07 (above)	(1,420,000)	(440,000)			(1,413,000)
Total liabilities and equities	(3,120,000)	(1,108,000)			(3,561,000)

Note: Parentheses indicate a credit balance.
*Boxed items highlight differences with consolidation in Exhibit 3.5.
Consolidation entries:
   (S)   Elimination of Sun's stockholders' equity accounts as of January 1, 2007, and book value portion of purchase price.
   (A)   Allocation of Parrot's cost in excess of Sun's book value.
   (I)   Elimination of parent's equity income accrual.
   (D)   Elimination of intercompany dividend payment.
   (E)   Recognition of excess amortization expenses on purchase price allocations.

Consolidation Entry D   When the cost method is applied, intercompany dividends are recorded by the parent as income. Because these distributions were already removed from the consolidated totals by Entry **I,** no separate Entry **D** is required.

Consolidation Entry E   Regardless of the parent's method of accounting, the reporting entity must recognize excess amortizations for the current year in connection with the original purchase price allocations. Thus, Entry **E** serves to bring the 2007 expenses into the consolidated financial statements.

Consequently, using the cost method rather than the equity method changes only Entries **I** and **D** in the year of acquisition. Despite the change in methods, reported figures are still derived by (1) eliminating all reciprocals, (2) allocating the excess portion of the purchase price, and (3) recording amortizations on these allocations. As indicated previously, the consolidated totals appearing in Exhibit 3.9 are identical to the figures produced previously in Exhibit 3.5.

Although the income and the investment accounts on the parent company's separate statements vary, the consolidated balances are not affected.

One significant difference between the cost method and equity method does exist: The parent's separate statements do not reflect consolidated income totals when the cost method is used. Because equity adjustments (such as excess amortizations) are ignored, neither Parrot's reported net income of $640,000 nor its retained earnings of $1,360,000 provides an accurate portrayal of consolidated figures.

Partial Equity Method Applied—2007 Consolidation

Exhibit 3.10 presents a worksheet to consolidate these two companies for 2007 (the year of acquisition) based on the assumption that Parrot applied the partial equity method. Again, the only changes from previous examples are found in (1) the parent's separate records for this investment and its related income and (2) worksheet Entries **I** and **D.**

As discussed earlier, under the partial equity approach, the parent's record-keeping is limited to two periodic journal entries: the annual accrual of subsidiary income and the receipt of dividends. Hence, within the parent's records, only a few differences exist when the partial equity method is applied rather than the cost method. The entries recorded by Parrot in connection with Sun's 2007 operations illustrate both of these approaches.

Parrot Company Cost Method 2007			**Parrot Company Partial Equity Method 2007**		
Cash	40,000		Cash	40,000	
Dividend Income		40,000	Investment in Sun Company		40,000
Dividends collected from subsidiary.			Dividends collected from subsidiary.		
			Investment in Sun Company	100,000	
			Equity in Subsidiary Earnings		100,000
			Accrual of subsidiary income.		

Therefore, by applying the partial equity method, the Investment account on the parent's balance sheet rises to $860,000 by the end of 2007. This total is composed of the original $800,000 purchase price adjusted for the $100,000 income recognition and the $40,000 cash dividend payment. The same $100,000 equity income figure appears within the parent's income statement. These two balances are appropriately found in Parrot's records in Exhibit 3.10.

Because of the handling of income recognition and dividend payments, Entries **I** and **D** again differ on the worksheet. For the partial equity method, the $100,000 equity income is eliminated (Entry **I**) by reversing the parent's entry. Removing this accrual allows the individual revenue and expense accounts of the subsidiary to be reported without double-counting. The $40,000 intercompany dividend payment must also be removed (Entry **D**). The Dividend Paid account is simply deleted. However, elimination of the dividend from the Investment in Sun Company actually causes an increase because receipt was recorded by Parrot as a reduction in that account. All other consolidation entries (Entries **S, A,** and **E**) are the same for all three methods.

Consolidation Subsequent to Year of Acquisition—Cost and Partial Equity Methods

By again incorporating the December 31, 2010, financial data for Parrot and Sun (presented in Exhibit 3.7), consolidation procedures for the cost method and the partial equity method can be examined for years subsequent to the date of acquisition. *In both cases, establishment of an appropriate beginning retained earnings figure becomes a significant goal of the consolidation.*

EXHIBIT 3.11

	Equity Method	Cost Method	Partial Equity Method
PARROT COMPANY AND SUN COMPANY			
Previous Years—2007–2009			
Equity accrual	$330,000	–0–	$330,000
Dividend income	–0–	$110,000	–0–
Excess amortization expenses	(21,000)	–0–	–0–
Increase in parent's retained earnings	$309,000	$110,000	$330,000

This concern was not faced previously when the equity method was adopted. Under that approach, the parent's Retained Earnings balance mirrors the consolidated total so that no adjustment is necessary. In the earlier illustration, the $330,000 income accrual for the 2007–2009 period as well as the $21,000 amortization expense were recognized by the parent based on employment of the equity method (see Exhibit 3.6). Having been recorded in this manner, these two balances form a permanent part of Parrot's retained earnings and are included automatically in the consolidated total. Consequently, if the equity method is applied, the process is simplified; no worksheet entries are needed to adjust the parent's Retained Earnings to record subsidiary operations or amortization for past years.

Conversely, if a method other than the equity method is used, a worksheet change must be made to the parent's beginning Retained Earnings (in every subsequent year) to equate this balance with the consolidated total. To quantify this adjustment, the parent's recognized income for these past three years under each method is first determined (Exhibit 3.11). For consolidation purposes, beginning Retained Earnings must then be increased or decreased to create the same effect as the equity method.

Cost Method Applied—Subsequent Consolidation

As shown in Exhibit 3.11, if the cost method is applied by Parrot during the 2007–2009 period, $199,000 less income is recognized than under the equity method ($309,000 − $110,000). This difference has two causes. First, Parrot has not accrued the $220,000 increase in the subsidiary's book value in the period prior to the current year. Although the $110,000 in dividends was recorded as income, the remainder of the $330,000 earned by the subsidiary was never recognized by the parent.[7] Second, no accounting has been made of the $21,000 excess amortization expenses. Thus, the parent's beginning Retained Earnings is $199,000 ($220,000 − $21,000) below the appropriate consolidated total and must be adjusted.[8]

To simulate the equity method so that the parent's beginning Retained Earnings agree with that of the combination, this $199,000 increase is recorded through a worksheet entry. The cost method figures reported by the parent are effectively being converted into equity method balances.

Consolidation Entry *C

Investment in Sun Company	199,000	
Retained Earnings, 1/1/10 (Parrot Company)		199,000
To convert parent's beginning retained earnings from cost method to equity method.		

---

[7] Two different methods are indicated here for determining the $220,000 in nonrecorded income for prior years: (1) subsidiary income less dividends paid and (2) the change in the subsidiary's book value as of the first day of the current year. The second method works only if the subsidiary has had no other equity transactions such as the issuance of new stock or the purchase of treasury shares. Unless otherwise stated, the assumption is made that no such transactions have occurred.

[8] Since neither the income in excess of dividends nor excess amortization is recorded by the parent under the cost method, its beginning Retained Earnings is $199,000 less than the $2,044,000 reported under the equity method (Exhibit 3.7). Thus, a $1,845,000 balance is shown in Exhibit 3.12 ($2,044,000 − this $199,000). Conversely, if the partial equity method had been applied, Parrot's failure to record amortization would cause Retained Earnings to be $21,000 higher than the figure derived by the equity method. For this reason, Exhibit 3.13 shows the parent with beginning Retained Earnings of $2,065,000 rather than $2,044,000.

This adjustment has been labeled Entry *C. The C refers to the conversion being made to equity method totals. The asterisk indicates that this equity simulation relates solely to transactions of prior periods. Thus, *Entry *C should be recorded before the other worksheet entries to align the beginning balances for the year.*

Exhibit 3.12 provides a complete presentation of the consolidation of Parrot and Sun as of December 31, 2010, based on the parent's application of the cost method. After Entry *C has been recorded on the worksheet, the remainder of this consolidation follows the same pattern as previous examples. Sun's stockholders' equity accounts are eliminated (Entry **S**) while the allocations stemming from the $800,000 purchase price are recorded (Entry **A**) at their

EXHIBIT 3.12

Consolidation: Purchase Method
Investment: Cost Method

PARROT COMPANY AND SUN COMPANY
Consolidated Worksheet
For Year Ending December 31, 2010

Accounts	Parrot Company	Sun Company	Consolidation Entries Debit	Consolidation Entries Credit	Consolidated Totals
Income Statement					
Revenues	(2,100,000)	(600,000)			(2,700,000)
Cost of goods sold	1,000,000	380,000			1,380,000
Depreciation expense	300,000	60,000	(E) 7,000		367,000
Dividend income	(70,000) *	–0–	(I) 70,000 *		–0–
Net income	(870,000)	(160,000)			(953,000)
Statement of Retained Earnings					
Retained earnings, 1/1/10:					
Parrot Company	(1,845,000)† *			(*C) 199,000 *	(2,044,000)
Sun Company		(600,000)	(S) 600,000		–0–
Net income (above)	(870,000)	(160,000)			(953,000)
Dividends paid	420,000	70,000		(I) 70,000 *	420,000
Retained earnings, 12/31/10	(2,295,000)	(690,000)			(2,577,000)
Balance Sheet					
Current assets	1,705,000	500,000		(P) 40,000	2,165,000
Investment in Sun Company	800,000 *	–0–	(*C) 199,000	(S) 820,000	–0–
				(A) 179,000	
Land	600,000	240,000	(A) 20,000		860,000
Buildings (net)	540,000	420,000	(A) 91,000	(E) 13,000	1,038,000
Equipment (net)	420,000	210,000	(E) 6,000	(A) 12,000	624,000
Goodwill	–0–	–0–	(A) 80,000		80,000
Total assets	4,065,000	1,370,000			4,767,000
Liabilities	(1,050,000)	(460,000)	(P) 40,000		(1,470,000)
Common stock	(600,000)	(200,000)	(S) 200,000		(600,000)
Additional paid-in capital	(120,000)	(20,000)	(S) 20,000		(120,000)
Retained earnings, 12/31/10 (above)	(2,295,000)	(690,000)			(2,577,000)
Total liabilities and equities	(4,065,000)	(1,370,000)			(4,767,000)

Note: Parentheses indicate a credit balance.
*Boxed items highlight differences with consolidation in Exhibit 3.7.
†See footnote 8.
Consolidation entries:
(*C) To recognize additional earnings and amortization relating to ownership of subsidiary for years prior to 2010.
(S)   Elimination of Sun's stockholders' equity accounts as of January 1, 2010, and book value portion of Investment account.
(A)   Allocation of Parrot's cost in excess of Sun's book value, unamortized values as of January 1, 2010.
(I)   Elimination of intercompany dividends recognized by parent as income.
(D)   Entry is not needed when cost method is applied because Entry I eliminates intercompany dividend income.
(E)   Recognition of excess amortization expenses on purchase price allocations.
(P)   Elimination of intercompany receivable/payable balances.

EXHIBIT 3.13

			Consolidation Entries		

PARROT COMPANY AND SUN COMPANY
Consolidated Worksheet
Consolidation: Purchase Method
Investment: Partial Equity Method
For Year Ending December 31, 2010

Accounts	Parrot Company	Sun Company	Consolidation Entries Debit	Consolidation Entries Credit	Consolidated Totals
Income Statement					
Revenues	(2,100,000)	(600,000)			(2,700,000)
Cost of goods sold	1,000,000	380,000			1,380,000
Depreciation expense	300,000	60,000	(E) 7,000		367,000
Equity in subsidiary earnings	(160,000) *	–0–	(I) 160,000 *		–0–
Net income	(960,000)	(160,000)			(953,000)
Statement of Retained Earnings					
Retained earnings, 1/1/10:					
Parrot Company	(2,065,000)† *		(*C) 21,000 *		(2,044,000)
Sun Company		(600,000)	(S) 600,000		–0–
Net income (above)	(960,000)	(160,000)			(953,000)
Dividends paid	420,000	70,000		(D) 70,000	420,000
Retained earnings, 12/31/10	(2,605,000)	(690,000)			(2,577,000)
Balance Sheet					
Current assets	1,705,000	500,000		(P) 40,000	2,165,000
Investment in Sun Company	1,110,000 *	–0–	(D) 70,000	(*C) 21,000 *	–0–
				(S) 820,000	
				(A) 179,000	
				(I) 160,000 *	
Land	600,000	240,000	(A) 20,000		860,000
Buildings (net)	540,000	420,000	(A) 91,000	(E) 13,000	1,038,000
Equipment (net)	420,000	210,000	(E) 6,000	(A) 12,000	624,000
Goodwill	–0–	–0–	(A) 80,000		80,000
Total assets	4,375,000	1,370,000			4,767,000
Liabilities	(1,050,000)	(460,000)	(P) 40,000		(1,470,000)
Common stock	(600,000)	(200,000)	(S) 200,000		(600,000)
Additional paid-in capital	(120,000)	(20,000)	(S) 20,000		(120,000)
Retained earnings, 12/31/10 (above)	(2,605,000)	(690,000)			(2,577,000)
Total liabilities and equities	(4,375,000)	(1,370,000)			(4,767,000)

Note: Parentheses indicate a credit balance.
*Boxed items highlight differences with consolidation in Exhibit 3.7.
†See footnote 8.
Consolidation entries:
(*C)   To record amortization of acquisition price allocations for years prior to 2010.
(S)   Elimination of Sun's stockholders' equity accounts as of January 1, 2010, and book value portion of investment account.
(A)   Allocation of Parrot's cost in excess of Sun's book value, unamortized values as of January 1, 2010.
(I)   Elimination of parent's equity income accrual.
(D)   Elimination of intercompany dividend payment.
(E)   Recognition of excess amortization expenses on purchase price allocations.
(P)   Elimination of intercompany receivable/payable balances.

unamortized balances as of January 1, 2010 (see Exhibit 3.8). Intercompany dividend income is removed (Entry **I**) and current year excess amortization expenses are recognized (Entry **E**). To complete this process, the intercompany debt of $40,000 is offset (Entry **P**).

In retrospect, the only new element introduced here is the adjustment of the parent's beginning Retained Earnings. For a consolidation produced after the initial year of acquisition, an Entry ***C** is required if the equity method has not been applied by the parent.

Partial Equity Method Applied—Subsequent Consolidation

Exhibit 3.13 demonstrates the worksheet consolidation of Parrot and Sun as of December 31, 2010, when the investment accounts have been recorded by the parent using the partial equity method. This approach accrues subsidiary income each year but records no other equity adjustments. Therefore, as of December 31, 2010, Parrot's Investment in Sun Company account has a balance of $1,110,000:

Purchase price		$ 800,000
Sun Company's 2007–2009 increase in book value:		
Accrual of Sun Company's Income	$330,000	
Collection of Sun Company's Dividends	(110,000)	220,000
Sun Company's 2010 operations:		
Accrual of Sun Company's income	$160,000	
Collection of Sun Company's dividends	(70,000)	90,000
Investment in Sun Company, 12/31/10 (Partial equity method)		$1,110,000

As indicated here and in Exhibit 3.11, the yearly equity income accrual has been properly recognized by Parrot, but amortization has not. Consequently, if the partial equity method is in use, the parent's beginning Retained Earnings must be adjusted to include this expense. The $21,000 amortization is recorded through Entry ***C** to simulate the equity method and, hence, consolidated totals.

Consolidation Entry *C

Retained Earnings, 1/1/10 (Parrot Company)	21,000	
Investment in Sun Company		21,000
To convert parent's beginning Retained Earnings from partial equity method to equity method by including excess amortizations.		

By recording Entry ***C** on the worksheet, all of the subsidiary's operational results for the 2007–2009 period are included in the consolidation. As shown in Exhibit 3.13, the remainder of the worksheet entries follow the same basic pattern as that illustrated previously for the year of acquisition (Exhibit 3.10).

Summary of Investment Methods

Having three investment methods available to the parent means that three sets of entries must be understood to arrive at reported figures appropriate for a business combination. The process can initially seem to be a confusing overlap of procedures. However, at this point in the coverage, only three worksheet entries actually are affected by the choice of either the equity method, partial equity method, or cost method: Entries ***C, I,** and **D.** Furthermore, accountants should never get so involved with a worksheet and its entries that they lose sight of the balances that this process is designed to calculate. These figures are never impacted by the parent's choice of an accounting method.

Consolidated Totals Subsequent to Acquisition—Purchase Method*

Current revenues	Parent revenues are included.
	Subsidiary revenues are included but only for the period since the acquisition.
Current expenses	Parent expenses are included.
	Subsidiary expenses are included but only for the period since the acquisition.
	Excess amortization expenses on the purchase price allocations are included by recognition on the worksheet.
Investment (or dividend) income	Income recognized by parent is eliminated on the worksheet so that the balance is not included in consolidated figures.

(*continued*)

Retained earnings, beginning balance	Parent balance is included.
	Subsidiary balance since the acquisition is included either as a regular accrual by the parent or through a worksheet entry to increase parent balance.
	Past excess amortization expenses on the purchase price allocations are included either as a part of parent balance or through a worksheet entry.
Assets and liabilities	Parent balances are included.
	Subsidiary balances are included.
	Remaining undepreciated purchase price allocations are included.
	Intercompany receivable/payable balances are eliminated.
Goodwill	Original purchase price allocation is included.
Investment in subsidiary	Asset account recorded by parent is eliminated on the worksheet so that the balance is not included in consolidated figures.
Capital stock and additional paid-in capital	Parent balances only are included although they will have been adjusted at date of purchase if stock was issued.

*The next few chapters discuss the necessity of altering some of these balances for consolidation purposes. Thus, this table is not definitive but is included only to provide a basic overview of the consolidation process as it has been described to this point.

EXHIBIT 3.14   Consolidation Worksheet Entries—Purchase Method

Equity Method Applied		Cost Method Applied	Partial Equity Method Applied
Any time during year of acquisition:			
Entry **S**	Beginning stockholders' equity of subsidiary is eliminated against book value portion of investment account.	Same as equity method.	Same as equity method.
Entry **A**	Excess purchase price is allocated to assets and liabilities based on difference in book values and fair values; residual is assigned to goodwill.	Same as equity method.	Same as equity method.
Entry **I**	Equity income accrual (including amortization expense) is eliminated.	Dividend income is eliminated.	Equity income accrual is eliminated.
Entry **D**	Intercompany dividends paid by subsidiary are eliminated.	No entry—intercompany dividends are eliminated in Entry **I**.	Same as equity method.
Entry **E**	Current year excess amortization expenses of cost allocations are recorded.	Same as equity method.	Same as equity method.
Entry **P**	Intercompany payable/receivable balances are offset.	Same as equity method.	Same as equity method.
Any time following year of acquisition:			
Entry ***C**	No entry—equity income for prior years has already been recognized along with amortization expenses.	Increase in subsidiary's book value during prior years as well as excess amortization expenses are recognized (conversion is made to equity method).	Excess amortization expenses for prior years are recognized (conversion is made to equity method).
Entry **S**	Same as initial year.	Same as initial year.	Same as initial year.
Entry **A**	Unamortized cost at beginning of year is allocated to specific accounts and to goodwill.	Same as equity method.	Same as equity method.
Entry **I**	Same as initial year.	Same as initial year.	Same as initial year.
Entry **D**	Same as initial year.	Same as initial year.	Same as initial year.
Entry **E**	Same as initial year.	Same as initial year.	Same as initial year.
Entry **P**	Same as initial year.	Same as initial year.	Same as initial year.

HOW DOES A COMPANY REALLY DECIDE WHICH INVESTMENT METHOD TO APPLY?

During the early stages of 2007, Pilgrim Products, Inc., buys a controlling interest in the common stock of Crestwood Corporation. Shortly after the acquisition, a meeting of Pilgrim's accounting department is convened to discuss the internal reporting procedures required by the ownership of this subsidiary. Each member of the staff has a definite opinion as to whether the equity method, cost method, or partial equity method should be adopted. To resolve this issue, Pilgrim's chief financial officer outlines several of her concerns about the decision.

"I already understand how each method works. I know the general advantages and disadvantages of all three. I realize, for example, that the equity method provides more detailed information whereas the cost method is much easier to apply. What I need to know are the factors specific to our situation that should be considered in deciding which method to adopt. I must make a recommendation to the president on this matter, and he will want firm reasons for my favoring a particular approach. I don't want us to select a method and then find out in six months that the information is not adequate for our needs or that the cost of adapting our system to monitor Crestwood outweighs the benefits derived from the data."

What are the factors that Pilgrim's officials should evaluate when making this decision?

Once the appropriate balance for each account is understood, worksheet entries assist the accountant in deriving these figures. To help clarify the consolidation process required under each of the three accounting methods, Exhibit 3.14 describes the purpose of each worksheet entry: first during the year of acquisition and second for any period following the year of acquisition.

INTANGIBLES ACQUIRED IN BUSINESS COMBINATIONS AND RELATED AMORTIZATIONS

As discussed in Chapter 2, *SFAS 141,* "Business Combinations," does not alter significantly the purchase price allocation procedures required in a business acquisition. *SFAS 141* does, however, suggest several categories of purchased intangible assets for possible recognition in a business combination. Examples include noncompetition agreements, customer lists, patents, subscriber databases, trademarks, lease agreements, and licenses.[9]

If fair values can be measured reliably for the identified intangibles in a business combination, they are separately recognized and subsequently amortized if appropriate. If a separate fair value estimation is unavailable or unreliable for a particular intangible, then any remaining unallocated purchase price is simply recognized as goodwill.

SFAS 142, "Goodwill and Other Intangible Assets," requires that all identified intangible assets be amortized over their economic useful life unless such life is considered *indefinite.* The term *indefinite life* is defined as a life that extends beyond the foreseeable future. A recognized intangible asset with an indefinite life should not be amortized unless and until its life is determined to be finite. Importantly, indefinite does not mean infinite. Also, the useful life of an intangible asset should not be considered indefinite because a precise finite life is not known.

For those intangible assets with finite lives, the method of amortization should reflect the pattern of decline in the economic usefulness of the asset. If no such pattern is apparent, the straight-line method of amortization should be used. The amount to be amortized should be the value assigned to the intangible asset less any residual value. In most cases the residual value is presumed to be zero. However, that presumption can be overcome if the acquiring enterprise has a commitment from a third party to purchase the intangible at the end of its

---

[9] The application guidance recommended in the 2005 FASB Exposure Draft, *Business Combinations,* remains basically the same as in *SFAS 141* with relatively few clarifications.

useful life, or an observable market exists for the intangible asset that provides a basis for estimating a terminal value.

The length of the amortization period for identifiable intangibles (i.e., those not included in goodwill) depends primarily on the assumed economic life of the asset. Factors that should be considered in determining the useful life of an intangible asset include

- Legal, regulatory, or contractual provisions.
- The effects of obsolescence, demand, competition, industry stability, rate of technological change, and expected changes in distribution channels.
- The expected use of the intangible asset by the enterprise.
- The level of maintenance expenditure required to obtain the asset's expected future benefits.

Any recognized intangible assets considered to possess indefinite lives are not amortized but instead are tested for impairment on an annual basis.[10] To test for impairment, the carrying amount of the intangible asset is compared to its fair value. If the fair value is less than the carrying amount, then the intangible asset is considered impaired and an impairment loss is recognized. The asset's carrying value is reduced accordingly.

SFAS 142—GOODWILL IMPAIRMENT

A major change in accounting for goodwill is the *SFAS 142* requirement of an annual test for impairment. The FASB reasoned that while goodwill can decrease over time, it does not do so in the "rational and systematic" manner that periodic amortization suggests.[11] Thus, amortization was not viewed as representationally faithful of the pattern of goodwill decline. Moreover, because *SFAS 141* provides more guidelines for recognizing identifiable intangibles, it was argued that future amounts included in goodwill were more likely to be nonwasting. Ultimately, the FASB decided to record a decline in the value of goodwill only when

- It is apparent that goodwill becomes impaired—that is, when the carrying amount of goodwill exceeds its implied fair value, an impairment loss is recognized equal to that excess.
- The operating unit where goodwill resides is partially or completely sold.

Importantly, goodwill impairment testing is performed at the *reporting unit* level. As discussed shortly, all assets (including goodwill) acquired and liabilities assumed in a business combination must be assigned across reporting units within a consolidated enterprise. For example, Wendy's International recently noted the following in its annual report:

> For purposes of testing goodwill for impairment, the Company has determined that its reporting units are Wendy's U.S., Wendy's Canada, Hortons Canada, Hortons U.S., Baja Fresh and Cafe Express. Each constitutes a business and has discrete financial information available which is regularly reviewed by management.

The goodwill residing in each reporting unit is then separately subjected to periodic impairment testing. Recent evidence shows that goodwill impairment losses can be substantial. Exhibit 3.15 provides examples of goodwill impairment losses recognized under *SFAS 142* reporting rules.

Testing Goodwill for Impairment

The notion of an indefinite life for goodwill allows firms to report over time the original amount of goodwill acquired in a business combination at its assigned purchase value.

[10] Impairment tests should also be conducted on an interim basis if an event or circumstance occurs between annual tests indicating that an intangible asset could be impaired.
[11] L. Todd Johnson and Kimberly R. Petrone, *FASB Viewpoints*, "Why Did the Board Change Its Mind on Goodwill Amortization?" December 2000.

EXHIBIT 3.15
Goodwill Impairment Examples (in billions) 2002—First Year of *SFAS 142* Implementation

AOL Time Warner	$99.7 billion
Boeing	2.4
Blockbuster	1.8
SBC Communications	1.8
General Electric	1.0
Coca-Cola	926 million
AT&T	856
Safeway	700
Verizon Communications	500

However, such goodwill can, at some point in time, become impaired, requiring loss recognition and a reduction in the amount reported in the consolidated balance sheet. Unlike amortization, which periodically reduces goodwill, impairment must first be revealed before a write-down is justified. To detect when impairment has occurred, a two-step testing procedure is utilized.

Step 1—Goodwill Impairment Test: Is the Fair Value of a Reporting Unit Less Than Its Carrying Value?

In the first step of impairment testing, fair values of the consolidated entity's reporting units with allocated goodwill are compared with their carrying values *(including goodwill)*. If an individual reporting unit's total fair value exceeds its carrying value, its goodwill is not considered impaired, and the second step in testing is not performed. Goodwill remains at the amount assigned at the date of the business combination. However, if the fair value of a reporting unit has fallen below its carrying value, a potential for goodwill impairment exists. In this case, a second step must be performed to determine if goodwill has been impaired.

Step 2—Goodwill Impairment Test: Is Goodwill's Implied Value Less Than Its Carrying Value?

If Step 1 indicates a potential goodwill impairment for a reporting unit, goodwill's implied and carrying values are compared for that reporting unit. If the fair value of a reporting unit falls below its carrying value, a second step in testing is performed. The second test requires a determination of the fair value of the related goodwill. Then if goodwill's fair value has declined below its carrying value, an impairment loss is recognized for the excess carrying value over fair value. However, determining fair values for reporting units and goodwill can be complex, making implementation of the necessary comparisons costly. These complexities are described in terms of three key attributes that govern the process of testing goodwill for impairment:

1. The assignment of acquisition values to reporting units.
2. The periodic determination of the fair values of reporting units.
3. The determination of goodwill implied fair value.

Assigning Values to Reporting Units

In deciding to forgo amortization in favor of impairment testing for goodwill, the FASB noted that goodwill is primarily associated with individual *reporting units* within the consolidated entity. Such goodwill is often considered "synergistic" because it arises from the interaction of the assets of the acquired company with those of the acquirer in specific ways. To better assess potential declines in value for goodwill (in place of amortization), the most specific business level at which goodwill is evident was chosen as the appropriate level for impairment testing. This specific business level is referred to as the *reporting unit.* The FASB also noted that, in practice, goodwill is often assigned to reporting units either at the level of a reporting segment—as described in *SFAS 131,* "Disclosures about Segments of an Enterprise and Related Information"—or at a lower level within a segment of a combined enterprise. Consequently, the reporting unit became the designated enterprise component for tests of goodwill impairment. Reporting units may thus include the following:

- A component of an operating segment at a level below the operating segment. Segment management should review and assess performance at this level. Also, the component should be a business in which discrete financial information is available and should differ economically from other components of the operating segment.
- The segments of an enterprise.
- The entire enterprise.

For example, in its 2005 financial statements, Meade Instruments Corporation notes that the company's reporting units for purposes of applying the provisions of *SFAS 142* are Meade Europe, Simmons, and Coronado. The latter two reporting units represent Meade Instruments' business acquisitions of Simmons Outdoor (2002) and Coronado Technology Group (2004).

The Meade Instruments annual report also notes the following:

> *SFAS 142* requires the Company to compare the fair value of the reporting unit to its carrying amount on an annual basis to determine if there is potential impairment. If the fair value of the reporting unit is less than its carrying value, an impairment loss is recorded to the extent that the fair value of the goodwill within the reporting unit is less than its carrying value. If the carrying amount of the goodwill exceeds its fair value, an impairment loss is recognized.

The number of reporting units identified by companies varies widely. In their respective 2004 annual reports Berkshire Hathaway, Inc., revealed that it employs 40 reporting units while Iomega Corporation noted that its goodwill resided in only one reporting unit related to its Zip product line.

In implementing impairment tests, it is essential first to identify the reporting units resulting from the acquisition. The assets and liabilities (including goodwill) acquired in a business combination are then assigned to these identified reporting units. The assignment should consider where the acquired assets and liabilities will be employed and whether they will be included in determining the reporting unit's fair value. The goodwill should be assigned to those reporting units that are expected to benefit from the synergies of the combination. Overall, the objective of the assignment of acquired assets and liabilities to reporting units is to facilitate the required fair value/carrying value comparisons for periodic impairment testing.

Periodic Determination of the Fair Values of Reporting Units

The necessary comparisons to determine whether goodwill is impaired depend first on the fair-value computation of the reporting unit and then, if necessary, the fair-value computation for goodwill. But how are such values computed? How can fair values be known if the subsidiary is wholly owned and thus not traded publicly?

Several alternative methods exist for determining the fair values of the reporting units that comprise a consolidated entity. First, any quoted market prices that exist can provide a basis for assessing fair value—particularly for subsidiaries with actively traded noncontrolling interests. Second, comparable businesses could exist that can help indicate market values. Third, a variety of present value techniques assess the fair value of an identifiable set of future cash flow streams, or profit projections discounted for the riskiness of the future flows. Clearly, portions of consolidated entities are frequently bought and sold. In these transactions, parties do derive fair values. However, the required periodic assessment of fair value represents a new valuation exercise for many firms. These annual determinations of fair values will likely be a costly impact from implementing the provisions of *SFAS 141* and *SFAS 142.*

However, once a detailed determination of the fair value of a reporting unit is made, that fair value may be used in subsequent periods if *all* of the following criteria are met *(SFAS 142):*

- The assets and liabilities that compose the reporting unit have not changed significantly since the most recent fair-value determination. (A recent acquisition or a reorganization of an entity's segment reporting structure are examples of events that might significantly change the composition of a reporting unit.)
- The most recent fair-value determination resulted in an amount that exceeded the carrying amount of the reporting unit by a substantial margin.
- Based on an analysis of events that have occurred and circumstances that have changed since the most recent fair-value determination, it is remote that a current fair-value determination would be less than the current carrying amount of the reporting unit.

If any of these criteria are not met, an updated determination of the reporting unit's fair value is required.

Determination of Goodwill Implied Fair Value

If the fair value of a reporting unit, once determined, falls below its carrying value, the second step of the impairment test focuses in on the possibility that goodwill could be impaired. Just as in the initial test of the reporting unit, now the fair value of goodwill must be determined in order to make the relevant comparison to its carrying value. Because, by definition, goodwill is not separable from other assets, it is not possible to directly observe its market value. Therefore, an *implied* value for goodwill is calculated in a similar manner to the determination of goodwill in a business combination. The fair value of the reporting unit is treated as the "purchase price" as if the reporting unit were being acquired in a business combination. Then this "purchase price" is allocated to all of the reporting unit's identifiable assets and liabilities with any remaining excess considered as the fair value of goodwill. This procedure is used only for assessing the fair value of goodwill. None of the other values allocated to assets and liabilities in the testing comparison are used to adjust their reported amounts.

Example—Accounting and Reporting for a Goodwill Impairment Loss

To illustrate the procedure for recognizing goodwill impairment, assume that on January 1, 2007, Newcall Corporation was formed to consolidate the telecommunications operations of DSM, Inc., Rocketel Company, and Visiontalk Company in a deal valued at $2.9 billion. Each of the three former firms is considered an operating segment, and each will be maintained as a subsidiary of Newcall. Additionally, DSM comprises two divisions—DSM Wired and DSM Wireless—that along with Rocketel and Visiontalk are treated as independent reporting units for internal performance evaluation and management reviews. Following *SFAS 141,* "Business Combinations," Newcall allocated $221 million value to goodwill at the merger date to its reporting units. That information and each unit's purchase price were as follows:

Newcall's Reporting Units	Goodwill	Purchase Price January 1, 2007
DSM Wired	$ 22,000,000	$950,000,000
DSM Wireless	155,000,000	748,000,000
Rocketel	38,000,000	492,000,000
Visiontalk	6,000,000	710,000,000

In December 2007, Newcall tested each of its four reporting units for goodwill impairment. Accordingly, Newcall compared the fair market value of its reporting units to its carrying value. The comparisons revealed that the fair market value of each reporting unit exceeded its carrying value except for DSM Wireless, whose market value had fallen to $600 million, well below its current carrying value. The decline in value was attributed to a failure to realize expected cost-saving synergies with Rocketel.

As indicated by *SFAS 142*, Newcall then compared the implied fair value of the DSM Wireless goodwill to its carrying value. Newcall derived the implied fair value of goodwill through the following allocation of the fair value of DSM Wireless:

DSM Wireless Dec. 31, 2007, fair market value		$600,000,000
Fair values of DSM Wireless net assets at Dec. 31, 2007:		
Current assets	$ 50,000,000	
Property	125,000,000	
Equipment	265,000,000	
Subscriber list	140,000,000	
Patented technology	185,000,000	
Current liabilities	(44,000,000)	
Long-term debt	(125,000,000)	
Value assigned to identifiable net assets		596,000,000
Value assigned to goodwill		4,000,000
Carrying value before impairment		155,000,000
Impairment loss		$151,000,000

Thus, $151,000,000 is reported as a separate line item in the operating section of Newcall's consolidated income statement as a goodwill impairment loss. Additional disclosures are required describing (1) the facts and circumstances leading to the impairment and (2) the method of determining the fair value of the associated reporting unit (e.g., market prices, comparable business, present value technique).

Although the amount reported for goodwill changes, the amounts for the other assets and liabilities of DSM Wireless do not change. The reported values for all of DSM Wireless's remaining assets and liabilities continue to be based on amounts assigned at the business combination date.

PURCHASE PRICE—CONTINGENT CONSIDERATION

Contingency agreements frequently accompany business combinations. In fact, *Mergers & Acquisitions* reported 154 deals in 2004 totaling $13.9 billion of which $4.3 billion was in the form of a contingency. In many cases, the target firm asks for consideration based on projections of its future performance. The acquiring firm, however, may not share the projections and, thus, may be unwilling to pay now for uncertain future performance. To close the deal, agreements for the acquirer's future payments to the former owners of the target are common. Alternatively, when the acquirer's stock comprises the consideration transferred, the sellers of the target firm may request a guaranteed minimum market value of the stock for a period of time to ensure a fair price.

The accounting for contingencies in business combinations under *SFAS 141* differs significantly from that proposed by the FASB 2005 Exposure Draft, *Business Combinations*. In general, *SFAS 141* requires a resolution of the contingency before financial statement recognition. In contrast, as briefly presented in Chapter 2, the 2005 Exposure Draft considers contingent payments to have value and, therefore, includes them as part of the consideration transferred in the acquisition. We present both the *SFAS 141* and the FASB 2005 *Business Combination* Exposure Draft accounting for contingencies in business combinations next.

SFAS 141 Accounting for Contingent Consideration in Business Combinations

In its 2004 annual report, Brunswick Corporation noted the following contingency:

> The company acquired the outstanding stock of four aluminum boat companies for $191.0 million. These companies include: Minnesota-based Crestliner, Inc., and Lund Boat Company; Lowe Boats, Inc., based in Missouri; and Lund Boats Canada, Inc. . . . The purchase agreement provides for additional consideration of up to $30 million to be paid in three years based on the achievement of a minimum 10 percent after-tax cash flow return on total investment over that time period.

Discussion **Question**

IS THIS INCOME?

Artilio Corporation pays $1 million for all of the outstanding stock of Zepthan, Inc. Because of an urgent need for cash, the owners of Zepthan accept this price although the company's net assets have a fair value of $1.6 million.

Based on the guidelines for a bargain purchase, under *SFAS 141* the $600,000 reduction is assigned to the subsidiary's noncurrent assets (other than certain specific exceptions). Consequently, assume that the consolidated value of Zepthan's land is reduced by $50,000 with its buildings and equipment decreased by a total of $550,000. If the buildings and equipment have a life of 10 years, these negative allocations reduce depreciation expense by $55,000 per year and, hence, increase income by that amount. Consolidated net income for the combination is projected to be approximately $250,000 per year for the foreseeable future. Thus, 22 percent is attributable to the bargain purchase ($55,000/$250,000).

Because of the annual decrease from depreciation, a bargain purchase creates a consolidated entity that reports more income than the sum of the two component companies. As in the case of Artilio and Zepthan, the amount can be very significant.

Alternatively, as the FASB proposed in its 2005 Exposure Draft, *Business Combinations,* when a bargain purchase occurs, the acquirer measures and recognizes the fair values of each of the assets acquired and liabilities assumed at the date of combination, regardless of the purchase price. As a result (1) no assets are recorded at amounts below their fair values and (2) a gain on a bargain purchase (in this case $600,000) is recognized at the acquisition date. In contrast to *SFAS 141,* the entire gain is thus recognized up front, leaving future depreciation expenses unaffected.

Should a business combination be allowed to increase reported earnings based on paying a bargain price to acquire a new subsidiary? Does this practice distort earnings? Does the new FASB proposal improve financial reporting?

A business combination has been formed here but, as this note describes, a portion of the purchase price the parent pays will not be finalized for three years after the date of acquisition.

When a subsequent payment, such as that described by Brunswick, is based solely on future performance, according to *SFAS 141* the contingency has no initial impact on the purchase price or the consolidated figures. The potential disbursement should be disclosed only in a note to the financial statements similar to the one just presented. When the contingency is ultimately resolved, any further payment made by the parent is simply added to the purchase price.

Thus, if goodwill was recognized at the date of acquisition, any later disbursement is assigned to this same intangible asset. Should another $30 million be paid, for example, reported goodwill increases by this amount. Conversely, if the original price was below fair value so that the balances assigned to specific noncurrent assets were reduced, a subsequent payment serves to decrease the amount of these reductions. In either case, an increase in the initial purchase price resulting from a contingency of this type is not accounted for in a retrospective manner. Any resulting amortization expense is recorded only over the *remaining* life of the appropriate account.

A contingency can also result from the acquisition of a subsidiary if the price is based on the future value of the stock issued by the acquirer. Such arrangements are designed to ensure that the previous owners receive compensation that retains a minimum value for a specified period. For example, in discussing an earlier acquisition, financial statements of Munsingwear, Inc., once stated that "the Company is obligated to issue additional shares of common stock . . . in the event of a decline in the market value of the common stock." From an accounting perspective, this second type of extra payment is not viewed as an increase in the parent's purchase price. Rather, the possible distribution is a guarantee of the value of the consideration conveyed in the original transaction. Thus, no change is made in goodwill or any other allocations.

If additional shares of the parent's stock must be issued because of a subsequent drop in price, the parent records the new shares at fair market value. At the same time, the total attributed to the shares originally issued at the date of purchase is reduced by a corresponding amount to reflect the decrease in value. The net effect is that the parent's stock account is increased by the par value of the new shares issued with additional paid-in capital reduced by the same amount. The purchase price does not change.

To illustrate, assume that Large issues 10,000 shares of its $10 par value stock to acquire Small. This stock had a value on that date of $25 per share ($250,000 in total). In recording this transaction, Large increases

- Its Common Stock account by the $100,000 par value of these shares.
- Additional Paid-In Capital by $150,000 to reflect the value in excess of par ($25 − $10).

Subsequently, the market value of this stock drops to $20 per share. Assume that the purchase agreement specified that the market value of the shares issued could not be reduced for a given period. To maintain the total value at $250,000, 2,500 more shares are issued to Small's previous owners. At $20 per share, the new total of 12,500 shares has the appropriate value of $250,000. The new shares are recorded at par value ($25,000, or 2,500 shares at $10 per share) with an accompanying reduction in Additional Paid-In Capital. Therefore, total contributed capital from this purchase remains at $250,000.

Large's Financial Records—Subsequent Issuance of Shares		
Additional Paid-In Capital	25,000	
Common Stock (par value)		25,000
To record issuance of 2,500 new shares of stock in connection with previous acquisition of Small. Additional shares were required because of drop in market value of shares originally issued.		

FASB 2005 Exposure Draft *Business Combinations*—Accounting for Contingent Consideration in Business Combinations

Under the acquisition method, contingent consideration obligations are recognized as part of the purchase price, consistent with the fair value concept. Therefore, the acquiring firm must estimate the fair value of the contingent portion of the purchase price obligation. The fair value is recognized as part of the acquisition regardless of whether it is based on future performance of the target firm or the future stock prices of the acquirer.[12]

As an illustration, assume that Skeptical, Inc., acquires 100 percent of the voting stock of Rosy Pictures Company on January 1, 2007, for the following consideration:

- $550,000 market value of 10,000 shares of its no-par common stock.
- A contingent payment of $8,000 cash if Rosy Pictures generates cash flows from operations of $20,000 or more in the next year.
- A payment of sufficient shares of Skeptical common stock to ensure a total value of $550,000 if the price per share is less than $55 on January 1, 2008.

Under the acquisition method, each of the three elements of consideration represents a portion of the negotiated fair value of Rosy Pictures and therefore must be included in the recorded

---

[12] The FASB recommends that a probability weighted approach, such as the expected cash flow discussed in FASB *Concepts Statement No. 7*, "Using Cash Flow Information and Present Value in Accounting Measurements," may be useful in estimating the fair value of contingent consideration. This approach may include any or all of the following five elements:

1. An estimate of the future cash flow, or in more complex cases, series of future cash flows at different times.
2. Expectations about possible variations in the amount or timing of those cash flows.
3. The time value of money, represented by the risk-free rate of interest.
4. The price for bearing the uncertainty inherent in the asset or liability.
5. Other, sometimes unidentifiable, factors including illiquidity and market imperfections.

value entered on Skeptical's accounting records. For the cash contingency, Skeptical estimates that there is a 30 percent chance that the $8,000 payment will be required. For the stock contingency, Skeptical estimates that there is a 20 percent probability that the 10,000 shares issued will have a market value of $540,000 on January 1, 2008, and an 80 percent probability that the market value of the 10,000 shares will exceed $550,000. Skeptical uses an interest rate of 4 percent to incorporate the time value of money.

To determine the fair values of the contingent consideration, Skeptical computes the present value of the expected payments as follows:

- Cash contingency = $80,000 \times 30\% \times (1/(1 + .04)) = \$23,077$
- Stock contingency = $10,000 \times 20\% \times (1/(1 + .04)) = \$1,923$

Skeptical then records the acquisition of Rosy Pictures in Skeptical's accounting records as follows:

Investment in Rosy Pictures	575,000	
Common stock (no par)		550,000
Contingent performance obligation		23,077
APIC–Contingent equity outstanding		1,923
To record acquisition of Rosy Pictures at fair value of consideration transferred including performance and stock contingencies.		

Skeptical will report the contingent cash payment under its liabilities and the contingent stock payment as a component of stockholders' equity. Subsequent to acquisition, obligations for contingent consideration that meet the definition of a liability will continue to be measured at fair value with adjustments recognized in income. Those obligations classified as equity are not subsequently remeasured at fair value. Finally, the proposed effective date for the recommended changes in accounting for contingent consideration is for fiscal years beginning on or after December 15, 2006. These changes would be applied prospectively for new combinations.

PUSH-DOWN ACCOUNTING

External Reporting

In the analysis of business combinations to this point, discussion has focused on (1) the recording by the parent company and (2) required consolidation procedures. Unfortunately, official accounting pronouncements give virtually no guidance as to the impact of a purchase on the separate financial statements of the subsidiary.

This issue has become especially significant in recent years because of a rash of management-led buyouts as well as corporate reorganizations. An organization, for example, might acquire a company and subsequently offer the shares back to the public in hopes of making a large profit. What should be reported in the subsidiary's financial statements being distributed with this offering? Such deals have reheated a long-standing debate over the merits of *push-down accounting,* the direct recording of purchase price allocations and subsequent amortization by a subsidiary.

For this reason, the FASB continues to explore various methods of reporting by a company that has been acquired or reorganized. To illustrate, assume that Yarrow Company owns one asset: a building with a book value of $200,000 but a fair value of $900,000. Mannen Corporation pays exactly $900,000 in cash to acquire Yarrow. Consolidation offers no real problem here: The building will be reported by the business combination at $900,000.

However, if Yarrow continues to issue separate financial statements (for example, to its creditors or potential stockholders), should the building be reported at $200,000 or $900,000? If adjusted, should the $700,000 increase be reported as a gain by the subsidiary or as an addition to contributed capital? Should depreciation be based on $200,000 or $900,000? If the subsidiary is to be viewed as a new entity with a new basis for its assets and liabilities, should Retained Earnings be returned to zero? If the parent acquires only 51 percent of Yarrow, does that change the answers to the previous questions? These questions represent just a few of the difficult issues currently being explored.

Proponents of push-down accounting argue that a change in ownership creates a new basis for subsidiary assets and liabilities. An unadjusted balance ($200,000 in the preceding illustration) is a cost figure applicable to previous stockholders. That total is no longer relevant information. Rather, according to this argument, it is the historical cost *paid by the current owner* that is important, a figure that is best reflected by the expenditure made in acquiring the subsidiary. Balance sheet accounts should be reported at the cost incurred by the present stockholders ($900,000 in the illustration) rather than the cost incurred by the company.

Currently, primary guidance concerning push-down accounting for external reporting purposes is provided by the Securities and Exchange Commission (SEC). Through *Staff Accounting Bulletin No. 54* ("Application of 'Push Down' Basis of Accounting in Financial Statements of Subsidiaries Acquired by Purchase") and *Staff Accounting Bulletin No. 73* ("'Push Down' Basis of Accounting for Parent Company Debt Related to Subsidiary Acquisitions"), the SEC has indicated that

> push down accounting should be used in the separate financial statements of a "substantially wholly owned" subsidiary. . . . That view is based on the notion that when the form of ownership is within the control of the parent company, the accounting basis should be the same whether the entity continues to exist or is merged into the parent's operations. If a purchase of a "substantially wholly owned" subsidiary is financed by debt of the parent, that debt generally must be pushed down to the subsidiary. . . . As a general rule, the SEC requires push down accounting when the ownership change is greater than 95 percent and objects to push down accounting when the ownership change is less than 80 percent. However, if the acquired subsidiary has outstanding public debt or preferred stock, push down accounting is encouraged by the SEC but not required.[13]

Thus, the SEC requires the use of push-down accounting for the separate financial statements of any subsidiary where no substantial outside ownership exists of the company's common stock, preferred stock, and publicly held debt. Apparently, the SEC believes that a change in ownership of that degree justifies a new basis of reporting for the subsidiary's assets and liabilities. Until the FASB takes action, though, application is only required when the subsidiary desires to issue securities (stock or debt) to the public as regulated by the SEC.

Internal Reporting

Although the use of push-down accounting for external reporting is limited, this approach has gained significant popularity in recent years for internal reporting purposes.

> Subsidiaries owned by the Chesapeake Corporation are recorded using push-down accounting. Under this theory, the subsidiary adjusts its assets and liabilities to current value at the time of the acquisition while also recording the necessary goodwill. The subsidiary's net assets, as adjusted, would equal the amount recorded by the parent as the investment in subsidiary.[14]

> At the time of acquisition of each subsidiary, purchase method accounting is applied by James River Corporation on a push-down basis. The parent's investment equals the net book value of the subsidiary through an allocation of the purchase price to the net assets of the subsidiary on a fair market value basis.[15]

Push-down accounting has several advantages for internal reporting. For example, it simplifies the consolidation process. Because the allocations and amortization are already entered into the records of the subsidiary, worksheet Entries **A** (to recognize the allocations originating from the purchase price) and **E** (amortization expense) are not needed. Therefore, except for eliminating the effects of intercompany transactions, the assets, liabilities, revenues, and expenses of the subsidiary can be added directly to those of the parent to derive consolidated totals.

---

[13] FASB Discussion Memorandum, *An Analysis of Issues Related to New Basis Accounting,* December 18, 1991, p. 54.

[14] Letter from Timothy M. Harhan, senior corporate accountant with Chesapeake Corporation.

[15] Letter from Catherine M. Freeman, manager—financial projects with James River Corporation.

More importantly, push-down accounting provides better information for internal evaluation. Since the subsidiary's separate figures include amortization expense, the net income reported by the company is a good representation of the impact that the acquisition has on the earnings of the business combination. As an example, assume that Ace Corporation owns 100 percent of Waxworth, Inc. Waxworth uses push-down accounting and reports net income of $500,000: $600,000 from operations less $100,000 in amortization expense resulting from purchase price allocations. Thus, officials of Ace Corporation know that this acquisition has added $500,000 to the consolidated net income of the business combination. They can then evaluate whether these earnings provide a sufficient return for the parent's investment.

However, the recording of amortization expense by the subsidiary can lead to dissension. Members of the subsidiary's management could argue that they are being forced to record a large expense over which they have no control or responsibility. This amortization comes directly from the purchase price paid by the parent but is not a result of any action taken by the subsidiary. Chesapeake Corporation has considered this problem and resolved it in the following manner: "For internal reporting of income statement activity, earnings from operations are identified separately from amortization. This allows management to analyze the subsidiary's results without the effect of amortization."[16]

SUBSEQUENT CONSOLIDATIONS—POOLING OF INTERESTS

Although the FASB prohibits the pooling of interests method of accounting for business combinations initiated after June 30, 2001, this restriction is for prospective application only. Given the popularity of poolings in the last century, the financial statement effects of this method of accounting will likely be encountered for decades to come. Therefore, familiarity with the effects of poolings in consolidations subsequent to acquisition will continue to be an important part of understanding financial reporting for business combinations.

For consolidations prepared after the date of combination, the pooling of interests method requires a slightly less complex set of procedures than does the purchase method. By reflecting on the fundamental concepts of a pooling, the essential differences between the subsequent consolidation entries employed by these two methods can be understood.

Pooling of interests combinations were assumed to be formed by a union of two companies. Because a takeover had not occurred, no acquisition price was ever calculated for a pooling. All assets and liabilities were simply consolidated at their book values. No allocations based on fair market value were computed, nor was any goodwill recognized. Hence, amortization that could have been associated with such cost factors was not encountered in a pooling of interests.

In mechanical terms, the absence of a purchase price means that worksheet entries relating to cost allocations (Entry **A**) and subsequent amortization expense (Entry **E**) are never found in a pooling. Obviously, as with push-down accounting, alleviating the necessity of working with these entries simplifies the entire consolidation process.

The company that issued its stock to consummate a pooling of interests recorded these shares along with the resulting investment. This company must then have adopted a method to account for this investment. One possibility is to apply the equity method to accrue income as it is earned by the other company and to adjust for intercompany transactions (as discussed in Chapter 5). The partial equity method also might be selected so that recording is limited to the periodic accrual of income.

Any reference to a cost method of interests would be a misnomer in a pooling because no acquisition cost is ever established. Thus, for internal reporting purposes, the cost method is replaced by a *book value method* that has the same essential characteristics: The investment account permanently retains its initial balance (the book value of the other company), with any dividends received being recognized as income.

To illustrate the consolidation techniques employed in a pooling of interests, assume that Brother Company obtains 100 percent of the outstanding voting shares of Sister Company on

---

[16] Letter from Timothy H. Harhan.

January 1, 2001. To create this combination, Brother issued 10,000 shares of its own common stock in an exchange that met all 12 requirements for a pooling of interests. On that date, Sister reported a total book value of $700,000 although market value was $950,000. For reporting purposes, the additional $250,000 is unimportant; only book value is relevant in accounting for a pooling of interests. Consequently, $700,000 is recorded by Brother as an investment. The book value method is applied by Brother; thus, this balance remains unchanged over the years.

For this example, consolidated financial statements are prepared as of December 31, 2007. Sister's book value has risen by $610,000 to $1,310,000 as of the first day of 2007. Assume also that Sister owes $90,000 to Brother at the end of this year. Exhibit 3.16 presents the worksheet for the 2007 consolidation of these two companies under the pooling of interests concept. Once again, the entries have been labeled to parallel the earlier consolidation examples, although neither Entry **A** nor Entry **E** is applicable to a pooling.

Because Brother applies the book value method, no recognition has been made of the increase in Sister's book value since the date of combination. Consequently, Brother's retained earnings at January 1, 2007, do not reflect a consolidated total; the $610,000 increment is not included. An Entry ***C** must be recorded on the worksheet to accrue this income that has been earned by Sister in excess of dividends distributed (the increase in net book value). After

EXHIBIT 3.16

Consolidation: Pooling of Interests Method *Investment: Book Value Method*	**BROTHER COMPANY AND SISTER COMPANY** Consolidated Worksheet For Year Ending December 31, 2007				
Accounts	**Brother Company**	**Sister Company**	**Consolidation Entries**		**Consolidated Totals**
			Debit	**Credit**	
Income Statement					
Revenues	(1,600,000)	(550,000)			(2,150,000)
Expenses	1,220,000	440,000			1,660,000
Dividend income	(40,000)	–0–	(I) 40,000		–0–
Net income	(420,000)	(110,000)			(490,000)
Statement of Retained Earnings					
Retained earnings, 1/1/07	(2,260,000)	(910,000)	(S) 910,000	(*C) 610,000	(2,870,000)
Net income (above)	(420,000)	(110,000)			(490,000)
Dividends paid	60,000	40,000		(I) 40,000	60,000
Retained earnings, 12/31/07	(2,620,000)	(980,000)			(3,300,000)
Balance Sheet					
Cash and receivables	590,000	140,000		(P) 90,000	640,000
Inventory	940,000	480,000			1,420,000
Investment in Sister Company	700,000	–0–	(*C) 610,000	(S) 1,310,000	–0–
Land	600,000	340,000			940,000
Buildings (net)	970,000	270,000			1,240,000
Equipment (net)	730,000	520,000			1,250,000
Total assets	4,530,000	1,750,000			5,490,000
Liabilities	(810,000)	(370,000)	(P) 90,000		(1,090,000)
Common stock	(800,000)	(300,000)	(S) 300,000		(800,000)
Additional paid-in capital	(300,000)	(100,000)	(S) 100,000		(300,000)
Retained earnings, 12/31/07 (above)	(2,620,000)	(980,000)			(3,300,000)
Total liabilities and equities	(4,530,000)	(1,750,000)			(5,490,000)

Note: Parentheses indicate a credit balance.
Consolidation entries:
   (*C)   To recognize increase in book value of affiliate company during years prior to 2007.
   (S)   Elimination of Sister's stockholders' equity accounts as of January 1, 2007, and book value portion of Investment account.
   (I)   Elimination of intercompany dividends recognized by Brother as income.
   (P)   Elimination of intercompany receivable/payable balances.

Brother's beginning Retained Earnings have been properly adjusted in this manner, the remaining consolidation entries eliminate Sister's stockholders' equity (Entry **S**), the intercompany dividend income (Entry **I**), and the intercompany debt (Entry **P**).

Summary

1. The procedures used to consolidate financial information generated by the separate companies in a business combination are affected by both the passage of time and the method applied by the parent in accounting for the subsidiary. Thus, no single consolidation process can be described that is applicable to all business combinations.

2. The parent might elect to utilize the equity method to account for a subsidiary. As discussed in Chapter 1, income is accrued by the parent when earned by the subsidiary and dividend receipts are recorded as reductions in the Investment account. The effects of excess amortizations or any intercompany transactions also are reflected within the parent's financial records. The equity method provides the parent with accurate information concerning the subsidiary's impact on consolidated totals; however, it is usually somewhat complicated to apply.

3. The cost method and the partial equity method are two alternatives to the equity method. The cost method recognizes only the subsidiary's dividends as income while the asset balance remains at cost. This approach is simple and provides a measure of cash flows between the two companies. Under the partial equity method, the parent accrues the subsidiary's income as earned but does not record adjustments that might be required by excess amortizations or intercompany transfers. The partial equity method is easier to apply than the equity method, and, in many cases, the parent's income is a reasonable approximation of the consolidated total.

4. For a consolidation in any subsequent period, all reciprocal balances have to be eliminated. Thus, the subsidiary's equity accounts, the parent's investment balance, and intercompany income, dividends, and liabilities are removed. In addition, the remaining unamortized portions of the purchase price allocations are recognized along with excess amortization expenses for the period. If the equity method has not been applied, the beginning Retained Earnings of the parent also must be adjusted for any previous income or excess amortizations that have not yet been recorded.

5. For each purchase of a subsidiary, the parent must assign the acquired assets and liabilities (including goodwill) to individual reporting units of its combined operations. The reporting units should be at the level of operating segment or lower and must provide the basis for future assessments of fair value. Any value assigned to goodwill is not amortized but instead is tested annually for impairment. This test consists of two steps. First, if the fair values of any of the consolidated entity's reporting units fall below their carrying values, then the implied value of the associated goodwill must be recomputed. Second, the recomputed implied value of goodwill is compared to its carrying value. An impairment loss must then be recognized if the carrying value of goodwill exceeds its implied value.

6. Push-down accounting is the adjustment of the subsidiary's account balances to recognize allocations and goodwill stemming from the parent's purchase price. Subsequent amortization of these cost figures also is recorded by the subsidiary as an expense. At this time, push-down accounting is required by the SEC for the separate statements of the subsidiary only when no substantial outside ownership exists. The FASB is currently studying push-down accounting and may issue more specific rules on its application. However, for internal reporting purposes, push-down accounting is gaining popularity because it aids company officials in evaluating the impact that the subsidiary has on the business combination.

7. The purchase price of a subsidiary can be based, at least in part, on future income levels or stock prices. If a subsequent payment is made because a specified amount of income is earned, consolidated goodwill is increased. If additional shares are issued because of a drop in the price of the parent's stock, the Common Stock and Additional Paid-In Capital accounts are realigned to agree with the new price. Under the 2005 FASB Exposure Draft, *Business Combinations,* the fair value of any contingent consideration must be included in the recorded value of the acquisition.

Comprehensive Illustration

PROBLEM

(*Estimated Time: 40 to 65 Minutes*) On January 1, 2007, Top Company acquired all of the outstanding common stock of Bottom Company for $800,000 in cash. As of that date, one of Bottom's buildings with a five-year remaining life was undervalued on its financial records by $30,000. Equipment with a 10-year life was undervalued but only by $10,000. The book values of all of Bottom's other assets and liabilities were equal to their fair values at that time, except for an unrecorded licensing agreement with an assessed value of $40,000 and a 20-year remaining useful life. Bottom's book value at January 1, 2007, was $720,000.

During 2007, Bottom reported net income of $100,000 and paid $30,000 in dividends. Earnings were $120,000 in 2008 with $20,000 in dividends distributed by the subsidiary. As of December 31, 2009, the companies reported the following selected balances:

	Top Company December 31, 2009		Bottom Company December 31, 2009	
	Debit	Credit	Debit	Credit
Buildings	$1,540,000		$460,000	
Cash and receivables	50,000		90,000	
Common stock		$ 900,000		$400,000
Dividends paid	70,000		10,000	
Equipment	280,000		200,000	
Cost of goods sold	500,000		120,000	
Depreciation expense	100,000		60,000	
Inventory	280,000		260,000	
Land	330,000		250,000	
Liabilities		480,000		260,000
Retained earnings, 1/1/09 ...		1,360,000		490,000
Revenues		900,000		300,000

Required:

a. If Top applies the equity method, what is its investment account balance as of December 31, 2009?

b. If Top applies the cost method, what is its investment account balance as of December 31, 2009?

c. Regardless of the accounting method in use by Top, what are the consolidated totals as of December 31, 2009, for each of the following accounts?

Buildings	Revenues
Equipment	Net Income
Land	Investment in Bottom
Depreciation Expense	Dividends Paid
Amortization Expense	Cost of Goods Sold

d. If this combination had been initiated prior to June 30, 2001, and was recorded as a pooling of interests, what would be the consolidated totals as of December 31, 2009, for the accounts listed in requirement (c)?

e. Prepare the worksheet entries required on December 31, 2009, to consolidate the financial records of these two companies. Assume that Top applied the equity method to its investment accounts and that the combination is a purchase.

f. How would the worksheet entries in requirement (e) be altered if Top has used the cost method?

SOLUTION

a. To determine the investment balances under the equity method, four items must be known: the original cost, the income accrual, dividend payments, and amortization of excess cost. Although the first three are indicated in the problem, amortizations must be calculated separately.

An allocation of Top's purchase prices as well as the related amortization expense follows.

Purchase price paid by Top Company	$ 800,000
Book value of Bottom Company, 1/1/07	(720,000)
Excess cost over book value	$ 80,000

Excess cost allocated to specific accounts based on fair values:

		Life (years)	Annual Amortization
Buildings	30,000	5	$6,000
Equipment	10,000	10	1,000
Licensing agreement	40,000	20	2,000
Total annual expense	$80,000		$9,000

Thus, if Top adopts the equity method to account for this subsidiary, the Investment in Bottom account holds a December 31, 2009, balance of $1,053,000, computed as follows:

Purchase price		$ 800,000
Bottom Company's 2007–2008 increase in book value (income less dividends)		170,000
Excess amortizations for 2007–2008 ($9,000 per year for two years)		(18,000)
Current year recognition (2009):		
Equity income accrual (Bottom's revenues less its expenses)	$120,000	
Excess amortization expenses	(9,000)	
Dividend from Bottom	(10,000)	101,000
Investment in Bottom Company, 12/31/09		$1,053,000

The $120,000 income accrual for 2009 and the $9,000 excess amortization expenses indicate that an Equity in Subsidiary Earnings balance of $111,000 appears in Top's income statement for the current period.

b. If Top Company applies the cost method, the Investment in Bottom Company account permanently retains its original $800,000 balance and only the intercompany dividend of $10,000 is recognized by the parent as income in 2009.

c. • The consolidated Buildings account as of December 31, 2009, holds a balance of $2,012,000. Although the two book value figures total only $2 million, a $30,000 purchase price allocation was made to this account based on fair value at date of acquisition. Because this amount is being depreciated at the rate of $6,000 per year, the original allocation will have been reduced by $18,000 by the end of 2009, leaving only a $12,000 increase.

• On December 31, 2009, the consolidated Equipment account amounts to $487,000. The book values found in the financial records of Top and Bottom provide a total of $480,000. Once again, the allocation ($10,000) established by the purchase price must be included in the consolidated balance after being adjusted for three years of depreciation ($1,000 × 3 years, or $3,000).

• Land has a consolidated total of $580,000. Because the book value and fair value of Bottom's land were in agreement at the date of acquisition, no allocation of the purchase price was made to this account. Thus, the book values are simply added together to derive a consolidated figure.

• Cost of goods sold = $620,000. The cost of goods sold of the parent and subsidiary are added together.

• Depreciation expense = $167,000. The depreciation expenses of the parent and subsidiary are added together along with the $6,000 additional building depreciation and the $1,000 additional equipment depreciation as presented in the purchase price allocation schedule.

• Amortization expense = $2,000. An additional expense of $2,000 is recognized from the amortization of the licensing agreement acquired in the business combination.

• The Revenues account appears as $1.2 million in the consolidated income statement. None of the worksheet entries in this example affects the individual balances of either company. Consolidation results merely from the addition of the two book values.

• Net income for this business combination is $411,000: consolidated expenses of $789,000 subtracted from revenues of $1.2 million.

• The parent's Investment in Bottom account is removed entirely on the worksheet so that no balance is reported. For consolidation purposes, this account is always eliminated so that the individual assets and liabilities of the subsidiary can be included.

• Dividends paid by the combination should be reported as $70,000, the amount distributed by Top. Because Bottom's dividend payments are entirely intercompany, they are deleted in arriving at consolidated figures.

d. The consolidation of companies under the pooling of interests method is based primarily on the addition of book values. Therefore, consolidated totals for the first five accounts in this question can be determined merely by summing the separate balances:

- Buildings = $2,000,000 ($1,540,000 + $460,000)
- Equipment = $480,000 ($280,000 + $200,000)
- Land = $580,000 ($330,000 + $250,000)
- Cost of Goods Sold = $620,000 ($500,000 + $120,000)
- Depreciation Expense = $160,000 ($100,000 + $60,000)
- Amortization Expense = 0
- Revenues = $1,200,000 ($900,000 + $300,000)
- Consolidated net income is calculated by subtracting the $780,000 in expenses (just computed) from revenues of $1.2 million for a reported total of $420,000.
- As in a purchase, the Investment in Bottom account is eliminated so that the subsidiary's individual balances can be included.
- Only the parent's dividend ($70,000) is reported in the consolidated statements since Bottom's payment is an intercompany cash transfer.

e. Consolidation Entries Assuming Equity Method Used by Parent

Entry S

Common Stock (Bottom Company)	400,000	
Retained Earnings, 1/1/09		
(Bottom Company)	490,000	
Investment in Bottom Company		890,000

Elimination of subsidiary's beginning stockholders' equity accounts against book value portion of investment account.

Entry A

Buildings	18,000	
Equipment	8,000	
Licensing Agreement	36,000	
Investment in Bottom Company		62,000

To recognize allocation of parent's unamortized cost in excess of subsidiary's book value. Balances represent original allocations less two years of amortization for the 2007–08 period.

Entry I

Equity in Subsidiary Earnings	111,000	
Investment in Bottom Company		111,000

To eliminate parent's equity income accrual, balance is computed in requirement (a).

Entry D

Investment in Bottom	10,000	
Dividends Paid		10,000

To eliminate intercompany dividend payment made by subsidiary to the parent (and recorded as a reduction in the investment account since the equity method is in use).

Entry E

Depreciation expense	7,000	
Amortization expense	2,000	
Equipment		1,000
Buildings		6,000
Licensing Agreement		2,000

To recognize excess cost depreciation and amortization for 2009.

f. If Top utilizes the cost method rather than the equity method, three changes are required in the development of consolidation entries:

(1) An Entry ***C** is required to update the beginning Retained Earnings of the parent as if the equity method had been applied. Both an income accrual as well as excess amortizations for the prior two years must be recognized since these balances were not recorded by the parent.

Entry *C

Investment in Bottom Company	152,000	
Retained Earnings, 1/1/09 (Top Company)		152,000

To convert cost figures to the equity method by accruing the net effect of the subsidiary's operations (income less dividends) for the prior two years ($170,000) along with excess amortization expenses ($18,000) for this same period.

(2) An alteration is needed in Entry **I** since, under the cost method, only dividend payments are recorded by the parent as income.

Entry I

Dividend Income	10,000	
Dividends Paid		10,000

To eliminate intercompany dividend payments recorded by parent as income.

(3) Finally, because the intercompany dividends have been eliminated in Entry **I**, no separate Entry **D** is needed.

Questions

1. CCES Corporation acquires a controlling interest in Schmaling, Inc., in a purchase transaction. CCES may utilize any one of three methods to account for this investment. Describe each of these methods, indicating their advantages and disadvantages.
2. Maguire Company obtains 100 percent control over Williams Company. Several years after the takeover, consolidated financial statements are being produced. For each of the following accounts, briefly describe the values that should be included in consolidated totals. Assume that Maguire acquired Williams in a transaction that must be viewed as a purchase.
   a. Equipment.
   b. Investment in Williams Company.
   c. Dividends paid.
   d. Goodwill.
   e. Revenues.
   f. Expenses.
   g. Common stock.
   h. Net income.
3. Using the information presented in question (2), determine each of the consolidated totals if the combination was accounted for as a pooling of interests.
4. When a parent company uses the equity method to account for an investment in a subsidiary, why do both the parent's Net Income and Retained Earnings balances agree with the consolidated totals?
5. When a parent company uses the equity method to account for a purchased investment, the amortization expense entry recorded during the year is eliminated on a consolidation worksheet as a component of Entry **I**. What is the necessity of removing this amortization?
6. When a parent company is applying the cost method or the partial equity method to an investment, an adjustment must be made to the parent's beginning Retained Earnings (Entry ***C**) in every period after the year of acquisition. What is the necessity for this entry? Why is no similar entry found when the equity method is utilized by the parent?
7. Several years ago, Jenkins Company acquired a controlling interest in Lambert Company. Lambert recently borrowed $100,000 from Jenkins. In consolidating the financial records of these two companies, how will this debt be handled?
8. Benns Company acquires Waters Company in a combination accounted for as a purchase. Benns adopts the equity method. At the end of six years, Benns reports an investment in Waters of $920,000. What figures constitute this balance?

9. One company is acquired by another in a purchase transaction in which $100,000 of the acquisition price is assigned to goodwill. Several years later a worksheet is being produced to consolidate these two companies. How is the reported value of the goodwill determined at this date?

10. Remo Company purchases Albane Corporation on January 1, 2007. As part of the purchase agreement, the parent states that an additional $100,000 payment to the former owners of Albane could be required in 2008, depending on the outcome of specified conditions. If this payment is subsequently made, how will Remo account for the extra cost under *SFAS 141*?

11. When is the use of push-down accounting required, and what is the rationale for its application?

12. How are the individual financial records of both the parent and the subsidiary affected in cases when push-down accounting is being applied?

13. Why has push-down accounting gained popularity for internal reporting purposes?

14. The consolidation process applicable to a pooling of interests often is viewed as easier than that used for a purchase. What creates this perception?

15. When should a parent consider recognizing an impairment loss for goodwill associated with a purchased subsidiary? How should the loss be reported in the financial statements?

Problems

1. A company acquires a subsidiary on January 1, 2007, and will prepare consolidated financial statements for the year ending December 31, 2007. For internal reporting purposes, the company has decided to apply the cost method. Why might the company have made this decision?
   a. It is a relatively easy method to apply.
   b. Operating results appearing on the parent's financial records reflect consolidated totals.
   c. The FASB now requires the use of this particular method for internal reporting purposes.
   d. Consolidation is not required when the cost method is used by the parent.

2. A company acquires a subsidiary on January 1, 2007, and will prepare consolidated financial statements for the year ending December 31, 2007. For internal reporting purposes, the company has decided to apply the equity method. Why might the company have made this decision?
   a. It is a relatively easy method to apply.
   b. Operating results appearing on the parent's financial records reflect consolidated totals.
   c. The FASB now requires the use of this particular method for internal reporting purposes.
   d. Consolidation is not required when the equity method is used by the parent.

3. When should a consolidated entity recognize a goodwill impairment loss?
   a. If both the market value of a reporting unit and its associated implied goodwill fall below their respective carrying values.
   b. Whenever the market value of the entity declines significantly.
   c. If the market value of a reporting unit falls below its original acquisition price.
   d. Annually on a systematic and rational basis.

4. Willkom Corporation buys 100 percent of Szabo, Inc., on January 1, 2005, at a price in excess of the subsidiary's fair value. On that date, Willkom's equipment (10-year life) has a book value of $300,000 but a fair value of $400,000. Szabo has equipment (10-year life) with a book value of $200,000 but a fair value of $300,000. Willkom uses the partial equity method to record its investment in Szabo. On December 31, 2007, Willkom has equipment with a book value of $210,000 but a fair value of $330,000. Szabo has equipment with a book value of $140,000 but a fair value of $270,000. What is the consolidated balance for the Equipment account as of December 31, 2007?
   a. $600,000.
   b. $490,000.
   c. $480,000.
   d. $420,000.

5. How would the answer to problem (4) have been affected if the parent had applied the cost method rather than the partial equity method?
   a. No effect: The method used by the parent is for internal reporting purposes only and has no impact on consolidated totals.
   b. The consolidated Equipment account would have a higher reported balance.

   c. The consolidated Equipment account would have a lower reported balance.

   d. The balance in the consolidated Equipment account cannot be determined for the cost method using the information given.

6. According to *SFAS 142,* "Goodwill and Other Intangible Assets," purchased goodwill must be allocated among a firm's identified reporting units. If the fair value of a particular reporting unit with recognized goodwill falls below its carrying amount, which of the following is true?

   a. No goodwill impairment loss is recognized unless the implied value for goodwill exceeds its carrying amount.

   b. A goodwill impairment loss is recognized if the carrying amount for goodwill exceeds its implied value.

   c. A goodwill impairment loss is recognized for the difference between the reporting unit's fair value and carrying amount.

   d. The reporting unit reduces the values assigned to its long-term assets (including any unrecognized intangibles) to reflect its fair value.

7. According to *SFAS 142,* "Goodwill and Other Intangible Assets," if no legal, regulatory, contractual, competitive, economic, or other factors limit the life of an intangible asset, the asset's cost is allocated to expense over which of the following?

   a. 20 years.

   b. 20 years with an annual impairment review.

   c. Infinitely.

   d. Indefinitely (no amortization) with an annual impairment review until its life becomes finite.

8. Dosmann, Inc., buys all outstanding shares of Lizzi Corporation on January 1, 2006, for $700,000 in cash. This portion of the consideration transferred results in a $35,000 allocation to equipment and goodwill of $88,000. At the acquisition date, Dosmann also agrees to pay Lizzi's previous owners an additional $110,000 on January 1, 2008, if Lizzi earns a 10 percent return on Dosmann's initial price in 2006 and 2007. Lizzi's profits exceed this threshold in both years. Under *SFAS 141,* which of the following is true? How would your answer change following the 2005 FASB Exposure Draft on *Business Combinations?*

   a. The additional $110,000 payment is a reduction in consolidated retained earnings.

   b. The fair value of the expected contingent payment increases goodwill at the acquisition date.

   c. Consolidated goodwill as of January 1, 2008, increases by $110,000.

   d. The $110,000 is recorded as an expense in 2008.

9. Lauren Corporation purchases Sarah, Inc., on January 1, 2006, by issuing 13,000 shares of common stock with a $10 per share par value and a $23 market value. This transaction results in recording $62,000 of goodwill. Lauren also agrees to compensate Sarah's former owners for any difference if Lauren's stock is worth less than $23 on January 1, 2008. On January 1, 2008, Lauren issues an additional 3,000 shares to Sarah's former owners to honor the contingent consideration agreement. Under *SFAS 141,* which of the following is true? How would your answer change following the 2005 FASB Exposure Draft on *Business Combinations?*

   a. The fair value of the expected number of shares to be issued for the contingency increases the Goodwill account balance at the date of acquisition.

   b. The Investment balance is not affected, but the parent's Additional Paid-In Capital is reduced by the par value of the extra 3,000 shares when issued.

   c. All of the subsidiary's asset and liability accounts must be revalued for consolidation purposes based on their fair values as of January 1, 2008.

   d. The additional shares are assumed to have been issued on January 1, 2006, so that a retrospective adjustment is required.

10. What is push-down accounting?

   a. A requirement that a subsidiary must use the same accounting principles as a parent company.

   b. Inventory transfers made from a parent company to a subsidiary.

   c. A subsidiary's recording of the fair value allocations found within the purchase price paid by a parent as well as subsequent amortization.

   d. The adjustments required for consolidation when a parent has applied the cost method of accounting for internal reporting purposes.

11. Treadway Corporation purchases Hooker, Inc., on January 1, 2007. The parent pays more for it than the fair value of the subsidiary's net assets. On that date, Treadway has equipment with a book value of $420,000 and a fair value of $530,000. Hooker has equipment with a book value of $330,000 and a fair value of $390,000. Hooker is going to use push-down accounting. Immediately after the acquisition, what amounts in the Equipment account appear on Hooker's separate balance sheet and on the consolidated balance sheet?

    a. $330,000 and $750,000.

    b. $330,000 and $860,000.

    c. $390,000 and $810,000.

    d. $390,000 and $920,000.

12. Herbert, Inc., buys all of the outstanding stock of Rambis Company on January 1, 2006, for $574,000. Annual excess amortization of $12,000 results from this purchase transaction. On the date of the takeover, Herbert reported retained earnings of $400,000 while Rambis reported a $200,000 balance. Herbert reported internal income of $40,000 in 2006 and $50,000 in 2007 and paid $10,000 in dividends each year. Rambis reported net income of $20,000 in 2006 and $30,000 in 2007 and paid $5,000 in dividends each year.

    a. Assume that Herbert's internal income does not include any income derived from the subsidiary.

    • If the parent uses the equity method, what is the amount of consolidated Retained Earnings on December 31, 2007?

    • If the parent uses the partial equity method, what is the amount of consolidated Retained Earnings on December 31, 2007?

    • If the parent uses the cost method, what is the amount of consolidated Retained Earnings on December 31, 2007?

    b. Under each of the following situations, what is the Investment in Rambis account balance on Herbert's books on January 1, 2007?

    • The parent uses the equity method.

    • The parent uses the partial equity method.

    • The parent uses the cost method.

    c. Under each of the following situations, what is Entry *C on a 2007 consolidation worksheet?

    • The parent uses the equity method.

    • The parent uses the partial equity method.

    • The parent uses the cost method.

13. Haynes, Inc., obtains 100 percent of Turner Company's common stock on January 1, 2005, by issuing 9,000 shares of $10 par value common stock. Haynes's shares had a $15 per share fair value. On that date, Turner reported a net book value of $100,000. However, its equipment (with a five-year remaining life) was undervalued by $5,000 in the company's accounting records. Also, Turner had developed a customer list with an assessed value of $30,000, although no value had been recorded on Turner's books. The customer list had an estimated remaining useful life of 10 years.

    The following figures come from the individual accounting records of these two companies as of December 31, 2005:

	Haynes	Turner
Revenues	$(600,000)	$(230,000)
Expenses	440,000	120,000
Investment income	Not given	–0–
Dividends paid	80,000	50,000

    The following figures come from the individual accounting records of these two companies as of December 31, 2006:

	Haynes	Turner
Revenues	$(700,000)	$(280,000)
Expenses	460,000	150,000
Investment income	Not given	–0–
Dividends paid	90,000	40,000
Equipment	500,000	300,000

    a. What balance does Haynes's Investment in Turner account show on December 31, 2006, when the equity method is applied?

    b. What is the consolidated net income for the year ending December 31, 2006?

    c. What is the consolidated Equipment balance as of December 31, 2006? How would this answer be affected by the investment method applied by the parent?

    d. If Haynes has applied the cost method to account for its investment, what adjustment is needed to beginning Retained Earnings on a December 31, 2006, consolidation worksheet? How would this answer change if the partial equity method had been in use? How would this answer change if the equity method had been in use?

14. Acme Co., a consolidated enterprise, conducted an impairment review for each of its reporting units. One particular reporting unit, Martel, emerged as a candidate for possible goodwill impairment. Martel has recognized net assets of $780, including goodwill of $500. Martel's fair value is assessed at $650 and includes two internally developed unrecognized intangible assets (a patent and a customer list with fair values of $150 and $50, respectively). The following table summarizes current financial information for the Martel reporting unit:

	Carrying Amount	Fair Value
Tangible assets, net	$ 80	$110
Recognized intangible assets, net	200	230
Goodwill	500	??
Unrecognized intangible assets	NA	200
Total	$780	$650

    a. Show the two steps to determine the amount of any goodwill impairment for Acme's Martel reporting unit.

    b. After recognition of any goodwill impairment loss, what are the reported book values for the following assets of Acme's reporting unit Martel?

    • Tangible assets, net.

    • Goodwill.

    • Customer list.

    • Patent.

15. Destin Company recently purchased several businesses and recognized goodwill in each acquisition. In accordance with *SFAS 142,* Destin has allocated its purchased goodwill to its three reporting units Sand Dollar, Salty Dog, and Baytowne.

    In its 2007 annual review for goodwill impairment, Destin provides the following individual asset and liability values for each reporting unit:

	Carrying Value	Fair Value
Sand Dollar		
Tangible assets	$180,000	$190,000
Trademark	170,000	150,000
Customer list	90,000	100,000
Goodwill	120,000	?
Liabilities	(30,000)	(30,000)
Salty Dog		
Tangible assets	200,000	200,000
Unpatented technology	170,000	125,000
Licenses	90,000	100,000
Goodwill	150,000	?
Baytowne		
Tangible assets	140,000	150,000
Unpatented technology	–0–	100,000
Copyrights	50,000	80,000
Goodwill	90,000	?

The overall valuations for the entire reporting units (including goodwill) are $510,000 for Sand Dollar, $580,000 for Salty Dog, and $560,000 for Baytowne. To date, Destin has reported no goodwill impairments.

a. Which of Destin's reporting units require both steps to test for goodwill impairment?

b. How much goodwill impairment should Destin report for 2007?

c. What changes to the valuations of Destin's tangible assets and identified intangible assets should be reported based on the goodwill impairment tests?

16. Texas, Inc., obtains all of the outstanding stock of Chainsaw Corporation on January 1, 2005. At that date, Chainsaw owns only three assets and has no liabilities:

	Book Value	Fair Value
Inventory	$ 30,000	$ 40,000
Building (10-year life)	100,000	150,000
Equipment (5-year life)	70,000	50,000

a. If Texas pays $250,000 in cash for Chainsaw, what allocation should be assigned to the subsidiary's Building account and its Equipment account in a December 31, 2007, consolidation?

b. If Texas pays $220,000 in cash for Chainsaw, what allocation should be assigned to the subsidiary's Building account and its Equipment account in a December 31, 2007, consolidation?

c. If Texas pays $180,000 in cash for Chainsaw, what allocation should be assigned to the subsidiary's Building account and its Equipment account in a December 31, 2007, consolidation?

d. If Texas issued common stock valued at $180,000 (rather than paying cash) for Chainsaw in a pooling of interests on June 30, 2001, what allocation should be assigned to the subsidiary's Building account and its Equipment account in a December 31, 2007, consolidation?

Problems 17 through 20 should be viewed as independent situations. They are based on the following data:

Chapman Company obtains 100 percent of the stock of Abernethy Company on January 1, 2006. As of that date, Abernethy has the following trial balance:

	Debit	Credit
Accounts payable		$ 50,000
Accounts receivable	$ 40,000	
Additional paid-in capital		50,000
Buildings (net) (4-year life)	120,000	
Cash and short-term investments	60,000	
Common stock		250,000
Equipment (net) (5-year life)	200,000	
Inventory	90,000	
Land	80,000	
Long-term liabilities (mature 12/31/09)		150,000
Retained earnings, 1/1/06		100,000
Supplies	10,000	
Totals	$600,000	$600,000

During 2006, Abernethy reported income of $80,000 while paying dividends of $10,000. During 2007, Abernethy reported income of $110,000 while paying dividends of $30,000.

17. Assume that Chapman Company acquired the common stock of Abernethy for $490,000 in cash. As of January 1, 2006, Abernethy's land had a fair value of $90,000, its buildings were valued at $160,000, and its equipment was appraised at $180,000. Chapman uses the equity method for this investment. Prepare consolidation worksheet entries for December 31, 2006, and December 31, 2007.

18. Assume that Chapman Company acquired the common stock of Abernethy for $500,000 in cash. Assume that the equipment and long-term liabilities had fair values of $220,000 and $120,000, respectively, on that date. Chapman uses the cost method to account for its investment. Prepare consolidation worksheet entries for December 31, 2006, and December 31, 2007.

19. Assume that Chapman Company acquired the common stock of Abernethy by issuing 10,000 shares of its $30 par value common stock. The stock had a $42 per share market value on January 1, 2006. On January 1, 2006, Abernethy's inventory had a fair value of $150,000. All of this inventory is assumed to have been sold during 2006. Chapman applies the equity method to account for this investment. Prepare the consolidation worksheet entries for December 31, 2006, and December 31, 2007.

20. Assume that Chapman Company acquired the common stock of Abernethy by paying $520,000 in cash. All accounts of Abernethy are estimated to have a value approximately equal to present book values. Chapman uses the partial equity method to account for its investment. Prepare the consolidation worksheet entries for December 31, 2006, and December 31, 2007.

21. Jefferson, Inc., purchases Hamilton Corporation on January 1, 2007. Immediately after the acquisition, the two companies have the following account balances. Hamilton's equipment (with a five-year life) is actually worth $450,000. Credit balances are indicated by parentheses.

	Jefferson	Hamilton
Current assets	$ 300,000	$ 210,000
Investment in Hamilton	510,000	
Equipment	600,000	400,000
Liabilities	(200,000)	(160,000)
Common stock	(350,000)	(150,000)
Retained earnings	(860,000)	(300,000)

In 2007, Hamilton earns a net income of $55,000 and pays a $5,000 cash dividend. At the end of 2008, selected account balances for the two companies are as follows:

	Jefferson	Hamilton
Revenues	$(400,000)	$(240,000)
Expenses	290,000	180,000
Investment income	Not given	
Retained earnings, 1/1/08	Not given	(350,000)
Common stock	(350,000)	(150,000)
Current assets	360,000	140,000
Investment in Hamilton	Not given	
Equipment	520,000	420,000
Liabilities	(170,000)	(190,000)

a. What will be the December 31, 2008, balance in the Investment Income account and the Investment in Hamilton account under each of the three methods described in this chapter?

b. How is the consolidated Expenses account affected by the accounting method used by the parent to record ownership of this subsidiary?

c. How is the consolidated Equipment account affected by the accounting method used by the parent to record ownership of this subsidiary?

d. What is Jefferson's Retained Earnings balance as of January 1, 2008, under each of the three methods described in this chapter?

e. What is Entry ***C** on a consolidation worksheet for 2008 under each of the three methods described in this chapter?

f. What is Entry **S** on a consolidation worksheet for 2008 under each of the three methods described in this chapter?

g. What is consolidated net income for 2008?

22. Following are selected account balances from Profitt Company and Simon Corporation as of December 31, 2007:

	Profitt	Simon
Revenues	$(700,000)	$(400,000)
Cost of goods sold	250,000	100,000
Depreciation expense	150,000	200,000
Investment income	Not given	
Dividends paid	80,000	60,000
Retained earnings, 1/1/07	(600,000)	(200,000)
Current assets	400,000	500,000
Buildings (net)	900,000	400,000
Equipment (net)	600,000	1,000,000
Investment in Simon	Not given	
Liabilities	(500,000)	(1,380,000)
Common stock	(600,000) ($20 par)	(200,000) ($10 par)
Additional paid-in capital	(150,000)	(80,000)

On January 1, 2007, Profitt purchased all of the outstanding stock of Simon for $660,000 in cash and common stock. Profitt also paid $20,000 in lawyers' fees and other combination costs as well as $10,000 in stock issuance costs. At the date of acquisition, Simon's buildings (with a six-year remaining life) have a $440,000 book value but a fair value of $560,000.

a. As of December 31, 2007, what is the consolidated Buildings balance?

b. For the year ending December 31, 2007, what is consolidated Net Income?

c. As of December 31, 2007, what is the consolidated Retained Earnings balance?

d. As of December 31, 2007, what is the consolidated balance to be reported for goodwill?

23. Foxx Corporation purchases all of the outstanding stock of Greenburg Company on January 1, 2005, for $600,000. Greenburg had net assets on that date of $470,000, although equipment with a 10-year life was undervalued on the records by $90,000. Any recognized goodwill is considered to have an indefinite life.

Greenburg reports net income in 2005 of $90,000 and $100,000 in 2006. Dividends of $20,000 are paid by the subsidiary in each of these two years.

Financial figures for the year ending December 31, 2007, follow. Credit balances are indicated by parentheses.

	Foxx	Greenburg
Revenues	$ (800,000)	$ (600,000)
Cost of goods sold	100,000	150,000
Depreciation expense	300,000	350,000
Investment income	(20,000)	–0–
Net income	$ (420,000)	$ (100,000)
Retained earnings, 1/1/07	$(1,100,000)	$ (320,000)
Net income	(420,000)	(100,000)
Dividends paid	120,000	20,000
Retained earnings, 12/31/07	$(1,400,000)	$ (400,000)
Current assets	$ 300,000	$ 100,000
Investment in subsidiary	600,000	–0–
Equipment (net)	900,000	600,000
Buildings (net)	800,000	400,000
Land	600,000	100,000
Total assets	$ 3,200,000	$ 1,200,000
Liabilities	$ (900,000)	$ (500,000)
Common stock	(900,000)	(300,000)
Retained earnings	(1,400,000)	(400,000)
Total liabilities and equity	$(3,200,000)	$(1,200,000)

a. Determine the December 31, 2007, consolidated balance for each of the following accounts:

Depreciation Expense	Buildings
Dividends Paid	Goodwill
Revenues	Common Stock
Equipment	

b. How does the parent's choice of an accounting method for its investment affect the balances computed in requirement (*a*)?

c. Which method of accounting for this subsidiary is the parent actually using for internal reporting purposes?

d. If a different method of accounting for this investment had been used by the parent company, how could that method have been identified?

e. What would be Foxx's balance for retained earnings as of January 1, 2007, if each of the following methods had been in use?

Cost method

Partial equity method

Equity method

24. Big Corporation purchased Little Company on January 1, 2007, for $400,000 in cash. Little reported net assets at that time of $320,000. However, several of Little's accounts had fair values that differed from book values:

	Book Value	Fair Value
Land	$ 60,000	$ 50,000
Buildings (10-year life)	100,000	120,000
Equipment (6-year life)	60,000	90,000

Any goodwill is considered to have an indefinite life.

Following are financial statements for these two companies for the year ending December 31, 2007. Credit balances are indicated by parentheses.

	Big	Little
Revenues	$ (600,000)	$(300,000)
Cost of goods sold	300,000	110,000
Depreciation expense	100,000	70,000
Income of Little	(113,000)	–0–
Net income	$ (313,000)	$(120,000)
Retained earnings, 1/1/07	$ (700,000)	$(220,000)
Net income (above)	(313,000)	(120,000)
Dividends paid	142,000	80,000
Retained earnings, 12/31/07	$ (871,000)	$(260,000)
Cash	$ 176,000	$ 80,000
Receivables	210,000	90,000
Inventory	190,000	130,000
Investment in Little	433,000	–0–
Land	350,000	60,000
Buildings (net)	343,000	90,000
Equipment (net)	190,000	50,000
Goodwill	–0–	–0–
Total assets	$ 1,892,000	$ 500,000
Liabilities	$ (621,000)	$(140,000)
Common stock	(400,000)	(100,000)
Retained earnings (above)	(871,000)	(260,000)
Total liabilities and equity	$(1,892,000)	$(500,000)

a. Show how Big computed the $113,000 Income of Little balance.

b. Without preparing a worksheet or consolidation entries, determine the totals to be reported for this business combination for the year ending December 31, 2007.

c. Verify the totals determined in part (*b*) by producing a consolidation worksheet for Big and Little for the year ending December 31, 2007.

25. Following are separate financial statements for Mitchell Company and Andrews Company as of December 31, 2007. Credit balances are indicated by parentheses. Mitchell acquired all of the outstanding stock of Andrews on January 1, 2003, by issuing 9,000 shares of its own common stock. This stock was valued at $50 per share while having a par value of $30 per share. In addition, Mitchell paid $20,000 to lawyers, accountants, and other parties for costs incurred in creating the combination.

	Mitchell Company 12/31/07	Andrews Company 12/31/07
Revenues	$ (610,000)	$ (370,000)
Cost of goods sold	270,000	140,000
Depreciation expense	115,000	80,000
Dividend income	(5,000)	–0–
Net income	$ (230,000)	$ (150,000)
Retained earnings, 1/1/07	$ (880,000)	$ (490,000)
Net income (above)	(230,000)	(150,000)
Dividends paid	90,000	5,000
Retained earnings, 12/31/07	$(1,020,000)	$ (635,000)
Cash	$ 110,000	$ 15,000
Receivables	380,000	220,000
Inventory	560,000	280,000
Investment in Andrews Company	470,000	–0–
Land	460,000	340,000
Buildings and equipment (net)	920,000	380,000
Total assets	$ 2,900,000	$ 1,235,000
Liabilities	$ (780,000)	$ (470,000)
Preferred stock	(300,000)	–0–
Common stock	(500,000)	(100,000)
Additional paid-in capital	(300,000)	(30,000)
Retained earnings, 12/31/07	(1,020,000)	(635,000)
Total liabilities and equity	$(2,900,000)	$(1,235,000)

On the date of purchase, Andrews reported retained earnings of $230,000 and a total book value of $360,000. At that time its buildings and equipment were undervalued by $60,000. This property was assumed to have a six-year life with no salvage value. Additionally, Andrews owned a trademark with a fair value of $50,000 and a 10-year remaining life that was not reflected on its books.

a. Using the preceding information, prepare a consolidation worksheet for these two companies as of December 31, 2007.

b. Assuming that Mitchell applied the equity method to this investment, what account balances would differ on the parent's individual financial statements?

c. Assuming that Mitchell applied the equity method to this investment, what changes would be necessary in the consolidation entries found on a December 31, 2007, worksheet?

d. Assuming that Mitchell applied the equity method to this investment, what changes would be created in the consolidated figures to be reported by this combination?

26. Giant purchased all of the common stock of Small on January 1, 2005. Over the next few years, Giant applied the equity method to the recording of this investment. At the date of the original purchase, $90,000 of the price was attributed to undervalued land, while $50,000 was assigned to equipment having a 10-year life. The remaining $60,000 unallocated portion of the purchase price was viewed as goodwill.

Following are individual financial statements for the year ending December 31, 2009. On that date, Small owes Giant $10,000. Credits are indicated by parentheses.

a. How was the $135,000 Equity in Income of Small balance computed?

b. Without preparing a worksheet or consolidation entries, determine and explain the totals to be reported by this business combination for the year ending December 31, 2009.

	Giant	Small
Revenues	$(1,175,000)	$ (360,000)
Cost of goods sold	550,000	90,000
Depreciation expense	172,000	130,000
Equity in income of Small	(135,000)	–0–
Net income	$ (588,000)	$ (140,000)
Retained earnings, 1/1/09	$(1,417,000)	$ (620,000)
Net income (above)	(588,000)	(140,000)
Dividends paid	310,000	110,000
Retained earnings, 12/31/09	$(1,695,000)	$ (650,000)
Current assets	$ 398,000	$ 318,000
Investment in Small	995,000	–0–
Land	440,000	165,000
Buildings (net)	304,000	419,000
Equipment (net)	648,000	286,000
Goodwill	–0–	–0–
Total assets	$ 2,785,000	$ 1,188,000
Liabilities	$ (840,000)	$ (368,000)
Common stock	(250,000)	(170,000)
Retained earnings (above)	(1,695,000)	(650,000)
Total liabilities and equity	$(2,785,000)	$(1,188,000)

c. Verify the figures determined in part (b) by producing a consolidation worksheet for Giant and Small for the year ending December 31, 2009.

d. If Giant determined that the entire amount of goodwill from its investment in Small was impaired in 2009, how would the accounts of the parent reflect the impairment loss? How would the worksheet process change? What impact does an impairment loss have on consolidated financial statements?

27. Following are selected accounts for Mergaronite Company and Hill, Inc., as of December 31, 2007. Several of Mergaronite's accounts have been omitted. Credit balances are indicated by parentheses.

	Mergaronite	Hill
Revenues	$(600,000)	$(250,000)
Cost of goods sold	280,000	100,000
Depreciation expense	120,000	50,000
Investment income	Not given	NA
Retained earnings, 1/1/07	(900,000)	(600,000)
Dividends paid	130,000	40,000
Current assets	200,000	690,000
Land	300,000	90,000
Buildings (net)	500,000	140,000
Equipment (net)	200,000	250,000
Liabilities	(400,000)	(310,000)
Common stock	(300,000)	(40,000)
Additional paid-in capital	(50,000)	(160,000)

Assume that Mergaronite took over Hill on January 1, 2003, in a purchase by issuing 7,000 shares of common stock having a par value of $10 per share but a fair value of $100 each. On January 1, 2003, Hill's land was undervalued by $20,000, its buildings were overvalued by $30,000, and equipment was undervalued by $60,000. The buildings had a 10-year life; the equipment had a 5-year life. A customer list with an appraised value of $100,000 was developed internally by Hill and was to be written off over a 20-year period.

a. Determine and explain the December 31, 2007, consolidated totals for the following accounts:

Revenues

Cost of Goods Sold

Depreciation Expense

Amortization Expense

Buildings

Equipment

Customer List

Common Stock

Additional Paid-In Capital

b. In requirement (*a*), why can the consolidated totals be determined without knowing which method the parent has used to account for the subsidiary?

c. If the equity method is used by the parent, what consolidation entries would be used on a 2007 worksheet?

28. Alton Company acquired Zeidner, Inc., on January 1, 1997, in a business combination properly accounted for as a purchase. On that date, Zeidner held assets and liabilities with book values of $700,000 and $200,000, respectively. Alton paid a total of $670,000 to acquire all of the outstanding stock of Zeidner. At the date of this purchase, Zeidner possessed equipment (with a five-year life) that had a value $50,000 in excess of its book value. In addition, Zeidner had buildings worth $80,000 more than their book value. These buildings had a remaining life expectancy of 20 years.

Any goodwill that resulted from the acquisition was initially amortized over a 20-year period.

Following are the individual financial statements for these two companies for the year ending December 31, 2006. Alton owes Zeidner $30,000 at this point in time. Without preparing consolidation entries or setting up a worksheet, determine and explain the consolidated totals for Alton Company and Zeidner, Inc. Credit balances are indicated by parentheses.

	Alton Company	Zeidner, Inc.
Income Statement		
Revenues	$ (600,000)	$ (500,000)
Cost of goods sold	175,000	160,000
Depreciation expense	125,000	140,000
Investment income from Zeidner	(200,000)	–0–
Net income	$ (500,000)	$ (200,000)
Statement of Retained Earnings		
Retained earnings, 1/1/06	$(1,500,000)	$ (650,000)
Net income (above)	(500,000)	(200,000)
Dividends paid	200,000	50,000
Retained earnings, 12/31/06	$(1,800,000)	$ (800,000)
Balance Sheet		
Current assets	$ 230,000	$ 300,000
Investment in Zeidner	1,270,000	–0–
Land	100,000	200,000
Buildings	300,000	400,000
Equipment	600,000	300,000
Goodwill	–0–	–0–
Total assets	$ 2,500,000	$ 1,200,000
Liabilities	$ (300,000)	$ (100,000)
Common stock	(400,000)	(300,000)
Retained earnings, 12/31/06	(1,800,000)	(800,000)
Total liabilities and equity	$(2,500,000)	$(1,200,000)

29. On January 1, 2002, Romeo, Incorporated, exchanged 10,000 shares of previously unissued common stock for all of the outstanding shares of Juliet Company. This was accounted for as a pooling of interests that was initiated prior to June 30, 2001. Romeo's common stock had a $20 par value but a market value of $48 per share. On the date of the exchange, Juliet reported $370,000 in stockholders' equity:

Common stock	$200,000
Additional paid-in capital	50,000
Retained earnings	120,000

Romeo originally offered only 8,000 shares for Juliet's stock but raised that bid based on favorable earnings projections. In addition, equipment held by the subsidiary (with a 10-year remaining life) was estimated to be undervalued on the accounting records by $70,000.

Collectively, during the period 2002 through 2005, Juliet reported net income totaling $80,000 and paid dividends totaling $60,000. In accounting for this investment, Romeo utilized the equity method.

Following are the December 31, 2006, trial balances for these two companies.

	Romeo, Incorporated	Juliet Company
Debits		
Accounts receivable	$ 140,000	$ 40,000
Buildings	620,000	260,000
Cash	60,000	10,000
Dividends paid	130,000	60,000
Equipment	490,000	330,000
Expenses	390,000	110,000
Inventory	190,000	110,000
Investment in Juliet Company	420,000	–0–
Land	300,000	200,000
Total debits	$2,740,000	$1,120,000
Credits		
Additional paid-in capital	$ 190,000	$ 50,000
Common stock	600,000	200,000
Investment income from Juliet Company	90,000	–0–
Liabilities	580,000	530,000
Retained earnings, 1/1/06	680,000	140,000
Revenues	600,000	200,000
Total credits	$2,740,000	$1,120,000

Determine and explain the December 31, 2006 consolidated balances that would be reported by this combination.

30. Broome paid $430,000 cash for all of the outstanding common stock of Charlotte, Inc., on January 1, 2005. The subsidiary had a book value of $340,000 on that date (common stock of $200,000 and retained earnings of $140,000), although equipment recorded at $40,000 (with a five-year remaining life) was assessed as having an actual worth of $70,000.

During the subsequent three years, Charlotte reported the following balances:

	Net Income	Dividends Paid
2005	$65,000	$25,000
2006	75,000	35,000
2007	80,000	40,000

On January 1, 2007, Broome paid an additional $20,000 to the previous owners of Charlotte, an amount that was due because the subsidiary's earnings for the first two years had exceeded $120,000.

a. Prepare consolidation worksheet entries as of December 31, 2007, assuming that Broome has applied the cost method.

b. Prepare consolidation worksheet entries as of December 31, 2007, assuming that Broome has applied the partial equity method.

31. Palm Company acquired 100 percent of the voting stock of Storm Company on January 1, 2003, by issuing 10,000 shares of its $10 par value common stock (having a fair value of $13 per share). Palm also paid $10,000 in acquisition fees to lawyers and investment analysts. As of that date, Storm had stockholders' equity totaling $105,000. Land shown on Storm's accounting records was undervalued by $10,000. Equipment (with a five-year life) was undervalued by $5,000. A secret formula developed by Storm was appraised at $20,000 with an estimated life of 20 years.

Following are the separate financial statements for the two companies for the year ending December 31, 2007. Credit balances are indicated by parentheses.

	Palm Company	Storm Company
Revenues	$ (485,000)	$(190,000)
Cost of goods sold	160,000	70,000
Depreciation expense	130,000	52,000
Equity in subsidiary earnings	(66,000)	–0–
Net income	$ (261,000)	$ (68,000)
Retained earnings, 1/1/07	$ (659,000)	$ (98,000)
Net income (above)	(261,000)	(68,000)
Dividends paid	175,500	40,000
Retained earnings, 12/31/07	$ (744,500)	$(126,000)
Current assets	$ 268,000	$ 75,000
Investment in Storm Company	216,000	–0–
Land	427,500	58,000
Buildings and equipment (net)	713,000	161,000
Total assets	$ 1,624,500	$ 294,000
Current liabilities	$ (110,000)	$ (19,000)
Long-term liabilities	(80,000)	(84,000)
Common stock	(600,000)	(60,000)
Additional paid-in capital	(90,000)	(5,000)
Retained earnings, 12/31/07	(744,500)	(126,000)
Total liabilities and equity	$(1,624,500)	$(294,000)

a. How was the $66,000 balance in the Equity in Subsidiary Earnings account derived?

b. Prepare a worksheet to consolidate the financial information for these two companies.

c. How would Storm's individual financial records differ if the push-down method of accounting had been applied?

32. The Tyler Company acquired all of the outstanding stock of Jasmine Company on January 1, 2005, for $206,000 in cash. Jasmine had a book value of only $140,000 on that date. However, equipment (having an eight-year life) was undervalued by $54,400 on Jasmine's financial records. A building with a 20-year life was overvalued by $10,000. Subsequent to the acquisition, Jasmine reported the following:

	Net Income	Dividends Paid
2005	$50,000	$10,000
2006	60,000	40,000
2007	30,000	20,000

In accounting for this investment, Tyler has used the equity method. Selected accounts taken from the financial records of these two companies as of December 31, 2007, are as follows:

	Tyler Company	Jasmine Company
Revenues—operating	$(310,000)	$(104,000)
Expenses	198,000	74,000
Equipment (net)	320,000	50,000
Buildings (net)	220,000	68,000
Common stock	(290,000)	(50,000)
Retained earnings, 12/31/07 balance	(410,000)	(160,000)

Determine and explain the following account balances as of December 31, 2007:

a. Investment in Jasmine Company (on Tyler's individual financial records).

b. Equity in Subsidiary Earnings (on Tyler's individual financial records).

c. Consolidated Net Income.

d. Consolidated Equipment (net).

e. Consolidated Buildings (net).

f. Consolidated Goodwill (net).

g. Consolidated Common Stock.

h. Consolidated Retained Earnings, 12/31/07.

33. During 2001, Abbott Corporation issued shares of its common stock for all of the outstanding stock of Drexel, Inc., in a transaction accounted for as a pooling of interests. Drexel's book value was only $120,000 at the time, but Abbott issued 10,000 shares valued at $18 per share. Abbott was willing to convey these shares because it felt that buildings (10-year life) were undervalued on Drexel's records by $40,000 while equipment (5-year life) was undervalued by $20,000.

   Following are the individual financial records for these two companies for the year ending December 31, 2007. Credit balances are indicated by parentheses.

	Abbott	Drexel
Revenues	$ (310,000)	$ (90,000)
Operating expenses	220,000	60,000
Equity in subsidiary earnings	(30,000)	–0–
Net income	$ (120,000)	$ (30,000)
Retained earnings, 1/1/07	$ (640,000)	$ (85,000)
Net income	(120,000)	(30,000)
Less: Dividends paid	70,000	20,000
Retained earnings, 12/31/07	$ (690,000)	$ (95,000)
Current assets	$ 159,000	$ 57,000
Investment in Drexel	155,000	–0–
Buildings (net)	472,000	71,000
Equipment (net)	404,000	107,000
Total assets	$ 1,190,000	$ 235,000
Liabilities	$ (160,000)	$ (80,000)
Common stock	(300,000)	(60,000)
Additional paid-in capital	(40,000)	–0–
Retained earnings, 12/31/07 (above)	(690,000)	(95,000)
Total liabilities and equity	$(1,190,000)	$(235,000)

a. Without making consolidation entries or setting up a worksheet, determine and explain the consolidated totals for this business combination.

b. Verify the balances determined in part (a) by preparing a worksheet as of December 31, 2007.

34. On January 1, 2006, Picante Corporation purchased 100 percent of the outstanding voting stock of Salsa Corporation for $1,765,000 cash. On the purchase date, Salsa had the following balance sheet:

Cash	$ 14,000	Accounts payable	$ 120,000
Accounts receivable	100,000	Long-term debt	930,000
Land	700,000	Common stock	1,000,000
Equipment (net)	1,886,000	Retained earnings	650,000
	$2,700,000		$2,700,000

At the purchase date, the following cost allocation was prepared:

Purchase price		$1,765,000
Book value acquired		1,650,000
Excess cost		115,000
To in-process research and development	$44,000	
To equipment (8-yr. remaining life)	56,000	100,000
To goodwill (indefinite life)		$ 15,000

The in-process research and development projects had not yet reached technological feasibility, and the assets used in the projects had no alternative future uses.

On December 31, 2007, Picante and Salsa submitted the following trial balances for consolidation:

	Picante	Salsa
Sales	$ (3,500,000)	$(1,000,000)
Cost of goods sold	1,600,000	630,000
Depreciation expense	540,000	160,000
Subsidiary income	(203,000)	–0–
Net income	$ (1,563,000)	$ (210,000)
Retained earnings 1/1/07	$ (3,000,000)	$ (800,000)
Net income	(1,563,000)	(210,000)
Dividends paid	200,000	25,000
Retained earnings 12/31/07	$ (4,363,000)	$ (985,000)
Cash	$ 228,000	$ 50,000
Accounts receivable	840,000	155,000
Inventory	900,000	580,000
Investment in Salsa	2,042,000	–0–
Land	3,500,000	700,000
Equipment (net)	5,000,000	1,700,000
Goodwill	290,000	–0–
Total assets	$ 12,800,000	$ 3,185,000
Accounts payable	$ (193,000)	$ (400,000)
Long-term debt	(3,094,000)	(800,000)
Common stock	(5,150,000)	(1,000,000)
Retained earnings 12/31/07	(4,363,000)	(985,000)
Total liabilities and equities	$(12,800,000)	$(3,185,000)

a. Show how Picante derived its December 31, 2007, Investment in Salsa account balance.

b. Prepare a consolidated worksheet for Picante and Salsa as of December 31, 2007.

c. Assume instead that Picante had used the cost method for its Investment in Salsa account and that Picante relies on worksheet adjustments to account for purchased in-process research and development. Prepare the *C entry to convert Picante's January 1, 2007, Retained Earnings balance to a full accrual basis.

35. On January 1, 2007, Prine, Inc., purchased 100 percent of the common stock of Lydia Company for $120,000,000 in cash and stock. Lydia's assets and liabilities equaled their fair values except for its equipment, which was undervalued by $500,000 and had a 10-year remaining life.

Prine specializes in media distribution and viewed its acquisition of Lydia as a strategic move into content ownership and creation. Prine expected both cost and revenue synergies from controlling Lydia's artistic content (a large library of classic movies) and its sports programming specialty video operation. Accordingly, Prine allocated Lydia's assets and liabilities (including $50,000,000 of goodwill) to a newly formed operating segment appropriately designated as a reporting unit.

The fair values of the reporting unit's identifiable assets and liabilities through the first year of operations were as follows.

Account	Fair Values	
	1/1/07	12/31/07
Cash	$ 215,000	$ 109,000
Receivables (net)	525,000	897,000
Movie library (25-year life)	40,000,000	60,000,000
Broadcast licenses (indefinite life)	15,000,000	20,000,000
Equipment (10-year life)	20,750,000	19,000,000
Current liabilities	(490,000)	(650,000)
Long-term debt	(6,000,000)	(6,250,000)

However, Lydia's assets have taken longer than anticipated to produce the expected synergies with Prine's operations. At year-end, Prine reduced its assessment of the Lydia reporting unit's fair value to $110,000,000.

At December 31, 2007, Prine and Lydia submitted the following balances for consolidation:

	Prine, Inc.	Lydia Co.
Revenues	$ (18,000,000)	$(12,000,000)
Operating expenses	10,350,000	11,800,000
Equity in Lydia earnings	(150,000)	NA
Dividends paid	300,000	80,000
Retained earnings, 1/1/07	(52,000,000)	(2,000,000)
Cash	260,000	109,000
Receivables (net)	210,000	897,000
Investment in Lydia	120,070,000	NA
Broadcast licenses	350,000	14,014,000
Movie library	365,000	45,000,000
Equipment (net)	136,000,000	17,500,000
Current liabilities	(755,000)	(650,000)
Long-term debt	(22,000,000)	(7,250,000)
Common stock	(175,000,000)	(67,500,000)

a. What is the relevant initial test to determine whether goodwill could be impaired?

b. At what amount should Prine record an impairment loss for its Lydia reporting unit for 2007?

c. What is consolidated net income for 2007?

d. What is the December 31, 2007, consolidated balance for goodwill?

e. What is the December 31, 2007, consolidated balance for broadcast licenses?

f. Prepare a consolidated worksheet for Prine and Lydia (Prine's trial balance should first be adjusted for any appropriate impairment loss).

Develop Your Skills

FARS RESEARCH CASE

Jonas Tech Corporation recently acquired Innovation + Company. The combined firm consists of three related businesses that will serve as reporting units. In connection with the acquisition, Jonas requests your help with the following asset valuation and allocation issues. Support your answers with references to FASB standards as appropriate.

Jonas recognizes several identifiable intangibles from its acquisition of Innovation+. It expresses the desire to have these intangible assets written down to zero in the acquisition period.

The price paid by Jonas for Innovation + indicates that a large amount was paid for goodwill. However, Jonas worries that any future goodwill impairment may send the wrong signal to its investors about the wisdom of the Innovation+ acquisition. Jonas thus wishes to allocate the combined goodwill of all of its reporting units to one account called *Enterprise Goodwill*. In this way, Jonas hopes to minimize the possibility of goodwill impairment because a decline in goodwill in one business unit could be offset by an increase in the value of goodwill in another business unit.

Required:

1. Advise Jonas on the acceptability of its suggested immediate write-off of its identifiable intangibles.
2. Indicate the relevant factors to consider in allocating the cost of identifiable intangibles acquired in a business combination to expense over time.
3. Advise Jonas on the acceptability of its suggested treatment of goodwill.
4. Indicate the relevant factors to consider in allocating goodwill across an enterprise's business units.

WENDY'S ANALYSIS CASE

In 2004 Wendy's International recorded a $190 million goodwill impairment loss for its Baja Fresh reporting unit. Use the Web site *www.wendys-invest.com* to view the "Notice of 2005 Annual Meeting of Shareholders, Proxy Statement, Financial Statements and Other Information" for Wendy's International for the year ended January 2, 2005. Address the following issues related to Wendy's 2004 goodwill impairment loss:

1. How much did Wendy's pay for Baja Fresh in 2002? How did Wendy's allocate the purchase price to the net assets of Baja Fresh?
2. Why did Wendy's recognize a goodwill impairment loss for its Baja Fresh reporting unit in 2004?
3. How did the 2004 goodwill impairment charge affect the performance bonuses of Wendy's top executives? What ratios determined these performance bonuses? How will the 2004 goodwill impairment charge affect the executives' ability to earn future bonuses?

ANALYSIS CASE

In July 2001, the FASB issued *SFAS 142,* which changed the accounting for goodwill and intangible assets. Upon adoption of *SFAS 142,* many large publicly traded companies recognized large goodwill impairment losses. For example, in 2002 AOL Time Warner (now Time Warner) recorded a $99 billion reduction in the carrying value of its goodwill—one of the largest goodwill impairments under *SFAS 142.*

Please use the AOL Time Warner, Inc., 2002 SEC Form 10-K Annual Report and *SFAS 142* to address the following issues and questions.

Required:

1. How did AOL determine the initial amount of goodwill to recognize in its merger with Time Warner?
2. How did AOL Time Warner determine the $99 billion 2002 impairment charge to its goodwill? What procedures will Time Warner follow in the future to assess the value of its goodwill?
3. What business areas did AOL Time Warner designate as its reporting units? Why is it important to define the reporting units?
4. What effects did *SFAS 142* have on AOL Time Warner earnings performance both in the short term and in the long term?
5. What is the rationale behind the accounting treatment for goodwill (initial recognition and subsequent allocation to income) in *SFAS 142?*

EXCEL CASE 1

On January 1, 2006, Innovus, Inc., purchased 100 percent of the common stock of ChipTech Company for $670,000 in cash and other consideration. The purchase price was allocated among ChipTech's net assets as follows:

Cost		$670,000
Book value of ChipTech:		
Common stock and APIC	$130,000	
Retained earnings	370,000	500,000
Excess cost over book value to		170,000
Trademark (10-year remaining life)	40,000	
Existing technology (5-year remaining life)	80,000	120,000
Goodwill		$ 50,000

The December 31, 2007, trial balances for the parent and subsidiary follow:

	Innovus	ChipTech
Revenues	$ (990,000)	$(210,000)
Cost of goods sold	500,000	90,000
Depreciation expense	100,000	5,000
Amortization expense	55,000	18,000
Dividend income	(40,000)	–0–
Net income	$ (375,000)	$ (97,000)
Retained earnings 1/1/07	$(1,555,000)	$(450,000)
Net income	(375,000)	(97,000)
Dividends paid	250,000	40,000
Retained earnings 12/31/07	$(1,680,000)	$(507,000)
Current assets	$ 960,000	$ 355,000
Investment in ChipTech	670,000	
Equipment (net)	765,000	225,000
Trademark	235,000	100,000
Existing technology	–0–	45,000
Goodwill	450,000	–0–
Total assets	$ 3,080,000	$ 725,000
Liabilities	$ (780,000)	(88,000)
Common stock	(500,000)	(100,000)
Additional paid-in capital	(120,000)	(30,000)
Retained earnings 12/31/07	$(1,680,000)	$(507,000)
Total liabilities and equity	$(3,080,000)	$(725,000)

Required:

1. Using Excel, compute consolidated balances for Innovus and ChipTech. Either use a worksheet approach or compute the balances directly.
2. Prepare a second spreadsheet that shows a 2007 impairment loss for the entire amount of goodwill from the ChipTech acquisition.

EXCEL CASE 2

On January 1, 2005, Hi-Speed.com purchased 100 percent of the common stock of Wi-Free Co. for $730,000. The purchase price was allocated among Wi-Free's net assets as follows:

Cost		$730,000
Book value of Wi-Free:		
Common stock and APIC	$130,000	
Retained earnings	370,000	500,000
Excess cost over book value to		$230,000
In-process R&D	75,000	
Computer software (overvalued)	(30,000)	
Internet domain name	120,000	165,000
Goodwill		$ 65,000

At the acquisition date, the computer software had a 4-year remaining life, and the Internet domain name was estimated to have a 10-year life. The acquired in-process R&D was judged to have no alternative future uses. At December 31, 2006, Wi-Free's accounts payable include a $30,000 amount owed to Hi-Speed.

The December 31, 2006, trial balances for the parent and subsidiary follow:

	Hi-Speed.com	Wi-Free Co.
Revenues	$(1,100,000)	$(325,000)
Cost of goods sold	625,000	122,000
Depreciation expense	140,000	12,000
Amortization expense	50,000	11,000
Equity in subsidiary earnings	(175,500)	–0–
Net income	$ (460,500)	$(180,000)
Retained earnings 1/1/06	$(1,552,500)	$(450,000)
Net income	(460,500)	(180,000)
Dividends paid	250,000	50,000
Retained earnings 12/31/06	$(1,763,000)	$(580,000)
Current assets	$ 1,034,000	$ 345,000
Investment in Wi-Free	856,000	–0–
Equipment (net)	713,000	305,000
Computer software	650,000	130,000
Internet domain name	–0–	100,000
Goodwill	–0–	–0–
Total assets	$ 3,253,000	$ 880,000
Liabilities	$ (870,000)	$(170,000)
Common stock	(500,000)	(110,000)
Additional paid-in capital	(120,000)	(20,000)
Retained earnings 12/31/06	(1,763,000)	(580,000)
Total liabilities and equity	$(3,253,000)	$(880,000)

Required:

1. Using Excel, prepare calculations showing how Hi-Speed derived the $856,000 amount for its investment in Wi-Free.

2. Using Excel, compute consolidated balances for Hi-Speed and Wi-Free. Either use a worksheet approach or compute the balances directly.

COMPUTER PROJECT

Alternative Investment Methods, Goodwill Impairment, and Consolidated Financial Statements

In this project, you are to provide an analysis of alternative accounting methods for controlling interest investments and subsequent effects on consolidated reporting. The project requires the use of a computer and a spreadsheet software package (Microsoft Excel®, Lotus 123®, etc.). The use of these tools allows you to assess the sensitivity of alternative accounting methods on consolidated financial reporting without preparing several similar worksheets by hand. Also, by modeling a worksheet process, you can develop a better understanding of accounting for combined reporting entities.

Consolidated Worksheet Preparation

You will be creating and entering formulas to complete four worksheets. The first objective is to demonstrate the effect of different methods of accounting for the investments (equity, cost, and partial equity) on the parent company's trial balance and on the consolidated worksheet subsequent to acquisition. The second objective is to show the effect on consolidated balances and key financial ratios of recognizing a goodwill impairment loss.

The project requires preparation of the following four separate worksheets:

a. Consolidated information worksheet (provided below).

b. Equity method consolidation worksheet.

c. Cost method consolidation worksheet.

d. Partial equity method consolidation worksheet.

If your spreadsheet package has multiple worksheet capabilities (e.g., Excel), you can use separate worksheets; otherwise, each of the four worksheets can reside in a separate area of a single spreadsheet.

In formulating your solution, each worksheet should link directly to the first worksheet. Also, feel free to create supplemental schedules to enhance the capabilities of your worksheet.

Project Scenario

Pecos Company acquired 100 percent of Suaro's outstanding stock for $1,450,000 cash on January 1, 2005, when Suaro had the following balance sheet:

Assets		Liabilities and Equity	
Cash	$ 37,000	Liabilities	$(422,000)
Receivables	82,000		
Inventory	149,000	Common stock	(350,000)
Land	90,000	Retained earnings	(126,000)
Equipment (net)	225,000		
Software	315,000		
Total assets	$898,000	Total liabilities and equity	$(898,000)

At the purchase date, the fair values of each identifiable asset and liability that differed from book value were as follows:

Land	$ 80,000	
Brand name	60,000	(indefinite life—unrecognized on Suaro's books)
Software	415,000	(2-year estimated useful life)
In-Process R&D	300,000	(no alternative use for these R&D assets)

Additional Information

- Pecos expects future benefits from the purchased in-process research and development (R&D) of Suaro. However, if the benefits are not realized, there is no alternative use for any of the purchased R&D assets.

- During 2005, Suaro earns $75,000 and pays no dividends.

- Selected amounts from Pecos and Suaro's separate financial statements at December 31, 2006, are presented in the consolidated information worksheet. All consolidated worksheets are to be prepared as of December 31, 2006, two years subsequent to acquisition.

- Pecos's January 1, 2006, Retained Earnings balance—before any effect from Suaro's 2005 income— is $(930,000) (credit balance).

- Pecos has 500,000 common shares outstanding for EPS calculations and reported $2,943,100 for consolidated assets at the beginning of the period.

Following is the consolidated information worksheet.

	A	B	C	D
1	**December 31, 2006, trial balances**			
2				
3		**Pecos**	**Suaro**	
4	Revenues	($1,052,000)	($427,000)	
5	Operating expenses	$ 821,000	$262,000	
6	Goodwill impairment loss	?		
7	Income of Suaro	?		
8	Net income	?	($165,000)	
9				
10	Retained earnings—Pecos 1/1/06	?		
11	Retained earnings—Suaro 1/1/06		($201,000)	
12	Net income (above)	?	($165,000)	
13	Dividends paid	$ 200,000	$ 35,000	
14	Retained earnings 12/31/06	?	($331,000)	
15				
16	Cash	$ 195,000	$ 95,000	
17	Receivables	$ 247,000	$143,000	
18	Inventory	$ 415,000	$197,000	
19	Investment in Suaro	?		
20				
21				
22				
23	Land	$ 341,000	$ 85,000	
24	Equipment (net)	$ 240,100	$100,000	
25	Software		$312,000	
26	Other intangibles	$ 145,000		
27	Goodwill			
28	Total assets	?	$932,000	
29				
30	Liabilities	($1,537,100)	($251,000)	
31	Common stock	($ 500,000)	($350,000)	
32	Retained earnings (above)	?	($331,000)	
33	Total liabilities and equity	?	($932,000)	
34				
35	Cost allocation schedule			
36	Price paid	$1,450,000		
37	Book value	$ 476,000		
38	Excess cost	$ 974,000	Amortizations	
39	to land	($ 10,000)	2005	2006
40	to brand name	$ 60,000	?	?
41	to software	$ 100,000	?	?
42	to IPR&D	$ 300,000	?	?
43	to goodwill	$ 524,000	?	?
44				
45	Suaro's RE changes	Income	Dividends	
46	2005	$ 75,000	$0	
47	2006	$ 165,000	$ 35,000	

Project Requirements

Complete the four worksheets as follows:

1. Input the **consolidated information worksheet** provided and complete the cost allocation schedule by computing the excess amortizations for 2005 and 2006.

2. Using separate worksheets, prepare Pecos's trial balances for each of the indicated accounting methods (equity, cost, and partial equity). **Use only formulas for the Investment in Suaro, the Income of Suaro, and Retained Earnings accounts.**

3. **Using references to other cells only (either from the consolidated information worksheet or from the separate method sheets), prepare for each of the three consolidation worksheets:**
   - Adjustments and eliminations.
   - Consolidated balances.

4. Calculate and present the effects of a 2006 total goodwill impairment loss on the following ratios for the consolidated entity:
   - Earnings per share (EPS).
   - Return on assets.
   - Return on equity.
   - Debt to equity.

Your worksheets should have the capability to adjust immediately for the possibility that all acquisition goodwill can be considered impaired in 2006.

5. **Prepare a word-processed report that describes and discusses the following worksheet results:**
   a. The effects of alternative investment accounting methods on the parent's trial balances and the final consolidation figures.
   b. The relation between consolidated retained earnings and the parent's retained earnings under each of the three (equity, cost, partial equity) investment accounting methods.
   c. The effect on EPS, return on assets, return on equity, and debt-to-equity ratios of the recognition that all acquisition-related goodwill is considered impaired in 2006.

CPA Review

Please visit the text Web site for the online CPA Simulation: mhhe.com/hoyle8e

Situation: On January 1, Year One, Big Corporation purchases for $700,000 in cash all of the outstanding voting stock of Little Corporation. It was the first such purchase for either company. On the day prior to the transaction, Big and Little reported assets of $2 million and $800,000 respectively, liabilities of $900,000 and $330,000, contributed capital of $300,000 and $100,000, and retained earnings of $800,000 and $370,000. Unless otherwise stated, assume Little Corporation holds a building with a book value of $200,000 but a fair value of $300,000. The building has a 10-year remaining life. All of Little's other assets and liabilities are fairly valued in its financial records.

Topics to be covered in simulation:

- Goodwill to be reported.
- Consolidated assets and equities.
- Consolidated expenses.
- Unrecorded intangible assets.
- Goodwill impairment.
- Determination of control.
- Unconsolidated subsidiaries.
- Application of the equity method.

Chapter **Four**

Consolidated Financial Statements and Outside Ownership

A note to recent financial statements of Merck & Co., Inc., contains the following information:

> The consolidated financial statements include the accounts of the Company and all of its subsidiaries in which a controlling interest is maintained. . . . For those consolidated subsidiaries where Company ownership is less than 100%, the outside stockholders' interests are shown as Minority interests. Investments in affiliates over which the Company has significant influence but not a controlling interest . . . are carried on the equity basis.

Merck includes *all of the financial figures* generated by both its wholly and majority-owned subsidiaries within consolidated financial statements. How does Merck account for the partial ownership interest of the noncontrolling owners of its subsidiaries?

A number of reasons exist for one company to hold less than 100 percent ownership of a subsidiary. The parent could not have had sufficient resources available to obtain all of the outstanding stock. As a second possibility, a few stockholders of the subsidiary could have elected to retain their ownership, perhaps in hope of getting a better price at a later date.

Lack of total ownership is frequently encountered with foreign subsidiaries. The laws of some countries prohibit outsiders from maintaining complete control of domestic business enterprises. In other areas of the world, a parent can seek to establish better relations with a subsidiary's employees, customers, and local government by maintaining some percentage of native ownership.

Regardless of the reason for owning less than 100 percent, the parent consolidates the financial data of every subsidiary when control is present. As discussed in Chapter 2, *complete ownership is not a prerequisite for consolidation.* A single economic entity is formed whenever one company is able to control the decision-making process of another.

Although most parent companies do possess 100 percent ownership of their subsidiaries, a significant number, such as Merck & Co., establish control with a lesser amount of stock. The remaining outside owners are collectively referred to as a *noncontrolling interest* or by the more traditional term *minority interest.* The presence of these other stockholders poses a number of reporting questions for the accountant. Whenever less than 100 percent of a subsidiary's voting stock is held, how should the subsidiary's accounts be valued within consolidated financial statements? How should the presence of these additional owners be acknowledged?

In 2005, two FASB Exposure Drafts proposed significant changes in financial reporting for noncontrolling interests in consolidated financial statements: (1) *Business Combinations* and (2) *Consolidated Financial Statements, Including Accounting and Reporting of Noncontrolling Interests in Subsidiaries*. These two exposure drafts have potentially far-reaching effects on the accounting issues covered in this chapter. Therefore, this chapter provides additional discussion of several of these issues.

CONSOLIDATIONS INVOLVING A NONCONTROLLING INTEREST

In any combination in which a noncontrolling interest[1] remains, an intriguing theoretical controversy arises concerning (1) the appropriate consolidation values to assign to the subsidiary's assets and liabilities and (2) the method of valuing and disclosing the presence of the other owners. This debate involves more than a reporting problem; it ultimately concerns the fundamental objectives of consolidated financial statements.

When total ownership exists, the subsidiary's assets and liabilities are always consolidated based on their fair values at the date of acquisition with any excess cost assigned to goodwill.[2] Because no other owners exist, disclosure of a noncontrolling interest is not relevant. In contrast, when a company acquires less than 100 percent of a subsidiary, several different theoretical methods exist to calculate the consolidated values of the acquired accounts. Each of these approaches uses a different technique for reporting the presence of the noncontrolling interest.

To examine the alternative noncontrolling interest valuation theories, assume that Small Company possesses net assets with the following values:

Book value of net assets	$110,000
Fair value of identifiable net assets (excluding goodwill)	130,000

In the current year, Big Company purchases 7,000 of the 10,000 outstanding voting stock shares of Small for $20 per share. We assume that the price per share that Big paid represents the fair value of each of Small's 10,000 shares. Therefore, the fair value for Small, taken as a whole, is $200,000 (10,000 × $20 per share or $140,000 ÷ 70%).

Exhibit 4.1 provides a framework for introducing the fundamental valuation challenges in accounting and reporting for a noncontrolling interest in consolidated financial statements. First, what amounts should the parent report for the acquired subsidiary's assets and liabilities it assumed when it acquired less than 100 percent of the subsidiary? Second, how does the valuation for these acquired net assets affect the amount reported for the noncontrolling interest?

---

[1] The term *minority interest* has been used almost universally over the decades to identify the presence of other outside owners. However, in the FASB's October 27, 2000, Exposure Draft, *Accounting for Financial Instruments with Characteristics of Liabilities, Equity, or Both,* the term *noncontrolling interest* was applied. Because this term is more descriptive, it is used throughout this textbook.

[2] To avoid unnecessary complexities in analyzing this issue, bargain purchases are not illustrated. In addition, this controversy does not relate to a pooling of interests when accounts are always consolidated at their book values.

EXHIBIT 4.1
Noncontrolling Interest—
Date of Acquisition

| **BIG (PARENT) AND 70% OWNED SMALL (SUBSIDIARY) COMPANIES** |
| **Consolidated Balance Sheet** |
| **Date of Acquisition** |

Parent's assets	Parent's liabilities
Subsidiary's assets	**Subsidiary's liabilities**
	Parent company owners' equity
	• 100% of parent's net assets
	• **70% of subsidiary's net assets**
	Noncontrolling owners' interest
	• **30% of subsidiary net assets**

One view is that Small Company's entire $200,000 fair value should serve as the valuation basis for both the parent and the noncontrolling interest share of the subsidiary's net assets. Even though the parent exchanged only $140,000 of consideration for a partial (70 percent) interest, the evidence of fair value may be sufficient to provide relevant information to financial statement users. This view also recognizes that management effectively controls 100 percent of the net assets acquired and is thus accountable for the entire fair value. Recognizing the full fair value of partially owned acquisitions reflects the *economic unit concept*.

A second alternative simply values the noncontrolling interest and its share of the subsidiary net assets at zero. This approach reflects a strict interpretation of the cost principle by incorporating only the percentage acquired by the parent for the subsidiary's assets and liabilities. This view reflects the *proportionate consolidation concept*.

A third view continues to reflect the cost principle but also assigns a value to the noncontrolling interest shares. Because the parent purchased only 70 percent of the subsidiary's shares, only 70 percent of the subsidiary's net assets are valued at the parent's cost. The 30 percent held by the noncontrolling interest is not part of the exchange transaction, and therefore no new basis of accountability arises. Thus, 30 percent of the net assets remains at the subsidiary's former book value (carryover basis) and 70 percent of the net assets is valued at cost to the parent. This view reflects the *parent company concept*.

To date, official accounting pronouncements have not addressed the issue of valuation theory in combinations involving less than 100 percent ownership. Technically, therefore, firms can choose any concept for noncontrolling interest valuation. Nevertheless, note that the vast majority of consolidated financial statements in the United States are prepared under the parent company concept. However, the 2005 FASB Exposure Drafts on business combinations and noncontrolling interest propose to change consolidated financial reporting from the parent company concept to the economic unit concept. We next present each of the concepts of noncontrolling interest valuation and their related effects on asset valuation and income determination.[3]

The Economic Unit Concept

The 2005 FASB Exposure Drafts *Business Combinations* and *Consolidated Financial Statements, Including Accounting and Reporting of Noncontrolling Interests in Subsidiaries* clearly embrace the economic unit concept as applied to the total fair value of an acquired firm at acquisition date. This concept is founded on the proposition that the subsidiary and especially the subsidiary's individual accounts cannot be divided along ownership lines. A controlled company must always be consolidated as a whole regardless of the parent's level of ownership.

Proponents argue that this concept provides the most consistent perspective of the consolidation process. It also gives the best view of the assets and liabilities that have come under the control of the parent company. If, in the previous illustration, Small owns land with a book

---

[3] Variations of each approach presented here do exist. To avoid unnecessary complication, only three of the basic theories are described.

Discussion **Question**

HOW DO WE REPORT THIS OTHER OWNER?

The Hartstone Company was created 15 years ago and presently owns several large retail clothing stores in and around Lakeland, Minnesota. Its four founders, Scott Arnold, Janine Bostio, Garrison Cantleberry, and Ingrid Jorgesson, hold Hartstone's capital stock equally.

Until recently, Thomas Warwick was the sole owner of a competing business in the nearby city of Kalshburg. Because Warwick was nearing retirement age, he opted to sell 90 percent of his company (which encompassed only one store) to Hartstone. Because the business had been in Warwick's family for several generations, he wanted to retain 10 percent ownership. Hartstone paid cash for this acquisition. Based on past profitability, the negotiated price for the shares was set to indicate a total value of $2 million, although the current book value of the store was only $1.4 million.

At the end of the current year, the owners of Hartstone must produce consolidated financial statements for the first time. Consequently, they are having a discussion with their accountant concerning the appropriate method of reporting Thomas Warwick's 10 percent interest in the Kalshburg store.

Scott Arnold: These statements are designed to represent the Hartstone Company and our assets, liabilities, revenues, and expenses. Warwick owns none of our stock. I see no reason to include any figure at all for him. Readers would naturally assume that he controls a portion of Hartstone; we would be misleading them. He has nothing to do with our company.

Janine Bostio: I think you are wrong. Warwick owns 10 percent of one of our stores. He is a partial owner of this asset, and since we are consolidating the entire Kalshburg store, we have to recognize that he has an equity interest. The price indicates a $2,000,000 value; so his ownership should be recognized at $200,000.

Garrison Cantleberry: I agree with Scott; the statements are designed to represent Hartstone Company, and Warwick is certainly not a stockholder of Hartstone. However, we do have a legal obligation to him. If we ever liquidate the Kalshburg store, he would be entitled to a portion of the residual. Even now, when the store pays a dividend, he must be paid 10 percent of each distribution. We have an obligation to him that can be properly disclosed only as a liability.

Ingrid Jorgesson: I have trouble with recording a liability. I understand that we eventually might have a debt to Warwick, but at this point in time we are under no obligation to him. To me, a possible future claim should not be recorded as an actual liability. However, Warwick has retained a $140,000 investment in one of our assets. That is his cost. Since this amount doesn't seem to be either debt or equity, why don't we record it separately between our liabilities and the stockholders' equity? Anyone reading the statements can add this figure to either balance if desired or simply ignore it entirely.

As the accountant, what recommendation would you make to your clients and why? Should Warwick's interest be recognized? If so, where should the figure be reported and what amount should be disclosed?

value of $8,000 but a fair value of $10,000, the economic unit concept requires the $10,000 figure to be reported within consolidated statements whether the parent acquires 70 percent, 100 percent, or any other level of control. The owners of Big control all of the resources of both Big and Small despite holding only 70 percent of the subsidiary's voting stock.

Therefore, in accounting for Big's acquisition of Small, the economic unit concept bases consolidated totals on the fair value of Small taken as a whole. In this case, the $20 price per share paid by Big for its 7,000 share acquisition is assumed to be equivalent to the value of all 10,000 of Small's shares and determining the fair value of Small as a whole is straightforward

($20 × 10,000) = $200,000.[4] All of the subsidiary's assets and liabilities are included at their fair values with any excess assigned to goodwill. Because the individual fair values total only $130,000 but the fair value of the company as a whole equals $200,000, the excess $70,000 is assigned to goodwill.

Because the total value of every asset and liability is attributed to the consolidated entity, the partial ownership held by outside parties must also be acknowledged. *Including 100 percent of the value of a subsidiary's accounts when only 70 percent of the stock is owned creates an imbalance that requires the recognition of a 30 percent noncontrolling interest.* Hence, $60,000 (30 percent of the total fair value being included in the consolidation) is attributed to the other owners of Small.

Economic Unit Concept

Fair value of Small ($140,000/70%, or $20 × 10,000 shares)	$200,000
Fair value assigned to Small's accounts	130,000
Fair value not assigned to identifiable accounts—goodwill	$ 70,000
Noncontrolling interest (30% of the $200,000 fair value included in consolidated totals)	$ 60,000

Although Small's outside owners do not possess an equity interest in the parent company, the $60,000 balance is presented within the consolidated stockholders' equity section when the economic unit concept is in use. This placement is based on the assertion that the two companies should be viewed together as a single entity. The outside parties own a component part of the resulting business combination; thus, their interest is viewed as an equity (or ownership) balance to be reported within the consolidated balance sheet.

After the balance sheet valuations are established for the economic unit concept, a logical extension can be made to the construction of a consolidated income statement. Once again, this approach recognizes 100 percent of the subsidiary's revenue and expense balances. Its entire income is included. The fundamental objective of reporting the subsidiary as an indivisible unit within the consolidated entity is fulfilled by consolidating every account in total. Furthermore, this approach effectively reports the income generated by the net assets under the control of the parent company.

Consequently, for Big's acquisition of Small, 100 percent of the subsidiary's revenues and expenses are included in the consolidated figures. Because the parent owns only 70 percent of Small, a 30 percent claim to the subsidiary's earnings must be deducted separately in recognition of the noncontrolling interest. This portion of consolidated net income is viewed as an allocation to these other owners.

In computing the part of consolidated income to assign to the noncontrolling interest, a theoretical question arises concerning the impact of any excess amortization incurred in connection with the price paid by the parent. As shown in Chapter 3, expense recognition is necessitated by the allocations made to specific subsidiary accounts. Within the business combination, are these expenses attributed to the parent or to the subsidiary?

A logical extension of the economic unit concept is that each purchase price allocation is perceived as a revaluation of a subsidiary asset or liability to fair value. Subsequent amortization of these costs, therefore, relates to the subsidiary rather than the parent. Because the expense is viewed as an adjustment to the subsidiary's net income, it affects the computation of the noncontrolling interest's share of these earnings.

For example, what is the noncontrolling interest in the subsidiary's income in the following situation?

Portion of subsidiary owned by parent	90 percent
Subsidiary's reported net income	$300,000
Amortization expenses on purchase price allocations	$40,000

---

[4] If the acquisition price does not provide a reliable basis for assessing the fair value of the subsidiary as a whole, other market and income-based valuation techniques may be employed. For example, the presence of a control premium often results in an acquisition price that does not reflect a similar value for the shares not acquired.

The economic unit concept presumes that excess amortizations relate to the subsidiary's assets. Thus, the allocation of consolidated income made to the noncontrolling interest is $26,000 (or 10 percent of earnings less excess amortization expenses).

Under the economic unit theory, all consolidated asset and liability totals are identical regardless of the degree of parent ownership. The parent controls the entire decision-making process of the subsidiary whenever control exists. Therefore, the economic unit concept views the subsidiary as an indivisible unit within the business combination. As such, fair value serves as the basis for consolidating each asset and liability, even though the parent's interest could be significantly below 100 percent control. Any contrived division of the subsidiary accounts is thus avoided.

The Proportionate Consolidation Concept

The *proportionate consolidation concept* presumes that the ultimate objective of consolidated financial statements is to serve as a report to the stockholders of the parent company. These owners are perceived as being primarily interested in an accounting of parent company resources. Returning to the previous illustration, the accounting emphasis is placed on Big's $140,000 investment cost to acquire a 70 percent interest in Small.

Under proportionate consolidation, the values utilized for consolidation reflect the parent's payment attributed to each asset and liability. Big is paying for these assets, not for the company. Because Big has acquired 70 percent ownership, that percentage of every account's fair value at the date of purchase forms the basis for consolidated figures. If, for example, Small owns land with a book value of $8,000 but a fair value of $10,000, a $7,000 component of the price (70 percent of fair value) is considered to be Big's cost incurred in connection with this asset.

Under proportionate consolidation, goodwill of $49,000 is recognized: the amount of the purchase price in excess of the appropriate portion of the net assets' fair value.

Proportionate Consolidation Concept

Purchase price	$140,000
Fair value assigned to Small's accounts ($130,000 × 70%)	91,000
Cost in excess of fair value—goodwill	$ 49,000
Noncontrolling interest	–0–

Although goodwill is computed here as a residual cost element, a more consistent view of proportionate consolidation is that this figure represents 70 percent of the subsidiary's total goodwill. As shown in the previous section, a goodwill figure of $70,000 is appropriate for the subsidiary as a whole (the $200,000 fair value of the company as a whole less the $130,000 fair value of its net assets). Thus, the portion of this goodwill that is applicable to Big's investment is $49,000 ($70,000 × 70%).

A unique feature of proportionate consolidation is the reporting of the noncontrolling interest; consolidated statements totally ignore these outside owners. Proponents of this theory hold that the presence of a noncontrolling interest is irrelevant to the stockholders of the parent company. An outside owner of a subsidiary has no capital invested in the parent company; furthermore, the parent has no legal obligation to this group. Thus, including any type of balance within consolidated financial statements to reflect a noncontrolling interest is viewed as serving no purpose.

Before leaving this discussion of proportionate consolidation, we make a quick extension of this concept to income statement reporting. Not surprisingly, Big Company includes 70 percent of each of the subsidiary's revenue and expense accounts in the consolidated balances while showing no amount of the income total as associated with the noncontrolling interest. Within the framework of proportionate consolidation, this presentation is consistent. The parent's ownership entitles it to accrue only 70 percent of the subsidiary's income; the remaining 30 percent is applicable to outside owners. Any recording of this 30 percent share of Small's net income has no apparent relevance to the owners of Big Company.

In actual practice, little evidence exists to indicate significant usage of proportionate consolidation. Although omitting any mention of outside stockholders can be appealing, the division of each subsidiary account based on the ownership percentage is difficult to justify. The parent has achieved control over all assets and liabilities, not just a 70 percent interest of each.

However, this concept recently gained some support for use in cases in which control is present without majority ownership. As discussed in Chapter 2, a parent can effectively control a subsidiary although holding only 50 percent or even less of the outstanding voting stock. Proponents argue that proportionate consolidation would be a better reflection of the relationship between the two companies than the equity method that is currently required.

The Parent Company Concept

The *parent company concept* is sometimes viewed as a hybrid method because it incorporates a mixture of the assumptions found in the economic unit concept and proportionate consolidation. Two fundamental assertions underlie this approach to consolidation valuation:

1. Holding control of a subsidiary provides the parent an indivisible interest in that company. This statement is clearly derived from the economic unit concept.
2. The parent company primarily produces consolidated financial statements for the benefit of its stockholders. This idea is, of course, the basic argument used to substantiate proportionate consolidation.

Both of the assertions attributed to the parent company concept appear to have merit. However, as the previous sections showed, they lead to radically differing sets of consolidated financial statements: one based on the fair value of the entire subsidiary and the other on the cost incurred in a partial acquisition. The parent company approach combines both of these ideas in valuing the consolidated enterprise. The subsidiary's book value and the purchase price the parent paid are viewed as separate elements that can be accounted for individually within the consolidation process.

The book value of each subsidiary asset and liability is presumed to be indivisible and, therefore, not subject to an artificial allocation because of the specific level of ownership. Conversely, differences between the market value and underlying book value of these same accounts are recognized only because of the purchase price paid by the parent. Thus, if the parent acquires less than 100 percent of the subsidiary's voting stock, allocations attributed to individual accounts at the date of purchase should be based on the resulting ownership percentage. *The subsidiary's book value is consolidated in total whereas any cost in excess of book value is assumed to be a parent company expenditure appropriately allocated based on fair values.*

Returning to Big's acquisition of Small, the appropriate consolidation values to be assigned under the parent company concept are computed as follows:

Parent Company Concept

Purchase price		$140,000
Book value of Small (100%)	$110,000	
Less: Recognition of noncontrolling interest (30%)	(33,000)	(77,000)
Cost in excess of underlying book value		63,000
Allocation based on fair value in excess of book value ($130,000 − $110,000) × 70%		(14,000)
Goodwill		$ 49,000
Noncontrolling interest (30% × $110,000)		$ 33,000

The parent company concept includes the entire book value of each of Small's accounts within the consolidated statements but only 70 percent of the difference between fair value and book value. Proponents justify this approach by pointing out that the parent's purchase does not affect the subsidiary's cost figures and, therefore, they should be consolidated in total. In contrast, the various allocations result solely from the price paid by the parent in a transaction negotiated to acquire 70 percent ownership. Thus, the investment is assumed to reflect only 70 percent of the change in the value of individual accounts.

As a practical example, Small's land, with an $8,000 cost but a fair value of $10,000, is consolidated at a $9,400 balance: the entire $8,000 book value plus 70 percent of the $2,000 increase in its worth ($10,000 − $8,000). The subsidiary originally expended $8,000 for this land, and the parent has now paid an additional $1,400 within the purchase price as a reflection of this change in value. Thus, to the business combination, the land's cost totals $9,400.

In the valuation schedule presented earlier, a noncontrolling interest of $33,000 is computed on the basis of Small's $110,000 book value rather than on either the fair value of the net assets or the fair value of the company taken as a whole. Under the parent company concept, only the book value of the subsidiary's accounts is consolidated in total. Although Big holds just 70 percent ownership, 100 percent of each book value is brought into the consolidation. Consequently, the presence of a noncontrolling interest equivalent to 30 percent of that particular total must also be recognized. Big's payment in excess of book value, however, has no impact on the remaining outside owners and is not included in this calculation.

Some amount of disagreement exists among the users of the parent company concept as to the appropriate placement of the noncontrolling interest figure within the consolidated balance sheet. Arguments can be made for showing the balance as either a liability or an equity. However, proponents of this theory are most likely to isolate the noncontrolling interest between liabilities and stockholders' equity.

> The parent company concept views the consolidated financial statements as those of the parent—with the assets, liabilities, revenues, and expenses of the subsidiary merely substituting for the parent's investment on the balance sheet. . . . From that perspective, the noncontrolling (minority) interest is not a liability because the parent does not have a present obligation to pay cash or other assets. Nor does it appear to be owners' equity from a parent company perspective because the noncontrolling investors in a subsidiary do not have an ownership interest in the subsidiary's parent. . . . Thus, the parent company concept generally reports noncontrolling interest below liabilities but above stockholders' equity in consolidated statements.[5]

Currently, the appropriate placement of a noncontrolling interest balance remains an unresolved question in practice. The 2005 FASB Exposure Drafts *Business Combinations* and *Consolidated Financial Statements, Including Accounting and Reporting of Noncontrolling Interests in Subsidiaries* recommend inclusion in equity (pages viii and ix):

> This proposed Statement would result in greater consistency with the Board's conceptual framework because it would require noncontrolling interests to be accounted for and reported as equity, separately from the parent shareholders' equity. In current practice, noncontrolling interests in the equity of subsidiaries are reported most commonly as "mezzanine" items between liabilities and equity in the consolidated financial statements of the parent, but also as liabilities or as equity. The display of noncontrolling interests as liabilities has no conceptual support because noncontrolling interests do not meet the definition of liabilities as defined in paragraph 35 of FASB Concepts Statement No. 6, *Elements of Financial Statements.* Not one of the entities involved—the parent, the subsidiary, or the consolidated entity—is obligated to transfer assets or provide services to the owners that hold equity interests in the subsidiary. Also, Concepts Statement 6 defines three elements of a statement of financial position: assets, liabilities, and equity (or net assets). The display of noncontrolling interests as mezzanine items would require that a new element—noncontrolling interests in consolidated subsidiaries—be created specifically for consolidated financial statements. The Board believes that no compelling reason exists to create such a new element. A view of consolidated financial statements as those of a single economic entity supports classification as equity because noncontrolling shareholders, partners, or other equity holders in subsidiaries are owners of a residual interest in a component of the consolidated entity.

Today, the placement of a noncontrolling interest continues to vary with the reporting entity. Many companies disclose this figure as a single balance appearing directly after noncurrent liabilities. No accumulated total is provided for liabilities or equities, so that the reader is forced to decide whether the noncontrolling interest should be included in either classification or viewed as an item separate from both. Although this placement is often encountered in practice, no consensus currently exists as to the appropriate classification of this balance. However, if the FASB eventually takes action on consolidation policies and procedures, a specific location for the noncontrolling interest could well be required in the future.

---

[5] FASB Discussion Memorandum, *An Analysis of Issues Related to Consolidation Policy and Procedures,* September 10, 1991, paras. 69 and 70.

Discussion **Question**

WHAT DECISION SHOULD THE FASB MAKE?

Whenever the FASB studies an accounting issue, the Board always seems to get plenty of advice. In response to its discussion memorandum, "An Analysis of Issues Related to Consolidation Policy and Procedures," the FASB received more than 70 letters. A sampling of these letters includes the following recommendations:

M. R. Schools, Jr., Virginia Power: Virginia Power believes that accounting information prepared under the proportionate consolidation approach provides the most relevant accounting information because it includes the interests of only the parent company shareholders.

David K. Owens, Edison Electric Institute: We generally support the "Parent Company Concept" because it emphasizes the interests of the parent shareholders and is most consistent with current practice.

Richard G. Rademacher, Sara Lee Corporation: By purchasing a controlling interest in an entity, management obtains the control of 100 percent of all assets and liabilities. It does not control only a proportionate share of each asset (i.e., 70% of a building) and the value of an asset recorded in consolidation does not vary dependent upon the percentage of ownership obtained. Therefore, we strongly oppose the parent company and proportionate share concepts of consolidation.

J. Michael Kelly, GTE Corporation: GTE has consistently responded in support of the parent company concept. The thrust of our support stems from this concept's emphasis on the interests of the parent's shareholders.

P. J. Lynch, Texaco Inc.: It is Texaco's view that neither the economic unit nor the parent company concept can be applied exclusively to all the issues raised in the DM. Accordingly any future promulgation concerning consolidation policy should be a hybrid of the two concepts.

Joseph J. Martin, IBM: While we take a parent's view of deciding when to consolidate, we generally favor an economic unit theory approach on the mechanics of consolidation and financial statement presentation.

John J. Mesloh, Pfizer Inc.: You may note that we favor the Parent Company view (which is consistent with our view of current written GAAP) of consolidation, as identified by the FASB. In short, we do not have too many issues with the current state of consolidation accounting.

What should the FASB decide to do?

In constructing a consolidated income statement, the parent company theory again demonstrates characteristics applicable to both the economic unit concept and proportionate consolidation. As with the economic unit concept, the entire amount of each subsidiary revenue and expense account is included in the total. Because these revenues and expenses are consolidated at 100 percent of their recorded balances, a 30 percent share of the subsidiary's net income is identified with the noncontrolling interest.

However, similar to proportionate consolidation, excess amortization is associated solely with the parent's investment because the allocations that create the expense result from the original payment. Consequently, such amortizations do not affect the calculation of noncontrolling interest. The additional cost is presumed to be that of the parent company and, thus, the expense is not directly related to the subsidiary's operations. *For reporting purposes, the subsidiary's income is simply multiplied times the outside ownership percentage.*

Under the parent company concept, the resulting noncontrolling interest figure has traditionally appeared as a reduction in arriving at consolidated net income. For example, following is the bottom portion of a typical income statement as reported by Citicorp:

CITICORP
Year Ended December 31, 2004
(in millions)

Income before income taxes and minority interests	$24,405
Income taxes	7,294
Minority interests	203
Net income	$16,908

As mentioned earlier, the FASB is currently studying valuation theories with the possibility that one concept will be mandated. Until that time, companies are free to select any approach and are not even required to disclose their choice. Although evidence is not readily available, the parent company concept is generally considered to be most commonly used in current practice. Therefore, except when noted, the parent company concept is used throughout the remainder of this textbook. Knowledge of the alternatives is important, though; companies do apply these other approaches, and the FASB can promote or require their use in the future.

VALUATION THEORIES—OVERVIEW

To provide a complete illustration of these three concepts, assume that Anderson Company acquires 60 percent of the voting stock of Zebulon Company on January 1, 2006. Anderson purchases this interest for $360,000 in cash at a time when Zebulon's assets and liabilities have the following values:

	Book Value 1/1/06	Fair Value 1/1/06
Current assets less liabilities	$160,000	$160,000
Buildings and equipment (10-year life)	240,000	360,000
	$400,000	$520,000

Assuming Anderson's $360,000 payment to acquire a 60 percent interest provides a sufficient basis to indicate the value of 100 percent of its stock, Zebulon is apparently worth $600,000 when taken as a whole ($360,000/60%). In comparison to the $520,000 appraised value of the net assets, this fair value signifies *total* goodwill associated with Zebulon of $80,000.

Exhibit 4.2 presents alternative values that can be attributed to Zebulon's accounts on consolidated statements produced as of the date of acquisition. Quite obviously, each of the three valuation theories results in differing figures. The economic unit concept makes no division of any balance, whereas proportionate consolidation includes only 60 percent of subsidiary accounts because that portion represents the parent's ownership. The parent company concept adopts a compromise position: The book values of the subsidiary's assets and liabilities remain intact while all cost allocations (based on the difference in book values and fair values) are computed using the parent's ownership percentage.

To carry this illustration to a natural conclusion, assume that Zebulon reports the following condensed income statement for the year of 2006:

Revenues	$400,000
Expenses	300,000
Net income	$100,000

EXHIBIT 4.2   Valuation Theories in Practice—Balance Sheet

ANDERSON COMPANY AND ZEBULON COMPANY
Subsidiary Consolidation Figures
Balance Sheet
January 1, 2006

	Economic Unit Concept	Proportionate Consolidation Concept	Parent Company Concept
Current assets and liabilities:			
Book value	$160,000 (100%)	$ 96,000 (60%)	$160,000 (100%)
Allocation based on fair value	–0–	–0–	–0–
Consolidated value	$160,000	$ 96,000	$160,000
Buildings and equipment:			
Book value	$240,000 (100%)	$144,000 (60%)	$240,000 (100%)
Allocation based on fair value	120,000 (100%)	72,000 (60%)	72,000 (60%)
Consolidated value	$360,000	$216,000	$312,000
Goodwill*	$ 80,000 (100%)	$ 48,000 (60%)	$ 48,000 (60%)
Noncontrolling interest, 1/1/06	$240,000 (40% of fair value)*	–0–	$160,000 (40% of book value)
Annual amortizations of allocations:			
Buildings and equipment (10-year life)	$ 12,000	$ 7,200	$ 7,200
Goodwill (indefinite life)	–0–	–0–	–0–
Annual expense	$ 12,000	$ 7,200	$ 7,200

*Fair value of company is $600,000 ($360,000/60%) with the value of net assets only $520,000. Total goodwill is $80,000 ($600,000 − $520,000).

These balances permit an examination of the totals to be included in the 2006 consolidated income statement. Exhibit 4.3 presents these figures, again computed under each of the three theories described in this chapter. The economic unit concept consolidates all accounts and assumes that amortization expense relates to the subsidiary. Proportionate consolidation includes only 60 percent of each revenue and expense and discloses no balance for the noncontrolling

EXHIBIT 4.3   Valuation Theories in Practice—Income Statement

ANDERSON COMPANY AND ZEBULON COMPANY
Subsidiary Consolidation Figures
Income Statement
For Year Ending December 31, 2006

	Economic Unit Concept	Proportionate Consolidation Concept	Parent Company Concept
Revenues	$400,000 (100%)	$240,000 (60%)	$400,000 (100%)
Expenses	300,000 (100%)	180,000 (60%)	300,000 (100%)
Excess amortization expenses (see Exhibit 4.2)	12,000	7,200	7,200
Noncontrolling interest in subsidiary's net income			40,000 (40% of subsidiary income, no amortization)
Net effect on consolidated net income	$ 88,000	$ 52,800	$ 52,800
Allocation of net income:			
To controlling interest (60%)	$ 52,800		
To noncontrolling interest (40%)	$ 35,200		

interest. The parent company concept recognizes all of the subsidiary's income statement accounts but attributes amortization to the parent so that the noncontrolling interest is not affected.

CONSOLIDATIONS INVOLVING A NONCONTROLLING INTEREST SUBSEQUENT TO ACQUISITION (PARENT COMPANY CONCEPT)

Having reviewed the basic philosophies of each of these three theories, we now concentrate on the mechanical aspects of the consolidation process when an outside ownership is present. More specifically, we examine consolidations for time periods subsequent to the date of acquisition to analyze the full range of accounting complexities created by a noncontrolling interest. As indicated previously, this discussion centers on the parent company concept because it is the most prevalent method in practice.

The presence of a noncontrolling interest does not dramatically alter the consolidation procedures demonstrated in Chapter 3. The unamortized balance of each purchase price allocation must still be computed and included within the consolidated totals. Excess amortization expenses on these allocations are recognized each year as appropriate. Reciprocal balances are eliminated.

Beyond these basic steps, the valuation and recognition of four noncontrolling interest balances add a new dimension to the process of consolidating financial information. The accountant must determine and then enter each of these figures when constructing a worksheet:

- Noncontrolling interest in the subsidiary as of the beginning of the current year.
- Noncontrolling interest in the subsidiary's current year income.
- Noncontrolling interest in the subsidiary's dividend payments.
- Noncontrolling interest as of the end of the year (found by combining the three balances above).

To illustrate, assume that King Company acquires 80 percent of the outstanding stock of Pawn Company on January 1, 2006, for $980,000 in cash. Exhibit 4.4 presents the book value of Pawn's accounts as well as the fair value of each asset and liability on the date of purchase.

King's $980,000 purchase price is attributed to Pawn's accounts as shown in Exhibit 4.5. Annual amortization relating to these allocations also is included in this schedule. Although expense figures are computed for only the initial years, some amount of amortization is recognized in each of the 20 years following the acquisition (the life assumed for the buildings).

EXHIBIT 4.4
Subsidiary Accounts—
Date of Acquisition

PAWN COMPANY
Account Balances
January 1, 2006

	Book Value	Fair Value	Differences
Current assets	$ 440,000	$ 440,000	–0–
Land	260,000	320,000	+$ 60,000
Buildings (20-year life)	480,000	600,000	+ 120,000
Equipment (10-year life)	110,000	100,000	(10,000)
Long-term liabilities (8-year maturity)	(550,000)	(510,000)	+ 40,000
Net assets	$ 740,000	$ 950,000	+$210,000
Common stock	$(230,000)		
Retained earnings, 1/1/06	(510,000)		

Note: Parentheses indicate a credit balance.

EXHIBIT 4.5

		KING COMPANY AND PAWN COMPANY	
		Purchase Price Allocation and Amortization	
		January 1, 2006	
	Allocation	Estimated Life (years)	Annual Excess Amortizations
Purchase price paid by King Company	$980,000		
80% of subsidiary book value ($740,000)			
(King Company's ownership)*	592,000		
Cost in excess of book value	388,000		
Allocation to specific accounts based on difference between fair value and book value:			
Land ($60,000 × 80%)	48,000		
Buildings ($120,000 × 80%)	96,000	20	4,800
Equipment ($10,000 × 80%)	(8,000)	10	(800)
Long-term liabilities ($40,000 × 80%)	32,000	8	4,000
Goodwill	$220,000	Indefinite	–0–
Annual amortizations (initial years)			$8,000

*The parent company concept consolidates 100 percent of all asset and liability book values but also records an offsetting noncontrolling interest of 20 percent. The net effect is equal to 80 percent of the subsidiary's book value.

Consolidated financial statements will be produced for the year ending December 31, 2007. This date is arbitrary. Any time period subsequent to 2006 could have served to demonstrate the applicable consolidation procedures. Having already calculated the purchase price allocations and related amortization, the accountant can construct a consolidation of these two companies along the lines demonstrated in Chapter 3. Only the presence of the 20 percent noncontrolling interest alters the previously explained process.

To complete the information needed for this combination, assume that Pawn Company reports the following changes in retained earnings since King's acquisition:

Current year (2007)	
Net income	$ 90,000
Less: Dividends paid	(50,000)
Increase in retained earnings	$ 40,000
Prior years (only 2006 in this illustration):	
Increase in retained earnings	$ 70,000

Assuming that King Company applies the equity method, the Investment in Pawn Company account as of December 31, 2007, can be constructed as shown in Exhibit 4.6.

Exhibit 4.7 presents the separate financial statements for these two companies as of December 31, 2007, and the year then ended, based on the information provided.

Consolidated Totals

Although the inclusion of a 20 percent outside ownership complicates the consolidation process, the 2007 totals to be reported by this business combination can still be determined without the use of a worksheet:

- *Revenues* = $1,340,000. The revenues of the parent and the subsidiary are added together. Under the parent company concept, the subsidiary's book value is included in total although King owns only 80 percent of the stock.

- *Cost of Goods Sold* = $550,000. The balances for the parent and subsidiary are added together.

EXHIBIT 4.6

KING COMPANY Investment in Pawn Company Equity Method December 31, 2007		
Purchase price		$ 980,000
Prior year (2006):		
Increase in retained earnings (80% × $70,000)	$56,000	
Excess amortization expenses (Exhibit 4.5)	(8,000)	48,000
Current year (2007):		
Income accrual (80% × $90,000)	72,000	
Excess amortization expense (Exhibit 4.5)	(8,000)	
Equity in subsidiary earnings	64,000*	
Dividends received (80% × $50,000)	(40,000)	24,000
Balance, 12/31/07		$1,052,000

*This figure appears in King's 2007 income statement.

- *Depreciation Expense* = $259,000. The balances for the parent and subsidiary are added together along with the $4,800 additional building depreciation and the $800 reduction in equipment depreciation as indicated in Exhibit 4.5.
- *Interest Expense* = $119,000. The balances for the parent and subsidiary are added along with an additional $4,000. As indicated in Exhibit 4.5, a reduction to fair value of Pawn's long-term debt accounted for $32,000 of the excess purchase price. Because the maturity

EXHIBIT 4.7

KING COMPANY AND PAWN COMPANY Separate Financial Statements For December 31, 2007, and the Year Then Ended		
	King	**Pawn**
Revenues	$ (910,000)	$ (430,000)
Cost of goods sold	350,000	200,000
Depreciation expense	160,000	95,000
Interest expense	70,000	45,000
Equity in subsidiary earnings (see Exhibit 4.6)	(64,000)	–0–
Net income	$ (394,000)	$ (90,000)
Retained earnings, 1/1/07	$ (881,600)	$ (580,000)
Net income (above)	(394,000)	(90,000)
Dividends paid	60,000	50,000
Retained earnings, 12/31/07	$(1,215,600)	$ (620,000)
Current assets	$ 626,000	$ 445,000
Land	298,000	295,000
Buildings (net)	880,000	540,000
Equipment (net)	290,000	160,000
Investment in Pawn Company (see Exhibit 4.6)	1,052,000	–0–
Total assets	$ 3,146,000	$ 1,440,000
Long-term liabilities	$(1,080,400)	$ (590,000)
Common stock	(850,000)	(230,000)
Retained earnings, 12/31/07	(1,215,600)	(620,000)
Total liabilities and equities	$(3,146,000)	$(1,440,000)

value remains constant, the $32,000 represents a discount that is amortized to interest expense over the remaining eight-year life of the debt.

- *Equity in Subsidiary Earnings* = –0–. The parent's investment income is eliminated so that the subsidiary's revenues and expenses can be included in the consolidated totals.
- *Noncontrolling Interest in Subsidiary's Income* = $18,000. The outside owners are assigned 20 percent of Pawn's reported income of $90,000. According to the parent company concept, that amount is shown as a reduction within the consolidated income statement.
- *Net Income* = $394,000. Both consolidated expenses and the amount allocated to the noncontrolling interest are subtracted from consolidated revenues.
- *Retained Earnings, 1/1/07* = $881,600. The parent company figure equals the consolidated total because the equity method was applied. If the cost method or the partial equity method had been used, the parent's balance would require adjustment to include any omitted figures.
- *Dividends Paid* = $60,000. Only the parent company balance is reported. Part of the subsidiary's payments (80 percent) were intercompany to the parent and are eliminated. The remaining distribution was made to the outside owners and serves to reduce the balance attributed to them.
- *Retained Earnings, 12/31/07* = $1,215,600. The balance is found by adding consolidated net income to the beginning Retained Earnings balance and then subtracting the consolidated dividends paid. Because the equity method is utilized, the parent company figure reflects the total for the business combination.
- *Current Assets* = $1,071,000. The parent's and subsidiary's book values are added.
- *Land* = $641,000. The parent's book value is added to the subsidiary's book value plus the $48,000 allocation within the purchase price (see Exhibit 4.5).
- *Buildings* = $1,506,400. The parent's book value is added to the subsidiary's book value plus the $96,000 allocation within the purchase price less 2006 and 2007 excess amortization of $4,800 per year (see Exhibit 4.5).
- *Equipment* = $443,600. The parent's book value is added to the subsidiary's book value less the $8,000 cost reduction allocation plus the 2006 and 2007 expense reduction of $800 per year (see Exhibit 4.5).
- *Investment in Pawn Company* = –0–. The balance reported by the parent is eliminated so that the subsidiary's assets and liabilities can be included in the consolidated totals.
- *Goodwill* = $220,000. The original allocation shown in Exhibit 4.5 is reported.
- *Total assets* = $3,882,000. This balance is a summation of the consolidated assets.
- *Long-Term Liabilities* = $1,646,400. The parent's book value is added to the subsidiary's book value less the $32,000 allocation within the purchase price plus 2006 and 2007 amortization of $4,000 per year (see Exhibit 4.5).
- *Noncontrolling Interest in Subsidiary* = $170,000. The outside ownership is 20 percent of the subsidiary's year-end book value (common stock plus ending retained earnings) of $850,000. This $170,000 total can also be calculated as follows:

Noncontrolling interest at 1/1/07 (20% of $810,000 beginning book value—common stock plus 1/1/07 retained earnings)	$162,000
Noncontrolling interest in subsidiary's income (computed above)	18,000
Dividends paid to noncontrolling interest (20% of $50,000 total)	(10,000)
Noncontrolling interest at 12/31/07	$170,000

- *Common Stock* = $850,000. Only the parent's book value is reported.
- *Retained Earnings, 12/31/07* = $1,215,600. Computed above.
- *Total Liabilities and Equities* = $3,882,000. This total is a summation of consolidated liabilities, noncontrolling interest, and equities.

Worksheet Process—Parent Company Concept

The consolidated totals for King and Pawn also can be determined by means of a worksheet as shown in Exhibit 4.8. A comparison of the worksheet entries made in this example with the

EXHIBIT 4.8   Noncontrolling Interest Illustrated—Parent Company Concept

KING COMPANY AND PAWN COMPANY

Consolidation: Purchase Method

Investment: Equity Method

Consolidation Worksheet

For Year Ending December 31, 2007

Ownership: 80%

Accounts	King Company*	Pawn Company*	Consolidation Entries Debit	Consolidation Entries Credit	Noncontrolling Interest	Consolidated Totals
Income Statement						
Revenues	(910,000)	(430,000)				(1,340,000)
Cost of goods sold	350,000	200,000				550,000
Depreciation expense	160,000	95,000	(E) 4,000			259,000
Interest expense	70,000	45,000	(E) 4,000			119,000
Equity in subsidiary earnings	(64,000)	–0–	(I) 64,000			–0–
Noncontrolling interest in Pawn Company's income	–0–	–0–			(18,000)	18,000
Net income	(394,000)	(90,000)				(394,000)
Statement of Retained Earnings						
Retained earnings, 1/1/07:						
King Company	(881,600)					(881,600)
Pawn Company		(580,000)	(S) 580,000			–0–
Net income (above)	(394,000)	(90,000)				(394,000)
Dividends paid	60,000	50,000		(D) 40,000	10,000	60,000
Retained earnings, 12/31/07	(1,215,600)	(620,000)				(1,215,600)
Balance Sheet						
Current assets	626,000	445,000				1,071,000
Land	298,000	295,000	(A) 48,000			641,000
Buildings (net)	880,000	540,000	(A) 91,200	(E) 4,800		1,506,400
Equipment (net)	290,000	160,000	(E) 800	(A) 7,200		443,600
Investment in Pawn Company	1,052,000	–0–	(D) 40,000	(S) 648,000		–0–
				(A) 380,000		
				(I) 64,000		
Goodwill	–0–	–0–	(A) 220,000			220,000
Total assets	3,146,000	1,440,000				3,882,000
Long-term liabilities	(1,080,400)	(590,000)	(A) 28,000	(E) 4,000		(1,646,400)
Noncontrolling interest in Pawn Company, 1/1/07	–0–	–0–		(S) 162,000	(162,000)	
Noncontrolling interest in Pawn Company, 12/31/07	–0–	–0–			(170,000)	(170,000)
Common stock	(850,000)	(230,000)	(S) 230,000			(850,000)
Retained earnings, 12/31/07 (above)	(1,215,600)	(620,000)				(1,215,600)
Total liabilities and equities	(3,146,000)	(1,440,000)	1,310,000	1,310,000		(3,882,000)

*See Exhibit 4.7.

Note : Parentheses indicate a credit balance.

Consolidation entries:

(S)   Elimination of subsidiary's stockholders' equity accounts along with recognition of January 1, 2007, noncontrolling interest.

(A)   Allocation of parent's cost in excess of subsidiary's book value, unamortized balances as of January 1, 2007.

(I)   Elimination of intercompany income (equity accrual less amortization expenses).

(D)   Elimination of intercompany dividend payments.

(E)   Recognition of amortization expenses on purchase price allocations.

entries incorporated in Chapter 3 (Exhibit 3.7) indicates that the presence of a noncontrolling interest does not create a significant number of changes in the consolidation procedures.

The worksheet still includes elimination of the subsidiary's stockholders' equity accounts (Entry **S**) although, as explained next, this entry is expanded to record the beginning noncontrolling interest for the year. The second worksheet entry recognizes the purchase price allocations at January 1 after one year of amortization (Entry **A**). Intercompany income as well as dividend payments are removed also (Entries **I** and **D**) while current year excess amortization expenses are recognized (Entry **E**). The differences that can be cited with illustrations in Chapter 3 relate exclusively to the recognition of four noncontrolling interest balances. In addition, *a separate Noncontrolling Interest column is added to the worksheet to accumulate the components that form the year-end figure to be reported on the consolidated balance sheet.*

Noncontrolling Interest—Beginning of Year   As discussed previously, Pawn's stockholders' equity accounts (common stock and beginning Retained Earnings) indicate a January 1, 2007, book value of $810,000. Thus, the 20 percent outside ownership is valued at $162,000 ($810,000 × 20%) as of the first day of the current year. This balance is recognized on the worksheet by means of Entry **S**:

Consolidation Entry S

Common Stock (Pawn)	230,000	
Retained Earnings, 1/1/07 (Pawn)	580,000	
Investment in Pawn Company (80%)		648,000
Noncontrolling Interest in Pawn Company, 1/1/07 (20%)		162,000
To eliminate beginning stockholders' equity accounts of subsidiary along with book value portion of investment (equal to 80 percent ownership). Noncontrolling interest of 20 percent is also recognized.		

The $162,000 balance assigned here to the outside owners at the beginning of the year is extended on the worksheet into the Noncontrolling Interest column (see Exhibit 4.7).

Noncontrolling Interest—Current Year Income   Exhibit 4.3 indicates that the parent company concept calculates the noncontrolling interest's share of current year earnings based on the subsidiary's income without regard for amortization. Thus, $18,000 (20 percent) of Pawn's 2007 $90,000 of earnings is assigned to the outside owners. This figure then reduces consolidated net income. In effect, 100 percent of each subsidiary revenue and expense account is consolidated with an accompanying 20 percent allocation to the noncontrolling interest. The 80 percent net effect corresponds to King's ownership.

Because $18,000 of consolidated income accrues to the noncontrolling interest, this amount is added to the $162,000 beginning balance assigned (in Entry **S**) to these outside owners. The noncontrolling interest increases because the subsidiary generated a profit during the period.

Although this allocation could be recorded on the worksheet through an additional entry, the $18,000 is usually shown, as in Exhibit 4.8, by means of a columnar adjustment. The current year accrual is simultaneously entered in the consolidated Income Statement column as a *reduction* and in the Noncontrolling Interest column as an *increase*. This procedure indicates that a portion of the combined earnings is assigned to the outside owners rather than to the parent company owners.

Noncontrolling Interest—Dividend Payments   The $40,000 dividend paid to the parent company is eliminated routinely through Entry **D**, but the remainder of Pawn's dividend was paid to the noncontrolling interest. The impact of the dividend (20 percent of the subsidiary's total payment) distributed to the other owners must be acknowledged. As shown in Exhibit 4.8, this remaining $10,000 is extended directly into the Noncontrolling Interest column on the worksheet as a reduction. It represents the drop in the underlying book value of the outside ownership that resulted from the subsidiary's asset distribution.

Noncontrolling Interest—End of Year   The ending assignment for these other owners is calculated by a summation of

1. The beginning balance for the year ($162,000).
2. Plus the appropriate share of the subsidiary's current income ($18,000).
3. Less the dividends paid to the outside owners ($10,000).

EXHIBIT 4.9
Consolidated Statements
with Noncontrolling
Interest—Parent Company
Concept

KING COMPANY AND PAWN COMPANY
Consolidated Financial Statements
Income Statement for December 31, 2007, and the Year Then Ended

Revenues	$1,340,000
Cost of goods sold	(550,000)
Depreciation expense	(259,000)
Interest expense	(119,000)
Noncontrolling interest in subsidiary income	(18,000)
Consolidated net income	$ 394,000

Statement of Retained Earnings

Retained earnings, January 1, 2007	$ 881,600
Consolidated net income	394,000
Less: Dividends paid	(60,000)
Retained earnings, December 31, 2007	$1,215,600

Balance Sheet

Assets

Current assets	$1,071,000
Land	641,000
Buildings (net)	1,506,400
Equipment (net)	443,600
Goodwill	220,000
Total assets	$3,882,000

Liabilities and Equities

Long-term liabilities	$1,646,400
Noncontrolling interest in subsidiary	170,000
Common stock—King Company	850,000
Retained earnings	1,215,600
Total liabilities and equities	$3,882,000

The Noncontrolling Interest column on the worksheet in Exhibit 4.8 accumulates these figures. The $170,000 total is then transferred to the balance sheet where it appears in the consolidated statements.

Consolidated Financial Statements

Having successfully consolidated the information for King and Pawn, the resulting financial statements for these two companies are produced in Exhibit 4.9. These figures can be computed directly or can be taken from the consolidation worksheet.

Effects Created by Alternative Investment Methods

In the King and Pawn illustration, the parent uses the equity method and bases all worksheet entries on that approach. As discussed in Chapter 3, had King incorporated either the cost method or the partial equity method, a few specific changes in the consolidation process would be required although the reported figures are not affected.

Cost Method

As in Chapter 3, the parent omits two balances if it applies the cost method. First, the parent recognizes dividend income rather than an equity income accrual. Thus, the parent fails to accrue the percentage of the subsidiary's income earned in past years in excess of dividends (the increase in subsidiary retained earnings). Second, the parent does not record amortization expense under the cost method and therefore must include it in the consolidation process if proper totals are to be achieved. Because neither of these figures is recognized in applying the cost method, an Entry ***C** is added to the worksheet to convert the previously recorded balances to the equity method. The parent's beginning Retained Earnings is affected by this adjustment as well as the Investment in Subsidiary account. The exact amount is computed as follows.

Conversion to Equity Method from Cost Method (Entry *C)   Combine:

1. The increase (since acquisition) in the subsidiary's retained earnings during past years (income less dividends) times the parent's ownership percentage, and
2. Total amortization expense for these same past years.

The parent's use of the cost method requires an additional procedural change. Under this method, the parent recognizes income from its subsidiary only when a dividend is received. Entry **I** removes both intercompany dividend income and subsidiary dividends paid to the parent. Thus, when the cost method is used, Entry **D** is unnecessary.

Partial Equity Method

Again, an Entry ***C** is needed to convert the parent's retained earnings as of January 1 to the equity method. In this case, however, only the amortization expense for the prior years must be included. Under the partial equity method, the income accrual is appropriately recognized each period by the parent company so that no further adjustment is necessary.

CONSOLIDATIONS INVOLVING A NONCONTROLLING INTEREST SUBSEQUENT TO ACQUISITION (ECONOMIC UNIT CONCEPT)

We next illustrate the preparation of consolidated financial statement under the economic unit concept as proposed by the FASB in its 2005 Exposure Drafts. The economic unit concept focuses on incorporating in the consolidated financial statements 100 percent of the subsidiary's fair value *as of the date of acquisition*. Note that subsequent to acquisition, changes in fair value are not recorded.[6] Instead, similar to the parent company concept, the subsidiary assets acquired and liabilities assumed are reflected in future consolidated financial statements using their date of acquisition fair values that are subsequently amortized (or possibly reduced for impairment). Under the economic unit concept, initial and subsequent fair value allocations to the subsidiary's assets and liabilities recognize a corresponding proportionate value as part of the noncontrolling interest.

We demonstrate the procedures under the economic unit concept through the preparation of a consolidated worksheet using the same example previously employed to illustrate the parent company concept. Again, assume that King purchases 80 percent of Pawn for $980,000. Under the economic unit concept, however, the equivalent fair value of 100 percent of Pawn serves as the valuation basis for consolidation. Therefore, we add the assumption that the $980,000 purchase price represents the best available evidence for measuring the fair value of Pawn Company as a whole. Thus, an equivalent fair value of $1,225,000 ($980,000 ÷ 80%) is assigned to Pawn Company and provides a valuation basis for the assets acquired, liabilities assumed, and noncontrolling interest.

Exhibit 4.10 shows the allocation of the $1,225,000 fair value to Pawn's net assets as of the January 1, 2005, date of acquisition and the related excess amortizations for subsequent year consolidations. Note that all allocations of Pawn's fair value represent 100 percent adjustments to the assets and liabilities from book value to fair values. Under the economic unit concept, Pawn's values do not depend on the percentage ownership of the controlling versus the noncontrolling interest. Pawn Company's accounts will be combined as a single economic unit with a single valuation basis—fair value.

---

[6] Exceptions common to all firms (whether subject to consolidation or not) include write-ups of marketable equity securities and other financial instruments.

EXHIBIT 4.10

KING COMPANY AND PAWN COMPANY
Fair Value Allocation and Amortization—Economic Unit Concept*
January 1, 2005

	Allocation	Estimated Life (years)	Annual Excess Amortizations
Pawn's fair value	$1,225,000		
Pawn's book value at acquisition	740,000		
Fair value in excess of book value	$ 485,000		
Allocation to specific accounts based on difference between fair value and book value:			
Land	60,000		
Buildings	120,000	20	6,000
Equipment	(10,000)	10	(1,000)
Long-term liabilities	40,000	8	5,000
Goodwill	$ 275,000	Indefinite	–0–
Annual amortizations (initial years)			$10,000

*The economic unit concept consolidates 100 percent of all asset and liability book values but also records an offsetting noncontrolling interest of 20 percent. The net effect is equal to 80 percent of the subsidiary's fair value for the parent and 20 percent for the noncontrolling interest.

We again assume that King, in its internal accounting records, applies the equity method to its Investment in Pawn account with the same December 31, 2007, balance of $1,052,000 as provided in Exhibit 4.6. Note that King does not account for the noncontrolling interest in its internal accounting records—the noncontrolling interest emerges through preparation of the consolidated financial statement. Therefore, using the equity method, King recognizes only its 80 percent of Pawn's income less its 80 percent of dividends received and excess amortizations. Under the economic unit concept, the noncontrolling interest is introduced on the consolidated worksheet. The final consolidated amounts then reflect 100 percent of Pawn's fair value as of the acquisition date and subsequently amortized.

Worksheet Process—Economic Unit Concept

Exhibit 4.11 shows the December 31, 2007, consolidated worksheet for King and Pawn companies under the economic unit concept. Subsidiary assets and liabilities are adjusted to full fair value at the date of acquisition regardless of the corresponding noncontrolling interest percentage ownership.

Several comparisons between the economic unit worksheet in Exhibit 4.11 and the parent company worksheet in Exhibit 4.8 provide insights into the valuation differences across the two concepts. First note the fundamental fair value allocation to the noncontrolling interest provided by the economic unit concept as revealed in Consolidation Entry **A.**

Consolidation Entry A—Economic Unit Concept

Land	60,000	
Buildings	114,000	
Goodwill	275,000	
Liabilities	35,000	
Equipment		9,000
Investment in Pawn Company (80%)		380,000
Noncontrolling Interest in Subsidiary, 1/1/07 (20%)		95,000
To recognize unamortized excess fair value as of January 1, 2007, to Pawn's assets acquired and liabilities assumed in the combination. Also to allocate the unamortized fair value to the noncontrolling interest.		

EXHIBIT 4.11   Noncontrolling Interest Illustrated—Economic Unit Concept

KING COMPANY AND PAWN COMPANY
Consolidation Worksheet
For Year Ending December 31, 2007

Accounts	King Company	Pawn Company	Consolidation Entries Debit	Consolidation Entries Credit	Noncontrolling Interest	Consolidated Totals
Revenues	(910,000)	(430,000)				(1,340,000)
Cost of goods sold	350,000	200,000				550,000
Depreciation expense	160,000	95,000	(E) 5,000			260,000
Interest expense	70,000	45,000	(E) 5,000			120,000
Equity in subsidiary earnings (see Exhibit 4.6)	(64,000)	–0–	(I) 64,000			–0–
Noncontrolling interest in Pawn income					(16,000)	16,000
Net income to controlling interest	(394,000)	(90,000)				(394,000)
Retained earnings, 1/1/07	(881,600)	(580,000)	(S) 580,000			(881,600)
Net income (above)	(394,000)	(90,000)				(394,000)
Dividends paid	60,000	50,000		(D) 40,000	10,000	60,000
Retained earnings, 12/31/07	(1,215,600)	(620,000)				(1,215,600)
Current assets	626,000	445,000				1,071,000
Land	298,000	295,000	(A) 60,000			653,000
Buildings (net)	880,000	540,000	(A) 114,000	(E) 6,000		1,528,000
Equipment (net)	290,000	160,000	(E) 1,000	(A) 9,000		442,000
Investment in Pawn Company (see Exhibit 4.6)	1,052,000	–0–	(D) 40,000	(S) 648,000 (A) 380,000 (I) 64,000		–0–
Goodwill	–0–	–0–	(A) 275,000			275,000
Total assets	3,146,000	1,440,000				3,969,000
Long-term liabilities	(1,080,400)	(590,000)	(A) 35,000	(E) 5,000		(1,640,400)
Common stock	(850,000)	(230,000)	(S) 230,000			(850,000)
				(S) 162,000		
Noncontrolling interest in Pawn 1/1/07				(A) 95,000	(257,000)	
Noncontrolling interest in Pawn 12/31/07					(263,000)	(263,000)
Retained earnings, 12/31/07	(1,215,600)	(620,000)				(1,215,600)
Total liabilities and equities	(3,146,000)	(1,440,000)	1,409,000	1,409,000		(3,969,000)

Consolidation entries:
  (S) Elimination of subsidiary's stockholders' equity along with recognition of 1/1/07 noncontrolling interest.
  (A) Allocation of subsidiary total fair value in excess of book value, unamortized balances as of 1/1/07.
  (I)   Elimination of intercompany income (equity accrual less amortization expenses).
  (D) Elimination of intercompany dividend payments.
  (E) Recognition of amortization expenses on fair value allocations.

In Entry **A** under the economic unit concept, subsidiary assets and liabilities are adjusted to their full (unamortized) fair values as of the acquisition date. In contrast, under the parent company concept, only an 80 percent adjustment is made. The economic unit concept approach thus produces a higher net asset value; however, the entire extra amount is allocated to the noncontrolling interest.

The allocation of the combined incomes of King and Pawn also provides contrasts across the two valuation concepts. Note that the $394,000 income to the controlling interest shareholders is identical across the parent company and economic unit concepts as is reported consolidated retained earnings. In contrast, observe that the noncontrolling interest share of combined entity net income is $18,000 under the parent company concept but only $16,000 under the economic unit concept, computed as follows:

	Parent Company	Economic Unit
Pawn's reported net income	$90,000	$90,000
Allocated excess amortization expenses	–0–	(10,000)
Pawn's adjusted net income	90,000	80,000
Noncontrolling interest percentage	20%	20%
Noncontrolling interest share of combined entity net income	$18,000	$16,000

These income effects highlight the fact that the primary difference between the parent company and economic unit concepts rests with noncontrolling interest valuation. Under the parent company concept, the noncontrolling interest is valued at the carryover book value basis of the subsidiary and thus bears no excess cost amortization. Under the economic unit concept, because the noncontrolling interest receives an initial excess fair value allocation for the subsidiary's net assets (Entry **A**), it also bears a portion of the amortization of the fair value allocation.

The final reported values for the noncontrolling interest (NCI) for the parent company and economic unit concepts can be compared as follows:

	Parent Company	Economic Unit
NCI share of subsidiary book value 1/1/07	$162,000	$162,000
Allocated unamortized excess fair value 1/1/07	–0–	95,000
Adjusted NCI balance 1/1/07	162,000	257,000
NCI share of combined net income	18,000	16,000
NCI share of subsidiary dividends	(10,000)	(10,000)
NCI balance 12/31/07	$170,000	$263,000

As these figures show, the parent company concept values the noncontrolling interest at the carryover subsidiary book value basis whereas the economic unit concept employs a fair value basis for the entire subsidiary, effectively ignoring past subsidiary book values.

STEP ACQUISITIONS

PepsiAmericas, Inc., reported in its recent annual financial statements,

> In March 2004, we acquired 2,000 additional shares of Pepsi-Cola Bahamas for $3.3 million, which increased our ownership interest in the Bahamas from 30 percent to 70 percent. As a result, we have consolidated the Bahamas beginning in the first quarter of 2004.

In all previous consolidation illustrations, control over a subsidiary was assumed to have been achieved through a single transaction. Obviously, PepsiAmericas' takeover of Pepsi-Cola Bahamas shows that a combination also can be the result of a series of stock purchases. These step acquisitions further complicate the consolidation process. The financial information of the separate companies must still be brought together, but no single purchase price exists. How do the initial acquisitions affect this process?

> If a parent-subsidiary relationship is established in a step acquisition, a problem arises that does not exist if the parent-subsidiary relationship is established in a single transaction. *That problem is how to include in consolidated financial statements the portion of the parent's interest in the subsidiary that was purchased prior to the date the parent-subsidiary relationship is established* [emphasis added].[7]

[7] FASB, *An Analysis of Issues Related to Consolidation Policy and Procedures,* para. 289. The FASB's Project Summary *Business Combinations: Purchase Method Procedures,* April 1, 2003, also addresses the issue of step acquisitions.

EXHIBIT 4.12
Allocation of First Purchase

ART COMPANY AND ZIP COMPANY	
Purchase Price Allocation and Amortization	
January 1, 2005	
Purchase price	$ 164,000
Book value equivalent of Art's ownership ($400,000 × 30%)	(120,000)
Customer base	$ 44,000
Assumed life	20 years
Annual amortization expense	$ 2,200

For example, in consolidating the accounts of Pepsi-Cola Bahamas, the values to be reported could vary significantly depending on PepsiAmericas' handling of the 30 percent ownership that it held prior to gaining control.

The FASB's recommendation for the economic unit concept for consolidated financial reporting (2005 Exposure Draft, *Business Combinations*) extends to step acquisitions. However, the recommendation is for a prospective treatment, thus requiring coverage of both the parent company concept (GAAP projected until December 15, 2006) and the economic unit concept.

Step Acquisitions—Parent Company Concept

Under the parent company concept, each investment is viewed as an individual purchase (sometimes referred to as a *layer*) with its own cost allocations and related amortization. To illustrate, assume that Art Company purchases 30 percent of Zip Company on January 1, 2005, for $164,000 in cash. As of the date of this acquisition, Zip is reporting a net book value of $400,000.

Assuming that Art has gained the ability to significantly influence Zip's decision-making process, this investment, for external reporting purposes, is accounted for by means of the equity method as discussed in Chapter 1. Thus, Art must determine any allocations and amortization associated with its purchase price (see Exhibit 4.12). A customer base with a 20-year life represented the initial excess payment.

As discussed previously, application of the equity method requires the accrual of investee income by the parent while any dividends received are recorded as a decrease in the Investment account. Art must also reduce both the income and asset balances in recognition of the annual $2,200 amortization indicated in Exhibit 4.12. If, over the next two years, Zip reports a total of $140,000 in net income and pays dividends of $40,000, the subsidiary's book value rises from $400,000 to $500,000. At the same time, the parent's investment account grows to $189,600:

Purchase price—1/1/05	$164,000
Accrual of 2005–06 equity income ($140,000 × 30%)	42,000
Dividends received 2005–06 ($40,000 × 30%)	(12,000)
Amortization ($2,200 per year for 2 years)	(4,400)
Investment in Zip, 12/31/06	$189,600

On January 1, 2007, Art's ownership is raised to 80 percent by the purchase of another 50 percent of Zip Company's outstanding common stock for $350,000. Although the equity method can still be utilized for internal reporting, this second purchase necessitates the preparation of consolidated financial statements beginning in 2007. Art now controls Zip; the two companies should be viewed as a single economic entity for external reporting purposes.

Before computing any consolidated balances, Art must make a separate cost allocation for this second purchase (Exhibit 4.13). In this purchase, the excess is attributable to Zip's substantially expanded customer base. This schedule does not supersede the allocation made in Exhibit 4.12 but merely supplements it for the price paid in acquiring the 50 percent block of Zip's stock.

EXHIBIT 4.13
Allocation of Second
Purchase

ART COMPANY AND ZIP COMPANY Purchase Price Allocation and Amortization January 1, 2007	
Purchase price	$ 350,000
Book value equivalent of Art's ownership ($500,000 × 50%)	(250,000)
Customer base	$ 100,000
Assumed life	20 years
Annual amortization expense	$ 5,000

Worksheet Consolidation for a Step Acquisition

To complete this example, assume that the subsidiary earns $100,000 in net income during
2007 and distributes $20,000 as a cash dividend. If the parent company continues applying the
equity method to this investment, Art reports an Equity in Subsidiary Earnings balance of
$72,800 for 2007 and an Investment in Zip Company of $596,400:

Investment in Zip, 12/31/06 (computed above)		$189,600
January 1, 2007—Second acquisition		350,000
Dividends received—2007 ($20,000 × 80%)		(16,000)
Equity income accrual—2007 ($100,000 × 80%)	$80,000	
2007 amortization: First purchase (Exhibit 4.12)	(2,200)	
Second purchase (Exhibit 4.13)	(5,000)	72,800
Investment in Zip, 12/31/07		$596,400

After determining both investment balances, the worksheet shown in Exhibit 4.14 can be
developed. Although this step acquisition might appear to be more complex than a single purchase, the actual consolidation process is the same as in previous examples.

- No conversion to the equity method (Entry *C) is required because the parent has applied
  that method. If the parent used a different approach it would have recognized amortization
  expense for prior years along with, possibly, the proportionate increase in the subsidiary's
  book value for this same period.
- Entry S removes the stockholders' equity accounts of Zip. This worksheet entry also establishes the $100,000 beginning balance for the 20 percent noncontrolling interest that still
  remains (20 percent multiplied by the $500,000 stockholders' equity as of January 1 of the
  current year).
- Entry A brings the unamortized purchase price allocations into the consolidation. The
  $44,000 balance resulting from the first transaction has already undergone two years of
  amortization. Thus, a cost of only $39,600 remains at the beginning of the current period.
  Because the second allocation ($100,000) was made on January 1 of the current year, no
  expense has been recorded in prior years.
- Entry I on the worksheet eliminates the $72,800 equity income accrual calculated above.
- Entry D removes the $16,000 current year intercompany dividend paid to the parent. The
  remaining 20 percent ($4,000) was paid to the outside owners. Thus, that amount is ex-
  tended to the Noncontrolling Interest column on the worksheet as a reduction.
- The final consolidation entry (Entry E) recognizes total excess amortizations for the current period.
- The noncontrolling interest balances to be reported on the income statement and balance
  sheet must be computed before the worksheet can be completed. Because Art now holds
  80 percent of Zip, the outside owner's share of the subsidiary's income is 20 percent of the
  $100,000 reported earnings (or $20,000). Once again, this assignment is recorded on the
  worksheet through a columnar entry: The Noncontrolling Interest column is increased by
  that amount with a parallel decrease to consolidated net income.

EXHIBIT 4.14   Step Acquisition Illustrated—Parent Company Concept

ART COMPANY AND ZIP COMPANY
Consolidation Worksheet
For Year Ending December 31, 2007

Consolidation: Purchase Method
Investment: Equity Method

Accounts	Art Company	Zip Company	Consolidation Entries Debit	Consolidation Entries Credit	Noncontrolling Interest	Consolidated Totals
Income Statement						
Revenues	(600,000)	(260,000)				(860,000)
Expenses	425,000	160,000	(E) 7,200			592,200
Equity in subsidiary earnings	(72,800)	–0–	(I) 72,800			–0–
Noncontrolling interest in Zip Company's income	–0–	–0–			(20,000)	20,000
Net income	(247,800)	(100,000)				(247,800)
Statement of Retained Earnings						
Retained earnings, 1/1/07:						
Art Company	(757,800)					(757,800)
Zip Company		(230,000)	(S) 230,000			
Net income (above)	(247,800)	(100,000)				(247,800)
Dividends paid	126,400	20,000		(D) 16,000	4,000	126,400
Retained earnings, 12/31/07	(879,200)	(310,000)				(879,200)
Balance Sheet						
Current assets	505,800	280,000				785,800
Land	205,000	90,000				295,000
Buildings (net)	646,000	310,000				956,000
Investment in Zip Company	596,400	–0–	(D) 16,000	(A) 139,600		–0–
				(S) 400,000		
				(I) 72,800		
Customer base	–0–	–0–	(A) 39,600	(E) 2,200		132,400
			(A) 100,000	(E) 5,000		
Total assets	1,953,200	680,000				2,169,200
Liabilities	(459,000)	(100,000)				(559,000)
Noncontrolling interest in Zip Company, 1/1/07	–0–	–0–		(S) 100,000	(100,000)	
Noncontrolling interest in Zip Company, 12/31/07					(116,000)	(116,000)
Common stock	(355,000)	(200,000)	(S) 200,000			(355,000)
Additional paid-in capital	(260,000)	(70,000)	(S) 70,000			(260,000)
Retained earnings, 12/31/07 (above)	(879,200)	(310,000)				(879,200)
Total liabilities and equities	(1,953,200)	(680,000)	735,600	735,600		(2,169,200)

Note: Parentheses indicate a credit balance.
Consolidation entries:
(S) Elimination of subsidiary's stockholders' equity accounts along with recognition of January 1, 2007, noncontrolling interest.
(A) Allocation of parent's cost in excess of subsidiary's book value for unamortized balances as of January 1, 2007. Two separate allocations are shown because two purchases were made.
(I) Elimination of intercompany income (equity accrual less amortization expense).
(D) Elimination of intercompany dividend payments.
(E) Recognition of amortization expense on customer base resulting from purchase price.

For the balance sheet, the ending amount applicable to these outside owners is determined within the Noncontrolling Interest column: Assigned income of $20,000 is added to the $100,000 beginning balance with dividends of $4,000 being subtracted. The $116,000 total then is reported on the balance sheet between the liabilities and stockholders' equity.

Retrospective Treatment Created by Step Acquisition

Because the initial 30 percent acquisition gave Art the ability to exercise significant influence over Zip, the investment balances in 2005 and 2006 were recorded using the equity method.

For external reporting, the subsidiary's operations as well as related amortization were accounted for in those years in a manner that parallels the consolidation process. Thus, the financial statements that Art prepared and distributed in 2005 and 2006 are considered comparable with the consolidated statements produced for 2007. Consequently, no retrospective application of the earlier figures is required by Art's change in the method of reporting its investment in Zip.

Conversely, if Art had originally secured only a small percentage of Zip's shares (achieving less than significant influence), the fair-value method would have been applied during 2005 and 2006. Under this approach, except for amounts received in the form of dividends, the owner ignores subsidiary income and the recording of any amortization. However, gaining control of Zip in 2007 necessitates a transformation to consolidated statements, a change that strains the comparability of the results reported in the earlier years. Thus, to establish a proper degree of consistency, the parent restates both the investment and income accounts as if the equity method had been utilized from the date of the first acquisition.

ARB 51 (para. 9) does allow one exception to this restatement policy by indicating that "if small purchases are made over a period of time and then a purchase is made which results in control, the date of the latest purchase, as a matter of convenience, may be considered as the date of acquisition." Therefore, retrospective application is not required when initial acquisition levels are relatively small. The ARB apparently felt that the difficulties encountered in restating such minor amounts outweighed the benefits derived from establishing comparability.

Step Acquisitions—Economic Unit Concept

To illustrate a step acquisition using the economic unit concept, assume that on January 1, 2006, Amanda Co. purchases 70 percent of Zoe, Inc., for $350,000. We also assume that the $350,000 purchase price paid by Amanda represents the best available evidence for measuring the fair value of Zoe Company as a whole. Therefore, Zoe Company's fair value is assessed at $500,000 ($350,000 ÷ 70%). Because Zoe's net assets have book values equal to its fair value of $400,000, under the economic unit concept, goodwill of $100,000 is recognized as the difference between the fair value of $500,000 and net asset fair value of $400,000. On January 1, 2007, when Zoe's book value has increased to $420,000, Amanda buys another 20 percent of Zoe for $95,000, bringing its total ownership up to 90 percent.

Under the economic unit concept, the valuation basis for Zoe's net assets was established on January 1, 2006, the date Amanda obtained control. Subsequent transactions in the subsidiary's stock (purchases or sales) are now viewed as transactions in the economic unit's own stock. Therefore, no gains or losses are recognized, and differences between transaction prices and the underlying subsidiary book value are simply treated as adjustments to Additional Paid-In Capital. The difference between the $95,000 price and the underlying consolidated book value is computed as follows:

1/1/07 purchase price for 20 percent interest		$ 95,000
Noncontrolling interest (NCI) acquired:		
Book value (20%) 1/1/07	$84,000	
Goodwill (20%)	20,000	
Noncontrolling interest book value 1/1/07		104,000
Additional paid-in capital from 20 percent NCI acquisition . . .		$ 9,000

By purchasing 20 percent of Zoe for $95,000, the consolidated entity's owners have acquired a portion of their own firm at a price $9,000 less than consolidated book value. From a worksheet perspective, the $95,000 purchase price and the $9,000 credit to Additional Paid-In Capital offset the recognition of the additional $104,000 in consolidated net assets from the

20 percent purchase. Importantly, the $95,000 purchase price for the 20 percent interest in Zoe's net assets does not affect consolidated asset valuation. From the economic unit perspective, the basis for the reported values in the consolidated financial statements was established on the date control was obtained.

Finally, if a parent acquires control over a subsidiary in which it already held an investment, the investment account is adjusted to its fair value on the date that the parent obtains control. A gain or loss from this adjustment is recognized in current earnings.

REVENUE AND EXPENSE REPORTING FOR MID-YEAR ACQUISITIONS

In virtually all of our previous examples, the parent has gained control of the subsidiary on the first day of the fiscal year. How is the consolidation process affected if an acquisition occurs on a mid-year (any other than the first day of the fiscal year) date?

If a company gains control at a mid-year date, a few obvious changes are needed. The new parent must compute the subsidiary's book value as of that date so that an appropriate comparison with the purchase price can be made to determine excess cost allocations (e.g., intangibles). Excess amortization expenses as well as any equity accrual and dividend collections are recognized for a period of less than a year. A slightly more complex issue to be resolved, though, is determining the amount of subsidiary revenues and expenses to include in consolidated totals. One alternative typically applied in practice is to simply include only post-acquisition revenue and expenses from consolidated totals. Another approach includes *all* pre- and post-acquisition current year subsidiary revenues and expenses followed by a separate deduction for a *pre-acquisition earnings* figure. Each approach is discussed below.

Consolidate Only Post-Acquisition Subsidiary Revenue and Expenses

Typically, a parent company will exclude current year subsidiary revenue and expense amounts that have accrued prior to the acquisition date from its consolidated totals.[8] For example, on November 18, 2002, Comcast Corporation completed its acquisition of AT&T Broadband. Comcast, in its December 31 year-end income statement, included AT&T Broadband revenues and expenses only subsequent to the acquisition date. For fiscal year 2002 Comcast reported revenues on its income statement of $8.1 billion. In a pro forma schedule Comcast noted that had it included AT&T Broadband's revenues from January 1, 2002, total revenue for the year would have been $16.8 billion. However, because the $8.7 billion additional revenue ($16.8 billion − $8.1 billion) was not earned by Comcast owners, Comcast excluded this pre-acquisition revenue from its consolidated total.

To further illustrate the complexities of accounting for a mid-year acquisition, assume that Tyler Company purchases 90 percent of Stevens Company on July 1, 2006, for $900,000 and prepares the following cost allocation schedule:

Purchase price, 7/1/06		$900,000
Book value acquired (90%)		
Common stock	$600,000	
Retained earnings, 7/1/06	200,000	
Book value, 7/1/06	$800,000	
Ownership	90%	720,000
Excess cost		180,000
Adjust trademark to fair value (4-year life) . . .		180,000
		−0−

[8] The 2005 FASB Exposure Draft, *Consolidated Financial Statements, Including Accounting and Reporting of Noncontrolling Interests in Subsidiaries,* recommends that the consolidated income statement include subsidiary revenues and expenses only subsequent to the date of acquisition, consistent with much of current practice.

The affiliates report the following 2006 income statement amounts from their own separate operations:

	Tyler	Stevens
Revenues	$450,000	$200,000
Expenses	325,000	150,000
Dividends (paid quarterly)	100,000	20,000

Assuming that all revenues and expenses occurred evenly throughout the year and that Tyler excludes the pre-acquisition revenues and expenses of its newly acquired subsidiary, the December 31, 2006, consolidated income statement appears as follows:

TYLER COMPANY
Consolidated Income Statement
For the Year Ended December 31, 2006

Revenues	$550,000
Expenses	422,500
Net income before noncontrolling interest	127,500
Noncontrolling interest in Stevens Company income	2,500
Consolidated net income	$125,000

The consolidated income components are computed below:

- Revenues = $650,000 combined amounts less $100,000 ($^{1}/_{2}$ of Stevens's revenues).
- Expenses = $475,000 combined amounts less $75,000 ($^{1}/_{2}$ of Stevens's expenses) plus $22,500 excess amortization for $^{1}/_{2}$ year ($180,000 ÷ 4 years × $^{1}/_{2}$ year).
- Noncontrolling interest in Stevens's income = (10% × $50,000 × $^{1}/_{2}$ year) = $2,500.

In this example, pre-acquisition subsidiary revenue and expense accounts are simply eliminated from the consolidated totals. Note also that by excluding 100 percent of the pre-acquisition income accounts from consolidation, the noncontrolling interest is viewed as coming into being as of the parent's acquisition date.

A mid-year acquisition requires additional adjustments when preparing consolidating worksheets. The balances the subsidiary submits for consolidation typically include results for its entire fiscal period. Thus, in the December 31 financial statements, the book value of the firm acquired on a mid-year date is reflected by a January 1 retained earnings balance plus revenues, expenses, and dividends paid from the beginning of the year to the acquisition date. To effectively eliminate subsidiary book value as of the acquisition date, Consolidation Entry **S** includes these items in addition to the other usual elements of book value (i.e., stock accounts). To illustrate, assuming that both affiliates submit fiscal year financial statements for consolidation, Tyler would make the following 2006 consolidation worksheet entry:

Consolidation Worksheet Entry S

Common stock—Stevens	600,000	
Retained earnings—Stevens (1/1/06)*	185,000	
Revenues	100,000	
Dividends paid—Stevens		10,000
Expenses		75,000
Noncontrolling interest (7/1/06)		80,000
Investment in Stevens		720,000

*July 1 balance of $200,000 less income from first six months of $25,000 (1/2 of $50,000 annual Stevens income) plus $10,000 dividends paid.

Through Entry **S,** pre-acquisition subsidiary revenues, expenses, and dividends are effectively

- Included as part of the subsidiary book value elimination in the year of acquisition.
- Included as components of the beginning value of the noncontrolling interest.
- Excluded from the consolidated income statement and statement of retained earnings.

In subsequent years, the need to separate pre- and post-acquisition amounts is limited to ensuring that excess amortizations correctly reflect the mid-year acquisition date. Finally, if the parent employs the cost method of accounting for the investment in subsidiary on its books, the conversion to the equity method must also reflect only post-acquisition amounts.

Consolidate Pre- and Post-Acquisition Subsidiary Revenue and Expenses

ARB 51 allows a different reporting technique as an alternative to the elimination of current year pre-acquisition subsidiary revenues and expenses. This approach includes all subsidiary revenues and expenses as if the acquisition took place at the beginning of the year. Then a "preacquisition earnings" line item removes the parent's share of subsidiary income earned prior to the acquisition date from consolidated income. Paragraph 10 of *ARB 51* addresses the issue by stating

> When a subsidiary is purchased during the year, there are alternative ways of dealing with the results of its operations in the consolidated income statement. One method, which usually is preferable, especially where there are several dates of acquisition of blocks of shares, is to include the subsidiary in the consolidation as though it had been acquired at the beginning of the year, and to deduct at the bottom of the consolidated income statement the pre-acquisition earnings applicable to each block of stock. This method presents results which are more indicative of the current status of the group, and facilitates future comparison with subsequent years.

The establishment of a pre-acquisition earnings amount of the acquisition year consolidated income statement represented an attempt to provide comparability across current and future fiscal years for consolidated revenue and expense figures. Importantly, the ARB's suggested handling of this matter has no effect on the amount of consolidated net income. Rather, the pronouncement simply constructs the income statement in a manner that provides comparability with future periods.[9]

SALES OF SUBSIDIARY STOCK

Although this textbook has concentrated on the acquisition and ownership of large blocks of corporate securities, the business world also encounters the eventual sale of these stocks. For example, a note to the 2002 financial statements of Sara Lee Corporation states (dollar amounts in millions other than per share values):

> A tax-free gain of $967, or $1.13 of diluted earnings per share, was recognized on the disposition of the Coach business in 2001. This disposition took place in two steps. In October 2000, the corporation's Coach subsidiary completed an initial public offering of 19.5 percent (8,487,000 shares) of its common stock. Cash proceeds of $122 were received and a tax-free gain of $105 was recognized upon completion of the offering. In April 2001, the second step of the disposition was completed when the corporation's remaining 80.5 percent (35,026,333 shares) ownership interest in Coach was exchanged with third parties for 41,402,285 shares of Sara Lee common stock. The market value of the Coach shares disposed of was $998, and an $862 gain was recognized on this tax-free transaction.

Under the parent company concept, accounting for the disposition of such shares parallels the sale of any corporate asset: The investment is adjusted to the appropriate book value as of

---

[9] Current practice typically provides comparability across fiscal years through pro forma disclosures of various categories of revenue and expense as if the combination had occurred at the beginning of the reporting period. With the advent of modern information systems, separate cutoffs for revenues and expenses are readily available. A Lexis-Nexis™ search of SEC 10-K annual reports revealed that very few firms currently use a pre-acquisition earnings figure in acquisition year income statements.

the date of sale and then removed from the records of the parent company.[10] Any difference in the recorded balance and the consideration received is recognized as a gain or loss.

Establishment of Investment Book Value

Any necessary adjustment to the investment account depends on the accounting method that the parent uses for internal reporting purposes. If the equity method has been applied, little problem should exist in recording the transaction. The parent correctly reports the investment as of the beginning of the year so that only the normal equity method adjustments are needed to reflect operations and amortization for the current period.

However, if the parent has utilized either the cost or the partial equity method, the adjustment process is more complicated. As indicated previously, both of these alternatives offer a convenient means to monitor a subsidiary. Unfortunately, neither produces the accurate book value necessary for recording a sales transaction. Therefore, when either of these other methods has been applied, the parent's Investment in Subsidiary account must be updated as if the equity method had been applied since the date of acquisition.

To illustrate, assume that Giant Company owns 80 percent of Tiny Company. Initially, Giant acquires a 50 percent interest in 2003 for $600,000 and purchases the additional 30 percent in 2005 for $440,000. If Giant elects to account for this subsidiary using the equity method, the Investment in Tiny account contains a $1,245,000 balance as of January 1, 2007, based on the following assumed figures:

	Cost	Income Accrual Since Acquisition	Dividends	Excess Amortization	Investment Balance 1/1/07
2003 purchase	$ 600,000	$200,000	$(15,000)	$(40,000)	$ 745,000
2005 purchase	440,000	100,000	(6,000)	(34,000)	500,000
Totals	$1,040,000	$300,000	$(21,000)	$(74,000)	$1,245,000

Sale Made at Beginning of Year

Appropriate application of the equity method signifies that the $1,245,000 is a correctly recorded balance. Assuming that Giant sells this entire interest on January 1, 2007, for $1,400,000, the transaction is recorded as follows:[11]

Giant's Financial Records—January 1, 2007

Cash (or other assets)	1,400,000	
Investment in Tiny Company		1,245,000
Gain on Sale of Investment		155,000
To record January 1, 2007, sale of subsidiary.		

Because the sale occurs on the first day of the year, no adjustment is required to recognize the subsidiary's 2007 operations.

In contrast, if Giant has utilized one of the alternative methods, a preliminary entry is needed to establish the appropriate $1,245,000 balance.

Application of the cost method. The parent continues to report the $1,040,000 total of the two original payments for this investment so that a $205,000 increase is necessary (income in excess of dividends and amortization).

Application of the partial equity method. The parent recognizes a book value of $1,319,000 (income and dividends, but does not record the $74,000 amortization). An adjustment must be made to record the amortization.

[10] Unless control is surrendered, the economic unit concept views the sale of a subsidiary's stock as a treasury stock transaction so that no gain or loss is recognized.

[11] Under the guidelines of *SFAS 144*, Giant could have to report this sale as the disposal of a segment. Because this issue is covered in most intermediate accounting textbooks, it is not explored here.

Hence, depending on the method used, the parent must make one of the following entries prior to recording the sales transaction:

Giant's Financial Records—January 1, 2007 **Cost Method Has Been Applied**		
Investment in Tiny Company	205,000	
Retained Earnings, 1/1/07 (Giant)		205,000
To establish correct equity balance by recognizing income accrual (in excess of dividends) for previous years as well as amortization.		

Partial Equity Method Has Been Applied		
Retained Earnings, 1/1/07 (Giant)	74,000	
Investment in Tiny Company		74,000
To establish correct equity balance by recognizing amortization relating to previous years.		

These adjustments are equivalent to the Entry *C used in previous consolidations to update an investment account applying either the cost or partial equity method. However, for a sale, the parent must record this entry directly into its books rather than as a part of the worksheet process. Following the adjustment to $1,245,000, the parent records the sales transaction using the same journal entry presented in connection with the equity method.

Sale Made during the Year

If this sale had transpired *within* the fiscal year, Giant would still adjust the investment to $1,245,000 (if necessary) but then extend application of the equity method over the period that it holds the stock during 2007. The resulting book value must be correct as of the date of sale. The income accruing to Giant during this portion of the year is reported as a single-line item in the 2007 income statement. In this manner, subsidiary earnings continue to be recognized throughout the period of ownership even though consolidation is no longer applicable.

Cost-Flow Assumptions

If it sells less than an entire investment, the parent must select an appropriate cost-flow assumption when it has made more than one purchase. In the sale of securities, the use of specific identification based on serial numbers is acceptable, although averaging or FIFO assumptions often are applied. Use of the averaging method is especially appealing because all shares are truly identical, creating little justification for identifying different cost figures with individual shares.

Returning to Giant's ownership of Tiny Company, assume that the parent sold only a 20 percent portion of the subsidiary on January 1, 2007 (thereby reducing its holdings from 80 to 60 percent). Averaging dictates the removal of $311,250 ([20%/80%] × $1,245,000) from the investment account. Conversely, adoption of FIFO requires that $298,000 be written off based on the currently reported value of the initial 2003 acquisition ([20%/50%] × $745,000).

Accounting for Shares That Remain

If Giant sells only a portion of the investment, it also must determine the proper method of accounting for the shares that remain. Three possible scenarios can be envisioned:

1. Giant could have so drastically reduced its interest that the parent no longer controls the subsidiary or even has the ability to significantly influence its decision making. For example, assume that Giant's ownership drops from 80 to 5 percent. In the current period prior to the sale, the 80 percent investment is reported by means of the equity method with the market-value method used for the 5 percent that remains thereafter. Consolidated financial statements are no longer applicable.

2. Giant could still apply significant influence over Tiny's operations although it no longer maintains control. A drop in the level of ownership from 80 to 30 percent normally meets this condition. In this case, the parent utilizes the equity method for the entire year. Application is based on 80 percent until the time of sale and then on 30 percent for the remainder of the year. Again, consolidated statements cease to be appropriate because control has been lost.

3. The decrease in ownership could be relatively small so that the parent continues to maintain control over the subsidiary even after the sale. Giant's reduction of its ownership in Tiny from 80 to 60 percent is an example of this situation. After the disposal, consolidated financial statements are still required, but the process is based on the *end-of-year ownership percentage.* As with step acquisitions, the accounting emphasis here is on maintaining comparability with future years. However, because only the retained shares (60 percent in this case) are consolidated, the parent must separately recognize any current year income accruing to it from its terminated interest. Thus, Giant shows earnings on this portion of the investment (a 20 percent interest in Tiny for the time during the year that it is held) in the consolidated income statement as a single-line item computed by means of the equity method.

Parent Sales of Subsidiary Stock under the Economic Unit Concept

The 2005 FASB proposal to adopt the economic unit concept differs from the parent company concept in the parent's accounting and reporting for sales of its shares of subsidiary stock. Under the economic unit concept, transactions in the stock of a subsidiary, whether purchases or sales, are considered to be transactions in the equity of the consolidated entity. Thus, if the parent maintains control, it recognizes no gains or losses when it sells a portion of its stock in the subsidiary. If the sale of the parent's ownership interest results in the loss of control of a subsidiary, it recognizes any resulting gain or loss in consolidated net income.

Summary

1. A parent company need not acquire 100 percent of a subsidiary's stock to form a business combination. Only control over the decision-making process is necessary, a level that has historically been achieved by obtaining a majority of the voting shares. Ownership of any subsidiary stock that is retained by outside, unrelated parties is collectively referred to as a *noncontrolling interest.*

2. A purchase consolidation takes on an added degree of complexity when a noncontrolling interest is present. A decision must be made as to the theoretical approach by which subsidiary assets and liabilities are to be valued within the financial statements of the business combination. One alternative, the economic unit concept, presumes that the combination is composed of two identifiable companies and should be accounted for as such. Allocations associated with the subsidiary's assets and liabilities are determined using their total fair value regardless of the degree of parent ownership. The calculation of any noncontrolling interest is based on this total and reported by the business combination as a component of stockholders' equity.

3. The proportionate consolidation concept focuses on the parent company by stressing the cost of buying a portion of the subsidiary. Under this approach, allocations are computed using the ownership percentage of each account's fair value. No recognition of noncontrolling interest is reported in either the consolidated balance sheet or income statement.

4. In practice, the parent company concept appears to be most popular. According to this method, the book value of each subsidiary asset and liability is included in the total whereas the difference between fair value and book value is consolidated based on the parent's ownership percentage. Any noncontrolling interest is measured using only the subsidiary's book value and reported between the liabilities and stockholders' equity.

5. In its 2005 Exposure Draft, *Business Combinations,* the FASB recommends the adoption of the economic unit concept for consolidated financial reporting. Under the economic unit concept, subsidiary assets and liabilities are adjusted to full fair value at the date of acquisition regardless of the parent's percentage ownership interest. A corresponding proportionate amount of the subsidiary's full fair value serves as the valuation basis for the noncontrolling interest.

6. Four noncontrolling interest figures appear in the annual consolidation process. Each is derived by multiplying the percentage of outside ownership by the subsidiary's book value. A balance as of the beginning of the year is brought into the worksheet first (through Entry **S**) followed by the noncontrolling

interest's share of the subsidiary's income for the period (recorded by a columnar entry). A decrease is recognized because of any dividends paid to these unrelated owners (with the amount appearing on the worksheet as the subsidiary's dividends that were not eliminated as intercompany). The final balance for the year is found as a summation of the Noncontrolling Interest column and is presented on the consolidated balance sheet, usually between the Liability and Stockholders' Equity sections. The income figure appears as a reduction within the income statement.

7. A parent can obtain control of a subsidiary by means of several separate purchases occurring over time, a process often referred to as a *step acquisition.* Under the parent company concept each purchase is viewed as an individual investment with separate allocations and amortization.

8. When a business acquisition is made within a year, consolidated revenues and expenses should exclude current subsidiary revenues and expenses that occurred prior to the acquisition date. The parent's and noncontrolling interest's shares of subsidiary net income include only post-acquisition subsidiary revenues and expenses.

9. A parent company also can sell all, or a portion, of a subsidiary. The appropriate book value for the investment must be established within the parent's separate records so that the gain or loss can be computed accurately. If the equity method has not been applied, the parent's investment balance should be restated to recognize any income and amortization previously omitted. The resulting balance is then compared to the amount received for the stock to arrive at the gain or loss. Any shares still held will subsequently be reported by either consolidation, the equity method, or the market-value method, depending on the influence retained by the parent.

Comprehensive Illustration

PROBLEM

(Estimated Time: 60 to 75 Minutes) On January 1, 2003, Father Company purchased an 80 percent interest in Sun Company for $410,000. As of that date, Sun reported total stockholders' equity of $400,000: $100,000 in common stock and $300,000 in retained earnings. In setting the acquisition price, Father had appraised four accounts as having values different from the balances reported within Sun's financial records.

Buildings (8-year life)	Undervalued by $20,000
Land	Undervalued by $50,000
Equipment (5-year life)	Undervalued by $12,500
Royalty agreement (20-year life)	Not recorded, valued at $30,000

As of December 31, 2007, the trial balances of these two companies are as follows:

	Father Company	Sun Company
Debits		
Current assets	$ 620,000	$ 280,000
Investment in Sun Company	410,000	–0–
Land	200,000	300,000
Buildings (net)	640,000	290,000
Equipment (net)	380,000	160,000
Expenses	550,000	190,000
Dividends	90,000	20,000
Total debits	$2,890,000	$1,240,000
Credits		
Liabilities	$ 910,000	$ 300,000
Common stock	480,000	100,000
Retained earnings, 1/1/07	704,000	480,000
Revenues	780,000	360,000
Dividend income	16,000	–0–
Total credits	$2,890,000	$1,240,000

Included in these figures is a $20,000 debt that Sun owes to the parent company.

Required:

a. Determine consolidated totals for Father Company and Sun Company for the year 2007. Assume that the parent company concept is to be applied.

b. Prepare worksheet entries to consolidate the trial balances of Father Company and Sun Company for the year 2007.

c. Assume that Father uses the economic unit concept rather than the parent company concept. Also assume that Father Company paid $410,000, which appropriately indicates Sun Company's total fair value of $512,500. Discuss the effects of applying the economic unit concept on the consolidated figures computed in requirement (a).

SOLUTION

a. The consolidation of Father Company and Sun Company begins with the allocation of the purchase price as shown in Exhibit 4.15. This process is based on the parent company concept and the parent's $410,000 expenditure. Because this consolidation is taking place after several years, the unamortized balances for the various allocations at the start of the current year also should be determined (see Exhibit 4.16).

Next, the parent's method of accounting for its subsidiary should be ascertained. The continuing presence of the original $410,000 acquisition price in the investment account indicates that Father is applying the cost method. This same determination can be made from the Dividend Income account, which equals 80 percent of the subsidiary's dividends. Thus, Father's accounting records have ignored the increase in Sun's book value as well as the excess amortization expenses for the prior periods of ownership. These amounts have to be added to the parent's January 1, 2007, Retained Earnings account to arrive at a properly consolidated balance.

During the 2003–2006 period of ownership, Sun's Retained Earnings account increased by $180,000 ($480,000 − $300,000). Father's 80 percent interest necessitates an accrual of $144,000 ($180,000 × 80%) for these years. In addition, the purchase price allocations require the recognition of $20,800 in excess amortization expenses for this same period ($5,200 × 4 years). Thus, a net increase of $123,200 ($144,000 − $20,800) is needed to correct the parent's beginning Retained Earnings balance for the year.

EXHIBIT 4.15

FATHER COMPANY AND SUN COMPANY
Purchase Price Allocation and Amortization
January 1, 2003

	Allocation	Estimated Life (years)	Annual Excess Amortization
Purchase price paid by Father Company	$ 410,000		
80% of subsidiary's $400,000 book value (Father Company's ownership)	(320,000)		
Cost in excess of book value	90,000		
Allocation to specific accounts based on fair value:			
Buildings ($20,000 × 80%)	16,000	8	$ 2,000
Land ($50,000 × 80%)	40,000		
Equipment ($12,500 × 80%)	10,000	5	2,000
Royalty agreement ($30,000 × 80%)	24,000	20	1,200
	–0–		
Annual excess amortization and depreciation expense			$ 5,200
2003–2006 excess amortization and depreciation expense ($5,200 × 4)			$20,800

EXHIBIT 4.16

FATHER COMPANY AND SUN COMPANY
Unamortized Cost Allocation
January 1, 2007, Balances

Account	Excess Original Allocation	Excess Amortization 2003–2006	Balance 1/1/07
Buildings	$16,000	$ 8,000	$ 8,000
Land	40,000	–0–	40,000
Equipment	10,000	8,000	2,000
Royalty	24,000	4,800	19,200
Total	$90,000	$20,800	$69,200

Once the adjustment from the cost method to the equity method has been determined, the consolidated figures for 2007 can be calculated:

Current assets = $880,000. The parent's book value is added to the subsidiary's book value. The $20,000 intercompany balance is eliminated.

Investment in Sun Company = –0–. The intercompany ownership is eliminated so that the subsidiary's specific assets and liabilities can be consolidated.

Land = $540,000. The parent's book value is added to the subsidiary's book value plus the $40,000 purchase price allocation (see Exhibit 4.15).

Buildings (net) = $936,000. The parent's book value is added to the subsidiary's book value plus the $16,000 purchase price allocation (see Exhibit 4.16) and less five years of amortization (2003 through 2007).

Equipment (net) = $540,000. The parent's book value is added to the subsidiary's book value. The $10,000 purchase price allocation has been completely amortized after five years.

Expenses = $745,200. The parent's book value is added to the subsidiary's book value plus amortization expenses on the purchase price allocations for the year (see Exhibit 4.15).

Dividends Paid = $90,000. Only the parent company dividends are consolidated. The subsidiary's dividends that were paid to the parent are eliminated; the remainder serve as a reduction in the Noncontrolling Interest balance.

Royalty Agreement = $18,000. The original residual allocation from the purchase price is recognized after taking into account five years of amortization (see Exhibit 4.15).

Noncontrolling Interest in Subsidiary's Income = $34,000. The outside owners are assigned a 20 percent share of the subsidiary's income (revenues of $360,000 less expenses of $190,000, or $170,000).

Total of Consolidated Debit Balances = $3,783,200. This figure is a summation of the preceding balances.

Liabilities = $1,190,000. The parent's book value is added to the subsidiary's book value. The $20,000 intercompany balance is eliminated.

Common Stock = $480,000. Only the parent company balance is reported.

Retained Earnings, 1/1/07 = $827, 200. Only the parent company balance is reported after a $123,200 increase is made as explained earlier to convert the parent's use of the cost method to the equity method.

Revenues = $1,140,000. The parent's book value is added to the subsidiary's book value.

Dividend Income = –0–. The intercompany dividend receipts are eliminated.

Noncontrolling Interest in Subsidiary, 12/31/07 = $146,000. The beginning balance is $116,000, 20 percent of the subsidiary's 1/1/07 book value ($580,000 as shown by the stockholders' equity accounts). This figure is increased by the noncontrolling interest's share of net income ($34,000 as computed above). The dividends paid to the outside owners (20 percent of $20,000, or $4,000) serve to decrease the balance. The consolidated total is then derived from these three balances.

Total of Consolidated Credit Balances = $3,783,200. This figure is a summation of the preceding balances.

b. Six worksheet entries are necessary to produce a consolidation worksheet for Father Company and Sun Company.

Entry *C

Investment in Sun Company	123,200	
Retained Earnings, 1/1/07 (parent)		123,200

As discussed earlier, this increment is required to adjust the parent's Retained Earnings from the cost method to the equity method. The amount is $144,000 (80 percent of the $180,000 increase in the subsidiary's book value during previous years) less $20,800 in excess amortization over this same four-year period ($5,200 × 4 years).

Entry S

Common Stock (subsidiary)	100,000	
Retained Earnings, 1/1/07 (subsidiary)	480,000	
Investment in Sun Company (80 percent)		464,000
Noncontrolling Interest in Sun Company (20 percent)		116,000

To eliminate beginning stockholders' equity accounts of the subsidiary and recognize the beginning balance attributed to the outside owners (20 percent).

Entry A

Buildings	8,000	
Land	40,000	
Equipment	2,000	
Royalty Agreement	19,200	
Investment in Sun Company		69,200

To recognize unamortized purchase price allocations as of the first day of the current year (see Exhibit 4.16).

Entry I

Dividend Income	16,000	
Dividends Paid		16,000

To eliminate intercompany dividend payments recorded by parent (using the cost method) as income.

Entry E

Depreciation Expense	4,000	
Amortization Expense	1,200	
Buildings		2,000
Equipment		2,000
Royalty Agreement		1,200

To recognize excess amortization expenses for the current year (see Exhibit 4.15).

Entry P

Liabilities	$20,000	
Current Assets		20,000

To eliminate the intercompany debt.

c. Recall that under the economic unit concept, not only is the fair value for 100 percent of the subsidiary used in allocating fair values to subsidiary assets but also adjustments are made for 100 percent of the differences in fair and book values. The following cost allocation schedule reflects the economic unit concept for Father's purchase of Sun on January 1, 2003:

	Allocation	Estimated Life (years)	Annual Excess Amortization
Fair value	$512,500		
Sun book value (100%)	400,000		
Excess fair value	112,500		
Allocation to specific subsidiary accounts based on fair value:			
Buildings	$ 20,000	8	$2,500
Land	50,000		
Equipment	12,500	5	2,500
Royalty agreement	30,000	20	1,500
	–0–		
Annual excess amortization expenses (economic unit concept)			$6,500

Father's consolidated statements would therefore reflect the total fair values of the subsidiary at acquisition date less the preceding amortizations. To offset the increased asset values, a larger noncontrolling interest is recognized.

The noncontrolling interest reported in the December 31, 2007, stockholders' equity section of Father's consolidated balance sheet is $162,000, computed as follows:

NCI in Sun's 1/1/07 book value (20% × $580,000)	$116,000
NCI in unamortized excess allocations (20% × $86,500)	17,300
January 1, 2007, NCI in Sun fair value	133,300
NCI in Sun's economic unit income [20% × ($360,000 − 196,500)]	32,700
NCI dividend share (20% × $20,000)	(4,000)
Total noncontrolling interest December 31, 2007	$162,000

Note that the $162,000 noncontrolling interest amount is the same as the $146,000 amount reported in part (*a*), plus 20 percent of the $80,000 unamortized excess allocations at December 31, 2007 ($112,500 − 5 years × $6,500).

The noncontrolling interest's share of the subsidiary's net income is reported on the consolidated income statement. This amount is based on the subsidiary's net income after deducting amortization expense, which is attributed to the company's asset and liability accounts.

Questions

1. What does the term *noncontrolling interest* mean?
2. Atwater Company acquires 80 percent of the outstanding voting stock of Belwood Company. On that date, Belwood possesses a building with a $160,000 book value but a $220,000 fair value. Assuming that a bargain purchase has not been made, at what value would this building be consolidated under each of the following?

   a. Economic unit concept.
   b. Proportionate consolidation concept.
   c. Parent company concept.
3. How does the parent company concept merge the ideas put forth under the economic unit concept and proportionate consolidation?
4. Where should the noncontrolling interest's claims be reported in a consolidated set of financial statements?

5. How is the noncontrolling interest in a subsidiary company calculated as of the end of the current year?

6. December 31 consolidated financial statements are being prepared for Allsports Company and its new subsidiary acquired on July 1 of the current year. Should Allsports adjust its consolidated balances for the pre-acquisition subsidiary revenues and expenses?

7. Tree, Inc., has held a 10 percent interest in the stock of Limb Company for several years. Because of the level of ownership, this investment has been accounted for using the fair-value method. At the beginning of the current year, Tree acquires an additional 70 percent interest, which provides the company with control over Limb. In preparing consolidated financial statements for this business combination, how does Tree account for the previous 10 percent ownership interest?

8. Duke Corporation owns a 70 percent equity interest in UNCCH, a subsidiary corporation. During the current year, a portion of this stock is sold to an outside party. Before recording this transaction, Duke adjusts the book value of its investment account. What is the purpose of this adjustment?

9. In question (8), how would the parent record the sales transaction?

10. In question (8), how would the parent record the sales transaction if the economic unit concept is being used and control is retained?

11. In question (8), how would Duke account for the remainder of its investment subsequent to the sale of this partial interest?

Problems

Note: Unless otherwise stated, assume the parent company concept. The economic unit concept is used in problems 1, 7, 10, 22, 29, 33, 35, the Excel Case, and the Computer Project.

1. Bailey, Inc., buys 60 percent of the outstanding stock of Luebs, Inc., in a purchase that resulted in the recognition of goodwill. Luebs owns a piece of land that cost $200,000 but was worth $500,000 at the date of purchase. For each of the three concepts described in this chapter, what value should be attributed to this land in a consolidated balance sheet at the date of takeover?

	Economic Unit Concept	Proportionate Consolidation	Parent Company Concept
a.	$500,000	$300,000	$500,000
b.	$200,000	$120,000	$500,000
c.	$200,000	$120,000	$380,000
d.	$500,000	$300,000	$380,000

2. Jordan, Inc., holds 75 percent of the outstanding stock of Paxson Corporation. Paxson currently owes Jordan $400,000 for inventory acquired over the past few months. In preparing consolidated financial statements, what amount of this debt should be eliminated?

   a. –0–.

   b. $100,000.

   c. $300,000.

   d. $400,000.

3. On January 1, 2006, Brendan, Inc., reports net assets of $760,000 although equipment (with a four-year life) having a book value of $440,000 is worth $500,000 and an unrecorded patent is valued at $45,000. Hope Corporation pays $692,000 on that date for an 80 percent ownership in Brendan. If the patent is to be written off over a 10-year period, at what amount should the patent be reported on consolidated statements at December 31, 2007?

   a. $20,800.

   b. $28,800.

   c. $34,200.

   d. $67,200.

4. On January 1, 2005, Turner, Inc., reports net assets of $480,000 although a building (with a 10-year life) having a book value of $260,000 is now worth $310,000. Plaster Corporation pays $400,000 on that date for a 70 percent ownership in Turner. On December 31, 2007, Turner reports a Building

account of $245,000 and Plaster reports a Building account of $510,000. What is the consolidated balance of the Building account?

   a. $779,500.

   b. $783,500.

   c. $790,000.

   d. $805,000.

5. On January 1, 2005, Hygille, Inc., reports net assets of $880,000 although a building (with a 10-year life) having a book value of $330,000 is now worth $400,000. Nuyt Corporation pays $840,000 on that date for an 80 percent ownership in Hygille. On December 31, 2007, Hygille reports total expenses of $621,000 while Nuyt reports expenses of $714,000. What is the consolidated total expense balance?

   a. $1,335,000.

   b. $1,339,000.

   c. $1,345,300.

   d. $1,340,600.

6. On January 1, 2005, Chamberlain Corporation pays $388,000 for a 60 percent ownership in Neville. Annual excess amortization of $8,800 results from the purchase. On December 31, 2007, Neville reports revenues of $400,000 and expenses of $300,000 and Chamberlain reports revenues of $700,000 and expenses of $400,000. The parent figures contain no income from the subsidiary. What is the consolidated net income?

   a. $349,600.

   b. $351,200.

   c. $360,000.

   d. $391,200.

7. What is a basic premise of the economic unit concept?

   a. Consolidated financial statements should be primarily for the benefit of the stockholders of the parent company.

   b. Consolidated financial statements should be produced only if both the parent and the subsidiary are in the same basic industry.

   c. A subsidiary is an indivisible part of a business combination and should be included in whole regardless of the degree of ownership.

   d. Consolidated financial statements should not report a noncontrolling interest balance because these outside owners do not hold stock in the parent company.

8. James Company acquired 85 percent of Mark-Right Company on April 1, 2006. On its December 31, 2006, consolidated income statement, how should James account for Mark-Right's revenues and expenses that occurred before April 1, 2006?

   a. Include 100 percent of Mark-Right's revenues and expenses and deduct the pre-acquisition portion as noncontrolling interest in net income.

   b. Exclude 100 percent of the pre-acquisition revenues and 100 percent of the pre-acquisition expenses from their respective consolidated totals.

   c. Exclude 15 percent of the pre-acquisition revenues and 15 percent of the pre-acquisition expenses from consolidated expenses.

   d. Deduct 15 percent of the net combined revenues and expenses relating to the pre-acquisition period from consolidated net income.

9. Ames, Inc., had a book value of $400,000 on January 1, 2004, and $550,000 on January 1, 2006. On both dates, the book value of the company's assets and liabilities was the same as their fair value. Hitchcock Corporation acquired 30 percent of Ames on January 1, 2004, for $160,000 in cash. Hitchcock purchased an additional 40 percent of Ames on January 1, 2006, for $240,000. On a consolidated balance sheet as of December 31, 2006, what amount of goodwill is reported?

   a. $60,000.

   b. $54,000.

   c. $53,000.

   d. $52,000.

10. A parent buys 32 percent of a subsidiary in one year and then buys an additional 40 percent in the next year. In a step acquisition of this type, how does the economic unit concept differ from the parent company concept?

   a. In using the economic unit concept, all subsequent purchases are valued based on the fair value at the time of the first acquisition.

   b. In using the economic unit concept, the two purchases are recorded as separate acquisitions with their own allocations and goodwill.

   c. In using the economic unit concept, the first purchase is adjusted to its fair value based on the acquisition price of the second transaction with a resulting gain or loss being recorded.

   d. The economic unit concept views each company as a whole and, thus, cannot be applied unless 100 percent of the subsidiary's stock is held.

11. On April 1, 2006, Pujols, Inc., purchases 70 percent of the outstanding stock of Ramirez Corporation for $430,000. The subsidiary's book value on that date was $500,000. Any excess cost was attributable to goodwill. During the remainder of 2006, Ramirez generates revenues of $600,000 and expenses of $360,000. On a December 31, 2006, consolidated balance sheet, what should be reported as the noncontrolling interest?

   a. $150,000.

   b. $201,000.

   c. $222,000.

   d. $518,000.

Use the following information for Problems 12 through 14:

David Company acquired 60 percent of Mark Company for $300,000 when Mark's book value was $400,000. On that date, Mark had equipment (with a 10-year life) that was undervalued in the financial records by $60,000. Also, buildings (with a 20-year life) were undervalued by $40,000. Two years later, the following figures are reported by these two companies (stockholders' equity accounts have been omitted):

	David Company Book Value	Mark Company Book Value	Mark Company Fair Value
Current assets	$ 620,000	$ 300,000	$ 320,000
Equipment	260,000	200,000	280,000
Buildings	410,000	150,000	150,000
Liabilities	(390,000)	(120,000)	(120,000)
Revenues	(900,000)	(400,000)	
Expenses	500,000	300,000	
Investment income	Not given		

12. What is the consolidated net income prior to the reduction for the noncontrolling interest's share of the subsidiary's income?

   a. $455,200.

   b. $494,000.

   c. $497,000.

   d. $495,200.

13. What are the noncontrolling interest's share of the subsidiary's income and the ending balance of the noncontrolling interest in the subsidiary?

   a. $42,000 and $252,000.

   b. $40,000 and $212,000.

   c. $38,080 and $208,160.

   d. $35,200 and $207,200.

14. What is the consolidated balance of the Equipment account?

   a. $488,800.

   b. $498,400.

   c. $500,800.

   d. $508,000.

Use the following information for Problems 15 through 19:

On January 1, 2006, Polk Corporation and Strass Corporation had condensed balance sheets as follows:

	Polk	Strass
Current assets	$ 70,000	$20,000
Noncurrent assets	90,000	40,000
Total assets	$160,000	$60,000
Current liabilities	$ 30,000	$10,000
Long-term debt	50,000	—
Stockholders' equity	80,000	50,000
Total liabilities and equities	$160,000	$60,000

On January 2, 2006, Polk borrowed $60,000 and used the proceeds to purchase 90 percent of the outstanding common shares of Strass. This debt is payable in 10 equal annual principal payments, plus interest, beginning December 31, 2006. The excess cost of the investment over the underlying book value of the acquired net assets is allocated to inventory (60 percent) and to goodwill (40 percent). On a consolidated balance sheet as of January 2, 2006, what should be the amount for each of the following?

15. Current assets:
    a. $99,000.
    b. $96,000.
    c. $90,000.
    d. $79,000.

16. Noncurrent assets:
    a. $130,000.
    b. $134,000.
    c. $136,000.
    d. $140,000.

17. Current liabilities:
    a. $50,000.
    b. $46,000.
    c. $40,000.
    d. $30,000.

18. Noncurrent liabilities, including noncontrolling interest:
    a. $115,000.
    b. $109,000.
    c. $104,000.
    d. $55,000.

19. Stockholders' equity:
    a. $80,000.
    b. $85,000.
    c. $90,000.
    d. $130,000.
    (AICPA adapted)

20. On January 1, 2006, Harrison, Inc., purchased 90 percent of Starr Company. Annual amortization of $8,000 resulted from this transaction. Starr Company reported a Common Stock account of $100,000 and Retained Earnings of $200,000 at that date. The subsidiary earned $70,000 in 2006 and $90,000 in 2007 with dividend payments of $30,000 each year. Without regard for this investment, Harrison had income of $220,000 in 2006 and $260,000 in 2007.

    a. What is the consolidated net income in each of these two years?
    b. What is the ending noncontrolling interest balance as of December 31, 2007?

21. Parker, Inc., purchases 70 percent of Sawyer Company for $406,000. On that date, Sawyer had the following accounts:

	Book Value	Fair Value
Current assets	$ 210,000	$ 210,000
Land	170,000	180,000
Buildings	300,000	330,000
Liabilities	(280,000)	(280,000)

The buildings have a 10-year life. In addition, Sawyer holds a patent worth $140,000 that has a five-year life but is not recorded on its financial records. At the end of 2006, the two companies report the following balances:

	Parker	Sawyer
Revenues	$(900,000)	$(600,000)
Expenses	600,000	400,000

a. Assume that the purchase took place on January 1, 2006. What figures would appear in a consolidated income statement for this year?

b. Assume that the purchase took place on April 1, 2006. Sawyer's revenues and expenses occurred uniformly throughout the year. Parker excludes all pre-acquisition subsidiary income statement amounts from consolidated totals. What amounts would appear in a consolidated income statement for this year?

22. On January 1, Beckman, Inc., purchases 60 percent of the outstanding stock of Calvin for $36,000. Calvin Co. has one recorded asset, a specialized production machine with a book value of $10,000, and no liabilities. The fair value of the machine is $50,000, and the remaining useful life is estimated to be 10 years. Any remaining excess cost is attributable to an unrecorded process trade secret with an estimated future life of 4 years. The fair value of Calvin as a whole is $60,000.

At the end of the year, Calvin reports the following in its financial statements:

Revenues	$50,000	Machine	$ 9,000	Common stock	$10,000
Expenses	20,000	Other assets	26,000	Retained earnings	25,000
Net income	$30,000	Total assets	$35,000	Total equity	$35,000
Dividends paid	$ 5,000				

For each of the following noncontrolling interest concepts, determine the amounts that Beckman should report in its consolidated financial statements for noncontrolling interest in subsidiary income, end-of-year total noncontrolling interest, Calvin's machine (net of accumulated depreciation), and the process trade secret.

a. Parent company concept.

b. Proportionate consolidation concept.

c. Economic unit concept.

23. Mabry, Inc., purchases 60 percent of Thompson Corporation on August 1, 2005, and an additional 30 percent on October 1, 2006. Annual amortization of $6,000 relates to the first acquisition and $10,000 to the second. Thompson reports the following figures for 2006 (revenues and expenses occurred evenly throughout the year):

Revenues	$(600,000)
Expenses	420,000
Retained earnings, 1/1/06	(540,000)
Dividends paid, 12/1/06	70,000
Common stock	(310,000)

Without regard for this investment, Mabry earns $360,000 in net income during 2006.

a. What is the consolidated net income for 2006?

b. What is the noncontrolling interest as of December 31, 2006?

24. Martinez Corporation acquired 50 percent of Johnson, Inc., several years ago and an additional 30 percent on April 1 of the current year. An excess cost allocation of $60,000 to equipment was computed in connection with the first acquisition, and that amount is being amortized over a 20-year

life. No excess amortizations resulted from the second acquisition. The following figures are reported by these two companies for the current year. Investment income is not included within the balances for Martinez shown here. Income is assumed to have been earned evenly throughout the year, and no dividends were paid. Assume that Martinez consolidates subsidiary revenues and expenses only subsequent to the date it obtains control.

	Martinez Corporation	Johnson, Inc.
Revenues	$(600,000)	$(500,000)
Expenses	380,000	300,000

a. What is the noncontrolling interest's share of the subsidiary's net income?

b. What is the consolidated net income for these two companies?

c. Assume that Martinez had applied the equity method to account for its 50 percent investment in Johnson from January 1 to April 1, 2006. What is the total income from Johnson recognized by Martinez in 2006?

25. Wilson Company acquired 7,000 of the 10,000 outstanding shares of Green Company on January 1, 2002, for $800,000. The subsidiary's book value on that date was $1,000,000. Any cost of this purchase in excess of Green's book value was assigned to a patent with a 10-year life. On January 1, 2006, Wilson reported a $1,085,000 balance in the Investment in Green Company account based on application of the partial equity method. On October 1, 2006, Wilson sells 1,000 shares of the investment for $191,000. During 2006, Green reported net income of $120,000 and paid dividends of $40,000. These amounts are assumed to have been incurred evenly throughout the year.

a. How are the 1,000 shares reported for the period from January 1, 2006, until October 1, 2006?

b. What is the effect on net income of this sale of 1,000 shares?

c. What accounting is now made of the 6,000 shares that Wilson continues to hold?

26. Carter, Inc., holds 90 percent of the stock of Wade Corporation. On January 1, 2006, Wade reports $10,000 in common stock and $90,000 in retained earnings. During each month of 2006, the company earns $15,000 in net income and pays dividends of $5,000. At the end of the year, Wade's net income is $180,000 (revenues of $420,000 less $240,000 in expenses), while $60,000 in dividends have been paid. All revenues and expenses have occurred uniformly throughout the year.

The book value of Wade Corporation on December 1, 2006, is $210,000 ($100,000 beginning balance plus $10,000 growth for 11 months). On that date, Brookwood, Inc., buys all of Carter's interest. Brookwood pays exactly book value for these shares ($189,000 or 90 percent of $210,000). The individual fair values of Wade's assets and liabilities are equal to their book values.

Brookwood is currently preparing consolidated financial statements for the year ending December 31, 2006. Brookwood's policy is to include only post-acquisition subsidiary amounts in its consolidated statements.

a. What amount of Wade's revenues and expenses would be included in the consolidated income statement?

b. What is the beginning balance of the noncontrolling interest at the date of Brookwood's acquisition? What is the December 31 balance for the noncontrolling interest?

c. Prepare the worksheet entry to eliminate the subsidiary's stockholders' equity. Assume that Brookwood uses the cost method to account for its investment in Wade and that Wade did not close its books at the date of Brookwood's purchase of 90 percent of its stock.

27. Jeffries acquired 80 percent of the outstanding stock of Goldblom for $156,000. Just prior to this purchase, the following information is gathered from the two companies:

	Jeffries Book Value	Goldblom Book Value	Goldblom Fair Value
Current assets	$500,000	$150,000	$150,000
Land	100,000	30,000	40,000
Buildings and equipment (net)	600,000	160,000	180,000
Liabilities	(300,000)	(200,000)	(200,000)
Common stock	(400,000)	(40,000)	
Retained earnings	(500,000)	(100,000)	

The buildings and equipment have a 10-year remaining life; any goodwill is assumed to have an indefinite life.

Subsequently, on December 31, 2006, the two companies report the following account balances. Fair values are presented where applicable.

	Jeffries Book Value	Goldblom Book Value	Goldblom Fair Value
Current assets	$ 300,000	$ 90,000	$ 90,000
Investment in Goldblom	156,000	–0–	–0–
Land	150,000	60,000	74,000
Buildings and equipment (net)	570,000	180,000	216,000
Liabilities	(246,000)	(185,000)	(185,000)
Common stock	(400,000)	(40,000)	
Retained earnings, 1/1/06	(470,000)	(95,000)	
Revenues	(300,000)	(100,000)	
Expenses	200,000	90,000	
Dividends paid	40,000	–0–	

a. On consolidated financial statements as of the date of acquisition, what balances are reported for the Buildings and Equipment account and the Goodwill account?

b. Assume that the purchase was made on January 1, 2002. What would be the consolidated Buildings and Equipment balance on December 31, 2006?

c. Assume that the purchase was made during 2005. What is the consolidated net income for 2006 before subtracting the noncontrolling interest's share of the subsidiary's income?

d. Assume that the purchase was made during 2004. What is the noncontrolling interest's share of the subsidiary's income for the year ending December 31, 2006?

e. Assume that the purchase was made on July 1, 2006, and that Jeffries's policy is to include only post-acquisition subsidiary amounts in its consolidated statements. Prepare a consolidated income statement for the year ending December 31, 2006.

f. Assume that the purchase was made on January 1, 2005. On October 1, 2006, Jeffries sells one-fourth of these shares for $82,000 in cash. What income effects appear on the consolidated income statement for 2006?

28. On January 1, 2004, Thacker purchases 70 percent of Barker for $410,000 cash. The new subsidiary reported common stock of $300,000 on that date, with retained earnings of $180,000. A building was undervalued in the company's financial records by $20,000. This building had a 10-year remaining life. Goodwill of $60,000 was recognized.

Barker earns income and pays cash dividends as follows:

Year	Net Income	Dividends Paid
2004	$ 75,000	$39,000
2005	96,000	44,000
2006	110,000	60,000

On December 31, 2006, Thacker owes $22,000 to Barker.

a. If the equity method has been applied by Thacker, what are the consolidation entries needed as of December 31, 2006?

b. If the cost method has been applied by Thacker, what Entry *C is needed for a 2006 consolidation?

c. If the partial equity method has been applied by Thacker, what Entry *C is needed for a 2006 consolidation?

d. What noncontrolling interest balances will appear in consolidated financial statements for 2006?

29. The Hearts Company acquired an 80 percent interest in Dylan Company as of January 1, 2004. Hearts paid $620,000 to the owners of Dylan to purchase these shares. In addition, Hearts paid several lawyers and merger analysts $44,000 for assisting in the acquisition.

On January 1, 2004, Dylan reported a book value of $600,000 (Common Stock—$300,000; Additional Paid-In Capital—$90,000; Retained Earnings—$210,000). Several of Dylan's buildings were undervalued by a total of $80,000. These buildings had a remaining life of 20 years.

During the 2004–06 time period, Dylan reported the following figures:

Year	Net Income	Dividends Paid
2004	$ 70,000	$10,000
2005	90,000	15,000
2006	100,000	20,000

Determine the appropriate answers for each of the following questions:

a. What amount of amortization expense would be recognized in the consolidated financial statements for the initial years following this purchase?

b. If a consolidated balance sheet is prepared as of January 1, 2004, what amount of goodwill would be recognized?

c. If a consolidation worksheet is prepared as of January 1, 2004, what Entry **S** should be included?

d. On the separate financial records of the parent company, what amount of investment income would be reported for 2004 under each of the following accounting methods?

   (1) The equity method.

   (2) The partial equity method.

   (3) The cost method.

e. On the separate financial records of the parent company, what would be the December 31, 2006, balance for the Investment in Dylan Company account under each of the following accounting methods?

   (1) The equity method.

   (2) The partial equity method.

   (3) The cost method.

f. As of December 31, 2005, Hearts's Buildings account on its separate records has a balance of $800,000 and Dylan has a similar account with a $300,000 balance. What would be the consolidated balance for the Buildings account? What would be the balance if the economic unit concept is used?

g. What would be the balance of consolidated goodwill as of December 31, 2006?

h. Assume that the parent company has been applying the equity method to this investment. On December 31, 2006, the separate financial statements for the two companies present the following information:

	Hearts Company	Dylan Company
Common stock	$500,000	$300,000
Additional paid-in capital	280,000	90,000
Retained earnings, 12/31/06	620,000	425,000

What will be the consolidated balance of each of these accounts?

30. Following are several account balances taken from the records of Ortiz and Damon as of December 31, 2006. A few asset accounts have been omitted here. All revenues, expenses, and dividends occurred evenly throughout the year. Annual tests have indicated no goodwill impairment.

	Ortiz	Damon
Sales	$ (800,000)	$(500,000)
Cost of goods sold	400,000	280,000
Operating expenses	200,000	100,000
Investment income	not given	–0–
Retained earnings, 1/1/06	(1,400,000)	(700,000)
Dividends	80,000	20,000
Land	600,000	200,000
Buildings (net)	700,000	300,000
Equipment (net)	400,000	400,000
Liabilities	(500,000)	(200,000)
Common stock ($10 par value)	(400,000)	(100,000)
Additional paid-in capital	(500,000)	(600,000)

On July 1, 2006, Ortiz purchased 80 percent of Damon for $1,300,000 in cash. In addition, Ortiz paid $30,000 in direct consolidation costs. At that time, Damon's buildings (with a 10-year life) were undervalued on its books by $100,000.

Ortiz includes only post-acquisition subsidiary amounts in its consolidated statements. For a consolidation prepared at the end of 2006, what balances would be reported for the following?

Sales	Net Income
Expenses	Retained Earnings, 1/1/06
Noncontrolling Interest in	Buildings (net)
Subsidiary's Net Income	Land
	Goodwill

31. Monroe, Inc., acquires 60 percent of Sunrise Corporation for $414,000 cash on January 1, 2003. On that date, Sunrise had the following accounts:

	Book Value	Fair Value
Current assets	$150,000	$150,000
Land	200,000	200,000
Buildings (net) (6-year life)	300,000	360,000
Equipment (net) (4-year life)	300,000	280,000
Patent (10-year life)	–0–	100,000
Liabilities	(400,000)	(400,000)

The companies' financial statements for the year ending December 31, 2006, follow:

	Monroe	Sunrise
Revenues	$ (600,000)	$ (300,000)
Operating expenses	410,000	210,000
Investment income	(42,000)	–0–
Net income	$ (232,000)	$ (90,000)
Retained earnings, 1/1/06	$ (700,000)	$ (300,000)
Net income	(232,000)	(90,000)
Dividends paid	92,000	70,000
Retained earnings, 12/31/06	$ (840,000)	$ (320,000)
Current assets	$ 330,000	$ 100,000
Land	220,000	200,000
Buildings (net)	700,000	200,000
Equipment (net)	400,000	500,000
Investment in Sunrise	414,000	–0–
Total assets	$ 2,064,000	$ 1,000,000
Liabilities	$ (500,000)	$ (200,000)
Common stock	(724,000)	(480,000)
Retained earnings, 12/31/06	(840,000)	(320,000)
Total liabilities and equities	$(2,064,000)	$(1,000,000)

Answer the following questions:

a. How can the accountant determine that the cost method has been applied by the parent?

b. What is the annual excess amortization initially recognized in connection with this purchase?

c. If the partial equity method had been applied, what investment income would have been recorded by the parent in 2006? What if the equity method had been applied?

d. What is the consolidated balance for the Retained Earnings account as of January 1, 2006?

e. What is the Noncontrolling Interest in the Subsidiary's 2006 income?

f. What is the consolidated net income for 2006?

g. Within consolidated statements at January 1, 2003, what balance is included for the subsidiary's Buildings account?

h. What is the consolidated Buildings account as of December 31, 2006?

32. Father, Inc., buys 80 percent of the outstanding common stock of Sam Corporation on January 1, 2006, for $680,000 cash. Sam's total book value on that date was only $600,000. However, Sam possessed several accounts that had fair values differing from their book values:

	Book Value	Fair Value
Land	$ 60,000	$ 225,000
Buildings and equipment (10-year remaining life)	275,000	250,000
Copyright (20-year life)	100,000	200,000
Notes payable (due in 8 years)	(130,000)	(120,000)

For internal reporting purposes, Father, Inc., employs the equity method to account for this investment.

The following account balances are for the year ending December 31, 2006, for both companies. Determine consolidated balances for this business combination (through either individual computations or the use of a worksheet).

	Father	Sam
Revenues	$(1,360,000)	$(540,000)
Cost of goods sold	700,000	385,000
Depreciation expense	260,000	10,000
Amortization expense	–0–	5,000
Interest expense	44,000	5,000
Equity in income of Sam	(105,000)	–0–
Net income	$ (461,000)	$(135,000)
Retained earnings, 1/1/06	$(1,265,000)	$(440,000)
Net income (above)	(461,000)	(135,000)
Dividends paid	260,000	65,000
Retained earnings, 12/31/06	$(1,466,000)	$(510,000)
Current assets	$ 965,000	$ 528,000
Investment in Sam	733,000	–0–
Land	292,000	60,000
Buildings and equipment (net)	877,000	265,000
Copyright	–0–	95,000
Total assets	$ 2,867,000	$ 948,000
Accounts payable	$ (191,000)	$(148,000)
Notes payable	(460,000)	(130,000)
Common stock	(300,000)	(100,000)
Additional paid-in capital	(450,000)	(60,000)
Retained earnings (above)	(1,466,000)	(510,000)
Total liabilities and equities	$(2,867,000)	$(948,000)

Note: Credits are indicated by parentheses.

33. Answer Problem 32 again, this time using the economic unit concept. Assume that the fair value of Sam as a whole on the date of acquisition is $850,000.

34. Burke Corporation purchased 90 percent of the outstanding voting shares of Drexel, Inc., on December 31, 2004. Burke paid a total of $602,000 in cash for these shares. As of that date, Drexel had the following account balances:

	Book Value	Fair Value
Current assets	$ 160,000	$ 160,000
Land	120,000	150,000
Buildings (10-year life)	220,000	200,000
Equipment (5-year life)	160,000	200,000
Patents (10-year life)	–0–	50,000
Liabilities (5-year life)	(200,000)	(180,000)
Common stock	(180,000)	
Retained earnings, 12/31/04	(280,000)	

December 31, 2006, adjusted trial balances for the two companies follow:

	Burke Corporation	Drexel, Inc.
Debits		
Current assets	$ 611,000	$ 250,000
Land	380,000	150,000
Buildings	490,000	250,000
Equipment	873,000	150,000
Investment in Drexel, Inc.	701,000	–0–
Cost of goods sold	500,000	100,000
Depreciation expense	100,000	55,000
Interest expense	20,000	5,000
Dividends paid	110,000	70,000
Total debits	$3,785,000	$1,030,000
Credits		
Liabilities	$ 860,000	$ 230,000
Common stock	510,000	180,000
Retained earnings, 1/1/06	1,367,000	340,000
Revenues	940,000	280,000
Investment income	108,000	–0–
Total credits	$3,785,000	$1,030,000

a. Without using a worksheet or consolidation entries, determine the balances to be reported as of December 31, 2006, for this business combination.

b. To verify the figures determined in requirement (a), prepare a consolidation worksheet for Burke Corporation and Drexel, Inc., as of December 31, 2006.

eXcel

35. Using the information presented in Problem 34, produce a worksheet to consolidate the financial statements of Burke and Drexel incorporating the economic unit concept rather than the parent company concept. Assume that the fair value of Drexel as a whole on the date of acquisition is $668,889.

36. Following are the individual financial statements for Bowen and Duncan for the year ending December 31, 2006:

	Bowen	Duncan
Sales	$ (600,000)	$ (300,000)
Cost of goods sold	300,000	140,000
Operating expenses	174,000	60,000
Dividend income	(24,000)	–0–
Net income	$ (150,000)	$ (100,000)
Retained earnings, 1/1/06	$ (700,000)	$ (400,000)
Net income	(150,000)	(100,000)
Dividends paid	80,000	40,000
Retained earnings, 12/31/06	$ (770,000)	$ (460,000)
Cash and receivables	$ 250,000	$ 100,000
Inventory	500,000	190,000
Investment in Duncan	526,000	–0–
Buildings (net)	524,000	600,000
Equipment (net)	400,000	400,000
Total assets	$ 2,200,000	$ 1,290,000
Liabilities	(800,000)	(490,000)
Common stock	(630,000)	(340,000)
Retained earnings, 12/31/06	(770,000)	(460,000)
Total liabilities and stockholders' equity	$(2,200,000)	$(1,290,000)

Bowen acquired 60 percent of Duncan on April 1, 2006, for $526,000. On that date, equipment (with a six-year life) was overvalued by $30,000. Duncan earned income evenly during the year but the dividend was paid entirely on November 1, 2006. For mid-year acquisitions, Bowen includes only post-acquisition amounts in its consolidated statements.

a. Prepare a consolidated income statement for the year ending December 31, 2006.

b. Determine the consolidated balance for each of the following accounts as of December 31, 2006:

Goodwill	Buildings (net)
Equipment (net)	Dividends Paid
Common Stock	

37. Bon Air, Inc., acquired 70 percent (2,800 shares) of the outstanding voting stock of Creedmoor Corporation on January 1, 2004, for $250,000 cash. Creedmoor's net assets on that date totaled $230,000, but this balance included three accounts having fair values that differed from their book values:

	Book Value	Fair Value
Land	$30,000	$ 40,000
Equipment (14-year life)	50,000	118,000
Liabilities (10-year life)	(70,000)	(50,000)

As of December 31, 2007, the two companies report the following balances:

	Bon Air	Creedmoor
Revenues	$ (694,800)	$(250,000)
Operating expenses	630,000	180,000
Investment income	(44,200)	–0–
Net income	$ (109,000)	$ (70,000)
Retained earnings, 1/1/07	$ (760,000)	$(260,000)
Net income	(109,000)	(70,000)
Dividends paid	68,000	10,000
Retained earnings, 12/31/07	$ (801,000)	$(320,000)
Current assets	$ 72,000	$ 120,000
Investment in Creedmoor Corp.	321,800	–0–
Land	241,000	50,000
Buildings (net)	289,000	200,000
Equipment (net)	165,200	40,000
Total assets	$ 1,089,000	$ 410,000
Liabilities	$ (180,000)	$ (50,000)
Common stock	(50,000)	(40,000)
Additional paid-in capital	(58,000)	–0–
Retained earnings, 12/31/07	(801,000)	(320,000)
Total liabilities and equities	$(1,089,000)	$(410,000)

(Each of the following is an independent question.)

a. Consolidated financial statements are being prepared on December 31, 2007. What balance should be reported for each of the following accounts?

> Operating Expenses
> Noncontrolling Interest in Creedmoor's Net Income
> Revenues
> Retained Earnings, 1/1/07
> Net Income
> Dividends Paid
> Land
> Equipment
> Liabilities
> Common Stock
> Retained Earnings, 12/31/07
> Noncontrolling Interest in Creedmoor, 12/31/07

b. If Bon Air sells 400 shares of this stock on December 31, 2007, for $60,000 cash, what journal entry is recorded?

eXcel

38. The Roddick Corporation purchased 80 percent of the outstanding stock of Carlsen, Inc., for $384,000. An appraisal made on that date determined that all book values appropriately reflected the actual worth of the underlying accounts except that a building with a 10-year life was undervalued by $20,000 and a fully amortized trademark with an estimated 20-year remaining life had an $80,000 fair value.

Following are the separate financial statements for the year ending December 31, 2006. Carlsen's income is assumed to have been earned evenly throughout the year. In addition, the subsidiary's dividend payments have been made as four equal quarterly payments. Roddick has inappropriately included the receipt of dividends in its Sales account rather than the separate Dividend Income account.

	Roddick Corporation	Carlsen, Inc.
Sales	$ (600,000)	$(210,000)
Cost of goods sold	200,000	80,000
Operating expenses	246,000	70,000
Dividend income	–0–	–0–
Net income	$ (154,000)	$ (60,000)
Retained earnings, 1/1/06	$ (700,000)	$(280,000)
Net income (above)	(154,000)	(60,000)
Dividends paid	70,000	20,000
Retained earnings, 12/31/06	$ (784,000)	$(320,000)
Current assets	$ 400,000	$ 220,000
Investment in Carlsen, Inc.	384,000	–0–
Building (net)	320,000	180,000
Equipment (net)	360,000	210,000
Total assets	$ 1,464,000	$ 610,000
Liabilities	$ (470,000)	$(190,000)
Common stock	(210,000)	(100,000)
Retained earnings, 12/31/06 (above)	(784,000)	(320,000)
Total liabilities and equities	$(1,464,000)	$(610,000)

a. Prepare a worksheet to consolidate these two companies on the assumption that the purchase was made on January 1, 2006.

b. Without using a worksheet, determine consolidated totals for these two companies on the assumption that the purchase was made on October 1, 2006, for $408,000. Roddick's policy is to include only post-acquisition amounts in its consolidated financial statements.

39. Watson, Inc., acquires 60 percent of Houston, Inc., on January 1, 2004, for $400,000 in cash. On that date, assets and liabilities of the subsidiary had the following values:

	Book Value	Fair Value
Current assets	$320,000	$320,000
Equipment (net)(10-year life)	410,000	380,000
Buildings (net)(15-year life)	300,000	455,000
Current liabilities	(190,000)	(190,000)
Bonds payable (due in 10 years)	(370,000)	(350,000)

On December 31, 2007, these two companies report the following figures:

	Watson	Houston
Revenues	$ (640,000)	$ (280,000)
Operating expenses	480,000	210,000
Equity in subsidiary earnings	(36,400)	–0–
Net income	$ (196,400)	$ (70,000)
Retained earnings, 1/1/07	$ (683,400)	$ (380,000)
Net income	(196,400)	(70,000)
Dividends paid	60,200	40,000
Retained earnings, 12/31/07	$ (819,600)	$ (410,000)

	Watson	Houston
Current assets	$ 215,000	$ 260,000
Investment in Houston	491,600	–0–
Equipment (net)	500,000	420,000
Buildings (net)	413,000	520,000
Total assets	$ 1,619,600	$ 1,200,000
Current liabilities	$ (390,000)	$ (170,000)
Bonds payable	(100,000)	(370,000)
Common stock	(310,000)	(250,000)
Retained earnings, 12/31/07	(819,600)	(410,000)
Total liabilities and equities	$(1,619,600)	$(1,200,000)

Answer each of the following questions:

a. The parent is recognizing a $36,400 balance as its Equity in Subsidiary Earnings. How was this balance calculated?

b. Is an adjustment to the parent's Retained Earnings as of January 1, 2007, needed? Why or why not?

c. How much total amortization expense should be recognized for consolidation purposes in 2007?

d. What is the noncontrolling interest in the subsidiary's net income?

e. Prepare a consolidated income statement.

f. What allocations were made as a result of the purchase price? What amount of each allocation remains at the end of 2007?

g. What is the December 31, 2007, amount in Noncontrolling Interest in the Subsidiary? What three components make up this total?

h. Prepare a consolidated balance sheet as of December 31, 2007.

e**X**cel

40. Good Corporation acquired 80 percent of the outstanding stock of Morning, Inc., on January 1, 2004, for $1,400,000 in cash, debt, and stock. One of Morning's buildings, with a 10-year remaining life, was undervalued on the company's accounting records by $80,000. Also, Morning's newly developed unpatented technology, with an estimated 10-year life, was assessed to have a fair value of $550,000.

During subsequent years, Morning reports the following:

	Net Income	Dividends Paid
2004	$180,000	$100,000
2005	200,000	100,000
2006	300,000	100,000
2007	400,000	120,000

The following trial balances are for these two companies as of December 31, 2007. Morning owes Good $100,000 as of this date.

	Good	Morning
Debits		
Cash	$ 300,000	$ 200,000
Receivables	700,000	400,000
Inventory	400,000	500,000
Investment in Morning	1,400,000	–0–
Land	700,000	600,000
Buildings (net)	300,000	700,000
Operating expenses	400,000	100,000
Dividends paid	380,000	120,000
Total debits	$4,580,000	$2,620,000
Credits		
Liabilities	$ 200,000	$ 620,000
Common stock	1,000,000	460,000
Additional paid-in capital	600,000	40,000
Retained earnings, 1/1/07	1,800,000	1,000,000
Revenues	884,000	500,000
Dividend income	96,000	–0–
Total credits	$4,580,000	$2,620,000

Prepare consolidated financial statements for this business combination for 2007.

41. On January 1, 2005, Truman Company bought a 30 percent interest in Athens Company. The acquisition price was $257,000 and was negotiated under the assumption that all of Athens's accounts within the company's accounting records were fairly valued. Any remaining excess cost was attributable to goodwill.

    During 2005, Athens reported net income of $90,000 and paid cash dividends of $60,000. Truman believed that it had achieved the ability to significantly influence the operations of Athens and therefore accounted for this investment by means of the equity method.

    On April 1, 2006, Truman acquired an additional 30 percent interest in Athens for $309,000 in cash. As of this date, the parent believed that a patent developed by Athens was worth $100,000, even though it was not recorded within the financial records of the subsidiary. This patent is anticipated to have a remaining life of six years. Although the financial statements now have to be consolidated, Truman elects to continue applying the equity method to this investment for internal reporting purposes. For mid-year acquisitions, Truman includes subsidiary revenues and expenses in its consolidated totals only subsequent to the date on which it obtains control.

    The following financial information is for these two companies for 2006. In addition, all of the subsidiary's operations and dividend payments are considered to have occurred evenly throughout the year.

	Truman Company	Athens Company
Revenues	$ (660,000)	$ (400,000)
Operating expenses	398,000	280,000
Equity in Athens's earnings	(59,250)	–0–
Net income	$ (321,250)	$ (120,000)
Retained earnings, 1/1/06	$ (823,000)	$ (500,000)
Net income (above)	(321,250)	(120,000)
Cash dividends paid to stockholders	148,000	80,000
Retained earnings, ending balance	$ (996,250)	$ (540,000)
Current assets	$ 481,000	$ 410,000
Investment in Athens	592,250	–0–
Land	388,000	200,000
Buildings	700,900	630,000
Total assets	$ 2,162,150	$ 1,240,000
Liabilities	$ (660,900)	$ (380,000)
Common stock	(95,000)	(300,000)
Additional paid-in capital	(410,000)	(20,000)
Retained earnings, 12/31/06	(996,250)	(540,000)
Total liabilities and equities	$(2,162,150)	$(1,240,000)

Answer each of the following questions:

a. What allocation would Truman have made of the initial $257,000 acquisition price?

b. What is the book value of the Investment in Athens account at the end of 2005?

c. What allocation would Truman have made of the second $309,000 acquisition price?

d. On Truman's separate income statement for 2006, the Income of Subsidiary account has a balance of $59,250. How was this amount derived?

e. On Truman's separate balance sheet as of December 31, 2006, the Investment in Athens account reports a balance of $592,250. How was this balance derived?

f. What is the consolidated Retained Earnings balance as of January 1, 2006? How is this amount determined?

g. Prepare a worksheet to consolidate the financial statements of these two companies as of December 31, 2006.

42. On January 1, 2005, Adams, Incorporated, acquired 60 percent of the outstanding shares of Hart Company for $566,000 in cash. At the time of this purchase, Hart held a building (six-year remaining life) that was undervalued in the accounting records by $70,000. During 2005, Hart reported net income of $150,000 and paid cash dividends of $80,000. On May 1, 2006, Adams bought an additional 30 percent interest in Hart for $366,000. Adams reappraised Hart's assets and liabilities on this date and estimated that the company's buildings were currently undervalued by $260,000. At the time of this second purchase, these buildings had a five-year remaining life.

    The following financial information is for these two companies for 2006. Hart issued no additional capital stock during either 2005 or 2006. Income and dividends can be assumed as having been earned and paid evenly throughout each of the years.

	Adams, Incorporated	Hart Company
Revenues	$ (400,000)	$ (300,000)
Operating expenses	200,000	120,000
Investment income (partial equity method)	(144,000)	–0–
Net income	$ (344,000)	$ (180,000)
Retained earnings, 1/1/06	$ (800,000)	$ (500,000)
Net income (above)	(344,000)	(180,000)
Dividends paid	144,000	60,000
Retained earnings, 12/31/06	$(1,000,000)	$ (620,000)
Current assets	$ 200,000	$ 190,000
Investment in Hart Company	1,070,000	–0–
Land	100,000	600,000
Buildings (net)	210,000	300,000
Equipment (net)	380,000	110,000
Total assets	$ 1,960,000	$ 1,200,000
Liabilities	$ (500,000)	$ (200,000)
Common stock	(400,000)	(300,000)
Additional paid-in capital	(60,000)	(80,000)
Retained earnings, 12/31/06	(1,000,000)	(620,000)
Total liabilities and equities	$(1,960,000)	$(1,200,000)

    Determine the appropriate balances for consolidated financial statements for Adams, Incorporated, and Hart Company for December 31, 2006, and the year then ended. To account for the 30 percent ownership share of Hart prior to the May 1, 2006, purchase, Adams will remove 30 percent of Hart's revenues, expenses, and dividends occurring during the first four months of the year through a consolidated worksheet adjustment. Show supporting computations in good form.

43. On January 1, 2003, Wilbourne Company acquired 6,000 of the 10,000 outstanding shares of Hampton Corporation. The purchase price included an allocation of $120,000 for a customer base that was not reflected on Hampton's books. All other assets and liabilities of Hampton had fair values equal to their book values. The customer base was to be amortized over a 20-year life.

    On January 1, 2006, Wilbourne bought an additional 2,000 shares of Hampton, increasing ownership to an 80 percent interest. In making this second acquisition, Wilbourne assigned $40,000 of the purchase price to a patent (life of 10 years) held by Hampton. An additional $40,000 was attributed to Hampton's expanding customer base to be amortized at $2,000 per year.

    In need of raising cash, Wilbourne sold 1,000 shares of its investment in Hampton on April 1, 2007, for $140,000 in cash. A problem arose in connection with the recording of this sale. Wilbourne's accountants could not agree on the appropriate gain or loss to be recognized, so they simply debited cash for $140,000 and credited the Investment account for the same amount. Because of the confusion, Wilbourne prepared no other entries for the investment for the year of 2007, although the equity method had been properly applied through 2006.

The following individual financial records are for these two companies for 2007. Prepare a consolidation worksheet and the resulting financial statements. Assume that an averaging system is used to determine the appropriate book value of the shares that were sold.

	Wilbourne Company	Hampton Corporation
Revenues	$ (920,000)	$ (600,000)
Expenses	650,000	440,000
Equity income of Hampton Corporation	–0–	–0–
Net income	$ (270,000)	$ (160,000)
Retained earnings, 1/1/07	$(1,417,000)	$ (750,000)
Net income (above)	(270,000)	(160,000)
Dividends paid	150,000	–0–
Retained earnings, 12/31/07	$(1,537,000)	$ (910,000)
Cash	$ 60,000	$ 98,000
Receivables	430,000	210,000
Inventories	677,000	620,000
Investment in Hampton Corporation	870,000	–0–
Buildings and equipment (net)	620,000	514,000
Patents (net)	40,000	90,000
Total assets	$ 2,697,000	$ 1,532,000
Liabilities	$ (690,000)	$ (322,000)
Common stock	(470,000)	(300,000)
Retained earnings, 12/31/07	(1,537,000)	(910,000)
Total liabilities and equities	$(2,697,000)	$(1,532,000)

Develop Your Skills

FARS RESEARCH CASE *SFAS 141, SFAS 142*

Required:

1. Identify the prescribed method of accounting for the acquisition by a parent company of the non-controlling interests in its subsidiary.
2. What types of transactions qualify as an acquisition of a noncontrolling interest by a parent?
3. What procedures are appropriate for goodwill impairment testing in the presence of a noncontrolling interest? What complications are introduced by the parent company concept in applying a goodwill impairment test in the presence of a noncontrolling interest?

EXCEL CASE

Giant Company acquired a controlling interest in Small Company at the beginning of the year. Subsequently, Giant reports net income of $60,000 for the year (without regard for the investment in Small). For the same period, this subsidiary reports earnings of $30,000. In acquiring its interest, Giant paid a total of $224,000, although Small's book value was only $200,000 at the time. A building with a 10-year life was undervalued on Small's accounting records by $10,000. Any other excess cost was attributed to a copyright with a 20-year life.

Required:

Using an Excel spreadsheet, compute consolidated net income after reduction is made for the non-controlling interest claim under each of the following concepts. Formulate your solution to accommodate various controlling interest percentages. Assume that the price paid for Small can be used to compute varying amounts for Small's fair value as a whole.

1. Economic unit.
2. Proportionate consolidation.
3. Parent company.

Computer Project

A Comparison of Consolidated Financial Statements under the Economic Unit Concept and the Parent Company Concept

The purpose of this project is to assess the sensitivity of alternative concepts of noncontrolling interest valuation on consolidated financial reporting. The project requires the use of a computer and a spreadsheet software package (Microsoft Excel®, etc.). The use of these tools allows assessment of the sensitivity of alternative accounting methods on consolidated financial reporting without the necessity of preparing several similar worksheets by hand. Also, modeling a worksheet process can result in a better understanding of accounting for combined reporting entities.

The project involves preparing two consolidated worksheets for a parent and subsidiary. The first worksheet uses the economic unit concept for the consolidated entity. The second worksheet uses the parent company concept (most prevalent in current practice). Additional analysis is provided to assess the sensitivity of each approach to changes in the percentage of the subsidiary owned by the noncontrolling interest.

Project Scenario

On January 1, 2006, Pinter purchased a controlling interest in Strong, Inc., for $800,000. The price paid for this controlling interest was considered sufficient evidence to compute a fair value for Strong Co. as a whole. At that date Strong's book value was $600,000. Strong's assets and liabilities approximated their fair values except for the following items:

	Fair Value	Book Value
Land	$ 88,000	$100,000
Building (six-year remaining life)	170,000	140,000
Equipment (three-year remaining life)	370,000	325,000

Pinter accounts for its investment in Strong using the equity method. Strong declared a $25,000 dividend late in 2006. The dividend had not been paid as of December 31, 2006.

Pinter and Strong submit trial balances for consolidation as of December 31, 2006, as indicated in the accompanying worksheet template. Note that the trial balance for Pinter reflects an 80 percent ownership of Strong. However, to provide insights regarding varying levels of outside ownership, the trial balance must be programmed so that this percentage can vary.

Instructions:

1. Input the information from the **worksheet template** into your spreadsheet as a starting point for two separate consolidation worksheets: one for the economic unit concept and one for the parent company concept. Use either of the separate worksheets available in Excel or use distinct areas of a single spreadsheet for each consolidation.

2. Designate a single cell as the percentage of Strong acquired by Pinter. Use this cell (e.g., B38 in the worksheet template) as a reference in other cell formulas. **Your worksheets should automatically change when different percentages are entered in this designated cell.**

3. On each worksheet, prepare separate cost allocation schedules using formulas to allow for alternative ownership percentages.

4. To accommodate alternative ownership percentages, the following accounts in Pinter's trial balances require formulas: Equity Income of Strong, Dividends Receivable, Investment in Strong, as well as the carrydown figures (Income and Retained Earnings) and the totals. For example, in Excel, cell B17 in Pinter's trial balance can be entered as =C12*B38 so that it will change whenever cell B38 changes. No accounts in Strong's trial balances require formulas.

5. Complete the worksheet adjusting and eliminating entries, the noncontrolling interest amounts, and consolidated balances. Be sure to use formulas to enable the worksheets to automatically change when the percentage acquired is changed.

6. Prepare an accompanying written report that compares and explains the differences between the economic unit concept and parent company concept consolidated figures at 80 percent ownership. Describe the effects on the consolidated balances when 100 percent ownership exists. Indicate which concept you believe should be used in financial reporting and why.

	A	B	C	D	E	F	G
	Worksheet Template						
				Adjustments & Eliminations		Noncontrolling	
1	December 31, 2006			Debit	Credit	Interest	
2		**Pinter**	**Strong**	Debit	Credit	Interest	Consolidated
3	Revenues	(840,000)	(740,000)				
4	Operating expenses	690,000	550,000				
5	Equity income of Strong	(136,000)					
6	Noncontrolling interest in Strong's income						
7	Net income	(286,000)	(190,000)				
8							
9	Retained earnings—Pinter, 1/1/06	(775,000)					
10	Retained earnings—Strong, 1/1/06		(350,000)				
11	Net income (above)	(286,000)	(190,000)				
12	Dividends declared	115,000	25,000				
13	Retained earnings, 12/31/06	(946,000)	(515,000)				
14							
15	Cash	102,000	32,000				
16	Accounts receivable	96,000	140,000				
17	Dividends receivable	20,000					
18	Inventory	225,000	208,000				
19	Investment in Strong	916,000					
20							
21							
22							
23	Land	200,000	100,000				
24	Buildings (net)	550,000	120,000				
25	Equipment (net)	350,000	310,000				
26	Goodwill						
27	Total assets	2,459,000	910,000				
28							
29	Dividends payable		(25,000)				
30	Liabilities	(513,000)	(120,000)				
31	Common stock	(1,000,000)	(250,000)				
32	Noncontrolling interest						
33							
34							
35	Retained earnings (above)	(946,000)	(515,000)				
36	Total liabilities and equity	(2,459,000)	(910,000)				
37							
38	**Percentage acquired**	**80%**					

Chapter **Five**

Consolidated Financial Statements— Intercompany Asset Transactions

Questions to Consider

- How does the intercompany transfer of inventory or other assets between parent and subsidiary affect the consolidation process?

- Gains on intercompany transactions are considered unrealized until the assets are resold to outsiders or consumed. Prior to the realization of these gains, what adjustments are required in producing consolidated financial statements?

- How does the presence of intercompany transactions affect the balances reported for any noncontrolling interest? What impact does the direction of these transfers (upstream versus downstream) have on the reporting of a noncontrolling interest?

- The intercompany sale of land and depreciable assets also can occur between the members of a business combination. What impact does the specific type of property being conveyed have on the consolidation process?

- Why does the transfer of a depreciable asset frequently result in the recording of excess depreciation in subsequent years?

Chapter 1 analyzed the deferral and subsequent recognition of gains created by inventory transfers between two affiliated companies in connection with equity method accounting. The central theme of that discussion is that intercompany profits are not considered to be realized until the earning process is culminated by a sale to an unrelated party. This same accounting logic applies to transactions between companies within a business combination. Because a single economic entity is formed, such sales create neither profits nor losses. In reference to this issue, *ARB 51* (para. 7) states,

> As consolidated statements are based on the assumption that they represent the financial position and operating results of a single business enterprise, such statements should not include gain or loss on transactions among the companies in the group. Accordingly, any intercompany profit or loss on assets remaining within the group should be eliminated; the concept usually applied for this purpose is gross profit or loss.[1]

The elimination of the accounting effects created by intercompany transactions is one of the most significant problems encountered in the consolidation process. The volume of transfers within most large enterprises can be large. A recent annual report for the Ford Motor Company, for example, shows the elimination of intersegment revenues amounting to $6.83 billion.

Such transactions are especially common in companies that have been constructed as a vertically integrated chain of organizations. These entities reduce their costs by

---

[1] This statement is reiterated virtually verbatim in the 2005 FASB Exposure Draft *Consolidated Financial Statements, Including Accounting and Reporting of Noncontrolling Interests in Subsidiaries*, para. 10.

developing affiliations in which one operation furnishes products to another. As *Mergers & Acquisitions* observed,

> Downstream acquisitions . . . are aimed at securing critical sources of materials and components, streamlining manufacturing and materials planning, gaining economies of scale, entering new markets, and enhancing overall competitiveness. Manufacturers that combine with suppliers are often able to assert total control over such critical areas as product quality and resource planning.[2]

Intercompany asset transactions take several forms. In particular, inventory transfers are especially prevalent. However, the sale of land and depreciable assets also can occur between the parties within a combination. This chapter examines the consolidation procedures for each of these different types of intercompany asset transfers.

INTERCOMPANY INVENTORY TRANSACTIONS

As previous chapters discussed, companies that make up a business combination frequently retain their legal identities as separate operating centers and maintain their own record-keeping. Thus, any inventory sales between these companies trigger the independent accounting systems of both parties. The seller duly records revenue, and the buyer simultaneously enters the purchase into its accounts. For internal reporting purposes, recording an inventory transfer as a sale/purchase provides vital data to help measure the operational efficiency of each enterprise.[3]

Despite the internal information benefits of accounting for the transaction in this manner, from a consolidated perspective neither a sale nor a purchase has occurred. *An intercompany transfer is merely the internal movement of inventory, an event that creates no net change in the financial position of the business combination taken as a whole.* Thus, in producing consolidated financial statements, the recorded effects of these transfers are eliminated so that consolidated statements reflect only transactions with outside parties. Worksheet entries serve this purpose; they adapt the financial information reported by the separate companies to the perspective of the consolidated enterprise. The entire impact of the intercompany transactions must be identified and then removed. The deleting of the actual transfer is described here first.

The Sales and Purchases Accounts

To account for related companies as a single economic entity, all intercompany sales/purchases accounts are eliminated. For example, if Arlington Company makes an $80,000 inventory sale to Zirkin Company, an affiliated party within a business combination, both parties record the transfer in their internal records as a normal sale/purchase. The following consolidation worksheet entry is then necessary to remove the resulting balances from the externally reported figures. Cost of Goods Sold is reduced here under the assumption that the Purchases account usually is closed out prior to the consolidation process.

Consolidation Entry TI		
Sales	80,000	
Cost of Goods Sold (purchases component)		80,000
To eliminate effects of intercompany transfer of inventory. (Labeled **"TI"** in reference to the transferred inventory.)		

---

[2] "Acquiring along the Value Chain," *Mergers & Acquisitions,* June–July 1996, p. 8.

[3] For all intercompany transactions, the two parties involved view the events from different perspectives. Thus, the transfer is both a sale and a purchase, often creating both a receivable and a payable. To indicate the dual nature of such transactions, these accounts are indicated within this text as sales/purchases, receivables/payables, and so on.

In the preparation of consolidated financial statements, the preceding elimination must be made for all intercompany inventory transfers. The total recorded (intercompany) sales figure is deleted regardless of whether the transaction was downstream (from parent to subsidiary) or upstream (from subsidiary to parent).[4] Furthermore, any markup included in the transfer price does not affect the elimination. Because the entire amount of the transfer occurred between related parties, the total effect must be removed in preparing the consolidated statements.[5]

Unrealized Gains—Year of Transfer (Year 1)

Removal of the sale/purchase is often just the first in a series of consolidation entries necessitated by inventory transfers. Despite the previous elimination, unrealized gains created by such sales can still exist in the accounting records at year-end. These gains initially result when the merchandise is priced at more than historical cost. Actual transfer prices are established in several ways, including the normal sales price of the inventory, sales price less a specified discount, or at a predetermined markup above cost. In a footnote to recent financial statements, Ford Motor Company explains that

> Intercompany sales among geographic areas consist primarily of vehicles, parts, and components manufactured by the company and various subsidiaries and sold to different entities within the consolidated group; transfer prices for these transactions are established by agreement between the affected entities.

Regardless of the method used for this pricing decision, intercompany gains that remain unrealized at year-end must be removed in arriving at consolidated figures.

All Inventory Remains at Year-End

In the preceding illustration, assume that Arlington acquired or produced this inventory at a cost of $50,000 and then sold it to Zirkin, an affiliated party, at the indicated $80,000 price. From a consolidated perspective, the inventory still has a historical cost of only $50,000. However, Zirkin's records now report it as an asset at the $80,000 transfer price. In addition, because of the markup, Arlington has recorded a $30,000 gross profit as a result of this intercompany sale. Because the transaction did not occur with an outside party, recognition of this profit is not appropriate for the combination as a whole.

Thus, although the consolidation entry **TI** shown earlier eliminated the sale/purchase figures, the $30,000 inflation created by the transfer price still exists in two areas of the individual statements:

- Ending inventory remains overstated by $30,000.
- Gross profit is artificially overstated by this same amount.

Correcting the ending inventory requires only a reduction in the asset. However, before decreasing gross profit, the accounts affected by the unrealized gain must be identified. The ending inventory total serves as a negative component within the Cost of Goods Sold computation; it represents the portion of acquired inventory that was not sold. Thus, the $30,000 overstatement of the inventory that is still held incorrectly decreases this expense (the inventory that was sold). *Despite Entry **TI**, the inflated ending inventory figure causes cost of goods sold to be too low and, thus, profits to be too high by $30,000.* For consolidation purposes, the expense is increased by this amount through a worksheet adjustment that properly removes the unrealized gain from consolidated net income.

---

[4] Downstream and upstream transactions were introduced in Chapter 1. Although the direction of the transfer did not influence financial reporting under the equity method for significant influence investments (usually 20 to 50 percent), the distinction is significant when control exists and consolidated financial statements are subsequently prepared.

[5] As is shown in the appendix to this chapter, alternative theoretical approaches to consolidation that advocate removing only the parent's portion of intercompany sales/purchases when a noncontrolling interest is present can be identified. In current practice, elimination of all intercompany sales/purchases (as shown here) appears to predominate.

EARNINGS MANAGEMENT

Enron Corporation's 2001 third-quarter 10-Q report disclosed the following transaction with LJM2, a nonconsolidated special purpose entity (SPE) that was formed by Enron:

> In June 2000, LJM2 purchased dark fiber optic cable from Enron for a purchase price of $100 million. LJM2 paid Enron $30 million in cash and the balance in an interest-bearing note for $70 million. Enron recognized $67 million in pre-tax earnings in 2000 related to the asset sale. Pursuant to a marketing agreement with LJM2, Enron was compensated for marketing the fiber to others and providing operation and maintenance services to LJM2 with respect to the fiber. LJM2 sold a portion of the fiber to industry participants for $40 million, which resulted in Enron recognizing agency fee revenue of $20.3 million.

As investigations later discovered, LJM2 was in many ways controlled by Enron.

FASB Interpretation 46(R) now requires the consolidation of SPEs that are essentially controlled by their primary beneficiary.

By selling goods to SPEs that it controlled but did not consolidate, did Enron overstate its earnings? What effect does consolidation have on the financial reporting for transactions between a firm and its controlled entities?

Consequently, if all of the transferred inventory is retained by the business combination at the end of the year, the following worksheet entry also must be included to eliminate the effects of the gain that remains unrealized within ending inventory:

Consolidation Entry G—Year of Transfer (Year 1) All Inventory Remains		
Cost of Goods Sold (ending inventory component)	30,000	
Inventory (balance sheet account)		30,000
To remove unrealized gain created by intercompany sale.		

This entry (labeled **G** for gain) reduces the consolidated Inventory account to its original $50,000 historical cost. Furthermore, increasing Cost of Goods Sold by $30,000 effectively removes the unrealized gain from gross profit. Thus, both reporting problems created by the transfer price markup are resolved by this worksheet entry.

Only a Portion of Inventory Remains

Obviously, a company does not buy inventory to hold it for an indefinite time. It either uses the acquired items within the company's operations or resells them to unrelated, outside parties. Intercompany gains ultimately are realized by subsequently consuming or reselling these goods. Therefore, only the transferred inventory still held at year-end continues to be recorded in the separate statements at a value more than the historical cost. For this reason, *the elimination of unrealized gains (Entry G) is based not on total intercompany sales but only on the amount of transferred merchandise retained within the business at the end of the year.*

To illustrate, assume that Arlington transferred inventory costing $50,000 to Zirkin, a related company, for $80,000, thus recording a gross profit of $30,000. Assume further that by year-end Zirkin has resold $60,000 of these goods to unrelated parties but retains the other $20,000 (for resale in the following year). From the viewpoint of the consolidated company, it has now earned the gain on the $60,000 portion of the intercompany sale and need not make an adjustment for consolidation purposes.

Conversely, any gain recorded in connection with the $20,000 in merchandise that remains is still a component within Zirkin's Inventory account. Because the markup was $37\frac{1}{2}$ percent ($30,000 gross profit/$80,000 transfer price), this retained inventory is stated at a value $7,500 more than its original cost ($20,000 $\times$ $37\frac{1}{2}\%$). The required reduction

(Entry **G**) is not the entire $30,000 shown previously but only the $7,500 unrealized gain that remains in ending inventory.

Consolidation Entry G—Year of Transfer (Year 1) 40% of Inventory Remains (replaces previous entry)		
Cost of Goods Sold (ending inventory component)	7,500	
Inventory		7,500
To remove portion of intercompany gain that is unrealized in year of transfer.		

Unrealized Gains—Year Following Transfer (Year 2)

Whenever an unrealized intercompany gain is present in ending inventory, one further consolidation entry is eventually required. Although Entry **G** removes the gain from the *consolidated* inventory balances in the year of transfer, the $7,500 overstatement remains within the separate financial records of the buyer and seller. The effects of this gain are carried into their beginning balances in the subsequent year. Hence, another worksheet adjustment is necessary in the period following the transfer. For consolidation purposes, the unrealized portion of the intercompany gain must be adjusted in two successive years (from ending inventory in the year of transfer and from beginning inventory of the next period).

Referring again to Arlington's sale of inventory to Zirkin, the $7,500 unrealized gain is still in Zirkin's Inventory account at the start of the subsequent year. Once again, the overstatement is removed within the consolidation process but this time from the beginning inventory balance (which appears in the financial statements only as a positive component of cost of goods sold). This elimination is termed *Entry *G.* The asterisk indicates that a previous year transfer created the intercompany gain.

Consolidation Entry *G—Year Following Transfer (Year 2)		
Retained Earnings (beginning balance of seller)	7,500	
Cost of Goods Sold (beginning inventory component)		7,500
To remove unrealized gain from beginning figures so that it can be recognized currently in the period in which the earning process is completed.		

Reducing Cost of Goods Sold (beginning inventory) through this worksheet entry increases the gross profit reported for this second year. For consolidation purposes, the gain on the transfer is recognized in the period in which the items are actually sold to outside parties. As shown in the following diagram, Entry **G** initially deferred the $7,500 gain because this amount was unrealized in the year of transfer. Entry ***G** now increases consolidated net income (by decreasing cost of goods sold) to reflect the earning process in the current year.

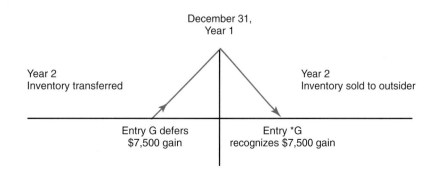

In Entry ***G,** removal of the $7,500 from beginning inventory (within Cost of Goods Sold) appropriately increases current income and should not pose a significant conceptual problem. However, the rationale for decreasing the seller's beginning Retained Earnings deserves further explanation. This reduction removes the unrealized gain (recognized by the seller in the year of transfer) so that the profit is reported in the period when it is earned. Despite the consolidation entries in Year 1, the $7,500 gain remained on this company's separate books and was closed to Retained Earnings at the end of the period. Recall that consolidation entries are never posted to the individual affiliate's books. Therefore, from a consolidated view, the buyer's Inventory and the seller's Retained Earnings accounts as of the beginning of Year 2 contain the unrealized profit, and must both be reduced in Entry ***G.**

Intercompany Beginning Inventory Gain Adjustment—Downstream Sales When Parent Uses Equity Method

The worksheet elimination of the sales/purchases balances (Entry **TI**) and the entry to remove the unrealized gain from ending Inventory in Year 1 (Entry **G**) are both standard, regardless of the circumstances of the consolidation. Conversely, in one specific situation, the procedure used to eliminate the intercompany gain from Year 2's beginning accounts differs from the Entry ***G** just presented. If (1) the original transfer is downstream (made by the parent) and (2) the equity method has been applied for internal accounting purposes, the Equity in Subsidiary Earnings account replaces beginning Retained Earnings in Entry ***G.**

When using the equity method, the parent maintains appropriate income balances within its own individual financial records. Thus, the parent defers any unrealized gain at the end of Year 1 through an equity method adjustment that also decreases the Investment in Subsidiary account. With the gain deferred, the Retained Earnings of the parent/seller at the beginning of the following year is correctly stated. The parent's Retained Earnings does not contain the unrealized gain and needs no adjustment.[6]

At the end of Year 2, both the Equity in Subsidiary Earnings and the Investment accounts are increased in recognition of the previously deferred intercompany gain. The Investment account—having been decreased in Year 1 and increased in Year 2 for the intercompany gain—thus no longer reflects any effects from the original deferral. For consolidation purposes, Entry ***G** simply transfers the income effect of the realized gain from the Equity in Subsidiary Earnings account to Cost of Goods Sold, appropriately increasing current consolidated income. The remaining balance in the Equity in Subsidiary Earnings account now reflects the same activity represented in the Investment account and is subsequently eliminated against the Investment account.

Consolidation Entry *G—Year Following Transfer (Year 2) (replaces previous Entry *G when transfers have been downstream and the equity method is in use)[7]

Equity in Subsidiary Earnings	7,500	
Cost of Goods Sold (beginning inventory component)		7,500

To recognize the previously deferred unrealized downstream inventory gain as part of current year income. The Equity in Subsidiary Earnings account replaces the Retained Earnings account (used for upstream profit adjustments) when adjusting for downstream sales. The parent's Retained Earnings account has already been corrected by application of the equity method.

[6] For upstream intercompany gains in beginning inventory, the subsidiary's retained earnings remain overstated and must be adjusted through Entry ***G.**

[7] A widely accepted alternative to recognizing realized intercompany inventory profits in the subsidiary's beginning inventory (downstream sale) when the parent uses the equity method (***G**) is as follows:

Investment in Subsidiary	7,500	
Cost of Goods Sold		7,500

In this case, the full amount of the Equity in Subsidiary Earnings is eliminated against the Investment in Subsidiaries account in Consolidation Adjustment **I.** In either alternative adjustment for recognizing realized intercompany inventory profits, the final consolidated balances remain exactly the same: Equity in Subsidiary Earnings = 0, Investment in Subsidiary = 0, and Cost of Goods Sold is reduced by $7,500.

EXHIBIT 5.1
Relationship between
Gross Profit Rate and
Markup on Cost

In determining appropriate amounts of intercompany profits for deferral and subsequent recognition in consolidated financial reports, two alternative—but mathematically related— profit percentages are often seen. Recalling that Gross Profit = Sales − Cost of Goods Sold, then

$$\textbf{Gross profit rate (GPR)} = \frac{\text{Gross profit}}{\text{Sales}} = \frac{MC}{1 + MC}$$

$$\textbf{Markup on cost (MC)} = \frac{\text{Gross profit}}{\text{Cost of goods sold}} = \frac{GPR}{1 - GPR}$$

Example: Sales (transfer price) $1,000
              Cost of goods sold   800
              Gross profit $ 200

Here the *GPR* = (200/1,000) = 20% and the *MC* = (200/800) = 25%. In most intercompany purchases and sales, the sales (transfer) price is known and therefore the *GPR* is the simplest percentage to use to determine the amount of intercompany profit.

$$\text{Intercompany profit} = \text{Transfer price} \times GPR$$

Instead, if the markup on cost is available, it readily converts to a *GPR* by the above formula. In this case (0.25/1.25) = 20%.

Finally, various markup percentages determine the dollar values for intercompany profit deferrals. Exhibit 5.1 shows formulas for both the gross profit rate and markup on cost and the relation between the two.

Unrealized Gains—Effect on Noncontrolling Interest Valuation

The worksheet entries just described appropriately account for the effects of intercompany inventory transfers on business combinations. However, one question remains: What impact do these procedures have on the valuation of a noncontrolling interest? In regard to this issue, paragraph 13 of *ARB 51* states,

> The amount of intercompany profit or loss to be eliminated in accordance with paragraph 7 is not affected by the existence of a minority interest. The complete elimination of the intercompany profit or loss is consistent with the underlying assumption that consolidated statements represent the financial position and operating results of a single business enterprise. The elimination of the intercompany profit or loss *may be allocated proportionately* between the majority and minority interests [emphasis added].

The last sentence indicates that alternative approaches are available in computing the noncontrolling interest's share of a subsidiary's net income. According to this pronouncement, unrealized gains resulting from intercompany transfers *may or may not* affect recognition of outside ownership. Because the amount attributed to a noncontrolling interest reduces consolidated net income, the handling of this issue can affect the reported profitability of a business combination.

To illustrate, assume that Large Company owns 70 percent of the voting stock of Small Company. To avoid extraneous complications, assume that no amortization expense resulted from this purchase. Assume further that Large reports current net income (from separate operations) of $500,000 while Small earns $100,000. During the current period, intercompany transfers of $200,000 occur with a total markup of $90,000. At the end of the year, an unrealized intercompany gain of $40,000 remains within the inventory accounts.

Clearly, the consolidated net income prior to the reduction for the 30 percent noncontrolling interest is $560,000, the two income balances less the unrealized gain. The problem facing the accountant is the computation of the noncontrolling interest's share of Small's income. Because of the flexibility allowed by *ARB 51*, this figure may be reported as either $30,000 (30 percent of the $100,000 earnings of the subsidiary) or $18,000 (30 percent of reported income after that figure is reduced by the $40,000 unrealized gain).

To determine an appropriate valuation for this noncontrolling interest allocation, the relationship between an intercompany transaction and the outside owners must be analyzed. If a transfer is downstream (the parent sells inventory to the subsidiary), a logical view would seem to be that the unrealized gain is that of the parent company. The parent made the original sale; therefore, the gross profit is included in its financial records. Because the subsidiary's income is unaffected, little justification exists for adjusting the noncontrolling interest to reflect the deferral of the unrealized gain. Consequently, in the example of Large and Small, if the transfers were downstream, the 30 percent noncontrolling interest would be $30,000 based on Small's reported income of $100,000.

In contrast, if the subsidiary sells inventory to the parent (an upstream transfer), the subsidiary's financial records would recognize the gross profit even though part of this income remains unrealized from a consolidation perspective. Because the outside owners possess their interest in the subsidiary, a reasonable conclusion would be that valuation of the noncontrolling interest is calculated on the income actually earned by this company. The 1995 FASB Exposure Draft, *Consolidated Financial Statements: Policy and Procedures,* supports allocating a proportionate amount of the intercompany profit adjustments (from upstream sales) to the noncontrolling interest:

> The effects on equity of eliminating intercompany profit and losses on assets that remain within the group shall be allocated between the controlling interest and the noncontrolling interest on the basis of their proportionate interest in the selling affiliate.

In this textbook, the noncontrolling interest's share of consolidated net income is computed based on *the reported income of the subsidiary after adjustment for any unrealized upstream gains.* Returning to Large Company and Small Company, if the $40,000 unrealized gain results from an upstream sale from subsidiary to parent, only $60,000 of Small's $100,000 reported income actually has been earned by the end of the year. The allocation to the noncontrolling interest is, therefore, reported as $18,000, or 30 percent of this realized income figure.

Alternative Concepts of a Noncontrolling Interest

Although the noncontrolling interest figure is based here on the subsidiary's reported income adjusted for the effects of upstream intercompany transfers, *ARB 51,* as quoted earlier, does not require this treatment. Giving effect to upstream transfers in this calculation but not to downstream transfers is no more than an attempt to select the most logical approach from among acceptable alternatives. Over the years a number of possible methods of consolidating the results of intercompany transfers have been considered. Several of these alternatives are discussed in the appendix at the end of this chapter.

Intercompany Inventory Transfers Summarized

To assist in overcoming the complications created by intercompany transfers, we demonstrate the consolidation process in three different ways:

- Before proceeding to a numerical example, the impact of intercompany transfers on consolidated figures is reviewed. Ultimately, the accountant must understand how the balances to be reported by a business combination are derived when unrealized gains result from either upstream or downstream sales.

- Next, two different consolidation worksheets are produced: one for downstream transfers and the other for upstream. The various consolidation procedures used in these worksheets are explained and analyzed.

- Finally, several of the worksheet entries used in developing a consolidation worksheet are shown side by side so that the differences created by the direction of the transfers can be better understood.

The Development of Consolidated Totals

The following summary discusses only the accounts impacted by intercompany transactions:

Revenues. The parent's balance is added to the subsidiary's balance, but all intercompany transfers are then removed.

Cost of Goods Sold. This expense is one of the most difficult figures computed within the consolidation process. The parent's balance is added to the subsidiary's balance but all intercompany transfers are removed. The resulting total is decreased by any beginning unrealized gain (thus raising net income) and increased by any ending unrealized gain (to reduce net income).

EXHIBIT 5.2
Intercompany Transfers

	2005	2006
Transfer prices	$80,000	$100,000
Historical cost	60,000	70,000
Gross profit	$20,000	$ 30,000
Inventory remaining at year's end (at transfer price)	$16,000	$ 20,000

Expenses. The parent's balance is added to the subsidiary's balance plus any amortization expense for the year recognized on the purchase price allocations.[8]

Noncontrolling Interest in Subsidiary's Net Income. The subsidiary's reported net income is adjusted for the effects of unrealized gains on upstream transfers (but not downstream transfers) and then multiplied by the percentage of outside ownership.

Retained Earnings at the Beginning of the Year. As discussed in previous chapters, if the equity method has been applied, the parent's balance mirrors the consolidated total. When any other method is used, the parent's beginning Retained Earnings must be converted to the equity method by Entry ***C**. Accruals for this purpose are based on the income actually earned by the subsidiary in previous years (reported income adjusted for any unrealized upstream gains).

Inventory. The parent's balance is added to the subsidiary's balance. Any unrealized gain remaining at the end of the current year is removed to adjust the reported balance to historical cost.

Land, Buildings, and Equipment. The parent's balance is added to the subsidiary's balance. This total is adjusted for any purchase price allocations and subsequent amortization.[9]

Noncontrolling Interest in Subsidiary at End of Year. The final total begins with the noncontrolling interest at the beginning of the year. This figure is based on the subsidiary's book value on that date after removing any unrealized gains on upstream sales. The beginning balance is updated by adding the portion of the subsidiary's income assigned to these outside owners (computed above) and subtracting the noncontrolling interest's share of the subsidiary's dividend payments.

Intercompany Inventory Transfers Illustrated

To examine the various consolidation procedures relative to intercompany inventory transfers, assume that Top Company purchases 80 percent of the voting stock of Bottom Company on January 1, 2005. The parent pays a total of $400,000, a price that includes all directly related consolidation costs. Allocation of $40,000 is made to a database, a figure amortized at the rate of $2,000 per year for 20 years.

The subsidiary reports net income of $30,000 in 2005 and $70,000 in 2006, the current year. Dividend payments are $20,000 in the first year and $50,000 in the second. Top applies the cost method so that dividend income of $16,000 ($20,000 × 80%) and $40,000 ($50,000 × 80%) is recorded by the parent during these two years. Using the cost method in this initial example avoids the problem of computing the parent's investment account balances. However, this illustration is extended to demonstrate the changes necessary if the parent applies the equity method.

After the takeover, intercompany inventory sales occurred between the two companies as shown in Exhibit 5.2. A $10,000 intercompany debt also exists as of December 31, 2006.

The 2006 consolidation of Top and Bottom is presented twice. First, the transfers are assumed to be downstream from parent to subsidiary. Second, consolidated figures are recomputed with the transfers being viewed as upstream. This distinction is significant only because of a noncontrolling interest.

---

[8] As discussed later in this chapter, consolidated expenses also have to be reduced to remove excess depreciation recognized whenever a depreciable asset is transferred between the companies within a business combination at a price more than the book value.

[9] As discussed later in this chapter, if land, buildings, or equipment have been transferred between parent and subsidiary, the separately reported balances must be returned to historical cost figures in deriving consolidated totals.

Downstream Sales

In the first example, all inventory transfers are assumed to have been *downstream* from Top to Bottom. Based on that perspective, the worksheet to consolidate these two companies for the year ending December 31, 2006, is in Exhibit 5.3.

Most of the worksheet entries found in Exhibit 5.3 are described and analyzed in previous chapters of this textbook. Thus, only four of these entries are examined in detail along with the computation of the noncontrolling interests in the subsidiary's income.

Entry *G   Entry *G removes the unrealized gains carried over from the previous period. Because $16,000 in transferred merchandise was retained by Bottom at the first of the current year, any related gain is unearned and must be deferred. The 2005 gross profit rate on these items was 25 percent ($20,000 gross profit/$80,000 transfer price), indicating an unrealized gain of $4,000 (25 percent of the remaining $16,000 in inventory). Thus, Entry *G reduces cost of goods sold (or the beginning inventory component of that expense) by that amount as well as the January 1, 2006, Retained Earnings of Top (the seller of the goods).

Two effects are created by Entry *G: First, last year's profits, as reflected in the seller's beginning Retained Earnings, are reduced because the $4,000 gain was not earned at that time. Second, the reduction in Cost of Goods Sold creates an increase in current year income. From a consolidation perspective, the gain is correctly recognized in 2006 when the inventory is sold to an outside party.

Entry *C   Entry *C is introduced in Chapter 3 as an initial consolidation adjustment required whenever the equity method is not applied by the parent company. Entry *C converts the parent's beginning Retained Earnings to a consolidated total. In the current illustration, Top did not accrue its portion of the 2005 increase in Bottom's book value [($30,000 income less $20,000 paid in dividends) × 80%, or $8,000] or record the $2,000 amortization expense for this same period. Because neither number has been recognized within the parent's individual records, both must be brought into the consolidation process through a $6,000 adjustment (Entry *C). The intercompany transfers do not affect this entry because they were downstream; the gains had no impact on the income recognized in connection with the subsidiary.

Entry TI   The intercompany sales/purchases for 2006 are eliminated by Entry **TI.** The entire $100,000 transfer recorded by the two parties during the current period is removed to arrive at consolidated figures for the business combination.

Entry G   Entry G defers the unrealized gain remaining at the end of 2006. The $20,000 in transferred merchandise that Bottom retained has a markup of 30 percent ($30,000 gross profit/$100,000 transfer price); thus, the unrealized gain amounts to $6,000. On the worksheet, Entry G eliminates this overstatement in the Inventory asset balance as well as the ending inventory (negative) component of Cost of Goods Sold. Because the gain remains unrealized, the increase in this expense account has the appropriate effect of decreasing consolidated income.

Noncontrolling Interest's Share of the Subsidiary's Income

In this first illustration, the intercompany transfers are downstream. Thus, the unrealized gains are considered to relate solely to the parent company, creating no effect on the subsidiary or the outside ownership. For this reason, the noncontrolling interest's share of consolidated income is recorded as a columnar entry of $14,000, 20 percent of the $70,000 net income reported by Bottom.

By including these entries along with the other routine worksheet eliminations and adjustments, the accounting information generated by Top and Bottom can be brought together into a single set of consolidated financial statements. However, this process does more than simply delete intercompany transactions; it also affects reported income. A $4,000 gain is being removed on the worksheet from 2005 figures so that it can be recognized in 2006 (Entry *G). A $6,000 gain is deferred in a similar fashion from 2006 (Entry G) and subsequently recognized in 2007. However, these changes do not affect the noncontrolling interest because the transfers were downstream.

EXHIBIT 5.3 Downstream Inventory Transfers

TOP COMPANY AND BOTTOM COMPANY

Consolidation: Purchase Method
Investment: Cost Method

Consolidation Worksheet
For Year Ending December 31, 2006

Ownership: 80%

Accounts	Top Company	Bottom Company	Consolidation Entries Debit	Consolidation Entries Credit	Noncontrolling Interest	Consolidated Totals
Income Statement						
Sales	(600,000)	(300,000)	(TI) 100,000			(800,000)
Cost of goods sold	320,000	180,000	(G) 6,000	(*G) 4,000		402,000
				(TI) 100,000		
Expenses	170,000	50,000	(E) 2,000			222,000
Dividend income	(40,000)	–0–	(I) 40,000			–0–
Noncontrolling interest in Bottom Company's income	–0–	–0–			(14,000) ‡	14,000
Net income	(150,000)	(70,000)				(162,000)
Statement of Retained Earnings						
Retained earnings, 1/1/06:						
Top Company	(650,000)		(*G) 4,000	(*C) 6,000		(652,000)
Bottom Company		(310,000)	(S) 310,000 †			–0–
Net income (above)	(150,000)	(70,000)				(162,000)
Dividends paid	70,000	50,000		(I) 40,000	10,000	70,000
Retained earnings, 12/31/06	(730,000)	(330,000)				(744,000)
Balance Sheet						
Cash and receivables	280,000	120,000		(P) 10,000		390,000
Inventory	220,000	160,000		(G) 6,000		374,000
Investment in Bottom Company	400,000	–0–	(*C) 6,000	(S) 368,000		–0–
				(A) 38,000		
Land	410,000	200,000				610,000
Plant assets (net)	190,000	170,000				360,000
Database	–0–	–0–	(A) 38,000	(E) 2,000		36,000
Total assets	1,500,000	650,000				1,770,000
Liabilities	(340,000)	(170,000)	(P) 10,000			(500,000)
Noncontrolling interest in Bottom Company, 1/1/06	–0–	–0–		(S) 92,000	(92,000)	
Noncontrolling interest in Bottom Company, 12/31/06					(96,000)	(96,000)
Common stock	(430,000)	(150,000)	(S) 150,000			(430,000)
Retained earnings, 12/31/06 (above)	(730,000)	(330,000)				(744,000)
Total liabilities and equities	(1,500,000)	(650,000)				(1,770,000)

Note: Parentheses indicate a credit balance.
†Boxed items highlight differences with upstream transfers examined in Exhibit 5.4.
‡Because intercompany sales are made downstream (by the parent), the subsidiary's earned income is the $70,000 reported figure with the 20% noncontrolling interest being allocated ($14,000).
Consolidation entries:
(*G) Removal of unrealized gain from beginning figures so that it can be recognized in current period. Downstream sales attributed to parent.
(*C) Recognition of increase in book value and amortization relating to ownership of subsidiary for year prior to 2006.
(S) Elimination of subsidiary's stockholders' equity accounts along with recognition of January 1, 2006, noncontrolling interest.
(A) Allocation of parent's cost in excess of subsidiary's book value, unamortized balance as of January 1, 2006.
(I) Elimination of intercompany dividends recorded by parent as income.
(E) Recognition of amortization expense for current year on database.
(P) Elimination of intercompany receivable/payable balances.
(TI) Elimination of intercompany sales/purchases balances.
(G) Removal of unrealized gain from ending figures so that it can be recognized in subsequent period.

Upstream Sales

A different set of consolidation procedures is necessary if the intercompany transfers are upstream from Bottom to Top. As previously discussed, upstream gains are attributed to the subsidiary rather than to the parent company. Therefore, had these transfers been upstream, the $4,000 gain moved from 2005 into the current year (Entry *G) and the $6,000 unrealized gain deferred from 2006 into the future (Entry G) are both considered adjustments to Bottom's reported totals.

Tying upstream gains to Bottom's income can be a logical perspective, but such treatment complicates the consolidation process in several ways:

- Deferring the $4,000 gain from 2005 into 2006 dictates the adjustment of the beginning Retained Earnings balance of the subsidiary (as the seller of the goods) to $306,000 rather than $310,000 found in the company's separate records on the worksheet.

- Because $4,000 of the income reported for 2005 was unearned at that time, Bottom's book value did not increase by $10,000 during the previous period (income less dividends as stated in the introduction) but only by an earned amount of $6,000.

- Bottom's earned income for the year 2006 is $68,000 rather than the $70,000 found within the company's separate financial statements. This $68,000 figure is based on adjusting the timing of the reported income to reflect the deferral and recognition of the intercompany gains.

Earned Income of Subsidiary—Upstream Transfers

Income Reported by Bottom Company, 2006	Add: Gain from Previous Period Realized in 2006	Less: Gain Reported in 2006 to Be Realized in Later Period	2006 Income of Bottom Company from Consolidated Perspective
$70,000	$4,000	$(6,000)	$68,000

Determining Bottom's beginning Retained Earnings (realized) to be $306,000 and its 2006 income as $68,000 are preliminary calculations made in anticipation of the consolidation process. These newly computed totals are significant because they serve as the basis for several worksheet entries. However, the subsidiary's financial records remain unaffected. In addition, because the cost method has been applied, no change is required in any of the parent's accounts on the worksheet.

To illustrate the effects of upstream inventory transfers, in Exhibit 5.4 we consolidate the financial statements of Top and Bottom once again. *The individual records of the two companies are unchanged from Exhibit 5.3: The only difference in this second worksheet is that the intercompany transfers are assumed to have been made upstream from Bottom to Top.* This single change creates several important differences between Exhibits 5.3 and 5.4:

1. Because the intercompany sales are made upstream, the $4,000 deferral of the beginning unrealized gain (Entry *G) is no longer a reduction in the retained earnings of the parent company. Bottom was the seller of the merchandise; thus, the elimination made in Exhibit 5.4 reduces that company's January 1, 2006, equity balance. Following this entry, Bottom's beginning Retained Earnings on the worksheet is $306,000, which is, as discussed earlier, the appropriate total from a consolidated perspective.

2. Because $4,000 of Bottom's 2005 income is being deferred into 2006, the increase in the subsidiary's book value in the previous year is only $6,000 rather than $10,000 as reported. Consequently, conversion to the equity method (Entry *C) requires an increase of just $2,800:

$6,000 earned increase in
 subsidiary's book value during 2005 × 80% $4,800
2005 amortization expense . . . . (2,000)
Increase in parent's beginning retained
 earnings (Entry *C) $2,800

3. Within Entry S, the valuation of the initial noncontrolling interest and the portion of the parent's investment account to be eliminated differ from the previous example. This worksheet entry removes the stockholders' equity accounts of the subsidiary as of the beginning of the

EXHIBIT 5.4   Upstream Inventory Transfers

TOP COMPANY AND BOTTOM COMPANY

Consolidation: Purchase Method
Investment: Cost Method

Consolidation Worksheet
For Year Ending December 31, 2006

Ownership: 80%

Accounts	Top Company	Bottom Company	Consolidation Entries Debit	Consolidation Entries Credit	Noncontrolling Interest	Consolidated Totals
Income Statement						
Sales	(600,000)	(300,000)	(TI) 100,000			(800,000)
Cost of goods sold	320,000	180,000	(G) 6,000	(*G) 4,000		402,000
				(TI) 100,000		
Expenses	170,000	50,000	(E) 2,000			222,000
Dividend income	(40,000)	–0–	(I) 40,000			–0–
Noncontrolling interest in Bottom Company's income	–0–	–0–			(13,600) ‡	13,600
Net income	(150,000)	(70,000)				(162,400)
Statement of Retained Earnings						
Retained earnings, 1/1/06:						
Top Company	(650,000)		(*G) 4,000	(*C) 2,800		(652,800)
Bottom Company		(310,000)	(S) 306,000 †			–0–
Net income (above)	(150,000)	(70,000)				(162,400)
Dividends paid	70,000	50,000		(I) 40,000	10,000	70,000
Retained earnings, 12/31/06	(730,000)	(330,000)				(745,200)
Balance Sheet						
Cash and receivables	280,000	120,000		(P) 10,000		390,000
Inventory	220,000	160,000		(G) 6,000		374,000
Investment in Bottom Company	400,000	–0–	(*C) 2,800	(S) 364,800		–0–
				(A) 38,000		
Land	410,000	200,000				610,000
Plant assets (net)	190,000	170,000				360,000
Database	–0–	–0–	(A) 38,000	(E) 2,000		36,000
Total assets	1,500,000	650,000				1,770,000
Liabilities	(340,000)	(170,000)	(P) 10,000			(500,000)
Noncontrolling interest in Bottom Company, 1/1/06	–0–	–0–		(S) 91,200	(91,200)	
Noncontrolling interest in Bottom Company, 12/31/06					(94,800)	(94,800)
Common stock	(430,000)	(150,000)	(S) 150,000			(430,000)
Retained earnings, 12/31/06 (above)	(730,000)	(330,000)				(745,200)
Total liabilities and equities	(1,500,000)	(650,000)				(1,770,000)

Note: Parentheses indicate a credit balance.

†Boxed items highlight differences with downstream transfers examined in Exhibit 5.3.

‡Because intercompany sales are made upstream (by the subsidiary), the subsidiary's realized income is the $68,000 ($70,000 reported balance plus $4,000 gain deferred from previous year less $6,000 deferred into next year) with the 20% noncontrolling interest being allocated $13,600.

Consolidation entries:

(*G)   Removal of unrealized gain from beginning figures so that it can be recognized in current period. Upstream sales attributed to subsidiary.

(*C)   Recognition of earned increase in book value and amortization relating to ownership of subsidiary for year prior to 2006.

(S)   Elimination of adjusted stockholders' equity accounts along with recognition of January 1, 2006, noncontrolling interest.

(A)   Allocation of parent's cost in excess of subsidiary's book value, unamortized balance as of January 1, 2006.

(I)   Elimination of intercompany dividends recorded by parent as income.

(E)   Recognition of amortization expense for current year on cost allocated to value of database.

(P)   Elimination of intercompany receivable/payable balances.

(TI)   Elimination of intercompany sales/purchases balances.

(G)   Removal of unrealized gain from ending figures so that it can be recognized in subsequent period.

current year. Thus, the $4,000 reduction made to Bottom's Retained Earnings to remove the 2005 unrealized gain must be taken into account in developing Entry **S.** After posting Entry ***G,** only $456,000 remains as the subsidiary's January 1, 2006, book value (the total of Common Stock and beginning Retained Earnings accounts after adjustment for Entry ***G**). This figure forms the basis for the 20 percent noncontrolling interest ($91,200) and the elimination of the 80 percent parent company investment ($364,800).

4. Finally, to complete the consolidation, the noncontrolling interest's share of the subsidiary's net income is recorded on the worksheet as $13,600. This balance represents a 20 percent allocation of the $68,000 earned income figure attributed to Bottom. Upstream transfers affect this computation although the downstream sales in the previous example did not. Thus, the noncontrolling interest balance reported previously in the income statement in Exhibit 5.3 differs from the allocation in Exhibit 5.4.

Consolidations—Downstream versus Upstream Transfers

To help clarify the effect of downstream and upstream transfers, the worksheet entries that differ can be examined in more detail.

Downstream Transfers	Upstream Transfers
(Exhibit 5.3)	(Exhibit 5.4)

Entry *G

Retained Earnings,			Retained Earnings,		
1/1/06—Top	4,000		1/1/06—Bottom	4,000	
Cost of Goods Sold		4,000	Cost of Goods Sold		4,000

To remove 2005 unrealized gain from beginning balances of the seller.

To remove 2005 unrealized gain from beginning balances of the seller.

Entry *C

Investment in Bottom	6,000		Investment in Bottom	2,800	
Retained Earnings,			Retained Earnings,		
1/1/06—Top		6,000	1/1/06—Bottom		2,800

To convert 1/1/06 cost figures to the equity method. Income accrual is 80% of $10,000 increase in Retained Earnings less $2,000 amortization.

To convert 1/1/06 cost figures to the equity method. Income accrual is 80% of $6,000 increase in Retained Earnings (after removal of unrealized gain) less $2,000 amortization.

Entry S

Common stock—			Common stock—		
Bottom	150,000		Bottom	150,000	
Retained Earnings,			Retaining Earnings,		
1/1/06—Bottom	310,000		1/1/06—Bottom (as		
Investment in			adjusted)	306,000	
Bottom (80%)		368,000	Investment in		
Noncontrolling			Bottom (80%)		364,800
interest—1/1/06			Noncontrolling		
(20%)		92,000	interest—1/1/06		
			(20%)		91,200

To remove subsidiary's stockholders' equity accounts and portion of investment balance. Book value at beginning of year is appropriate.

To remove subsidiary's stockholders' equity accounts (as adjusted in Entry ***G**) and portion of investment balance. Adjusted book value at beginning of year is appropriate.

Noncontrolling Interest in Subsidiary's Income = $14,000. 20% of Bottom's reported income.

Noncontrolling Interest in Subsidiary's Income = $13,600. 20% of Bottom's earned income (reported income after adjustment for unrealized gains).

WHAT PRICE SHOULD WE CHARGE OURSELVES?

Slagle Corporation is a large manufacturing organization. Over the past several years, Slagle has obtained an important component used in its production process exclusively from Harrison, Inc., a relatively small company in Topeka, Kansas. Harrison charges $90 per unit for this part:

Variable cost per unit	$40
Fixed cost assigned per unit	30
Markup	20
Total price	$90

In hope of reducing manufacturing costs, Slagle purchases all of Harrison's outstanding common stock. This new subsidiary continues to sell merchandise to a number of outside customers as well as to Slagle. Thus, for internal reporting purposes, Slagle views Harrison as a separate profit center.

A controversy has now arisen among company officials about the amount that Harrison should charge Slagle for each component. The administrator in charge of the subsidiary wants to continue with a $90 price as in the past. He believes this figure best reflects the profitability of the division: "If we are to be judged by our profits, why should we be punished for selling to our own parent company? If that occurs, my figures will look better if I forget Slagle as a customer and try to market my goods solely to outsiders."

In contrast, the vice president in charge of Slagle's production wants the price set at variable cost, total cost, or some derivative of these numbers. "We bought Harrison to bring our costs down. It only makes sense to reduce the transfer price, otherwise the benefits of acquiring this subsidiary are not apparent. I pushed the company to buy Harrison; if our operating results are not improved, I will get the blame."

Will the decision about the transfer price affect consolidated net income? Which method would be easiest for the company's accountant to administer? As the company's accountant, what advice would you give to these officials?

Effects of Alternative Investment Methods on Consolidation

Exhibits 5.3 and 5.4 utilized the cost method. However, when using either the equity method or the partial equity method, consolidation procedures normally continue to follow the same patterns analyzed in the previous chapters of this textbook. As described earlier, though, a variation in Entry *G is required when the equity method is applied and downstream transfers have occurred. The equity in subsidiary earnings account is decreased rather than recording a reduction in the beginning retained earnings of the parent/seller with the remaining amount in equity in subsidiary earnings eliminated in Entry I. Otherwise, the specific accounting method in use creates no unique impact on the consolidation process for intercompany transactions.

The major complication when the parent uses the equity method is not always related to a consolidation procedure. Frequently, the composition of the investment balances appearing on the parent's separate financial records proves to be the most complex element of the entire process. Under the equity method, the investment accounts are subjected to (1) income accrual, (2) amortization, (3) dividends, and (4) adjustments required by unrealized intercompany gains. Thus, if Top Company applies the equity method and the transfers are downstream, the Investment in Bottom Company account would increase from $400,000 to $414,000 by the end of 2006. For that year, the Equity Income—Bottom Company account registers a $52,000 balance. Both of these totals result from the accounting shown in Exhibit 5.5.

If transfers are upstream, the individual investment accounts that the parent reports can be determined in the same manner as in Exhibit 5.5. Because of the change in direction, the gains are now attributed to the subsidiary. Thus, both investment accounts hold balances that vary from the totals computed earlier. The Investment in Bottom Company balance becomes

EXHIBIT 5.5
Investment Balances—
Equity Method—
Downstream Sales

Investment in Bottom Company Analysis, 1/1/05 to 12/31/06		
Cost 1/1/05		$400,000
Top's share of Bottom Co. reported income for 2005 (80%) . . .	$24,000	
Database amortization	(2,000)	
Deferred profit from Top's 2005 unrealized gain	(4,000)	
Equity in earnings of Bottom Company, 2005		18,000
Top's share of Bottom Co. dividends, 2005 (80%)		(16,000)
Balance 12/31/05		$402,000
Top's share of Bottom Co. income for 2006 (80%)	$56,000	
Database amortization	(2,000)	
Recognized profit from Top's 2005 unrealized gain	4,000	
Deferred profit from Top's 2006 unrealized gain	(6,000)	
Equity in earnings of Bottom Company, 2006		$ 52,000
Top's share of Bottom Co. dividends, 2006 (80%)		(40,000)
Balance 12/31/06		$414,000

$415,200, whereas the Equity Income—Bottom Company account for the year is $52,400. The differences are the result of having upstream rather than downstream transactions. The components of these accounts are identified in Exhibit 5.6. Consolidated worksheets for downstream and upstream inventory transfers when Top uses the equity method are shown in Exhibit 5.7 and Exhibit 5.8.

The equity method procedures for downstream profits in Exhibit 5.5 differ from those presented in Chapter 1 for a significant influence (typically 20 to 50 percent ownership) investment. For significant influence investments, an investor company defers intercompany profits only to the extent of its percentage ownership, regardless of whether the profits resulted from upstream or downstream sales. In contrast, Exhibit 5.5 shows a 100 percent intercompany profit deferral in 2005 (with a subsequent 100 percent recognition in 2006) for downstream intercompany sales from Top to its 80 percent owned subsidiary.

EXHIBIT 5.6
Investment Balances—
Equity Method—
Upstream Sales

Investment in Bottom Company Analysis, 1/1/05 to 12/31/06		
Cost 1/1/05		$400,000
Bottom Co. reported income for 2005	$30,000	
Deferred profit from Bottom's 2005 unrealized gain	(4,000)	
Bottom Company adjusted earnings	26,000	
Top Company ownership	80%	
Top's share of Bottom's 2005 earnings	$20,800	
Database amortization	(2,000)	
Equity in earnings of Bottom Company, 2005		18,800
Top's share of Bottom Co. dividends, 2005 (80%)		(16,000)
Balance 12/31/05		$402,800
Bottom Co. reported income for 2006	$70,000	
Recognized profit from Bottom's 2005 unrealized gain	4,000	
Deferred profit from Bottom's 2006 unrealized gain	(6,000)	
Bottom Company adjusted earnings	68,000	
Top Company ownership	80%	
Top's share of Bottom's 2006 earnings	$54,400	
Database amortization	(2,000)	
Equity in earnings of Bottom Company, 2006		$ 52,400
Top's share of Bottom Co. dividends, 2006 (80%)		(40,000)
Balance 12/31/06		$415,200

EXHIBIT 5.7   Downstream Inventory Transfers

TOP COMPANY AND BOTTOM COMPANY

Consolidation: Purchase Method   **Consolidation Worksheet**

Investment: Equity Method   **For Year Ending December 31, 2006**   *Ownership: 80%*

Accounts	Top Company	Bottom Company	Consolidation Entries Debit	Consolidation Entries Credit	Noncontrolling Interest	Consolidated Totals
Income Statement						
Sales	(600,000)	(300,000)	(TI) 100,000			(800,000)
Cost of goods sold	320,000	180,000	(G) 6,000	(*G) 4,000		402,000
				(TI) 100,000		
Operating expenses	170,000	50,000	(E) 2,000			222,000
Noncontrolling interest in Bottom Company's income					(14,000) ‡	14,000
Equity in earnings of Bottom	(52,000)		(I) 48,000			
			(*G) 4,000 †			–0–
Net income	(162,000)	(70,000)				(162,000)
Statement of Retained Earnings						
Retained earnings, 1/1/06						
Top Company	(652,000)					(652,000)
Bottom Company		(310,000)	(S) 310,000			
Net income	(162,000)	(70,000)				(162,000)
Dividends paid	70,000	50,000		(D) 40,000	10,000	70,000
Retained earnings, 12/31/06	(744,000)	(330,000)				(744,000)
Balance Sheet						
Cash and receivables	280,000	120,000		(P) 10,000		390,000
Inventory	220,000	160,000		(G) 6,000		374,000
Investment in Bottom Company	414,000			(I) 48,000		–0–
			(D) 40,000	(S) 368,000		
				(A) 38,000		
Land	410,000	200,000				610,000
Plant assets (net)	190,000	170,000				360,000
Database			(A) 38,000	(E) 2,000		36,000
Total assets	1,514,000	650,000				1,770,000
Liabilities	(340,000)	(170,000)	(P) 10,000			(500,000)
Noncontrolling interest in Bottom Company, 1/1/06				(S) 92,000	(92,000)	
Noncontrolling interest in Bottom Company, 12/31/06					(96,000)	(96,000)
Common stock	(430,000)	(150,000)	(S) 150,000			(430,000)
Retained earnings, 12/31/06	(744,000)	(330,000)				(744,000)
Total liabilities and equities	(1,514,000)	(650,000)				(1,770,000)

Note: Parentheses indicate a credit balance.

†Boxed items highlight differences with upstream transfers examined in Exhibit 5.8.

‡Because intercompany sales are made downstream (by the parent), the subsidiary's earned income is the $70,000 reported figure with the 20% noncontrolling interest being allocated ($14,000).

Consolidation entries:

  (*G) Removal of unrealized gain from beginning figures so that it can be recognized in current period. Downstream sales attributed to parent.

  (S)   Elimination of subsidiary's stockholders' equity accounts along with recognition of January 1, 2006, noncontrolling interest.

  (A)   Allocation of parent's cost in excess of subsidiary's book value, unamortized balance as of January 1, 2006.

  (I)   Elimination of intercompany income remaining after *G elimination.

  (D)   Elimination of intercompany dividend.

  (E)   Recognition of amortization expense for current year on cost allocated to database.

  (P)   Elimination of intercompany receivable/payable balances.

  (TI) Elimination of intercompany sales/purchases balances.

  (G)   Removal of unrealized gain from ending figures so that it can be recognized in subsequent period.

EXHIBIT 5.8   Upstream Inventory Transfers

TOP COMPANY AND BOTTOM COMPANY

Consolidation: Purchase Method — **Consolidation Worksheet**

Investment: Equity Method — **For Year Ending December 31, 2006** — *Ownership: 80%*

Accounts	Top Company	Bottom Company	Consolidation Entries Debit	Consolidation Entries Credit	Noncontrolling Interest	Consolidated Totals
Income Statement						
Sales	(600,000)	(300,000)	(TI) 100,000			(800,000)
Cost of goods sold	320,000	180,000	(G) 6,000	(*G) 4,000		402,000
				(TI) 100,000		
Operating expenses	170,000	50,000	(E) 2,000			222,000
Noncontrolling interest in Bottom Company's income					(13,600) ‡	13,600
Equity in earnings of Bottom	(52,400)		(I) 52,400 †			
Net income	(162,400)	(70,000)				(162,400)
Statement of Retained Earnings						
Retained earnings, 1/1/06						
Top Company	(652,800)					(652,800)
Bottom Company		(310,000)	(*G) 4,000			
			(S) 306,000			
Net income	(162,400)	(70,000)				(162,400)
Dividends paid	70,000	50,000		(D) 40,000	10,000	70,000
Retained earnings, 12/31/06	(745,200)	(330,000)				(745,200)
Balance Sheet						
Cash and receivables	280,000	120,000		(P) 10,000		390,000
Inventory	220,000	160,000		(G) 6,000		374,000
Investment in Bottom Company	415,200			(I) 52,400		–0–
			(D) 40,000	(S) 364,800		
				(A) 38,000		
Land	410,000	200,000				610,000
Plant assets (net)	190,000	170,000				360,000
Database			(A) 38,000	(E) 2,000		36,000
Total assets	1,515,200	650,000				1,770,000
Liabilities	(340,000)	(170,000)	(P) 10,000			(500,000)
Noncontrolling interest in Bottom Company, 1/1/06				(S) 91,200	(91,200)	
Noncontrolling interest in Bottom Company, 12/31/06					(94,800)	(94,800)
Common stock	(430,000)	(150,000)	(S) 150,000			(430,000)
Retained earnings, 12/31/06	(745,200)	(330,000)				(745,200)
Total liabilities and equities	(1,515,200)	(650,000)				(1,770,000)

Note: Parentheses indicate a credit balance.

†Boxed items highlight differences with downstream transfers examined in Exhibit 5.7.

‡Because intercompany sales are made upstream (by the subsidiary), the subsidiary's realized income is the $68,000 ($70,000 reported balance plus $4,000 gain deferred from previous year less $6,000 deferred into next year) with the 20% noncontrolling interest being allocated $13,600.

Consolidation entries:

(*G)   Removal of unrealized gain from beginning figures so that it can be recognized in current period. Upstream sales attributed to subsidiary.

(S)   Elimination of adjusted stockholders' equity accounts along with recognition of January 1, 2006, noncontrolling interest.

(A)   Allocation of parent's cost in excess of subsidiary's book value, unamortized balance as of January 1, 2006.

(I)   Elimination of intercompany income.

(D)   Elimination of intercompany dividends.

(E)   Recognition of amortization expense for current year on database.

(P)   Elimination of intercompany receivable/payable balances.

(TI)   Elimination of intercompany sales/purchases balances.

(G)   Removal of unrealized gain from ending figures so that it can be recognized in subsequent period.

Why the distinction? Because control (rather than just significant influence) exists, 100 percent of all intercompany profits are eventually removed from consolidated income regardless of the direction of the underlying sale. The 100 percent deferral on Top's books for downstream sales explicitly recognizes that none of the deferral will be allocated to the noncontrolling interest. As discussed previously, when the parent is the seller in an intercompany transfer, little justification exists for it to allocate a portion of the deferral to the noncontrolling interest. In contrast, for an upstream sale, the subsidiary recognizes the gross profit. Because the noncontrolling interest owns a portion of the subsidiary (but not of the parent), allocating of intercompany profit deferrals and subsequent recognitions across the noncontrolling interest and the parent appear appropriate. Nonetheless, the appendix to this chapter discusses other alternatives to this approach for both downstream and upstream sales.

INTERCOMPANY LAND TRANSFERS

Although not as prevalent as inventory transactions, intercompany sales of other assets occur occasionally. The final two sections of this chapter examine the worksheet procedures that noninventory transfers necessitate. We first analyze land transactions followed by a discussion of the effects created by the intercompany sale of depreciable assets such as buildings and equipment.

Accounting for Land Transactions

The consolidation procedures necessitated by intercompany land transfers partially parallel those for intercompany inventory. As with inventory, the sale of land creates a series of effects on the individual records of the two companies. The worksheet process must then adjust the account balances to present all transactions from the perspective of a single economic entity.

By reviewing the sequence of events occurring in an intercompany land sale, the similarities to inventory transfers can be ascertained as well as the unique features of this transaction.

1. A gain (losses are rare in intercompany asset transfers) is reported by the original seller of the land, even though the transaction occurred between related parties. At the same time, the acquiring company capitalizes the inflated transfer price rather than the land's historical cost to the business combination.
2. The unrealized gain recorded by the seller is closed into Retained Earnings at the end of the year. From a consolidated perspective, this account has been artificially increased. Thus, both the buyer's Land account and the seller's Retained Earnings account continue to contain the unrealized profit.
3. Only when the land is subsequently disposed of to an outside party is the gain on the original transfer actually earned. Therefore, appropriate consolidation techniques must be designed to eliminate the intercompany gain each period until the time of resale.

Clearly, two characteristics encountered in inventory transfers also exist in intercompany land transactions: inflated book values and unrealized gains subsequently culminated through sales to outside parties. Despite these similarities, significant differences exist. Because of the nature of the transaction, the individual companies record no sales/purchases balances when land is transferred. Instead, the seller establishes a separate gain account. Because this gain is unearned, the balance has to be eliminated when preparing consolidated statements.

In addition, the subsequent resale of land to an outside party does not always occur in the year immediately following the transfer. Although inventory is normally disposed of within a relatively short time, the buyer often holds land for years if not permanently. Thus, the over-valued Land account can remain on the books of the acquiring company indefinitely. As long as the land is retained, elimination of the effects of the unrealized gain (the equivalent of Entry ***G** in inventory transfers) must be made for each subsequent consolidation. By repeating this worksheet entry every year, the consolidated financial statements properly state both the Land and the Retained Earnings accounts.

Eliminating Unrealized Gains—Land Transfers

To illustrate these worksheet procedures, assume that Hastings Company and Patrick Company are related parties. On July 1, 2005, Hastings sold land that originally cost $60,000 to Patrick at a $100,000 transfer price. The seller reports a $40,000 gain; the buyer records the land at the $100,000 acquisition price. At the end of this fiscal period, the intercompany effect of this transaction must be eliminated for consolidation purposes:

Consolidation Entry TL (year of transfer)		
Gain on Sale of Land	40,000	
Land		40,000
To eliminate effects of intercompany transfer of land. (Labeled **"TL"** in reference to the transferred land.)		

This worksheet entry eliminates the unrealized gain from the consolidated statements of 2005. However, as with the transfer of inventory, the effects created by the original transaction remain in the financial records of the individual companies for as long as the property is held. The gain recorded by Hastings carries through to Retained Earnings while Patrick's Land account retains the inflated transfer price. *Therefore, for every subsequent consolidation until the land is eventually sold, the elimination process must be repeated.* Including the following entry on each subsequent worksheet removes the unrealized gain from the asset and from the earnings reported by the combination:

Consolidation Entry *GL (every year following transfer)		
Retained Earnings (beginning balance of seller)	40,000	
Land		40,000
To eliminate effects of intercompany transfer of land made in a previous year. (Labeled "***GL**" in reference to the gain on a land transfer occurring in a prior year.)		

Note that the reduction in Retained Earnings is changed to an increase in the investment account whenever the original sale is downstream and the parent has applied the equity method. In that specific situation, equity method adjustments have already corrected the timing of the parent's unrealized gain. Removing the gain has created a reduction in the investment account that is appropriately allocated to the subsidiary's Land account on the worksheet. Conversely, if sales were upstream, the Retained Earnings of the seller (the subsidiary) continue to be overstated even if the parent applies the equity method.

One final consolidation concern exists in accounting for intercompany transfers of land. If the property is ever sold to an outside party, the company making the sale records a gain or loss based on its recorded book value. However, this cost figure is actually the internal transfer price. The gain or loss being recognized is incorrect for consolidation purposes; it has not been computed by comparison to the land's historical cost. Once again, the separate financial records fail to reflect the transaction from the perspective of the single economic entity.

Therefore, if the company eventually sells the land, it must recognize the gain deferred at the time of the original transfer. It has finally earned this profit by selling the property to outsiders. On the worksheet, the gain is removed one last time from beginning Retained Earnings (or the investment account, if applicable). In this instance, though, the entry is completed by reclassifying the amount as a realized gain. The timing of income recognition has been switched from the year of transfer into the fiscal period in which the land is sold to the unrelated party.

Returning to the previous illustration, Hastings acquired land for $60,000 and sold it to Patrick, a related party, for $100,000. Consequently, the $40,000 unrealized gain was eliminated on the consolidation worksheet in the year of transfer as well as in each succeeding period. However, if this land is subsequently sold to an outside party for $115,000, Patrick will recognize only a $15,000 gain. From the viewpoint of the business combination, the land (having been bought for $60,000) was actually sold at a $55,000 gain. To correct the reporting, the following consolidation entry must be made in the year that the property is sold to the unrelated party. This adjustment increases the $15,000 gain recorded by Patrick to the consolidated balance of $55,000:

Consolidation Entry *GL (year of sale to outside party)		
Retained Earnings (Hastings)	40,000	
Gain on Sale of Land		40,000
To remove intercompany gain from year of transfer so that total profit can be recognized in the current period when land is sold to an outside party.		

As in the accounting for inventory transfers, the entire consolidation process demonstrated here accomplishes two major objectives:

1. Reports historical cost for the transferred land for as long as it remains within the business combination.
2. Defers income recognition until the land is sold to outside parties.

Effect on Noncontrolling Interest Valuation—Land Transfers

The preceding discussion of intercompany land transfers has ignored the possible presence of a noncontrolling interest. In constructing financial statements for an economic entity that includes outside ownership, the guidelines already established for inventory transfers remain applicable.

If the original sale was a *downstream* transaction, neither the annual deferral nor the eventual recognition of the unrealized gain has any effect on the noncontrolling interest. The rationale for this treatment, as previously indicated, is that profits from downstream transfers relate solely to the parent company.

Conversely, if the transfer is made *upstream,* deferral and recognition of gains are attributed to the subsidiary and, hence, to the valuation of the noncontrolling interest. As with inventory, all noncontrolling interest balances are to be computed on the reported earnings of the subsidiary after adjustment for any upstream transfers.

To reiterate, the accounting consequences stemming from land transfers are these:

1. In the year of transfer, any unrealized gain is deferred and the Land account is reduced to historical cost. When an upstream sale creates the gain, the amount also is excluded in calculating the noncontrolling interest's share of the subsidiary's net income for that year.
2. Each year thereafter, the unrealized gain will be removed from the seller's beginning Retained Earnings. If the transfer was upstream, eliminating this earlier gain directly affects the balances recorded within both Entry *C (if conversion to the equity method is required) and Entry S. The additional equity accrual (Entry *C, if needed) as well as the elimination of beginning Stockholders' Equity (Entry S) must be based on the newly adjusted balance in the subsidiary's Retained Earnings. This deferral process also has an impact on the noncontrolling interest's share of the subsidiary's income, but only in the year of transfer and the eventual year of sale.
3. In the event that the land is ever sold to an outside party, the original gain is earned and must be reported by the consolidated entity.

INTERCOMPANY TRANSFER OF DEPRECIABLE ASSETS

Just as related parties can transfer land, the intercompany sale of a host of other assets is possible. Equipment, patents, franchises, buildings, and other long-lived assets can be involved. Accounting for these transactions resembles that demonstrated for land sales. However, the subsequent calculation of depreciation or amortization provides an added challenge in the development of consolidated statements.[10]

---

[10] To avoid redundancy within this analysis, all further references are made to depreciation expense alone, although this discussion is equally applicable to the amortization of intangible assets or the depletion of wasting assets.

The Deferral of Unrealized Gains

When faced with intercompany sales of depreciable assets, the accountant's basic objective remains unchanged: *to defer unrealized gains to establish both historical cost balances and recognize appropriate income within the consolidated statements.* More specifically, accountants defer gains created by these transfers until such time as the subsequent use or resale of the asset consummates the original transaction. For inventory sales, the culminating disposal normally occurs currently or in the year following the transfer. In contrast, transferred land is quite often never resold, thus permanently deferring the recognition of the intercompany profit.

For depreciable asset transfers, the ultimate realization of the gain normally occurs in a different manner; the property's use within the buyer's operations is reflected through depreciation. Recognition of this expense reduces the asset's book value every year and, hence, the overvaluation within that balance.

The depreciation systematically eliminates the unrealized gain not only from the asset account but also from Retained Earnings. For the buyer, excess expense results each year because the computation is based on the inflated transfer cost. This depreciation is then closed annually into Retained Earnings. *From a consolidated perspective, the extra expense gradually offsets the unrealized gain within this equity account. In fact, over the life of the asset, the depreciation process eliminates all effects of the transfer from both the asset balance and the Retained Earnings account.*

Depreciable Asset Transfers Illustrated

To examine the consolidation procedures required by the intercompany transfer of a depreciable asset, assume that Able Company sells equipment to Baker Company at the current market value of $90,000. Able originally acquired the equipment for $100,000 several years ago; since that time, it has recorded $40,000 in accumulated depreciation. The transfer is made on January 1, 2005, when the equipment has a 10-year remaining life.

Year of Transfer

The 2005 effects on the separate financial accounts of the two companies can be quickly enumerated:

1. Baker, as the buyer, enters the equipment into its records at the $90,000 transfer price. However, from a consolidated view, the $60,000 book value ($100,000 cost less $40,000 accumulated depreciation) is still appropriate.
2. Able, as the seller, reports a profit of $30,000, although the combination has as yet not earned anything. Able then closes this gain into the company's Retained Earnings account at the end of 2005.
3. Assuming application of the straight-line method of depreciation with no salvage value, Baker records expense of $9,000 at the end of 2005 ($90,000 transfer price/10 years). The buyer recognizes this amount rather than the $6,000 depreciation figure applicable to the consolidated entity ($60,000 book value/10 years).

To report these events as seen by the business combination, both the $30,000 unrealized gain and the $3,000 overstatement in depreciation expense must be eliminated on the worksheet. For clarification purposes, two separate consolidation entries for 2005 follow. However, they can be combined into a single adjustment:

Consolidation Entry TA (year of transfer)		
Gain on Sale of Equipment	30,000	
Equipment	10,000	
Accumulated Depreciation		40,000
To remove unrealized gain and return equipment accounts to balances based on original historical cost. (Labeled **"TA"** in reference to transferred asset.)		

Consolidation Entry ED (year of transfer)

Accumulated Depreciation	3,000	
Depreciation Expense		3,000

To eliminate overstatement of depreciation expense caused by inflated transfer price. (Labeled **"ED"** in reference to excess depreciation.) *Entry must be repeated for all 10 years of the equipment's life.*

From the viewpoint of a single entity, these entries accomplish several objectives:

- Reinstate the asset's historical cost of $100,000.
- Return the January 1, 2005, book value to the appropriate $60,000 figure by recognizing accumulated depreciation of $40,000.
- Eliminate the $30,000 unrealized gain recorded by Able so that this intercompany profit does not appear in the consolidated income statement.
- Reduce depreciation for the year from $9,000 to $6,000, the appropriate expense based on historical cost.

In the year of the intercompany depreciable asset transfer, the preceding consolidation entries **TA** and **ED** are applicable regardless of whether the transfer was upstream or downstream. They are likewise applicable regardless of whether the parent applies the equity method, cost method, or partial equity method of accounting for its investment. As discussed subsequently, however, in the years following the intercompany transfer, a slight modification must be made to the consolidation entry ***TA** when the equity method is applied and the transfer was downstream.

Years Following Transfer

Once again, the preceding worksheet entries do not actually remove the effects of the inter-company transfer from the individual records of these two organizations. Both the unrealized gain and the excess depreciation expense remain on the separate books and are closed into Retained Earnings of the respective companies at year-end. Similarly, the Equipment account along with the related accumulated depreciation continue to hold balances based on the transfer price, not historical cost. *Thus, for every subsequent period, the separately reported figures must be adjusted on the worksheet to present the consolidated totals from the perspective of a single entity.*

To derive worksheet entries at any future point, the balances in the accounts of the individual companies must be ascertained and compared to the figures appropriate for the business combination. As an illustration, the separate records of Able and Baker two years after the transfer (December 31, 2006) follow. Consolidated totals are calculated based on the original historical cost of $100,000 and accumulated depreciation of $40,000.

Account	Individual Records	Consolidated Perspective	Worksheet Adjustments
Equipment 12/31/06	$90,000	$100,000	$10,000
Accumulated Depreciation 12/31/06	(18,000)	(52,000)*	(34,000)
Depreciation Expense 12/31/06	9,000	6,000	(3,000)
1/1/06 Retained Earnings effect	(21,000)†	6,000	27,000

*Accumulated depreciation before transfer $(40,000) plus 2 years × $(6,000).

†Intercompany transfer gain $(30,000) less one year's depreciation of $9,000.

Note: Parentheses indicate a credit.

Because effects of the transfer continue to exist in the separate financial records, the various accounts have to be corrected in each succeeding consolidation. However, the amounts involved must be updated every period because of the continual impact that depreciation has on these balances. As an example, to adjust the individual figures to the consolidated totals derived earlier, the 2006 worksheet must include the following entries:

Consolidation Entry *TA (year following transfer)		
Equipment	10,000	
Retained Earnings, 1/1/06 (Able)	27,000	
Accumulated Depreciation		37,000
To return the Equipment account to original historical cost and correct the 1/1/06 balances of Retained Earnings and Accumulated Depreciation.		

Consolidation Entry ED (year following transfer)		
Accumulated Depreciation	3,000	
Depreciation Expense		3,000
To remove excess depreciation expense on the intercompany transfer price and adjust Accumulated Depreciation to its correct 12/31/06 balance.		
Note that the $34,000 increase in 12/31/06 consolidated Accumulated Depreciation is accomplished by a $37,000 credit in Entry *TA and a $3,000 debit in Entry ED.		

Although adjustments of the asset and depreciation expense remain constant, the change in beginning Retained Earnings and Accumulated Depreciation varies with each succeeding consolidation. At December 31, 2005, the individual companies closed out both the unrealized gain of $30,000 and the initial $3,000 overstatement of depreciation expense. Therefore, as reflected in Entry *TA, the beginning Retained Earnings account for 2006 is overvalued by a net amount of only $27,000 rather than $30,000. *Over the life of the asset, the unrealized gain in retained earnings will be systematically reduced to zero as excess depreciation expense ($3,000) is closed out each year.* Hence, on subsequent consolidation worksheets, the beginning Retained Earnings account decreases by $27,000 in 2006, $24,000 in 2007, and $21,000 in the following period. This reduction continues until the effect of the unrealized gain no longer exists at the end of 10 years.

If this equipment is ever resold to an outside party, the remaining portion of the gain would be consummated. As in the previous discussion of land, the intercompany profit that exists at that date must be recognized on the consolidated income statement to arrive at the appropriate amount of gain or loss on the sale.

Depreciable Intercompany Asset Transfers—Downstream Transfers When the Parent Uses the Equity Method

A slight modification to consolidation entry *TA is required when the intercompany depreciable asset transfer is downstream and the parent uses the equity method. In applying the equity method, the parent adjusts its book income for both the original transfer gain and periodic depreciation expense adjustments. Thus, in downstream intercompany transfers when the equity method is used, from a consolidated view, the book value of the parent's Retained Earnings balance has been already reduced for the gain. Therefore, continuing with the previous example, the following worksheet consolidation entries would be made for a downstream sale assuming that (1) Able is the parent and (2) Able has applied the equity method to account for its investment in Baker.

Consolidation Entry *TA (year following transfer)		
Equipment	10,000	
Investment in Baker	27,000	
Accumulated Depreciation		37,000

Consolidation Entry ED (year following transfer)		
Accumulated Depreciation	3,000	
Depreciation Expense		3,000

In Entry ***TA,** note that the Investment in Baker account replaces the parent's Retained Earnings. The debit to the investment account effectively allocates the write-down necessitated by the intercompany transfer to the appropriate subsidiary equipment and accumulated depreciation accounts.

Effect on Noncontrolling Interest Valuation—Depreciable Asset Transfers

Because of the lack of official guidance, no easy answer exists as to the assignment of any income effects created within the consolidation process. Consistent with the previous sections of this chapter, all income is assigned here to the original seller. In Entry ***TA,** for example, the beginning Retained Earnings account of Able (the seller) is reduced. Both the unrealized gain on the transfer and the excess depreciation expense subsequently recognized are assigned to that party.

Thus, once again, downstream sales are assumed to have no effect on any noncontrolling interest values. The parent rather than the subsidiary made the sale. Conversely, the impact on income created by upstream sales must be taken into account in computing the balances attributed to these outside owners. Currently, this approach is one of many acceptable alternatives. However, in its future deliberations on consolidation policies and procedures, the FASB could mandate a specific allocation pattern.

Summary

1. The transfer of assets, especially inventory, between the members of a business combination is a common practice. In producing consolidated financial statements, any effects on the separate accounting records created by such transfers must be removed because the transactions did not occur with an outside, unrelated party.

2. Inventory transfers are the most prevalent form of intercompany asset transaction. Despite being only a transfer, one company records a sale while the other reports a purchase. These balances are reciprocals that have to be offset on the worksheet in the process of producing consolidated figures.

3. Additional accounting problems result if inventory is transferred at a markup. Any portion of the merchandise still held at year-end would be valued at more than historical cost because of the inflation in price. Furthermore, the gross profit that the seller reports on these goods is unrealized from a consolidation perspective. Thus, this gain must be removed from the ending Inventory account, a figure that appears as an asset on the balance sheet and as a negative component within cost of goods sold.

4. Unrealized inventory gains also create a consolidation problem in the year following the transfer. Within the separate accounting systems, the seller closes the gross profit to Retained Earnings. The buyer's ending Inventory balance becomes the beginning balance (within Cost of Goods Sold) of the next period. Therefore, the inflation must be removed again but this time in the subsequent year. The seller's beginning Retained Earnings is decreased to eliminate the unrealized gain while Cost of Goods Sold is reduced to remove the overstatement from the beginning inventory component. Through this process, the intercompany profit is deferred from the year of transfer so that recognition can be made at the point of disposal or consumption.

5. The deferral and subsequent realization of intercompany gains raises a question concerning the valuation of noncontrolling interest balances: Does the change in the period of recognition alter these calculations? Although the issue is currently under debate, no formal answer to this question is yet found in official accounting pronouncements. In this textbook, the deferral of gains from upstream transfers (from subsidiary to parent) is assumed to affect the noncontrolling interest whereas downstream transactions (from parent to subsidiary) do not. When upstream transfers are involved, noncontrolling interest values are based on the earned figures remaining after adjustment for any unrealized gains.

6. Inventory is not the only asset that can be sold between the members of a business combination. For example, transfers of land sometimes occur. Once again, if the price exceeds original cost, the buyer's records state the asset at an inflated value while the seller recognizes an unrealized gain. As with inventory, the consolidation process must return the asset's recorded balance to cost while deferring

the gain. Repetition of this procedure is necessary in every consolidation for as long as the land remains within the business combination.

7. The consolidation process required by the intercompany transfer of depreciable assets differs somewhat from that demonstrated for inventory and land. Unrealized gain created by the transaction must still be eliminated along with the overstatement of the asset. However, because of subsequent depreciation, these adjustments systematically change from period to period. Following the transfer, the buyer computes depreciation based on the new inflated transfer price. Thus, an expense that reduces the carrying value of the asset at a rate in excess of appropriate depreciation is recorded; the book value moves closer to the historical cost figure each time that depreciation is recorded. Additionally, because the excess depreciation is closed annually to Retained Earnings, the overstatement of the equity account resulting from the unrealized gain is constantly reduced. To produce consolidated figures at any point in time, the remaining inflation in these figures (as well as in the current depreciation expense) must be determined and removed.

Comprehensive Illustration

PROBLEM

(Estimated Time: 45 to 65 Minutes) On January 1, 2001, Daisy Company purchased 80 percent of Rose Company for $594,000 in cash. Rose's total book value on that date was $610,000. The newly acquired subsidiary possessed equipment (10-year remaining life) undervalued by $75,000 in the company's accounting records and land undervalued by $15,000. Any excess intangibles within the purchase will be amortized over 10 years.

Daisy decided to acquire Rose so that the subsidiary could furnish component parts for the parent's production process. During the ensuing years, Rose sold inventory to Daisy as follows:

Year	Cost to Rose Company	Transfer Price	Markup on Transfer Price	Transferred Inventory Being Held at End of Year (at transfer price)
2001	$ 60,000	$ 90,000	33.3%	$10,000
2002	80,000	100,000	20.0	15,000
2003	90,000	120,000	25.0	10,000
2004	100,000	140,000	28.6	20,000
2005	100,000	150,000	33.3	30,000
2006	96,000	160,000	40.0	40,000

Any transferred merchandise that Daisy retained at the end of a year was always put into production during the following period.

On January 1, 2004, Daisy sold several pieces of equipment to Rose. These assets had a 10-year remaining life and were being depreciated on the straight-line method with no salvage value. This equipment was transferred at an $80,000 price, although it had an original cost to Daisy of $100,000 and a book value at the date of exchange of $44,000.

On January 1, 2006, Daisy sold land to Rose for $60,000, the fair value at that date. The original cost had been only $40,000. By the end of 2006, Rose had made no payment for the land.

The following separate financial statements are for Daisy and Rose as of December 31, 2006. Daisy has applied the equity method to account for this investment.

	Daisy Company	Rose Company
Sales	$ (900,000)	$ (500,000)
Cost of goods sold	600,000	300,000
Operating expenses	210,000	80,000
Gain on sale of land	(20,000)	–0–
Income of Rose Company	(65,400)	–0–
Net income	$ (175,400)	$ (120,000)
Retained earnings, 1/1/06	$ (620,000)	$ (430,000)
Net income	(175,400)	(120,000)
Dividends paid	55,400	50,000
Retained earnings, 12/31/06	$ (740,000)	$ (500,000)
Cash and accounts receivable	$ 380,000	$ 410,000
Inventory	421,600	190,000
Investment in Rose Company	711,600	–0–
Land	452,800	280,000

	Daisy Company	Rose Company
Equipment	270,000	190,000
Accumulated depreciation	(180,000)	(50,000)
Total assets	$ 2,056,000	$ 1,020,000
Liabilities	(716,000)	(120,000)
Common stock	(600,000)	(400,000)
Retained earnings, 12/31/06	(740,000)	(500,000)
Total liabilities and equities	$(2,056,000)	$(1,020,000)

Required:

Answer the following questions:

a. By how much did Rose's book value increase during the period from January 1, 2001, through December 31, 2005?

b. During the initial years after the takeover, what annual amortization expense was recognized in connection with the parent's purchase price?

c. What amount of unrealized gain exists within the parent's inventory figures at the beginning and at the end of 2006?

d. Equipment has been transferred between the companies. What amount of excess depreciation is recognized in 2006 because of this transfer?

e. The parent reports Income of Rose Company of $65,400 for 2006. How was this figure calculated?

f. Without using a worksheet, determine consolidated totals.

g. Prepare the worksheet entries required at December 31, 2006, by the transfer of inventory, land, and equipment.

SOLUTION

a. The subsidiary's book value on the date of purchase was given as $610,000. At the beginning of 2006, the company's common stock and retained earnings total is $830,000 ($400,000 and $430,000, respectively). In the previous years, Rose's book value has apparently grown by $220,000 ($830,000 − $610,000).

b. To determine amortization, an allocation of the purchase price must first be made. The following allocations to equipment ($60,000) and intangibles (residual $34,000) lead to additional annual expenses of $9,400 for the initial years of the combination. The $12,000 assigned to land is not subject to amortization.

Cost Allocation and Excess Amortization Schedule

Purchase price	$ 594,000
Book value of Rose Company ($610,000 × 80%)	(488,000)
Excess cost over book value	106,000

	Life (years)	Annual Excess Amortizations	Excess Amortizations 2001–2006	Unamortized Value, 12/31/06
Equipment undervaluation ($75,000 × 80%) .. 60,000	10	$6,000	$36,000	$24,000
Land undervaluation ($15,000 × 80%) .. 12,000		–0–	–0–	12,000
Intangibles $34,000	10	3,400	20,400	13,600
		$9,400		

c. Of the inventory transferred to Daisy during 2005, $30,000 is still held at the beginning of 2006. This merchandise contains an unrealized gain of $10,000 ($30,000 × 33.3% [rounded] markup for that year). At year-end, $16,000 ($40,000 remaining inventory × 40% markup) is viewed as an unrealized gain.

d. Excess depreciation for 2006 is $3,600. Equipment with a book value of $44,000 was transferred at a price of $80,000. The addition of $36,000 to this asset's account balance would be written off over 10 years for an extra $3,600 per year.

e. According to the separate statements given, the subsidiary reports net income of $120,000. However, in determining the income allocation between the parent and the noncontrolling interest, this reported figure must be adjusted for the effects of *any upstream transfers*. Because Rose sold the inventory upstream to Daisy, the $10,000 gain deferred in requirement (c) from 2005 into the current period is attributed to the subsidiary (as the seller). Likewise, the $16,000 unrealized gain at year-end is viewed as a reduction in Rose's income.

    All other transfers are downstream and not considered to have an effect on the subsidiary. Therefore, the Income of Rose Company balance can be verified as follows:

Rose Company's reported income—2006	$120,000
Recognition of 2005 unrealized gain	10,000
Deferral of 2006 unrealized gain	(16,000)
Earned income of subsidiary from consolidated perspective	114,000
Parent's ownership percentage	80%
Equity income accrual	$ 91,200
Adjustments attributed to parent's ownership:	
Excess amortization expense—2006 (see requirement [b])	(9,400)
Deferral of unrealized gain—land	(20,000)
Removal of excess depreciation (see requirement [d])	3,600
Income of Rose Company—2006	$ 65,400

f. Each of the 2006 consolidated totals for this business combination can be determined as follows:

Sales = $1,240,000. The parent's balance is added to the subsidiary's balance less the $160,000 in intercompany transfers for the period.

Cost of Goods Sold = $746,000. The computation begins by adding the parent's balance to the subsidiary's balance less the $160,000 in intercompany transfers for the period. The $10,000 unrealized gain from the previous year is deducted to recognize this income currently. Next, the $16,000 ending unrealized gain is added to cost of goods sold to defer the income until a later year when the goods are sold to an outside party.

Operating Expenses = $295,800. The parent's balance is added to the subsidiary's balance. Annual amortization of $9,400 on the purchase price allocations (see requirement [b]) must also be included. Excess depreciation of $3,600 resulting from the transfer of equipment (see requirement [e]) is removed.

Gain on Sale of Land = –0–. This amount is eliminated for consolidation purposes because the transaction was intercompany.

Income of Rose Company = 0. The equity income figure is removed so that the actual revenues and expenses of the subsidiary can be included in the financial statements without double-counting.

Noncontrolling Interest in Subsidiary's Income = $22,800. In requirement (e), the subsidiary's earned income was computed as $114,000 after adjustments were made for unrealized upstream gains. Because outsiders hold 20 percent of the subsidiary, a $22,800 allocation ($114,000 × 20%) is necessary.

Net Income = $175,400. This total is derived from the previous consolidated balances. Because the equity method has been applied, consolidated net income is also equal to the balance reported by the parent.

Retained Earnings, 1/1/06 = $620,000. The equity method has been applied; therefore, the parent's balance is equal to the consolidated total.

Dividends Paid = $55,400. Only the amount the parent paid is shown in the consolidated statements. Distributions that the subsidiary made to the parent are eliminated as intercompany transfers. Any payment to the noncontrolling interest reduces the ending balance attributed to these outside owners.

Cash and Accounts Receivable = $730,000. The two balances are added after removal of the $60,000 intercompany receivable created by the transfer of land.

Inventory = $595,600. The two balances are added after removal of the $16,000 ending unrealized gain (see requirement [c]).

Investment in Rose Company = –0–. The investment balance is eliminated so that the actual assets and liabilities of the subsidiary can be included.

Land = $724,800. The two balances are added. The $20,000 unrealized gain created by the transfer is removed. The $12,000 allocation from the purchase price is added.

Equipment = $540,000. The two balances are added. Because of the intercompany transfer, $20,000 must also be included to adjust the $80,000 transfer price to the original $100,000 cost of the asset. A $60,000 allocation within the purchase price must also be recognized.

Accumulated Depreciation = $311,200. The balances are added together along with the $36,000 that has been written off in connection with the purchase price allocation to equipment ($6,000 per year for six years). The $56,000 in accumulated depreciation on the equipment (before its transfer) must also be reinstated. A reduction of $10,800 is made to remove the excess depreciation subsequently recorded on this same equipment ($3,600 per year for three years).

Intangibles = $13,600. The $34,000 allocation is recognized less six years of amortization ($20,400, or $3,400 per year for six years).

Total Assets = $2,292,800. This figure is a summation of the preceding consolidated assets.

Liabilities = $776,000. The two balances are added after removal of the $60,000 intercompany payable created by the transfer of land.

Noncontrolling Interest in Subsidiary, 12/31/06 = $176,800. This figure is composed of several different balances:

Book value of subsidiary, 1/1/06 (common stock and beginning retained earnings)	$830,000
Unrealized gain on upstream transfer as of beginning of year	(10,000)
Earned book value of subsidiary, 1/1/06	$820,000
Noncontrolling interest	20%
Noncontrolling interest, 1/1/06	$164,000
Noncontrolling interest in subsidiary's income (see above)	22,800
Less: Dividends paid to noncontrolling interest ($50,000 × 20%)	(10,000)
Noncontrolling interest, 12/31/06	$176,800

Common Stock = $600,000. Only the parent company balance is reported within the consolidated statements.

Retained Earnings, 12/31/06 = $740,000. The retained earnings amount is found by adding consolidated net income to the beginning Retained Earnings balance and then subtracting the dividends paid. All of these figures have been computed previously.

Total Liabilities and Equities = $2,292,800. This figure is the summation of all consolidated liabilities and equities.

g.

Consolidation Worksheet Entries
Intercompany Transactions
December 31, 2006

Inventory

Entry *G

Retained Earnings, 1/1/06—Subsidiary	10,000	
Cost of Goods Sold		10,000

To remove 2005 unrealized gain from beginning balances of the current year. Because transfers were upstream, retained earnings of the subsidiary (as the original seller) are being reduced. Balance is computed in requirement (c).

Entry TI

Sales	160,000	
Cost of Goods Sold		160,000

To eliminate current year intercompany transfer of inventory.

Entry G

Cost of Goods Sold	16,000	
Inventory		16,000

To remove 2006 unrealized gain from ending accounts of the current year. Balance is computed in requirement (c).

Land

Entry TL

Gain on Sale of Land	20,000	
Land		20,000

To eliminate gain created on first day of current year by an intercompany transfer of land.

Equipment

Entry *TA

Equipment	20,000	
Investment in Rose Company	28,800	
Accumulated Depreciation		48,800

To remove unrealized gain (as of January 1, 2006) created by intercompany transfer of equipment and to adjust equipment and accumulated depreciation to historical cost figures.

Equipment is increased from the $80,000 transfer price to $100,000 cost.

Accumulated depreciation of $56,000 was eliminated at time of transfer. Excess depreciation of $3,600 per year has been recorded for the two prior years ($7,200); thus, the accumulated depreciation is now only $48,800 less than cost-based figure.

The unrealized gain on the transfer was $36,000 ($80,000 less $44,000). That figure has now been reduced by two years of excess depreciation ($7,200). Because the parent used the equity method and this transfer was downstream, the adjustment here is to the investment account rather than the parent's beginning Retained Earnings.

Entry ED

Accumulated Depreciation	3,600	
Operating Expenses (depreciation)		3,600

To eliminate the current year overstatement of depreciation created by inflated transfer price.

Appendix

Transfers—Alternative Approaches

In this chapter, we use one method to consolidate the effects of intercompany transfers and unrealized gains when a noncontrolling interest is present. This approach was chosen because it is consistent with the guidelines put forth in *ARB 51*. Over the years, several other possibilities have been devised and considered. The FASB's discussion memorandum, *An Analysis of Issues Related to Consolidation Policy and Procedures,* describes eight methods of consolidating intercompany transactions (three for downstream transfers and five for upstream). The following table indicates the range of potential effects on consolidated totals by demonstrating six of these approaches (two for downstream and four for upstream). All methods except for proportionate consolidation have been included.

The figures used in this illustration are the same as in the Large Company and Small Company example in the first section of this chapter:

Large owns 70 percent of the outstanding stock of Small.

Intercompany inventory transfers during the year amount to $200,000.

The remaining unrealized gain at the end of the year is $40,000.

Subsidiary reported income is $100,000.

DOWNSTREAM TRANSFERS (FROM PARENT TO SUBSIDIARY)

	ARB 51* Economic Unit Concept One Variation of Parent Company Concept (method used in this textbook)	Another Variation of Parent Company Concept
Sales	Eliminate all $200,000 transfers	Eliminate $140,000 (70%) of the transfers
Purchases	Eliminate all $200,000 transfers	Eliminate $140,000 (70%) of the transfers
Unrealized gain	Eliminate all $40,000	Eliminate $28,000 (70%)
Income assigned to noncontrolling interests	30% of $100,000 reported income, or $30,000	30% of $100,000 reported income, or $30,000

*Titles indicate authority for each approach.

UPSTREAM TRANSFERS (FROM SUBSIDIARY TO PARENT)

	ARB 51 Economic Unit Concept (method used in this textbook)	One Variation of Parent Company Concept	Another Approach Based on *ARB 51*	Another Variation of Parent Company Concept
Sales	Eliminate all $200,000 transfers	Eliminate $140,000 (70%) of the transfers	Eliminate all $200,000 transfers	Eliminate all $200,000 transfers
Purchases	Eliminate all $200,000 transfers	Eliminate $140,000 (70%) of the transfers	Eliminate all $200,000 transfers	Eliminate all $200,000 transfers
Unrealized gain	Eliminate all $40,000	Eliminate $28,000 (70%)	Eliminate all $40,000	Eliminate $28,000 (70%)
Income assigned to noncontrolling interests	30% of $100,000 realized income less $40,000 unrealized gain, or $18,000	30% of $100,000 reported income, or $30,000	30% of $100,000 reported income, or $30,000	30% of $100,000 reported income, or $30,000

Questions

1. Intercompany transfers between the component companies of a business combination are quite common. Why do these intercompany transactions occur so frequently?
2. Barker Company owns 80 percent of the outstanding voting stock of Walden Company. During the current year, intercompany sales amount to $100,000. These transactions were made with a markup equal to 40 percent of the transfer price. In consolidating the two companies, what amount of these sales would be eliminated?

3. Padlock Corp. owns 90 percent of Safeco, Inc. During the year, Padlock sold 3,000 locking mecha-nisms to Safeco for $900,000. By the end of the year, Safeco had sold all but 500 of the locking mechanisms to outside parties. Padlock marks up the cost of its locking mechanisms by 60 percent in computing its sales price to affiliated and nonaffiliated customers. How much intercompany profit remains in Safeco's inventory at year-end?

4. How are unrealized inventory gains created, and what consolidation entries does the presence of these gains necessitate?

5. James, Inc., sells inventory to Matthews Company, a related party, at James's standard markup. At the end of the current fiscal year, Matthews still holds some portion of this inventory. If consolidated fi-nancial statements are to be prepared, why are worksheet entries required in two different fiscal periods?

6. How do intercompany gains that are present in any year affect the noncontrolling interest calculations?

7. A worksheet is being developed to consolidate Williams, Incorporated, and Brown Company. These two organizations have made considerable intercompany transactions. How would the consolidation process be affected if these transfers were downstream? How would the consolidation process be af-fected if these transfers were upstream?

8. King Company owns a 90 percent interest in the outstanding voting shares of Pawn Company. Pawn reports a net income of $110,000 for the current year. Intercompany sales occur at regular intervals between the two companies. Unrealized gains of $30,000 were present in the beginning inventory balances, whereas $60,000 in similar gains were recorded at the end of the year. What is the non-controlling interest's share of the subsidiary's net income?

9. When a subsidiary sells inventory to a parent, the intercompany profit is removed from the subsidiary's income and reduces the income allocation to the noncontrolling interest. Is the profit permanently eliminated from the noncontrolling interest, or is it merely shifted from one period to the next? Explain.

10. The consolidation process that is applicable when intercompany land transfers have occurred differs somewhat from that used for intercompany inventory sales. What differences should be noted?

11. A subsidiary sells land to the parent company at a significant gain. The parent holds the land for two years and then sells it to an outside party, also for a gain. How does the business combination account for these events?

12. Why does an intercompany sale of a depreciable asset (such as equipment or a building) require sub-sequent adjustments to depreciation expense within the consolidation process?

13. If a seller makes an intercompany sale of a depreciable asset at a price above book value, the seller's beginning Retained Earnings is reduced when preparing each subsequent consolidation. Why does the amount of the adjustment change from year to year?

Problems

1. What is the impact on consolidated financial statements of upstream and downstream transfers?
   a. No difference exists in consolidated financial statements between upstream and downstream transfers.
   b. Downstream transfers affect the computation of the noncontrolling interest's share of the sub-sidiary's income but upstream transfers do not.
   c. Upstream transfers affect the computation of the noncontrolling interest's share of the sub-sidiary's income but downstream transfers do not.
   d. Downstream transfers can be ignored since they are made by the parent company.

2. King Corporation owns 80 percent of Lee Corporation's common stock. During October 2006, Lee sold merchandise to King for $100,000. At December 31, 2006, 50 percent of this merchandise re-mains in King's inventory. For 2006, gross profit percentages were 30 percent for King and 40 per-cent for Lee. The amount of unrealized intercompany profit in ending inventory at December 31, 2006, that should be eliminated in the consolidation process is
   a. $40,000.
   b. $20,000.
   c. $16,000.
   d. $15,000.
   (AICPA adapted)

3. When intercompany transfers occur, how is the noncontrolling interest's share of the subsidiary's in-come computed?
   a. The subsidiary's reported income is adjusted for the impact of upstream transfers prior to com-puting the noncontrolling interest's allocation.

    b. The subsidiary's reported income is adjusted for the impact of all transfers prior to computing the noncontrolling interest's allocation.

    c. The subsidiary's reported income is not adjusted for the impact of transfers prior to computing the noncontrolling interest's allocation.

    d. The subsidiary's reported income is adjusted for the impact of downstream transfers prior to computing the noncontrolling interest's allocation.

4. Bellgrade, Inc., acquired a 60 percent interest in Hansen Company several years ago. During 2006, Hansen sold inventory costing $75,000 to Bellgrade for $100,000. A total of 16 percent of this inventory was not sold to outsiders until 2007. During 2007, Hansen sold inventory costing $96,000 to Bellgrade for $120,000. A total of 35 percent of this inventory was not sold to outsiders until 2008. In 2007, Bellgrade reported cost of goods sold of $380,000 while Hansen reported $210,000. What is the consolidated cost of goods sold in 2007?

    a. $465,600.

    b. $473,440.

    c. $474,400.

    d. $522,400.

5. Top Company holds 90 percent of the common stock of Bottom Company. In the current year, Top reports sales of $800,000 and cost of goods sold of $600,000. For this same period, Bottom has sales of $300,000 and cost of goods sold of $180,000. During the current year, Top sold merchandise to Bottom for $100,000. The subsidiary still possesses 40 percent of this inventory at the end of the current year. Top had established the transfer price based on its normal markup. What are the consolidated sales and cost of goods sold?

    a. $1,000,000 and $690,000.

    b. $1,000,000 and $705,000.

    c. $1,000,000 and $740,000.

    d. $970,000 and $696,000.

6. Use the same information as in Problem 5 except assume that the transfers were from Bottom Company to Top Company. What are the consolidated sales and cost of goods sold?

    a. $1,000,000 and $720,000.

    b. $1,000,000 and $755,000.

    c. $1,000,000 and $696,000.

    d. $970,000 and $712,000.

7. Hardwood, Inc., holds a 90 percent interest in Pittstoni Company. During 2005, Pittstoni sold inventory costing $77,000 to Hardwood for $110,000. A total of $40,000 of this inventory was not sold to outsiders until 2006. During 2006, Pittstoni sold inventory costing $72,000 to Hardwood for $120,000. A total of $50,000 of this inventory was not sold to outsiders until 2007. In 2006, Hardwood reported net income of $150,000 while Pittstoni reported $90,000. What is the noncontrolling interest in the 2006 income of the subsidiary?

    a. $8,000.

    b. $8,200.

    c. $9,000.

    d. $9,800.

8. Dunn Corporation owns 100 percent of Grey Corporation's common stock. On January 2, 2006, Dunn sold to Grey for $40,000 machinery with a carrying amount of $30,000. Grey is depreciating the acquired machinery over a five-year life by the straight-line method. The net adjustments to compute 2006 and 2007 consolidated net income would be an increase (decrease) of

	2006	2007
a.	$(8,000)	$2,000
b.	$(8,000)	–0–
c.	$(10,000)	$2,000
d.	$(10,000)	–0–

(AICPA adapted)

9. Wallton Corporation owns 70 percent of the outstanding stock of Hastings, Incorporated. On January 1, 2004, Wallton acquired a building with a 10-year life for $300,000. Wallton anticipated no salvage value, and the building was to be depreciated on the straight-line method. On January 1, 2006, Wallton sold this building to Hastings for $280,000. At that time, the building had a remaining life of eight years but still no expected salvage value. In preparing financial statements for 2006, how does this transfer affect the computation of consolidated net income?

a. Income must be reduced by $32,000.

b. Income must be reduced by $35,000.

c. Income must be reduced by $36,000.

d. Income must be reduced by $40,000.

Use the following data for Problems 10–15:

On January 1, 2006, Jarel bought 80 percent of the outstanding voting stock of Suarez for $260,000. Of this payment, $20,000 was allocated to equipment (with a five-year life) that had been undervalued on Suarez's books by $25,000. Any excess purchase price was allocated to unrecorded secret formulas and amortized over a 20-year life.

As of December 31, 2006, the financial statements appeared as follows:

	Jarel	Suarez
Revenues	$ (300,000)	$(200,000)
Cost of goods sold	140,000	80,000
Expenses	20,000	10,000
Net income	$ (140,000)	$(110,000)
Retained earnings, 1/1/06	$ (300,000)	$(150,000)
Net income	(140,000)	(110,000)
Dividends paid	–0–	–0–
Retained earnings, 12/31/06	$ (440,000)	$(260,000)
Cash and receivables	$ 210,000	$ 90,000
Inventory	150,000	110,000
Investment in Jarel	260,000	–0–
Equipment (net)	440,000	300,000
Total assets	$ 1,060,000	$ 500,000
Liabilities	$ (420,000)	$(140,000)
Common stock	(200,000)	(100,000)
Retained earnings, 12/31/06	(440,000)	(260,000)
Total liabilities and equities	$(1,060,000)	$(500,000)

During 2006, Jarel bought inventory for $80,000 and sold it to Suarez for $100,000. Suarez had paid for only half of this purchase by the end of the year. Of these goods, Suarez still purchases 60 percent on December 31.

10. What is the total of consolidated revenues?

a. $500,000.

b. $460,000.

c. $420,000.

d. $400,000.

11. What is the total of consolidated expenses?

a. $30,000.

b. $36,000.

c. $33,000.

d. $39,000.

12. What is the total of consolidated cost of goods sold?

a. $140,000.

b. $152,000.

c. $132,000.

d. $145,000.

13. What is the consolidated total of noncontrolling interest appearing on the balance sheet?
    a. $72,000.
    b. $69,600.
    c. $67,000.
    d. $70,600.

14. What is the consolidated total for equipment (net) at December 31?
    a. $680,000.
    b. $756,000.
    c. $764,000.
    d. $848,000.

15. What is the consolidated total for inventory at December 31?
    a. $240,000.
    b. $248,000.
    c. $250,000.
    d. $260,000.

16. Following are several figures reported for Pop and Sam as of December 31, 2006:

	Pop	Sam
Inventory	$300,000	$100,000
Sales	700,000	500,000
Investment income	not given	
Cost of goods sold	300,000	200,000
Operating expenses	200,000	200,000

    Pop acquired 80 percent of Sam on January 1, 1999. An excess $180,000 is allocated to an intangible asset and amortized over a 20-year life. During 2006, Sam sells inventory costing $100,000 to Pop for $150,000. Of this inventory, 10 percent remains at year-end. On a 2006 consolidation, determine the totals that would be reported for the following accounts:

    Inventory
    Sales
    Cost of Goods Sold
    Operating Expenses
    Noncontrolling Interest in the Subsidiary's Net Income

17. On January 1, 2005, Corgan Company purchased 80 percent of the outstanding voting stock of Smashing, Inc., for $980,000 in cash and other consideration. At the purchase date, Smashing had common stock of $700,000 and retained earnings of $250,000. Corgan attributed the excess of cost over Smashing's book value to various covenants with a 20-year life. Corgan uses the equity method to account for its investment in Smashing.

    During the next two years Smashing reported the following:

	Net Income	Dividends	Inventory Purchases from Corgan
2005	$150,000	$35,000	$100,000
2006	130,000	45,000	120,000

    Corgan sells inventory to Smashing using a 60 percent markup on cost. At the end of 2005 and 2006, 40 percent of the current year purchases remain in Smashing's inventory.

    a. Compute the equity method balance in Corgan's Investment in Smashing, Inc., account as of December 31, 2006.
    b. Prepare the worksheet adjustments for the December 31, 2006, consolidation of Corgan and Smashing.

18. Smith Corporation acquired 80 percent of the outstanding voting stock of Kane, Inc., on January 1, 1999, when Kane had a net book value of $400,000. Any unexplained excess purchase price was assigned to intangible assets and amortized at a rate of $5,000 per year.

Smith reported net income for 2006 of $300,000 while Kane reported $110,000. Smith distributed $100,000 in dividends during this period; Kane paid $40,000. At the end of the year, selected figures from the two companies' balance sheets were as follows:

	Smith Corporation	Kane, Inc.
Inventory	$140,000	$ 90,000
Land	600,000	200,000
Equipment (net)	400,000	300,000
Common stock	400,000	200,000
Retained earnings, 12/31/06	600,000	400,000

During 2005, intercompany sales of $90,000 (original cost of $54,000) were made. Only 20 percent of this inventory was still held at the end of 2005. In 2006, $120,000 in intercompany sales were made with an original cost of $66,000. Of this merchandise, 30 percent had not been resold to outside parties by the end of the year.

Each of the following questions should be considered as an independent situation.

a. If the intercompany sales were upstream, what would be the noncontrolling interest's share of the subsidiary's 2006 net income?

b. What is the consolidated balance in the ending Inventory account?

c. If the intercompany sales were downstream, what would be the noncontrolling interest's share of the subsidiary's 2006 net income?

d. If the intercompany sales were downstream, what would be the consolidated net income prior to the reduction for the noncontrolling interest's share of the subsidiary's income? Assume that Smith uses the cost method to account for this investment.

e. If the intercompany sales were downstream, what would be the consolidated balance of the Retained Earnings account as of the end of 2006? Assume that Smith uses the partial equity method to account for this investment.

f. If the intercompany sales were upstream, what would be the consolidated balance for Retained Earnings as of the end of 2006? Assume that Smith uses the partial equity method to account for this investment.

g. Assume that no intercompany inventory sales occurred between Smith and Kane. Instead, in 2003, Kane sold land costing $30,000 to Smith for $50,000. On the 2006 consolidated balance sheet, what value should be reported for land?

h. Assume that no intercompany inventory or land sales occurred between Smith and Kane. Instead, on January 1, 2005, Kane sold equipment (that originally cost $100,000 but had a $60,000 book value on that date) to Smith for $80,000. At the time of sale, the equipment had a remaining useful life of five years. What worksheet entries are made for a December 31, 2006, consolidation of these two companies to eliminate the impact of the intercompany transfer? For 2006, what is the noncontrolling interest's share of Kane's net income?

19. Rockney owns 60 percent of the outstanding stock of Dabney. Dabney reports net income of $120,000 for 2006. Since being acquired, the subsidiary has regularly supplied inventory to Rockney at 20 percent more than cost. Sales to Rockney amounted to $252,000 in 2005 and $288,000 in 2006. Approximately one-tenth of the inventory purchased during any one year is not used until the following period.

a. What is the noncontrolling interest's share of Dabney's income in 2006?

b. Prepare the 2006 consolidation entries required by the preceding intercompany inventory transfers.

20. Several years ago Penguin, Inc., purchased an 80 percent interest in Snow Company. The book values of Snow's asset and liability accounts at that time were considered to be equal to their fair values. Penguin paid an amount corresponding to the underlying book value of Snow so that no allocations or goodwill resulted from the purchase price.

The following selected account balances are from the individual financial records of these two companies as of December 31, 2006:

	Penguin	Snow
Sales	$640,000	$360,000
Cost of goods sold	290,000	197,000
Operating expenses	150,000	105,000

	Penguin	**Snow**
Retained earnings, 1/1/06	740,000	180,000
Inventory	346,000	110,000
Buildings (net)	358,000	157,000
Investment income	Not given	–0–

Each of the following problems is an independent situation:

a. Assume that Penguin sells inventory to Snow at a markup equal to 40 percent of cost. Intercompany transfers were $90,000 in 2005 and $110,000 in 2006. Of this inventory, Snow retained and then sold $28,000 of the 2005 transfers in 2006 and held $42,000 of the 2006 transfers until 2007.

On consolidated financial statements for 2006, determine the balances that would appear for the following accounts:

Cost of Goods Sold
Inventory
Noncontrolling Interest in Subsidiary's Net Income

b. Assume that Snow sells inventory to Penguin at a markup equal to 40 percent of cost. Intercompany transfers were $50,000 in 2005 and $80,000 in 2006. Of this inventory, $21,000 of the 2005 transfers were retained and then sold by Penguin in 2006, whereas $35,000 of the 2006 transfers were held until 2007.

On consolidated financial statements for 2006, determine the balances that would appear for the following accounts:

Cost of Goods Sold
Inventory
Noncontrolling Interest in Subsidiary's Net Income

c. Penguin sells a building to Snow on January 1, 2005, for $80,000, although its book value was only $50,000 on this date. The building had a five-year remaining life and was to be depreciated using the straight-line method with no salvage value.

On consolidated financial statements for 2006, determine the balances that would appear for the following accounts:

Buildings (net)
Operating Expenses
Noncontrolling Interest in Subsidiary's Net Income

21. Allen, Inc., owns all of the outstanding stock of Bowen Corporation. Amortization expense of $9,000 per year resulted from the original purchase. For 2007, the companies had the following account balances:

	Allen	**Bowen**
Sales	$900,000	$500,000
Cost of goods sold	400,000	300,000
Operating expenses	300,000	120,000
Investment income	Not given	–0–
Dividends paid	60,000	40,000

Intercompany sales of $200,000 occurred during 2006 and again in 2007. This merchandise cost $140,000 each year. Of the total transfers, $60,000 was still held on December 31, 2006, with $45,000 unsold on December 31, 2007.

a. For consolidation purposes, does the direction of the transfers (upstream or downstream) affect the balances to be reported here?

b. Prepare a consolidated income statement for the year ending December 31, 2007.

22. On January 1, 2005, PortFast Company purchased 90 percent of the outstanding voting stock of SpeedNet, Inc., for $1,400,000 in cash and stock options. At the purchase date, SpeedNet had Common Stock of $900,000 and Retained Earnings of $300,000. PortFast attributed the excess of cost over SpeedNet's book value to a database with a five-year life. PortFast uses the equity method to account for its investment in SpeedNet.

During the next two years, SpeedNet reported the following:

	Income	Dividends
2005	$ 80,000	$5,000
2006	115,000	8,000

On July 1, 2005, PortFast sold communication equipment to SpeedNet for $42,000. The equipment originally cost $48,000 and had accumulated depreciation of $9,000 and an estimated remaining life of three years at the date of the intercompany transfer.

a. Compute the equity method balance in PortFast's Investment in SpeedNet, Inc., account as of December 31, 2006.

b. Prepare the worksheet adjustments for the December 31, 2006, consolidation of PortFast and SpeedNet.

23. Plimpton holds 100 percent of the outstanding shares of Stanger. On January 1, 2005, Plimpton transferred equipment to Stanger for $70,000. The equipment had cost $110,000 originally but had a $40,000 book value and five-year remaining life at the date of transfer. Depreciation expense is computed according to the straight-line method with no salvage value.

Consolidated financial statements for 2007 currently are being prepared. What worksheet entries are needed in connection with the consolidation of this asset? Assume that the parent applies the partial equity method.

24. On January 1, 2007, Slaughter sold equipment to Bennett (a wholly owned subsidiary) for $120,000 in cash. The equipment had originally cost $100,000 but had a book value of only $70,000 when transferred. On that date, the equipment had a five-year remaining life. Depreciation expense is computed using the straight-line method.

Slaughter earned $220,000 in net income in 2007 (not including any investment income) while Bennett reported $90,000.

a. What is the consolidated net income for 2007?

b. What is the consolidated net income for 2007 if Slaughter owns only 90 percent of Bennett?

c. What is the consolidated net income for 2007 if Slaughter owns only 90 percent of Bennett and the equipment transfer was upstream?

d. What is the consolidated net income for 2008 if Slaughter reports $240,000 (does not include investment income) and Bennett $100,000 in income? Assume that Bennett is a wholly owned subsidiary and the equipment transfer was downstream.

25. Anchovy purchased 90 percent of Yelton on January 1, 2004. Of the original price paid by the parent, $60,000 was allocated to undervalued equipment (with a 10-year life) and $80,000 was attributed to franchises (to be written off over a 20-year period).

Since the takeover, Yelton has transferred inventory to its parent as follows:

Year	Cost	Transfer Price	Remaining at Year-End
2004	$20,000	$ 50,000	$20,000 (at transfer price)
2005	49,000	70,000	30,000 (at transfer price)
2006	50,000	100,000	40,000 (at transfer price)

On January 1, 2005, Anchovy sold a building to Yelton for $50,000. The building had originally cost $70,000 but had a book value at the date of transfer of only $30,000. The building is estimated to have a five-year remaining life (straight-line depreciation is used with no salvage value).

Selected figures from the December 31, 2006, trial balances of these two companies are as follows:

	Anchovy	Yelton
Sales	$600,000	$500,000
Cost of goods sold	400,000	260,000
Operating expenses	120,000	80,000
Investment income	Not given	–0–
Inventory	220,000	80,000
Equipment (net)	140,000	110,000
Buildings (net)	350,000	190,000

Determine consolidated totals for each of these account balances.

26. On January 1, 2006, Sledge had common stock of $120,000 and retained earnings of $260,000. During that year, Sledge reported sales of $130,000, cost of goods sold of $70,000, and operating expenses of $40,000.

    On January 1, 2001, 80 percent of Sledge's outstanding voting stock was acquired by Percy, Inc. At that date, $60,000 of the purchase price was assigned to contracts (with a 20-year life) and $20,000 to an undervalued building (with a 10-year life).

    In 2005, Sledge sold inventory costing $9,000 to Percy for $15,000. Of this merchandise, Percy continued to hold $5,000 at the end of that period. During 2006, Sledge transferred inventory costing $11,000 to Percy for $20,000. Percy still held half of these items at year-end.

    On January 1, 2005, Percy sold equipment to Sledge for $12,000. This asset originally cost $16,000 but had a January 1, 2005, book value of $9,000. At the time of transfer, the equipment's remaining life was estimated to be five years.

    Percy has properly applied the equity method to the investment in Sledge.

    a. Prepare worksheet entries to consolidate these two companies as of December 31, 2006.

    b. Compute the noncontrolling interest in the subsidiary's income for 2006.

27. Big purchased 90 percent of the outstanding shares of Little on January 1, 2004, for $345,000 in cash. The subsidiary's stockholders' equity accounts totaled $330,000 on that day. However, a building held by Little (with a nine-year remaining life) was undervalued in the accounting records by $20,000. Any excess purchase price is assigned to patented technology to be amortized over a 10-year period.

    Little reported net income of $60,000 in 2004 and $80,000 in 2005. The company followed a policy of paying dividends each year equal to 30 percent of income.

    Little sells inventory to Big as follows:

Year	Cost to Little	Transfer Price to Big	Inventory Remaining at Year-End (at transfer price)
2004	$69,000	$115,000	$25,000
2005	81,000	135,000	37,500
2006	92,800	160,000	50,000

    At December 31, 2006, Big owes Little $16,000 for inventory acquired during the current period.

    The following separate account balances are for these two companies for December 31, 2006, and the year then ended. Credits are indicated by parentheses.

	Big	Little
Sales revenues	$ (862,000)	$(366,000)
Cost of goods sold	515,000	209,000
Expenses	186,600	67,000
Investment income—Little	(70,600)	—
Net income	$ (231,000)	$ (90,000)
Retained earnings, 1/1/06	$ (488,000)	$(278,000)
Net income (above)	(231,000)	(90,000)
Dividends paid	136,000	27,000
Retained earnings, 12/31/06	$ (583,000)	$(341,000)
Cash and receivables	$ 146,000	$ 98,000
Inventory	255,000	136,000
Investment in Little	456,000	—
Land, buildings, and equipment (net)	959,000	328,000
Total assets	$ 1,816,000	$ 562,000
Liabilities	$ (718,000)	$ (71,000)
Common stock	(515,000)	(150,000)
Retained earnings, 12/31/06	(583,000)	(341,000)
Total liabilities and equities	$(1,816,000)	$(562,000)

Answer each of the following questions:

a. How much did the book value of the subsidiary increase during the previous two years of ownership (2004 and 2005)?

b. What was the annual amortization resulting from the purchase price allocations?

c. Were the intercompany transfers upstream or downstream?

d. What unrealized gain existed as of January 1, 2006?

e. What was the subsidiary's realized retained earnings as of January 1, 2006?

f. What unrealized gain existed as of December 31, 2006?

g. What was the subsidiary's realized net income for 2006?

h. What amounts make up the $70,600 Investment Income—Little account balance for 2006?

i. What was the noncontrolling interest's share of the subsidiary's net income for 2006?

j. What amounts make up the $456,000 Investment in Little account balance as of December 31, 2006?

k. What Entry **S** is required in producing a 2006 consolidation worksheet?

l. Without preparing a worksheet or consolidation entries, determine the consolidation balances for these two companies.

28. Asphalt acquired 70 percent of Broadway on June 11, 1995. Based on the purchase price, an intangible of $300,000 was recognized and is being amortized at the rate of $10,000 per year. The 2006 financial statements are as follows:

	Asphalt	Broadway
Sales	$ (800,000)	$ (600,000)
Cost of goods sold	535,000	400,000
Operating expenses	100,000	100,000
Dividend income	(35,000)	–0–
Net income	$ (200,000)	$ (100,000)
Retained earnings, 1/1/06	$(1,300,000)	$ (850,000)
Net income	(200,000)	(100,000)
Dividends paid	100,000	50,000
Retained earnings, 12/31/06	$(1,400,000)	$ (900,000)
Cash and receivables	$ 400,000	$ 300,000
Inventory	298,000	700,000
Investment in Broadway	902,000	–0–
Fixed assets	1,000,000	600,000
Accumulated depreciation	(300,000)	(200,000)
Totals	$ 2,300,000	$ 1,400,000
Liabilities	$ (600,000)	$ (400,000)
Common stock	(300,000)	(100,000)
Retained earnings	(1,400,000)	(900,000)
Totals	$(2,300,000)	$(1,400,000)

Asphalt sells inventory costing $72,000 to Broadway during 2005 for $120,000. At year-end, 30 percent is left. Asphalt sells inventory costing $200,000 to Broadway during 2006 for $250,000. At year-end, 20 percent is left. Under these circumstances, determine the consolidated balances for the following accounts:

Sales
Cost of Goods Sold
Operating Expenses
Dividend Income
Noncontrolling Interest in Consolidated Income
Inventory
Noncontrolling Interest in Subsidiary, 12/31/06

29. Compute the balances in Problem 28 again, assuming that the intercompany transfers were all made from Broadway to Asphalt.

30. Following are financial statements for Topper Company and Kirby Company for 2006:

	Topper	Kirby
Sales and other income	$ (800,000)	$ (600,000)
Cost of goods sold	500,000	400,000
Operating and interest expense	100,000	160,000
Net income	$ (200,000)	$ (40,000)
Retained earnings, 1/1/06	$ (990,000)	$ (500,000)
Net income	(200,000)	(40,000)
Dividends paid	130,000	–0–
Retained earnings, 12/31/06	$(1,060,000)	$ (540,000)
Cash and receivables	$ 220,000	$ 170,000
Inventory	224,000	160,000
Investment in Kirby	654,000	–0–
Equipment (net)	600,000	400,000
Buildings	1,000,000	800,000
Accumulated depreciation—buildings	(100,000)	(200,000)
Other assets	200,000	100,000
Total assets	$ 2,798,000	$ 1,430,000
Liabilities	$(1,138,000)	$ (590,000)
Common stock	(600,000)	(300,000)
Retained earnings, 12/31/06	(1,060,000)	(540,000)
Total liabilities and equity	$(2,798,000)	$(1,430,000)

- Topper purchased 90 percent of Kirby on January 1, 1995, for $654,000 in cash. On the date of acquisition, Kirby held equipment (5-year life) that was undervalued on the financial records by $50,000 and liabilities (20-year life) that were overvalued by $30,000. Any excess price was assigned to brand names and amortized over a 40-year life.

- Between January 1, 1995, and December 31, 2005, Kirby earned a net income of $600,000 and paid dividends of $340,000.

- Kirby sells inventory to Topper each year with a markup equal to 20 percent of the transfer price. Intercompany sales were $145,000 in 2005 and $160,000 in 2006. On January 1, 2006, 30 percent of the 2005 transfers were still on hand and, on December 31, 2006, 40 percent of the 2006 transfers remained in inventory. Topper still owes $20,000 on the final shipment.

- Topper sold a building to Kirby on January 1, 2005. It had cost Topper $100,000 but had $90,000 in accumulated depreciation at the time of this transfer. The price was $25,000 in cash. At that time, the building had a five-year remaining life.

Determine all consolidated balances either computationally or by the use of a worksheet.

31. Atkins, Inc., and Smith, Inc., formed a business combination on January 1, 2000, when Atkins acquired a 60 percent interest in the common stock of Smith for $372,000. Smith's book value on that day was $350,000. The subsidiary held patents (with a 12-year remaining life) that were undervalued within the company's accounting records by $120,000. Any remaining excess purchase price is assigned to a customer list to be amortized over 10 years.

Intercompany inventory sales between the two companies have been made as follows:

Year	Cost to Atkins	Transfer Price to Smith	Ending Balance (at transfer price)
2000	$ 60,000	$ 72,000	$15,000
2001	70,000	84,000	25,000
2002	80,000	100,000	20,000
2003	100,000	125,000	40,000
2004	90,000	120,000	30,000
2005	120,000	150,000	50,000
2006	112,000	160,000	40,000

Smith sold a building to Atkins on January 1, 2004, for $80,000. The building had a net book value of $30,000 on that date and a five-year life. No salvage value was expected for this asset, which was being depreciated by the straight-line method.

The individual financial statements for these two companies as of December 31, 2006, and the year then ended follow:

	Atkins, Inc.	Smith, Inc.
Sales	$ (700,000)	$(300,000)
Cost of goods sold	460,000	205,000
Operating expenses	170,000	70,000
Income of Smith	(15,000)	–0–
Net income	$ (85,000)	$ (25,000)
Retained earnings, 1/1/06	$ (690,000)	$(400,000)
Net income (above)	(85,000)	(25,000)
Dividends paid	45,000	5,000
Retained earnings, 12/31/06	$ (730,000)	$(420,000)
Cash and receivables	$ 185,000	$ 142,000
Inventory	233,000	229,000
Investment in Smith	474,000	–0–
Buildings (net)	308,000	202,000
Equipment (net)	220,000	86,000
Patents (net)	–0–	20,000
Total assets	$ 1,420,000	$ 679,000
Liabilities	$ (390,000)	$(159,000)
Common stock	(300,000)	(100,000)
Retained earnings, 12/31/06	(730,000)	(420,000)
Total liabilities and equities	$(1,420,000)	$(679,000)

For each of the following accounts, determine the 2006 consolidated balance:

a. Cost of Goods Sold.

b. Operating Expenses.

c. Net Income.

d. Retained Earnings, 1/1/06.

e. Inventory.

f. Buildings (net).

g. Patents (net).

h. Common Stock.

i. Noncontrolling Interest in Smith, 12/31/06.

32. Tall Company purchased 60 percent of the outstanding stock of Short, Inc., on January 1, 2004. A $70,000 portion of the purchase price was allocated to equipment with a 10-year remaining life, and $40,000 was attributed to a building having a 20-year life. A huge database was assigned $60,000 and has been amortized over a 30-year period.

Short sells inventory to Tall at a markup equal to 25 percent of the transfer price. Sales have been as follows:

Year	Transfer Price to Tall	Inventory Remaining at Year-End (at transfer price)
2004	$ 90,000	$30,000
2005	120,000	20,000
2006	140,000	40,000

Tall still owes $30,000 to Short for the last inventory shipment.

Following are the account balances at December 31, 2006, for both companies. Credit balances are indicated with parentheses.

	Tall	Short
Revenues	$ (984,000)	$(438,000)
Cost of goods sold	551,000	286,000
Operating expenses	198,000	112,000
Equity earnings of Short	(10,000)	–0–
Net income	$ (245,000)	$ (40,000)
Retained earnings, 1/1/06	$ (871,000)	$(350,000)
Net income (above)	(245,000)	(40,000)
Dividends paid	110,000	25,000
Retained earnings, 12/31/06	$(1,006,000)	$(365,000)
Cash and receivables	$ 239,000	$ 57,000
Inventory	454,000	95,000
Investment in Short	440,000	–0–
Land and buildings (net)	722,000	394,000
Equipment (net)	328,000	257,000
Total assets	$ 2,183,000	$ 803,000
Liabilities	$ (686,000)	$(288,000)
Common stock	(320,000)	(90,000)
Additional paid-in capital	(171,000)	(60,000)
Retained earnings	(1,006,000)	(365,000)
Total liabilities and stockholders' equity	$(2,183,000)	$(803,000)

a. How was the $10,000 balance in the Equity Earnings of Short account determined?

b. Construct a worksheet to arrive at consolidated figures to be used for external reporting purposes.

33. On December 31, 2003, Silvey Company acquired 70 percent of the outstanding common stock of Young Company for $665,000. Young reported stockholders' equity accounts on that date as follows:

Common stock—$10 par value	$300,000
Additional paid-in capital	90,000
Retained earnings	410,000

In establishing the purchase price, Silvey appraised Young's assets and ascertained that the accounting records undervalued a building (with a five-year life) by $50,000. Any remaining excess purchase price is allocated to a franchise agreement to be amortized over 10 years.

During the subsequent years, Young sold inventory to Silvey at a 30 percent markup on the transfer price. Silvey consistently resold this merchandise in the year of acquisition or in the period immediately following. Transfers for the three years after this business combination was created amounted to the following:

Year	Transfer Price	Inventory Remaining at Year-End (at transfer price)
2004	$60,000	$10,000
2005	80,000	12,000
2006	90,000	18,000

In addition, Silvey sold several pieces of fully depreciated equipment to Young on January 1, 2005, for $20,000. The equipment had originally cost Silvey $50,000. Young plans to depreciate the cost of these assets over a five-year period.

In 2006, Young earns a net income of $160,000 and distributes $50,000 in cash dividends. These figures increase the subsidiary's Retained Earnings to a $740,000 balance at the end of 2006. During this same year, Silvey reported dividend income of $35,000 and an investment account containing the original cost balance of $665,000.

Prepare the 2006 consolidation worksheet entries for Silvey and Young. In addition, compute the noncontrolling interest's share of the subsidiary's net income for 2006.

34. Assume the same basic information as presented in Problem 33 except that Silvey has employed the equity method of accounting. Hence, it reports investment income for 2006 as $100,740 with an Investment account balance of $838,220. Under these circumstances, prepare the worksheet entries required for the consolidation of Silvey Company and Young Company.

35. The individual financial statements for Bumpus Company and Keller Company for the year ending December 31, 2006, follow. Bumpus acquired a 60 percent interest in Keller on January 1, 2001. An internally developed customer list was assigned $100,000 within the original purchase price. This intangible asset is being amortized over 20 years.

Bumpus sold Keller land with a book value of $60,000 on January 1, 2003, for $100,000. Keller still holds this land at the end of the current year.

Keller annually transfers inventory to Bumpus. In 2006, it shipped inventory costing $100,000 to Bumpus at a price of $150,000. During 2006, intercompany shipments totaled $200,000, although the original cost to Keller was only $140,000. In each of these years, 20 percent of the merchandise was not resold to outside parties until the period following the transfer. Bumpus owes Keller $40,000 at the end of 2006.

	Bumpus Company	Keller Company
Sales	$ (800,000)	$ (500,000)
Cost of goods sold	500,000	300,000
Operating expenses	100,000	60,000
Income of Keller Company	(84,000)	–0–
Net income	$ (284,000)	$ (140,000)
Retained earnings, 1/1/06	$(1,116,000)	$ (620,000)
Net income (above)	(284,000)	(140,000)
Dividends paid	115,000	60,000
Retained earnings, 12/31/06	$(1,285,000)	$ (700,000)
Cash	$ 177,000	$ 90,000
Accounts receivable	316,000	410,000
Inventory	440,000	320,000
Investment in Keller Company	766,000	–0–
Land	180,000	390,000
Buildings and equipment (net)	496,000	300,000
Total assets	$ 2,375,000	$ 1,510,000
Liabilities	$ (480,000)	$ (400,000)
Common stock	(610,000)	(320,000)
Additional paid-in capital	–0–	(90,000)
Retained earnings, 12/31/06	(1,285,000)	(700,000)
Total liabilities and equities	$(2,375,000)	$(1,510,000)

a. Prepare a worksheet to consolidate the separate 2006 financial statements for Bumpus and Keller.

b. How would the consolidation entries in requirement (a) have differed if Bumpus had sold a building with a $60,000 book value (cost of $140,000) to Keller for $100,000 instead of land, as the problem reports? Assume that the building had a 10-year remaining life at the date of transfer.

36. Greene, Inc., obtained 100 percent of Meadow Corporation on January 1, 2003. Meadow reported total stockholders' equity on this date of $300,000 although the stock issued by Greene in the transaction had a $170,000 par value but a fair value of $450,000. On January 1, 2003, Meadow held land that was undervalued in the company's accounting records by $30,000. Any excess purchase price is assigned to a franchise contract that is to be amortized over a 40-year life.

Meadow regularly transferred inventory to Greene. In 2006, Meadow sold merchandise costing $60,000 to Greene for $100,000. Of this total, 30 percent was not resold to unrelated parties until the following year. In 2007, Meadow shipped $75,000 in inventory to Greene for $150,000 with $20,000 (transfer price) still held at the end of the period.

On June 19, 2007, Greene sold land costing $12,000 to Meadow for $17,000. This money has not yet been paid.

The following account balances are for both companies as of December 31, 2007, and the year then ended. The parent has used the equity method to record this investment. Produce a worksheet to arrive at consolidated financial statements for this business combination. Credit balances are indicated by parentheses.

	Greene	Meadow
Revenues	$ (477,000)	$(358,000)
Cost of goods sold	289,000	195,000
General and administrative expenses	170,000	75,000
Gain on sale of land	(5,000)	–0–
Investment income	(82,000)	–0–
Net income	$ (105,000)	$ (88,000)
Retained earnings, 1/1/07	$ (365,000)	$(292,000)
Net income	(105,000)	(88,000)
Dividends distributed	70,000	20,000
Retained earnings, 12/31/07	$ (400,000)	$(360,000)
Cash and receivables	$ 169,000	$ 210,000
Inventory	281,000	232,000
Investment in Meadow	630,000	–0–
Land, buildings, and equipment (net)	487,000	284,000
Total assets	$ 1,567,000	$ 726,000
Liabilities	$ (466,000)	$(216,000)
Common stock	(410,000)	(120,000)
Additional paid-in capital	(291,000)	(30,000)
Retained earnings, 12/31/07	(400,000)	(360,000)
Total liabilities and stockholders' equity	$(1,567,000)	$(726,000)

Develop Your Skills

EXCEL CASE

On January 1, 2006, Patrick Company purchased 100 percent of the outstanding voting stock of Shawn, Inc., for $1,000,000 in cash and other consideration. At the purchase date, Shawn had common stock of $500,000 and retained earnings of $185,000. Patrick attributed the excess of cost over Shawn's book value to a trade name with a 25-year life. Patrick uses the equity method to account for its investment in Shawn.

During the next two years, Shawn reported the following:

	Income	Dividends	Inventory Transfers to Patrick at Transfer Price
2006	$78,000	$25,000	$190,000
2007	85,000	27,000	210,000

Shawn sells inventory to Patrick after a markup based on a gross profit rate. At the end of 2006 and 2007, 30 percent of the current year purchases remain in Patrick's inventory.

Required:

Create an Excel spreadsheet that computes the following:

1. Equity method balance in Patrick's Investment in Shawn, Inc., account as of December 31, 2007.

2. Worksheet adjustments for the December 31, 2007, consolidation of Patrick and Shawn.

Formulate your solution so that Shawn's gross profit rate on sales to Patrick is treated as a variable.

ANALYSIS AND RESEARCH CASE: ACCOUNTING INFORMATION AND SALARY NEGOTIATIONS

Granger Eagles Players' Association and Mr. Doublecount, the CEO of Granger Eagles Baseball Company, ask your help in resolving a salary dispute. Mr. Doublecount presents the following income statement to the player representatives.

GRANGER EAGLES BASEBALL COMPANY
Income Statement

Ticket revenues		$2,000,000
Stadium rent expense	$1,400,000	
Ticket expense	25,000	
Promotion	35,000	
Player salaries	400,000	
Staff salaries and miscellaneous	200,000	2,060,000
Net income (loss)		$ (60,000)

Mr. Doublecount argues that the Granger Eagles really lose money and, until things turn around, a salary increase is out of the question.

As a result of your inquiry, you discover that Granger Eagles Baseball Company owns 91 percent of the voting stock in Eagle Stadium, Inc. This venue is specifically designed for baseball and is where the Eagles play their entire home game schedule. However, Mr. Doublecount does not wish to consider the profits of Eagle Stadium in the negotiations with the players. He claims that "the stadium is really a separate business entity that was purchased separately from the team" and therefore does not concern the players. The Eagles Stadium income statement appears as follows:

EAGLES STADIUM, INC.
Income Statement

Stadium rent revenue	$1,400,000	
Concession revenue	800,000	
Parking revenue	100,000	$2,300,000
Cost of goods sold	250,000	
Depreciation	80,000	
Staff salaries and miscellaneous	150,000	480,000
Net income (loss)		$1,820,000

Required:

1. What advice would you provide the negotiating parties regarding the issue of considering the Eagles Stadium income statement in their discussions? What authoritative literature could you cite in supporting your advice?

2. What other pertinent information would you need to provide a specific recommendation regarding players' salaries?

Please visit the text Web site for the online CPA Simulation: mhhe.com/hoyle8e

Situation: Giant Company acquired all of the outstanding common stock of Tiny Corporation 4 years ago for $240,000 more than book value. This excess was assigned equally to a building (10-year life), inventory (sold within 1 year), and goodwill. On its separate financial statements for the current year, Giant reported sales of $900,000, cost of goods sold of $500,000, and operating expenses of $200,000. No investment income was included in these figures. On its separate financial statements for the current year, Tiny reported sales of $500,000, cost of goods sold of $200,000, and operating expenses of $100,000. Both companies paid dividends of $20,000 this year. Both companies reported positive current ratios of above 1 to 1.

Topics to be covered in simulation:

- Intercompany inventory transfers.
- Intercompany equipment transfer.
- Intercompany land transfer.
- Intercompany debts.
- Equity method.
- Push-down accounting.
- Minority interest.
- Negative goodwill.

Chapter **Six**

Variable Interest Entities, Intercompany Debt, Consolidated Cash Flows, and Other Issues

The consolidation of financial information can be a highly complex process often encompassing a number of practical challenges. This chapter examines the procedures required by several additional issues:

- Variable interest entities.
- Intercompany debt.
- Subsidiary preferred stock.
- The consolidated statement of cash flows.
- Computation of consolidated earnings per share.
- Subsidiary stock transactions.

Each of these can create potential difficulties for an accountant attempting to produce fairly presented financial statements for a business combination.

Questions to Consider

- What is a variable interest entity and when must such an entity be consolidated? How are consolidated values determined for variable interest entities?

- When a company buys an affiliate's debt instrument *from an outside party*, the reciprocal balances (investment and debt, interest revenue and expense, etc.) usually do not agree. How do intercompany debt and related interest affect the consolidation process in the year of acquisition as well as in succeeding periods?

- Some preferred stocks are viewed as equity interests but others are considered to be equivalent to debts. What impact does the nature of a subsidiary's preferred stock have on the consolidation process?

- What effect does a business combination have on the consolidated statement of cash flows?

- How are basic and diluted earnings per share computed for business combinations?

- Why would a subsidiary buy or sell more shares of its own stock after coming under the control of a parent company? What effect do such transactions have on consolidated financial statements?

FIN 46R—CONSOLIDATION OF VARIABLE INTEREST ENTITIES

Starting in the late 1970s, many firms began establishing separate business structures to help finance their operations at favorable rates. These structures became commonly known as *special purpose entities* (SPEs), *special purpose vehicles*, or *off-balance sheet structures*. In this text, we will refer to all such entities collectively as *variable interest entities* or VIEs. Many firms have routinely included their VIEs in their consolidated financial reports. However, others have sought to avoid consolidation. As we discussed, FASB *Interpretation 46R,* "Consolidation of Variable Interest Entities," December 2003 (*FIN 46R*), addresses financial reporting for enterprises involved with VIEs.[1]

What Is a VIE?

A VIE can take the form of a trust, partnership, joint venture, or corporation although sometimes it has neither independent management nor employees. Most are established for valid business purposes, and transactions involving VIEs have become widespread. Common examples of VIE activities include transfers of financial assets, leasing, hedging financial instruments, research and development, and other transactions. An enterprise often sponsors a VIE to accomplish a well-defined and limited business activity and to provide low-cost financing.

Low-cost financing of asset purchases is frequently a main benefit available through VIEs. Rather than engaging in the transaction directly, the business may sponsor a VIE to purchase and finance an asset acquisition. The VIE then leases the asset to the sponsor. This strategy saves the business money because the VIE is often eligible for a lower interest rate. This advantage is achieved for several reasons. First, the VIE typically operates with a very limited set of assets—in many cases just one asset. By isolating an asset in a VIE, the risk of the asset is isolated from the overall risk of the sponsoring firm. Thus the VIE creditors remain protected by the specific collateral in the asset. Second, the business activities of a VIE can be strictly limited by its governing documents. These limits further protect lenders by preventing the VIE from engaging in any activities not specified in its agreements. As noted by a major public accounting firm,

> The borrower/transferor gains access to a source of funds less expensive than would otherwise be available. This advantage derives from isolating the assets in an entity prohibited from undertaking any other business activity or taking on any additional debt, thereby creating a better security interest in the assets for the lender/investor.[2]

Because governing agreements limit activities and decision making in most VIEs, there is often little need for voting stock. In fact, a sponsoring enterprise may own very little, if any, of its VIE's voting stock. Prior to *FIN 46R* because these businesses were technically not majority owners of their VIEs, they often left such entities unconsolidated in their financial reports. In utilizing the VIE as a conduit to provide financing, the related assets and debt were effectively removed from the enterprise's balance sheet.

Characteristics of Variable Interest Entities

Like all business entities, VIEs generally have assets, liabilities, and investors with equity interests. Unlike most businesses, because a VIE's activities can be strictly limited, the role of the equity investors can be fairly minor. The VIE may have been created specifically to benefit its sponsoring firm with low-cost financing. Thus, the equity investors may serve simply as a technical requirement to allow the VIE to function as a legal entity. Because they bear relatively low economic risk, equity investors are typically provided only a small rate of return.

The small equity investments normally are insufficient to induce lenders to provide a low-risk interest rate for the VIE. As a result, another party (often the sponsoring firm that benefits from the VIE's activities) must contribute substantial resources—often loans and/or guarantees—to enable the VIE to secure additional financing needed to accomplish its purpose. For example, the sponsoring firm may guarantee the VIE's debt, thus assuming risk of default. Other contractual arrangements may limit returns to equity holders while participation rights provide increased profit potential and risks to the sponsoring firm. Risks and rewards such as these cause the sponsor's economic interest to vary depending on the success of the created entity—hence the term *variable interest entity*. In contrast to a traditional entity, a VIE's risks and rewards are distributed not according to stock ownership but according to other variable interests. Exhibit 6.1 describes variable interests further and provides several examples presented in *FIN 46R*.

---

[1] *FIN 46R* represents a revision of *FIN 46* originally issued in January 2003. Although several elements of implementation guidance have been clarified and/or revised, the fundamental concepts of *FIN 46* remain intact.
[2] KPMG, "Defining Issues: New Accounting for SPEs," March 1, 2002.

EXHIBIT 6.1
FIN 46R **Examples of**
Variable Interests

Variable interests in a variable interest entity are contractual, ownership, or other pecuniary interests in an entity that change with changes in the entity's net asset value. Variable interests will absorb portions of a variable interest entity's expected losses if they occur or receive portions of the entity's expected residual returns if they occur.

Expected losses and expected residual returns include

- the expected variability in the entity's net income or loss
- the expected variability in the fair value of the entity's assets

The following are some examples of variable interests and the related potential losses or returns:

Variable interests	Potential losses or returns
• Guarantees of debt	• If a VIE cannot repay liabilities, honoring a debt guarantee will produce a loss
• Subordinated debt instruments	• If a VIE's cash flow is insufficient to repay all senior debt, subordinated debt may be required to absorb the loss
• Lease residual value guarantees	• If leased asset declines below the residual value, honoring the guarantee will produce a loss
• Participation rights	• Entitles holder to residual profits
• Asset purchase options	• Entitles holder to benefit from increases in asset fair values

A firm with variable interests in a VIE increases its risk with the level (or potential level in the case of a guarantee) of resources provided. With increased risks come increased incentives to exert greater influence over the decision making of the VIE. In fact, a firm with variable interests will regularly limit the decision-making power of the equity investors through the governance documents that establish the VIE. As noted in *FIN 46R,*

> If the total equity investment at risk is not sufficient to permit the entity to finance its activities, the parties providing the necessary additional subordinated financial support will not permit an equity investor to make decisions that may be counter to their interests (para. E20).

Although technically the equity investors are the owners of the VIE, in reality they may retain little of the traditional responsibilities, risks, and benefits of ownership. In fact, the equity investors often cede financial control of the VIE to those with variable interest in exchange for a guaranteed rate of return.

VIEs can help accomplish legitimate business purposes. Nonetheless, their use was widely criticized in the aftermath of the 2001 collapse of Enron Corporation. Because many firms used VIEs for off-balance sheet financing, such entities were often characterized as vehicles to hide debt and mislead investors. Other critics observed that firms with variable interests recorded questionable profits on sales to their VIEs that were not arm's length transactions.[3]

Consolidation of Variable Interest Entities

Prior to FASB *Interpretation No. 46R,* "Consolidation of Variable Interest Entities," December 2003 (*FIN 46R*), the assets, liabilities, and results of operations for VIEs and other entities frequently were not consolidated with those of the firm that controlled the entity. These firms invoked *ARB 51*'s reliance on voting interests, as opposed to variable interests, to indicate a lack of a controlling financial interest. As *FIN 46R* observes,

> ARB 51 requires that an enterprise's consolidated financial statements include subsidiaries in which the enterprise has a controlling financial interest. That requirement usually has been applied to subsidiaries in which an enterprise has a majority voting interest, but in

[3] In its 2001 fourth quarter 10-Q, Enron recorded earnings restatements of over $400 million related to its failure to properly consolidate several of its SPEs (e.g., Chewco and LMJ1). Enron also admitted an improper omission of $700 million of its SPE's debt. Within a month of the restatements, Enron filed for bankruptcy.

many circumstances, the enterprise's consolidated financial statements do not include variable interest entities with which it has similar relationships. The voting interest approach is not effective in identifying controlling financial interests in entities that are not controllable through voting interests or in which the equity investors do not bear residual economic risk. (Summary, page 2)

FIN 46R first describes how to identify a VIE that is not subject to control through voting ownership interests but is nonetheless controlled by another enterprise and therefore subject to consolidation. Each enterprise involved with a VIE must determine whether the financial support it provides makes it the primary beneficiary of the VIE's activities. The VIE's primary beneficiary is then required to include the assets, liabilities, and results of the activities of the VIE in its consolidated financial statements.[4]

According to *FIN 46R*, an entity qualifies as a VIE if either of the following conditions exists:

- The total equity at risk is not sufficient to permit the entity to finance its activities without additional subordinated financial support provided by any parties, including equity holders. In most cases, if equity at risk is less than 10 percent of total assets, the risk is deemed insufficient.[5]

- The equity investors in the VIE lack any one of the following three characteristics of a controlling financial interest:

  1. The direct or indirect ability to make decisions about an entity's activities through voting rights or similar rights.
  2. The obligation to absorb the expected losses of the entity if they occur (e.g., another firm may guarantee a return to the equity investors).
  3. The right to receive the expected residual returns of the entity (e.g., the investors' return may be capped by the entity's governing documents or other arrangements with variable interest holders).

In assessing whether an enterprise should consolidate the assets, liabilities, revenues, and expenses of a VIE, *FIN 46R* next relies on an expanded notion of a controlling financial interest. The following characteristics indicate an enterprise qualifying as a primary beneficiary with a controlling financial interest in a VIE:

- The direct or indirect ability to make decisions about the entity's activities.
- The obligation to absorb the expected losses of the entity if they occur.
- The right to receive the expected residual returns of the entity if they occur.

Note that these characteristics mirror those that the equity investors lack in a VIE. Instead, the primary beneficiary is subject to the majority of risks of losses or entitled to receive a majority of the entity's residual returns or both. The fact that the primary beneficiary may own no voting shares whatsoever becomes inconsequential because such shares do not effectively allow the equity investors to exercise control. Thus, in assessing control, a careful examination of the VIE's governing documents and the contractual arrangements among the parties involved is necessary to determine who bears the majority risk.

The magnitude of the effect of consolidating an enterprise's VIEs can be large. For example, Walt Disney Company disclosed that two of its major investments qualified as VIEs and that it now will consolidate them. In its 2004 annual report, Disney stated the following:

> The Company manages and has ownership interests in the Disneyland Resort Paris in France (also referred to as Euro Disney) and Hong Kong Disneyland, which is under construction and

---

[4] An exception to consolidation requirements is made for firms that employ "qualifying special-purpose entities" that fall under FASB 140, *Accounting for Transfers and Servicing of Financial Assets and Extinguishments of Liabilities*. An enterprise must still report its rights and obligations related to the qualifying SPE.

[5] Alternatively, a 10 percent or greater equity interest may also be insufficient. According to *FIN 46R*, "Some entities may require an equity investment greater than 10 percent of their assets to finance their activities, especially if they engage in high-risk activities, hold high-risk assets, or have exposure to risks that are not reflected in the reported amounts of the entities' assets or liabilities" (para. 10).

scheduled to open in fiscal 2005. The Company's ownership interests in Disneyland Resort Paris and Hong Kong Disneyland are 41 percent and 43 percent, respectively. The Company adopted Financial Accounting Standards Board (FASB) *Interpretation No. 46R* "Consolidation of Variable Interest Entities" (*FIN 46R*) in fiscal 2004 and as a result, consolidated the balance sheets of Euro Disney and Hong Kong Disneyland as of March 31, 2004, and the income and cash flow statements beginning April 1, 2004.

As a result of the consolidation of these two VIEs, Disney's total assets increased by $3.9 billion while its total debt increased by $3.6 billion. *FIN 46R* emphasizes that its objective is to improve financial reporting by companies involved with VIEs, not to restrict the use of VIEs. *FIN 46R* reasons that if a "business enterprise has a controlling financial interest in a variable interest entity, assets, liabilities, and results of the activities of the variable interest entity should be included with those of the business enterprise."

Example of a Primary Beneficiary and Consolidated Variable Interest Entity

Assume that Twin Peaks Power Company seeks to acquire a generating plant for a negotiated price of $400 million from Ace Electric Company. Twin Peaks wishes to expand its market share and expects to be able to sell the electricity generated by the plant acquisition at a profit to its owners.

In reviewing financing alternatives, Twin Peaks observed that its general credit rating allowed for a 4 percent annual interest rate on a debt issue. Twin Peaks also explored the establishment of a separate legal entity whose sole purpose would be to own the electric generating plant and lease it back to Twin Peaks. Because the separate entity would isolate the electric generating plant from Twin Peaks' other risky assets and liabilities, and provide specific collateral, an interest rate of 3 percent on the debt is available producing before tax savings of $4 million per year. To obtain the lower interest rate, however, Twin Peaks must guarantee the separate entity's debt. Twin Peaks must also maintain certain of its own predefined financial ratios and restrict the amount of additional debt it can assume.

To take advantage of the lower interest rate, on January 1, 2007, Twin Peaks establishes Power Finance Co., a special purpose entity (SPE) designed solely to own, finance, and lease the electric generating plant to Twin Peaks.[6] The documents governing the SPE specify the following:

- The sole purpose of Power Finance is to purchase the Ace electric generating plant, provide equity and debt financing, and lease the plant to Twin Peaks.
- An outside investor will provide $16 million in exchange for a 100 percent nonvoting equity interest in Power Finance.
- Power Finance will issue debt in exchange for $384 million. Because the $16 million equity investment by itself is insufficient to attract low-interest debt financing, the debt will be guaranteed by Twin Peaks.
- Twin Peaks will lease the electric generating plant from Power Finance in exchange for payments of $12 million per year based on a 3 percent fixed interest rate for both the debt and equity investors for an initial lease term of five years.
- At the end of the five-year lease term (or any extension), Twin Peaks must do one of the following:
  - Renew the lease for five years subject to the approval of the equity investor.
  - Purchase the electric generating plant for $400 million.
  - Sell the electric generating plant to an independent third party. If the proceeds of the sale are insufficient to repay the equity investor, Twin Peaks is required to make a payment of $16 million to the equity investor.

---

[6] This arrangement is similar to a "synthetic lease" commonly used in utility companies. Synthetic leases also can have tax advantages because the sponsoring firm accounts for tax purposes as capital leases.

EXHIBIT 6.2
Variable Interest Entity to Facilitate Financing

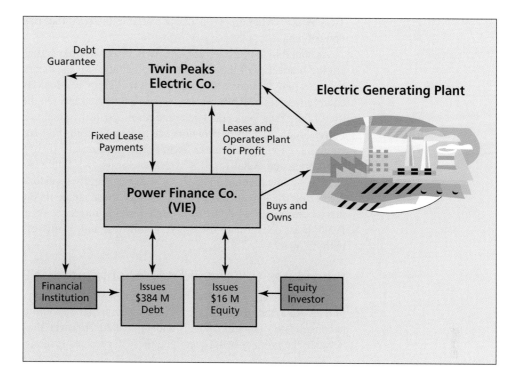

Once the purchase of the electric generating plant is complete and the equity and debt are issued, Power Finance Company reports the following balance sheet:

POWER FINANCE COMPANY
Balance Sheet
January 1, 2007

Electric Generating Plant	$400M	Long-Term Debt	$384M
		Owner's Equity	16M
Total Assets	$400M	Total Liabilities and OE	$400M

Exhibit 6.2 shows the relationships between Twin Peaks, Power Finance, the electric generating plant, and the parties financing the asset purchase.

In evaluating whether Twin Peaks Electric Company must consolidate Power Finance Company, two conditions must be met. First, Power Finance must qualify as a VIE by either (a) an inability to secure financing without additional subordinated support or (b) a lack of either the risk of losses or entitlement to residual returns (or both). Second, Twin Peaks must qualify as the primary beneficiary of Power Finance.

In assessing the first condition, several factors point to VIE status for Power Finance. Its owner's equity comprises only 4 percent of total assets, far short of the 10 percent benchmark provided by *FIN 46R*. Moreover, Twin Peaks guarantees Power Finance's debt, suggesting insufficient equity to finance its operations without additional support. Finally, the equity investor appears to bear almost no risk with respect to the operations of the Ace electric plant. These characteristics indicate that the Power Finance SPE qualifies as a VIE.

In evaluating the second condition for consolidation, an assessment is made to determine if Twin Peaks qualifies as the primary beneficiary of Power Finance. According to *FIN 46R*, an enterprise must consolidate a VIE if that enterprise has a variable interest that will absorb a majority of the entity's expected losses if they occur, receive a majority of the entity's expected residual returns if they occur, or both.[7] But what possible losses or returns would accrue to

---

[7] *FIN 46R* refers to expected losses and expected residual returns as amounts derived from expected cash flows as described in FASB Concept Statement 7, *Using Cash Flow Information and Present Value in Accounting Measurements.*

Twin Peaks? What are Twin Peaks' variable interests that rise and fall with the fortunes of Power Finance?

As stated in the SPE agreement, Twin Peaks will pay a fixed fee to lease the electric generating plant. It will then operate the plant and sell the electric power in its markets. If the business plan is successful, Twin Peaks will enjoy residual profits from operating while the equity investors of Power Finance receive the fixed fee. On the other hand, if prices for electricity fall, Twin Peaks may generate revenues insufficient to cover its lease payments while Power Finance's equity investors are protected from this risk. Moreover, if the plant's fair value increases significantly, Twin Peaks can exercise its option to purchase the plant at a fixed price and either resell it or keep it for its own future use. Alternatively, if Twin Peaks were to sell the plant at a loss, it must pay the equity investors all of their initial investment, furthering the loss to Twin Peaks. Each of these elements points to Twin Peaks as the primary beneficiary of its SPE through variable interests. As the primary beneficiary, Twin Peaks must consolidate the assets, liabilities, and results of operations of Power Finance with its own.

Procedures to Consolidate Variable Interest Entities

As the balance sheet of Power Finance exemplifies, VIEs typically possess few assets and liabilities. Also, their business activities usually are strictly limited. Thus, the actual procedures to consolidate VIEs are relatively uncomplicated. However, the close nature of the relationship between the primary beneficiary and the VIE presents several measurement issues.

Initial Measurement Issues

The financial reporting principles for consolidating variable interest entities require asset, liability, and noncontrolling interest valuations. These valuations initially are based on fair values with two notable exceptions. First, if any of the VIE's assets have been transferred from the primary beneficiary, these assets will continue to be measured as if they had not been transferred. Second, the asset valuation procedures in *FIN 46R* also rely in part on the allocation principles described in *SFAS 141, Business Combinations.*[8] Recall that *SFAS 141* requires an allocation of the cost of an acquisition based on the underlying fair values of its assets and liabilities. However, unlike a voting interest acquisition, in a VIE control is not obtained by incurring a cost, but through governance agreements and contractual arrangements. Therefore, an *implied value* substitutes for the acquisition cost in determining the valuation of a VIE.

In determining the total amount to consolidate for a variable interest entity, the implied value of the entity is considered as the sum of

- Consideration paid by the primary beneficiary (plus the reported values of any previously held interests).
- The fair value of the newly consolidated liabilities and noncontrolling interests.

If the assessed fair values of the assets exceed the implied value of the VIE, then the assets are proportionately reduced as specified in *SFAS 141.* On the other hand, if the implied fair value of the VIE exceeds the assessed fair values of the assets, the difference is reported as goodwill, if the variable interest entity is a business.[9] Alternatively, if the activities of the VIE are so restricted that it does not qualify as a business, the excess fair value paid into the VIE is considered an extraordinary loss, as opposed to goodwill.

For example, assume that Vax Company invests $5 million in TLH Property, a variable interest business entity. In agreements completed July 1, 2007, Vax establishes itself as the primary

[8] The 2005 FASB Exposure Draft, *Business Combinations,* proposes that "Acquisitions of variable interest entities that are businesses that previously were accounted for under the provisions of FASB Interpretation 46 (revised 2003), *Consolidation of Variable Interest Entities,* would be accounted for consistent with the provisions of this proposed Statement."

[9] *FIN 46R* (Appendix C) defines a *business* as a self-sustaining integrated set of activities and assets conducted and managed for the purpose of providing a return to investors. A business consists of (a) inputs, (b) processes applied to those inputs, and (c) resulting outputs that are used to generate revenues. For a set of activities and assets to be a business, it must contain all of the inputs and processes necessary for it to conduct normal operations, which include the ability to sustain a revenue stream by providing its outputs to customers.

beneficiary of TLH Property. Previously, Vax had no interest in TLH. After Vax's investment, TLH presents the following financial information at assessed fair values:

Cash	$ 5 million
Land.	20 million
Production facility.	60 million
Long-term debt	65 million
Vax equity investment	5 million
Noncontrolling interest.	(See below for alternative valuations)

The allocations to be used in the consolidation of Vax and TLH Property depend on the relation between the implied value of the VIE and the assessed fair values of its assets. To demonstrate these valuation principles, we use three brief examples, each with a different implied value depending on alternative assessed fair values of the noncontrolling interest.

Implied Value of VIE Equals Assessed Values of Assets

In this case, assume that the noncontrolling interest fair value equals $15 million. The VIE's implied value is then $85 million ($5 million consideration paid + $65 million fair values for liabilities and $15 million for the noncontrolling interest). Because the implied value is identical to the total assessed fair values for the assets (including cash), the land and production facility are consolidated at their individual fair values of $20 million and $60 million, respectively.

Implied Value of VIE Less Than Assessed Asset Values

Alternatively, assume that the value of the noncontrolling interest was assessed at only $11 million. In this case, the implied value of TLH Property would be calculated at $81 million ($5 million consideration paid + $65 million fair values for liabilities and $11 million for the noncontrolling interest). The $81 million implied value compared to the $85 assessed fair value of TLH Property's assets (including cash) produces an excess fair value of $4 million. In this case, the fair values of the VIE's long-term assets are reduced proportionately below their fair values by the $4 million excess. The Land account, with an assessed fair value of $20 million (¼ of the $80 million total asset assessed value), will be reduced to a $19 million valuation. Similarly, the Production Facility account, with an assessed fair value of $60 million (¾ of the $80 million total asset assessed value), will be reduced to a $57 million valuation. As noted in *FIN 46R,* "this provision is intended to prevent intentional creation of a gain by arranging to become the primary beneficiary of a carefully structured entity, especially if the entity's assets are difficult to measure."

Implied Value of VIE Greater Than Assessed Asset Values

Finally, assume that the value of the noncontrolling interest is assessed at $20 million. In this case, the implied value of TLH Property would be calculated at $90 million ($5 million consideration paid + $65 million fair values for liabilities and $20 million for the noncontrolling interest). The $90 million implied value compared to the $85 assessed fair value of TLH Property's assets produces an excess implied value of $5 million. According to *FIN 46R,* because TLH is a business entity, Vax Company records the excess $5 million implied value as goodwill in the year it became the primary beneficiary. If TLH did not qualify as a business entity, Vax Company would have recorded an extraordinary loss of $5 million instead of goodwill.

For example, General Electric Company now consolidates Penske Truck Leasing Company as a VIE under the provisions of *FIN 46R.* In its 2004 annual report, GE recognized an additional $1.055 billion in goodwill and more than $9 billion in property, plant, and equipment from the Penske consolidation. Prior to 2004, General Electric's investment in Penske was accounted for under the equity method.

Consolidation of VIEs Subsequent to Initial Measurement

After the initial measurement, consolidations of VIEs with their primary beneficiaries should follow the same process as if the entity were consolidated based on voting interests. Importantly, all intercompany transactions between the primary beneficiary and the VIE including fees, other sources of income or loss, and intercompany inventory purchases) must be eliminated in consolidation. Finally, the income of the VIE must be allocated among the parties involved (i.e., equity holders and the primary beneficiary). For a VIE, contractual arrangements, as opposed to ownership percentages, typically specify the distribution of its income. Therefore, a close examination of these contractual arrangements is needed to determine the appropriate allocation of VIE income to its equity owners and those holding variable interests.

Other *FIN 46R* Disclosure Requirements

In addition to consolidated financial statements, primary beneficiaries of VIEs must also provide the following in footnotes to the financial statements:

- The VIE's nature, purpose, size, and activities.
- The carrying amount and classification of consolidated assets that are collateral for the VIE's obligations.
- Lack of recourse if creditors (or beneficial interest holders) of a consolidated VIE have no recourse to the general credit of the primary beneficiary.

Enterprises that hold a significant variable interest in a VIE but are not the primary beneficiary must disclose the following in footnotes to the financial statements:

- The nature of the involvement with the VIE and when that involvement began.
- The nature, purpose, size, and activities of the VIE.
- The enterprise's maximum exposure to loss as a result of its involvement with the VIE.

Clearly the FASB wishes to enhance disclosures for all VIEs. Because in the past VIEs were often created in part to keep debt off a sponsoring firm's balance sheet, these enhanced disclosures are a significant improvement in financial reporting transparency.

INTERCOMPANY DEBT TRANSACTIONS

The previous chapter explored the consolidation procedures required by the intercompany transfer of inventory, land, and depreciable assets. In consolidating these transactions, all resulting gains were deferred until earned through either the use of the asset or its resale to outside parties. Deferral was necessary because these gains, although legitimately recognized by the individual companies, were unearned from the perspective of the consolidated entity. The separate financial information of each company was adjusted on the worksheet to be consistent with the view that the related companies actually composed a single economic concern.

This same objective applies in consolidating all intercompany transactions: The financial statements must represent the business combination as one enterprise rather than as a group of independent organizations. Consequently, in designing consolidation procedures for intercompany transactions, the effects recorded by the individual companies first must be isolated. After the impact of each action is analyzed, the worksheet entries necessary to recast these events from the vantage point of the business combination are developed. Although this process involves a number of nuances and complexities, the desire for reporting financial information solely from the perspective of the consolidated entity remains constant.

We introduced the intercompany sales of inventory, land, and depreciable assets together (in Chapter 5) because these transfers result in similar consolidation procedures. In each case, one of the affiliated companies recognizes a gain prior to when the consolidated entity actually earned it. The worksheet entries required by these transactions simply realign the separate financial information to agree with the viewpoint of the business combination. The gain is removed and the inflated asset value is reduced to historical cost.

The next section of this chapter examines the intercompany acquisition of bonds and notes. Although accounting for the related companies as a single economic entity continues to be the central goal, the consolidation procedures applied to intercompany debt transactions are in diametric contrast to the process utilized in Chapter 5 for asset transfers.

Before delving into this topic, note that *direct* loans used to transfer funds between affiliated companies create no unique consolidation problems. Regardless of whether bonds or notes generate such amounts, the resulting receivable/payable balances are necessarily identical. Because no money is owed to or from an outside party, these reciprocal accounts must be eliminated in each subsequent consolidation. A worksheet entry simply offsets the two corresponding balances. Furthermore, the interest revenue/expense accounts associated with direct loans also agree and are removed in the same fashion.

Acquisition of Affiliate's Debt from an Outside Party

The difficulties encountered in consolidating intercompany liabilities relate to a specific type of transaction: the purchase from an outside third party of an affiliate's debt instrument. A parent company, for example, could acquire a bond previously issued by a subsidiary on the open market. Despite the intercompany nature of this transaction, the debt remains an outstanding obligation of the original issuer but is recorded as an investment by the acquiring company. Thereafter, even though related parties are involved, interest payments pass periodically between the two organizations.

Although the individual companies continue to report both the debt and the investment, from a consolidation viewpoint this liability is retired as of the date of acquisition. From that time forward, the debt is no longer owed to a party outside of the business combination. Subsequent interest payments are simply intercompany cash transfers. To create consolidated statements, worksheet entries must be developed to adjust the various balances to report the effective retirement of the debt.

Acquiring an affiliate's bond or note from an unrelated party poses no significant consolidation problems if the purchase price equals the corresponding book value of the liability. Reciprocal balances within the individual records would always be identical in value and easily offset in each subsequent consolidation.

Realistically, though, such reciprocity is rare when a debt is purchased from a third party. A variety of economic factors typically produce a difference between the price paid for the investment and the carrying amount of the obligation. The debt is originally sold under market conditions at a particular time. Any premium or discount associated with this issuance is then amortized over the life of the bond, creating a continuous adjustment to book value. The acquisition of this instrument at a later date is made at a price influenced by current economic conditions, prevailing interest rates, and myriad other financial and market factors.

Therefore, the cost paid to purchase the debt could be either more or less than the book value of the liability currently found within the issuing company's financial records. *To the business combination, this difference is a gain or loss because the acquisition effectively retires the bond; the debt is no longer owed to an outside party.* For external reporting purposes, this gain or loss must be recognized immediately by the consolidated entity.

Accounting for Intercompany Debt Transactions— Individual Financial Records

The accounting problems encountered in consolidating intercompany debt transactions are fourfold:

1. Both the investment and debt accounts have to be eliminated now and for each future consolidation despite containing differing balances.
2. Subsequent interest revenue/expense (as well as any interest receivable/payable accounts) must be removed although these balances also fail to agree in amount.
3. Changes in all of the preceding accounts occur constantly because of the amortization process.
4. The gain or loss on retirement of the debt must be recognized by the business combination, even though this balance does not appear within the financial records of either company.

To illustrate, assume that Alpha Company possesses an 80 percent interest in the outstanding voting stock of Omega Company. On January 1, 2005, Omega issues $1 million in 10-year bonds paying cash interest of 9 percent annually. Because of market conditions prevailing on that date, Omega sells the debt for $938,555 to yield an effective interest rate of 10 percent per year. Shortly thereafter, the prime interest rate begins to fall, and by January 1, 2007, Omega makes the decision to retire this debt prematurely and refinance it at the currently lower rates. To carry out this plan, Alpha purchases all of these bonds in the open market on January 1, 2007, for $1,057,466. This price was based on an effective yield of 8 percent, which is assumed to be in line with the interest rates at the time.

Many reasons could exist for having Alpha, rather than Omega, reacquire this debt. For example, company cash levels at that date could necessitate Alpha's role as the purchasing agent. Also, contractual limitations can prohibit Omega from repurchasing its own bonds.

In accounting for this business combination, an early extinguishment of the debt has occurred. Thus, the difference between the $1,057,466 payment and the January 1, 2007, book value of the liability must be recognized in the consolidated statements as a gain or loss. The exact account balance reported for the debt on that date depends on the amortization process. Although the issue was recorded initially at the $938,555 exchange price, after two years the carrying value has increased to $946,651, calculated as follows:[10]

Bonds Payable—Book Value—January 1, 2007

Year	Book Value	Effective Interest (10 percent rate)	Cash Interest	Amortization	Year-End Book Value
2005	$938,555	$93,855	$90,000	$3,855	$942,410
2006	942,410	94,241	90,000	4,241	946,651

Because Alpha paid $110,815 in excess of the recorded liability ($1,057,466 − $946,651), a loss of this amount must be recognized by the consolidated entity. After the loss has been acknowledged, the bond is considered to be retired and no further reporting would be necessary by the *business combination* after January 1, 2007.

Despite the simplicity of this approach, neither company accounts for the event in this manner. Omega retains the $1 million debt balance within its separate financial records and amortizes the remaining discount each year. Annual cash interest payments of $90,000 (9 percent) continue to be made. At the same time, Alpha records the investment at the historical cost of $1,057,466, an amount that also requires periodic amortization. Furthermore, as the owner of these bonds, Alpha receives the $90,000 interest payments made by Omega.

To organize the accountant's approach to this consolidation, a complete analysis of the subsequent financial recording made by each of these companies should be produced. Omega would record only two journal entries during 2007 if the assumption is made that interest is paid each December 31:

	Omega Company's Financial Records		
12/31/07	Interest Expense.	90,000	
	Cash.		90,000
	To record payment of annual cash interest on $1 million, 9 percent bonds payable.		
12/31/07	Interest Expense.	4,665	
	Bonds Payable (or Discount on Bonds Payable)		4,665
	To adjust interest expense to effective rate based on original yield rate of 10 percent ($946,651 book value for 2007 × 10% = $94,665). Book value increases to $951,316.		

[10] The effective rate method of amortization is demonstrated here because this approach is theoretically preferable. However, the straight-line method can be applied if the resulting balances are not materially different than the figures computed using the effective rate method.

Concurrently, Alpha journalizes entries to record its ownership of this investment:

	Alpha Company's Financial Record		
1/1/07	Investment in Omega Company Bonds	1,057,466	
	Cash		1,057,466
	To record acquisition of $1,000,000 in Omega Company bonds paying 9 percent cash interest, acquired to yield an effective rate of 8 percent.		
12/31/07	Cash.	90,000	
	Interest Income		90,000
	To record receipt of cash interest from Omega Company bonds ($1,000,000 × 9%).		
12/31/07	Interest Income.	5,403	
	Investment in Omega Company Bonds		5,403
	To reduce $90,000 interest income to effective rate based on original yield rate of 8 percent ($1,057,466 book value for 2007 × 8% = $84,597). Book value decreases to $1,052,063.		

Even a brief review of these entries indicates that the reciprocal accounts to be eliminated within the consolidation process do not agree in amount. You can see the dollar amounts appearing in each set of financial records in Exhibit 6.3. Despite the presence of these recorded balances, none of the four intercompany accounts (the liability, investment, interest expense, and interest revenue) appears in the consolidated financial statements. *The only figure that the business combination reports is the $110,815 loss created by the extinguishment of this debt.*

Effects on Consolidation Process

As previous discussions indicated, consolidation procedures convert information generated by the individual accounting systems to the perspective of a single economic entity. A worksheet entry is therefore required on December 31, 2007, to eliminate the intercompany balances shown in Exhibit 6.3 and to recognize the loss resulting from the repurchase. Mechanically, the differences in the liability and investment balances as well as the interest expense and interest income accounts stem from the $110,815 deviation between the purchase price of the investment and the book value of the liability. Recognition of this loss, in effect, bridges the gap between the divergent figures.

Consolidation Entry B (December 31, 2007)		
Bonds Payable	951,316	
Interest Income	84,597	
Loss on Retirement of Bond	110,815	
Investment in Omega Company Bonds		1,052,063
Interest Expense		94,665
To remove intercompany bonds and related interest accounts and record loss on the early extinguishment of this debt. (Labeled **"B"** in reference to bonds.)		

The preceding entry successfully transforms the separate financial reporting of Alpha and Omega to that appropriate for the business combination. The objective of the consolidation process has been met: The statements present the bonds as having been retired on January 1, 2007. The debt and the corresponding investment are eliminated along with both interest accounts. Only the loss now appears on the worksheet to be reported within the consolidated financial statements.

EXHIBIT 6.3

ALPHA COMPANY AND OMEGA COMPANY
Effects of Intercompany Debt Transaction
2007

	Omega Company Reported Debt	Alpha Company Investment
2007 interest expense*	$ 94,665	$ –0–
2007 interest income†	–0–	(84,597)
Bonds payable*	(951,316)	–0–
Investment in bonds, 12/31/07†	–0–	1,052,063
Loss on retirement	–0–	–0–

Note: Parentheses indicate credit balances.
*Company total is adjusted for 2007 amortization of $4,665 (see journal entry).
†Adjusted for 2007 amortization of $5,403 (see journal entry).

Assignment of Retirement Gain or Loss

Perhaps the most intriguing issue to be addressed in accounting for intercompany debt transactions concerns the assignment of any gains and losses created by the retirement. Should the $110,815 loss just reported be attributed to Alpha or to Omega? From a practical perspective, this assignment is important only in calculating and reporting noncontrolling interest figures. However, at least four different possible allocations can be identified, each of which demonstrates theoretical merit.

First, a strong argument can be made that the liability being extinguished is that of the issuing company and, thus, any resulting income relates solely to that party. This approach assumes that the retirement of any obligation affects only the debtor. Proponents of this position hold that the acquiring company is merely serving as a purchasing agent for the original issuer of the bonds. Accordingly, in the previous illustration, the benefits derived from paying off the liability should accrue to Omega because that company's interest rate has been reduced through refinancing. The loss was incurred solely to obtain these lower rates. Therefore, under this assumption, the entire $110,815 is assigned to Omega, the issuer of the debt. This assignment is usually considered to be consistent with the economic unit concept and was recommended in the FASB Exposure Draft, *Consolidated Financial Statements: Policy and Procedures*.

Second, other accountants argue that the loss should be assigned solely to the investor (Alpha). According to proponents of this approach, the acquisition of the bonds and the price negotiated by the buyer created the income effect.

A third hypothesis is that the resulting gain or loss should be split in some manner between the two companies. This approach is consistent with both the parent company concept and proportionate consolidation. Because both parties are involved with the debt, this proposition contends that assigning income to only one company is arbitrary and misleading. Normally, such a division is based on the original face value of the debt. Hence, $57,466 of the loss would be allocated to Alpha with the remaining $53,349 assigned to Omega:

Alpha		Omega	
Purchase price	$1,057,466	Book value	$ 946,651
Face value	1,000,000	Face value	1,000,000
Loss—Alpha	$ 57,466	Loss—Omega	$ 53,349

Allocating the loss in this manner is an enticing solution; the subsequent accounting process creates an identical division within the individual financial records. Because both Alpha's premium and Omega's discount must be amortized, the loss figures eventually affect the respective companies' reported earnings. Over the life of the bond, Alpha records the $57,466 as an interest income reduction, and Omega increases its own interest expense by $53,349 because of the amortization of the discount.

Discussion **Question**

WHO LOST THIS $300,000?

Several years ago, Penston Company purchased 90 percent of the outstanding shares of Swansan Corporation. Penston made the acquisition because Swansan produced a vital component used in Penston's manufacturing process. Penston wanted to ensure an adequate supply of this item at a reasonable price. The former owner, James Swansan, retained the remaining 10 percent of Swansan's stock and agreed to continue managing this organization. He was given responsibility over the subsidiary's daily manufacturing operations but not for any financial decisions.

Swansan's takeover has proven to be a successful undertaking for Penston. The subsidiary has managed to supply all of the parent's inventory needs and distribute a variety of items to outside customers.

At a recent meeting, Penston's president and the company's chief financial officer began discussing Swansan's debt position. The subsidiary had a debt-to-equity ratio that seemed unreasonably high considering the significant amount of cash flows being generated by both companies. Payment of the interest expense, especially on the subsidiary's outstanding bonds, was a major cost, one that the corporate officials hoped to reduce. However, the bond indenture specified that Swansan could retire this debt prior to maturity only by paying 107 percent of face value.

This premium was considered prohibitive. Thus, to avoid contractual problems, Penston acquired a large portion of Swansan's liability on the open market for 101 percent of face value. Penston's purchase created an effective loss on the debt of $300,000: the excess of the price over the book value of the debt as reported on Swansan's books.

Company accountants currently are computing the noncontrolling interest's share of consolidated net income to be reported for the current year. They are unsure about the impact of this $300,000 loss. The subsidiary's debt was retired, but the decision was made by officials of the parent company. Who lost this $300,000?

A fourth perspective takes a more practical view of intercompany debt transactions: All repurchases are ultimately orchestrated by the parent company. As the controlling party in a business combination, the ultimate responsibility for retiring any obligation lies with the parent. The gain or loss resulting from the decision should thus be assigned solely to the parent regardless of the specific identity of the debt issuer or the acquiring company. In the current example, Alpha maintains control over Omega. Therefore, according to this theory, the financial consequences of reacquiring these bonds rest with Alpha so that the entire $110,815 loss must be attributed to it.

Each of these arguments has conceptual merit, and if the FASB eventually sets an official standard, any one approach (or possibly a hybrid) could be required. Unless otherwise stated, however, all income effects in this textbook relating to intercompany debt transactions are assigned solely to the parent company, as discussed in the final approach. Consequently, the results of extinguishing debt always are attributed to the party most likely to have been responsible for the action.

Intercompany Debt Transactions—Subsequent to Year of Acquisition

Even though the preceding Entry **B** correctly eliminates Omega's bonds in the year of retirement, the debt remains within the financial accounts of both companies until maturity. Therefore, in each succeeding time period, all balances must again be consolidated so that the liability is always reported as having been extinguished on January 1, 2007. Unfortunately, a simple repetition of Entry **B** is not possible. Developing the appropriate worksheet entry is complicated by the amortization process that produces continual change in the various account balances. Thus, as a preliminary step in each subsequent consolidation, current book values, as reported by the two parties, must be identified.

To illustrate, the 2008 journal entries for Alpha and Omega follow. Exhibit 6.4 (on the following page) shows the resulting account balances as of the end of that year.

Omega Company's Financial Records—December 31, 2008		
Interest Expense	90,000	
Cash		90,000
To record payment of annual cash interest on $1 million, 9 percent bonds payable.		
Interest Expense	5,132	
Bonds Payable (or Discount on Bonds Payable)		5,132
To adjust interest expense to effective rate based on an original yield rate of 10 percent ($951,316 book value for 2008 × 10% = $95,132). Book value increases to $956,448.		

Alpha Company's Financial Records—December 31, 2008		
Cash	90,000	
Interest Income		90,000
To record receipt of cash interest from Omega Company bonds.		
Interest Income	5,835	
Investment in Omega Company Bonds		5,835
To reduce $90,000 interest income to effective rate based on an original yield rate of 8 percent ($1,052,063 book value for 2008 × 8% = $84,165). Book value decreases to $1,046,228.		

After the information in Exhibit 6.4 has been assembled, the necessary consolidation entry as of December 31, 2008, can be produced. This entry removes the balances reported at that date for the intercompany bonds, along with both of the interest accounts, to reflect the extinguishment of the debt on January 1, 2007. Because retirement took place in a prior period, the adjustment on the worksheet must also create a $110,815 reduction in Retained Earnings to represent the original loss.

Consolidation Entry *B (December 31, 2008)		
Bonds Payable	956,448	
Interest Income	84,165	
Retained Earnings, 1/1/08 (Alpha)	100,747	
Investment in Omega Company Bonds		1,046,228
Interest Expense		95,132
To eliminate intercompany bond and related interest accounts and to adjust Retained Earnings from $10,068 (currently recorded net debit balance) to $110,815. (Labeled "*B" in reference to prior year bond transaction.)		

In analyzing this latest consolidation entry, several important factors should be emphasized:

1. The individual account balances change during the present fiscal period so that the current consolidation entry differs from Entry **B.** These alterations are a result of the amortization process. To ensure the accuracy of the worksheet entry, the adjusted balances are isolated in Exhibit 6.4.

2. As indicated previously, all income effects arising from intercompany debt transactions are assigned to the parent company. For this reason, the adjustment to beginning Retained

EXHIBIT 6.4

<table>
<tr><td colspan="3" align="center">**ALPHA COMPANY AND OMEGA COMPANY**
Effects of Intercompany Debt Transactions
2008</td></tr>
<tr><td></td><td align="center">**Omega Company Reported Debt**</td><td align="center">**Alpha Company Investment**</td></tr>
<tr><td>2008 interest expense* . . . .</td><td align="center">$95,132</td><td align="center">–0–</td></tr>
<tr><td>2008 interest income† . . . .</td><td align="center">–0–</td><td align="center">$(84,165)</td></tr>
<tr><td>Bonds payable* . . . .</td><td align="center">(956,448)</td><td align="center">–0–</td></tr>
<tr><td>Investment in bonds, 12/31/08† . . . .</td><td align="center">–0–</td><td align="center">1,046,228</td></tr>
<tr><td>Income effect within retained earnings, 1/1/08‡ . . . .</td><td align="center">94,665</td><td align="center">(84,597)</td></tr>
</table>

Note: Parentheses indicate credit balances.
*Company total is adjusted for 2008 amortization of $5,132 (see journal entry).
†Adjusted for 2008 amortization of $5,835 (see journal entry).
‡The balance shown for the Retained Earnings account of each company represents the 2007 reported interest figures.

Earnings in Entry ***B** is attributed to Alpha as is the $10,967 increase in current income ($95,132 interest expense elimination less the $84,165 interest revenue elimination).[11] Consequently, the noncontrolling interest balances are not altered by Entry ***B.**

3. The 2008 reduction to beginning Retained Earnings in Entry ***B** ($100,747) does not agree with the original $110,815 retirement loss. The individual companies have recorded a net deficit balance of $10,068 (the amount by which previous interest expense exceeds interest revenue) at the start of 2008. To achieve the proper consolidated total, an adjustment of only $100,747 is required ($110,815 − $10,068).

<table>
<tr><td>Retained earnings balance—consolidation perspective
  (loss on retirement of debt) . . . .</td><td></td><td align="right">$110,815</td></tr>
<tr><td>Individual retained earnings balances, 1/1/08:</td><td></td><td></td></tr>
<tr><td> Omega Company (interest expense—2007). . . . .</td><td align="right">$ 94,665</td><td></td></tr>
<tr><td> Alpha Company (interest income—2007) . . . .</td><td align="right">(84,597)</td><td align="right">10,068</td></tr>
<tr><td>Adjustment to consolidated retained earnings, 1/1/08. . . . .</td><td></td><td align="right">$100,747</td></tr>
</table>

Parentheses indicate a credit balance.

The periodic amortization of both the bond payable discount and the premium on the investment impacts the interest expense and revenue recorded by the two companies. As this schedule shows, these two interest accounts do not offset exactly; a $10,068 net residual amount remains in Retained Earnings after the first year. Because this balance continues to increase each year, the subsequent consolidation adjustments to record the loss decrease to $100,747 in 2008 and constantly get smaller thereafter. *Over the life of the bond, the amortization process gradually brings the totals in the individual Retained Earnings accounts into agreement with the consolidated balance.*

4. Entry ***B** as shown is appropriate for consolidations in which the parent has applied either the cost or the partial equity method. However, a deviation is required if the parent uses the equity method for internal reporting purposes. As discussed in Chapter 5, proper application of the equity method ensures that the parent's income and, hence, its retained earnings are correctly stated prior to consolidation. Alpha would have already recognized the loss in accounting for this investment. Consequently, no adjustment to Retained Earnings would be needed. In this one case, the $100,747 debit in Entry ***B** is made to the Investment in Omega Company because the loss has become a component of that account.

---

[11] Had the effects of the retirement been attributed solely to the original issuer of the bonds, the $10,967 addition to current income would have been assigned to Omega (the subsidiary), thus creating a change in the noncontrolling interest computations.

SUBSIDIARY PREFERRED STOCK

When Kohlberg Kravis Roberts & Company purchased the outstanding common stock of Owens-Illinois, Inc., for $60.50 per share, the company also acquired all of the preferred stock of Owens-Illinois for $363 per share, or a total of $25.8 million. Although both small and large corporations routinely issue preferred shares, their presence within the equity structure of a subsidiary adds a new dimension to the consolidation process. What accounting should be made of a subsidiary's preferred stock and the parent's payments, such as this $25.8 million, that are made to acquire these shares?

The consolidation measures required to report the preferred stock of a subsidiary depend on the specific nature of the shares. Controversy has long existed as to whether such issues are more akin to equity or debt, a distinction that depends on the specified rights granted to the holders. The characteristics of many preferred shares resemble those attributed to long-term liabilities rather than to equity securities. For example, a stock with a call value and no rights except for a set, cumulative dividend is in substance almost identical to a bond payable. Conversely, preferred shares that offer voting and/or participation rights clearly demonstrate essential characteristics associated with an ownership interest.

However, not all preferred stocks lend themselves to easy classification: The legal rights given to shareholders often vary significantly from issue to issue. For example, Ford Motor Company in a recent annual report shows both Series A and Series B preferred stock outstanding, each with specific rights as to dividends, convertibility to common stock, and redemption prices. Such attributes can make the distinction between debt and equity quite nebulous. Because of this identification problem, the FASB has plans to study the issue within its financial instruments project. However, until a guideline is established to utilize in earnings per share computations, determining the true nature of many types of preferred stock still requires considerable individual judgment.

In consolidating subsidiary preferred stock, the accountant must evaluate whether the shares are more similar to debt or to equity. If the stock resembles a debt, any shares acquired by the parent are recorded as if retired. Conversely, if a preferred stock is truly an equity instrument, the combination accounts for the purchased shares in the same manner as common stock: Allocations are made to specific assets and liabilities with any residual payment assigned to goodwill.

Preferred Stock Viewed as a Debt Instrument

If a subsidiary's preferred stock has characteristics that primarily resemble a liability, consolidation techniques should parallel the process previously demonstrated for intercompany debt. To illustrate, assume that on January 1, 2006, High Company acquires control over Low Company by purchasing 80 percent of its outstanding common stock and 60 percent of its nonvoting, cumulative, preferred stock. Low owns land that is undervalued in its records by $100,000.

High paid a purchase price of $1 million for the common shares and $62,400 for the preferred. On the date of acquisition, Low reported the following stockholders' equity balances. Note that the 1,000 shares of preferred stock outstanding have a $100 par value but can be called (retired) by Low for $110 per share.

Common stock, $20 par value (20,000 shares outstanding)	$ 400,000
Preferred stock, 6% cumulative with a par value of $100 and a	
$110 call value (1,000 shares outstanding)	100,000
Additional paid-in capital	200,000
Retained earnings	516,400
Total stockholders' equity (book value)	$1,216,400

Low's preferred stock carries no rights other than its cumulative dividend; thus, this issue is considered a debt instrument in nature. The $62,400 price that High paid is handled in a manner consistent with that of an intercompany bond. The payment made for these shares has no influence on the valuation of specific subsidiary accounts (such as the undervalued land) or the recognition of goodwill. Instead, the preferred stock acquired by the parent is eliminated on each subsequent worksheet as if the shares had been retired.

Although this handling parallels that of a long-term liability, one important distinction must be drawn. Preferred stock is legally an equity; thus, its retirement cannot result in the reporting of a gain or loss to the consolidated entity. Instead, the difference between the stock's par value and the acquisition price paid by the parent must be recorded as an adjustment to Additional Paid-In Capital (or to Retained Earnings if a reduction is required and the Additional Paid-In Capital account is not of sufficient size).

The consolidation entry to account for this preferred stock acquisition follows. *Because the stock is viewed as the equivalent of debt, these shares (60 percent of the 1,000 outstanding) are simply eliminated as if retired.*

Preferred Stock (the 60% owned by High)	60,000	
Additional Paid-In Capital	2,400	
Investment in Low Company's Preferred Stock		62,400
To eliminate preferred stock of Low Company acquired by the parent company.		

This entry assumes that no part of the cumulative dividend is in arrears at the date of purchase. If a dividend had been owed on the preferred stock, a reduction in the subsidiary's Retained Earnings equal to that amount would have been included here rather than assigning the entire $2,400 difference to Additional Paid-In Capital. This alteration presumes that a portion of the purchase price is paid to reimburse the former owners for the missed dividends.

Although the preceding worksheet entry removes the effects of High's acquisition, it ignores the residual 40 percent noncontrolling interest in the preferred stock. In recording an allocation to these outside owners, the appropriate amount to be recognized must be determined. When preferred stock is viewed as a debt, the call value (if present) is considered to be more relevant to the consolidated entity than par value. Thus, the outside owners are assigned a balance equal to the call value of the securities (plus any dividends in arrears). In the current illustration, the $110 figure reflects the cost required to retire each of the remaining 400 shares (40 percent of 1,000). Thus, the worksheet entry to recognize this noncontrolling interest is as follows:

Preferred Stock (40% owned by outsiders)	40,000	
Additional Paid-In Capital	4,000	
Noncontrolling Interest in Low Company (call value)		44,000
To recognize the outside ownership of 40 percent of Low Company's preferred stock.		

We have presented these entries separately to clarify the difference in consolidating parent-owned and outside-owned shares. In practice, these figures are combined to eliminate all of the subsidiary's preferred stock. Thus, a single consolidation entry actually should be incorporated in this illustration:

Consolidation Entry PS		
Preferred Stock	100,000	
Additional Paid-In Capital	6,400	
Investment in Low Company's Preferred Stock		62,400
Noncontrolling Interest in Low Company		44,000
To eliminate preferred stock of subsidiary (viewed as a debt) and record noncontrolling interest. (Labeled **"PS"** in reference to preferred stock.)		

Having accounted for Low's preferred stock, the elimination of the company's remaining stockholders' equity accounts can now be made. As with any purchase combination, a preliminary

EXHIBIT 6.5

HIGH COMPANY AND LOW COMPANY	
Allocation of Common Stock Purchase Price	
January 1, 2006	
Purchase price paid for common stock	$1,000,000
Common stock book value equivalent to High's ownership ($1,110,000 × 80%)	(888,000)
Cost in excess of book value	112,000
Allocation to specific accounts based on fair value: Land ($100,000 × 80%)	80,000
Excess cost not identified with specific accounts—goodwill	$ 32,000

allocation of the purchase price paid for the common stock is essential. Because of the amounts attributed to preferred stock, only $1,110,000 of Low's total book value is assigned to the common stock at the date of acquisition:

Total book value of Low Company, 1/1/06		$1,216,400
Allocated to preferred stock ownership:		
Acquisition price of High Company's interest	$62,400	
Call value of noncontrolling interest	44,000	(106,400)
Book value allocated to common stock		$1,110,000

Based on this book value, High's $1 million payment for 80 percent of Low's common stock is allocated as shown in Exhibit 6.5. As indicated previously, we assume here that land owned by Low is undervalued on the subsidiary's records by $100,000.

By utilizing the information from Exhibit 6.5, we can construct basic worksheet entries as of January 1, 2006 (the date of purchase). After Entry **PS** removes the preferred shares and recognizes the noncontrolling interest in that stock, Entry **S** eliminates the remainder of Low's stockholders' equity accounts. In addition, a 20 percent noncontrolling interest in Low's common stock is established as $222,000 (20 percent of the $1,110,000 book value). Entry **A** then recognizes the allocations made to the undervalued land and to goodwill. No other consolidation entries are needed because no time has passed since the acquisition took place.

Consolidation Entry S		
Common Stock (Low Company)	400,000	
Additional Paid-In Capital (Low Company)	193,600	
Retained Earnings (Low Company)	516,400	
Investment in Low Company's Common Stock (80%)		888,000
Noncontrolling Interest in Low Company (20%)		222,000
To eliminate remaining stockholders' equity accounts after removal of preferred stock and to recognize noncontrolling interest in common stock.		

Consolidation Entry A		
Land	80,000	
Goodwill	32,000	
Investment in Low Company's Common Stock		112,000
To allocate excess cost paid for Low's common stock to specific account based on fair value and to goodwill (see Exhibit 6.5).		

In working with this illustration, note the structure that is followed in consolidating a subsidiary's preferred stock. First, a determination is made of the nature of the stock. Identifying Low Company's issue as a debt-type instrument significantly influenced the development of the consolidation process. Second, the subsidiary's book value is divided between the preferred and common stock interests. Assigning $106,400 of Low's book value to the preferred stock (the price of the purchased shares plus the call value of remainder) and the residual $1,110,000 to common stock led directly to the valuations and eliminations incorporated in this consolidation. As we subsequently demonstrate, this book value allocation can vary considerably, depending on the specific rights granted to the preferred shareholders.

Allocation of Subsidiary Income

The final factor influencing a consolidation that includes subsidiary preferred shares is the allocation of the company's income between the two types of stock. A division must be made for every period subsequent to the takeover (1) to compute the noncontrolling interest's share and (2) for the parent's own recognition purposes. For a cumulative, nonparticipating preferred stock such as the one presently being examined, only the specified annual dividend is attributed to the preferred stock with all remaining income assigned to common stock. Consequently, if we assume that Low reports earnings of $100,000 in 2006 while paying the annual $6,000 dividend on its preferred stock, we allocate income for consolidation purposes as follows:

	Income
Subsidiary total	$100,000
Preferred stock (6% dividend × $100,000 par value of the stock)	$ 6,000
Common stock (residual amount)	94,000

During 2006, High Company, as the parent, would be entitled to $3,600 in dividends from Low's preferred stock because of its 60 percent ownership. In addition, High holds 80 percent of Low's common stock so that another $75,200 of the income ($94,000 × 80%) is attributed to the parent. The noncontrolling interest in the subsidiary's income can be calculated in a similar fashion:

		Percentage Outside Ownership	Noncontrolling Interest
Preferred stock dividend	$ 6,000	40%	$ 2,400
Income attributed to common stock	94,000	20	18,800
Noncontrolling interest in subsidiary's income . . .			$21,200

Preferred Stock Viewed as an Equity Interest

Having established basic principles for a consolidation that includes subsidiary preferred stock that resembles debt, we present a second example in which the stock is considered an equity. Continuing to employ High's acquisition of Low, we assume now that the dividends of the subsidiary's preferred stock are fully participating and cumulative. Furthermore, the stock is not callable. Because the preferred shares convey additional rights, the relative values of the two classes of stock differ from those of the previous example. Therefore, High is assumed to have paid only $894,496 for an 80 percent interest in Low's common stock but $149,968 for 60 percent of the preferred.

The ability to participate in the earnings of Low Company provides the preferred shareholders an ownership interest akin to that of common stock. Thus, altering the rights of this issue has changed its essential nature to that of an equity interest rather than a debt. When subsidiary preferred stock is viewed as an equity, the consolidation process differs significantly from that examined in the previous illustration. *The preferred stock is handled in the same*

EXHIBIT 6.6

HIGH COMPANY AND LOW COMPANY
Allocation of Preferred and Common Stock Purchase Prices
January 1, 2006

Preferred Stock

Purchase price paid for preferred stock	$ 149,968
Preferred stock book value equivalent to High's ownership ($203,280 × 60%)	(121,968)
Cost in excess of book value	$ 28,000
Allocation to specific accounts:	
Land ($20,000 × 60%)	12,000
Excess cost not identified with specific accounts—goodwill	$ 16,000

Common Stock

Purchase price paid for common stock	$ 894,496
Common stock book value equivalent to High's ownership ($1,013,120 × 80%)	(810,496)
Cost in excess of book value	$ 84,000
Allocation to specific accounts:	
Land ($80,000 × 80%)	64,000
Excess cost not identified with specific accounts—goodwill	$ 20,000

---

manner as common stock: Any purchase price in excess of underlying book value is allocated to specific accounts as well as to goodwill. Income is accrued by the owners based on subsidiary earnings rather than on dividends.

The cumulative participation rights entitle the holders of Low's preferred shares to a portion of the subsidiary's earnings each year. The specific division of income would be stipulated on the preferred stock certificate. That percentage is often based on the ratio of the total par values of the two classes of equity. Thus, 20 percent ($100,000 par value of the preferred stock divided by $500,000 total par value) of Low's annual income is assigned to the preferred shares. Additionally, because of the cumulative right, 20 percent of the subsidiary's retained earnings should also be attributed to the preferred stock (assuming that both classes of stock were originally issued on the same date). With these particular rights in force, allocation of the January 1, 2006, book value of Low Company is as follows:

Total book value of Low Company, 1/1/06		$1,216,400
Allocated to preferred stock ownership:		
Par value of preferred stock (no call value)	$100,000	
20% of total retained earnings ($516,400) based on cumulative participation rights.	103,280	(203,280)
Book value allocated to common stock (residual)		$1,013,120

Once the division of the subsidiary's book value has been established, High must allocate each of the acquisition payments. In this manner, the preferred stock is being accounted for as a true equity interest. Exhibit 6.6 analyzes both purchases: The $149,968 price paid for the preferred stock appears first followed by the $894,496 amount invested in common stock. To complete this allocation, we must address one theoretical question: How is the undervaluation of the subsidiary's land to be treated? Because both stocks are considered equity interests, the $100,000 undervaluation is assumed to be reflected in each purchase price. Because of the participation feature of the preferred shares, the logical approach is to divide this $100,000 unrealized gain between the two stocks according to the par value ratio (20:80) or $20,000 to preferred stock and $80,000 to common.

From the information produced in Exhibit 6.6, the following consolidation entries for January 1, 2006 (the date of purchase), can be developed. Note that Entry **A** has been split into **A1** and **A2** to identify the allocations resulting from the preferred stock and common stock, respectively. The purpose of this segregation is merely to clarify the process; these two worksheet entries could easily be combined.

Consolidation Entry PS

Preferred Stock (Low Company)	100,000	
Retained Earnings (Low Company) (20%)	103,280	
Investment in Low Company Preferred Stock (60% ownership)		121,968
Noncontrolling Interest in Low Company (40%)		81,312

To eliminate subsidiary's preferred stockholders' equity accounts ($203,280) and recognize noncontrolling interest in preferred stock. Retained earnings is based on par value assignment.

Consolidation Entry S

Common Stock (Low Company)	400,000	
Additional Paid-In Capital (Low Company)	200,000	
Retained Earnings (Low Company) (80%)	413,120	
Investment in Low Company Common Stock (80% ownership)		810,496
Noncontrolling Interest in Low Company (20%)		202,624

To eliminate subsidiary's remaining stockholders' equity accounts ($1,013,120) and recognize noncontrolling interest in common stock. Retained earnings reflects Entry **PS.**

Consolidation Entry A1

Land	12,000	
Goodwill	16,000	
Investment in Low Company Preferred Stock		28,000

To allocate cost paid for preferred stock in excess of book value. (See Exhibit 6.6.)

Consolidation Entry A2

Land	64,000	
Goodwill	20,000	
Investment in Low Company Common Stock		84,000

To allocate cost paid for common stock in excess of book value. (See Exhibit 6.6.)

Allocation of Subsidiary Income

The specific rights granted to the owners of the preferred stock also affect the subsequent allocation of the subsidiary's income each year. If the assumption is again made that Low reports net income for 2006 of $100,000, this amount must be divided between the two ownership interests based on the cumulative, participating rights of the preferred stock. These shares constitute 20 percent of the subsidiary's total par value with the remaining 80 percent coming from the holders of the common stock. Thus, net income is prorated according to this same ratio.

	Income
Subsidiary total	$100,000
Preferred stock—possesses rights to 20% of total (based on relative par values)	$ 20,000
Common stock—residual 80% interest	80,000

Based on this allocation of the subsidiary's income for 2006, the noncontrolling interest's share of consolidated income can be determined:

		Percentage Outside Ownership	Noncontrolling Interest
Income attributed to preferred stock	$20,000	40%	$ 8,000
Income attributed to common stock	80,000	20	16,000
Noncontrolling interest in subsidiary's income . . .			$24,000

2005 FASB *Business Combinations* Exposure Draft and Subsidiary Preferred Stock

Finally, the FASB, in its Exposure Draft *Business Combinations,* recommends the economic unit method using a fair value approach for all business acquisitions. The economic unit method would value all business acquisitions (whether 100 percent or less than 100 percent acquired) at their full fair values. Thus, the existence of subsidiary preferred stock would not affect the values assigned to the subsidiary's assets and liabilities in consolidation. If the subsidiary preferred stock is viewed as a debt instrument, consolidation techniques continue to parallel those applied to intercompany debt. If the subsidiary preferred stock is viewed as equity, no separate allocation of preferred and common stock purchase prices is necessary. Instead, each subsidiary asset and liability is simply consolidated at its fair value. Preferred stock equity not owned by the parent would simply form part of the fair value assigned to the noncontrolling interest.

CONSOLIDATED STATEMENT OF CASH FLOWS

The Financial Accounting Standards Board *Statement No. 95,* "Statement of Cash Flows," mandates that companies include a statement of cash flows among their financial statements. Because of this pronouncement, an organization must report details of its cash flows for each period in which it presents an income statement.

It is important that the consolidated statement of cash flows is not prepared from the individual cash flows of the separate companies. Instead, the income statements and balance sheets are first brought together on the worksheet. The cash flows statement is then based on the resulting consolidated figures. *Thus, this statement is not actually produced by consolidation but is created from numbers generated by that process.*

However, preparing a statement of cash flows for a business combination does introduce several accounting issues. Preparation of this statement involves properly handling noncontrolling interest balances, amortization, and intercompany transactions.

Noncontrolling Interest

The consolidated income statement reflects the outside ownership of a noncontrolling interest as a decrease in net income. This reduction represents the earnings accrual assigned to these other owners. However, the only cash actually distributed to the noncontrolling interest is the portion of dividends the subsidiary paid to these outside owners. Although the income statement presents the accrual rather than the dividend, the opposite is true of the cash flow statement: Only cash transactions are included. *Thus, for this statement, two adjustments are made. First, the noncontrolling interest's share of the subsidiary's net income must be eliminated; second, the dividends paid to the outside owners are included.*

The noncontrolling interest's income accrual can be removed from the statement of cash flows in either of two ways. If the business combination is using the direct approach to disclose cash generated by operations, the specific cash inflows and outflows are identified. For example, the cash collected from customers is disclosed along with the cash paid for inventory and expenses. Because the noncontrolling interest's share of consolidated income is a noncash item, the statement simply omits this balance.

The business combination could instead determine the cash from operations by applying the indirect approach. This alternative removes noncash and nonoperational items from net income, which leaves a residual figure representing the increase or decrease in cash resulting from operations. Use of the indirect approach must eliminate the noncontrolling interest's share of consolidated income from net income because this reduction in earnings is a noncash amount. The noncontrolling interest balance does not represent an actual cash payment or collection. Because the earnings assigned to these outside owners are a decrease (or negative) within consolidated income, adding the number to net income eliminates the amount.

Regardless of which approach is used, the noncontrolling interest income accrual is removed in computing the cash derived from operations. However, any dividend paid to the other owners during the period is an actual cash outflow incurred by the combination and must be included on the statement. Because this distribution is made to an owner, the amount is listed separately under the Cash Flows from Financing Activities section of the statement of cash flows.

Amortizations

A worksheet adjustment (Entry **E**) includes in the consolidation process the amortizations of allocations made to specific accounts. These expenses appear not on either set of individual records but in the business combination's income statement. As a noncash decrease in income, this expense impacts the statement of cash flows in the same manner as the noncontrolling interest's share of consolidated income. If the business combination uses the direct approach, it omits the balance because this expense does not affect the amount of cash. In contrast, application of the indirect approach removes the amortization expense by adding the balance to net income.

Intercompany Transactions

As this text previously discussed, a significant volume of transfers often occur between the related companies composing a business combination. The resulting effects of this intercompany activity must be eliminated on the worksheet so that the consolidated income statement and balance sheet reflect only transactions with outside parties. Likewise, the consolidated statement of cash flows should not include the impact of these transfers. Although the cash flows can be large, intercompany sales and purchases do not change the amount of cash being held by the business combination when viewed as a whole.

Because the statement of cash flows is derived from the consolidated balance sheet and income statement, the impact of all transfers has been removed prior to producing this last statement. Therefore, no special adjustments are needed to arrive at a proper presentation of cash flows. The elimination entries made on the worksheet have the added effect of providing correct data for the consolidated statement of cash flows.

Acquisition Year Cash Flow Adjustments

In the year of a business acquisition the consolidated cash flow statement must properly reflect several additional considerations that arise. For many business combinations, the following issues frequently are present:

- Cash purchases of businesses must be accounted for as an investing activity. Importantly, the *net cash outflow* (cash paid less subsidiary cash acquired) is reported as the amount paid in a business acquisition.
- For intraperiod purchase acquisitions, *SFAS No. 95* requires that any adjustments from changes in operating balance sheet accounts (Accounts Receivable, Inventory, Accounts Payable, etc.) reflect the amounts acquired in the combination. Therefore, any changes in operating assets and liabilities are reported net of effects of acquired businesses in computing the necessary adjustments to convert consolidated net income to operating cash flows. Use of the direct approach of presenting operating cash flows also reports the separate computations of cash collected from customers and cash paid for inventory net of effects of any acquired businesses.

- Any adjustments arising from the subsidiary's revenues or expenses (e.g., depreciation, amortization) must reflect only postacquisition amounts. Closing the subsidiary's books at the date of acquisition facilitates the determination of the appropriate postacquisition subsidiary effects on the consolidated entity's cash flows.

- Acquired in-process research and development can represent an allocation of the purchase price that is expensed in the consolidated income statement in the acquisition year. Such in-process research and development costs are considered cash outflows from investing activities.[12] Therefore, under the indirect method, the expense is added back to consolidated net income in determining cash flows from operating activities.

Consolidated Statement of Cash Flows Illustration

Assume that on July 1, 2006, Pinto Company purchases 90 percent of the outstanding stock of Salida Company for $775,000 in cash. At the acquisition date Pinto prepares the following cost allocation schedule based on the fair values of Salida's assets and liabilities:

Acquisition cost, July 1, 2006.		$775,000
Cash	$ 35,000	
Accounts receivable	145,000	
Inventory	90,000	
Land	100,000	
Buildings	136,000	
Equipment.	259,000	
Accounts payable.	(15,000)	
Net book value	$750,000	
Percent acquired	× 90%	675,000
		100,000
Excess cost over book value allocation		
Equipment (four-year life).	$ 40,000	
In-process research and development.	22,000	
Database (four-year life).	38,000	100,000
		–0–

At the end of 2006, the following comparative balance sheets and consolidated income statement are available:

PINTO COMPANY AND SUBSIDIARY SALIDA COMPANY
Comparative Balance Sheets

	Pinto Co. January 1, 2006	Consolidated December 31, 2006
Cash	$ 170,000	$ 449,500
Accounts receivable (net)	118,000	319,000
Inventory	310,000	395,000
Land	250,000	350,000
Buildings (net)	350,000	426,000
Equipment (net)	1,145,000	1,379,000
Database		33,250
Total assets	$2,343,000	$3,351,750
Accounts payable	$ 50,000	$ 45,000
Long-term liabilities	18,000	519,500
Common stock	1,500,000	1,500,000
Noncontrolling interest		87,500
Retained earnings	775,000	1,199,750
Total liabilities and equities	$2,343,000	$3,351,750

---

[12] See Compaq's acquisition of Digital or several of DuPont's acquisitions in the late 1990s for examples of acquired in-process research and development classified as an investing activity.

PINTO COMPANY AND SUBSIDIARY SALIDA COMPANY
Consolidated Income Statement
For the Year Ended December 31, 2006

Revenues		$1,255,000
Cost of goods sold	$600,000	
Depreciation	125,000	
Database amortization	4,750	
In-process research and development	22,000	
Interest and other expenses	13,500	
Noncontrolling interest in Salida's income	15,000	780,250
Net income		$ 474,750

Additional Information

- At the date of acquisition, Salida Company closed its books. Consequently, the consolidated income statement totals include Salida's postacquisition revenues and expenses.
- During 2006, Pinto paid $50,000 in dividends. On August 1, 2006, Salida paid a $25,000 dividend.
- During 2006, Pinto issued $501,500 in long-term debt at par value.
- No other asset purchases or dispositions occurred during 2006 other than the purchase of Salida.
- The acquired in-process research and development was judged not to have reached technological feasibility and to have no alternative future uses.

In preparing the consolidated statement of cash flows, note that each adjustment derives from the consolidated income statement or changes from Pinto's January 1, 2006, balance sheet to the consolidated balance sheet at December 31, 2006.

Depreciation and Amortization   These expenses do not represent current operating cash outflows and thus are added back to convert accrual basis income to cash provided by operating activities.

Increase in Accounts Receivable, Inventory, and Accounts Payable (net of acquisition)
SFAS No. 95 requires that changes in balance sheet accounts affecting operating cash flows reflect amounts acquired in business acquisitions. In this case, note that the changes in Accounts Receivable, Inventory, and Accounts Payable are computed as follows:

	Accounts Receivable	Inventory	Accounts Payable
Pinto's balance 1/1/06	$118,000	$310,000	$50,000
Increase from Salida acquisition	145,000	90,000	15,000
Adjusted beginning balance	263,000	400,000	65,000
Consolidated balance 12/31/06	319,000	395,000	45,000
Operating cash flow adjustment	$ 56,000	$ 5,000	$20,000

Acquired In-Process Research and Development   The purchase price for Salida Company includes $22,000 for in-process research and development, which the combined entity is expensing immediately upon acquisition. The $22,000 is added back to net income and included as part of cash outflows from investing activities.

Noncontrolling Interest   The noncontrolling interest's share of the combined entity's net income represents neither a distribution nor a collection of cash and therefore is added back to consolidated net income. Ownership divisions between the noncontrolling and controlling interests do not affect reporting for the entity's operating cash flows.

Purchase of Salida Company   The Investing Activities section of the cash flow statement shows increases and decreases in assets purchased or sold involving cash. The cash outflow from the purchase of Salida Company's assets is determined as follows:

Purchase price for 90 percent interest in Salida...............	$775,000
Cash acquired	(35,000)
Net cash paid for Salida investment	$740,000

Note here that although Pinto acquires only 90 percent of Salida, 100 percent of Salida's cash is offset against the purchase price in determining the investing cash outflow. Ownership divisions between the noncontrolling and controlling interests do not affect reporting for the entity's investing cash flows.

Issue of Long-Term Debt   Pinto Company's issuance of long-term debt represents a cash inflow from financing activities.

Dividends   The dividends paid to Pinto Company owners ($50,000) combined with the dividends paid to the noncontrolling interest ($2,500) represent cash outflows from financing activities.

Based on the consolidated totals from the comparative balance sheets and the consolidated income statement, the following consolidated statement of cash flows is then prepared. Pinto chooses to use the indirect method of reporting cash flows from operating activities.

PINTO COMPANY AND SUBSIDIARY SALIDA COMPANY
Consolidated Statement of Cash Flows
For the Year Ended December 31, 2006

Consolidated net income		$474,750
Depreciation expense	$125,000	
Amortization expense	4,750	
Increase in accounts receivable (net of acquisition effects)	(56,000)	
Decrease in inventory (net of acquisition effects)	5,000	
Decrease in accounts payable (net of acquisition effects)	(20,000)	
Acquired in-process research and development	22,000	
Noncontrolling interest in income	15,000	95,750
Net cash provided by operations		570,500
Purchase of Salida Company (net of cash acquired)		
Net cash used in investing activities	(740,000)	(740,000)
Issue long-term debt	501,500	
Dividends	(52,500)	
Net cash provided by financing activities		449,000
Increase in Cash 1/1/06 to 12/31/06		**$279,500**

CONSOLIDATED EARNINGS PER SHARE

The consolidation process affects one other intermediate accounting topic, the computation of earnings per share (EPS). As *Statement of Financial Accounting Standards No. 128* (March 1997), "Earnings per Share," requires, publicly held companies must disclose EPS each period. The following steps calculate such figures:

• Determine basic earnings per share by dividing net income (after reduction for preferred stock dividends) by the weighted average number of common stock shares outstanding for the period. If the reporting entity has no dilutive options, warrants, or other convertible items, only basic EPS is presented on the face of the income statement. However, diluted earnings per share also must be presented if any dilutive convertibles are present.

- Compute diluted earnings per share by combining the effects of *any dilutive securities* with basic earnings per share. Stock options, stock warrants, convertible debt, and convertible preferred stock often qualify as dilutive securities.[13]

In most instances, the computation of earnings per share for a business combination follows the same general pattern. Consolidated net income along with the number of outstanding parent shares provides the basis for calculating basic EPS. Any convertibles, warrants, or options for the parent's stock that can possibly dilute the reported figure must be included as described earlier in determining diluted EPS.

However, a problem arises if warrants, options, or convertibles that can dilute the subsidiary's earnings are outstanding. Although the parent company is not directly affected, the potential impact of these items on consolidated net income must be given weight in computing diluted earnings per share for the business combination as a whole. Because of possible conversion, the subsidiary earnings figure included in consolidated net income is not necessarily applicable to the diluted earnings per share computation. *Thus, the accountant must separately determine the amount of subsidiary income that should be used in deriving diluted earnings per share for the business combination.*

Earnings per Share Illustration

Assume that Big Corporation has 100,000 shares of its common stock outstanding during the current year. The company also has issued 20,000 shares of nonvoting preferred stock, paying an annual cumulative dividend of $5 per share ($100,000 total). Each of these preferred shares is convertible into two shares of Big's common stock.

Assume also that Big owns 90 percent of Little's common stock and 60 percent of its preferred stock (which pays $12,000 in dividends per year). Annual amortization is $24,000 attributable to various intangibles. EPS computations currently are being made for 2007. During the year, Big reported separate income of $600,000 and Little earned $100,000. A simplified consolidation of the figures for the year indicates net income for the business combination of $662,400:

Big's separate income for 2007		$600,000
Amortization expense resulting from original purchase price		(24,000)
Little's separate income for 2007	$100,000	
Noncontrolling interest in Little—common stock		
(10% of income after $12,000 in preferred stock dividends)	(8,800)	
Noncontrolling interest in Little—		
preferred stock (40% of dividends).	(4,800)	86,400
Consolidated net income		$662,400

Little has 20,000 shares of common stock and 4,000 shares of preferred stock outstanding. The preferred shares pay a $3 per year dividend, and each can be converted into two shares of common stock (or 8,000 shares in total). Because Big owns only 60 percent of Little's preferred stock, a $4,800 dividend is distributed each year to the outside owners (40 percent of $12,000 total payment).

Assume finally that the subsidiary also has $200,000 in convertible bonds outstanding that were originally issued at face value. This debt has a cash and an effective interest rate of 10 percent ($20,000 per year) and can be converted by the owners into 9,000 shares of Little's common stock. Big owns none of these bonds. The tax rate applicable to Little is 30 percent.

---

[13] Complete coverage of the earnings per share computation can be found in virtually any intermediate accounting textbook. To adequately understand this process, a number of complex procedures must be mastered, including these:
- Calculation of the weighted average number of common shares outstanding.
- Understanding the method of including stock rights, convertible debt, and convertible preferred stock within the computation of diluted earnings per share.

EXHIBIT 6.7
Subsidiary's Diluted Earnings per Share

LITTLE COMPANY
Diluted Earnings per Common Share
For Year Ending December 31, 2007

	Earnings	Shares	
As reported	$100,000	20,000	
Preferred stock dividends	(12,000)		
Effect of possible preferred stock conversion:			
Dividends saved	12,000 New shares	8,000	$1.50 impact (12,000/8,000)
Effect of possible bond conversion:			
Interest saved (net of taxes)	14,000	9,000	$1.56 impact (14,000/9,000)
Diluted EPS	$114,000	37,000	$3.08 (rounded)

To better visualize these factors, the convertible items are scheduled as follows:

Company	Item	Interest or Dividend	Conversion	Big Owns
Big	Preferred stock	$100,000/year	40,000 shares	Not applicable
Little	Preferred stock	12,000/year	8,000 shares	60%
Little	Bonds	14,000/year*	9,000 shares	–0–

*Interest on the bonds is shown net of the 30 percent tax effect ($20,000 interest less $6,000 tax savings). No tax is computed for the preferred shares because distributed dividends do not create a tax impact.

Because the subsidiary has convertible items that can affect the company's outstanding shares and net income, Little's diluted earnings per share must be derived *before* consolidated diluted EPS can be determined. As shown in Exhibit 6.7, Little's diluted earnings per share are $3.08. Two aspects of this schedule should be noted:

- The individual impact of the convertibles ($1.50 for the preferred stock and $1.56 for the bonds) did not raise the earnings per share figures. Thus, neither the preferred stock nor the bonds are antidilutive, and both are properly included in these computations.

- Determining diluted earnings per share of the subsidiary is necessary only because of the possible dilutive impact. Without the subsidiary's convertible bonds and preferred stock, consolidated net income would form the basis for computing EPS for the business combination, and only basic EPS would be reported.

According to Exhibit 6.7, Little's income is $114,000 for diluted EPS. The issue for the accountant is how much of this amount should be included in computing consolidated diluted earnings per share. This allocation is based on the percentage of shares controlled by the parent. Note that if the subsidiary's preferred stock and bonds are converted into common shares, Big's ownership falls from 90 to 62 percent. For diluted EPS, 37,000 shares are appropriate. Big's 62 percent ownership (22,800/37,000) is the basis for allocating the subsidiary's $114,000 income to the parent.

Supporting Calculations for Diluted Earnings per Share

	Little Company Shares	Big's Percentage	Big's Ownership
Common stock	20,000	90%	18,000
Possible new shares—preferred stock	8,000	60	4,800
Possible new shares—bonds	9,000	–0–	–0–
Total	37,000		22,800

Big's ownership (diluted): 22,800/37,000 = 62% (rounded)
Income assigned to Big (diluted earnings per share computation):
    $114,000 × 62% = $70,680

EXHIBIT 6.8

BIG COMPANY AND CONSOLIDATED SUBSIDIARY
Consolidated Basic Earnings per Common Share
For Year Ending December 31, 2007

	Earnings	Shares	
Consolidated net income	$662,400		
Big's shares outstanding		100,000	
Preferred stock dividends (Big)	(100,000)		
Basic EPS	$562,400	100,000	$5.62

Consolidated Diluted Earnings per Common Share
For Year Ending December 31, 2007

	Earnings	Shares	
Computed below	$646,680*		
Big's shares outstanding		100,000	
Preferred stock dividends (Big)	(100,000)		
Effect of possible preferred stock (Big) conversion:			
Dividends saved	100,000 New shares	40,000	$2.50 impact (100,000/40,000)
Diluted EPS	$646,680	140,000	$4.62 (rounded)

*Net income computation:

Big's separate income	$600,000
Amortization expense resulting from original purchase price	(24,000)
Portion of Little's income assigned to diluted earnings per share calculation	70,680 (computed previously)
Earnings of the business combination applicable to diluted earnings per share	$646,680

We can now determine consolidated earnings per share. Only $70,680 of subsidiary income is appropriate for the diluted EPS computation. Because two different income figures are utilized, basic and diluted calculations are made separately as in Exhibit 6.8. Consequently, these schedules determine that this business combination should report basic earnings per share of $5.62, with diluted earnings per share of $4.62.

SUBSIDIARY STOCK TRANSACTIONS

A footnote to the financial statements of Gerber Products Company disclosed a transaction carried out by one of the organization's subsidiaries: "The Company's wholly owned Mexican subsidiary sold previously unissued shares of common stock to Grupo Coral, S.A., a Mexican food company, at a price in excess of the shares' net book value." The footnote went on to state that Gerber had increased consolidated Additional Paid-In Capital by $432,000 as a result of this stock sale.

As this illustration shows, subsidiary stock transactions can alter the level of parent ownership. A subsidiary, for example, can decide to sell previously unissued stock to raise needed capital. Although the parent company can acquire a portion or even all of these new shares, such issues frequently are marketed entirely to outsiders. A subsidiary could also be legally forced to sell additional shares of its stock. As an example, companies holding control over foreign subsidiaries occasionally encounter this problem because of laws in the individual localities. Regulations requiring a certain percentage of local ownership as a prerequisite for operating within a country can mandate issuance of new shares. Of course, changes in the level of parent ownership do not result solely from stock sales: A subsidiary also can repurchase its own stock. The acquisition, as well as the possible retirement, of such treasury shares serves as a means of reducing the percentage of outside ownership.

Changes in Subsidiary Book Value—Stock Transactions

When a subsidiary subsequently buys or sells its own stock, a nonoperational increase or decrease occurs in the company's book value. Because the transaction need not involve the parent, the parent's investment account does not automatically reflect the effect of this change. *Thus, a separate adjustment must be recorded to maintain reciprocity between the subsidiary's stockholders' equity accounts and the parent's investment balance.* The accountant measures the impact that the stock transaction has on the parent to ensure that this effect is appropriately recorded within the consolidation process.

An example demonstrates the mechanics of this issue. Assume that on January 1, 2007, Small Company's book value is $700,000 as follows:

Common stock ($1.00 par value with 70,000 shares issued and outstanding)	$ 70,000
Retained earnings	630,000
Total stockholders' equity	$700,000

Based on the 70,000 outstanding shares, Small's book value at this time is $10 per common share ($700,000/70,000 shares).

On this same date, Giant Company acquired in the open market an 80 percent interest in Small Company (56,000 of the outstanding shares). To avoid unnecessary complications, we assume that the price of this stock is $560,000, or $10 per share, exactly equivalent to the book value of the purchased shares. We also assume that this acquisition involves no goodwill or other revaluations.

Under these conditions, the consolidation process is uncomplicated. On the purchase date, only a single worksheet entry is required. The investment account is eliminated and the 20 percent noncontrolling interest recognized through the following routine entry:

Consolidation Entry S (January 1, 2007)		
Common Stock (Small Company)	70,000	
Retained Earnings (Small Company)	630,000	
Investment in Small Company (80%)		560,000
Noncontrolling Interest in Small Company (20%)		140,000
To eliminate subsidiary's stockholders' equity accounts and record noncontrolling interest balance on this date.		

We now introduce a subsidiary stock transaction to demonstrate the effect created on the consolidation process. Assume that on January 2, 2007, Small sells 10,000 previously unissued shares of its common stock to outside parties for $16 per share.[14] Because of this transaction, Giant no longer possesses an 80 percent interest in a subsidiary having a $700,000 net book value. Instead, the parent now holds 70 percent (56,000 shares of a total of 80,000) of a company with a book value of $860,000 ($700,000 previous book value plus $160,000 capital generated by the sale of additional shares). *Independent of any action by the parent company, the book value equivalency of this investment has risen from $560,000 to $602,000 (70 percent of $860,000).* Small's ability to sell shares of stock at $6.00 more than the book value has created this increase.

Small's new stock issuance has increased the underlying book value component of Giant's investment by $42,000 ($602,000 − $560,000). Thus, even with the rise in outside ownership, the business combination has grown in size by this amount, a change that the consolidated financial figures must reflect. As the Gerber example indicates, this adjustment is frequently recorded to Additional Paid-In Capital. Because the subsidiary's stockholders' equity is eliminated on the

---

[14] This example is solely for demonstration purposes. Obviously, having the parent acquire stock at book value on one day with an outsider paying $6 per share more than book value on the following day is an unlikely situation. Normally, the prices would be similar or more time would transpire between the two acquisitions. In either case, the consolidation process is fundamentally unchanged.

worksheet, the parent must recognize any equity increase accruing to the business combination. Therefore, the $42,000 increment is entered into Giant's financial records as an adjustment in both the investment account (because the underlying book value of the subsidiary has increased) and Additional Paid-In Capital:

Giant Company's Financial Records—January 2, 2007		
Investment in Small Company	42,000	
Additional Paid-In Capital (Giant Company)		42,000
To recognize change in equity of business combination created by issuance of 10,000 additional shares of common stock by Small Company, the subsidiary, at above book value.		

After the change in the parent's records has been made, the consolidation process can proceed in a normal fashion. If, for example, the financial statements are brought together immediately following the sale of these additional shares, the following worksheet Entry **S** can be constructed. *Although the investment and subsidiary equity accounts are removed here, the change recorded earlier in Giant's Additional Paid-In Capital remains within the consolidated figures.* Thus, the subsidiary's issuance of stock at more than the book value has increased the reported equity of the business combination:

Consolidation Entry S—January 2, 2007—After Subsidiary's Stock Issuance		
Common Stock (Small Company)	80,000	
Additional Paid-In Capital (Small Company)	150,000	
Retained Earnings (Small Company)	630,000	
Investment in Small Company (70%)		602,000
Noncontrolling Interest in Small Company (30%)		258,000
To eliminate subsidiary's stockholders' equity accounts and record noncontrolling interest balance on this date. Small's capital accounts have been updated to reflect the issuance of 10,000 shares of $1 par value common stock at $16 per share. The investment balance has also been adjusted for the $42,000 increment recorded earlier by the parent.		

In 1983, because of a lack of formal guidance, the staff of the SEC decided that an adjustment necessitated by subsidiary stock transactions could be made to either Additional Paid-In Capital or to a gain or loss account. For example, Atlantic Richfield Company disclosed that a previously wholly owned subsidiary had "completed an initial public offering of 19,550,000 shares of its common stock, thereby decreasing ARCO's percentage ownership to 80.4 percent. The Company recognized an after-tax gain of $185 million from this transaction."

In its October 2000 Exposure Draft, *Accounting for Financial Instruments with Characteristics of Liabilities, Equity, or Both,* however, the FASB reiterated its support for the view that the effects on a parent of a subsidiary's transactions in its own stock should be reported as adjustments to Additional Paid-In Capital, not gains and losses. As stated in the Exposure Draft (para. 234):

> Having reached a decision that the noncontrolling interest in a subsidiary constitutes part of the equity of a consolidated group, the Board concluded that sales of shares of that subsidiary are sales of the consolidated entity's equity and, therefore, should not result in gain or loss recognition as long as the subsidiary remains consolidated.
>
> The Board believes that [sales of] the stock of a subsidiary by any of the affiliates, whether . . . by the parent or another subsidiary . . . are transactions in the equity of the reporting entity. The stock of the subsidiary is neither an asset nor a liability of the reporting entity comprising a parent and its subsidiaries. Rather, it is part of the residual interest remaining after subtracting consolidated liabilities from consolidated assets. Therefore, no gains or losses should be recognized on those transactions.

The 2005 FASB Exposure Draft, *Consolidated Financial Statements, Including Accounting and Reporting of Noncontrolling Interests in Subsidiaries,* similarly recommends that the effects from any changes in ownership (that do not result in a loss of control) should be accounted for as capital transactions. Consistent with the recommendations of this Exposure Draft, this textbook treats the effects from subsidiary stock transactions on the consolidated entity as adjustments to Additional Paid-In Capital.

Subsidiary Stock Transactions—Illustrated

No single example can demonstrate the many possible variations that different types of subsidiary stock transactions could create. To provide a working knowledge of this process, we analyze several additional cases briefly. The original balances presented for Small (the 80 percent–owned subsidiary) and Giant (the parent) at the beginning of the current year serve as the basis for these illustrations:

Small Company (subsidiary):		
Shares outstanding	70,000	
Book value of company	$700,000	
Book value per share	$ 10.00	
Giant Company (parent):		
Shares owned of Small Company	56,000	
Book value of investment	$560,000	(80%)

View each of the following cases as an independent situation. Also, all adjustments are made here to Additional Paid-In Capital although, as discussed, recognition of a gain or loss remains a possible alternative.

Case 1

Assume that Small Company sells 10,000 shares of previously unissued common stock to outside parties for $8 per share.

Small is issuing its stock here at a price below the company's current book value of $10 per share. Selling shares to outsiders at a discount necessitates a drop in the recorded value of consolidated Additional Paid-In Capital. The parent's ownership interest is being diluted, thus creating a decrease in the underlying book value of the parent's investment. This reduction can be measured as follows:

Adjusted book value of subsidiary ($700,000 + $80,000)	$780,000
Current parent ownership (56,000 shares/80,000 shares)	70%
Book value equivalency of ownership	546,000
Current book value of investment account	560,000
Required *reduction*	$ 14,000

In the original illustration, the subsidiary sold new shares at $6 more than book value, thus increasing consolidated equity. Here the opposite transpires: It issues the shares at a price less than book value, creating a decrease:

Giant Company's Financial Records		
Additional Paid-In Capital (or Retained Earnings) (Giant Company)	14,000	
Investment in Small Company		14,000
To recognize change in equity of business combination created by issuance of 10,000 additional shares of Small's common stock at less than book value.		

Case 2

Assume that Small issues 10,000 new shares of common stock for $16 per share. Of this total, Giant acquires 8,000 shares to maintain its 80 percent level of ownership. Giant pays a total of $128,000 (8,000 × $16) for this additional stock. Outside parties bought the remaining shares.

Under these circumstances, the stock transaction alters both the parent's investment account and the book value of the subsidiary. Thus, both figures must be updated prior to determining the necessity of an equity revaluation:

Adjusted book value of subsidiary ($700,000 + $160,000)	$860,000
Current parent ownership (64,000 shares/80,000 shares)	80%
Book value equivalency of ownership	688,000
Current book value of investment (after including additional $128,000 acquisition)	688,000
Required *change*	$ –0–

This case requires no adjustment because Giant's underlying interest remains properly aligned with the subsidiary's book value. Any purchase of new stock by the parent in the same ratio as previous ownership does not affect consolidated Additional Paid-In Capital. The transaction creates no proportionate increase or decrease.

Case 3

Assume that Small issues 10,000 additional shares of common stock solely to Giant for $16 per share.

A different type of situation occurs here. As the following computational schedule shows, this issuance causes the parent's investment account again to be in excess of the subsidiary's underlying book value (as in Case 1). However, in this latest example, a parent company purchase creates the $10,500 difference rather than the subsidiary's sale of common stock to outside parties. Thus, reporting this impact has to be altered to reflect Giant's acquisition of these new shares:

Adjusted book value of subsidiary ($700,000 + $160,000)	$860,000
Current parent ownership (66,000 shares/80,000 shares)	82.5%
Book value equivalency of ownership	709,500
Current book value of investment (after including additional $160,000 acquisition)	720,000
Differences in subsidiary book value and investment book value after second purchase	$ 10,500

The subsidiary's sale of stock to outsiders at a price less than book value, a transaction that mathematically diluted the value of the parent's investment, caused the $14,000 reduction in Case 1. Because this action realigned the ownership interests to the apparent detriment of the business combination, it reduced Additional Paid-In Capital. This result was achieved for consolidation purposes through a decrease in the parent's equity account and in the Investment in Small Company.

Conversely, in Case 3, an expenditure made by the parent solely created the $10,500 difference. Because the price paid was more than the corresponding book value of the subsidiary, the excess is attributed to goodwill (unless the amount can be traced to specific asset or liability accounts). As in any purchase combination, Giant records the entire $160,000 payment as an investment and then utilizes Entry **A** on the consolidation worksheet to report the allocation. Because the parent made the acquisition, the transaction is handled differently than a subsidiary's sale of stock to outsiders at less than book value.

Case 4

Assume that instead of issuing new stock, Small reacquires 10,000 shares from outside owners. It pays $16 per share for this treasury stock.

This illustration presents another type of subsidiary stock transaction: the acquisition of treasury stock. Although the subsidiary's actions have changed, the basic accounting procedures are unaffected.

Adjusted book value of subsidiary ($700,000 − $160,000)	$540,000
Current parent ownership (56,000 shares/60,000 shares)	93⅓%
Book value equivalency of ownership	504,000
Current book value of investment	560,000
Required *reduction*	$ 56,000

The subsidiary paid an amount in excess of the treasury stock's $10 per share book value. Consequently, this once again dilutes the parent's interest. A transaction between the subsidiary and the noncontrolling interest created this effect; the reduction does not result from a purchase made by the parent. As in Case 1, the parent must report the change as an adjustment in its Additional Paid-In Capital accompanied by a corresponding decrease in its investment account (to $504,000 in this case). Again, for reporting purposes, this transaction results in lowering consolidated Additional Paid-In Capital:

Giant Company's Financial Records

Additional Paid-In Capital (Giant Company)	56,000	
Investment in Small Company		56,000
To recognize change in equity of business combination created by acquisition of 10,000 treasury shares by Small at above book value.		

This fourth illustration represents a different subsidiary stock transaction, the purchase of treasury stock. Therefore, display of consolidation Entry **S** should also be presented. This entry demonstrates the worksheet elimination required when the subsidiary holds treasury shares:

Consolidation Entry S

Common Stock (Small Company)	70,000	
Retained Earnings (Small Company)	630,000	
Treasury Stock (Small Company) (at cost)		160,000
Investment in Small Company (93⅓%—subsequent to adjustment)		504,000
Noncontrolling Interest (6⅔% of net book value)		36,000
To eliminate equity accounts of Small Company and recognize appropriate noncontrolling interest. Book value of Small is now $540,000.		

Case 5

Assume that Small issues a 10 percent stock dividend (7,000 new shares) to its owners when the stock's fair value is $16 per share.

This final case illustrates that not all subsidiary stock transactions produce discernible effects on the consolidation process. A stock dividend, whether large or small, capitalizes a portion of the issuing company's retained earnings and, thus, does not alter book value. Shareholders recognize the receipt of a stock dividend only as a change in the recorded cost of each share rather than as any type of adjustment in the investment balance. Because neither party perceives a net effect, the consolidation process proceeds in a routine fashion. Therefore, a subsidiary stock dividend requires no special treatment prior to development of a worksheet.

Book value of subsidiary (no adjustment required)	$700,000
Current parent ownership (adjusted for 10% stock dividend— 61,600 shares/77,000 shares)	80%
Book value equivalency of ownership	560,000
Current book value of investment	560,000
Adjustment required by stock dividend	$ –0–

The consolidation Entry **S** made just after the issuance of this stock dividend follows. The $560,000 component of the investment account continues to be offset against the stockholders' equity of the subsidiary. Although the dividend did not affect the parent's investment, the equity accounts of the subsidiary have been realigned in recognition of the $112,000 stock dividend (7,000 shares of $1 par value stock valued at $16 per share):

Consolidation Entry S		
Common Stock (Small Company)	77,000	
Additional Paid-In Capital (Small Company)	105,000	
Retained Earnings (Small Company)	518,000	
Investment in Small Company (80%)		560,000
Noncontrolling interest (20%)		140,000
To eliminate stockholders' equity accounts of subsidiary and recognize noncontrolling interest following issuance of stock dividend.		

Summary

1. Variable interest entities (VIEs) typically take the form of a trust, partnership, joint venture, or corporation. In most cases, a sponsoring firm creates these entities to engage in a limited and well-defined set of business activities. Control of VIEs, by design, often does not rest with its equity holders. Instead, control is exercised through contractual arrangements with the sponsoring firm that becomes the entity's "primary beneficiary." These contracts can take the form of leases, participation rights, guarantees, or other residual interests. Through contracting, the primary beneficiary bears a majority of the risks and receives a majority of the rewards of the entity, often without owning any voting shares. *FIN 46R* requires a business that has a controlling financial interest in a VIE to consolidate the financial statements of the VIE with its own.

2. If one member of a business combination acquires an affiliate's debt instrument (e.g., a bond or note) from an outside party, the purchase price usually differs from the book value of the liability. Thus, a gain or loss has been incurred from the perspective of the business combination. However, both the debt and investment remain in the individual financial accounts of the two companies but the gain or loss goes unrecorded. The consolidation process must adjust all balances to reflect the effective retirement of the debt.

3. Following a related party's acquisition of a company's debt, Interest Income and Expense are recognized. Because these accounts result from intercompany transactions, they also must be removed in every subsequent consolidation along with the debt and investment figures. Retained Earnings also requires adjustment in each year after the purchase to record the impact of the gain or loss.

4. Amortization of intercompany debt/investment balances often is necessary because of discounts and/or premiums. Consequently, the interest income and interest expense figures reported by the two parties will not agree. The closing of these two accounts into Retained Earnings each year gradually reduces the consolidation adjustment that must be made to this equity account.

5. When acquired, many subsidiaries have preferred stock outstanding as well as common stock. The method of handling any subsidiary preferred shares within the consolidation process depends on the nature of the stock. Preferred issues that have a call value, no voting rights, and a set cumulative dividend are not easily distinguished from a debt. Conversely, preferred shares with a voting or participation right are clearly an ownership interest resembling common stock.

6. If a subsidiary's preferred stock is viewed as a debt-type instrument, any shares acquired by the parent are eliminated on the worksheet as if the stock had been retired. Because a gain or loss cannot be recognized in connection with a company's own stock transactions, the difference between par value and the parent's cost is adjusted through Additional Paid-In Capital or Retained Earnings. Any shares still held by outside parties are reported as a noncontrolling interest based on the call value of the stock.

7. A subsidiary preferred stock perceived as an equity interest is accounted for in the same manner as a common stock purchase. Any excess acquisition price paid for the preferred stock is assigned to specific accounts based on fair value with any residual reported as goodwill. As a prerequisite to this process, the book value of the subsidiary must be divided between the two equity interests. This calculation is based on the rights specified for the preferred shareholders.

8. Every business combination must prepare a statement of cash flows. This statement is not created by consolidating the individual cash flows of the separate companies. Instead, both a consolidated income statement and balance sheet are produced, and the cash flows statement is developed from these figures. Within this statement, the noncontrolling interest's share of the subsidiary's income is not included because no cash flows result. However, the dividends paid to these outside owners must be listed as a financing activity.

9. For most business combinations, the determination of consolidated earnings per share follows the normal pattern presented in intermediate accounting textbooks. However, if the subsidiary has potentially dilutive items outstanding (stock warrants, convertible preferred stock, convertible bonds, etc.), a different process must be followed. The subsidiary's own diluted earnings per share are computed as a preliminary procedure. The parent and the outside owners then allocate the earnings used in each of these calculations based on the ownership levels of the subsidiary's shares and the dilutive items. The determination of the diluted earnings per share figures to be reported for the business combination includes the portion of income assigned to the parent.

10. After the combination is created, a subsidiary may enter into stock transactions such as issuing additional shares or acquiring treasury stock. Such actions normally create a proportional increase or decrease in the subsidiary's equity when compared with the parent's investment. The change is measured and then reflected in the consolidated statements through the Additional Paid-In Capital account. Recognition of a gain or loss is also a possibility. To achieve the appropriate accounting, the parent adjusts the Investment in Subsidiary account as well as its own Additional Paid-In Capital. Because the worksheet does not eliminate this equity balance, the required increase or decrease is created in the consolidated figures.

Comprehensive Illustration

PROBLEM: CONSOLIDATED STATEMENT OF CASH FLOWS AND EARNINGS PER SHARE

(Estimated Time: 35 to 45 Minutes) Pop, Inc., acquires 90 percent of the 20,000 shares of Son Company's outstanding common stock on December 31, 2005. Of the purchase price, it allocates $80,000 to covenants, a figure amortized at the rate of $2,000 per year. Comparative consolidated balance sheets for 2007 and 2006 are as follow:

	2007	2006
Cash	$ 210,000	$ 130,000
Accounts receivable	350,000	220,000
Inventory	320,000	278,000
Land, buildings, and equipment (net)	1,090,000	1,120,000
Covenants	78,000	80,000
Total assets	$2,048,000	$1,828,000
Accounts payable	$ 290,000	$ 296,000
Long-term liabilities	650,000	550,000
Noncontrolling interest	38,000	34,000
Preferred stock (2,000 shares outstanding)	100,000	100,000
Common stock (26,000 shares outstanding)	520,000	520,000
Retained earnings, 12/31	450,000	328,000
Total liabilities and stockholders' equity	$2,048,000	$1,828,000

Additional Information for 2007

- Consolidated net income (after adjustments for all intercompany items) was $172,000.
- Consolidated depreciation and amortization equaled $52,000.

- On April 10, Son sold a building with a $40,000 book value receiving cash of $50,000. Later that month, Pop borrowed $100,000 from a local bank and purchased equipment for $60,000. These transactions were all with outside parties.

- During the year, Pop paid $50,000 dividends on its common stock and $10,000 on its preferred stock, and Son paid a $20,000 dividend on its common stock.

- Son has long-term convertible debt of $180,000 outstanding included in consolidated liabilities. It recognized interest expense of $16,000 (net of taxes) on this debt during the year. This debt can be exchanged for 10,000 shares of the subsidiary's common stock. Pop owns none of this debt.

- Son recorded $60,000 net income from its own operations. Noncontrolling interest in Son's income was $6,000.

- Pop recorded $4,000 in profits on sales of goods to Son. These goods remain in Son's warehouse at December 31.

- Pop applies the equity method to account for its investment in Son. On its own books, Pop recognized $48,000 equity in earnings from Son (90% × $60,000 less $2,000 amortization and $4,000 unrealized intercompany profit on its sales to Son).

Required:

a. Prepare a consolidated statement of cash flows for Pop, Inc., and Son Company for the year ending December 31, 2007. Use the indirect approach for determining the amount of cash generated by normal operations.[15]

b. Compute basic earnings per share and diluted earnings per share for this business combination.

SOLUTION

a. Consolidated Statement of Cash Flows

The problem specifies that the indirect approach should be used in preparing the consolidated statement of cash flows. Therefore, all items that do not represent cash flows from operations must be removed from the $172,000 consolidated net income. For example, the depreciation and amortization both are eliminated (noncash items) as well as the gain on the sale of the building (a nonoperational item). As the chapter discussed, the noncontrolling interest's share of Son's net income is another noncash reduction that also is removed. In addition, each of the changes in consolidated Accounts Receivable, Inventory, and Accounts Payable produces a noncash impact on net income. The increase in accounts receivable, for example, indicates that the sales figure for the period was larger than the amount of cash collected so that adjustment is required in producing this statement.

From the information given, only five nonoperational changes in cash can be determined: the bank loan, the acquisition of equipment, the sale of a building, the dividend paid by Son to the minority interest, and the dividend paid by the parent. Each of these transactions is included in the consolidated statement of cash flows shown on the next page in Exhibit 6.9, which explains the $80,000 increase in cash experienced by the entity during 2007.

b. Consolidated Earnings per Share

The subsidiary's convertible debt has a potentially dilutive effect on earnings per share. Therefore, diluted EPS cannot be determined for the business combination directly from consolidated net income. First, the diluted EPS figure must be calculated for the subsidiary. This information then is used in the computations made by the consolidated entity.

Diluted earnings per share of $2.53 for the subsidiary is determined as follows:

Son Company—Diluted Earnings per Share

	Earnings		Shares	
As reported	$60,000		20,000	$3.00
Effect of possible debt conversion:				
Interest saved (net of taxes)	16,000	New shares	10,000	$1.60 impact
				(16,000/10,000)
Diluted EPS	$76,000		30,000	$2.53 (rounded)

[15] Prior to attempting this problem, a review of an intermediate accounting textbook might be useful to obtain a complete overview of the production of a statement of cash flows.

EXHIBIT 6.9

POP, INC., AND SON COMPANY
Consolidated Statement of Cash Flows
Year Ending December 31, 2007

Cash flows from operating activities			
Net income			$ 172,000
Adjustments to reconcile net income to net cash provided by operating activities:			
Depreciation and amortization		$ 52,000	
Gain on sale of building		(10,000)	
Noncontrolling interest in Son's income		6,000	
Increase in accounts receivable		(130,000)	
Increase in inventory		(42,000)	
Decrease in accounts payable		(6,000)	(130,000)
Net cash provided by operations			42,000
Cash flows from investing activities			
Purchase of equipment		(60,000)	
Sale of building		50,000	
Net cash used in investing activities			(10,000)
Cash flows from financing activities			
Payment of cash dividend—Pop		(50,000)	
Payment of cash dividend to noncontrolling owners of Son		(2,000)	
Borrowed from bank		100,000	
Net cash provided by financing activities			48,000
Net increase in cash			80,000
Cash, January 1, 2007			130,000
Cash, December 31, 2007			$ 210,000

EXHIBIT 6.10

POP, INC., AND SON COMPANY
Consolidated Earnings per Share
Year Ending December 31, 2007

	Earnings		Shares	
	Basic Earnings per Share			
Basic EPS	$172,000		26,000	$6.62 (rounded)
	Diluted Earnings per Share			
Pop's reported income	$172,000			
Remove equity income	(48,000)			
Remove unrealized gain	(4,000)			
Recognize amortization expense	(2,000)			
Preferred stock dividend	(10,000)			
Common shares outstanding (Pop, Inc.)				
Common stock income—Pop (for EPS computations)	$108,000		26,000	
Income of Son (for diluted EPS)	45,600			
	$153,600		26,000	$5.91 (rounded)
Effect of possible preferred stock conversion:				
Dividends saved	10,000	New shares	6,000	$1.67 impact
				(10,000/6,000)
Diluted EPS	$163,600		32,000	$5.11

The parent owns none of the convertible debt included in computing diluted earnings per share. Pop holds only 18,000 (90 percent of the outstanding common stock) of the 30,000 shares used in this EPS calculation. Consequently, in determining diluted EPS for the entire business combination, just $45,600 of the subsidiary's income is applicable:

$$\$76,000 \times 18,000/30,000 = \$45,600$$

Exhibit 6.10 reveals consolidated basic earnings per share of $6.62 and diluted EPS of $5.11. Because the subsidiary's earnings figure is included separately in the computation of diluted EPS, the individual income of the parent must be identified in the same manner. Thus, the effect of the equity income, intercompany (downstream) transactions, and amortization are taken into account in arriving at the parent's earnings alone.

Questions

1. What is a variable interest entity (VIE)?
2. What are variable interests in an entity and how might they provide financial control over an entity?
3. When is a sponsoring firm required to consolidate the financial statements of a VIE with its own financial statements?
4. A parent company acquires from a third party bonds that had been issued originally by one of its subsidiaries. What accounting problems are created by this purchase?
5. In Question 4, why is the consolidation process simpler if the bonds had been acquired directly from the subsidiary than from a third party?
6. When a company acquires an affiliated company's debt instruments from a third party, how is the gain or loss on extinguishment of the debt calculated? When should this balance be recognized?
7. Several years ago, Bennett, Inc., bought a portion of the outstanding bonds of Smith Corporation, a subsidiary organization. The acquisition was made from an outside party. In the current year, how should these intercompany bonds be accounted for within the consolidation process?
8. One company purchases the outstanding debt instruments of an affiliated company on the open market. This transaction creates a gain that is appropriately recognized in the consolidated financial statements of that year. Thereafter, a worksheet adjustment is required to correct the beginning balance of the consolidated Retained Earnings. Why is the amount of this adjustment reduced from year to year?
9. A parent acquires the outstanding bonds of a subsidiary company directly from an outside third party. For consolidation purposes, this transaction creates a gain of $45,000. Should this gain be allocated to the parent or the subsidiary? Why?
10. Some preferred stocks possess characteristics that resemble an equity or ownership interest. Others, however, demonstrate traits similar to a debt instrument. How do you draw the distinction as to whether the preferred stock is actually an equity or a debt?
11. Perkins Company acquires 90 percent of the outstanding common stock of the Butterfly Corporation as well as 55 percent of its preferred stock. Because of the rights being conveyed, the preferred stock is considered to be a debt-type instrument. How should these preferred shares be accounted for within the consolidation process? How should the book value of Butterfly be allocated between the common and the preferred stock?
12. Assume the same information as in Question 11 except that the preferred stock is viewed as an equity interest. How is the preferred stock now accounted for within the consolidation process? How should the book value of Butterfly be allocated between the common and the preferred stock?
13. The income statement and the balance sheet are produced using a worksheet, but a consolidated statement of cash flows is not. What process is followed in preparing a consolidated statement of cash flows?
14. How do noncontrolling interest balances affect the consolidated statement of cash flows?
15. In many cases, consolidated earnings per share is computed based on consolidated net income and parent company shares and convertibles. However, a different process must be used for some business combinations. When is this alternative approach required?
16. A subsidiary has (1) a convertible preferred stock and (2) a convertible bond. How are these items factored into the computation of earnings per share for the business combination?
17. Why might a subsidiary decide to issue new shares of common stock to parties outside of the business combination?
18. Washburn Company owns 75 percent of the outstanding common stock of Metcalf Company. During the current year, Metcalf issues additional shares to outside parties at a price more than book

value. How does this transaction affect the business combination? How is this impact recorded within the consolidated statements?

19. Assume the same information as in Question 18 except that the new shares are issued primarily to Washburn. How does this transaction affect the business combination?

20. Assume the same information as in Question 18 except that Metcalf issues a 10 percent stock dividend instead of selling new shares of stock. How does this transaction affect the business combination?

21. If a parent must increase its investment because a subsidiary issues additional shares of stock, in what two ways can the adjustment be recorded?

Problems

1. A subsidiary has a debt outstanding that was originally issued at a discount. At the beginning of the current year, the parent company acquired the debt at a slight premium from outside parties. Which of the following statements is true?

   a. Whether the balances agree or not, both the subsequent interest income and interest expense should be reported in a consolidated income statement.

   b. The interest income and interest expense will agree in amount and should be offset for consolidation purposes.

   c. In computing any noncontrolling interest allocation, the interest income should be included but not the interest expense.

   d. Although subsequent interest income and interest expense will not agree in amount, both balances should be eliminated for consolidation purposes.

2. A subsidiary acquired a bond that had been issued by a parent company at a discount several years ago from an outside party at a premium. Which of the following statements is true?

   a. The bond has no impact on a current consolidation because the acquisition was made in the past.

   b. The original loss would be reported in the current year's consolidated income statement.

   c. For consolidation purposes, retained earnings must be reduced at the beginning of the current year but by an amount smaller than the original loss.

   d. The various interest balances exactly offset so that no adjustment to retained earnings or to income is necessary.

3. A parent company acquires all of a subsidiary's common stock but only 70 percent of its preferred shares. This preferred stock is callable and pays a 7 percent annual cumulative dividend. No dividends are in arrears at the current time. How is the noncontrolling interest's share of the subsidiary's income computed?

   a. As 30 percent of the subsidiary's preferred dividend.

   b. No allocation is made since the dividends have been paid.

   c. As 30 percent of the subsidiary's income after all dividends have been subtracted.

   d. Income is assigned to the preferred stock based on total par value and 30 percent of that amount is allocated to the noncontrolling interest.

4. Aceton Corporation owns 80 percent of the outstanding stock of Voctax, Inc. During the current year, Voctax made $140,000 in sales to Aceton. How does this transfer affect the consolidated statement of cash flows?

   a. The transaction should be included if payment has been made.

   b. Only 80 percent of the transfers should be included because the sales were made by the subsidiary.

   c. Because the transfers were from a subsidiary organization, the cash flows are reported as investing activities.

   d. Because of the intercompany nature of the transfers, the amount is not reported in the consolidated cash flow statement.

5. Warrenton, Inc., owns 80 percent of Aminable Corporation. On a consolidated income statement, the Noncontrolling Interest in the Subsidiary's Income is reported as $37,000. Aminable paid a total cash dividend of $100,000 for the year. How does this impact the consolidated statement of cash flows?

   a. The dividends paid to the outside owners are reported as a financing activity, but the noncontrolling interest figure is not viewed as a cash flow.

   b. The noncontrolling interest figure is reported as an investing activity, but the dividends amount paid to the outside owners is omitted entirely.

    c. Neither figure is reported on the statement of cash flows.

    d. Both dividends paid and the noncontrolling interest are viewed as financing activities.

Problems 6 and 7 are based on the following information:

Comparative consolidated balance sheet data for Iverson, Inc., and its 80 percent–owned subsidiary Oakley Co. follow:

	2007	2006
Cash	$ 7,000	$ 20,000
Accounts receivable (net)	55,000	38,000
Merchandise inventory	85,000	45,000
Buildings and equipment (net)	95,000	105,000
Trademark	85,000	100,000
Totals	$327,000	$308,000
Accounts payable	$ 75,000	$ 63,000
Notes payable, long-term	–0–	25,000
Noncontrolling interest	39,000	35,000
Common stock, $10 par	200,000	200,000
Retained earnings (deficit)	13,000	(15,000)
Totals	$327,000	$308,000

Additional Information for Fiscal Year 2007

- Iverson and Oakley's consolidated net income was $40,000.
- Oakley paid $5,000 in dividends during the year.
- Oakley sold $11,000 worth of merchandise to Iverson during the year.
- There were no purchases or sales of long-term assets during the year.

In the 2007 consolidated statement of cash flows for Iverson Company:

  6. Net cash flows from operating activities were

    a. $12,000.

    b. $20,000.

    c. $24,000.

    d. $25,000.

  7. Net cash flows from financing activities were

    a. $(25,000).

    b. $(37,000).

    c. $(38,000).

    d. $(42,000).

  8. Thuoy Corporation is computing consolidated earnings per share. One of its subsidiaries has stock warrants outstanding. How do these convertible items affect the consolidated earnings per share computation?

    a. No effect is created because the stock warrants were for the shares of the subsidiary company.

    b. The stock warrants are not included in the computation unless they are antidilutive.

    c. The effect of the stock warrants must be computed in deriving the amount of subsidiary income that is to be included in making the consolidated diluted earnings per share calculation.

    d. The stock warrants are included only in basic earnings per share but never in diluted earnings per share.

  9. A parent company owns a controlling interest in a subsidiary whose stock has a book value of $31 per share. At the end of the current year, the subsidiary issues new shares entirely to outside parties at $45 per share. The parent still holds control over this subsidiary. Which of the following statements is true?

    a. Because the shares were all sold to outside parties, the parent's investment account is not affected.

    b. Because the parent now owns a smaller percentage of the subsidiary, the parent's investment account must be reduced.

    c. Because the shares were sold for more than book value, the parent's investment account must be increased.

    d. Because the sale was made at the end of the year, the parent's investment account is not affected.

10. Rodgers, Inc., owns Ferdinal Corporation. For 2007, Rodgers reports net income (without consideration of its investment in Ferdinal) of $200,000 and the subsidiary reports $80,000. The parent had a bond payable outstanding on January 1, 2007, with a book value of $212,000. The subsidiary acquired the bond on that date for $199,000. During 2007, Rodgers reported interest income of $22,000 while Ferdinal reported interest expense of $21,000. What is the consolidated net income?

    a. $266,000.

    b. $268,000.

    c. $292,000.

    d. $294,000.

11. Thompkins, Inc., owns Pastimer Company. The subsidiary had a bond payable outstanding on January 1, 2006, with a book value of $189,000. The parent acquired the bond on that date for $206,000. Subsequently, Pastimer reported interest income of $18,000 in 2006 and Thompkins reported interest expense of $21,000. Consolidated financial statements are being prepared for 2007. What adjustment is needed for the Retained Earnings balance as of January 1, 2007?

    a. Reduction of $20,000.

    b. Reduction of $14,000.

    c. Reduction of $3,000.

    d. Reduction of $22,000.

12. Ace Company reports current earnings of $400,000 while paying $40,000 in cash dividends. Byrd Company earns $100,000 in net income and distributes $10,000 in dividends. Ace has held a 70 percent interest in Byrd for several years, an investment that it originally purchased at a price equal to the book value of the underlying net assets. Ace uses the cost method to account for these shares.

    On January 1 of the current year, Byrd acquired in the open market $50,000 of Ace's 8 percent bonds. The bonds had originally been issued several years ago for 92, reflecting a 10 percent effective interest rate. On the date of purchase, the book value of the bonds payable was $48,300. Byrd paid $46,600 based on a 12 percent effective interest rate over the remaining life of the bonds.

    What is consolidated net income for this year prior to reduction for the noncontrolling interest's share of the subsidiary's net income?

    a. $492,160.

    b. $493,938.

    c. $499,160.

    d. $500,258.

13. Using the same information presented in Problem 12, what is the noncontrolling interest's share of the subsidiary's net income?

    a. $27,000.

    b. $28,290.

    c. $28,620.

    d. $30,000.

14. Able Company possesses 80 percent of the outstanding voting stock of Baker Company. Able uses the partial equity method to account for this investment. On January 1, 2003, Able sold 9 percent bonds payable with a $10 million face value (maturing in 20 years) on the open market at a premium of $600,000. On January 1, 2006, Baker acquired 40 percent of these same bonds from an outside party at 96.6 of face value. Both companies use the straight-line method of amortization. For a 2007 consolidation, what adjustment should be made to Able's beginning Retained Earnings as a result of this bond acquisition?

    a. $320,000 increase.

    b. $326,000 increase.

    c. $331,000 increase.

    d. $340,000 increase.

15. On January 1, 2006, Top Company spent a total of $4,384,000 to acquire control over Bottom Company. This price was based on paying $424,000 for 20 percent of Bottom's preferred stock and

$3,960,000 for 90 percent of its outstanding common stock. As of the date of purchase, Bottom's stockholders' equity accounts were as follows:

Preferred stock—9%, $100 par value, cumulative and participating; 10,000 shares outstanding	$1,000,000
Common stock—$50 par value; 40,000 shares outstanding	2,000,000
Retained earnings	3,000,000
Total stockholders' equity	$6,000,000

The owners of the preferred stock vote on any issues considered by the owners of the common stock.

Top believes that all of Bottom's accounts are correctly valued within the company's financial statements. What amount of consolidated goodwill should be recognized?

a. $300,000.

b. $316,000.

c. $364,000.

d. $384,000.

16. On January 1, 2006, Mitchell Company has a net book value of $1,500,000 as follows:

1,000 shares of preferred stock; par value $100 per share; cumulative, nonparticipating, nonvoting; call value $108 per share	$ 100,000
20,000 shares of common stock; par value $40 per share	800,000
Retained earnings	600,000
Total	$1,500,000

Andrews Company acquires all of the outstanding preferred shares for $106,000 and 60 percent of the common stock for $916,400. Andrews believed that one of Mitchell's buildings, with a 12-year life, was undervalued on the company's financial records by $50,000.

What amount of consolidated goodwill would be recognized from this purchase?

a. $50,000.

b. $51,200.

c. $52,400.

d. $56,000.

17. Aedion Company owns control over Breedlove, Inc. Aedion reports sales of $300,000 during 2007 and Breedlove reports $200,000. Inventory costing $20,000 was transferred from Breedlove to Aedion (upstream) during the year for $40,000. Of this amount, 25 percent is still in ending inventory at year's end. Total receivables on the consolidated balance sheet were $80,000 at the first of the year and $110,000 at year-end. No intercompany debt existed at the beginning or ending of the year. Using the direct approach, what is the consolidated amount of cash collected by the business combination from its customers?

a. $430,000.

b. $460,000.

c. $490,000.

d. $510,000.

18. Ames owns 100 percent of Nestlum, Inc. Although the Investment in Nestlum account has a balance of $596,000, the subsidiary's 12,000 shares have an underlying book value of only $40 per share. On January 1, 2007, Nestlum issues 3,000 new shares to the public for $50 per share. How does this transaction affect the Investment in Nestlum account?

a. It is not affected since the shares were sold to outside parties.

b. It should be increased by $24,000.

c. It should be decreased by $119,200.

d. It should be increased by $30,000.

Problems 19 through 21 are based on the following information:

Chapman Company purchases 80 percent of the common stock of Russell Company on January 1, 2001, when Russell has the following stockholders' equity accounts:

Common stock—40,000 shares outstanding	$100,000
Additional paid-in capital	75,000
Retained earnings	340,000
Total stockholders' equity	$515,000

To acquire this interest in Russell, Chapman pays a total of $487,000 with any excess cost being allocated to goodwill.

On January 1, 2007, Russell reports a net book value of $795,000. Chapman has accrued the increase in Russell's book value through application of the equity method.

View the following problems as independent situations:

19. On January 1, 2007, Russell issues 10,000 additional shares of common stock for $25 per share. Chapman acquires 8,000 of these shares. How will this transaction affect the Additional Paid-In Capital account of the parent company?

    a. Has no effect on it.
    b. Increases it by $20,500.
    c. Increases it by $36,400.
    d. Increases it by $82,300.

20. On January 1, 2007, Russell issues 10,000 additional shares of common stock for $15 per share. Chapman does not acquire any of this newly issued stock. How would this transaction affect the Additional Paid-In Capital account of the parent company?

    a. Has no effect on it.
    b. Increases it by $16,600.
    c. Decreases it by $31,200.
    d. Decreases it by $48,750.

21. On January 1, 2007, Russell reacquires 8,000 of the outstanding shares of its own common stock for $24 per share. None of these shares belonged to Chapman. How would this transaction affect the parent company's Additional Paid-In Capital account?

    a. Has no effect on it.
    b. Decreases it by $22,000.
    c. Decreases it by $30,500.
    d. Decreases it by $33,000.

22. The following describes a set of arrangements between TecPC Company and a special purpose entity as of December 31, 2007:

    TecPC Company has entered into agreements with a special purpose entity (SPE) to develop, construct, finance, and lease a computer chip research and development (R&D) facility. The SPE will own the R&D facility and lease it to TecPC Company after construction is completed. Payments under the operating lease are expected to commence in the first quarter of 2009.

    The SPE has an aggregate financing commitment from equity and debt participants (Investors) of $4 million and $42 million, respectively. TecPC Company, in its role as construction agent for the SPE, is responsible for completing construction by December 31, 2008. In the event the project is terminated before completion of construction, TecPC Company has the option to either purchase the project for 100 percent of project costs or terminate the project and make a payment to the SPE for 89.9 percent of project costs. Total project cost is estimated at $48 million.

    The term of the operating lease between the SPE and the TecPC Company is five years with multiple extension options. The lease is a variable rate obligation indexed to a three-month market rate. Consequently as market interest rates increase, the payments under this operating lease will also increase.

    If all extension options are exercised, the total term of the lease would be 35 years. TecPC's lease payments to the SPE are sufficient to provide a return to the Investors. TecPC Company has guaranteed a portion of the obligations of the SPE during the construction and post-construction periods.

At the end of the first five-year lease term or any extension, TecPC Company may

- Renew the lease at fair market value subject to Investor approval.
- Purchase the facility at its original construction cost.
- Sell the facility, on behalf of the SPE, to an independent third party. If the project is sold and the proceeds from the sale are insufficient to repay the Investors, TecPC Company may be required to make a payment to the SPE of up to 85 percent of the project's cost.

a. What is the purpose of a parent company consolidating its financial statements with a subsidiary?

b. When should an SPE be consolidated into another company's financial statements?

c. Identify the risks of the construction project that TecPC has effectively shifted to the owners of the SPE and those risks that remain with TecPC.

d. According to *FIN 46R* what characteristics of a primary beneficiary does TecPC possess?

23. On December 31, 2007, Pantech Company invests $20,000 in Softplus, a variable interest business entity. In contractual agreements completed on that date, Pantech established itself as the primary beneficiary of Softplus. Previously, Pantech had no interest in Softplus. Immediately after Pantech's investment, Softplus presents the following balance sheet:

Cash	$ 20,000	Long-term debt	$120,000
Marketing software	140,000	Noncontrolling interest	60,000
Computer equipment . . .	40,000	Pantech equity interest	20,000
Total assets	$200,000	Total liabilities and equity . .	$200,000

Each of the above amounts represents an assessed fair value at December 31, 2007, except for the marketing software.

a. If the marketing software was undervalued by $20,000, what reported amounts for Softplus's financial statement items would appear in Pantech's December 31, 2007, consolidated balance sheet and income statement?

b. If the marketing software was overvalued by $20,000, what reported amounts for Softplus's financial statement items would appear in Pantech's December 31, 2007, consolidated balance sheet and income statement?

24. Darges owns 51 percent of the voting stock of Walrus, Inc. The parent's interest was acquired several years ago on the date that the subsidiary was formed. Consequently, no goodwill or other allocation was recorded in connection with the purchase price.

   On January 1, 2005, Walrus sold $1,000,000 in 10-year bonds to the public at 105. The bonds had a cash interest rate of 9 percent payable every December 31. Darges acquired 40 percent of these bonds on January 1, 2007, for 96 percent of face value. Both companies utilize the straight-line method of amortization.

a. What consolidation entry would be recorded in connection with these intercompany bonds on December 31, 2007?

b. What consolidation entry would be recorded in connection with these intercompany bonds on December 31, 2008?

c. What consolidation entry would be recorded in connection with these intercompany bonds on December 31, 2009?

25. Highlight, Inc., owns all of the outstanding stock of Kiort Corporation. The two companies report the following balances for the year ending December 31, 2007:

	Highlight	Kiort
Revenues and interest income	$(670,000)	$(390,000)
Operating and interest expense	540,000	221,000
Other gains and losses	(120,000)	(32,000)
Net income	$(250,000)	$(201,000)

   On January 1, 2007, Highlight acquired bonds on the open market for $108,000 originally issued by Kiort. This investment had an effective rate of 8 percent. The bonds had a face value of $100,000 and a cash interest rate of 9 percent. At the date of acquisition, these bonds were shown as liabilities by Kiort with a book value of $84,000 (based on an effective rate of 11 percent). Determine the balances that should appear on a consolidated income statement for 2007.

26. Several years ago Absalom, Inc., sold $800,000 in bonds to the public. Annual cash interest of 8 percent ($64,000) was to be paid on this debt. The bonds were issued at a discount to yield 10 percent. At the beginning of 2007, McDowell Corporation (a wholly owned subsidiary of Absalom) purchased $100,000 of these bonds on the open market for $121,655, a price that was based on an effective interest rate of 6 percent. The bond liability had a book value on that date of $668,778.

   a. What consolidation entry would be required for these bonds on December 31, 2007?

   b. What consolidation entry would be required for these bonds on December 31, 2009?

27. Opus, Incorporated, owns 90 percent of Bloom Company. On December 31, 2007, Opus acquires half of Bloom's $500,000 in outstanding bonds. These bonds had been sold on the open market on January 1, 2005, at a 12 percent effective rate. The bonds pay a cash interest rate of 10 percent every December 31 and are scheduled to come due on December 31, 2015. Bloom issued this debt originally for $435,763. Opus paid $283,550 for this investment indicating an 8 percent effective yield.

   a. Assuming that both parties use the effective rate method, what gain or loss should be reported on the consolidated income statement for 2007 from the retirement of this debt?

   b. Assuming that both parties use the effective rate method, what balances should appear in the Investment in Bloom Bonds account on Opus's records and the Bonds Payable account of Bloom as of December 31, 2008?

   c. Assuming that both parties use the straight-line method, what consolidation entry would be required on December 31, 2008, because of these bonds? Assume that the parent is not applying the equity method.

28. Hapinst Corporation has the following stockholders' equity accounts:

Preferred stock (6% cumulative dividend)	$500,000
Common stock	750,000
Additional paid-in capital	300,000
Retained earnings	950,000

   The preferred stock is participating and, therefore, is considered an equity instrument. Westyln Corporation buys 90 percent of this common stock for $1,600,000 and 70 percent of the preferred stock for $800,000. All of the subsidiary's assets and liabilities are viewed as having fair values equal to their book values. What amount is attributed to goodwill on the date of acquisition?

29. On January 1, 2006, Mace, Inc., acquires 90 percent of the outstanding common stock of Blade Company from the company's president for $2,520,000 and 40 percent of the preferred stock for $250,000. On the date of purchase, Blade had the following stockholders' equity accounts:

Common stock	$ 800,000
Preferred stock	200,000
Retained earnings	2,000,000
Total	$3,000,000

   a. Assume that the preferred stock is both cumulative and fully participating and is, therefore, considered an equity interest. What is the total amount of goodwill to be recognized within consolidated financial statements?

   b. Assume that the preferred stock is callable at 120 percent of par value and is, therefore, considered a debt instrument. What is the total amount of goodwill to be recognized within consolidated financial statements?

   c. Assume that the preferred stock is callable at 120 percent of par value and is, therefore, considered a debt instrument. What is the total value assigned to the noncontrolling interest on the date of acquisition?

30. Smith, Inc., has the following stockholders' equity accounts as of January 1, 2007:

Preferred stock—$100 par, nonvoting and nonparticipating, 8 percent cumulative dividend	$ 2,000,000
Common stock—$20 par value	4,000,000
Retained earnings	10,000,000

   Haried Company purchases all of the common stock of Smith on January 1, 2007, for $14,040,000. The preferred stock (which is callable at 108) remains in the hands of outside parties. Any excess purchase price will be assigned to franchise contracts with a 40-year life.

During 2007, Smith reports earning $450,000 in net income and pays $360,000 in cash dividends. Haried applies the equity method to this investment.

a. What is the noncontrolling interest's share of consolidated net income for this period?

b. What is the balance in the Investment in Smith account as of December 31, 2007?

c. What consolidation entries would be needed for 2007?

31. Through the payment of $10,468,000 in cash, Drexel Company acquires voting control over Young Company. This price was paid for 60 percent of the subsidiary's 100,000 outstanding common shares ($40 par value) as well as all 10,000 shares of 8 percent, cumulative, $100 par value preferred stock. Of the total payment, $3.1 million was attributed to the fully participating and fully voting preferred stock with the remainder paid for the common. This purchase is carried out on January 1, 2006, when Young reports retained earnings of $10 million and a total book value of $15 million. On this same date, a building owned by Young (with a 5-year remaining life) is undervalued in the financial records by $200,000, while equipment with a 10-year life is overvalued by $100,000. Any excess payment is assigned to a brand name with a 20-year life.

   During 2006, Young reports net income of $900,000 while paying $400,000 in cash dividends. Drexel has used the cost method to account for both of these investments.

   Prepare consolidation entries that would be appropriate for the year of 2006.

32. The following information has been taken from the consolidation worksheet of Peak and its 90 percent–owned subsidiary, Valley:

   • Peak reports a $12,000 gain on the sale of a building. The building had a book value of $32,000 but was sold for $44,000 cash.
   • The noncontrolling interest in Valley's income is reported as $23,000.
   • Intercompany inventory transfers of $129,000 occurred during the current period.
   • A $30,000 dividend was paid by Valley during the year with $27,000 of this amount going to Peak.
   • Amortization of an intangible asset recognized by Peak's purchase was $16,000 for the current period.
   • Consolidated accounts payable decreased by $11,000 during the year.

   Indicate how each of these events is reflected on a consolidated statement of cash flows.

33. Ames Company and its 80 percent–owned subsidiary, Wallace, have the following income statements for 2007:

	Ames	Wallace
Revenues	$(500,000)	$(230,000)
Cost of goods sold	300,000	140,000
Depreciation and amortization	40,000	10,000
Other expenses	20,000	20,000
Gain on sale of equipment	(30,000)	–0–
Equity in earnings of Wallace	(48,000)	–0–
Net income	$(218,000)	$ (60,000)

Additional Information

   • Intercompany transfers during 2007 amounted to $90,000 and were downstream from Ames to Wallace.
   • Unrealized inventory gains at January 1, 2007, were $6,000, but at December 31, 2007, unrealized gains are $9,000.
   • Annual amortization expense resulting from the purchase price is $11,000.
   • Wallace paid dividends totaling $20,000.
   • The noncontrolling interest's share of the subsidiary's income is $12,000.
   • During 2007, consolidated inventory rose by $11,000 while accounts receivable and accounts payable declined by $8,000 and $6,000, respectively.

   Using either the direct or the indirect approach, determine the amount of cash generated from operations during the period by this business combination.

34. Parent Corporation owns all 30,000 shares of the common stock of Subsid, Inc. Parent has 60,000 shares of its own common stock outstanding. In 2007, Parent earns income (without any consideration of its investment in Subsid) of $150,000 while Subsid reports $130,000. Annual amortization of $10,000 is recognized each year on the consolidation worksheet based on allocations within the

original purchase price. Both companies have convertible bonds outstanding. During 2007, interest expense (net of taxes) is $32,000 for Parent and $24,000 for Subsid. Parent's bonds can be converted into 10,000 shares of common stock; Subsid's bonds can be converted into 12,000 shares. Parent owns 20 percent of Subsid's bonds (bought directly from Subsid). What are the basic and diluted earnings per share for this business combination?

35. Primus, Inc., owns all of the outstanding stock of Sonston, Inc. For 2007, Primus reports income (exclusive of any investment income) of $600,000. Primus has 100,000 shares of common stock outstanding. Sonston reports net income of $200,000 for the period with 40,000 shares of common stock outstanding. Sonston also has 10,000 stock warrants outstanding that allow the holder to acquire shares at $10 per share. The value of this stock was $20 per share throughout the year. Primus owns 2,000 of these warrants. What are the consolidated diluted earnings per share?

36. Garfun, Inc., owns all of the stock of Simon, Inc. For 2007, Garfun reports income (exclusive of any investment income) of $480,000. Garfun has 80,000 shares of common stock outstanding. Garfun also has 5,000 shares of preferred stock outstanding that pay a dividend of $15,000 per year. Simon reports net income of $290,000 for the period with 80,000 shares of common stock outstanding. Simon also has a liability for 10,000 $100 bonds that pay annual interest of $8 per bond. Each of these bonds can be converted into three shares of common stock. Garfun owns none of these bonds. Assume a tax rate of 30 percent. What is the consolidated diluted earnings per share?

37. The following separate income statements are for Mason and its 80 percent–owned subsidiary, Dixon:

	Mason	Dixon
Revenues	$(400,000)	$(300,000)
Expenses	290,000	225,000
Gain on sale of equipment	–0–	(15,000)
Equity earnings of subsidiary	(72,000)	–0–
Net income	$(182,000)	$ (90,000)
Outstanding common shares	50,000	30,000

Additional Information

- Amortization expense resulting from the purchase price paid by Mason is $20,000 per year.

- Mason has convertible preferred stock outstanding. Each of these 5,000 shares is paid a dividend of $4.00 per year. Each share can be converted into four shares of common stock.

- Stock warrants to buy 10,000 shares of Dixon are also outstanding. For $20, each warrant can be converted into a share of Dixon's common stock. The fair value of this stock is $25 throughout the year. Mason owns none of these warrants.

- Dixon has convertible bonds payable that paid interest of $30,000 (after taxes) during the year. These bonds can be exchanged for 20,000 shares of common stock. Mason holds 15 percent of these bonds, which it bought directly from Dixon.

Compute the basic and diluted earnings per share for this business combination.

38. Alice, Inc., owns 100 percent of Rughty, Inc. On Alice's books, the Investment in Rughty account currently is shown as $731,000 although the subsidiary's 40,000 shares have an underlying book value of only $12 per share.

Rughty issues 10,000 new shares to the public for $15.75 per share. How does this transaction affect the Investment in Rughty account that appears on Alice's financial records?

39. Davis, Incorporated, acquired 16,000 shares of Maxwell Company several years ago. At the present time, Maxwell is reporting $800,000 as total stockholders' equity, which is broken down as follows:

Common stock ($10 par value)	$200,000
Additional paid-in capital	230,000
Retained earnings	370,000
Total	$800,000

View the following cases as independent situations:

a. Maxwell issues 5,000 shares of previously unissued common stock to the public for $50 per share. Davis purchased none of this stock. What journal entry should Davis make to recognize the impact of this stock transaction?

b. Maxwell issues 4,000 shares of previously unissued common stock to the public for $25 per share. Davis purchased none of this stock. What journal entry should Davis make to recognize the impact of this stock transaction?

c. Maxwell issues 5,000 shares of previously unissued common stock for $42 per share. Davis purchased all of these shares. How would this transaction affect a consolidation prepared immediately thereafter?

40. On January 1, 2005, Abraham Company purchased 90 percent of the outstanding shares of Sparks Company. Sparks had a net book value on that date of $480,000: common stock ($10 par value) of $200,000 and retained earnings of $280,000. Sparks also possessed a tract of land that was undervalued by $80,000 on its financial statements.

    Abraham paid $584,000 for this investment. Any excess payment is assigned to copyrights, which are to be amortized over a 20-year period. Subsequent to the purchase, Abraham applied the cost method to its investment accounts.

    In the 2005–2006 period, the subsidiary's book value rose by $100,000. During 2007, Sparks earned income of $80,000 while paying $20,000 in dividends. Also, at the beginning of the year, Sparks issued 4,000 new shares of common stock for $36 per share to finance the expansion of its corporate facilities. None of these additional shares was sold to Abraham and, hence, it recorded no entry.

    a. Prepare the consolidation entries that would be appropriate for these two companies for the year of 2007.

    b. Assume that Sparks actually issued 5,000 new shares of stock (rather than 4,000 shares) at the beginning of 2007 for $25 per share. Abraham purchased 4,500 of these shares and recorded the acquisition at cost. Under these altered circumstances, prepare consolidation entries for 2007.

41. Giant purchases all of the outstanding shares of Little on January 1, 2004, for $460,000 in cash. Of this price, $30,000 was attributed to equipment with a 10-year remaining life and $40,000 was assigned to trademarks that will be expensed over a 20-year period. Giant applies the partial equity method so that income is accrued each period based solely on the earnings reported by the subsidiary.

    On January 1, 2007, Giant reports $200,000 in bonds outstanding with a book value of $188,000. Little purchases half of these bonds on the open market for $97,000.

    During 2007, Giant begins to sell merchandise to Little. During that year, inventory costing $80,000 was transferred at a price of $100,000. All but $10,000 (at sales price) of these goods were resold to outside parties by year-end. Little still owes $36,000 for inventory shipped from Giant during December.

    The following financial figures are for the two companies for the year ending December 31, 2007. Prepare a worksheet to produce consolidated balances. (Credits are indicated by parentheses.)

	Giant	Little
Revenues	$ (639,000)	$(466,000)
Cost of goods sold	345,000	198,000
Expenses	134,000	161,000
Interest expense—bonds	24,000	–0–
Interest income—bond investment	–0–	(11,000)
Equity in income of Little	(118,000)	–0–
Net income	$ (254,000)	$(118,000)
Retained earnings, 1/1/07	$ (345,000)	
Retained earnings, 1/1/07		$(361,000)
Net income (above)	(254,000)	(118,000)
Dividends paid	155,000	61,000
Retained earnings, 12/31/07	$ (444,000)	$(418,000)
Cash and receivables	$ 133,000	$ 78,000
Inventory	171,000	87,000
Investment in Little	608,000	–0–
Investment in Giant bonds	–0–	98,000
Land, buildings, and equipment (net)	249,000	541,000
Total assets	$ 1,161,000	$ 804,000
Accounts payable	$ (225,000)	$(166,000)
Bonds payable	(200,000)	(100,000)
Discount on bonds	8,000	–0–
Common stock	(300,000)	(120,000)
Retained earnings (above)	(444,000)	(418,000)
Total liabilities and stockholders' equity	$(1,161,000)	$(804,000)

42. Fred, Inc., and Bub Corporation formed a business combination on January 1, 2003, when Fred purchased a 60 percent interest in the common stock of Bub for $310,000 in cash. The book value of Bub's assets and liabilities on that day totaled $300,000. Patents being held by Bub (with a 12-year remaining life) were undervalued by $100,000 within the company's financial records. Any excess indicated by this acquisition is assigned to a customer list to be amortized over a 10-year period.

Intercompany inventory transfers have been made between the two companies on a regular basis. Merchandise that is carried over from one year to the next is always sold in the subsequent period.

Year	Original Cost to Bub	Transfer Price to Fred	Ending Balance at Transfer Price
2003	$ 60,000	$ 72,000	$15,000
2004	70,000	84,000	25,000
2005	80,000	100,000	20,000
2006	100,000	125,000	40,000
2007	90,000	120,000	30,000

Fred had not paid for half of the 2007 inventory transfers by the end of the year.

On January 1, 2004, Fred sold $15,000 in land to Bub for $22,000. Bub is still holding this land.

On January 1, 2007, Bub acquired $20,000 (face value) of Fred's bonds on the open market. These bonds had an 8 percent cash interest rate. On the date of repurchase, the liability was shown within Fred's records at $21,386, indicating an effective yield of 6 percent. Bub's acquisition price was $18,732 based on an effective interest rate of 10 percent.

Bub indicated earning a net income of $15,000 within its 2007 financial statements. The subsidiary also reported a beginning Retained Earnings balance of $300,000, dividends paid of $5,000, and common stock of $100,000. Bub has not issued any additional common stock since its takeover. The parent company has applied the equity method to record its investment in Bub.

a. Prepare consolidation worksheet adjustments for 2007.

b. Calculate the 2007 balance for the noncontrolling interest's share of consolidated net income. In addition, determine the ending 2007 balance for noncontrolling interest in the consolidated balance sheet.

c. Determine the consolidation worksheet adjustments needed in 2008 in connection with the intercompany bonds.

43. On January 1, 2006, Mona, Inc., purchased 80 percent of Lisa Company's common stock as well as 60 percent of its preferred shares. Mona paid $65,000 in cash for the preferred stock, which is considered a debt-type instrument (because no voting rights were granted and the stock has a call value of 110 percent of the $50 per share par value). Mona also paid $552,800 for the common stock, a price that recognized franchise contracts of $40,000. This intangible asset is being amortized over a 40-year period. Lisa pays all preferred stock dividends (a total of $8,000 per year) on an annual basis. During 2006, Lisa's book value increased by $50,000.

On January 2, 2006, Mona acquired one-half of Lisa's outstanding bonds payable to reduce the debt position of the business combination. Lisa's bonds had a face value of $100,000 and paid cash interest of 10 percent per year. These bonds had been issued to the public to yield 14 percent. Interest is paid each December 31. On January 2, 2006, these bonds payable had a total book value of $88,350. Mona paid $53,310, an amount indicating an effective interest rate of 8 percent.

On January 3, 2006, Mona sold fixed assets to Lisa. These assets had originally cost $100,000 but had accumulated depreciation of $60,000 when transferred. The transfer was made at a price of $120,000. These assets were estimated to have a remaining useful life of 10 years.

The individual financial statements for these two companies for the year ending December 31, 2007, are as follows:

	Mona, Inc.	Lisa Company
Sales and other revenues	$ (500,000)	$ (200,000)
Expenses	220,000	120,000
Dividend income—Lisa common stock	(8,000)	–0–
Dividend income—Lisa preferred stock	(4,800)	–0–
Net income	$ (292,800)	$ (80,000)
Retained earnings, 1/1/07	$ (700,000)	$ (500,000)
Net income (above)	(292,800)	(80,000)

	Mona, Inc.	Lisa Company
Dividends paid—common stock	92,800	10,000
Dividends paid—preferred stock	–0–	8,000
Retained earnings, 12/31/07	$ (900,000)	$ (562,000)
Current assets	$ 130,419	$ 500,000
Investment in Lisa—common stock	552,800	–0–
Investment in Lisa—preferred stock	65,000	–0–
Investment in Lisa—bonds	51,781	–0–
Fixed assets	1,100,000	800,000
Accumulated depreciation	(300,000)	(200,000)
Total assets	$ 1,600,000	$ 1,100,000
Accounts payable	$ (400,000)	$ (144,580)
Bonds payable	–0–	(100,000)
Discount on bonds payable	–0–	6,580
Common stock	(300,000)	(200,000)
Preferred stock	–0–	(100,000)
Retained earnings, 12/31/07	(900,000)	(562,000)
Total liabilities and equities	$(1,600,000)	$(1,100,000)

a. What consolidation worksheet adjustments would have been required as of January 1, 2006, to eliminate the subsidiary's common and preferred stocks?

b. What consolidation worksheet adjustments would have been required as of December 31, 2006, to account for Mona's purchase of Lisa's bonds?

c. What consolidation worksheet adjustments would have been required as of December 31, 2006, to account for the intercompany sale of fixed assets?

d. Assume that consolidated financial statements are being prepared for the year ending December 31, 2007. Calculate the consolidated balance for each of the following accounts:

    Franchises

    Fixed Assets

    Accumulated Depreciation

    Expenses

44. Rogers Company holds 80 percent of the common stock of Andrews, Inc., and 40 percent of this subsidiary's convertible bonds. The following consolidated financial statements are for 2007 and 2008:

Rogers Company Consolidated Subsidiary

	2007	2008
Revenues	$ (760,000)	$ (880,000)
Cost of goods sold	510,000	540,000
Depreciation and amortization	90,000	100,000
Gain on sale of building	–0–	(20,000)
Interest expense	30,000	30,000
Noncontrolling interest	9,000	11,000
Net income	$ (121,000)	$ (219,000)
Retained earnings, 1/1	$ (300,000)	$ (371,000)
Net income	(121,000)	(219,000)
Dividends paid	50,000	100,000
Retained earnings, 12/31	$ (371,000)	$ (490,000)
Cash	$ 80,000	$ 140,000
Accounts receivable	150,000	140,000
Inventory	200,000	340,000
Buildings and equipment (net)	640,000	690,000
Databases	150,000	145,000
Total assets	$1,220,000	$1,455,000

	2007	2008
Accounts payable	$ (140,000)	$ (100,000)
Bonds payable	(400,000)	(500,000)
Noncontrolling interest in Andrews	(32,000)	(41,000)
Common stock	(100,000)	(120,000)
Additional paid-in capital	(177,000)	(204,000)
Retained earnings	(371,000)	(490,000)
Total liabilities and equities	$(1,220,000)	$(1,455,000)

Additional Information

- The parent issued bonds during 2008 for cash.

- Amortization of databases amounts to $5,000 per year.

- The parent sold a building with a cost of $60,000 but a $30,000 book value for cash on May 11, 2008.

- The subsidiary purchased equipment on July 23, 2008, using cash.

- Late in November of 2008, the parent issued stock for cash.

- During 2008, the subsidiary paid dividends of $10,000.

Prepare a consolidated statement of cash flows for this business combination for the year ending December 31, 2008. Either the direct or the indirect approach may be used.

45. Following are separate income statements for Alexander, Inc., and Raleigh Corporation as well as a consolidated statement for the business combination as a whole.

	Alexander	Raleigh	Consolidated
Revenues	$(700,000)	$(500,000)	$(1,000,000)
Cost of goods sold	400,000	300,000	495,000
Operating expenses	100,000	70,000	190,000
Equity in earnings of Raleigh	(104,000)	–0–	–0–
Noncontrolling interest in			
Raleigh's income	–0–	–0–	26,000
Net income	$(304,000)	$(130,000)	$ (289,000)

Additional Information

- Intercompany inventory transfers are all downstream.

- The parent applies the partial equity method to this investment.

- Alexander has 50,000 shares of common stock and 10,000 shares of preferred stock outstanding. Owners of the preferred stock are paid an annual dividend of $40,000, and each share can be exchanged for two shares of common stock.

- Raleigh has 30,000 shares of common stock outstanding. The company also has 5,000 stock warrants outstanding. For $10, each warrant can be converted into a share of Raleigh's common stock. Alexander holds half of these warrants. The price of Raleigh's common stock was $20 per share throughout the year.

- Raleigh also has convertible bonds, none of which Alexander owned. During the current year, total interest expense (net of taxes) was $22,000. These bonds can be exchanged for 10,000 shares of the subsidiary's common stock.

Determine the basic and diluted earnings per share for this business combination.

46. On January 1, 2007, Paisley, Inc., paid $560,000 for all of the outstanding stock of Skyler Corporation. This cash payment was based on a price of $180 per share for Skyler's $100 par value preferred stock and $38 per share for the company's $20 par value common stock. The preferred shares are voting, cumulative, and fully participating; they have no set call value. At the date of purchase, the book values of Skyler's accounts equaled their fair values. Any excess payment is assigned to an intangible asset and will be amortized over a 10-year period.

During 2007, Skyler sold inventory costing $60,000 to Paisley for $90,000. All but $18,000 (measured at transfer price) of this merchandise has been resold to outsiders by the end of the year. At the end of 2007, Paisley continues to owe Skyler for the last shipment of inventory priced at $28,000.

Also, on January 2, 2007, Paisley sold equipment to Skyler for $20,000 although it had a book value of only $12,000 (original cost of $30,000). Both companies depreciate such property according to the straight-line method with no salvage value. The remaining life at this date was four years.

The following financial statements are for each company for the year ending December 31, 2007. Determine consolidated financial totals for this business combination.

	Paisley, Inc.	Skyler Corporation
Sales	$ (800,000)	$(400,000)
Costs of goods sold	528,000	260,000
Expenses	180,000	130,000
Gain on sale of equipment	(8,000)	–0–
Net income	$ (100,000)	$ (10,000)
Retained earnings, 1/1/07	$ (400,000)	$(150,000)
Net income	(100,000)	(10,000)
Dividends paid	60,000	–0–
Retained earnings, 12/31/07	$ (440,000)	$(160,000)
Cash	$ 30,000	$ 40,000
Accounts receivable	300,000	100,000
Inventory	260,000	180,000
Investment in Skyler Corporation	560,000	–0–
Land, buildings, and equipment	680,000	500,000
Accumulated depreciation	(180,000)	(90,000)
Total assets	$ 1,650,000	$ 730,000
Accounts payable	$ (140,000)	$ (90,000)
Long-term liabilities	(240,000)	(180,000)
Preferred stock	–0–	(100,000)
Common stock	(620,000)	(200,000)
Additional paid-in capital	(210,000)	–0–
Retained earnings, 12/31/07	(440,000)	(160,000)
Total liabilities and equity	$(1,650,000)	$(730,000)

Note: Parentheses indicate a credit balance.

47. On June 30, 2006, Plaster, Inc., paid $916,000 for 80 percent of the outstanding stock of Stucco Company. At the date of acquisition, Stucco Company closed its books and reported the following assets and liabilities:

Cash	$ 60,000
Accounts receivable	127,000
Inventory	203,000
Land	65,000
Buildings	175,000
Equipment	300,000
Accounts payable	(35,000)

On June 30, Plaster allocated the excess cost over book value of Stucco's net assets as follows:

Equipment (three-year life)	$ 75,000
Database (10-year life)	125,000

At the end of 2006, the following comparative (2005 and 2006) balance sheets and consolidated income statement were available:

	Plaster, Inc. December 31, 2005	Consolidated December 31, 2006
Cash	$ 43,000	$ 242,850
Accounts receivable (net)	362,000	485,400
Inventory	415,000	720,000
Land	300,000	365,000
Buildings (net)	245,000	370,000
Equipment (net)	1,800,000	2,037,500
Database	–0–	118,750
Total assets	$3,165,000	$4,339,500
Accounts payable	$ 80,000	$ 107,000
Long-term liabilities	400,000	1,200,000
Common stock	1,800,000	1,800,000
Noncontrolling interest	–0–	209,750
Retained earnings	885,000	1,022,750
Total liabilities and equities	$3,165,000	$4,339,500

PLASTER, INC., AND SUBSIDIARY STUCCO COMPANY
Consolidated Income Statement
For the Year Ended December 31, 2006

Revenues		$1,217,500
Cost of goods sold	$737,500	
Depreciation	187,500	
Database amortization	6,250	
Interest and other expenses	9,750	
Noncontrolling interest in Stucco's income	38,750	979,750
Net income		$ 237,750

Additional Information

- On December 1, 2006, Stucco paid a $40,000 dividend. During 2006, Plaster paid $100,000 in dividends.

- During 2006, Plaster issued $800,000 in long-term debt at par.

- Plaster reported no other asset purchases or dispositions during 2006 other than the acquisition of Stucco.

Prepare a 2006 consolidated statement of cash flows for Plaster and Stucco. Use the indirect method of reporting cash flows from operating activities.

Develop Your Skills

EXCEL CASE: INTERCOMPANY BONDS

Place Company owns a majority voting interest in Sassano, Inc. On January 1, 2005, Place issued $1,000,000 of 11 percent 10-year bonds at $943,497.77 to yield 12 percent. On January 1, 2007, Sassano purchased all of these bonds in the open market at a price of $904,024.59 with an effective yield of 13 percent.

Required:

Using an Excel spreadsheet, do the following:

1. Prepare amortization schedules for the Place Company bonds payable and the Investment in Place Bonds for Sassano, Inc.

2. Using the values from the amortization schedules, compute the worksheet adjustment for a December 31, 2007, consolidation of Place and Sassano to reflect the effective retirement of the

Place bonds. Formulate your solution to be able to accommodate various yield rates (and therefore prices) on the repurchase of the bonds.

Hints:

Present value of $1 = 1/(1 + r)^n$

Present value of an annuity of $1 = (1 - 1/(1 + r)^n)/r$

Where r = effective yield and n = years remaining to maturity

RESEARCH CASE

Find a recent annual report for a firm with business acquisitions (e.g., Compaq, GE) accounted for under the purchase method. Locate the firm's consolidated statement of cash flows and answer the following:

- Does the firm employ the direct or indirect method of accounting for operating cash flows?
- How does the firm account for the balances in balance sheet operating accounts (e.g., accounts receivable, inventory, accounts payable) in determining operating cash flows?
- Describe the accounting for cash paid for business acquisitions in the statement of cash flows.
- Describe the accounting for any noncontrolling subsidiary interest, acquired in-process research and development costs, and any other business combination–related items in the consolidated statement of cash flows.

FARS RESEARCH AND ANALYSIS CASE

Financial Interpretation No. 46R, "Consolidation of Variable Interest Entities," references several of the FASB Concepts Statements in motivating the need to identify and consolidate variable interest entities. *FIN 46R* also expands the traditional definition of control as provided in *Accounting Research Bulletin 51,* "Consolidated Financial Statements." Review the Summary to *FIN 46R* and explain the following:

- In what ways do the conclusions in *FIN 46R* relate to the concepts of relevance and reliability?
- How do the definitions of assets and liabilities relate to the consolidation of VIEs?
- Why is a majority voting interest insufficient evidence of a controlling financial interest in a VIE?

FINANCIAL REPORTING RESEARCH AND ANALYSIS CASE

FIN 46R affects thousands of business enterprises that now, as primary beneficiaries, consolidate entities that qualify as controlled VIEs. Retrieve the annual reports of one or more of the following companies (or any others you may find) that consolidate VIEs:

- The Walt Disney Company.
- Wyndham International.
- ConAgra Foods.
- AutoBytel.
- Monongahela Power Company.

Required:

Write a brief report that describes

1. The reasons for consolidation of the company's VIE(s).
2. The effect of the consolidation of the VIE(s) on the company's financial statements.

Chapter **Seven**

Consolidated Financial Statements— Ownership Patterns and Income Taxes

Chapter 7 concludes coverage of the accounting for business combinations by analyzing two additional aspects of consolidated financial statements. First, the various patterns of ownership that can exist within a combination are presented. We examine indirect control of a subsidiary, connecting affiliations, and mutual ownership as well as the consolidation procedures applicable to each of these organizational structures. The chapter then presents an overview of the income tax considerations relevant to the members of a business combination. We discuss income tax accounting for both consolidated and separate corporate returns in light of current laws.

> ## Questions to Consider
>
> - If a parent holds control over a subsidiary, which, in turn, owns a majority of the voting stock of another company, the parent indirectly controls both of these subsidiaries. How does this type of ownership pattern affect the consolidation process for a business combination?
>
> - If a subsidiary possesses stock of its parent company, what impact does the mutual ownership have on consolidated financial statements?
>
> - How does a business combination qualify to file a consolidated income tax return? What advantages are gained by filing in this manner?
>
> - Why does the filing of separate tax returns by the members of a business combination frequently create the need to recognize deferred income taxes?

INDIRECT SUBSIDIARY CONTROL

Previous chapters presented only one type of relationship for every business combination. Specifically, a parent has always held a direct financial interest in a single subsidiary. This ownership pattern has been assumed to expedite the explanation of consolidation theories and techniques. In actual practice, though, much more elaborate corporate structures commonly exist. General Electric Company (GE), for example, controls literally scores of subsidiaries. However, GE owns voting stock in a relatively small number of these companies. It often maintains control through indirect ownership as GE's subsidiaries hold the stock of many of the companies within this business combination. For example, GE, the parent company, owns a controlling interest in voting stock of NBC Universal, Inc., which in turn has total ownership of CNBC and other companies. This type of corporate configuration is often referred to as a *father-son-grandson relationship* (or sometimes as a *pyramid*) because of the pattern the descending tiers create.

Forming a business combination as a series of indirect ownerships is not an unusual practice. Many businesses organize their operations in this manner to group individual companies along product lines, geographic districts, or some other logical criteria. The philosophy behind this structuring is that placing direct control in proximity to each subsidiary can develop clearer lines of communication and responsibility reporting. However, other indirect ownership patterns are simply the result of years of acquisition and growth. As an example, in purchasing General Foods, Philip Morris Companies, Inc., actually gained control over a number of corporations (including Oscar Mayer Foods Corporation, Maxwell House Coffee Company, and Birds Eye, Inc.). Philip Morris did not achieve this control directly but indirectly through the acquisition of their parent company.

The Consolidation Process When Indirect Control Is Present

Regardless of a company's reason for establishing indirect control over a subsidiary, a new accounting problem occurs: The financial information generated by several connecting corporations must be consolidated into a single set of financial statements. Fortunately, indirect ownership does not introduce any new conceptual issues but affects only the mechanical elements of this process. For example, a purchase price allocation, as well as an annual amortization expense figure, must be computed and recognized for every investment. In addition, all of the worksheet entries previously demonstrated continue to apply. For business combinations involving indirect control, the entire consolidation process is basically repeated for each separate acquisition.

Calculation of Realized Income

Although the presence of an indirect ownership does not change most consolidation procedures, the isolation of each subsidiary's realized income does pose an added degree of difficulty. Appropriate determination of this figure is essential because it serves as the basis for calculating (1) equity income accruals and (2) the noncontrolling interest's share of consolidated income.

Previous chapters determined the subsidiary's realized income by adjusting reported earnings for the effects of any upstream intercompany transfers. *However, when indirect control is involved, at least one company within the business combination (and possibly many) holds both a parent and a subsidiary position.* Any company in that position must first properly recognize the equity income accruing from its subsidiaries before computing its own realized income total. This guideline is not a theoretical doctrine but merely a necessary arrangement for calculating income totals in a predetermined order. The process begins with the grandson, then moves to the son, and finishes with the father. Only by following this systematic approach can the correct amount of realized income be determined for each individual company.

Realized Income Computation Illustrated

For example, assume that three companies form a business combination: Top Company owns 70 percent of Midway Company, which, in turn, possesses 60 percent of Bottom Company. As the following display indicates, Top controls both subsidiaries, although the parent's relationship with Bottom is only of an indirect nature.

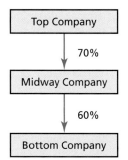

For illustration purposes, assume that the following information comes from the 2007 individual financial records of the three companies making up this combination:

	Top Company	Midway Company	Bottom Company
Operating income	$600,000	$300,000	$100,000
Dividend income from investment in subsidiary (based on cost method)	80,000	50,000	
Reported net income	$680,000	$350,000	$100,000
Additional information: Net unrealized intercompany gains within current year income	$110,000	$ 80,000	$ 20,000
Amortization expense relating to purchase price of investment	20,000	15,000	–0–

Beginning, as specified, with the grandson of the organization, we calculate each company's 2007 realized income. For example, from the perspective of the business combination, Bottom's income for the period is only $80,000 after removing the $20,000 effect of the company's unrealized intercompany gains. Thus, $80,000 is the basis for the equity accrual by its parent as well as any noncontrolling interest recognition:

Once the grandson's income has been derived, this figure then can be used to compute the realized earnings of the son, Midway:

Operating income—Midway Company	$300,000
Equity income accruing from Bottom Company— 60% of *realized* income of $80,000	48,000
Recognition of amortization expense relating to purchase of Bottom Company (above)	(15,000)
Removal of Midway's unrealized intercompany gain (above)	(80,000)
Realized income of Midway Company	$253,000

The $253,000 realized income figure determined for Midway varies significantly from the company's reported profit of $350,000. This difference is not unusual and merely results from establishing an appropriate consolidation perspective in viewing both the investment in its subsidiary and the effects of intercompany transfers. The recognition of all transactions is being brought into line with the company's vantage point within this business combination.

Continuing with this systematic calculation of each company's earnings, we now can determine Top's realized income. Only after the appropriate figure is computed for the son can the father's earnings within the business combination be derived:

Operating income—Top Company	$600,000
Equity income accruing from Midway Company— 70% of *realized* income of $253,000	177,100
Recognition of amortization expense relating to purchase of Midway Company (above)	(20,000)
Removal of Top's unrealized intercompany gain (above)	(110,000)
Realized income of Top	$647,100

Having established realized income figures for each of these three companies, we should note several aspects of these data:

1. The 2007 income statement reported for Top Company and its consolidated subsidiaries discloses a $107,900 balance as the "noncontrolling interests' share of subsidiary income."

This total is based on the realized income figures of the two subsidiaries and is computed as follows:

	Realized Income	Outside Ownership	Noncontrolling Interest in Income
Bottom Company	$ 80,000	40%	$ 32,000
Midway Company	253,000	30	75,900
Total			$107,900

2. Although this illustration applied the cost method to both of the investments, the parent's individual accounting is not a factor in determining realized income totals. The cost figures were omitted and replaced with equity accruals in preparation for consolidation. The selection of a particular method is relevant only for internal reporting purposes; computation of realized earnings, as shown here, is based entirely on the equity income accruing from each subsidiary.

3. As demonstrated previously, if appropriate equity accruals are recognized, the parent's realized income can serve as a "proof figure" for the consolidated total. Parent earnings calculated in this manner equal the net income for the entire business combination. Thus, if the consolidation process is carried out correctly, the earnings to be reported by this entire organization should equal $647,100, as indicated previously for Top.

4. Whenever indirect control is established, a discrepancy exists between the percentage of stock being held and the income contributed to the business combination by a subsidiary. In this illustration, Midway possesses 60 percent of Bottom's voting stock but, mathematically, only 42 percent of Bottom's income is attributed to Top's controlling interest (70% direct ownership of Midway × 60% indirect ownership of Bottom). The remaining income earned by this subsidiary is assigned to the owners outside of the combination.

The validity of this 42 percent accrual is one aspect of the consolidation that is not readily apparent. Therefore, we construct an elementary example to demonstrate the mathematical accuracy of this percentage. Assume that neither Top nor Midway reports any earnings during the year but that Bottom has $100 in realized income. If Bottom declares a $100 cash dividend, $60 goes to Midway and the remaining $40 goes to Bottom's noncontrolling interest. Assuming then that Midway uses this $60 to pay its own dividend, $42 (70 percent) is transferred to Top with $18 going to Midway's outside owners.

Thus, 58 percent of Bottom's income should be attributed to parties outside the business combination. An initial 40 percent belongs to Bottom's own noncontrolling interest and an additional 18 percent accrues eventually to Midway's other shareholders. Consequently, only 42 percent of Bottom's original income is considered as having been earned by the combination. Consolidated financial statements reflect this allocation by including 100 percent of the subsidiary's revenues and expenses and simultaneously recognizing a reduction for the 58 percent of the subsidiary's net income that is attributed to noncontrolling interests.

Consolidation Process—Indirect Control

Having analyzed the calculation of realized income within a father-son-grandson configuration, a full-scale consolidation now can be produced. As is demonstrated, this type of ownership pattern does not significantly alter the worksheet process. In reality, most worksheet entries are simply made twice: first for the son's investment in the grandson and then for the father's ownership of the son. Although this sudden doubling of entries can initially seem overwhelming, close examination reveals that the individual procedures remain unaffected.

As an illustration, assume that on January 1, 2005, Big purchases 80 percent of the outstanding common stock of Middle for $640,000. On that date, Middle has a book value (total stockholders' equity) of $700,000, which indicates the parent paid $80,000 in excess of the subsidiary's underlying $560,000 book value ($700,000 × 80%). This $80,000 is assigned to franchises and amortized at the rate of $2,000 per year.

EXHIBIT 7.1

Consolidation: Purchase Method
Investment: Partial Equity Method

BIG COMPANY AND CONSOLIDATED SUBSIDIARIES
Consolidation Worksheet
For Year Ending December 31, 2007

Accounts	Big Company	Middle Company	Little Company	Consolidation Entries Debit	Consolidation Entries Credit	Noncontrolling Interest	Consolidated Totals
Income Statement							
Sales	(800,000)	(500,000)	(300,000)	(LTI) 120,000 (BTI) 250,000			(1,230,000)
Cost of goods sold	300,000	220,000	140,000	(LG) 25,000	(L*G) 20,000 (LTI) 120,000 (B*G) 30,000 (BTI) 250,000		305,000
Expenses	200,000	80,000	60,000	(BG) 40,000			342,500
Income of Little Company	(216,000)			(LE) 500			-0-
Income of Middle Company		(70,000)		(BE) 2,000			-0-
Noncontrolling interest in Little Company's net income				(LI) 70,000		(28,500)	28,500
Noncontrolling interest in Middle Company's net income				(BI) 216,000		(51,200)	51,200
Net income	(516,000)	(270,000)	(100,000)				(502,800)
Statement of Retained Earnings							
Retained earnings, 1/1/07:							
Big Company	(900,000)	-0-	-0-	(B*C) 39,600 (B*G) 30,000			(860,400)
Middle Company		(800,000)		(L*C) 14,500 (BS) 755,500			-0-
Little Company			(600,000)	(L*G) 20,000 (LS) 580,000			-0-
Net income (from above)	(516,000)	(270,000)	(100,000)				(502,800)
Dividends paid:							
Big Company	120,000	-0-	-0-				120,000
Middle Company		90,000			(BD) 72,000	18,000	-0-
Little Company			50,000		(LD) 35,000	15,000	-0-
Retained earnings, 12/31/07	(1,296,000)	(980,000)	(650,000)				(1,243,200)

continued from page 318

Balance Sheet

	Big	Middle	Little	Consolidation Entries Debit	Consolidation Entries Credit	Noncontrolling Interest	Consolidated Totals
Cash and receivables	600,000	300,000	280,000				1,180,000
Investment in Middle Company	944,000	-0-	-0-	(BD) 72,000	(B*C) 39,600 (BS) 684,400 (BI) 216,000 (BA) 76,000		-0-
Investment in Little Company	-0-	566,000	-0-	(LD) 35,000	(L*C) 14,500 (LS) 497,000 (LI) 70,000 (LA) 19,500		-0-
Inventory	300,000	260,000	290,000		(LG) 25,000 (BG) 40,000		785,000
Land, buildings, equipment	192,000	154,000	510,000				856,000
Franchises	-0-	-0-	-0-	(LA) 19,500 (BA) 76,000	(LE) 500 (BE) 2,000		93,000
Total assets	2,036,000	1,280,000	1,080,000				2,914,000
Liabilities	(340,000)	(200,000)	(300,000)				(840,000)
Noncontrolling interest in Little Company, 1/1/07	-0-	-0-	-0-		(LS) 213,000	(213,000)	
Noncontrolling interest in Middle Company, 1/1/07	-0-	-0-	-0-		(BS) 171,100	(171,100)	
Total noncontrolling interest, 12/31/07	-0-	-0-	-0-			(430,800)	(430,800)
Common stock: Big Company	(400,000)						(400,000)
Middle Company	-0-	(100,000)		(BS) 100,000			-0-
Little Company	-0-	-0-	(130,000)	(LS) 130,000			-0-
Retained earnings (above)	(1,296,000)	(980,000)	(650,000)				(1,243,200)
Total liabilities and equities	(2,036,000)	(1,280,000)	(1,080,000)				(2,914,000)

Note: Parentheses indicate a credit balance.

Consolidation entries: Entries labeled with a "B" refer to the investment relationship between Big and Middle. Entries with an "L" refer to Middle's ownership of Little.

(*G) Removal of unrealized gain from beginning inventory figures so that it can be recognized in current period.

(*C) Conversion of partial equity method to equity method. Amortization for prior years is recognized along with effects of beginning unrealized upstream gains.

(S) Elimination of subsidiaries' stockholders' equity accounts along with recognition of January 1, 2007, noncontrolling interests.

(A) Allocation to franchises, unamortized balance being recognized as of January 1, 2007.

(I) Elimination of intercompany income accrued during the period.

(D) Elimination of intercompany dividends.

(E) Recognition of amortization expense for the current period.

(TI) Elimination of intercompany sales/purchases balances created by the transfer of inventory.

(G) Removal of unrealized inventory gain from ending figures so that it can be recognized in subsequent period.

Following the acquisition, Middle's book value rises to $1,080,000 by the end of 2007, denoting a $380,000 increment during this three-year period ($1,080,000 − $700,000). Big applies the partial equity method; therefore, the parent accrues a $304,000 ($380,000 × 80%) increase in the investment account (to $944,000) over this same time span.

On January 1, 2006, Middle acquires 70 percent of Little for $461,000. Little's stockholders' equity accounts total $630,000, indicating that Middle has paid $20,000 more than the applicable book value of $441,000 ($630,000 × 70%). Middle allocates this entire $20,000 to franchises so that, over a 40-year assumed life, the business combination amortization recognizes an expense of $500 each year. During 2006–2007, Little's book value increases by $150,000, to a $780,000 total. Because Middle also applies the partial equity method, it adds $105,000 ($150,000 × 70%) to the investment account to arrive at a $566,000 balance ($461,000 + $105,000).

To complete the introductory information for this illustration, assume that a number of intercompany upstream transfers occurred over the past two years. The dollar volume of these transactions is chronicled here as well as the unrealized gain in each year's ending inventory:

Year	Little Company Transfers to Middle Company		Middle Company Transfers to Big Company	
	Transfer Price	Year-End Unrealized Gain	Transfer Price	Year-End Unrealized Gain
2006	$ 75,000	$20,000	$200,000	$30,000
2007	120,000	25,000	250,000	40,000

Exhibit 7.1, on pages 318–319, presents the worksheet to consolidate these three companies for the year ending December 31, 2007. The first three columns represent the individual statements for each of the organizations. The entries required to consolidate the various balances follow this information. To help identify the separate procedures, entries concerning the relationship between Big (father) and Middle (son) are marked with a "B," whereas an "L" denotes Middle's ownership of Little (grandson). The duplication of entries in this exhibit is primarily to facilitate a clearer understanding of this consolidation. A number of these dual entries can be combined later.

To arrive at consolidated figures, Exhibit 7.1 incorporates the worksheet entries described next. Analyzing each of these adjustments and eliminations can identify the consolidation procedures necessitated by a father-son-grandson ownership pattern. Despite the presence of indirect control over Little, financial statements can be created for the business combination as a whole utilizing the process described in previous chapters.

Consolidation Entry *G

Entry *G defers the unrealized intercompany gains contained in the beginning financial figures. Within their separate accounting systems, two of the companies prematurely recorded income ($20,000 by Little and $30,000 by Middle) in 2006 at the time of transfer. For consolidation purposes, a worksheet entry must be included in 2007 to eliminate these unrealized gains from both beginning Retained Earnings as well as Cost of Goods Sold (the present location of the beginning inventory). Consequently, gross profit is appropriately recognized on the consolidated income statement of the current period.

Consolidation Entry *C

Neither Big nor Middle has applied the full equity method to its investments; therefore, the figures recognized during the years prior to the current period (2007) must now be updated on the worksheet. This process begins with the son's ownership of the grandson. Hence, Middle must reduce its 2006 income (now closed into Retained Earnings) by $500 to reflect the amortization applicable to that year. This expense would not have been recorded by Middle in applying the partial equity method.

In addition, because $20,000 of Little's previously reported earnings have just been deferred (in preceding Entry *G), the effect of this reduction on Middle's ownership must also be recognized. The parent's original equity accrual for 2006 was based on reported rather than realized profit; thus, too much income was recorded. Little's deferral necessitates a parallel $14,000 decrease ($20,000 × 70%) by Middle. Consequently, the worksheet reduces Middle's Retained Earnings balance as of January 1, 2007, as well as the Investment in Little account by a total of $14,500:

Reduction in Middle's Beginning Retained Earnings

2006 amortization expense	$ 500
Income effect created by Little's deferral of 2006 unrealized gain (reduction of previous accrual) ($20,000 × 70%)	14,000
Required reduction to Middle's beginning retained earnings (Entry **L*C**)	$14,500

A similar equity adjustment also must be made in connection with Big's ownership of Middle. The calculation of the specific amount to be recorded follows the same procedural path identified earlier for Middle's investment in Little. Once again, amortization expense for all prior years (2005 and 2006, in this case) must be brought into the consolidation as well as the income reduction created by the deferral of Middle's $30,000 unrealized gain (Entry ***G**). *However, recognition also must be given to the effects associated with the $14,500 decrease in Middle's pre-2007 earnings described in the previous paragraph.* Although recorded only on the worksheet, this adjustment is a change in Middle's originally reported income. To reflect Big's ownership of Middle, the effect of this reduction must be included in arriving at the income balances actually accruing to the parent company. Thus, a decrease of $39,600 is needed in Big's beginning Retained Earnings to establish the proper accounting for its subsidiaries:

Reduction in Big's Beginning Retained Earnings

Amortization expense relating to acquisition of Middle Company— 2005–2006 ($2,000 per year)	$ (4,000)
Income effect created by Middle Company's deferral of unrealized gain ($30,000 × 80%)	(24,000)
Income effect created by Middle Company's adjustment to its prior year's investment income ($14,500 × 80%) (above)	(11,600)
Required reduction to Big's beginning retained earnings (Entry **B*C**)	$(39,600)

Consolidation Entry S

The beginning stockholders' equity accounts of each subsidiary are eliminated here and noncontrolling interest balances as of the beginning of the year are recognized. As in previous chapters, the preliminary adjustments described earlier have directly affected the amounts involved in this entry. Because Entry ***G** removed a $20,000 beginning unrealized gain, Little's January 1, 2007, book value on the worksheet is $710,000, not $730,000. This realized total is the basis for recording a $213,000 beginning noncontrolling interest (30 percent) as well as the $497,000 elimination (70 percent) from the parent's investment account.

In a similar vein, Entries ***G** ($30,000) and ***C** ($14,500) have already decreased Middle's book value by $44,500. Thus, the beginning stockholders' equity accounts for this company are now adjusted to a total of $855,500 ($900,000 − $44,500). This balance leads to a $171,100 initial noncontrolling interest valuation (20 percent) and a $684,400 (80 percent) offset against Big's Investment in Middle account.

Consolidation Entry A

The unamortized franchise balances remaining as of January 1, 2007, are removed from the two investment accounts so that this intangible asset can be identified separately on the consolidated balance sheet. Because amortization expense for the previous periods is already recognized in Entry ***C**, only beginning totals for the year of $19,500 ($20,000 − $500) and $76,000 ($80,000 − $4,000) still remain from the original amounts paid.

Consolidation Entry I

This entry eliminates the current intercompany income figures accrued by each parent through its application of the partial equity method.

Consolidation Entry D

Intercompany dividends distributed during the year are removed here from the consolidated financial totals.

Consolidation Entry E

The annual amortization expense relating to each of the franchise balances is recorded.

Consolidation Entry TI

The intercompany sales/purchases figures created by the transfer of inventory during 2007 are eliminated on the worksheet.

Consolidation Entry G

This final consolidation entry defers the intercompany inventory gains that remain unrealized as of December 31, 2007. The profit on these transfers is removed until the merchandise is subsequently sold to unrelated parties.

Noncontrolling Interests' Share of Consolidated Income

To complete the steps that constitute this consolidation worksheet, recognition must be given to the 2007 income accruing to owners outside the business combination. This allocation is based on the realized earnings of the two subsidiaries, which, as previously discussed, is calculated beginning with the grandson (Little) followed by the son (Middle):

Little Company's Realized Income and Noncontrolling Interest

Reported operating income (from Exhibit 7.1)	$100,000
Realization of gains previously deferred from 2006 (Entry L*G)	20,000
Deferral of gains unrealized as of 12/31/07 (Entry LG)	(25,000)
Little Company's realized income, 2007	95,000
Outside ownership	30%
Noncontrolling interest in Little Company's income	$ 28,500

Middle Company's Realized Income and Noncontrolling Interest

Reported operating income (from Exhibit 7.1 after removing income of Little Company)	$200,000
Amortization expense relating to acquisition of Little Company, current year	(500)
Realization of gains previously deferred from 2006 (Entry B*G)	30,000
Deferral of gains unrealized as of 12/31/07 (Entry BG)	(40,000)
Equity income accruing from Little Company (70% of $95,000 realized income [above])	66,500
Middle Company's realized income, 2007	256,000
Outside ownership	20%
Noncontrolling interest in Middle Company's income	$ 51,200

Although computation of Big's realized earnings is not required here, as previously noted, this figure does provide a means of verifying the accuracy of the income total reported for the consolidated entity:

Big Company's Realized Income

Reported operating income (from Exhibit 7.1 after removing income of Middle Company)	$300,000
Amortization expense relating to acquisition of Middle Company, current year	(2,000)
Equity income accruing from Middle Company (80% of $256,000 realized income [above])	204,800
Big Company's realized income, 2007	$502,800

This $502,800 figure represents the income derived by the parent from its own operations plus the earnings accrued from the company's two subsidiaries (one directly owned and the other indirectly controlled). If calculated correctly, this balance equals the consolidated income of the business combination. As Exhibit 7.1 shows, the income reported by Big Company and consolidated subsidiaries does, indeed, net to this same total: $502,800. Although not completely conclusive, the agreement of these balances serves as strong evidence of the validity of the final figures on the consolidation worksheet.

INDIRECT SUBSIDIARY CONTROL—CONNECTING AFFILIATION

The father-son-grandson organization is hardly the only corporate ownership pattern that can be encountered. The number of possible configurations found in the modern world of business is almost limitless. To assist in illustrating the consolidation procedures necessitated by these alternative patterns, we briefly discuss a second basic ownership structure referred to as a *connecting affiliation.*

A connecting affiliation exists whenever two or more companies within a business combination own an interest in another member of that organization. The simplest form of this configuration is frequently drawn as a triangle:

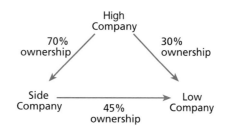

In this example, both High Company and Side Company maintain an ownership interest in Low Company, thus creating a connecting affiliation. Although neither of these individual companies possesses enough voting stock to establish direct control over Low's operations, members of the combination hold a total of 75 percent of the outstanding shares. Consequently, control lies within the boundaries of the single economic entity, and the inclusion of Low's financial information as a part of consolidated statements is necessary.

Despite the potential for numerous variations in this basic ownership pattern, the process for consolidating a connecting affiliation is essentially unchanged from that demonstrated for a father-son-grandson organization. Perhaps the most noticeable alteration is that more than two investments are always going to be present. In this triangular business combination, High possesses an ownership interest in both Side and Low while Side also maintains an investment in Low. Thus, unless combined in some manner, three separate sets of consolidation entries would appear on the worksheet. Although the added quantity of entries certainly provides a degree of mechanical complication, the basic concepts involved in the consolidation process remain the same regardless of the number of investments involved.

As with the father-son-grandson structure, one key aspect of the consolidation process warrants additional illustration: the determination of realized income figures for the individual companies. Therefore, assume that High, Side, and Low have separate operating incomes (without inclusion of any earnings from their subsidiaries) of $300,000, $200,000, and $100,000, respectively. Each company also retains a $30,000 net unrealized gain in its current year income figures. Assume further that annual amortization expense of $10,000 has been identified within the purchase price paid for each of the three investments.

In the same manner as a father-son-grandson organization, determining realized earnings should begin with any companies that are solely in a subsidiary position (Low, in this case). Next, realized income is computed for companies that are both parents as well as subsidiaries (Side). Finally, this same calculation should be made for the one company (High) that has ultimate control over the entire combination. Realized income figures for the three companies in this combination would be derived as follows:

Low Company's Realized Income and Noncontrolling Interest

Reported operating income	$100,000
Deferral of Low Company's net unrealized gain	(30,000)
Low Company's realized income	70,000
Outside ownership	25%
Noncontrolling interest in Low Company's income	$ 17,500

Side Company's Realized Income and Noncontrolling Interest

Reported operating income	$200,000
Deferral of Side Company's net unrealized gain	(30,000)
Equity income accruing from Low Company (45% of $70,000 realized income)	31,500
Amortization expense relating to Side Company's acquisition of Low Company	(10,000)
Side Company's realized income	191,500
Outside ownership	30%
Noncontrolling interest in Side Company's income	$ 57,450

High Company's Realized Income

Reported operating income	$300,000
Deferral of High Company's net unrealized gain	(30,000)
Equity income accruing from Side Company (70% of $191,500 realized income)	134,050
Amortization expense relating to High Company's acquisition of Side Company	(10,000)
Equity income accruing from Low Company—direct ownership (30% of $70,000 realized income)	21,000
Amortization expense relating to High Company's acquisition of Low Company	(10,000)
High Company's realized income (and consolidated net income)	$405,050

Even though a connecting affiliation exists in this illustration, the basic tenets of the consolidation process remain the same:

- All effects from intercompany transfers are removed.
- The parents' beginning Retained Earnings figures are adjusted to recognize the equity income resulting from ownership of the subsidiaries in prior years. The determination of realized earnings for this period is necessary to properly align the balances with the perspective of a single economic entity.
- The beginning stockholders' equity accounts of each subsidiary are eliminated and the noncontrolling interests' figures as of the first day of the year are recognized.
- All unamortized allocation balances created by the original purchase prices are entered onto the worksheet.
- Amortization expense for the current year is recorded.
- Intercompany income and dividends are removed.
- The noncontrolling interests' share of the subsidiaries' net income is computed (as just shown) and included in the financial statements of the business combination.

MUTUAL OWNERSHIP

One specific corporate structure that does require further analysis is a mutual ownership. This type of configuration exists whenever two companies within a business combination hold an equity interest in each other. This ownership pattern is sometimes created as a result of financial battles that occur during takeover attempts. A defensive strategy (often referred to as the *Pac-Man Defense*) is occasionally adopted whereby the target company attempts to avoid takeover by reversing roles and acquiring shares of its investor. Consequently, the two parties hold shares of each other with one usually gaining control.

Two typical mutual ownership patterns follow. In situation A, the parent and the subsidiary possess a percentage of each other's voting shares; in situation B, the mutual ownership exists between two subsidiary companies:

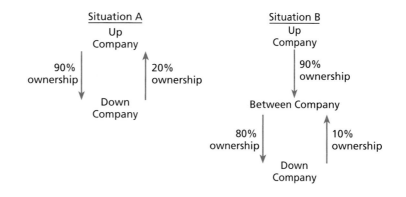

Accounting for mutual ownership raises unique conceptual issues. These concerns center on the handling of any parent company stock owned by a subsidiary. *ARB 51* (para. 12) states that "shares of the parent held by a subsidiary should not be treated as outstanding stock in the consolidated balance sheet." The 2005 FASB Exposure Draft, *Consolidated Financial Statements, Including Accounting and Reporting of Noncontrolling Interests in Subsidiaries,* agrees with this approach and recommends that "shares of the parent held by the subsidiary should be eliminated in consolidated financial statements and, therefore, should not be treated as outstanding shares in the consolidated statement of financial position" (para. 13). This guidance is theoretically appropriate because parties outside the business combination do not own the shares. Unfortunately, the actual reporting of such internally held stock can vary significantly, depending on the perspective taken as to the substance of the subsidiary's purchase. Until standard setters provide formal guidance, variations in practice will continue.

Treasury Stock Approach

Interestingly, when a subsidiary obtains parent shares, both of the prevalent methods of accounting take the same perspective: Financial reporting should not vary based on the specific identity of the purchasing agent. For consolidation purposes, no legitimate accounting distinction can be drawn between an acquisition by the parent and the same transaction if it is made by a subsidiary. However, these two methods disagree as to the underlying nature of a subsidiary's purchase of the parent's stock: Should the shares be viewed as treasury stock or as an investment?

The *treasury stock approach* assumes that both parties should account for this transaction because the parent would record a purchase of its own stock. Conversely, according to the *conventional approach,* both the parent and the subsidiary must record all intercompany investments in the same manner. Because the parent recognizes income based on its ownership of the subsidiary, the subsidiary should recognize income from an investment in the parent. Although the distinction between these two approaches seems subtle, the resulting financial figures can vary appreciably.

The treasury stock approach to mutual ownership focuses on the parent's control over the subsidiary. Even though the companies maintain separate legal incorporation, only a single economic entity actually exists, and the parent dominates it. Hence, according to proponents, either company can purchase stock or other items, but all reporting for the business combination has to be from the parent's perspective. Although the subsidiary may serve as the purchasing agent, the acquisition of parent shares is still viewed as treasury stock in the consolidated statements. This perspective is firmly grounded in the parent company concept (discussed in Chapter 4), which accounts for all transactions from the vantage point of the parent's stockholders.

Discussion **Question**

MUTUAL OWNERSHIP: WHAT DO THOSE SHARES REPRESENT?

During 2007, Pierpont Corporation began a plan to acquire control over Sandstone, Inc., a competing company of similar size. Pierpont initially made an offer of $27 per share (to be paid in a combination of cash and stock) for Sandstone's common stock. In an attempt to maintain its independence, Sandstone began a counterattack by purchasing the outstanding common stock of Pierpont on the open market. Pierpont increased its offer to $31 and, finally, to $38 per share before successfully winning control over Sandstone. Eventually, Pierpont obtained 80 percent of Sandstone's shares. However, during the takeover struggle, Sandstone managed to acquire 30 percent of Pierpont's stock (75,000 shares) at a total cost of $8 million.

Following the purchase, Sandstone remained a relatively autonomous organization. The president and administrative officers retained their positions with the company, and Sandstone's principal stockholder before the takeover is now on Pierpont's board of directors.

Sandstone's separate accounting records reported the investment in Pierpont's stock using the equity method. Thus, by the end of 2007, the asset's balance has risen to $8.7 million. Pierpont accounting officials, who currently are preparing consolidated financial statements, are attempting to determine the proper accounting for these 75,000 shares. According to the controller, "These shares are our own stock and they are being held within the business combination. The acquisition is no more than the intercompany purchase of treasury shares. Reporting should be simple; we show $8 million as the cost of treasury stock and eliminate all other related figures."

The assistant vice president for finance does not agree. "If we just remove all the balances, we will be using an income for Sandstone that has not been correctly calculated. Sandstone owns this investment and it generates a profit; that profit must be assigned to Sandstone in some manner or we are understating the income that this subsidiary's assets are producing."

The controller is not convinced: "Sandstone has no earnings from this investment. The dividends that we pay it are just intercompany cash transfers, and Sandstone should not even be recognizing equity income accruals. We control it; Sandstone certainly does not have significant influence over us."

In computing the noncontrolling interest in Sandstone's income, how should the ownership of these 75,000 shares affect the determination of the subsidiary's realized income?

In present accounting practice, the treasury stock approach appears to predominate, although this popularity is undoubtedly based as much on the ease of application as on theoretical merit. *The cost of parent shares held by the subsidiary is merely reclassified on the worksheet into a treasury stock account.* Any dividend payments on this stock are considered intercompany cash transfers that must be eliminated. This reporting technique is simple and the shares are, indeed, no longer accounted for as if they were outstanding.

Conventional Approach

The conventional approach provides a different view of a subsidiary's ownership of parent shares. This alternative theory presumes that the acquisition of parent stock is no more than another equity purchase made in one of the affiliated companies within a business combination. Thus, the consolidation of a mutual ownership should parallel the process that has been demonstrated already for a connecting affiliation: Two investments are present rather than one. *In effect, this argument contends that accounting for the parent's investment and a subsidiary's investment by totally different methods is inconsistent.*

Proponents of the conventional approach believe that introducing a unique process, such as the treasury stock approach, simply because of the subsidiary's location within the corporate structure is not justified. To rectify this situation, the internally held shares of the parent company are consolidated in the same manner as an investment in a subsidiary. The conventional approach is aligned with the economic unit concept, which contends that each company should be accounted for as an individual component within the business combination.

Probably the most distinctive aspect of the conventional approach is the determination of realized income figures. Because of the mutual ownership, each company occupies both a parent and a subsidiary position within the combination. Immediately, this relationship creates a paradox. The income of neither company can be computed first; each partially depends on the final balance of the other. Unlike the previous indirect ownership examples, no systematic calculation of earnings is possible. Rather, only by solving two simultaneous equations can we derive mutual income accruals.

Clearly, these two approaches represent alternative perceptions of the same event: the subsidiary's purchase of parent stock. However, the underlying question here concerns the theoretical concept that should provide the basis for consolidated statements. What is the purpose of a consolidation and for whom are the financial statements prepared? After these central issues have been resolved, the handling of mutual ownerships (as well as other theoretical concerns) should follow as logical extensions of the selected concept.

Mutual Ownership Illustrated

To illustrate both the treasury stock and the conventional approaches, assume that on January 1, 2005, Sun Company purchased 10 percent of Pop Company. Sun paid $120,000 for these shares, an amount that exactly equaled the proportionate book value of Pop. Many possible reasons exist for this transaction. The acquisition could be simply an investment or an attempt to forestall a takeover move by Pop. Regardless, Sun subsequently accounts for these shares according to *SFAS 115*. To simplify the illustration, it is assumed that Pop's shares are not traded actively and therefore continuous market values are unavailable. Under these circumstances, Sun's books appropriately carry the investment in Pop at original cost.

On January 1, 2006, Pop managed to gain control over Sun by acquiring a 70 percent ownership interest, thus creating a business combination. Details of Pop's purchase are as follows:

Purchase price of 70% interest, 1/1/06 . . . . $500,000
Sun Company's reported book value, 1/1/06 600,000
Excess cost over book value—assumed to be paid for franchise contracts . . . . . . 40-year life
   Investment is being accounted for internally by means of the cost method.

During the ensuing years, these two companies report the following balances and transactions:

	Sun Company			Pop Company		
Year	Reported Operating Income	Dividend Income (10 percent ownership)	Dividends Paid	Reported Operating Income	Dividend Income (70 percent ownership)	Dividends Paid
2005	$20,000	$3,000	$ 8,000	$ 90,000	–0–	$30,000
2006	30,000	5,000	10,000	130,000	$ 7,000	50,000
2007	40,000	7,000	15,000	160,000	10,500	70,000

Treasury Stock Approach Illustrated

Exhibit 7.2 presents one possible consolidation of Pop and Sun for the year 2007. This worksheet has been developed under the treasury stock approach to mutual ownerships so that Pop's investment in Sun is consolidated along routine lines. This process begins with the determination of the excess purchase price to be assigned to franchise contracts:

Purchase price . . . . $ 500,000
Proportionate interest in Sun's book value ($600,000 × 70%) . . . . (420,000)
Franchises, January 1, 2006 . . . . $ 80,000
Annual amortization—40-year life . . . . $ 2,000
Unamortized balance, January 1, 2007 . . . . $ 78,000

EXHIBIT 7.2

Investment: Cost Method
Mutual Ownership:
Treasury Stock Approach

POP AND CONSOLIDATED SUBSIDIARY
Consolidation Worksheet
For Year Ending December 31, 2007

Accounts	Pop Company	Sun Company	Consolidation Entries Debit	Consolidation Entries Credit	Noncontrolling Interest	Consolidated Totals
Income Statement						
Revenues	(900,000)	(400,000)				(1,300,000)
Expenses	740,000	360,000	(E) 2,000			1,102,000
Dividend income	(10,500)	(7,000)	(I) 17,500			–0–
Noncontrolling interest in Sun Company's income ($47,000 × 30%)	–0–	–0–			(14,100)	14,100
Net income	(170,500)	(47,000)				(183,900)
Statement of Retained Earnings						
Retained earnings, 1/1/07:						
Pop Company	(747,000)	–0–	(*C) 15,500			(762,500)
Sun Company	–0–	(425,000)	(S) 425,000			–0–
Net income (above)	(170,500)	(47,000)				(183,900)
Dividends paid:						
Pop Company	70,000	–0–	(I) 7,000			63,000
Sun Company	–0–	15,000	(I) 10,500	4,500		–0–
Retained earnings, 12/31/07	(847,500)	(457,000)				(883,400)
Balance Sheet						
Current assets	855,500	331,000				1,186,500
Investment in Sun Company	500,000	–0–	(*C) 15,500	(S) 437,500		–0–
				(A) 78,000		
Investment in Pop Company	–0–	120,000		(TS) 120,000		–0–
Land, buildings, equipment (net)	642,000	516,000				1,158,000
Franchises	–0–	–0–	(A) 78,000	(E) 2,000		76,000
Total assets	1,997,500	967,000				2,420,500
Liabilities	(550,000)	(310,000)				(860,000)
Noncontrolling interest in Sun Company, 1/1/07	–0–	–0–		(S) 187,500	(187,500)	
Noncontrolling interest in Sun Company, 12/31/07	–0–	–0–			(197,100)	(197,100)
Common stock	(600,000)	(200,000)	(S) 200,000			(600,000)
Retained earnings, 12/31/07 (above)	(847,500)	(457,000)				(883,400)
Treasury stock	–0–	–0–	(TS) 120,000			120,000
Total liabilities and equities	(1,997,500)	(967,000)				(2,420,500)

Note: Parentheses indicate a credit balance.
Consolidation entries:
(*C) Conversion of cost method to equity method. This entry recognizes 70 percent of the 2006 increase in Sun Company's book value ($25,000 × 70% = $17,500) less $2,000 amortization expense applicable to that year.
(S) Elimination of subsidiary's stockholders' equity accounts along with recognition of January 1, 2007, noncontrolling interest.
(TS) Reclassification of Sun Company's ownership in Pop Company into a treasury stock account.
(A) Allocation to franchises, unamortized balance being recorded as of January 1, 2007.
(I) Elimination of intercompany dividend income for the period.
(E) Recognition of amortization expense for the current year.

Following the calculation of the franchise value and amortization, regular worksheet entries can be developed for Pop's investment. Because the cost method is applied, the $7,000 dividend income recognized in the prior years of ownership (only 2006, in this case) is converted to an equity accrual in Entry ***C**. The parent should recognize 70 percent of the subsidiary's $35,000 income for 2006, or $24,500.[1] However, inclusion of the $2,000 amortization expense (computed earlier) dictates that $22,500 is the appropriate equity accrual. Because the parent has already recognized $7,000 in dividend income, Entry ***C** records the necessary increase as $15,500 ($22,500 − $7,000).[2]

The remaining entries relating to Pop's investment are standard: The stockholders' equity accounts of the subsidiary are eliminated (Entry **S**), the franchises' allocation is recognized (Entry **A**), and so on. The existence of the mutual ownership actually affects only two facets of Exhibit 7.2. First, the $120,000 payment made by Sun for the parent's shares is reclassified into a treasury stock account (through Entry **TS**). Second, the $7,000 intercompany dividend flowing from Pop to Sun during the current year of 2007 is eliminated within Entry **I** (Entry **I** is used because the collection was recorded as income). The simplicity of applying the treasury stock approach should be apparent from this one example.

Before leaving the treasury stock approach, a final comment needs to be made in connection with the computation of the noncontrolling interest's share of Sun's income. In Exhibit 7.2, this balance is recorded as $14,100, or 30 percent of the subsidiary's $47,000 net income figure. A question can be raised as to the validity of including the $7,000 dividend within this income total since that payment is eliminated within the consolidation.

These dividends, although intercompany in nature, do increase the subsidiary company's book value (see footnote 1). Therefore, the increment must be reflected in some manner to indicate the change in the amount attributed to the outside owners. For example, the increase could be recognized as a direct adjustment of $2,100 (30 percent of $7,000) in the noncontrolling interest balance being reported. More often, as shown here, such cash transfers are considered to be income *when viewed from the perspective of these other unrelated parties.*

Conventional Approach Illustrated

Exhibit 7.3 presents the consolidation of this same business combination based on the conventional method of reporting mutual holdings. Although many aspects of the worksheet also are routine, several entries involve procedures unique to the conventional approach. These distinctive elements concern the investment income accruals recorded for both Pop and Sun. According to the conventional approach, these figures must be calculated by identical methods to avoid any inconsistency.

Because each of the stock purchases is maintained at cost, equity accruals (Entry ***C**) must be established to correct the recording of all pre-2007 investment earnings. This process should begin with the earliest acquisition: the purchase made by Sun. According to the schedule presented previously, Sun reported $23,000 in total earnings (operating income plus dividends) for 2005. However, based on the data given, Sun's *realized* income for that year was actually $29,000: its own $20,000 operating profit plus an accrual of 10 percent of Pop's earnings ($9,000, or 10 percent of $90,000). To record the appropriate investment income for this

---

[1] Although an intercompany transfer, the $5,000 dividend received from Pop is included here in measuring the subsidiary's previous income. This cash distribution increased Sun's book value; thus, some accounting must be made within the consolidation process. In addition, at the time of payment, the parent reduced its Retained Earnings. Hence, the intercompany portion of this dividend has to be reinstated or consolidated Retained Earnings will be too low.

[2] The necessary adjustment to beginning retained earnings also can be computed as follows:

Income of subsidiary—2006	$ 35,000
Dividends paid	(10,000)
Increase in book value	$ 25,000
Ownership percentage	70%
Income accrual	$ 17,500
Amortization—2006	(2,000)
Increase in beginning retained earnings	$ 15,500

EXHIBIT 7.3

			Consolidation Entries			
Investment: Cost Method *Mutual Ownership:* *Conventional Approach*	**POP AND CONSOLIDATED SUBSIDIARY** **Consolidation Worksheet** **For Year Ending December 31, 2007**					

POP AND CONSOLIDATED SUBSIDIARY
Consolidation Worksheet
For Year Ending December 31, 2007

Accounts	Pop Company	Sun Company	Debit	Credit	Noncontrolling Interest	Consolidated Totals
Income Statement						
Revenues	(900,000)	(400,000)				(1,300,000)
Expenses	740,000	360,000	(E) 1,895			1,101,895
Dividend income	(10,500)	(7,000)	(I) 17,500			–0–
Noncontrolling interest in Sun Company's income	–0–	–0–			(18,003)	18,003
Net income	(170,500)	(47,000)				(180,102)
Statement of Retained Earnings						
Retained earnings, 1/1/07:						
Pop Company	(747,000)	–0–	(SS) 77,033	(*C2) 23,328		(693,295)
Sun Company	–0–	(425,000)	(S) 442,033	(*C1) 17,033		–0–
Net income (above)	(170,500)	(47,000)				
	(180,102)					
Dividends paid:						
Pop Company	70,000	–0–		(I) 7,000		63,000
Sun Company	–0–	15,000		(I) 10,500	4,500	–0–
Retained earnings, 12/31/07	(847,500)	(457,000)				(810,397)
Balance Sheet						
Current assets	855,500	331,000				1,186,500
Investment in Sun Company	500,000	–0–	(*C2) 23,328	(S) 449,423		–0–
				(A) 73,905		
Investment in Pop Company	–0–	120,000	(*C1) 17,033	(SS) 137,033		–0–
Land, buildings, equipment (net)	642,000	516,000				1,158,000
Franchises	–0–	–0–	(A) 73,905	(E) 1,895		72,010
Total assets	1,997,500	967,000				2,416,510
Liabilities	(550,000)	(310,000)				(860,000)
Noncontrolling interest in Sun Company, 1/1/07	–0–	–0–		(S) 192,610	(192,610)	
Noncontrolling interest in Sun Company, 12/31/07					(206,113)	(206,113)
Common stock:						
Pop Company	(600,000)		(SS) 60,000			(540,000)
Sun Company		(200,000)	(S) 200,000			–0–
Retained earnings, 12/31/07 (above)	(847,500)	(457,000)				(810,397)
Total liabilities and equities	(1,997,500)	(967,000)				(2,416,510)

Note: Parentheses indicate a credit balance.

Consolidation entries:

(*C1)   Conversion of cost method to equity method for Sun's investment in Pop. This accrual for prior years (2005–2006) is computed by solving a set of simultaneous equations.

(*C2)   Conversion of cost method to equity method for Pop's investment in Sun. This accrual for the prior year (2006) is computed by solving a set of simultaneous equations.

(S)   Elimination of subsidiary's stockholders' equity accounts along with recognition of January 1, 2007, noncontrolling interest.

(SS)   Elimination of 10 percent of Pop's stockholders' equity in recognition of intercompany holdings of Sun.

(A)   Allocation to franchises, unamortized balance being recorded as of January 1, 2007.

(I)   Elimination of intercompany dividend income for the period.

(E)   Recognition of amortization expense for the current year.

initial period, the worksheet must include a $6,000 ($29,000 − $23,000) increase in Sun's beginning Retained Earnings. No special difficulty is encountered in arriving at this first amount because the mutual ownership did not yet exist in 2005.

Before leaving this 2005 adjustment, the validity of making an equity income accrual for a time period in which only 10 percent ownership was maintained warrants an explanation. The business combination formed by these two companies did not come into existence until Pop's subsequent purchase on January 1, 2006.

Despite the limited level of ownership at the time, a $6,000 equity accrual is still required for 2005 to report the subsequently created combination. As discussed in Chapter 1, retrospective adjustment to the equity method is mandated when such changes occur in the relationship between two companies. Only by applying this approach consistently can comparable financial statements be produced from year to year. Consequently, this $6,000 income accrual is recorded within the 2007 consolidation as an increase in the subsidiary's beginning Retained Earnings. The amount is included as a component of Entry ***C1** found on the worksheet.

The creation of the mutual ownership makes computation of equity income accruals significantly more involved in 2006. Because neither company's realized earnings can be determined first, they must be solved simultaneously. The following set of equations provides the appropriate realized income figures for each company:

Sun's realized income

$$= \text{Sun's operating income} + 10\% \text{ of Pop's realized income}$$

and

Pop's realized income

$$= \text{Pop's operating income} + 70\% \text{ of Sun's realized income}$$

Only two of the balances needed in these equations are available for 2006. Sun's operating income for this year already has been reported as $30,000, and Pop's profits amounted to $128,105. The total for Pop comes from the $130,000 figure indicated previously for 2006 less $1,895 in amortization expense relating to its investment in Sun. This expense differs from the annual $2,000 charge previously derived in producing Exhibit 7.2. The change is necessary because the $6,000 accrual attributed earlier to Sun for 2005 alters the realized book value of the subsidiary to $606,000 on the date of the parent's purchase. This adjustment, based on application of the conventional approach, was not made in the treasury stock approach.

Purchase price—70% of Sun Company		$ 500,000
Proportionate interest in Sun Company's book value:		
Reported book value, 1/1/06	$600,000	
Adjustment to book value—2005 equity income		
accrual relating to investment	6,000	
Adjusted book value, 1/1/06	606,000	
Ownership interest	70%	(424,200)
Excess assumed to be paid for franchises		$ 75,800
Annual amortization—40-year life		$ 1,895

By inserting the two operating income figures, the simultaneous equations can be restated as follows. SRI and PRI are used here to indicate Sun's realized income and Pop's realized income, respectively:

$$\text{SRI} = \$30,000 + 10\% \text{ of PRI}$$

and

$$\text{PRI} = \$128,105 + 70\% \text{ of SRI}$$

To arrive at a single equation containing only one unknown, the equivalency of PRI formulated in the second equation can be used as a replacement within the first. In addition, to facilitate making the necessary mathematical computations, all percentages are restated in their decimal equivalents. Through these two alterations, the first equation can be solved to derive Sun's realized income for 2006 (note ownership percentages are expressed in decimal form):

$$SRI = \$30,000 + 0.10\ (\$128,105 + 0.70\ SRI)$$
$$SRI = \$30,000 + \$12,810.50 + 0.07\ SRI$$
$$0.93\ SRI = \$42,810.50$$
$$SRI = \$46,033\ (rounded)$$

A quick comparison of Sun's 2006 realized income of $46,033 with the reported earnings of $35,000 (from operations and dividends) indicates a required increase in the subsidiary's Retained Earnings of $11,033. *This increment properly records Sun's 2006 income derived from the investment in the parent company.* Thus, to consolidate the pre-2007 earnings of Sun, a total increase of $17,033 is recognized in Entry ***C1** as of January 1, 2007, $6,000 in connection with 2005, and $11,033 for 2006.

Accrual of Sun's Equity Income for Years Prior to 2007

Year	Sun's Realized Income	Sun's Reported Income	Accrual
2005	$29,000	$23,000	$ 6,000
2006	46,033	35,000	11,033
Total increase in subsidiary's 2007 beginning retained earnings—Entry ***C1**			$17,033

The conventional approach also requires a 2006 equity accrual for Pop's income because of the mutual ownership at that time. This adjustment must be determined in an identical manner. The second simultaneous equation is incorporated for this purpose along with the appropriate replacement from the first:

$$PRI = \$128,105 + 0.70\ (\$30,000 + 0.10\ PRI)$$
$$PRI = \$128,105 + \$21,000 + 0.07\ PRI$$
$$0.93\ PRI = \$149,105$$
$$PRI = \$160,328\ (rounded)$$

Based on this calculated total of $160,328, Pop's originally reported income of $137,000 (operations plus dividends) must be updated on the worksheet by $23,328 (Entry ***C2**). This adjustment correctly includes the 2006 income earned from the investment in the subsidiary in the consolidated Retained Earnings.

Having accounted for the pre-2007 operations of this business combination, the remaining consolidation entries utilized in Exhibit 7.3 are mostly routine. However, the elimination of Sun's Investment in Pop (Entry **SS**) merits further attention. The worksheet shows the parent with beginning Stockholders' Equity for 2007 of $1,370,328: Common Stock of $600,000 plus a January 1 Retained Earnings balance of $770,328 (after increasing the previously recorded income through Entry ***C2**). Because Sun's original purchase price was equal to Pop's proportionate book value, the newly adjusted investment balance of $137,033 necessarily equates to 10 percent of this same total. The investment was 10 percent of Pop's book value when acquired, and Entry ***C1** (based on the solution of the simultaneous equations) maintains this agreement.

Consequently, we can eliminate Sun's investment account through a direct write-off against this portion of Pop's Stockholders' Equity; 10 percent of the company's Common Stock, and 10 percent of its beginning Retained Earnings are eliminated on the worksheet (Entry **SS**). Although this process is more complicated than recording the cost of the intercompany purchase as treasury stock, the same goal is achieved: Parent shares that the subsidiary holds are not reported as outstanding on the consolidated statements. However, income is assigned to the subsidiary in the same manner that Pop used in recognizing income on its investment.

One final aspect of the consolidation process presented in Exhibit 7.3 should be analyzed: the 2007 computation of the noncontrolling interest in Sun's income (shown on the worksheet as $18,003). As in all previous illustrations, this allocation is based on the realized income of the subsidiary. However, under the conventional approach, the figure must be determined by solving two simultaneous equations. For this computation, Pop's operating income for the period ($160,000) has, once again, been reduced by $1,895 of amortization:

$$SRI = \$40{,}000 + 10\% \text{ of PRI}$$

and

$$PRI = \$158{,}105 + 70\% \text{ of SRI}$$

therefore

$$SRI = \$40{,}000 + 0.10 \,(\$158{,}105 + 0.70\,SRI)$$
$$SRI = \$40{,}000 + \$15{,}810.50 + 0.07\,SRI$$
$$0.93\,SRI = \$55{,}810.50$$
$$SRI = \$60{,}011 \text{ (rounded)}$$

The subsidiary's realized income is $60,011. Because the noncontrolling interest possesses 30 percent of Sun's voting stock, $18,003 ($60,011 × 30%) of the consolidated income is assigned to these outside owners. This balance varies significantly from the $14,100 allocation calculated under the treasury stock approach and recognized in Exhibit 7.2. Indeed, several consolidated totals (retained earnings, net income, etc.) will differ depending on the method adopted. Under the conventional approach, a portion of the parent's income is being assigned to the subsidiary. Consequently, a higher realized earnings figure is normally calculated for the subsidiary each year, an increase that produces an impact on the consolidated income balances.

Although the discussion here focuses exclusively on mutual ownerships between a parent and a subsidiary, similar relationships can exist between two subsidiaries within a business combination. The consolidation principles applicable in this circumstance remain substantially unaltered. The only major difference created by this configuration is that the treasury stock approach is no longer a viable option because parent shares are not being held. Rather, the conventional approach must be utilized based, once again, on determining realized income figures through the solution of two simultaneous equations.

INCOME TAX ACCOUNTING FOR A BUSINESS COMBINATION

Up to this point, this textbook has not attempted to analyze the income tax implications involved in corporate mergers and acquisitions. Numerous complexities inherent in the tax laws in this area necessitate that only a comprehensive tax course can provide complete coverage. Furthermore, essential accounting issues can become overshadowed by intermingling an explanation of the financial reporting process with an in-depth study of related tax consequences.

Thus, coverage to this point of business combinations and consolidated financial statements has been designed solely to develop a basic understanding of the reporting required when one company gains control over another. The effort to isolate the examination of conceptual accounting matters is not intended to minimize the importance of the tax laws as they concern consolidated entities. In reality, one of the motives behind the creation of many business combinations is the reduction of tax liabilities.

Despite the desire to focus attention on basic accounting issues, income taxes can never be ignored. Certain elements of the tax laws have a direct impact on the financial reporting of any business combination. At a minimum, recognition of current income tax expense figures as well as deferred income taxes is required to present fairly the financial statements of the consolidated entity. Therefore, an introduction to the income taxation of a business combination is necessary for a complete understanding of the financial reporting process.

Affiliated Groups

A central issue in accounting for the income taxes of a business combination is the method by which to file the entity's tax returns. Many combinations require only a single consolidated return whereas in other cases, some, or even all, of the component corporations prepare separate returns. According to current tax laws, a business combination may elect to file a consolidated return encompassing all companies that compose an *affiliated group* as defined by the Internal Revenue Code. The Code automatically requires all other corporations to submit separate income tax returns. Consequently, a first step in working with the taxation process is to delineate the boundaries of an affiliated group. Because of specific requirements outlined in the tax laws, this designation does not necessarily cover the same constituents as a business combination.

According to the Internal Revenue Code, the essential criterion for including a subsidiary within an affiliated group is the parent's ownership of at least 80 percent of the voting stock as well as at least 80 percent of each class of nonvoting stock. This ownership may be direct or indirect, although the parent must meet these requirements in connection with at least one directly owned subsidiary. As another condition, each company included in the affiliated group must be a domestic (rather than a foreign) corporation. A company's options can be described as follows:

- Domestic subsidiary, 80 percent to 100 percent owned: May file as part of consolidated return or may file separately.
- Domestic subsidiary, less than 80 percent owned: Must file separately.
- Foreign subsidiary: Must file separately.

Clearly, a distinction can be drawn between business combinations (identified for financial reporting) and affiliated groups as defined for tax purposes. Chapter 2 described a business combination as containing all subsidiaries controlled by a parent company unless control was only temporary. The possession (either directly or indirectly) of a mere majority of voting stock normally supports control. Conversely, the 80 percent rule established by the Internal Revenue Code creates a smaller circle of companies qualifying for inclusion in an affiliated group.

For the companies that compose an affiliated group, the filing of a consolidated tax return provides several distinct benefits:

- Intercompany profits are not taxed until realized (through use or sale to an outside party), and in a similar manner, intercompany losses (which are rare) are not deducted until finally culminated.
- Intercompany dividends are nontaxable (this exclusion applies to all dividends between members of an affiliated group regardless of whether a consolidated return is filed).
- Losses incurred by one affiliated company can be used to reduce taxable income earned by other members of that group.

Many companies can't resist the lure of consolidated tax returns. When corporate parent companies file such returns, they can offset profits with losses from any members of their affiliated groups.[3]

Deferred Income Taxes

Some of the deviations between generally accepted accounting principles and income tax laws create *temporary differences* whereby (1) a variation between an asset or liability's recorded book value and its tax basis exists and (2) this difference results in taxable or deductible amounts in future years. Whenever a temporary difference is present, the recognition of a deferred tax asset or liability is required for financial reporting purposes. The specific amount of this income tax deferral depends somewhat on whether consolidated or separate returns are being filed. Thus, we analyze here the tax consequences of several

---

[3] *Journal of Accountancy,* Tax Briefs, October 1993.

common transactions as a means of demonstrating the recording of income tax expense by a business combination.

Intercompany Dividends

For financial reporting, dividends between the members of a business combination always are eliminated; they represent intercompany transfers of cash. In tax accounting, dividends also are removed from income but only if at least 80 percent of the subsidiary's stock is held. Consequently, with this level of ownership, no difference exists between financial and tax reporting; all intercompany dividends are eliminated in both cases. Income tax expense is not recorded. Deferred tax recognition is also ignored because no temporary difference has been created.

However, if less than 80 percent of a subsidiary's stock is held, tax recognition becomes necessary. Any intercompany dividends are taxed partially because, at that level of ownership, 20 percent is taxable. The dividends-received deduction on the tax return (the nontaxable portion) is only 80 percent.[4] Thus, an income tax liability is immediately created for the recipient. *In addition, deferred income taxes are required for any of the subsidiary's income not paid currently as a dividend.* A temporary difference has been created because tax payments will be necessary in future years when the earnings of this investment eventually are distributed to the parent. Hence, a current tax liability is recorded based on the dividends collected, and a deferred tax liability is recorded for the taxable portion of any income not paid to the parent during the year.

The Impact of Goodwill

Prior to 1993, goodwill costs were not deductible for tax purposes. However, the Revenue Reconciliation Act of 1993 allowed the amortization of goodwill and other purchased intangibles (referred to as *Section 197 property*) over a 15-year period. For financial reporting, goodwill is written off if it is impaired or if the related business is disposed of in some manner. Because of the difference in the periods in which taxable income and financial income are reduced, the presence of goodwill creates a temporary difference that necessitates the recognition of deferred income taxes. The same is true for other purchased intangibles if a life other than 15 years is used for financial reporting.

Unrealized Intercompany Gains

Taxes on the unrealized gains that can result from transfers made between the related companies within a business combination create a special accounting problem. On consolidated financial statements, the impact of all such transactions is deferred. The same handling is true for a consolidated tax return; the gains are removed until realized. No temporary difference is created.

If separate returns are filed, though, tax laws require the profits to be reported in the period of transfer even though unearned by the business combination. Thus, the income is taxed immediately, prior to being earned from a financial reporting perspective. This "prepayment" of the tax creates a deferred income tax asset.[5]

Consolidated Tax Returns—Illustration

As an illustration of the accounting effects created by the filing of a consolidated tax return, assume that Great Company possesses 90 percent of Small Company's voting and nonvoting stocks. Subsequent to the acquisition, the two companies continued normal operations, which included significant intercompany transactions. Each company's operational and dividend

---

[4] If less than 20 percent of a company's stock is owned, the dividends-received deduction is only 70 percent. However, this level of ownership is not applicable to a subsidiary within a business combination.

[5] In *SFAS 109,* the FASB required deferral of the amount of taxes paid on the unrealized gain by the seller. This approach was taken rather than computing the deferral based on the future tax effect caused by the difference between the buyer's book value and tax basis, a procedure consistent with the rest of the pronouncement. According to paragraph 124, this decision was made to help "eliminate the need for complex cross-currency deferred tax computations" when the parties are in separate tax jurisdictions.

incomes for the current time period follow, as well as the effects of unrealized gains. No income tax accruals have been recognized within these totals:

	Great Company	Small Company (90% owned)
Operating income (excludes equity or dividend income from subsidiary)	$160,000	$40,000
Net unrealized gains in current year income (included in operating income above)	30,000	8,000
Dividend income (from Small)	9,000	–0–
Dividends paid	20,000	10,000

From the perspective of the single economic entity, Great's individual income for the period amounts to $130,000, $160,000 in operational earnings less $30,000 in unrealized gains. Using this same approach, Small's income is $32,000 after removing the effects of the intercompany transfers ($40,000 operating income less $8,000 in unrealized gains). Thus, the income to be reported in consolidated financial statements before the reduction for noncontrolling interest is $162,000 ($130,000 + $32,000). For financial reporting, both intercompany dividends and unrealized gains have been omitted in arriving at this total. Income prior to the noncontrolling interest has been computed here because any allocation to these other owners is not deductible for tax purposes.

Because the parent owns more than 80 percent of Small's stock, the dividends collected from the subsidiary are tax free. Likewise, the intercompany gains are not taxable presently since a consolidated return is being filed. Hence, *financial and tax accounting are the same for both items;* neither of these figures produces a temporary difference so that recognition of a deferred income tax is ignored.

The affiliated group pays taxes on $162,000 and, assuming an effective rate of 30 percent, must convey $48,600 ($162,000 × 30%) to the government this year. Because no temporary differences are present, deferred income tax recognition is not applicable. Consequently, $48,600 is the only expense reported in connection with current income. This amount should be recorded as the income tax expense for the consolidated entity by means of a worksheet entry or through an individual accrual recorded by each company.

Assigning Income Tax Expense—Consolidated Return

Whenever a consolidated tax return is filed, an allocation of the total expense between the two parties must be determined. This figure is especially important to the subsidiary if it has to produce separate financial statements for a loan or a future issuance of equity. The subsidiary's expense also is needed as a basis for calculating the noncontrolling interest's share of consolidated income.

Several techniques exist to accomplish this proration. For example, the expense charged to the subsidiary often is based on the percentage of the total taxable income that comes from each company (the percentage allocation method) or on the taxable income figures that would be appropriate if separate returns were filed (the separate return method).

To illustrate, we again use the figures from Great and Small shown in the previous example. Great owned 90 percent of Small's outstanding stock. Based on filing a consolidated return, total income tax expense of $48,600 was recognized. How should these two companies allocate this figure?

Percentage Allocation Method

Total taxable income on this consolidated return was $162,000. Of this amount, $130,000 applied to the parent (operating income after deferral of unrealized gain), and $32,000 came from the subsidiary (computed in the same manner). Thus, 19.753 percent ($32,000/$162,000) of total expense should be assigned to the subsidiary, an amount that equals $9,600 (19.753 percent of $48,600).

Separate Return Method

On separate returns, intercompany gains are taxable. Therefore, the separate returns of these two companies would appear as follows:

	Great	Small	Total
Operating income	$160,000	$40,000	
Assumed tax rate	30%	30%	
Income tax expense—separate returns	$ 48,000	$12,000	$60,000

By filing a consolidated return, an expense of only $48,600 is recorded for the business combination. Because 20 percent of income tax expense on the separate returns ($12,000/$60,000) came from the subsidiary, $9,720 of the expense ($48,600 × 20%) should be assigned to Small.

Under this second approach, the noncontrolling interest's share of this subsidiary's income is computed as follows:

Small Company—reported income	$40,000
Less: Unrealized intercompany gains	(8,000)
Less: Assigned income tax expense	(9,720)
Small Company—realized income	22,280
Outside ownership	10%
Noncontrolling interest in Small Company's income	$ 2,228

Filing Separate Tax Returns

Despite the advantages of filing as an affiliated group, a single consolidated return cannot always encompass every member of a business combination. Separate returns are mandatory for foreign subsidiaries and for domestic corporations not meeting the 80 percent ownership rule. However, even if it meets the conditions for inclusion within an affiliated group, a company may still elect to file separately. If all companies in an affiliated group are profitable and few intercompany transactions occur, they could prefer separate returns. By filing in this manner, the various companies have more flexibility in their choice of accounting methods as well as fiscal tax years.[6] Tax laws, though, do not allow a company to switch back and forth between consolidated and separate returns. Once a company elects to file a consolidated tax return as part of an affiliated group, obtaining permission from the Internal Revenue Service to file separately can be difficult.

The filing of a separate tax return by a member of a business combination often creates temporary differences because of (1) the immediate taxation of unrealized gains (and losses) and (2) the possible future tax effect of any subsidiary income in excess of dividend payments. Because temporary differences can result, recognition of a deferred tax asset or liability can be necessary. For example, as mentioned previously, intercompany gains and losses must be included on a separate return at the time of transfer rather than when the earning process is culminated. These gains and losses appear on both sets of records but, if unrealized at year's end, in different time periods. The temporary difference produced between the transferred asset's book value and tax basis affects future tax computations; thus, deferred taxes must be reported.

For dividend payments, deferred taxes are not required if 80 percent or more of the subsidiary's stock is owned. The transfer is nontaxable even on a separate return; no expense recognition is required.

If the amount distributed by a subsidiary that is less than 80 percent owned is equal to current earnings, 20 percent of the collection is taxed immediately, but no temporary difference

---

[6] At one time, the filing of separate returns was especially popular as a means of taking advantage of reduced tax rates on lower income levels. However, Congress eliminated the availability of this tax savings.

is created because no future tax effect is produced. Hence, again, deferred income tax recognition is not appropriate.

Conceptually, though, as discussed in Chapter 1, questions arise about the recognition of deferred taxes when a subsidiary less than 80 percent owned pays less in dividends than its current income. If a subsidiary earns $100,000, for example, but pays dividends of only $60,000, will the parent's share of the $40,000 remainder ever become taxable income? Do these undistributed earnings represent temporary differences? If so, immediate recognition of the associated tax effect is required even though payment of this $40,000 is not anticipated for the foreseeable future.

In response to these concerns, *FASB Statement No. 109*, "Accounting for Income Taxes," February 1992 (para. 32), states that "a deferred tax liability shall be recognized for . . . an excess of the amount for financial reporting over the tax basis of an investment in a domestic subsidiary." Therefore, other than one exception noted later in this chapter, any portion of the subsidiary's income not distributed in the form of dividends creates a temporary difference. These earnings would not be taxed until a later date; thus, a deferred tax liability is created. Because many companies retain a substantial portion of their income to finance growth, an expense is recognized here that could never be paid.

Deferred Tax on Undistributed Earnings—Illustrated

Accounting for the income tax effect created by undistributed earnings probably is demonstrated best through a practical example. Assume that Parent Company owns 70 percent of Child Company. Because ownership is less than 80 percent, filing separate tax returns for the two companies is mandatory. In the current year, Parent's operational earnings (excluding taxes and any income from this investment) amount to $200,000, and Child reports a pretax net income of $100,000. During the period, the subsidiary paid a total of $20,000 in cash dividends, $14,000 (70 percent) to Parent, and the remainder going to the other owners. To avoid complications in this initial example, the assumption is made that no unrealized intercompany gains and losses are present.

The reporting of Child's income taxes does not provide a significant difficulty because it involves no temporary differences. Using an assumed tax rate of 30 percent, the subsidiary accrues income tax expense of $30,000 ($100,000 × 30%), leaving an after-tax profit of $70,000. *Because only $20,000 in dividends was paid, undistributed earnings for the period amount to $50,000.*

For Parent, Child's undistributed earnings represent a temporary tax difference. The following schedules have been developed to calculate Parent's current tax liability and deferred tax liability:

Income Tax Currently Payable—Parent Company

Reported operating income—Parent Company		$200,000
Dividends received	$ 14,000	
Less: Dividend deduction (80%)	(11,200)	2,800
Taxable income—current year		202,800
Tax rate		30%
Income tax payable—current period (Parent)		$ 60,840

Deferred Income Tax Payable—Parent Company

Undistributed earnings of Child Company	$ 50,000
Parent Company's ownership	70%
Undistributed earnings accruing to Parent	35,000
Dividend deduction upon eventual distribution (80%)	(28,000)
Income to be taxed—subsequent dividend payments	7,000
Tax rate	30%
Deferred income tax payable	$ 2,100

These computations indicate a total income tax expense of $62,940: a current liability of $60,840 and a deferred liability of $2,100. The deferred balance results entirely from Child's undistributed earnings. Although the subsidiary had an after-tax income of $70,000, it distributed only $20,000 in the form of dividends. According to *FASB Statement 109,* just quoted, the $50,000 that Child retained represents a temporary tax difference to the stockholders. Thus, recognition of the deferred income tax associated with these undistributed earnings is required. The income is earned now; therefore, the liability must be recorded in the current period.

FASB Statement 109 is not completely inflexible on this matter; in connection with a subsidiary's undistributed income, it provides one important exception to the recognition of deferred income taxes. The pronouncement (para. 31) states that a deferred tax liability is not recognized for the excess of the amount for financial reporting over the tax basis of an investment in a *foreign* subsidiary unless the reversal of those temporary differences in the foreseeable future becomes apparent.

Thus, in the previous example, if the subsidiary is foreign and if the retention of these excess earnings seems to be permanent, the $2,100 deferred tax liability is omitted, reducing the total reported expense to $60,840.

Separate Tax Returns Illustrated

The full accounting impact created by the filing of separate tax returns is demonstrated best by a complete example. As a basis for this illustration, assume that Lion Corporation reported the following data with its 60 percent owned subsidiary, Cub Company (a domestic corporation), for the year 2007:

	Lion Corporation	Cub Company (60% owned by Lion)
Operating income	$500,000	$200,000
Unrealized intercompany inventory gains (included in operating income)	40,000	30,000
Dividend income from Cub Company	24,000	Not applicable
Dividends paid	Not applicable	40,000
Applicable tax rate	30%	30%

Subsidiary's Income Tax Expense   Because the companies must file separate tax returns, they do not defer the unrealized gains but leave them in both companies' operating incomes. Thus, Cub's taxable income for 2007 is $200,000, an amount that creates a current payable of $60,000 ($200,000 × 30%). The unrealized gain is a temporary difference for financial reporting purposes, creating a deferred income tax asset (payment of the tax comes before the income actually is earned) of $9,000 ($30,000 × 30%). Therefore, the appropriate expense to be recognized by the subsidiary for the period is only $51,000:

Income Tax Expense—Cub

Income currently taxable	$200,000	
Tax rate	30%	$60,000
Temporary difference (unrealized gain is taxed before being earned)	(30,000)	
Tax rate	30%	(9,000)
Income tax expense—Cub		$51,000

Consequently, Cub reports after-tax income of $119,000 ($200,000 operating income less $30,000 unrealized gain less $51,000 in income tax expense). This profit figure serves as the basis for recognizing $47,600 ($119,000 × 40% outside ownership) as the noncontrolling interest's share of consolidated income.

Parent's Income Tax Expense   On Lion's separate return, its own unrealized gains remain within income. The taxable portion of the dividends received from Cub also must be included. Hence, the parent's taxable earnings for 2007 would be $504,800, a balance that creates a $151,440 current tax liability for the company:

Income Tax Currently Payable—Lion

Operating income—Lion Corporation (includes $40,000 unrealized gains)		$500,000
Dividends received from Cub Company (60%)	$24,000	
Less: 80% dividend deduction	(19,200)	4,800
Taxable income		504,800
Tax rate		30%
Income tax payable—current (Lion)		$151,440

Although Lion's tax return information is presented here, the total tax expense to be reported for the period can be determined only by accounting for the impact of the two temporary differences: the parent's $40,000 in unrealized gains and the undistributed earnings of the subsidiary. The undistributed earnings amount to $47,400, computed as follows:

After-tax income of Cub (above)	$119,000
Dividends paid	(40,000)
Undistributed earnings	79,000
Lion's ownership	60%
Lion's portion of undistributed earnings	$ 47,400

The deferred income tax effects to be recorded by the parent now can be derived:

Deferred Income Taxes—Lion Company

Unrealized Gains

Amount taxable now prior to being earned	$40,000
Tax rate	30%
Deferred income tax asset	$12,000

Undistributed Earnings of Subsidiary

Undistributed earnings of Cub—to be taxed later (computed above)	$ 47,400
Dividend-received deduction upon distribution (80%)	(37,920)
Income eventually taxable	9,480
Tax rate	30%
Deferred income tax liability	$ 2,844

The two temporary differences exert opposite effects on Lion's reported income taxes. Because separate returns are filed, the unrealized gains are taxable in the current period despite not actually having been earned. From an accounting perspective, paying the tax on these gains now creates a deferred income tax asset of $12,000 ($40,000 × 30%). In contrast, the parent currently recognizes the undistributed earnings (through consolidation of the investment). However, this portion of the subsidiary's income is not yet taxable to the parent. Because the tax payment is not required until the dividends are received, a deferred income tax liability of $2,844 is necessary ($9,480 × 30%).

The deferred tax asset is reported as a current asset because it relates to inventory whereas the deferred tax liability is long-term because ownership of the investment created it. Lion's reported income tax expense results from the creation of these three accounts:

Lion's Financial Records		
Deferred Income Tax Asset—Current	12,000	
Income Tax Expense	142,284	
Deferred Income Tax Liability—Long-Term		2,844
Income Tax Currently Payable		151,440
To record current and deferred taxes of parent company.		

Temporary Differences Generated by Business Combinations

Based on the nature of the transaction, the tax laws deem some purchase combinations to be tax free (to the seller) whereas they deem others to be taxable. In most tax-free purchases and in a few taxable purchases, the resulting book values of the acquired company's assets and liabilities differ from their tax bases. Such differences result because the subsidiary's cost is retained for tax purposes (in tax-free exchanges) or because the allocations for tax purposes vary from those used for financial reporting (a situation found in some taxable transactions).

Thus, formation of a business combination can create temporary differences. Any deferred income tax assets and liabilities previously recorded by the subsidiary are not at issue; these accounts are consolidated in the same manner as other assets and liabilities. The question addressed here concerns differences in book value and tax basis that stem from the takeover.

As an illustration, assume that Son Company owns a single asset, a building. This property has a tax basis of $150,000 (cost less accumulated depreciation), but it presently has a fair value of $210,000. Pop Corporation conveys a total value of $300,000 to acquire this company. The exchange is structured to be tax free. After this transaction, the building continues to have a tax basis of only $150,000. However, its consolidated book value is $210,000, an amount $60,000 more than the figure applicable for tax purposes. How does this $60,000 difference affect the consolidated statements?

In 1992, the FASB issued *Statement of Financial Accounting Standards No. 109*, "Accounting for Income Taxes," which established guidelines for the reporting of deferred income tax assets and liabilities created in a business combination. According to paragraph 127:

> Values are assigned to identified assets and liabilities when a business combination is accounted for as a purchase. The assigned values frequently will be different from the tax bases of those assets and liabilities. The Board concluded that a liability or asset should be recognized for the deferred tax consequences of differences between the assigned values and the tax bases of the assets and liabilities (other than goodwill and leveraged leases) recognized in a purchase business combination.

Thus, according to this pronouncement, any temporary difference such as is found in Pop's purchase of Son creates a deferred tax asset or liability. Because the tax basis of the asset is $150,000 but its recorded value within consolidated statements is $210,000, a temporary difference of $60,000 exists. Assuming that a 30 percent tax rate is appropriate, a deferred income tax liability of $18,000 ($60,000 × 30%) must be recognized by the newly formed business combination. Before *Statement 109*, this $18,000 would have been reported as a reduction in the consolidated value of the Buildings account. However, a liability is recorded now to reflect the future effect of recognizing lower depreciation for tax purposes (thus creating higher taxable income and additional payments). The FASB also apparently believed that this placement was more consistent with the asset and liability approach required by *Statement 109*.

Consequently, in a consolidated balance sheet prepared immediately after Pop obtains control over Son, the building would be recorded at fair value of $210,000. In addition, the new deferred tax liability of $18,000 computed earlier is recognized. Because the net value of these two accounts is $192,000, goodwill of $108,000 also is recorded as the figure remaining from the $300,000 purchase price.

This $18,000 liability systematically declines to zero over the life of the building. Depreciation for tax purposes must be computed on the $150,000 cost figure and would, therefore, be less each year than the expense shown for financial reporting purposes (based on $210,000). With less expense, taxable income would be more than book income for the remaining years of the asset's life. However, according to *Statement 109,* the extra payment that results is not charged to expense. Rather, the deferred tax liability (initially established at the date of purchase) is reduced by the additional amount:

To illustrate, assume that revenues of $40,000 per year are generated from this building. Assume also that it has a life of 10 years and that the straight-line method of depreciation is in use:

	Financial Reporting	Income Tax Reporting
Revenues	$40,000	$40,000
Depreciation expense:		
10% of $210,000	21,000	
10% of $150,000		15,000
Income	19,000	25,000
Tax rate	30%	30%
Tax effect	$ 5,700	$ 7,500

Although $7,500 must be paid to the government, currently reported income would have caused only $5,700 of that amount. The other $1,800 ($6,000 reversal of temporary difference × 30%) resulted because of the use of the previous basis for tax purposes. Therefore, the following entry is made:

Income Tax Expense	5,700	
Deferred Income Tax Liability (to remove part of balance created at date of purchase)	1,800	
Income Tax Currently Payable		7,500
To accrue current income taxes as well as impact of temporary difference in asset of subsidiary.		

Business Combinations and Operating Loss Carryforwards

Tax laws in the United States provide a measure of relief for companies incurring net operating losses (NOLs) when filing current tax returns. Such losses may be carried back for two years and applied as a reduction to taxable income figures previously reported. This procedure generates a cash refund of income taxes paid by the company during these earlier periods.

If a loss still exists after the carryback (or if the taxpayer elects not to carry the loss back), a carryforward for the subsequent 20 years also is allowed.[7] Carrying the loss forward reduces subsequent taxable income levels until the NOL is eliminated entirely or the time period expires. *Thus, NOL carryforwards can benefit the company only if taxable income can be generated in the future.* The immediate recognition of NOL carryforwards has always been controversial because it requires the company to anticipate making profits. *Statement 109* of the Financial Accounting Standards Board establishes reporting rules for the appropriate recognition of such carryforwards.

---

[7] If a taxpayer believes that tax rates will be higher in the future, choosing not to carry a loss back in favor of only a carryforward could be financially preferable.

Until recently, some business combinations were created, at least in part, to take advantage of tax carryforwards. If an acquired company had an unused NOL while the parent projected significant profitability, the carryforward was used on a consolidated return to reduce income taxes after the acquisition. U.S. laws have now been changed so that virtually all of an NOL carryforward can be used only by the company that reported the loss. Hence, the acquisition of companies with an NOL carryforward has ceased to be a popular business strategy. However, because the practice has not disappeared, reporting rules for a subsidiary's NOL carryforward are still needed.

Statement 109 requires the recording of a deferred income tax asset for any NOL carryforward. In addition, though, a valuation allowance also must be recognized

> if, based on the weight of available evidence, it is *more likely than not* (a likelihood of more than 50 percent) that some portion or all of the deferred tax assets will not be realized. The valuation allowance should be sufficient to reduce the deferred tax asset to the amount that is more likely than not to be realized. (para. 17e)

As an example, assume that a company has one asset (a building) worth $500,000. Because of recent losses, this company has an NOL carryforward of $200,000. The assumed tax rate is 30 percent so that a benefit of $60,000 ($200,000 × 30%) will be derived if future taxable profits are earned.

Assume that the parent purchased this company for $640,000. In accounting for the acquisition, the parent must anticipate the likelihood that some portion or all of the NOL carryforward will ever be utilized by the new subsidiary. If it is more likely than not that the benefit will be realized, goodwill of $80,000 results:

Purchase price		$640,000
Subsidiary assets:		
Building	$500,000	
Deferred income tax asset	60,000	560,000
Goodwill		$ 80,000

Conversely, if the chances that this subsidiary will use the NOL carryforward are only 50 percent or less, a valuation allowance must be recognized and consolidated goodwill is $140,000:

Purchase price			$640,000
Subsidiary assets:			
Building		$500,000	
Deferred income tax asset	$ 60,000		
Valuation allowance	(60,000)	–0–	500,000
Goodwill			$140,000

In this second case, a question arises if this carryforward successfully reduces future taxes: How should the valuation allowance be removed? *Statement 109* requires that these subsequent benefits be recorded as a reduction to goodwill. Only if this asset is decreased to zero should income tax expense be reduced.

Summary

1. For consolidation purposes, a parent need not possess majority ownership of each of the component companies constituting a business combination. Often control is indirect: One subsidiary owns a majority of an affiliated subsidiary's shares. Although the parent might own stock in only one of these companies, control has been established over both. Such an arrangement often is referred to as a *father-son-grandson* or a *pyramid configuration.*

2. The consolidation of financial information for a father-son-grandson business combination does not differ conceptually from a consolidation involving only direct ownership. All intercompany, reciprocal balances are eliminated. Goodwill, other allocations, and amortization usually must be recognized if a purchase has taken place. Because more than one investment is involved, the quantity of worksheet entries increases, but that is more of a mechanical inconvenience than a conceptual concern.

3. One aspect of a father-son-grandson consolidation that does warrant attention is the determination of realized income figures for each of the subsidiaries. Any company within a business combination that holds both a parent and subsidiary position must determine the income accruing from ownership of its subsidiary before computing its own realized earnings. This procedure is important because realized income is the basis for each parent's equity accruals as well as noncontrolling interest allocations.

4. If a subsidiary possesses shares of its parent, a mutual affiliation exists. Although this investment is intercompany in nature and must be eliminated for consolidation purposes, the amount to be removed and the income allocated to the subsidiary can be computed in two different ways. The treasury stock approach simply reclassifies the cost of these shares as treasury stock with no equity accrual being recorded. In contrast, the conventional approach accounts for the shares as a regular investment in a related party. Under this second method, equity income accruals are attributed to the subsidiary in connection with ownership of the parent. Because the companies are both in parent and subsidiary positions, the amount of realized income cannot be directly derived by either party. These figures can be found only by solving two simultaneous equations.

5. Under present tax laws, a single consolidated income tax return can be filed by an affiliated group. Only domestic corporations are included, and 80 percent of the voting stock as well as 80 percent of the nonvoting stock must be controlled (either directly or indirectly) by the parent. A consolidated return allows the companies to defer recognition of intercompany gains until realized. Furthermore, losses incurred by one member of the group reduce taxable income earned by the others. Intercompany dividends are also nontaxable on a consolidated return, although such distributions are never taxable when paid between companies within an affiliated group.

6. For some members of a business combination, separate tax returns are applicable. Foreign corporations, as an example, must report in this manner as well as any company not meeting the 80 percent ownership rule. In addition, a company might simply elect to file in this manner if no advantages are gained from a consolidated return. For financial reporting purposes, a separate return often necessitates recognition of deferred income taxes because temporary differences can result from unrealized transfer gains as well as intercompany dividends (if 80 percent ownership is not held).

7. When a purchase combination is created, the subsidiary's assets and liabilities sometimes have a tax basis that differs from their assigned values. In such cases, a deferred tax asset or liability must be recognized at the time of acquisition to reflect the tax impact of these differences.

Comprehensive Illustration

PROBLEM

(Estimated Time: 60 to 75 Minutes) On January 1, 2005, Gold Company purchased 90 percent of Silver Company for $570,000. Within the price, $30,000 was assigned to an intangible asset, a cost that is to be expensed over a 15-year period at the rate of $2,000 per year.

Subsequently, on January 1, 2006, Silver acquired 10 percent of Gold for $150,000. This price equaled the appropriately adjusted book value of Gold's underlying net assets. Consequently, no allocation was made to either goodwill or any specific accounts.

On January 1, 2007, Gold and Silver each purchased 30 percent of the outstanding shares of Bronze for $105,000 apiece. Bronze had a book value on that date of $300,000, so the underlying book value of each acquisition was $90,000 ($300,000 × 30%). The excess $15,000 in each investment is assigned to an intangible asset and is to be amortized over a 15-year period, necessitating an annual expense of $1,000 for Gold and Silver.

After the formation of this business combination, significant intercompany inventory sales were made from Silver to Gold. The volume of these transfers has been as follows:

Year	Transfer Price to Gold Company	Markup on Transfer Price	Inventory Retained at End of Year (at transfer price)
2005	$100,000	30%	$ 60,000
2006	160,000	25	90,000
2007	200,000	28	120,000

In addition, on July 1, 2007, Gold sold a tract of land to Bronze for $25,000. This property originally had cost $12,000 when acquired by the parent several years ago.

The cost method is used to account for all investments. The individual firms recognize income from the investments when dividends are received. Because consolidated statements are prepared for the business combination, accounting for the investments affects internal reporting only. During 2005 and 2006, Gold and Silver individually reported the following information:

	Gold Company	Silver Company
2005:		
Operational income	$180,000	$120,000
Dividend income—Silver Company (90%)	36,000	–0–
Dividends paid	80,000	40,000
2006:		
Operational income	240,000	150,000
Dividend income—Gold Company (10%)	–0–	9,000
Dividend income—Silver Company (90%)	27,000	–0–
Dividends paid	90,000	30,000

The 2007 financial statements for each of the three companies comprising this business combination are presented in Exhibit 7.4. Income tax effects have been ignored in deriving these figures.

Required:

a. Prepare worksheet entries to consolidate the 2007 financial statements for this combination. Assume that the mutual ownership between Gold and Silver is accounted for by means of the conventional approach. Compute the noncontrolling interests in Bronze's income and in Silver's income.

b. Assume that consolidated net income (before deducting any balance for the noncontrolling interests) amounts to $501,900. Assume further that the effective tax rate is 40 percent and that Gold and Silver file a consolidated tax return but Bronze files separately. Calculate the income tax expense to be recognized within the consolidated income statement for 2007.

EXHIBIT 7.4
Individual Financial Statements—2007

	Gold Company	Silver Company	Bronze Company
Sales	$ (800,000)	$ (600,000)	$ (300,000)
Cost of goods sold	380,000	300,000	120,000
Operating expenses	193,000	100,000	90,000
Gain on sale of land	(13,000)	–0–	–0–
Dividend income from Gold Company	–0–	(10,000)	–0–
Dividend income from Silver Company	(36,000)	–0–	–0–
Dividend income from Bronze Company	(6,000)	(6,000)	–0–
Net income	$ (282,000)	$ (216,000)	$ (90,000)
Retained earnings, 1/1/07	$ (923,200)	$ (609,000)	$ (200,000)
Net income (above)	(282,000)	(216,000)	(90,000)
Dividends paid	100,000	40,000	20,000
Retained earnings, 12/31/07	$(1,105,200)	$ (785,000)	$ (270,000)
Cash and receivables	$ 295,000	$ 190,000	$ 130,000
Inventory	459,000	410,000	110,000
Investment in Silver Company	570,000	–0–	–0–
Investment in Gold Company	–0–	150,000	–0–
Investment in Bronze Company	105,000	105,000	–0–
Land, buildings, and equipment (net)	980,000	670,000	380,000
Total assets	$ 2,409,000	$ 1,525,000	$ 620,000
Liabilities	$ (603,800)	$ (540,000)	$ (250,000)
Common stock	(700,000)	(200,000)	(100,000)
Retained earnings, 12/31/07	(1,105,200)	(785,000)	(270,000)
Total liabilities and equities	$(2,409,000)	$(1,525,000)	$ (620,000)

SOLUTION

a. The 2007 consolidation entries for Gold, Silver, and Bronze follow.

Entry *G

The consolidation process begins with Entry ***G,** which recognizes the intercompany gain (on transfers from Silver to Gold) created in the previous period. The unrealized gain within ending inventory is deferred from the previous period into the current period:

Consolidation Entry *G

Retained earnings, 1/1/07 (Silver Company)	22,500	
Cost of goods sold		22,500

To recognize gains on intercompany sales made from Silver to Gold during the preceding year (25% markup × $90,000).

Entry *C1

Gold's ownership of Silver has been recorded using the cost method. This worksheet entry converts that number to a balance appropriate for the equity method. According to the information provided, Gold has recognized dividend income from its 90 percent investment in Silver in the amounts of $36,000 (2005) and $27,000 (2006). However, Silver's total operational income for these prior years, after adjustment for intercompany transfers, amounted to $102,000 and $145,500, respectively:

2005 reported operational income—Silver	$120,000
Less: Unrealized gains (30% markup × $60,000)	(18,000)
2005 operational income—Silver	$102,000
2006 reported operational income—Silver	$150,000
Add: 2005 gains actually realized in 2006 (from above)	18,000
Less: 2006 unrealized gains (25% markup × $90,000)	(22,500)
2006 operational income—Silver	$145,500

Because the mutual relationship between these two companies did not exist in 2005, the solving of simultaneous equations is not applicable for this initial period. Gold's equity income can be computed directly: 90 percent of Silver's $102,000 in realized earnings ($91,800) less the $2,000 amortization expense associated with this acquisition. The resulting $89,800 balance indicates the need for an additional accrual of $53,800 on the worksheet to correct the $36,000 figure recognized by Gold.

In contrast, Gold's 2006 equity accrual should reflect the mutual relationship that has come into existence. As the conventional approach is to be applied, simultaneous equations will be incorporated. These equations include Silver's 2006 operational income of $145,500 (calculated above) and the $238,000 operational income of Gold (reported earnings for the year less the annual amortization expense):

Gold's 2006 realized income = $238,000 + 90% of Silver's realized income

and

Silver's 2006 realized income = $145,500 + 10% of Gold's realized income

therefore

GRI = $238,000 + 0.90 ($145,500 + 0.10 GRI)
GRI = $238,000 + $130,950 + 0.09 GRI
0.91 GRI = $368,950
Gold's realized income = $405,440 (rounded)

Gold recorded income in 2006 of only $267,000 ($240,000 from operations plus $27,000 in dividend income). Its realized income is computed to be $405,440 here; therefore, an additional accrual of $138,440 ($405,440 − $267,000) is required to reflect ownership in Silver during this period. Combined with the $53,800 accrual calculated previously for 2005, a total worksheet adjustment of $192,240 must be made for Gold (Entry ***C1**) to recognize the appropriate equity income for these two prior years:

Consolidation Entry *C1 (Gold)

Investment in Silver Company	192,240	
Retained Earnings, 1/1/07 (Gold Company)		192,240

To convert Gold's investment income figures for the two preceding
years to equity income accruals.

*Entry *C2*

At the beginning of 2006, Silver obtained a 10 percent interest in Gold, an investment that also has been recorded using the cost method. To apply the conventional approach, Silver must solve the same simultaneous equations as Gold to determine the correct equity accrual. Using these equations, a realized income figure for Silver of $186,044 can be calculated for 2006:

$$SRI = \$145,500 + 10\% \text{ of GRI}$$

and

$$GRI = \$238,000 + 90\% \text{ of SRI}$$

therefore

$$SRI = \$145,500 + 0.10 (\$238,000 + 0.90 \text{ SRI})$$
$$SRI = \$145,500 + \$23,800 + 0.09 \text{ SRI}$$
$$0.91 \text{ SRI} = \$169,300$$
$$\text{Silver's 2006 realized income} = \$186,044 \text{ (rounded)}$$

Consequently, total investment income of $40,544 ($186,044 realized earnings less $145,500 operating income) should be recognized by Silver for 2006. However, only the $9,000 received in the form of dividends actually was recorded during that period. Therefore, Entry *C2 is included on the worksheet to rectify the consolidated figures for this preceding year by recording $31,544 in additional earnings ($40,544 − $9,000):

Consolidation Entry *C2 (Silver)

Investment in Gold Company	31,544	
Retained Earnings, 1/1/07 (Silver Company)		31,544

To convert Silver's investment income figures for the prior year
to equity income.

Remaining Consolidation Entries

After the three previous entries have been recorded, the remainder of the worksheet entries to consolidate these companies are relatively uncomplicated:

Consolidation Entry S1

Common Stock (Silver Company)	200,000	
Retained Earnings, 1/1/07 (Silver Company) (as adjusted above)	618,044	
Investment in Silver Company (90%)		736,240
Noncontrolling Interest in Silver Company, 1/1/07 (10%)		81,804

To eliminate the beginning stockholders' equity accounts of Silver and
to recognize a 10 percent noncontrolling interest in the subsidiary.
Retained Earnings has been adjusted for Entry *G and Entry *C2.

Consolidation Entry S2

Common Stock (Gold Company) (10%)	70,000	
Retained Earnings (Gold Company) (10% of 1/1/07 balance as adjusted above)	111,544	
Investment in Gold Company (as adjusted above)		181,544

To eliminate the January 1, 2007, equity of Gold Company's shares being
held by Silver Company. Retained Earnings has been adjusted for Entry
*C1. Investment in Gold Company has been adjusted for Entry *C2.

Consolidation Entry S3

Common Stock (Bronze Company)	100,000	
Retained Earnings, 1/1/07 (Bronze Company)	200,000	
Investment in Bronze Company (60%)		180,000
Noncontrolling Interest in Bronze Company, 1/1/07 (40%)		120,000

To eliminate beginning stockholders' equity accounts of Bronze and to recognize outside ownership of the company's remaining shares. The investments of both Gold and Silver are accounted for concurrently through this one entry.

Consolidation Entry A

Intangible Asset	56,000	
Investment in Silver Company		26,000
Investment in Bronze Company		30,000

To recognize January 1, 2007, intangible asset balances. Although $30,000 was originally allocated within the purchase of Silver, the recognition of amortization for 2005 and 2006 has reduced that figure by $4,000 ($2,000 per year). Conversely, as of the beginning of 2007, no expense has been recorded yet on the $30,000 associated with the acquisition of Bronze. Thus, a total allocation of $56,000 is appropriate as of January 1, 2007.

Consolidation Entry I

Dividend Income from Gold Company	10,000	
Dividend Income from Silver Company	36,000	
Dividend Income from Bronze Company	12,000	
Dividends Paid (Gold Company)		10,000
Dividends Paid (Silver Company)		36,000
Dividends Paid (Bronze Company)		12,000

To eliminate dividend payments made between the companies and recorded as income based on application of the cost method.

Consolidation Entry E

Amortization Expense	4,000	
Intangible Asset		4,000

To recognize the 2007 amortization expense for the various intangible asset balances. Amortization of $2,000 is recognized on the $30,000 allocation made in the acquisition of Silver, and an additional $1,000 expense is associated with each of the two investments made in Bronze.

Consolidation Entry TI

Sales	200,000	
Cost of Goods Sold		200,000

To eliminate the intercompany transfer of inventory made in 2007 by Silver.

Consolidation Entry G

Cost of Goods Sold	33,600	
Inventory		33,600

To eliminate intercompany gains remaining in the December 31, 2007, inventory of Gold. The unrealized gain is 28 percent (the markup for 2007) of the $120,000 ending inventory balance held by the parent.

Consolidation Entry GL

Gain on Sale of Land	13,000	
Land		13,000

To eliminate gain on intercompany transfer of land made from Gold
Company to Bronze during the year.

Noncontrolling Interest in Bronze Company's Income

As in all past examples, the noncontrolling interest's claim to a portion of consolidated income must be calculated based on the realized income of the subsidiary. In this illustration, the combination is a father-son-grandson configuration; therefore, computation of income must begin with Bronze. Because this subsidiary has neither unrealized intercompany gains nor amortization expense, the $90,000 income figure reported in Exhibit 7.4 is applicable. Thus, $36,000 ($90,000 × 40%) should be reported as the noncontrolling interest's share of Bronze's 2007 income.

Noncontrolling Interest in Silver Company's Income

Because of the mutual ownership with Gold, Silver's realized income for 2007 can be determined only by solving two simultaneous equations (since the conventional approach is being applied). Operational income figures for both parties are required as a prerequisite for this procedure:

Silver's Operational Income

Sales	$ 600,000
Cost of goods sold	(300,000)
Operating expenses	(100,000)
Amortization expense—purchase of Bronze	(1,000)
Equity in earnings of Bronze (30%)	27,000
2006 intercompany gains currently realized (Entry *G)	22,500
2007 intercompany unrealized gains being deferred (Entry G)	(33,600)
Operational income	$ 214,900

Gold's Operational Income

Sales	$ 800,000
Cost of goods sold	(380,000)
Operating expenses	(193,000)
Amortization expense—purchase of Silver	(2,000)
Amortization expense—purchase of Bronze	(1,000)
Equity in earnings of Bronze (30%)	27,000
Operational income	$ 251,000

Using these two income balances, the simultaneous equations can be constructed to determine Silver's realized income for the current year. This total serves as the basis for making the noncontrolling interest calculation:

$$SRI = \$214,900 + 10\% \text{ of GRI}$$

and

$$GRI = \$251,000 + 90\% \text{ of SRI}$$

therefore

$$SRI = \$214,900 + 0.10 (\$251,000 + 0.90 \text{ SRI})$$
$$SRI = \$214,900 + \$25,100 + 0.09 \text{ SRI}$$
$$0.91 \text{ SRI} = \$240,000$$
$$\text{Silver's realized income} = \$263,736$$
$$\text{Noncontrolling interest in Silver's income (10\%)} = \$26,374 \text{ (rounded)}$$

b. For Bronze, no differences exist between book values and tax basis. No computation of deferred income taxes is required; thus, this company's separate tax return is relatively straightforward. The $90,000 income figure being reported creates a current tax liability of $36,000 (based on the 40 percent tax rate).

In contrast, the consolidated tax return filed for Gold and Silver must include the following financial information. Where applicable, figures reported in Exhibit 7.4 have been combined for the two companies.

Tax Return Information—Consolidated Return

Sales	$1,400,000	
Less: Intercompany sales (2007)	(200,000)	$1,200,000
Cost of goods sold	680,000	
Less: 2007 intercompany purchases	(200,000)	
Less: 2006 intercompany gains recognized in 2007 (90,000 × 25%)	(22,500)	
Add: 2007 unrealized intercompany gains (120,000 × 28%)	33,600	491,100
Gross profit		708,900
Operating expenses (including amortization)		297,000
Operating income		411,900
Other income (since Bronze is not part of affiliated group):		
Gain on sale of land		13,000
Dividend income—Bronze Company	12,000	
Less: 80% deduction	(9,600)	2,400
Taxable income		$ 427,300
Tax rate		40%
Income tax payable by Gold Company and Silver Company for 2007		$ 170,920

Members of this business combination must pay a total of $206,920 to the government in 2007 ($36,000 for Bronze and $170,920 in connection with the consolidated return of Gold and Silver). However, according to *FASB Statement 109,* any temporary differences that originate or reverse during the year necessitate accounting for deferred income tax assets and/or liabilities. *In this illustration, only the dividend payments from Bronze and the unrealized gain on the sale of land to Bronze actually create such differences.* For example, amortization of the intangible asset would be the same for book and tax purposes. Other items encountered do not lead to deferred income taxes:

- Because Gold and Silver are filing a consolidated return, the unrealized inventory gains are deferred for both tax purposes and financial reporting so that no difference is created.
- The dividends that Silver paid to Gold are not subject to taxation because these distributions were made between members of an affiliated group.

However, recognition of a deferred tax liability is required because Bronze's realized income ($54,000 after income tax expense of $36,000) is greater than its $20,000 dividend distribution. Gold and Silver own 60 percent of this subsidiary, indicating that $32,400 ($54,000 × 60%) of its income is included on the consolidated income statement. Because this figure is $20,400 more than the amount of dividends paid to Gold and Silver ($12,000, or 60% of $20,000), a deferred tax liability is required. The temporary difference is actually $4,080 (20% of $20,400) because of the 80 percent dividend deduction. The future tax effect on this difference is $1,632 based on the 40 percent tax rate being applied.

A deferred tax asset also is needed in connection with the intercompany sale of land from Gold to Bronze. Separate returns are being filed by these companies. Thus, the gain is taxed immediately, although this $13,000 will not be realized for reporting purposes until a future resale occurs. From an accounting perspective, the tax of $5,200 ($13,000 × 40%) is being prepaid in 2007.

Recognition of the current payable as well as the two deferrals leads to an income tax expense of $203,352:

Income Tax Expense	203,352	
Deferred Income Tax—Asset	5,200	
Income Taxes Payable—Current		206,920
Deferred Income Tax—Liability		1,632

Questions

1. What is meant by a father-son-grandson relationship?

2. When an indirect ownership is present, why is a specific ordering necessary for determining the realized incomes of the component corporations?

3. Able Company owns 70 percent of the outstanding voting stock of Baker Company, which, in turn, holds 80 percent of Carter Company. Carter possesses 60 percent of the capital stock of Dexter Company. How much income actually accrues to the consolidated entity from each of these companies after giving consideration to the various noncontrolling interests?

4. How does the presence of an indirect ownership (such as a father-son-grandson relationship) affect the mechanical aspects of the consolidation process?

5. What is the difference between a connecting affiliation and a mutual ownership?

6. When a mutual ownership exists, two different views of this relationship can be adopted. What are these two views, and how do they differ?

7. In accounting for mutual ownerships, why is the treasury stock approach more prevalent in practice than the conventional approach?

8. Alexander Company holds 80 percent of the outstanding common stock of Baxter Company. Baxter, in turn, owns 30 percent of the stock of Alexander. How is the realized income of these two companies computed if the conventional approach is being utilized?

9. For income tax purposes, how is an affiliated group defined?

10. What are the advantages to a business combination filing a consolidated tax return? Considering these advantages, why do some members of a business combination file separate tax returns?

11. Why is the allocation of the income tax expense figure between the members of a business combination important? By what methods can this allocation be made?

12. If a parent and its subsidiary file separate income tax returns, why will the parent frequently have to recognize deferred income taxes? Why might the subsidiary have to recognize deferred income taxes?

13. In a recent acquisition, the consolidated value of a subsidiary's assets exceeded the basis appropriate for tax purposes. How does this difference affect the consolidated balance sheet?

14. Jones acquires Wilson, in part because the new subsidiary has an unused net operating loss carryforward for tax purposes. How does this carryforward affect the consolidated figures at the date of acquisition?

15. A subsidiary is acquired that has a net operating loss carryforward. The related deferred income tax asset is $230,000. Because the parent believes that a portion of this carryforward likely will never be used, a valuation allowance of $150,000 also is recognized. At the end of the first year of ownership, the parent reassesses the situation and determines that the valuation allowance should be reduced to $110,000. What effect does this change have on the reporting of the business combination?

Problems

1. In a father-son-grandson business combination, which of the following statements is true?

   a. The father company always must have its realized income computed first.

   b. The computation of a company's realized income has no effect on the realized income of other companies within a business combination.

   c. A father-son-grandson configuration does not require consolidation unless one company owns shares in all of the other companies.

   d. All companies that are solely in subsidiary positions must have their realized income computed first within the consolidation process.

2. A subsidiary owns shares of its parent company. Which of the following is true concerning the treasury stock approach?

   a. It is considered to be more difficult to apply than the conventional approach.

   b. The original cost of the subsidiary's investment is a reduction in consolidated stockholders' equity.

   c. The subsidiary accrues income on its investment by using the equity method.

   d. The treasury stock approach eliminates these shares entirely within the consolidation process.

3. On January 1, 2007, a subsidiary buys 10 percent of the outstanding shares of its parent company. Although the total book value and fair value of the parent's net assets were $4 million, the purchase price for these shares was $420,000. An intangible asset is amortized in this business combination

over a 40-year period. During 2007, the parent reported operational income (no investment income was included) of $510,000 while paying dividends of $140,000. How are these shares reported at December 31, 2007, if the treasury stock approach is used?

  a. The investment is recorded as $457,000 at the end of 2007 and then eliminated for consolidation purposes.

  b. Consolidated stockholders' equity is reduced by $457,000.

  c. The investment is recorded as $456,500 at the end of 2007 and then eliminated for consolidation purposes.

  d. Consolidated stockholders' equity is reduced by $420,000.

4. Which of the following is correct for two companies that want to file a consolidated tax return as an affiliated group?

  a. One company must hold at least 51 percent of the other company's voting stock.

  b. One company must hold at least 65 percent of the other company's voting stock.

  c. One company must hold at least 80 percent of the other company's voting stock.

  d. They cannot file a consolidated tax return unless one company owns 100 percent of the voting stock of the other.

5. How does the amortization of goodwill affect the computation of income taxes on a consolidated tax return?

  a. It is a deductible expense but only if the parent owns 80 percent of the voting stock of the subsidiary.

  b. It is deductible only if it is impaired.

  c. It is a deductible item over a 15-year period.

  d. It is deductible for tax purposes but only if a consolidated tax return is being filed.

6. Which of the following is not a reason for two companies to file separate tax returns?

  a. The parent owns 68 percent of the subsidiary.

  b. They have no intercompany transactions.

  c. Intercompany dividends are tax free only on separate returns.

  d. Neither company historically has had an operating tax loss.

7. Bassett Company owns 80 percent of Crimson Corporation. Crimson Corporation owns 90 percent of Damson, Inc. Operational income totals for 2007 follow; these figures contain no investment income. Amortization expense was not required by any of these purchases. Included in Damson's income is a $40,000 unrealized gain on intercompany transfers to Crimson.

	Bassett	Crimson	Damson
Operational income	$300,000	$200,000	$200,000

What is Bassett's realized income for the year?

  a. $575,200.

  b. $588,000.

  c. $596,400.

  d. $604,000.

8. Gardner Corporation holds 80 percent of Healthstone, which, in turn, owns 80 percent of Icede. Operational income figures (without investment income) as well as unrealized upstream gains included in the income for the current year follow:

	Gardner	Healthstone	Icede
Operational income	$400,000	$300,000	$220,000
Unrealized gains	50,000	30,000	60,000

On a consolidated income statement for the year, what balance is reported for the noncontrolling interest in the subsidiaries' income?

  a. $86,000.

  b. $100,000.

  c. $111,600.

  d. $120,800.

9. Nesbitt Corporation owns 90 percent of Jones, Inc., and Jones owns 10 percent of the outstanding shares of Nesbitt. No goodwill or any other allocations were recognized in connection with either of these acquisitions. Nesbitt reports operational income of $190,000 for 2007, and Jones earned $70,000 during the same period. No investment income is included within either of these income totals. On a consolidated income statement, what is the noncontrolling interest in Jones's income if the conventional approach is being used?

   a. $7,000.

   b. $7,740.

   c. $8,900.

   d. $9,780.

10. Horton, Inc., owns 90 percent of the voting stock of Juvyn Corporation. The purchase price was in excess of book value and fair value by $80,000. Juvyn holds 20 percent of the voting stock of Horton. That purchase price was in excess of book value and fair value by $20,000. Any excess price is assigned to copyrights to be amortized over a 20-year period.

    During the current year, Horton reported operational income of $160,000 and dividend income from Juvyn of $27,000. At the same time, Juvyn reported operational income of $50,000 and dividend income from Horton of $14,000.

    If the treasury stock approach is utilized, what will be reported as the Noncontrolling Interest in Juvyn's Net Income?

    a. $5,000.

    b. $5,400.

    c. $6,300.

    d. $6,400.

11. What would be the answer to Problem 10 if the conventional approach were being used?

    a. $9,781.

    b. $9,964.

    c. $10,414.

    d. $11,864.

12. Cremmins, Inc., owns 60 percent of Anderson. During the current year, Anderson reported net income of $200,000 but paid a total cash dividend of only $40,000. What deferred income tax liability must be recognized in the consolidated balance sheet? Assume the tax rate is 30 percent.

    a. $5,760.

    b. $9,600.

    c. $12,840.

    d. $28,800.

13. Prybylos, Inc., owns 90 percent of Station Corporation. Both companies have been profitable for many years. During the current year, the parent sold merchandise costing $70,000 to the subsidiary for $100,000. At the end of the year, 20 percent of this merchandise was still being held. Assume that the tax rate is 25 percent and that separate tax returns are filed. What deferred income tax asset is created?

    a. –0–.

    b. $300.

    c. $1,500.

    d. $7,500.

14. What would be the answer to Problem 13 if a consolidated tax return were filed?

    a. –0–.

    b. $300.

    c. $1,500.

    d. $7,500.

15. Hastoon Company purchases all of Zedner Company for $420,000 in cash. On that date, the subsidiary has net assets with a $400,000 fair value but a $300,000 book value and tax basis.

The tax rate is 30 percent. Neither company has reported any deferred income tax assets or liabilities. What amount of goodwill should be recognized on the date of the acquisition?

a. $20,000.

b. $36,000.

c. $50,000.

d. $120,000.

16. On January 1, 2005, Tree Company purchased 70 percent of Limb Company's outstanding voting stock for $250,000. Limb had a $300,000 reported book value on that date. Subsequently, on January 1, 2006, Limb Company acquired 70 percent of Leaf Company for $90,000 when Leaf had a $100,000 book value. Any excess purchase price is to be assigned to a trade name with a 40-year life.

These companies report the following financial information. Investment income figures are not included.

	2005	2006	2007
Sales:			
Tree Company	$400,000	$500,000	$650,000
Limb Company	200,000	280,000	400,000
Leaf Company	Not available	160,000	210,000
Expenses:			
Tree Company	$310,000	$420,000	$510,000
Limb Company	160,000	220,000	335,000
Leaf Company	Not available	150,000	180,000
Dividends paid:			
Tree Company	$20,000	$40,000	$50,000
Limb Company	10,000	20,000	20,000
Leaf Company	Not available	2,000	10,000

Assume that the following questions are each independent:

a. If all companies use the equity method for internal reporting purposes, what is the December 31, 2006, balance in the Tree's Investment in Limb Company account?

b. If all companies use the cost method to account for their investments, what adjustments must Limb and Tree make to their beginning Retained Earnings balances on the 2007 consolidation worksheet?

c. What is the consolidated net income for this business combination for the year of 2007 prior to any reduction for the noncontrolling interests' share of the subsidiaries' net income?

d. What is the noncontrolling interests' share of the consolidated net income in 2007?

e. Assume that Limb made intercompany inventory transfers to Tree that have resulted in the following unrealized gains at the end of each year:

Date	Amount
12/31/05	$10,000
12/31/06	16,000
12/31/07	25,000

What is the realized income of Limb in 2006 and 2007, respectively?

f. Assuming the same unrealized gains as presented in part (e), what worksheet adjustment must be made to the January 1, 2007, Retained Earnings account of Tree if that company has applied the cost method to its investment?

17. On January 1, 2006, Uncle Company purchased 80 percent of Nephew Company's capital stock for $500,000 in cash and other assets. Nephew had a book value of $600,000 on that date.

On January 1, 2005, Nephew had acquired 30 percent of Uncle for $280,000. Uncle's appropriately adjusted book value as of that date was $900,000.

Operational income figures (includes no investment income) for these two companies follow. In addition, Uncle pays $20,000 in dividends to shareholders each year while Nephew distributes $5,000 annually. Any purchase price allocations are amortized over a 10-year period.

Year	Uncle Company	Nephew Company
2006	$ 90,000	$30,000
2007	120,000	40,000
2008	140,000	50,000

Each of the following questions should be viewed as independent:

a. Assume that the treasury stock approach is utilized and that Uncle applies the equity method to account for this investment in Nephew. What is the income of the subsidiary recognized by Uncle in 2008?

b. If the treasury stock approach is applied, what is the noncontrolling interest's share of the subsidiary's 2008 income?

c. Assume that the conventional approach is utilized and that Uncle applies the equity method to this investment in Nephew. What is the income of the subsidiary recognized by Uncle in 2008?

d. If the conventional approach is applied, what is the noncontrolling interest's share of the subsidiary's 2008 net income?

18. Gaddy, Inc., obtained 60 percent of Mabry Corporation on January 1, 2006. Annual amortization of $25,000 is to be recorded on the allocations made in connection with this purchase. On January 1, 2007, Mabry acquired 90 percent of Tucson Company's voting stock. Amortization on this second purchase amounted to $2,000 per year.

For the year of 2008, these three companies reported the following information as accumulated by their separate accounting systems. Operating income figures do not include any investment or dividend income.

	Operating Income	Dividends Paid
Gaddy	$220,000	$120,000
Mabry	160,000	50,000
Tucson	90,000	10,000

a. On consolidated financial statements for 2008, what is the noncontrolling interests' share of the subsidiaries' income?

b. What is consolidated net income for 2008?

c. If Mabry's operating income figures for 2008 include a net unrealized gain of $12,000, what is consolidated net income for that year?

19. Fonseca owns 80 percent of the voting stock of Carson. The purchase price exceeded the underlying book value of Carson's assets and liabilities by $60,000. At the same time, Carson holds a 30 percent interest in the outstanding shares of Fonseca. This stock was bought at a price $10,000 in excess of underlying book value. All excess amounts are assigned to patented technology with a 10-year life.

Both of these companies use the cost method to record their investments for internal reporting purposes. During the current year, the following information was reported:

	Operating Income	Dividend Income	Total Reported Income
Fonseca	$80,000	$16,000 (all from Carson)	$96,000
Carson	30,000	15,000 (all from Fonseca)	45,000

a. If the conventional approach is to be utilized, what reduction should be recorded in the consolidated income statement as the noncontrolling interest in Carson's net income?

b. If the treasury stock approach is applied, what reduction should be recorded in the consolidated income statement as the noncontrolling interest in Carson's net income?

20. Baxter, Inc., owns 90 percent of Wisconsin, Inc., and 20 percent of the Cleveland Company. Wisconsin, in turn, holds 60 percent of the outstanding stock of Cleveland. Total annual amortization of $17,000 resulted from purchases that Baxter made. During the current year, Cleveland sold a variety of inventory items to Wisconsin for $40,000 although the original cost was $30,000. Of this total, $12,000 in inventory (at transfer price) was still held by Wisconsin at year-end.

During this same period, Wisconsin sold merchandise to Baxter for $100,000 although the original cost was only $70,000. At the end of the year, $40,000 of these goods (at the transfer price) was still on hand.

The cost method was used to record each of these investments. None of the companies hold any other investments.

Using the following separate income statements, determine the figures that would appear on a consolidated income statement:

	Baxter	Wisconsin	Cleveland
Sales	$(1,000,000)	$ (450,000)	$ (280,000)
Cost of goods sold	670,000	280,000	190,000
Expenses	110,000	60,000	30,000
Dividend income:			
Wisconsin	(36,000)	–0–	–0–
Cleveland	(4,000)	(12,000)	–0–
Net income	$ (260,000)	$ (122,000)	$ (60,000)

21. Alice Corporation bought 90 percent of the outstanding shares of Wonderland, Inc., several years ago for $610,000. Wonderland, in turn, acquired 10 percent of Alice for $111,000. Annual amortization expense of $12,000 resulted from Alice's purchase. The cost method was used to record each of these investments. Neither company holds other investments.

   a. Based on the following separate income statements, produce the figures that would appear on a consolidated income statement. Assume that the treasury stock approach is being used.

	Alice	Wonderland
Sales	$(1,300,000)	$ (500,000)
Cost of goods sold	750,000	270,000
Expenses	220,000	120,000
Dividend income	(45,000)	(16,000)
Net income	$ (375,000)	$ (126,000)

   b. Assuming that the treasury stock approach is still in use, what are the consolidated totals for the following two accounts?

	Alice	Wonderland
Common stock	$880,000	$350,000
Treasury stock	–0–	–0–

22. The following figures are reported by Up and its 80 percent owned subsidiary (Down) for the year ending December 31, 2007. Down paid dividends of $30,000 during this period.

	Up	Down
Sales	$(600,000)	$(300,000)
Cost of goods sold	300,000	140,000
Operating expenses	174,000	60,000
Dividend income	(24,000)	–0–
Net income	$(150,000)	$(100,000)

   In 2006, unrealized gains of $30,000 on upstream transfers of $90,000 were deferred into 2007. In 2007, unrealized gains of $40,000 on upstream transfers of $110,000 were deferred into 2008.

   a. What figures appear in a consolidated income statement?

   b. What income tax expense should be shown in the consolidated income statement if separate returns are filed? Assume that the tax rate is 30 percent.

23. Clarke has a controlling interest in the outstanding stock of Rogers. At the end of the current year, the following information has been accumulated for these two companies:

	Operating Income	Dividends Paid
Clarke	$500,000 (includes a $90,000 net unrealized gain on intercompany inventory transfers)	$90,000
Rogers	240,000	80,000

Clarke uses the cost method to account for the investment in Rogers. Neither dividend nor other investment income is included in the operating income figures just presented. The effective tax rate for both companies is 40 percent.

a. Assume that Clarke owns 100 percent of the voting stock of Rogers and is filing a consolidated tax return. What amount of income taxes would this affiliated group pay in connection with the current period?

b. Assume that Clarke owns 92 percent of the voting stock of Rogers and is filing a consolidated tax return. What amount of income taxes would this affiliated group pay in connection with the current period?

c. Assume that Clarke owns 80 percent of the voting stock of Rogers but the companies have elected to file separate tax returns. What is the total amount of income taxes that these two companies pay for the current period?

d. Assume that Clarke owns 70 percent of the voting stock of Rogers so that separate tax returns are required. What is the total amount of income tax expense to be recognized in the consolidated income statement for the current period?

e. Assume that Clarke owns 70 percent of the voting stock of Rogers so that separate tax returns are required. What amount of income taxes does Clarke have to pay in connection with the current year?

24. On January 1, 2006, Piranto acquires 90 percent of the outstanding shares of Slinton. Financial information for these two companies for the years of 2006 and 2007 is as follows:

	2006	**2007**
Piranto Company:		
Sales	$(600,000)	$(800,000)
Operational expenses	400,000	500,000
Unrealized gains as of end of year		
(included in above figures)	(120,000)	(150,000)
Dividend income—Slinton Company	(18,000)	(36,000)
Slinton Company:		
Sales	(200,000)	(250,000)
Operational expenses	120,000	150,000
Dividends paid	(20,000)	(40,000)

Assume that a tax rate of 40 percent is applicable to both companies.

a. On consolidated financial statements for 2007, what would be the income tax expense and the income tax currently payable if Piranto and Slinton file a consolidated tax return as an affiliated group?

b. On consolidated financial statements for 2007, what would be the income tax expense and income tax currently payable for each company if they choose to file separate returns?

25. Lake acquired a controlling interest in Boxwood several years ago. During the current fiscal period, these two companies have individually reported the following income figures (exclusive of any investment income):

Lake	$300,000
Boxwood	100,000

Lake paid a cash dividend of $90,000 during the current year while Boxwood distributed $10,000.

Boxwood sells inventory to Lake each period. Unrealized intercompany gains of $18,000 were present in Lake's beginning inventory for the current year, and its ending inventory carried $32,000 in unrealized profits.

Each of the following questions should be viewed as an independent situation. The effective tax rate for both companies is 40 percent.

a. If Lake owns a 60 percent interest in Boxwood, what total income tax expense must be reported on a consolidated income statement for this period?

b. If Lake owns a 60 percent interest in Boxwood, what total amount of income taxes must be paid by these two companies for the current year?

c. If Lake owns a 90 percent interest in Boxwood and a consolidated tax return is being filed, what amount of income tax expense would be reported on a consolidated income statement for the year?

d. Assume that Lake owns a 90 percent interest in Boxwood and that Boxwood possesses a 20 percent interest in Lake. Using the conventional approach to mutual ownership, determine the noncontrolling interest in Boxwood's income for the year. Ignore income taxes.

26. Garrison holds a controlling interest in the outstanding stock of Robertson. For the current year, the following information has been gathered about these two companies:

	Garrison	Robertson
Operating income	$300,000	$200,000
	(includes a $50,000 net unrealized gain on an intercompany transfer)	
Dividends paid	32,000	50,000
Tax rate	40%	40%

Garrison uses the cost method to account for the investment in Robertson. Dividend income for the current year is not included in Garrison's operating income figure.

   a. Assume that Garrison owns 80 percent of the voting stock of Robertson. On a consolidated tax return, what amount of income taxes would be paid?
   b. Assume that Garrison owns 80 percent of the voting stock of Robertson. On separate tax returns, what is the total amount of income taxes to be paid?
   c. Assume that Garrison owns 70 percent of the voting stock of Robertson. What is the total amount of income tax expense to be recognized on a consolidated income statement?
   d. Assume that Garrison holds 60 percent of the voting stock of Robertson. On a separate income tax return, what amount of income taxes would Garrison have to pay?

27. Leftwich recently purchased all of the stock of Kew Corporation and is now in the process of consolidating the financial data of this new subsidiary. Leftwich paid a total of $650,000 for the company, which has the following accounts:

	Fair Value	Tax Basis
Accounts receivable	$110,000	$110,000
Inventory	130,000	130,000
Land	100,000	100,000
Buildings	180,000	140,000
Equipment	200,000	150,000
Liabilities	(220,000)	(220,000)

Assume that the effective tax rate is 30 percent. On a consolidated balance sheet prepared immediately after this takeover, what impact would the acquisition of Kew have on the individual asset and liability accounts reported by the business combination?

28. House Corporation was created in 1950 and has been operating profitably since that time. At the beginning of 2005, House purchased a 70 percent ownership in Room Company. Room's financial accounts as of that date were as follows:

	Book Value	Fair Value
Cash and receivables	$300,000	$300,000
Inventory	380,000	380,000
Buildings (20-year life)	200,000	260,000
Equipment (4-year life)	160,000	140,000
Land	260,000	260,000
Liabilities	(510,000)	(510,000)

House paid $701,000 in cash for this investment. Any excess purchase price is attributed to franchise contracts to be amortized over a 40-year life.

During 2005 and 2006, Room earned net income totaling $160,000 while paying cash dividends of $50,000.

House has made regular acquisitions of inventory from Room at a markup of 25 percent more than cost. House's purchases during 2005 and 2006 as well as related ending inventory balances are as follows:

Year	Intercompany Purchases	Retained Intercompany Inventory—End of Year (at transfer price)
2005	$120,000	$40,000
2006	150,000	60,000

On January 1, 2007, House and Room acted together as coacquirers of 80 percent of Wall Company's outstanding common stock. The total price of these shares was $200,000, indicating that no goodwill or other specific valuation allocations were needed. Each company put up one-half of this purchase price.

During 2007, House acquired additional inventory at a price of $200,000 from Room. Of this merchandise, 45 percent is still being held at year-end.

Room loaned Wall $40,000 on a 10 percent note on October 1, 2007. Although interest has been properly recorded, no part of this debt has been repaid as of December 31, 2007.

Wall's preferred stock is owned entirely by outside parties. This stock pays an 8 percent annual cumulative dividend. The stock is neither participating nor voting although it does have a call value of 106 percent of par value. No dividends are currently in arrears on these shares.

Following are the financial records for these three companies for 2007. Prepare a consolidation worksheet. The partial equity method based on *operational earnings* has been applied to each investment.

	House Corporation	Room Company	Wall Company
Sales and other revenues	$(900,000)	$(700,000)	$(300,000)
Cost of goods sold	551,120	300,000	140,000
Operating expenses	218,400	268,400	90,000
Income of Room Company	(92,120)	–0–	–0–
Income of Wall Company	(26,400)	(26,400)	–0–
Net income	$(249,000)	$(158,000)	$ (70,000)
Retained earnings, 1/1/07	$(820,000)	$(590,000)	$(153,000)
Net income (above)	(249,000)	(158,000)	(70,000)
Dividends paid	100,000	96,000	50,000
Retained earnings, 12/31/07	$(969,000)	$(652,000)	$(173,000)
Cash and receivables	$ 244,880	$ 354,000	$ 70,000
Inventory	390,200	320,000	103,000
Investment in Room Company	802,920	–0–	–0–
Investment in Wall Company	108,000	108,000	–0–
Buildings	385,000	320,000	144,000
Equipment	310,000	130,000	88,000
Land	180,000	300,000	16,000
Liabilities	(632,000)	(570,000)	(98,000)
Preferred stock	–0–	–0–	(50,000)
Common stock	(820,000)	(310,000)	(100,000)
Retained earnings, 12/31/07	(969,000)	(652,000)	(173,000)

29. Mighty Company purchased a 60 percent interest in Lowly Company on January 1, 2001, for $400,000 in cash. Lowly's book value at that date was reported as $500,000. Any excess purchase price is assigned to trademarks to be amortized over 20 years. Subsequently, on January 1, 2002, Lowly acquired a 20 percent interest in Mighty. The price of $240,000 was equivalent to 20 percent of Mighty's book value.

Neither company has paid dividends since these acquisitions occurred. On January 1, 2007, Lowly's book value was $800,000, a figure that rises to $840,000 (Common Stock of $300,000 and Retained Earnings of $540,000) by the end of the year. Mighty's book value was $1.7 million at the beginning of 2007 and $1.8 million (Common Stock of $1 million and Retained Earnings of $800,000) at December 31, 2007. No intercompany transactions have occurred and no additional stock has been sold. Each company applies the cost method in accounting for the individual investments.

a. What worksheet entries are required to consolidate these two companies for 2007? What is the noncontrolling interest in the subsidiary's net income for this year? Assume that the treasury stock approach is utilized.

b. Answer the same questions as in requirement (a) but assume that the conventional approach is being applied to the mutual ownership.

c. How do the answers in requirement (b) differ if, on January 1, 2005, Mighty sold equipment (costing $80,000) with a remaining life of 10 years and a $20,000 book value to Lowly for $50,000 in cash?

30. On January 1, 2006, Travers Company purchased 90 percent of the outstanding stock of Yarrow Company. On the same date, Yarrow acquired an 80 percent interest in Stookey Company. Although both of these investments are to be accounted for by applying the cost method, no dividends are distributed by either Yarrow or Stookey during 2006 or 2007. Travers follows a policy of paying out cash dividends each year equal to 40 percent of operational earnings. Reported income totals for 2006 are as follows:

Travers Company	$300,000
Yarrow Company	160,000
Stookey Company	120,000

Any excess payments are attributed to a customer list to be amortized over 15 years.

Following are the 2007 financial statements for these three companies. Stookey has made numerous transfers of inventory to Yarrow since the takeover: $80,000 (2006) and $100,000 (2007). These transactions include the same markup applicable to Stookey's outside sales. In each of these years, Yarrow has carried 20 percent of this inventory into the succeeding year before disposing of it.

An effective tax rate of 45 percent is applicable to all companies.

	Travers Company	Yarrow Company	Stookey Company
Sales	$ (900,000)	$ (600,000)	$(500,000)
Cost of goods sold	480,000	320,000	260,000
Operating expenses	100,000	80,000	140,000
Net income	$ (320,000)	$ (200,000)	$(100,000)
Retained earnings, 1/1/07	$ (700,000)	$ (600,000)	$(300,000)
Net income (above)	(320,000)	(200,000)	(100,000)
Dividends paid	128,000	–0–	–0–
Retained earnings, 12/31/07	$ (892,000)	$ (800,000)	$(400,000)
Current assets	$ 423,000	$ 375,000	$ 280,000
Investment in Yarrow Company	741,000	–0–	–0–
Investment in Stookey Company	–0–	349,000	–0–
Land, buildings, and equipment (net) .	949,000	836,000	520,000
Total assets	$ 2,113,000	$ 1,560,000	$ 800,000
Liabilities	$ (721,000)	$ (460,000)	$(200,000)
Common stock	(500,000)	(300,000)	(200,000)
Retained earnings, 12/31/07	(892,000)	(800,000)	(400,000)
Total liabilities and equities	$(2,113,000)	$(1,560,000)	$(800,000)

a. Prepare the 2007 consolidation worksheet for this business combination. Ignore income tax effects.

b. Determine the amount of income taxes to be paid by Travers and Yarrow on a consolidated tax return for the year 2007.

c. Determine the amount of income taxes to be paid by Stookey on a separate tax return for the year 2007.

d. Based on the answers to requirements (b) and (c), what journal entry would be made by this combination to record 2007 income taxes?

31. Several years ago, Daniel Company purchased 90 percent of the outstanding voting stock of Murphy, Inc. At approximately the same time, Murphy acquired 10 percent of Daniel's common stock. In both cases, the price paid was equal to the book value and fair value of the underlying net assets. No allocations were made to either goodwill or specific asset or liability accounts.

Prior to the current year, Daniel's book value has increased by $400,000 since the date of acquisition, and Murphy's book value has risen by $150,000.

Both companies use the cost method to account for their investments.

Using the following information for the year 2007, prepare a consolidation worksheet based on the conventional approach to mutual holdings:

	Daniel	Murphy
Sales	$ (600,000)	$(220,000)
Expenses	400,000	126,000
Dividend income	(18,000)	(9,000)
Net income	$ (218,000)	$(103,000)
Retained earnings, 1/1/07	$ (850,000)	$(200,000)
Net income	(218,000)	(103,000)
Dividends paid	90,000	20,000
Retained earnings, 12/31/07	$ (978,000)	$(283,000)
Cash	$ 20,000	$ 40,000
Receivables	178,000	96,000
Inventory	125,000	108,000
Investment in Murphy	189,000	–0–
Investment in Daniel	–0–	50,000
Property, plant, and equipment (net)	651,000	361,000
Total assets	$ 1,163,000	$ 655,000
Liabilities	$ (135,000)	$(212,000)
Common stock	(50,000)	(160,000)
Retained earnings, 12/31/07	(978,000)	(283,000)
Total liabilities and equities	$(1,163,000)	$(655,000)

32. Politan Company acquired an 80 percent interest in Soludan several years ago. Any portion of the purchase price in excess of the corresponding book value of Soludan Company was assigned to trademarks. This intangible asset has subsequently undergone annual amortization based on a 15-year life. In recent years, regular intercompany inventory sales have transpired between the two companies. No payment has yet been made on the latest transfer.

Following are the individual financial statements for the two companies as well as consolidated totals for the current year:

	Politan Company	Soludan Company	Consolidated Totals
Sales	$ (800,000)	$(600,000)	$(1,280,000)
Cost of goods sold	500,000	400,000	784,000
Operating expenses	100,000	100,000	202,000
Income of Soludan	(80,000)	–0–	–0–
Noncontrolling interest in Soludan Company's income	–0–	–0–	19,200
Net income	$ (280,000)	$(100,000)	$ (274,800)
Retained earnings, 1/1	$ (620,000)	$(290,000)	$ (607,600)
Net income (above)	(280,000)	(100,000)	(274,800)
Dividends paid	70,000	20,000	70,000
Retained earnings, 12/31	$ (830,000)	$(370,000)	$ (812,400)
Cash and receivables	$ 290,000	$ 90,000	$ 360,000
Inventory	190,000	160,000	338,000
Investment in Soludan Company	390,000	–0–	–0–
Land, buildings, and equipment	380,000	260,000	640,000
Trademarks	–0–	–0–	22,000
Total assets	$ 1,250,000	$ 510,000	$ 1,360,000
Liabilities	$ (270,000)	$ (60,000)	$ (310,000)
Noncontrolling interest in Soludan Company	–0–	–0–	(87,600)
Common stock	(120,000)	(80,000)	(120,000)
Additional paid-in capital	(30,000)	–0–	(30,000)
Retained earnings (above)	(830,000)	(370,000)	(812,400)
Total liabilities and equities	$(1,250,000)	$(510,000)	$(1,360,000)

    a. By what method is Politan accounting for its investment in Soludan?

    b. What is the balance of the unrealized inventory gain being deferred at the end of the current period?

    c. What amount was originally allocated to the trademarks?

    d. What was the amount of the current year intercompany inventory sales?

    e. Were the intercompany inventory sales made upstream or downstream?

    f. What was the balance of the intercompany liability at the end of the current year?

    g. What unrealized gain was deferred into the current year from the preceding period?

    h. The consolidated Retained Earnings account shows a balance of $607,600 rather than the $620,000 reported by the parent. What creates this difference?

    i. How was the ending Noncontrolling Interest in Soludan Company computed?

    j. Assuming a tax rate of 40 percent, what income tax journal entry is recorded if these two companies prepare a consolidated tax return?

    k. Assuming a tax rate of 40 percent, what income tax journal entry is recorded if these two companies prepare separate tax returns?

33. On January 1, 2002, Alpha acquired 80 percent of Delta. Of the total purchase price, $100,000 was allocated to copyrights. Subsequently, on January 1, 2003, Delta obtained 70 percent of the outstanding voting shares of Omega. In this second acquisition, $80,000 of the payment was assigned to copyrights. All copyright balances are being amortized over a 20-year life. Delta had a book value of $490,000 at January 1, 2002, whereas Omega reported a book value of $140,000 on January 1, 2003.

    Delta has made numerous inventory transfers to Alpha since the business combination was formed. Unrealized gains of $15,000 were present in Alpha's inventory as of January 1, 2007. During the year, $200,000 in additional intercompany sales were made with $22,000 in gains remaining unrealized at the end of the period.

    Both Alpha and Delta have utilized the partial equity method to account for their investment balances.

    Following are the individual financial statements for these three companies for the year 2007, along with consolidated totals. Develop the worksheet entries necessary to derive these reported balances:

	Alpha Company	Delta Company	Omega Company	Consolidated Totals
Sales	$ (900,000)	$ (500,000)	$(200,000)	$(1,400,000)
Cost of goods sold	500,000	240,000	80,000	627,000
Operating expenses.	294,000	129,000	50,000	482,000
Income of subsidiary	(144,000)	(49,000)	–0–	–0–
Noncontrolling interest in income of Delta Company	–0–	–0–	–0–	33,800
Noncontrolling interest in income of Omega Company	–0–	–0–	–0–	21,000
Net income	$ (250,000)	$ (180,000)	$ (70,000)	$ (236,200)
Retained earnings, 1/1/07	$ (600,000)	$ (400,000)	$(100,000)	$ (550,200)
Net income (above)	(250,000)	(180,000)	(70,000)	(236,200)
Dividends paid.	50,000	40,000	50,000	50,000
Retained earnings, 12/31/07	$ (800,000)	$ (540,000)	$(120,000)	$ (736,400)
Cash and receivables	$ 262,000	$ 210,000	$ 70,000	$ 522,000
Inventory.	290,000	310,000	160,000	738,000
Investment in Delta Company	628,000	–0–	–0–	–0–
Investment in Omega Company.	–0–	234,000	–0–	–0–
Property, plant, and equipment	420,000	316,000	270,000	1,006,000
Copyrights.	–0–	–0–	–0–	130,000
Total assets	$1,600,000	$1,070,000	$ 500,000	$ 2,396,000

Liabilities	$ (600,000)	$ (410,000)	$(280,000)	$(1,270,000)
Common stock	(200,000)	(120,000)	(100,000)	(200,000)
Retained earnings, 12/31/07	(800,000)	(540,000)	(120,000)	(736,400)
Noncontrolling interest in Delta Company, 12/31/07	–0–	–0–	–0–	(123,600)
Noncontrolling interest in Omega Company, 12/31/07.	–0–	–0–	–0–	(66,000)
Total liabilities and equities	$(1,600,000)	$(1,070,000)	$(500,000)	$(2,396,000)

Develop Your Skills

EXCEL CASE: INDIRECT SUBSIDIARY CONTROL

Summit Corporation owns a 90 percent majority voting interest in Treeline, Inc. Treeline, Inc., in turn, owns a 70 percent majority voting interest in Basecamp Company. In the current year, each of these firms reports the following income and dividends. Operating income figures do not include any investment or dividend income.

	Operating Income	Dividends Paid
Summit	$345,000	$150,000
Treeline	280,000	100,000
Basecamp	175,000	40,000

In addition, in computing its income on a full accrual basis, Treeline's acquisition of Basecamp necessitates excess cost amortizations of $25,000 per year. Similarly, Summit's acquisition of Treeline requires $17,000 of excess cost amortizations.

Required:

Prepare an Excel spreadsheet that computes the following:

1. Treeline's income including its equity in Basecamp earnings.
2. Summit's income including its equity in Treeline's total earnings.
3. Total entity net income for the three companies.
4. Total noncontrolling interest in the total entity's net income.
5. Difference between these elements:
   - Summit's net income.
   - Total entity net income for the three companies less noncontrolling interest in the total entity's net income.

(*Hint:* The difference between these two amounts should be zero.)

RESEARCH CASE: CONSOLIDATED TAX EXPENSE

Using the Web, access the current financial statements of Coca-Cola Company at www.coca-cola.com. Identify and discuss the following aspects of consolidated tax expense disclosed in the firm's financial statements:

1. Loss carryforwards and carrybacks.
2. Components of deferred tax assets and liabilities.
3. Deferred tax impacts of stock sales by equity investees.
4. Deferred tax impacts of sales of interests in investees.
5. Valuation allowances on deferred taxes.
6. Differences between statutory and effective tax rates.

Chapter **Eight**

Segment and Interim Reporting

As one of the largest industrial firms in the United States, Altria Group, Inc., reported consolidated net revenues of $89.6 billion in 2004. As the parent company of Philip Morris and Kraft Foods, Altria Group is well known as a maker of cigarettes and food products. How much of the company's consolidated revenues did these different lines of business generate? Knowing this could be very useful to potential investors as opportunities for future growth and profitability in these different industries could differ significantly.

To comply with U.S. GAAP, Altria Group disaggregated its 2004 consolidated net revenues and reported that the company's revenues were generated by these different ventures; approximately $57.0 billion came from tobacco, $32.2 billion from food, and $395 million from financial services. Altria Group disclosed additional information indicating that $41.2 billion of the 2004 consolidated net revenues were generated in the United States, $36.2 billion in Europe, and $12.2 billion in other parts of the world. Such information, describing the various components of Altria Group's operations (both by line of business and by geographic area), often can be more useful to an analyst than the single sales figures reported in the consolidated income statement. "All investors like segment reporting—separate financials for each division—because it enables them to analyze how well each part of a corporation is doing."[1]

In its 2004 Annual Report, the Boeing Company reported earnings of $1.9 billion for the year ended December 31, 2004. This information was not made available to the public until early in 2005 after the company had closed the books on 2004. To provide more timely information on which investors could base their decisions about the company, Boeing published separate interim reports for each of the first three quarters of 2004. Earnings were $623 million in the first quarter, $607 million in the second quarter, and $456 million in the third quarter, and then earnings dropped precipitously in the fourth quarter to $186 million. Information about the reports of operations for time intervals of less than one year can be very useful to an analyst.

Questions to Consider

- The consolidation process brings together the many, varied components of a business combination to form a single set of financial statements. How can a reader of such statements evaluate the results and prospects of the individual segments that make up the organization?

- How are the operating segments of a company identified, and how is the significance of each of these units determined?

- What information must a company disclose in its financial statements about its various operating segments?

- What information must a company disclose about its products and services and about its operations in foreign countries?

- What guidance has the FASB provided to reporting entities concerning disclosure of major customers?

- What approach should a company take in preparing financial statements for time periods of less than one year?

- What minimum information should a company disclose in its interim financial reports?

[1] Robert A. Parker, "How Do You Play the New Annual Report Game?" *Communication World,* September 1990, p. 26.

In the first part of this chapter, we examine the specific requirements for disaggregating financial statement information as required by the FASB. New rules for reporting segment information went into effect in 1998. Before examining those rules, we trace the history of segment reporting in the United States to better explain the importance of disaggregated information for financial analysts. In the second part of the chapter, we concentrate on the special rules that are required to be applied in the preparation of interim reports. All publicly traded companies in the United States are required to prepare interim reports on a quarterly basis.

SEGMENT REPORTING

To facilitate the analysis and evaluation of financial data, in the 1960s several groups began to push the accounting profession to require disclosure of segment information such as Altria Group reported. Not surprisingly, the timing of this movement corresponded to a period of significant corporate merger and acquisition activity. As business organizations expanded through ever-widening diversification, financial statement analysis became increasingly difficult. The broadening of an enterprise's activities into different products, industries, or geographic areas complicates the analysis of conditions, trends, and ratios and, therefore, the ability to predict. The various industry segments or geographic areas of operations of an enterprise can have different rates of profitability, degrees and types of risk, and opportunities for growth.

Because of the increasingly diverse activities of many organizations, disclosure of additional information was sought to help the readers of financial statements. The identity of the significant elements of an entity's operations was viewed as an important complement to consolidated totals. Thus, organizations such as the Financial Analysts Federation and the Financial Executives Institute supported the inclusion of data describing the major components (or segments) of an enterprise as a means of enhancing the informational content of corporate financial statements.

As a result of the demand for disaggregated information, a number of official steps have been taken since the 1960s to encourage or mandate such presentation within financial statements. During this period, the Accounting Principles Board (APB) and the New York Stock Exchange both urged companies to present such data voluntarily. The Securities and Exchange Commission as well as the Federal Trade Commission required the reporting of certain line-of-business information within documents filed with those bodies.

Because of the cost to generate these data and the fear that confidential information would be disclosed to competitors, however, not all reporting corporations agreed with these requirements. "Segment reporting came into being after a vicious battle waged between the Federal Trade Commission and big corporations in the mid-1970s. The corporations fought the FTC's demands for income statements and balance sheets on each of their different lines of business all the way to the Supreme Court, and they lost."[2]

The move toward dissemination of disaggregated information culminated in December 1976 with the FASB's release of *SFAS 14*, "Financial Reporting for Segments of a Business Enterprise." This pronouncement established guidelines for the presentation within corporate financial statements of information to describe the various segments that constitute each reporting entity.

SFAS 14

Specifically, *SFAS 14* required financial information to be presented portraying as many as four distinct aspects of a company's operations.

1. *Industry segments*. To disclose for each reportable industry segment:

Revenues
Operating profit or loss

[2] Dana Wechsler and Katarzyna Wandycz, "'An Innate Fear of Disclosure,'" *Forbes*, February 5, 1990.

Identifiable assets
Aggregate amount of depreciation, depletion, and amortization expense
Capital expenditures
Equity in the net income from an investment in the net assets of equity investees

2. *Domestic and foreign operations.* To disclose for domestic operations as well as for operations in each significant foreign geographic area:

Revenues
Operating profit or loss
Identifiable assets

3. *Export sales.* To report for domestic operations the amount of revenue derived from exporting products to unaffiliated customers in foreign countries.

4. *Major customers.* To disclose the amount of revenue derived from sales to each major customer.

Most companies made this information available within the notes to the financial statements. *SFAS 14* also allowed companies to report segment data in the body of the statements or as a separate schedule attached to the financial statements. In addition, some companies, such as the Colgate-Palmolive Company, provided this information in Management's Discussion and Analysis.

As an illustration of the industry segment disclosures required, a note to the 1996 financial statements of General Electric Company indicated that total consolidated revenues of $79.18 billion were generated by the following separately identifiable industry segments (in millions):

GE
Aircraft engines	$ 6,302
Appliances	6,375
Broadcasting	5,232
Industrial products and systems	10,412
Materials	6,509
Power generation	7,257
Technical products and services	4,692
All other	3,108
Corporate items and eliminations	(322)
Total GE	49,565

GECS
Financing	23,742
Specialty insurance	8,966
All other	5
Total GECS	32,713
Eliminations	(3,099)
Consolidated revenues	$79,179

General Electric reported information that gave the operating profit, assets, depreciation and amortization, and the total amount of capital expenditures for each of these segments.

The 1996 annual report of the Hewlett-Packard Company disclosed the following information about its operations in several different geographic areas (in millions):

	Net Revenues	Earnings from Operations	Identifiable Assets
United States	$24,304	$2,470	$14,321
Europe	14,895	769	7,991
Japan, other Asia Pacific, Canada, Latin America	13,597	1,173	7,200

Data describing industry segments and foreign operations were not the only disaggregated information to be disclosed based on the standards set by *SFAS 14*. As required by this same pronouncement, the financial statements of Caterpillar, Inc., reported that $5.13 billion of its 1995 sales came from exporting products to customers outside the United States (the largest amount was $1.527 billion to the Asia/Pacific area). The toy manufacturer Hasbro, Inc., also complied with *SFAS 14* by disclosing that "sales to the Company's two largest customers, Toys R Us, Inc., and Wal-Mart Stores, Inc., amounted to 21 percent and 12 percent, respectively, of consolidated net revenues during each year of 1995 and 1994 and 20 percent and 11 percent, respectively, in 1993."[3]

USEFULNESS OF SEGMENT INFORMATION

As these illustrations indicate, *SFAS 14* had a significant impact on the financial reporting process. The goal of reporting segment information is to enhance the usefulness of a corporation's financial statements. With disaggregation, the past and present operational success of each corporate component can be analyzed on an ongoing basis. Lockheed Martin, as an example, disclosed an overall decrease of $53 million in its revenues between 1994 and 1995. However, during that time, three of its five industry segments actually had an increase in revenues totaling more than $1,180 million. Although of significant interest to anyone evaluating the company, this information is not evident from the single revenue figure presented on the consolidated income statement.[4]

Just as important, segment data can assist analysts in predicting the effects of future changes in an organization's environment. For example, if textile manufacturing anticipates a recession, the degree of a company's involvement in that industry is vital information to a present or potential investor. Similarly, data describing operations in a particular area of the world are of immediate interest if political turbulence becomes prevalent there.

In its 1993 position paper entitled *Financial Reporting in the 1990s and Beyond,* the Association for Investment Management and Research (AIMR), formerly the Financial Analysts Federation, left no doubt as to the importance of segment reporting (59, 60):

> It is vital, essential, fundamental, indispensable, and integral to the investment analysis process. Analysts need to know and understand how the various components of a multifaceted enterprise behave economically. One weak member of the group is analogous to a section of blight on a piece of fruit; it has the potential to spread rot over the entirety. Even in the absence of weakness, different segments will generate dissimilar streams of cash flows to which are attached disparate risks and which bring about unique values. Thus, without disaggregation, there is no sensible way to predict the overall amounts, timing, or risks of a complete enterprise's cash flows. There is little dispute over the analytic usefulness of disaggregated financial data.

A substantial body of academic research has empirically investigated the usefulness of *SFAS 14* disclosures. Some of the major findings are these:

- Industry segment data improve analysts' accuracy in predicting consolidated sales and earnings; this is true for both large and small firms.
- The availability of industry segment data leads to greater consensus among analysts regarding their forecasts of sales and earnings.
- Segment *revenue* data (both industry and geographic) appear to be more useful than segment *earnings* data in making forecasts.
- The initial disclosure of geographic area data was used by stock market participants in assessing the riskiness of companies with foreign operations.[5]

When considered as a whole, the extant research clearly indicates that *SFAS 14* segment data have been useful to investors and creditors in evaluating the risk and return associated with investment or lending alternatives.

[3] Hasbro, Inc. 1995 Annual Report, Note 16 Segment Reporting.

[4] Lockheed Martin Corporation, 1995 Annual Report, Note 15—Information on Industry Segments and Major Customers.

[5] For an extensive review of the relevant literature, see Paul Pacter, *Reporting Disaggregated Information* (Stamford, CT: FASB, February 1993), pp. 131–202.

Notwithstanding the fact that in complying with *SFAS 14* companies provided information useful to external users of financial statements, financial analysts have consistently requested that information be disaggregated to a much greater degree than was done in practice. In its 1993 position paper referred to earlier, the AIMR indicated, "There is no disagreement among AIMR members that segment information is totally vital to their work. There also is general agreement among them that the current segment reporting standard, *Financial Accounting Standard No. 14,* is inadequate."[6] The AICPA's Special Committee on Financial Reporting echoed this sentiment by stating that "[users] believe that many companies define industry segments too broadly for business reporting and thus report on too few industry segments."[7]

One area of concern was the flexibility with which industry segments could be identified, especially when management determined that the company had a "dominant industry segment." *SFAS 14* provided that when a single segment made up more than 90 percent of a company's revenues, operating profit or loss, and identifiable assets, industry segment disclosures were not required. As an example, McDonald's Corporation, one of the largest corporations in the world, reported in its 1996 annual report that the company "operates exclusively in the food service industry," and thereby avoided providing industry segment information.[8]

Despite the apparent diversity of U.S. businesses, companies with dominant industry segments have been very common. In a survey of 600 companies, the AICPA's *Accounting Trends & Techniques* found that only 306 of these organizations reported industry segment revenues in their 1997 annual report.[9] The remainder must have viewed themselves as operating primarily in only one industry.

Both the AIMR and the AICPA's special committee recommended aligning segment reporting with internal reporting with segments defined on the basis of how an enterprise is organized and managed. Segments based on an enterprise's internal organization structure would have four advantages:

1. Knowledge of an enterprise's organization structure is valuable because it reflects the risks and opportunities that management believes to be important.
2. The ability to see the company the way management views it improves an analyst's ability to predict management actions that can significantly affect future cash flows.
3. Because segment information already is generated for management's use on the basis of the company's internal structure, the incremental cost of providing that information externally should be minimal.
4. Segments based on an existing internal structure should be less subjective than segments based on the term *industry*.[10]

Other recommendations for improving segment reporting that the AIMR made include these:

- Disclose segment information in interim financial statements.
- Disclose revenues and profit by product or service line, even if the company is deemed to operate in only one industry.
- Provide additional guidance as to how segments should be identified with the objectives to (1) disaggregate the company into more segments, (2) enhance the comparability of segments across companies, and (3) make segments consistent with the segmentation used by management in making decisions.
- Disclose more information—such as cash flows, liabilities, net assets, cost of goods sold, and interest expense.

[6] Association for Investment Management and Research, *Financial Reporting in the 1990s and Beyond* (Charlottesville, VA: AIMR, 1993), p. 5.

[7] American Institute of Certified Public Accountants, *Improving Business Reporting—A Customer Focus* (New York: AICPA, 1994). p. 69.

[8] McDonald's Corporation, 1996 Annual Report, p. 39.

[9] American Institute of Certified Public Accountants, *Accounting Trends and Techniques*—1997, 52nd ed. (New York: AICPA, 1998), p. 27.

[10] FASB, Proposed Statement of Financial Accounting Standards, "Reporting Disaggregated Information about a Business Enterprise," 1996, para. 66–67.

- Disclose what is in segments designated as "other."
- Provide more descriptive information about the segments.

In 1992, at the request of the AIMR, the AICPA Special Committee on Financial Reporting, and others, the FASB and the Accounting Standards Board (AcSB) in Canada decided to jointly reconsider segmental reporting with the objective of developing common standards that would apply in both the United States and Canada. After several years of study, in January 1996, the FASB issued an exposure draft for a Proposed Statement of Financial Accounting Standards entitled "Reporting Disaggregated Information about a Business Enterprise." The AcSB also issued an exposure draft identical in its applicable requirements to the FASB's proposed statement. In addition, the International Accounting Standards Committee (IASC) issued an exposure draft on this topic which, while not identical, is similar to the FASB's. Members of both the FASB and the AcSB participated in IASC meetings on segment reporting to exchange views.

In June 1997, *SFAS 131*, "Disclosures about Segments of an Enterprise and Related Information," was approved. Effective for fiscal years beginning after December 15, 1997, this statement makes substantial changes to the segment disclosures required to be provided by U.S. companies. There is a significant change in *how reportable segments are determined,* as well as in the *amount and types of information* to be provided.

SFAS 131

According to *SFAS 131,* the objective of segment reporting is to provide information about the different business activities in which an enterprise engages and the different economic environments in which it operates to help users of financial statements

- Better understand the enterprise's performance.
- Better assess its prospects for future net cash flows.
- Make more informed judgments about the enterprise as a whole (para. 3).

The Management Approach

To achieve this objective, *SFAS 131* has adopted the so-called management approach for determining segments. The management approach is based on the way that management disaggregates the enterprise for making operating decisions. These disaggregated components are *operating segments,* which will be evident from the enterprise's organization structure. More specifically, an operating segment is a component of an enterprise if

- It engages in business activities from which it earns revenues and incurs expenses.
- Its operating results are regularly reviewed by the chief operating decision maker to assess performance and make resource allocation decisions.
- Discrete financial information is available for it.

An organizational unit can be an operating segment even if all of its revenue or expense results from transactions with other segments as might be the case in a vertically integrated company. However, not all parts of a company are necessarily included in an operating segment. For example, a research and development unit that incurs expenses but does not earn revenues would not be an operating segment. Similarly, corporate headquarters might not earn revenues or might earn revenues that are only incidental to the activities of the enterprise and therefore would not be considered an operating segment.

For many companies, only one set of organizational units qualifies as operating segments. In some companies, however, business activities are disaggregated in more than one way and the chief operating decision maker uses multiple sets of reports. For example, a company might generate reports by geographic region *and* by product line. In those cases, two additional criteria must be considered to identify operating segments:

1. An operating segment has a segment manager who is directly accountable to the chief operating decision maker for its financial performance. If more than one set of organizational

units exists, but segment managers are held responsible for only one set, that set constitutes the operating segments.

2. If segment managers exist for two or more overlapping sets of organizational units (as in a matrix form of organization), the nature of the business activities must be considered, and the organizational units based on products and services constitute the operating segments. For example, if certain managers are responsible for different product lines and other managers are responsible for different geographic areas, the enterprise components based on products would constitute the operating segments.

DETERMINING REPORTABLE OPERATING SEGMENTS

After a company has identified its operating segments based on its internal reporting system, management must decide which of these segments should be reported separately. Generally, information must be reported separately for each operating segment that meets one or more quantitative thresholds established in *SFAS 131. However, if two or more operating segments have essentially the same business activities in essentially the same economic environments, information for those individual segments may be combined.* "For example, a retail chain may have 10 stores that individually meet the definition of an operating segment, but each store is essentially the same as the others."[11] In that case, the Board believes that the benefit to be derived from separately reporting each operating segment would not justify the cost of disclosure. In determining whether business activities and environments are similar, management must consider these aggregation criteria:

1. The nature of the products and services provided by each operating segment.
2. The nature of the production process.
3. The type or class of customer.
4. The distribution methods.
5. If applicable, the nature of the regulatory environment.

Segments must be similar in each and every one of these areas to be combined. However, aggregation of similar segments is not required.

Quantitative Thresholds

After determining whether any segments are to be aggregated, management next must determine which of its operating segments are significant enough to justify separate disclosure. In *SFAS 131,* the FASB decided to retain the three tests introduced in *SFAS 14* for identifying operating segments for which separate disclosure is required:

- A revenue test.
- A profit or loss test.
- An asset test.

An operating segment needs to satisfy only one of these tests to be considered of significant size to necessitate separate disclosure.

To apply these three tests, a segment's revenues, profit or loss, and assets must be determined. *SFAS 131* does not stipulate a specific measure of profit or loss, such as operating profit or income before taxes, to be used in applying these tests. Instead, the measure of profit that the chief operating decision maker applies in evaluating operating segments is to be used. An operating segment is considered to be significant if it meets any one of the following tests:

1. *Revenue test.* Segment revenues, both external and intersegment, are 10 percent or more of the combined revenue, internal and external, of all reported operating segments.

---

[11] *FASB Statement 131,* "Disclosures about Segments of an Enterprise and Related Information," June 1997, para. 73.

2. *Profit or loss test.* Segment profit or loss is 10 percent or more of the higher (in absolute terms) of the combined reported profit of all profitable segments or the combined reported loss of all segments incurring a loss.

3. *Asset test.* Segment assets are 10 percent or more of the combined assets of all operating segments.

Application of the revenue and asset tests would seem to pose few problems. In contrast, the profit or loss test is more complicated and warrants illustration. For this purpose, assume that Durham Company has five separate operating segments with the following profits or losses:

Durham Company Segments—Profits and Losses

Soft drinks	$1,700,000
Wine	(600,000)
Food products	240,000
Paper packaging	880,000
Recreation parks	(130,000)
Net operating profit	$2,090,000

Three of these industry segments (soft drinks, food products, and paper packaging) report profits that total $2,820,000. The two remaining segments have losses for the year in the amount of $730,000.

Profits		**Losses**	
Soft drinks	$1,700,000	Wine	$600,000
Food products	240,000	Recreation parks	130,000
Paper packaging	880,000		
Total	$2,820,000	Total	$730,000

Consequently, $2,820,000 serves as the basis for the profit or loss test because that figure is higher in absolute terms than $730,000. Based on the 10 percent threshold, any operating segment with either a profit *or loss* of more than $282,000 (10% × $2,820,000) is considered material and, thus, must be disclosed separately. According to this one test, the soft drink and paper packaging segments (with operating profits of $1.7 million and $880,000, respectively) are both judged to be reportable as is the wine segment, despite having a loss of $600,000.

Operating segments that do not meet any of the quantitative thresholds may be combined to produce a reportable segment if they share *a majority* of the aggregation criteria listed earlier. Durham Company's food products and recreation parks operating segments do not meet any of the aggregation criteria. Operating segments that are not individually significant and that cannot be aggregated with other segments are combined and disclosed in an *all other* category. The sources of the revenues included in the All Other category must be disclosed.

TESTING PROCEDURES—COMPLETE ILLUSTRATION

To provide a comprehensive example of all three of these testing procedures, assume that Atkinson Company is a large business combination comprising six operating segments: automotive, furniture, textbook, motion picture, appliance, and finance. Complete information about each of these segments, as reported internally to the chief operating decision maker, appears in Exhibit 8.1.

The Revenue Test

In applying the revenue test to the operating segments of Atkinson Company, the combined revenue of all segments must be determined:

EXHIBIT 8.1   Reportable Segment Testing

				Motion		
ATKINSON COMPANY						
	Automotive	**Furniture**	**Textbook**	**Picture**	**Appliance**	**Finance**
Revenues:						
Sales to outsiders	$32.6*	$6.9	$ 6.6	$22.2	$3.1	–0–
Intersegment transfers	6.6	1.2	–0–	–0–	1.9	–0–
Interest revenue—outsiders	2.4	0.9	0.2	0.6	0.3	8.7
Interest revenue—						
intersegment loans	–0–	–0–	–0–	–0–	–0–	3.6
Total revenues	$41.6	$9.0	$ 6.8	$22.8	$5.3	$12.3
Expenses:						
Operating expenses—						
outsiders	$17.1	$3.6	$ 7.3	$24.0	$3.6	$ 2.3
Operating expenses—						
intersegment transfers	4.8	1.0	–0–	–0–	0.8	0.8
Interest expense	2.1	1.0	2.2	4.6	–0–	6.1
Income taxes	6.6	1.4	(1.5)	(3.1)	0.4	0.1
Total expenses	$30.6	$7.0	$ 8.0	$25.5	$4.8	$ 9.3
Assets:						
Tangible	$ 9.6	$1.1	$.8	$10.9	$0.9	$ 9.2
Intangible	1.8	0.2	0.7	3.6	0.1	–0–
Intersegment loans	–0–	–0–	–0–	–0–	–0–	5.4
Total assets	$11.4	$1.3	$ 1.5	$14.5	$1.0	$14.6

*All figures in millions.

Operating Segment	**Total Revenues**
Automotive	$41.6*
Furniture	9.0
Textbook	6.8
Motion picture	22.8
Appliance	5.3
Finance	12.3
Combined total	$97.8

*All figures are in millions.

Because these six segments have total revenues of $97.8 million, that figure is used in applying the revenue test. Based on the 10 percent significance level, any segment with revenues of more than $9.78 million qualifies for required disclosure. Accordingly, the automotive, motion picture, and finance segments all have satisfied this particular criterion. Atkinson must present appropriate disaggregated information for each of these three operating segments, therefore, within its financial statements.

The Profit or Loss Test

The profit or loss of each operating segment is determined by subtracting segment expenses from total segment revenues. *SFAS 131* does not require common costs to be allocated to individual segments to determine segment profit or loss if this is not normally done for internal purposes. For example, an enterprise that accounts for pension expense only on a consolidated basis is not required to allocate pension expense to each operating segment. Any allocations that are made must be done on a reasonable basis. Moreover, segment profit or loss does not have to be calculated in accordance with generally accepted accounting principles if the measure reported internally is calculated on another basis. To assist the readers of financial statements in understanding segment disclosures, *SFAS 131* does require disclosure of any differences in the basis of measurement between segment and consolidated amounts.

Each operating segment's profit or loss is calculated as follows:

Operating Segment	Total Revenues	Total Expenses	Profit	Loss
Automotive	$41.6*	$30.6	$11.0	–0–
Furniture	9.0	7.0	2.0	–0–
Textbook	6.8	8.0	–0–	$ 1.2
Motion picture	22.8	25.5	–0–	2.7
Appliance	5.3	4.8	0.5	–0–
Finance	12.3	9.3	3.0	–0–
Totals	$97.8	$85.2	$16.5	$ 3.9

*All figures are in millions.

The $16.5 million total (the four profit figures) is higher in an absolute sense than the $3.9 million in losses. Therefore, this larger balance serves as the basis for the second quantitative test. Because the FASB has again established a 10 percent criterion, either a profit or loss of $1.65 million or more qualifies a segment for disaggregation. According to the income totals just calculated, Atkinson Company's automotive, furniture, motion picture, and finance segments are large enough to warrant separate disclosure.

The Asset Test

The final test designed by the FASB is based on the operating segments' combined total assets:

Operating Segment	Assets
Automotive	$11.4*
Furniture	1.3
Textbook	1.5
Motion picture	14.5
Appliance	1.0
Finance	14.6
Combined total	$44.3

*All figures are in millions.

Because 10 percent of the combined total equals $4.43 million, any segment holding at least that amount of assets is viewed as a reportable segment. Consequently, according to this final significance test, the automotive, motion picture, and finance segments are all considered of sufficient size to require disaggregation. The three remaining segments do not have sufficient assets to pass this particular test.

Analysis of Test Results

A summary of all three significance tests as applied to Atkinson Company is as follows:

Operating Segments	Revenue Test	Profit or Loss Test	Asset Test
Automotive	✔	✔	✔
Furniture		✔	
Textbook			
Motion picture	✔	✔	✔
Appliance			
Finance	✔	✔	✔

Four of this company's operating segments (automotive, furniture, motion picture, and finance) have been determined to be separately reportable. Because neither the appliance nor the textbook segment has met any of these three tests, disaggregated information describing their *individual* operations is not required. However, the financial data accumulated from these two nonsignificant segments still have to be presented. The figures can be combined and disclosed as aggregate amounts in an All Other category with appropriate disclosure of the source of revenues.

OTHER GUIDELINES

Several other FASB guidelines apply to the disclosure of operating segment information. These rules are designed to ensure that the disaggregated data are consistent from year to year and relevant to the needs of financial statement users. For example, any operating segment that has been reportable in the past and is judged by management to be of continuing significance should be disclosed separately in the current statements regardless of the outcome of the testing process. This degree of flexibility is included within the rules to ensure the ongoing usefulness of the disaggregated information, especially for comparison purposes.

In a similar manner, if an operating segment newly qualifies for disclosure in the current year, prior period segment data presented for comparative purposes must be restated to reflect the newly reportable segment as a separate segment. Once again, the comparability of information has been given high priority in setting the standards for disclosure.

One final issue that *SFAS 131* raised concerns the number of operating segments that should be disclosed. To enhance the value of the disaggregated information, a substantial portion of a company's operations should be presented individually. Thus, the FASB has stated that a sufficient number of segments is presumed to be included only if their combined sales to unaffiliated customers are at least 75 percent of total company sales made to outsiders. If this lower limit is not achieved, additional segments must be disclosed separately despite their failure to satisfy even one of the three quantitative thresholds.

As an illustration, assume that Brendan Corporation has identified seven industry segments that have generated revenues as follows (in millions):

Operating Segments	Sales to Unaffiliated Customers	Intersegment Transfers	Segment Revenues (and percentage of total)	
Housewares	$ 5.5	$ 1.6	$ 7.1	(9.3%)
Toys	6.2	–0–	6.2	(8.1)
Pottery	3.4	7.9	11.3	(14.8) ✔
Lumber	6.6	10.4	17.0	(22.3) ✔
Lawn mowers	7.2	–0–	7.2	(9.4)
Appliances	2.1	6.2	8.3	(10.9) ✔
Construction	19.2	–0–	19.2	(25.2) ✔
Totals	$50.2	$26.1	$76.3	(100%)

Based on the 10 percent revenue test, four of these segments are reportable (because each has total revenues of more than $7.63 million): pottery, lumber, appliances, and construction. Assuming that none of the other segments qualifies as significant in either of the two remaining tests, disclosure of disaggregated data is required only for these four segments. However, the FASB's 75 percent rule has not been met; the reportable segments generate just 62.4 percent of the company's total sales to unrelated parties (in millions):

Reportable Segments	Sales to Unaffiliated Customers
Pottery	$ 3.4
Lumber	6.6
Appliances	2.1
Construction	19.2
Total	$31.3

Information being disaggregated: $31.3 million/$50.2 million = 62.4%

To satisfy the 75 percent requirement, Brendan Corporation must also include the lawn mower segment within the disaggregated data being presented. With the addition of this nonsignificant segment, sales of \$38.5 million (\$31.3 + \$7.2) to outside parties now are disclosed. This figure amounts to 76.7 percent of the company total (\$38.5 million/ \$50.2 million). The two remaining segments—housewares and toys—could still be included separately within the disaggregated data; disclosure is not prohibited. However, information for these two segments would probably be combined and reported as aggregate figures.

One final aspect of these reporting requirements should be mentioned. Some companies might be organized in such a fashion that a relatively large number of operating segments exist. The FASB suggests there could be a practical limit to the number of operating segments that should be reported separately. Beyond that limit, the information becomes too detailed to be useful. *SFAS 131* (para. 24) indicates that "Although no precise limit has been determined, as the number of segments that are reportable . . . increases above 10, the enterprise should consider whether a practical limit has been reached."

INFORMATION TO BE DISCLOSED BY OPERATING SEGMENT

Consistent with requests from the financial analyst community, *SFAS 131* has significantly expanded the amount of information to be disclosed for each operating segment:

1. *General information* about the operating segment:
   - Factors used to identify operating segments.
   - Types of products and services from which each operating segment derives its revenues.

2. *Segment profit or loss* and the following revenues and expenses included in segment profit or loss:
   - Revenues from external customers.
   - Revenues from transactions with other operating segments.
   - Interest revenue and interest expense (reported separately); net interest revenue may be reported for finance segments if this measure is used internally for evaluation.
   - Depreciation, depletion, and amortization expense.
   - Other significant noncash items included in segment profit or loss.
   - Unusual items (discontinued operations and extraordinary items).
   - Income tax expense or benefit.

3. *Total segment assets* and the following related items:
   - Investment in equity method affiliates.
   - Expenditures for additions to long-lived assets.

Although the AIMR requested its reporting, the FASB does not specifically require cash flow information to be reported for each operating segment because this information often is not generated by segment for internal reporting purposes. The requirement to disclose noncash items other than depreciation is an attempt to provide information that might enhance users' ability to estimate cash flow from operations.

SFAS 131 need not be applied to immaterial items. For example, some segments do not have material amounts of interest revenue and expense, and therefore disclosure of these items of information would not be necessary. In addition, if an item of information is not generated by the internal financial reporting system on a segment basis, that item need not be disclosed. This is consistent with the FASB's desire that segment reporting create as little additional cost to an enterprise as possible.

To demonstrate how the operating segment information might be disclosed, let us return to the Atkinson Company example referred to earlier in this chapter. Application of the quantitative threshold tests resulted in four separately reportable segments (automotive, furniture, motion picture, and finance). The nonsignificant operating segments (textbook and appliance) are

EXHIBIT 8.2   Operating Segment Disclosures

ATKINSON COMPANY

	Operating Segment				
	Automotive	**Furniture**	**Motion Picture**	**Finance**	**All Other**
Revenues from external customers	$32.6*	$6.9	$22.2	—	$ 9.7
Intersegment revenues	6.6	1.2	—	—	1.9
Segment profit (loss)	11.0	2.0	(2.7)	$3.0	(0.7)
Interest revenue	2.4	0.9	0.6	—	0.5
Interest expense	2.1	1.0	4.6	—	2.2
Net interest revenue	—	—	—	6.2	—
Depreciation and amortization	2.7	1.5	2.4	0.9	0.4
Other significant noncash items:					
Cost in excess of billings on long-term contracts	0.8	—	—	—	—
Income tax expense (benefit)	6.6	1.4	(3.1)	0.1	(1.1)
Segment assets	11.4	1.3	14.5	14.6	2.5
Expenditures for segment assets	3.5	0.4	3.7	1.7	1.3

*All figures in millions.

combined in an All Other category. Exhibit 8.2 shows the operating segment disclosures included in Atkinson Company's financial statements.

In addition to information provided in Exhibit 8.1, information on depreciation and amortization, other significant noncash items, and expenditures for long-lived segment assets has been gathered for each operating segment to comply with the disclosure requirements. Only the automotive segment has other significant noncash items, and none of the segments has equity method investments. Atkinson Company had no unusual items during the year.

To determine whether a sufficient number of segments is included, the ratio of combined sales to unaffiliated customers for the separately reported operating segments must be compared with total company sales made to outsiders. The combined amount of revenues from external customers disclosed for the automotive, furniture, motion picture, and finance segments is $61.7 million. Total revenues from external customers is $71.4 million:

$$\$61.7 \text{ million}/\$71.4 \text{ million} = 86.4\%$$

Because 86.4 percent exceeds the lower limit of 75 percent that the FASB imposed, the level of disaggregation that Atkinson Company reports is adequate.

Reconciliations to Consolidated Totals

As noted earlier, *SFAS 131* does not require that disaggregated information be provided in accordance with generally accepted accounting principles. Instead, information is to be provided as it is prepared by the company's internal reporting system even if not based on GAAP. "Preparing segment information in accordance with the generally accepted accounting principles used at the consolidated level would be difficult because some generally accepted accounting principles are not intended to apply at a segment level" (*SFAS 131,* para. 84). Examples are the accounting for inventory on a LIFO basis when inventory pools include items in more than one segment, accounting for companywide pension plans, and accounting for purchased goodwill. Accordingly, allocation of these items to individual operating segments is not required.

However, the total of the reportable segments' revenues must be reconciled to consolidated revenues, and the total of reportable segments' profit or loss must be reconciled to income before tax for the company as a whole. Adjustments and eliminations that have been made to develop enterprise financial statements in compliance with generally accepted accounting principles must be identified. Examples would be the elimination of intersegment revenues

EXHIBIT 8.3
Reconciliation of Segment Results to Consolidated Totals

ATKINSON COMPANY	
Revenues:	
Total segment revenues	$ 97.8*
Elimination of intersegment revenues	(13.3)
Total consolidated revenues	$ 84.5
Profit or loss:	
Total segment profit or loss	$ 12.6
Total segment income taxes	3.9
Total segment profit before income taxes	$ 16.5
Elimination of intersegment profits	(5.9)
Unallocated amounts:	
Litigation settlement received	3.6
Other corporate expenses	(2.7)
Adjustment to pension expense in consolidation	(0.8)
Consolidated income before income taxes	$ 10.7
Assets:	
Total for reported segments	$ 44.3
Elimination of intersegment loans	(5.4)
Goodwill not allocated to segments	3.2
Other unallocated amounts	2.6
Total consolidated assets	$ 44.7

*All figures in millions.

and an adjustment for companywide pension expense. The same is true for reconciliation of total segments' assets to the enterprise's total assets.

In addition, in reconciling the total of segments' revenues, profit or loss, and assets to the enterprise totals, the aggregate amount of revenues, profit or loss, and assets from immaterial operating segments must be disclosed. The company also must disclose assets, revenues, expenses, gains, losses, interest expense, and depreciation, depletion, and amortization expense for components of the enterprise that are not operating segments. This would include, for example, assets and expenses associated with corporate headquarters. An example of how Atkinson Company might make these reconciliations is presented in Exhibit 8.3.

Atkinson Company must make three adjustments in reconciling segment results with consolidated totals. The first adjustment is the elimination of intercompany revenues, profit or loss, and assets that are not included in consolidated totals. The elimination of intersegment revenues includes intersegment transfers amounting to $9.7 million plus $3.6 million of intersegment interest revenue generated by the finance segment. The second adjustment relates to corporate items that have not been allocated to the operating segments. These include purchased goodwill, a litigation settlement received by the company, and corporate headquarters expenses and assets. The third adjustment reconciles differences in segment accounting practices from accounting practices used in the consolidated financial statements. The only adjustment of this nature that Atkinson Company made relates to the accounting for pension expense. Individual operating segments measure pension expense based on cash payments made to the pension plan. Because GAAP requires pension expense to be measured on an accrual basis, an adjustment for the amount of pension expense to be recognized in the consolidated statements is necessary.

In addition to the operating segment disclosures and reconciliation of segment results to consolidated totals, companies also must provide an explanation of the measurement of segment profit or loss and segment assets. This explanation should include a description of any differences in measuring segment profit or loss and consolidated income before tax, any differences in measuring segment assets and consolidated assets, and any differences in measuring segment profit or loss and segment assets. An example of this last item would be the allocation of depreciation expense to segments but not of the related depreciable assets. The basis of accounting for intersegment transactions also must be described.

EXHIBIT 8.4   Operating Segment Disclosures in Wyeth's 2004 Annual Report

15. Company Data by Segment

The Company has four reportable segments: Pharmaceuticals, Consumer Health Care, Animal Health, and Corporate. The Company's Pharmaceuticals, Consumer Health Care, and Animal Health reportable segments are strategic business units that offer different products and services. Beginning in the 2003 fourth quarter, the Company changed its reporting structure to include the Animal Health business as a separate reportable segment. The Animal Health business was previously reported within the Pharmaceuticals segment. Prior period information presented herein has been restated to be on a comparable basis. The reportable segments are managed separately because they manufacture, distribute, and sell distinct products and provide services that require differing technologies and marketing strategies.

The accounting policies of the segments described above are the same as those described in *Summary of Significant Accounting Policies* in Note 1. The Company evaluates the performance of the Pharmaceuticals, Consumer Health Care, and Animal Health reportable segments based on income (loss) before income taxes, which includes gains on the sales of noncorporate assets and certain other items. Corporate includes interest expense and interest income, gains on the sales of investments and other corporate assets, gains relating to Immunex/Amgen common stock transactions, certain litigation provisions, including the *Redux* and *Pondimin* litigation charges, special charges, and other miscellaneous items.

Company Data by Reportable Segment

(in millions)

Year Ended December 31,	2004	2003	2002
Net Revenue from Customers			
Pharmaceuticals	$13,964.1	$12,622.7	$11,733.3
Consumer Health Care	2,557.4	2,434.5	2,197.4
Animal Health	836.5	793.4	653.3
Consolidated total	$17,358.0	$15,850.6	$14,584.0
Income (Loss) before Income Taxes			
Pharmaceuticals	$ 4,040.1	$ 3,798.5	$ 3,441.4
Consumer Health Care	578.6	592.4	608.0
Animal Health	134.8	127.4	64.1
Corporate	(4,883.3)	(2,156.7)	1,983.7
Consolidated total	$ (129.8)	$ 2,361.6	$ 6,097.2
Depreciation and Amortization Expense			
Pharmaceuticals	$ 529.5	$ 458.0	$ 409.6
Consumer Health Care	45.7	34.9	32.1
Animal Health	29.9	25.9	25.2
Corporate	17.3	19.1	17.8
Consolidated total	$ 622.4	$ 537.9	$ 484.7
Expenditures for Long-Lived Assets			
Pharmaceuticals	$ 1,226.5	$ 1,742.1	$ 1,758.2
Consumer Health Care	33.2	53.8	40.1
Animal Health	40.0	28.4	31.2
Corporate	83.4	126.3	126.3
Consolidated total	$ 1,383.1	$ 1,950.6	$ 1,955.8
Total Assets at December 31,			
Pharmaceuticals	$15,771.2	$14,513.7	$12,608.7
Consumer Health Care	1,701.4	1,742.8	1,709.8
Animal Health	1,340.9	1,328.4	1,293.1
Corporate	14,816.2	13,447.0	10,431.0
Consolidated total	$33,629.7	$31,031.9	$26,042.6

EXAMPLES OF OPERATING SEGMENT DISCLOSURES

A majority of companies are organized along product and/or service lines. For example, we show operating segment disclosures for Wyeth (formerly American Home Products) in Exhibit 8.4. Wyeth does not disclose interest revenue and interest expense by operating segment because these relate only to Corporate. Nor does it report income tax expense or benefit by segment because the company evaluates the performance of its operating segments based on income before taxes.

A study of 106 companies with reportable segments based on line of business found that 52 percent of the companies disclosed more segments under *SFAS 131* than they did under *SFAS 14*, 42 percent disclosed the same number of segments, and only 6 percent reported fewer segments.[12] Notwithstanding these results, the Securities and Exchange Commission (SEC) has expressed concern about the number of segments reported by companies. In 2001, SEC Chief Accountant Robert Bayless warned companies that they should expect his staff to "review the company's Web site, financial analysts' reports, and other public documents to assess whether segments included in the footnotes appear reasonably disaggregated."[13]

Some companies, such as McDonald's, Coca-Cola, and Nike, are organized geographically and define operating segments as regions of the world. McDonald's has six operating segments: United States, Europe, APMEA (Asia, Pacific, Middle East, Africa), Latin America, Canada, and Other.

Some companies report a combination of products or services and international segments. Wal-Mart has four operating segments: Wal-Mart Stores, Sam's Club, International, and Other. Anheuser-Busch Companies, Inc., has five reportable segments: Domestic Beer, International Beer, Packaging, Entertainment, and Other. The nature of the segmentation of these companies provides considerable insight into the manner in which upper management views and evaluates the various parts that make up the consolidated enterprise.

ENTERPRISEWIDE DISCLOSURES

Information about Products and Services

The FASB recognizes that some enterprises are not organized along product or service lines. For example, some enterprises organize by geographic areas. Moreover, some enterprises may have only one operating segment yet provide a range of different products and services. To provide some comparability between enterprises, *SFAS 131* requires *disclosure of revenues derived from transactions with external customers from each product or service* if operating segments have not been determined based on differences in products or services. An enterprise with only one operating segment also would have to disclose revenues from external customers on the basis of product or service. However, providing this information is not required if impracticable—that is, the information is not available and the cost to develop it would be excessive.

Lowe's Companies, Inc., operates in only one segment; nevertheless, it reported "sales by product category" as required under *SFAS 131* in its 2004 annual report. See Exhibit 8.5 for that information.

Information about Geographic Areas

In addition, the following two items of information must be reported *(1) for the domestic country, (2) for all foreign countries in which the enterprise derives revenues or holds assets, and (3) for each foreign country in which a material amount of revenues is derived or assets are held:*

- Revenues from external customers.
- Long-lived assets.

---

[12] Donna L. Street, Nancy B. Nichols, and Sidney J. Gray, "Segment Disclosures under *SFAS No. 131:* Has Business Segment Reporting Improved?" *Accounting Horizons,* September 2000, pp. 259–85.

[13] "SEC's Bayless Warns: 10-K Audits Likely to Rise in 2001," *Accounting Today,* April 2–15, 2001, p. 3.

EXHIBIT 8.5
Sales by Product Category in Lowe's Companies, Inc., 2004 Annual Report

	Sales by Product Category					
	2004		**2003**		**2002**	
Product Category	**Total Sales***	**%**	**Total Sales***	**%**	**Total Sales***	**%**
Appliances	$ 4,078	11%	$ 3,518	11%	$ 2,995	11%
Lumber	3,288	9	2,652	9	2,232	9
Seasonal living	2,442	7	2,008	7	1,738	7
Millwork	2,439	7	2,043	7	1,724	7
Flooring	2,370	6	1,998	6	1,651	6
Paint	2,317	6	2,048	7	1,737	7
Nursery	2,201	6	1,954	6	1,656	6
Tools	2,150	6	1,822	6	1,576	6
Fashion plumbing	2,128	6	1,820	6	1,556	6
Lighting	2,089	6	1,857	6	1,586	6
Building materials	2,025	6	1,666	5	1,408	5
Hardware	1,980	5	1,667	5	1,417	5
Outdoor power equipment . .	1,511	4	1,202	4	983	4
Cabinets and countertops . . .	1,369	4	1,029	3	790	3
Rough plumbing	1,161	3	982	3	847	3
Rough electrical	977	3	791	3	683	3
Walls/windows	951	3	848	3	707	3
Home organization	793	2	670	2	528	2
Furniture	163	0	213	1	243	1
Other	32	0	50	0	55	0
Totals	**$36,464**	**100%**	**$30,838**	**100%**	**$26,112**	**100%**

* Dollars in millions.

Even if the company has only one operating segment and therefore does not otherwise provide segment information, it must report geographic area information. The previous requirement under *SFAS 14* to disclose *profit or loss* by geographic area no longer exists.

Note that the FASB requires companies to disclose information for *each material country*. Requiring disclosure at the country level is a significant change from *SFAS 14*. The FASB believes that reporting information about individual countries rather than larger areas has two benefits. First, it reduces the burden on preparers of financial statements because most operating segments are likely to have material operations in only a few countries. Second, the information is easier to interpret and therefore more useful because individual countries within a geographic area often experience very different rates of economic growth and economic conditions.

Although the FASB considered using a 10 percent rule for determining when a country is material, ultimately it decided to leave this determination to management's judgment. In determining materiality, management should apply the concept that an item is material if its omission could change a user's decision about the enterprise as a whole. The FASB does not provide more specific guidance on this issue.

The change in geographic area reporting under *SFAS 131* has caused some companies to provide more information than under *SFAS 14* and other companies to provide less information. Exhibit 8.6 presents the geographic area disclosures made by E.I. du Pont de Nemours and Company in its 1997 (last year of *SFAS 14*) and 1998 (first year of *SFAS 131*) annual reports. In complying with *SFAS 131*, DuPont has defined materiality at a very low amount; for example, Mexico generated less than 2 percent of total net sales. By reporting by individual country in 1998, DuPont clearly provides more detailed information than it provided previously. A limitation in the requirements of *SFAS 131*, however, is the fact that operating income is no longer required to be reported by geographic area.

International Business Machines Corporation's geographic area information reported in its 1997 and 1998 annual reports is presented in Exhibit 8.7. As a result of the change from reporting by geographic segment under *SFAS 14* to reporting by material country under *SFAS 131*, IBM provided less detail with regard to the location of non-U.S. revenues. In 1998,

EXHIBIT 8.6
Comparison of DuPont's
1997 and 1998 Geographic
Area Disclosures

E. I. DU PONT DE NEMOURS AND COMPANY

1997 Geographic Information

	United States	Europe	Other Regions	Consolidated
Sales to unaffiliated customers	$24,648*	$15,389	$5,042	$45,079
Transfers between geographic areas	3,108	625	832	–0–
Total	$27,756	$16,014	$5,874	$45,079
After-tax operating income	$ 1,346	$ 1,306	$ 126	$ 2,778
Identifiable assets at December 31	20,015	11,346	5,242	36,603

1998 Geographic Information

	Net Sales	Net Property
North America		
United States	$13,075	$ 8,454
Canada	881	459
Mexico	421	117
Other	93	135
Total	$14,470	$ 9,165
Europe, Middle East, and Africa		
Germany	$ 1,450	$ 388
United Kingdom	988	1,078
France	904	181
Italy	902	5
Other	2,108	1,188
Total	$ 6,352	$ 2,840
Asia Pacific		
Japan	$ 820	$ 159
Taiwan	591	707
China	398	208
Singapore	86	635
Other	947	244
Total	$ 2,842	$ 1,953
South America		
Brazil	$ 659	$ 83
Other	444	90
Total	$ 1,103	$ 173
Total	$24,767	$14,131

*Dollars in millions.

the company disclosed the fact that it generated 44 percent of its revenue in the United States and 10 percent in Japan, but it does not disclose the location of the remaining 46 percent of revenues generated in other foreign countries.

Information about Major Customers

SFAS 131 retained one final but important disclosure requirement that *SFAS 14* originally established. A reporting entity must indicate its reliance on any major customer. *Presentation of this information is required whenever 10 percent or more of a company's revenues is derived from a single customer.* The existence of all major customers must be disclosed along with the related amount of revenues and the identity of the operating segment generating the revenues. Interestingly enough, the company need not reveal the identity of the customer.

INTERNATIONAL BUSINESS MACHINES CORPORATION

1997 Geographic Information

United States
Revenue—customers	$32,663*
Interarea transfers	9,426
Total	$42,089
Net earnings	2,354
Assets at December 31	41,633

Europe, Middle East, Africa
Revenue—customers	$23,919
Interarea transfers	2,513
Total	$26,432
Net earnings	1,343
Assets at December 31	21,006

Asia Pacific
Revenue—customers	$15,246
Interarea transfers	3,475
Total	$18,721
Net earnings	1,788
Assets at December 31	11,984

Americas
Revenue—customers	$ 6,680
Interarea transfers	4,407
Total	$11,087
Net earnings	586
Assets at December 31	7,628

1998 Geographic Information

	Revenues	Long-Lived Assets
United States	$35,303*	$18,450
Japan	8,567	4,310
Other non-U.S. countries	37,797	12,343
Total	$81,667	$35,103

*Dollars in millions.

An example of how this information is disclosed can be found in the 2004 annual report for the Briggs & Stratton Corporation. Note 5 to the financial statements indicated that it had made significant sales to three "major engine customers that exceeded 40 percent of our business and in certain years they individually exceeded 10 percent of total Company net sales. The sales to these customers are summarized below (in thousands of dollars and percent of total Company sales)."

Customer	2004 Net Sales	%	2003 Net Sales	%	2002 Net Sales	%
A	$318,705	16%	$260,253	16%	$255,155	17%
B	334,748	17	253,066	15	299,864	19
C	169,002	9	168,928	10	165,097	11
	$822,455	42%	$682,247	41%	$720,116	47%

Discussion Question

Of 600 companies surveyed in *Accounting Trends & Techniques*, 137 indicated the existence of a major customer in their 2002 annual reports.[14]

Statement 131 requires major customer disclosures even if a company operates in only one segment and therefore does not provide segment information (as is the case for Briggs and Stratton). Also, to avoid any confusion, "a group of entities under common control shall be considered as a single customer, and the federal government, a state government, a local government (for example, a county or municipality), or a foreign government shall each be considered as a single customer" (*SFAS 131,* para. 39).

In addition to requiring information about major customers, *SFAS 14* also required information about export sales. Providing information on export sales, however, is no longer necessary under *Statement 131. Accounting Trends & Techniques* indicates that the number of companies reporting export sales dropped from 168 in 1997 to only 33 in 2002.[15]

INTERIM REPORTING

To give investors and creditors more timely information than an annual report provides, companies show financial information for periods of less than one year. The U.S. Securities and Exchange Commission requires publicly traded companies in the United States to provide financial statements on a quarterly basis. Unlike annual financial statements, financial statements included in quarterly reports filed with the SEC need not be audited. This allows companies to disseminate the information to investors and creditors as quickly as possible.

APB Opinion No. 28 issued in 1973 provides guidance to companies as to how to prepare interim statements. That opinion has stood the test of time with only two subsequent authoritative pronouncements related to interim reporting. *FASB Statement No. 3* amended *APB Opinion No. 28*

---

[14] AICPA, *Accounting Trends & Techniques,* 2003, p. 31.
[15] Ibid., p. 31.

with regard to the reporting of accounting changes in interim statements, and *FASB Interpretation No. 18* clarifies the application of *APB Opinion No. 28* with regard to income taxes.

Some inherent problems are associated with determining the results of operations for time periods of less than one year, especially with regard to expenses that do not occur evenly throughout the year. Two approaches can be followed in preparing interim reports: (1) treat the interim period as a **discrete** accounting period, standing on its own, or (2) treat it as an **integral** portion of a longer period. Considering the annual bonus a company pays to key employees in December of each year illustrates the distinction between these two approaches. Under the *discrete* period approach, the company reports the entire bonus as an expense in December, reducing fourth quarter income only. Under the *integral* part of an annual period approach, a company accrues a portion of the bonus to be paid in December as an expense in each of the first three quarters of the year. Obviously, application of the integral approach requires estimating the annual bonus early in the year and developing a method for allocating the bonus to the four quarters of the year. The advantage of this approach is that there is less volatility in quarterly earnings as irregularly occurring costs are spread out over the entire year.

APB Opinion No. 28 requires companies to treat interim periods as integral parts of an annual period rather than as discrete accounting periods in their own right. Generally speaking, companies should prepare interim financial statements following the same accounting principles and practices it uses in preparing annual statements. However, deviation from this general rule is necessary for several items so that the interim statements better reflect the expected annual amounts. Special rules related to revenues, inventory and cost of goods sold, other costs and expenses, extraordinary items, income taxes, accounting changes, and seasonal items are discussed in turn in the following sections.

Revenues

Companies should recognize revenues in interim periods in the same way they recognize revenues on an annual basis. For example, a company that accounts for revenue from long-term construction projects under the percentage of completion method for annual purposes should also recognize revenue in interim statements on a percentage of completion basis. Moreover, a company should recognize projected losses on long-term contracts to their full extent in the interim period in which it becomes apparent that a loss will arise.

Inventory and Cost of Goods Sold

Interim period accounting for inventory and cost of goods sold requires several modifications to procedures used on an annual basis. The modifications relate to (1) a LIFO liquidation, (2) application of the lower-of-cost-or-market rule, and (3) standard costing.

1. *LIFO liquidation:* Companies using the last-in, first-out (LIFO) cost-flow assumption to value inventory experience a LIFO liquidation at the end of an interim period when the number of units of inventory sold exceeds the number of units added to inventory during the period. When prices are rising, the matching of beginning inventory cost (carried at low LIFO amounts) against the current period's sales revenue results in an unusually high amount of gross profit. If, by year-end, the company expects to replace the units of beginning inventory sold, there will be no LIFO liquidation on an annual basis. In that case, gross profit for the interim period should not reflect the temporary LIFO liquidation, and inventory reported on the interim balance sheet should include the expected cost to replace the beginning inventory sold.

To illustrate, assume that Liquid Products Company began the first quarter with 100 units of inventory that cost $10 per unit. During the first quarter, it purchased 200 units at a cost of $15 per unit, and sold 240 units at $20 per unit. During the first quarter, the company experienced a liquidation of 40 units of beginning inventory. It calculates gross profit as follows:

Sales (240 units @ $20)		$4,800
Cost of goods sold:		
200 units @ $15	$3,000	
40 units @ $10 (LIFO historical cost)	400	3,400
Gross profit		$1,400

However, during the second quarter, the company expects to replace the units of beginning inventory sold at a cost of $17 per unit and that inventory at year-end will be at least 100 units. Therefore, it calculates gross profit for the first quarter as follows:

Sales (240 units @ $20)		$4,800
Cost of goods sold:		
200 units @ $15	$3,000	
40 units @ $17 (replacement cost)	680	3,680
Gross profit		$1,120

The journal entry to record cost of goods sold in the first quarter is as follows:

Cost of goods sold	3,680	
Inventory		3,400
Excess of replacement cost over historical cost of LIFO liquidation . . .		280

To record cost of goods sold with a historical cost of $3,400 and an excess of replacement cost over historical cost for beginning inventory liquidated of $280 [($17 − $10) × 40 units].

2. *Lower-of-cost-or-market rule:* If at the end of an interim period, the fair value of inventory is less than its cost, the company should write down inventory and recognize a loss so long as it deems the decline in fair value to be permanent. However, if it expects the fair value to recover above the inventory's original cost by the end of the year, it should not write down inventory at the interim balance sheet date. Instead, it should continue to carry inventory at cost.

3. *Standard costing:* A company should not reflect in interim financial statements planned price, volume, or capacity variances arising from the use of a standard cost system that are expected to be absorbed by the end of the annual period. However, it should report unplanned variances at the end of the interim period in the same fashion as it would in the annual financial statements.

Other Costs and Expenses

A company should charge costs and expenses not directly matched with revenues to income in the interim period in which they occur unless they can be identified with activities or benefits of other interim periods. In that case, the cost should be allocated among interim periods on a reasonable basis through the use of accruals and deferrals. For example, assume that a company required to prepare quarterly financial statements pays annual property taxes of $100,000 on April 10. One-fourth of the estimated property tax should be accrued as expense in the first quarter of the year. When it makes the payment, it should apply one-fourth against the accrued property tax payable from the previous quarter and charge one-fourth to second-quarter income. The company should defer one-half of the payment as a prepaid expense to be allocated to the third and fourth quarters of the year. The following journal entries demonstrate the procedures for ensuring that the company recognizes one-fourth of the annual payment as expense in each quarter of the year:

March 31

Property Tax Expense	25,000	
Accrued Property Tax Payable		25,000

To accrue one-fourth of the estimated annual property tax as expense for the quarter ended March 31.

April 10

Accrued Property Tax Payable	25,000	
Property Tax Expense	25,000	
Prepaid Property Tax (Current Asset)	50,000	
Cash		100,000
To record the payment of the annual property tax, recognize one-fourth as property tax expense for the quarter ending June 30, and defer one-half as a prepaid expense.		

September 30

Property Tax Expense	25,000	
Prepaid Property Tax		25,000
To record property tax expense for the quarter ended September 30.		

December 31

Property Tax Expense	25,000	
Prepaid Property Tax		25,000
To record property tax expense for the quarter ended December 31.		

Other items requiring similar treatment include annual major repairs and advertising. In addition, a number of adjustments such as bad debt expense, executive bonuses, and quantity discounts based on annual sales volume that are normally made at year-end actually relate to the entire year. To the extent that the company can estimate annual amounts, it should make adjustments at the end of each interim period so that the interim periods bear a reasonable portion of the expected annual amount.

Extraordinary Items

Companies should report extraordinary gains and losses separately and in full in the interim period in which they occur. Companies should deem gains and losses extraordinary if they are (1) unusual in nature, (2) infrequent in occurrence, and (3) material in amount. The materiality of extraordinary items should be determined by comparing the amount of the gain or loss to the expected income for the full year. Companies should separately disclose unusual and infrequent gains and losses that are material to the interim period but not to the year as a whole. Likewise, they should separately disclose gains and losses on the disposal of a segment of the business in the interim period in which the disposal takes place.

For example, assume that Charleston Company incurred a hurricane loss of $100,000 in the first quarter that it deems to be both unusual and infrequent. First-quarter income before subtracting the hurricane loss is $800,000, and annual income is expected to be $10 million. The loss is clearly material with respect to first-quarter income (12.5 percent) but is not material for the year as a whole (1 percent). Charleston Company should not label this loss as an extraordinary item on its first-quarter income statement, but it nevertheless should separately disclose the loss (either as a separate line item on the income statement or in the notes).

Companies should disclose contingencies in interim reports the same way they disclose them in annual reports. The contingency should continue to be reported in subsequent interim and annual reports until it is resolved or becomes immaterial. Materiality should be judged with respect to the year as a whole.

Income Taxes

Companies should compute income tax related to ordinary income at an estimated *annual* effective tax rate. At the end of each interim period, a company makes its best estimate of the effective tax rate for the entire year. The effective tax rate reflects anticipated tax credits, foreign tax rates, and tax planning activities for the year. It then applies this rate to the pretax ordinary income earned to date during the year, resulting in the cumulative income tax expense to recognize to date. The difference between the cumulative income tax recognized to date and income tax recognized in earlier interim periods is the amount of income tax expense recognized in the current interim period.

Assume that Viertel Company estimated its effective annual tax rate at 42 percent in the first quarter of 2007. Pretax income for the first quarter was $500,000. At the end of the second quarter of 2007, the company expects its effective annual tax rate will be only 40 percent because of the planned usage of foreign tax credits. Pretax income in the second quarter of 2007 is also $500,000. There are no items requiring net-of-tax presentation in either quarter. The income tax expense recognized in each of the first two quarters of 2007 is determined as follows:

First Quarter

Pretax income for first quarter of 2007	$500,000
Estimated annual income tax rate	42%
Income tax expense	$210,000

Second Quarter

Pretax income for first quarter of 2007	$500,000	
Pretax income for second quarter of 2007	500,000	
Year-to-date income statement		$1,000,000
Estimated annual income tax rate		40%
Year-to-date income tax expense		$ 400,000
Income tax expense recognized in first quarter		210,000
Income tax expense recognized in second quarter		$ 190,000

The same process is followed for the third and fourth quarters of the year.

Companies should compute income tax related to those special items reported net of tax (extraordinary items and discontinued operations) and recognize them when the item occurs. *FASB Interpretation No. 18* explains that the income tax on an interim period special item is calculated at the margin as the difference between income tax on income including this item and income tax on income excluding this item.

Change in Accounting Principle

Until 2005, *APB Opinion No. 20,* "Accounting Changes," and FASB *SFAS 3,* "Reporting Accounting Changes in Interim Financial Statements," governed the treatment of the effect of a change in accounting principle in interim reports. Generally, under *APBO 20,* a change in accounting principle required a company to recalculate previous years' income based on the new accounting principle and include the cumulative effect in income in the year of change. When a cumulative effect type of accounting change occurred in the first interim period, *SFAS 3* required the entire cumulative effect to be included in income of the first interim period. If an accounting change was made in other than the first interim period, no cumulative effect was included in income for that period. Instead, income for the first interim period of the year was restated to include the cumulative effect of the accounting change.

FASB *Statement of Financial Accounting Standards No. 154,* "Accounting Changes and Error Corrections," issued in May 2005, replaces both *APBO 20* and *SFAS 3* and amends the accounting for a change in accounting principle. *SFAS 154* requires retrospective application of the new accounting principle to prior periods' financial statements. Retrospective application means that comparative financial statements will be restated as if the new accounting principle had always been used. Whether an accounting change occurs in the first or in a subsequent interim period has no bearing on the manner in which the change is reflected in the interim financial statements. According to *Statement 154,* changes in accounting principle, regardless of when the accounting change is made, are handled as follows:

a. The cumulative effect of the change to the new accounting principle on periods prior to those presented shall be reflected in the carrying amounts of assets and liabilities as of the beginning of the first period presented.

b. An offsetting adjustment, if any, shall be made to the opening balance of retained earnings (or other appropriate components of equity or net assets in the statement of financial position) for that period.

c. Financial statements for each individual prior period shall be adjusted to reflect the period-specific effects of applying the new accounting principle.[16]

When the accounting change takes place in other than the first interim period, *SFAS 154* requires information for the interim periods prior to the change to be reported by retrospectively applying the new accounting principle to those prechange interim periods. If retrospective application of the new accounting principle to interim periods prior to the change is impracticable, the accounting change is not allowed to be made in an interim period but may be made only at the beginning of the next fiscal year. The FASB expects that situations in which the retrospective application of a new accounting principle to prechange interim periods is not feasible will be rare.

Illustration of Accounting Change Made in Other Than First Interim Period

Modal Company began operations on January 1, 2006. The company's interim income statements as originally reported under the LIFO inventory valuation method are presented below:

	2006				2007
	1stQ	**2ndQ**	**3rdQ**	**4thQ**	**1stQ**
Sales	$2,000	$2,000	$2,000	$2,000	$2,200
Cost of goods sold (LIFO)	900	950	1,000	1,000	1,050
Operating expenses	500	500	500	500	600
Income before income taxes	600	550	500	500	550
Income taxes (40%)	240	220	200	200	220
Net income	$ 360	$ 330	$ 300	$ 300	$ 330

Modal Company has 500 shares of common stock outstanding. The company's interim report for the first quarter of 2007 included the following information:

	Three Months Ended March 31	
	2006	**2007**
Net income	$360	$330
Net income per common share	$0.72	$0.66

In June 2007, Modal Company decides to adopt the FIFO method of inventory valuation for both financial reporting and tax purposes. Retrospective application of the FIFO method to previous quarters results in the following amounts of cost of goods sold:

	2006				2007
	1stQ	**2ndQ**	**3rdQ**	**4thQ**	**1stQ**
Cost of goods sold (FIFO)	$800	$850	$1,000	$920	$950

---

[16] FASB *Statement 154,* "Accounting Changes and Error Corrections," May 2005, para. 7.

Retrospective application of the FIFO method results in the following restatements of income:

	2006				2007
	1stQ	**2ndQ**	**3rdQ**	**4thQ**	**1stQ**
Sales	$2,000	$2,000	$2,000	$2,000	$2,200
Cost of goods sold (FIFO)	800	850	1,000	900	950
Operating expenses	500	500	500	500	600
Income before income taxes	700	650	500	600	650
Income taxes (40%)	280	260	200	240	260
Net income	$ 420	$ 390	$ 300	$ 360	$ 390

Sales for the second quarter of 2007 are $2,400, cost of goods sold under the FIFO method is $1,000, and operating expenses are $600. Income before income taxes in the second quarter of 2007 is $800, income taxes are $320, and net income is $480.

To prepare interim statements for the second quarter of 2007 in accordance with *SFAS 154*, net income as originally reported in the first and second quarters of 2006, as well as in the first quarter of 2007, is restated to reflect the change to FIFO. The manner in which the accounting change would be reflected in the second quarter of 2007, with year-to-date information, and comparative information for similar periods in 2006 is as follows:

	Three Months Ended June 30		Six Months Ended June 30	
	2006	**2007**	**2006**	**2007**
Net income	$390	$480	$810	$870
Net income per common share	$0.78	$0.96	$1.62	$1.74

Seasonal Items

The sales volume of some companies experiences significant seasonal variation. Manufacturers of summer sports equipment, for example, are likely to have a significant upward spike in sales during the second quarter of the year. To avoid the risk that investors and creditors will be misled into believing that second-quarter earnings indicate earnings for the entire year, *APB Opinion No. 28* requires companies to disclose the seasonal nature of their business operations. In addition, such companies should supplement their interim reports with reports on the 12-month period ended at the interim date for both the current and preceding years.

MINIMUM DISCLOSURES IN INTERIM REPORTS

Many companies provide summary financial statements and notes in their interim reports that contain less information than is included in the annual financial statements. *APB Opinion No. 28* requires companies to provide the following minimum information in their interim reports:

- Sales or gross revenues, provision for income taxes, extraordinary items, and net income.
- Earnings per share.
- Seasonal revenues and expenses.
- Significant changes in estimates or provisions for income taxes.
- Disposal of a segment of a business and unusual or infrequently occurring items.
- Contingent items.
- Changes in accounting principles or estimates.
- Significant changes in financial position.

APB Opinion No. 28 also encourages, but does not require, companies to publish balance sheet and cash flow information in interim reports. If they do not include this information they

QUARTERLY FINANCIAL DATA (Unaudited)

(in millions, except per share amounts)	Three Months Ended			
	March 31	June 30	September 30	December 31
2004				
Operating revenues	$1,484	$1,716	$1,674	$1,655
Operating income	46	197	191	120
Income before income taxes	41	179	181	89
Net income	26	113	119	56
Net income per share, basic	0.03	0.14	0.15	0.07
Net income per share, diluted	0.03	0.14	0.15	0.07

must disclose significant changes since the last period in cash and cash equivalents, net working capital, long-term liabilities, and stockholders' equity.

Companies that provide interim reports on a quarterly basis are not required to publish a fourth-quarter report because this coincides with the end of the annual period. When they do not provide separate fourth-quarter financial statements, they should disclose special accounting items occurring in the fourth quarter in the notes to the annual financial statements. These items include extraordinary or unusual and infrequently occurring items, disposals of a segment of the business, and the aggregate effect of year-end adjustments that are material to the results of the fourth quarter.

The SEC requires companies to include selected quarterly financial data in their annual report to shareholders. Southwest Airlines Co. provided quarterly data in its 2004 annual report as shown in Exhibit 8.8.

SEGMENT INFORMATION IN INTERIM REPORTS

The management approach to determining operating segments should result in less costly disclosure because, by definition, management already collects this information. Because the information is readily available, *Statement 131* also requires the inclusion of segment disclosures in interim reports. This was one of the major recommendations that the AIMR made for improving segment reporting. *Statement 131* requires the following items of information to be included in interim reports for each operating segment:

- Revenues from external customers.
- Intersegment revenues.
- Segment profit or loss.
- Total assets, if there has been a material change from the last annual report.

In addition, an enterprise must reconcile total segments' profit or loss to the company's total income before taxes and disclose any change from the last annual report in the basis for measuring segment profit or loss. Requiring only a few items of information in interim reports is a compromise between the desire of users to have the same information as is provided in annual financial statements and the cost to preparers who must report the information.

The FASB does not require segment information to be provided in interim financial statements until the second year that a company applies *SFAS 131*. Without a full set of segment information in an annual report for comparison, the Board believes that segment information in interim reports would be less meaningful. There is no requirement to provide information about geographic areas or major customers in interim reports.

Summary

1. The consolidation of information from many, varied companies into a set of consolidated financial statements tends to camouflage the characteristics of the individual components. Consequently, during the 1960s, several groups made a strong push to require that disaggregated information be included as an integral part of financial reporting to provide a means for analyzing the components of a business combination.

2. The move toward dissemination of disaggregated information culminated in 1976 with the FASB release of *SFAS 14,* "Financial Reporting for Segments of a Business Enterprise." This pronouncement established guidelines for the required presentation of information describing the various segments that make up a reporting entity. *SFAS 14* required disclosure of information on as many as four distinct aspects of a company's operations: industry segments, geographic segments, export sales, and sales to major customers.

3. Over the years after *SFAS 14* was introduced, financial analysts consistently requested that financial statements be disaggregated to a much greater degree than was done in practice. In direct response to the criticisms and suggestions made by the financial analyst community, the FASB issued a new standard for segment reporting in 1997—*SFAS 131.*

4. *SFAS 131* adopts a so-called management approach in which operating segments are based on a company's organization structure and internal reporting system. The management approach should enhance the usefulness of segment information because it highlights the risks and opportunities that management believes are important and allows the analyst to see the company through the eyes of management. This approach also has the advantage of reducing the cost of providing segment information because that information already is being produced for internal use.

5. Once operating segments have been identified, a company must determine which of these segments are of significant magnitude to warrant separate disclosure. *SFAS 131* contains three quantitative threshold tests to apply to identify reportable segments: a revenue test, a profit or loss test, and an asset test. A segment need satisfy only one of these tests to be considered of sufficient size to necessitate disclosure. Each test is based on identifying segments that meet a 10 percent minimum of the related combined total. The profit and loss test has a 10 percent criterion based on the higher (in an absolute sense) of the total profit from all segments with profits or the total loss from all segments with losses.

6. Companies must report several types of information for each reportable operating segment, including selected revenues, profit or loss, selected expenses, assets, capital expenditures, and equity method investment and income. Companies must report revenues from external customers separately from intersegment revenues. In addition, the types of products and services from which each segment derives its revenues must be disclosed.

7. *SFAS 131* establishes a set of parameters for the number of segments that should be reported by an enterprise. As a minimum, the separately disclosed units must generate at least 75 percent of the total sales made to unaffiliated parties. For an upper limit, the pronouncement suggests that the disclosure of more than 10 operating segments reduces the usefulness of the information.

8. Companies must reconcile the total of all segments' revenues, profit or loss, and assets to the consolidated totals. The major reconciliation adjustments relate to intercompany revenues, profit or loss, and assets eliminated in consolidation; revenues, profit or loss, and assets that have not been allocated to individual operating segments; and differences in accounting methods used by segments and in preparing consolidated financial statements.

9. *SFAS 131* requires several enterprisewide disclosures. If an enterprise does not define operating segments internally on a product line basis or has only one operating segment, disclosure of revenues derived from each product or service is required.

10. In addition, companies must report revenues from external customers and long-lived assets for the domestic country, for each foreign country in which a material amount of revenues is generated or assets are held, and for all foreign countries in total. *SFAS 131* does not provide any threshold tests for determining when operations in a foreign country are material.

11. *SFAS 131* requires disclosure of one other type of information. The reporting entity must indicate the existence of major customers whenever 10 percent or more of consolidated revenues are derived from a single unaffiliated party.

12. For interim reporting purposes, *APB Opinion No. 28* requires time intervals of less than one year to be treated as an integral part of the annual period.

13. Costs and expenses that are not directly matched with revenues should be charged to income in the interim period in which they occur unless they can be identified with activities or benefits of other interim periods. In that case, the cost should be allocated among interim periods on a reasonable basis through the use of accruals and deferrals. Items related to the whole year but recorded as an adjustment only at year-end should be estimated and accrued in each interim period of the year.

14. Companies must report extraordinary gains and losses separately and in full in the interim period in which they occur. The materiality of extraordinary items should be determined by comparing the amount of the gain or loss to the expected income for the full year. Unusual and infrequent gains and losses that are material to the interim period but not to the year as a whole should be disclosed separately.

15. Companies determine interim period income tax expense by applying the estimated annual effective income tax rate to year-to-date pretax ordinary income, resulting in the cumulative income tax expense to be recognized to date. The cumulative income tax to be recognized to date less income tax recognized in earlier interim periods is the amount of income tax expense recognized in the current interim period.

16. When an accounting change is made in other than the first interim period, information for the pre-change interim periods should be reported based on retrospective application of the new accounting principle to those periods. An accounting change may be made only at the beginning of a fiscal year if retrospective application of the new accounting principle to prechange interim periods is not practicable.

17. *APB Opinion No. 28* outlines the minimum information to be included in interim reports, including sales, income taxes, extraordinary items, net income, earnings per share, seasonal revenues and expenses, and significant changes in financial position. Publication of balance sheet and cash flow information in interim reports is not required. If this information is not included, significant changes since the last period in cash and cash equivalents, net working capital, long-term liabilities, and stockholders' equity must be disclosed.

18. At financial analysts' request, *SFAS 131* requires certain items of information to be disclosed in interim reports. Specifically, companies must disclose revenues from outside customers, intersegment revenues, and segment profit or loss in interim reports for each operating segment. In addition, companies must report total assets by segment if a material change occurred since the last annual report.

Comprehensive Illustration

PROBLEM

(Estimated Time: 25 to 40 Minutes) Battey Corporation, an enterprise located in the United States, manufactures several different products: natural fibers, synthetic fibers, leather, plastics, and wood. The company is organized into five operating divisions based on these different products. The company has developed a number of subsidiaries that carry on operations throughout the world. At the end of 2007 as part of the internal reporting process, Battey reported the following revenues, profits, and assets (in millions) to the chief operating decision maker:

Revenues by Operating Segment	United States	Canada	Mexico	France	Italy	Brazil
Natural fibers:						
Sales to external customers	$1,739	—	$342	$606	—	$1,171
Intersegment sales	—	—	—	—	—	146
Synthetic fibers:						
Sales to external customers	290	116	—	—	—	37
Intersegment sales	12	5	—	—	—	—
Leather:						
Sales to external customers	230	—	57	—	278	55
Intersegment sales	22	—	9	—	34	9
Plastics:						
Sales to external customers	748	286	—	83	92	528
Intersegment sales	21	12	—	—	—	72
Wood:						
Sales to external customers	116	22	—	—	—	149
Intersegment sales	17	3	—	—	—	28

Operating Profit or Loss by Operating Segment	United States	Canada	Mexico	France	Italy	Brazil
Natural fibers	$ 526	—	$ 92	$146	—	$ 404
Synthetic fibers	21	8	—	—	—	10
Leather	70	—	27	—	94	24
Plastics	182	74	—	18	24	68
Wood	18	5	—	—	—	37

Assets by Operating Segment	United States	Canada	Mexico	France	Italy	Brazil
Natural fibers	$1,005	—	$223	$296	—	$ 817
Synthetic fibers	163	50	—	—	—	74
Leather	146	—	41	—	150	38
Plastics	425	173	—	54	58	327
Wood	66	19	—	—	—	143

Required

a. Determine the operating segments that should be reported separately in Battey's 2007 financial statements using the criteria established in *SFAS 131*.

b. Determine the geographic areas for which Battey should report revenues separately in its 2007 financial statements. Assume that Battey has elected to define a material country as one in which sales to external customers are 10 percent or more of consolidated sales.

c. Determine the volume of revenues that must be generated from a single customer to necessitate disclosure of a major customer under *SFAS 131*.

SOLUTION

a. Battey Corporation determines its reportable operating segments by following the three-step process established in *SFAS 131*. First, it identifies operating segments. Second, it examines aggregation criteria to determine whether any operating segments may be combined. Third, it determines reportable operating segments by applying the three quantitative threshold tests.

   Identification of Operating Segments   Battey's internal reporting system provides information to the chief operating decision maker by operating division and by country. Either of these components conceivably could be identified as operating segments for segment reporting purposes. However, *SFAS 131* stipulates that, in this type of situation, the components based on products and services constitute the operating segments. Thus, the five operating divisions are identified as Battey's operating segments.

   Aggregation Criteria   The aggregation criteria included in *SFAS 131* are examined next to determine whether any operating segments can be combined. Management determines the economic characteristics of the Natural Fibers and Synthetic Fibers operating divisions to be very similar. In addition, these two divisions are considerably similar with regard to the nature of the product, production process, customers, and distribution methods. Because each of *SFAS 131*'s aggregation criteria are met, Battey elects to combine these two segments into a single Fibers category.

   Quantitative Threshold Tests   Determination of Battey's reportable operating segments depends on the three materiality tests described in this chapter. The revenue test can be performed directly from the information provided. Any operating segment with total revenues (including intersegment sales) equal to 10 percent or more of combined revenue (internal and external) must be reported separately:

Revenue Test (in millions)

Operating Segments	Total Revenues (including intersegment)	
Fibers	$4,464	60.8%
Leather	694	9.5
Plastics	1,842	25.1
Wood	335	4.6
Total combined revenues	$7,335	100.0%

Reportable segments are Fibers and Plastics.

   The profit or loss test can be performed next. Battey must separately report any operating segment with profit or loss equal to 10 percent or more of the higher, in absolute amount, of combined segment profit (for those segments with a profit) or combined segment loss (for those segments with a loss). Because each of Battey's operating segments generated a profit in 2007, this test can be applied by determining the total combined profit:

Profit or Loss Test (in millions)

Operating Segments	Total Profit or Loss	
Fibers	$1,207	65.3%
Leather	215	11.6
Plastics	366	19.8
Wood	60	3.3
Total combined segment profit	$1,848	100.0%

Reportable segments are Fibers, Leather, and Plastics.

Finally, Battey performs the asset test:

Asset Test (in millions)

Operating Segments	Total Assets	
Fibers	$2,628	61.6%
Leather	375	8.8
Plastics	1,037	24.3
Wood	228	5.3
Total combined segment assets	$4,268	100.0%

Reportable segments are Fibers and Plastics.

Based on these three tests, information about the Fibers, Leather, and Plastics operating segments must be reported separately. Information on the immaterial Wood segment need not be reported. However, the revenues, profit, and assets of this segment would be included in reconciliations to consolidated totals.

b. Battey must report revenues from external customers for the United States, for all foreign countries, and for each foreign country in which the company generates a material amount of revenues. *SFAS 131* provides no quantitative tests for determining when a foreign country is material; this is left to management's judgment. Battey has decided to define *materiality* as sales to external customers equal to 10 percent or more of consolidated revenues. This was one of two criteria that *SFAS 14* established for determining significant geographic areas.

Revenue Test (in millions)

Country	Sales to External Customers	
United States	$3,123	45.0%
Canada	424	6.1
Mexico	399	5.8
France	689	9.9
Italy	370	5.3
Brazil	1,940	27.9
Total consolidated revenues	$6,945	100.0%

Using this criterion, Battey reports results for the United States and Brazil separately and combines the remaining countries into an All Other category. Alternatively, if Battey had established a materiality threshold of 5 percent, it would report separately each of the foreign countries in which it generates revenues. Once again, determination of materiality is left to management's judgment.

c. The significance test for disclosure of a major customer is 10 percent of consolidated revenues. Under the guidelines of *SFAS 131,* Battey must report the existence of any major customer from which $694.5 million or more in revenues was generated during 2007.

Questions

1. How does the consolidation process tend to disguise information needed to analyze the financial operations of a diversified organization?
2. What is disaggregated financial information?
3. *SFAS 14* required many companies to present disaggregated information about several different aspects of current operations. What were the various types of segments that could have required disclosure?
4. What was *SFAS 14*'s dominant industry segment rule and what problem could this rule generate?
5. According to the FASB, what is the major objective of segment reporting?
6. *SFAS 131*'s management approach requires firms to define segments on the basis of the firm's internal organization structure. What are the advantages in defining segments on this basis?
7. What is an operating segment?
8. How should companies determine operating segments when business activities are disaggregated in more than one way and the chief operating decision maker uses multiple sets of reports?
9. Describe the three tests for identifying reportable operating segments.
10. What information must an enterprise report for each of its material operating segments?
11. Under what conditions must an enterprise provide information about products and services?
12. Under what conditions must an enterprise provide information about geographic areas?
13. What information must an enterprise report by geographic area?
14. To satisfy *SFAS 131*'s geographic area disclosure requirements, what are the minimum number and the maximum number of countries for which information should be reported separately?
15. Under what conditions should a company disclose the amount of sales from a major customer?
16. Why are publicly traded companies in the United States required to prepare interim reports on a quarterly basis?
17. What approach does *APB Opinion 28* require companies to follow in preparing interim financial statements?
18. How should a company handle LIFO liquidation in an interim period when the liquidated inventory is expected to be replaced by year-end?
19. How does a company determine the amount of income tax expense to report in an interim period?
20. According to *SFAS 154*, what procedures must companies follow to account for a change in accounting principle made in other than the first interim period of the year?
21. In accordance with *APB Opinion No. 28*, what minimum information must an enterprise provide in an interim report?
22. According to *SFAS 131*, what type of segment information must companies provide in interim financial statements?

Problems

1. Which of the following does the FASB *not* consider to be an objective of segment reporting?
   a. It helps users better understand the enterprise's performance.
   b. It helps users better assess the enterprise's prospects for future cash flows.
   c. It helps users make more informed judgments about the enterprise as a whole.
   d. It helps users make comparisons between a segment of one enterprise and a similar segment of another enterprise.

2. Under *SFAS 131*, which of the following items of information is Most Company *not* required to disclose, even if it were material in amount?
   a. Revenues generated from sales of its Consumer Products line of goods.
   b. Revenues generated by its Japanese subsidiary.
   c. Revenues generated from export sales.
   d. Revenues generated from sales to Wal-Mart.

3. Which of the following operating segment disclosures does *SFAS 131 not* require?
   a. Liabilities.
   b. Interest expense.
   c. Intersegment sales.
   d. Unusual items (extraordinary items and discontinued operations).

4. In determining whether a particular operating segment is of significant size to warrant disclosure, which of the following statements is true?

    a. Three tests are applied, and all three must be met.

    b. Four tests are applied, and only one must be met.

    c. Three tests are applied, and only one must be met.

    d. Four tests are applied, and all four must be met.

5. Which of the following statements is not true under *SFAS 131?*

    a. Operating segments can be determined by looking at a company's organization chart.

    b. Companies may combine individual foreign countries into geographic areas for purposes of complying with the geographic area disclosure requirements.

    c. If companies define their operating segments by product lines, the companies must provide revenue and asset information for the domestic country and each material foreign country.

    d. Companies must disclose total assets, investment in equity method affiliates, and total expenditures for long-lived assets by operating segment.

6. Which of the following is not necessarily true for an operating segment?

    a. An operating segment earns revenues and incurs expenses.

    b. The chief operating decision maker regularly reviews an operating segment to assess performance and make resource allocation decisions.

    c. Discrete financial information generated by the internal accounting system is available for an operating segment.

    d. An operating segment regularly generates a profit from its normal, ongoing operations.

7. Which of the following is a criterion for determining whether an operating segment is separately reportable?

    a. Segment liabilities are 10 percent or more of consolidated liabilities.

    b. Segment profit or loss is 10 percent or more of consolidated net income.

    c. Segment assets are 10 percent or more of combined segment assets.

    d. Segment revenues from external sales are 5 percent or more of combined segment revenues from external sales.

8. Which of the following statements is true?

    a. *SFAS 131* does not require segment information to be reported in accordance with generally accepted accounting principles.

    b. *SFAS 131* does not require a reconciliation of segment assets to consolidated assets.

    c. *SFAS 131* requires geographic area information to be disclosed in interim financial statements.

    d. *SFAS 131* requires disclosure of the identity of a major customer.

9. Plume Company has a paper products operating segment. Which of the following items does Plume *not* have to report for this segment?

    a. Interest expense.

    b. Research and development expense.

    c. Depreciation and amortization expense.

    d. Interest income.

10. Which of the following items is required to be disclosed by geographic area?

    a. Total assets.

    b. Revenues from external customers.

    c. Profit or loss.

    d. Capital expenditures.

11. According to *SFAS 131,* which of the following is an acceptable grouping of countries for providing information by geographic area?

    a. United States, Mexico, Japan, Spain, All Other Countries.

    b. United States, Canada and Mexico, Germany, Italy.

    c. United States, Taiwan, Japan, Europe.

    d. Canada, Germany, France, All Other Countries.

12. What information about revenues by geographic area should a company present?
    a. Disclose separately the amount of sales to unaffiliated customers and the amount of intracompany sales between geographic areas.
    b. Disclose as a combined amount sales to unaffiliated customers and intracompany sales between geographic areas.
    c. Disclose separately the amount of sales to unaffiliated customers but not the amount of intracompany sales between geographic areas.
    d. No disclosure of revenues from foreign operations need be reported.

13. Which of the following items of information must be disclosed with regard to a major customer?
    a. The identity of the customer.
    b. The percentage of total sales derived from the major customer.
    c. The operating segment making the sale.
    d. The geographic area from which the sale was made.

14. In considering interim financial reporting, how did the Accounting Principles Board conclude that such reporting should be viewed?
    a. As a special type of reporting that need not follow generally accepted accounting principles.
    b. As useful only if activity is evenly spread throughout the year so that estimates are unnecessary.
    c. As reporting for a basic accounting period.
    d. As reporting for an integral part of an annual period.

15. How should material seasonal variations in revenue be reflected in interim financial statements?
    a. The seasonal nature should be disclosed, and the interim report should be supplemented with a report on the 12-month period ended at the interim date for both the current and preceding years.
    b. The seasonal nature should be disclosed, but no attempt should be made to reflect the effect of past seasonality on financial statements.
    c. The seasonal nature should be reflected by providing pro forma financial statements for the current interim period.
    d. There should be no attempt to reflect seasonality in interim financial statements.

16. For interim financial reporting, an extraordinary gain occurring in the second quarter should be
    a. Recognized ratably over the last three quarters.
    b. Recognized ratably over all four quarters, with the first quarter being restated.
    c. Recognized in the second quarter.
    d. Disclosed by footnote only in the second quarter.

17. Which of the following items must be disclosed in interim reports?
    a. Total assets.
    b. Total liabilities.
    c. Cash flow from operating activities.
    d. Gross revenues.

18. Which of the following items is *not* required to be reported in interim financial statements for each material operating segment?
    a. Revenues from external customers.
    b. Intersegment revenues.
    c. Segment assets.
    d. Segment profit or loss.

19. Estilo Company has three operating segments with the following information:

	Paper	Pencils	Hats
Sales to outsiders	$8,000	$4,000	$6,000
Intersegment transfers	600	1,000	1,400

In addition, corporate headquarters generates revenues of $1,000.

What is the minimum amount of revenue that each of these segments must generate to be considered separately reportable?

a. $1,800.

b. $1,900.

c. $2,000.

d. $2,100.

20. The Carson Company has four separate operating segments:

	Apples	Oranges	Pears	Peaches
Sales to outsiders	$123,000	$81,000	$95,000	$77,000
Intersegment transfers	31,000	26,000	13,000	18,000

What amount of revenues must one customer generate before that party must be identified as a major customer?

a. $37,600.

b. $41,200.

c. $46,400.

d. $56,400.

21. Jarvis Corporation has six different operating segments reporting the following operating profit and loss figures:

K	$ 80,000 loss		N	$440,000 profit
L	140,000 profit		O	90,000 profit
M	940,000 loss		P	100,000 profit

With respect to the profit or loss test, which of the following statements is not true?

a. K is not a reportable segment based on this one test.

b. L is a reportable segment based on this one test.

c. O is not a reportable segment based on this one test.

d. P is a reportable segment based on this one test.

22. Quatro Corp. engages solely in manufacturing operations. The following data pertain to the operating segments for the current year:

Operating Segment	Total Revenues	Profit	Assets at 12/31
A	$10,000,000	$1,750,000	$20,000,000
B	8,000,000	1,400,000	17,500,000
C	6,000,000	1,200,000	12,500,000
D	3,000,000	550,000	7,500,000
E	4,250,000	675,000	7,000,000
F	1,500,000	225,000	3,000,000
Total	$32,750,000	$5,800,000	$67,500,000

In its segment information for the current year, how many reportable segments does Quatro have?

a. Three.

b. Four.

c. Five.

d. Six.

23. What is the minimum number of operating segments that must be separately reported?

a. Ten.

b. Segments with at least 75 percent of revenues as measured by the revenue test.

c. At least 75 percent of the segments must be separately reported.

d. Segments with at least 75 percent of the revenues generated from outside parties.

24. Medford Company has seven operating segments but only four (G, H, I, and J) are of significant size to warrant separate disclosure. Segments K, L, and M are not large enough. As a whole, these segments have revenues of $710,000 ($520,000 + $190,000) generated from outside parties. In addition, the segments had $260,000 in intersegment transfers ($220,000 + $40,000).

	Outside Sales	Intersegment Sales
G	$120,000	$ 80,000
H	150,000	50,000
I	160,000	20,000
J	90,000	70,000
Totals	$520,000	$220,000

	Outside Sales	Intersegment Sales
K	$ 60,000	–0–
L	70,000	$20,000
M	60,000	20,000
Totals	$190,000	$40,000

Which of the following statements is true?

a. A sufficient number of segments is being reported because those segments have $740,000 in revenues of a total of $970,000 for the company as a whole.

b. Not enough segments are being reported because those segments have $520,000 in outside sales of a total of $710,000 for the company as a whole.

c. Not enough segments are being reported because those segments have $740,000 in revenues of a total of $970,000 for the company as a whole.

d. A sufficient number of segments is being reported because those segments have $520,000 in outside sales of a total of $710,000 for the company as a whole.

25. Philo Company estimates that total depreciation expense for the year ending December 31 will amount to $60,000 and that year-end bonuses to employees will amount to $120,000. What is the total amount of expense relating to these two items that Philo should report in its quarterly income statement for the three months ended June 30?

a. $15,000.

b. $30,000.

c. $45,000.

d. $90,000.

26. Ming Company's $100,000 income for the quarter ended September 30 included the following after-tax items:

• $20,000 of a $40,000 extraordinary loss, realized on August 15; the other $20,000 was allocated to the fourth quarter of the year.

• A $16,000 cumulative effect loss resulting from a change in inventory valuation method made on September 1.

• $12,000 of the $48,000 annual property taxes paid on February 1.

For the quarter ended September 30, the correct amount of net income that Ming should report is

a. $80,000.

b. $88,000.

c. $96,000.

d. $116,000.

27. In March 2007, Archibald Company estimated that its year-end bonus to executives would be $1,000,000. The bonus paid to executives in 2006 was $950,000. What amount of bonus expense, if any, should Archibald Company recognize in determining net income for the first quarter of 2007?

a. –0–.

b. $237,500.

c. $250,000.

d. $1,000,000.

Use the following information for Problems 28 and 29:
On March 15, 2007, Calloway, Inc., paid property taxes of $480,000 for the calendar year 2007.

28. How much of this expense should be reflected in Calloway's income statement for the quarter ending March 31, 2007?

a. –0–.

b. $40,000.

c. $120,000.

d. $480,000.

29. The journal entry at March 15, 2007, to record the payment of property taxes would include which of the following?

a. A debit to Property Tax Expense of $480,000.

b. A credit to Cash of $120,000.

c. A debit to Prepaid Property Taxes of $360,000.

d. A credit to Prepaid Property Taxes of $40,000.

Use the following information for Problems 30 and 31:
Lifetime Sports, Inc., uses the LIFO cost-flow assumption to value inventory. The company began the year 2007 with 1,000 units of inventory carried at LIFO cost of $50 per unit. During the first quarter of 2007, the company purchased 5,000 units at an average cost of $80 per unit and sold 5,300 units at $100 per unit.

30. The company does not expect to replace the units of beginning inventory sold; it plans to reduce inventory by year-end 2007 to 500 units. What is the amount of cost of goods sold to be recorded for the quarter ended March 31, 2007?

a. $415,000.

b. $424,000.

c. $424,600.

d. $434,600.

31. The company expects to replace the units of beginning inventory sold in April 2007 at a cost of $82 per unit and expects inventory at year-end to be between 1,500 and 2,000 units. What is the amount of cost of goods sold to be recorded for the quarter ended March 31, 2007?

a. $415,000.

b. $424,000.

c. $424,600.

d. $434,600.

32. Fireside Corporation is organized into four operating segments. The internal reporting system generated the following segment information:

	Revenues from Outsiders	Intersegment Transfers	Operating Expenses
Cards	$1,200,000	$100,000	$ 900,000
Calendars	900,000	200,000	1,350,000
Clothing	1,000,000	—	700,000
Books	800,000	50,000	770,000

Additional operating expenses (of a general nature) incurred by the company amounted to $700,000.

What is the profit or loss of each of these segments? Carry out the profit or loss test to determine which of these segments is separately reportable.

33. Ecru Company has identified five industry segments: plastics, metals, lumber, paper, and finance. Ecru appropriately consolidated each of these segments in producing its annual financial statements. Information describing each segment is presented here (in thousands):

	Plastics	Metals	Lumber	Paper	Finance
Sales to outside parties	$6,319	$2,144	$636	$347	–0–
Intersegment transfers	106	131	96	108	–0–
Interest income from outside parties	–0–	19	6	–0–	$ 27
Interest income from intersegment loans	–0–	–0–	–0–	–0–	159
Operating expenses	3,914	1,612	916	579	16
Interest expense	61	16	51	31	87
Tangible assets	1,291	2,986	314	561	104
Intangible assets	72	361	–0–	48	–0–
Intersegment loans	–0–	–0–	–0–	–0–	664

In addition, Ecru has $1,250,000 in common expenses that it does not allocate to the various segments.

Perform the testing procedures designed by the FASB to determine Ecru Company's reportable operating segments.

34. Following is financial information describing the six operating segments that make up Fairfield, Inc. (in thousands):

	Red	Blue	Green	Pink	Black	White
Sales to outside parties	$1,811	$812	$514	$309	$121	$ 99
Intersegment revenues	16	91	109	–0–	16	302
Salary expense	614	379	402	312	317	62
Rent expense	139	166	81	92	42	31
Interest expense	65	59	82	49	14	5
Income tax expense (savings) .	141	87	61	(86)	(64)	–0–

The following questions should be considered independently. Unless specified, none of the six segments has a primarily financial nature.

a. What minimum amount of revenue must any one segment generate to be of significant size to require disaggregated disclosure?

b. If only Red, Blue, and Green are of sufficient size to necessitate separate disclosure, is Fairfield disclosing disaggregated data for enough segments?

c. What volume of revenues must a single client generate to necessitate disclosing the existence of a major customer?

d. If each of these six segments has a profit or loss (in thousands) as follows, which is of significant size to warrant separate disclosure?

Red	$1,074	Pink	$ (94)
Blue	449	Black	(222)
Green	140	White	308

35. Mason Company has prepared consolidated financial statements for the current year and is now gathering information in connection with the following five operating segments it has identified.

Determine the reportable segments by carrying out each of the applicable tests. Also describe the procedure utilized to ensure that a sufficient number of segments are being separately disclosed. (Figures are in thousands.)

	Company Total	Books	Computers	Maps	Travel	Finance
Sales to outside parties . . .	$1,547	$121	$ 696	$416	$314	–0–
Intersegment sales	421	24	240	39	118	–0–
Interest income— external	97	60	–0–	–0–	–0–	$ 37
Interest income— intersegment loans	147	–0–	–0–	–0–	–0–	147
Assets	3,398	206	1,378	248	326	1,240

(continued)

	Company Total	Books	Computers	Maps	Travel	Finance
Operating expenses	1,460	115	818	304	190	33
Expenses— intersegment sales	198	70	51	31	46	–0–
Interest expense— external	107	–0–	–0–	–0–	–0–	107
Interest expense— intersegment loans	177	21	71	38	47	–0–
Income tax expense (savings)	21	12	(41)	27	31	(8)
General corporate expenses	55					
Unallocated operating costs	80					

36. Slatter Corporation operates primarily in the United States. However, a few years ago, the company opened a plant in Spain to produce merchandise that it sells within that country. This foreign operation has been so successful that during the past 24 months, the company also started a manufacturing plant in Italy and another in Greece. Financial information for each of these facilities follows:

	Spain	Italy	Greece
Sales	$395,000	$272,000	$463,000
Intersegment transfers	–0–	–0–	62,000
Operating expenses	172,000	206,000	190,000
Interest expense	16,000	29,000	19,000
Income taxes	67,000	19,000	34,000
Long-lived assets	191,000	106,000	72,000

The company's domestic (U.S.) operations reported the following information for the current year:

Sales to unaffiliated customers	$4,610,000
Intersegment transfers	427,000
Operating expenses	2,410,000
Interest expense	136,000
Income taxes	819,000
Long-lived assets	1,894,000

Slatter has adopted the following criteria for determining the materiality of an individual foreign country: (1) sales to unaffiliated customers within a country are 10 percent or more of consolidated sales or (2) long-lived assets within a country are 10 percent or more of consolidated long-lived assets.

Apply the materiality tests that Slatter adopted to determine those countries to be reported separately.

37. Noventis Corporation prepared the following estimates for the four quarters of the current year:

	First Quarter	Second Quarter	Third Quarter	Fourth Quarter
Sales	$1,000,000	$1,200,000	$1,400,000	$1,600,000
Cost of goods sold	400,000	480,000	550,000	600,000
Administrative costs	250,000	155,000	160,000	170,000
Advertising costs	–0–	100,000	–0–	–0–
Executive bonuses	–0–	–0–	–0–	80,000
Provision for bad debts	–0–	–0–	–0–	52,000
Annual maintenance costs ...	60,000	–0–	–0–	–0–

Additional Information

- First-quarter administrative costs include the annual insurance premium of $100,000.

- Advertising costs paid in the second quarter relate to television advertisements that will be broadcast throughout the entire year.

- There are no special items affecting income during the year.
- Noventis estimates an effective income tax rate for the year of 40 percent.
    - *a.* Assuming that actual results do not vary from the estimates provided, determine the amount of income to be reported each quarter of the current year.
    - *b.* Assume that actual results do not vary from the estimates provided except for that in the third quarter, the estimated annual effective income tax rate is revised downward to 38 percent. Determine the amount of income to be reported each quarter of the current year.

38. Cambi Company began operations on January 1, 2006. In the second quarter of 2007, Cambi Company adopted the FIFO method of inventory valuation. In the past, the LIFO method was used. The company's interim income statements as originally reported under the LIFO method are as follows:

	2006				2007
	1stQ	**2ndQ**	**3rdQ**	**4thQ**	**1stQ**
Sales	$10,000	$12,000	$14,000	$16,000	$18,000
Cost of goods sold (LIFO)	4,000	5,000	5,800	7,000	8,500
Operating expenses	2,000	2,200	2,600	3,000	3,200
Income before income taxes ...	4,000	4,800	5,600	6,000	6,300
Income taxes (40%)	1,600	1,920	2,240	2,400	2,520
Net income	$ 2,400	$ 2,880	$ 3,360	$ 3,600	$ 3,780

If the FIFO method had been used since the company began operations, cost of goods sold in each of the previous quarters would have been as follows:

	2006				2007
	1stQ	**2ndQ**	**3rdQ**	**4thQ**	**1stQ**
Cost of goods sold (FIFO)	$3,800	$4,600	$5,200	$6,000	$7,400

Sales for the second quarter of 2007 are $20,000, cost of goods sold under the FIFO method is $9,000, and operating expenses are $3,400. The effective tax rate remains 40 percent. Cambi Company has 1,000 shares of common stock outstanding.

Prepare a schedule showing the calculation of net income and earnings per share to be reported by Cambi Company for the three-month period and the six-month period ended June 30, 2007.

39. The following information for Quadrado Corporation relates to the three-month period ending September 30, 2007:

	Units	Price per Unit
Sales	110,000	$20
Beginning inventory	20,000	12
Purchases	100,000	14
Ending inventory	10,000	

Quadrado Corporation expects to purchase 150,000 units of inventory in the fourth quarter of 2007 at a cost of $15 per unit, and to have on hand 30,000 units of inventory at year-end. Quadrado uses the last-in, first-out (LIFO) method to account for inventory costs.

Determine the amount of cost of goods sold and gross profit to be recorded for the three months ending September 30, 2007. Prepare journal entries to reflect these amounts.

Develop Your Skills

RESEARCH CASE 1—SEGMENT REPORTING

Many companies make annual reports available on their corporate Internet home page. Annual reports also can be accessed through the SEC's EDGAR system at www.sec.gov (under Forms, search for ARS or 10-K) or in your school's library. Access the most recent annual report for a company with which you are familiar to complete the following requirements.

Required:

Prepare a one-page report describing your findings for the following:

1. Determine the company's reported operating segments and identify whether they are based on product lines, geographic areas, or some other basis.
2. Determine the importance of each operating segment for the company as a whole in terms of revenues, income, and assets.
3. Determine whether the company provides any enterprisewide disclosures in addition to disclosures related to its operating segments.
4. Determine whether the company provides disclosures about major customers.

RESEARCH CASE 2—INTERIM REPORTING

Many companies make quarterly reports available on their corporate Internet home page. Quarterly reports also can be accessed through the SEC's EDGAR system at www.sec.gov (under Forms, search for 10-Q) or in your school's library. Access the most recent quarterly report for a company with which you are familiar to complete the following requirements.

Required:

Prepare a one-page report describing your findings for the following:

1. Assess whether the company provides the minimum disclosures required by *APB Opinion No. 28* for interim reports.
2. Identify any additional disclosures the company provides that exceed the minimum disclosures required by *APB Opinion No. 28.*
3. Determine the various year-to-year comparisons that can be made using the disclosures provided in the quarterly report.

RESEARCH CASE 3—OPERATING SEGMENTS

Many companies make annual reports available on their corporate Internet home page. Annual reports also can be accessed through the SEC's EDGAR system at www.sec.gov (under Forms, search for ARS or 10-K) or in your school's library. Access the most recent annual report for each of the following companies:

    Abbott Laboratories
    Anheuser-Busch
    Cisco Systems
    General Electric
    Lockheed Martin

Complete the following requirements for each company.

Required:

Prepare a one-page report summarizing your findings for the following:

1. Determine the two most important operating segments in terms of percentage of total revenues.
2. Determine the two operating segments with the largest growth in revenues.
3. Determine the two most profitable operating segments in terms of profit margin.

RESEARCH CASE 4—COMPARABILITY OF GEOGRAPHIC AREA INFORMATION

Many companies make annual reports available on their corporate Internet home page. Annual reports also can be accessed through the SEC's EDGAR system at www.sec.gov (under Forms, search for ARS or 10-K) or in your school's library. Access the most recent annual report for each of the following companies:

    Bristol-Myers-Squibb
    Eli Lilly
    Merck
    Pfizer

Required:

Prepare a one-page report describing the comparability of the geographic area information provided by these companies.

RESEARCH CASE 5—WITHIN INDUSTRY COMPARISON OF SEGMENT INFORMATION

Many companies make annual reports available on their corporate Internet home page. Annual reports also can be accessed through the SEC's EDGAR system at www.sec.gov (under Forms, search for ARS or 10-K) or in your school's library. Access the most recent annual report for two companies generally considered to be competitors. Possible companies include these:

Automobile: Ford, General Motors

Beverages: Coca-Cola, PepsiCo

Chemical: Dow Chemical, DuPont, Monsanto, Union Carbide

Computer: Apple Computer, Hewlett-Packard, IBM

Food products: Campbell Soup, Heinz, Sara Lee

Petroleum: Chevron-Texaco, ExxonMobil

Pharmaceutical: Eli Lilly, Merck, Pfizer, Schering-Plough

Required:

Based solely on the segment information provided, prepare a one-page report describing and comparing the two companies.

ANALYSIS CASE 1—AIRLINE INDUSTRY INTERIM REPORTING

In addition to a tragic loss of life, the terrorist attacks in the United States on September 11, 2001, severely disrupted the nation's commercial, financial, and transportation activities. The effect of this disruption on financial position and profitability was not uniform across all companies. Airlines were hit especially hard. On the other hand, companies involved in providing security experienced an upswing in activity.

Required:

1. Access the interim report for the third quarter 2001 for a company in the airline industry.
2. Determine the impact, if any, that the events of September 11, 2001, appear to have had on the company's operations.

FARS CASE 1—INTERIM REPORTING

Some firms experience material seasonal variations in revenues. U.S. GAAP requires firms to disclose the seasonal nature of their activities in their interim financial statements. Search the FASB's *Original Pronouncements* using either hard copy or the Financial Accounting Research System (FARS) database to complete the following requirements.

Required:

1. Identify the authoritative pronouncement and the paragraph within that pronouncement that require disclosure of material seasonal variations in interim financial statements.
2. Summarize the requirements with respect to this issue.

FARS CASE 2—SEGMENT REPORTING

In establishing new rules for segment reporting, the FASB considered allowing companies an exemption from providing segment disclosures if such disclosure would result in competitive harm for the company. The FASB ultimately decided not to provide a competitive harm exemption to companies. Search the FASB's *Original Pronouncements* using either hard copy or the Financial Accounting Research System (FARS) to complete the following requirements.

Required:

1. Identify the authoritative pronouncement and paragraphs within that pronouncement that discuss the issue of competitive harm from providing segment disclosures.
2. Summarize the specific illustrations of competitive harm that the FASB received that have resulted from disclosing segment information.
3. Summarize the FASB's reason for not granting a competitive harm exemption.
4. Explain how the possibility of competitive harm influenced the FASB's decision regarding the disclosure of research and development costs by segment.

ANALYSIS CASE 2—WAL-MART INTERIM AND SEGMENT REPORTING

The following information was extracted from quarterly reports for Wal-Mart Stores, Inc.:

Operating Income	Three Months Ended April 30,		Three Months Ended July 31,		Three Months Ended October 31,	
	2004	2003	2004	2003	2004	2003
Wal-Mart Stores	$3,121	$2,752	$3,685	$3,317	$3,115	$2,967
Sam's Club	267	204	352	309	306	270
International	563	384	748	561	698	564

The following information was extracted from the notes to the financial statements in the Wal-Mart Stores, Inc., 2005 annual report (for the fiscal year ended January 31, 2005):

11 Segments
Fiscal Year Ended January 31, 2005

	Wal-Mart Stores	SAM'S Club	International	Other	Consolidated
Revenues from external customers	$191,826	$37,119	$56,277	—	$285,222
Operating income (loss)	14,163	1,280	2,988	(1,340)	17,091
Total assets of continuing operations	29,489	5,685	40,981	44,068	120,223

12 Quarterly Financial Data (Unaudited)
Amounts in Millions except per share information

	Quarters Ended			
2004/2005	April 30	July 31	October 31	January 31
Net sales	$64,763	$69,722	$68,520	$82,216
Cost of sales	49,969	53,533	52,567	63,723
Net income	2,166	2,651	2,286	3,164
Net income per common share	$ 0.50	$ 0.62	$ 0.54	$ 0.75

Required:

1. Assess the seasonal nature of Wal-Mart's sales and income for the company as a whole and by operating segment.
2. Assess Wal-Mart's profitability by quarter and by operating segment.

EXCEL CASE 1—ALTRIA GROUP OPERATING SEGMENT INFORMATION

The following information was extracted from Note 15 (Segment Reporting) in the Altria Group, Inc., 2004 annual report:

Segment data were as follows:
(in millions)

For the Years Ended December 31,	2004	2003	2002
Net revenues:			
Domestic tobacco	$17,511	$17,001	$18,877
International tobacco	39,536	33,389	28,672
North American food	22,060	20,937	20,489
International food	10,108	9,561	8,759
Beer			2,641
Financial services	395	432	495
Net revenues	$89,610	$81,320	$79,933
Earnings from continuing operations before income taxes and minority interest:			
Operating companies income:			
Domestic tobacco	$ 4,405	$ 3,889	$ 5,011
International tobacco	6,566	6,286	5,666
North American food	3,870	4,658	4,664
International food	933	1,393	1,466
Beer			276
Financial services	144	313	55
Amortization of intangibles	(17)	(9)	(7)
General corporate expenses	(721)	(771)	(683)
Operating income	15,180	15,759	16,448
Gain on Miller transaction			2,631
Interest and other debt expenses, net	(1,176)	(1,150)	(1,134)
Earnings from continuing operations before income taxes and minority interest	$14,004	$14,609	$17,945

In addition, Note 19 (Contingencies) to the consolidated financial statements consists of nine pages of information on legal proceedings against the company, primarily class action lawsuits filed in the United States related to disease allegedly caused by smoking tobacco products.

Required:

1. Use an electronic spreadsheet to calculate the following for each reportable operating segment for 2004 and 2003:

    Percentage of total net revenues.

    Percentage change in total net revenues.

    Percentage of total operating companies income.

    Operating companies income as a percentage of net revenues (profit margin).

2. Evaluate the relative importance of the various reportable operating segments to Altria's overall profitability. Determine how the relative importance of the various operating segments changed from 2003 to 2004.

3. Assess the impact that the information provided in Note 19 might have on the company's future prospects.

EXCEL CASE 2—COCA-COLA GEOGRAPHIC SEGMENT INFORMATION

The Coca-Cola Company is organized geographically and defines reportable operating segments as regions of the world. The following information was extracted from Note 19 (Operating Segments) in the Coca-Cola Company 2004 annual report:

Information about our Company's operations by operating segment is as follows (in millions):

	North America	Africa	Asia	Europe, Eurasia, and Middle East	Latin America	Corporate	Consolidated
2004							
Net operating revenues	$6,643	$1,067	$4,691	$7,195	$2,123	$ 243	$21,962
Operating income (loss)	1,606	340	1,758	1,898	1,069	(973)	5,698
Interest income						157	157
Interest expense						196	196
Depreciation and amortization	345	28	133	245	42	100	893
Equity income (loss)—net	11	12	83	85	185	245	621
Income (loss) before income taxes and cumulative effect of accounting change	1,629	337	1,841	1,916	1,270	(771)	6,222
Identifiable operating assets	4,731	789	1,722	5,373	1,405	11,055	25,075
Investments	116	162	1,401	1,323	1,580	1,670	6,252
Capital expenditures	247	28	92	233	38	117	755
2003							
Net operating revenues	$6,344	$827	$5,052	$6,556	$2,042	$ 223	$21,044
Operating income (loss)	1,282	249	1,690	1,908	970	(878)	5,221
Interest income						176	176
Interest expense						178	178
Depreciation and amortization	305	27	124	230	52	112	850
Equity income (loss)—net	13	13	65	78	(5)	242	406
Income (loss) before income taxes and cumulative effect of accounting change	1,326	249	1,740	1,921	975	(716)	5,495
Identifiable operating assets	4,953	721	1,923	5,222	1,440	7,545	21,804
Investments	109	156	1,345	1,229	1,348	1,351	5,538
Capital expenditures	309	13	148	198	35	109	812
2002							
Net operating revenues	$6,264	$684	$5,054	$5,262	$2,089	$ 211	$19,564
Operating income (loss)	1,531	224	1,820	1,612	1,033	(762)	5,458
Interest income						209	209
Interest expense						199	199
Depreciation and amortization	266	37	133	193	57	120	806
Equity income (loss)—net	15	(25)	60	(18)	131	221	384
Income (loss) before income taxes and cumulative effect of accounting change	1,552	187	1,848	1,540	1,081	(709)	5,499
Identifiable operating assets	4,999	565	2,370	4,481	1,205	5,795	19,415
Investments	142	115	1,150	1,211	1,352	1,021	4,991
Capital expenditures	334	18	209	162	37	91	851

Required:

1. Use an electronic spreadsheet to calculate the following measures for each of Coca-Cola's reportable operating segments:

    Percentage of total net operating revenues (excluding Corporate), 2003 and 2004.

    Percentage growth in net operating revenues, 2002 to 2003 and 2003 to 2004.

    Operating income as a percentage of net operating revenues (profit margin), 2003 and 2004.

2. Determine whether there is a particular region of the world in which you believe Coca-Cola should attempt to expand its operations to increase operating revenues and operating income.

3. List any additional information you would like to have to conduct your analysis.

Chapter **Nine**

Foreign Currency Transactions and Hedging Foreign Exchange Risk

Questions to Consider

- How does a company that has transactions in a foreign currency determine the amounts to report in the financial statements?

- Does a change in the value of a foreign currency asset or liability held by a company represent a gain or loss that should be reported in income?

- What is foreign exchange risk? How does a company become exposed to foreign exchange risk?

- How do foreign currency derivatives such as forward contracts and options hedge foreign exchange risk?

- What is hedge accounting? What are the conditions that must be met for hedge accounting to be applied?

- What is the difference in accounting for a cash flow hedge and a fair value hedge?

- How do hedges of foreign currency denominated assets and liabilities, hedges of foreign currency firm commitments, and hedges of forecasted foreign currency transactions differ? How does the accounting for these different types of hedges differ?

Today, international business transactions are a regular occurrence. In its 2004 annual report, Lockheed Martin Corporation reported export sales of $6 billion, representing 17 percent of total sales. Even small businesses are significantly involved in transactions occurring throughout the world as evidenced by this excerpt from Cirrus Logic, Inc.'s, 2004 annual report: "Export sales to customers located in Asia were 59 percent, 68 percent, and 78 percent of net sales in fiscal years 2004, 2003, and 2002, respectively." Collections from export sales or payments for imported items may be made not in U.S. dollars but in pesos, pounds, yen, and the like depending on the negotiated terms of the transaction. As the foreign currency exchange rate fluctuates, so does the U.S. dollar value of these export sales and import purchases. Companies often find it necessary to engage in some form of hedging activity to reduce losses arising from fluctuating exchange rates. At the end of fiscal year 2004 as part of its foreign currency hedging activities, Hewlett-Packard Company reported having outstanding foreign currency forward contracts and options with a notional value of $4.9 billion.

This chapter covers accounting issues related to foreign currency transactions and foreign currency hedging activities. To provide background for subsequent discussions of the accounting issues, the chapter begins with a description of foreign exchange markets. The chapter then discusses accounting for import and export transactions, followed by coverage of various hedging techniques. Because they are most popular, the discussion concentrates on forward contracts and options. Understanding how to account for these items is important for any company engaged in international transactions.

FOREIGN EXCHANGE MARKETS

Each country uses its own currency as the unit of value for the purchase and sale of goods and services. The currency used in the United States is the U.S. dollar, the currency used in Mexico is the Mexican peso, and so on. If a U.S. citizen travels to Mexico and wishes to purchase local goods, Mexican merchants require payment to be made in Mexican pesos. To make a purchase, a U.S. citizen has to purchase pesos using U.S. dollars. The *foreign exchange rate* is the price at which the foreign currency can be acquired. A variety of factors determines the exchange rate between two currencies; unfortunately for those engaged in international business, the exchange rate can fluctuate over time.[1]

Exchange Rate Mechanisms

Exchange rates have not always fluctuated. During the period 1945–1973, countries fixed the par value of their currency in terms of the U.S. dollar, and the value of the U.S. dollar was fixed in terms of gold. Countries agreed to maintain the value of their currency within 1 percent of the par value. If the exchange rate for a particular currency began to move outside this 1 percent range, the country's central bank was required to intervene by buying or selling its currency in the foreign exchange market. Because of the law of supply and demand, a central bank's purchase of currency would cause the price of the currency to stop falling, and its sale of currency would cause the price to stop rising.

The integrity of the system hinged on the U.S. dollar maintaining its value in gold and the ability of foreign countries to convert their U.S. dollar holdings into gold at the fixed rate of $35 per ounce. As the United States began to incur balance of payment deficits in the 1960s, a glut of U.S. dollars arose worldwide, and foreign countries began converting their U.S. dollars into gold. This resulted in a decline in the U.S. government's gold reserve from a high of $24.6 billion in 1949 to a low of $10.2 billion in 1971. In that year, the United States suspended the convertibility of the U.S. dollar into gold, signaling the beginning of the end for the fixed exchange rate system. In March 1973, most currencies were allowed to float in value.

Today, several different currency arrangements exist. Some of the more important ones and the countries affected follow:

1. *Independent float:* The value of the currency is allowed to fluctuate freely according to market forces with little or no intervention from the central bank (Canada, Japan, Sweden, Switzerland, United States).
2. *Pegged to another currency:* The value of the currency is fixed (pegged) in terms of a particular foreign currency and the central bank intervenes as necessary to maintain the fixed value. For example, 25 countries peg their currency to the U.S. dollar (including the Bahamas and Syria).
3. *European Monetary System (euro):* In 1998, the countries comprising the European Monetary System adopted a common currency called the *euro* and established a European Central Bank.[2] Until 2002, local currencies such as the German mark and French franc continued to exist but were fixed in value in terms of the euro. On January 1, 2002, local currencies disappeared, and the euro became the currency in 12 European countries. The value of the euro floats against other currencies such as the U.S. dollar.

Foreign Exchange Rates

Exchange rates between the U.S. dollar and most foreign currencies are published on a daily basis in *The Wall Street Journal* and major U.S. newspapers. To better illustrate exchange rates and the foreign currency market, next we examine the exchange rates published in *The Wall Street Journal* for Wednesday, April 20, 2005, as shown in Exhibit 9.1.

---

[1] Several theories attempt to explain exchange rate fluctuations but with little success, at least in the short term. An understanding of the causes of exchange rate changes is not necessary to comprehend the concepts underlying the accounting for changes in exchange rates.

[2] Most members of the European Union (EU) are "euro zone" countries. The major exception is the United Kingdom, which elected not to participate. Switzerland is another important European country not part of the euro zone because it is not a member of the EU.

EXHIBIT 9.1 *The Wall Street Journal* **Foreign Exchange Quotes, Wednesday, April 20, 2005**

Source: Reuters

Exchange Rates   April 20, 2005

The foreign exchange mid-range rates below apply to trading among banks in amounts of $1 million and more, as quoted at 4 p.m. Eastern time by Reuters and other sources. Retail transactions provide fewer units of foreign currency per dollar.

Country	U.S. $ Equivalent		Currency per U.S. $	
	Wed.	Tue.	Wed.	Tue.
Argentina (Peso)-y	.3450	.3444	2.8986	2.9036
Australia (Dollar)	.7760	.7717	1.2887	1.2958
Bahrain (Dinar)	2.6525	2.6524	.3770	.3770
Brazil (Real)	.3907	.3893	2.5595	2.5687
Canada (Dollar)	.8067	.8080	1.2396	1.2376
1-month forward	.8071	.8083	1.2390	1.2372
3-months forward	.8078	.8090	1.2379	1.2361
6-months forward	.8094	.8107	1.2355	1.2335
Chile (Peso)	.001723	.001726	580.38	579.37
China (Renminbi)	.1208	.1208	8.2765	8.2764
Colombia (Peso)	.0004267	.0004251	2343.57	2352.39
Czech. Rep. (Koruna)				
Commercial rate	.04336	.04303	23.063	23.240
Denmark (Krone)	.1757	.1754	5.6915	5.7013
Ecuador (US Dollar)	1.0000	1.0000	1.0000	1.0000
Egypt (Pound)-y	.1724	.1724	5.8001	5.8001
Hong Kong (Dollar)	.1282	.1282	7.8003	7.8003
Hungary (Forint)	.005285	.005238	189.21	190.91
India (Rupee)	.02288	.02286	43.706	43.745
Indonesia (Rupiah)	.0001044	.0001045	9579	9569
Israel (Shekel)	.2289	.2287	4.3687	4.3725
Japan (Yen)	.009365	.009367	106.78	106.76
1-month forward	.009390	.009392	106.50	106.47
3-months forward	.009439	.009441	105.94	105.92
6-months forward	.009524	.009523	105.00	105.01
Jordan (Dinar)	1.4114	1.4114	.7085	.7085
Kuwait (Dinar)	3.4245	3.4245	.2920	.2920
Lebanon (Pound)	.0006603	.0006603	1514.46	1514.46
Malaysia (Ringgit)-b	.2632	.2632	3.7994	3.7994

Country	U.S. $ Equivalent		Currency per U.S. $	
	Wed.	Tue.	Wed.	Tue.
Malta (Lira)	3.0440	3.0407	.3285	.3289
Mexico (Peso)				
Floating rate	.0903	.0903	11.0693	11.0693
New Zealand (Dollar)	.7279	.7244	1.3738	1.3805
Norway (Krone)	.1602	.1594	6.2422	6.2735
Pakistan (Rupee)	.01683	.01684	59.418	59.382
Peru (new Sol)	.3072	.3068	3.2552	3.2595
Philippines (Peso)	.01839	.01839	54.377	54.377
Poland (Zloty)	.3141	.3120	3.1837	3.2051
Russia (Ruble)-a	.03605	.03603	27.739	27.755
Saudi Arabia (Riyal)	.2667	.2666	3.7495	3.7509
Singapore (Dollar)	.6077	.6067	1.6455	1.6483
Slovak Rep. (Koruna)	.03317	.03283	30.148	30.460
South Africa (Rand)	.1643	.1620	6.0864	6.1728
South Korea (Won)	.0009945	.0009896	1005.53	1010.51
Sweden (Krona)	.1426	.1423	7.0126	7.0274
Switzerland (Franc)	.8494	.8477	1.1773	1.1797
1-month forward	.8511	.8494	1.1750	1.1773
3-months forward	.8545	.8528	1.1703	1.1726
6-months forward	.8605	.8587	1.1621	1.1646
Taiwan (Dollar)	.03185	.03177	31.397	31.476
Thailand (Baht)	.02540	.02531	39.370	39.510
Turkey (New Lira)-d	.7364	.7334	1.3580	1.3635
U.K. (Pound)	1.9200	1.9194	.5208	.5210
1-month forward	1.9170	1.9163	.5216	.5218
3-months forward	1.9117	1.9112	.5231	.5232
6-months forward	1.9048	1.9044	.5250	.5251
United Arab (Dirham)	.2723	.2723	3.6724	3.6724
Uruguay (Peso) Financial	.03990	.03980	25.063	25.126
Venezuela (Bolivar)	.000466	.000466	2145.92	2145.92
SDR	1.5175	1.5137	.6590	.6606
Euro	1.3093	1.3075	.7638	.7648

Special Drawing Rights (SDR) are based on exchange rates for the U.S., British, and Japanese currencies. Source: International Monetary Fund.
a-Russian Central Bank rate. b-Government rate. d-Rebased as of Jan. 1, 2005.
y-Floating rate.

These exchange rates were quoted in New York at 4:00 P.M. Eastern time. The U.S. dollar price for one Argentinian peso on Wednesday, April 20, at 4:00 P.M. in New York was 0.3450. The U.S. dollar price for a peso at 4:01 P.M. Eastern time in New York was probably something different, as was the U.S. dollar price for a peso in Buenos Aires at 4:00 P.M. Eastern time. These exchange rates are for trades between banks in amounts of $1 million or more; that is, these are interbank or wholesale prices. Prices charged to retail customers, such as companies engaged in international business, are higher. These are selling rates, the rates at which banks in New York will sell currency to one another. The prices that banks are willing to pay to buy foreign currency (buying rates) are somewhat less than the selling rates. The difference between the buying and selling rates is the spread through which the banks earn a profit on foreign exchange trades.

There are two columns of information for each day exchange rates are published. The first column, U.S. $ equivalent, indicates the number of U.S. dollars needed to purchase one unit of foreign currency. These are known as *direct quotes*. The direct quote for the Swedish krona on April 20 was $0.1426; in other words, 1.0 krona could be purchased with $0.1426. The second column, Currency per U.S. $, indicates the number of foreign currency units that could be purchased with one U.S. dollar. These are called *indirect quotes,* which are simply the inverse of direct quotes. If one krona can be purchased with $0.1426, then 7.0126 kroner can be purchased with $1.00. (The arithmetic does not always work out perfectly because the direct quotes for the Swedish krona published in *The Wall Street Journal* are carried out to only four decimal points.) To avoid confusion, direct quotes are used exclusively in this chapter.

For each currency, comparative exchange rates for two days are presented. In most cases, there has been a change in the exchange rate from Tuesday, April 19, 2005, to Wednesday, April 20, 2005. Some currencies, such as the Swiss franc, increased in value or appreciated against the U.S. dollar (from $0.8477 to $0.8494). Other currencies, such as the Canadian dollar, decreased in value or depreciated against the U.S. dollar (from $0.8080 to $0.8067).

Spot and Forward Rates

Foreign currency trades can be executed on a spot or forward basis. The *spot rate* is the price at which a foreign currency can be purchased or sold today. In contrast, the *forward rate* is the price today at which foreign currency can be purchased or sold sometime in the future. Because many international business transactions take some time to be completed, the ability to lock in a price today at which foreign currency can be purchased or sold at some future date has definite advantages.

Most of the quotes published in *The Wall Street Journal* are *spot rates*. In addition, it publishes forward rates quoted by New York banks for the major currencies (British pound, Canadian dollar, Japanese yen, and Swiss franc) on a daily basis. This is only a partial listing of possible forward contracts. A firm and its bank can tailor forward contracts in other currencies and for other time periods to meet the needs of the firm. There is no up-front cost to enter into a forward contract.

The forward rate can exceed the spot rate on a given date, in which case the foreign currency is said to be selling at a *premium* in the forward market, or the forward rate can be less than the spot rate, in which case it is selling at a *discount*. Currencies sell at a premium or a discount because of differences in interest rates between two countries. When the interest rate in the foreign country exceeds the interest rate domestically, the foreign currency sells at a discount in the forward market. Conversely, if the foreign interest rate is less than the domestic rate, the foreign currency sells at a premium.[3] Forward rates are said to be unbiased predictors of the future spot rate.

The spot rate for British pounds on April 20, 2005, indicates that 1 pound could have been purchased on that date for $1.9200. On the same day, the one-month forward rate was $1.9170. By entering into a forward contract on April 20, it was possible to guarantee that pounds could be purchased on May 20 at a price of $1.9170, regardless of what the spot rate turned out to be on May 20. Entering into the forward contract to purchase pounds would have been beneficial if the spot rate on May 20 was more than $1.9170. On the other hand, such a forward contract would have been detrimental if the spot rate was less than $1.9170. In either case, the forward contract must be honored and pounds must be purchased on May 20 at $1.9170.

Option Contracts

To provide companies more flexibility than exists with a forward contract, a market for *foreign currency options* has developed. A foreign currency option gives the holder of the option *the right but not the obligation* to trade foreign currency in the future. A *put* option is for the sale of foreign currency by the holder of the option; a *call* is for the purchase of foreign currency by the holder of the option. The *strike price* is the exchange rate at which the option will be executed if the holder of the option decides to exercise the option. The strike price is similar to a

---

[3] This relationship is based on the theory of interest rate parity that indicates the difference in national interest rates should be equal to, but opposite in sign to, the forward rate discount or premium. This topic is covered in detail in international financial textbooks.

forward rate. There are generally several strike prices to choose from at any particular time. Foreign currency options can be purchased either on the Philadelphia Stock Exchange or directly from a bank in the so-called over-the-counter market.

Unlike a forward contract, for which banks earn their profit through the spread between buying and selling rates, options must actually be purchased by paying an *option premium*. The option premium is a function of two components: intrinsic value and time value. The *intrinsic value* of an option is equal to the gain that could be realized by exercising the option immediately. For example, if a spot rate for a foreign currency is $1.00, a *call* option (to purchase foreign currency) with a strike price of $0.97 has an intrinsic value of $0.03, whereas a *put* option with a strike price of $0.97 has an intrinsic value of zero. An option with a positive intrinsic value is said to be "in the money." The *time value* of an option relates to the fact that the spot rate can change over time and cause the option to become in the money. Even though a 90-day call option with a strike price of $1.00 has zero intrinsic value when the spot rate is $1.00, it will still have a positive time value if there is a chance that the spot rate could increase over the next 90 days and bring the option into the money.

The value of a foreign currency option can be determined by applying an adaptation of the Black-Scholes option pricing formula. This formula is discussed in detail in international finance books. In very general terms, the value of an option is a function of the difference between the current spot rate and strike price, the difference between domestic and foreign interest rates, the length of time to expiration, and the potential volatility of changes in the spot rate. For purposes of this book, the premium originally paid for a foreign currency option and its subsequent fair value up to the date of expiration derived from applying the pricing formula will be given.

Option quotes reported in *The Wall Street Journal* on April 20, 2005, indicated that a May call option in euros with a strike price of $1.31 could have been purchased by paying a premium of $0.0159 per euro. Thus, the right to purchase 125,000 euros in May 2005 at a price of $1.31 per euro could have been acquired by paying $1,987.50 ($0.0159 × 125,000 euros). If the spot rate for euros in May is more than $1.31, the option would be exercised and euros purchased at the strike price of $1.31. If, on the other hand, the May spot rate is less than $1.31, the option would not be exercised; instead, euros would be purchased at the lower spot rate. The option contract establishes the maximum amount that would have to be paid for euros but does not lock in a disadvantageous price should the spot rate fall below the option strike price.

FOREIGN CURRENCY TRANSACTIONS

Export sales and import purchases are international transactions; they are components of what is called *trade*. When two parties from different countries enter into a transaction, they must decide which of the two countries' currencies to use to settle the transaction. For example, if a U.S. computer manufacturer sells to a customer in Japan, the parties must decide whether the transaction will be denominated (payment will be made) in U.S. dollars or Japanese yen.

Assume that a U.S. exporter (Amerco) sells goods to a German importer that will pay in euros (€). In this situation, Amerco has entered into a foreign currency transaction. It must restate the euro amount that it actually will receive into U.S. dollars to account for this transaction. This happens because Amerco keeps its books and prepares financial statements in U.S. dollars. Although the German importer has entered into an international transaction, it does not have a foreign currency transaction (payment will be made in its currency) and no restatement is necessary.

Assume that, as is customary in its industry, Amerco does not require immediate payment and allows its German customer 30 days to pay for its purchases. By doing this, Amerco runs the risk that the euro might depreciate against the U.S. dollar between the sale date and the date of payment. Then, the sale generates fewer U.S. dollars than it would have had the euro not decreased in value, and the sale is less profitable because it was made on a credit basis.

In this situation Amerco is said to have an *exposure to foreign exchange risk*. Specifically, Amerco has a transaction exposure that can be summarized as follows:

- *Export sale:* A transaction exposure exists when the exporter allows the buyer to pay in a foreign currency and allows the buyer to pay sometime after the sale has been made. The exporter is exposed to the risk that the foreign currency might depreciate (decrease in value) between the date of sale and the date of payment, thereby decreasing the U.S. dollars ultimately collected.

- *Import purchase:* A transaction exposure exists when the importer is required to pay in foreign currency and is allowed to pay sometime after the purchase has been made. The importer is exposed to the risk that the foreign currency might appreciate (increase in price) between the date of purchase and the date of payment, thereby increasing the U.S. dollars that have to be paid for the imported goods.

Accounting Issue

The major issue in accounting for foreign currency transactions is how to deal with the change in U.S. dollar value of the sales revenue and account receivable resulting from the export when the foreign currency changes in value. (The corollary issue is how to deal with the change in the U.S. dollar value of the account payable and goods being acquired in an import purchase.) For example, assume that Amerco, a U.S. company, sells goods to a German customer at a price of 1 million euros when the spot exchange rate is $0.92 per euro. If payment were received at the date of sale, Amerco could have converted 1 million euros into $920,000; this amount clearly would be the amount at which the sales revenue would be recognized. Instead, Amerco allows the German customer 30 days to pay for its purchase. At the end of 30 days, the euro has depreciated to $0.90 and Amerco is able to convert the 1 million euros received on that date into only $900,000. How should Amerco account for this $20,000 decrease in value?

Accounting Alternatives

Conceptually, the two methods of accounting for changes in the value of a foreign currency transaction are the one-transaction perspective and the two-transaction perspective. The *one-transaction perspective* assumes that an export sale is not complete until the foreign currency receivable has been collected and converted into U.S. dollars. Any change in the U.S. dollar value of the foreign currency is accounted for as an adjustment to Accounts Receivable and to Sales. Under this perspective, Amerco would ultimately report Sales at $900,000 and an increase in the Cash account of the same amount. This approach can be criticized because it hides the fact that the company could have received $920,000 if the German customer had been required to pay at the date of sale. The company incurs a $20,000 loss because of the depreciation in the euro, but that loss is buried in an adjustment to Sales. This approach is not acceptable under U.S. GAAP.

Instead, FASB *Statement No. 52* requires companies to use a *two-transaction perspective* in accounting for foreign currency transactions.[4] This perspective treats the export sale and the subsequent collection of cash as two separate transactions. Because management has made two decisions—(1) to make the export sale and (2) to extend credit in foreign currency to the customer—the company should report the income effect from each of these decisions separately. The U.S. dollar value of the sale is recorded at the date the sale occurs. At that point the sale has been completed; there are no subsequent adjustments to the Sales account. Any difference between the number of U.S. dollars that could have been received at the date of sale and the number of U.S. dollars actually received at the date of collection due to fluctuations in the exchange rate is a result of the decision to extend foreign currency credit to the customer. This difference is treated as a foreign exchange gain or loss that is reported separately from Sales in the income statement. Using the

---

[4] FASB, *Statement of Financial Accounting Standards No. 52,* "Foreign Currency Translation" (Stamford, CT: FASB, December 1981).

two-transaction perspective to account for its export sale to Germany, Amerco would make the following journal entries:

Date of Sale:	Accounts Receivable (€)	920,000	
	Sales		920,000
	To record the sale and euro receivable at the spot rate of $0.92.		
Date of Collection:	Foreign Exchange Loss	20,000	
	Accounts Receivable (€)		20,000
	To adjust the value of the euro receivable to the new spot rate of $0.90 and record a foreign exchange loss resulting from the depreciation in the euro.		
	Cash	900,000	
	Accounts Receivable (€)		900,000
	To record the receipt of 1 million euros and conversion at the spot rate of $0.90.		

Sales are reported in income at the amount that would have been received if the customer had not been given 30 days to pay the 1 million euros—that is, $920,000. A separate Foreign Exchange Loss of $20,000 is reported in income to indicate that because of the decision to extend foreign currency credit to the German customer and because the euro decreased in value, Amerco actually received fewer U.S. dollars.[5]

Note that Amerco keeps its Account Receivable (€) account separate from its U.S. dollar receivables. Companies engaged in international trade need to keep separate payable and receivable accounts in each of the currencies in which they have transactions. Each foreign currency receivable and payable should have a separate account number in the company's chart of accounts.

We can summarize the relationship between fluctuations in exchange rates and foreign exchange gains and losses as follows:

		Foreign Currency (FC)	
Transaction	**Type of Exposure**	**Appreciates**	**Depreciates**
Export sale	Asset	Gain	Loss
Import purchase	Liability	Loss	Gain

A foreign currency receivable arising from an export sale creates an *asset exposure* to foreign exchange risk. If the foreign currency appreciates, the foreign currency asset increases in U.S. dollar value and a foreign exchange gain arises; depreciation of the foreign currency causes a foreign exchange loss. A foreign currency payable arising from an import purchase creates a *liability exposure* to foreign exchange risk. If the foreign currency appreciates, the foreign currency liability increases in U.S. dollar value and a foreign exchange loss results; depreciation of the currency results in a foreign exchange gain.

Balance Sheet Date before Date of Payment

The question arises as to what accounting should be done if a balance sheet date falls between the date of sale and the date of payment. For example, assume that Amerco shipped goods to its German customer on December 1, 2007, with payment to be received on March 1, 2008. Assume that at December 1, the spot rate for the euro is $0.92, but by December 31, the euro has appreciated to $0.93. Is any adjustment needed at December 31, 2007, when the books are closed to account for the fact that the foreign currency receivable has changed in U.S. dollar value since December 1?

---

[5] Note that the foreign exchange loss results because the customer is allowed to pay in euros and is given 30 days to pay. If the transaction were denominated in U.S. dollars, no loss would result. Nor would there be a loss if the euros had been received at the date the sale was made.

The general consensus worldwide is that a foreign currency receivable or foreign currency payable should be revalued at the balance sheet date to account for the change in exchange rates. Under the two-transaction perspective, this means that a foreign exchange gain or loss arises at the balance sheet date. The next question then is what should be done with these foreign exchange gains and losses that have not yet been realized in cash. Should they be included in net income?

The two approaches to accounting for unrealized foreign exchange gains and losses are the deferral approach and the accrual approach. Under the *deferral approach,* unrealized foreign exchange gains and losses are deferred on the balance sheet until cash is actually paid or received. When cash is paid or received, a *realized* foreign exchange gain or loss is included in income. This approach is not acceptable under U.S. GAAP.

SFAS 52 requires U.S. companies to use the *accrual approach* to account for unrealized foreign exchange gains and losses. Under this approach, a firm reports unrealized foreign exchange gains and losses in net income in the period in which the exchange rate changes. *SFAS 52* says, "This is consistent with accrual accounting; it results in reporting the effect of a rate change that will have cash flow effects when the event causing the effect takes place."[6] Thus, any change in the exchange rate from the date of sale to the balance sheet date results in a foreign exchange gain or loss to be reported in income in that period. Any change in the exchange rate from the balance sheet date to the date of payment results in a second foreign exchange gain or loss that is reported in the second accounting period. Amerco makes the following journal entries under the accrual approach:

12/1/07	Accounts Receivable (€)	920,000	
	Sales		920,000
	To record the sale and euro receivable at the spot rate of $0.92.		
12/31/07	Accounts Receivable (€)	10,000	
	Foreign Exchange Gain		10,000
	To adjust the value of the euro receivable to the new spot rate of $0.93 and record a foreign exchange gain resulting from the appreciation in the euro since December 1.		
3/1/08	Foreign Exchange Loss	30,000	
	Accounts Receivable (€)		30,000
	To adjust the value of the euro receivable to the new spot rate of $0.90 and record a foreign exchange loss resulting from the depreciation in the euro since December 31.		
	Cash	900,000	
	Accounts Receivable (€)		900,000
	To record the receipt of 1 million euros and conversion at the spot rate of $0.90.		

The net impacts on income in 2007 are a sale of $920,000 and a foreign exchange gain of $10,000; in 2008, Amerco records a foreign exchange loss of $30,000. This results in a net increase of $900,000 in Retained Earnings that is balanced by an equal increase in Cash.

One criticism of the accrual approach is that it leads to a violation of conservatism when an unrealized foreign exchange gain arises at the balance sheet date. In fact, this is one of only two situations in U.S. GAAP in which it is acceptable to recognize an unrealized gain in income. (The other situation relates to trading marketable securities reported at fair value.) Germany, Austria, and several other countries more strictly adhere to the concept of conservatism than does the United States. In those countries, if at the balance sheet date the exchange rate has changed so that an unrealized gain arises, the change in exchange rate is ignored, and the

[6] *SFAS 52,* para. 124.

foreign currency account receivable or payable continues to be carried on the balance sheet at the exchange rate that existed at the date of the transaction. On the other hand, if the exchange rate had changed to cause a foreign exchange loss, the accounting receivable would be revalued, and an unrealized loss would have been recorded and reported in income. This is a classic application of conservatism.

SFAS 52 requires restatement at the balance sheet date of all foreign currency assets and liabilities carried on a company's books. In addition to foreign currency payables and receivables arising from import and export transactions, companies might have dividends receivable from foreign subsidiaries, loans payable to foreign lenders, or lease payments receivable from foreign customers that are denominated in a foreign currency and therefore must be restated at the balance sheet date. Each of these foreign currency denominated assets and liabilities is exposed to foreign exchange risk; therefore, fluctuation in the exchange rate results in foreign exchange gains and losses.

Many U.S. companies report foreign exchange gains and losses on the income statement in a line item often titled Other Income (Expense). Companies include other incidental gains and losses such as gains and losses on sales of assets in this line item as well. *SFAS 52* requires companies to disclose the magnitude of foreign exchange gains and losses if material. For example, in the Notes to Financial Statements in its 2004 annual report, Merck indicated that the income statement item Other (Income) Expense, Net included exchange gains of $18.4 million, $28.4 million, and $7.8 million in 2004, 2003, and 2002, respectively.

HEDGING FOREIGN EXCHANGE RISK

In the preceding example, Amerco has an asset exposure in euros when it sells goods to the German customer and allows the customer three months to pay for its purchase. If the euro depreciates over the next three months, Amerco will incur a foreign exchange loss. For many companies, the uncertainty of not knowing exactly how many U.S. dollars an export sale will generate is of great concern. To avoid this uncertainty, companies often use foreign currency derivatives to hedge against the effect of unfavorable changes in the value of foreign currencies. The two most common derivatives used to hedge foreign exchange risk are *foreign currency forward contracts* and *foreign currency options*. Through a forward contract, Amerco can lock in the price at which it will sell the euros it receives in three months. An option establishes a price at which Amerco will be able, but is not required, to sell the euros it receives in three months. If Amerco enters into a forward contract or purchases an option on the date the sale is made, the derivative is being used as a *hedge of a recognized foreign currency denominated asset* (the euro account receivable).

Companies engaged in foreign currency activities often enter into hedging arrangements as soon as they receive a noncancelable sales order or place a noncancelable purchase order. A noncancelable order that specifies the foreign currency price and date of delivery is known as a *foreign currency firm commitment*. Assume that on June 1, Amerco accepts an order to sell parts to a customer in Korea at a price of 5 million Korean won. The parts will be delivered and payment will be received on August 15. On June 1, before the sale has been made, Amerco enters into a forward contract to sell 5 million Korean won on August 15. In this case, Amerco is using a foreign currency derivative as a *hedge of an unrecognized foreign currency firm commitment*.

Some companies have foreign currency transactions that occur on a regular basis and can be reliably forecasted. For example, Amerco regularly purchases materials from a supplier in Hong Kong for which it pays in Hong Kong dollars. Even if Amerco has no contract to make future purchases, it has an exposure to foreign currency risk if it plans to continue making purchases from the Hong Kong supplier. Assume that on October 1, Amerco forecasts that it will make a purchase from the Hong Kong supplier in one month. To hedge against a possible increase in the price of the Hong Kong dollar, Amerco acquires a call option on October 1 to purchase Hong Kong dollars in one month. The foreign currency option represents a *hedge of a forecasted foreign currency denominated transaction*.

ACCOUNTING FOR DERIVATIVES

SFAS 133, "Accounting for Derivative Instruments and Hedging Activities," which went into effect in 2001, governs the accounting for all derivatives, including those used to hedge foreign exchange risk. In response to concerns expressed by many companies, *SFAS 138*, "Accounting for Certain Derivative Instruments and Certain Hedging Activities," amends *SFAS 133* with respect to the accounting for hedges of recognized foreign currency denominated assets and liabilities.

SFAS 133 (as amended by *SFAS 138*) provides guidance for hedges of the following sources of foreign exchange risk:

1. Recognized foreign currency denominated assets and liabilities.
2. Unrecognized foreign currency firm commitments.
3. Forecasted foreign currency denominated transactions.
4. Net investments in foreign operations.

Different accounting applies to each different type of foreign currency hedge. This chapter demonstrates the accounting for the first three types of hedge. Chapter 10 covers hedges of net investments in foreign operations.

Fundamental Requirement of Derivatives Accounting

The fundamental requirement of *SFAS 133* (and *SFAS 138*) is that companies carry all derivatives on the balance sheet at their fair value. Derivatives are reported on the balance sheet as assets when they have a positive fair value and as liabilities when they have a negative fair value. The first issue in accounting for derivatives is the determination of fair value.

The fair value of derivatives can change over time, causing adjustments to be made to the carrying values of the assets and liabilities. The second issue in accounting for derivatives is the treatment of the gains and losses that arise from these adjustments.

Determining the Fair Value of Derivatives

The *fair value of a foreign currency forward contract* is determined by reference to changes in the forward rate over the life of the contract, discounted to the present value. Three pieces of information are needed to determine the fair value of a forward contract at any point in time:

1. The forward rate when the forward contract was entered into.
2. The current forward rate for a contract that matures on the same date as the forward contract entered into.
3. A discount rate—typically, the company's incremental borrowing rate.

Assume that Exim Company enters into a forward contract on December 1 to sell 1 million Mexican pesos on March 1 at a forward rate of $0.085 per peso, or a total of $85,000. Exim Company incurs no cost to enter into the forward contract, which has no value on December 1. On December 31, when Exim closes its books to prepare financial statements, the forward rate to sell Mexican pesos on March 1 has changed to $0.082. On that date, a forward contract for the delivery of 1 million pesos could be negotiated, resulting in a cash inflow of only $82,000 on March 1. This represents a favorable change in the value of Exim Company's forward contract of $3,000 ($85,000 − $82,000). The fair value of the forward contract on December 31 is $3,000, discounted to its present value. Assuming that the company's incremental borrowing rate is 12 percent per annum, the fair value of the forward contract must be discounted at the rate of 1 percent per month for two months (from the current date of December 31 to the settlement date of March 1). The fair value of the forward contract at December 31 is $2,940.90 ($3,000 × 0.9803).[7]

The manner in which the *fair value of a foreign currency option* is determined depends on whether the option is traded on an exchange or has been acquired in the over-the-counter

---

[7] The present value factor for two months at 1 percent per month is calculated as $1/1.01^2$, or 0.9803.

market. The fair value of an exchange-traded foreign currency option is its current market price quoted on the exchange. For over-the-counter options, fair value can be determined by obtaining a price quote from an option dealer (such as a bank). If dealer price quotes are unavailable, the company can estimate the value of an option using the modified Black-Scholes option pricing model (briefly mentioned earlier). Regardless of who does the calculation, principles similar to those of the Black-Scholes pricing model can be used to determine the fair value of the option.

Accounting for Changes in the Fair Value of Derivatives

Changes in the fair value of derivatives must be included in *comprehensive income*. The FASB introduced the reporting of comprehensive income in 1997.[8] *Comprehensive income* is defined as all changes in equity from nonowner sources and consists of two components: *net income* and *other comprehensive income*. Other comprehensive income consists of income items that previous FASB statements required to be deferred in stockholders' equity such as gains and losses on available-for-sale marketable securities. Other comprehensive income is accumulated and reported as a separate line in the stockholders' equity section of the balance sheet. This book uses the account title *Accumulated Other Comprehensive Income* to describe this stockholders' equity line item.

In accordance with *SFAS 133* (as amended by *SFAS 138*), gains and losses arising from changes in the fair value of derivatives are recognized initially either (1) on the income statement as a part of net income or (2) on the balance sheet as a component of other comprehensive income. Recognition treatment depends partly on whether the company uses derivatives for hedging purposes or for speculation.[9] For speculative derivatives, the company recognizes the change in the fair value of the derivative (the gain or loss) immediately in net income. The accounting for changes in the fair value of derivatives used for hedging depends on the nature of the foreign exchange risk being hedged and on whether the derivative qualifies for *hedge accounting*.

HEDGE ACCOUNTING

Companies enter into hedging relationships to minimize the adverse effect that changes in exchange rates have on cash flows and net income. As such, companies would like to account for hedges in such a way to recognize the gain or loss from the hedge in net income in the same period as the loss or gain on the risk being hedged. This approach is known as *hedge accounting*. *SFAS 133* and *SFAS 138* allow hedge accounting for foreign currency derivatives only if three conditions are satisfied:

1. The derivative is used to hedge either a fair value exposure or cash flow exposure to foreign exchange risk.
2. The derivative is highly effective in offsetting changes in the fair value or cash flows related to the hedged item.
3. The derivative is properly documented as a hedge.

Each of these conditions is discussed in turn.

Nature of the Hedged Risk

A *fair value exposure* exists if changes in exchange rates can affect the fair value of an asset or liability reported on the balance sheet. To qualify for hedge accounting, the fair value risk must have the potential to affect net income if it is not hedged. For example, a fair value risk

[8] FASB *SFAS 130*, "Reporting Comprehensive Income," issued in June 1997.

[9] Companies can acquire derivative financial instruments as investments for speculative purposes. For example, assume that the three-month forward rate for British pounds is $1.50, and a speculator believes the British pound spot rate in three months will be $1.47. In that case, the speculator would enter into a three-month forward contract to sell British pounds. At the future date, the speculator purchases pounds at the spot rate of $1.47 and sells them at the contracted forward rate of $1.50, reaping a gain of $0.03 per pound. Of course, such an investment might just as easily generate a loss if the spot rate does not move as expected.

is associated with a foreign currency account receivable. If the foreign currency depreciates, the receivable must be written down with an offsetting loss recognized in net income. The FASB has determined that a fair value exposure also exists for foreign currency firm commitments.

A *cash flow exposure* exists if changes in exchange rates can affect the amount of cash flow to be realized from a transaction with changes in cash flow reflected in net income. A foreign currency account receivable, for example, has both a fair value exposure and a cash flow exposure. A cash flow exposure exists for (1) recognized foreign currency assets and liabilities, (2) foreign currency firm commitments, and (3) forecasted foreign currency transactions.

Derivatives for which companies wish to use hedge accounting must be designated as either a *fair value hedge* or a *cash flow hedge*. For hedges of recognized foreign currency assets and liabilities and hedges of foreign currency firm commitments, companies must choose between the two types of designation. Hedges of forecasted foreign currency transactions can qualify only as cash flow hedges. Accounting procedures differ for the two types of hedges. In general, gains and losses on fair value hedges are recognized immediately in net income, and gains and losses on cash flow hedges are included in other comprehensive income.

Hedge Effectiveness

For hedge accounting to be used initially, the hedge must be expected to be highly effective in generating gains and losses that offset losses and gains on the item being hedged. The hedge actually must be effective in generating offsetting gains and losses for hedge accounting to continue to be applied.

At inception, a foreign currency derivative can be considered an effective hedge if the critical terms of the hedging instrument match those of the hedged item. Critical terms include the currency type, currency amount, and settlement date. For example, a forward contract to purchase 100,000 Canadian dollars in 30 days would be an effective hedge of a 100,000 Canadian dollar liability that is payable in 30 days. Assessing hedge effectiveness on an ongoing basis can be accomplished using a cumulative dollar offset method.

Hedge Documentation

For hedge accounting to be applied, *SFAS 133* requires formal documentation of the hedging relationship at the inception of the hedge (i.e., on the date a foreign currency forward contract is entered into or a foreign currency option is acquired). The hedging company must prepare a document that identifies the hedged item, the hedging instrument, the nature of the risk being hedged, how the hedging instrument's effectiveness will be assessed, and the risk management objective and strategy for undertaking the hedge.

HEDGES OF FOREIGN CURRENCY DENOMINATED ASSETS AND LIABILITIES

Hedges of foreign currency denominated assets and liabilities, such as accounts receivable and accounts payable, can qualify as either *cash flow hedges* or *fair value hedges*. To qualify as a cash flow hedge, the hedging instrument must completely offset the variability in the cash flows associated with the foreign currency receivable or payable. If the hedging instrument does not qualify as a cash flow hedge or if the company elects not to designate the hedging instrument as a cash flow hedge, the hedge is designated as a fair value hedge. The following summarizes the basic accounting for the two types of hedges.

Cash Flow Hedge

At each balance sheet date, the following procedures are required:

1. The hedged asset or liability is adjusted to fair value based on changes in the spot exchange rate, and a foreign exchange gain or loss is recognized in net income.
2. The derivative hedging instrument is adjusted to fair value (resulting in an asset or liability reported on the balance sheet) with the counterpart recognized as a change in Accumulated Other Comprehensive Income (AOCI).

3. An amount equal to the foreign exchange gain or loss on the hedged asset or liability is then transferred from AOCI to net income; the net effect is to offset any gain or loss on the hedged asset or liability.

4. An additional amount is removed from AOCI and recognized in net income to reflect (a) the current period's amortization of the original discount or premium on the forward contract (if a forward contract is the hedging instrument) or (b) the change in the *time value* of the option (if an option is the hedging instrument).

Fair Value Hedge

At each balance sheet date, the following procedures are required:

1. The hedged asset or liability is adjusted to fair value based on changes in the spot exchange rate, and a foreign exchange gain or loss is recognized in net income.

2. The derivative hedging instrument is adjusted to fair value (resulting in an asset or liability reported on the balance sheet), with the counterpart recognized as a gain or loss in net income.

FORWARD CONTRACT USED TO HEDGE A FOREIGN CURRENCY DENOMINATED ASSET

We now return to the Amerco example in which the company has a foreign currency account receivable to demonstrate the accounting for a recognized foreign currency denominated asset.[10] In the preceding example, Amerco has an asset exposure in euros when it sells goods to the German customer and allows the customer three months to pay for its purchase. To hedge its exposure to a decline in the U.S. dollar value of the euro, Amerco decides to enter into a forward contract.

Assume that on December 1, 2007, the three-month forward rate for euros is $0.905 and Amerco signs a contract with New Manhattan Bank to deliver 1 million euros in three months in exchange for $905,000. No cash changes hands on December 1, 2007. Because the spot rate on December 1 is $0.92, the euro (€) is selling at a discount in the three-month forward market (the forward rate is less than the spot rate). Because the euro is selling at a discount of $0.015 per euro, Amerco receives $15,000 less than it would had payment been received at the date the goods are delivered ($905,000 versus $920,000). This $15,000 reduction in cash flow can be considered as an expense; it is the cost of extending foreign currency credit to the foreign customer.[11] Conceptually, this expense is similar to the transaction loss that arises on the export sale. It exists only because the transaction is denominated in a foreign currency. The major difference is that Amerco knows the exact amount of the discount expense at the date of sale, whereas when it is left unhedged, Amerco does not know the size of the transaction loss until three months pass. (In fact, it is possible that the unhedged receivable could result in a transaction gain rather than a transaction loss.)

Because the future spot rate turns out to be only $0.90, selling euros at a forward rate of $0.905 is obviously better than leaving the euro receivable unhedged: Amerco will receive $5,000 more as a result of the hedge. This can be viewed as a gain resulting from the use of the forward contract. Unlike the discount expense, the exact size of this gain is not known until three months pass. (In fact, it is possible that use of the forward contract could result in an additional loss. This would occur if the spot rate on March 1, 2008, is more than the forward rate of $0.905.)

Amerco must account for its foreign currency transaction and the related forward contract simultaneously but separately. The process can be better understood by referring to the steps

---

[10] The comprehensive illustration at the end of this chapter demonstrates the accounting for the hedge of a foreign currency denominated liability.

[11] This should not be confused with the cost associated with normal credit risk—that is, the risk that the customer will not pay for its purchase. That is a separate issue unrelated to the currency in which the transaction is denominated.

EXHIBIT 9.2
**Hedge of a Foreign
Currency Account
Receivable with a
Forward Contract**

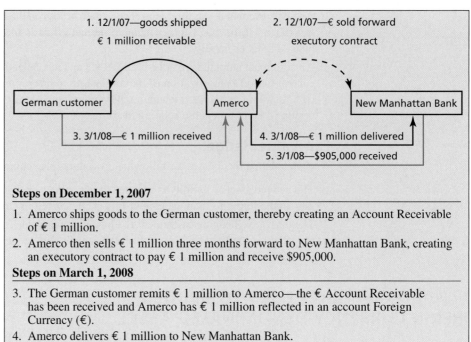

Steps on December 1, 2007

1. Amerco ships goods to the German customer, thereby creating an Account Receivable of € 1 million.
2. Amerco then sells € 1 million three months forward to New Manhattan Bank, creating an executory contract to pay € 1 million and receive $905,000.

Steps on March 1, 2008

3. The German customer remits € 1 million to Amerco—the € Account Receivable has been received and Amerco has € 1 million reflected in an account Foreign Currency (€).
4. Amerco delivers € 1 million to New Manhattan Bank.
5. New Manhattan Bank pays Amerco $905,000.

involving the three parties—Amerco, the German customer, and New Manhattan Bank—shown in Exhibit 9.2.

Because the settlement date, currency type, and currency amount of the forward contract match the corresponding terms of the account receivable, the hedge is expected to be highly effective. If Amerco properly designates the forward contract as a hedge of its euro account receivable position, it may apply hedge accounting. Because it completely offsets the variability in the cash flows related to the account receivable, Amerco may designate the forward contract as a cash flow hedge. Alternatively, because changes in the spot rate affect not only the cash flows but also the fair value of the foreign currency receivable, Amerco may elect to account for this forward contract as a fair value hedge.

In either case, Amerco determines the fair value of the forward contract by referring to the change in the forward rate for a contract maturing on March 1, 2008. The relevant exchange rates, U.S. dollar value of the euro receivable, and fair value of the forward contract are determined as follows:

Date	Spot Rate	Account Receivable (€)		Forward Rate to 3/1/08	Forward Contract	
		U.S. Dollar Value	Change in U.S. Dollar Value		Fair Value	Change in Fair Value
12/1/07	$0.92	$920,000	—	$0.905	–0–	—
12/31/07	0.93	930,000	+$10,000	0.916	$(10,783)*	−$10,783
3/1/08	0.90	900,000	−$30,000	0.90	5,000†	+ 15,783

*$905,000 − $916,000 = $(11,000) × 0.9803 = $(10,783), where 0.9803 is the present value factor for two months at an annual interest rate of 12 percent (1 percent per month) calculated as $1/1.01^2$.
†$905,000 − $900,000 = $5,000.

Amerco pays nothing to enter into the forward contract at December 1, 2007, and the forward contract has a fair value of zero on that date. At December 31, 2007, the forward rate for a contract to deliver euros on March 1, 2008, is $0.916. Amerco could enter into a forward contract on December 31, 2007, to sell 1 million euros for $916,000 on March 1, 2008. Because Amerco is committed to sell 1 million euros for $905,000, the nominal value of the forward contract is $(11,000). The fair value of the forward contract is the present value of this amount. Assuming that Amerco has an incremental borrowing rate of 12 percent per year (1 percent per month) and discounting for two months (from December 31, 2007, to March 1, 2008), the fair value of the forward contract at December 31, 2007, is $(10,783), a liability. On March 1, 2008, the forward rate to sell euros on that date is the spot rate, $0.90. At that rate, Amerco could sell 1 million euros for $900,000. Because Amerco has a contract to sell euros for $905,000, the fair value of the forward contract on March 1, 2008, is $5,000. This represents an increase of $15,783 in fair value from December 31, 2007. The original discount on the forward contract is determined by the difference in the euro spot rate and three-month forward rate on December 1, 2007: ($0.905 − $0.92) × € 1 million = $15,000.

Forward Contract Designated as Cash Flow Hedge

Assume that Amerco designates the forward contract as a *cash flow hedge* of a foreign currency denominated asset. In this case, it allocates the original forward discount or premium to net income over the life of the forward contract using an effective interest method. The company prepares the following journal entries to account for the foreign currency transaction and the related forward contract:

2007 Journal Entries—Forward Contract Designated as a Cash Flow Hedge

12/1/07	Accounts Receivable (€)	920,000	
	Sales		920,000
	To record the sale and € 1 million account receivable at the spot rate of $.920 (Step 1 in Exhibit 9.2).		

Amerco makes no formal entry for the forward contract because it is an executory contract (no cash changes hands) and has a fair value of zero (Step 2 in Exhibit 9.2).

Amerco prepares a memorandum designating the forward contract as a hedge of the risk of changes in the cash flow to be received on the foreign currency account receivable resulting from changes in the U.S. dollar–euro exchange rate.

12/31/07	Accounts Receivable (€)	10,000	
	Foreign Exchange Gain		10,000
	To adjust the value of the € receivable to the new spot rate of $0.93 and record a foreign exchange gain resulting from the appreciation of the € since December 1.		
	Accumulated Other Comprehensive Income (AOCI)	10,783	
	Forward Contract		10,783
	To record the forward contract as a liability at its fair value of $10,783 with a corresponding debit to AOCI.		
	Loss on Forward Contract	10,000	
	Accumulated Other Comprehensive Income (AOCI)		10,000
	To record a loss on forward contract to offset the foreign exchange gain on account receivable with a corresponding credit to AOCI.		
	Discount Expense	5,028	
	Accumulated Other Comprehensive Income (AOCI)		5,028
	To allocate the forward contract discount to net income over the life of the contract using the effective interest method with a corresponding credit to AOCI.		

The company calculates the implicit interest rate associated with the forward contract by considering the fact that the forward contract will generate cash flow of $905,000 from a foreign currency asset with an initial value of $920,000. Because the discount of $15,000 accrues over a three-month period, the effective interest rate is calculated as $[1 - \sqrt[3]{\$905{,}000/\$920{,}000}] = 0.0054647$. The amount of discount to be allocated to net income for the month of December 2004 is $920,000 × 0.0054647 = $5,028.

The impact on net income for the year 2007 follows:

Sales.		$920,000
Foreign exchange gain	$ 10,000	
Loss on forward contract	(10,000)	
Net gain (loss).		–0–
Discount expense		(5,028)
Impact on net income.		$914,972

The effect on the December 31, 2007, balance sheet is as follows:

Assets		Liabilities and Stockholders' Equity	
Accounts receivable (€)	$930,000	Forward contract	$ 10,783
		Retained earnings	914,972
		AOCI	4,245
			$930,000

2008 Journal Entries—Forward Contract Designated as Cash Flow Hedge

3/1/08	Foreign Exchange Loss	30,000	
	Accounts Receivable (€)		30,000
	To adjust the value of the € receivable to the new spot rate of $0.90 and record a foreign exchange loss resulting from the depreciation of the € since December 31.		
	Forward Contract	15,783	
	Accumulated Other Comprehensive Income (AOCI)		15,783
	To adjust the carrying value of the forward contract to its current fair value of $5,000 with a corresponding credit to AOCI.		
	Accumulated Other Comprehensive Income (AOCI)	30,000	
	Gain on Forward Contract		30,000
	To record a gain on forward contract to offset the foreign exchange loss on account receivable with a corresponding debit to AOCI.		
	Discount Expense	9,972	
	Accumulated Other Comprehensive Income (AOCI)		9,972
	To allocate the remaining forward contract discount to net income ($15,000 − 5,028 = $9,972) with a corresponding credit to AOCI.		

(As a result of these entries, the balance in AOCI is zero: $4,245 + $15,783 − $30,000 + $9,972 = $0.)

	Foreign Currency (€)	900,000	
	Accounts Receivable (€)		900,000
	To record receipt of € 1 million from the German customer as an asset (Foreign Currency) at the spot rate of $0.90 (Step 3 in Exhibit 9.2).		

Cash	905,000	
Foreign Currency (€)		900,000
Forward Contract		5,000
To record settlement of the forward contract (i.e., record receipt of $905,000 in exchange for delivery of € 1 million) and remove the forward contract from the accounts (Steps 4 and 5 in Exhibit 9.2).		

The impact on net income for the year 2008 follows:

Foreign exchange loss	$(30,000)	
Gain on forward contract	30,000	
Net gain (loss)		–0–
Discount expense		$(9,972)
Impact on net income		$(9,972)

The net effect on the balance sheet over the two years is a $905,000 increase in cash with a corresponding increase in Retained Earnings of $905,000 ($914,972 − $9,972). The cumulative amount recognized as Discount Expense of $15,000 reflects the cost of extending credit to the German customer.

The net benefit from having entered into the forward contract is $5,000. This "gain" is reflected in net income as the difference between the net gain on the forward contract and the cumulative amount of discount expense ($20,000 − $15,000 = $5,000) recognized over the two periods.

Effective Interest versus Straight-Line Methods

Use of the effective interest method results in allocation of the forward contract discount of $5,028 at the end of the first month and $9,972 at the end of the next two months. Straight-line allocation of the $15,000 discount on a monthly basis results in a reasonable approximation of these amounts:

$$12/31/07 \qquad \$15,000 \times 1/3 = \$5,000$$
$$3/1/08 \qquad \$15,000 \times 2/3 = \$10,000$$

Determining the effective interest rate is complex and provides no conceptual insights. For the remainder of this chapter, we use straight-line allocation of forward contract discounts and premiums, as is allowed by the FASB's Derivatives Implementation Group. The important thing to keep in mind in this example is that with a cash flow hedge, an expense equal to the original forward contract discount is recognized in net income over the life of the contract.

What if the forward rate on December 1, 2007, had been $0.926 (i.e., the euro was selling at a premium in the forward market)? In that case, Amerco would receive $6,000 more through the forward sale of euros ($926,000) than had it received the euros at the date of sale ($920,000). Amerco allocates the forward contract premium as an increase in net income at the rate of $2,000 per month: $2,000 at December 31, 2007, and $4,000 at March 1, 2008.

Forward Contract Designated as Fair Value Hedge

Assume that Amerco decides to designate the forward contract not as a cash flow hedge but as a fair value hedge. In that case, it takes the gain or loss on the forward contract directly to net income and does not separately amortize the original discount on the forward contract.

2007 Journal Entries—Forward Contract Designated as a Fair Value Hedge

12/1/07	Accounts Receivable (€)	920,000	
	Sales		920,000
	To record the sale and € 1 million account receivable at the spot rate of $0.920.		

The forward contract requires no formal entry. A memorandum designates the forward contract as a hedge of the risk of changes in the fair value of the foreign currency account receivable resulting from changes in the U.S. dollar–euro exchange rate.

12/31/07	Accounts Receivable (€)	10,000	
	Foreign Exchange Gain		10,000
	To adjust the value of the € receivable to the new spot rate of $0.93 and record a foreign exchange gain resulting from the appreciation of the € since December 1.		
	Loss on Forward Contract	10,783	
	Forward Contract		10,783
	To record the forward contract as a liability at its fair value of $10,783 and record a forward contract loss for the change in the fair value of the forward contract since December 1.		

The impact on net income for the year 2007 is as follows:

Sales		$920,000
Foreign exchange gain	$10,000	
Loss on forward contract	(10,783)	
Net gain (loss)		(783)
Impact on net income		$919,217

The effect on the December 31, 2007, balance sheet follows:

Assets		Liabilities and Stockholders' Equity	
Accounts receivable (€)	$930,000	Forward contract	$ 10,783
		Retained earnings	919,217
			$930,000

2008 Journal Entries—Forward Contract Designated as a Fair Value Hedge

3/1/08	Foreign Exchange Loss	30,000	
	Accounts Receivable (€)		30,000
	To adjust the value of the € receivable to the new spot rate of $0.90 and record a foreign exchange loss resulting from the depreciation of the € since December 31.		
	Forward Contract	15,783	
	Gain on Forward Contract		15,783
	To adjust the carrying value of the forward contract to its current fair value of $5,000 and record a forward contract gain for the change in the fair value since December 31.		
	Foreign Currency (€)	900,000	
	Accounts Receivable (€)		900,000
	To record receipt of € 1 million from the German customer as an asset at the spot rate of $0.90.		
	Cash	905,000	
	Foreign Currency (€)		900,000
	Forward Contract		5,000
	To record settlement of the forward contract (i.e., record receipt of $905,000 in exchange for delivery of € 1 million) and remove the forward contract from the accounts.		

Discussion **Question**

DO WE HAVE A GAIN OR WHAT?

Ahnuld Corporation, a health juice producer, recently expanded its sales through exports to foreign markets. Earlier this year, the company negotiated the sale of several thousand cases of turnip juice to a retailer in the country of Tcheckia. The customer is unwilling to assume the risk of having to pay in U.S. dollars. Desperate to enter the Tcheckian market, the vice president for international sales agrees to denominate the sale in tchecks, the national currency of Tcheckia. The current exchange rate for tchecks is $2.00. In addition, the customer indicates that it cannot pay until it sells all of the juice. Payment is scheduled for six months from the date of sale.

Fearful that the tcheck might depreciate in value over the next six months, the head of the risk management department at Ahnuld Corporation enters into a forward contract to sell tchecks in six months at a forward rate of $1.80. The forward contract is designated as a fair value hedge of the tcheck receivable. Six months later, when Ahnuld receives payment from the Tcheckian customer, the exchange rate for the tcheck is $1.70. The corporate treasurer calls the head of the risk management department into her office.

Treasurer: I see that your decision to hedge our foreign currency position on that sale to Tcheckia was a bad one.

Department head: What do you mean? We have a gain on that forward contract. We're $10,000 better off from having entered into that hedge.

Treasurer: That's not what the books say. The accountants have recorded a net loss of $20,000 on that particular deal. I'm afraid I'm not going to be able to pay you a bonus this year. Another bad deal like this one and I'm going to have to demote you back to the interest rate swap department.

Department head: Those bean counters have messed up again. I told those guys in international sales that selling to customers in Tcheckia was risky, but at least by hedging our exposure, we managed to receive a reasonable amount of cash on that deal. In fact, we ended up with a gain of $10,000 on the hedge. Tell the accountants to check their debits and credits again. I'm sure they just put a debit in the wrong place or some accounting thing like that.

Have the accountants made a mistake? Does the company have a loss, a gain, or both from this forward contract?

The impact on net income for the year 2008 follows:

Foreign exchange loss	$(30,000)
Gain on forward contract.	15,783
Impact on net income	$(14,217)

The net effect on the balance sheet for the two periods is an increase of $905,000 in Cash with a corresponding increase in Retained Earnings of $905,000 ($919,217 − $14,217).

Under fair value hedge accounting, the company does not amortize the original forward contract discount systematically over the life of the contract. Instead, it recognizes the discount in income as the difference between the foreign exchange Gain (Loss) on the account receivable and the Gain (Loss) on the forward contract—that is, $(783) in 2007 and $(14,217) in 2008. The net impact on net income over the two years is $(15,000), which reflects the cost of extending credit to the German customer. The net gain on the forward contract of $5,000 ($10,783 loss in 2007 and $15,783 gain in 2008) reflects the net benefit (i.e., increase in cash inflow) from Amerco's decision to hedge the euro receivable.

Companies often cannot or do not bother to designate as hedges the forward contracts they use to hedge foreign currency denominated assets and liabilities. In those cases, the company accounts for the forward contract in exactly the same way it would if it had designated it as a fair value hedge. The company reports an undesignated forward contract on the balance sheet at fair value as an asset or liability and immediately recognizes changes in the fair value of the forward contract in income. The only difference between a forward contract designated as a fair value hedge of a foreign currency denominated asset or liability and an undesignated forward contract is the manner in which the company discloses it in the notes to the financial statements. E.I. du Pont de Nemours and Company provided the following disclosure related to this in its 2004 Form 10-K (page F-43):

Derivatives Not Designated in Hedging Relationships

The company uses forward exchange contracts to reduce its net exposure, by currency, related to foreign currency-denominated monetary assets and liabilities. The netting of such exposures precludes the use of hedge accounting. However, the required revaluation of the forward contract and the associated foreign currency-denominated monetary assets and liabilities results in a minimal earnings impact, after taxes.

Cash Flow Hedge versus Fair Value Hedge

A forward contract used to hedge a foreign currency denominated asset or liability can be designated as either a cash flow hedge or a fair value hedge when it completely offsets the variability in cash flows associated with the hedged item. The total impact on income is the same regardless of whether the forward contract is designated as a fair value hedge or as a cash flow hedge. In our example, Amerco recognized an expense (or loss) of $15,000 in both cases, and the company knew what the total expense was going to be as soon as the contract was signed.

A benefit to designating a forward contract as a cash flow hedge is that the company knows the forward contract's effect on net income *each year* as soon as the contract is signed. The net impact on income is the periodic amortization of the forward contract discount or premium. In our example, Amerco knew on December 1, 2007, that it would recognize a discount expense of $5,000 in 2007 and $10,000 in 2008. The impact on each year's income is not as systematic when the forward contract is designated as a fair value hedge—loss of $783 in 2007 and $14,217 in 2008. Moreover, the company does not know what the net impact on 2007 income will be until December 31, 2007, when the euro account receivable and the forward contract are revalued. Because of the potential for greater volatility in periodic net income that results from a fair value hedge, companies may prefer to designate forward contracts as cash flow hedges.

FOREIGN CURRENCY OPTION USED TO HEDGE A FOREIGN CURRENCY DENOMINATED ASSET

As an alternative to a forward contract, Amerco could hedge its exposure to foreign exchange risk arising from the euro account receivable by purchasing a foreign currency put option. A put option would give Amerco the right but not the obligation to sell 1 million euros on March 1, 2008, at a predetermined strike price. Assume that on December 1, 2007, Amerco purchases an over-the-counter option from its bank with a strike price of $0.92 when the spot rate is $0.92 and pays a premium of $0.009 per euro.[12] Thus, the purchase price for the option is $9,000 (€1 million × $0.009).

Because the strike price and spot rate are the same, no intrinsic value is associated with this option. The premium is based solely on time value; that is, it is possible that the euro will depreciate and the spot rate on March 1, 2008, will be less than $0.92, in which case the option will be "in the money." If the spot rate for euros on March 1, 2008, is less than the strike price of $0.92, Amerco will exercise its option and sell its 1 million euros at the strike price of $0.92. If the spot rate for euros in three months is more than the strike price of $0.92, Amerco

[12] The seller of the option determined the price of the option (the premium) by using a variation of the Black-Scholes option pricing formula.

will not exercise its option but will sell euros at the higher spot rate. By purchasing this option, Amerco is guaranteed a minimum cash flow from the export sale of $911,000 ($920,000 from exercising the option less the $9,000 cost of the option). There is no limit to the maximum number of U.S. dollars that Amerco could receive.

As is true for other derivative financial instruments, *SFAS 133* requires foreign currency options to be reported on the balance sheet at fair value. The fair value of a foreign currency option at the balance sheet date is determined by reference to the premium quoted by banks on that date for an option with a similar expiration date. Banks (and other sellers of options) determine the current premium by incorporating relevant variables at the balance sheet date into the modified Black-Scholes option pricing model. Changes in value for the euro account receivable and the foreign currency option are summarized as follows:

| Date | Spot Rate | Account Receivable (€) | | Option Premium for 3/1/08 | Foreign Currency Option | |
		U.S. Dollar Value	Change in U.S. Dollar Value		Fair Value	Change in Fair Value
12/1/07	$0.92	$920,000	—	$0.009	$ 9,000	—
12/31/07	0.93	930,000	+ $10,000	0.006	6,000	− $ 3,000
3/1/08	0.90	900,000	− 30,000	0.020	20,000	+ 14,000

We can decompose the fair value of the foreign currency option into its intrinsic value and time value components as follows:

Date	Fair Value	Intrinsic Value	Time Value	Change in Time Value
12/1/07	$ 9,000	–0–	$9,000	—
12/31/07	6,000	–0–	6,000	− $3,000
3/1/08	20,000	$20,000	–0–	− 6,000

Because the option strike price is less than or equal to the spot rate at both December 1 and December 31, the option has no intrinsic value at those dates. The entire fair value is attributable to time value only. On March 1, the date of expiration, no time value remains, and the entire amount of fair value is attributable to intrinsic value.

Option Designated as Cash Flow Hedge

Assume that Amerco designates the foreign currency option as a *cash flow hedge* of a foreign currency denominated asset. In this case, Amerco recognizes the change in the option's time value immediately in net income. The company prepares the following journal entries to account for the foreign currency transaction and the related foreign currency option:

2007 Journal Entries—Option Designated as a Cash Flow Hedge

12/1/07	Accounts Receivable (€)	920,000	
	Sales		920,000
	To record the sale and € 1 million account receivable at the spot rate of $0.92.		
	Foreign Currency Option	9,000	
	Cash		9,000
	To record the purchase of the foreign currency option as an asset at its fair value of $9,000.		
12/31/07	Accounts Receivable (€)	10,000	
	Foreign Exchange Gain		10,000
	To adjust the value of the € receivable to the new spot rate of $0.93 and record a foreign exchange gain resulting from the appreciation of the € since December 1.		

Accumulated Other Comprehensive Income (AOCI)		3,000	
Foreign Currency Option			3,000
To adjust the fair value of the option from $9,000 to $6,000 with a corresponding debit to AOCI.			
Loss on Foreign Currency Option		10,000	
Accumulated Other Comprehensive Income (AOCI)			10,000
To record a loss on foreign currency option to offset the foreign exchange gain on the € account receivable with a corresponding credit to AOCI.			
Option Expense		3,000	
Accumulated Other Comprehensive Income (AOCI)			3,000
To recognize the change in the time value of the option as a decrease in net income with a corresponding credit to AOCI.			

The impact on net income for the year 2007 follows:

Sales		$920,000
Foreign exchange gain	$ 10,000	
Loss on foreign currency option	(10,000)	
Net gain (loss)		0
Option expense		(3,000)
Impact on net income		$917,000

The effect on the December 31, 2007, balance sheet is as follows:

Assets		**Liabilities and Stockholders' Equity**	
Cash	$ (9,000)	Retained earnings	$917,000
Accounts receivable (€)	930,000	AOCI	10,000
Foreign currency option	6,000		$927,000
	$927,000		

At March 1, 2008, the option has increased in fair value by $14,000—time value decreases by $6,000 and intrinsic value increases by $20,000. The accounting entries made in 2008 are presented next:

2008 Journal Entries—Option Designated as a Cash Flow Hedge

3/1/08	Foreign Exchange Loss	30,000	
	Accounts Receivable (€)		30,000
	To adjust the value of the € receivable to the new spot rate of $0.90 and record a foreign exchange loss resulting from the depreciation of the € since December 31.		
	Foreign Currency Option	14,000	
	Accumulated Other Comprehensive Income (AOCI)		14,000
	To adjust the fair value of the option from $6,000 to $20,000 with a corresponding credit to AOCI.		
	Accumulated Other Comprehensive Income (AOCI)	30,000	
	Gain on Foreign Currency Option		30,000
	To record a gain on foreign currency option to offset the foreign exchange gain on account receivable with a corresponding debit to AOCI.		

Option Expense	6,000	
Accumulated Other Comprehensive Income (AOCI)		6,000
To recognize the change in the time value of the option as a decrease in net income with a corresponding credit to AOCI.		
Foreign Currency (€)	900,000	
Accounts Receivable (€)		900,000
To record receipt of € 1 million from the German customer as an asset at the spot rate of $.90.		
Cash	920,000	
Foreign Currency (€)		900,000
Foreign Currency Option		20,000
To record exercise of the option (i.e., record receipt of $920,000 in exchange for delivery of € 1 million) and remove the foreign currency option from the accounts.		

The impact on net income for the year 2008 follows:

Foreign exchange loss	$(30,000)	
Gain on foreign currency option	30,000	
Net gain (loss)		–0–
Option expense		(6,000)
Impact on net income		$(6,000)

Over the two accounting periods, Amerco reports Sales of $920,000 and a cumulative Option Expense of $9,000. The net effect on the balance sheet is an increase in the Cash account of $911,000 ($920,000 − $9,000) with a corresponding increase in the Retained Earnings account of $911,000 ($917,000 − $6,000).

The net benefit from having acquired the option is $11,000. Amerco reflects this "gain" in net income as the net Gain on Foreign Currency Option less the cumulative Option Expense ($20,000 − $9,000 = $11,000) recognized over the two accounting periods.

Option Designated as Fair Value Hedge

Assume that Amerco decides not to designate the foreign currency option as a cash flow hedge but to treat it as a fair value hedge. In that case, it takes the gain or loss on the option directly to net income and does not separately recognize the change in the time value of the option.

2007 Journal Entries—Option Designated as a Fair Value Hedge

12/1/07	Accounts Receivable (€)	920,000	
	Sales		920,000
	To record the sale and € 1 million account receivable at the spot rate of $.92.		
	Foreign Currency Option	9,000	
	Cash		9,000
	To record the purchase of the foreign currency option as an asset at its fair value of $9,000.		
12/31/07	Accounts Receivable (€)	10,000	
	Foreign Exchange Gain		10,000
	To adjust the value of the € receivable to the new spot rate of $0.93 and record a foreign exchange gain resulting from the appreciation of the € since December 1.		
	Loss on Foreign Currency Option	3,000	
	Foreign Currency Option		3,000
	To adjust the fair value of the option from $9,000 to $6,000 and record a loss on foreign currency option for the change in the fair value of the option since December 1.		

The impact on net income for the year 2007 follows:

Sales		$920,000
Foreign exchange gain	$10,000	
Loss on foreign currency option	(3,000)	
Net gain (loss)		7,000
Impact on net income		$927,000

2008 Journal Entries—Option Designated as a Fair Value Hedge

3/1/08	Foreign Exchange Loss	30,000	
	Accounts Receivable (€)		30,000
	To adjust the value of the € receivable to the new spot rate of $0.90 and record a foreign exchange loss resulting from the depreciation of the € since December 31.		
	Foreign Currency Option	14,000	
	Gain on Foreign Currency Option		14,000
	To adjust the fair value of the option from $6,000 to $20,000 and record a gain on foreign currency option for the change in fair value since December 31.		
	Foreign Currency (€)	900,000	
	Accounts Receivable (€)		900,000
	To record receipt of € 1 million from the German customer as an asset at the spot rate of $0.90.		
	Cash	920,000	
	Foreign Currency (€)		900,000
	Foreign Currency Option		20,000
	To record exercise of the option (i.e., record receipt of $920,000 in exchange for delivery of € 1 million) and remove the foreign currency option from the accounts.		

The impact on net income for the year 2008 follows:

Foreign exchange loss	$(30,000)
Gain on foreign currency option	14,000
Impact on net income	$(16,000)

Over the two accounting periods, Amerco reports Sales of $920,000 and a cumulative net loss of $9,000 ($7,000 net gain in 2007 and $16,000 net loss in 2008). The net effect on the balance sheet is an increase in Cash of $911,000 ($920,000 − $9,000) with a corresponding increase in Retained Earnings of $911,000 ($927,000 − $16,000). The net benefit from having acquired the option is $11,000. Amerco reflects this in net income through the net Gain on Foreign Currency Option ($3,000 loss in 2007 and $14,000 gain in 2008) recognized over the two accounting periods.

The accounting for an option used as a fair value hedge of a foreign currency denominated asset or liability is the same as if the option had been considered a speculative derivative. The only advantage to designating the option as a fair value hedge relates to the disclosures made in the notes to the financial statements.

Spot Rate Exceeds Strike Price

If the spot rate at March 1, 2008, had been more than the strike price of $0.92, Amerco would allow its option to expire unexercised. Instead it would sell its foreign currency (€) at the spot rate. The fair value of the foreign currency option on March 1, 2008, would be zero. The journal entries for 2007 to reflect this scenario would be the same as the preceding ones. The option would be reported as an asset on the December 31, 2007, balance sheet at $6,000 and the € receivable would have a carrying value of $930,000. The entries on March 1, 2008, assuming a spot rate on that date of $0.925 (rather than $0.90), would be as follows:

3/1/08	Foreign Exchange Loss	5,000	
	Accounts Receivable (€)		5,000
	To adjust the value of the € receivable to the new spot rate of $0.925 and record a foreign exchange loss resulting from the depreciation of the € since December 31.		
	Loss on Foreign Currency Option	6,000	
	Foreign Currency Option		6,000
	To adjust the fair value of the option from $6,000 to $0 and record a loss on foreign currency option for the change in fair value since December 31.		
	Foreign Currency (€)	925,000	
	Accounts Receivable (€)		925,000
	To record receipt of € 1 million from the German customer as an asset at the spot rate of $0.925.		
	Cash	925,000	
	Foreign Currency (€)		925,000
	To record the sale of € 1 million at the spot rate of $0.925.		

The overall impact on net income for the year 2008 is as follows:

Foreign exchange loss	$ (5,000)
Loss on foreign currency option	(6,000)
Impact on net income	$(11,000)

HEDGES OF UNRECOGNIZED FOREIGN CURRENCY FIRM COMMITMENTS

In the examples thus far, Amerco does not enter into a hedge of its export sale until it actually makes the sale. Assume now that on December 1, 2007, Amerco receives and accepts an order from a German customer to deliver goods on March 1, 2008, at a price of 1 million euros. Assume further that under the terms of the sales agreement, Amerco will ship the goods to the German customer on March 1, 2008, and will receive immediate payment on delivery. In other words, Amerco will not allow the German customer time to pay. Although Amerco will not make the sale until March 1, 2008, it has a firm commitment to make the sale and receive 1 million euros in three months. This creates a euro asset exposure to foreign exchange risk as of December 1, 2007. On that date, Amerco wants to hedge against an adverse change in the value of the euro over the next three months. This is known as a *hedge of a foreign currency firm commitment*. Although *SFAS 133* indicated that only fair value hedge accounting is appropriate for hedges of foreign currency firm commitments, the FASB's Derivatives Implementation Group subsequently concluded that cash flow hedge accounting also could be used. However, because the results of fair value hedge accounting are intuitively more appealing, we do not cover cash flow hedge accounting for firm commitments.

Under fair value hedge accounting, (1) the gain or loss on the hedging instrument is recognized currently in net income and (2) the gain or loss (that is, the change in fair value) on the firm commitment attributable to the hedged risk is also recognized currently in net income. This accounting treatment requires (1) measuring the fair value of the firm commitment, (2) recognizing the change in fair value in net income, and (3) reporting the firm commitment on the balance sheet as an asset or liability. This raises the conceptual question of how to measure the fair value of the firm commitment. Two possibilities are (1) through reference to changes in the spot exchange rate or (2) through reference to changes in the forward rate. The examples that follow demonstrate these two approaches.

Forward Contract Used as Fair Value Hedge of a Firm Commitment

To hedge its firm commitment exposure to a decline in the U.S. dollar value of the euro, Amerco decides to enter into a forward contract on December 1, 2007. Assume that on that date, the three-month forward rate for euros is $0.905 and Amerco signs a contract with New Manhattan Bank to deliver 1 million euros in three months in exchange for $905,000. No cash changes hands on December 1, 2007. Amerco elects to measure the fair value of the firm commitment through changes in the forward rate. Because the fair value of the forward contract is also measured using changes in the forward rate, the gains and losses on the firm commitment and forward contract exactly offset. The fair value of the forward contract and firm commitment are determined as follows:

Date	Forward Rate to 3/1/08	Forward Contract		Firm Commitment	
		Fair Value	Change in Fair Value	Fair Value	Change in Fair Value
12/1/07	$0.905	–0–	—	–0–	—
12/31/07	0.916	$(10,783)*	– $10,783	$10,783*	+ $10,783
3/1/08	0.90 (spot)	5,000†	+ 15,783	(5,000)†	– 15,783

*($905,000 − $916,000) = $(11,000) × 0.9803 = $(10,783), where 0.9803 is the present value factor for two months at an annual interest rate of 12 percent (1 percent per month) calculated as $1/1.01^2$.
†($905,000 − $900,000) = $5,000.

Amerco pays nothing to enter into the forward contract at December 1, 2007. Both the forward contract and the firm commitment have a fair value of zero on that date. At December 31, 2007, the forward rate for a contract to deliver euros on March 1, 2008, is $0.916. A forward contract could be entered into on December 31, 2007, to sell 1 million euros for $916,000 on March 1, 2008. Because Amerco is committed to sell 1 million euros for $905,000, the value of the forward contract is $(11,000); present value is $(10,783), a liability. The fair value of the firm commitment is also measured through reference to changes in the forward rate. As a result, the fair value of the firm commitment is equal in amount but of opposite sign to the fair value of the forward contract. At December 31, 2007, the firm commitment is an asset of $10,783.

On March 1, 2008, the forward rate to sell euros on that date is the spot rate, $0.90. At that rate, Amerco could sell 1 million euros for $900,000. Because Amerco has a contract to sell euros for $905,000, the fair value of the forward contract on March 1, 2008, is $5,000 (an asset). The firm commitment has a value of $(5,000), a liability. The journal entries to account for the forward contract fair value hedge of a foreign currency firm commitment are as follows:

2007 Journal Entries—Forward Contract Fair Value Hedge of Firm Commitment

12/1/07	No entry records either the sales agreement or the forward contract because both are executory contracts. A memorandum would be prepared to designate the forward contract as a hedge of the risk of changes in the fair value of the firm commitment resulting from changes in the U.S. dollar–euro forward exchange rate.		
12/31/07	Loss on Forward Contract	10,783	
	Forward Contract		10,783
	To record the forward contract as a liability at its fair value of $(10,783) and record a forward contract loss for the change in the fair value of the forward contract since December 1.		

Firm Commitment	10,783	
Gain on Firm Commitment		10,783
To record the firm commitment as an asset at its fair value of $10,783 and record a firm commitment gain for the change in the fair value of the firm commitment since December 1.		

Consistent with the objective of hedge accounting, the gain on the firm commitment offsets the loss on the forward contract, and the impact on 2007 net income is zero. Amerco reports the forward contract as a liability and reports the firm commitment as an asset on the December 31, 2007, balance sheet. This achieves the FASB's objective of making sure that derivatives are reported on the balance sheet and ensures that there is no impact on net income.

2008 Journal Entries—Forward Contract Fair Value Hedge of Firm Commitment

3/1/08	Forward Contract	15,783	
	Gain on Forward Contract		15,783
	To adjust the fair value of the forward contract from $(10,783) to $5,000 and record a forward contract gain for the change in fair value since December 31.		
	Loss on Firm Commitment	15,783	
	Firm Commitment		15,783
	To adjust the fair value of the firm commitment from $10,783 to $(5,000) and record a firm commitment loss for the change in fair value since December 31.		
	Foreign Currency (€)	900,000	
	Sales		900,000
	To record the sale and the receipt of € 1 million as an asset at the spot rate of $0.90.		
	Cash	905,000	
	Foreign Currency (€)		900,000
	Forward Contract		5,000
	To record settlement of the forward contract (receipt of $905,000 in exchange for delivery of € 1 million) and remove the forward contract from the accounts.		
	Firm Commitment	5,000	
	Adjustment to Net Income		5,000
	To close the firm commitment as an adjustment to net income.		

Once again, the gain on forward contract and the loss on firm commitment offset. As a result of the last entry, the export sale increases 2008 net income by $905,000 ($900,000 in sales plus a $5,000 adjustment to net income). This exactly equals the amount of cash received. In practice, companies use a variety of account titles for the adjustment to net income that results from closing the firm commitment account.

The net gain on forward contract of $5,000 ($10,783 loss in 2007 plus $15,783 gain in 2008) measures the net benefit to the company from hedging its firm commitment. Without the forward contract, Amerco would have sold the 1 million euros received on March 1, 2008, at the spot rate of $0.90, generating cash flow of $900,000. Through the forward contract, Amerco is able to sell the euros for $905,000, a net gain of $5,000.

Option Used as Fair Value Hedge of Firm Commitment

Now assume that to hedge its exposure to a decline in the U.S. dollar value of the euro, Amerco purchases a put option to sell 1 million euros on March 1, 2008, at a strike price of $0.92. The premium for such an option on December 1, 2007, is $0.009 per euro. With this option, Amerco is guaranteed a minimum cash flow from the export sale of $911,000 ($920,000 from option exercise less $9,000 cost of the option).

Amerco elects to measure the fair value of the firm commitment by referring to changes in the U.S. dollar–euro spot rate. In this case, Amerco must discount the fair value of the firm commitment to its present value. The fair value and changes in fair value for the firm commitment and foreign currency option are summarized here:

Date	Option Premium for 3/1/08	Foreign Currency Option		Spot Rate	Firm Commitment	
		Fair Value	Change in Fair Value		Fair Value	Change in Fair Value
12/1/07	$0.009	$9,000	—	$0.92	—	—
12/31/07	0.006	6,000	− $3,000	0.93	$9,803*	+ $9,803
3/1/08	0.020	20,000	+ 14,000	0.90	(20,000)†	− 29,803

*$930,000 − $920,000 = $10,000 × 0.9803 = $9,803, where 0.9803 is the present value factor for two months at an annual interest rate of 12 percent (1 percent per month) calculated as $1/1.01^2$.

†$900,000 − $920,000 = $(20,000).

At December 1, 2007, given the spot rate of $0.92, the firm commitment to receive 1 million euros in three months would generate a cash flow of $920,000. At December 31, 2007, the cash flow that the firm commitment could generate increases by $10,000 to $930,000. The fair value of the firm commitment at December 31, 2007, is the present value of $10,000 discounted at 1 percent per month for two months. Amerco determines the fair value of the firm commitment on March 1, 2008, by referring to the change in the spot rate from December 1, 2007, to March 1, 2008. Because the spot rate declines by $0.02 over that period, the firm commitment to receive 1 million euros has a fair value of $(20,000) on March 1, 2008. The journal entries to account for the foreign currency option and related foreign currency firm commitment are discussed next:

2007 Journal Entries—Option Fair Value Hedge of Firm Commitment

12/1/07	Foreign Currency Option	9,000	
	Cash		9,000
	To record the purchase of the foreign currency option as an asset.		

There is no entry to record the sales agreement because it is an executory contract. Amerco prepares a memorandum to designate the option as a hedge of the risk of changes in the fair value of the firm commitment resulting from changes in the spot exchange rate.

12/31/07	Firm Commitment	9,803	
	Gain on Firm Commitment		9,803
	To record the firm commitment as an asset at its fair value of $9,803 and record a firm commitment gain for the change in the fair value of the firm commitment since December 1.		
	Loss on Foreign Currency Option	3,000	
	Foreign Currency Option		3,000
	To adjust the fair value of the option from $9,000 to $6,000 and record the change in the value of the option as a loss.		

The impact on net income for the year 2007 is as follows:

Gain on firm commitment	$ 9,803
Loss on foreign currency option	(3,000)
Impact on net income	$ 6,803

The effect on the December 31, 2007, balance sheet follows:

Assets		Liabilities and Stockholders' Equity	
Cash	$(9,000)	Retained earnings	$6,803
Foreign currency option	6,000		
Firm commitment	9,803		
	$ 6,803		

2008 Journal Entries—Option Fair Value Hedge of Firm Commitment

3/1/08	Loss on Firm Commitment	29,803	
	Firm Commitment		29,803
	To adjust the fair value of the firm commitment from $9,803 to $(20,000) and record a firm commitment loss for the change in fair value since December 31.		
	Foreign Currency Option	14,000	
	Gain on Foreign Currency Option		14,000
	To adjust the fair value of the foreign currency option from $6,000 to $20,000 and record a gain on foreign currency option for the change in fair value since December 31.		
	Foreign Currency (€)	900,000	
	Sales		900,000
	To record the sale and the receipt of € 1 million as an asset at the spot rate of $.90.		
	Cash	920,000	
	Foreign Currency (€)		900,000
	Foreign Currency Option		20,000
	To record exercise of the foreign currency option (receipt of $920,000 in exchange for delivery of € 1 million) and remove the foreign currency option from the accounts.		
	Firm Commitment	20,000	
	Adjustment to Net Income		20,000
	To close the firm commitment as an adjustment to net income.		

The following is the impact on net income for the year 2008:

Sales	$900,000
Loss on firm commitment	(29,803)
Gain on foreign currency option	14,000
Adjustment to net income	20,000
Impact on net income	$904,197

The net increase in net income over the two accounting periods is $911,000 ($6,803 in 2007 plus $904,197 in 2008), which exactly equals the net cash flow realized on the export sale ($920,000 from exercising the option less $9,000 to purchase the option). The net gain on the option of $11,000 (loss of $3,000 in 2007 plus gain of $14,000 in 2008) reflects the net benefit from having entered into the hedge. Without the option, Amerco would have sold the 1 million euros received on March 1, 2008, at the spot rate of $0.90 for $900,000.

HEDGE OF FORECASTED FOREIGN CURRENCY DENOMINATED TRANSACTION

SFAS 133 also allows the use of cash flow hedge accounting for foreign currency derivatives used to hedge the cash flow risk associated with a forecasted foreign currency transaction. For hedge accounting to apply, the forecasted transaction must be probable (likely to occur), the hedge must be highly effective in offsetting fluctuations in the cash flow associated with the foreign currency risk, and the hedging relationship must be properly documented.

The accounting for a hedge of a forecasted transaction differs from the accounting for a hedge of a foreign currency firm commitment in two ways:

1. Unlike the accounting for a firm commitment, there is no recognition of the forecasted transaction or gains and losses on the forecasted transaction.

2. The company reports the hedging instrument (forward contract or option) at fair value, but because no gain or loss occurs on the forecasted transaction to offset against, the company does not report changes in the fair value of the hedging instrument as gains and losses in net income. Instead, it reports them in other comprehensive income. On the projected date of the forecasted transaction, the company transfers the cumulative change in the fair value of the hedging instrument from other comprehensive income (balance sheet) to net income (income statement).

Forward Contract Cash Flow Hedge of a Forecasted Transaction

To demonstrate the accounting for a hedge of a forecasted foreign currency transaction, assume that Amerco has a long-term relationship with its German customer and can reliably forecast that the customer will require delivery of goods costing 1 million euros in March 2008. Confident that it will receive 1 million euros on March 1, 2008, Amerco enters into a forward contract on December 1, 2007, to sell 1 million euros on March 1, 2008, at a rate of $0.905. The facts are essentially the same as those for the hedge of a firm commitment except that Amerco does not receive a sales order from the German customer until late February 2008. Relevant exchange rates and the fair value of the forward contract are as follows:

Date	Forward Rate to 3/31/08	Forward Contract Fair Value	Change in Fair Value
12/1/07	$0.905	–0–	—
12/31/07	0.916	$(10,783)*	– $10,783
3/1/08	0.90 (spot)	5,000	+ $15,783

*($905,000 − $916,000) = $(11,000) × 0.9803 = $(10,783), where 0.9803 is the present value factor for two months at an annual interest rate of 12 percent (1 percent per month) calculated as $1/1.01^2$. The original discount on the forward contract is determined by the difference in the € spot rate and the three-month forward rate on December 31, 2007: ($.905 − $.92) × € 1 million = $15,000.

2007 Journal Entries—Forward Contract Hedge of a Forecasted Transaction

12/1/07	No entry to record either the forecasted sale or the forward contract. A memorandum designates the forward contract as a hedge of the risk of changes in the cash flows related to the forecasted sale resulting from changes in the spot rate.		
12/31/07	Accumulated Other Comprehensive Income	10,783	
	Forward Contract		10,783
	To record the forward contract as a liability at its fair value of $10,783 with a corresponding debit to AOCI.		
	Discount Expense	5,000	
	Accumulated Other Comprehensive Income		5,000
	To record straight-line allocation of the forward contract discount: $15,000 × ⅓ = $5,000.		

Discount expense reduces 2007 net income by $5,000. The impact on the December 31, 2007, balance sheet is as follows:

Assets	Liabilities and Stockholders' Equity	
No effect	Forward contract	$10,783
	Retained earnings	(5,000)
	AOCI	(5,783)
		$ 0

2008 Journal Entries—Forward Contract Hedge of a Forecasted Transaction

3/1/08	Forward Contract	15,783	
	Accumulated Other Comprehensive Income		15,783
	To adjust the carrying value of the forward contract to its current fair value of $5,000 with a corresponding credit to AOCI.		
	Discount Expense	10,000	
	Accumulated Other Comprehensive Income		10,000
	To record straight-line allocation of the forward contract discount: $15,000 × ²/₃ = $10,000.		
	Foreign Currency (€)	900,000	
	Sales		900,000
	To record the sale and the receipt of € 1 million as an asset at the spot rate of $0.90.		
	Cash	905,000	
	Foreign Currency (€)		900,000
	Forward Contract		5,000
	To record settlement of the forward contract (receipt of $905,000 in exchange for delivery of € 1 million) and remove the forward contract from the accounts.		
	Accumulated Other Comprehensive Income	20,000	
	Adjustment to Net Income		20,000
	To close AOCI as an adjustment to net income.		

The impact on net income for the year 2008 follows:

Sales	$900,000
Discount expense	(10,000)
Adjustment to net income	20,000
Impact on net income	$910,000

Over the two accounting periods, the net impact on net income is $905,000, which equals the amount of net cash inflow realized from the sale.

Option Designated as a Cash Flow Hedge of a Forecasted Transaction

Now assume that Amerco hedges its forecasted foreign currency transaction by purchasing a 1 million euro put option on December 1, 2007. The option, which expires on March 1, 2008, has a strike price of $0.92 and a premium of $0.009 per euro. The fair value of the option at relevant dates is as follows:

	Option Premium for 3/1/08	Foreign Currency Option				
Date		Fair Value	Change in Fair Value	Intrinsic Value	Time Value	Change in Time Value
12/1/07	$0.009	$ 9,000	—	–0–	$9,000	—
12/31/07	0.006	6,000	– $ 3,000	–0–	6,000	– $3,000
3/1/08	0.020	20,000	+ 14,000	$20,000	–0–	– 6,000

2007 Journal Entries—Option Hedge of a Forecasted Transaction

12/1/07	Foreign Currency Option	9,000	
	Cash		9,000
	To record the purchase of the foreign currency option as an asset.		

No entry records the forecasted sale. A memorandum designates the foreign currency option as a hedge of the risk of changes in the cash flows related to the forecasted sale.

12/31/07	Option Expense	3,000	
	Foreign Currency Option		3,000
	To adjust the carrying value of the option to its fair value and recognize the change in the time value of the option as an expense.		

The impact on net income for the year 2007 follows:

Option expense .... $(3,000)

Impact on net income .... $(3,000)

A foreign currency option of $6,000 is reported as an asset on the December 31, 2007, balance sheet. Cash decreases by $9,000, and Retained Earnings decreases by $3,000.

2008 Journal Entries—Option Hedge of a Forecasted Transaction

3/1/08	Foreign Currency Option	14,000	
	Option Expense	6,000	
	Accumulated Other Comprehensive Income (AOCI)		20,000
	To adjust the carrying value of the option to its fair value and recognize the change in the time value of the option as an expense with a corresponding credit to AOCI.		
	Foreign Currency (€)	900,000	
	Sales		900,000
	To record the sale and the receipt of € 1 million as an asset at the spot rate of $0.90.		
	Cash	920,000	
	Foreign Currency (€)		900,000
	Foreign Currency Option		20,000
	To record the exercise of the foreign currency option (receipt of $920,000 in exchange for delivery of € 1 million) and remove the foreign currency option from the accounts.		
	Accumulated Other Comprehensive Income (AOCI)	20,000	
	Adjustment to Net Income		20,000
	To close AOCI as an adjustment to net income.		

The following is the impact on net income for the year 2008:

Sales	$900,000
Option expense	(6,000)
Adjustment to net income	20,000
Impact on net income	$914,000

Over two periods, net income increases by $911,000, equal to the net cash inflow realized from the export sale (Sales of $920,000 − Option purchase price of $9,000).

USE OF HEDGING INSTRUMENTS

There are probably as many different corporate strategies regarding hedging foreign exchange risk as there are companies exposed to that risk. Some companies simply require hedges of all foreign currency transactions. Others require the use of a forward contract hedge when the forward rate results in a larger cash inflow or smaller cash outflow than with the spot rate. Still other companies have proportional hedging policies that require hedging on some predetermined percentage (e.g., 50 percent, 60 percent, or 70 percent) of transaction exposure.

Companies are required to provide information on the use of derivative financial instruments to hedge foreign exchange risk in the notes to financial statements. Exhibit 9.3 presents disclosures made by Abbott Laboratories in its 2004 annual report. Abbott Labs uses forward contracts to hedge foreign exchange risk associated with anticipated foreign currency transactions, foreign currency denominated payables and receivables, and foreign currency borrowings. Much of its hedging activity relates to intercompany transactions involving foreign

EXHIBIT 9.3 **Disclosures Related to Hedging Foreign Exchange Risk in Abbott Laboratories' 2004 Annual Report**

Foreign Currency Sensitive Financial Instruments

Abbott enters into foreign currency forward exchange contracts to manage its exposure to foreign currency denominated intercompany loans and trade payables and third-party trade payables and receivables. The contracts are marked-to-market, and resulting gains or losses are reflected in income and are generally offset by losses or gains on the foreign currency exposure being managed. At December 31, 2004 and 2003, Abbott held $3.3 billion and $3.0 billion, respectively, of such contracts, which all mature in the next calendar year.

In addition, certain Abbott foreign subsidiaries enter into foreign currency forward exchange contracts to manage exposures to changes in foreign exchange rates for anticipated intercompany purchases by those subsidiaries whose functional currencies are not the U.S. dollar. These contracts are designated as cash flow hedges of the variability of the cash flows due to changes in foreign exchange rates and are marked-to-market with the resulting gains or losses reflected in Accumulated other comprehensive income (loss). Gains or losses will be included in Cost of products sold at the time the products are sold, generally within the next calendar year. At December 31, 2004 and 2003, Abbott held $984 million and $602 million, respectively, of such contracts, which all mature in the next calendar year.

The following table reflects the total foreign currency forward contracts outstanding at December 31, 2004 and 2003:

(dollars in millions)	Contract Amount	Average Exchange Rate	Fair and Carrying Value Receivable/ (Payable)
Receive primarily U.S. Dollars in exchange for the following currencies:			
Euro	$1,688	1.2843	$(39.1)
British Pound	1,112	0.542	(26.7)
Japanese Yen	533	107.300	9.2
Canadian Dollar	301	0.785	(20.0)
All other currencies	601	N/A	(3.3)
Total	$4,235		$(79.9)

subsidiaries. The table included in Exhibit 9.3 discloses that (1) Abbott's forward contracts primarily are to sell foreign currencies for U.S. dollars, (2) 40 percent of Abbott's $4.235 billion in forward contracts at December 31, 2004, was in euros, and (3) with the exception of contracts in Japanese yen, all of Abbott's forward contracts had a negative fair value and it reported these on the balance sheet as liabilities.

Abbott Labs uses forward contracts exclusively in its management of foreign exchange risk. In contrast, the Coca-Cola Company reported using a combination of forward contracts and currency options in its foreign exchange risk hedging strategy. In its 2004 annual report, Coca-Cola reported recording an increase (decrease) to AOCI of approximately $(31) million, $(151) million, and $92 million, respectively, in 2004, 2003, and 2002, on foreign currency cash flow hedges. The company had forward contracts and options with a fair value of $39 million at December 31, 2004, which it reflected in the prepaid expenses and other assets section on the consolidated balance sheet.

The Euro

The introduction of the euro as a common currency throughout much of Europe reduced the need for hedging in that region of the world. For example, a German company purchasing goods from a Spanish supplier no longer has an exposure to foreign exchange risk because both countries use a common currency. This is also true for German subsidiaries of U.S. parent companies. However, any euro-denominated transactions between the U.S. parent and its German (or other euro zone) subsidiary continue to be exposed to foreign exchange risk.

One advantage of the euro for U.S. companies is that a euro account receivable from sales to a customer in, say, the Netherlands, acts as a natural hedge of a euro account payable on purchases from, say, a supplier in Italy. Assuming that similar amounts and time periods are involved, any foreign exchange loss (gain) arising from the euro payable is offset by a foreign exchange gain (loss) on the euro receivable. A company does not need to hedge the euro account payable with a hedging instrument such as a foreign currency option.

FOREIGN CURRENCY BORROWING

In addition to the receivables and payables that arise from import and export activities, companies often must account for foreign currency borrowings, another type of foreign currency transaction. Companies borrow foreign currency from foreign lenders either to finance foreign operations or perhaps to take advantage of more favorable interest rates. The facts that both the principal and interest are denominated in foreign currency and both create an exposure to foreign exchange risk complicate accounting for a foreign currency borrowing.

To demonstrate the accounting for foreign currency debt, assume that on July 1, 2007, Multicorp International borrowed 1 billion Japanese yen (¥) on a one-year note at a per annum interest rate of 5 percent. Interest is payable and the note comes due on July 1, 2008. The following exchange rates apply:

Date	U.S. Dollars per Japanese Yen Spot Rate
July 1, 2007	$0.00921
December 31, 2007	0.00932
July 1, 2008	0.00937

On July 1, 2007, Multicorp borrows ¥ 1 billion and converts it into $9,210,000 in the spot market. Over the life of the note, Multicorp must record accrued interest expense at year-end and interest payments on the anniversary date of July 1. In addition, the firm must revalue the Japanese yen note payable at year-end, with foreign exchange gains and losses reported in income. These journal entries account for this foreign currency borrowing:

7/1/07	Cash	9,210,000	
	Note Payable (¥)		9,210,000
	To record the ¥ note payable at the spot rate of $0.00921 and the conversion of ¥ 1 billion into U.S. dollars.		
12/31/07	Interest Expense	233,000	
	Accrued Interest Payable (¥)		233,000
	To accrue interest for the period July 1–December 31, 2007: ¥ 1 billion × 5% × ½ year = ¥ 25 million × $0.00932 = $233,000.		
	Foreign Exchange Loss	110,000	
	Note Payable (¥)		110,000
	To revalue the ¥ note payable at the spot rate of $0.00932 and record a foreign exchange loss of $110,000 [¥ 1 billion × ($0.00932 − $0.00921)].		
7/1/08	Interest Expense	234,250	
	Accrued Interest Payable (¥)	233,000	
	Foreign Exchange Loss	1,250	
	Cash		468,500
	To record the interest payment of ¥ 50 million acquired at the spot rate of $0.00937 for $468,500; interest expense for the period of January 1–July 1, 2008: ¥ 25 million × $0.00937; and a foreign exchange loss on the ¥ accrued interest payable: ¥ 25 million × ($0.00937 − $0.00932).		
	Foreign Exchange Loss	50,000	
	Note Payable (¥)		50,000
	To revalue the ¥ note payable at the spot rate of $0.00937 and record a foreign exchange loss of $50,000 [¥ 1 billion × ($0.00937 − $0.00932)].		
	Note Payable (¥)	9,370,000	
	Cash		9,370,000
	To record repayment of the ¥ 1 billion note through purchase of ¥ at the spot rate of $.00937.		

Foreign Currency Loan

At times companies lend foreign currency to related parties, creating the opposite situation from a foreign currency borrowing. The accounting involves keeping track of a note receivable and interest receivable, both of which are denominated in foreign currency. Fluctuations in the U.S. dollar value of the principal and interest generally give rise to foreign exchange gains and losses that would be included in income. Under *SFAS 52,* an exception arises when the foreign currency loan is being made on a long-term basis to a foreign branch, subsidiary, or equity method affiliate. Foreign exchange gains and losses on "intercompany foreign currency transactions that are of a long-term investment nature (that is, settlement is not planned or anticipated in the foreseeable future)" are deferred in other comprehensive income until the loan is repaid.[13] Only the foreign exchange gains and losses related to the interest receivable are recorded currently in net income.

Summary

1. Several exchange rate mechanisms are used around the world. Most national currencies fluctuate in value against other currencies over time.

2. Exposure to foreign exchange risk exists when a payment to be made or to be received is denominated (stated) in terms of a foreign currency. Appreciation in a foreign currency results in a foreign exchange gain when the foreign currency is to be received and a foreign exchange loss when the foreign currency is to be paid. Conversely, a decrease in the value of a foreign currency results in a foreign exchange loss when the foreign currency is to be received and a foreign exchange gain when the foreign currency is to be paid.

[13] *SFAS 52,* para. 20(b).

3. Under *SFAS 52*, companies record foreign exchange gains and losses on foreign currency balances in income in the period in which an exchange rate change occurs; this is a two-transaction perspective, accrual approach. Companies must revalue foreign currency balances to their current U.S. dollar equivalent using current exchange rates when financial statements are prepared. This approach violates the conservatism principle when unrealized foreign exchange gains are recognized as income.

4. Exposure to foreign exchange risk can be eliminated through hedging. Hedging involves establishing a price today at which a foreign currency to be received in the future can be sold in the future or at which a foreign currency to be paid in the future can be purchased in the future.

5. The two most popular instruments for hedging foreign exchange risk are foreign currency forward contracts and foreign currency options. A *forward contract* is a binding agreement to exchange currencies at a predetermined rate. An *option* gives the buyer the right, but not the obligation, to exchange currencies at a predetermined rate.

6. *SFAS 133* (as amended by *SFAS 138*) governs the accounting for derivative instruments used in hedging foreign exchange risk. Hedge accounting is appropriate if the derivative is used to hedge either a fair value exposure or cash flow exposure to foreign exchange risk, the derivative is highly effective in offsetting changes in the fair value or cash flows related to the hedged item, and the derivative is properly documented as a hedge. Hedge accounting requires reporting gains and losses on the hedging instrument in net income in the same period as gains and loss on the item being hedged.

7. Companies must report all derivatives, including forward contracts and options, on the balance sheet at their fair value. Changes in fair value are included in other comprehensive income if the derivative is designated as a cash flow hedge and in net income if it is designated as a fair value hedge.

8. *SFAS 133* (as amended by *SFAS 138*) provides guidance for hedges of (a) recognized foreign currency denominated assets and liabilities, (b) unrecognized foreign currency firm commitments, and (c) forecasted foreign currency denominated transactions. Cash flow hedge accounting can be used for all three types of hedge; fair value hedge accounting can be used only for (a) and (b).

9. If a company hedges a foreign currency firm commitment (fair value hedge), it should recognize gains and losses on the hedging instrument as well as on the underlying firm commitment in net income. The firm commitment account created to offset the gain or loss on firm commitment is treated as an adjustment to the underlying transaction when it takes place.

10. If a company hedges a forecasted transaction (cash flow hedge), it reports changes in the fair value of the hedging instrument in other comprehensive income. The cumulative change in fair value reported in other comprehensive income is included in net income in the period in which the forecasted transaction was originally anticipated to take place.

Comprehensive Illustration

PROBLEM

(Estimated Time: 60 to 75 minutes) Zelm Company is a U.S. company that produces electronic switches for the telecommunications industry. Zelm regularly imports component parts from a supplier located in Guadalajara, Mexico, and makes payments in Mexican pesos. The following spot exchange rates, forward exchange rates, and call option premia for Mexican pesos exist during the period August to October.

		U.S. Dollar per Mexican Peso	
Date	**Spot Rate**	**Forward Rate to October 31**	**Call Option Premium for October 31 (strike price $0.080)**
August 1	$0.080	$0.085	$0.0052
September 30	0.086	0.088	0.0095
October 31	0.091	0.091	0.0110

Part A

On August 1, Zelm imports parts from its Mexican supplier at a price of 1 million Mexican pesos. It receives the parts on August 1 but does not pay for them until October 31. In addition, on August 1, Zelm enters into a forward contract to purchase 1 million pesos on October 31. It appropriately designates the forward contract as a *cash flow hedge* of the Mexican peso liability exposure. Zelm's incremental borrowing rate is 12 percent per annum (1 percent per month), and the company uses a straight-line method on a monthly basis for allocating forward discounts and premia.

Part B

The facts are the same as in Part A, with the exception that Zelm designates the forward contract as a *fair value hedge* of the Mexican peso liability exposure.

Part C

On August 1, Zelm imports parts from its Mexican supplier at a price of 1 million Mexican pesos. It receives the parts on August 1 but does not pay for them until October 31. In addition, on August 1, Zelm purchases a three-month call option on 1 million Mexican pesos with a strike price of $0.080. The option is appropriately designated as a *cash flow hedge* of the Mexican peso liability exposure.

Part D

On August 1, Zelm orders parts from its Mexican supplier at a price of 1 million Mexican pesos. It receives the parts and pays for them on October 31. On August 1, Zelm enters into a forward contract to purchase 1 million Mexican pesos on October 31. It designates the forward contract as a *fair value hedge* of the Mexican peso firm commitment. Zelm determines the fair value of the firm commitment by referring to changes in the forward exchange rate.

Part E

On August 1, Zelm orders parts from its Mexican supplier at a price of 1 million Mexican pesos. It receives the parts and pays for them on October 31. On August 1, Zelm purchases a three-month call option on 1 million Mexican pesos with a strike price of $0.080. The option is appropriately designated as a *fair value hedge* of the Mexican peso firm commitment. The fair value of the firm commitment is determined through reference to changes in the spot exchange rate.

Part F

Zelm anticipates that it will import component parts from its Mexican supplier in the near future. On August 1, Zelm purchases a three-month call option on 1 million Mexican pesos with a strike price of $0.080. It appropriately designates the option as a *cash flow hedge* of a forecasted Mexican peso transaction. Zelm receives and pays for parts costing 1 million Mexican pesos on October 31.

Required:

Prepare journal entries for each of these independent situations in accordance with *SFAS 52, SFAS 133,* and *SFAS 138,* and determine the impact each situation has on the September 30 and October 31 trial balances.

SOLUTION

Part A. Forward Contract Cash Flow Hedge of a Recognized Foreign Currency Liability

8/1	Parts Inventory	80,000	
	Accounts Payable (Mexican pesos)		80,000
	To record the purchase of parts and a Mexican peso account payable at the spot rate of $0.080.		

The forward contract requires no formal entry. Zelm prepares a memorandum to designate the forward contract as a hedge of the risk of changes in the cash flow to be paid on the foreign currency payable resulting from changes in the U.S. dollar–Mexican peso exchange rate.

9/30	Foreign Exchange Loss	6,000	
	Accounts Payable (Mexican pesos)		6,000
	To adjust the value of the Mexican peso payable to the new spot rate of $0.086 and record a foreign exchange loss resulting from the appreciation of the peso since August 1.		
	Forward Contract	2,970	
	Accumulated Other Comprehensive Income (AOCI)		2,970
	To record the forward contract as an asset at its fair value of $2,970 with a corresponding credit to AOCI.		
	Accumulated Other Comprehensive Income (AOCI)	6,000	
	Gain on Forward Contract		6,000
	To record a gain on forward contract to offset the foreign exchange loss on account payable with a corresponding debit to AOCI.		

Zelm determines the fair value of the forward contract by referring to the change in the forward rate for a contract that settles on October 31: ([$0.088 − $0.085] × 1 million pesos = $3,000. The present value of $3,000 discounted for one month [from October 31 to September 30] at an interest rate of 12 percent per year [1 percent per month] is calculated as follows: $3,000 × 0.9901 = $2,970.)

	Debit	Credit
Premium Expense	3,333	
Accumulated Other Comprehensive Income (AOCI)		3,333

To allocate the forward contract premium to income over the life of the contract using a straight-line method on a monthly basis ($5,000 × ⅔ = $3,333).

The original premium on the forward contract is determined by the difference in the peso spot rate and three-month forward rate on August 1: ($0.085 − $0.080) × 1 million pesos = $5,000.

Trial Balance—September 30	Debit	Credit
Parts Inventory	$80,000	
Accounts Payable (Mexican pesos)		$86,000
Forward Contract (asset)	2,970	
AOCI		303
Foreign Exchange Loss	6,000	
Gain on Forward Contract		6,000
Premium Expense	3,333	
	$92,303	$92,303

		Debit	Credit
10/31	Foreign Exchange Loss	5,000	
	Accounts Payable (Mexican pesos)		5,000

To adjust the value of the Mexican peso payable to the new spot rate of $0.091 and record a foreign exchange loss resulting from the appreciation of the peso since September 30.

	Debit	Credit
Forward Contract	3,030	
Accumulated Other Comprehensive Income (AOCI)		3,030

To adjust the carrying value of the forward contract to its current fair value of $6,000 with a corresponding credit to AOCI.

	Debit	Credit
Accumulated Other Comprehensive Income (AOCI)	5,000	
Gain on Forward Contract		5,000

To record a gain on forward contract to offset the foreign exchange loss on account payable with a corresponding debit to AOCI.

The current fair value of the forward contract is determined by referring to the difference in the spot rate on October 31 and the original forward rate: ($0.091 − $0.085) × 1 million pesos = $6,000. The forward contract adjustment on October 31 is calculated as the difference in the current fair value and the carrying value at September 30: $6,000 − $2,970 = $3,030.

	Debit	Credit
Premium Expense	1,667	
Accumulated Other Comprehensive Income (AOCI)		1,667

To allocate the forward contract premium to income over the life of the contract using a straight-line method on a monthly basis ($5,000 × ⅓ = $1,667).

	Debit	Credit
Foreign Currency (Mexican pesos)	91,000	
Cash		85,000
Forward Contract		6,000

To record settlement of the forward contract: Record payment of $85,000 in exchange for 1 million pesos, record the receipt of 1 million pesos as an asset at the spot rate of $0.091, and remove the forward contract from the accounts.

Accounts Payable (pesos)   91,000

     Foreign Currency (pesos)   91,000

To record remittance of 1 million pesos to the Mexican supplier.

Trial Balance—October 31	Debit	Credit
Cash		$85,000
Parts Inventory	$80,000	
Retained Earnings, 9/30	3,333	
Foreign Exchange Loss	5,000	
Gain on Forward Contract		5,000
Premium Expense	1,667	
	$90,000	$90,000

Part B. Forward Contract Fair Value Hedge of a Recognized Foreign Currency Liability

8/1   Parts Inventory   80,000

             Accounts Payable (Mexican pesos)   80,000

             To record the purchase of parts and a peso account payable
             at the spot rate of $0.080.

The forward contract requires no formal entry. A memorandum designates the forward contract as a hedge of the risk of changes in the cash flow to be paid on the foreign currency payable resulting from changes in the U.S. dollar–peso exchange rate.

9/30   Foreign Exchange Loss   6,000

             Accounts Payable (Mexican pesos)   6,000

             To adjust the value of the peso payable to the new spot rate
             of $0.086 and record a foreign exchange loss resulting from
             the appreciation of the peso since August 1.

      Forward Contract   2,970

             Gain on Forward Contract   2,970

             To record the forward contract as an asset at its fair value of
             $2,970 and record a forward contract gain for the change in
             the fair value of the forward contract since August 1.

Trial Balance—September 30	Debit	Credit
Parts Inventory	$80,000	
Accounts Payable (Mexican pesos)		$86,000
Forward Contract (asset)	2,970	
Foreign Exchange Loss	6,000	
Gain on Forward Contract		2,970
	$88,970	$88,970

10/31   Foreign Exchange Loss   5,000

             Accounts Payable (Mexican pesos)   5,000

             To adjust the value of the peso payable to the new spot rate
             of $0.091 and record a foreign exchange loss resulting from
             the appreciation of the peso since September 30.

      Forward Contract   3,030

             Gain on Forward Contract   3,030

             To adjust the carrying value of the forward contract to its
             current fair value of $6,000 and record a forward contract
             gain for the change in fair value since September 30.

Foreign Currency (Mexican pesos)	91,000	
Cash		85,000
Forward Contract		6,000

To record settlement of the forward contract: Record payment of $85,000 in exchange for 1 million pesos, record the receipt of 1 million pesos as an asset at the spot rate of $0.091, and remove the forward contract from the accounts.

Accounts Payable (pesos)	91,000	
Foreign Currency (pesos)		91,000

To record remittance of 1 million pesos to the Mexican supplier.

Trial Balance—October 31	Debit	Credit
Cash		$85,000
Parts Inventory	$80,000	
Retained Earnings, 9/30	3,030	
Foreign Exchange Loss	5,000	
Gain on Forward Contract		3,030
	$88,030	$88,030

Part C. Option Cash Flow Hedge of a Recognized Foreign Currency Liability

The following schedule summarizes the changes in the components of the fair value of the peso call option with a strike price of $0.080:

Date	Spot Rate	Option Premium	Fair Value	Change in Fair Value	Intrinsic Value	Time Value	Change in Time Value
8/1	$0.080	$0.0052	$ 5,200	—	–0–	$5,200*	—
9/30	0.086	0.0095	9,500	+ $4,300	$ 6,000†	3,500†	− $1,700
10/31	0.091	0.0110	11,000	+ 1,500	11,000	–0–‡	− 3,500

*Because the strike price and spot rate are the same, the option has no intrinsic value. Fair value is attributable solely to the time value of the option.
†With a spot rate of $0.086 and a strike price of $0.08, the option has an intrinsic value of $6,000. The remaining $3,500 of fair value is attributable to time value.
‡The time value of the option at maturity is zero.

8/1	Parts Inventory	80,000	
	Accounts Payable (Mexican pesos)		80,000
	To record the purchase of parts and a peso account payable at the spot rate of $0.080.		
	Foreign Currency Option	5,200	
	Cash		5,200
	To record the purchase of a foreign currency option as an asset.		
9/30	Foreign Exchange Loss	6,000	
	Accounts Payable (pesos)		6,000
	To adjust the value of the peso payable to the new spot rate of $0.086 and record a foreign exchange loss resulting from the appreciation of the peso since August 1.		
	Foreign Currency Option	4,300	
	Accumulated Other Comprehensive Income (AOCI)		4,300
	To adjust the fair value of the option from $5,200 to $9,500 with a corresponding credit to AOCI.		
	Accumulated Other Comprehensive Income (AOCI)	6,000	
	Gain on Foreign Currency Option		6,000
	To record a gain on forward currency option to offset the foreign exchange loss on account payable with a corresponding debit to AOCI.		

	Option Expense	1,700	
	Accumulated Other Comprehensive Income (AOCI)		1,700
	To recognize the change in the time value of the foreign currency option as an expense with a corresponding credit to AOCI.		

Trial Balance—September 30	Debit	Credit
Cash		$ 5,200
Parts Inventory	$80,000	
Foreign Currency Option (asset)	9,500	
Accounts Payable (Mexican pesos)		86,000
Foreign Exchange Loss	6,000	
Gain on Foreign Currency Option		6,000
Option Expense	1,700	
	$97,200	$97,200

10/31	Foreign Exchange Loss	5,000	
	Accounts Payable (Mexican pesos)		5,000
	To adjust the value of the peso payable to the new spot rate of $0.091 and record a foreign exchange loss resulting from the appreciation of the peso since September 30.		
	Foreign Currency Option	1,500	
	Accumulated Other Comprehensive Income (AOCI)		1,500
	To adjust the carrying value of the foreign currency option to its current fair value of $11,000 with a corresponding credit to AOCI.		
	Accumulated Other Comprehensive Income (AOCI)	5,000	
	Gain on Foreign Currency Option		5,000
	To record a gain on foreign currency option to offset the foreign exchange loss on account payable with a corresponding debit to AOCI.		
	Option Expense	3,500	
	Accumulated Other Comprehensive Income (AOCI)		3,500
	To recognize the change in the time value of the foreign currency option as an expense with a corresponding credit to AOCI.		
	Foreign Currency (Mexican pesos)	91,000	
	Cash		80,000
	Foreign Currency Option		11,000
	To record exercise of the foreign currency option: Record payment of $80,000 in exchange for 1 million pesos, record the receipt of 1 million pesos as an asset at the spot rate of $0.091, and remove the option from the accounts.		
	Accounts Payable (pesos)	91,000	
	Foreign Currency (pesos)		91,000
	To record remittance of 1 million pesos to the Mexican supplier.		

Trial Balance—October 31	Debit	Credit
Cash ($5,200 credit balance + $80,000 credit) ...		$85,200
Parts Inventory	$80,000	
Retained Earnings, 9/30	1,700	
Foreign Exchange Loss	5,000	
Gain on Foreign Currency Option		5,000
Option Expense	3,500	
	$90,200	$90,200

Part D. Forward Contract Fair Value Hedge of a Foreign Currency Firm Commitment

8/1	The forward contract or the purchase order requires no formal entry. A memorandum would be prepared designating the forward contract as a fair value hedge of the foreign currency firm commitment.		
9/30	Forward Contract	2,970	
	Gain on Forward Contract		2,970
	To record the forward contract as an asset at its fair value of $2,970 and record a forward contract gain for the change in the fair value of the forward contract since August 1.		
	Loss on Firm Commitment	2,970	
	Firm Commitment		2,970
	To record the firm commitment as a liability at its fair value of $2,970 based on changes in the forward rate and record a firm commitment loss for the change in fair value since August 1.		

Trial Balance—September 30	Debit	Credit
Forward Contract (asset)	$2,970	
Firm Commitment (liability)		$2,970
Gain on Forward Contract		2,970
Loss on Firm Commitment	2,970	
	$5,940	$5,940

10/31	Forward Contract	3,030	
	Gain on Forward Contract		3,030
	To adjust the carrying value of the forward contract to its current fair value of $6,000 and record a forward contract gain for the change in fair value since September 30.		
	Loss on Firm Commitment	3,030	
	Firm Commitment		3,030
	To adjust the value of the firm commitment to $6,000 based on changes in the forward rate and record a firm commitment loss for the change in fair value since September 30.		
	Foreign Currency (Mexican pesos)	91,000	
	Cash		85,000
	Forward Contract		6,000
	To record settlement of the forward contract: Record payment of $85,000 in exchange for 1 million pesos, record the receipt of 1 million pesos as an asset at the spot rate of $0.091, and remove the forward contract from the accounts.		
	Parts Inventory	91,000	
	Foreign Currency (Mexican pesos)		91,000
	To record the purchase of parts through the payment of 1 million pesos to the Mexican supplier.		
	Firm Commitment	6,000	
	Adjustment to Net Income		6,000
	To close the firm commitment account as an adjustment to net income.		

(*Note:* The final entry to close the Firm Commitment account to Adjustment to Net Income must be made *only* in the period in which Parts Inventory affects net income through Cost of Goods Sold. The Firm Commitment account remains on the books as a liability until that point in time.)

Trial Balance—October 31	Debit	Credit
Cash		$85,000
Parts Inventory (Cost of Goods Sold)	$91,000	
Gain on Forward Contract		3,030
Loss on Firm Commitment	3,030	
Adjustment to Net Income		6,000
	$94,030	$94,030

Part E. Option Fair Value Hedge of a Foreign Currency Firm Commitment

8/1	Foreign Currency Option		5,200	
	Cash			5,200
	To record the purchase of a foreign currency option as an asset.			
9/30	Foreign Currency Option		4,300	
	Gain on Foreign Currency Option			4,300
	To adjust the fair value of the option from $5,200 to $9,500 and record an option gain for the change in fair value since August 1.			
	Loss on Firm Commitment		5,940	
	Firm Commitment			5,940
	To record the firm commitment as a liability at its fair value of $5,940 based on changes in the spot rate and record a firm commitment loss for the change in fair value since August 1.			

The fair value of the firm commitment is determined by referring to changes in the spot rate from August 1 to September 30: ($0.080 − $0.086) × 1 million pesos = $(6,000). This amount must be discounted for one month at 12 percent per annum (1 percent per month): $(6,000) × 0.9901 = $(5,940).

Trial Balance—September 30	Debit	Credit
Cash		$ 5,200
Foreign Currency Option (asset)	$ 9,500	
Firm Commitment (liability)		5,940
Gain on Foreign Currency Option		4,300
Loss on Firm Commitment	5,940	
	$15,440	$15,440

10/31	Foreign Currency Option		1,500	
	Gain on Foreign Currency Option			1,500
	To adjust fair value of the option from $9,500 to $11,000 and record an option gain for the change in fair value since September 30.			
	Loss on Firm Commitment		5,060	
	Firm Commitment			5,060
	To adjust the fair value of the firm commitment from $5,940 to $11,000 and record a firm commitment loss for the change in fair value since September 30.			

The fair value of the firm commitment is determined by referring to changes in the spot rate from August 1 to October 31: ($0.080 − $0.091) × 1 million pesos = $(11,000).

	Debit	Credit
Foreign Currency (Mexican pesos)	91,000	
Cash		80,000
Foreign Currency Option		11,000
To record exercise of the foreign currency option: Record payment of $80,000 in exchange for 1 million pesos, record the receipt of 1 million pesos as an asset at the spot rate of $0.091, and remove the option from the accounts.		
Parts Inventory	91,000	
Foreign Currency (pesos)		91,000
To record the purchase of parts through the payment of 1 million pesos to the Mexican supplier.		
Firm Commitment	11,000	
Adjustment to Net Income		11,000
To close Firm Commitment account to Adjustment to Net Income.		

(*Note:* The final entry to close the Firm Commitment to Adjustment to Net Income is made *only* in the period in which Parts Inventory affects net income through Cost of Goods Sold. The Firm Commitment account remains on the books as a liability until that point in time.)

Trial Balance—October 31	Debit	Credit
Cash ($5,200 credit balance + $80,000 credit)...		$85,200
Parts Inventory (Cost of Goods Sold)...........	$91,000	
Retained Earnings, 9/30	1,640	
Gain on Foreign Currency Option		1,500
Loss on Firm Commitment	5,060	
Adjustment to Net Income		11,000
	$97,700	$97,700

Part F. Option Cash Flow Hedge of a Forecasted Foreign Currency Transaction

		Debit	Credit
8/1	Foreign Currency Option	5,200	
	Cash		5,200
	To record the purchase of a foreign currency option as an asset.		
9/30	Foreign Currency Option	4,300	
	Accumulated Other Comprehensive Income (AOCI)		4,300
	To adjust the fair value of the option from $5,200 to $9,500 with a corresponding adjustment to AOCI.		
	Option Expense	1,700	
	Accumulated Other Comprehensive Income (AOCI)		1,700
	To recognize the change in the time value of the foreign currency option as an expense with a corresponding credit to AOCI.		

Trial Balance—September 30	Debit	Credit
Cash		$ 5,200
Foreign Currency Option (asset)	$ 9,500	
Accumulated Other Comprehensive Income ...		6,000
Option Expense	1,700	
	$11,200	$11,200

10/31	Foreign Currency Option	1,500	
	Accumulated Other Comprehensive Income (AOCI)		1,500
	To adjust the fair value of the option from $9,500 to $11,000 with a corresponding adjustment to AOCI.		
	Option Expense	3,500	
	Accumulated Other Comprehensive Income (AOCI)		3,500
	To recognize the change in the time value of the foreign currency option as an expense with a corresponding credit to AOCI.		
	Foreign Currency (Mexican pesos)	91,000	
	Cash		80,000
	Foreign Currency Option		11,000
	To record exercise of the foreign currency option: Record payment of $80,000 in exchange for 1 million pesos, record the receipt of 1 million pesos as an asset at the spot rate of $0.091, and remove the option from the accounts.		
	Parts Inventory	91,000	
	Foreign Currency (Mexican pesos)		91,000
	To record the purchase of parts through the payment of 1 million pesos to the Mexican supplier.		
	Accumulated Other Comprehensive Income (AOCI)	11,000	
	Adjustment to Net Income		11,000
	To close AOCI as an adjustment to net income.		

(*Note:* The final entry to close AOCI to Adjustment to Net Income is made at the date that the forecasted transaction was expected to occur, regardless of when the parts inventory affects net income.)

Trial Balance—October 31	Debit	Credit
Cash ($5,200 credit balance + $80,000 credit)		$85,200
Parts Inventory (Cost of Goods Sold)	$91,000	
Retained Earnings, 9/30.	1,700	
Foreign Currency Option expense	3,500	
Adjustment to Net Income		11,000
	$96,200	$96,200

Questions

1. What concept underlies the two-transaction perspective in accounting for foreign currency transactions?
2. A company makes an export sale denominated in a foreign currency and allows the customer one month to pay. Under the two-transaction perspective, accrual approach, how does the company account for fluctuations in the exchange rate for the foreign currency?
3. What factors create a foreign exchange gain on a foreign currency transaction? What factors create a foreign exchange loss?
4. What does the term *hedging* mean? Why do companies elect to follow this strategy?
5. How does a foreign currency option differ from a foreign currency forward contract?
6. How does the timing of hedges of (a) foreign currency denominated assets and liabilities, (b) foreign currency firm commitments, and (c) forecasted foreign currency transactions differ?
7. Why would a company prefer a foreign currency option over a forward contract in hedging a foreign currency firm commitment? Why would a company prefer a forward contract over an option in hedging a foreign currency asset or liability?
8. How do companies report foreign currency derivatives, such as forward contracts and options, on the balance sheet?
9. How does a company determine the fair value of a foreign currency forward contract? How does it determine the fair value of an option?

10. What is hedge accounting?

11. Under what conditions can companies use hedge accounting to account for a foreign currency option used to hedge a forecasted foreign currency transaction?

12. What are the differences in accounting for a forward contract used as (a) a cash flow hedge and (b) a fair value hedge of a foreign currency denominated asset or liability?

13. What are the differences in accounting for a forward contract used as a fair value hedge of (a) a foreign currency denominated asset or liability and (b) a foreign currency firm commitment?

14. What are the differences in accounting for a forward contract used as a cash flow hedge of (a) a foreign currency denominated asset or liability and (b) a forecasted foreign currency transaction?

15. How are changes in the fair value of an option accounted for in a cash flow hedge? In a fair value hedge?

16. In what way is the accounting for a foreign currency borrowing more complicated than the accounting for a foreign currency account payable?

Problems

1. Which of the following combinations correctly describes the relationship between foreign currency transactions, exchange rate changes, and foreign exchange gains and losses?

Type of Transaction	Foreign Currency	Foreign Exchange Gain or Loss
a. Export sale	Appreciates	Loss
b. Import purchase	Appreciates	Gain
c. Import purchase	Depreciates	Gain
d. Export sale	Depreciates	Gain

2. In accounting for foreign currency transactions, which of the following approaches is used in the United States?

a. One-transaction perspective; accrue foreign exchange gains and losses.

b. One-transaction perspective; defer foreign exchange gains and losses.

c. Two-transaction perspective; defer foreign exchange gains and losses.

d. Two-transaction perspective; accrue foreign exchange gains and losses.

3. On October 1, 2007, Mud Co., a U.S. company, purchased parts from Terra, a Portuguese company, with payment due on December 1, 2007. If Mud's 2007 operating income included no foreign exchange gain or loss, the transaction could have

a. Resulted in an extraordinary gain.

b. Been denominated in U.S. dollars.

c. Generated a foreign exchange gain to be reported as a deferred charge on the balance sheet.

d. Generated a foreign exchange loss to be reported as a separate component of stockholders' equity.

4. Post, Inc., had a receivable from a foreign customer that is payable in the customer's local currency. On December 31, 2007, Post correctly included this receivable for 200,000 local currency units (LCU) in its balance sheet at $110,000. When Post collected the receivable on February 15, 2008, the U.S. dollar equivalent was $95,000. In Post's 2008 consolidated income statement, how much should it report as a foreign exchange loss?

a. $0.

b. $10,000.

c. $15,000.

d. $25,000.

5. On July 1, 2007, Houghton Company borrowed 200,000 euros from a foreign lender evidenced by an interest-bearing note due on July 1, 2008. The note is denominated in euros. The U.S. dollar equivalent of the note principal is as follows:

Date	Amount
July 1, 2007 (date borrowed)	$195,000
December 31, 2007 (Houghton's year-end)	220,000
July 1, 2008 (date repaid)	230,000

In its 2008 income statement, what amount should Houghton include as a foreign exchange gain or loss on the note?

a. $35,000 gain.

b. $35,000 loss.

c. $10,000 gain.

d. $10,000 loss.

6. Slick Co. had a Swiss franc receivable resulting from exports to Switzerland and a Mexican peso payable resulting from imports from Mexico. Slick recorded foreign exchange gains related to both its franc receivable and peso payable. Did the foreign currencies increase or decrease in dollar value from the date of the transaction to the settlement date?

	Franc	Peso
a.	Increase	Increase
b.	Decrease	Decrease
c.	Decrease	Increase
d.	Increase	Decrease

7. Grete Corp. had the following foreign currency transactions during 2007:

- Purchased merchandise from a foreign supplier on January 20, 2007, for the U.S. dollar equivalent of $60,000 and paid the invoice on April 20, 2007, at the U.S. dollar equivalent of $68,000.

- On September 1, 2007, borrowed the U.S. dollar equivalent of $300,000 evidenced by a note that is payable in the lender's local currency on September 1, 2008. On December 31, 2007, the U.S. dollar equivalent of the principal amount was $320,000.

In Grete's 2007 income statement, what amount should be included as a foreign exchange loss?

a. $4,000.

b. $20,000.

c. $22,000.

d. $28,000.

8. A U.S. exporter has a Thai baht account receivable resulting from an export sale on April 1 to a customer in Thailand. The exporter signed a forward contract on April 1 to sell Thai baht and designated it as a cash flow hedge of a recognized Thai baht receivable. The spot rate was $0.022 on that date, and the forward rate was $0.023. Which of the following did the U.S. exporter report in net income?

a. Discount expense.

b. Discount revenue.

c. Premium expense.

d. Premium revenue.

9. Lawrence Company ordered parts costing FC100,000 from a foreign supplier on May 12 when the spot rate was $0.20 per FC. A one-month forward contract was signed on that date to purchase FC100,000 at a forward rate of $0.21. The forward contract is properly designated as a fair value hedge of the FC100,000 firm commitment. On June 12, when the company receives the parts, the spot rate is $0.23. At what amount should Lawrence Company carry the parts inventory on its books?

a. $20,000.

b. $21,000.

c. $22,000.

d. $23,000.

10. On December 1, 2007, Barnum Company (a U.S.-based company) entered into a three-month forward contract to purchase 1,000,000 ringgits on March 1, 2008. The following U.S. dollar per ringgit exchange rates apply:

Date	Spot Rate	Forward Rate (to March 1, 2008)
December 1, 2007	$0.044	$0.042
December 31, 2007	0.040	0.037
March 1, 2008	0.038	N/A

Barnum's incremental borrowing rate is 12 percent. The present value factor for two months at an annual interest rate of 12 percent (1 percent per month) is 0.9803.

Which of the following correctly describes the manner in which Barnum Company will report the forward contract on its December 31, 2007, balance sheet?

a. As an asset in the amount of $1,960.60.

b. As an asset in the amount of $3,921.20.

c. As a liability in the amount of $6,862.10.

d. As a liability in the amount of $4,901.50.

Use the following information for Problems 11 and 12.
MNC Corp. (a U.S.-based company) sold parts to a Korean customer on December 1, 2007, with payment of 10 million Korean won to be received on March 31, 2008. The following exchange rates apply:

Date	Spot Rate	Forward Rate (to March 31, 2008)
December 1, 2007	$0.0035	$0.0034
December 31, 2007	0.0033	0.0032
March 31, 2008	0.0038	N/A

MNC's incremental borrowing rate is 12 percent. The present value factor for three months at an annual interest rate of 12 percent (1 percent per month) is 0.9706.

11. Assuming that MNC entered into no forward contract, how much foreign exchange gain or loss should it report on its 2007 income statement with regard to this transaction?

a. $5,000 gain.

b. $3,000 gain.

c. $2,000 loss.

d. $1,000 loss.

12. Assuming that MNC entered into a forward contract to sell 10 million Korean won on December 1, 2007, as a fair value hedge of a foreign currency receivable, what is the net impact on its net income in 2007 resulting from a fluctuation in the value of the won?

a. No impact on net income.

b. $58.80 decrease in net income.

c. $2,000 decrease in net income.

d. $1,941.20 increase in net income.

13. On March 1, Pimlico Corporation (a U.S.-based company) expects to order merchandise from a supplier in Sweden in three months. On March 1, when the spot rate is $0.10 per Swedish krona, Pimlico enters into a forward contract to purchase 500,000 Swedish kroner at a three-month forward rate of $0.12. At the end of three months, when the spot rate is $0.115 per Swedish krona, Pimlico orders and receives the merchandise, paying 500,000 kroner. What amount does Pimlico report in net income as a result of this cash flow hedge of a forecasted transaction?

a. $10,000 Premium Expense plus a $7,500 positive Adjustment to Net Income when the merchandise is purchased.

b. $10,000 Discount Expense plus a $5,000 positive Adjustment to Net Income when the merchandise is purchased.

c. $2,500 Premium Expense plus a $5,000 negative Adjustment to Net Income when the merchandise is purchased.

d. $2,500 Premium Expense plus a $2,500 positive Adjustment to Net Income when the merchandise is purchased.

14. Palmer Corporation operates as a U.S. corporation. Palmer expects to order goods from a foreign supplier at a price of 200,000 pounds, with delivery and payment to be made on April 15. On January 15, Palmer purchased a three-month call option on 200,000 pounds and designated this option

as a cash flow hedge of a forecasted foreign currency transaction. The option has a strike price of $0.25 per pound and costs $2,000. The spot rate for pounds is $0.25 on January 15 and $0.22 on April 15. What amount will Palmer Corporation report as an option expense in net income during the period January 15 to April 15?

a. $600.

b. $1,000.

c. $2,000.

d. $4,400.

Use the following information for Problems 15 through 17.
On September 1, 2007, Jensen Company received an order to sell a machine to a customer in Canada at a price of 100,000 Canadian dollars. Jensen shipped the machine and received payment on March 1, 2008. On September 1, 2007, Jensen purchased a put option giving it the right to sell 100,000 Canadian dollars on March 1, 2008, at a price of $80,000. Jensen properly designated the option as a fair value hedge of the Canadian dollar firm commitment. The option cost $2,000 and had a fair value of $2,300 on December 31, 2007. The fair value of the firm commitment was measured by referring to changes in the spot rate. The following spot exchange rates apply:

Date	U.S. Dollar per Canadian Dollar
September 1, 2007	$0.80
December 31, 2007	0.79
March 1, 2008	0.77

Jensen Company's incremental borrowing rate is 12 percent. The present value factor for two months at an annual interest rate of 12 percent (1 percent per month) is 0.9803.

15. What was the net impact on Jensen Company's 2007 income as a result of this fair value hedge of a firm commitment?

a. –0–.

b. $680.30 decrease in income.

c. $300 increase in income.

d. $980.30 increase in income.

16. What was the net impact on Jensen Company's 2008 income as a result of this fair value hedge of a firm commitment?

a. –0–.

b. $1,319.70 decrease in income.

c. $77,980.30 increase in income.

d. $78,680.30 increase in income.

17. What was the net increase or decrease in cash flow from having purchased the foreign currency option to hedge this exposure to foreign exchange risk?

a. –0–.

b. $1,000 increase in cash flow.

c. $1,500 decrease in cash flow.

d. $3,000 increase in cash flow.

Use the following information for Problems 18 through 20.
On March 1, 2007, Werner Corp. received an order for parts from a Mexican customer at a price of 500,000 Mexican pesos with a delivery date of April 30, 2007. On March 1, when the U.S. dollar–Mexican peso spot rate is $0.115, Werner Corp. entered into a two-month forward contract to sell 500,000 pesos at a forward rate of $0.12 per peso. It designates the forward contract as a fair value hedge of the firm commitment to receive pesos, and the fair value of the firm commitment is measured by referring to changes in the peso forward rate. Werner delivers the parts and receives payment on April 30, 2007, when the peso spot rate is $0.118. On March 31, 2007, the Mexican peso spot rate is $0.123, and the forward contract has a fair value of $1,250.

18. What is the net impact on Werner's net income for the quarter ended March 31, 2007, as a result of this forward contract hedge of a firm commitment?

    a. –0–.

    b. $1,250 increase in net income.

    c. $1,500 decrease in net income.

    d. $1,500 increase in net income.

19. What is the net impact on Werner's net income for the quarter ended June 30, 2007, as a result of this forward contract hedge of a firm commitment?

    a. –0–.

    b. $59,000 increase in net income.

    c. $60,000 increase in net income.

    d. $61,500 increase in net income.

20. What is the net increase or decrease in cash flow from having entered into this forward contract hedge?

    a. –0–.

    b. $1,000 increase in cash flow.

    c. $1,500 decrease in cash flow.

    d. $2,500 increase in cash flow.

Use the following information for Problems 21 and 22.
On November 1, 2007, Dos Santos Company forecasts the purchase of raw materials from a Brazilian supplier on February 1, 2008, at a price of 200,000 Brazilian reals. On November 1, 2007, Dos Santos pays $1,500 for a three-month call option on 200,000 reals with a strike price of $0.40 per real. Dos Santos properly designates the option as a cash flow hedge of a forecasted foreign currency transaction. On December 31, 2007, the option has a fair value of $1,100. The following spot exchange rates apply:

Date	U.S. Dollar per Brazilian Real
November 1, 2007	$0.40
December 31, 2007	0.38
February 1, 2008	0.41

21. What is the net impact on Dos Santos Company's 2007 net income as a result of this hedge of a forecasted foreign currency purchase?

    a. –0–.

    b. $400 decrease in net income.

    c. $1,000 decrease in net income.

    d. $1,400 decrease in net income.

22. What is the net impact on Dos Santos Company's 2008 net income as a result of this hedge of a forecasted foreign currency purchase? Assume that the raw materials are consumed and become a part of the cost of goods sold in 2008.

    a. $80,000 decrease in net income.

    b. $80,600 decease in net income.

    c. $81,100 decrease in net income.

    d. $83,100 decrease in net income.

23. Rabato Corporation acquired merchandise on account from a foreign supplier on November 1, 2007, for 60,000 LCU (local currency units). It paid the foreign currency account payable on January 15, 2008. The following exchange rates for 1 LCU are known:

November 1, 2007	$0.345
December 31, 2007	0.333
January 15, 2008	0.359

    a. How does the fluctuation in exchange rates affect Rabato's 2007 income statement?

    b. How does the fluctuation in exchange rates affect Rabato's 2008 income statement?

24. On December 20, 2007, Butanta Company (a U.S. company headquartered in Miami, Florida) sold parts to a foreign customer at a price of 50,000 ostras. Payment is received on January 10, 2008. Currency exchange rates for 1 ostra are as follows:

December 20, 2007	$1.05
December 31, 2007	1.02
January 10, 2008	0.98

    a. How does the fluctuation in exchange rates affect Butanta's 2007 income statement?

    b. How does the fluctuation in exchange rates affect Butanta's 2008 income statement?

25. New Colony Corporation (a U.S. company) made a sale to a foreign customer on September 15, 2007, for 100,000 foreign currency units (FCU). It received payment on October 15, 2007. The following exchange rates for 1 FCU apply:

September 15, 2007	$0.40
September 30, 2007	0.42
October 15, 2007	0.37

    Prepare all journal entries for New Colony in connection with this sale, assuming that the company closes its books on September 30 to prepare interim financial statements.

26. On December 1, 2007, Dresden Company (a U.S. company located in Albany, New York) purchases inventory from a foreign supplier for 60,000 local currency units (LCU). Dresden will pay in 90 days, after it sells this merchandise. It makes sales rather quickly and pays this entire obligation on January 28, 2008. Currency exchange rates for 1 LCU are as follows:

December 1, 2007	$0.88
December 31, 2007	0.82
January 28, 2008	0.90

    Prepare all journal entries for Dresden Company in connection with the purchase and payment.

27. Acme Corporation (a U.S. company located in Sarasota, Florida) has the following import/export transactions in 2007:

March 1	Bought inventory costing 50,000 pesos on credit.
May 1	Sold 60 percent of the inventory for 45,000 pesos on credit.
August 1	Collected 40,000 pesos from customers.
September 1	Paid 30,000 pesos to creditors.

    Currency exchange rates for 1 peso for 2007 are as follows:

March 1	$0.17
May 1	0.18
August 1	0.19
September 1	0.20
December 31	0.21

    For each of the following accounts, how much will Acme report on its 2007 financial statements?

    a. Inventory.

    b. Cost of Goods Sold.

    c. Sales.

    d. Accounts Receivable.

    e. Accounts Payable.

    f. Cash.

28. Bartlett Company, which has its headquarters in Cincinnati, Ohio, has occasional transactions with companies in a foreign country whose currency is the lira. Prepare journal entries for the following transactions in U.S. dollars. Also prepare any necessary adjusting entries at December 31 caused by fluctuations in the value of the foreign currencies. Assume that the company uses a perpetual inventory system.

Transactions in 2007

February 1	Bought equipment for 40,000 lire on credit.
April 1	Paid for the equipment purchased February 1.
June 1	Bought inventory for 30,000 lire on credit.
August 1	Sold 70 percent of inventory purchased June 1 for 40,000 lire on credit.
October 1	Collected 30,000 lire from the sales made on August 1, 2007.
November 1	Paid 20,000 lire on the debts incurred on June 1, 2007.

Transactions in 2008

February 1	Collected remaining 10,000 lire from August 1, 2007, sales.
March 1	Paid remaining 10,000 lire on the debts incurred on June 1, 2007.

Currency exchange rates for 1 lira for 2007

February 1	$0.44
April 1	0.45
June 1	0.47
August 1	0.48
October 1	0.49
November 1	0.50
December 31	0.52

Currency exchange rates for 1 lira for 2008

February 1	$0.54
March 1	0.55

29. Benjamin, Inc., operates an export/import business. The company, located in Mobile, Alabama, has considerable dealings with companies in the country of Camerrand. The denomination of all transactions with these companies is alaries (AL), the Camerrand currency. During 2007, Benjamin acquires 20,000 widgets at a price of 8 alaries per widget. It will pay for them when it sells them. Currency exchange rates for 1 AL are as follows:

September 1, 2007	$0.46
December 1, 2007	0.44
December 31, 2007	0.48
March 1, 2008	0.45

a. Assume that Benjamin acquired the widgets on December 1, 2007, and made payment on March 1, 2008. What is the effect of the exchange rate fluctuations on reported income in 2007 and in 2008?

b. Assume that Benjamin acquired the widgets on September 1, 2007, and made payment on December 1, 2007. What is the effect of the exchange rate fluctuations on reported income in 2007?

c. Assume that Benjamin acquired the widgets on September 1, 2007, and made payment on March 1, 2008. What is the effect of the exchange rate fluctuations on reported income in 2007 and in 2008?

30. On September 30, 2007, Ericson Company negotiated a two-year, 1,000,000 dudek loan from a foreign bank at an interest rate of 2 percent per year. It makes interest payments annually on September 30, and will repay the principal on September 30, 2009. Ericson prepares U.S.-dollar financial statements and has a December 31 year-end. Prepare all journal entries related to this foreign currency borrowing assuming the following exchange rates for 1 dudek:

September 30, 2007	$0.100
December 31, 2007	0.105
September 30, 2008	0.120
December 31, 2008	0.125
September 30, 2009	0.150

Determine the effective cost of borrowing in dollars in each of the three years 2007, 2008, and 2009.

31. Brandlin Company of Anaheim, California, sells parts to a foreign customer on December 1, 2007, with payment of 20,000 korunas to be received on March 1, 2008. Brandlin enters into a forward contract on December 1, 2007, to sell 20,000 korunas on March 1, 2008. Relevant exchange rates for the koruna on various dates are as follows:

Date	Spot Rate	Forward Rate (to March 1, 2008)
December 1, 2007	$2.00	$2.075
December 31, 2007	2.10	2.200
March 1, 2008	2.25	N/A

Brandlin's incremental borrowing rate is 12 percent. The present value factor for two months at an annual interest rate of 12 percent (1 percent per month) is 0.9803. Brandlin must close its books and prepare financial statements at December 31.

  a. Assuming that Brandlin designates the forward contract as a cash flow hedge of a foreign currency receivable and recognizes any premium or discount using the straight-line method, prepare journal entries for these transactions in U.S. dollars. What is the impact on 2007 net income? What is the impact on 2008 net income? What is the impact on net income over the two accounting periods?

  b. Assuming that Brandlin designates the forward contract as a fair value hedge of a foreign currency receivable and recognizes any premium or discount using the straight-line method, prepare journal entries for these transactions in U.S. dollars. What is the impact on 2007 net income? What is the impact on 2008 net income? What is the impact on net income over the two accounting periods?

32. Use the same facts as in Problem 31 except that Brandlin Company purchases parts from a foreign supplier on December 1, 2007, with payment of 20,000 korunas to be made on March 1, 2008. On December 1, 2007, Brandlin enters into a forward contract to purchase 20,000 korunas on March 1, 2008.

  a. Assuming that Brandlin designates the forward contract as a cash flow hedge of a foreign currency payable, prepare journal entries for these transactions in U.S. dollars. What is the impact on 2007 net income? What is the impact on 2008 net income? What is the impact on net income over the two accounting periods?

  b. Assuming that Brandlin designates the forward contract as a fair value hedge of a foreign currency payable, prepare journal entries for these transactions in U.S. dollars. What is the impact on 2007 net income? What is the impact on 2008 net income? What is the impact on net income over the two accounting periods?

33. On June 1, Alexander Corporation sold goods to a foreign customer at a price of 1,000,000 pesos. It will receive payment in three months on September 1. On June 1, Alexander acquired an option to sell 1,000,000 pesos in three months at a strike price of $0.045. Relevant exchange rates and option premia for the peso are as follows:

Date	Spot Rate	Call Option Premium for September 1 (strike price $0.045)
June 1	$0.045	$0.0020
June 30	0.048	0.0018
September 1	0.044	N/A

Alexander Corporation must close its books and prepare its second-quarter financial statements on June 30.

  a. Assuming that Alexander designates the foreign currency option as a cash flow hedge of a foreign currency receivable, prepare journal entries for these transactions in U.S. dollars. What is the impact on net income over the two accounting periods?

  b. Assuming that Alexander designates the foreign currency option as a fair value hedge of a foreign currency receivable, prepare journal entries for these transactions in U.S. dollars. What is the impact on net income over the two accounting periods?

34. On June 1, Hamilton Corporation purchased goods from a foreign supplier at a price of 1,000,000 markkas. It will make payment in three months on September 1. On June 1, Hamilton acquired an

option to purchase 1,000,000 markkas in three months at a strike price of $0.085. Relevant exchange rates and option premia for the markka are as follows:

Date	Spot Rate	Call Option Premium for September 1 (strike price $0.085)
June 1	$0.085	$0.002
June 30	0.088	0.004
September 1	0.090	N/A

Hamilton Corporation must close its books and prepare its second-quarter financial statements on June 30.

a. Assuming that Hamilton designates the foreign currency option as a cash flow hedge of a foreign currency payable, prepare journal entries for these transactions in U.S. dollars. What is the impact on net income over the two accounting periods?

b. Assuming that Hamilton designates the foreign currency option as a fair value hedge of a foreign currency payable, prepare journal entries for these transactions in U.S. dollars. What is the impact on net income over the two accounting periods?

35. On November 1, 2007, Ambrose Company sold merchandise to a foreign customer for 100,000 FCUs with payment to be received on April 30, 2008. At the date of sale, Ambrose entered into a six-month forward contract to sell 100,000 LCUs. It properly designates the forward contract as a cash flow hedge of a foreign currency receivable. The following exchange rates apply:

Date	Spot Rate	Forward Rate (to April 30, 2008)
November 1, 2007	$0.53	$0.52
December 31, 2007	0.50	0.48
April 30, 2008	0.49	N/A

Ambrose Company's incremental borrowing rate is 12 percent. The present value factor for four months at an annual interest rate of 12 percent (1 percent per month) is 0.9610.

a. Prepare all journal entries, including December 31 adjusting entries, to record the sale and forward contract.

b. What is the impact on net income in 2007?

c. What is the impact on net income in 2008?

36. Eximco Corporation (based in Champaign, Illinois) has a number of transactions with companies in the country of Mongagua, where the currency is the mong. On November 30, 2007, Eximco sold equipment at a price of 500,000 mongs to a Mongaguan customer that will make payment on January 31, 2008. In addition, on November 30, 2007, Eximco purchased raw materials from a Mongaguan supplier at a price of 300,000 mongs; it will make payment on January 31, 2008. To hedge its net exposure in mongs, Eximco entered into a two-month forward contract on November 30, 2007, to deliver 200,000 mongs to the foreign currency broker in exchange for $104,000. Eximco properly designates its forward contract as a fair value hedge of a foreign currency receivable. The following rates for the mong apply:

Date	Spot Rate	Forward Rate (to January 31, 2008)
November 30, 2007	$0.53	$0.52
December 31, 2007	0.50	0.48
January 31, 2008	0.49	N/A

Eximco Corporation's incremental borrowing rate is 12 percent. The present value factor for one month at an annual interest rate of 12 percent (1 percent per month) is 0.9901.

a. Prepare all journal entries, including December 31 adjusting entries, to record these transactions and forward contract.

b. What is the impact on net income in 2007?

c. What is the impact on net income in 2008?

37. On October 1, 2007, Hanks Company entered into a forward contract to sell 100,000 LCUs in four months (on January 31, 2008) and receive $65,000 in U.S. dollars. Exchange rates for the LCU are as follows:

Date	Spot Rate	Forward Rate (to January 31, 2008)
October 1, 2007	$0.69	$0.65
December 31, 2007	0.71	0.74
January 31, 2008	0.72	N/A

Hanks Company's incremental borrowing rate is 12 percent. The present value factor for one month at an annual interest rate of 12 percent (1 percent per month) is 0.9901. Hanks must close its books and prepare financial statements on December 31.

a. Prepare journal entries, assuming that Hanks entered into the forward contract as a fair value hedge of a 100,000 LCU receivable arising from a sale made on October 1, 2007. Include entries for both the sale and the forward contract.

b. Prepare journal entries, assuming that Hanks entered into the forward contract as a fair value hedge of a firm commitment related to a 100,000 LCU sale that will be made on January 31, 2008. Include entries for both the firm commitment and the forward contract. The fair value of the firm commitment is measured referring to changes in the forward rate.

38. On August 1, Jackson Corporation (a U.S.-based importer) placed an order to purchase merchandise from a foreign supplier at a price of 200,000 rupees. Jackson will receive and make payment for the merchandise in three months on October 31. On August 1, Jackson entered into a forward contract to purchase 200,000 rupees in three months at a forward rate of $0.30. It properly designates the forward contract as a fair value hedge of a foreign currency firm commitment. The fair value of the firm commitment is measured by referring to changes in the forward rate. Relevant exchange rates for the rupee are as follows:

Date	Spot Rate	Forward Rate (to October 31)
August 1	$0.300	$0.300
September 30	0.305	0.325
October 31	0.320	N/A

Jackson's incremental borrowing rate is 12 percent. The present value factor for one month at an annual interest rate of 12 percent (1 percent per month) is 0.9901. Jackson Corporation must close its books and prepare its third-quarter financial statements on September 30.

a. Prepare journal entries for the forward contract and firm commitment.

b. What is the impact on net income over the two accounting periods?

c. What is the net cash outflow resulting from the purchase of merchandise from the foreign customer?

39. On June 1, Vandervelde Corporation (a U.S.-based manufacturing firm) received an order to sell goods to a foreign customer at a price of 500,000 leks. Vandervelde will ship the goods and receive payment in three months on September 1. On June 1, Vandervelde purchased an option to sell 500,000 leks in three months at a strike price of $1.00. It properly designated the option as a fair value hedge of a foreign currency firm commitment. The fair value of the firm commitment is measured by referring to changes in the spot rate. Relevant exchange rates and option premiums for the lek are as follows:

Date	Spot Rate	Call Option Premium for September 1 (strike price $1.00)
June 1	$1.00	$0.010
June 30	0.99	0.016
September 1	0.97	N/A

Vandervelde's incremental borrowing rate is 12 percent. The present value factor for two months at an annual interest rate of 12 percent (1 percent per month) is 0.9803. Vandervelde Corporation must close its books and prepare its second-quarter financial statements on June 30.

a. Prepare journal entries for the foreign currency option and firm commitment.

b. What is the impact on net income over the two accounting periods?

c. What is the net cash inflow resulting from the sale of goods to the foreign customer?

40. Big Arber Company ordered parts from a foreign supplier on November 20 at a price of 50,000 pijios when the spot rate was $0.20 per pijio. Delivery and payment were scheduled for December 20. On November 20, Big Arber acquired a call option on 50,000 pijios at a strike price of $0.20, paying a premium of $0.008 per pijio. It designates the option as a fair value hedge of a foreign currency firm commitment. The fair value of the firm commitment is measured by referring to changes in the spot rate. The parts arrive and Big Arber makes payment according to schedule. Big Arber does not close its books until December 31.

a. Assuming a spot rate of $0.21 per pijio on December 20, prepare all journal entries to account for the option and firm commitment.

b. Assuming a spot rate of $0.18 per pijio on December 20, prepare all journal entries to account for the option and firm commitment.

41. Based on past experience, Leickner Company expects that it will need to purchase raw materials from a foreign supplier at a cost of 1,000,000 marks on March 15, 2008. To hedge this forecasted transaction, the company acquires a three-month call option to purchase 1,000,000 marks on December 15, 2007. Leickner selects a strike price of $0.58 per mark, paying a premium of $0.005 per unit, when the spot rate is $0.58. The spot rate increases to $0.584 at December 31, 2007, causing the fair value of the option to increase to $8,000. By March 15, 2008, when the raw materials are purchased, the spot rate has climbed to $0.59, resulting in a fair value for the option of $10,000.

a. Prepare all journal entries for the option hedge of a forecasted transaction and for the purchase of raw materials, assuming that December 31 is Leickner's year-end and that the raw materials are included in the cost of goods sold in 2008.

b. What is the overall impact on net income over the two accounting periods?

c. What is the net cash outflow to acquire the raw materials?

42. Vino Veritas Company, a U.S.-based importer of wines and spirits, placed an order with a French supplier for 1,000 cases of wine at a price of 200 euros per case. The total purchase price is 200,000 euros. Relevant exchange rates for the euro are as follows:

Date	Spot Rate	Forward Rate to October 31, 2007	Call Option Premium for October 31, 2007 (strike price $1.00)
September 15, 2007	$1.00	$1.06	$0.035
September 30, 2007	1.05	1.09	0.070
October 31, 2007	1.10	1.10	0.100

Vino Veritas Company has an incremental borrowing rate of 12 percent (1 percent per month) and closes the books and prepares financial statements at September 30.

a. Assume that the wine arrived on September 15, 2007, and the company made payment on October 31, 2007. There was no attempt to hedge the exposure to foreign exchange risk. Prepare journal entries to account for this import purchase.

b. Assume that the wine arrived on September 15, 2007, and the company made payment on October 31, 2007. On September 15, Vino Veritas Corporation entered into a 45-day forward contract to purchase 200,000 euros. It properly designated the forward contract as a fair value hedge of a foreign currency payable. Prepare journal entries to account for the import purchase and foreign currency forward contract.

c. Vino Veritas ordered the wine on September 15, 2007. The wine arrived and the company paid for it on October 31, 2007. On September 15, Vino Veritas Corporation entered into a 45-day forward contract to purchase 200,000 euros. The company properly designated the forward contract as a fair value hedge of a foreign currency firm commitment. The fair value of the firm commitment is measured by referring to changes in the forward rate. Prepare journal entries to account for the foreign currency forward contract, firm commitment, and import purchase.

d. The wine arrived on September 15, 2007, and the company made payment on October 31, 2007. On September 15, Vino Veritas Corporation purchased a 45-day call option for 200,000 euros. It properly designated the option as a cash flow hedge of a foreign currency payable. Prepare journal entries to account for the import purchase and foreign currency option.

e. The company ordered the wine on September 15, 2007. It arrived on October 31, 2007, and the company made payment on that date. On September 15, Vino Veritas Corporation purchased a 45-day call option for 200,000 euros. It properly designated the option as a fair value hedge of a foreign currency firm commitment. The fair value of the firm commitment is measured by referring to changes in the spot rate. Prepare journal entries to account for the foreign currency option, firm commitment, and import purchase.

Develop Your Skills

RESEARCH CASE 1—INTERNATIONAL FLAVORS AND FRAGRANCES

Many companies make annual reports available on their corporate Internet home page. Annual reports also can be accessed through the SEC's EDGAR system at www.sec.gov (under Forms, search for ARS or 10-K) or in your school's library. Access the most recent annual report for International Flavors and Fragrances (IFF).

Required:

1. Identify the location(s) in the annual report where IFF provides disclosures related to its management of foreign exchange risk.
2. Determine the types of hedging instruments the company uses and the types of hedges in which it engages.
3. Determine the manner in which the company discloses the fact that its foreign exchange hedges are effective in offsetting gains and losses on the underlying items being hedged.

RESEARCH CASE 2—DISCLOSURE OF HEDGING ACTIVITIES

Many companies make annual reports available on their corporate Internet home page. Annual reports also can be accessed through the SEC's EDGAR system at www.sec.gov (under Forms, search for ARS or 10-K) or in your school's library. Access the most recent annual report for the following U.S.-based multinational corporations:

Federal-Mogul Corporation
Ford Motor Company
General Motors Corporation

Required:

1. Identify the location(s) in the annual report that provides disclosures related to foreign exchange risk management (hedging).
2. Determine the types of hedging instrument each company uses and the types of hedges in which it engages.
3. Identify whether each company reports a concentration of foreign exchange exposure in any particular currency or currencies.
4. Determine whether each company discloses the aggregate amount of foreign exchange gains/losses included in income, and if so, whether this amount is reported as a separate line item in the income statement.

FARS CASE 1—HEDGE OF FORECASTED FOREIGN CURRENCY TRANSACTION

The French subsidiary of a U.S. parent corporation forecasts that it will purchase parts from a Swiss supplier in six months. The U.S. parent contemplates purchasing a Swiss franc call option to hedge this foreign exchange risk. Whether it is acceptable for the U.S. parent corporation to use hedge accounting for the hedge of a forecasted foreign currency transaction of its French subsidiary is in question. Search the FASB's *Original Pronouncements* using either hard copy or the Financial Accounting Research System (FARS) database.

Required:

1. Identify the authoritative pronouncement and paragraph(s) within it that provide an answer to the issue in question.
2. Summarize the FASB's response with respect to the question that has arisen.

FARS CASE 2—FOREIGN CURRENCY DENOMINATED DEBT

CPA *skills*

Many companies issue fixed-rate foreign currency denominated debt in which the principal and interest payments are made in a foreign currency. There is some question as to whether a foreign currency denominated interest payment should be considered (a) an unrecognized firm commitment that could be designated as a hedged item in a foreign currency fair value hedge or (b) a forecasted transaction that could be designated as the hedged item in a foreign currency cash flow hedge. The FASB's Derivatives Implementation Group (DIG) has addressed many implementation issues including this question. Search the Derivative Instruments and Hedging Activities database in the FASB's Financial Accounting Research System (FARS).

Required:

1. Identify the number of the *Statement 133* Implementation Issue that provides an answer to this issue.
2. Summarize the DIG's response with respect to the issue.

EXCEL CASE—DETERMINE FOREIGN EXCHANGE GAINS AND LOSSES

CPA *skills*

Import/Export Company made a number of import purchases and export sales denominated in foreign currency in 2004. Information related to these transactions is summarized in the following table. The company made each purchase or sale on the date in the Transaction Date column and made payment in foreign currency or received payment on the date in the Settlement Date column.

Foreign Currency	Type of Transaction	Amount in Foreign Currency	Transaction Date	Settlement Date
Brazilian real (BRL)	Import purchase	$ (147,700)	2/2/2004	8/2/2004
Swiss franc (CHF)	Import purchase	(63,600)	3/1/2004	4/30/2004
Euro (EUR)	Export sale	40,500	4/1/2004	7/2/2004
South African rand (ZAR)	Export sale	347,200	4/30/2004	11/1/2004
Chinese yuan (CNY)	Export sale	413,900	6/1/2004	8/31/2004
Thai baht (THB)	Import purchase	(2,045,000)	7/2/2004	10/1/2004
British pound (GBP)	Import purchase	(27,400)	8/2/2004	11/1/2004
South Korean won (KRW)	Import purchase	(57,700,000)	8/31/2004	11/30/2004

Required:

1. Create an electronic spreadsheet with the information from the preceding table. Label columns as follows:

   Foreign Currency
   Type of Transaction
   Amount in Foreign Currency
   Transaction Date
   Exchange Rate at Transaction Date
   $ Value at Transaction Date
   Settlement Date
   Exchange Rate at Settlement Date
   $ Value at Settlement Date
   Foreign Exchange Gain (Loss)

2. Use historical exchange rate information available on the Internet at www.x-rates.com, Historic Lookup, to find the 2004 exchange rates between the U.S. dollar and each foreign currency on the relevant transaction and settlement dates.

3. Complete the electronic spreadsheet to determine the foreign exchange gain (loss) on each transaction. Determine the total net foreign exchange gain (loss) reported in Import/Export Company's 2004 income statement.

ANALYSIS CASE—CASH FLOW HEDGE

On February 1, 2007, Linber Company forecasted the purchase of component parts on May 1, 2007, at a price of 100,000 euros. On that date, Linber Company entered into a forward contract to purchase 100,000 euros on May 1, 2007. It designated the forward contract as a cash flow hedge of the forecasted transaction. The spot rate for euros on February 1, 2007, is $1 per euro. On May 1, 2007, the forward contract was settled, and the component parts were received and paid for. The parts were consumed in the second quarter of 2007.

Linber Company's financial statements reported the following amounts related to this cash flow hedge (credit balances in parentheses):

Income Statement	First Quarter 2007	Second Quarter 2007
Premium expense	$4,000	$ 2,000
Cost of goods sold	—	103,000
Adjustment to net income	—	3,000

Balance Sheet	3/31/07	5/1/07
Forward contract (liability)	$(1,980)*	—
AOCI (credit)	(2,020)	—
Change in cash	N/A	$(106,000)

*$2,000 × 0.9901 = $1,980, where 0.9901 is the present value factor for one month at an annual interest rate of 12 percent calculated as 1/1.01.

Required:

1. On January 15, 2007, what was the U.S. dollar per euro forward rate to May 1, 2007?

2. On March 31, 2007, what was the U.S. dollar per euro forward rate to May 1, 2007?

3. Was Linber Company better off or worse off as a result of having entered into this cash flow hedge of a forecasted transaction? By what amount?

4. What does the total premium expense of $6,000 reflect?

INTERNET CASE—HISTORICAL EXCHANGE RATES

The Pier Ten Company made credit sales to three customers in Asia on December 15, 2004, and received payment on January 14, 2005. Information related to these sales is as follows:

Customer	Location	Invoice Price
Hang Fung Trading Ltd.	Hong Kong, China	500,000 Hong Kong dollars
Daeron Industrial Company	Seoul, South Korea	66,350,000 Korean won
Siam Commercial Ltd.	Bangkok, Thailand	2,500,000 Thai baht

The Pier Ten Company's fiscal year ends December 31.

Required:

1. Use historical exchange rate information available on the Internet at www.x-rates.com, Historic Lookup, to find exchange rates between the U.S. dollar and each foreign currency for December 15, 2004, December 31, 2004, and January 14, 2005.

2. Determine the foreign exchange gains and losses that Pier Ten would have recognized in net income in 2004 and 2005, and the overall foreign exchange gain or loss for each transaction. Determine for which transaction it would have been most important for Pier Ten to hedge its foreign exchange risk.

3. Pier Ten could have acquired a one-month put option on December 15, 2004, to hedge the foreign exchange risk associated with each of the three export sales. In each case, the put option would have cost $100 with the strike price equal to the December 15, 2004, spot rate. Determine for which hedges, if any, Pier Ten would have recognized a net gain on the foreign currency option.

COMMUNICATION CASE—FORWARD CONTRACTS AND OPTIONS

Palmetto Bug Extermination Corporation (PBEC) regularly purchases chemicals from a supplier in Switzerland with the invoice price denominated in Swiss francs. PBEC has experienced several foreign exchange losses in the past year due to increases in the U.S. dollar price of the Swiss currency. As a result, Dewey Nukem, PBEC's CEO, has asked you to investigate the possibility of using derivative financial instruments, specifically foreign currency forward contracts and foreign currency options, to hedge the company's exposure to foreign exchange risk.

Required:

Draft a memo to CEO Nukem comparing the advantages and disadvantages of using forward contracts and options to hedge foreign exchange risk. Recommend the type of hedging instrument you believe the company should employ and justify this recommendation.

Chapter **Ten**

Translation of Foreign Currency Financial Statements

Questions to Consider

- What is a translation adjustment? How is it computed? Where should it be reported in a set of consolidated financial statements?

- What is balance sheet exposure and how does it compare with transaction exposure to foreign exchange risk?

- What are the different concepts underlying the temporal and current rate methods of translation? How does balance sheet exposure differ under these two methods of translation?

- What is a company's functional currency? How is this functional currency identified?

- When is remeasurement appropriate rather than translation of foreign currency balances?

- How does a remeasurement differ from a translation?

- Why would a company hedge a balance sheet exposure and how is this accounted for?

- In one of the biggest foreign investments in Russia outside the energy sector, Coca-Cola Co. and one of its bottlers said they agreed to buy Multon Co., the No. 2 juice maker in Russia, the fifth-largest juice market in the world.[1]

- UPS today announced it has agreed to acquire Messenger Service Stolica S.A., one of the leading parcel and express delivery companies in Poland.[2]

- In an acquisition described as both the largest ever undertaken by a Mexican company and the most expensive takeover in the global construction materials business, Monterrey's Cemex SA, the world's third-largest cement producer, has agreed to purchase U.K.-based ready mixed giant RMC Group Plc for $4.15 billion in cash.[3]

- Kuwaiti wireless operator Mobile Telecommunications Co. said it will buy pan-African telecommunications company Celtel International BV for $3.4 billion gaining access to one of the world's fastest-growing regions.[4]

Recent announcements such as these have become more the norm than the exception in today's global economy. Companies establish operations in foreign countries for a variety of reasons including the development of new markets for their products, taking advantage of lower production costs, or gaining access to raw materials. Some multinational companies have reached a stage in their development in which domestic operations are no longer considered to be of higher priority than international operations. For example, U.S.-based International Flavors and Fragrances, Inc., has operations in 43 countries and has 66 percent of its segment assets outside North America. Coca-Cola Company generates more than 69 percent of its sales and 75 percent of its operating profit from foreign operations.

---

[1] *The Wall Street Journal,* April 1, 2005, p. A3.

[2] UPS Press Release, February 7, 2005, www.pressroom.ups.com.

[3] *Cement Americas,* September 1, 2004, cementamericas.com.

[4] *The Wall Street Journal,* March 30, 2005, p. B3.

Foreign operations create numerous managerial problems for the parent company that do not exist for domestic operations. Some of these problems arise from cultural differences between the home and foreign countries. Other problems exist because foreign operations generally are required to comply with the laws and regulations of the foreign country. For example, most countries require companies to prepare financial statements in the local currency using local accounting rules.

To prepare worldwide consolidated financial statements, a U.S. parent company must (1) convert the foreign GAAP financial statements of its foreign operations into U.S. GAAP and (2) translate the financial statements from the foreign currency into U.S. dollars. This conversion and translation process must be carried out regardless of whether the foreign operation is a branch, joint venture, majority-owned subsidiary, or affiliate accounted for under the equity method. Differences in GAAP and problems associated with those differences are discussed in the next chapter. This chapter deals with the issue of translating foreign currency financial statements into the parent's reporting currency.

Two major theoretical issues are related to the translation process: (1) which **translation method** should be used and (2) where the resulting **translation adjustment** should be reported in the consolidated financial statements. In this chapter, these two issues are examined first from a conceptual perspective and second by the manner in which the FASB in the United States has resolved these issues.

EXCHANGE RATES USED IN TRANSLATION

Two types of exchange rates are used in translating financial statements:

1. **Historical exchange rate**—the exchange rate that exists when a transaction occurs.
2. **Current exchange rate**—the exchange rate that exists at the balance sheet date.

Translation methods differ as to which balance sheet and income statement accounts to translate at historical exchange rates and which to translate at current exchange rates.

Assume that the company described in the discussion question on the next page began operations in Gualos on December 31, 2007, when the exchange rate was $0.20 per vilsek. When Southwestern Corporation prepares its consolidated balance sheet at December 31, 2007, it had no choice about the exchange rate it uses to translate the Land account into U.S. dollars. It translates the Land account carried on the foreign subsidiary's books at 150,000 vilseks at an exchange rate of $0.20; $0.20 was both the *historical* and *current* exchange rate for the Land account at December 31, 2007.

Consolidated Balance Sheet: 12/31/07
Land (150,000 vilseks × $0.20) $30,000

During the first quarter of 2008, the vilsek appreciates relative to the U.S. dollar by 15 percent; the exchange rate at March 31, 2008, is $0.23 per vilsek. In preparing its balance sheet at the end of the first quarter of 2008, Southwestern now must decide whether the Land account carried on the subsidiary's balance sheet at 150,000 vilseks should be translated into dollars using the *historical exchange rate* of $0.20 or the *current exchange rate* of $0.23.

If the historical exchange rate is used at March 31, 2008, Land continues to be carried on the consolidated balance sheet at $30,000 with no change from December 31, 2007.

Historical Rate—Consolidated Balance Sheet: 3/31/08
Land (150,000 vilseks × $0.20) $30,000

HOW DO WE REPORT THIS?

The Southwestern Corporation operates throughout Texas buying and selling widgets. In hopes of expanding into more profitable markets, the company recently decided to open a small subsidiary in the nearby country of Gualos. The currency in Gualos is the vilsek. For some time, the government of that country held the exchange rate constant: 1 vilsek equaled $0.20 (or 5 vilseks equaled $1.00). Initially, Southwestern invested cash in this new operation; its $90,000 was converted into 450,000 vilseks ($90,000 × 5). Southwestern used one-third of this money (150,000 vilseks, or $30,000) to purchase land to hold for the possible construction of a plant, invested one-third in short-term marketable securities, and spent one-third in acquiring inventory for future resale.

Shortly thereafter, the Gualos government officially revalued the currency so that 1 vilsek was worth $0.23. Because of the strength of the local economy, the vilsek gained buying power in relation to the U.S. dollar. The vilsek then was considered more valuable than in the past. The accountants for Southwestern realized that a change had occurred; each of the assets was now worth more in U.S. dollars than the original $30,000 investment: 150,000 vilseks × $0.23 = $34,500. Two of the company's top officers met to determine the appropriate method for reporting this change in currency values.

Controller: Nothing has changed. Our cost is still $30,000 for each item. That's what we spent. Accounting uses historical cost wherever possible. Thus, we should do nothing.

Finance director: Yes, but the old rates are meaningless now. We would be foolish to report figures based on a rate that no longer exists. The cost is still 150,000 vilseks for each item. You are right, the cost has not changed. However, the vilsek is now worth $0.23, so our reported value must change.

Controller: The new rate affects us only if we take money out of the country. We don't plan to do that for many years. The rate will probably change 20 more times before we remove money from Gualos. We've got to stick to our $30,000 historical cost. That's our cost and that's good, basic accounting.

Finance director: You mean that for the next 20 years we will be translating balances for external reporting purposes using an exchange rate that has not existed for years? That doesn't make sense. I have a real problem using an antiquated rate for the investments and inventory. They will be sold for cash when the new rate is in effect. These balances have no remaining relation to the original exchange rate.

Controller: You misunderstand the impact of an exchange rate fluctuation. Within Gualos, no impact occurs. One vilsek is still one vilsek. The effect is realized only when an actual conversion takes place into U.S. dollars at a new rate. At that point, we will properly measure and report the gain or loss. That is when realization takes place. Until then our cost has not changed.

Finance director: I simply see no value at all in producing financial information based entirely on an exchange rate that does not exist. I don't care when realization takes place.

Controller: You've got to stick with historical cost, believe me. The exchange rate today isn't important unless we actually convert vilseks to dollars.

How should Southwestern report each of these three assets on its current balance sheet? Does the company have a gain because the value of the vilsek has increased relative to the U.S. dollar?

If the current exchange rate is used, Land is carried on the consolidated balance sheet at $34,500, an increase of $4,500 from December 31, 2007.

Current Rate—Consolidated Balance Sheet: 3/31/08	
Land (150,000 vilseks × $0.23)	$34,500

Translation Adjustments

To keep the accounting equation (A = L + OE) in balance, the increase of $4,500 on the asset (A) side of the consolidated balance sheet when the current exchange rate is used must be offset by an equal $4,500 *increase* in owners' equity (OE) on the other side of the balance sheet. The increase in owners' equity is called a **positive translation adjustment.** It has a *credit* balance.

The increase in dollar value of the Land due to appreciation of the vilsek creates a positive translation adjustment. This is true for any asset on the Gualos subsidiary's balance sheet that is translated at the *current* exchange rate. *Assets translated at the current exchange rate when the foreign currency has appreciated generate a positive (credit) translation adjustment.*

Liabilities on the Gualos subsidiary's balance sheet that are translated at the current exchange rate also increase in dollar value when the vilsek appreciates. For example, Southwestern would report Notes Payable of 10,000 vilseks at $2,000 on the December 31, 2007, balance sheet and at $2,300 on the March 31, 2008, balance sheet. To keep the accounting equation in balance, the increase in liabilities (L) must be offset by a *decrease* in owners' equity (OE), giving rise to a **negative translation adjustment.** This has a *debit* balance. *Liabilities translated at the current exchange rate when the foreign currency has appreciated generate a negative (debit) translation adjustment.*

Balance Sheet Exposure

Balance sheet items (assets and liabilities) translated at the *current* exchange rate change in dollar value from balance sheet to balance sheet as a result of the change in exchange rate. These items are *exposed* to translation adjustment. Balance sheet items translated at *historical* exchange rates do not change in dollar value from one balance sheet to the next. These items are *not* exposed to translation adjustment. Exposure to translation adjustment is referred to as *balance sheet, translation,* or *accounting exposure.* **Balance sheet exposure** can be contrasted with the **transaction exposure** discussed in Chapter 9 that arises when a company has foreign currency receivables and payables in the following way: *Transaction exposure gives rise to foreign exchange gains and losses that are ultimately realized in cash; translation adjustments arising from balance sheet exposure do not directly result in cash inflows or outflows.*

Each item translated at the current exchange rate is exposed to translation adjustment. In effect, a separate translation adjustment exists for each of these exposed items. However, negative translation adjustments on liabilities offset positive translation adjustments on assets when the foreign currency appreciates. If total exposed assets equal total exposed liabilities throughout the year, the translation adjustments (although perhaps significant on an individual basis) net to a zero balance. The *net* translation adjustment needed to keep the consolidated balance sheet in balance is based solely on the *net asset* or *net liability* exposure.

A foreign operation has a **net asset balance sheet exposure** when assets translated at the current exchange rate are larger in amount than liabilities translated at the current exchange rate. A **net liability balance sheet exposure** exists when liabilities translated at the current exchange rate are larger than assets translated at the current exchange rate. The following summarizes the relationship between exchange rate fluctuations, balance sheet exposure, and translation adjustments:

Balance Sheet Exposure	Foreign Currency (FC)	
	Appreciates	**Depreciates**
Net asset	Positive translation adjustment	Negative translation adjustment
Net liability	Negative translation adjustment	Positive translation adjustment

Exactly how to handle the translation adjustment in the consolidated financial statements is a matter of some debate. The major issue is whether the translation adjustment should be treated as a *translation gain or loss reported in net income* or whether the translation adjustment should be treated as a *direct adjustment to owners' equity without affecting net income.* We consider this issue in more detail later after examining methods of translation.

TRANSLATION METHODS

Two major methods of translation are currently used: (1) the current rate (or closing rate) method and (2) the temporal method. We discuss these methods from the perspective of a U.S.-based multinational company translating foreign currency financial statements into U.S. dollars.

Current Rate Method

The basic assumption underlying the **current rate method** is that a company's *net investment* in a foreign operation is *exposed* to foreign exchange risk. In other words, a foreign operation represents a foreign currency net asset and if the foreign currency *decreases* in value against the U.S. dollar, a *decrease in the U.S. dollar value of the foreign currency net asset* occurs. This decrease in U.S. dollar value of the net investment will be reflected by reporting a *negative* (debit balance) translation adjustment in the consolidated financial statements. If the foreign currency *increases* in value, an *increase in the U.S. dollar value of the net asset* occurs and will be reflected through a *positive* (credit balance) translation adjustment.

To measure the net investment's exposure to foreign exchange risk, *all assets and all liabilities* of the foreign operation are translated at the *current* exchange rate. Stockholders' equity items are translated at historical rates. *The balance sheet exposure under the current rate method is equal to the foreign operation's net asset (total assets minus total liabilities) position.*[5]

$$\text{Total assets} > \text{Total liabilities} \rightarrow \text{Net asset exposure}$$

A positive translation adjustment arises when the foreign currency appreciates, and a negative translation adjustment arises when the foreign currency depreciates.

As mentioned earlier, the major difference between the translation adjustment and a foreign exchange gain or loss is that the translation adjustment is not necessarily realized through inflows and outflows of cash. The translation adjustment arising when using the current rate method is unrealized. It can become a realized gain or loss only if the foreign operation is sold (for its book value) and the foreign currency proceeds from the sale are converted into U.S. dollars.

The current rate method requires translation of all income statement items at the exchange rate in effect at the date of accounting recognition. In most cases, an assumption can be made that the revenue or expense is incurred evenly throughout the accounting period and a weighted average-for-the-period exchange rate can be used for translation. However, when an income account, such as a gain or loss, occurs at a specific point in time, the exchange rate at that date should be used for translation.[6]

Temporal Method

The basic objective underlying the **temporal method** of translation is to produce a set of U.S. dollar–translated financial statements as if the foreign subsidiary had actually used U.S. dollars in conducting its operations. Continuing with the Gualos subsidiary example presented earlier, Southwestern, the U.S. parent, should report the Land account on the consolidated balance sheet at the amount of U.S. dollars that it would have spent if it had sent dollars to the subsidiary to purchase land. Because the land had a cost of 150,000 vilseks at a time when one vilsek could be acquired with $0.20, the parent would have sent $30,000 to the subsidiary to acquire the land; this is the land's historical cost *in U.S. dollar terms*. The following rule is consistent with the temporal method's underlying objective:

1. Assets and liabilities carried on the foreign operation's balance sheet at *historical cost* are translated at *historical* exchange rates to yield an equivalent historical cost in U.S. dollars.
2. Conversely, assets and liabilities carried at a *current or future value* are translated at the *current* exchange rate to yield an equivalent current value in U.S. dollars.

---

[5] In rare cases, a foreign subsidiary could have liabilities greater than assets (negative stockholders' equity). In those cases, a net liability exposure exists under the current rate method.

[6] Alternatively, all income statement items may be translated at the current exchange rate. Later we demonstrate that translation at the current rate has a slight advantage over translation at the average-for-the-period rate.

Application of this rule maintains the underlying valuation method (current value or historical cost) that the foreign subsidiary uses in accounting for its assets and liabilities. In addition, stockholders' equity accounts are translated at historical exchange rates.

Cash, marketable securities, receivables, and most liabilities are carried at current or future value and translated at the *current* exchange rate under the temporal method.[7] The temporal method generates either a net asset or a net liability balance sheet exposure, depending on whether cash plus marketable securities plus receivables are more than or less than liabilities.

$$\text{Cash} + \text{Marketable securities} + \text{Receivables} > \text{Liabilities} \rightarrow \text{Net asset exposure}$$

$$\text{Cash} + \text{Marketable securities} + \text{Receivables} < \text{Liabilities} \rightarrow \text{Net liability exposure}$$

Because liabilities (current plus long term) usually are more than assets translated at the current exchange rate, *a net liability exposure generally exists when the temporal method is used.*

One way to understand the concept of exposure underlying the temporal method is to pretend that the parent actually carries the foreign operation's cash, marketable securities, receivables, and payables on the parent's balance sheet. For example, consider the Japanese subsidiary of a U.S. parent company. The Japanese yen receivables of the Japanese subsidiary that result from sales in Japan may be thought of as Japanese yen receivables of the U.S. parent that result from export sales to Japan. If the U.S. parent had yen receivables on its balance sheet, a decrease in the value of the yen would result in a *foreign exchange loss*. A foreign exchange loss also occurs on the Japanese yen held in cash by the U.S. parent and on the Japanese yen denominated marketable securities. A foreign exchange gain on the parent's Japanese yen payables resulting from foreign purchases would offset these foreign exchange losses. Whether a net gain or a net loss exists depends on the relative amount of yen cash, marketable securities, and receivables versus yen payables. Under the temporal method, the translation adjustment measures the "net foreign exchange gain or loss" on the foreign operation's cash, marketable securities, receivables, and payables, *as if those items were actually carried on the books of the parent.*

Again, the major difference between the translation adjustment resulting from the use of the temporal method and a foreign exchange gain or loss is that the translation adjustment is not necessarily realized through inflows or outflows of cash. The U.S. dollar translation adjustment in this case *could be realized* only if (1) the parent sends U.S. dollars to the Japanese subsidiary to pay off all its yen liabilities and (2) the Japanese subsidiary converts its yen receivables and marketable securities into yen cash and then sends this amount plus the amount in its yen cash account to the parent in the United States where it is converted into U.S. dollars.

The temporal method translates income statement items at exchange rates that exist when the revenue is generated or the expense is incurred. For most items, an assumption can be made that the revenue or expense is incurred evenly throughout the accounting period and an average-for-the-period exchange rate can be used for translation. However, some expenses are related to assets carried at historical cost—for example, cost of goods sold, depreciation of fixed assets, and amortization of intangibles. Because the related assets are translated at historical exchange rates, these expenses must be translated at historical rates as well.

The current rate method and temporal method are the two methods currently used in the United States. They are also the predominant methods used worldwide. A summary of the appropriate exchange rate for selected financial statement items under these two methods is presented in Exhibit 10.1.

Translation of Retained Earnings

Stockholders' equity items are translated at historical exchange rates under both the temporal and current rate methods. This creates somewhat of a problem in translating retained

---

[7] Under *SFAS 105*, all marketable equity securities and marketable debt securities that are classified as "trading" or "available for sale" are carried at current market value. Marketable debt securities classified as "hold to maturity" are carried at cost. Throughout the remainder of this chapter, we will assume that all marketable securities are reported at current value.

EXHIBIT 10.1
Exchange Rates for Selected Financial Statement Items

	Temporal Method Exchange Rate	Current Rate Method Exchange Rate
Balance Sheet		
Assets		
Cash and receivables	Current	Current
Marketable securities	Current*	Current
Inventory at market	Current	Current
Inventory at cost	Historical	Current
Prepaid expenses	Historical	Current
Property, plant, and equipment	Historical	Current
Intangible assets	Historical	Current
Liabilities		
Current liabilities	Current	Current
Deferred income	Historical	Current
Long-term debt	Current	Current
Stockholders' equity		
Capital stock	Historical	Historical
Additional paid-in capital	Historical	Historical
Retained earnings	Composite	Composite
Dividends	Historical	Historical
Income Statement		
Revenues	Average	Average
Most expenses	Average	Average
Cost of goods sold	Historical	Average
Depreciation of property, plant, and equipment	Historical	Average
Amortization of intangibles	Historical	Average

*Marketable debt securities classified as hold to maturity are carried at cost and translated at the historical exchange rate under the temporal method.

earnings. This figure is actually a composite of many previous transactions: all revenues, expenses, gains, losses, and declared dividends occurring over the life of the company. At the end of the first year of operations, foreign currency (FC) retained earnings is translated as follows:

Net income in FC	[translated per method used to translate income statement items]	= Net income in $
− Dividends in FC	× historical exchange rate when declared	= − Dividends in $
Ending R/E in FC		Ending R/E in $

The ending dollar amount of retained earnings in Year 1 becomes the beginning dollar retained earnings for Year 2, and the translated retained earnings in Year 2 (and subsequent years) is then determined as follows:

Beginning R/E in FC	(from last year's translation)	= Beginning R/E in $
+ Net income in FC	[translated per method used to translate income statement items]	= + Net income in $
− Dividends in FC	× historical exchange rate when declared	= − Dividends in $
Ending R/E in FC		Ending R/E in $

The same approach translates retained earnings under both the current rate and the temporal methods. The only difference is that translation of the current period's net income is calculated differently under the two methods.

COMPLICATING ASPECTS OF THE TEMPORAL METHOD

Under the temporal method, keeping a record of the exchange rates is necessary when acquiring inventory, prepaid expenses, fixed assets, and intangible assets because these assets, carried at historical cost, are translated at historical exchange rates. Keeping track of the historical rates for these assets is not necessary under the current rate method. Translating these assets at historical rates makes the application of the temporal method more complicated than the current rate method.

Calculation of Cost of Goods Sold (COGS)

Under the *current rate method,* the account COGS in foreign currency (FC) is simply translated using the average-for-the-period exchange rate (ER):

$$\text{COGS in FC} \times \text{Average ER} = \text{COGS in \$}$$

Under the *temporal method,* COGS must be decomposed into beginning inventory, purchases, and ending inventory, and each component of COGS must then be translated at its appropriate historical rate. For example, if a company acquires beginning inventory (FIFO basis) in the year 2007 evenly throughout the fourth quarter of 2006, then it uses the average exchange rate in the fourth quarter of 2006 to translate beginning inventory. Likewise, it uses the fourth quarter (4thQ) 2007 exchange rate to translate ending inventory. When purchases can be assumed to have been made evenly throughout 2007, the average 2007 exchange rate is used to translate purchases:

Beginning inventory in FC	×	Historical ER (4thQ 2006)	=	Beginning inventory in $
+ Purchases in FC	×	Average ER (2007)	=	+ Purchases in $
− Ending inventory in FC	×	Historical ER (4thQ 2007)	=	− Ending inventory in $
COGS in FC				COGS in $

No single exchange rate can be used to directly translate COGS in FC into COGS in dollars.

Application of the Lower-of-Cost-or-Market Rule

Under the *current rate method,* the ending inventory reported on the foreign currency balance sheet is translated at the current exchange rate regardless of whether it is carried at cost or a lower market value. Application of the *temporal method* requires the foreign currency cost and foreign currency market value of the inventory to be translated into U.S. dollars at appropriate exchange rates, and the *lower of the dollar cost and dollar market value* is reported on the consolidated balance sheet. As a result of this procedure, inventory can be carried at cost on the foreign currency balance sheet and at market value on the U.S. dollar consolidated balance sheet, and vice versa.

Fixed Assets, Depreciation, Accumulated Depreciation

The *temporal method* requires translating fixed assets acquired at different times at different (historical) exchange rates. The same is true for depreciation of fixed assets and accumulated depreciation related to fixed assets.

For example, assume that a company purchases a piece of equipment on January 1, 2007, for FC 1,000 when the exchange rate is $1.00 per FC. It purchases another item of equipment on January 1, 2008, for FC 5,000 when the exchange rate is $1.20 per FC. Both pieces of equipment have a five-year useful life. The temporal method would report the amount of the equipment on the consolidated balance sheet on December 31, 2009, when the exchange rate is $1.50 per FC, as follows:

$$
\begin{array}{rll}
\text{FC } 1,000 \times \$1.00 = & \$1,000 \\
5,000 \times \ \ 1.20 = & \underline{6,000} \\
\text{FC } 6,000 & \$7,000
\end{array}
$$

Depreciation expense for 2009 under the temporal method is calculated as shown here:

$$
\begin{array}{rl}
\text{FC} \quad 200 \times \$1.00 = & \$ \ \ 200 \\
\underline{1,000} \times \ \ 1.20 = & \underline{1,200} \\
\text{FC } 1,200 & \$1,400 \\
\end{array}
$$

Accumulated depreciation under the temporal method is calculated as shown:

$$
\begin{array}{rl}
\text{FC} \quad 600 \times \$1.00 = & \$ \ \ 600 \\
\underline{2,000} \times \ \ 1.20 = & \underline{2,400} \\
\text{FC } 2,600 & \$3,000 \\
\end{array}
$$

Similar procedures apply for intangible assets as well.

The *current rate method* would report equipment on the December 31, 2009, balance sheet at FC 6,000 × $1.50 = $9,000. Depreciation expense would be translated at the average exchange rate of $1.40, FC 1,200 × $1.40 = $1,680, and accumulated depreciation would be FC 2,600 × $1.50 = $3,900.

In this example, the foreign subsidiary has only two fixed assets requiring translation. The temporal method can require substantial additional work for subsidiaries that own hundreds and thousands of fixed assets as compared to the current rate method.

Gain or Loss on the Sale of an Asset

Assume that a foreign subsidiary sells land that cost FC 1,000 at a selling price of FC 1,200. The subsidiary reports a gain on the sale of land of FC 200 on its income statement. It acquired the land when the exchange rate was $1.00 per FC; it made the sale when the exchange rate was $1.20 per FC; and the exchange rate at the balance sheet date is $1.50 per FC.

The *current rate method* translates the gain on sale of land at the exchange rate in effect at the date of sale:

$$
\text{FC } 200 \times \$1.20 = \$240
$$

The *temporal method* cannot translate the gain on the sale of land directly. Instead, it requires translating the cash received and the cost of the land sold into U.S. dollars separately, with the difference being the U.S. dollar value of the gain. In accordance with the rules of the temporal method, the Cash account is translated at the exchange rate on the date of sale, and the Land account is translated at the historical rate:

$$
\begin{array}{llr}
\text{Cash} & \text{FC } 1,200 \times \$1.20 = & \$1,440 \\
\text{Land} & \underline{1,000} \times \ \ 1.00 = & \underline{1,000} \\
\text{Gain} & \text{FC} \quad 200 & \$ \ \ 440 \\
\end{array}
$$

DISPOSITION OF TRANSLATION ADJUSTMENT

The *first issue* related to the translation of foreign currency financial statements is selecting the appropriate method. The *second issue* in financial statement translation relates to deciding *where to report the resulting translation adjustment in the consolidated financial statements.* There are two prevailing schools of thought with regard to this issue:

1. **Translation gain or loss:** This treatment considers the translation adjustment to be a gain or loss analogous to the gains and losses arising from foreign currency transactions and reports it in net income in the period in which the fluctuation in the exchange rate occurs.

The first of two conceptual problems with treating translation adjustments as gains or losses in income is that the gain or loss is unrealized; that is, no cash inflow or outflow accompanies it. The second problem is that the gain or loss could be inconsistent with economic reality. For example, the depreciation of a foreign currency can have a *positive* impact on the foreign operation's export sales and income, but the particular translation method used gives rise to a translation *loss*.

2. **Cumulative translation adjustment in other comprehensive income:** The alternative to reporting the translation adjustment as a gain or loss in net income is to include it in Other Comprehensive Income. In effect, this treatment defers the gain or loss in stockholders' equity until it is realized in some way. As a balance sheet account, the cumulative translation adjustment is not closed at the end of an accounting period and will fluctuate in amount over time.

The two major translation methods and the two possible treatments for the translation adjustment give rise to these four possible combinations:

Combination	Translation Method	Treatment of Translation Adjustment
A	Temporal	Gain or loss in Net Income
B	Temporal	Deferred in Other Comprehensive Income
C	Current rate	Gain or loss in Net Income
D	Current rate	Deferred in Other Comprehensive Income

U.S. RULES

Prior to 1975, the United States had no authoritative rules about which translation method to use or where to report the translation adjustment in the consolidated financial statements. Different companies used different combinations. As an indication of the importance of this particular accounting issue, the first official pronouncement issued by the newly created FASB in 1974 was *SFAS 1,* "Disclosure of Foreign Currency Translation Information." *SFAS 1* did not express a preference for any particular combination but simply required disclosure of the method used and the treatment of the translation adjustment.

The use of different combinations by different companies created a lack of comparability across companies. To eliminate this noncomparability, in 1975 the FASB issued *SFAS 8,* "Accounting for the Translation of Foreign Currency Transactions and Foreign Currency Financial Statements." *SFAS 8* mandated use of the *temporal method* with all companies reporting *translation gains or losses* in net income for all foreign operations (Combination A).

U.S. multinational companies (MNCs) were strongly opposed to *SFAS 8.* Specifically, they considered reporting translation gains and losses in income to be inappropriate because they are unrealized. Moreover, because currency fluctuations often reversed themselves in subsequent quarters, artificial volatility in quarterly earnings resulted.

After releasing two exposure drafts proposing new translation rules, the FASB finally issued *SFAS 52,* "Foreign Currency Translation," in 1981. This resulted in a complete overhaul of U.S. GAAP with regard to foreign currency translation. A narrow four-to-three vote of the Board approving *SFAS 52* indicates how contentious the issue of foreign currency translation has been.

SFAS 52

Implicit in the **temporal method** is the assumption that foreign subsidiaries of U.S. MNCs have very close ties to their parent companies and that they would actually carry out their day-to-day operations and keep their books in the U.S. dollar if they could. To reflect the integrated nature of the foreign subsidiary with its U.S. parent, the translation process should create a set of U.S. dollar–translated financial statements as if the foreign subsidiary had actually used the dollar in carrying out its activities. This is the **U.S. dollar perspective** to translation that *SFAS 8* adopted.

In *SFAS 52,* the FASB recognized two types of foreign entities. First, some foreign entities are so closely integrated with their parents that they do conduct much of their business in U.S. dollars. *Second, other foreign entities are relatively self-contained and integrated with the local economy; primarily, they use a foreign currency in their daily operations.* For the first type of entity, the FASB determined that the U.S. dollar perspective still applies and, therefore, *SFAS 8* rules are still relevant.

For the second relatively independent type of entity, a **local currency perspective** to translation is applicable. For this type of entity, the FASB determined that a different translation methodology, namely the *current rate method,* should be used for translation and that translation adjustments should be reported as a *separate component in other comprehensive income*

(Combination D on page 478). In addition, the FASB requires using the *average-for-the-period* exchange rate in translating income when the current rate method is used.

In rationalizing the placement of the translation adjustment in stockholders' equity rather than net income, *SFAS 52* (paras. 113, 114) offered two contrasting positions on the conceptual nature of the translation adjustment. One view is that the "change in the dollar equivalent of the net investment is an unrealized enhancement or reduction, having no effect on the functional currency net cash flow generated by the foreign entity which may be currently reinvested or distributed to the parent." Philosophically, this position holds that even though changes in the exchange rate create gains and losses, they are unrealized in nature and should, therefore, not be included within net income.

The alternative perspective put forth by the FASB "regards the translation adjustment as merely a mechanical by-product of the translation process." This second contention argues that exchange rate fluctuation creates no meaningful effect; the resulting translation adjustment merely serves to keep the balance sheet in equilibrium.

Interestingly enough, the FASB chose not to express preference for either of these theoretical views. The Board felt no need to offer a hint of guidance as to the essential nature of the translation adjustment because both explanations point to its exclusion from net income. Thus, a balance sheet figure that can amount to millions of dollars is basically undefined.

Functional Currency

To determine whether a specific foreign operation is integrated with its parent or self-contained and integrated with the local economy, *SFAS 52* created the concept of the **functional currency.** The functional currency is the primary currency of the foreign entity's operating environment. It can be either the parent's currency (U.S.$) or a foreign currency (generally the local currency). *SFAS 52*'s functional currency orientation results in the following rule:

Functional Currency	Translation Method	Translation Adjustment
U.S. dollar	Temporal method	Gain (loss) in Net Income
Foreign currency	Current rate method	Separate component of Other Comprehensive Income (Stockholders' Equity)

In addition to introducing the concept of the *functional currency, SFAS 52* introduced some new terminology. The **reporting currency** is the currency in which the entity prepares its financial statements. For U.S.-based corporations, this is the U.S. dollar. If a foreign operation's functional currency is the U.S. dollar, foreign currency balances must be **remeasured** into U.S. dollars using the temporal method with translation adjustments reported as **remeasurement gains and losses** in income. When a foreign currency is the functional currency, foreign currency balances are **translated** using the current rate method and a **translation adjustment** is reported on the balance sheet.

The functional currency is essentially a matter of fact. However, *SFAS 52* (para. 8) states that for many cases, "management's judgment will be required to determine the functional currency in which financial results and relationships are measured with the greatest degree of relevance and reliability." *SFAS 52* provides a list of indicators to guide parent company management in its determination of a foreign entity's functional currency (see Exhibit 10.2). *SFAS 52* provides no guidance as to how to weight these indicators in determining the functional currency. Leaving the decision about identifying the functional currency up to management allows some leeway in this process. Different companies approach this selection in different ways:

> "For us it was intuitively obvious," versus "It was quite a process. We took the six criteria and developed a matrix. We then considered the dollar amount and the related percentages in developing a point scheme. Each of the separate criteria was given equal weight (in the analytical methods applied)."[8]

[8] Jerry L. Arnold and William W. Holder, *Impact of Statement 52 on Decisions, Financial Reports and Attitudes* (Morristown, NJ: Financial Executives Research Foundation, 1986), p. 89.

Indicator	Indication That Functional Currency Is the	
	Foreign Currency	**Parent's Currency**
Cash flow	Primarily in FC and does not affect parent's cash flows	Directly impacts parent's cash flows on a current basis
Sales price	Not affected on short-term basis by changes in exchange rate	Affected on short-term basis by changes in exchange rate
Sales market	Active local sales market	Sales market mostly in parent's country or sales denominated in parent's currency
Expenses	Primarily local costs	Primarily costs for components obtained from parent's country
Financing	Primarily denominated in foreign currency and FC cash flows adequate to service obligations	Primarily from parent or denominated in parent currency or FC cash flows not adequate to service obligations
Intercompany transactions	Low volume of intercompany transactions, not extensive interrelationship with parent's operations	High volume of intercompany transactions and extensive interrelationship with parent's operations

Research has shown that the weighting schemes used by U.S. multinationals for determining the functional currency might be biased toward selection of the *foreign currency* as the functional currency.[9] This would be rational behavior for multinationals because, when the foreign currency is the functional currency, the translation adjustment is reported in stockholders' equity and does not affect net income.

Highly Inflationary Economies

Multinationals do not need to determine the functional currency of those foreign entities located in a **highly inflationary economy**; *SFAS 52* mandates the use of the *temporal method with remeasurement gains or losses reported in income.*

A country is defined has having a *highly inflationary economy* when its cumulative three-year inflation exceeds 100 percent. With compounding, this equates to an average of approximately 26 percent per year for three years in a row. Countries that have met this definition at some time since *SFAS 52* was implemented include Argentina, Brazil, Israel, Mexico, and Turkey. In any given year, a country may or may not be classified as highly inflationary, depending on its most recent three-year experience with inflation.

One reason for this rule is to avoid a "disappearing plant problem" caused by using the current rate method in a country with high inflation. Remember that under the current rate method, all assets (including fixed assets) are translated at the current exchange rate. To see the problem this creates in a highly inflationary economy, consider the following hypothetical example.

The Brazilian subsidiary of a U.S. parent purchased land at the end of 1984 for 10,000,000 cruzeiros (Cr$) when the exchange rate was $0.001 per Cr$. Under the *current rate method,* the land would be reported in the parent's consolidated balance sheet at $10,000:

	Historical Cost		Current ER		Consolidated B.S.
1984	Cr$ 10,000,000	×	$0.001	=	$10,000

In 1985, Brazil experienced roughly 200 percent inflation. Accordingly, with the forces of purchasing power parity at work, the cruzeiro plummeted against the U.S. dollar to a

[9] Timothy S. Doupnik and Thomas G. Evans, "Functional Currency as a Strategy to Smooth Income," *Advances in International Accounting,* 1988.

value of $0.00025 at the end of 1985. Under the current rate method, the parent's consolidated balance sheet now would report land at $2,500, and a negative translation adjustment of $7,500 would result:

$$1985 \quad Cr\$ \ 10,000,000 \times \$0.00025 = \$2,500$$

Using the current rate method, the land has lost 75 percent of its U.S. dollar value in one year—and land is not even a depreciable asset!

High rates of inflation continued in Brazil and reached the high point of roughly 1,800 percent in 1993. As a result of applying the current rate method, the land originally reported on the 1984 consolidated balance sheet at $10,000 was carried on the 1993 balance sheet at less than $1.00.

In the exposure draft leading to *SFAS 52,* the FASB proposed requiring companies with operations in highly inflationary countries to first **restate** the historical costs for inflation and then **translate** using the current rate method. For example, with 200 percent inflation in 1985, the Land account would have been written up to Cr$ 40,000,000 and then translated at the current exchange rate of $0.00025. This would have produced a translated amount of $10,000, the same as in 1984.

Companies objected to making inflation adjustments, however, because of a lack of reliable inflation indices in many countries. The FASB backed off from requiring the **restate/translate** approach; instead *SFAS 52* requires using the temporal method in highly inflationary countries. In the previous example, under the *temporal method,* a firm would use the historical rate of $0.001 to translate the land value year after year. The firm would carry land on the consolidated balance sheet at $10,000 each year, thereby avoiding the disappearing plant problem.

THE PROCESS ILLUSTRATED

To provide a basis for demonstrating the translation and remeasurement procedures prescribed by *SFAS 52,* assume that USCO (a U.S.-based company) forms a wholly owned subsidiary in Switzerland (SWISSCO) on December 31, 2006. On that date, USCO invested $300,000 in exchange for all of the subsidiary's common stock. Given the exchange rate of $0.60 per Swiss franc (CHF), the initial capital investment was CHF 500,000, of which CHF 150,000 was immediately invested in inventory and the remainder held in cash. Thus, SWISSCO began operations on January 1, 2007, with stockholders' equity (net assets) of CHF 500,000 and net monetary assets of CHF 350,000.

SWISSCO Opening Balance Sheet January 1, 2007			
Assets	**CHF**	**Liabilities and Equity**	**CHF**
Cash	CHF 350,000	Common stock	CHF 100,000
Inventory	150,000	Additional paid-in capital	400,000
	CHF 500,000		CHF 500,000

During 2007, SWISSCO purchased property and equipment, acquired a patent, and purchased additional inventory, primarily on account. It negotiated a five-year loan to help finance the purchase of equipment. It sold goods, primarily on account, and incurred expenses. It generated income after taxes of CHF 470,000 and declared dividends of CHF 150,000 on October 1, 2007.

As a company incorporated in Switzerland, SWISSCO must account for its activities using Swiss accounting rules, which differ from U.S. GAAP in many respects. As noted in the introduction to this chapter, to prepare consolidated financial statements, USCO must first convert SWISSCO's financial statements to a U.S. GAAP basis.[10] SWISSCO's U.S. GAAP financial statements for the year 2007 in Swiss francs appear in Exhibit 10.3.

[10] Differences in accounting rules across countries are discussed in more detail in Chapter 11.

EXHIBIT 10.3
Foreign Currency
Financial Statements

SWISSCO
Income Statement
For Year Ending December 31, 2007

	CHF
Sales	4,000,000
Cost of goods sold	(3,000,000)
Gross profit	1,000,000
Depreciation expense	(100,000)
Amortization expense	(10,000)
Other expenses	(220,000)
Income before income taxes	670,000
Income taxes	(200,000)
Net income	470,000

Statement of Retained Earnings
For Year Ending December 31, 2007

	CHF
Retained earnings, 1/1/07	–0–
Net income, 2007	470,000
Less: Dividends, 10/1/07	(150,000)
Retained earnings, 12/31/07	320,000

Balance Sheet
December 31, 2007

Assets	CHF	Liabilities and Equity	CHF
Cash	130,000	Accounts payable	600,000
Accounts receivable	200,000	Total current liabilities	600,000
Inventory*	400,000	Long-term debt	250,000
Total current assets	730,000	Total liabilities	850,000
Property and equipment	1,000,000	Common stock	100,000
Accumulated depreciation	(100,000)	Additional paid-in capital	400,000
Patents, net	40,000	Retained earnings	320,000
Total assets	1,670,000	Total equity	820,000
		Total liabilities and equity	1,670,000

*Inventory is valued at FIFO cost under the lower-of-cost-or-market-value rule; ending inventory was acquired evenly throughout the fourth quarter.

Statement of Cash Flows
For Year Ending December 31, 2007

	CHF
Operating activities:	
Net income	470,000
Add: Depreciation expense	100,000
Amortization expense	10,000
Increase in accounts receivable	(200,000)
Increase in inventory	(250,000)
Increase in accounts payable	600,000
Net cash from operations	730,000
Investing activities:	
Purchase of property and equipment	(1,000,000)
Acquisition of patent	(50,000)
Net cash from investing activities	(1,050,000)
Financing activities:	
Proceeds from long-term debt	250,000
Payment of dividends	(150,000)
Net cash from financing activities	100,000
Decrease in cash	(220,000)
Cash at 12/31/06	350,000
Cash at 12/31/07	130,000

To properly translate the Swiss franc financial statements into U.S. dollars, USCO must gather exchange rates between the Swiss franc and U.S. dollar at various points in time. Relevant exchange rates are as follows:

January 1, 2007	$0.60
Rate when property and equipment were acquired and long-term debt was incurred, March 15, 2007	$0.61
Rate when patent was acquired, April 10, 2007	$0.62
Average 2007	$0.65
Rate when dividends were declared, October 1, 2007	$0.67
Average fourth quarter 2007	$0.68
December 31, 2007	$0.70

As you can see, the Swiss franc steadily appreciated against the dollar during the year.

TRANSLATION OF FINANCIAL STATEMENTS—CURRENT RATE METHOD

The first step in translating foreign currency financial statements is determining the functional currency. Assuming that the Swiss franc is the functional currency, the income statement and statement of retained earnings would be translated into U.S. dollars using the current rate method as shown in Exhibit 10.4.

All revenues and expenses are translated at the exchange rate in effect at the date of accounting recognition. We utilize the weighted average exchange rate for 2007 here because each revenue and expense in this illustration would have been recognized evenly throughout the year. However, when an income account, such as a gain or loss, occurs at a specific point in time, the exchange rate as of that date is applied. Depreciation and amortization expense also are translated at the average rate for the year. These expenses accrue evenly throughout the year even though the journal entry could have been delayed until year-end for convenience.

EXHIBIT 10.4
Translation of Income Statement and Statement of Retained Earnings—Current Rate Method

Income Statement
For Year Ending December 31, 2007

	CHF	Translation Rate*	US$
Sales	CHF 4,000,000	0.65 A	$ 2,600,000
Cost of goods sold	(3,000,000)	0.65 A	(1,950,000)
Gross profit	1,000,000		650,000
Depreciation expense	(100,000)	0.65 A	(65,000)
Amortization expense	(10,000)	0.65 A	(6,500)
Other expenses	(220,000)	0.65 A	(143,000)
Income before income taxes	670,000		435,500
Income taxes	(200,000)	0.65 A	(130,000)
Net income	CHF 470,000		$ 305,500

Statement of Retained Earnings
For Year Ending December 31, 2007

	CHF	Translation Rate*	US$
Retained earnings, 1/1/07	CHF –0–		$ –0–
Net income, 2007	470,000	Above	305,500
Dividends, 10/1/07	(150,000)	0.67 H	(100,500)
Retained earnings, 12/31/07	CHF 320,000		$ 205,000

*Indicates the exchange rate used and whether the rate is the current (C), average (A), or a historical (H) rate.

EXHIBIT 10.5
Translation of Balance Sheet—Current Rate Method

		Balance Sheet December 31, 2007		
	CHF		Translation Rate	US$
Assets				
Cash	CHF	130,000	0.70 C	$ 91,000
Accounts receivable		200,000	0.70 C	140,000
Inventory		400,000	0.70 C	280,000
Total current assets		730,000		511,000
Property and equipment		1,000,000	0.70 C	700,000
Less: Accumulated depreciation		(100,000)	0.70 C	(70,000)
Patents, net		40,000	0.70 C	28,000
Total assets	CHF	1,670,000		$1,169,000
Liabilities and Equities				
Accounts payable	CHF	600,000	0.70 C	$ 420,000
Total current liabilities		600,000		420,000
Long-term debt		250,000	0.70 C	175,000
Total liabilities		850,000		595,000
Common stock		100,000	0.60 H	60,000
Additional paid-in capital		400,000	0.60 H	240,000
Retained earnings		320,000	Above	205,000
Cumulative translation adjustment .			To balance	69,000
Total equity		820,000		574,000
Total liabilities and equity	CHF	1,670,000		$1,169,000

The translated amount of net income for 2007 is brought down from the income statement into the statement of retained earnings. Dividends are translated at the exchange rate on the date of declaration.

Translation of the Balance Sheet

Looking at SWISSCO's translated balance sheet in Exhibit 10.5, note that all assets and liabilities are translated at the current exchange rate. Common stock and additional paid-in capital are translated at the exchange rate on the day the common stock was originally sold. Retained earnings at December 31, 2007, is brought down from the statement of retained earnings. Application of these procedures results in total assets of $1,169,000 and total liabilities and equities of $1,100,000. The balance sheet is brought back into balance by creating a positive translation adjustment of $69,000 that is treated as an increase in Stockholders' Equity.

Note that the translation adjustment for 2007 is a *positive* $69,000 (credit balance). The sign of the translation adjustment (positive or negative) is a function of two factors: (1) the nature of the balance sheet exposure (asset or liability) and (2) the change in the exchange rate (appreciation or depreciation). In this illustration, SWISSCO has a *net asset exposure* (total assets translated at the current exchange rate are more than total liabilities at the current exchange rate), and the Swiss franc has *appreciated*, creating a *positive translation adjustment*.

The translation adjustment can be derived as the amount needed to bring the balance sheet back into balance. The translation adjustment also can be calculated by considering the impact of exchange rate changes on the beginning balance and subsequent changes in the net asset position summarized as follows:

1. Translate the net asset balance of the subsidiary at the beginning of the year at the exchange rate in effect on that date.

2. Translate individual increases and decreases in the net asset balance during the year at the rates in effect when those increases and decreases occurred. Only a few events, such as net income, dividends, stock issuance, and the acquisition of treasury stock, actually change net assets. Transactions such as the acquisition of equipment or the payment of a liability have no effect on total net assets.

3. Combine the translated beginning net asset balance (*a*) and the translated value of the individual changes (*b*) to arrive at the relative value of the net assets being held prior to the impact of any exchange rate fluctuations.

4. Translate the ending net asset balance at the current exchange rate to determine the reported value after all exchange rate changes have occurred.

5. Compare the translated value of the net assets prior to any rate changes (*c*) with the ending translated value (*d*). The difference is the result of exchange rate changes during the period. If (*c*) is greater than (*d*), a negative (debit) translation adjustment arises. If (*d*) is greater than (*c*), a positive (credit) translation adjustment results.

Computation of Translation Adjustment

Based on the process just described, the translation adjustment for SWISSCO in this example is calculated as follows:

Net asset balance, 1/1/07	CHF 500,000	× 0.60	=	$ 300,000
Change in net assets:				
Net income, 2007	470,000	× 0.65	=	305,500
Dividends declared, 10/1/07	(150,000)	× 0.67	=	(100,500)
Net asset balance, 12/31/07	CHF 820,000			$ 505,000
Net asset balance, 12/31/07				
at current exchange rate	CHF 820,000	× 0.70	=	(574,000)
Translation adjustment, 2007 (positive)				$ (69,000)

Because this subsidiary began operations at the beginning of the current year, the $69,000 translation adjustment is the only amount applicable for reporting purposes. If translations had already created a balance in previous years, that beginning balance would have been combined with the $69,000 to arrive at an appropriate year-end total to be presented as other comprehensive income within stockholders' equity.

The translation adjustment is reported in other comprehensive income only until the foreign operation is sold or liquidated. *SFAS 52* (para. 14) stipulates that, *in the period in which sale or liquidation occurs, the cumulative translation adjustment related to the particular entity must be removed from other comprehensive income and reported as part of the gain or loss on the sale of the investment.* In effect, the accumulated unrealized foreign exchange gain or loss that has been deferred in other comprehensive income becomes realized when the entity is disposed of.

Translation of the Statement of Cash Flows

The current rate method requires translating all operating items in the statement of cash flows at the average-for-the-period exchange rate (see Exhibit 10.6). This is the same rate used for translating income statement items. Although the ending balances in Accounts Receivable, Inventory, and Accounts Payable on the balance sheet are translated at the current exchange rate, the average rate is used for the *changes* in these accounts because those changes are caused by operating activities (such as sales and purchases) that are translated at the average rate.

Investing and financing activities are translated at the exchange rate on the day the activity took place. Although long-term debt is translated in the balance sheet at the current rate, in the statement of cash flows it is translated at the historical rate when the debt was incurred.

The $(4,500) "effect of exchange rate change on cash" is a part of the overall translation adjustment of $69,000. It represents that part of the translation adjustment attributable to a decrease in Cash and is derived as a plug figure.

EXHIBIT 10.6
Translated Statement of Cash Flows—Current Rate Method

Statement of Cash Flows
For Year Ending December 31, 2007

	CHF	Translation Rate	US$
Operating activities:			
Net income	CHF 470,000	0.65 A	$ 305,500
Add: Depreciation	100,000	0.65 A	65,000
Amortization	10,000	0.65 A	6,500
Increase in accounts receivable	(200,000)	0.65 A	(130,000)
Increase in inventory	(250,000)	0.65 A	(162,500)
Increase in accounts payable	600,000	0.65 A	390,000
Net cash from operations	730,000		474,500
Investing activities:			
Purchase of property and equipment	(1,000,000)	0.61 H	(610,000)
Acquisition of patent	(50,000)	0.62 H	(31,000)
Net cash from investing activities	(1,050,000)		(641,000)
Financing activities:			
Proceeds from long-term debt	250,000	0.61 H	152,500
Payment of dividends	(150,000)	0.67 H	(100,500)
Net cash from financing activities	100,000		52,000
Decrease in cash	(220,000)		(114,500)
Effect of exchange rate change on cash		To balance	(4,500)
Cash at December 31, 2006	CHF 350,000	0.60 H	210,000
Cash at December 31, 2007	CHF 130,000	0.70 C	$ 91,000

REMEASUREMENT OF FINANCIAL STATEMENTS—TEMPORAL METHOD

Now assume that a careful examination of the functional currency indicators outlined in *SFAS 52* leads USCO's management to conclude that SWISSCO's functional currency is the U.S. dollar. In that case, the Swiss franc financial statements must be remeasured into U.S. dollars using the temporal method and the remeasurement gain or loss reported in income. To ensure that the remeasurement gain or loss is reported in income, it is easiest to remeasure the balance sheet first (as shown in Exhibit 10.7).

According to the procedures outlined in Exhibit 10.1, the temporal method remeasures cash, receivables, and liabilities into U.S. dollars using the current exchange rate of $0.70. Inventory (carried at FIFO cost), property and equipment, patents, and the contributed capital accounts (Common Stock and Additional Paid-In Capital) are remeasured at historical rates. These procedures result in total assets of $1,076,800 and liabilities and contributed capital of $895,000. To balance the balance sheet, Retained Earnings must total $181,800. We verify the accuracy of this amount later.

Remeasurement of the Income Statement

Exhibit 10.8 shows the remeasurement of SWISSCO's income statement and statement of retained earnings. Revenues and expenses incurred evenly throughout the year (sales, other expenses, and income taxes) are remeasured at the average exchange rate. Expenses related to assets remeasured at historical exchange rates (depreciation expense and amortization expense) are remeasured at relevant historical rates.

The following procedure remeasures cost of goods sold at historical exchange rates. Beginning inventory acquired on January 1 is remeasured at the exchange rate from that date ($0.60). Purchases made evenly throughout the year are remeasured at the average rate for the

EXHIBIT 10.7
Remeasurement of Balance Sheet—Temporal Method

Balance Sheet
December 31, 2007

	CHF	Remeasurement Rate	US$
Assets			
Cash	CHF 130,000	0.70 C	$ 91,000
Accounts receivable	200,000	0.70 C	140,000
Inventory	400,000	0.68 H	272,000
Total current assets	730,000		503,000
Property and equipment	1,000,000	0.61 H	610,000
Less: Accumulated depreciation	(100,000)	0.61 H	(61,000)
Patents, net	40,000	0.62 H	24,800
Total assets	CHF 1,670,000		$1,076,800
Liabilities and Equities			
Accounts payable	CHF 600,000	0.70 C	$ 420,000
Total current liabilities	600,000		420,000
Long-term debt	250,000	0.70 C	175,000
Total liabilities	850,000		595,000
Common stock	100,000	0.60 H	60,000
Additional paid-in capital	400,000	0.60 H	240,000
Retained earnings	320,000	To balance	181,800
Total equity	820,000		481,800
Total liabilities and equity	CHF 1,670,000		$1,076,800

EXHIBIT 10.8
Remeasurement of Income Statement and Statement of Retained Earnings—Temporal Method

Income Statement
For Year Ending December 31, 2007

	CHF	Remeasurement Rate	US$
Sales	CHF 4,000,000	0.65 A	$ 2,600,000
Cost of goods sold	(3,000,000)	Calculation	(1,930,500)
Gross profit	1,000,000		669,500
Depreciation expense	(100,000)	0.61 H	(61,000)
Amortization expense	(10,000)	0.62 H	(6,200)
Other expenses	(220,000)	0.65 A	(143,000)
Income before income taxes	670,000		459,300
Income taxes	(200,000)	0.65 A	(130,000)
Remeasurement Loss		To balance	(47,000)
Net income	CHF 470,000		$ 282,300

Statement of Retained Earnings
For Year Ending December 31, 2007

	CHF	Remeasurement Rate	US$
Retained earnings, 1/1/07	CHF –0–		$ –0–
Net income, 2007	470,000	Above	282,300
Dividends	(150,000)	0.67 H	(100,500)
Retained earnings, 12/31/07	CHF 320,000	To balance	$ 181,800

year ($0.65). Ending inventory (at FIFO cost) purchased evenly throughout the fourth quarter of 2007 and the average exchange rate for the quarter ($0.68) are used to remeasure that component of cost of goods sold. These procedures result in Cost of Goods Sold of $1,930,500, calculated as follows:

Beginning inventory, 1/1/07	CHF 150,000	×	0.60	=	$ 90,000
Plus: Purchases, 2007	3,250,000	×	0.65	=	2,112,500
Less: Ending inventory, 12/31/07	(400,000)	×	0.68	=	(272,000)
Cost of goods sold, 2007	CHF 3,000,000				$1,930,500

The ending balances in Retained Earnings on the balance sheet and on the statement of retained earnings must reconcile with one another. Because dividends are remeasured into a U.S. dollar equivalent of $100,500 and the ending balance in Retained Earnings on the balance sheet is $181,800, net income must be $282,300.

Reconciling the amount of income reported in the statement of retained earnings and in the income statement requires a remeasurement loss of $47,000 in calculating income. Without this remeasurement loss, the income statement, statement of retained earnings, and balance sheet are not consistent with one another.

The remeasurement loss can be calculated by considering the impact of exchange rate changes on the subsidiary's balance sheet exposure. Under the temporal method, SWISSCO's balance sheet exposure is defined by its net monetary asset or net monetary liability position. SWISSCO began 2007 with net monetary assets (cash) of CHF 350,000. During the year, however, expenditures of cash and the incurrence of liabilities caused monetary liabilities (accounts payable + long-term debt = CHF 850,000) to exceed monetary assets (cash + accounts receivable = CHF 330,000). A net monetary liability position of CHF 520,000 exists at December 31, 2007. The remeasurement loss is computed by translating the beginning net monetary asset position and subsequent changes in monetary items at appropriate exchange rates and then comparing this with the dollar value of net monetary liabilities at year-end based on the current exchange rate:

Computation of Remeasurement Loss					
Net monetary assets, 1/1/07	CHF 350,000	×	0.60	=	$ 210,000
Increase in monetary items:					
Sales, 2007	4,000,000	×	0.65	=	2,600,000
Decreases in monetary items:					
Purchases, 2007	(3,250,000)	×	0.65	=	(2,112,500)
Other expenses, 2007	(220,000)	×	0.65	=	(143,000)
Income taxes, 2007	(200,000)	×	0.65	=	(130,000)
Purchase of property and equipment, 3/15/07 . . .	(1,000,000)	×	0.61	=	(610,000)
Acquisition of patent, 4/10/07	(50,000)	×	0.62	=	(31,000)
Dividends, 10/1/07	(150,000)	×	0.67	=	(100,500)
Net monetary liabilities, 12/31/07	CHF (520,000)				$ (317,000)
Net monetary liabilities, 12/31/07, at the current exchange rate	CHF (520,000)	×	0.70	=	(364,000)
Remeasurement loss					$ 47,000

If SWISSCO had maintained its net monetary asset position (cash) of CHF 350,000 for the entire year, a remeasurement gain of $35,000 would have resulted. The CHF held in cash was worth $210,000 (CHF 350,000 × $0.60) at the beginning of the year and $245,000 (CHF 350,000 × $0.70) at year-end. However, the net monetary asset position is not maintained. Indeed, a net monetary liability position arises. The *appreciation* of the foreign currency coupled with an increase in *net monetary liabilities* generates a *remeasurement loss* for the year.

EXHIBIT 10.9
Remeasurement of Statement of Cash Flows— Temporal Method

Statement of Cash Flows
For Year Ending December 31, 2007

	CHF	Remeasurement Rate	US$
Operating activities:			
Net income	CHF 470,000	From I/S	$ 282,300
Add: Depreciation expense	100,000	0.61 H	61,000
Amortization expense	10,000	0.62 H	6,200
Remeasurement loss		From I/S	47,000
Increase in accounts receivable	(200,000)	0.65 A	(130,000)
Increase in inventory	(250,000)	*	(182,000)
Increase in accounts payable	600,000	0.65 A	390,000
Net cash from operations	730,000		474,500
Investing activities:			
Purchase of property and equipment	(1,000,000)	0.61 H	(610,000)
Acquisition of patent	(50,000)	0.62 H	(31,000)
Net cash from investing activities	(1,050,000)		(641,000)
Financing activities:			
Proceeds from long-term debt	250,000	0.61 H	152,500
Payment of dividends	(150,000)	0.67 H	(100,500)
Net cash from financing activities	100,000		52,000
Decrease in cash	(220,000)		(114,500)
Effect of exchange rate changes on cash		To balance	(4,500)
Cash at December 31, 2006	CHF 350,000	0.6 H	$ 210,000
Cash at December 31, 2007	CHF 130,000	0.7 C	$ 91,000

*In remeasuring cost of goods sold earlier, beginning inventory was remeasured as $90,000 and ending inventory was remeasured as $272,000: an increase of $182,000.

Remeasurement of the Statement of Cash Flows

In remeasuring the statement of cash flows (shown in Exhibit 10.9), the U.S. dollar value for net income comes directly from the remeasured income statement (I/S). Depreciation and amortization are remeasured at the rates used in the income statement, and the remeasurement loss is added back to net income because it is a noncash item. The increases in accounts receivable and accounts payable relate to sales and purchases and therefore are remeasured at the average rate. The U.S. dollar value for the increase in inventory is determined by referring to the remeasurement of the cost of goods sold.

The resulting U.S. dollar amount of "net cash from operations" ($474,500) is exactly the same as when the current rate method was used in translation. In addition, the investing and financing activities are translated in the same manner under both methods. This makes sense; the amount of cash inflows and outflows is a matter of fact and is not affected by the particular translation methodology employed.

Nonlocal Currency Balances

One additional issue related to the translation of foreign currency financial statements needs to be considered. If any of the accounts of the Swiss subsidiary are denominated in a currency other than the Swiss franc, those balances would first have to be restated into francs in accordance with the rules discussed in Chapter 9. Both the foreign currency balance and any related foreign exchange gain or loss would then be translated (or remeasured) into U.S. dollars. For example, a note payable of 10,000 British pounds first would be remeasured into Swiss francs before the translation process could commence.

COMPARISON OF THE RESULTS FROM APPLYING THE TWO DIFFERENT METHODS

The determination of the foreign subsidiary's functional currency (and the use of different translation methods) can have a significant impact on consolidated financial statements. The following chart shows differences for SWISSCO in several key items under the two different translation methods:

| | Translation Method | | |
Item	Current Rate	Temporal	Difference
Net income	$ 305,500	$ 282,300	+ 8.2%
Total assets	1,169,000	1,076,800	+ 8.6
Total equity	574,000	481,800	+19.1
Return on equity	53.2%	58.6%	− 9.2

In this illustration if the Swiss franc is determined to be SWISSCO's functional currency (and the current rate method is applied), net income reported in the consolidated income statement would be 8.2 percent more than if the U.S. dollar is the functional currency (and the temporal method is applied). In addition, total assets would be 8.6 percent more and total equity would be 19.1 percent more using the current rate method. Because of the larger amount of equity, return on equity using the current rate method is 9.2 percent less.

Note that the current rate method does not always result in higher net income and a higher amount of equity than the temporal method. For example, if SWISSCO had maintained its net monetary asset position, it would have computed a remeasurement gain under the temporal method leading to higher income than under the current rate method. Moreover, if the Swiss franc had depreciated during 2007, the temporal method would have resulted in higher net income.

The important point is that the determination of the functional currency and resulting translation method can have a significant impact on the amounts a parent company reports in its consolidated financial statements. The appropriate determination of the functional currency is an important issue.

> "Within rather broad parameters," says Peat, Marwick, Mitchell partner James Weir, choosing the functional currency is basically a management call. So much so, in fact, that Texaco, Occidental, and Unocal settled on the dollar as the functional currency for most of their foreign operations, whereas competitors Exxon, Mobil, and Amoco chose primarily the local currencies as the functional currencies for their foreign businesses.[11]

Different functional currencies selected by different companies in the same industry could have a significant impact on the comparability of financial statements within that industry. Indeed, one concern that those FASB members dissenting on *SFAS 52* raised was that the functional currency rules might not result in similar accounting for similar situations.

In addition to differences in amounts reported in the consolidated financial statements, the results of the SWISSCO illustration demonstrate several conceptual differences between the two translation methods.

Underlying Valuation Method

Using the temporal method, SWISSCO remeasured its property and equipment as follows:

$$\text{Property and equipment CHF } 1,000,000 \times \$0.61 \text{ H} = \$610,000$$

By multiplying the historical cost in Swiss francs by the historical exchange rate, $610,000 represents the U.S. dollar equivalent historical cost of this asset. It is the amount of U.S. dollars that the parent company would have had to pay to acquire assets having a cost of CHF 1,000,000 when the exchange rate was $0.61 per Swiss franc.

---

[11] John Heins, "Plenty of Opportunity to Fool Around," *Forbes,* June 2, 1986, p. 139.

Property and equipment were translated under the current rate method as follows:

Property and equipment CHF 1,000,000 $\times$ $0.70 C = $700,000

The $700,000 amount is not readily interpretable. It does not represent the U.S. dollar equivalent historical cost of the asset; that amount is $610,000. Nor does it represent the U.S. dollar equivalent current cost of the asset because CHF 1,000,000 is not the current cost of the asset in Switzerland. The $700,000 amount is simply the product of multiplying two numbers together!

Underlying Relationships

The following table reports the values for selected financial ratios calculated from the original foreign currency financial statements and from the U.S. dollar–translated statements using the two different translation methods:

Ratio	CHF	US$ Temporal	US$ Current Rate
Current ratio (current assets/current liabilities)	1.22	1.20	1.22
Debt/equity ratio (total liabilities/total equities)	1.04	1.23	1.04
Gross profit ratio (gross profit/sales)	25%	25.8%	25%
Return on equity (net income/total equity)	57.3%	58.6%	53.2%

The temporal method distorts all of the ratios as measured in the foreign currency. The subsidiary appears to be less liquid, more highly leveraged, and more profitable than it does in Swiss franc terms.

The current rate method maintains the first three ratios but distorts return on equity. The distortion occurs because income was translated at the average-for-the-period exchange rate whereas total equity was translated at the current exchange rate. In fact, the use of the average rate for income and the current rate for assets and liabilities distorts any ratio combining balance sheet and income statement figures, such as turnover ratios.

Conceptually, when the current rate method is employed, income statement items can be translated at either the average or the current exchange rate. *SFAS 52* requires using the average exchange rate. In this illustration, if revenues and expenses had been translated at the current exchange rate, net income would have been $329,000 (CHF 470,000 $\times$ $0.70), and the return on equity would have been 57.3 percent ($329,000/$574,000), exactly the amount reflected in the Swiss franc financial statements. In several countries in which the current rate method is used, companies are allowed to choose between the average exchange rate and the current exchange rate in translating income. This is true, for example, in France and the United Kingdom.

HEDGING BALANCE SHEET EXPOSURE

When the U.S. dollar is the functional currency or when a foreign operation is located in a highly inflationary economy, remeasurement gains and losses are reported in the consolidated income statement. Management of U.S. multinational companies could wish to avoid reporting remeasurement losses in net income because of the perceived negative impact this has on the company's stock price. Likewise, when the foreign currency is the functional currency, management could wish to avoid negative translation adjustments because of the adverse impact on the debt to equity ratio.

> More and more corporations are hedging their translation exposure—the recorded value of international assets such as plant, equipment and inventory—to prevent gyrations in their quarterly accounts. Though technically only paper gains or losses, translation adjustments can play havoc with balance-sheet ratios and can spook analysts and creditors alike.[12]

[12] Ida Picker, "Indecent Exposure," *Institutional Investor,* September 1991, p. 82.

Translation adjustments and remeasurement gains or losses are functions of two factors: (1) changes in the exchange rate and (2) balance sheet exposure. Although a company can do little if anything to influence exchange rates, parent companies can use several techniques to hedge the balance sheet exposures of their foreign operations.

Parent companies can hedge balance sheet exposure by using a derivative financial instrument, such as a forward contract or foreign currency option, or a nonderivative hedging instrument, such as a foreign currency borrowing. To illustrate, assume that SWISSCO's functional currency is the Swiss franc; this creates a net asset balance sheet exposure. USCO believes that the Swiss franc will depreciate, thereby generating a negative translation adjustment that will reduce consolidated stockholders' equity. USCO could hedge this balance sheet exposure by borrowing Swiss francs for a period of time, thus creating an offsetting Swiss franc liability exposure. As the Swiss franc depreciates, a foreign exchange gain will occur on the Swiss franc liability that offsets the negative translation adjustment arising from the translation of SWISSCO's financial statements. As an alternative to the Swiss franc borrowing, USCO might have acquired a Swiss franc call option to hedge its balance sheet exposure. As the Swiss franc depreciates, the fair value of the call option should increase, resulting in a gain. *SFAS 133* provides that the gain or loss on a hedging instrument designated and effective as a *hedge of the net investment in a foreign operation* should be reported in the same manner as the translation adjustment being hedged. Thus, the foreign exchange gain on the Swiss franc borrowing or the gain on the foreign currency option would be included in Other Comprehensive Income along with the negative translation adjustment arising from the translation of SWISSCO's financial statements. In the event that the gain on the hedging instrument is larger than the translation adjustment being hedged, the excess is taken to net income.

The paradox of hedging a balance sheet exposure is that in the process of avoiding an unrealized translation adjustment, realized foreign exchange gains and losses can result. Consider USCO's foreign currency borrowing to hedge a Swiss franc exposure. At the initiation of the loan, USCO will convert the borrowed Swiss francs into U.S. dollars at the spot exchange rate. When the liability matures, USCO will purchase Swiss francs at the spot rate prevailing at that date to repay the loan. The change in exchange rate over the life of the loan will generate a realized gain or loss. If the Swiss franc depreciates as expected, a realized foreign exchange gain that will offset the negative translation adjustment in Other Comprehensive Income will result. Although the net effect on Other Comprehensive Income is zero, a net increase in cash occurs as a result of the hedge. If the Swiss franc unexpectedly appreciates, a realized foreign exchange loss will occur. This will be offset by a positive translation adjustment in Other Comprehensive Income, but a net decrease in cash will exist. While a hedge of a net investment in a foreign operation eliminates the possibility of reporting a negative translation adjustment in Other Comprehensive Income, gains and losses realized in cash can result.

DISCLOSURES RELATED TO TRANSLATION

SFAS 52 (para. 31) requires firms to present an analysis of the change in the cumulative translation adjustment account in the financial statements or notes thereto. Many companies comply with this requirement by including an Other Comprehensive Income column in their statement of stockholders' equity. Other companies provide separate disclosure in the notes; see Exhibit 10.10 for an example of this disclosure for the Gillette Company.

An analysis of the Foreign Currency Translation column indicates positive translation adjustments in each year 2002–2004. From the sign of these adjustments, one can infer that, in aggregate, the foreign currencies in which Gillette has operations appreciated against the U.S. dollar in each of those years. On the whole, Gillette's management might be disappointed that the translation adjustment is not reflected in income. Before-tax income would have been 17 percent higher in 2002, 20 percent higher in 2003, and 8 percent higher in 2004 if translation adjustments had been included in net income.

Note that Gillette's Foreign Currency Translation account includes not only "net exchange gains or losses resulting from the translation of assets and liabilities of foreign subsidiaries" but also gains and losses on "intercompany transactions of a long-term investment nature"

EXHIBIT 10.10
The Gillette Company and Subsidiary Companies, 2004 Annual Report

4. Accumulated Other Comprehensive Loss

An analysis of accumulated other comprehensive loss follows:

(millions)	Foreign Currency Translation	Pension Adjustment	Cash Flow Hedges	Accumulated Other Comprehensive Loss
Balance at December 31, 2001	$(1,373)	$ (56)	$ (8)	$(1,437)
Change in period	196	(183)	(10)	3
Reclassification to earnings, pre-tax	—	—	15	15
Income tax benefit (expense)	(155)	53	(2)	(104)
Balance at December 31, 2002	(1,332)	(186)	(5)	(1,523)
Change in period	398	(10)	8	396
Reclassification to earnings, pre-tax	11	—	4	15
Income tax benefit (expense)	25	3	(4)	24
Balance at December 31, 2003	(898)	(193)	3	(1,088)
Change in period	293	(3)	5	295
Reclassification to earnings, pre-tax	30	—	(4)	26
Income tax benefit (expense)	7	1	(1)	7
Balance at December 31, 2004	(568)	(195)	3	(760)

Net exchange gains or losses resulting from the translation of assets and liabilities of foreign subsidiaries, except those in highly inflationary economies, are accumulated in a separate section of stockholders' equity. Also included are the effects of foreign exchange rate changes on intercompany balances of a long-term investment nature and transactions designated as hedges of net foreign investments. The Company recorded pre-tax gains of $293 million in accumulated foreign currency translation in 2004, due primarily to the strength of the Euro and the U.K. Pound Sterling. The pre-tax gains of $398 million in 2003 were due primarily to the strength of the Euro. Pre-tax gains of $196 million in 2002 were due primarily to strengthening European currencies, which were partially offset by weakening Latin American currencies.

Included in "Other charges (income)—net" in the Consolidated Statement of Income are a net exchange loss of $35 million in 2004, and net exchange gains of $14 million and $16 million in 2003 and 2002, respectively, for the foreign currency effects of transactions (including translation of hyper-inflationary entities) in those years. In 2004 and 2003, the Company reclassified $30 million and $11 million, respectively, in exchange losses from accumulated other comprehensive loss upon liquidation of foreign subsidiaries.

(as mentioned in Chapter 9) and on "transactions designated as hedges of net foreign investments." Gillette reports its remeasurement gains and losses in a line item titled "Other charges (income)—net" on the income statement.

Although not specifically required to do so, many companies include a description of their translation procedures in their "summary of significant accounting policies" in the notes to the financial statements. The following excerpt from International Business Machines Corporation's 2004 annual report illustrates this type of disclosure:

Translation of Non-U.S. Currency Amounts—Assets and liabilities of non-U.S. subsidiaries that operate in a local currency environment are translated to U.S. dollars at year-end exchange rates. Income and expense items are translated at weighted average rates of exchange prevailing during the year. Translation adjustments are recorded in Accumulated gains and losses not affecting retained earnings within stockholders' equity.

Inventories, plant, rental machines and other properties—net, and other nonmonetary assets and liabilities of non-U.S. subsidiaries and branches that operate in U.S. dollars or whose economic environment is highly inflationary, are translated at approximate exchange rates prevailing when the company acquired the assets or liabilities. All other assets and liabilities are translated at year-end exchange rates. Cost of sales and depreciation are translated at historical exchange rates. All other income and expense items are translated at the weighted average rates of exchange prevailing during the year. Gains and losses that result from translation are included in net income.

CONSOLIDATION OF A FOREIGN SUBSIDIARY

The final section of this chapter demonstrates the procedures used to consolidate the financial statements of a foreign subsidiary with those of its parent. The treatment of the excess of cost over book value requires special attention. As an item denominated in foreign currency, translation of the excess gives rise to a translation adjustment recorded on the consolidation worksheet.

On January 1, 2006, Altman, Inc., a U.S.-based manufacturing firm, purchased 100 percent of Bradford Ltd. in Great Britain. Altman paid £25,000,000 for its purchase. On January 1, 2006, Bradford had the following balance sheet:

Cash	£ 925,000	Accounts payable	£ 675,000
Accounts receivable	1,400,000	Long-term debt	4,000,000
Inventory	6,050,000	Common stock	20,000,000
Plant and equipment (net)	19,000,000	Retained earnings	2,700,000
Total	£27,375,000	Total	£27,375,000

The excess of cost over book value of £2,300,000 resulted from undervalued land (part of plant and equipment) and therefore is not subject to amortization. Altman uses the equity method to account for its investment in Bradford.

On December 31, 2007, two years after the date of acquisition, Bradford submitted the following trial balance for consolidation (credit balances are in parentheses):

Cash	£ 600,000
Accounts Receivable	2,700,000
Inventory	9,000,000
Plant and Equipment (net)	17,200,000
Accounts Payable	(500,000)
Long-Term Debt	(2,000,000)
Common Stock	(20,000,000)
Retained Earnings, 1/1/07	(3,800,000)
Sales	(13,900,000)
Cost of Goods Sold	8,100,000
Depreciation Expense	900,000
Other Expenses	950,000
Dividends Declared, 6/30/07	750,000
	£ –0–

Although Bradford generated net income of £1,100,000 in 2006, it declared or paid no dividends that year. Other than the payment of dividends in 2007, no intercompany transactions occurred between the two affiliates. Altman has determined the British pound to be Bradford's functional currency.

Relevant exchange rates for the British pound were as follows:

	January 1	June 30	December 31	Average
2006	$1.51	—	$1.56	$1.54
2007	1.56	$1.58	1.53	1.55

Translation of Foreign Subsidiary Trial Balance

The initial step in consolidating the foreign subsidiary is to translate its trial balance from British pounds into U.S. dollars. Because the British pound has been determined to be the functional currency, this is done using the current rate method. The historical exchange rate for translating Bradford's common stock and January 1, 2006, retained earnings is the exchange rate that existed at the date of acquisition—$1.51.

	British Pounds	Rate	U.S. Dollars
Cash	£ 600,000	1.53 C	$ 918,000
Accounts Receivable	2,700,000	1.53 C	4,131,000
Inventory	9,000,000	1.53 C	13,770,000
Plant and Equipment (net)	17,200,000	1.53 C	26,316,000
Accounts Payable	(500,000)	1.53 C	(765,000)
Long-Term Debt	(2,000,000)	1.53 C	(3,060,000)
Common Stock	(20,000,000)	1.51 H	(30,200,000)
Retained Earnings, 1/1/07	(3,800,000)	*	(5,771,000)
Sales	(13,900,000)	1.55 A	(21,545,000)
Cost of Goods Sold	8,100,000	1.55 A	12,555,000
Depreciation Expense	900,000	1.55 A	1,395,000
Other Expenses	950,000	1.55 A	1,472,500
Dividends Declared, 6/30/07	750,000	1.58 H	1,185,000
Cumulative translation adjustment			(401,500)
	£ –0–		$ –0–
*Retained Earnings, 1/1/06	£2,700,000	1.51 H	$4,077,000
Net Income, 2006	1,100,000	1.54 A	1,694,000
Retained Earnings, 12/31/06	£3,800,000		$5,771,000

A positive (credit balance) cumulative translation adjustment is required to make the trial balance actually balance. The cumulative translation adjustment is calculated as follows:

Net assets, 1/1/06	£22,700,000	1.51 H	$34,277,000	
Change in net assets, 2006				
Net income, 2006	1,100,000	1.54 A	1,694,000	
Net assets, 12/31/06	£23,800,000		$35,971,000	
Net assets, 12/31/06, at current exchange rate	£23,800,000	1.56 C	37,128,000	
Translation adjustment, 2006 (positive)				$(1,157,000)
Net assets, 1/1/07	£23,800,000	1.56 H	$37,128,000	
Change in net assets, 2007				
Net income, 2007	3,950,000	1.55 A	6,122,500	
Dividends 6/30/07	(750,000)	1.58 H	(1,185,000)	
Net assets, 12/31/07	£27,000,000		$42,065,500	
Net assets, 12/31/07, at current exchange rate	£27,000,000	1.53 C	41,310,000	
Translation adjustment, 2007 (negative)				755,500
Cumulative translation adjustment, 12/31/07 (positive)				$ (401,500)

The translation adjustment in 2006 is positive because the British pound appreciated that year; the translation adjustment in 2007 is negative because the British pound depreciated.

Determination of Balance in Investment Account—Equity Method

The original cost of the investment in Bradford, the net income earned by Bradford, and the dividends paid by Bradford are all denominated in British pounds. Relevant amounts must be translated from pounds into U.S. dollars so Altman can account for its investment in Bradford under the equity method. In addition, the translation adjustment calculated each year is included in the Investment in Bradford account to update the foreign currency investment to its U.S. dollar equivalent. The counterpart is recorded as a translation adjustment on Altman's books:

12/31/06	Investment in Bradford	$1,157,000	
	Cumulative Translation Adjustment		$1,157,000
	To record the positive translation adjustment related to the investment in a British subsidiary when the British pound appreciated.		
12/31/07	Cumulative Translation Adjustment	$ 755,500	
	Investment in Bradford		$ 755,500
	To record the negative translation adjustment related to the investment in a British subsidiary when the British pound depreciated.		

The carrying value of the investment account in U.S. dollar terms at December 31, 2007, is determined as follows:

Investment in Bradford	British Pounds	Exchange Rate	U.S. Dollars
Original cost	£25,000,000	1.51 H	$37,750,000
Bradford net income, 2006	1,100,000	1.54 A	1,694,000
Translation adjustment, 2006			1,157,000
Balance, 12/31/06	£26,100,000		$40,601,000
Bradford net income, 2007	3,950,000	1.55 A	6,122,500
Bradford dividends, 6/30/07	(750,000)	1.58 H	(1,185,000)
Translation adjustment, 2007			(755,500)
Balance, 12/31/07	£29,300,000		$44,783,000

In addition to Altman's investment in Bradford of $44,783,000, it also has equity income on its December 31, 2007, trial balance in the amount of $6,122,500.

Consolidation Worksheet

Once the subsidiary's trial balance has been translated into dollars and the carrying value of the investment is known, the consolidation worksheet at December 31, 2007, can be prepared. As is true in the consolidation of domestic subsidiaries, the investment account, the subsidiary's equity accounts, and the effects of intercompany transactions must be eliminated. The excess of cost over book value at the date of acquisition also must be allocated to the appropriate accounts (in this example, plant and equipment).

Unique to the consolidation of foreign subsidiaries is the fact that the excess of cost over book value, which is denominated in foreign currency, also must be translated into the parent's reporting currency. When the foreign currency is the functional currency, the excess is translated at the current exchange rate with a resulting translation adjustment. The excess is not carried on either the parent's or the subsidiary's books but is recorded only in the consolidation worksheet. *Neither the parent nor the subsidiary has recognized the translation adjustment related to the excess, and it must be recorded in the consolidation worksheet.* Exhibit 10.11 presents the consolidation worksheet of Altman and Bradford at December 31, 2007.

Explanation of Consolidation Entries

S—Eliminates the subsidiary's stockholders' equity accounts as of the beginning of the current year along with the equivalent book value component within the parent's purchase price in the Investment in Bradford account.

A—Allocates the excess of cost over book value at the date of acquisition to land (plant and equipment) and eliminates that amount within the parent's purchase price from the Investment account.

I—Eliminates the amount of equity income recognized by the parent in the current year and included in the Investment in Bradford account under the equity method.

EXHIBIT 10.11 Consolidation Worksheet—Parent and Foreign Subsidiary

ALTMAN, INC., AND BRADFORD LTD.
Consolidation Worksheet
For Year Ending December 31, 2007

Accounts	Altman	Bradford	Consolidated Entries Debits	Consolidated Entries Credits	Consolidated Totals
Income Statement					
Sales	$ (32,489,000)	$(21,545,000)			$ (54,034,000)
Cost of goods sold	16,000,000	12,555,000			28,555,000
Depreciation expense	9,700,000	1,395,000			11,095,000
Other expenses	2,900,000	1,472,500			4,372,500
Equity income	(6,122,500)		(I) 6,122,500		–0–
Net income	$ (10,011,500)	$ (6,122,500)			$ (10,011,500)
Statement of Retained Earnings					
Retained earnings, 1/1/07	$ (25,194,000)	$ (5,771,000)	(S) 5,771,000		$ (25,194,000)
Net income (above)	(10,011,500)	(6,122,500)			(10,011,500)
Dividends paid	1,500,000	1,185,000		(D) 1,185,000	1,500,000
Retained earnings, 12/31/07	$ (33,705,500)	$(10,708,500)			$ (33,705,500)
Balance Sheet					
Cash	$ 3,649,800	$ 918,000			$ 4,567,800
Accounts receivable	3,100,000	4,131,000			7,231,000
Inventory	11,410,000	13,770,000			25,180,000
Investment in Bradford	44,783,000			(S) 35,971,000	–0–
				(A) 3,473,000	
			(D) 1,185,000	(I) 6,122,500	
				(T) 401,500	
Plant and equipment (net)	39,500,000	26,316,000	(A) 3,473,000		
			(E) 46,000		69,335,000
Total assets	$ 102,442,800	$ 45,135,000			$ 106,313,800
Accounts payable	$ (2,500,000)	$ (765,000)			$ (3,265,000)
Long-term debt	(22,728,800)	(3,060,000)			(25,788,800)
Common stock	(43,107,000)	(30,200,000)	(S) 30,200,000		(43,107,000)
Retained earnings, 12/31/07 (above)	(33,705,500)	(10,708,500)			(33,705,500)
Cumulative translation adjustment	(401,500)	(401,500)	(T) 401,500	(E) 46,000	(447,500)
Total liabilities and equities	$(102,422,800)	$(45,135,000)	$47,199,000	$(47,199,000)	$(106,313,800)

D—Eliminates the subsidiary's dividend payment that was a reduction in the Investment in Bradford account under the equity method.

T—Eliminates the cumulative translation adjustment included in the Investment in Bradford account under the equity method and eliminates the cumulative translation adjustment carried on the parent's books.

E—Revalues the excess of cost over book value for the change in exchange rate since the date of acquisition with the counterpart recognized as an increase in the consolidated cumulative translation adjustment. The revaluation is calculated as follows:

Excess of Cost over Book Value

U.S. dollar equivalent at 12/31/07	£2,300,000 × $1.53 =	$3,519,000
U.S. dollar equivalent at 1/1/06	2,300,000 × $1.51 =	3,473,000
Cumulative translation adjustment related to excess, 12/31/07		$ 46,000

Summary

1. Because many companies have significant financial involvement in foreign countries, the process by which foreign currency financial statements are translated into U.S. dollars has special accounting importance. The two major issues related to the translation process are (1) which method to use and (2) where to report the resulting translation adjustment in the consolidated financial statements.

2. Translation methods differ on the basis of which accounts are translated at the current exchange rate and which are translated at historical rates. Accounts translated at the current exchange rate are exposed to translation adjustment. Different translation methods give rise to different concepts of balance sheet exposure and translation adjustments of differing signs and magnitude.

3. The temporal method translates assets carried at current value (cash, marketable securities, receivables) and liabilities at the current exchange rate. This method translates assets carried at historical cost and stockholders' equity at historical exchange rates. When liabilities are more than the sum of cash, marketable securities, and receivables, a net liability balance sheet exposure exists. Appreciation in the foreign currency results in a negative translation adjustment (remeasurement loss). Depreciation in the foreign currency results in a positive translation adjustment (remeasurement gain). By translating assets carried at historical cost at historical exchange rates, the temporal method maintains the underlying valuation method used by the foreign operation but distorts relationships in the foreign currency financial statements.

4. The current rate method translates all assets and liabilities at the current exchange rate, giving rise to a net asset balance sheet exposure. Appreciation in the foreign currency results in a positive translation adjustment. Depreciation in the foreign currency results in a negative translation adjustment. By translating assets carried at historical cost at the current exchange rate, the current rate method maintains relationships in the foreign currency financial statements but distorts the underlying valuation method used by the foreign operation.

5. From 1975 through 1981, the temporal method—as prescribed by *SFAS 8* of the Financial Accounting Standards Board—was used to translate the financial statements of foreign operations. Translation adjustments were reported as gains and losses in income. Because this approach came under increasing attack from the business community as well as from many accountants, the FASB eventually replaced it with *SFAS 52*.

6. *SFAS 52* creates two separate procedures for translating foreign currency financial statements into the parent's reporting currency. *Translation* through use of the current rate method is appropriate when the foreign operation's functional currency is a foreign currency. In this case, the translation adjustment is reported in Other Comprehensive Income and reflected on the balance sheet as a separate component of stockholders' equity. *Remeasurement* by using the temporal method is appropriate when the operation's functional currency is the U.S. dollar. Remeasurement also is applied when the operation is in a country with a highly inflationary economy. In these situations, the translation adjustment is treated as a remeasurement gain or loss in net income.

7. Some companies hedge their balance sheet exposures to avoid reporting remeasurement losses in net income and/or negative translation adjustments in Other Comprehensive Income. Gains and losses on derivative or nonderivative instruments used to hedge net investments in foreign operations are reported in the same manner as the translation adjustment being hedged.

Comprehensive Illustration

PROBLEM

(Estimated Time: 55 to 65 Minutes) Arlington Company is a U.S.-based organization with numerous foreign subsidiaries. As a preliminary step in preparing consolidated financial statements for 2007, it must translate the financial information from each of these foreign operations into its reporting currency, the U.S. dollar.

Arlington owns a subsidiary in Sweden that has been in business for several years. On December 31, 2006, this entity's balance sheet was translated from Swedish kroner (SKr) (its functional currency) into U.S. dollars as prescribed by *SFAS 52*. Equity accounts at that date were as follows (all credit balances):

Common stock	SKr 110,000	= $21,000
Retained earnings	194,800	= 36,100
Cumulative translation adjustment		3,860

At the end of 2007, the Swedish subsidiary produced the trial balance that follows. These figures include all of the entity's transactions for the year except for the results of several transactions related to sales made to a Chinese customer. A separate ledger has been maintained for these transactions denominated in Chinese renminbi (RMB). This ledger follows the company's trial balance.

Trial Balance—Swedish Subsidiary
December 31, 2007

	Debit	Credit
Cash	SKr 41,000	
Accounts Receivable	126,000	
Inventory	128,000	
Land	160,000	
Fixed Assets	228,000	
Accumulated Depreciation		SKr 98,100
Accounts Payable		39,000
Notes Payable		56,000
Bonds Payable		125,000
Common Stock		110,000
Retained Earnings, 1/1/07		194,800
Sales		350,000
Cost of Goods Sold	165,000	
Depreciation Expense	10,900	
Salary Expense	36,000	
Rent Expense	12,000	
Other Expenses	41,000	
Dividends Paid, 7/1/07	25,000	
Totals	SKr 972,900	SKr 972,900

Ledger—Transactions in Chinese Renminbi
December 31, 2007

	Debit	Credit
Cash	RMB 10,000	
Accounts Receivable	28,000	
Fixed Assets	20,000	
Accumulated Depreciation		RMB 4,000
Notes Payable		15,000
Sales		44,000
Depreciation Expense	4,000	
Interest Expense	1,000	
Totals	RMB 63,000	RMB 63,000

Additional Information

- The Swedish subsidiary began selling to the Chinese customer at the beginning of the current year. At that time, it borrowed 20,000 RMB to acquire a truck for delivery purposes. It paid one-fourth of that debt before the end of the year. The subsidiary made sales to China evenly during the period.

- The U.S. dollar exchange rates for 1 SKr are as follows:

January 1, 2007	$0.200 = 1.00 SKr
Weighted average rate for 2007	0.192 = 1.00
July 1, 2007	0.190 = 1.00
December 31, 2007	0.182 = 1.00

- The exchange rates applicable for the remeasurement of 1 RMB into Swedish kroner are as follows:

January 1, 2007	1.25 SKr = 1.00 RMB
Weighted average rate for 2007	1.16 = 1.00
December 1, 2007	1.10 = 1.00
December 31, 2007	1.04 = 1.00

- The Swedish subsidiary expended SKr 10,000 during the year for research and development. In accordance with Swedish accounting rules, this cost has been capitalized within the Fixed Assets account. This expenditure had no effect on the depreciation recognized for the year.

Required:

Prepare financial statements for the year ending December 31, 2007, for the Swedish subsidiary. Translate these statements according to *SFAS 52* into U.S. dollars to facilitate the preparation of consolidated statements. The Swedish krona is the subsidiary's functional currency.

SOLUTION

Remeasurement of Foreign Currency Balances

A portion of the Swedish subsidiary's operating results are presently stated in Chinese renminbi. These balances must be remeasured into the functional currency, the Swedish krona, before the translation process can begin. In remeasuring these accounts using the temporal method, the krona value of the monetary assets and liabilities is determined by using the current (C) exchange rate (1.04 SKr per RMB) whereas all other accounts are remeasured at historical (H) or average (A) rates.

Remeasurement of Foreign Currency Balances

	Renminbi		Rate		Kroner
Sales	RMB 44,000	×	1.16 A	=	SKr 51,040
Interest Expense	(1,000)	×	1.16 A	=	(1,160)
Depreciation Expense	(4,000)	×	1.25 H	=	(5,000)
Income from renminbi transactions	39,000				44,880
Cash	10,000	×	1.04 C	=	10,400
Accounts Receivable	28,000	×	1.04 C	=	29,120
Fixed Assets	20,000	×	1.25 H	=	25,000
Accumulated Depreciation	(4,000)	×	1.25 H	=	(5,000)
Total assets	54,000				59,520
Notes Payable	15,000	×	1.04 C	=	15,600
Income from renminbi transactions	39,000		From above		44,880
	54,000				60,480
Remeasurement Loss					(960)
Total					59,520

Remeasurement Loss for 2007

Net monetary asset balance, 1/1/07		–0–			–0–
Increases in net monetary items:					
Operations (sales less interest expense)	RMB 43,000	×	1.16	=	SKr 49,880
Decreases in net monetary items:					
Purchased truck, 1/1/07	(20,000)	×	1.25	=	(25,000)
Net monetary assets, 12/31/07	RMB 23,000				SKr 24,880
Net monetary assets, 12/31/07, at current exchange rate	RMB 23,000	×	1.04	=	SKr 23,920
Remeasurement loss (gain)					SKr 960

The net monetary asset exposure (cash and accounts receivable > notes payable) and depreciation of the Chinese renminbi create a remeasurement loss of SKr 960.

The remeasured figures from the Chinese operation must be combined in some manner with the subsidiary's trial balance denominated in Swedish kroner. For example, the accounts can simply be added together on a worksheet. As an alternative, a year-end adjustment can be recorded in the accounting system of the Swedish subsidiary to add the remeasured balances for financial reporting purposes:

12/31/07 Adjustment	Debit	Credit
Cash	10,400	
Accounts receivable	29,120	
Fixed assets	25,000	
Depreciation expense	5,000	
Interest expense	1,160	
Remeasurement loss	960	
Accumulated depreciation		5,000
Notes payable		15,600
Sales		51,040

To record in Swedish kroner the foreign currency transactions originally denominated in renminbi.

One more adjustment is necessary before translating the subsidiary's Swedish krona financial statements into the parent's reporting currency. The research and development costs incurred by the Swedish entity should be reclassified as an expense as required by *SFAS 2*, "Accounting for Research and Development Costs," December 1974. After this adjustment, the Swedish subsidiary's statements conform with U.S. generally accepted accounting principles.

12/31/07 Adjustment	Debit	Credit
Other expenses	10,000	
Fixed assets		10,000

To adjust fixed assets and expenses in Swedish kroner to be in compliance with U.S. GAAP.

Combining all remeasured and adjusted balances with the Swedish subsidiary's trial balance allows totals to be derived. For example, total sales for the subsidiary are SKr 401,040 (350,000 + 51,040), cash is SKr 51,400 (41,000 + 10,400), and so on. Having established all account balances in the functional currency (Swedish kroner), the subsidiary's statements now can be translated into U.S. dollars. Under the current rate method, the dollar values to be reported for income statement items are based on the average exchange rate for the current year. All assets and liabilities are based on the current exchange rate at the balance sheet date, and equity accounts are based on historical rates in effect at the date of accounting recognition.

SWEDISH SUBSIDIARY
Income Statement for Year Ending December 31, 2007

Sales	SKr 401,040	× 0.192 A =	$ 76,999.68
Cost of goods sold	(165,000)	× 0.192 A =	(31,680.00)
Gross profit	236,040		45,319.68
Depreciation expense	(15,900)	× 0.192 A =	(3,052.80)
Salary expense	(36,000)	× 0.192 A =	(6,912.00)
Rent expense	(12,000)	× 0.192 A =	(2,304.00)
Other expenses	(51,000)	× 0.192 A =	(9,792.00)
Interest expense	(1,160)	× 0.192 A =	(222.72)
Remeasurement loss	(960)	× 0.192 A =	(184.32)
Net income	SKr 119,020		$ 22,851.84

Statement of Retained Earnings for Year Ending December 31, 2007

Retained earnings, 1/1/ 07	SKr 194,800	Given above	$ 36,100.00
Net income, 2007	119,020		22,851.84
Dividends paid, 7/1/07	(25,000)	× 0.190 H =	(4,750.00)
Retained earnings, 12/31/07	SKr 288,820		$ 54,201.84

Balance Sheet
December 31, 2007

Cash	SKr 51,400	× 0.182 C =	$ 9,354.80
Accounts receivable	155,120	× 0.182 C =	28,231.84
Inventory	128,000	× 0.182 C =	23,296.00
Land	160,000	× 0.182 C =	29,120.00
Fixed assets	243,000	× 0.182 C =	44,226.00
Accumulated depreciation	(103,100)	× 0.182 C =	(18,764.20)
Total	SKr 634,420		$115,464.44
Accounts payable	SKr 39,000	× 0.182 C =	$ 7,098.00
Notes payable	71,600	× 0.182 C =	13,031.20
Bonds payable	125,000	× 0.182 C =	22,750.00
Common stock	110,000	Given above	21,000.00
Retained earnings	288,820		54,201.84
Cumulative translation adjustment			(2,616.60)
Total	SKr 634,420		$115,464.44

The cumulative translation adjustment at 12/31/07 comprises the beginning balance (given) plus the translation adjustment for the current year:

Cumulative Translation Adjustment

Balance, 1/1/07	$ 3,860.00
Translation adjustment for 2007	(6,476.60)
Balance, 12/31/07	$(2,616.60)

The negative translation adjustment for 2007 of $6,476.60 is calculated by considering the effect of exchange rate changes on net assets:

Translation Adjustment for 2007

Net assets, 1/1/07	SKr 304,800*	×	0.200	=	$60,960.00
Increase in net assets:					
Net income, 2007	119,020	×	0.192	=	22,851.84
Decrease in net assets:					
Dividends, 7/1/07	(25,000)	×	0.190	=	(4,750.00)
Net assets, 12/31/07	SKr 398,820†				$79,061.84
Net assets, 12/31/07, at current exchange rate	SKr 398,820	×	0.182	=	72,585.24
Translation adjustment, 2007—negative					$ 6,476.60

*Indicated by January 1, 2007, stockholders' equity balances—Common Stock, SKr 110,000; Retained Earnings, SKr 194,800.
†Indicated by December 31, 2007, stockholders' equity balances—Common Stock, SKr 110,000; Retained Earnings, SKr 288,820.

Questions

1. What are the two major issues related to the translation of foreign currency financial statements?
2. What causes balance sheet (or translation) exposure to foreign exchange risk? How does balance sheet exposure compare with transaction exposure?
3. Why might a company want to hedge its balance sheet exposure? What is the paradox associated with hedging balance sheet exposure?
4. Under *SFAS 133*, how are gains and losses on financial instruments used to hedge the net investment in a foreign operation reported in the consolidated financial statements?
5. What is the concept underlying the temporal method of translation? What is the concept underlying the current rate method of translation? How does balance sheet exposure differ under these two methods?

6. In translating the financial statements of a foreign subsidiary, why is the value assigned to retained earnings especially difficult to determine? How is this problem normally resolved?

7. What are the major procedural differences in applying the current rate and temporal methods of translation?

8. Clarke Company has a subsidiary operating in a foreign country. In relation to this subsidiary, what does the term *functional currency* mean? How is the functional currency determined?

9. A translation adjustment must be calculated and disclosed whenever financial statements of a foreign subsidiary are translated into the parent's reporting currency. How is this figure computed, and where is the amount reported in the financial statements?

10. The FASB put forth two theories about the underlying nature of a translation adjustment. What are these theories, and which one did the FASB consider correct?

11. When is remeasurement rather than translation appropriate? How does remeasurement differ from translation?

12. Which translation method does FASB *SFAS 52* require for operations in highly inflationary countries? What is the rationale for mandating use of this method?

Problems

1. What is a subsidiary's functional currency?
   a. The parent's reporting currency.
   b. The currency in which transactions are denominated.
   c. The currency in which the entity primarily generates and expends cash.
   d. Always the currency of the country in which the company has its headquarters.

2. In comparing the translation process and the remeasurement process, which of the following statements is true?
   a. The reported balance of inventory is normally the same under both methods.
   b. The reported balance of equipment is normally the same under both methods.
   c. The reported balance of sales is normally the same under both methods.
   d. The reported balance of depreciation expense is normally the same under both methods.

3. Which of the following statements is true for the translation process (as opposed to remeasurement)?
   a. A translation adjustment can affect consolidated net income.
   b. Equipment is translated at the historical exchange rate in effect at the date of its purchase.
   c. A translation adjustment is created by the change in the relative value of a subsidiary's net assets caused by exchange rate fluctuations.
   d. A translation adjustment is created by the change in the relative value of a subsidiary's monetary assets and monetary liabilities caused by exchange rate fluctuations.

4. A subsidiary of Byner Corporation has one asset (inventory) and no liabilities. The functional currency for this subsidiary is the peso. The inventory was acquired for 100,000 pesos when the exchange rate was $0.16 = 1$ peso. Consolidated statements are to be produced, and the current exchange rate is $0.19 = 1$ peso. Which of the following statements is true for the consolidated financial statements?
   a. A remeasurement gain must be reported.
   b. A positive translation adjustment must be reported.
   c. A negative translation adjustment must be reported.
   d. A remeasurement loss must be reported.

5. At what rates should the following balance sheet accounts in foreign statements be translated (rather than remeasured) into U.S. dollars?

	Accumulated Depreciation—Equipment	Equipment
a.	Current	Current
b.	Current	Average for year
c.	Historical	Current
d.	Historical	Historical

Problems 6 and 7 are based on the following information.

Certain balance sheet accounts of a foreign subsidiary of the Rose Company have been stated in U.S. dollars as follows:

	Stated at	
	Current Rates	**Historical Rates**
Accounts receivable, current	$200,000	$220,000
Accounts receivable, long term	100,000	110,000
Prepaid insurance	50,000	55,000
Goodwill	80,000	85,000
	$430,000	$470,000

6. A foreign currency is the functional currency of this subsidiary. What total should Rose's balance sheet include for the above items?

    a. $430,000.

    b. $435,000.

    c. $440,000.

    d. $450,000.

7. The U.S. dollar is the functional currency of this subsidiary. What total should Rose's balance sheet include for the above items?

    a. $430,000.

    b. $435,000.

    c. $440,000.

    d. $450,000.

Problems 8 and 9 are based on the following information.

A subsidiary of Salisbury, Inc., is located in a foreign country. This subsidiary's functional currency is the schweikart (SWK). The subsidiary acquires inventory on credit on November 1, 2006, for SWK 100,000 that is sold on January 17, 2007, for SWK 130,000. The subsidiary pays for the inventory on January 31, 2007. Currency exchange rates for 1 SWK are as follows:

November 1, 2006	$0.16 = 1 SWK
December 31, 2006	0.17 = 1
January 17, 2007	0.18 = 1
January 31, 2007	0.19 = 1
Average for 2007	0.20 = 1

8. What amount does Salisbury's consolidated balance sheet report for this inventory at December 31, 2006?

    a. $16,000.

    b. $17,000.

    c. $18,000.

    d. $19,000.

9. What amount does Salisbury's consolidated income statement report for cost of goods sold for the year ending December 31, 2007?

    a. $16,000.

    b. $17,000.

    c. $18,000.

    d. $19,000.

Problems 10 and 11 are based on the following information.

A subsidiary of Clarke Corporation buys marketable equity securities and inventory on April 1, 2007, for 100,000 pesos each. It pays for both of these items on June 1, 2007, and they are still on hand at year-end.

Inventory is carried at cost under the lower-of-cost-or-market rule. Currency exchange rates for 1 peso are as follows:

> January 1, 2007 .... $0.15 = 1 peso
> April 1, 2007 .... 0.16 = 1
> June 1, 2007 .... 0.17 = 1
> December 31, 2007 .... 0.19 = 1

10. Assume that the peso is the subsidiary's functional currency. What balances does a consolidated balance sheet report as of December 31, 2007?
    a. Marketable equity securities = $16,000 and Inventory = $16,000.
    b. Marketable equity securities = $17,000 and Inventory = $17,000.
    c. Marketable equity securities = $19,000 and Inventory = $16,000.
    d. Marketable equity securities = $19,000 and Inventory = $19,000.

11. Assume that the U.S. dollar is the subsidiary's functional currency. What balances does a consolidated balance sheet report as of December 31, 2007?
    a. Marketable equity securities = $16,000 and Inventory = $16,000.
    b. Marketable equity securities = $17,000 and Inventory = $17,000.
    c. Marketable equity securities = $19,000 and Inventory = $16,000.
    d. Marketable equity securities = $19,000 and Inventory = $19,000.

12. A U.S. company's foreign subsidiary had the following amounts in foreign currency units (FCU) in 2007:

> Cost of goods sold .... FCU 10,000,000
> Ending inventory 500,000
> Beginning inventory 200,000

    The average exchange rate during 2007 was $0.80 = FCU 1. The beginning inventory was acquired when the exchange rate was $1.00 = FCU 1. Ending inventory was acquired when the exchange rate was $0.75 = FCU 1. The exchange rate at December 31, 2007, was $0.70 = FCU 1. Assuming that the foreign country is highly inflationary, at what amount should the foreign subsidiary's cost of goods sold be reflected in the U.S. dollar income statement?
    a. $7,815,000.
    b. $8,040,000.
    c. $8,065,000.
    d. $8,090,000.

13. Ace Corporation starts a subsidiary in a foreign country; the subsidiary has the peso as its functional currency. On January 1, 2007, Ace buys all of the subsidiary's common stock for 20,000 pesos. On April 1, 2007, the subsidiary purchases inventory for 20,000 pesos with payment made on May 1, 2007, and sells this inventory on August 1, 2007, for 30,000 pesos, which it collects on October 1, 2007. Currency exchange rates for 1 peso are as follows:

> January 1, 2007 .... $0.15 = 1 peso
> April 1, 2007 .... 0.17 = 1
> May 1, 2007 .... 0.18 = 1
> August 1, 2007 .... 0.19 = 1
> October 1, 2007 .... 0.20 = 1
> December 31, 2007 .... 0.21 = 1

    In preparing consolidated financial statements, what translation adjustment will Ace report at the end of 2007?
    a. $400 positive (credit).
    b. $600 positive (credit).
    c. $1,400 positive (credit).
    d. $1,800 positive (credit).

14. In the translated financial statements, which method of translation maintains the underlying valuation methods used in the foreign currency financial statements?

    a. Current rate method; income statement translated at average exchange rate for the year.

    b. Current rate method; income statement translated at exchange rate at the balance sheet date.

    c. Temporal method.

    d. Monetary/nonmonetary method.

15. Houston Corporation operates a branch operation in a foreign country. Although this branch deals in pesos, the U.S. dollar is viewed as its functional currency. Thus, a remeasurement is necessary to produce financial information for external reporting purposes. The branch began the year with 100,000 pesos in cash and no other assets or liabilities. However, the branch immediately used 60,000 pesos to acquire equipment. On May 1, it purchased inventory costing 30,000 pesos for cash. It sold this merchandise on July 1 for 50,000 pesos cash. The branch transferred 10,000 pesos to the parent on October 1 and recorded depreciation on the equipment of 6,000 pesos for the year. Currency exchange rates for 1 peso follow:

January 1	$0.16 = 1 peso
May 1	0.18 = 1
July 1	0.20 = 1
October 1	0.21 = 1
December 31	0.22 = 1
Average for the year	0.19 = 1

    What is the remeasurement gain to be recognized in the consolidated income statement?

    a. $2,100.

    b. $2,400.

    c. $2,700.

    d. $3,000.

16. Which of the following items is *not* remeasured using historical exchange rates under the temporal method?

    a. Accumulated depreciation on equipment.

    b. Cost of goods sold.

    c. Marketable equity securities.

    d. Retained earnings.

17. In accordance with U.S. generally accepted accounting principles, which translation combination is appropriate for a foreign operation whose functional currency is the U.S. dollar?

	Method	Treatment of Translation Adjustment
a.	Temporal	Other comprehensive income
b.	Temporal	Gain or loss in net income
c.	Current rate	Other comprehensive income
d.	Current rate	Gain or loss in net income

18. A foreign subsidiary's functional currency is its local currency, which has not experienced significant inflation. The weighted average exchange rate for the current year is the appropriate exchange rate for translating

	Wages Expense	Wages Payable
a.	Yes	Yes
b.	Yes	No
c.	No	Yes
d.	No	No

19. The functional currency of DeZoort, Inc.'s, British subsidiary is the British pound. DeZoort borrowed British pounds as a partial hedge of its investment in the subsidiary. In preparing consolidated financial statements, DeZoort's negative translation adjustment on its investment in the subsidiary exceeded its foreign exchange gain on the borrowing. How should the effects of the negative translation adjustment and foreign exchange gain be reported in DeZoort's consolidated financial statements?

a. Report the translation adjustment in Other Comprehensive Income on the balance sheet and the foreign exchange gain in the income statement.

b. Report the translation adjustment in the income statement and defer the foreign exchange gain in Other Comprehensive Income on the balance sheet.

c. Report the translation adjustment less the foreign exchange gain in Other Comprehensive Income on the balance sheet.

d. Report the translation adjustment less the foreign exchange gain in the income statement.

20. Gains from remeasuring a foreign subsidiary's financial statements from the local currency, which is not the functional currency, into the parent's currency should be reported as a(n)

a. Deferred foreign exchange gain.

b. Translation adjustment in Other Comprehensive Income.

c. Extraordinary item, net of income taxes.

d. Part of continuing operations.

21. The foreign currency is the functional currency for a foreign subsidiary. At what exchange rate should each of the following accounts be translated?

a. Rent Expense.

b. Dividends Paid.

c. Equipment.

d. Notes Payable.

e. Sales.

f. Depreciation Expense.

g. Cash.

h. Accumulated Depreciation.

i. Common Stock.

22. On January 1, 2007, Dandu Corporation started a subsidiary in a foreign country. On April 1, 2007, the subsidiary purchased inventory at a cost of 120,000 local currency units (LCU). One-fourth of this inventory remained unsold at the end of 2007 while 40 percent of the liability from the purchase had not yet been paid. The exchange rates for $1 were as follows:

January 1, 2007	$1 = LCU 2.5
April 1, 2007	1 = 2.8
Average for 2007	1 = 2.7
December 31, 2007	1 = 3.0

What should be the December 31, 2007, Inventory and Accounts Payable balances for this foreign subsidiary as translated into U.S. dollars using the current rate method?

23. The following accounts are denominated as of December 31, 2007, in pesos. For reporting purposes, these amounts need to be stated in U.S. dollars. For each balance, indicate the exchange rate that would be used if a translation is made. Then, again for each account, provide the exchange rate that would be necessary if a remeasurement is being made. The company was started in 2000. The buildings were acquired in 2002 and the patents in 2003.

	Translation	Remeasurement
Accounts payable		
Accounts receivable		
Accumulated depreciation		
Advertising expense		
Amortization expense (patents)		
Buildings		
Cash		
Common stock		
Depreciation expense		
Dividends paid (10/1/07)		
Notes payable—due in 2009		
Patents (net)		
Salary expense		
Sales		

Exchange rates for 1 peso are as follows:

2000	1 peso = $0.28
2002	1 = 0.26
2003	1 = 0.25
January 1, 2007	1 = 0.24
April 1, 2007	1 = 0.23
July 1, 2007	1 = 0.22
October 1, 2007	1 = 0.20
December 31, 2007	1 = 0.16
Average for 2007	1 = 0.19

24. On December 18, 2007, Stephanie Corporation acquired 100 percent of a Swiss company for CHF 3.7 million Swiss francs (CHF). At the date of acquisition, the exchange rate was $0.70 = CHF 1. The acquisition price is attributable to the following assets and liabilities:

Cash	CHF 500,000
Inventory	1,000,000
Fixed assets	3,000,000
Notes payable	(800,000)

Stephanie Corporation prepares consolidated financial statements on December 31, 2007. By that date, the Swiss franc has appreciated to $0.75 = CHF 1. Because of the year-end holidays, no transactions took place prior to consolidation.

   a. Determine the translation adjustment to be reported on Stephanie's December 31, 2007, consolidated balance sheet, assuming that the Swiss franc is the Swiss subsidiary's functional currency. What is the economic relevance of this translation adjustment?

   b. Determine the remeasurement gain or loss to be reported in Stephanie's 2007 consolidated net income, assuming that the U.S. dollar is the functional currency. What is the economic relevance of this remeasurement gain or loss?

25. Fenwicke Company began operating a subsidiary in a foreign country on January 1, 2007, by acquiring all of its common stock for LCU 40,000. This subsidiary immediately borrowed LCU 100,000 on a five-year note with 10 percent interest payable annually beginning on January 1, 2008. The subsidiary then purchased a building for LCU 140,000. This property had a 10-year anticipated life and no salvage value and is to be depreciated using the straight-line method. The subsidiary rents the building for three years to a group of local doctors for LCU 5,000 per month. By year-end, payments totaling LCU 50,000 had been received. On October 1, LCU 4,000 was paid for a repair made on that date. The subsidiary transferred a cash dividend of LCU 5,000 back to Fenwicke on December 31, 2007. The functional currency for the subsidiary is the LCU. Currency exchange rates for 1 LCU are as follows:

January 1, 2007	$2.00 = LCU 1
October 1, 2007	1.85 = 1
Average for 2007	1.90 = 1
December 31, 2007	1.80 = 1

Prepare an income statement, statement of retained earnings, and balance sheet for this subsidiary in LCU and then translate these amounts into U.S. dollars.

26. Refer to the information in Problem 25. Prepare a statement of cash flows in LCU for Fenwicke's foreign subsidiary and then translate these amounts into U.S. dollars.

27. Watson Company has a subsidiary in the country of Alonza where the local currency unit is the kamel (KM). On December 31, 2006, the subsidiary has the following balance sheet:

Cash	KM 16,000	Notes payable (due 2008) ...	KM 19,000
Inventory	10,000	Common stock	20,000
Land	4,000	Retained earnings	10,000
Building	40,000		
Accumulated depreciation ..	(21,000)		
	KM 49,000		KM 49,000

The subsidiary acquired the inventory on August 1, 2006, and the land and buildings in 2000. It issued the common stock in 1998. During 2007, the following transactions took place:

2007

Feb. 1	Paid 5,000 KM on the note payable.
May 1	Sold entire inventory for 15,000 KM on account.
June 1	Sold land for 5,000 KM cash.
Aug. 1	Collected all accounts receivable.
Sept. 1	Signed long-term note to receive 6,000 KM cash.
Oct. 1	Bought inventory for 12,000 KM cash.
Nov. 1	Bought land for 4,000 KM on account.
Dec. 1	Paid 3,000 KM cash dividend to parent.
Dec. 31	Recorded depreciation for the entire year of 2,000 KM.

The exchange rates for 1 KM are as follows:

1998	1 KM = $0.24
2000	1 = 0.21
August 1, 2006	1 = 0.31
December 31, 2006	1 = 0.32
February 1, 2007	1 = 0.33
May 1, 2007	1 = 0.34
June 1, 2007	1 = 0.35
August 1, 2007	1 = 0.37
September 1, 2007	1 = 0.38
October 1, 2007	1 = 0.39
November 1, 2007	1 = 0.40
December 1, 2007	1 = 0.41
December 31, 2007	1 = 0.42
Average for 2007	1 = 0.37

a. If this is a translation, what is the translation adjustment determined solely for 2007?

b. If this is a remeasurement, what is the remeasurement gain or loss determined solely for 2007?

28. Aerkion Company starts the year of 2007 with two assets: cash of 22,000 LCU (local currency units) and land that originally cost 60,000 LCU when acquired on April 4, 2000. On May 1, 2007, the company rendered services to a customer for 30,000 LCU, an amount immediately paid in cash. On October 1, 2007, the company incurred an operating expense of 18,000 LCU that was immediately paid. No other transactions occurred during the year. Currency exchange rates for 1 LCU were as follows:

April 4, 2000	1 LCU = $0.23
January 1, 2007	1 = 0.24
May 1, 2007	1 = 0.25
October 1, 2007	1 = 0.26
Average for 2007	1 = 0.27
December 31, 2007	1 = 0.29

a. Assume that Aerkion is a foreign subsidiary of a U.S. multinational company that uses the U.S. dollar as its reporting currency. Assume also that the LCU is the functional currency of the subsidiary. What is the translation adjustment for this subsidiary for the year 2007?

b. Assume that Aerkion is a foreign subsidiary of a U.S. multinational company that uses the U.S. dollar as its reporting currency. Assume also that the U.S. dollar is the functional currency of the subsidiary. What is the remeasurement gain or loss for 2007?

c. Assume that Aerkion is a foreign subsidiary of a U.S. multinational company. On the December 31, 2007, balance sheet, what is the translated value of the Land account? On the December 31, 2007, balance sheet, what is the remeasured value of the Land account?

29. Lancer, Inc., starts a subsidiary in a foreign country on January 1, 2006. The following account balances are for the year ending December 31, 2007, and are stated in kanquo (KQ), the local currency:

Sales	KQ 200,000
Inventory (bought on 3/1/07)	100,000
Equipment (bought on 1/1/06)	80,000
Rent expense	10,000
Dividends (paid on 10/1/07)	20,000
Notes receivable (to be collected in 2010)	30,000
Accumulated depreciation—equipment	24,000
Salary payable	5,000
Depreciation expense	8,000

The following exchange rates for $1 are applicable:

January 1, 2006	13 KQ
January 1, 2007	18
March 1, 2007	19
October 1, 2007	21
December 31, 2007	22
Average for 2006	14
Average for 2007	20

Lancer is preparing account balances to produce consolidated financial statements.

a. Assuming that the kanquo is the functional currency, what exchange rate would be used to report each of these accounts in U.S. dollar consolidated financial statements?

b. Assuming that the U.S. dollar is the functional currency, what exchange rate would be used to report each of these accounts in U.S. dollar consolidated financial statements?

30. Board Company has a foreign subsidiary that began operations at the start of 2007 with assets of 132,000 kites (the local currency unit) and liabilities of 54,000 kites. During this initial year of operation, the subsidiary reported a profit of 26,000 kites. Two dividends were distributed; each was for 5,000 kites with one dividend paid on March 1 and the other on October 1. Applicable exchange rates for 1 kite are as follows:

January 1, 2007 (start of business)	$0.80
March 1, 2007	0.78
Weighted average rate for 2007	0.77
October 1, 2007	0.76
December 31, 2007	0.75

a. Assume that the kite is the functional currency for this subsidiary. What translation adjustment would Board report for the year 2007?

b. Assume that on October 1, 2007, Board entered into a forward exchange contract to hedge the net investment in this subsidiary. On that date, Board agreed to sell 200,000 kites in three months at a forward exchange rate of $0.76/1 kite. Prepare the journal entries required by this forward contract.

c. Compute the net translation adjustment for Board to report in Other Comprehensive Income for the year 2007 under this second set of circumstances.

31. Kingsfield starts a subsidiary operation in a foreign country on January 1, 2007. The currency in this country is the kumquat (KQ). To start this business, Kingsfield invests 10,000 kumquats. Of this amount, it spends 3,000 kumquats immediately to acquire equipment. Later, on April 1, 2007, it also purchases land. All subsidiary operational activities occur at an even rate throughout the year. The currency exchange rates for the kumquat for this year are as follows:

January 1, 2007	$1.71
April 1, 2007	1.59
June 1, 2007	1.66
Weighted average—2007	1.64
December 31, 2007	1.62

As of December 31, 2007, the subsidiary reports the following trial balance:

	Debits	Credits
Cash	KQ 8,000	
Accounts Receivable	9,000	
Equipment	3,000	
Accumulated Depreciation		KQ 600
Land	5,000	
Accounts Payable		3,000
Notes Payable (due 2009)		5,000
Common Stock		10,000
Dividends Paid (6/1/07)	4,000	
Sales		25,000
Salary Expense	5,000	
Depreciation Expense	600	
Miscellaneous Expenses	9,000	
Totals	KQ 43,600	KQ 43,600

Kingsfield is a corporation based in East Lansing, Michigan, and, therefore, uses the U.S. dollar as its reporting currency.

a. Assume that the functional currency of the subsidiary is the kumquat. Prepare a trial balance for the subsidiary in U.S. dollars so that consolidated financial statements can be prepared.

b. Assume that the subsidiary's functional currency is the U.S. dollar. Prepare a trial balance for the subsidiary in U.S. dollars so that consolidated financial statements can be prepared.

32. Livingston Company is a wholly owned subsidiary of Rose Corporation. Livingston operates in a foreign country with financial statements recorded in goghs (GH), the company's functional currency. Financial statements for the year of 2007 are as follows:

Income Statement
For Year Ending December 31, 2007

Sales	GH 270,000
Cost of goods sold	(155,000)
Gross profit	115,000
Less: Operating expenses	(54,000)
Gain on sale of equipment	10,000
Net income	GH 71,000

Statement of Retained Earnings
For Year Ending December 31, 2007

Retained earnings, 1/1/07	GH 216,000
Net income	71,000
Less: Dividends paid	(26,000)
Retained earnings, 12/31/07	GH 261,000

Balance Sheet
December 31, 2007

Assets

Cash	GH 44,000
Receivables	116,000
Inventory	58,000
Fixed assets (net)	339,000
Total assets	GH 557,000

Liabilities and Equities

Liabilities	GH 176,000
Common stock	120,000
Retained earnings, 12/31/07	261,000
Total liabilities and equities	GH 557,000

Additional Information

- The common stock was issued in 1999 when the exchange rate was $1.00 = 0.48 GH; fixed assets were acquired in 2000 when the rate was $1.00 = 0.50 GH.
- As of January 1, 2007, the Retained Earnings balance was translated as $395,000.
- The currency exchange rates for $1 for the current year are as follows:

January 1, 2007	0.60 goghs
April 1, 2007	0.62
September 1, 2007	0.58
December 31, 2007	0.65
Weighted average rate for 2007	0.63

- Inventory was acquired evenly throughout the year.
- A translation adjustment was reported on the December 31, 2006, balance sheet with a debit balance of $85,000.
- Dividends were paid on April 1, 2007, and a piece of equipment was sold on September 1, 2007.

  Translate the foreign currency statements into the parent's reporting currency, the U.S. dollar.

33. The following account balances are for the Agee Company as of January 1, 2007, and again as of December 31, 2007. All figures are denominated in kroner (Kr).

	January 1, 2007	December 31, 2007
Accounts payable	(18,000)	(24,000)
Accounts receivable	35,000	79,000
Accumulated depreciation—buildings	(20,000)	(25,000)
Accumulated depreciation—equipment	–0–	(5,000)
Bonds payable—due 2012	(50,000)	(50,000)
Buildings	118,000	97,000
Cash	35,000	8,000
Common stock	(70,000)	(80,000)
Depreciation expense	–0–	15,000
Dividends (10/1/07)	–0–	32,000
Equipment	–0–	30,000
Gain on sale of building	–0–	(6,000)
Rent expense	–0–	14,000
Retained earnings	(30,000)	(30,000)
Salary expense	–0–	20,000
Sales	–0–	(80,000)
Utilities expense	–0–	5,000

Additional Information

- Additional shares of common stock were issued during the year on April 1, 2007. Common stock at January 1, 2007, also was sold at the start of operations in 2000.
- Buildings were purchased in 2002. One building with a book value of Kr 16,000 was sold on July 1 of the current year.
- Equipment was acquired on April 1, 2007.
- Retained earnings as of January 1, 2007, was reported as $62,319.

  Relevant exchange rates for 1 Kr were as follows:

2000	$2.40
2002	2.20
January 1, 2007	2.50
April 1, 2007	2.60
July 1, 2007	2.80
October 1, 2007	2.90
December 31, 2007	3.00
Average for 2007	2.70

  a. If a remeasurement is being carried out, what would be the remeasurement gain or loss for 2007?

  b. If a translation is being carried out, what would be the translation adjustment for 2007?

34. Sendelbach Corporation is a U.S.-based organization with operations throughout the world. One of the company's subsidiaries is headquartered in Toronto. Although this wholly owned company operates primarily in Canada, some transactions are carried out through a branch in Mexico. Therefore, the subsidiary maintains a ledger denominated in Mexican pesos (Ps) as well as a general ledger in Canadian dollars (C$). As of December 31, 2007, the Canadian subsidiary is preparing financial statements in anticipation of consolidation with the U.S. parent corporation. Both ledgers for the subsidiary are as follows:

Main Operation—Canada

	Debit	Credit
Accounts payable		C$ 35,000
Accumulated depreciation		27,000
Buildings and equipment	C$167,000	
Cash	26,000	
Common stock		50,000
Cost of goods sold	203,000	
Depreciation expense	8,000	
Dividends paid, 4/1/07	28,000	
Gain on sale of equipment, 6/1/07		5,000
Inventory	98,000	
Notes payable—due in 2009		76,000
Receivables	68,000	
Retained earnings, 1/1/07		135,530
Salary expense	26,000	
Sales		312,000
Utility expense	9,000	
Branch operation	7,530	
Totals	C$640,530	C$640,530

Branch Operation—Mexico

	Debit	Credit
Accounts payable		Ps 49,000
Accumulated depreciation		19,000
Building and equipment	Ps 40,000	
Cash	59,000	
Depreciation expense	2,000	
Inventory (beginning—income statement)	23,000	
Inventory (ending—income statement)		28,000
Inventory (ending—balance sheet)	28,000	
Purchases	68,000	
Receivables	21,000	
Salary expense	9,000	
Sales		124,000
Main office		30,000
Totals	Ps 250,000	Ps 250,000

Additional Information

- The functional currency for the Canadian subsidiary is the Canadian dollar, and the reporting currency for Sendelbach is the U.S. dollar. The Canadian and Mexican operations are not viewed as separate accounting entities.
- The building and equipment used in the Mexican operation were acquired in 1998 when the currency exchange rate was C$0.25 = Ps 1.
- Purchases should be assumed as having been made evenly throughout the fiscal year.
- Beginning inventory was acquired evenly throughout 2006; ending inventory was acquired evenly throughout 2007.
- The Main Office account found on the Mexican records should be considered an equity account. This balance was remeasured into C$7,530 on December 31, 2006, and no further transactions have occurred.

- Currency exchange rates for 1 Ps applicable to the Mexican operation are as follows:

Weighted average, 2006	C$0.30
January 1, 2007	0.32
Weighted average rate for 2007	0.34
December 31, 2007	0.35

- On the December 31, 2006, consolidated balance sheet, a cumulative translation adjustment was reported with a $36,950 credit (positive) balance.
- The subsidiary's common stock was issued in 1996 when the exchange rate was $0.45 = C$1.
- The December 31, 2006, Retained Earnings balance for this subsidiary was C$135,530, a figure that has been translated into US$70,421.
- The applicable currency exchange rates for 1 C$ for translation purposes are as follows:

January 1, 2007	US$0.70
April 1, 2007	0.69
June 1, 2007	0.68
Weighted average rate for 2007	0.67
December 31, 2007	0.65

    a. Remeasure the Mexican peso operation's figures into Canadian dollars (*Hint:* Back into the beginning net monetary asset or liability position.)

    b. Prepare financial statements (income statement, statement of retained earnings, and balance sheet) for the Canadian subsidiary in its functional currency.

    c. Translate the Canadian dollar functional currency financial statements into U.S. dollars so that Sendelbach can prepare consolidated financial statements.

35. On January 1, 2007, Cayce Corporation purchased 100 percent of Simbel Company at a cost of $126,000. Cayce is a U.S.-based company headquartered in Buffalo, New York, and Simbel is in Cairo, Egypt. Cayce accounts for its investment in Simbel under the cost method. Any excess of purchase price over book value is attributable to undervalued land on Simbel's books. Simbel had no retained earnings at the date of acquisition. Following are the 2008 financial statements for the two operations. Cayce's information is in U.S. dollars ($), and Simbel's statements are in Egyptian pounds (£E).

	Cayce Corporation	Simbel Company
Sales	$200,000	£E 800,000
Cost of goods sold	(93,800)	(420,000)
Salary expense	(19,000)	(74,000)
Rent expense	(7,000)	(46,000)
Other expenses	(21,000)	(59,000)
Dividend income—from Simbel	13,750	–0–
Gain on sale of fixed asset, 10/1/08	–0–	30,000
Net income	$ 72,950	£E 231,000
Retained earnings, 1/1/08	$318,000	£E 133,000
Net income	72,950	231,000
Dividends paid	(24,000)	(50,000)
Retained earnings, 12/31/08	$366,950	£E 314,000
Cash and receivables	$110,750	£E 146,000
Inventory	98,000	297,000
Prepaid expenses	30,000	–0–
Investment in Simbel (cost)	126,000	–0–
Fixed assets (net)	398,000	455,000
Total assets	$762,750	£E 898,000
Accounts payable	$ 60,800	£E 54,000
Notes payable—due in 2011	132,000	140,000
Common stock	120,000	240,000
Additional paid-in capital	83,000	150,000
Retained earnings, 12/31/08	366,950	314,000
Total liabilities and equities	$762,750	£E 898,000

Additional Information

- During 2007, the first year of joint operation, Simbel reported income of £E 163,000 earned evenly throughout the year. Simbel paid a dividend of £E 30,000 to Cayce on June 1 of that year. Simbel also paid the 2008 dividend on June 1.

- On December 9, 2008, Simbel classified a £E 10,000 expenditure as a rent expense, although this payment related to prepayment of rent for the first few months of 2009.

- The exchange rates for 1 £E are as follows:

January 1, 2007	$0.300
June 1, 2007	0.290
Weighted average rate for 2007	0.288
December 31, 2007	0.280
June 1, 2008	0.275
October 1, 2008	0.273
Weighted average rate for 2008	0.274
December 31, 2008	0.270

Translate Simbel's 2008 financial statements into U.S. dollars and prepare a consolidation worksheet for Cayce Corporation and its Egyptian subsidiary. Assume that the Egyptian pound is the subsidiary's functional currency.

36. Diekmann Company, a U.S.-based company, acquired a 100 percent interest in Rakona A.S. in the Czech Republic on January 1, 2007, when the exchange rate for the Czech koruna (Kčs) was $0.05. The financial statements of Rakona as of December 31, 2008, two years later, are as follows:

Balance Sheet
December 31, 2008

Assets

Cash	Kčs	2,000,000
Accounts receivable (net)		3,300,000
Inventory		8,500,000
Equipment		25,000,000
Less: Accumulated depreciation		(8,500,000)
Building		72,000,000
Less: Accumulated depreciation		(30,300,000)
Land		6,000,000
Total assets	Kčs	78,000,000

Liabilities and Stockholders' Equity

Accounts payable	Kčs	2,500,000
Long-term debt		50,000,000
Common stock		5,000,000
Additional paid-in capital		15,000,000
Retained earnings		5,500,000
Total liabilities and stockholders' equity	Kčs	78,000,000

Income Statement
For Year Ending December 31, 2008

Sales	Kčs	25,000,000
Cost of goods sold		(12,000,000)
Depreciation expense—equipment		(2,500,000)
Depreciation expense—building		(1,800,000)
Research and development expense		(1,200,000)
Other expenses (including taxes)		(1,000,000)
Net income	Kčs	6,500,000
Plus: Retained earnings, 1/1/08		500,000
Less: Dividends, 2008		(1,500,000)
Retained earnings, 12/31/08	Kčs	5,500,000

Additional Information

- The January 1, 2008, beginning inventory of Kčs 6,000,000 was acquired on December 18, 2007, when the exchange rate was $0.043. Purchases of inventory during 2008 were acquired uniformly throughout the year. The December 31, 2008, ending inventory of Kčs 8,500,000 was acquired in the latter part of 2008 when the exchange rate was $0.032. All fixed assets were on the books when the subsidiary was acquired except for Kčs 5,000,000 of equipment acquired on January 3, 2008, when the exchange rate was $0.036, and Kčs 12,000,000 in buildings acquired on March 5, 2008, when the exchange rate was $0.034. Straight-line depreciation is 10 years for equipment and 40 years for buildings. A full year's depreciation is taken in the year of acquisition.

- Dividends were declared and paid on December 15, 2008, when the exchange rate was $0.031.

- Other exchange rates for 1 Kčs follow:

January 1, 2008	$0.040
Average 2008	0.035
December 31, 2008	0.030

Part I. Translate the Czech koruna financial statements into U.S. dollars in accordance with *SFAS 52* at December 31, 2008, in the following three situations:

a. The Czech koruna is the functional currency. The December 31, 2007, U.S. dollar translated balance sheet reported retained earnings of $22,500. The December 31, 2007, cumulative translation adjustment was negative $202,500 (debit balance).

b. The U.S. dollar is the functional currency. The December 31, 2007, Retained Earnings account in U.S. dollars (including a 2007 remeasurement gain) that appeared in Rakona's remeasured financial statements was $353,000.

c. The U.S. dollar is the functional currency, but Rakona has no long-term debt. Instead, Rakona has common stock of Kčs 20,000,000 and additional paid-in capital of Kčs 50,000,000. The December 31, 2007, U.S. dollar translated balance sheet reported a negative balance in retained earnings of $147,000 (including a 2007 remeasurement loss).

Part II. Explain the positive or negative sign of the translation adjustment in Part I(*a*) and explain why a remeasurement gain or loss in Parts I(*b*) and I(*c*) exists.

Develop Your Skills

RESEARCH CASE 1—FOREIGN CURRENCY TRANSLATION AND HEDGING ACTIVITIES

Many companies make annual reports available on their corporate Internet home page. Annual reports also can be accessed through the SEC's EDGAR system at www.sec.gov (under Forms, search for ARS or 10-K) or in your school's library.

Access the most recent annual report for a U.S.-based multinational company with which you are familiar.

Required:

1. Identify the location(s) in the annual report that provides disclosures related to the translation of foreign currency financial statements and foreign currency hedging.

2. Determine whether the company's foreign operations have a predominant functional currency.

3. Determine the amount of remeasurement gain or loss, if any, reported in net income in each of the three most recent years.

4. Determine the amount of translation adjustment, if any, reported in other comprehensive income in each of the three most recent years. Explain the sign (positive or negative) of the translation adjustment in each of the three most recent years.

5. Determine whether the company hedges net investments in foreign operations. If so, determine the type(s) of hedging instrument used.

RESEARCH CASE 2—FOREIGN CURRENCY TRANSLATION DISCLOSURES IN THE COMPUTER INDUSTRY

Many companies make annual reports available on their corporate Internet home page. Annual reports also can be accessed through the SEC's EDGAR system at www.sec.gov (under Forms, search for ARS or 10-K) or in your school's library.

Access the most recent annual report for the following U.S.-based multinational corporations:

Dell Computer Company.

International Business Machines Corporation.

Required:

1. Identify the location(s) in the annual report that provides disclosures related to foreign currency translation and foreign currency hedging.
2. Determine whether the company's foreign operations have a predominant functional currency. Discuss the implication this has for the comparability of financial statements of the two companies.
3. Determine the amount of translation adjustment, if any, reported in other comprehensive income in each of the three most recent years. Explain the sign (positive or negative) of the translation adjustment in each of the three most recent years. Compare the relative magnitude of these translation adjustments for the two companies.
4. Determine whether each company hedges the net investment in foreign operations. If so, determine the type(s) of hedging instrument used.
5. Prepare a brief report comparing and contrasting the foreign currency translation and foreign currency hedging policies of these two companies.

RESEARCH CASE 3—FOREIGN CURRENCY TRANSLATION DISCLOSURES IN THE SEMICONDUCTOR INDUSTRY

Many companies make annual reports available on their corporate Internet home page. Annual reports also can be accessed through the SEC's EDGAR system at www.sec.gov (under Forms, search for ARS or 10-K) or in your school's library.

Access the most recent annual report for the following U.S.-based multinational corporations:

Intel Corporation.

Advanced Micro Devices, Inc.

Required:

1. Identify the location(s) in the annual report that provides disclosures related to foreign currency translation and foreign currency hedging.
2. Determine whether foreign operations have a predominant functional currency. Discuss the implication this has for the comparability of financial statements of the two companies.
3. Determine the amount of translation adjustment, if any, reported in other comprehensive income in each of the three most recent years.

FARS CASE 1—MORE THAN ONE FUNCTIONAL CURRENCY

A foreign subsidiary of a U.S.-based parent company can have more than one distinct and separable operation. For example, a foreign subsidiary can have one operation that sells products produced by the parent company and another operation that manufactures and sells its own products. The question arises whether a single foreign entity could be considered to have more than one functional currency. Search the FASB's *Original Pronouncements* using either hard copy or the Financial Accounting Research System (FARS) database.

Required:

1. Identify the authoritative pronouncement and paragraph(s) within that pronouncement that address whether a foreign entity can have different functional currencies.
2. Summarize the guidance the FASB provided with respect to this particular issue.

FARS CASE 2—CHANGE IN FUNCTIONAL CURRENCY

A U.S.-based parent company must determine the functional currency of each of its foreign entities to determine the appropriate translation method to use in translating the financial statements of each entity. The question arises as to whether the functional currency of an entity could be considered to change over time, and if so, how this change should be handled. Search the FASB's *Original Pronouncements* using either hard copy or the Financial Accounting Research System (FARS) database.

Required:

1. Identify the authoritative pronouncement and paragraph(s) within that pronouncement that address whether the determination of functional currency of a foreign entity can change over time.
2. Summarize the guidance provided by the FASB with respect to this particular issue.

ANALYSIS CASE—BELLSOUTH CORPORATION

BellSouth Corporation invested in two wireless communications operations in Brazil in the mid-1990s that it accounted for under the equity method. The following note is taken from BellSouth Corporation's interim report for the quarter ended March 31, 1999:

> *Note E—Devaluation of Brazilian Currency*
>
> *We hold equity interests in two wireless communications operations in Brazil. During January 1999, the government of Brazil allowed its currency to trade freely against other currencies. As a result, the Brazilian Real experienced a devaluation against the U.S. Dollar. The devaluation resulted in the entities recording exchange losses related to their net U.S. Dollar-denominated liabilities. Our share of the foreign exchange rate losses for the first quarter was $280.*
>
> *These exchange losses are subject to further upward or downward adjustment based on fluctuations in the exchange rates between the U.S. Dollar and the Brazilian Real.*

In a press release announcing first quarter 1999 results, BellSouth Corporation provided the following information (as found on the company's Web site):

> *BellSouth Corporation (NYSE: BLS) reported a 15 percent increase in first quarter earnings per share (EPS) before special items. EPS was 46 cents before a non-cash expense of 14 cents related to Brazil's currency devaluation.*

BELLSOUTH CORPORATION
Normalized Earnings Summary ($ in millions, except per share amounts)
(unaudited)

	Quarter Ended		
	3/31/99	3/31/98	%Change
Reported Net Income	$615	$892	(31.1%)
Foreign currency loss (a)	280	—	
Gain on sale of ITT World Directories (b)	—	(96)	
Normalized Net Income	$895	$796	12.4%

	Quarter Ended		
	3/31/99	3/31/98	%Change
Reported Diluted Earnings per Share	$0.32	$0.45	(28.9%)
Foreign currency loss (a)	0.14	—	
Gain on sale of ITT World Directories (b)	—	(0.05)	
Normalized Diluted Earnings per Share	$0.46	$0.40	15.0%

(a) Represents our share of foreign currency losses recorded during first quarter 1999 as a result of the devaluation of the Brazilian Real during January 1999.

(b) Represents the after-tax gain associated with additional proceeds received in first quarter 1998 on the July 1997 sale of ITT World Directories.

Required:

Based on the disclosure provided by BellSouth Corporation presented here, answer these questions:

1. Why did the company report a foreign currency loss as a result of the devaluation of the Brazilian real?
2. What does the company mean when it states, "These exchange losses are subject to further upward or downward adjustment based on fluctuations in the exchange rates between the U.S. Dollar and the Brazilian Real"?
3. What is the company's objective in reporting Normalized Net Income?
4. Do you agree with the company's assessment that it had a 15 percent increase in first-quarter earnings per share?

EXCEL CASE—TRANSLATING FOREIGN CURRENCY FINANCIAL STATEMENTS

Charles Edward Company established a subsidiary in a foreign country on January 1, 2007, by investing FC 3,200,000 when the exchange rate was $0.50/FC. Charles Edward negotiated a bank loan of FC 3,000,000 on January 5, 2007, and purchased plant and equipment in the amount of FC 6,000,000 on January 8, 2007. It depreciated plant and equipment on a straight-line basis over a 10-year useful life. It purchased its beginning inventory of FC 1,000,000 on January 10, 2007, and acquired additional inventory of FC 4,000,000 at three points in time during the year at an average exchange rate of $0.43/FC. It uses the first-in, first-out (FIFO) method to determine cost of goods sold. Additional exchange rates per FC 1 during the year 2007 follow:

January 1–31, 2007	$0.50
Average 2007	0.45
December 31, 2007	0.38

The foreign subsidiary's income statement for 2007 and balance sheet at December 31, 2007, follow:

INCOME STATEMENT
For the Year Ended December 31, 2007
FC (in thousands)

Sales	FC 5,000
Cost of goods sold	3,000
Gross profit	2,000
Selling expense	400
Depreciation expense	600
Income before tax	1,000
Income taxes	300
Net income	700
Retained earnings, 1/1/07	0
Retained earnings, 12/31/07	FC 700

BALANCE SHEET
At December 31, 2007
FC (in thousands)

Cash	FC 1,000
Inventory	2,000
Fixed assets	6,000
Less: Accumulated depreciation	(600)
Total assets	FC 8,400
Current liabilities	FC 1,500
Long-term debt	3,000
Contributed capital	3,200
Retained earnings	700
Total liabilities and stockholders' equity	FC 8,400

As the controller for Charles Edward Company, you have evaluated the characteristics of the foreign subsidiary to determine that the FC is the subsidiary's functional currency.

Required:

1. Use an electronic spreadsheet to translate the foreign subsidiary's FC financial statements into U.S. dollars at December 31, 2007, in accordance with *SFAS 52*. Insert a row in the spreadsheet after retained earnings and before total liabilities and stockholders' equity for the cumulative translation adjustment. Calculate the translation adjustment separately to verify the amount obtained as a balancing figure in the translation worksheet.

2. Use an electronic spreadsheet to remeasure the foreign subsidiary's FC financial statements in U.S. dollars at December 31, 2007, assuming that the U.S. dollar is the subsidiary's functional currency. Insert a row in the spreadsheet after depreciation expense and before income before taxes for the remeasurement gain (loss).

3. Prepare a report for James Edward, CEO of Charles Edward Company, summarizing the differences that will be reported in the company's 2007 consolidated financial statements because the FC, rather than the U.S. dollar, is the foreign subsidiary's functional currency. In your report, discuss the relationship between the current ratio, the debt-to-equity ratio, and profit margin calculated from the FC financial statements and from the translated U.S. dollar financial statements. Also discuss the meaning of the translated U.S. dollar amounts for inventory and for fixed assets.

EXCEL AND ANALYSIS CASE—PARKER, INC., AND SUFFOLK PLC

On January 1, 2006, Parker, Inc., a U.S.-based firm, purchased 100 percent of Suffolk PLC located in Great Britain. Parker paid 52,000,000 British pounds (£) for its purchase. The excess of cost over book value is attributable to land (part of property, plant, and equipment) and is not subject to depreciation. Parker accounts for its investment in Suffolk at cost. On January 1, 2006, Suffolk reported the following balance sheet:

Cash	£ 2,000,000	Accounts payable	£ 1,000,000
Accounts receivable	3,000,000	Long-term debt	8,000,000
Inventory	14,000,000	Common stock	44,000,000
Property, plant, and equipment (net)	40,000,000	Retained earnings	6,000,000
	£ 59,000,000		£59,000,000

Suffolk's 2006 income was recorded at £2,000,000. No dividends were declared or paid by Suffolk in 2006.

On December 31, 2007, two years after the date of acquisition, Suffolk submitted the following trial balance to Parker for consolidation:

Cash	£ 1,500,000
Accounts Receivable	5,200,000
Inventory	18,000,000
Property, Plant, and Equipment (net)	36,000,000
Accounts Payable	(1,450,000)
Long-Term Debt	(5,000,000)
Common Stock	(44,000,000)
Retained Earnings (1/1/07)	(8,000,000)
Sales	(28,000,000)
Cost of Goods Sold	16,000,000
Depreciation	2,000,000
Other Expenses	6,000,000
Dividends Paid (1/30/07)	1,750,000
	–0–

Other than the payment of dividends, no intercompany transactions occurred between the two companies. Relevant exchange rates for the British pound were as follows:

	January 1	January 30	Average	December 31
2006	$1.60	$1.61	$1.62	$1.64
2007	1.64	1.65	1.66	1.68

December 31, 2007, financial statements (before consolidation with Suffolk) follow. Dividend income is the U.S. dollar amount of dividends received from Suffolk translated at the $1.65/£ exchange rate at January 30, 2007. The amounts listed for dividend income and all affected accounts (i.e., net income, December 31 retained earnings, and cash) reflect the $1.65/£ exchange rate at January 30, 2007. Credit balances are in parentheses.

Parker	
Sales	$ (70,000,000)
Cost of goods sold	34,000,000
Depreciation	20,000,000
Other expenses	6,000,000
Dividend income	(2,887,500)
Net income	$ (12,887,500)
Retained earnings, 1/1/07	$ (48,000,000)
Net income, 2007	(12,887,500)
Dividends, 1/30/07	4,500,000
Retained earnings, 12/31/07	$ (56,387,500)
Cash	$ 3,687,500
Accounts receivable	10,000,000
Inventory	30,000,000
Investment in Suffolk	83,200,000
Plant and equipment (net)	105,000,000
Accounts payable	(25,500,000)
Long-term debt	(50,000,000)
Common stock	(100,000,000)
Retained earnings, 12/31/07	(56,387,500)
	–0–

Parker's chief financial officer (CFO) wishes to determine the effect that a change in the value of the British pound would have on consolidated net income and consolidated stockholders' equity. To help assess the foreign currency exposure associated with the investment in Suffolk, the CFO requests assistance in comparing consolidated results under actual exchange rate fluctuations with results that would have occurred had the dollar value of the pound remained constant or declined during the first two years of Parker's ownership.

Required:

Use an electronic spreadsheet to complete the following four parts:

Part I. Given the relevant exchange rates presented,

1. Translate Suffolk's December 31, 2007, trial balance from British pounds to U.S. dollars. The British pound is Suffolk's functional currency.
2. Prepare a schedule that details the change in Suffolk's cumulative translation adjustment (beginning net assets, income, dividends, etc.) for 2006 and 2007.
3. Prepare the December 31, 2007, consolidation worksheet for Parker and Suffolk.
4. Prepare the 2007 consolidated income statement and the December 31, 2007, consolidated balance sheet.

Note: Worksheets should possess the following qualities:

- Each spreadsheet should be programmed so that all relevant amounts adjust appropriately when different values of exchange rates (subsequent to January 1, 2006) are entered into it.
- Be sure to program Parker's dividend income, cash, and retained earnings to reflect the dollar value of alternative January 30, 2007, exchange rates.

Part II. Repeat tasks (1), (2), (3), and (4) from Part I to determine consolidated net income and consolidated stockholders' equity if the exchange rate had remained at $1.60/£ over the period 2006 to 2007.

Part III. Repeat tasks (1), (2), (3), and (4) from Part I to determine consolidated net income and consolidated stockholders' equity if the following exchange rates had existed:

	January 1	January 30	Average	December 31
2006	$1.60	$1.59	$1.58	$1.56
2007	1.56	1.55	1.54	1.52

Part IV. Prepare a report that provides Parker's CFO with the risk assessments requested. Focus on profitability, cash flow, and the debt-to-equity ratio.

CPA Review

Please visit the text Web site for the online CPA Simulation: mhhe.com/hoyle8e

Situation: The Texas Corporation is located in San Antonio and has transactions both in the United States and in Mexico although the United States dollar is its functional currency. In addition, this company has a wholly owned subsidiary (Mexico, Inc.) located in Mexico. Consolidated financial statements are being prepared for Year One. The currency exchange rates are as follows for the current year (Year One):

- January 1, Year One: 1 peso equals $0.088.
- Average for Year One: 1 peso equals $0.090.
- November 1, Year One: 1 peso equals $0.092.
- December 1, Year One: 1 peso equals $0.094.
- December 31, Year One: 1 peso equals $0.095.
- January 31, Year Two: 1 peso equals $0.098.

Topics to be covered in simulation:

- Remeasurement process.
- Translation process.
- Foreign currency balances—impact on net income.
- Foreign currency balances—impact on comprehensive income.
- Translation adjustment.
- Functional currency.
- Forward exchange contracts as a cash flow hedge.
- Forward exchange contracts as a fair value hedge.

Chapter Eleven

Worldwide Accounting Diversity and International Standards

Questions to Consider

- Why do accounting and reporting practices differ throughout the world? What problems does worldwide accounting diversity cause?

- What are the major classes of accounting systems internationally?

- What benefits would be derived from the use of a single set of financial reporting standards across countries?

- What progress has the IASB achieved in establishing worldwide financial reporting standards? How many countries require or allow domestic companies to use the IASB's international financial reporting standards (IFRSs) in preparing financial statements?

- What differences exist between IFRSs and U.S. GAAP? What is the so-called Norwalk Agreement?

- What differences exist in the structure of the financial statements prepared by companies in Germany, Japan, and the United Kingdom?

Considerable differences exist across countries in the accounting treatment of many items. As discussed in Chapter 3, for example, goodwill is an asset subject to annual impairment testing in the United States; however, it must be amortized over a period not to exceed 20 years in Brazil. For the most part, U.S. companies are not allowed to report assets at amounts higher than historical cost. Mexican companies, on the other hand, must write up their assets on the balance sheet to inflation-adjusted amounts. Research and development costs must be expensed as incurred in the United States, but development costs must be capitalized in European Union countries when certain criteria are met. Numerous other differences exist across countries. In its 2004 annual report, the Dutch electronics firm Philips described six significant differences between U.S. and Dutch accounting rules.[1] If Philips had used U.S. GAAP in 2004, its net income would have been 21 percent higher than the amount the firm actually reported in conformity with Dutch GAAP. In its 2004 annual report, the British beverage company Cadbury Schweppes listed 11 significant differences between U.S. and U.K. GAAP.[2] If Cadbury Schweppes had used U.S. accounting rules, its 2004 net income would have been 12 percent higher than the amount the firm actually reported in accordance with U.K. GAAP, and its shareholders' equity would have been 32 percent higher.

This chapter is divided into three parts. Part 1 presents evidence of accounting diversity, explores the reasons for accounting diversity, and describes international patterns or models of accounting. Part 2 discusses and evaluates accounting harmonization efforts. Regarding harmonization, we concentrate on the effort undertaken in the European Union and, more importantly, on the standards developed by the International Accounting Standards Board. We also describe current efforts to converge IASB standards with U.S. GAAP.

---

[1] The adjustments related to differences in accounting for goodwill, gains on sale of securities, impairment charges, and other items.

[2] The accounting difference requiring the largest adjustment was related to goodwill/intangibles amortization.

Part 3 provides a description of the accounting environment in several major countries. We focus on the accounting profession and the presentation of financial statements in those countries.

EVIDENCE OF ACCOUNTING DIVERSITY

Exhibit 11.1 presents the 2004 balance sheet for the British company Imperial Chemical Industries PLC (ICI). A quick examination of this statement reveals several differences in format and terminology used between statements in the United Kingdom and the United States. Noncurrent assets in general are called *fixed assets* in the United Kingdom, whereas property, plant, and equipment are referred to as *tangible assets*. Liabilities are called *creditors,* and accounts receivable are *debtors*. Unless one is fluent in the language of U.K. accounting, stocks might be thought to be marketable securities, when actually stocks are *inventories*. Called Up Share Capital is the par value, and Share Premium Account is the Paid-In Capital in Excess of Par on Common Stock. Retained earnings are not reported separately but are included in the item labeled Profit and Loss Account. Rather than being treated as an asset, goodwill is included in the Profit and Loss Account as a negative item. Goodwill written off to shareholders' equity exceeds the amount of retained earnings, resulting in a negative balance in the Profit and Loss Account.

From the perspective of U.S. financial reporting, the U.K. balance sheet has an unusual structure. Rather than the U.S. norm of Assets = Liabilities + Shareholders' Equity, ICI's balance sheet is presented as Total Assets − Current Liabilities = Long-Term Liabilities + Shareholders' Equity. Listed in reverse order of liquidity, assets start with tangible assets and move down to cash. Current liabilities follow current assets to arrive at net working capital.

All of these superficial differences would probably cause a financial analyst no problem in analyzing the company's financial statements. More important than the format and terminology differences are the differences in measurement rules employed to value assets and calculate income. Because ICI's common stock is listed on the New York Stock Exchange, the company is required to be registered and file financial statements with the U.S. Securities and Exchange Commission (SEC). For foreign registrants, the SEC requires income and stockholders' equity reported under foreign GAAP to be reconciled with U.S. GAAP. ICI's 2004 reconciliation to U.S. GAAP is in Exhibit 11.2. This reconciliation provides significant insight into the major differences in accounting principles between the United States and the United Kingdom. Note that although only eight items required adjustments, the aggregate effect on income and stockholders' equity was highly significant. Net income in 2004 under U.K. GAAP was twice as high as under U.S. GAAP. Stockholders' equity under U.K. GAAP was less than one-third the amount reported under U.S. accounting rules.

Magnitude of Accounting Diversity

Although it is generally assumed that accounting diversity results in significant differences in the measurement of income and equity across countries, until the 1990s there was very little systematic empirical documentation of the effect that these differences have on published financial statements. In 1993, the SEC published a survey that examined the U.S. GAAP reconciliations made by 444 foreign entities from 36 countries.[3] The results of that survey indicate that approximately two-thirds of the foreign companies showed material differences between net income and owners' equity reported on the basis of home GAAP and U.S. GAAP. Of those with material differences, net income would have been lower under U.S. GAAP for about two-thirds of the companies (higher using U.S. GAAP for about one-third). Similar results were found with regard to owners' equity. At the extremes, income was 29 times higher under U.S. GAAP for one foreign entity, and 178 times higher using British GAAP for another entity. In addition, the study found that significant differences are spread relatively evenly

---

[3] United States Securities and Exchange Commission, *Survey of Financial Statement Reconciliations by Foreign Registrants* (Washington, D.C., 1993).

EXHIBIT 11.1   Imperial Chemical Industries PLC U.K. Balance Sheet

Balance Sheets at 31 December 2004

	Notes	Group 2004 £m	Group 2003 £m	Company 2004 £m	Company 2003 £m
Assets employed					
Fixed assets					
Intangible assets—goodwill	11	**480**	532	—	—
Tangible assets	4,12	**1,659**	1,794	**66**	68
Investments					
Subsidiary undertakings	13	**—**	—	**11,854**	10,489
Participating and other interests	14	**61**	57	**1**	1
		2,200	2,383	**11,921**	10,558
Current assets					
Stocks	15	**648**	626	**37**	27
Debtors	16	**1,587**	1,605	**2,187**	2,438
Investments and short-term deposits	17	**105**	345	**—**	—
Cash	33	**396**	249	**9**	9
		2,736	2,825	**2,233**	2,474
Total assets		**4,936**	5,208	**14,154**	13,032
Creditors due within one year					
Short-term borrowings	18	**(137)**	(29)	**—**	—
Current installments of loans	20	**(165)**	(534)	**(105)**	—
Other creditors	19	**(1,775)**	(1,663)	**(5,877)**	(4,725)
		(2,077)	(2,226)	**(5,982)**	(4,725)
Net current assets (liabilities)		**659**	599	**(3,749)**	(2,251)
Total assets less current liabilities	4	**2,859**	2,982	**8,172**	8,307
Financed by					
Creditors due after more than one year					
Loans	20	**1,117**	1,353	**26**	133
Other creditors	19	**20**	18	**3,335**	3,450
		1,137	1,371	**3,361**	3,583
Provisions for liabilities and charges	21	**914**	1,092	**185**	207
Minority interests—equity		87	69	—	—
Shareholders' fund—equity					
Called-up share capital	23	**1,191**	1,191	**1,191**	1,191
Reserves					
Share premium account		**933**	933	**933**	933
Associates' reserves		**15**	13	**—**	—
Profit and loss account		**(1,418)**	(1,687)	**2,502**	2,393
Total reserves	24	**(470)**	(741)	**3,435**	3,326
Total shareholders' funds		**721**	450	**4,626**	4,517
		2,859	2,982	**8,172**	8,307

across countries. In other words, material differences are as likely to exist for a British or Canadian company as for a company in South America, Asia, or Continental Europe.

Focusing on the U.S. GAAP reconciliations of British companies, a separate study found that all 39 companies examined reported material differences in income or equity. Over 90 percent reported lower income under U.S. GAAP and approximately 60 percent reported higher equity. The average difference in income, even after including those with higher U.S.

EXHIBIT 11.2
**Imperial Chemical
Industries PLC
Reconciliation to
U.S. GAAP**

	2004 £m	2003 £m	2002 £m
Net income (loss) after exceptional items—U.K. GAAP	**210**	20	179
Continuing operations	**224**	23	166
Discontinued operations	**(14)**	(3)	13
Adjustments to conform with U.S. GAAP			
Pension expense	**(24)**	(7)	(14)
Purchase accounting adjustments			
Amortisation/impairment of goodwill and amortisation of intangibles	**(10)**	(249)	(117)
Disposals and other adjustments	**(67)**	72	(31)
Capitalisation of interest less amortisation and disposals	**(4)**	(5)	(5)
Derivative instruments and hedging activities	**(10)**	(15)	(41)
Restructuring costs	**(47)**	46	(6)
Share compensation expense	**(7)**	(7)	(3)
Others	**—**	—	(2)
Tax effect of U.S. GAAP adjustments	**64**	(21)	49
Total U.S. GAAP adjustments	**(105)**	(186)	(170)
Net income (loss)—U.S. GAAP	**105**	(166)	9
Continuing operations	**129**	(181)	(124)
Discontinued operations	**(24)**	15	133
	Pence	**Pence**	**Pence**
Basic and diluted net earnings (net loss) per Ordinary Share in accordance with U.S. GAAP	**8.9**	(14.0)	0.8
Continuing operations	**10.9**	(15.3)	(11.1)
Discontinued operations	**(2.0)**	1.3	11.9
	2004 £m	2003 £m	
Shareholders' funds—equity, as shown in the Group balance sheet—U.K. GAAP	**721**	450	
Adjustments to conform with U.S. GAAP			
Pension costs	**(510)**	(482)	
Pension costs—minimum pension liability	**(582)**	(601)	
Purchase accounting adjustments, including goodwill and intangibles	**2,489**	2,778	
Disposal accounting adjustments	**(100)**	(29)	
Capitalisation of interest less amortisation and disposals	**27**	31	
Derivative instruments and hedging activities	**24**	25	
Restructuring—contract terminations	**(2)**	8	
Restructuring—asset impairment	**2**	39	
Ordinary dividends	**46**	42	
Deferred taxation and tax effects of U.S. GAAP adjustments ..	**(225)**	(421)	
Deferred taxation and tax effects of U.S. GAAP adjustments ..	**389**	519	
Total U.S. GAAP adjustments	**1,558**	1,909	
Shareholders' equity in accordance with U.S. GAAP	**2,279**	2,359	

GAAP income, was a 42 percent reduction in income when reconciling to U.S. GAAP.[4] It is clear that differences in accounting principles can have a material impact on amounts reported in financial statements.

[4] Vivian Periar, Ron Paterson, and Allister Wilson, *UK/US GAAP Comparison,* 2nd ed. (London: Kogan Page Limited, 1992), pp. 384–93.

REASONS FOR ACCOUNTING DIVERSITY

Why do differences in financial reporting practices exist across countries? Accounting scholars have hypothesized numerous influences on a country's accounting system, including factors as varied as the nature of the political system, the stage of economic development, and the state of accounting education and research. A survey of the relevant literature identified the following five items as commonly accepted factors influencing a country's financial reporting practices: (1) legal system, (2) taxation, (3) providers of financing, (4) inflation, and (5) political and economic ties.[5]

Legal System

The two major types of legal systems used around the world are common law and codified Roman law. Common law began in England and is found primarily in the English-speaking countries of the world. Common law countries rely on a limited amount of statute law that is interpreted by the courts. Court decisions establish precedents, thereby developing case law that supplements the statutes. A system of code law, followed in most non-English-speaking countries, originated in the Roman *jus civile* and was developed further in European universities during the Middle Ages. Code law countries tend to have relatively more statute or codified law governing a wider range of human activity.

What does a country's legal system have to do with accounting? Code law countries generally have a corporation law (sometimes called a *commercial code* or *companies act*) that establishes the basic legal parameters governing business enterprises. Corporation law often stipulates which financial statements must be published in accordance with a prescribed format. Additional accounting measurement and disclosure rules are included in an accounting law that has been debated and passed by the national legislature. The accounting profession tends to have little influence on the development of accounting standards. In countries with a tradition of common law, although a corporation law laying the basic framework for accounting might exist (such as in the United Kingdom), the profession or an independent, nongovernmental body representing a variety of constituencies establishes specific accounting rules. Thus, the type of legal system in a country determines whether the primary source of accounting rules is the government or the accounting profession.

In code law countries, the accounting law is rather general; it does not provide much detail regarding specific accounting practices and may provide no guidance at all in certain areas. Germany is a good example of a code law country. The German accounting law passed in 1985 is only 47 pages in length and is silent with regard to issues such as leases, foreign currency translation, and a cash flows statement.[6] In those situations where no guidance is provided in the law, German companies must refer to other sources, including tax law and opinions of the German auditing profession, to decide how to do their accounting. Common law countries, where a nongovernment organization is likely to develop accounting standards, have much more detailed rules. The extreme case might be the FASB in the United States. The Board provides very specific detail in its Statements of Financial Accounting Standards about how to apply the rules and has been accused of producing a standards overload.

Taxation

In some countries, published financial statements form the basis for taxation, whereas in other countries, financial statements are adjusted for tax purposes and submitted to the government separately from the reports sent to stockholders. Continuing to focus on Germany, its so-called conformity principle (*Massgeblichkeitsprinzip*) requires that, in most cases, an expense also must be used in calculating financial statement income to be deductible for tax purposes. Well-managed German companies attempt to minimize income for tax purposes, for example, through the use of accelerated depreciation to reduce their tax liability. As a result of the conformity principle, accelerated depreciation also must be taken in the calculation of accounting income.

---

[5] Gary K. Meek and Sharokh M. Saudagaran, "A Survey of Research on Financial Reporting in a Transnational Context," *Journal of Accounting Literature,* 1990, pp. 145–82.

[6] Jermyn Paul Brooks and Dietz Mertin, *Neues Deutsches Bilanzrecht* (Düsseldorf: IDW-Verlag GmbH, 1986).

In the United States, on the other hand, conformity between the tax statement and financial statements is required only for the use of the LIFO inventory cost-flow assumption. U.S. companies are allowed to use accelerated depreciation for tax purposes and straight-line depreciation in the financial statements. All else being equal, a U.S. company is likely to report higher income than its German counterpart.

Providers of Financing

The major providers of financing for business enterprises are family members, banks, governments, and shareholders. In those countries in which company financing is dominated by families, banks, or the state, there is less pressure for public accountability and information disclosure. Banks and the state often are represented on the board of directors and therefore are able to obtain information necessary for decision making from inside the company. As companies depend more on financing from the general populace through the public offering of shares of stock, the demand for more information made available outside the company increases. It simply is not feasible for the company to allow the hundreds, thousands, or hundreds of thousands of shareholders access to internal accounting records. The information needs of those financial statement users can be satisfied only through extensive disclosures in accounting reports.

There also can be a difference in orientation, with stockholders more interested in profit (emphasis on the income statement) and banks more interested in solvency and liquidity (emphasis on the balance sheet). Bankers prefer companies to practice rather conservative accounting with regard to assets and liabilities.

Inflation

Countries with chronically high rates of inflation have been forced to adopt accounting rules that require the inflation adjustment of historical cost amounts. This has been especially true in Latin America, which as a region has had more inflation than any other part of the world. For example, prior to economic reform in the mid-1990s, Brazil regularly experienced annual inflation rates exceeding 100 percent. The high point was reached in 1993 when annual inflation was nearly 1,800 percent. Double- and triple-digit inflation rates render historical costs meaningless. This factor primarily distinguishes accounting in Latin America from the rest of the world.

Political and Economic Ties

Accounting is a technology that can be borrowed relatively easily from or imposed on another country. Through political and economic linkages, accounting rules have been conveyed from one country to another. For example, through previous colonialism, both England and France have transferred their accounting frameworks to a variety of countries around the world. British accounting systems can be found in countries as far-flung as Australia and Zimbabwe. French accounting is prevalent in the former French colonies of western Africa. More recently, economic ties with the United States have had an impact on accounting in Canada, Mexico, and Israel.

Correlation of Factors

Whether by coincidence or not, there is a high degree of correlation between the legal system, tax conformity, and source of financing. Common law countries separate taxation from accounting and rely more heavily on the stock market as a source of capital. Code law countries link taxation to accounting statements and rely less on financing provided by shareholders.

PROBLEMS CAUSED BY DIVERSE ACCOUNTING PRACTICES

The diversity in accounting practices across countries causes problems that can be quite serious for some parties. One problem relates to the preparation of consolidated financial statements by companies with foreign operations. Consider The Coca-Cola Company, which has subsidiaries in more than 100 countries around the world. Each subsidiary incorporated in the country in which it is located is required to prepare financial statements in accordance with local regulations. These regulations usually require companies to keep books in the local currency and follow local accounting principles. Thus, Coca-Cola Italia SRL prepares financial statements in euros using Italian accounting rules, and Coca-Cola Amatil Ltd. prepares financial statements in Australian dollars using Australian standards. To prepare consolidated financial statements in the United States, in addition to translating the foreign currency financial statements into U.S. dollars, the parent company must also convert the financial statements of its foreign subsidiaries into U.S. GAAP. Each foreign subsidiary must either maintain two sets of books prepared in accordance with both local and U.S. GAAP or, as is more common, make reconciliations from local GAAP to U.S. GAAP at the balance sheet date. In either case, considerable effort and cost are involved; company personnel must develop an expertise in more than one country's accounting standards.

A second problem relates to companies gaining access to foreign capital markets. If a company desires to obtain capital by selling stock or borrowing money in a foreign country, it might be required to present a set of financial statements prepared in accordance with the accounting standards in the country in which the capital is being obtained. Consider the case of the Swedish appliance manufacturer Electrolux. The equity market in Sweden is so small (there are fewer than 9 million Swedes) and Electrolux's capital needs are so great that the company has found it necessary to have its common shares listed on foreign stock exchanges in London and Frankfurt and on NASDAQ in the United States. To have their stock traded in the United States, foreign companies must reconcile financial statements to U.S. accounting standards. This can be quite costly. To prepare for a New York Stock Exchange (NYSE) listing in 1993, the German automaker Daimler-Benz estimated it spent $60 million to initially prepare U.S. GAAP financial statements; it planned to spend $15 to 20 million each year thereafter.[7]

A third problem relates to the lack of comparability of financial statements between companies from different countries. This can significantly affect the analysis of foreign financial statements for making investment and lending decisions. In 2001 alone, U.S. investors bought nearly $95 billion in debt and equity of foreign entities while foreign investors pumped approximately $408 billion into U.S. entities through similar acquisitions.[8] In recent years there has been an explosion in mutual funds that invest in the stock of foreign companies—from 123 in 1989 to 534 at the end of 1995.[9] T. Rowe Price's New Asia Fund, for example, invests exclusively in stocks and bonds of companies located in Asian countries other than Japan. The job of deciding which foreign company to invest in is complicated by the fact that foreign companies use accounting rules that differ from those used in the United States, and those rules differ from country to country. It is very difficult, if not impossible, for a potential investor to directly compare the financial position and performance of chemical companies in Germany (BASF), China (Sinopec), and the U.S. (DuPont) because these three countries have different financial accounting and reporting standards. According to Ralph E. Walters, former chairman of the steering committee of the International Accounting Standards Committee, "Either international investors have to be extremely knowledgeable about multiple reporting methods or they have to be willing to take greater risk."[10]

A lack of comparability of financial statements also can have an adverse effect on corporations when making foreign acquisition decisions. As a case in point, consider the experience of foreign investors in Eastern Europe. After the fall of the Berlin Wall in 1989, officials invited Western companies to acquire newly privatized companies in Poland, Hungary, and other countries in the former communist bloc. The concept of profit and accounting for assets in those countries under communism was so much different from accounting practice in the West that most Western investors found financial statements useless in helping them determine the most attractive acquisition targets. Many investors asked the then Big 5 public accounting firms to convert financial statements to a Western basis before acquisition of a company could be seriously considered.

---

[7] Allan B. Afterman, *International Accounting, Financial Reporting, and Analysis* (New York: Warren, Gorham & Lamont, 1995), pp. C1–17 and C1–22.

[8] U.S. Department of Commerce, *Survey of Current Business,* January 2003, p. 38.

[9] James L. Cochrane, James E. Shapiro, and Jean E. Tobin, "Foreign Equities and U.S. Investors: Breaking Down the Barriers Separating Supply and Demand," NYSE Working Paper 95–04, 1995.

[10] Stephen H. Collins, "The Move to Globalization, *Journal of Accountancy,* March 1989, p. 82.

EXHIBIT 11.3
A Hypothetical Classification of Accounting Systems

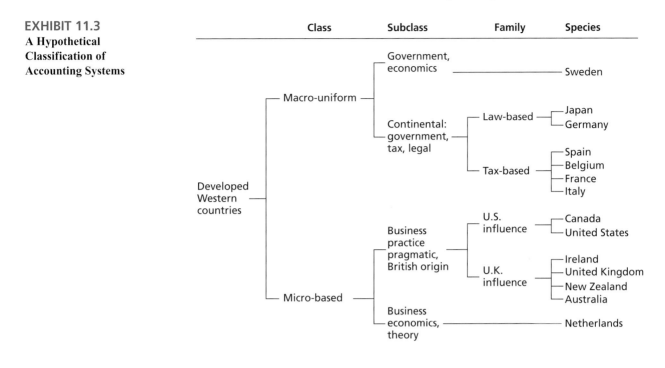

Because of the problems associated with worldwide accounting diversity, attempts to reduce accounting differences across countries have been ongoing for more than three decades. This process is known as *harmonization*. The ultimate goal of harmonization is to have all companies around the world follow one set of international accounting standards.

ACCOUNTING CLUSTERS

Given the discussion regarding factors influencing accounting practice worldwide, it should not be surprising to learn that clusters of countries share common accounting practices. One classification scheme identifies four major accounting models: British–American, Continental, South American, and Mixed Economy.[11] **British–American** describes the approach used in the United Kingdom and United States where accounting is oriented toward the decision needs of large numbers of investors and creditors. Dutch accounting is quite similar. This model is used in most of the English-speaking countries, and other countries heavily influenced by the United Kingdom or United States. Most of these countries follow a common law legal system. Most of continental Europe and Japan use the **Continental** model. Companies in this group usually are tied quite closely to banks that serve as the primary suppliers of financing. Because these are code law countries, accounting is legalistic, designed to provide information for taxation or government planning purposes. The **South American** model resembles the Continental model in its legalistic, tax, and government planning orientation. This model distinguishes itself, however, through the extensive use of adjustments for inflation. The **Mixed Economy** model describes the approach recently developed in Eastern Europe and the former Union of Soviet Socialist Republics that combines elements of the former planned economic system and the recent market economy reforms.

Concentrating on the British–American and Continental model countries, Professor Chris Nobes has developed a more refined classification scheme that shows how the financial reporting systems in 14 developed countries relate to one another. An adaptation of Nobes's classification is in Exhibit 11.3.[12]

---

[11] Gerhard G. Mueller, Helen Gernon, and Gary Meek, *Accounting—An International Perspective,* 3rd ed. (Burr Ridge, Ill.: Richard D. Irwin, 1994), pp. 8–12.

[12] Source: C. W. Nobes, "A Judgemental International Classification of Financial Reporting Practices," *Journal of Business Finance and Accounting,* Spring 1983, p. 7.

A Hypothetical Model of Accounting Diversity

The terms *micro-based* and *macro-uniform* describe the British–American and Continental models, respectively. Each of these classes is divided into two subclasses that are further divided into families. Within the micro-based class of accounting system is a subclass heavily influenced by business economics and accounting theory. The Netherlands is the only country in this subclass. One manifestation of the influence of theory is that Dutch companies may use current replacement cost accounting in their primary financial statements. The other micro-based subclass is of British origin and is more pragmatic and oriented toward business practice, relying less on economic theory in the development of accounting rules. The British origin subclass can be split into two families: one dominated by the United States and one dominated by the United Kingdom. Nobes does not indicate how these two families differ.

On the macro-uniform side of the model, a government, economics subclass has only one country, Sweden. Swedish accounting distinguishes itself from the other macro-uniform countries in being closely aligned with national economic policies. For example, income smoothing is allowed to promote economic stability, and social accounting has developed to meet macroeconomic concerns. The Continental government, tax, legal subclass contains Continental European countries divided into two families. Led by Germany, the law-based family includes Japan. The tax-based family consists of several Romance-language countries. The major difference between these families is that the accounting law is the primary determinant of accounting practice in Germany, whereas the tax law dominates in the Southern European countries.

The importance of this hierarchical model is that it shows the comparative distances between countries and could be used as a blueprint for determining where financial statement comparability is likely to be greater. For example, comparisons of financial statements in the United States and those in Canada (which are in the same family) are likely to be more valid than comparisons between those in the United States and in the United Kingdom (which are not in the same family). However, the United States and the United Kingdom (which are in the same subclass) are more comparable than are the United States and the Netherlands (which are in different subclasses). Finally, comparisons between the United States and the Netherlands (which are in the same class) might be more meaningful than comparisons between the United States and any of the macro-uniform countries.

The hypothetical model in Exhibit 11.3 was empirically tested in 1993.[13] Data gathered on 100 financial reporting practices in 50 countries (including the 14 countries in Exhibit 11.3) were analyzed using the statistical procedure of hierarchical cluster analysis. The significant clusters arising from the analysis are in Exhibit 11.4.

The large size of the U.K. influence cluster (Cluster 1) clearly shows the influence of British colonialism on accounting worldwide. In contrast, Cluster 2, which includes the United States, is quite small. The emergence of Cluster 4, which includes several Latin American countries, is evidence of the importance of inflation as a factor affecting accounting practice.

The two classes of accounting reflected in Exhibit 11.4 differ significantly on 66 of the 100 financial reporting practices examined.[14] Differences exist for 41 of the 56 disclosure practices studied. In all but one case, the micro class of countries provided a higher level of disclosure than the macro class of countries. There were also significant differences for 25 of the 44 practices examined affecting income measurement. Of particular importance is the item asking whether accounting practice adhered to tax requirements. The mean level of agreement with this statement among macro countries was 72 percent, whereas it was only 45 percent among micro countries. To summarize, companies in the micro-based countries provide more extensive disclosure than do companies in the macro-uniform countries, and companies in the macro countries are more heavily influenced by taxation than are companies in the micro countries. These results are consistent with the relative importance of equity finance and relatively weak link between accounting and taxation in the micro countries.

---

[13] Timothy S. Doupnik and Stephen B. Salter, "An Empirical Test of a Judgemental International Classification of Financial Reporting Practices," *Journal of International Business Studies,* First Quarter 1993, pp. 41–60.

[14] Ibid., 1993, p. 56.

EXHIBIT 11.4
Results of Cluster
Analysis on 100 Financial
Reporting Practices

Micro Class			Macro Class		
Cluster 1	**Cluster 2**		**Cluster 3**	**Cluster 5**	**Cluster 7**
Australia	Bermuda		Costa Rica	Colombia	Finland
Botswana	Canada			Denmark	Sweden
Hong Kong	Israel		**Cluster 4**	France	
Ireland	United States		Argentina	Italy	**Cluster 8**
Jamaica			Brazil	Norway	Germany
Luxembourg			Chile	Portugal	
Malaysia			Mexico	Spain	**Cluster 9**
Namibia					Japan
Netherlands				**Cluster 6**	
Netherlands Antilles				Belgium	
Nigeria				Egypt	
New Zealand				Liberia	
Philippines				Panama	
Papua New Guinea				Saudi Arabia	
South Africa				Thailand	
Singapore				United Arab Emirates	
Sri Lanka					
Taiwan					
Trinidad and Tobago					
United Kingdom					
Zambia					
Zimbabwe					

Source: Timothy S. Doupnik and Stephen B. Salter, "An Empirical Test of a Judgemental International Classification of Financial Reporting Practices," *Journal of International Business Studies,* First Quarter 1993, p. 53.

INTERNATIONAL HARMONIZATION OF FINANCIAL REPORTING

The preceding sections make clear the significant, systematic differences in accounting practices across countries. As noted in the introduction, these differences cause complications for those preparing and using financial statements. Several organizations around the world are involved in an effort to harmonize financial reporting practices.

Harmonization is the process of reducing differences in financial reporting practices across countries, thereby increasing the comparability of financial statements. Ultimately, harmonization implies the development of a set of international accounting standards that would be applied in all countries.

Arguments for Harmonization

Proponents of accounting harmonization argue that comparability of financial statements worldwide is necessary for the globalization of capital markets. Financial statement comparability would make it easier for investors to evaluate potential investments in foreign securities and thereby take advantage of the risk reduction possible through international diversification. It also would simplify the evaluation by multinational companies of possible foreign takeover targets. From the other side, with harmonization, companies could gain access to all capital markets in the world with one set of financial statements. This would allow companies to lower their cost of capital and would make it easier for foreign investors to acquire the company's stock.

One set of universally accepted accounting standards would reduce the cost of preparing worldwide consolidated financial statements and would simplify the auditing of these statements. Multinational companies would find it easier to transfer accounting staff to other countries. This would be true for the international auditing firms as well.

Arguments against Harmonization

One obstacle to harmonization is the magnitude of the differences between countries and the fact that the political cost of eliminating those differences could be quite high. As stated by Dennis Beresford, former chairman of the FASB, "High on almost everybody's list of obstacles is nationalism. Whether out of deep-seated tradition, indifference born of economic power, or resistance to intrusion of foreign influence, some say that national entities will not bow to any international body."[15] Arriving at principles that satisfy all of the parties involved throughout the world seems an almost Herculean task.

Harmonization is difficult to achieve, and the need for such standards is not universally accepted. As Richard Karl Goeltz stated, "Full harmonization of international accounting standards is probably neither practical nor truly valuable. . . . It is not clear whether significant benefits would be derived in fact. A well-developed global capital market exists already. It has evolved without uniform accounting standards."[16] Opponents of harmonization argue that it is unnecessary to force all companies worldwide to follow a common set of rules. The international capital market will force those companies that benefit from accessing the market to provide the required accounting information without harmonization.

Another argument against harmonization is that because of different environmental influences, differences in accounting across countries might be appropriate and necessary. For example, countries at different stages of economic development or that rely on different sources of financing perhaps should have differently oriented accounting systems.

Regardless of the arguments against harmonization, substantial effort to reduce differences in accounting practice and to develop a set of international accounting standards has been ongoing for several decades. The question is no longer *whether* harmonization should be strived for, but *to what extent* accounting practices can be harmonized and *how fast*.

MAJOR HARMONIZATION EFFORTS

While numerous organizations are involved in harmonization on either a regional or worldwide basis, the two most important players in this effort have been the European Union on a regional basis and the International Accounting Standards Board on a global basis.

European Union

The major objective embodied in the Treaty of Rome that created the European Economic Community in 1957 (now called the *European Union*) was the establishment of free movement of persons, goods and services, and capital across member countries. To achieve a common capital market, the European Union (EU) has attempted to harmonize financial reporting practices within the community. To do this, the EU issues directives that must be incorporated into the laws of member nations. Two directives have helped harmonize accounting. The Fourth Directive, issued in 1978, deals with valuation rules, disclosure requirements, and the format of financial statements. The Seventh Directive, issued in 1983, relates to the preparation of consolidated financial statements.

The Seventh Directive requires companies to prepare consolidated financial statements and outlines the procedures for their preparation. This directive has had a significant impact on European accounting because consolidations were previously uncommon on the Continent.

The Fourth Directive provides considerable flexibility with dozens of provisions beginning with the expression "member states may require or permit companies to"; these allow countries to choose from among acceptable alternatives. One manifestation of this flexibility is that under Dutch and British law, companies may write up assets to higher market values, whereas in Germany this is strictly forbidden. Notwithstanding this flexibility, implementation of the directives into local law caused extensive change in accounting practice in several countries.

Given that EU countries are in four of the nine clusters in Exhibit 11.4, the Fourth and Seventh Directives clearly did not create complete harmonization within the European Union. As an illustration of the effects of differing principles within the EU, the profits of one case study

[15] Dennis R. Beresford, "Accounting for International Operations," *CPA Journal,* October 1988, pp. 79–80.
[16] Richard Karl Goeltz, "International Accounting Harmonization: The Impossible (and Unnecessary?) Dream," *Accounting Horizons,* March 1991, pp. 85–86.

company were measured in European currency units (ECUs) using the accounting principles of various member states. The results are almost startling:

Most Likely Profit—Case Study Company

Country	ECUs (millions)
Spain	131
Germany	133
Belgium	135
Netherlands	140
France	149
Italy	174
United Kingdom	192

Source: Anthony Carey, "Harmonization: Europe Moves Forward," *Accountancy,* March 1990, pp. 92–93.

Part of the difference in profit across EU countries is the result of several important topics not being covered in the directives including lease accounting, foreign currency translation, accounting changes, contingencies, income taxes, and long-term construction contracts. In 1990, the EU Commission indicated that there would be no further accounting directives. Instead, the Commission indicated in 1995 that it would associate the EU with efforts undertaken by the International Accounting Standards Committee toward a broader international harmonization of accounting standards. We will return to the EU harmonization effort later in this chapter.

INTERNATIONAL ACCOUNTING STANDARDS COMMITTEE

In hopes of eliminating the diversity of principles used throughout the world, the International Accounting Standards Committee (IASC) was formed in June 1973 by accountancy bodies in Australia, Canada, France, Germany, Japan, Mexico, the Netherlands, the United Kingdom and Ireland, and the United States. The IASC operated until April 1, 2001, when it was succeeded by the International Accounting Standards Board (IASB).

Based in London, the IASC's primary objective was the development of international accounting standards (IASs). The IASC had no power to require the use of its standards, but member accountancy bodies pledged to work toward adoption of IASs in their countries. IASs were approved by a board consisting of representatives from 14 countries. The part-time board members normally met only three times a year for three or four days. The publication of a final IAS required approval of at least 11 of the 14 board members.

Early IASs tended to follow a lowest common denominator approach and often allowed at least two methods for dealing with a particular accounting issue. For example, IAS 2, originally issued in 1975, allowed the use of specific identification, FIFO, LIFO, average cost, and the base stock method for valuing inventories, effectively sanctioning most of the alternative methods in worldwide use. For the same reason, the IASC initially allowed both the traditional U.S. treatment of expensing goodwill over a period of up to 40 years and the U.K. approach of writing off goodwill directly to stockholders' equity. Although perhaps necessary from a political perspective, such compromise brought the IASC under heavy criticism.

A study conducted by the IASC in 1988 found that all or most companies listed on the stock exchange in the countries in Exhibit 11.3 (except Italy and Germany) were in compliance with IASC standards.[17] Given that research has shown that these countries were following at least four significantly different models of accounting at that time, it is obvious that IASC standards existing in 1988 introduced little if any comparability of financial statements across countries.

[17] International Accounting Standards Committee, *Survey of the Use and Application of International Accounting Standards* (1988), p. 5.

THE IOSCO AGREEMENT

In 1987, the International Organization of Securities Commissions (IOSCO) became a member of the IASC's Consultative Group. IOSCO's membership is composed of the stock exchange regulators in more than 100 countries, including the U.S. SEC. As one of its objectives, IOSCO works to facilitate cross-border securities offerings and listings by multinational issuers. To this end, IOSCO has supported the IASC's efforts at developing IASs that could be used by foreign issuers in lieu of local accounting standards when entering capital markets outside of their home country. "This could mean, for example, that if a French company has a simultaneous stock offering in the United States, Canada, and Japan, financial statements prepared in accordance with international standards could be used in all three nations."[18]

IOSCO supported the IASC's Comparability Project (begun in 1987), the purpose of which was "to eliminate most of the choices of accounting treatment currently permitted under International Accounting Standards."[19] As a result of the Comparability Project, 10 revised IASs were approved in 1993 to become effective in 1995. In 1993, IOSCO and the IASC agreed upon a list of "core" standards for use in financial statements of companies involved in cross-border securities offerings and listings. Upon their completion, IOSCO agreed to evaluate the core standards for possible endorsement for cross-border listing purposes.

The IASC accelerated its pace of standards development, issuing or revising 16 standards in the period 1997–1998. With the publication of IAS 39 in December 1998, the IASC completed its work program to develop the core set of standards. In 2000, IOSCO's Technical Committee recommended that securities regulators permit foreign issuers to use IASC standards to gain access to a country's capital market as an alternative to using local standards. The Technical Committee consists of securities regulators representing the 14 largest and most developed capital markets including Australia, France, Germany, Japan, the United Kingdom, and the United States.

INTERNATIONAL ACCOUNTING STANDARDS BOARD

Upon completion of its core set of standards, the IASC proposed a new structure that would allow it and national standard setters to better work together toward global harmonization. The restructuring created the International Accounting Standards Board (IASB). In April 2001, the IASB assumed accounting standard-setting responsibilities from its predecessor body, the IASC.

The IASB consists of 14 members—12 full-time and 2 part-time. To ensure independence of the IASB, all full-time members are required to sever their employment relationships with former employers and are not allowed to hold any position giving rise to perceived economic incentives that might call their independence into question. Seven of the full-time IASB members have a formal liaison responsibility with one or more national standard setters; the other seven do not have such a responsibility. A minimum of five IASB members must have a background as practicing auditors, three must have a background as preparers of financial statements and three as users of financial statements, and at least one member must come from academia. The most important criterion for selection as an IASB member is technical competence. The initial IASB members came from nine countries: Australia, Canada, France, Germany, Japan, South Africa, Switzerland, the United Kingdom (4), and the United States (3).

International Financial Reporting Standards (IFRSs)

In April 2001, the IASB adopted all international accounting standards issued by the IASC and announced that its accounting standards would be called *international financial reporting standards* (IFRSs). *IAS 1,* "Presentation of Financial Statements," was amended in 2003 and

---

[18] Stephen H. Collins, "The SEC on Full and Fair Disclosure," *Journal of Accountancy,* January 1989, p. 84.

[19] International Accounting Standards Committee, *International Accounting Standards* 1990 (London: IASC, 1990), p. 13.

defines IFRSs as standards and interpretations adopted by the IASB. The authoritative pronouncements that make up IFRSs consist of these:

- International Financial Reporting Standards issued by the IASB.
- International Accounting Standards issued by the IASC (and adopted by the IASB).
- Interpretations originated by the International Financial Reporting Interpretations Committee (IFRIC).

Under the new structure, the IASB has sole responsibility for establishing IFRSs.

The IASC issued 41 IASs from 1975 to 2001, and the IASB had issued five international financial reporting standards (IFRSs) as of January 1, 2005. Several IASs have been withdrawn or superseded by subsequent standards. For example, later standards dealing with property, plant, and equipment, and intangible assets have superseded *IAS 4,* "Depreciation Accounting," originally issued in 1976. Other IASs have been revised one or more times since their original issuance. For example, *IAS 2,* "Inventories," was originally issued in 1975 and then revised as part of the comparability project in 1993. As part of an improvements project undertaken by the IASB, *IAS 2* was again updated in 2003. Unlike the U.S. FASB, which creates a uniquely numbered statement of financial accounting standards to amend a previous standard, the IASC and IASB recycle existing numbers.[20] Of 41 IASs issued by the IASC, only 31 were still in force as of January 1, 2005. The IASB issued the first IFRS in 2003; it deals with the important question of how a company should restate its financial statements when it adopts IFRSs for the first time.

Exhibit 11.5 provides a complete list of the 36 IASs and IFRSs in force as of January 1, 2005. Together these two sets of standards create what the IASB refers to as *IFRSs* and what can be thought of as IASB GAAP. IFRSs constitute a comprehensive set of financial reporting standards that cover the major accounting issues. In addition, the IASB's Framework for the Preparation and Presentation of Financial Statements, which is very similar in scope to the FASB's Conceptual Framework, provides a basis for determining the appropriate accounting treatment for those items not covered by a specific standard or interpretation. As was true for its predecessor, the IASB does not have the ability to enforce its standards. It develops IFRSs for the public good and makes them available to any organization or nation that might wish to use them.

Use of IFRSs

A country can use IFRSs in a number of different ways. For example, a country could (1) adopt IFRSs as its national GAAP, (2) require domestic listed companies to use IFRSs in preparing their consolidated financial statements, (3) allow domestic listed companies to use IFRSs, and/or (4) require or allow foreign companies listed on a domestic stock exchange to use IFRSs. See Exhibit 11.6 for a summary of the extent to which IFRSs are required or permitted to be used by domestic listed companies in countries around the world.

Of the 132 countries included in Exhibit 11.6, 66 require all domestic listed companies to use IFRSs. Perhaps most significant among this group are the 25 countries of the European Union. All publicly traded companies in the EU have been required to use IFRSs to prepare their consolidated financial statements since January 1, 2005. The only exceptions are those companies that were already using U.S. GAAP, which several jurisdictions allowed, or that have publicly traded debt securities only.[21] These companies will begin using IFRSs in 2007. EU companies continue to use domestic GAAP to prepare parent company financial statements, which often serve as the basis for taxation.

In addition to the EU, many developing countries require the use of IFRSs. This is especially true for countries in Eastern Europe and the former Union of Soviet Socialist Republics (USSR), which may have found adoption of IFRSs an inexpensive means of switching from a Soviet-style accounting system to one oriented toward a free market.

---

[20] In December 2004, the FASB broke with its tradition of using new numbers for revisions to standards when it issued *SFAS 123* (revised 2004) to supersede *SFAS 123*, originally issued in 1995.

[21] One of the best-known examples of a European company using U.S. GAAP prior to the introduction of IFRSs in the EU was Daimler-Chrysler, the largest manufacturing firm in Germany.

EXHIBIT 11.5
International Financial Reporting Standards as of January 2005

Title		Issued
IAS 1	Presentation of Financial Statements	1975 (revised 1997, 2003)
IAS 2	Inventories	1975 (revised 1993, 2003)
IAS 7	Cash Flow Statements	1977 (revised 1992)
IAS 8	Net Profit or Loss for the Period, Fundamental Errors and Changes in Accounting Policies	1978 (revised 1993, 2003)
IAS 10	Events after the Balance Sheet Date	1978 (revised 1999, 2003)
IAS 11	Construction Contracts	1979 (revised 1993)
IAS 12	Accounting for Taxes on Income	1979 (revised 1997, 2000)
IAS 14	Segment Reporting	1981 (revised 1997)
IAS 16	Property, Plant, and Equipment	1982 (revised 1993,1998, 2003)
IAS 17	Leases	1982 (revised 1997)
IAS 18	Revenue	1982 (revised 1993)
IAS 19	Employee Benefits	1983 (revised 1997, 2000)
IAS 20	Accounting for Government Grants and Disclosure of Government Assistance	1983
IAS 21	The Effects of Changes in Foreign Exchange Rates	1983 (revised 1993, 2003)
IAS 23	Borrowing Costs	1984 (revised 1993)
IAS 24	Related Party Disclosures	1984 (revised 2003)
IAS 26	Accounting and Reporting by Retirement Benefit Plans	1987
IAS 27	Consolidated Financial Statements and Accounting for Investments in Subsidiaries	1989 (revised 2003)
IAS 28	Accounting for Investments in Associates	1989 (revised 1998, 2003)
IAS 29	Financial Reporting in Hyperinflationary Economies	1989
IAS 30	Disclosures in the Financial Statements of Banks and Similar Financial Institutions	1990
IAS 31	Financial Reporting of Interests in Joint Ventures	1990 (revised 1998, 2003)
IAS 32	Financial Instruments: Disclosure and Presentation	1995 (revised 2003)
IAS 33	Earnings per Share	1997 (revised 2003)
IAS 34	Interim Financial Reporting	1998
IAS 36	Impairment of Assets	1998 (revised 2004)
IAS 37	Provisions, Contingent Liabilities and Contingent Assets	1998
IAS 38	Intangible Assets	1998 (revised 2004)
IAS 39	Financial Instruments: Recognition and Measurement	1998 (revised 2000, 2003)
IAS 40	Investment Property	2000 (revised 2003)
IAS 41	Agriculture	2001
IFRS 1	First-Time Adoption of IFRS	2003
IFRS 2	Share-Based Payment	2004
IFRS 3	Business Combinations	2004
IFRS 4	Insurance Contracts	2004
IFRS 5	Non-Current Assets Held for Sale and Discontinued Operations	2004

Few countries in the Western Hemisphere require or permit domestic listed companies to use IFRSs in preparing their financial statements, and those that do tend to be the smaller economies. None of the largest economies in the Americas—the United States, Canada, Brazil, Mexico, Argentina, Chile—allows the use of IFRSs by domestic companies. This situation is unlikely to continue for very long. In March 2005, the Accounting Standards Board in Canada issued an invitation to comment on a strategic plan for converging Canadian GAAP with IFRSs. The plan proposes to converge Canadian standards with IFRSs over a period of five years, and at the end of that period, "Canadian GAAP will cease to exist as a separate, distinct basis of financial reporting for public companies."[22]

[22] Accounting Standards Board (Canada), "Accounting Standards in Canada: Future Directions Draft Strategic Plan," page i, accessed at www.acsbcanada.org, May 6, 2005.

EXHIBIT 11.6
Use of IFRSs in Preparing
Consolidated Financial
Statements

IFRSs Required for All Domestic Listed Companies

Armenia	Finland*	Kyrgyzstan	Peru
Austria*	France*	Latvia*	Poland*
Bahamas	Georgia	Lebanon	Portugal*
Barbados	Germany*	Liechtenstein	Slovak Republic*
Bangladesh	Greece*	Lithuania*	Slovenia*
Belgium*	Guatemala	Luxembourg*	South Africa
Bosnia & Herzegovina	Guyana	Macedonia	Spain*
Bulgaria	Haiti	Malawi	Sweden*
Costa Rica	Honduras	Malta*	Tajikistan
Croatia	Hungary*	Mauritius	Tanzania
Cyprus*	Iceland	Nepal	Trinidad & Tobago
Czech Republic*	Ireland*	Netherlands*	Ukraine
Denmark*	Italy*	Nicaragua	United Kingdom*
Dominican Republic	Jamaica	Norway	Venezuela
Ecuador	Jordan	Oman	Yugoslavia
Egypt	Kenya	Panama	
Estonia*	Kuwait	Papua New Guinea	

IFRSs Required for Some Domestic Listed Companies

Bahrain	Kazakhstan	Russian Federation	United Arab Emirates
China	Romania		

IFRSs Permitted for Domestic Listed Companies

Aruba	Dominica	Myanmar	Turkey
Bermuda	El Salvador	Namibia	Uganda
Bolivia	Gibraltar	Netherlands Antilles	Uruguay
Botswana	Hong Kong†	Sri Lanka	Virgin Is. (British)
Brunei	Laos	Swaziland	Zambia
Cayman Islands	Lesotho	Switzerland	Zimbabwe

IFRSs Not Permitted for Domestic Listed Companies

Argentina	Cote d'Ivoire	Mali	Singapore‡
Australia#	Fiji	Mexico	Syria
Benin	Ghana	Moldova	Taiwan
Bhutan	India	Mozambique	Thailand
Brazil	Indonesia	New Zealand#	Togo
Burkina Faso	Israel	Niger	Tunisia
Canada	Japan	Pakistan	United States
Chile	Korea (S)	Philippines†	Uzbekistan
Colombia	Malaysia	Saudi Arabia	Vietnam

*Denotes EU membership.
†Hong Kong and Philippines have adopted national standards that are identical to IFRSs.
‡Singapore has adopted many IFRSs word for word but has changed several IFRSs when adopting them as national standards.
#Australia and New Zealand have national standards described as IFRS equivalents; some options permitted in IFRSs are not available under the equivalent national standard.

Source: Deloitte Touche Tohmatsu, "Use of IFRSs for Reporting by Domestic Listed Companies, by Country—Status as of 2005," www.iasplus.com, accessed May 5, 2005.

A number of countries that do not allow domestic listed companies to use IFRSs nevertheless allow *foreign* companies listed on domestic stock exchanges to use them as recommended by IOSCO. For example, Japan allows foreign companies listing on the Tokyo Stock Exchange to prepare IFRS-based financial statements without reconciling them to Japanese GAAP. The SEC in the United States also allows foreign registrants to prepare their financial statements in accordance with IFRSs, or any other non-U.S. GAAP for that matter. However, in those cases, the foreign company must also provide a reconciliation of net income and stockholders' equity to U.S. GAAP in the notes to the financial statements included in its annual report filed on Form 20–F with the SEC. The SEC has been under pressure for a number of years to eliminate its GAAP reconciliation requirement for those foreign registrants that use IFRSs. With the adoption of IFRSs in the EU in 2005, pressure from Europe has intensified.

As the IASC was completing its core set of standards under the IOSCO agreement in the 1990s, the SEC put the IASC and the rest of the world on notice that it would not necessarily approve the use of IASs simply because IOSCO recommended that it do so. In 1996, the SEC announced that to be acceptable for cross-listing purposes, IASs would have to meet three key criteria. The core set of standards would have to

- Constitute a comprehensive, generally accepted basis of accounting.
- Be of high quality, resulting in comparability and transparency, and providing for full disclosure.
- Be rigorously interpreted and applied.

The SEC began its assessment of the IASC's core set of standards in 1999 and issued a Concept Release in 2000 to solicit comments on whether it should modify its GAAP reconciliation requirement. The GAAP reconciliation requirement has not yet been changed, but in April 2005, SEC Chairman Donaldson discussed a road map with EU Internal Market Commissioner McCreevy to eliminate the U.S. GAAP reconciliation requirement "as early as possible between now and 2009 at the latest."[23] The extent to which EU companies are faithful and consistent in their application and interpretation of IFRSs in preparing their financial statements from 2005 on will be of great interest to the SEC.

FASB–IASB CONVERGENCE

At a joint meeting in Norwalk, Connecticut, in September 2002, the FASB and IASB agreed to "use their best efforts to (a) make their existing financial reporting standards fully compatible as soon as is practicable and (b) to coordinate their work program to ensure that once achieved, compatibility is maintained."[24] Both the SEC chairman and the EU's commissioner for the internal market immediately welcomed the so-called Norwalk Agreement.

The six key FASB initiatives to further convergence[25] between IFRSs and U.S. GAAP follow:

1. *Short-term convergence project.* The objective of the short-term convergence project is to eliminate those differences between U.S. GAAP and IFRSs in which convergence is likely to be achievable in the short term. Convergence is expected to occur by selecting either existing U.S. GAAP or IASB requirements as the high-quality solution.
2. *Joint projects.* Joint projects involve sharing FASB and IASB staff resources and working on a similar time schedule.
3. *The convergence research project.* The FASB staff embarked on a project to identify all of the substantive differences between U.S. GAAP and IFRSs and catalog differences based on the FASB's strategy for resolving them.
4. *Liaison IASB member on site at the FASB offices.* To facilitate information exchange and foster cooperation, a full-time IASB member is in residence at the FASB offices. Former FASB Vice-Chair James Leisenring was the first IASB member to serve in this capacity.
5. *Monitoring IASB projects.* The FASB monitors IASB projects based on the level of interest in the topic being addressed.
6. *Explicit consideration of convergence potential in board agenda decisions.* As part of the process for considering topics to add to its agenda, the FASB explicitly considers the potential for cooperation with the IASB.

Short-Term Convergence Project

The short-term convergence project is intended to remove a variety of individual differences between IFRSs and U.S. GAAP that are not covered in broader projects and for which a

[23] SEC Press Release, "Chairman Donaldson Meets with EU Internal Market Commissioner McCreevy," April 21, 2005, available at www.sec.gov.

[24] FASB–IASB, Memorandum of Understanding, "The Norwalk Agreement," available at www.iasplus.com.

[25] Extensive information on the FASB's international convergence project can be found on the organization's Web site at www.fasb.org.

high-quality solution appears to be achievable in a short period of time. The short-term convergence project already has resulted in several changes to U.S. GAAP. Topics covered under this project include these:

1. *Inventory costs.* The FASB issued *SFAS 151,* "Inventory Costs—An Amendment of ARB 43, Chapter 4," in December 2004, to converge with the IASB's treatment of items such as idle facility expenses, excessive spoilage, double freight, and rehandling costs as current period expenses.

2. *Asset exchanges. APB Opinion 29* provided an exception to the general rule that asset exchanges should be measured at fair value. That exception related to nonmonetary exchanges of similar assets. To converge with IFRSs, *SFAS 153,* "Exchanges of Nonmonetary Assets—An Amendment of APB Opinion 29," issued in December 2004, eliminates this exception.

3. *Accounting changes.* The FASB issued *SFAS 154,* "Accounting Changes and Error Corrections—A Replacement of APB Opinion No. 20 and FASB Statement No. 3," in May 2005. This statement changes the reporting of certain accounting changes to be consistent with their treatment under IFRSs. Reporting the cumulative effect of a change in accounting principle in current period net income is no longer permissible. Instead, retrospective application of the new accounting principle is required.

4. *Earnings per share.* In December 2003, the FASB issued the Exposure Draft, "Earnings per Share—An Amendment of FASB Statement No. 128," which would amend the guidance for computing earnings per share. The FASB indicates that this proposed standard would improve financial reporting by enhancing the comparability of financial statements prepared under U.S. GAAP and IFRSs.

Although not formally a part of the short-term convergence project, the issuance of *SFAS 123* (revised 2004), "Share-Based Payment," in December 2004, which requires share-based payments to be measured at fair value, was at least partially justified through convergence with IFRSs. As one of the principal reasons for issuing this statement, the FASB provided the following explanation:

> **Converging with international accounting standards.** This Statement will result in greater international comparability in the accounting for share-based payment transactions. In February 2004, the International Accounting Standards Board (IASB), whose standards are followed by entities in many countries, issued International Financial Reporting Standard (IFRS) 2, *Share-Based Payment.* IFRS 2 requires that all entities recognize an expense for all employee services received in share-based payment transactions, using a fair-value-based method that is similar in most respects to the fair-value-based method established in Statement 123 and the improvements made to it by this Statement. Converging to a common set of high-quality financial accounting standards for share-based payment transactions with employees improves the comparability of financial information around the world and makes the accounting requirements for entities that report financial statements under both U.S. GAAP and international accounting standards less burdensome.[26]

Joint Projects

The IASB and FASB are jointly working on several projects that deal with broader issues expected to take longer to resolve than those topics covered by the short-term project. We describe four of these projects.

Business Combinations Project

After separately eliminating the pooling of interests method, the FASB and IASB developed common exposure drafts to revise existing guidance on the application of the purchase method. As a result of this project, the two boards developed common solutions with respect to the measurement at full fair value of an acquired company's assets and liabilities and the

---

[26] FASB, *Statement of Financial Accounting Standards No. 123* (revised 2004), "Share-Based Payment," page ii.

measurement and presentation of noncontrolling interests. The FASB's exposure draft was discussed in Chapter 2.

Performance Reporting Project

This project deals with the presentation of information in the financial statements. The objective is to enhance the usefulness of information in assessing the financial performance of the reporting enterprise. The FASB issued an initial proposal related to this project in August 2001. In April 2004, the FASB and IASB agreed to work together on this project in the future. Issues being considered in this project include whether a single statement of comprehensive income should be required to be presented as a primary financial statement, whether the direct method should be mandated for reporting cash flow from operations in the statement of cash flows, how many years should be included in comparative financial statements, and which totals and subtotals should be reported on each required financial statement.

Revenue Recognition Project

This project's objective is to develop a common, comprehensive standard on revenue recognition that is grounded in conceptually based principles. More than 140 authoritative pronouncements in the United States relate to revenue recognition.[27] Finding the answer to a specific revenue recognition question can be difficult, and gaps exist. Unlike U.S. GAAP, IFRSs contain a single, general standard on revenue recognition (*IAS 19,* "Revenue"). However, this standard is of limited use in determining the appropriate recognition of revenue in many cases. This project is expected to result in a single standard that will (1) eliminate inconsistencies in existing literature, (2) fill the gaps that have developed in recent years as new business models have emerged, and (3) provide a conceptual basis for addressing issues that arise in the future.

Conceptual Framework Project

This project seeks to develop a common conceptual framework that both boards could use as a basis for future standards. Although the IASB Framework and the FASB's Conceptual Framework (as embodied in its *Statements of Financial Accounting Concepts*) are substantially similar, differences do exist. More importantly, the existing frameworks have internal inconsistencies and are not comprehensive.

DIFFERENCES BETWEEN IFRSs AND U.S. GAAP

In a comparison of IFRSs and U.S. GAAP conducted in January 2005, Deloitte Touche Tohmatsu identified some 120 key differences in the two sets of standards. A few of these differences are summarized in Exhibit 11.7. Note that a number of these differences are within the scope of the FASB–IASB convergence projects and therefore are likely to be eliminated over time.

The types of differences that exist between IFRSs and U.S. GAAP can be generally classified as follows:

1. Recognition differences.
2. Measurement differences.
3. Presentation and disclosure differences.

Examples of each type of difference are described next.

Recognition Differences

Several differences between IFRSs and U.S. GAAP relate to (1) whether an item is recognized or not, (2) how it is recognized, or (3) when it is recognized. A good example of this type of difference relates to the accounting for research and development costs. Under U.S. GAAP, research and development costs must be expensed immediately. The only exception relates to

---

[27] FASB, "The Revenue Recognition Project," *The FASB Report,* December 24, 2002.

EXHIBIT 11.7
Some Key Differences between IFRSs and U.S. GAAP at January 2005

Accounting Item	IFRSs	U.S. GAAP
Inventory		
Cost-flow assumption	LIFO not allowed	LIFO allowed
"Market" in lower-of-cost-or-market rule	Net realizable value	Replacement cost (with ceiling and floor)
Reversal of inventory writedown	Required if certain criteria are met	Not allowed
Property, plant, and equipment		
Measurement subsequent to acquisition	Based on historical cost or a revalued amount	Based on historical cost
Major inspection or overhaul costs	Generally capitalized	Generally expensed
Capitalization of interest on qualifying assets	Permitted but not required	Required
Asset impairment		
Indication of impairment	Asset's carrying value exceeds the greater of its (1) value in use (discounted expected future cash flows) or (2) fair value less costs to sell	Asset's carrying value exceeds the undiscounted expected future cash flows from the asset
Subsequent reversal of an impairment loss	Required if certain criteria are met	Not allowed
Construction contracts		
Method used when percentage of completion not appropriate	Cost recovery method	Completed contract method
Research and development costs		
Development costs	Capitalized if certain criteria are met	Expensed immediately (except computer software development)
Leases		
Recognition of gain on sale and leaseback on an operating lease	Recognized immediately	Amortized over the lease term
Pensions		
Recognition of past service costs related to benefits that have vested	Recognized immediately	Amortized over the remaining service period of life expectancy
Recognition of minimum liability	No minimum liability requirement	Unfunded accumulated benefit obligation must be recognized as a minimum
Income taxes		
Recognition of deferred tax assets	Recognized only if realization of tax benefit is probable	Always recognized but a valuation allowance is provided
Consolidated financial statements		
Different accounting policies of parent and subsidiaries	Must conform policies	No requirement to conform policies
Presentation of minority interest	In equity	Between liabilities and equity
Purchased in-process R&D	Recognized as intangible asset if separately measurable, otherwise as part of goodwill	Expensed immediately

(continued)

EXHIBIT 11.7
(continued)

Accounting Item	IFRSs	U.S. GAAP
Negative goodwill	Recognize immediately as a gain	Allocate on a pro rata basis as reduction in certain acquired nonfinancial assets, with any excess recognized as an extraordinary gain
Presentation of "extraordinary" items	Not allowed	Required when certain criteria are met
Definition of a "discontinued operation"	A reportable business or geographic segment	A reportable segment, operating segment, reporting unit, subsidiary, or asset group
Interim reporting	Interim period is treated as discrete accounting period	Interim period treated as integral part of full year
Segment reporting	Disclosures required for both industry and geographic segments, one of which is "primary" and the other "secondary"	Disclosures required for operating segments, plus certain "enterprise-wide" disclosures

Source: Deloitte Touche Tohmatsu, "Status of Some Key Differences between IFRSs and U.S. GAAP as of January 2005," www.iasplus.com, accessed May 5, 2005.

costs incurred in developing computer software, which must be capitalized when several restrictive criteria are met. *IAS 38,* "Intangible Assets," also requires immediate expensing of all research costs. Development costs, on the other hand, must be recognized as an internally generated intangible asset when certain criteria are met. Deferred development costs are amortized over their useful life but not to exceed 20 years. Development costs include all costs directly attributable to or that can be reasonably allocated to development activities including personnel costs, materials and services costs, depreciation on fixed assets, amortization of patents and licenses, and overhead costs other than general administration. The types of development costs that might qualify as an internally generated intangible asset under *IAS 38* include computer software costs, patents and copyrights, customer or supplier relationships, market share, fishing licenses, and franchises. Brands, advertising costs, training costs, and customer lists are specifically excluded from recognition as an intangible asset.

Other recognition differences relate to (1) gains on sale and leaseback transactions, (2) past service costs related to vested pension benefits, (3) deferred tax assets, (4) purchased in-process R&D, and (5) negative goodwill.

Measurement Differences

Measurement differences result in the recognition of different amounts in the financial statements under IFRSs and U.S. GAAP. In some cases, these differences result from different measurement methods required under the two sets of standards. For example, although both IFRSs and U.S. GAAP require the use of a lower-of-cost-or-market rule in valuing inventory, the two sets of standards measure "market" differently. Under U.S. GAAP, market value is measured as *replacement cost* (with net realizable value as a ceiling and net realizable value minus a normal profit as a floor). *IAS 2,* "Inventory," requires inventory to be carried on the balance sheet at the lower of cost or *net realizable value.*

In other cases, measurement differences can exist because of alternatives allowed by one set of standards but not the other. Permitting the use of LIFO under U.S. GAAP but not allowing its use under IFRSs is an example of this type of difference. Another example can be found in *IAS 23,* "Borrowing Costs," which establishes a benchmark and an allowed alternative treatment for the accounting for interest and other costs associated with borrowings. The benchmark treatment is to expense all borrowing costs immediately. This treatment is inconsistent with U.S. GAAP, which requires the capitalization of interest on qualifying self-constructed assets. A company using the benchmark treatment under *IAS 23* would measure the cost of its qualifying self-constructed assets differently from a company using U.S. GAAP. However, as an allowed alternative, companies may capitalize interest as part of the cost of a qualifying asset in much the same manner as is required under U.S. GAAP.

One of the greatest potential differences between the application of IFRSs and U.S. GAAP is found in *IAS 16,* "Property, Plant, and Equipment." In measuring fixed assets subsequent to acquisition, *IAS 16* establishes cost less accumulated depreciation and impairment losses as the benchmark treatment. This is consistent with U.S. GAAP. The allowed alternative provided in *IAS 16* allows fixed assets to be measured and reported on the balance sheet subsequent to acquisition at a revalued amount, which is measured as fair value at the date of revaluation less any subsequent accumulated depreciation and impairment losses. If a company elects to follow the allowed alternative, it must make revaluations regularly enough that the carrying value reported on the balance sheet does not differ materially from fair value. Companies following the allowed alternative need not adopt this treatment for all classes of property, plant, and equipment. However, they must apply it to all items within a class of assets. A company could choose to revalue land but not buildings, for example, but it would need to revalue each and every parcel of land it owns at the same time.

Presentation and Disclosure Differences

Presentation and disclosure differences relate to the manner in which items are presented on the financial statements or disclosed in the notes to the financial statements. Presentation of certain gains and losses as *extraordinary items* under U.S. GAAP, which is not allowed under IFRSs, is one example. The difference between the two sets of standards in what is considered a discontinued operation and therefore presented separately in the income statement is another example. The definition of a discontinued operation is less restrictive under U.S. GAAP.

Differences exist in the reporting of segments under the two sets of standards. U.S. GAAP requires a management approach in which extensive disclosures must be made for operating segments, which can be based on either product line or geography. If operating segments are based on product line, additional disclosures must be provided for all foreign operations and for each material foreign country. *IAS 14,* "Segment Reporting," requires disclosures to be provided for both industry segments and geographic segments, one of which is designated as the primary reporting format and for which more extensive information must be provided. Geographic segments typically are defined as regions of the world rather than as individual countries.

U.S. GAAP Reconciliations

A good source of information for understanding the differences between IFRSs and U.S. GAAP and their impact on financial statements are the U.S. GAAP reconciliations prepared by foreign companies listed on U.S. stock exchanges in compliance with SEC regulations. Studying these reconciliations was instrumental in determining which were the most important issues to address in the FASB–IASB convergence project.[28] Exhibit 11.8 provides an excerpt from the U.S. GAAP reconciliation included in the 2003 Form 20–F of China Eastern Airlines Corporation Limited (CEA). CEA is one of several Chinese companies listed on the New York Stock Exchange that prepares its consolidated financial statements in accordance with IFRSs.

Note 40, "Significant Differences between IFRS and U.S. GAAP," indicates that CEA made four adjustments to both net income and owners' equity as stated under IFRSs to reconcile to U.S. GAAP. Adjustments (a) and (b) relate to the fact that CEA uses the allowed alternative treatment of *IAS 16,* "Property, Plant, and Equipment," to revalue fixed assets subsequent to initial recognition. CEA revalued fixed assets in 1996 as part of the process of transforming from a state-owned enterprise to a publicly traded company. An additional revaluation of assets occurred in 2002. The net result of these revaluations was an increase in the carrying value of fixed assets accompanied by an increase in owner's equity. The revaluation of fixed assets also resulted in an increase in the amount of annual depreciation expense.

[28] International Accounting Standards Committee Foundation (IASCF), Annual Report 2003, p. 5. The IASCF oversees, funds, and selects the members of the IASB.

EXHIBIT 11.8   China Eastern Airlines Corporation Limited Form 20-F Excerpt from Note 40

Note 40. Significant Differences between IFRS and U.S. GAAP

Differences between IFRS and U.S. GAAP which have significant effects on the consolidated profits/(loss) attributable to shareholders and consolidated owners' equity of the Group are summarized as follows:

Consolidated profit/(loss) attributable to shareholders
(Amounts in thousands except per share data)

	Note	Year Ended December 31,			
		2001 RMB	2002 RMB	2003 RMB	2003 US$ (note 2a)
As stated under IFRS		541,713	86,369	(949,816)	(114,758)
U.S. GAAP adjustments:					
Reversal of difference in depreciation charges arising from revaluation of fixed assets	(a)	94,140	20,370	63,895	7,720
Reversal of revaluation deficit of fixed assets	(a)	—	171,753	—	—
Gain/(loss) on disposal of aircraft and related assets	(b)	5,791	(26,046)	(10,083)	(1,218)
Others	(c)	(11,295)	23,767	6,860	829
Deferred tax effect on U.S. GAAP adjustments	(d)	(155,877)	(28,477)	(9,101)	(1,100)
As stated under U.S. GAAP		474,472	247,736	(898,245)	(108,527)

Consolidated owners' equity
(Amounts in thousands)

	Note	December 31,		
		2002 RMB	2003 RMB	2003 US$ (note 2a)
As stated under IFRS		7,379,103	6,382,151	771,099
U.S. GAAP adjustments:				
Reversal of net revaluation surplus of fixed assets	(a)	(908,873)	(908,873)	(109,811)
Reversal of difference in depreciation charges and accumulated depreciation and loss on disposals arising from the revaluation of fixed assets	(a), (b)	637,423	691,235	83,516
Others	(c)	29,111	35,971	4,346
Deferred tax effect on U.S. GAAP adjustments	(d)	20,844	9,225	1,115
As stated under U.S. GAAP		7,157,608	6,209,709	750,264

Notes:

(a) Revaluation of fixed assets

Under IFRS, fixed assets of the Group are initially recorded at cost and are subsequently restated at revalued amounts less accumulated depreciation. Fixed assets of the Group were revalued as of June 30, 1996, as part of the restructuring of the Group for the purpose of listing. In addition, as of December 31, 2002, a revaluation of the Group's aircraft and engines was carried out and difference between the valuation and carrying amount was recognized. Under U.S. GAAP, the revaluation surplus or deficit and the related difference in depreciation are reversed since fixed assets are required to be stated at cost.

(b) Disposals of aircraft and related assets

This represents the loss on disposals of aircraft and related assets during the years. Under U.S. GAAP, fixed assets are required to be stated at cost. Accordingly, the accumulated depreciation and the gain or loss on disposals of aircraft is different between IFRS and U.S. GAAP, which is attributable to the surplus or deficit upon valuation associated with the assets disposed of.

(c) Other U.S. GAAP adjustments

The application of U.S. GAAP differs in certain other respects from IFRS, mainly relating to sale and leaseback transactions, post retirement benefits and goodwill. Under US GAAP: (i) recognition of gain on sale and leaseback transactions is deferred and amortized, (ii) transitional obligation for post retirement benefits is amortized over the average remaining service period of active plan participants, and (iii) goodwill is reviewed for impairment and is not amortized.

(d) Deferred tax effect

These represent the corresponding deferred tax effect as a result of the adjustments stated in (a), (b), and (c) above.

Adjustment (a) reverses the additional depreciation taken under IFRSs on the revaluation amount that would not be allowed under U.S. GAAP. In 2003, this resulted in an increase in net income of US$7,720 to reconcile to U.S. GAAP. Also in 2003, IFRS–based owner's equity is decreased by US$109,811 to remove the revaluation surplus that was recognized under IFRSs.

The profit(loss) effect of adjustment (b) relates to the difference in the amount of loss recognized on the disposal of aircraft and related assets because of different carrying values under IFRSs and U.S. GAAP. Due to revaluation, fixed assets have a larger carrying value under IFRSs, which results in a smaller loss being recognized upon disposal. To reconcile to U.S. GAAP, an additional amount of loss based on the original cost of the assets must be subtracted from net income. The owners' equity account affected by adjustment (b) is retained earnings. Because additional depreciation expense on the revaluation amount has been taken under IFRSs, net income has been smaller in each year since 1996 under IFRSs than it would have been if U.S. GAAP had been used. The cumulative amount of the difference in income must be added back to retained earnings to reconcile to a U.S. GAAP basis.

The company explains that adjustment (c) is composed of adjustments related to the difference between IFRSs and U.S. GAAP in the accounting for (1) gains on sale and leaseback transactions, (2) post-retirement benefit obligations, and (3) goodwill. Prior to the publication of *IFRS 3*, "Business Combinations," in 2004, a difference existed between IFRSs and U.S. GAAP in the accounting for goodwill. Under IFRSs, goodwill was capitalized and amortized systematically over its useful life, whereas goodwill is not amortized but instead is subject to annual impairment under U.S. GAAP. *IFRS 3* removed this difference, converging IFRSs with U.S. GAAP.

Adjustment (d) arises because of the difference in reported profit(loss) under IFRSs and U.S. GAAP. This adjustments reflects the net deferred tax effect of adjustments (a), (b), and (c).

Exhibit 11.9 presents the net income reconciliation provided by Swiss pharmaceutical giant Novartis AG in its 2004 Form 20–F. Novartis made 12 adjustments to convert net income under IFRSs to a U.S. GAAP basis. Net income in 2004 on a U.S. GAAP basis was 13.5 percent smaller than under IFRSs; this difference was 24.5 percent the previous year.

Three adjustments made in 2004 relate to the use of the pooling method and the manner in which goodwill was recognized and amortized prior to 2004 under IFRSs. These differences from U.S. GAAP were removed with the issuance of *IFRS 3* in late 2004. Another adjustment

EXHIBIT 11.9
Novartis AG 2004
Form 20–F Excerpt
from Note 32

32. Significant Differences between IFRS and United States Generally Accepted Accounting Principles (U.S. GAAP) ($ millions)

	Notes	2004	2003	2002
Net income under IFRS		**5,767**	**5,016**	**4,725**
U.S. GAAP adjustments:				
Purchase accounting: Ciba-Geigy	a	(366)	(339)	(294)
Purchase accounting: other acquisitions	b	17	(175)	(298)
Purchase accounting: IFRS goodwill amortization	c	170	172	140
Available-for-sale securities and derivative financial instruments	d	(183)	(240)	(273)
Pension provisions	e	(6)	(18)	27
Share-based compensation	f	(326)	(273)	(120)
Consolidation of share-based employee compensation foundation	g	(4)	(3)	(20)
Deferred taxes	h	100	(63)	(93)
In-process research and development	i	(55)	(260)	(11)
Reversal of currency translation gain	j	(301)		
Other	l	13	(20)	(95)
Deferred tax effect on U.S. GAAP adjustments		163	(9)	141
Net income under U.S. GAAP		**4,989**	**3,788**	**3,829**

arising from business combinations relates to in-process research and development, which is expensed immediately under U.S. GAAP but treated as an asset under IFRSs. This type of adjustment is likely to continue in the future because neither the IASB nor the FASB has yet addressed this difference.

Adjustment (j) pertains to a portion of the cumulative translation adjustment in equity being transferred to net income under IFRSs as a result of the partial repayment of the capital of a foreign subsidiary. Under U.S. GAAP, the cumulative translation adjustment is recognized in income only upon disposal of a subsidiary.

THE ACCOUNTING PROFESSION AND FINANCIAL STATEMENT PRESENTATION

As discussed earlier in this chapter, accounting has evolved differently in different countries in response to environmental factors such as the nature of the legal system, the relationship between financial reporting and taxation, and the importance of the equity market as a source of financing. The final section of this chapter describes the accounting environment in three key countries, focusing on the accounting profession and the presentation of financial statements in these countries.

United Kingdom

"The United Kingdom has the oldest accounting profession in the world today, and its reputation is second to none."[29] As this quotation indicates, no discussion of world accounting principles would be complete without a study of the United Kingdom, a world leader in commerce and accounting. The legal foundation for accounting is provided by the Companies Acts, a series of legislation culminating in the Companies Act of 1989. The Companies Acts are basic commercial legislation designed to provide legal rules for U.K. corporations concerning issues dealing with management, administration, and dissolution. However, these laws also cover the issuance and content of financial statements. Prior to the 1980s, the law provided little more than a framework within which the accounting profession could set more detailed principles.[30] In 1981, the Companies Act was amended to incorporate the European Union's Fourth Directive, and in 1989 it was amended to implement the Seventh Directive, thereby increasing the importance of legislation in determining GAAP. Although the law prescribes some specific accounting procedures consistent with the EU directives, the law also requires companies to present a "true and fair view" of their results and financial position. This principle overrides the detailed requirements of the law. That is, if strict compliance with legislated accounting rules (or professional accounting standards) would not allow for a true and fair view to be presented, U.K. companies should deviate from the rules. A survey of some 450 U.K. companies in 1993 found that 10 percent used the true and fair view override.[31] The EU adopted the concept of true and fair view in its accounting directives.

In the United Kingdom, professional accounting organizations are quite important; membership now nears 200,000. A person may be a chartered accountant only through membership in the Institutes of Chartered Accountants in England and Wales, of Scotland, or in Ireland. Normally, once required exams have been passed, a license to practice is available to members after two years of approved experience.

In total, six different professional groups exist; and the largest is the Institute of Chartered Accountants in England and Wales. Until 1990, these organizations collectively controlled the accounting standard-setting process. Together, they formally created the Consultative Committee of Accountancy Bodies. A subcommittee of this group, the Accounting Standards

---

[29] Geoffrey Alan Lee, "Accounting in the United Kingdom," *International Accounting* (New York: Harper & Row, 1984), p. 261.

[30] Lee H. Radebaugh and Sidney J. Gray, *International Accounting and Multinational Enterprises*, 3rd ed. (New York: John Wiley and Sons, 1993), p. 83.

[31] J. M. Samuels, R. E. Brayshaw, and J. M. Cramer, *Financial Statement Analysis in Europe* (London: Chapman and Hall, 1995), p. 361.

Committee (ASC), produced 25 statements of standard accounting practice (SSAPs) between 1971 and 1990.

The ASC was originally created "to reduce and regularize the range of permissable accounting treatments applicable to comparable transactions and situations."[32] Over the years, the ASC gradually branched into a standard-setting role. However, the committee experienced difficulty because its pronouncements had to be accepted by each of the six professional organizations before being issued. Thus, the creation of accounting standards was agonizingly slow at times.

Consequently, the Accounting Standards Board (ASB) was formed on August 1, 1990, to replace the ASC as the standard-setting organization in the United Kingdom. The ASB is an independent body styled somewhat along the lines of the FASB in the United States. The ASB issues financial reporting standards (FRSs) on its own authority. The ASB has sanctioned all of the SSAPs and has issued several FRSs, including one that requires cash flow information. Any deviation from the ASB's standards must be explained and the financial effects disclosed.

A second body, the Financial Reporting Review Panel (FRRP), was created along with the ASB. The FRRP monitors compliance with the accounting standards. This panel has the authority to seek a court order against companies producing financial statements that fail to provide a true and fair view.

Financial statements must be submitted to the shareholders at the annual meeting. They include a directors' report describing the directors' activities for the period, post-balance sheet events, the business year in general, research and development activities, and a host of other information. The financial statements themselves are normally the balance sheet, profit and loss account, and cash flows statement. In addition, a statement of total recognized gains and losses often is presented that among other things reports the amount of translation adjustments included in stockholders' equity but not in income. In contrast to practice in the United States, separate parent company financial statements are provided along with the consolidated statements.

For the balance sheet and profit and loss account, two different formats (allowed under the EU's Fourth Directive) are available: a vertical and a horizontal presentation. Most British companies provide a vertical balance sheet; an example is that of Imperial Chemical Industries PLC in Exhibit 11.1. An example of a British profit and loss account is in Exhibit 11.10.

In the United Kingdom, the group profit and loss account is the equivalent of a consolidated income statement. The statement begins with *turnover* (the British term for *net sales*) followed by operating expenses, interest, and then taxes. Exceptional items related to continuing operations and discontinued operations appear in separate columns. Exceptional items primarily consist of restructuring costs (operating costs) and gains on closure of operations. Similar to the U.S. practice, British companies must report earnings per share at the bottom of the profit and loss account. Also as in the United States, reported figures tend to be highly condensed with much of the information provided in the notes to the statements. On the face of the financial statements, specific references relate the notes to particular line items.

Germany

Accounting principles in Germany are set by the national legislature. Currently, these mandatory principles are outlined in detail in the Third Book of the Commercial Code. Tax laws have had a significant influence on the reporting principles established by the code. In addition, because the code is silent with regard to many accounting issues, German companies refer to tax law, professional pronouncements, academic commentaries, and international accounting standards to fill in the gaps. Actual changes in the accounting laws are rare because they must be passed by the legislature. A major change to the accounting law was passed in December 1985 to bring German accounting principles in line with the directives of the European Union. Although this law introduced the notion of a true and fair view into German accounting practice, application of this principle differs from that in the United Kingdom. Günter Seckler found, "It still seems to be the dominant opinion in Germany that compliance with legal requirements ensures a true and fair presentation."[33]

[32] Emile Woolf, "The ASC at the Crossroads," *Accountancy,* September 1988, p. 72.

[33] Günter Seckler, "Germany," in *European Accounting Guide,* 3d ed., ed. David Alexander and Simon Archer (New York: Harcourt Brace & Company, 1998), p. 361.

EXHIBIT 11.10   United Kingdom Income Statement

IMPERIAL CHEMICAL INDUSTRIES PLC
Group Profit and Loss Account for the Year Ended 31 December 2004

	Notes	Continuing Operations Before Exceptional Items £m	Continuing Operations Exceptional Items £m	Discontinued Operations £m	Total £m
Turnover	4,5	5,601	—	—	5,601
Operating costs	3,5	(5,192)	(5)	—	(5,197)
Other operating income	5	35	—	—	35
Trading profit (loss)	3,4,5	444	(5)	—	439
After deducting goodwill amortisation	4	*(35)*	—	—	*(35)*
Share of operating profits less losses of associates	6	4	—	—	4
		448	(5)	—	443
Profits less losses on sale or closure of operations	3		(23)	(20)	3
Profits less losses on disposals of fixed assets	3		(1)	—	(1)
Amounts written off investments	3		—	—	—
Profit (loss) on ordinary activities before interest	4	448	17	(20)	445
Net interest payable	7				
Group		(86)	—	—	(86)
Associates		—	—	—	—
		(86)	—	—	(86)
Profit (loss) on ordinary activities before taxation		362	17	(20)	359
Taxation on profit (loss) on ordinary activities	8	(111)	11	6	(116)
Profit (loss) on ordinary activities after taxation		251	6	14	243
Attributable to minorities		(27)	(6)	—	(33)
Net profit (loss) for the financial year		224	—	(14)	210
Dividends	9				(86)
Profit (loss) retained for the year	24				124
Earnings (loss) per £1 Ordinary Share	10				
Basic		18.9p	—	(1.1)p	17.8p
Diluted		18.8p	—	(1.1)p	17.7p

Financial statements must be prepared in accordance with the code. If this does not result in a true and fair view, additional information must be presented in the notes to the financial statements.

As in many countries where legislated accounting rules exist, German accounting is considered quite conservative. This is true for two major reasons. One is the so-called tax conformity principle that is not found in many other countries. In Germany, commercial financial statements are the basis for taxation. Thus, for an item to be deducted for tax purposes, it must be recorded as an expense in calculating income in the financial statements. Companies interested in taking advantage of provisions in the tax law to reduce taxable income are required to report lower financial income as well. The second is that German accounting "is greatly influenced by the German banks, because they provide the major investment and mandate the reporting requirements for many industries in Germany. . . . When individuals in other countries analyze the financial statements, they generally write up the figures because of the extreme conservatism of German policies and procedures."[34] In fact, the German Association of Financial Analysts (DVFA) has developed a standardized procedure for adjusting reported earnings to assess the real profitability of German companies. The adjustments include adding back to income special depreciation allowed for tax purposes and excess amounts transferred to provisions.

The accounting profession in Germany is well established. The *Wirtschaftsprüfer* is the equivalent of a certified public accountant. A person can use this designation only after passing a series of difficult examinations and gaining six years of relevant experience. Only college graduates with degrees in economics, law, or a related subject may sit for the exams. "Because of the comprehensive requirements for entry to the profession, it is almost impossible to fulfill all of them before the age of 30, and most are 35 before they are admitted."[35] The profession's self-governing body is the *Wirtschaftsprüferkammer,* which enforces strict rules on independence and ethics.

In Germany, companies must produce a balance sheet each year as well as an income statement and notes to the financial statements. Also required is a management report to discuss issues such as current business position, significant subsequent events, future prospects, and research and development activities. Many companies fulfill a disclosure requirement regarding changes in fixed assets by providing a statement of fixed assets in addition to the balance sheet and income statement. A law passed in 1998 requires publicly traded companies to prepare a statement of cash flows.

The income statement must be produced according to one of two formats. The cost of sales approach, which has increased in popularity in recent years with Germany's larger multinationals, is similar to the structure of the income statement typically found in the United States. In contrast, the type-of-cost statement is more traditional in Germany. The consolidated statement of income for Brau und Brunnen AG for the year ending December 31, 2003, is an example of this format (see Exhibit 11.11).

In the traditional cost of sales format used in the United States, manufacturing costs (materials, labor, overhead) are included in the cost of sales line item in the income statement, and administrative costs are reported in a separate line. Under this approach, the total wages and salaries paid by a company are disaggregated into two parts: Manufacturing wages are reported in cost of sales, and administrative wages are reported in administrative expense. The same is true for depreciation and other operating expenses. Using the type-of-cost approach, Brau und Brunnen reports total wages and salaries (manufacturing and administrative) in a single line. Similarly, it reports total depreciation and amortization as well as total other operating expenses in one line. Brau und Brunnen reports the materials component of cost of sales in two parts: Purchases are reported as an expense in cost of materials, and the difference between beginning and ending Work in Process and Finished Goods Inventory is treated as an adjustment to sales. Although quite unique in appearance when compared to a U.S. income statement, the type-of-cost approach and the cost of sales approach result in the same calculation of earnings. One analytical limitation of this approach, however, is that it is not possible to calculate the cost of sales; therefore, gross profit cannot be determined.

Note the 2004 consolidated balance sheet for the chemical company BASF AG in Exhibit 11.12. Similar to the financial reporting in the United Kingdom, the German balance sheet begins with noncurrent assets followed by current assets. Deferred taxes and prepaid expenses are not classified as either current or noncurrent. Stockholders' equity usually appears next before the reporting of any liabilities, and minority interest is specifically included in equity.

German companies do not classify obligations on the balance sheet as current and noncurrent. Instead, they classify obligations as either provisions or liabilities. The major distinction between the two is that provisions are generally estimated whereas liabilities are of a fixed, contractual nature. German companies have traditionally considered liabilities due within the

[34] Roger K. Doost and Karen M. Ligon, "How U.S. and European Accounting Practices Differ," *Management Accounting,* October 1986, p. 40.

[35] Thomas G. Evans, Martin E. Taylor, and Robert J. Rolfe, *International Accounting and Reporting,* 3d ed. (Houston, Texas: Dame Publications, 1999), p. 38.

EXHIBIT 11.11
German Income Statement

BRAU UND BRUNNEN AG
Consolidated Profit and Loss Account
For the Year Ended December 31, 2003

		2003 (EUR)
Sales revenues		647,810,090.56
Decrease in work-in-process, finished goods, and uninvoiced services		−1,448,721.92
		646,361,368.64
Other manufacturing costs capitalised		536,047.73
Other operating income		99,373,867.52
		746,271,283.89
Cost of materials		
Expenses for raw materials, supplies, and merchandise purchased	131,426,366.79	
Expenses for services purchased	10,262,787.12	
		141,689,173.91
Staff expenses		
Wages and salaries	123,161,388.42	
Social security levies and cost of pension schemes and related benefits	43,200,577.32	
of which for pension schemes EUR 19,260,172.47		
		166,361,965.74
Depreciation and amortisation		
Depreciation and amortisation of intangible fixed assets and of tangible assets		74,343,753.87
Other operating expenses		269,491,754.64
		94,384,635.73
Income from profit transfer agreements		6,274.78
Income from equity interests		178,493.63
of which from affiliated companies EUR 91,977.72		
Income from other securities and from loans forming part of the financial assets		1,328,218.96
Other interest and similar income		782,502.50
of which from affiliated companies EUR 3,626.55		
		96,680,125.60
Depreciation of financial assets and of securities held as current assets		10,011,559.19
Expenses for the assumption of losses		68,891.69
Losses from shares in associated companies		51,421.26
Interest and similar expenses		8,272,004.58
of which for affiliated companies EUR 2,685,267.02		
Results from ordinary activities		78,276,248.88
Extraordinary income	6,442,269.00	
Extraordinary expenses	12,337,349.28	
Extraordinary results		−5,895,080.28
		72,381,168.60
Taxes on income and profit		209,017.00
Other taxes		64,699,005.52
NET PROFIT FOR THE YEAR		7,473,146.08

EXHIBIT 11.12
German Balance Sheet

BASF AG
Consolidated Balance Sheets
December 31, 2004

Million EUR	Explanations in Note	2004	2003
Assets			
Intangible assets	(11)	3.338.1	3,793.2
Property, plant, and equipment	(12)	12,444.2	13,069.9
Financial assets	(13)	1,911.9	2,599.6
Fixed assets		**17,694.2**	**19,462.7**
Inventories	(14)	**4,626.4**	**4,151.1**
Accounts receivable, trade		5,511.0	4,954.0
Receivables from affiliated companies		443.9	575.5
Miscellaneous receivables and other assets		2,008.4	2,069.5
Receivables and other assets	(15)	**7,963.3**	**7,599.0**
Marketable securities	(16)	162.8	146.9
Cash & cash equivalents		2,085.9	480.6
Liquid funds		**2,248.7**	**627.5**
Current assets		**14,838.4**	**12,377.6**
Deferred taxes	(8)	**1,210.9**	**1,247.0**
Prepaid expenses	(17)	**172.1**	**514.3**
Total assets		**33,915.6**	**33,601.6**
Stockholders' Equity and Liabilities			
Subscribed capital	(18)	1,383.5	1,425.0
Capital surplus	(18)	3,021.8	2,982.4
Retained earnings	(19)	12,252.7	12,054.8
Currency translation adjustment		(1,224.8)	(971.9)
Minority interests	(20)	331.8	388.1
Stockholders' equity		**15,765.0**	**15,878.4**
Provisions for pensions and similar obligations	(21)	3,866.3	3,862.4
Provisions for taxes		1,303.9	1,078.8
Other provisions	(22)	4,557.7	4,246.2
Provisions		**9,727.9**	**9,187.4**
Bonds and other liabilities to capital market	(23)	2,525.0	2,610.6
Liabilities to credit institutions	(23)	778.3	896.1
Accounts payable, trade		2,220.1	2,056.3
Liabilities to affiliated companies		381.0	400.6
Miscellaneous liabilities	(23)	2,167.4	2,202.4
Liabilities		**8,071.8**	**8,166.0**
Deferred income		**350.9**	**369.8**
Total stockholders' equity and liabilities		**33,915.6**	**33,601.6**

next five years as short term. However, the 1985 accounting law requires companies to disclose in the notes the amount of liabilities due within one year; many companies also continue to indicate those liabilities due in more than five years.

BASF's provisions include estimates for items such as pensions, taxes, warranties, and other identifiable risks. In addition to being extremely conservative, German companies are notorious for their use of provisions to conceal profits and create hidden reserves. In profitable years, provisions are created for items such as deferred repairs (that is, repairs the company plans to make sometime in the future) and for undetermined obligations resulting from general business risks that might occur in the future. The counterpart to the balance sheet provision is an expense or loss reported in income. In years in which profits are below expectations, provisions are released with an offsetting increase to income. This income smoothing is an acceptable practice, done within the law, and very much a part of German business culture.

One of the most dramatic examples of the use of hidden reserves was carried out by Daimler-Benz AG in 1989. In 1988, the company reported income of 1.7 billion deutschemarks (DM). Because 1989 was a bad year for automobile sales, analysts expected Daimler-Benz's 1989 income to be somewhat lower than the year before. It created quite a stir in the German business community when the company reported 1989 income as DM6.8 billion, a fourfold increase over the prior year. The notes to the 1989 financial statements provide the following explanation:

> Provisions for old-age pensions and similar obligations are actuarially computed in accordance with the tax regulation of Section 6a of the Income Tax Act, at an interest rate of 6 percent per annum. Previously, a rate of 3.5 percent was used. Using the higher interest rate resulted in higher income of about DM4.9 billion and is shown in the income statement under "Other Operating Income."

Through the selection of a low (and therefore more conservative) discount rate from a range accepted by tax law, Daimler-Benz was able to report higher expenses in years prior to 1989 and thus establish hidden reserves. The release of those reserves in 1989 through a change in the discount rate significantly affected net income. Without the change, income would have been only DM1.9 billion.

In 1992, Daimler-Benz reported net income of DM1.45 billion after creating provisions for loss contingencies of DM774 million. Otherwise, 1992 profit would have been DM2.22 billion. In 1993, reported income was DM615 million but included the release of previous provisions of DM4.26 billion, thus masking a loss of some DM3.65 billion.

Perhaps the ultimate in income smoothing was done by the electrical equipment manufacturer AEG, which reported net income of exactly zero in each of the three years 1985, 1986, and 1987. The odds of a company generating net income of zero in any given year, let alone three years in a row, without the help of income smoothing are extremely small.

Recently, German accounting has undergone considerable change. German law was amended in 1998 to allow German companies to use IASs in their consolidated financial statements. In fact, German companies could choose to use U.S. GAAP, U.K. GAAP, or any other internationally accepted standards in lieu of German law in preparing consolidated statements. Also in 1998, the German Accounting Standards Committee was created to develop standards for consolidated financial reporting, represent German interests in international meetings, and advise the Ministry of Justice on accounting legislation. Since 2005, German publicly traded companies have been required to use IFRSs in preparing consolidated financial statements. Parent company financial statements continue to be prepared in accordance with German GAAP.

Japan

In Japan and most other code law countries, basic accounting principles are set primarily by the government. The Japanese Commercial Code requires annual audited financial statements of joint stock corporations (known as *Kabushiki Kaisha,* or KK) that have stated capital of at least 500 million yen or total liabilities of 20 billion yen or more. The Securities and Exchange Law imposes a similar reporting requirement on companies listed on Japanese stock exchanges as well as companies issuing stocks and bonds in the amount of 100 million yen or more. Consequently, many Japanese companies must produce two sets of financial statements: one to fulfill the requirements of the Commercial Code and the other based on the securities law. The two sets of statements are very similar except that the securities law requires more disclosure, and its requirements are more precisely defined.

The Commercial Code prescribes a few basic accounting principles (valuation of assets and liabilities, recording of deferred assets, and the like). These rules are supplemented by the

Financial Accounting Standards for Business Enterprises developed by the Business Accounting Deliberation Council (BADC). The BADC is, therefore, the single most important source of accounting principles in Japan. The BADC is made up of individuals drawn from the government, business, education, and the accounting profession. Membership in this council is by appointment of the Ministry of Finance, which, therefore, allows government control.

In 2001, a private sector accounting standard-setting body was established. The Accounting Standards Board of Japan (ASBJ) is modeled on the U.S. FASB and derives its standard-setting authority from the BADC. The BADC reserves the right, however, to override ASBJ pronouncements.

Tax laws quite heavily influence financial reporting in Japan. Companies usually follow the tax guidelines in producing their statements unless absolutely prohibited from doing so. Fortunately, the tax laws are written so that actual differences with official accounting pronouncements are few.

The Japanese Institute of Certified Public Accountants (JICPA) has not been a powerful force in establishing accounting principles. The Audit Committee of the JICPA, though, does issue papers describing preferable accounting practices. More recently, the JICPA has been involved in standard setting through members serving on the ASBJ and its various technical committees.

To become a certified public accountant in Japan, applicants must pass three examinations: the first (from which college graduates are exempted) consists of mathematics, the Japanese language, and a thesis. The second comprises accounting, cost accounting, auditing, management, economics, and commercial law. Passing this second test qualifies one as a Junior CPA. Then, after three years of experience, a third examination is required to become a CPA. This final test is made up of accounting practice, auditing practice, and financial analysis. Although the population of Japan is about one-third the size of the population in the United States, Japan has only about one-sixteenth as many CPAs.

Financial statements required by the Japanese Commercial Code consist of the following:

- Balance sheet.
- Income statement.
- Proposal of appropriation of profit or disposition of loss.
- Business report.

Although a statement of cash flows is not specifically required, companies must provide extensive cash flow information in supplementary information filed with the Ministry of Finance. It is not uncommon for companies to voluntarily provide a cash flows statement in their annual reports.

Large Japanese companies commonly prepare an English language version of their annual report, known as *convenience translations.* (The same is true for the larger European companies.) In their English language convenience translations, Japanese companies usually translate yen amounts into U.S. dollars for the benefit of foreign readers. Note 2 to Nippon Light Metal's financial statements indicates how this is carried out.

> The rate of ¥133.25 = U.S. $1, the approximate current rate prevailing at March 31, 2002, has been used to present the U.S. dollar amounts in the accompanying consolidated financial statements. These amounts are included solely for convenience and should not be construed as representations that the yen amounts actually represent or have been or could be converted into U.S. dollars. The amounts shown in U.S. dollars are not intended to be computed in accordance with generally accepted accounting principles.

Because each financial statement item is translated using the same rate, no translation adjustment arises.

The Japanese balance sheet is similar in appearance to that used in the United States. Assets and liabilities usually are classified as current or long term.

The Japanese income statement is divided into two sections to arrive at income before income taxes: ordinary income and special items. The income statement of Nippon Light Metal Company, Ltd., in Exhibit 11.13 is an example of this structure. The first part of this statement includes operating revenues and expenses as well as nonoperating items such as interest and equity method income. The definition of a special item in Japan is not as restrictive as the definition of an extraordinary item in the United States. Japanese companies are

EXHIBIT 11.13
Japanese Income Statement

NIPPON LIGHT METAL COMPANY, LTD.
Consolidated Statement of Income
For the Year Ended March 31, 2004

	Millions of Yen 2004	Thousands of U.S. Dollars (Note 2) 2004
Net sales	¥532,201	$5,035,490
Cost of sales (Note 13)	419,908	3,973,015
Gross profit	112,293	1,062,475
Selling, general, and administrative expenses (Note 13)	85,938	813,114
Operating profit	26,355	249,361
Nonoperating income:		
Interest income	80	757
Amortization of negative goodwill	1,409	13,332
Equity in earnings of associates	304	2,876
Other	3,484	32,964
Total nonoperating income	5,277	49,929
Nonoperating expenses:		
Interest expense	5,438	51,452
Amortization of transition obligation for employee retirement benefits (Note 7)	2,130	20,153
Loss on disposal of inventories	1,292	12,224
Other	6,680	63,204
Total nonoperating expenses	15,540	147,033
Ordinary profit	16,092	152,257
Special gains:		
Gain on sale of fixed assets	3,699	34,999
Gain on sale of investment securities (Note 5)	1,231	11,647
Total special gains	4,930	46,646
Special losses:		
Loss on devaluation of investment securities	1,914	18,110
Additional retirement allowance for early retirement program (Note 7)	—	—
Loss on disposal of fixed assets	—	—
Prior years' severance costs for directors and statutory auditors	—	—
Total special losses	1,914	18,110
Income before income taxes and minority interest	19,108	180,793
Income taxes (Note 8)—current	4,562	43,164
—deferred	2,309	21,847
	6,871	65,011
Minority interest in income of consolidated subsidiaries	712	6,737
Net income	¥ 11,525	$ 109,045

Per share of common stock:	Yen	U.S. dollars (Note 2)
Net income	¥ 21.24	$ 0.20
Cash dividends	¥ 2.50	$ 0.02

Discussion **Question**

WHICH ACCOUNTING METHOD REALLY IS APPROPRIATE?

In this era of rapidly changing technology, research and development expenditures represent one of the most important factors in the future success of many companies. Organizations that spend too little on R&D risk being left behind by the competition. Conversely, companies that spend too much may waste money or not be able to make efficient use of the results.

In the United States, all research and development expenditures are expensed as incurred. Mexico uses this same treatment. However, expensing all research and development costs is not an approach used in much of the world. Firms using IFRSs must capitalize development costs as an intangible asset when they can demonstrate (1) the technical feasibility of completing the project, (2) the intention to complete the project, (3) the ability to use or sell the intangible asset, (4) how the intangible asset will generate future benefits, (5) the availability of adequate resources to complete the asset, and (6) the ability to measure development costs associated with the intangible asset. Similarly, Canadian companies must capitalize development costs when certain criteria are met. Japanese accounting allows research and development costs to be capitalized if the research is directed toward new goods or techniques, development of markets, or exploitation of resources. Korean businesses capitalize their research and development costs when they are incurred in relation to a specific product or technology, when costs can be separately identified, and when the recovery of costs is reasonably expected. Brazil also allows research and development costs to be capitalized under certain conditions.

Should any portion of research and development costs be capitalized? Is the expensing of all research and development expenditures the best method of reporting these vital costs? Is the U.S. system necessarily the best approach? Which approach provides the best representation of the company's activities?

required to report earnings per share calculated as net income divided by the weighted average number of shares outstanding during the period. There is no requirement to present earnings per share on a fully diluted basis.

In March 2005, the ASBJ and the IASB held an initial meeting to discuss a project with a goal of converging their respective standards. Subsequent to that meeting, the chairman of the U.S. SEC and the Japan Minister of State for Financial Services met to discuss convergence between the United States and Japan. Japan appears to be firmly committed to international convergence of financial reporting.

Summary

1. The world is rapidly developing a global economy with numerous multinational corporations. U.S. companies are expanding into other countries while foreign investors are acquiring businesses in the United States. Thus, a knowledge of the accounting principles applied throughout the world is necessary to be an efficient decision maker, especially when dealing with international capital markets. The wide diversity of these accounting principles can make understanding reported financial information and comparing companies a difficult task.

2. Accounting rules differ significantly across countries partially because of environmental factors such as the type of legal system followed in the country, the importance of equity as a source of capital, and the extent to which accounting statements serve as the basis for taxation. The two major classes of accounting systems in the world are the macro-uniform and the micro-based classes. Each class is composed of several families, the largest of which is heavily influenced by accounting development in the United Kingdom.

3. The International Accounting Standards Committee (IASC) was formed in 1973 to develop accounting standards universally acceptable in all countries. In 2001, the International Accounting Standards Board (IASB) replaced the IASC. As a private organization, the IASB does not have the ability to require the use of its standards. However, an increasing number of countries either require or allow the use of IFRSs for domestic companies. All publicly traded companies in the EU began using

IFRSs in 2005. The International Organization of Securities Commissions (IOSCO) recommends that securities regulators permit foreign issuers to use IAS for cross-listing. Most major stock exchanges comply with this recommendation.

4. In 2002 the FASB and the IASB announced the Norwalk Agreement to converge their financial reporting standards as soon as practicable. The FASB's initiatives to further convergence include a short-term project to eliminate those differences in which convergence is likely to be achievable in the short term by selecting either existing U.S. GAAP or IASB requirements. The FASB and IASB also are jointly working on several projects that deal with broader issues, including a project to converge the two boards' conceptual frameworks. In addition, a full-time member of the IASB serves as a liaison with the FASB.

5. Numerous differences exist between IFRSs and U.S. GAAP. These differences can be categorized as relating to (a) recognition, (b) measurement, or (c) presentation and disclosure. Recognizing development costs as an asset when certain criteria are met under IFRSs while requiring they be expensed immediately under U.S. GAAP is an example of a recognition difference. Writing inventory down to net realizable value under IFRSs versus replacement cost under U.S. GAAP when applying the lower-of-cost-or-market rule is a measurement difference. Presenting certain gains and losses in the income statement as extraordinary items in accordance with U.S. GAAP, which is not allowed by IFRSs, is an example of a presentation difference. The U.S. GAAP reconciliations prepared by foreign companies that have securities registered with the SEC are a good source of information about the practical importance of differences between IFRSs and U.S. GAAP.

6. The accounting standards in Japan, Germany, and other macro-uniform countries are based on government regulation and are quite conservative. Financial institutions and tax authorities are considered the primary users of published financial data. In the United Kingdom, a micro-based country, individual investors are the main users of statements. Accounting standards are set by the accounting profession, and measurement rules are less conservative. The financial statements of each of these countries exhibit a number of unique characteristics when viewed from the perspective of a U.S. company. For example, the profit and loss statement in Japan labels a wide variety of transactions as extraordinary (or special). In both Germany and the United Kingdom, the balance sheet begins with fixed assets.

Comprehensive Illustration

PROBLEM

(Estimated Time: 20 to 30 minutes)

Part A

The following information pertains to inventory held by a company on December 31, 2007:

Historical cost	$20,000
Replacement cost	18,000
Net realizable value	19,000
Normal profit margin	20%

At what amount should the inventory be reported on the December 31, 2007, balance sheet and what amount, if any, should be reported in net income related to this inventory using (a) U.S. GAAP and (b) IFRSs?

Part B

A company acquired a new piece of construction equipment on January 1, 2006, at a cost of $100,000. The equipment is expected to have a useful life of 10 years and a residual value of $20,000, and is being depreciated on a straight-line basis. On January 1, 2008, the equipment was appraised and determined to have a fair value of $97,000, a salvage value of $25,000, and a remaining useful life of eight years.

What amount of depreciation expense should the company recognize in determining 2010 income and at what amount should the company report the equipment on its December 31, 2010, balance sheet using (a) U.S. GAAP and (b) IFRSs?

Part C

A company incurs research and development costs of $100,000 in 2007, of which $60,000 relates to development activities subsequent to a point in time when certain criteria have been met that suggest that an intangible asset has been created.

What amount should the company recognize as research and development expense in 2007 using (*a*) U.S. GAAP and (*b*) IFRSs?

Part D

A company sells a building to a bank in 2007 at a gain of $50,000 and immediately leases the building back for a period of five years. The lease is accounted for as an operating lease.

What amount should be recognized in 2007 as a gain on the sale of the building using (*a*) U.S. GAAP and (*b*) IFRSs?

SOLUTION

Part A

a. Under U.S. GAAP, the company reports inventory on the balance sheet at the lower of cost or market, where market is defined as replacement cost (with net realizable value as a ceiling and net realizable value less a normal profit as a floor).

In this case, inventory will be written down to replacement cost and reported on the December 31, 2007, balance sheet at $18,000. A $2,000 loss will be included in 2007 income.

b. In accordance with *IAS 2,* the company reports inventory on the balance sheet at the lower of cost or net realizable value. The inventory will be reported on the December 31, 2007, balance sheet at net realizable value of $19,000 and a loss on the write-down of inventory of $1,000 will be reflected in income.

As a result of this difference between U.S. GAAP and IFRSs, IFRS-based income in 2007 would be $1,000 larger than U.S. GAAP income.

Part B

a. Under U.S. GAAP, the company would report the equipment at its depreciated historical cost (book value). Straight-line deprecation expense is $8,000 per year [($100,000 − $20,000)/10 years]. Five years after acquisition, the equipment would be reported on the December 31, 2010, balance sheet at $60,000 ($100,000 − [$8,000 × 5 years]).

b. Under *IAS 16*'s benchmark treatment, the equipment would be reported on the December 31, 2010, balance sheet at its depreciated historical cost of $60,000, and depreciation expense of $8,000 would be subtracted in determining 2010 income.

Under *IAS 16*'s allowed alternative treatment, the equipment would have been revalued on January 1, 2008, to its fair value of $97,000. Depreciation expense on a straight-line basis in 2008 and beyond would be $9,000 per year ([$97,000 − $25,000]/8 years). The equipment would be reported on the December 31, 2010, balance sheet at $70,000 ($97,000 − [$9,000 × 3 years]).

As a result of this difference between U.S. GAAP and IFRSs, IFRS-based income in 2007 would be $1,000 less than U.S. GAAP income (assuming the allowed alternative in IFRSs is used).

Part C

a. Under U.S. GAAP, research and development expense in the amount of $100,000 would be recognized to determine 2007 income.

b. In accordance with *IAS 38,* $40,000 of research and development costs would be expensed in 2007, and $60,000 of development costs would be capitalized as an intangible asset.

As a result of this difference between U.S. GAAP and IFRSs, IFRS-based income in 2007 would be $60,000 higher than U.S. GAAP income.

Part D

a. Under U.S. GAAP, the gain on the sale and leaseback transaction of $50,000 is recognized in income over the life of the lease. With a lease period of five years, $10,000 of the gain would be recognized in 2007.

b. IFRSs recognize the entire gain on the sale and leaseback in income in the year of the sale. A gain of $50,000 is recognized in 2007.

As a result of this difference between U.S. GAAP and IFRSs, IFRS-based income in 2007 would be $40,000 more than U.S. GAAP income.

Questions

1. Why would the knowledge of accounting principles used throughout the world be important to a businessperson in the United States?

2. Because a multitude of different sets of accounting principles exists in the world, which sets of principles are applicable to a particular company?

3. What factors contribute to the diversity of accounting principles worldwide?

4. What are the major classes of accounting systems used throughout the world? What are the major influences on these different accounting systems?

5. What major accounting families comprise the macro-uniform class of accounting system? What families make up the micro-based class?

6. What arguments can be made in favor of international harmonization? What arguments can be made against it?

7. What are the Fourth and Seventh Directives?

8. Why were several of the original standards issued by the IASC revised in 1993?

9. Why has interest in international accounting standards increased in recent years?

10. In which regions of the world have IFRSs been most and least accepted?

11. What are the FASB's key initiatives in its international convergence project?

12. What are three potentially significant differences between IFRSs and U.S. GAAP with respect to the recognition and measurement of assets?

13. What has been the U.S. SEC's reaction with respect to the recommendation that foreign companies be allowed to file financial statements prepared in accordance with IFRSs without providing a reconciliation to U.S. GAAP?

14. What is the basis for the accounting principles used in the United Kingdom, Japan, and Germany?

15. How does a balance sheet prepared by a U.K. company differ from that produced by a U.S. company?

16. Why is the net income figure computed by a German company often assumed to be understated?

17. How does an income statement produced by a Japanese company differ from that produced by a U.S. company?

Problems

1. Which of the following could explain why accounting is more conservative in some countries than in others?
   a. Accounting is oriented toward stockholders as a major source of financing.
   b. Published financial statements are the basis for taxation.
   c. A common law legal system is used.
   d. Full disclosure in financial statements is emphasized.

2. Which of the following is *not* a problem caused by differences in financial reporting practices across countries?
   a. Consolidation of financial statements by firms with foreign operations is more difficult.
   b. Firms incur additional costs when attempting to obtain financing in foreign countries.
   c. Firms face double taxation on income earned by foreign operations.
   d. Comparisons of financial ratios across firms in different countries may not be meaningful.

3. How does the macro-uniform class differ from the micro-based class of accounting system?
   a. The micro-based class is more heavily influenced by taxation.
   b. In the macro-uniform class, accounting rules tend to be set by the government.
   c. The macro-uniform class consists primarily of countries in the U.S.-influence and U.K.-influence accounting families.
   d. The micro-based class provides lower levels of disclosure in financial statements than the macro-uniform class.

4. Which of the following is *not* in the micro-based class of accounting systems?
   a. Hong Kong.
   b. Spain.
   c. Australia.
   d. Canada.

5. Which of the following is *not* a reason for establishing international accounting standards?

a. Some countries do not have the resources to develop accounting standards on their own.

b. Comparability is needed between companies operating in different areas of the world.

c. Some of the accounting principles allowed in various countries report markedly different results for similar transactions.

d. Demand in the United States is heavy for an alternative to U.S. generally accepted accounting principles.

6. The International Accounting Standards Committee (IASC) was formed by representatives of several different

   a. Government agencies.

   b. Accountancy bodies.

   c. Legislative organizations.

   d. Academic organizations.

7. According to critics, what is the major problem with the original standards produced by the IASC?

   a. Too many popular methods were eliminated.

   b. Too many optional methods were allowed.

   c. They failed to examine and report on key accounting issues.

   d. The pronouncements tend to be too similar to U.S. GAAP.

8. The goal of the IASB is to

   a. Formulate and publish accounting standards as well as harmonize accounting standards.

   b. Establish a quality review process for all international financial statements.

   c. Promote adequate reporting disclosure so that unique accounting standards can continue to be employed around the world.

   d. Require that all financial standards be consistent with the standards used in the United States because of its central role in the capital markets of the world.

9. Why does the IASB currently have only limited powers?

   a. The IASB is a private organization and, thus, cannot enforce the use of its official pronouncements.

   b. The IASB has always refused to mandate that its pronouncements be followed.

   c. International capital markets establish and use their own accounting principles that must be followed in all cases.

   d. The IASB is a new organization that has not yet had time to exert significant influence in the world of accounting.

10. Why might Japanese companies prefer to follow the accounting standards of the IASB?

    a. Japanese accounting principles are extremely complicated so that appropriate financial statements can be difficult to produce.

    b. The Japanese have tended to follow U.S. generally accepted accounting principles rather than develop their own accounting principles.

    c. The use of IASB standards allows Japanese companies to be more easily compared with companies from other countries.

    d. Japan has almost no accounting principles, so comparison between companies within the country is virtually impossible.

11. According to the IASB, IFRSs are composed of

    a. International financial reporting standards issued by the IASB only.

    b. International accounting standards issued by the IASC only.

    c. International financial reporting standards issued by the IASB and international accounting standards issued by the IASC.

    d. International financial reporting standards issued by the IASB and statements of financial accounting standards issued by the FASB.

12. Which of the following countries or groups of countries does not permit any domestic listed companies to use IFRSs in preparing consolidated financial statements?

    a. European Union.

    b. Mexico.

    c. Russian Federation.

    d. Switzerland.

13. What is the so-called Norwalk Agreement?

   a. An agreement between the FASB and SEC to allow foreign companies to use IFRSs in their filing of financial statements with the SEC.

   b. An agreement between the U.S. FASB, the U.K. ASB, and Japan's ASBJ to converge their respective accounting standards as soon as practicable.

   c. An agreement between the SEC chairman and the EU Internal Market commissioner to allow EU companies to list securities in the United States without providing a U.S. GAAP reconciliation.

   d. An agreement between the FASB and the IASB to make their existing standards compatible as soon as practicable and to work together to ensure compatibility in the future.

14. Which of the following is not one of the FASB's initiatives to converge with IASB standards?

   a. The FASB eliminates differences between FASB and IASB standards by adopting IASB requirements, or vice versa, in a short-term convergence project.

   b. The FASB considers the possibility of convergence with IASB standards when deciding which topics to add to its work agenda.

   c. A member of the FASB serves as a liaison with the IASB by working out of the IASB's offices in London.

   d. A joint project develops a common conceptual framework that both the FASB and IASB could use as a basis for future standards.

15. Which of the following describes an IASB requirement that the FASB has adopted as part of the short-term convergence project?

   a. Following the IASB format for presentation of a statement of comprehensive income.

   b. Treating items such as idle facility expense, excessive spoilage, and rehandling costs as current period expenses rather than as part of the cost of inventory.

   c. Using the cost recovery method when the percentage of completion method is not appropriate for long-term construction contracts.

   d. Eliminating LIFO as an acceptable inventory cost flow method.

16. In which of the following areas does the IASB allow firms to choose between a benchmark treatment and an allowed alternative treatment?

   a. Measuring property, plant, and equipment subsequent to acquisition.

   b. Presenting gains and losses as extraordinary on the face of the income statement.

   c. Recognizing development costs that meet criteria for capitalization as an asset.

   d. Recognizing past service costs related to pension benefits that have already vested.

17. In Japan, special items are

   a. Never reported.

   b. More limited than in the United States.

   c. Items not necessarily considered extraordinary in the United States.

   d. Unusual and infrequent.

18. In the United Kingdom, a balance sheet

   a. Begins with fixed assets and then reports current assets less current liabilities.

   b. Is not required except for companies of a specific size.

   c. Begins with stockholders' equity.

   d. Is similar to a balance sheet that a U.S. company would produce.

19. In the United Kingdom, one encounters stocks and debtors accounts. What do these balances represent?

	Stocks	Debtors
a.	Investments	Minority interest
b.	Treasury stock	Notes payable
c.	Capital stock	Notes receivable
d.	Inventory	Receivables

20. In the financial reporting utilized in the United Kingdom, to what does the term *turnover* refer?
    a. Net sales.
    b. Age of inventory.
    c. Length of time needed to collect accounts receivable.
    d. Profit as a percentage of net assets.

21. In German accounting, *hidden reserves* are
    a. Assets invested for specified future use.
    b. Created to be able to smooth income from one period to the next.
    c. Equity balances used to record adjustments not included in computing net income.
    d. Annual adjustments to net income caused by the effects of inflation.

22. Which of the following is a major influence on German financial reporting?
    a Financial analysts and investors in equity securities.
    b. The Securities Transactions Committee.
    c. German banks because they provide a major portion of the financial capital.
    d. The Financial Accounting Standards Board.

23. Which of the following is true for the German type-of-cost format income statement?
    a. All income items other than revenues from the sale of inventory are labeled as extraordinary gains and losses.
    b. Changes in inventory levels are reported as adjustments to sales.
    c. Cost of goods sold is shown prior to revenues.
    d. Income taxes are not viewed as expenses.

24. In reporting research and development costs,
    a. Most countries capitalize research costs but expense development costs when incurred.
    b. Some countries capitalize some portion of development costs.
    c. Usually only one approach is found throughout the world.
    d. Most countries record all research and development costs as expenses when incurred.

25. Answer the following questions about the IASC (now IASB):
    a. What was the IASC's comparability project? What was its objective? What was the outcome of the project?
    b. What evidence is there that IASB standards are becoming acceptable around the world?

26. A multinational company is planning to raise a significant amount of capital funds by issuing stocks and bonds in the United States, the United Kingdom, Japan, and Canada. What impact might the IASB's international accounting standards have on the reporting of this company?

27. Compare and contrast a balance sheet produced by a German company with a balance sheet developed by a British company.

28. Compare and contrast an income statement prepared by a German company with an income statement prepared by a Japanese company.

Develop Your Skills

ANALYSIS CASE 1—APPLICATION OF *IAS 16*

Abacab Company's shares are listed on the New Market Stock Exchange, which allows the use of either international financial reporting standards (IFRSs) or U.S. GAAP. On January 1, Year 1, Abacab Company acquired a building at a cost of $10 million. The building has a 20-year useful life and no residual value and is depreciated on a straight-line basis. On January 1, Year 3, the company hired an appraiser who determines the fair value of the building (net of any accumulated depreciation) to be $12 million.

IAS 16, "Property, Plant, and Equipment," requires assets to be initially measured at cost. Subsequent to initial recognition, assets may be carried either at cost less accumulated depreciation and any impairment losses (benchmark treatment) or at a revalued amount equal to fair value at the date of the revaluation less any subsequent accumulated depreciation and impairment losses (allowed alternative treatment).

If a firm chooses to use the allowed alternative treatment, the counterpart to the revaluation of the asset is recorded as an increase in Accumulated Other Comprehensive Income (stockholders' equity). Subsequent depreciation is based on the revalued amount less any residual value.

APB Opinion No. 6 (U.S. GAAP) requires items of property, plant, and equipment to be initially measured at cost. *APB Opinion No. 6* does not allow property, plant, and equipment to be revalued above original cost at subsequent balance sheet dates. The cost of property, plant, and equipment must be depreciated on a systematic basis over its useful life. Subsequent to initial recognition, assets must be carried at cost less accumulated depreciation and any impairment losses.

Required:

1. Determine the amount of depreciation expense recognized in Year 2, Year 3, and Year 4 under (*a*) the allowed alternative treatment of *IAS 16* and (*b*) U.S. GAAP.
2. Determine the book value of the building under the two different sets of accounting rules at January 2, Year 3; December 31, Year 3; and December 31, Year 4.
3. Summarize the difference in net income and in stockholders' equity over the 20-year life of the building using the two different sets of accounting rules.

ANALYSIS CASE 2—APPLICATION OF *IAS 23*

Buckner Company's shares are listed on the New Market Stock Exchange, which allows the use of either international financial reporting standards (IFRSs) or U.S. GAAP. Buckner Company begins construction of a building for its own use on January 1, Year 1. Construction is complete and Buckner Company moves into the building on December 31, Year 1. The total cost of construction is $12 million dollars, incurred evenly throughout Year 1. A 20-year loan of $8 million at 10 percent was obtained on January 1, Year 1. Buckner Company has no other borrowings. The building has a 20-year life, has no residual value, and is depreciated on a straight-line basis.

SFAS No. 34, "Capitalization of Interest Cost" (U.S. GAAP), requires interest to be capitalized on qualifying assets, which are assets constructed or otherwise produced for a company's own use that require a period of time to prepare them for their intended use. The amount of interest to be capitalized is determined by multiplying an appropriate interest rate by the average accumulated expenditures for the asset during the period. The capitalization of interest ends when the asset is ready for its intended use.

The benchmark treatment in *IAS 23*, "Borrowing Costs," requires interest costs to be recognized as an expense in the period in which they are incurred.

Required:

1. Determine the amount of interest expense recognized in Year 1, Year 2, and Year 3 under (*a*) the benchmark treatment of *IAS 23* and (*b*) U.S. GAAP.
2. Determine the amount of depreciation expense recognized in Year 1, Year 2, and Year 3 under (*a*) the benchmark treatment of *IAS 23* and (*b*) U.S. GAAP.
3. Determine the book value of the building at the end of Year 1, Year 2, and Year 3 under the two different sets of accounting rules.
4. Summarize the difference in net income and stockholders' equity over the 20-year life of the building under the two different sets of accounting rules.

RESEARCH CASE—RECONCILIATION TO U.S. GAAP

Foreign companies with securities listed in the United States (in the form of ADRs) are required to reconcile their net income and stockholder's equity to U.S. GAAP in the annual report (Form 20–F) they file with the Securities and Exchange Commission (SEC). Lists of foreign SEC registrants are available on the Internet at www.bankofny.com; search for ADRs. Annual reports of foreign SEC registrants may be accessed through the SEC's EDGAR system at www.sec.gov (under Forms, search for 20–F). However, not all foreign registrants file their reports with the SEC electronically. Many non-U.S. companies make annual reports available on their corporate Internet home page. Access a recent annual report (Form 20–F) for a foreign company listed on the New York Stock Exchange to complete the following requirements.

Required:

1. Determine the nationality of the company selected and the accounting rules and regulations it used (company GAAP) to prepare its financial statements.

2. Summarize the major differences in measuring net income between company GAAP and U.S. GAAP.

3. Compare the profitability of the company using company GAAP and U.S. GAAP.

COMMUNICATION CASE—SEC CONCEPT RELEASE

Pursuant to its agreement with IOSCO, the International Accounting Standards Committee completed its core set of standards in 1999. The U.S. Securities and Exchange Commission subsequently issued *Concept Release: International Accounting Standards* in 2000, in which the SEC asked for public comment on a list of questions including the following:

- Do the core standards provide a sufficiently comprehensive accounting framework to provide a basis to address the fundamental accounting issues that are encountered in a broad range of industries and a variety of transactions without the need to look to other accounting regimes? Do additional topics need to be addressed to provide a comprehensive set of standards?

Required:

Draft a memo to the secretary of the U.S. Securities and Exchange Commission providing your response to these questions.

INTERNET CASE 1—CHINA PETROLEUM AND CHEMICAL CORPORATION

China Petroleum and Chemical Corporation (Sinopec) is a major Chinese company with shares listed on the New York Stock Exchange. Access the company's most recent annual report (not Form 20–F) at www.english.sinopec.com to complete this assignment.

Required:

1. Identify the different sets of financial statements presented by the company in its annual report.
2. Identify the major differences between IFRSs and accounting rules and regulations in the People's Republic of China for the company.
3. Determine what kind of information "Supplemental Information for North American Shareholders" provides.
4. Identify the major differences between IFRSs and U.S. GAAP for the company.
5. Assess the company's profitability based on the measures of profit reported under different sets of accounting standards.

INTERNET CASE 2—FOREIGN COMPANY ANNUAL REPORT

Many non-U.S. companies make annual reports available on their corporate Internet home page. Access the financial statements from the most recent annual report for a foreign company with which you are familiar to complete this assignment.

Required:

1. Determine the set of accounting rules (GAAP) the company uses to prepare its financial statements.
2. Determine whether the company provides a set of financial statements comparable to the set of financial statements provided by U.S. companies (consolidated balance sheet, consolidated income statement, consolidated cash flow statement).
3. List five differences between the company's income statement and the income statement of a typical U.S. corporation.
4. List five differences between the company's balance sheet and the balance sheet of a typical U.S. corporation.
5. Determine whether the scope and content of the information provided in the notes to the financial statements are comparable to the information provided in the notes to the financial statements by a typical U.S. corporation.
6. Evaluate the overall presentation of financial statements and notes to financial statements by the company in comparison with a typical U.S. corporation.

Chapter **Twelve**

Financial Reporting and the Securities and Exchange Commission

Questions to Consider

- How has the Sarbanes-Oxley Act of 2002 affected the regulation of public accounting firms and the issuance of financial statements by publicly held organizations?

- How do government agencies work to ensure that adequate reliable information is available to encourage investors to buy and sell securities so that businesses can raise sufficient capital for financing purposes?

- What companies are subject to the rules and regulations of the Securities and Exchange Commission?

- What is the purpose of the registration statements filed with the SEC? What various periodic filings must also be made?

- What steps usually occur in the registration process, and what is the CPA's role in this process?

- Which types of securities are exempt from registration with the SEC?

The Securities and Exchange Commission was born on June 6, 1934—a time of despair in the markets. Americans were still suffering from the 1929 market crash after a roaring 1920s when they bought about $50 billion in new securities—half of which turned out to be worthless. Their confidence also was eroded by the 1932 indictment (later acquittal) of Samuel Insull for alleged wrongs in the collapse of his utility "empire," and by the 1933–34 Senate hearings on improper market activity.[1]

The financing of the U.S. industrial complex depends very much on raising vast amounts of monetary capital. During every business day in the United States, tens of billions of dollars of stocks, bonds, and other securities are sold to thousands of individuals, corporations, trust funds, pension plans, mutual funds, and other institutions. Such investors cannot be expected to venture their money without forethought. They have to be able to assess the risks involved: the possibility of either a profit or loss being returned to them as well as the expected amount.

Consequently, disclosure of sufficient, accurate information is absolutely necessary to stimulate the inflow of large quantities of capital. Enough data must be available to encourage investors to consider buying and selling securities in hopes of generating profits. Without adequate information on which to base these decisions, investing becomes no more than gambling.

THE WORK OF THE SECURITIES AND EXCHANGE COMMISSION

In the United States, the responsibility for ensuring that complete and reliable information is available to investors lies with the Securities and Exchange Commission (SEC), an independent agency of the federal government created by the Securities Exchange Act of 1934. Although the SEC's authority applies mainly to publicly held companies, the commission's

---

[1] "D-Day for the Securities Industry, 1934," *The Wall Street Journal,* May 9, 1989, p. B1.

guidelines and requirements surely have been a major influence in the United States on the development of all generally accepted accounting principles.

> The primary mission of the U.S. Securities and Exchange Commission (SEC) is to protect investors and maintain the integrity of the securities markets. As more and more first-time investors turn to the markets to help secure their futures, pay for homes and send children to college, these goals are more compelling than ever. The world of investing is fascinating, complex, and can be very fruitful. But unlike the banking world, where deposits are guaranteed by the federal government, stocks, bonds and other securities can lose value. There are no guarantees. That's why investing should not be a spectator sport; indeed, the principal way for investors to protect the money they put into the securities markets is to do research and ask questions. The laws and rules that govern the securities industry in the United States derive from a simple and straightforward concept: all investors, whether large institutions or private individuals, should have access to certain basic facts about an investment prior to buying it. To achieve this, the SEC requires public companies to disclose meaningful financial and other information to the public, which provides a common pool of knowledge for all investors to use to judge for themselves if a company's securities are a good investment. Only through the steady flow of timely, comprehensive and accurate information can people make sound investment decisions.[2]

The SEC is headed by five commissioners appointed by the president of the United States (with the consent of the Senate) to serve five-year staggered terms. To ensure the bipartisan nature of this group, no more than three of these individuals can belong to the same political party. The chairman is from the same political party as the president. The commissioners provide leadership for an agency that has grown over the years into an organization with approximately 3,100 employees in 11 regional and district locations. Despite its importance, the SEC is a relatively small component of the federal government. However, the SEC generates significant fees primarily from issuers, relative to 8–K, 10–K, 10–Q, and registration statement fees. In 2003, the SEC deposited $1.076 billion in the United States Treasury.

The SEC is composed of four divisions and 18 offices including the following:

- The *Division of Corporation Finance* has responsibility to ensure that publicly held companies meet disclosure requirements. This division reviews registration statements, annual and quarterly filings, proxy materials, annual reports, and tender offers.

- The *Division of Market Regulation* oversees the securities markets in this country and is responsible for registering and regulating brokerage firms. This division also oversees the Securities Investor Protection Corporation (SIPC), a nonprofit corporation that provides insurance for cash and securities held by customers in member brokerage firms. This insurance protects ("insures") against the failure of the member brokerage firms.

- The *Division of Enforcement* helps to ensure compliance with federal securities laws. This division investigates possible violations of securities laws and recommends appropriate remedies. The most common issues facing this division are insider trading, misrepresentation or omission of important information about securities, manipulation of the market price of a security, and issuance of securities without proper registration. According to the SEC's annual report, 679 investigations of possible violations were opened during 2003.

- The *Division of Investment Management* oversees the $15 trillion investment management industry and administers the securities laws affecting investment companies including mutual funds and investment advisers. This division also interprets laws and regulations for the public and the SEC staff.

- The *Office of Information Technology* supports the SEC and its staff in all aspects of information technology. This office operates the Electronic Data Gathering Analysis and Retrieval (EDGAR) system, which electronically receives, processes, and disseminates more than half a million financial statements every year. This office also maintains a very active Web site that contains a tremendous amount of data about the SEC and the securities industry and free access to EDGAR.[3]

---

[2] The U.S. Securities and Exchange Commission, SEC Web site, June 2005. Available at http://www.SEC/about/whatwedo.shtml.

[3] http://www.sec.gov/edgar/shtml.

- The *Office of Compliance Inspections and Examinations* determines whether brokers, dealers, and investment companies and advisers comply with federal securities laws.
- The *Office of the Chief Accountant* is the principal adviser to the commission on accounting and auditing matters that arise in connection with the securities laws. The office also works closely with private sector bodies such as the FASB and the AICPA that set various accounting and auditing standards.

This chapter provides an overview of the workings of the Securities and Exchange Commission as well as the agency's relationship to the accounting profession. Because complete examination of the organization is beyond the scope of this textbook, we discuss only a portion of the SEC's functions here. This coverage introduces the role the agency currently plays in the world of U.S. business.

Purpose of the Federal Securities Laws

Before examining the SEC and its various functions in more detail, a historical perspective should be established. The development of laws regulating companies involved in interstate commerce were discussed as early as 1885. In fact, the Industrial Commission created by Congress suggested in 1902 that all publicly held companies should be required to disclose material information including annual financial reports. However, the crisis following the stock market crash of 1929 and the widespread fraud that was subsequently discovered were necessary to prompt Congress to act in hope of reestablishing the trust and stability needed for the capital markets.

> Before the Great Crash of 1929, there was little support for federal regulation of the securities markets. This was particularly true during the post-World War I surge of securities activity. Proposals that the federal government require financial disclosure and prevent the fraudulent sale of stock were never seriously pursued. Tempted by promises of "rags to riches" transformations and easy credit, most investors gave little thought to the dangers inherent in uncontrolled market operation. During the 1920s, approximately 20 million large and small shareholders took advantage of post-war prosperity and set out to make their fortunes in the stock market. It is estimated that of the $50 billion in new securities offered during this period, half became worthless. When the stock market crashed in October 1929, the fortunes of countless investors were lost. . . . With the Crash and ensuing depression, public confidence in the markets plummeted. There was a consensus that for the economy to recover, the public's faith in the capital markets needed to be restored.[4]

As a result, Congress enacted two primary pieces of securities legislation designed to restore investor trust in the capital markets by providing more structure and government oversight:

- The Securities Act of 1933, often referred to as the *truth in securities law,* regulates the initial offering of securities by a company or underwriter.
- The Securities Exchange Act of 1934, which actually created the SEC, regulates the subsequent trading of securities through brokers and exchanges.

These laws put an end to the legality of many abuses that had been common practices such as the manipulation of stock market prices and the misuse of corporate information by officials and directors (often referred to as *inside parties*[5]) for their own personal gain. Just as important, these two legislative actions were designed to help rebuild public confidence in the capital market system. Because of the large losses suffered during the 1929 market crash and subsequent depression, many investors had begun to avoid buying stocks and bonds.

---

[4] U.S. Securities and Exchange Commission, SEC Web site, May 2005. Available at http//www.sec.gov/about/whatwedo.shtml/at 2.

[5] *Inside parties* usually are identified as the officers of a company as well as its directors and any owners of more than 10 percent of any class of equity security. An individual's level of ownership is measured by a person's own holdings of equity securities as well as ownership by a spouse, minor children, relatives living in the same house as the person in question, and a trust in which the person is the beneficiary.

This reduction in the pool of available capital dramatically compounded the economic problems of the day.

The creation of federal securities laws did not end with the 1933 Act and the 1934 Act. During the decades since the first commissioners were appointed, the SEC has administered rules and regulations created by a number of different congressional actions. Despite the passage of subsequent legislation, the major objectives of this organization have remained relatively constant. Over the years, the SEC has attempted to achieve several interconnected goals that include these:

- Ensuring that full and fair information is disclosed to all investors before the securities of a company are allowed to be bought and sold.
- Prohibiting the dissemination of materially misstated information.
- Preventing the misuse of information especially by inside parties.
- Regulating the operation of securities markets such as the New York Stock Exchange, American Stock Exchange, and the various over-the-counter exchanges.

In many ways, the work of the SEC has been a huge success. The value of the securities that have been registered as well as the volume of these securities bought and sold each business day are staggering by any standard. Over the decades, the number of individuals and institutions (from both inside and outside the United States) willing to take the risk of making financial investments has grown to incredible numbers. In 2004 alone, more than 750 billion shares were exchanged. However, a cloud recently has rested over the entire U.S. capital market system. During 2001 and 2002, a number of highly publicized corporate scandals shook public confidence in the financial information available for decision-making purposes. Where once most investors appeared to believe in the overall integrity of the stock markets, that faith has clearly been diminished although the problem has not reached the magnitude seen in the 1930s. This lack of confidence has been a drag on the general willingness to invest and, thus, on the economy as a whole.

Almost an unlimited number of reasons can be put forth for these scandals:

- Greed by corporate executives.
- Failure in the corporate governance process as practiced by many boards of directors.
- Failure of public accounting firms to provide appropriate quality control measures to ensure independent judgments.
- Shortcomings in promulgated standards used to self-regulate the accounting profession.
- Unreasonable market expectations brought on by years of skyrocketing stock values fueled in part by technology stocks.
- A workload that overburdened the Securities and Exchange Commission, which the relatively small agency could not handle in an adequate fashion.

As a result, on July 30, 2002, President George W. Bush signed the Sarbanes-Oxley Act of 2002. This wide-ranging legislation was designed to end many of the problems that have plagued corporate reporting and the securities markets in recent years in the hope of restoring public confidence. As discussed later in this chapter, this new law has had an enormous impact on public accounting as well as the reporting required in connection with the issuance of securities. However, as with most new legislation, it will take a considerable period of time for the overall implementation of the Sarbanes-Oxley Act.

Full and Fair Disclosure

Probably no responsibility of the SEC is more vital than the task of ensuring that sufficient, reliable information is disclosed by a company before its stocks, bonds, or other securities can be publicly traded. Recent problems with companies such as Enron, WorldCom, Global Crossing, and Tyco have drawn increased attention to this role.

Unless specifically exempted, all publicly held companies (frequently referred to as *registrants*) must periodically file detailed reports with the SEC. The Securities and Exchange

Commission requires and regulates these filings as a result of a number of laws passed by Congress over the years:

1. *Securities Act of 1933.* Requires the registration of new securities offered for public sale so that potential investors can have adequate information. The act is also intended to prevent deceit and misrepresentation in connection with the sale of securities.[6]

2. *Securities Exchange Act of 1934.* Created the SEC and empowered it to require reporting by publicly owned companies and registration of securities, security exchanges, and certain brokers and dealers. This act prohibits fraudulent and unfair behavior such as sales practice abuses and insider trading.

3. *Public Utility Holding Company Act of 1935.* Requires registration of interstate holding companies of public utilities covered by this law. This act was passed because of abuses in the 1920s in which huge, complex utility empires were created to minimize the need for equity financing.

4. *Trust Indenture Act of 1939.* Requires registration of trust indenture documents and supporting data in connection with the public sale of bonds, debentures, notes, and other debt securities.

5. *Investment Company Act of 1940.* Requires registration of investment companies, including mutual funds, that engage in investing and trading in securities. This act is designed in part to minimize conflicts of interest that arise with fund management.

6. *Investment Advisers Act of 1940 and Securities Investor Protection Act of 1970.* Require investment advisers to register and to follow certain standards created to protect investors.

7. *Foreign Corrupt Practices Act of 1977.* Affects registration indirectly through amendment to the Securities Exchange Act of 1934. This act requires the maintenance of accounting records and adequate internal accounting controls.

8. *Insider Trading Sanctions Act of 1984 and Insider Trading and Securities Fraud Enforcement Act of 1988.* Also affect registration indirectly. Increase the penalties against persons who profit from illegal use of inside information and who are associated with market manipulation and securities fraud.

9. *Sarbanes-Oxley Act of 2002.* As discussed in a later section of this chapter, designed as an answer to the numerous corporate accounting scandals that came to light in 2001 and 2002. This act mandated a number of reforms to bolster corporate responsibility, strengthen disclosure, and combat fraud. It also created the Public Company Accounting Oversight Board (PCAOB) to oversee the accounting profession.

SEC Requirements

As is obvious from the previous list of statutes, the filing requirements administered by the SEC are extensive. Thus, accountants who specialize in working with the federal securities laws must develop a broad knowledge of a great many reporting rules and regulations. The SEC specifies most of these disclosure requirements in two basic documents, *Regulation S–K* and *Regulation S–X,* which are supplemented by periodic releases and staff bulletins.

Regulation S–K establishes requirements for all nonfinancial information contained in filings with the SEC. Descriptions of the registrant's business and its securities are just two items covered by these regulations. A partial list of other nonfinancial data to be disclosed includes specified data about the company's directors and management, management's discussion and analysis of the current financial condition and the results of operations, and descriptions of both legal proceedings and the company's properties.

Regulation S–X prescribes the form and content of the financial statements (as well as the accompanying notes and related schedules) included in the various reports filed with the SEC. Thus, before being accepted, all financial information must meet a number of clearly specified requirements.

[6] Interestingly, one of the provisions originally suggested for this act would have created a federal corps of auditors. The defeat of this proposal (after some debate) has allowed for the rise of the independent auditing profession as it is currently structured in the United States. For more information, see Mark Moran and Gary John Previts, "The SEC and the Profession, 1934–1984: The Realities of Self-Regulation," *Journal of Accountancy,* July 1984.

The SEC's Impact on Financial Reporting to Stockholders

The SEC's disclosure and accounting requirements are not limited to the filings made directly with that body. *Rule 14c–3* of the 1934 act states that the annual reports of publicly held companies should include financial statements that have been audited. This information (referred to as *proxy information* because it accompanies the management's request to cast votes for the stockholders at the annual meeting) must present balance sheets as of the end of the two most recent fiscal years along with income statements and cash flow statements for the three most recent years. *Rule 14c–3* also states that additional information, as specified in *Regulation S–K,* should be included in this annual report.

Over the years, the SEC has moved toward an *integrated disclosure system.* Under this approach, much of the same reported information that the SEC requires must also go to the shareholders. Thus, the overall reporting process is simplified because only a single set of information must be generated in most cases. The integrated disclosure system is also intended as a way to improve the quality of the disclosures received directly by the shareholders.

Information required in proxy statements, which the shareholders receive directly, includes the following:

1. Five-year summary of operations including sales, total assets, income from continuing operations, and cash dividends per share.
2. Description of the business activities including principal products and sources and availability of raw materials.
3. Three-year summary of industry segments, export sales, and foreign and domestic operations.
4. List of company directors and executive officers.
5. Market price of the company's common stock for each quarterly period within the two most recent fiscal years.
6. Any restrictions on the company's ability to continue paying dividends.
7. Management's discussion and analysis of financial condition, changes in financial condition, and results of operations. This discussion should include liquidity, trends and significant events, causes of material changes in the financial statements, and the impact on the company of inflation.

In addition, even prior to passage of the Sarbanes-Oxley Act, the SEC required certain disclosures in proxy statements describing the services provided by the registrant's independent external auditor. This information was intended to help ensure that true independence was not endangered. Apparently, mere disclosure was not adequate in all cases.

Such disclosure must include the following:

1. All nonaudit services provided by the independent auditing firm.
2. A statement as to whether the board of directors (or its audit committee) approved all nonaudit services after considering the possibility that such services might impair the external auditor's independence.
3. The percentage of nonaudit fees to the total annual audit fee. This disclosure helps indicate the importance of the audit work to the firm versus the reward from any other services provided to the registrant.
4. Individual nonaudit fees that are more than 3 percent of the annual audit fee.

CORPORATE ACCOUNTING SCANDALS AND THE SARBANES-OXLEY ACT

"When William H. Donaldson enters his cavernous corner office on the sixth floor of the Securities and Exchange Commission early next year, he will head an agency at one of its lowest points since its creation nearly 70 years ago."[7]

"Enron's former chairman and chief executive, Kenneth Lay, received $152.7 million in payments and stock in the year leading up to the company's collapse amid revelations that

[7] Stephen Labaton, "Can a Bloodied S.E.C. Dust Itself Off and Get Moving," *The New York Times,* December 16, 2002, p. C-2.

it hid debt and inflated profit for years. Lay's take in 2001 was more than 11,000 times the maximum amount of severance paid to laid-off workers.

"Former WorldCom CEO Bernard Ebbers borrowed $408 million from the telecommunications company that had improperly accounted for $9 billion and was forced into bankruptcy. Ebbers had pledged company shares as collateral, but with those shares, once valued at $286 million, worthless, he was said to be considering forgoing his $1.5 million annual pension to help settle the debt.

"Adelphia Communications' founder and former CEO, John J. Rigas, allegedly conspired with four other executives to loot the company, leading prosecutors to seek the forfeiture of more than $2.5 billion."[8]

Hardly a day passed during 2002 without a new revelation of corporate wrongdoing. The list of companies whose executives virtually robbed the corporate treasury or whose accounting practices ranged from dubious to outrageous would be long, indeed. Throughout this excruciating disclosure process, many in the investing public began to raise two related questions:

Why didn't the independent auditor stop these practices?

How can the SEC allow such activities to occur?

As indicated previously, a number of theories can suggest the cause of the ethical meltdown during this period, ranging from human greed to sloppy auditing practices. In truth, when the history of this time is finally written, a variety of culprits will probably share the blame for such reprehensible behavior on both the corporate and the individual levels.

Regardless of the reasons, drastic actions had to be taken to reduce or eliminate future abuses (actual and perceived) to begin restoring public confidence in publicly traded entities and their disclosed accounting information. A capitalistic economy needs freely given investments, and that is possible only if investors believe they can make wise decisions to buy and sell securities based on the information available. Thus, Congress passed the Sarbanes-Oxley Act in July 2002[9] by a virtually unanimous vote. The scope and potential consequences of this legislation are extremely broad; the actual impact will probably not be determined for years, if not decades. "The Sarbanes-Oxley Act of 2002 is a major reform package mandating the most far-reaching changes Congress has imposed on the business world since FDR's New Deal."[10]

The act is so wide ranging that we describe only a general overview of some of the more discussed elements here.

Creation of the Public Company Accounting Oversight Board

The public accounting profession has long taken pride in its own self-regulation. Through its major professional body, the American Institute of Certified Public Accountants (AICPA), the profession has established and enforced its own code of conduct and created its own auditing standards for decades. The maintenance of public trust was often heard as a litany for the creation of such professional guidelines. Unfortunately, self-regulation has obviously not succeeded in recent times. One of the inherent flaws in the system was that the professional body, the AICPA, was considerably smaller than many of the international auditing firms that it sought to control. Discipline and conformity are simply difficult to maintain when the students are many times bigger, richer, and more powerful than the principal.

The Sarbanes-Oxley Act created the Public Company Accounting Oversight Board to oversee public accountants. The creation of the Oversight Board effectively minimizes self-regulation in the accounting profession. The board

- Has five members appointed by the SEC to staggered five-year terms.[11]
- Allows only two members to be accountants, past or present.[12]

[8] Brad Foss, "Unearthing of Corporate Scandals Exposed Market's Vulnerabilities," Associated Press Newswires, December 12, 2002.

[9] Public Law 107-204; 107th Congress, July 30, 2002.

[10] Richard I. Miller and Paul H. Pashkoff, "Regulations under the Sarbanes-Oxley Act," *Journal of Accountancy,* October 2002, p. 33.

[11] Sarbanes-Oxley Act of 2002, Sec. 101(e)(1).

[12] Ibid., at Sec. 101(e)(2).

- Enforces auditing, quality control, and independence standards and rules.
- Is under the oversight and enforcement authority of the SEC.
- Is funded from fees levied on all publicly traded companies.

These few provisions show that this Oversight Board rather than the accounting profession is now in charge of regulating public accounting for publicly traded companies. Although the board itself is not a government agency, the SEC has control of it and, thus, will be a much more active participant in the work of the independent auditor. For example, the SEC is to pick the five members of the board (after consultation with the chair of the Board of Governors of the Federal Reserve System and the Secretary of the United States Department of the Treasury). The act requires the board members to be prominent individuals of integrity and good reputation who must cease all other professional and business activities to help ensure independence and adequate time commitment.

One of the most interesting issues to be resolved is whether the new Oversight Board will continue to allow the Auditing Standards Board (ASB) to promulgate auditing and attest standards. For years, the AICPA has authorized the ASB to issue such pronouncements. However, the mandate of the Sarbanes-Oxley Act requires the Oversight Board to play a significant role in this process in the future. Although the board is directed to cooperate with the accounting profession, the board has the authority to amend, modify, repeal, or reject any auditing standard.[13] Thus, the eventual relationship that develops between the ASB and the board will have a huge impact on the extent to which the profession will retain some authority in establishing its own auditing standards.

Conversely, the future of the Financial Accounting Standards Board (FASB) is much less in doubt at this time. From its inception, the FASB has been a free-standing organization entirely separate from the AICPA. As we discuss later, the SEC has always held the ability to significantly impact accounting standards. Furthermore, the problems that led to the recent corporate scandals have been less about accounting issues and more about auditing lapses. Some observers, however, contend that the rule-based orientation of U.S. generally accepted accounting principles encourages income manipulation, which could also encourage more activity by the SEC in this area.

Registration of Public Accounting Firms

Registration of public accounting firms is required only of firms that prepare, issue, or participate in the preparation of an audit report for an issuer—basically an entity that issues securities. Consequently, virtually all public accounting firms of significant size must register, but most small firms do not need to register. Even foreign firms that play a substantial role in the audit of an organization that has securities registered in the United States must register with the Public Company Accounting Oversight Board and follow the rules of the Sarbanes-Oxley Act. The act has a significant impact on the activities of foreign companies that sell their securities on U.S. markets, an impact not necessarily appreciated outside the United States. "Under the law, CEOs are required to vouch for financial statements, boards must have audit committees drawn from independent directors, and companies can no longer make loans to corporate directors. All of that conflicts with some other countries' rules and customs."[14]

The application process provides the Oversight Board a significant amount of information about the auditing firms, which must identify each of their audit clients that qualifies as an issuer. Interestingly, the Oversight Board then assesses an annual fee on these issuers based on the size of its market capitalization. These fees serve, in part, as the financial support for the work of the Oversight Board.[15]

Other information required of the accounting firms in this application process includes the following:

- A list of all accountants participating in the audit report of any client qualifying as an issuer.
- Annual fees received from each issuer with the amounts separated as to audit and nonaudit services.

[13] Ibid., at Sec. 103(a)(1).

[14] Louis Lavelle and Mike McNamee, "Will Overseas Boards Play by American Rules?" *BusinessWeek*, December 16, 2002, p. 36.

[15] Sarbanes-Oxley Act of 2002, at Sec. 102(b)(2).

- Information about any criminal, civil, or administrative actions pending against the firm or any person associated with the firm.
- Information regarding disagreements between the issuer and the auditing firm during the previous year.

Inspections of Registered Firms

After registration, each auditing firm is subject to periodic inspections by the Public Company Accounting Oversight Board. This process is to eliminate the need for peer reviews that have been conducted by one firm on another. Now any firm that audits more than 100 issuers per year will be inspected annually. All other registered firms will be inspected every three years. The Oversight Board has the power to take disciplinary action as a result of the findings of these inspections. In addition, deficiencies can be made public if the firm does not address them in an appropriate fashion within 12 months.

The Oversight Board's power is not limited just to reacting to the findings of annual inspections. "The new board has a full range of sanctions at its disposal, including suspension or revocation of registration, censure, and significant fines. It has authority to investigate any act or practice that may violate the act, the new board's rules, the provisions of the federal securities laws relating to audit reports or applicable professional standards."[16] Clearly, Congress intended to give the new Oversight Board extensive powers to enable it to clean up any problems discovered in public accounting.

Auditor Independence

One of the most discussed issues surrounding the current accounting scandals is the failure of auditing firms to act independently in dealing with audit clients. Not surprisingly, a significant portion of the Sarbanes-Oxley Act is intended to ensure that public accounting firms are, indeed, independent. Certain services that could previously be provided to an audit client are now forbidden. These include financial information system design and implementation as well as internal audit outsourcing. The client's audit committee must preapprove any allowed services and disclose them in reports to the SEC.

Audit committees have long been considered an important element in maintaining an appropriate distance between the external auditors and the management of the client. The committee has been composed of members of the company's board of directors and served as a liaison with the auditors. However, in actual practice, the work and the composition of the audit committee have tended to vary greatly from company to company. The Sarbanes-Oxley Act has formalized that role by making the audit committee responsible for the appointment and compensation of the external auditor. To help ensure impartiality, the committee must be made up of individuals who are independent from the management. The act directs the auditor to report to the audit committee rather than to company management. To further ensure independence from management, the lead partner of the auditing firm must be rotated off the job after five years.

These provisions, as well as the many other elements of the Sarbanes-Oxley Act, have begun to change public accounting as it has been known in the past. Drastic action was needed and has been taken. This act should strengthen the independent audit to help eliminate the dubious practices that have haunted public accounting in recent years. Some of these steps may not have been necessary, but the need to reestablish public confidence in the capital market system forced the legislators to avoid any "quick-fix" solutions.

The SEC's Authority over Generally Accepted Accounting Principles

The primary focus of the Sarbanes-Oxley Act was on the regulation of independent auditing and auditing standards. Therefore, it had little impact on accounting standards and the registration of securities. Those regulations continue to evolve over time. Because financial reporting standards can be changed merely by amending *Regulation S–X,* the SEC holds the ultimate legal authority for establishing accounting principles for most publicly held companies in this country. In the past, the SEC has usually restricted the application of this power to disclosure

---

[16] Miller and Pashkoff, "Relations under the Sarbanes-Oxley Act," pp. 35 and 36.

issues while looking to the private sector (with the SEC's oversight) to formulate accounting principles. For this reason, the FASB rather than the SEC is generally viewed as the main standards-setting body for financial accounting in the United States. "Under federal law, the SEC has the mandate to determine accounting principles for publicly traded companies. But it has generally ceded that authority to private-sector accounting bodies such as the Financial Accounting Standards Board."[17]

However, the Securities and Exchange Commission does retain the ability to exercise its power with regard to the continuing evolution of accounting principles. The chief accountant of the SEC is responsible for providing the commissioners and the commission staff with advice on all current accounting and auditing matters and helps to draft rules for the form and content of financial statement disclosure and other reporting requirements. Because he or she is the principal adviser to the SEC on all accounting and auditing matters,[18] the most powerful accounting position in the United States is that of Chief Accountant of the SEC. The work of the chief accountant can lead the SEC to pass amendments as needed to alter various aspects of *Regulation S–X.*

Currently the SEC issues *Financial Reporting Releases (FRRs)* as needed to supplement *Regulation S–X* and *Regulation S–K.* They explain desired changes in the reporting requirements. By the end of 1998, 50 FRRs had been issued.[19] By 2004 this number was 72. In addition, the staff of the SEC publishes a series of *Staff Accounting Bulletins (SABs)* as a means of informing the financial community of its positions.

> Staff Accounting Bulletins reflect the SEC staff's views regarding accounting-related disclosure practices. They represent interpretations and policies followed by the Division of Corporation Finance and the Office of the Chief Accountant in administering the disclosure requirements of the federal securities laws.[20]

For example, *SAB 101* was released late in 1999 to provide guidance in connection with the recognition of revenue. The bulletin first stated that any transaction that fell within the scope of specific authoritative literature (e.g., an FASB statement) should be reported based on that pronouncement. *SAB 101* then established guidelines for revenue recognition situations when authoritative standards were not available. In such cases, a reporting entity should recognize revenue when realized (or realizable) and earned. However, *SAB 101* then went further to establish four criteria for revenue recognition: evidence that an arrangement exists, delivery has occurred or services have been rendered, the price is fixed or can be determined, and collectibility is reasonably assured. To help apply these criteria in actual practice, *SAB 101* included nine examples to show how to judge revenue recognition in such cases as the receipt of money in layaway programs and annual membership fees received by discount retailers.

Additional Disclosure Requirements

Historically, the SEC has tended to restrict use of its authority (as in *SAB 101*) to the gray areas of accounting for which official guidance is not available. New reporting problems arise each year while no authoritative body has ever completely addressed many other accounting issues, even after years of discussion. As another response to such problems, the SEC often requires the disclosure of additional data if current rules are viewed as insufficient.

> It was in the 1970s that the SEC seemed to single out disclosure as the area in which it would take the standard-setting lead, leaving measurement issues to the FASB. This was when the SEC was expanding the coverage of Management's Discussion & Analysis (MD&A), an extensive narrative disclosure that is required to be appended to the financial statements.[21]

[17] Kevin G. Salwen and Robin Goldwyn Blumenthal, "Tackling Accounting, SEC Pushes Changes with Broad Impact," *The Wall Street Journal,* September 27, 1990, p. A1.

[18] http://www.SEC/about/whatwedo.shtml@8, June 2005.

[19] From 1937 until 1982, the SEC issued more than 300 *Accounting Series Releases* (ASRs) to (1) amend *Regulation S-X,* (2) express interpretations regarding specific accounting and auditing issues, and (3) report disciplinary actions against public accountants. The ASRs that dealt with financial reporting matters of continuing interest were codified by the SEC in 1982 and issued as *Financial Reporting Release No. 1.*

[20] See footnote 2.

[21] Stephen A. Zeff, "A Perspective on the U.S. Public/Private-Sector Approach to the Regulation of Financial Reporting," *Accounting Horizons,* March 1995, pp. 58–59.

For example, in the early part of 1997, while the FASB worked on a project concerning the accounting for derivatives, the SEC approved rules so that more information would be available immediately. Footnote disclosure had to include more information about accounting policies in use. In addition, information was required about the risk of loss from market rate or price changes inherent in derivatives and other financial instruments. By means of these disclosures, the SEC enabled investors to have data about the potential consequences of the company's financial position.

Moratorium on Specific Accounting Practices

The commission also can exert its power by declaring a moratorium on the use of specified accounting practices. When authoritative guidance is not present, the SEC can simply prohibit a particular method from being applied. As an example, in the 1980s, companies utilized a variety of procedures to account for internal computer software costs because no official pronouncement had yet been issued. Consequently, the SEC

> imposed a moratorium that will prohibit companies that plan to go public from capitalizing the internal costs of developing computer software for sale or lease or marketed to customers in other ways. . . . The decision doesn't prevent companies currently capitalizing internal software expenses from continuing, but the companies must disclose the effect of not expensing such costs as incurred. The moratorium continues until the Financial Accounting Standards Board issues a standard on the issue.[22]

When the FASB eventually arrived at a resolution of this question by issuing *SFAS 86,* "Accounting for the Costs of Computer Software to Be Sold, Leased, or Otherwise Marketed," the SEC dropped the moratorium. Hence, the FASB was allowed to set the accounting rule, but the SEC ensured appropriate reporting until that time.

Challenging Individual Statements

As described, officially requiring additional disclosure and prohibiting the application of certain accounting practices are two methods the SEC uses to control the financial reporting process. Forcing a specific registrant to change its filed statements is another, less formal approach that can create the same effect. For example:

> Advanced Micro Devices, Inc., agreed to settle an investigation by the Securities and Exchange Commission of the semiconductor company's public disclosures. The SEC found AMD "made inaccurate and misleading statements" concerning development of its 486 microprocessor. In 1992 and 1993, AMD "led the public to believe that it was independently designing the microcode for its 486 microprocessor without access" to the code of its rival chipmaker, Intel Corp., the SEC said, "when, in fact, AMD had provided its engineers . . . with Intel's copyright 386 microcode to accelerate the company's development efforts." Without admitting or denying the commission's findings, AMD, based in Sunnyvale, California, consented to an order barring it from committing future violations of SEC rules. No fines were imposed.[23]

Following the action taken by the SEC, any company involved in a similar event would certainly be well advised to provide the suggested disclosure. Failing to do so could result in the SEC's refusal to approve an issuer's future registrations.

Overruling the FASB

The SEC's actions are not necessarily limited, however, to the gray areas of accounting. Although the commission generally has allowed the FASB (and previous authoritative groups) to establish accounting principles, the SEC retains the authority to override or negate any pronouncements produced in the private sector. This power was dramatically demonstrated in 1977 when the FASB issued *SFAS 19,* "Financial Accounting and Reporting by Oil and Gas Producing Companies." After an extended debate over the merits of alternative methods, the FASB issued this statement requiring oil- and gas-producing companies to apply the successful-efforts method when accounting for unsuccessful exploration and drilling costs.

[22] "SEC Imposes 'Software Costs' Moratorium," *Journal of Accountancy,* September 1983, p. 3.
[23] "SEC Inquiry on Disclosure to Public Is Being Settled," *The Wall Street Journal,* October 1, 1996, p. B4.

In response, the SEC almost immediately invoked a moratorium on the use of this practice until an alternative approach could be evaluated. Thus, companies filing with the SEC were not allowed to follow the method established by the FASB (after years of formal study and deliberation by that body). Although the commission's reaction toward the accounting profession was a unique instance, the handling of this one issue clearly demonstrates the veto power that the SEC maintains over the work of the FASB.[24]

Filings with the SEC

Because of legal regulations, registrants may be required to make numerous different filings with the SEC. The SEC actually receives hundreds of thousands of filings per year. However, for the overview being presented here, the reporting process is divided into two very broad categories:

- Registration statements.
- Periodic filings.

Registration statements ensure the disclosure of sufficient, relevant financial data before either a company or its underwriters can *initially offer* a security to the public. The Securities Act of 1933 mandates dissemination of such information. Registration is necessary except in certain situations described at a later point in this chapter. The SEC charges a registration fee based on the value of the securities offered. This fee is a very small fraction of the value of the securities being issued. In 1999, it was 0.0264 of 1 percent of the value of the securities offered. In 2003, the SEC collected more than $2.0 billion in fees, an amount that vastly exceeded its operating costs.

For years, the existence of this surplus has caused debate. Some viewed it as a source of general revenue for the federal government, and others have argued that it indicated that corporations were being overcharged for the registration process. However, another possibility emerged as a result of the corporate accounting scandals in 2001 and 2002: The surplus probably meant that the resources being invested in the work of the SEC were not adequate. In other words, the agency could simply not meet its responsibilities with the money allotted. Not surprisingly, the Sarbanes-Oxley Act authorized a 77 percent increase in the agency's budget and a substantial jump in the size of its staff. However, this authorization does not necessarily mean that the SEC will actually receive more money in the budgeting process. "Instead of supporting the 77 percent budget hike promised by Congress, the White House wants the SEC to make do with a more modest $568 million next year. The Commission's 2002 budget was $438 million. While this might seem like a lot, Harvey Goldschmid [SEC Commissioner] said that it is not enough to pay for the effective policing of 17,000 companies, 34,000 investment portfolios, and 7,500 financial advisers, especially in a climate where so much emphasis is placed on the quality of oversight."[25]

After initial registration, periodic filings with the SEC are required of registrants by a number of federal laws, the most important of which is the Securities Exchange Act of 1934. This legislation has resulted in the *continual reporting of specified data* by all companies that have securities publicly traded on either a national securities exchange or an over-the-counter market.[26]

For registration statements as well as periodic filings, the SEC has established forms that provide the format and content to be followed in providing required information. "These forms contain no blanks to be filled in as do tax forms. Instead, they are narrative in character, giving general instructions about the items of information to be furnished. Detailed information must be assembled by the companies using the form designed for the type of security being offered as well as the type of company making the offer."[27]

---

[24] For a detailed account of the activities surrounding the SEC's rejection of *SFAS 19*, see Donald Gorton, "The SEC Decision Not to Support SFAS 19: A Case Study of the Effect of Lobbying on Standard Setting," *Accounting Horizons*, March 1991.

[25] Howard Stock, "Don't Short-Change SEC, Goldschmid Tells Bush," *Investors Relations Business*, December 16, 2002.

[26] A company that has securities traded on an over-the-counter market does not have to file under the 1934 Act unless it has at least $10 million in assets and 500 shareholders.

[27] K. Fred Skousen, *An Introduction to the SEC* (Cincinnati: South-Western Publishing, 1991), p. 47.

Registration Statements (1933 Act)

As indicated, a registration statement must be filed with and made effective by the Securities and Exchange Commission before a company can offer a security publicly. A security is very broadly defined to include items such as a note, stock, treasury stock, bond, debenture, investment contract, evidence of indebtedness, or transferable share.

The SEC's role is not to evaluate the quality of the investment. Rather, the SEC seeks to ensure that the content and disclosure of the filing comply with all applicable regulations. The responsibility for the information always rests with corporate officials. The SEC is charged with ensuring full and fair disclosure of relevant financial information. The registrant has the responsibility to provide such data, but the decision to invest must remain with the public.

A number of different forms are available for this purpose, depending on the specific circumstances. Some of the most commonly encountered registration statement forms follow:

- S–1 Used when no other form is prescribed. Usually used by new registrants or by companies that have been filing reports with the SEC for less than 36 months.
- S–2 Used by companies that have filed with the SEC for 36 months or longer but are not large enough to file a Form S–3.
- S–3 Used by companies that are large and already have a significant following in the stock market (at least $75 million of the voting stock is held by nonaffiliates). Disclosure is reduced for these organizations because the public is assumed to already have access to a considerable amount of information. Form F–3 is used if registration is by a foreign issuer.
- S–4 Used for securities issued in connection with business combination transactions.
- S–8 Used as a registration statement for employee stock plans.
- S–11 Used for the registration of securities by certain real estate companies.
- SB–1 Used by small business issuers to register up to $10 million of securities but only if the company has not registered more than $10 million of securities offerings during the previous 12 months. A small business issuer has annual revenues of less than $25 million and less than $25 million of voting securities held by nonaffiliates.
- SB–2 Used by small business issuers to register securities to be sold for cash.

The use of several of these forms, especially Form S–3, offers a distinct advantage to established companies that are issuing securities. Rather than duplicate voluminous information already disclosed in other filings with the SEC—frequently the annual report to shareholders—the registrant can simply indicate the location of the data in these other documents, a process referred to as *incorporation by reference.*

Registration Procedures

The actual registration process is composed of a series of events leading up to the permission to "go effective" by the SEC. Because the registrant is seeking to obtain significant financial resources through the issuance of new securities in public markets, each of these procedures is vitally important.

After selecting the appropriate form, the company accumulates information according to the requirements of *Regulation S–K* and *Regulation S–X.* If it anticipates problems or questions, the company may request a prefiling conference with the SEC staff to seek guidance prior to beginning the registration. For example, if uncertainty exists concerning the handling or disclosure of an unusual transaction, a prefiling conference can save all parties considerable time and effort.

> The Commission has a long-established policy of holding its staff available for conferences with prospective registrants or their representatives in advance of filing a registration statement. These conferences may be held for the purpose of discussing generally the problems confronting a registrant in effecting registration or to resolve specific problems of an unusual nature which are sometimes presented by involved or complicated financial transactions.[28]

---

[28] Stanley Weinstein, Daniel Schechtman, and Michael A. Walker, *SEC Compliance,* vol. 4 (Englewood Cliffs, NJ: Prentice-Hall, 1999), para. 30,641.

When the SEC receives it, the Division of Corporation Finance[29] reviews the registration statement. An analyst determines whether all nonfinancial information complies with the SEC's disclosure requirements in *Regulation S–K*. At the same time, an accountant verifies that the financial statement data included in the filing meet the standards of *Regulation S–X* and have been prepared according to generally accepted accounting principles. *Because the SEC does not conduct a formal audit, the report of the company's independent CPA is essential to this particular evaluation.* In addition, an SEC lawyer reviews the registration statement to verify the legal aspects of the document.

The Division of Corporation Finance regularly requests clarifications, changes, or additional information, especially for those filings involving an initial registration. A *letter of comments* (also known as a *deficiency letter*) is issued to the company to communicate these findings. In most cases, the registrant attempts to provide the necessary data or changes to expedite the process. However, in controversial areas, the issuer may begin discussions directly with the SEC staff in hope of resolving the problem without making the requested adjustments or disclosure or, at least, with limited inconvenience.

When the Division of Corporate Finance is eventually satisfied that the company has fulfilled all SEC regulations, the registration statement is made effective and the securities can be sold. *Effectiveness does not, however, indicate an endorsement of the securities by the SEC.* With most offerings, the company actually sells the stock using one or more underwriters (stock brokerage firms) that market the shares to their clients to earn commissions.

For convenience and to save time and money, large companies are allowed to use a process known as *shelf registration.* They file once with the SEC and are then allowed to offer those securities at any time over the subsequent two years without having to go back to the SEC. For example, "Enterprise Products Partners L. P. announced today that it has filed an $800 million universal shelf registration statement with the Securities and Exchange Commission for the proposed sale of debt and equity securities over the next two years."[30]

The registration statement is physically composed of two parts. Part I, referred to as a *prospectus,* contains extensive information that includes these items:

1. Financial statements for the issuing company audited by an independent CPA along with appropriate supplementary data.
2. An explanation of the intended use of the proceeds to be generated by the sale of the new securities.
3. A description of the risks associated with the securities.
4. A description of the business and the properties owned by the company.

The registrant must furnish every potential buyer of the securities with a copy of this prospectus, thus ensuring the adequate availability of information for their investment analysis.

Part II of the registration statement is primarily for the informational needs of the SEC staff. Additional data should be disclosed about the company and the securities being issued such as marketing arrangements, expenses of issuance, sales to special parties, and the like. The registrant is not required to provide this information to prospective buyers, although the entire registration statement is available to the public through the SEC.

Securities Exempt from Registration   According to the 1933 act, not all securities issued by companies and their underwriters require registration prior to their sale. For example, securities sold to the residents of the state in which the issuing company is chartered and principally doing business are exempted. However, these offerings may still be regulated by the securities laws of the individual states (commonly known as *blue sky laws*), which vary significantly across the country.[31]

---

[29] All registration statements filed by issuers offering securities to the public for the first time are reviewed. Subsequent registration statements and periodic filings are reviewed only on a selective basis.

[30] "Enterprise Files $800 Million Universal Shelf Registration with SEC," *Business Wire,* December 27, 1999.

[31] "These early laws became known as 'blue sky' laws after a judicial decision characterized some transactions as 'speculative schemes which have no more basis than so many feet of blue sky.'" (Skousen, *An Introduction to the SEC,* p. 3.)

Other exempt offerings include but are not limited to the following:

- Securities issued by governments, banks, and savings and loan associations.
- Securities issued that are restricted to a company's own existing stockholders for which no commission is paid to solicit the exchange.
- Securities issued by nonprofit organizations such as religious, educational, or charitable groups.
- Small offerings of no more than $5 million within a 12-month period. In most cases, though, a Regulation A offering circular must still be filed with the SEC and given to prospective buyers. However, much less information is required of a company in an offering circular than in a registration statement.
- Offerings of no more than $1 million made to any number of investors within a 12-month period. No specific disclosure of information is required. General solicitations are allowed. The issuer must give notice of the offering to the SEC within 15 days of the first sale.
- Offerings of no more than $5 million made to 35 or fewer purchasers in a 12-month period. No general solicitation is allowed for securities issued in this manner. Accredited investors (such as banks, insurance companies, and individuals with net worth of more than $1 million) are not included in the restriction on the number of buyers. Unaccredited investors must still be furnished with an audited balance sheet and other specified information. Parties making purchases have to hold the securities for at least two years or the filing exemption is lost.
- The private placement of securities to no more than 35 sophisticated investors (having knowledge and experience in financial matters) who already have sufficient information available to them about the issuing company. Again, the number of accredited investors is unlimited and general solicitation is not permitted. These private placement rules have become quite important in recent years. Private placements in the United States rose from $16 billion in 1980 to more than $200 billion in 1996. By 2004 private equity placements nearly approached this figure, approximating $177 billion. For example, "SYS Technologies, a leading provider of real time information technology solutions to industrial and U.S. government customers, announced today that it has completed a private placement with institutional investors raising gross proceeds of $3.35 million on June 3, 2005."[32]

Periodic Filings with the SEC

Once a company has issued securities that are publicly traded on a securities exchange or an over-the-counter market, it must continually file information with the SEC so that adequate disclosure is available. As with registration statements, several different forms are utilized for this purpose. However, for most companies with actively traded securities, three of these are common: Form 10–K (an annual report), Form 10–Q (a quarterly report), and Form 8–K (disclosure of significant events). Smaller businesses use Form 10–KSB for annual reports and Form 10–QSB for quarterly reports.

In addition, as mentioned previously, proxy statements must be filed with the SEC. Management or another interested party issues these statements to a company's owners in hope of securing voting rights to be used at stockholders' meetings.

Form 10–K   A 10–K form is an annual report filed with the SEC to provide information and disclosures required by *Regulation S–K* and *Regulation S–X*. Fortunately, because of the integrated disclosure system, the annual report distributed by companies to their stockholders now includes most of the basic financial disclosures required by the SEC in Form 10–K. Thus, many companies simply attach the stockholders' annual report to the Form 10–K each year and use the incorporation by reference procedure to meet most of the SEC's filing requirements. This process is sometimes known as a *wraparound filing*.

Form 10–K, as with the various other SEC filings, is constantly undergoing assessment to determine whether investor needs are being met.[33] Thus, the SEC's reporting requirements are evolutionary and change over time.

---

[32] "SYS Technologies Completes Private Placement Transaction," http://freshnews.com/news/fresh-money/article_24429.html.

[33] The current Form 10–K instructions can be viewed at http://www.sec.gov/about/forms/form10-K.pdf.

The Securities and Exchange Commission issued guidelines aimed at making public companies provide a more detailed look at the trends and business changes that management expects in the future. . . . In the main part of yesterday's interpretation, the commissioners said that in the 10–K reports, companies must discuss "trends, demands, commitments or events" that it knows are "reasonably likely" to occur and have a material effect on financial condition or results.[34]

As this quote indicates, the SEC is especially interested in the quality of the information provided by the Management's Discussion and Analysis (MD&A) section of a registrant's filings. Basically, management should describe verbally the company's past, present, and future. This information can furnish investors with a feel for the prospects of the company; it is a candid narrative to provide statement readers with a sense of management's priorities, accomplishments, and concerns. The SEC staff carefully reviews the MD&A feature. "If the management of a company knows something that could have a material impact on earnings in the future, officials have an obligation to share that information with shareholders."[35]

Form 10–Q A 10–Q form contains condensed interim financial statements for the registrant and must be filed with the SEC shortly after the end of each quarter. However, no Form 10–Q is required following the fourth quarter of the year since a Form 10–K is forthcoming shortly thereafter. A Form 10–Q does not have to be audited by an independent CPA.

Information to be contained in each Form 10–Q includes the following:

- Income statements must be included for the most recent quarter and for the year to date as well as for the comparative periods in the previous year.
- A statement of cash flows is also necessary, but only for the year to date as well as for the corresponding period in the preceding year.
- Two balance sheets are reported: one as of the end of the most recent quarter and the second showing the company's financial position at the end of the previous fiscal year.
- Each Form 10–Q should also include any needed disclosures pertaining to the current period including the management's discussion and analysis of the financial condition of the company and results of operations.

Form 8–K An 8–K form is used to disclose a unique or significant happening. Consequently, the 8–K is not filed at regular time intervals but within 15 calendar days of the event (or within 5 business days in certain specified instances). The SEC receives thousands of 8–K reports each year. According to the SEC's guidelines, Form 8–K may be filed to report any action that company officials believe is important to security holders. However, the following events are designated for required disclosure in this manner:

- Resignation of a director.
- Changes in control of the registrant.
- Acquisition or disposition of assets.
- Changes in the registrant's certified accountants (independent auditors).
- Bankruptcy or receivership.

Proxy Statements As previously mentioned, most of the significant actions undertaken by a company first must be approved at stockholders' meetings. For example, the members of the board of directors are elected in this manner to oversee the operations of the company. Although such votes are essential to the operations of a business, few major companies could possibly assemble enough shareholders at any one time and place for a voting quorum. The geographic distances are simply too great. Hence, before each of the periodic meetings, the management (or any other interested party) usually requests signed proxies from shareholders granting the legal authority to cast votes for the owners in connection with the various actions to be taken at such stockholders' meetings.[36]

[34] Paul Duke, Jr., "SEC Issues Guidelines for 10–K Filings Seeking More Details on Trends, Changes," *The Wall Street Journal*, May 19, 1989, p. A2.

[35] Kevin G. Salwen, "SEC Charges Caterpillar Failed to Warn Holders of Earnings Risk Posed by Unit," *The Wall Street Journal*, April 2, 1992, p. A3.

[36] Any person who owns at least 5 percent of the company's stock or has been an owner for six months or longer has the right to look at a list of shareholders to make a proxy solicitation.

Because of the power conveyed by a proxy, any such solicitation sent to shareholders (by any party) must include specific information as required by the SEC in its *Regulation 14A.* This proxy statement has to be filed with the SEC at least 10 days before being distributed. A number of the disclosed items were described previously. Other data that must be reported to the owners include these:

- The proxy statement needs to indicate on whose behalf the solicitation is being made.
- The proxy statement must disclose fully all matters that are to be voted on at the meeting.
- In most cases, the proxy statement has to be accompanied (or preceded) by an annual report to the shareholders.

As with all areas of disclosure, the SEC's regulation of proxy statements has greatly enhanced the information available to investors. Historically, shareholders have not always been able to get adequate information.

> Thus was the president of one company able to respond cavalierly to a shareholder's request for information, "I can assure you that the company is in a good financial position. I trust that you will sign and mail your proxy at an early date." Quaint. But that was nothing. One unlisted company printed its proxy on the back of the dividend check—so when you endorsed the check you voted for management.[37]

> From a 1902 annual report to shareholders: "The settled plan has been to withhold all information from stockholders and others that is not called for by the stockholders in a body. So far no request for information has been made in the manner prescribed by the directors."[38]

Electronic Data Gathering, Analysis, and Retrieval System (EDGAR)

During recent years, the SEC has become almost overwhelmed by the sheer mountains of documents that it receives, reviews, and makes available to the public. Filings with the SEC are estimated to contain 5 million pieces of paper each year. Not surprisingly, some of the problems in the capital markets during the last few years have been blamed, in part, on this overload. "(The SEC's) corporation finance division cannot keep up with the deluge of company filings."[39]

In 1984, the SEC began to develop an electronic data gathering, analysis, and retrieval system nicknamed EDGAR. As originally envisioned, all filings would arrive at the SEC on disks or through some other electronic transmission. Each filing could be reviewed, analyzed, and stored by SEC personnel on a computer so they would no longer constantly have to sift through stacks of paper. Perhaps more importantly, investors would have the ability to access this data through the Internet. Thus, investors throughout the world could have information available for their decisions literally minutes after the documents are made effective by the SEC.

Because of the ambitious nature of the EDGAR project, approximately a decade was required to get the system effectively operational. For years, EDGAR was the object of much scorn; "one member of the House Energy and Commerce Committee suggested renaming the project Mr. Ed, 'since the SEC has a much better chance of finding a talking horse than it does of achieving an efficient computer filing system'."[40] However, the beginning of the explosive use of the Internet in the mid-1990s corresponded with the widescale availability of information on EDGAR. Not surprisingly, EDGAR's popularity has expanded.

> If you're suspicious about a certain stock, then go to the Securities and Exchange Commission's EDGAR database—chockablock with annual reports, prospectuses and all the other paperwork demanded of public companies.[41]

---

[37] Laura Jereski, "You've Come a Long Way, Shareholder," *Forbes,* July 13, 1987, p. 282.

[38] Skousen, *An Introduction to the SEC,* p. 75.

[39] Labaton, "Can a Bloodied S.E.C. Dust Itself Off and Get Moving."

[40] Sandra Block, "SEC Gets Closer to Electronic Filing," *The Wall Street Journal,* August 30, 1991, p. C1.

[41] The address for EDGAR is www.sec.gov. A quick EDGAR tutorial is available at www.sec.gov/edgar/quickedgar.htm to familiarize users with the retrieval system. Joseph R. Garber, "Click Before You Leap," *Forbes,* February 24, 1997, p. 162.

Discussion **Question**

IS THE DISCLOSURE WORTH THE COST?

Filing with the SEC requires a very significant amount of time and effort on the part of the registrant. Companies frequently resist attempts by the commission to increase the levels of disclosure. Usually, they argue that additional information will not necessarily be useful to a great majority of investors. Regardless of the issue being debated, critics claim that the cost of the extra data far outweighs any benefits that might be derived from this disclosure.

Such contentions are not necessarily made just to avoid disclosing information. One survey estimated the cost of SEC disclosures to be more than $400 million in 1975 alone. "The table reports an estimated $213,500,000 for the fully variable costs of 10–K, 10–Q and 8–K disclosures in 1975. To this should be added the separate estimate (not shown) of $191,900,000 for disclosure related to new issues in 1975, for a total estimate of about $400,000,000 for SEC disclosure costs in 1975. These estimates are biased downward because they do not include various fixed costs."* Such costs are either passed along to the consumer in the form of higher prices or serve to retard the growth of the reporting company.

Additional SEC requirements continue to concern issuers, many of which conclude that "the cost of mandatory SEC disclosures outweigh the benefits" and accept delisting from the various exchanges, rather than incurring the costs of such disclosure.† SEC revenues, which constitute real out-of-pocket costs to issuers, exceeded $2 billion in 2003. This represents a ten-fold increase in the past 30 years.

The author of one survey (that has been widely discussed and debated over the years) held that federal securities laws are not actually helpful to investors.

> I found that there was little evidence of fraud related to financial statements in the period prior to the enactment of the Securities Acts. Nor was there a widespread lack of disclosure. . . . Hence, I conclude that there was little justification for the accounting disclosure required by the Acts. . . . These findings indicate that the data required by the SEC do not seem to be useful to investors.‡

The SEC was created, in part, to ensure that the public has fair and full disclosure about companies that have their securities publicly traded. However, the commission must be mindful of the cost of such disclosures. How can the SEC determine whether the cost of a proposed disclosure is more or less than the benefits that will be derived by the public?

*J. Richard Zecher, "An Economic Perspective of SEC Corporate Disclosure," *The SEC and Accounting: The First 50 Years,* ed. Robert H. Mundheim and Noyes E. Leech (Amsterdam: North-Holland, 1985), pp. 75–76.

†Brian J. Bushee and Christian Leuz, "Economic Consequences of SEC Disclosure Regulation," The Wharton School, University of Pennsylvania, February 2004, p. 3.

‡George J. Benston, "The Value of the SEC's Accounting Disclosure Requirements," *The Accounting Review,* July 1969, p. 351.

Since Congress went to all the trouble in the 1930s of creating the SEC and requiring these corporate disclosures, it seems like somebody should give them an occasional good read. The Edgar database at the SEC's Web site gives any individual free access to the filings of thousands of public companies. . . . It's sometimes amazing what kind of information typing someone's name, address or phone number into an Edgar search engine can generate.[42]

Today, virtually all publicly held companies are required to file their SEC reports electronically. Paper filings, when permitted, are also converted to electronic files and available to the general public.[43] The resultant EDGAR filings are typically available via the SEC's Web site within 24 hours of filings. These public filings, combined with the ease of access via the Internet, have resulted in the virtually immediate dissemination of vital investment-related

[42] John Emshwiller, "Financial Filings Hold Key to Investigative Pieces, Big and Small" *The Wall Street Journal,* May 31, 2005.

[43] www.sec.gov/edgar/quickedgar.htm.

data to accounting professionals, financial advisers, government regulators, and the investing public. EDGAR users can locate filings based on entity names, standard industrial classification (SIC) codes, central index keys (CIK), addresses, date–time frames, and a variety of other variables. This extensive database has helped move financial reporting to a significantly higher level of transparency.

Summary

1. In the United States, the Securities and Exchange Commission (SEC) has been entrusted with the responsibility for ensuring that complete and reliable information is available to investors who buy and sell securities in public capital markets. Since being created in 1934, this agency has administered numerous reporting rules and regulations created by congressional actions starting with the Securities Act of 1933 and the Securities Exchange Act of 1934.

2. The corporate accounting scandals that rocked the U.S. financial community during 2001 and 2002 led Congress to pass the Sarbanes-Oxley Act. This legislation addressed a number of problems. Its main provision was the creation of the Public Company Accounting Oversight Board to monitor and regulate the public accounting profession. Auditing firms of public companies must register with this board and are subject to periodic inspections as well as various types of possible disciplinary actions. This act also contains rules to help ensure the absolute independence of the external auditor.

3. Before a company's securities (such as either equity or debt) can be publicly traded, appropriate filings must be made with the SEC to ensure that sufficient data are made available to potential investors. Disclosure requirements for this process are outlined in two documents: *Regulation S–K* (for nonfinancial information) and *Regulation S–X* (describing the form and content of all included financial statements).

4. The ability to require the reporting of special information gives the SEC enormous legal power over the accounting standards in the United States. Traditionally, this authority has been wielded only to increase disclosure requirements and to provide guidance where none was otherwise available. However, in a significant demonstration of its authority, the SEC overruled the FASB's decision in 1977 as to the appropriate method to account for unsuccessful exploration and drilling costs incurred by oil- and gas-producing companies.

5. Filings with the SEC are divided generally into two broad categories: registration statements and periodic filings. Registration statements are designed to provide information about a company prior to its issuance of a security to the public. Depending on the circumstances, several different registration forms are available for this purpose. After the statement is produced by the registrant and initially reviewed by the SEC, a letter of comments is furnished describing desired explanations or changes. These concerns must be resolved before the security can be sold.

6. Not all securities issued in the United States require registration with the SEC. As an example, formal registration is not necessary for securities sold by either government units or banks. Certain issues for relatively small amounts are also exempt although some amount of disclosure is normally required. Securities sold solely within the state in which the business operates are not subject to federal securities laws but must comply with state laws frequently referred to as *blue sky laws.*

7. Companies whose stocks or bonds are publicly traded on a securities exchange must also submit periodic filings to the SEC to ensure that adequate disclosure is constantly maintained. Among the most common of these filings are Form 10–K (an annual report) and Form 10–Q (condensed interim financial information). Form 8–K also is required to report any significant events that occur. In addition, proxy statements (documents that are used to solicit votes at stockholders' meetings) also come under the filing requirements monitored by the SEC.

8. The SEC has created the EDGAR database to allow companies to make electronic filings with the commission. More importantly, EDGAR allows any person with access to the Internet to review these documents in a timely fashion. Thus, access to financial and other information about filing entities has become much more widely available.

Questions

(Students may wish to visit the SEC Web site, www.sec.gov, for supplemental resources.)

1. Why were federal securities laws originally enacted by Congress?
2. What are some of the possible reasons for the numerous corporate accounting scandals discovered during 2001 and 2002?
3. List several provisions of the Sarbanes-Oxley Act that are designed to restore public confidence in the U.S. capital market system.

4. What is the relationship of the SEC to the Public Company Accounting Oversight Board?

5. Who must register with the Public Company Accounting Oversight Board?

6. What is the impact of being registered with this board?

7. How has the Sarbanes-Oxley Act attempted to ensure that external auditors will be completely independent in the future?

8. What is the purpose of the inspection process created by the Sarbanes-Oxley Act?

9. What is covered by *Regulation S–K?*

10. What is covered by *Regulation S–X?*

11. What are some of the major divisions within the SEC?

12. What does the Securities Act of 1933 cover?

13. What does the Securities Exchange Act of 1934 cover?

14. What are the goals of the SEC?

15. What information is required in a proxy statement?

16. Why is the content of a proxy statement considered to be so important?

17. How does the SEC affect the development of generally accepted accounting principles in the United States?

18. What is the purpose of *Financial Reporting Releases* and *Staff Accounting Bulletins?*

19. What was the SEC's response to the FASB's handling of accounting for oil- and gas-producing companies, and why was this action considered so significant?

20. What is the purpose of a registration statement?

21. Under what law is a registration statement filed?

22. What are the two parts of a registration statement? What is contained in each part?

23. How does the SEC generate revenues?

24. Three forms commonly used in the registration process are Form S–1, Form S–3, and Form SB–2. Which registrants should use each of these forms?

25. What is incorporation by reference?

26. What is a prefiling conference, and why might it be helpful to a registrant?

27. What is a letter of comments? By what other name is a letter of comments often called?

28. What is a prospectus? What does a prospectus contain?

29. Under what circumstances is a company exempt from filing a registration statement with the SEC prior to the issuance of securities?

30. What is a private placement of securities?

31. What are blue sky laws?

32. What is a wraparound filing?

33. When is a Form 8–K issued by a company? What specific information does a Form 8–K convey?

34. What is the purpose of the Management's Discussion and Analysis?

35. What is the difference between a Form 10–K and a Form 10–Q?

36. What was the purpose of creating the EDGAR system?

Problems

1. Which of the following statements is true?
   a. The Securities Exchange Act of 1934 regulates intrastate stock offerings made by a company.
   b. The Securities Act of 1933 regulates the subsequent public trading of securities through brokers and markets.
   c. The Securities Exchange Act of 1934 is commonly referred to as blue sky legislation.
   d. The Securities Act of 1933 regulates the initial offering of securities by a company.

2. What is the purpose of *Regulation S–K?*
   a. Defines generally accepted accounting principles in the United States.
   b. Establishes required disclosure of nonfinancial information with the SEC.
   c. Establishes required financial disclosures with the SEC.
   d. Indicates which companies must file with the SEC on an annual basis.

3. What is the difference between *Regulation S–K* and *Regulation S–X?*

   a. *Regulation S–K* establishes reporting requirements for companies in their initial issuance of securities whereas *Regulation S–X* is directed toward the subsequent issuance of securities.

   b. *Regulation S–K* establishes reporting requirements for companies smaller than a certain size whereas *Regulation S–X* is directed toward companies larger than that size.

   c. *Regulation S–K* establishes regulations for nonfinancial information filed with the SEC whereas *Regulation S–X* prescribes the form and content of financial statements included in SEC filings.

   d. *Regulation S–K* establishes reporting requirements for publicly held companies whereas *Regulation S–X* is directed toward private companies.

4. The Securities Exchange Act of 1934

   a. Regulates the public trading of previously issued securities through brokers and exchanges.

   b. Prohibits blue sky laws.

   c. Regulates the initial offering of securities by a company.

   d. Requires the registration of investment advisers.

5. Which of the following is a requirement of the Sarbanes-Oxley Act of 2002?

   a. Registration of all auditing firms with the Public Company Accounting Oversight Board.

   b. Annual inspection of all auditing firms registered with the Public Company Accounting Oversight Board.

   c. A monetary fee assessed on organizations issuing securities.

   d. Overall assessment of the work of the SEC each year.

6. Which of the following is *not* correct in connection with the Public Company Accounting Oversight Board?

   a. The board can expel a registered auditing firm without SEC approval.

   b. All registered auditing firms must be inspected at least every three years.

   c. The board members must be appointed by Congress.

   d. The board has the authority to set auditing standards rather than utilize the work of the Auditing Standards Board.

7. Which of the following is *not* a way by which the Sarbanes-Oxley Act attempts to ensure auditor independence from an audit client?

   a. The auditing firm must be appointed by the client's audit committee.

   b. Audit fees must be approved by the Public Company Accounting Oversight Board.

   c. The audit committee must be composed of members of the client's board of directors who are independent of the management.

   d. The external auditor cannot also perform financial information system design and implementation work.

8. What is a registration statement?

   a. A statement that must be filed with the SEC before a company can begin an initial offering of securities to the public.

   b. A required filing with the SEC before a large amount of stock can be obtained by an inside party.

   c. An annual filing made with the New York Stock Exchange.

   d. A filing made by a company with the SEC to indicate that a significant change has occurred.

9. Which of the following is a registration statement used by large companies that already have a significant following in the stock market?

   a. Form 8–K.

   b. Form 10–K.

   c. Form S–1.

   d. Form S–3.

10. What was the significance of the controversy in 1977 over the appropriate accounting principles to be used by oil- and gas-producing companies?

    a. Several major lawsuits resulted.

    b. Companies refused to follow the SEC's dictates.

c. Partners of a major accounting firm were indicted on criminal charges.

d. The SEC overruled the FASB on the handling of this matter.

11. Which of the following must be provided to every potential buyer of a new security?

    a. A letter of comments.

    b. A deficiency letter.

    c. A prospectus.

    d. A Form S–16.

12. What is meant by the term *incorporation by reference?*

    a. The legal incorporation of a company in more than one state.

    b. Filing information with the SEC by indicating that the information is already available in another document.

    c. A reference guide indicating informational requirements specified in *Regulation S–X.*

    d. Incorporating a company in a state outside of its base of operations.

13. What is a letter of comments?

    a. A letter sent to a company by the SEC indicating needed changes or clarifications in a registration statement.

    b. A questionnaire supplied to the SEC by a company suggesting changes in *Regulation S–X.*

    c. A letter included in a Form 10–K to indicate the management's assessment of the company's financial position.

    d. A letter composed by a company asking for information or clarification prior to the filing of a registration statement.

14. What is a prospectus?

    a. A document attached to a Form 8–K.

    b. A potential stockholder as defined by *Regulation S–K.*

    c. A document filed with the SEC prior to the filing of a registration statement.

    d. The first part of a registration statement that must be furnished by a company to all potential buyers of a new security.

15. Which of the following is *not* exempt from registration with the SEC under the Securities Act of 1933?

    a. Securities issued by a nonprofit religious organization.

    b. Securities issued by a government unit.

    c. A public offering of no more than $5.9 million.

    d. An offering made to only 26 sophisticated investors.

16. Which of the following is usually not filed with the SEC on a regular periodic basis?

    a. A Form 10–Q.

    b. A prospectus.

    c. A proxy statement.

    d. A Form 10–K.

17. What is a shelf registration?

    a. A registration statement that is formally rejected by the SEC.

    b. A registration statement that is rejected by the SEC due to the lapse of a specified period of time.

    c. A registration process for large companies that allows them to offer securities over a period of time without seeking additional approval by the SEC.

    d. A registration form that is withdrawn by the registrant without any action having been taken.

18. What is EDGAR?

    a. A system used by the SEC to reject registration statements that do not contain adequate information.

    b. The enforcement arm of the SEC.

    c. A system designed by the SEC to allow electronic filings.

    d. A branch of the government that oversees the work of the SEC.

19. Identify each of the following as they pertain to the SEC.
    a. Blue sky laws.
    b. S–8 Statement.
    c. Letter of deficiencies.
    d. Public Company Accounting Oversight Board.
    e. Prospectus.
20. Discuss the objectives of the Securities Act of 1933 and the Securities Exchange Act of 1934. How are these objectives accomplished?
21. What are the general steps involved in filing a registration statement with the SEC?
22. Discuss the methods by which the SEC can influence the development of generally accepted accounting principles in the United States.
23. Which forms do most companies file with the SEC on a periodic basis? Explain the purpose of each form and its primary contents.
24. Which forms do most companies file with the SEC in connection with the offering of securities to the public?
25. What is the importance of a Form 8–K? What is the importance of a proxy statement?
26. Describe the provisions of the Sarbanes-Oxley Act as they relate to the creation and responsibilities of the Public Company Accounting Oversight Board.
27. Explain each of the following items:
    a. *Staff Accounting Bulletins.*
    b. Wraparound filing.
    c. Incorporation by reference.
    d. Division of corporation finance.
    e. Integrated disclosure system.
    f. Management's discussion and analysis.
    g. Chief accountant of the SEC.
28. Which organizations are normally exempted from the registration requirements imposed by the SEC?

Develop Your Skills

RESEARCH CASE 1

Domer Corporation is preparing to issue a relatively small amount of securities and does not want to go to the trouble of filing a registration statement with the SEC. Company officials hope to be exempt under provisions of Regulation A. These officials want to be certain that they meet these provisions precisely so that no later legal problems will be encountered.

Required:

Go to the Web site http://www.sec.gov/divisions/corpfin/forms/rega.htm. Based on the information provided for Regulation A, prepare a report for the officials of Domer Corporation as to the requirements for exemption and advise as to the maximum amount of capital that may be raised through such issuance. Assuming that Domer Corporation is a development stage company, revise the report.

RESEARCH CASE 2

Tasch Corporation, a multilevel marketing and sales organization, plans to sell approximately $10,000,000 worth of "service agreements" to many of its customers. These service agreements guarantee a set return to the customer in exchange for an up-front purchase price, with Tasch Corporation managing the various business interests of its customers. Jerry Tasch, the corporation's president, needs advice concerning the necessity of SEC filings prior to the sale of these service agreements.

Required:

Assume that the only (initial) question to be addressed is whether the service agreements constitute securities under the Securities Act of 1933. Perform research utilizing an Internet search engine to determine whether the service agreements are in fact securities. Note that courts interpret statutes and regulations, so it is often useful to look at judicial determinations to reach a conclusion. To that end, consider locating and reviewing the following case: *SEC v. Alpha Telcom, Inc.,* 187 F.Supp.2d 1250 (D. Ore. 2002). This case can be located using many Web links including FINDLAW and LexisNexis.

ANALYSIS CASE 1

Go to the Web site www.sec.gov and, under the Filings & Forms (EDGAR) heading, click on "Search for Company Filings" and then click on "Companies & Other Filers." Enter the name of a well-known company such as Dell or Ford Motor Co. A list of available documents should be shown for that company.

Required:

Using these available documents, answer the following questions:

1. Has the company filed an 8–K during the recent time period? If so, open that document and determine the reason that the form was filed with the SEC.
2. Has the company filed a 10–K during the recent time period? If so, open that document and determine the total reported net income for the latest period of time.
3. Has the company filed a 14A (a proxy statement) during the recent time period? If so, open that document and determine what issues were to be voted on at the annual meeting.

COMMUNICATION CASE 1

The senior partner of Wojtysiak & Co., CPAs, has been approached by a small, publicly traded corporation wishing to change auditors. The Wojtysiak firm does not audit any other public companies. Because of the Sarbanes-Oxley Act of 2002, Mike Wojtysiak, the senior partner, needs to know the regulatory issues facing his firm if it accepts the new engagement.

Required:

Draft a report that outlines the Sarbanes-Oxley considerations for a firm such as the Wojtysiak firm. Locate the actual act (Public Law 107-204) or a thorough summary and review it prior to preparing the report. The full act may be found at http://news.findlaw.com/hdocs/docs/gwbush/sarbanesoxley072302.pdf.

Chapter **Thirteen**

Accounting for Legal Reorganizations and Liquidations

Questions to Consider

- What is the difference between a voluntary and an involuntary bankruptcy petition?

- How does the liquidation of an insolvent company (a Chapter 7 bankruptcy) differ from a reorganization (a Chapter 11 bankruptcy)?

- Why would the creditors of an insolvent company allow it to reorganize rather than attempt to force a liquidation of its assets?

- What assistance can an accountant provide to an insolvent company?

- What provisions are frequently included in a bankruptcy reorganization plan?

- What financial reporting is made for a company while it goes through reorganization?

- What financial reporting does a company that successfully leaves bankruptcy reorganization make?

- If an insolvent company is liquidated, how are the assets that result distributed? How is a fair and equitable settlement produced?

One common thread that runs throughout a significant portion of this textbook is the accounting for an organization when viewing it as a whole.[1] Several chapters, for example, examine the consolidation of financial information generated by two or more companies that have been united in a business combination. Although that coverage included the handling of specific accounts, the primary emphasis was on reporting these companies as a single economic entity.

Likewise, the analysis of foreign currency translation demonstrated the procedures to use in consolidating the financial position and operating results of a subsidiary doing business anywhere in the world. The various reporting requirements for disaggregated information have been presented as another means of disclosing complete information to describe an entity. Once again, the accounting goal was to convey data about the entire operation.

Continuing with this theme, subsequent chapters present the specialized accounting procedures that partnerships, state and local government units, not-for-profit organizations, estates, and trusts utilize.

The method by which financial data should be accumulated and disclosed to describe an organization is not a rigid structure. Accounting is adaptable; several factors influence its development in specific circumstances: the purpose of the information, the nature of the organization, the environment in which the entity operates, and so on. Thus, in reporting the operations and financial position of a business combination, a foreign subsidiary, an industry segment, a partnership, a government unit, an estate, or a not-for-profit organization, accountants must develop unique reporting techniques that address particular needs and problems.

The current chapter extends this coverage by presenting the accounting procedures required in bankruptcy cases. A financially troubled company and its owners and creditors

---

[1] Intermediate accounting textbooks, in contrast, tend to examine the reporting of specific assets and liabilities such as leases, pensions, deferred income taxes, and bonds.

face the prospect of incurring significant losses. Thus, the accountant must adapt financial reporting to meet many and varied informational needs. The large number of failed businesses in recent years has made this accounting process especially important.

ACCOUNTING FOR LEGAL REORGANIZATIONS AND LIQUIDATIONS

Centuries ago in Italy the bankrupt merchant would be forced into an odd form of pillory. He would have the table he did business at in the town square broken. At least one source says the word *bankruptcy* derives from the Italian words for this practice, which translate to *broken bench.*[2]

A basic assumption of accounting is that a business is considered a *going concern* unless evidence to the contrary is discovered. As a result, assets such as inventory, land, buildings, and equipment are reported based on historical cost rather than net realizable value. Unfortunately, not all companies prove to be going concerns.

Since the beginning of 2001, more than 60,000 companies have sought bankruptcy protection, and the number of affected employees is rising fast. In 2001, the 10 largest companies filing for bankruptcy reported employing about 140,500 people in their most recent annual report before the filing.[3]

Not only is the number of bankruptcies increasing but also the size of some of the bankruptcies is becoming astronomical in size. Notice how many of the top 15 U.S. bankruptcies have occurred since 2001:

- WorldCom Inc., July 21, 2002; $103.9 billion in assets.
- Enron Corp., December 2, 2001; $63.4 billion.
- Conseco Inc., December 17, 2002; $61.4 billion.
- Texaco Inc., April 12, 1987; $35.9 billion.
- Financial Corp. of America, September 9, 1988; $33.9 billion.
- Global Crossing Ltd., January 28, 2002; $30.2 billion.
- Pacific Gas and Electric Co., April 6, 2001; $29.8 billion.
- UAL Corp., December 9, 2002; $25.2 billion.
- Adelphia, June 25, 2002; $21.5 billion.
- MCorp., March 31, 1989; $20.2 billion.
- Mirant Corporation, July 14, 2003; $19.4 billion.
- First Executive Corp., May 31, 1991; $15.2 billion.
- Gibraltar Financial Corp., February 8, 1990; $15 billion.
- Kmart Corp., January 22, 2002; $14.6 billion.
- The FINOVA Group Inc., March 7, 2001; $14.1 billion.[4]

What happens to these businesses after they fail? Who gets the assets? Are the creditors protected? How does the accountant reflect the economic plight of the company?

Virtually all businesses undergo financial difficulties at various times. Economic downturns, poor product performance, or litigation losses can create cash flow difficulties for even the best-managed organizations. Most companies take remedial actions and work to return their operations to normal profitability. However, as the preceding list indicates, not all companies are able to solve their monetary difficulties. If problems persist, a company can eventually become *insolvent,* unable to pay debts as the obligations come due. When creditors are not paid, they obviously attempt to protect their financial interests in hope of reducing the possibility of loss.

[2] "In Pursuit of a Balanced Bankruptcy Law," *ABA Banking Journal,* May 1993, p. 50.

[3] Shawn Young, "In Bankruptcy, Getting Laid Off Hurts Even Worse," *The Wall Street Journal,* September 30, 2002, p. A-1.

[4] http://www.bankruptcydata.com/Research/15_Largest.htm.

They may seek recovery from the distressed company in several ways: repossessing assets, filing lawsuits, foreclosing on loans, and so on. An insolvent company can literally become besieged by its creditors.

If left unchecked, pandemonium would be the possible outcome of a company's insolvency. As a result, some of the creditors and stockholders as well as the company itself could find themselves treated unfairly. One party might be able to collect in full while another is left with a total loss. *Thus, bankruptcy laws have been established in the United States to structure this process, provide protection for all parties, and ensure fair and equitable treatment.*

Although a complete coverage of bankruptcy statutes is more appropriate for a business law textbook, significant aspects of this process directly involve accountants.

> In many small business situations, the company accountant is the sole outside financial adviser and the first to recognize that the deteriorating financial picture mandates consideration of bankruptcy in one form or another. In many such situations, the accountant's role in convincing management that a timely reorganization under the bankruptcy law is the sole means of salvaging any part of the business may be critical.[5]

Bankruptcy Reform Act of 1978

> Over the ages debtors who found themselves unable to meet obligations were dealt with harshly. Not only were all their assets taken from them, but they were given little or no relief through legal forgiveness of debts. Many of them ended up in debtors' prisons with all means of rehabilitation removed. A large number of the early settlers in this country left their homelands to escape such a fate.[6]

Based on an original provision of the U.S. Constitution, Congress must create all bankruptcy laws. However, virtually no federal bankruptcy laws were actually passed until the Bankruptcy Act of 1898 (subsequently revised in 1938 by the Chandler Act). Later, following a decade of study and debate by Congress, the Bankruptcy Reform Act of 1978 replaced these laws. Congress subsequently revised and updated that act by passing the Bankruptcy Reform Act of 1994.

The adoption of the Bankruptcy Abuse and Prevention and Consumer Protection Act of 2005 made additional changes to the law. Most of the new regulations dealt with personal bankruptcy provisions because of the significant and steady increase in such cases. However, a few provisions applied to business bankruptcy cases although little push for sweeping changes in this area of bankruptcy law has been evident.

Consequently, the Bankruptcy Reform Act of 1978 as amended continues to provide the legal structure for most bankruptcy proceedings. *To this end, it strives to achieve two goals in connection with insolvency cases: (1) the fair distribution of assets to creditors and (2) the discharge of an honest debtor from debt.*

Voluntary and Involuntary Petitions

When insolvency occurs, any interested party has the right to seek protection under the Bankruptcy Reform Act.[7] Thus, the company itself can file a petition with the court to begin bankruptcy proceedings. If the company is the instigator, the process is referred to as a *voluntary* bankruptcy. In such cases, the company's petition must be accompanied by exhibits listing all debts and assets (reported at fair value). Company officials also must respond to questions concerning various aspects of the business's affairs. Such questions include these:

- When did the business commence?
- In whose possession are the books of account and records?
- When was the last inventory of property taken?

---

[5] John K. Pearson, "The Role of the Accountant in Business Bankruptcies," *The National Public Accountant,* November 1982, p. 22.

[6] Homer A. Bonhiver, *The Expanded Role of the Accountant under the 1978 Bankruptcy Code* (New York: Deloitte Haskins & Sells, 1980), p. 7.

[7] As is discussed later in this chapter, insolvency (not being able to pay debts as they come due) is not necessary for filing a bankruptcy petition. Such companies as Manville Corporation, Texaco, and A. H. Robins have filed for protection under the Bankruptcy Reform Act in hope of settling massive litigation claims.

Creditors also can seek to force a debtor into bankruptcy (known as an *involuntary* bankruptcy) in hope of reducing their potential losses. To avoid nuisance actions, bankruptcy laws regulate the filing of involuntary petitions. If a company has 12 or more unsecured creditors, at least 3 must sign the petition. In addition, under current rules, the creditors that sign must have unsecured debts of at least $12,300.[8] If fewer than 12 unsecured creditors exist, only a single signer is required but the $12,300 minimum debt limit remains. "L. L. Knickerbocker Co., of Lake Forest, California, said three Asian creditors filed an involuntary bankruptcy petition seeking to force the company to liquidate its assets. Knickerbocker didn't identify the creditors further, but said 'the company is currently evaluating its options,' including opposing the petition."[9]

Neither a voluntary nor an involuntary petition automatically creates a bankruptcy case. The court rejects voluntary petitions if the action is considered detrimental to the creditors. Involuntary petitions also can be rejected unless evidence exists to indicate that the debtor is not actually able to meet obligations as they come due. Merely being slow to pay is not sufficient. The debtor may well fight an involuntary petition fearing that it will taint its reputation in the business community.

If the court accepts the petition, it grants an *order for relief.* This order halts all actions against the debtor, thus providing time for the various parties involved to develop a course of action. In addition, the company comes under the authority of the bankruptcy court so that any distributions must be made in a fair manner.

> To prevent creditors from seizing whatever is handy once the bankruptcy is filed, the Bankruptcy Code provides for an automatic stay or injunction that prohibits actions by creditors to collect debts from the debtor or the debtor's property without the court's permission. The automatic stay bars any creditor (including governmental creditors such as the Internal Revenue Service) from taking any action against the debtor or the debtor's property.[10]

Classification of Creditors

Following the issuance of an order for relief, the possible risk of loss obviously influences each creditor's view of a bankruptcy case. However, many creditors may have already obtained some measure of security for themselves. At the time a debt is created, the parties can agree to attach a mortgage lien or security interest to specified assets (known as *collateral*) owned by the debtor. Such action is most likely when the amounts involved are great or the debtor is experiencing financial difficulty. In the event that the liability is not paid when due, the creditor has the right to force the sale (or, in some cases, the return) of the pledged property with the proceeds being used to satisfy all or part of the obligation. Thus, in bankruptcy proceedings, a secured creditor is in a much less vulnerable position than an unsecured creditor.

Because of the possible presence of liens, all loans and other liabilities are reported to the court according to their degree of protection against loss. Some debts are identified as *fully secured* to indicate that the net realizable value of the collateral exceeds the amount of the obligation. Despite the debtor's insolvency, these creditors will not suffer loss; they are completely protected by the pledged property. Any money received from the asset that is in excess of the balance of the debt is used to pay unsecured creditors.

Conversely, if a liability is *partially secured,* the value of the collateral covers only a portion of the obligation. The remainder is considered *unsecured* so that the creditor risks losing some or all of this additional amount. As an example, a bank might have a $90,000 loan due from an insolvent party protected by a lien attached to land valued at $64,000. This debt is only partially secured; the asset would not satisfy $26,000 of the balance so that this residual portion must be reported to the court as unsecured.

All other liabilities are unsecured; these creditors have no legal right to any of the debtor's specific assets. They are entitled to share in any funds that remain after all secured claims have been settled. Obviously, unsecured creditors are in a precarious position. Unless a debtor's

---

[8] Throughout the bankruptcy laws, a number of monetary standards such as this exist. Such dollar amounts were last adjusted for inflation on April 1, 2004. These balances are to be adjusted every three years based on the Consumer Price Index for All Urban Consumers.

[9] "Three Creditors Petition to Liquidate the Company," *The Wall Street Journal,* August 26, 1999, p. C15.

[10] Pearson, "The Role of the Accountant," p. 24.

assets greatly exceed secured liabilities (which is unlikely in most insolvency cases), these creditors can expect significant losses if liquidation is necessary. Hence, one of the most important aspects of the bankruptcy laws is the ranking of unsecured claims. Only in this manner is a systematic distribution of any remaining assets possible.

The Bankruptcy Reform Act identifies several types of unsecured liabilities that have priority and must be paid before other unsecured debts are settled. *These obligations are ranked with each level having to be satisfied in full before any payment is made to the next.*

Unsecured Liabilities Having Priority   The following liabilities have priority:[11]

1. Claims for administrative expenses such as the costs of preserving and liquidating the estate. All trustee expenses and the costs of outside attorneys, accountants, or other consultants are included in this category. Without this high-priority ranking, insolvent companies would have problems convincing qualified individuals to serve in these essential positions. However, in recent years, the amounts assessed for such services have come under fire from many critics: "The protests follow a recent court filing by Enron, the fallen energy company, projecting that professional fees for the first 13 months of the bankruptcy will total $306 million. All told, according to the projections, administrative costs during the period will be $773 million, or nearly $60 million a month."[12]

2. Obligations arising between the date that a petition is filed with the bankruptcy court and the appointment of a trustee or the issuance of an order for relief. In voluntary cases, such claims are quite rare because an order for relief is usually entered when the petition is filed. This provision is important, however, in helping the debtor continue operations if an involuntary petition is presented but no legal action is immediately taken. Without this ranking, suppliers would stop supplying merchandise to the debtor until the matter was resolved. With this high ranking, the debtor can continue to buy goods and stay in business while resisting an involuntary petition.

3. Employee claims for wages earned during the 90 days preceding the filing of a petition. The amount of this priority is limited, though, to $4,925 (previously $4,650) per individual. This priority ranking does not include officers' salaries. It is designed to prevent employees from being penalized by the company's problems and encourages them to continue working until the bankruptcy issue is settled. In addition, employees are not company creditors in the traditional sense of that term. They did not enter employment to serve as lenders to the corporation. However, employees can still be financially damaged by bankruptcy. "After 9½ years as a manager in technical training, the 44-year-old father of four had $22,354 in severance coming to him. And under the company policy, he was slated to get health insurance coverage for 13 weeks. But then WorldCom filed for bankruptcy protection in the wake of a massive accounting scandal—and with that, much of Mr. Wehmeier's financial safety net vanished. Instead of his expected severance, he received just $4,650."[13]

4. Employee claims for contributions to benefit plans earned during the 180 days preceding the filing of a petition. Once again, a $4,925 limit per individual (reduced by certain specified payments) is enforced.

5. Claims for the return of deposits made by customers to acquire property or services that the debtor never delivered or provided. The priority figure, in this case, is limited to $2,225. These claimants did not intend to be creditors; they were merely trying to make a purchase.

6. Government claims for unpaid taxes.

All other obligations of an insolvent company are classified as general unsecured claims that can be repaid only after the creditors with priority have been satisfied. *If the funds that remain for the general unsecured debts are not sufficient to settle all claims, the available money must be divided proportionally.* Periodic changes in this priority listing are made and can impact the

---

[11] Only the most significant unsecured liabilities given priority are included here. For a complete list, check a current business law textbook.

[12] "Michael Orey, "Group of Enron Creditors Say Court Costs Grow Unwieldly," *The Wall Street Journal,* November 4, 2002, p. B3.

[13] Young, "In Bankruptcy."

Discussion **Question**

WHAT DO WE DO NOW?

The Toledo Shirt Company manufactures men's shirts sold to department stores and other outlets throughout Ohio, Illinois, and Indiana. For the past 14 years, one of Toledo's major customers has been Abraham and Sons, a chain of nine stores selling men's clothing. Unfortunately, 18 months ago, Mr. Abraham retired and his two sons took complete control of the organization. Since that time, they have invested enormous sums of money in an attempt to expand each store by also selling women's clothing. Success in this new market has been difficult; Abraham and Sons is not known for selling women's clothing, and no one in the company has much expertise in the area.

Approximately seven months ago, James Thurber, the chief financial officer of the Toledo Shirt Company, began to notice that it was taking longer than usual to collect payments from Abraham and Sons. Instead of the normal 30 days, the retailer was taking at least 45 days—and frequently longer—to pay each invoice. Because of the amount of money involved, Thurber began to monitor the balance daily. When the age of the receivable ($97,000) hit 65 days, he placed a call to Abraham and Sons. The treasurer assured him that the company was merely having seasonal cash flow issues but that payments would soon be back on a normal schedule.

Thurber was still concerned and shortly thereafter placed Abraham and Sons on a "cash and carry" basis; no sales were to be made unless cash was collected in advance. The company's treasurer immediately called Thurber to complain bitterly. "We have been one of your best customers for well over a decade, but now that we have gotten into a bit of trouble you stab us in the back. When we straighten things out here, we will remember this. We can get our shirts from someone else. Our expansions are now complete; we have hired an expert to help us market women's clothing. We can see the light at the end of the tunnel. Abraham and Sons will soon be more profitable than ever." In hope of appeasing the customer while still protecting his own position, Thurber agreed to sell merchandise to Abraham and Sons on a very limited credit basis.

A few days later, Thurber received a disturbing phone call from a vice president with another clothing manufacturer. "We've got to force Abraham and Sons into bankruptcy immediately to protect ourselves. Those guys are running the company straight into the ground. They owe me $49,000, and I can hope to collect only a small portion of it now. I need two other creditors to sign the petition and I want Toledo Shirt to be one of them. Abraham and Sons has already mortgaged all of its buildings and equipment so we can't get anything from those assets. Inventory stocks are dwindling and sales have disappeared since they've tried to change the image of their stores. We can still get some of our money but if we wait much longer nothing will be left but the bones."

Should the Toledo Shirt Company be loyal to a good customer or start the bankruptcy process to protect itself? What actions should Thurber take?

amounts various types of creditors will receive. For example, in 2005, Congress reclassified prior rent still due as an administrative expense rather than as an unsecured claim as it had previously been classified. Consequently, such rental debts are now more likely to be paid in full, leaving less for the remaining unsecured creditors.

Liquidation versus Reorganization

The most important decision in any bankruptcy filing (either voluntary or involuntary) is the method by which the debtor will be discharged from its obligations. One obvious option is to liquidate the company's assets with the proceeds being distributed to creditors based on their secured positions and the priority ranking system just outlined. However, a very important alternative to liquidation does exist. The debtor company may survive insolvency and continue operations if the parties involved accept a proposal for *reorganization*. Not everyone agrees with the wisdom of allowing reorganization; this argument holds that keeping inefficient organizations alive and competing does not serve the economy well.

There are many reasons why a business gets sick, but they don't necessarily mean it should be destroyed. Hundreds of thousands of businesses that at one time or another had financial difficulties survive today as the result of Chapter 11 proceedings. They continue to contribute to employment, to tax revenues, to overall growth. It's counterproductive to destroy the business value of an asset by liquidating it and paying it out in a Chapter 7 if that company shows signs of being able to recover in a reorganization.[14]

Contrast that statement with the following:

The efficiency of Chapter 11 is under growing scrutiny. A particular concern, in industries such as telecoms and now airlines, is that bankrupt firms will return with manageable debts and thus be better able to compete, with the result that they force hitherto healthier rivals into bankruptcy in their turn. Does Chapter 11 create zombie companies that live on, only to drag other firms into their graves?[15]

Under most reorganization plans, the creditors agree to absorb a partial loss rather than force the insolvent company to liquidate. Before accepting such an arrangement, the creditors (as well as the bankruptcy court) must be convinced that helping to rehabilitate the debtor will lead to a higher return. One benefit associated with reorganizations is that the creditor may be able to retain the insolvent company as a customer. In many cases, continuation of this relationship is an important concern if the debtor historically has been a good client. Furthermore, the priority ranking system often leaves the general unsecured creditors very little to lose in trying to avoid a liquidation.

Legal guidelines for the liquidation of a debtor are contained in Chapter 7 of Title I of the Bankruptcy Reform Act; Chapter 11 describes the reorganization process. Consequently, the proceedings have come to be referred to as a *Chapter 7 bankruptcy* (liquidation) or a *Chapter 11 bankruptcy* (reorganization). Accountants face two entirely different reporting situations depending on the type of bankruptcy encountered. However, in both cases, accountants must obtain sufficient data and report them adequately to keep all parties informed about the events as they occur.

Statement of Financial Affairs

Like other companies in bankruptcy, WorldCom is required to file schedules of assets and liabilities, of executory contracts and unexpired leases, lists of shareholders, and statements of financial affairs within 15 days of its Chapter 11 filing.[16]

At the start of bankruptcy proceedings, the debtor normally prepares a statement of financial affairs. This schedule provides information about the current financial position of the company and helps all parties as they consider what actions to take. This statement is especially important in assisting the unsecured creditors as they decide whether to push for reorganization or liquidation. The debtor's assets and liabilities are reported according to the classifications relevant to a liquidation.

Consequently, assets are labeled as follows:

1. Pledged with fully secured creditors.
2. Pledged with partially secured creditors.
3. Available for priority liabilities and unsecured creditors (often referred to as *free assets*).

The debts of the company are then listed in a parallel fashion:

1. Liabilities with priority.
2. Fully secured creditors.
3. Partially secured creditors.
4. Unsecured creditors.

Stockholders are included in this final group.

The statement of financial affairs is produced under the assumption that liquidation will occur. Thus, historical cost figures are not relevant. The various parties to the bankruptcy desire

---

[14] James A. Goodman as interviewed by Robert A. Mamis, "Why Bankruptcy Works," *Inc.*, October 1996, p. 39.

[15] "The Night of the Killer Zombies," *The Economist*, December 14, 2002.

[16] "WorldCom Gets Judge's Approval for $750 Million in Financing," *The Wall Street Journal*, July 23, 2002, p. A-3.

Discussion **Question**

HOW MUCH IS THAT BUILDING REALLY WORTH?

Viron, Inc., was created in 1997 to recycle plastic products and manufacture a variety of new items. The actual production process was quite complex because the old plastic had to be divided into categories and then reclaimed based on the composition. Viron made new products based on the type of plastic available and the market demand.

In December 2004, the company spent $3.3 million to construct a building for manufacturing purposes. The facility was designed specifically to meet Viron's needs. The building was constructed near Gaffney, South Carolina, to take advantage of a large labor force available because of high unemployment in the area.

Unfortunately, the company was not able to generate revenues quickly enough to reach a break-even point and was forced to file for bankruptcy. An accountant was hired to produce a statement of financial affairs to aid the parties in deciding whether to liquidate or reorganize.

In producing the statement of financial affairs, the accountant needed to establish a liquidation value for the building that was the company's largest asset. A real estate appraiser was brought in and made the following comments about the building:

> The building is well made and practically new. It is clearly worth in excess of $2 million. However, I doubt that anyone is going to pay that much for it. We don't get a lot of new industry in this area, so not many companies need to buy large buildings. Even if a company did buy the building, it would have to spend a significant amount of money for conversion. Unless a company just wanted to recycle plastics, the building would have to be completely adapted to any other purpose. To tell you the truth, I am not sure it can be sold at any price. Of course, if someone wants to recycle plastics, it just might bring $2 million.

In producing the statement of financial affairs, how should the accountant report this building?

information that reflects (1) the net realizable value of the debtor's assets and (2) the ultimate application of these proceeds to specific liabilities. Based on this information, both creditors and stockholders can estimate the monetary resources that will be available after all secured claims and priority liabilities have been settled. By comparing this total with the amount of unsecured liabilities, any interested parties can approximate the potential loss they face.

The information found in a statement of financial affairs can affect the outcome of the bankruptcy. If, for example, the statement indicates that unsecured creditors are destined to suffer a material loss in a liquidation, this group will probably favor reorganizing the company in hope of averting such a consequence. Conversely, if the statement shows that all creditors will be paid in full and that a distribution to the stockholders is also possible, liquidation becomes a much more viable option. Thus, all parties involved with an insolvent company should consult a statement of financial affairs before deciding the fate of the operation.

Statement of Financial Affairs Illustrated

We demonstrate the preparation of this statement for Chaplin Company, which has experienced severe financial difficulties in recent times and is currently insolvent. Chaplin will soon file a voluntary bankruptcy petition, and company officials are trying to decide whether to seek liquidation or reorganization. Consequently, they have asked their accountant to produce a statement of financial affairs to assist them in formulating an appropriate strategy. A current balance sheet for Chaplin, prepared as if the company were a going concern, is presented in Exhibit 13.1.

Prior to the creation of a statement of financial affairs, additional data must be ascertained concerning the insolvent company and its assets and liabilities. In this illustration, the following information about Chaplin Company has been accumulated:

- The investment reported on the balance sheet has appreciated in value since being acquired and is now worth $20,000. Dividends of $500 are currently due from this investment, although Chaplin has not yet recognized the revenue.

EXHIBIT 13.1
Financial Position Prior to Bankruptcy Petition

CHAPLIN COMPANY
Balance Sheet
June 30, 2007

Assets

Current assets:		
Cash	$ 2,000	
Investment (equity method)	15,000	
Accounts receivable (net)	23,000	
Inventory	41,000	
Prepaid expenses	3,000	$ 84,000
Land, building, equipment, and other assets:		
Land	100,000	
Building (net)	110,000	
Equipment (net)	80,000	
Intangible assets	15,000	305,000
Total assets		$389,000

Liabilities and Stockholders' Equity

Current liabilities:		
Notes payable (secured by inventory)	$ 75,000	
Accounts payable	60,000	
Accrued expenses	18,000	$153,000
Long-term liabilities:		
Notes payable (secured by lien on land and buildings)		200,000
Stockholders' equity:		
Common stock	100,000	
Retained earnings (deficit)	(64,000)	36,000
Total liabilities and stockholders' equity		$389,000

- Officials estimate that $12,000 of the company's accounts receivable can still be collected despite the bankruptcy proceedings.
- By spending $5,000 for repairs and marketing, Chaplin can sell the inventory it currently holds for $50,000.
- The company will receive a refund of $1,000 from the various prepaid expenses, but its intangible assets have no resale value.
- The land and building are in an excellent location and can be sold for a figure 10 percent more than book value. However, the equipment was specially designed for Chaplin. Company officials anticipate having trouble finding a buyer unless the price is reduced considerably. Hence, they expect to receive only 40 percent of current book value for these assets.
- Administrative costs of $21,500 are projected if the company does liquidate.
- Accrued expenses include salaries of $13,000. Of this figure, one person is owed a total of $5,925 but is the only employee due an amount in excess of $4,925. Payroll taxes withheld from wages but not yet paid to the government total $3,000. However, company records currently show only a $1,000 portion of this liability.
- Interest of $5,000 on the company's long-term liabilities has not been accrued for the first six months of 2007.

From this information, the statement of financial affairs presented in Exhibit 13.2 for Chaplin Company was prepared. Several aspects of this statement should be specifically noted:

1. The current and long-term distinctions usually applied to assets and liabilities are omitted. Because the company is on the verge of going out of business, such classifications are meaningless. Instead, the statement is designed to separate the secured and unsecured balances.

EXHIBIT 13.2

CHAPLIN COMPANY
Statement of Financial Affairs
June 30, 2007

Book Values		Available for Unsecured Creditors
	Assets	
	Pledged with fully secured creditors:	
$210,000	Land and building . . . . $ 231,000	
	Less: Notes payable (long term) . . . . (200,000)	
	Interest payable . . . . (5,000)	$ 26,000
	Pledged with partially secured creditors:	
41,000	Inventory . . . . $ 45,000	
	Less: Notes payable (current) . . . . (75,000)	–0–
	Free assets:	
2,000	Cash	2,000
15,000	Investment in marketable securities	20,000
–0–	Dividends receivable	500
23,000	Accounts receivable	12,000
3,000	Prepaid expenses	1,000
80,000	Equipment	32,000
15,000	Intangible assets	–0–
	Total available to pay liabilities with priority and unsecured creditors	93,500
	Less: Liabilities with priority (see Ⓐ)	(36,500) Ⓑ
	Available for unsecured creditors	57,000 Ⓓ
	Estimated deficiency	38,000 Ⓔ
$389,000		$ 95,000

Book Values		Unsecured— Nonpriority Liabilities
	Liabilities and Stockholders' Equity	
	Liabilities with priority:	
–0–	Administrative expenses (estimated) . . . . $ 21,500	
$ 13,000	Salaries payable (accrued expenses) 12,000	$ 1,000 Ⓒ
1,000	Payroll taxes payable (accrued expenses) 3,000	
	Total . . . . $ 36,500 Ⓐ	
	Fully secured creditors:	
200,000	Notes payable . . . . $ 200,000	
–0–	Interest payable 5,000	
	Less: Land and building. . . . . (231,000)	–0–
	Partially secured creditors:	
75,000	Notes payable . . . . $ 75,000	
	Less: Inventory . . . . (45,000)	30,000
	Unsecured creditors:	
60,000	Accounts payable	60,000
4,000	Accrued expenses (other than salaries and payroll taxes)	4,000
36,000	Stockholders' equity	–0–
$389,000		$ 95,000

2. Book values are included on the left side of the schedule but only for informational purposes. These figures are not relevant in a bankruptcy. *All assets are reported at estimated net realizable value, whereas liabilities are shown at the amount required for settlement.*

3. Both the dividend receivable and the interest payable are included in Exhibit 13.2, although neither has been recorded on the balance sheet. The payroll tax liability also is reported at the amount the company presently owes. Because these balances represent future cash flows, the statement of financial affairs must disclose currently updated figures.

4. Liabilities having priority are individually identified within the liability section (point A). Because these claims will be paid before other unsecured creditors, the $36,500 total also is subtracted directly from the free assets (point B). Although not yet incurred, estimated administrative costs are included in this category because such expenses will be necessary for a liquidation. Salaries payable are also considered priority liabilities. However, the $1,000 owed to one employee in excess of the individual $4,925 limit is separated as an unsecured claim (point C).

5. According to this statement, if liquidation occurs, Chaplin expects to have $57,000 in free assets remaining after settling all liabilities with priority (point D). Unfortunately, the liability section shows unsecured claims with a total of $95,000. These creditors, therefore, face a $38,000 loss ($95,000 − $57,000) if the company is liquidated (point E). This final distribution is often stated as a percentage:

$$\frac{\text{Free assets}}{\text{Unsecured claims}} = \frac{\$57,000}{\$95,000} = 60\%$$

Thus, unsecured creditors can anticipate receiving only 60 percent of their claims. An individual, for example, to whom this company owes $400 should anticipate collecting only $240 ($400 × 60%) following liquidation.

6. If the statement of financial affairs had shown the company with more free assets (after subtracting liabilities with priority) than unsecured claims, all creditors could expect to be paid in full with any excess money going to Chaplin's stockholders.

LIQUIDATION—CHAPTER 7 BANKRUPTCY

When an insolvent company is to be liquidated, the provisions found in Chapter 7 of the Bankruptcy Reform Act regulate the process. This set of laws was written to provide an orderly and equitable structure for selling assets and paying debts. To this end, several events occur after the court has entered an order for relief in either a voluntary or involuntary liquidation case.

To begin, the court appoints an interim trustee to oversee the company and its liquidation. This individual is charged with preserving the assets and preventing loss of the estate. Thus, creditors are protected from any detrimental actions that management, the ownership, or any of the other creditors might undertake. The interim trustee (as well as the permanent trustee, if one is subsequently selected by the creditors) must perform a number of tasks shortly after being appointed. These functions include (but are not limited to) the following:

- Changing locks and moving all assets and records to locations the trustee controls.
- Posting notices that the U.S. trustee now possesses all business assets and that tampering with or removing any contents is a violation of federal law.
- Compiling all financial records and placing them in the custody of the trustee's own accountant.
- Obtaining possession of any corporate records including minute books and other official documents.[17]

---

[17] Bonhiver, *The Expanded Role of the Accountant,* pp. 50–51.

The court then calls for a meeting of all creditors who have appropriately filed a proof of claim against the debtor. This group may choose to elect a permanent trustee to replace the person temporarily appointed by the court. A majority (in number as well as in dollars due from the company) of the unsecured, nonpriority creditors must agree to this new trustee. If the creditors cannot reach a decision, the interim trustee is retained.

As an additional action taken to ensure fairness, a committee of between 3 and 11 unsecured creditors is selected to help protect the group's interests. This committee of creditors does the following:

- Consults with the trustee regarding the administration of the estate.
- Makes recommendations to the trustee regarding the performance of the trustee's duties.
- Submits to the court any questions affecting the administration of the estate.[18]

Role of the Trustee

In the liquidation of any company, the trustee is a central figure. This individual must recover all property belonging to the insolvent company, preserve the estate from any further deterioration, liquidate noncash assets, and make distributions to the proper claimants. Additionally, the trustee may even need to continue operating the company to complete business activities that were in progress when the order for relief was entered. To accomplish such a multitude of objectives, this individual holds wide-ranging authority in bankruptcy matters, including the right to obtain professional assistance from attorneys and accountants.

The trustee can also void any transfer of property (known as a *preference)* made by the debtor within 90 days *prior* to filing the bankruptcy petition if the company was already insolvent at the time. The recipient must then return these payments so that they can be included in the debtor's free assets.[19]

> Drexel Burnham Lambert Group Inc. made more than $600 million in payments that may be recoverable under bankruptcy law because the transactions occurred during the three months immediately prior to the company's bankruptcy-court filing. The payments were disclosed in the company's statement of financial affairs, . . . such payments, with certain exceptions, can be recovered if it is shown that a company gave preference to some creditors and if the debtor was insolvent at the time.[20]

This rule is intended to prevent one party from gaining advantage over another in the sometimes hectic period just before a bankruptcy petition is filed. Return of the asset is not necessary, however, if the transfer was for no more than would have been paid to this party in a liquidation.

Not surprisingly, the trustee must properly record all activities and report them periodically to the court and other interested parties. Interestingly, the actual reporting rules that the Bankruptcy Reform Act created are quite general: "Each trustee, examiner, and debtor-in-possession is required to file 'such reports as are necessary or as the court orders.' . . . In the past there have been no specific guidelines or forms used in the preparation of these reports."[21] Consequently, a wide variety of statements and reports may be encountered in liquidations. However, the trustee commonly uses *a statement of realization and liquidation* to report the major aspects of the liquidation process. This statement is designed to convey the following information:

- The account balances reported by the company at the date on which the order for relief was filed.
- The cash receipts generated by the sale of the debtor's property.
- The cash disbursements the trustee made to wind up the affairs of the business and to pay the secured creditors.
- Any other transactions of the company such as the write-off of assets and the recognition of unrecorded liabilities.

Any cash that remains after this series of events is paid to the unsecured creditors after the priority claims have first been settled.

Statement of Realization and Liquidation Illustrated

To demonstrate the production of a statement of realization and liquidation, we again use the information previously presented for Chaplin Company. Assume that company officials have decided to liquidate the business, a procedure regulated by Chapter 7 of the Bankruptcy Reform Act. The court appointed an interim trustee whom the creditors then confirmed to oversee the liquidation of assets and distribution of cash.

The dollar amounts resulting from this liquidation will not necessarily agree with the balances used in creating the statement of financial affairs in Exhibit 13.2. The previous statement was based on projected sales and other estimations, whereas a statement of realization and liquidation reports the actual transactions and other events as they occur. Consequently, discrepancies should be expected. Assume the following transactions occur in liquidating this company:

Liquidation Transactions of Chaplin Company—2007

July 1	The accounting records in Exhibit 13.1 are adjusted to the correct balances as of June 30, 2007, the date on which the order for relief was entered. Hence, the dividends receivable, interest payable, and additional payroll tax liability are recognized.
July 23	The trustee expends $7,000 to dispose of the company's inventory at a negotiated price of $51,000. The net cash results are applied to the notes payable for which the inventory served as partial security.
July 29	Cash dividend of $500, accrued as of June 30, is collected. The related investments (being reported at $15,000) are then sold for $19,600.
Aug. 17	Accounts receivable of $16,000 are collected. The remaining balances are written off as bad debts.
Aug. 30	The trustee determines that no refund is available from any of the company's prepaid expenses. The intangible assets also are removed from the financial records because they have no cash value. The land and building are sold for $208,000. The trustee immediately uses $205,000 of this money to pay off the secured creditors.
Oct. 9	After an extended search for a buyer, the equipment is sold for $42,000 in cash.
Nov. 1	An invoice of $24,900 is received for various administrative expenses incurred in liquidating the company. The trustee also reclassifies the remaining partially secured liabilities as unsecured.
Nov. 9	Noncash assets have now been converted into cash and all secured claims settled, so the trustee begins to plan to distribute any remaining funds. The liabilities with priority are paid first. The excess is then applied to the claims of unsecured nonpriority creditors.

The physical structure used to prepare a statement of realization and liquidation can vary significantly. One popular form presents the various account groups on a horizontal plane with the liquidating transactions shown vertically. In this manner, accountants can record the events as they occur and their effects on each account classification. Exhibit 13.3 has been constructed in this style to display the liquidation of Chaplin Company.

EXHIBIT 13.3 **Final Statement**

CHAPLIN COMPANY
Statement of Realization and Liquidation
June 30, 2007, to November 9, 2007

Date	Cash	Noncash Assets	Liabilities with Priority	Fully Secured Creditors	Partially Secured Creditors	Unsecured— Nonpriority Liabilities	Stockholders' Equity (Deficit)
6/30/07	Book balances	$ 2,000	$ 387,000	$13,000*	$ 200,000	$ 75,000	$65,000†	$ 36,000
7/1/07	Adjustments for dividends, interest, and payroll taxes			2,000	5,000			(6,500)
7/1/07	Adjusted book balances	2,000	387,500	15,000	205,000	75,000	65,000	29,500
7/23/07	Inventory sold—recorded net of disposal costs	44,000	(41,000)					3,000
7/23/07	Proceeds from inventory paid to secured creditors	(44,000)				(44,000)		
7/29/07	Investments sold and dividends received	20,100	(15,500)					4,600
8/17/07	Receivables collected with remainder written off	16,000	(23,000)					(7,000)
8/30/07	Intangible assets and prepaid expenses written off		(18,000)					(18,000)
8/30/07	Land and building sold	208,000	(210,000)					(2,000)
	Proceeds from land and building paid to secured creditors	(205,000)			(205,000)			
10/9/07	Equipment sold	42,000	(80,000)					(38,000)
11/1/07	Administrative expenses accrued			24,900				(24,900)
11/1/07	Excess of partially secured liabilities reclassified as an unsecured claim					(31,000)	31,000	
11/9/07	Final balances remaining for unsecured creditors	$ 83,100	–0–	$39,900	–0–	–0–	$96,000	$(52,800)

*Includes salary payable of $12,000 (amount due employees but limited to $4,925 per individual) and $1,000 in payroll taxes owed to the government.

†Accounts payable plus accrued expenses other than salary payable (within $4,925 per person limitation) and payroll tax liability.

Probably the most significant information presented in this statement is the measurement and classification of the insolvent company's liabilities. In the same manner as the statement of financial affairs, this statement reports fully and partially secured claims separately from liabilities with priority and unsecured nonpriority claims.

For Chaplin Company, Exhibit 13.3 discloses that $135,900 in debts remain as of November 9 ($39,900 in priority claims and $96,000 in unsecured nonpriority liabilities). Unfortunately, after satisfying all secured liabilities, the company retains only $83,100 in cash. The trustee must first use this money to pay the three liabilities with priority according to the following ranking:

Administrative expenses	$24,900
Salaries payable (within the $4,925 per person limitation)	12,000
Payroll taxes payable	3,000
Total	$39,900

These disbursements leave the company with $43,200 ($83,100 − $39,900) in cash but $96,000 in unsecured liabilities. Consequently, the remaining creditors can collect only 45 percent of their claims against Chaplin Company:

$$\frac{\$43,200}{\$96,600} = 45\%$$

Because all liabilities have not been paid in full, the stockholders receive nothing from the liquidation process.

Interestingly, the unsecured nonpriority creditors are receiving a smaller percentage of their claims than the 60 percent figure projected in the statement of financial affairs (produced in Exhibit 13.2). Although this earlier statement plays an important role in bankruptcy proceedings, the preparer's ability to foretell future events limits its accuracy.

REORGANIZATION—CHAPTER 11 BANKRUPTCY

Reorganization under the federal Bankruptcy Code is a way to salvage a company rather than liquidate it. Although the original owners of a company rescued in this way are often left without anything, others whose livelihoods depend on the company's fortunes may come out with their interests intact. The company's creditors, for example, may take over as the new owners. Its suppliers might be able to maintain the company as a customer. Its customers still may count on the company as a supplier. And perhaps most important, many of its employees may be able to keep the jobs that otherwise would have been sacrificed in a liquidation.[22]

For the 12 months ended June 2004, 11,048 Chapter 11 reorganizations were begun in the United States.[23] Of these reorganizations, only 84 companies were publicly owned.[24] Reorganizations attempt to salvage the company so that operations can continue. Although this legal procedure offers the company some hope of survival, reorganization is certainly not a guarantee of future prosperity. Most companies that attempt to reorganize eventually are liquidated. In practice, however, reorganization appears to be biased in favor of large organizations. One expert estimates that 90 percent of big corporations that attempt to reorganize emerge as functioning entities but fewer than 20 percent of smaller companies survive.[25]

Many reorganizations may actually fail because the debtor struggles too long before filing a petition:

Seeking bankruptcy because disaster looms—not after it has arrived—helps (gives the corporation time and provides equality of treatment). . . . Once a company files under the bankruptcy

[22] John Robbins, Al Goll, and Paul Rosenfield, "Accounting for Companies in Chapter 11 Reorganization," *Journal of Accountancy,* January 1991, p. 75.

[23] "Chapter 11 Filings Up; Total Filings Down," *BCD News and Comment,* September 7, 2004.

[24] Matt Krantz, "Chapter 11 Bankruptcies on Verge of Surge?" *USA Today,* February 23, 2005, p. 3B.

[25] Michael Selz, "For Many Small Businesses, Chapter 11 Closes the Book," *The Wall Street Journal,* November 4, 1992, p. B2.

laws, suppliers are likely to demand cash on delivery. So management that moves before liquid assets are depleted has a better chance of making a go of reorganization.[26]

Obviously, the activities and events surrounding a reorganization differ significantly from a liquidation. One important distinction is that the ownership normally retains control over the company (referred to as a *debtor in possession*). However, if fraud or gross mismanagement can be proven, the court has the authority to appoint an independent trustee to assume control. Unless replaced, the debtor in possession continues to operate the company and has the primary responsibility for developing an acceptable plan of reorganization. Not everyone, though, agrees with the wisdom of leaving the current management in charge of the company: "One philosophical objection raised increasingly often is the rule that puts the debtor in control of the bankruptcy process, an idea that often leaves foreigners 'stunned,' says one bankruptcy lawyer. This typically means that the managers who bankrupt a firm can have a go at restructuring it to keep it alive."[27]

While a reorganization is in process, the owners and managers are legally required to preserve the company's estate as of the date that the order for relief is entered. In this way, the bankruptcy regulations seek to reduce the losses that creditors and stockholders may have to absorb when either reorganization or liquidation eventually occurs. For this reason, a newsletter distributed by the A. H. Robins Company to employees a few days after the corporation filed for Chapter 11 protection specified that "the company cannot pay any creditor or supplier for goods delivered or services rendered before August 21, 1985. The company is prohibited from making such payments unless there is a special court order. Monthly bills will have to be prorated to assure all creditors are treated the same."[28]

The Plan for Reorganization

> The plan is the heart of every Chapter 11 reorganization. The provisions of the plan specify the treatment of all creditors and equity holders upon its approval by the Bankruptcy Court. Moreover, the plan shapes the financial structure of the entity that emerges.[29]

The most intriguing aspect of a Chapter 11 bankruptcy is the plan developed to rescue the company from insolvency. Initially, only the debtor in possession can file proposals with the court. However, if a plan for reorganization is not put forth within 120 days of the order for relief or accepted within 180 days (unless the court grants an extension), any interested party has the right to prepare and file a proposal. Creditors of Revco D. S., Inc., had the quandary of choosing between three different reorganization plans: one backed by the company's management, one proposed by Rite Aid Corporation, and one submitted by Jack Eckerd Corporation.[30]

A reorganization plan may contain an unlimited number of provisions: proposed changes in the company, additional financing arrangements, alterations in the debt structure, and the like.[31] Regardless of the specific contents, the intent of all such plans is to provide a feasible long-term solution to the company's monetary difficulties. However, to gain acceptance by the parties involved, a plan must present convincing evidence that it will enable the business to emerge from bankruptcy as a viable going concern.

Although a definitive list of elements that could be included in a reorganization proposal is not possible, some of the most common follow:

1. *Plans proposing changes in the company's operations.* In hope of improving liquidity, officials may decide to introduce new product lines or sell off unprofitable assets or even entire businesses. The closing of failing operations is especially common. A debtor in possession

---

[26] Daniel B. Moskowitz and Mark Ivey, "You Don't Have to Be Broke to Need Chapter 11," *BusinessWeek,* April 27, 1987, p. 108.

[27] "The Night of the Killer Zombies."

[28] Thomas R. Morris, "Some Questions Went Unasked," *Richmond Times-Dispatch,* May 18, 1986, p. B1.

[29] AICPA Statement of Position 90–7, *Financial Reporting by Entities in Reorganization Under the Bankruptcy Code,* November 19, 1990, para. 3.

[30] Gabriella Stern, "Timing of Revco Status Change Stays Uncertain," *The Wall Street Journal,* January 6, 1992, p. A3.

[31] See, for example, "When Will Somebody—Anybody—Rescue Battered Allegheny?" *The Wall Street Journal,* April 19, 1990, p. A1.

bears the burden of proving that it can eliminate the problems that led to insolvency and then avoid them in the future. As an example, before emerging from Chapter 11 reorganization, House of Fabrics, Inc., made a number of significant business changes:

> Since it opted to reorganize under bankruptcy court protection, the company, among other things, has closed more than 200 stores, reduced debt, secured a new three-year $60 million credit facility and disposed of surplus real estate. Earlier this week, the retail fabric and craft store operator announced the addition of three new board members.[32]

2. *Plans for generating additional monetary resources.* Companies faced with insolvency must develop new sources of cash, often in a short time period. Loans and the sale of both common and preferred stocks are frequently negotiated during reorganization to provide funding for the continuation of the business. For example, as part of the initial reorganization plan put forth by Orion Pictures, its majority owner, Metromedia Company, agreed to invest $15 million in cash. Without the willingness of the owners to back the company, creditors would probably be hesitant to agree to a reorganization.

3. *Plans for changes in company management.* Frequently, a financial crisis is blamed on poor management. In that situation, proposing to reorganize a company with the management team intact is probably not a practical suggestion. Therefore, many plans include hiring new individuals to implement the reorganization and run important aspects of the company. These changes may even affect the board of directors elected by the stockholders to oversee the company and its operations: "Manville Corporation agreed to let creditors have the final say in any board appointments, eliminating the last major obstacle in gaining approval of its 3½ year bankruptcy-law reorganization."[33]

4. *Plans to settle the debts of the company that existed when the order for relief was entered.* No element of a reorganization plan is more important than the proposal for satisfying the various creditors of the company. In most cases, their agreement is necessary before the court will confirm any plan of reorganization. The actual proposal to settle these debts may take one of several forms:

- Assets can be transferred to creditors who accept this payment in exchange for extinguishing a specified amount of debt. The book value of the liability being canceled is usually higher than the fair value of the assets rendered. "Dow Corning Corp. made public a $4.4 billion bankruptcy-reorganization plan, its third attempt to forge a solution for exiting from bankruptcy court and hammering out a way to resolve thousands of claims that silicone breast implants cause diseases and injuries. The company, which for years was the leading maker of silicone implants in the United States, offered $3 billion of that total to resolve an estimated 200,000 existing silicone claims."[34]

- An equity interest (such as common stock, preferred stock, or stock rights) can be conveyed to creditors to settle an outstanding debt. For example, the announcement that Garden Ridge was moving to exit from bankruptcy indicated that the "reorganization plan will call for the distribution of preferred stock to general unsecured creditors."[35]

- The terms of the outstanding liabilities can be modified: maturity dates extended, interest rates lowered, face values reduced, accrued interest forgiven, and so on.

One recent development is the use of prepackaged or prearranged bankruptcies. In such cases, the company and its debtors agree on some or all of the terms of the reorganization plan before a bankruptcy petition is signed. Thus, the parties go into the bankruptcy with a complete or partial agreement to present to the court. In this manner, all parties can avoid extensive legal fees. Furthermore, the parties have more protection because the Bankruptcy

---

[32] "Bankruptcy Period Ends; Stock to Resume Trading," *The Wall Street Journal,* August 1, 1996, p. B4.

[33] Cynthia F. Mitchell, "Manville Is Said to Have Agreed to Let Creditors Decide Board Appointments," *The Wall Street Journal,* April 25, 1986, p. 5.

[34] Thomas M. Burton, "Dow Corning Has $4.4 Billion Plan on Chapter 11 and Implant Claims," *The Wall Street Journal,* February 18, 1998, p. B2.

[35] "Garden Ridge Gets Bankruptcy Plans OK'd," *Home Textiles Today,* April 4, 2005, p. 8.

Court is likely to accept the plan without requiring extensive changes or revisions. To illustrate, note the timing of the negotiations in this announcement that Trump Hotels & Casino Resorts had won confirmation of its plan to exit Chapter 11: "Bondholders who negotiated the Chapter 11 restructuring before the Nov. 21 filing for bankruptcy protection voted overwhelmingly in favor of the Chapter 11 plan."[36]

Acceptance and Confirmation of Reorganization Plan

The creation of a plan for reorganization does not guarantee its implementation. The Bankruptcy Reform Act specifies that a plan must be voted on by both the company's creditors and stockholders before the court confirms. *To be accepted, each class of creditors must vote for the plan.* Acceptance requires the approval of two-thirds in dollar amount and more than one-half in the number of claims that cast votes. A separate vote is also required of each class of shareholders. For approval, at least two-thirds (measured by the number of shares held) of the owners who vote must agree to the proposed reorganization. In fact, convincing any of the parties to support a specific plan is not an easy task because agreement often means accepting a significant loss.

Although the plan may gain creditor and stockholder approval, court confirmation is still required. The court reviews the proposal and can reject the reorganization plan if a claimant (who did not vote for acceptance) would receive more through liquidation. The court also has the authority to confirm a reorganization plan that was not accepted by a particular class of creditors or stockholders. This provision is referred to as a *cram down;* it occurs when the court determines that the plan is fair and equitable. As an alternative, the court may convert a Chapter 11 reorganization into a Chapter 7 liquidation at any time if the development of an acceptable plan does not appear to be possible. That threat often encourages the parties to work together to achieve a workable resolution.

Financial Reporting during Reorganization

Developing and gaining approval for a reorganization plan can take years. During that period, the company continues operating under the assumption that it is eventually going to emerge from the bankruptcy proceedings. While going through reorganization, the company faces several specific accounting questions:

- Should the income effects resulting from operating activities be differentiated from transactions connected solely with the reorganization process?
- How should liabilities be reported? Because some debts may not be paid for years and then may require payment of an amount considerably less than face value, how should this information be conveyed?
- Does reorganization necessitate a change in the reporting basis of the company's assets?

In 1990, the AICPA Task Force on Financial Reporting by Entities in Reorganization Under the Bankruptcy Code issued *Statement of Position 90–7* ("Financial Reporting by Entities in Reorganization Under the Bankruptcy Code") (referred to as *SOP 90–7*). This pronouncement provides standards for the preparation of financial statements at two times:

1. During the period when a company is going through reorganization.
2. At the point that the company emerges from reorganization.

The Income Statement during Reorganization

According to *SOP 90–7,* any gains, losses, revenues, and expenses resulting from the reorganization of the business should be reported separately. Such items are placed on the income statement before any income tax expense or benefits.[37]

These separately reported reorganization items would include any gains and losses on the sale of assets necessitated by the reorganization. In addition, as mentioned previously,

[36] "Trump Hotels & Casino Resorts: Court Overseeing Bankruptcy Clears Plan to Exit," *The Wall Street Journal,* April 6, 2005, p. 1.

[37] In a similar manner, the statement of cash flows should be constructed so that reorganization items are shown separately within the operating, investing, and financing categories.

enormous amounts of professional fees may be incurred. *SOP 90–7* requires that these costs be expensed as incurred.

> What's the proper way to account for lawyers' and investment bankers' fees that can run to millions monthly for large cases like LTV? It makes sense to expense them along the way—and that's what the new rules call for. In the past, some clever companies capitalized the fees on the theory that part of the work would benefit the company as a going concern.[38]

SOP 90–7 also examined the reporting of interest expense and interest revenue. During reorganization, interest expense usually does not accrue on debts owed at the date on which the order for relief is granted. The amount of liability on that date is frozen. Thus, recognition of interest is necessary only if payment will be made during the proceeding (for example, on debts incurred during the bankruptcy) or if the interest will probably be an allowed claim (for example, if the amount was owed but unrecorded prior to the granting of the order for relief). Any interest expense to be recognized is not really a result of the reorganization process and should not be separately reported as a reorganization item.

In contrast, interest revenue can increase to quite a substantial amount during reorganization. Because the company is not forced to pay the debts incurred prior to the date of the order for relief, cash reserves can tend to grow, and the resulting interest can become a significant source of income. Any interest revenue that would not have been earned except for the proceeding is reported separately as a reorganization item.

For example, the 2001 financial statements for AMF Bowling Worldwide disclosed the following in connection with its Chapter 11 reorganization:

> Reorganization items, net for the year ended December 31, 2001, consist of the following (in thousands):

Provision for center closings	$22,396
Professional fees	19,783
Write-off deferred financing costs	9,068
Employee retention program	2,447
Other	3,037
Total	$56,731

To illustrate, assume that Crawford Corporation files a voluntary bankruptcy petition and is granted an order for relief on January 1, 2007. Thereafter, the ownership and management of the company begin to (1) work on a reorganization plan and (2) rehabilitate the company. Several branch operations are closed and accountants, lawyers, and other professionals are hired to assist in the reorganization. At the end of 2007, the bankruptcy is still in progress. The company prepares the income statement, which is structured so that the reader can distinguish the results of operating activities from the reorganization items (see Exhibit 13.4).

The Balance Sheet during Reorganization

A new entity is not created when a company moves *into* reorganization. Therefore, traditional generally accepted accounting principles continue to apply. Assets, for example, should still be reported at their book values. However, the final reorganization plan will likely reduce many liabilities. In addition, because of the order for relief, the current/noncurrent classification system is no longer applicable; payments may be delayed for years.

Thus, in reporting the liabilities of a company being reorganized, debts subject to compromise (reduction by the court through acceptance of a reorganization plan) must be disclosed separately. Unsecured and partially secured obligations existing as of the granting of the order for relief fall into this category. Fully secured liabilities and all debts incurred since that date are not subject to compromise and must be reported in a normal manner as either a current or noncurrent liability.

According to *SOP 90–7* (para. 24), liabilities subject to compromise "should be reported on the basis of the expected amount of the allowed claims . . . as opposed to the amounts for

---

[38] Laura Jereski, "Starting Fresh," *Forbes,* April 15, 1991, p. 105.

EXHIBIT 13.4
Income Statement during Reorganization

CRAWFORD CORPORATION
(Debtor in Possession)
Income Statement
For Year Ended December 31, 2007

Revenues:		
Sales		$650,000
Cost and expenses:		
Cost of goods sold	$346,000	
General and administrative expenses	165,000	
Selling expenses	86,000	
Interest expense	4,000	601,000
Earnings before reorganization items and tax effects		49,000
Reorganization items:		
Loss on closing of branches	(86,000)	
Professional fees	(75,000)	
Interest revenue	26,000	(135,000)
Loss before income tax benefit		(86,000)
Income tax benefit		18,800
Net loss		$ (67,200)
Loss per common share		$ (0.56)

which those allowed claims may be settled." Thus, the company does not attempt to antici-pate the payment required by a final plan but simply discloses the amount of these claims. For example, the December 31, 2002, balance sheet for US Airways Group, Inc. (as debtor and debtor in possession), reported current liabilities of $2.2 billion and noncurrent liabilities of $3.7 billion. The company then reported also having liabilities subject to compromise of $5.5 billion.

Financial Reporting for Companies Emerging from Reorganization

Is a company that successfully leaves Chapter 11 status considered a new entity so that current values should be assigned to its asset and liability accounts (referred to as *fresh start report-ing*)? Or is the company simply a continuation of the organization that entered bankruptcy so that historical figures are still applicable? *SOP 90–7* holds that these accounts should be ad-justed to current value if two criteria are met (para. 36):

- The reorganization (or fair) value of the assets of the emerging company is less than the total of the allowed claims as of the date of the order for relief plus the liabilities incurred subsequently.
- The original owners of the voting stock are left with less than 50 percent of the voting stock of the company when it emerges from bankruptcy.

Meeting the first criterion shows that the old company could not have continued in business as a going concern. The second criterion indicates that control of the company has changed.

Many, if not most, Chapter 11 bankruptcies meet these two criteria. Consequently, the en-tity is reported as if it were a brand new business. For example, Golden Books Entertainment reported that "on January 27, 2000, the Company formally emerged from protection under the Bankruptcy Code upon the consummation of the Amended Joint Plan of Reorganization. The Company has applied the reorganization and fresh-start reporting adjustments as required by *SOP 90–7* to the consolidated balance sheet as of December 25, 1999. . . . Under fresh start accounting, a new reporting entity is deemed to be created and the recorded amounts of assets and liabilities are adjusted to reflect their estimated fair values."

In applying fresh start accounting, the reorganization value of the entity that emerges from bankruptcy must first be determined. According to paragraph 9 of *SOP 90–7,* "reorganization value generally approximates fair value of the entity before considering liabilities and approximates the amount a willing buyer would pay for the assets of the entity immediately after the restructuring . . . generally it is determined by discounting future cash flows for the reconstituted business that will emerge." This total value is then assigned to the specific tangible and intangible assets of the company in the same way as in a purchase combination.

Unfortunately, determining the reorganization value for a large and complex corporation can be a difficult assignment. The 10–K filed by Kmart Holdings for the year ending January 26, 2005, describes its attempt at this computation:

> To facilitate the calculation of the enterprise value of the Successor Company, we developed a set of financial projections. Based on these financial projections and with the assistance of a financial adviser, we determined the enterprise value using various valuation methods, including (i) a comparison of the Company and its projected performance to the market value of comparable companies, (ii) a review and analysis of several recent transactions of companies in similar industries to the Company, and (iii) a calculation of the present value of the future cash flows under the projections. The estimated enterprise value was highly dependent upon achieving the future financial results set forth in the projections as well as the realization of certain other assumptions which were not guaranteed. The estimated enterprise value of the Company was calculated to be approximately $2.3 billion to $3.0 billion. We selected the midpoint of the range, $2.6 billion, as the estimated enterprise value.

After the reorganization value has been determined, an allocation to individual asset accounts should be carried out in the same manner as with the purchase price that establishes a business combination. In applying fresh start accounting, the assets held by a company on the day when it exits from reorganization should be reported based on current values, not historical book values. The entity is viewed as a newly created organization. That is the reason that the 10–K for Kmart Holdings indicates the "fair value adjustments included the recognition of approximately $2.2 billion of intangible assets that were previously not recorded in the Predecessor Company's financial statements, such as favorable leasehold interests, Kmart brand rights, pharmacy customer relationships and other lease and license agreements." As with a consolidation, any unallocated portion of the total value is reported as goodwill.

The reporting of liabilities following a reorganization also creates a concern because many of these balances will be reduced and the payment period extended. *SOP 90–7* requires reporting all liabilities (except for deferred income taxes, which should be accounted for according to the provisions of FASB *SFAS 109*) at the present value of the future cash payments.

To make the necessary asset adjustments to fresh start accounting, Additional Paid-In Capital is normally increased or decreased. However, any write-down of a liability creates a recognized gain. Finally, because the company is viewed as a new entity, it must leave reorganization with a zero balance reported for retained earnings.

Fresh Start Accounting Illustrated

Assume that a company has the following trial balance just prior to emerging from bankruptcy:

	Debit	Credit
Current assets	$ 50,000	
Land	100,000	
Buildings	400,000	
Equipment	250,000	
Accounts payable (incurred since the order for relief was granted)		$ 100,000
Liabilities when the order for relief was granted:		
Accounts payable		60,000
Accrued expenses		50,000
Notes payable (due in 3 years)		300,000
Bonds payable (due in 5 years)		600,000
Common stock (50,000 shares with a $1 par value)		50,000
Additional paid-in capital		40,000
Retained earnings (deficit)	400,000	
Totals	$1,200,000	$1,200,000

Other Information

- *Assets.* The company's land has a market value of $120,000; the building is worth $500,000. Other assets are valued at their book values. The reorganization value of the company's assets is assumed to be $1,000,000 based on discounted future cash flows.
- *Liabilities.* The $100,000 of accounts payable incurred since the order for relief was granted must be paid in full as the individual balances come due. The accounts payable and accrued expenses that were owed when the order for relief was granted will be converted into one-year notes payable of $70,000, paying interest of 10 percent. The $300,000 in notes payable on the trial balance will be converted into a 10-year, 8 percent note of $100,000. These creditors also get 20,000 shares of stock that the common stockholders are to turn in to the company. Finally, the $600,000 bonds payable will be converted into eight-year, 9 percent notes totaling $430,000. The bondholders also get 15,000 shares of common stock turned in by the current owners.
- *Stockholders' equity.* The owners of the common stock will return 70 percent of their stock (35,000 shares) to the company to be issued as specified above. The reorganization value of the assets is $1,000,000, and the debts of the company after the proceeding total $700,000 ($100,000 + $70,000 + $100,000 + $430,000). Thus, stockholders' equity must be the $300,000 difference. Because shares with a $50,000 par value would still be outstanding, Additional Paid-In Capital (APIC) needs to be adjusted to $250,000.

In accounting for this reorganization, the initial question to be resolved is whether fresh start accounting is appropriate. The first criterion is met because the reorganization value of the assets ($1,000,000) is less than the sum of all postpetition liabilities ($100,000 in Accounts Payable) plus allowed claims (the $1,010,000 total of liabilities remaining from the date of the order for relief before any write-down). The second criterion is also met because the original stockholders retain less than 50 percent of the shares after the plan takes effect. At that point, they will hold only 15,000 of the 50,000 outstanding shares.

Because fresh start accounting is appropriate, the assets must be adjusted to fair value rather than retain their historical book value. The reorganization value is $1 million, but the assets' fair value is only $920,000 (current assets $50,000, land $120,000 [adjusted], buildings $500,000 [adjusted], and equipment $250,000). In addition, goodwill is recognized for the $80,000 reorganization value of the company in excess of the value assigned to specific assets.

The accounts are already recorded at book value; thus, adjustment is necessary only when fair value differs from this book value:

Land	20,000	
Buildings	100,000	
Goodwill	80,000	
Additional Paid-In Capital		200,000
To adjust asset accounts to fresh start accounting and to recognize excess value as goodwill.		

Next, the 35,000 shares of common stock (with a $1 per share par value) returned to the company by the original owners should be recorded as follows:

Common Stock	35,000	
Additional Paid-In Capital		35,000
To record shares of common stock returned to the company by owners as part of the reorganization agreement.		

The liability accounts on the records at the date of the order for relief must now be adjusted for the provisions of the bankruptcy reorganization plan. Because all new debts bear a reasonable interest rate, present value computations are not necessary. The first entry is a straight conversion with a gain recorded for the difference between the old debt and the new:

Accounts Payable	60,000	
Accrued Expenses	50,000	
Notes Payable (1 year)		70,000
Gain on Debt Discharge		40,000
To convert liabilities to a one-year note as per reorganization plan.		

The two remaining debts (the note payable and the bond payable) will be exchanged, at least in part, for shares of common stock. Each of these entries will require a computation of the amount to be assigned to Additional Paid-In Capital (APIC). The calculated total APIC for the company derived previously is $250,000. Because the holders of the notes receive 20,000 shares of stock (or 40 percent of the company's 50,000 share total), this stock is assigned APIC of $100,000 (40 percent). The holders of the bonds are to receive 15,000 shares (30 percent of the total). Hence, APIC of $75,000 (30 percent) is recorded:

Notes Payable (3 years)	300,000	
Notes Payable (10 years)		100,000
Common Stock (par value of 20,000 shares)		20,000
Additional Paid-In Capital (40 percent of company total)		100,000
Gain on Debt Discharge		80,000
To record exchange with gain recorded for difference between book value of old note and the amount recorded for new note and shares of stock.		
Bonds Payable	600,000	
Notes Payable (8 years)		430,000
Common Stock (par value of 15,000 shares)		15,000
Additional Paid-In Capital (30 percent of company total)		75,000
Gain on Debt Discharge		80,000
To record exchange with gain recorded for difference between book value of old bonds and the amount recorded for new notes and shares of stock.		

At this point, all asset, liability, and common stock amounts are reported based on the amounts for the company as it leaves reorganization. Only additional paid-in capital and retained earnings remain to be finalized. Additional Paid-In Capital now has a balance of $450,000 ($40,000 beginning balance plus $200,000 for adjusting assets plus $35,000 for shares returned by owners plus $100,000 because of shares issued for note and $75,000 because of shares issued for bonds). Therefore, this balance is $200,000 more than the amount to be reported as established through the provisions of the reorganization agreement. In addition, the Gain on Debt Discharge account has a balance of $200,000 ($40,000 + $80,000 + $80,000), a figure that must be closed out. Adjusting and closing these accounts eliminates the deficit in Retained Earnings so that the emerging company has no balance in this equity account:

Additional Paid-In Capital	200,000	
Gain on Debt Discharge	200,000	
Retained Earnings (Deficit)		400,000
To adjust Additional Paid-In Capital balance to correct amount, close out Gain account, and eliminate deficit balance.		

After posting these entries, this company emerges from bankruptcy with the following:

1. Its assets are reported at fair value except for goodwill, which is a residual figure.
2. Its debts equal the present value of the future cash payments (except for any deferred income taxes).
3. It has no deficit balance.

Discussion **Question**

IS THIS THE REAL PURPOSE OF THE BANKRUPTCY LAWS?

Insolvency is not a necessary condition for bankruptcy. Moreover a firm may petition the court for protection under Chapter 11 even though it is not insolvent. If the business can demonstrate real financial trouble, the court will generally not dismiss the petition. In recent years, Chapter 11 has been looked upon as a safe harbor for gaining time to restructure the business and to head off more serious financial problems. *For example, when Johns Manville filed a petition under Chapter 11, it was a profitable, financially sound company.* Yet it faced numerous lawsuits for damages resulting from asbestos products it sold. Reorganization helped Johns Manville deal with its financial problems [emphasis added].*

During recent years, the filing of a voluntary Chapter 11 bankruptcy petition has become a tool that companies sometimes use to settle significant financial problems. Just as Johns Manville reorganized to settle the claims of asbestos victims, A. H. Robins followed a similar path to resolve thousands of lawsuits stemming from injuries resulting from the Dalkon Shield intrauterine device. The Wilson Foods Corporation managed to reduce union wages by filing under Chapter 11 as did Continental Airlines Corporation.

Not surprisingly, seeking protection under Chapter 11 to force a bargained resolution of a financial difficulty is a controversial legal maneuver. Creditors and claimants often argue that this procedure is used to avoid responsibility. Companies counter that bankruptcy can become the only realistic means of achieving any settlement.

Should companies be allowed to use the provisions of Chapter 11 in this manner?

*Paul J. Corr and Donald D. Bourque, "Managing in a Reorganization," *Management Accounting*, January 1988, p. 34.

	Debit	Credit
Current assets	$ 50,000	
Land	120,000	
Buildings	500,000	
Equipment	250,000	
Goodwill	80,000	
Accounts payable		$ 100,000
Note payable (due in 1 year)		70,000
Note payable (due in 10 years)		100,000
Notes payable (due in 8 years)		430,000
Common stock (50,000 shares with a $1 par value)		50,000
Additional paid-in capital		250,000
Retained earnings	–0–	–0–
Totals	$1,000,000	$1,000,000

Summary

1. Every year a significant number of businesses in the United States become insolvent, unable to pay debts as they come due. Because creditors and owners hold financial interests in each failed company, bankruptcy laws provide protection for all parties. The Bankruptcy Reform Act of 1978 (as amended) currently serves as the primary structure for these legal proceedings. This act was designed to ensure a fair distribution of all remaining properties while discharging the obligations of an honest debtor.

2. Bankruptcy proceedings can be voluntary (instigated by the insolvent debtor) or involuntary (instigated by a group of creditors). In either case, the court usually grants an order for relief to halt all actions against the debtor. Some creditors may have already gained protection for themselves by having a mortgage lien or security interest attached to specific assets. A creditor is considered fully secured if the value of any collateral exceeds the related debt balance but is only partially secured if the obligation is larger. All other liabilities are unsecured; these creditors have legal rights but not to any specific assets of the debtor. The Bankruptcy Reform Act lists several types of unsecured liabilities (including administrative expenses and government claims for unpaid taxes) that have priority and must be paid before other unsecured debts are settled.

3. The parties involved in a bankruptcy want, and need, to be informed of the possible outcome, especially if liquidation is being considered. Thus, a statement of financial affairs can be prepared for an insolvent company. This document lists the net realizable value of all remaining assets and indicates any property pledged to specific creditors. In addition, the liabilities of the business are segregated and disclosed within four classifications: fully secured, partially secured, unsecured with priority, and unsecured. Prior to filing a bankruptcy petition, the parties can use this information to help decide whether either liquidation or reorganization is the best course of action. However, this statement should be viewed as a projection because many reported values are merely estimations.

4. If the assets of the insolvent company will be liquidated to satisfy obligations (a Chapter 7 bankruptcy), a trustee is appointed to oversee the process. This individual must recover all property belonging to the company, liquidate noncash assets, possibly continue running operations to complete any business in progress, and make appropriate payments. To convey information about these events and transactions, the trustee commonly prepares a statement of realization and liquidation. This statement provides a current report of all account balances and transactions to date.

5. Liquidation is not the only alternative available to an insolvent business. The company may seek to survive by developing a reorganization plan (a Chapter 11 bankruptcy). Reorganization is possible only if creditors, shareholders, and the court accept the plan. While a reorganization is in process, the owners and management must preserve the company's estate as of the date on which the order of relief was entered. Although the ownership has the initial opportunity for creating a proposal for action, any interested party has the right to file a reorganization plan after a period of time.

6. Reorganization plans usually contain a number of provisions for modifying operations, generating new financing by equity or debt, and settling the liabilities existing when the order for relief was entered. To be accepted, each class of creditors and shareholders must support the agreement. Thereafter, the court must confirm the reorganization plan.

7. During reorganization, a company reports its liabilities as being subject to compromise or not subject to compromise. The first category includes all unsecured and partially secured debts that existed on the day the order for relief was granted. The balance to be reported is the expected amount of allowed claims rather than the estimated amount of settlement. Liabilities not subject to compromise are those debts fully secured or incurred following the granting of the order for relief.

8. An income statement prepared during the reorganization period should disclose operating activities separately from reorganization items. Professional fees associated with the reorganization such as lawyers' fees are reorganization items and are expensed as incurred. Any interest revenue earned during this period because of an increase in the company's cash reserves should also be reported as a reorganization item.

9. Many companies that emerge from reorganization proceedings must apply fresh start accounting. The AICPA *SOP 90–7* provides authoritative guidance. Companies record assets at fair value, and recognition of intangible assets and goodwill might also be necessary. Liabilities (except for deferred income taxes) are reported at the present value of required cash flows. Retained earnings (or a deficit) are eliminated. Additional Paid-In Capital is adjusted to keep the balance sheet in equilibrium.

Comprehensive Illustration

PROBLEM

(Estimated Time: 50 to 65 Minutes) Roth Company is insolvent and in the process of filing for relief under the provisions of the Bankruptcy Reform Act of 1978. Roth has no cash, and the company's balance sheet currently shows Accounts Payable of $48,000. Roth owes an additional $8,000 in connection with various expenses but has not yet recorded these amounts. The company's assets with an indication of both book value and anticipated net realizable value follow:

	Book Value	Expected Net Realizable Value
Accounts receivable	$ 31,000	$ 9,000
Inventory	48,000	36,000
Investments	10,000	18,000
Land	80,000	75,000
Buildings	90,000	60,000
Accumulated depreciation	(38,000)	
Equipment	110,000	20,000
Accumulated depreciation	(61,000)	
Other assets	5,000	–0–
Totals	$275,000	$218,000

Roth has three notes payable, each with a different maturity date:

- Note 1 due in 5 years—$120,000, secured by a mortgage lien on Roth's land and buildings.
- Note 2 due in 8 years—$30,000, secured by Roth's investments.
- Note 3 due in 10 years—$35,000, unsecured.

Of the accounts payable that Roth owes, $10,000 represents salaries to employees. However, no individual is entitled to receive more than $1,300. An additional $3,000 due to the U.S. government in connection with taxes is included in this liability amount.

The company reported the stockholders' equity balance of $42,000 at the current date: common stock of $140,000 and a deficit of $98,000. Liquidating the company will lead to administrative expenses of approximately $20,000.

Required:

a. Prepare a statement of financial affairs for Roth to indicate the expected availability of funds if the company is liquidated.

b. Assume that Roth owes Philip, Inc., a total of $2,000. This liability is unsecured. If Roth is liquidated, what amount of money can Philip expect to receive?

c. What amount will be paid on note 2 if Roth is liquidated?

d. Assume that Roth is immediately reorganized. Assume that the company has a reorganization value of $230,000, and the net realizable value is to be the assigned value for each asset. The accounts payable and accrued expenses are reduced to $20,000. Note 1 is reduced to a $30,000 note due in four years with a 7 percent annual interest rate. This creditor also receives half of the company's outstanding stock from the owners. Note 2 is reduced to a $12,000 note due in five years with an 8 percent annual interest rate. This creditor also receives 10 percent of the outstanding stock of the company from the owners. Note 3 is reduced to $5,000 due in three years with a 9 percent annual interest rate.

Prepare a trial balance for this company after it emerges from bankruptcy.

SOLUTION

a. To develop a statement of financial affairs for this company, the following preliminary actions must be taken:

- Enter the $8,000 in unrecorded accounts payable into the company's accounting records. Because these debts were incurred in connection with expenses, the deficit is increased by a corresponding amount.
- The unsecured liabilities that have priority are identified:

Administrative costs (estimated)	$20,000
Salary payable	10,000
Amount due to government for taxes	3,000
Total liabilities with priority	$33,000

- The secured claims should be appropriately classified:

  Note 1 is fully secured because Roth's land and buildings can be sold for an amount in excess of the $120,000 balance.

  Note 2 is only partially secured because Roth's investments are worth less than $30,000.

With this information, the statement of financial affairs in Exhibit 13.5 can be produced.

b. Based on the information provided by the statement of financial affairs, Roth anticipates having $47,000 in free assets remaining at the end of the liquidation. This amount must be distributed to unsecured creditors with total claims of $90,000. Therefore, only 52.2 percent of each obligation can be paid:

$$\frac{\$47,000}{\$90,000} = 52.2\% \text{ (rounded)}$$

Philip, Inc., should receive 52.2 percent of its $2,000 unsecured claim, or $1,044.

c. The $30,000 note payable is partially secured by Roth's investments, an asset having a net realizable value of only $18,000. The remaining $12,000 is an unsecured claim, which (as computed in the

EXHIBIT 13.5

ROTH COMPANY
Statement of Financial Affairs

Book Values	Assets		Available for Unsecured Creditors
	Pledged with fully secured creditors:		
$132,000	Land and buildings	$ 135,000	
	Less: Note payable	(120,000)	$ 15,000
	Pledged with partially secured creditors:		
10,000	Investments	18,000	
	Less: Note payable	(30,000)	–0–
	Free assets:		
31,000	Accounts receivable		9,000
48,000	Inventory		36,000
49,000	Equipment		20,000
5,000	Intangible assets		–0–
	Total available for liabilities with priority and unsecured creditors		80,000
	Less: Liabilities with priority (listed below)		(33,000)
	Available for unsecured creditors		47,000
	Estimated deficiency		43,000
$275,000			$ 90,000

Book Values	Liabilities and Stockholders' Equity		Available for Nonpriority Liabilities
	Liabilities with priority:		
–0–	Administrative expenses (estimated)	$ 20,000	
	Accounts payable:		
$ 10,000	Salaries payable	10,000	
3,000	Taxes payable	3,000	
	Total	$ 33,000	
	Fully secured creditors:		
120,000	Note payable	120,000	
	Less: Land and buildings	(135,000)	–0–
	Partially secured creditors:		
30,000	Note payable	30,000	
	Less: investments	(18,000)	$12,000
	Unsecured creditors:		
35,000	Note payable		35,000
43,000	Accounts payable (other than salaries and taxes, plus unrecorded liabilities have been included)		43,000
34,000	Stockholders' equity (adjusted for unrecorded liabilities)		–0–
$275,000			$90,000

previous requirement) will be paid 52.2 percent of face value. Thus, the holder of this note can expect to receive $24,264:

Net realizable value of investments	$18,000
Payment on $12,000 unsecured claim (52.2 percent)	6,264
Amount to be received	$24,264

d. Fresh start accounting is appropriate. The reorganization value of $230,000 is less than the $241,000 total amount of claims (no liabilities after the issuance of the order for relief are indicated).

Accounts payable	$ 48,000
Accrued expenses	8,000
Note 1	120,000
Note 2	30,000
Note 3	35,000
Total claims	$241,000

In addition, the original owners of the stock retain only 40 percent of the shares after the company leaves the bankruptcy proceeding.

The company's assets are assigned values equal to their net realizable value based on the information provided. Because the reorganization value of $230,000 is $12,000 in excess of the total net realizable value of $218,000, goodwill is recognized for that amount.

Each liability is adjusted to the newly agreed-on amounts. Present value computations are not required because a reasonable interest rate is included in each case. These debts now total $67,000 ($20,000 + $30,000 + $12,000 + $5,000).

Because the reorganization value is $230,000, stockholders' equity must be $163,000 ($230,000 − $67,000). The number of outstanding shares of common stock has not changed, so that account retains its balance of $140,000. The other $23,000 of stockholders' equity is recorded as additional paid-in capital.

	Debit	Credit
Accounts receivable	$ 9,000	
Inventory	36,000	
Investments	18,000	
Land	75,000	
Buildings	60,000	
Equipment	20,000	
Goodwill	12,000	
Accounts payable and accrued expenses		$ 20,000
Note payable one		30,000
Note payable two		12,000
Note payable three		5,000
Common stock		140,000
Additional paid-in capital		23,000
Totals	$230,000	$230,000

Questions

1. What does the term *insolvent* mean?
2. At present, what federal legislation governs most bankruptcy proceedings?
3. What are the primary objectives of a bankruptcy proceeding?
4. A bankruptcy case may begin with either a voluntary or an involuntary petition. What is the difference? What are the requirements for an involuntary petition?
5. A bankruptcy court enters an order for relief. How does this action affect an insolvent company and its creditors?
6. What is the difference between fully secured liabilities, partially secured liabilities, and unsecured liabilities?
7. In a bankruptcy proceeding, what is the significance of a liability with priority? What are the general categories of liabilities that have priority in a liquidation?
8. Why are the administrative expenses incurred during a liquidation classified as liabilities having priority?
9. What is the difference between a Chapter 7 bankruptcy and a Chapter 11 bankruptcy?
10. Why might unsecured creditors favor reorganizing an insolvent company rather than forcing it into liquidation?

11. What is the purpose of a statement of financial affairs? Why might this statement be prepared before a bankruptcy petition has been filed?

12. In the liquidation of a company, what actions does the trustee perform?

13. A trustee for a company that is being liquidated voids a preference transfer. What has happened, and why did the trustee take this action?

14. A statement of realization and liquidation is prepared for a company that is being liquidated. What information can be ascertained from this statement?

15. What does the term *debtor in possession* mean?

16. Who can develop reorganization plans in a Chapter 11 bankruptcy?

17. What types of proposals might a reorganization plan include?

18. Under normal conditions, how does a reorganization plan become effective?

19. In a bankruptcy proceeding, what is a *cram down?*

20. While a company goes through reorganization, how should its liabilities be reported?

21. During reorganization, how should a company's income statement be structured?

22. What accounting is made of the professional fees incurred during a reorganization?

23. What does *fresh start accounting* mean?

24. Under what conditions does a company emerging from a bankruptcy reorganization use fresh start accounting?

25. When fresh start accounting is utilized, how are a company's assets reported? How are its liabilities reported?

26. How is goodwill computed if fresh start accounting is applied to a reorganized company?

Problems

1. What are the objectives of the bankruptcy laws in the United States?
   a. Provide relief for the court system in this country and ensure that all debtors are treated the same.
   b. Distribute assets fairly and discharge honest debtors from their obligations.
   c. Protect the economy and stimulate growth.
   d. Prevent insolvency and protect shareholders.

2. In a bankruptcy, which of the following statements is true?
   a. An order for relief results only from a voluntary petition.
   b. Creditors entering an involuntary petition must have debts totaling at least $20,000.
   c. Secured notes payable are considered liabilities with priority on a statement of affairs.
   d. A liquidation is referred to as a *Chapter 7 bankruptcy,* and a reorganization is referred to as a *Chapter 11 bankruptcy.*

3. In the reporting for a company that is to be liquidated, assets are shown at
   a Present value calculated using an appropriate effective rate.
   b. Net realizable value.
   c. Historical cost.
   d. Book value.

4. An involuntary bankruptcy petition must be filed by
   a. The insolvent company's attorney.
   b. The holders of the insolvent company's debenture bonds.
   c. Unsecured creditors with total debts of at least $12,300.
   d. The management of the company.

5. An order for relief
   a. Prohibits creditors from taking action to collect from an insolvent company without court approval.
   b. Calls for the immediate distribution of free assets to unsecured creditors.
   c. Can be entered only in an involuntary bankruptcy proceeding.
   d. Gives an insolvent company time to file a voluntary bankruptcy petition.

6. Which of the following is *not* a liability that has priority in a liquidation?
   a. Administrative expenses incurred in the liquidation.
   b. Salary payable of $800 per person owed to 26 employees.
   c. Payroll taxes due to the federal government.
   d. Advertising expense incurred before the company became insolvent.

7. Which of the following is the minimum limitation necessary for filing an involuntary bankruptcy petition?
   a. The signature of 12 creditors to whom the debtor owes at least $4,925 in unsecured debt.
   b. The signature of six creditors to whom the debtor owes at least $20,000 in unsecured debt.
   c. The signature of three creditors to whom the debtor owes at least $12,300 in unsecured debt.
   d. The signature of nine creditors to whom the debtor owes at least $25,000 in unsecured debt.

8. On a statement of financial affairs, how are liabilities classified?
   a. Current and noncurrent.
   b. Secured and unsecured.
   c. Monetary and nonmonetary.
   d. Historic and futuristic.

9. What is a *debtor in possession?*
   a. The holder of a note receivable issued by an insolvent company prior to granting an order for relief.
   b. A fully secured creditor.
   c. The ownership of an insolvent company that continues to control the organization during a bankruptcy reorganization.
   d. The stockholders in a Chapter 7 bankruptcy.

10. How are anticipated administrative expenses reported on a statement of financial affairs?
    a. As a footnote until actually incurred.
    b. As a liability with priority.
    c. As a partially secured liability.
    d. As an unsecured liability.

11. Prior to filing a voluntary Chapter 7 bankruptcy petition, Haynes Company pays a supplier $1,000 to satisfy an unsecured claim. Haynes was insolvent at the time. Subsequently, the trustee appointed to oversee this liquidation forces the return of this $1,000. Which of the following is correct?
    a. A preference transfer has been voided.
    b. All transactions just prior to a voluntary bankruptcy proceeding must be nullified.
    c. The supplier should sue for the return of this money.
    d. The $1,000 claim becomes a liability with priority.

12. Which of the following is *not* an expected function of a bankruptcy trustee?
    a. Filing a plan of reorganization.
    b. Recovering all property belonging to a company.
    c. Liquidating noncash assets.
    d. Distributing assets to the proper claimants.

13. What is an inherent limitation of the statement of financial affairs?
    a. Many of the amounts reported are only estimations that might prove to be inaccurate.
    b. The statement is applicable only to a Chapter 11 bankruptcy.
    c. The statement covers only a short time, whereas a bankruptcy may last much longer.
    d. The figures on the statement vary as to a voluntary and an involuntary bankruptcy.

14. What is a *cram down?*
    a. An agreement about the total amount of money to be reserved to pay creditors who have priority.
    b. The bankruptcy court's confirmation of a reorganization even though a class of creditors or stockholders did not accept it.

c. The filing of an involuntary bankruptcy petition, especially by the holders of partially secured debts.

d. The court's decision as to whether a particular creditor has priority.

15. On a balance sheet prepared for a company during its reorganization, how are liabilities reported?

a. As current and long term.

b. As monetary and nonmonetary.

c. As subject to compromise and not subject to compromise.

d. As equity related and debt related.

16. On a balance sheet prepared for a company during its reorganization, at what balance are liabilities reported?

a. At the expected amount of the allowed claims.

b. At the present value of the expected future cash flows.

c. At the expected amount of the settlement.

d. At the amount of the anticipated final payment.

17. Which of the following is not a reorganization item for purposes of reporting a company's income statement during a Chapter 11 bankruptcy?

a. Professional fees.

b. Interest income.

c. Interest expense.

d. Gains and losses on closing facilities.

18. What accounting is made for professional fees incurred during a bankruptcy reorganization?

a. They must be expensed immediately.

b. They must be capitalized and written off over 40 years or less.

c. They must be capitalized until the company emerges from the reorganization.

d. They are either expensed or capitalized, depending on the nature of the expenditure.

19. Which of the following is necessary for a company to use fresh start accounting?

a. The original owners must hold at least 50 percent of the stock of the company when it emerges from bankruptcy.

b. The reorganization value of the company must exceed the value of all assets.

c. The reorganization value of the company must exceed the value of all liabilities.

d. The original owners must hold less than 50 percent of the stock of the company when it emerges from bankruptcy.

20. If the reorganization value of a company emerging from bankruptcy is larger than the values that can be assigned to specific assets, what accounting is made of the difference?

a. Because of conservatism, the difference is simply ignored.

b. The difference is expensed immediately.

c. The difference is capitalized as an intangible asset.

d. The difference is recorded as a professional fee.

21. For a company emerging from bankruptcy, how are its liabilities (other than deferred income taxes) reported?

a. At their historical value.

b. At zero because of fresh start accounting.

c. At the present value of the future cash flows.

d. At the negotiated value less all professional fees incurred in the reorganization.

22. A company is to be liquidated and has the following liabilities:

Income taxes	$ 8,000
Notes payable (secured by land)	120,000
Accounts payable	85,000
Salary payable (evenly divided between two employees)	6,000
Bonds payable	70,000
Administrative expenses for liquidation	20,000

The company has the following assets:

	Book Value	Fair Value
Current assets	$ 80,000	$ 35,000
Land	100,000	90,000
Buildings and equipment	100,000	110,000

How much money will the holders of the notes payable collect following the liquidation?

23. Xavier Company is going through a Chapter 7 bankruptcy. All assets have been liquidated, and the company retains only $15,000 in free cash. The following debts, totaling $27,950, remain:

Government claims to unpaid taxes	$5,000
Salary during last month owed to Mr. Key (not an officer)	7,300
Administrative expenses	2,450
Salary during last month owed to Ms. Rankin (not an officer)	5,650
Unsecured accounts payable	7,550

Indicate how much money will be paid to the creditor of each debt.

24. Ataway Company has had severe financial difficulties and is considering filing a bankruptcy petition. At this time, the company has the following assets (stated at net realizable value) and liabilities:

Assets (pledged against debts of $70,000)	$116,000
Assets (pledged against debts of $130,000)	50,000
Other assets	80,000
Liabilities with priority	42,000
Unsecured creditors	200,000

In a liquidation, how much money would be paid on the partially secured debt?

25. Chesterfield Company has cash of $50,000, inventory worth $90,000, and a building worth $130,000. Unfortunately, the company also has accounts payable of $180,000, a note payable of $80,000 (secured by the inventory), liabilities with priority of $20,000, and a bond payable of $150,000 (secured by the building). In a Chapter 7 bankruptcy, how much money will the holders of the bond expect to receive?

26. Mondesto Company has the following:

Unsecured creditors	$230,000
Liabilities with priority	110,000
Secured liabilities:	
Debt 1, $210,000; value of pledged asset	180,000
Debt 2, $170,000; value of pledged asset	100,000
Debt 3, $120,000; value of pledged asset	140,000

The company also has a number of other assets that are not pledged in any way. The creditors holding debt 2 want to receive at least $142,000. For how much do these free assets have to be sold so that debt 2 would receive exactly $142,000?

27. A statement of financial affairs created for an insolvent corporation that is beginning the process of liquidation discloses the following data (assets are shown at net realizable values):

Assets pledged with fully secured creditors	$200,000
Fully secured liabilities	150,000
Assets pledged with partially secured creditors	380,000
Partially secured liabilities	490,000
Assets not pledged	300,000
Unsecured liabilities with priority	160,000
Accounts payable (unsecured)	390,000

a. This company owes $3,000 to an unsecured creditor (without priority). How much money can this creditor expect to collect?

b. This company owes $100,000 to a bank on a note payable that is secured by a security interest attached to property with an estimated net realizable value of $80,000. How much money can this bank expect to collect?

28. A company preparing for a Chapter 7 liquidation has the following liabilities:
    - Note payable A of $90,000 secured by land having a book value of $50,000 and a fair value of $70,000.
    - Note payable B of $120,000 secured by a building having a $60,000 book value and a $40,000 fair value.
    - Note payable C of $60,000, unsecured.
    - Administrative expenses payable of $20,000.
    - Accounts payable of $120,000.
    - Income taxes payable of $30,000.

    It has these other assets:
    - Cash of $10,000.
    - Inventory of $100,000 but with fair value of $60,000.
    - Equipment of $90,000 but with fair value of $50,000.

    How much will each of the company's liabilities be paid after liquidation?

29. Olds Company declares Chapter 7 bankruptcy. The following are the accounts at that time; administrative expenses are estimated to be $12,000:

Cash	$ 24,000	
Accounts receivable	60,000	(worth $28,000)
Inventory	70,000	(worth $56,000)
Land (secures note A)	200,000	(worth $160,000)
Building (secures bonds)	400,000	(worth $320,000)
Equipment	120,000	(worth unknown)
Accounts payable	180,000	
Taxes payable to government	20,000	
Note payable A	170,000	
Note payable B	250,000	
Bonds payable	300,000	

    The holders of note payable B want to collect at least $125,000. To achieve that goal, how much does the company have to receive in the liquidation of its equipment?

30. A company is going through a Chapter 7 bankruptcy and has the following account balances:

Cash	$ 30,000
Receivables (30% collectible)	50,000
Inventory (worth $39,000)	90,000
Land (worth $120,000) (secures note payable)	100,000
Buildings (worth $180,000) (secures bonds payable)	200,000
Salary payable (7 workers owed equal amounts for last 2 weeks)	10,000
Accounts payable	90,000
Note payable (secured by land)	110,000
Bonds payable (secured by building)	300,000
Common stock	100,000
Retained earnings	(140,000)

    How much will it pay on each of the following?
    Salary payable
    Accounts payable
    Note payable
    Bonds payable

31. Pumpkin Company is going through bankruptcy reorganization. It has a note payable for $200,000 that was incurred prior to the order for relief. The company believes that the note will be settled for $60,000 in cash. It is also possible that the creditor will instead take a piece of land that cost the company $50,000 but is worth $72,000. On a balance sheet during the reorganization period, how will this debt be reported?

32. A company is coming out of reorganization with the following accounts:

	Book Value	Fair Value
Receivables	$ 80,000	$ 90,000
Inventory	200,000	210,000
Buildings	300,000	400,000
Liabilities	300,000	300,000
Common stock	330,000	
Additional paid-in capital	20,000	
Retained earnings (deficit)	(70,000)	

The company's assets have a $760,000 reorganization value. Before the reorganization, the owners of the company transferred 80 percent of the outstanding stock to the creditors.

Prepare the journal entry that is necessary to adjust the company's records to fresh start accounting.

33. Addison Corporation is currently going through a Chapter 11 bankruptcy. The company has the following account balances. Prepare an income statement for this organization. The effective tax rate is 20 percent (realization of any tax benefits is anticipated).

	Debit	Credit
Advertising expense	$ 24,000	
Cost of goods sold	211,000	
Depreciation expense	22,000	
Interest expense	4,000	
Interest revenue		$ 32,000
Loss on closing of branch	109,000	
Professional fees	71,000	
Rent expense	16,000	
Revenues		467,000
Salary expense	70,000	

34. Kansas City Corporation holds three assets when it comes out of Chapter 11 bankruptcy:

	Book Value	Fair Value
Inventory	$ 86,000	$ 50,000
Land and buildings	250,000	400,000
Equipment	123,000	110,000

The company has a reorganization value of $600,000.

a. Describe the rules to determine whether to apply fresh start accounting to Kansas City Corporation.

b. If fresh start accounting is appropriate, how will this company's assets be reported?

c. If a Goodwill account is recognized in a reorganization, where should it be reported? What happens to this balance?

35. Jaez Corporation is in the process of going through a reorganization. As of December 31, 2007, the company's accountant has determined the following information although the company is still several months away from emerging from the bankruptcy proceeding. Prepare a balance sheet in appropriate form.

	Book Value	Fair Value
Assets		
Cash	$ 23,000	$ 23,000
Inventory	45,000	47,000
Land	140,000	210,000
Buildings	220,000	260,000
Equipment	154,000	157,000

	Allowed Claims	Expected Settlement
Liabilities as of the date of the order for relief		
Accounts payable	$ 123,000	$ 20,000
Accrued expenses	30,000	4,000
Income taxes payable	22,000	18,000
Note payable (due 2010, secured by land)	100,000	100,000
Note payable (due 2012)	170,000	80,000
Liabilities since the date of the order for relief		
Accounts payable	$60,000	
Note payable (due 2009)	110,000	
Stockholders' equity		
Common stock	$ 200,000	
Deficit	(233,000)	

36. Ristoni Company is in the process of emerging from a Chapter 11 bankruptcy. The company will apply fresh start accounting as of December 31, 2007. The company currently has 30,000 shares of common stock outstanding with a $240,000 par value. As part of the reorganization, the owners will contribute 18,000 shares of this stock back to the company. A deficit balance of $330,000 is also being reported.

   The company has the following asset accounts:

	Book Value	Fair Value
Accounts receivable	$100,000	$ 80,000
Inventory	112,000	90,000
Land and buildings	420,000	500,000
Equipment	78,000	65,000

   The company's liabilities will be settled as follows. Assume that all notes will be issued at reasonable interest rates.
   - Accounts payable of $80,000 will be settled with a note for $5,000. These creditors will also get 1,000 shares of the stock contributed by the owners.
   - Accrued expenses of $35,000 will be settled with a note for $4,000.
   - Note payable (due 2011) of $100,000 was fully secured and has not been renegotiated.
   - Note payable (due 2010) of $200,000 will be settled with a note for $50,000 and 10,000 shares of the stock contributed by the owners.
   - Note payable (due 2008) of $185,000 will be settled with a note for $71,000 and 7,000 shares of the stock contributed by the owners.
   - Note payable (due 2009) of $200,000 will be settled with a note for $110,000.

   The company has a reorganization value of $780,000.

   Prepare all journal entries for Ristoni so that the company can emerge from the bankruptcy proceeding.

37. Smith Corporation has gone through bankruptcy and is ready to emerge as a reorganized entity on December 31, 2007. On this date, the company has the following assets (fair value is based on the discounted future cash flows that are anticipated):

	Book Value	Fair Value
Accounts receivable	$ 20,000	$ 18,000
Inventory	143,000	111,000
Land and buildings	250,000	278,000
Machinery	144,000	121,000
Patents	100,000	125,000

   The company has a reorganization value of $800,000.

   The company has 50,000 shares of $10 par value common stock outstanding. A deficit Retained Earnings balance of $670,000 also is reported. The owners will distribute 30,000 shares of this stock as part of the reorganization plan.

   The company's liabilities will be settled as follows:
   - Accounts payable of $180,000 (existing at the date on which the order for relief was granted) will be settled with an 8 percent, two-year note for $35,000.

- Accounts payable of $97,000 (incurred since the date on which the order for relief was granted) will be paid in the regular course of business.
- Note payable—First Metropolitan Bank of $200,000 will be settled with an 8 percent, five-year note for $50,000 and 15,000 shares of the stock contributed by the owners.
- Note payable—Northwestern Bank of Tulsa of $350,000 will be settled with a 7 percent, eight-year note for $100,000 and 15,000 shares of the stock contributed by the owners.

  a. How does Smith Corporation's accountant know that fresh start accounting must be utilized?

  b. Prepare a balance sheet for Smith Corporation upon its emergence from reorganization.

38. Ambrose Corporation reports the following information:

	Book Value	Liquidation Value
Assets pledged with fully secured creditors	$220,000	$245,000
Assets pledged with partially secured creditors	111,000	103,000
Other assets	140,000	81,000
Liabilities with priority	36,000	
Fully secured liabilities	200,000	
Partially secured liabilities	180,000	
Accounts payable (unsecured)	283,000	

   In liquidation, what amount of cash should each class of liabilities expect to collect?

39. The following balance sheet has been prepared by the accountant for Limestone Company as of June 3, 2007, the date on which the company is to file a voluntary petition of bankruptcy:

LIMESTONE COMPANY
Balance Sheet
June 3, 2007

Assets

Cash	$ 3,000
Accounts receivable (net)	65,000
Inventory	88,000
Land	100,000
Buildings (net)	300,000
Equipment (net)	180,000
Total assets	$736,000

Liabilities and Equities

Accounts payable	$ 98,000
Notes payable—current (secured by equipment)	250,000
Notes payable—long term (secured by land and buildings)	190,000
Common stock	120,000
Retained earnings	78,000
Total liabilities and equities	$736,000

Additional Information:

- If the company is liquidated, administrative expenses are estimated at $18,000.
- The Accounts Payable figure includes $10,000 in wages earned by the company's 12 employees during May. No one earned more than $2,200.
- Liabilities do not include taxes of $14,000 owed to the U.S. government.
- Company officials estimate that 40 percent of the accounts receivable will be collected in a liquidation and that the inventory disposal will bring $80,000. The land and buildings are to be sold together for approximately $310,000; the equipment should bring $130,000 at auction.

Prepare a statement of financial affairs for Limestone Company as of June 3, 2007.

40. Creditors of Jones Corporation are considering petitioning the courts to force the company into Chapter 7 bankruptcy. The following information has been determined. Administrative expenses in

connection with the liquidation are estimated to be $22,000. Indicate the amount of money that each class of creditors can anticipate receiving.

	Book Value	Net Realizable Value
Cash	$ 6,000	$ 6,000
Accounts receivable	32,000	18,000
Inventory	45,000	31,000
Supplies	3,000	–0–
Investments	2,000	8,000
Land	60,000	72,000
Buildings	90,000	68,000
Equipment	50,000	35,000
Notes payable (secured by land)	65,000	
Notes payable (secured by buildings)	78,000	
Bonds payable (secured by equipment)	115,000	
Accounts payable	70,000	
Salary payable (two weeks' salary for the four employees)	6,000	
Taxes payable	10,000	

41. Anteium Company owes $80,000 on a note payable that is currently due. The note is held by a local bank and is secured by a mortgage lien attached to three acres of land worth $48,000. The land originally cost Anteium $31,000 when acquired several years ago. The only other account balances for this company are Investments of $20,000 (but worth $25,000), Accounts Payable of $20,000, Common Stock of $40,000, and a deficit of $89,000. Anteium is insolvent and attempting to arrange a reorganization so that the business can continue to operate. The reorganization value of the company is $82,000.

View each of the following as an independent situation:

a. On a statement of financial affairs, how would this note be reported? How would the land be shown?

b. Assume that Anteium develops an acceptable reorganization plan. Sixty percent of the common stock is transferred to the bank to settle that particular obligation. A 7 percent, three-year note payable for $5,000 is used to settle the accounts payable. How would Anteium record the reorganization?

c. Assume that Anteium is liquidated. The land and investments are sold for $50,000 and $26,000, respectively. Administrative expenses amount to $11,000. How much will the various parties collect?

42. The following balance sheet has been produced for Litz Corporation as of August 8, 2007, the date on which the company is to begin selling assets as part of a corporate liquidation:

LITZ CORPORATION
Balance Sheet
August 8, 2007

Assets

Cash	$ 16,000
Accounts receivable (net)	82,000
Investments	32,000
Inventory (net realizable value is expected to approximate cost)	69,000
Land	30,000
Buildings (net)	340,000
Equipment (net)	210,000
Total assets	$779,000

Liabilities and Equities

Accounts payable	$150,000
Notes payable—current (secured by inventory)	132,000
Notes payable—long term (secured by land and buildings [valued at $300,000])	259,000
Common stock	135,000
Retained earnings	103,000
Total liabilities and equities	$779,000

The following events occur during the liquidation process:

- The investments are sold for $39,000.
- The inventory is sold at auction for $48,000.
- The money derived from the inventory is applied against the current notes payable.
- Administrative expenses of $15,000 are incurred in connection with the liquidation.
- The land and buildings are sold for $315,000. The long-term notes payable are paid.
- The accountant determines that $34,000 of the accounts payable are liabilities with priority.
- The company's equipment is sold for $84,000.
- Accounts receivable of $34,000 are collected. The remainder of the receivables are considered uncollectible.
- The administrative expenses are paid.

a. Prepare a statement of realization and liquidation for the period just described.

b. What percentage of their claims should the unsecured creditors receive?

43. The following balance sheet has been prepared by the accountant of Becket Corporation as of November 10, 2007, the date on which the company is to release a plan for reorganizing operations under Chapter 11 of the Bankruptcy Reform Act:

BECKET CORPORATION
Balance Sheet
November 10, 2007

Assets

Cash	$ 12,000
Accounts receivable (net)	61,000
Investments	26,000
Inventory (net realizable value is expected to approximate 80% of cost)	80,000
Land	57,000
Buildings (net)	248,000
Equipment (net)	117,000
Total assets	$ 601,000

Liabilities and Equities

Accounts payable	$ 129,000
Notes payable—current (secured by equipment)	220,000
Notes payable—(due in 2010) (secured by land and buildings)	325,000
Common stock ($10 par value)	60,000
Retained earnings (deficit)	(133,000)
Total liabilities and equities	$ 601,000

The company presented the following proposal:

- The reorganization value of the company's assets just prior to emerging from bankruptcy is set at $650,000.
- Accounts receivable of $20,000 are written off as uncollectible. Investments are worth $40,000, land is worth $80,000, the buildings are worth $300,000, and the equipment is worth $86,000.
- An outside investor has been found to buy 7,000 shares of common stock at $11 per share.
- The company's investments are to be sold for $40,000 in cash with the proceeds going to the holders of the current note payable. The remainder of these short-term notes will be converted into $130,000 of notes due in 2011 and paying 10 percent annual cash interest.
- All accounts payable will be exchanged for $40,000 in notes payable due in 2008 that pay 8 percent annual interest.
- Title to land costing $20,000 but worth $50,000 will be transferred to the holders of the note payable due in 2010. In addition, these creditors will receive $180,000 in notes payable (paying 10 percent annual interest) coming due in 2014. These creditors also are issued 3,000 shares of previously unissued common stock.

Prepare journal entries for Becket to record the transactions as put forth in this reorganization plan.

44. Oregon Corporation has filed a voluntary petition to reorganize the company under Chapter 11 of the Bankruptcy Reform Act. The creditors are considering an attempt to force liquidation. The company currently holds cash of $6,000 and accounts receivable of $25,000. In addition, the company owns four plots of land. The first two (labeled A and B) cost $8,000 each. Plots C and D cost the company $20,000 and $25,000, respectively. A mortgage lien is attached to each parcel of land as security for four different notes payable of $15,000 each. Presently, the land can be sold for the following:

Plot A	$16,000
Plot B	$11,000
Plot C	$14,000
Plot D	$27,000

Another $25,000 note payable is unsecured. Accounts payable at this time total $32,000. Of this amount, $12,000 is salary owed to the company's workers. No employee is due more than $1,800.

The company expects to collect $12,000 from the accounts receivable if liquidation becomes necessary. Administrative expenses required for liquidation are anticipated to be $16,000.

a. Prepare a statement of financial affairs for Oregon Corporation.

b. If the company is liquidated, how much cash would be paid on the note payable secured by plot B?

c. If the company is liquidated, how much cash would be paid on the note payable that is unsecured?

d. If the company is liquidated and plot D is sold for $30,000, how much cash would be paid on the note payable secured by plot B?

45. Lynch, Inc., is a hardware store operating in Boulder, Colorado. Management recently made some poor inventory acquisitions that have loaded the store with unsalable merchandise. Because of the drop in revenues, the company is now insolvent. The entire inventory can be sold for only $33,000. Following is a trial balance as of March 14, 2007, the day the company files for a Chapter 7 liquidation:

	Debit	Credit
Accounts payable		$ 33,000
Accounts receivable	$ 25,000	
Accumulated depreciation, building		50,000
Accumulated depreciation, equipment		16,000
Additional paid-in capital		8,000
Advertising payable		4,000
Building	80,000	
Cash	1,000	
Common stock		50,000
Equipment	30,000	
Inventory	100,000	
Investments	15,000	
Land	10,000	
Note Payable—Colorado Savings and Loan (secured by lien on land and building)		70,000
Note Payable—First National Bank (secured by equipment)		150,000
Payroll taxes payable		1,000
Retained earnings (deficit)	126,000	
Salary payable (owed equally to two employees)		5,000
Totals	$387,000	$387,000

Company officials believe that 60 percent of the accounts receivable can be collected if the company is liquidated. The building and land have a fair value of $75,000, and the equipment is worth $19,000. The investments represent shares of a nationally traded company that can be sold at the current time for $21,000. Administrative expenses necessary to carry out a liquidation would approximate $16,000.

Prepare a statement of financial affairs for Lynch, Inc., as of March 14, 2007.

46. Use the trial balance presented for Lynch, Inc., in Problem 45. Assume that the company will be liquidated and the following transactions will occur:

    - Accounts receivable of $18,000 are collected with remainder written off.
    - All of the company's inventory is sold for $40,000.
    - Additional accounts payable of $10,000 incurred for various expenses such as utilities and maintenance are discovered.
    - The land and building are sold for $71,000.
    - The note payable due to the Colorado Savings and Loan is paid.
    - The equipment is sold at auction for only $11,000 with the proceeds applied to the note owed to the First National Bank.
    - The investments are sold for $21,000.
    - Administrative expenses total $20,000 as of July 23, 2007, but no payment has yet been made.

    a. Prepare a statement of realization and liquidation for the period from March 14, 2007, through July 23, 2007.

    b. How much cash would be paid to an unsecured, nonpriority creditor that Lynch, Inc., owes a total of $1,000?

47. Holmes Corporation has filed a voluntary petition with the bankruptcy court in hopes of reorganizing the company. A statement of financial affairs has been prepared for the company showing the following debts:

Liabilities with priority:	
Salary payable	$ 18,000
Fully secured creditors:	
Notes payable (secured by land and buildings valued at $84,000)	70,000
Partially secured creditors:	
Notes payable (secured by inventory valued at $30,000)	140,000
Unsecured creditors:	
Notes payable	50,000
Accounts payable	10,000
Accrued expenses	4,000

    Holmes has 10,000 shares of common stock outstanding with a par value of $5 per share. In addition, the company is currently reporting a deficit balance of $132,000.

    Company officials have proposed the following reorganization plan:

    - The company's assets have a total book value of $210,000, an amount considered to be equal to fair value. The reorganization value of the assets as a whole, though, is set at $225,000.
    - Employees will receive a one-year note in lieu of all salaries owed. Interest will be 10 percent, a normal rate for this type of liability.
    - The fully secured note will have all future interest dropped from a 15 percent rate, which is now unrealistic, to a 10 percent rate.
    - The partially secured note payable will be satisfied by signing a new six-year $30,000 note paying 10 percent annual interest. In addition, this creditor will receive 5,000 new shares of Holmes's common stock.
    - An outside investor has been enlisted to buy 6,000 new shares of common stock at $6 per share.
    - The unsecured creditors will be offered 20 cents on the dollar to settle the remaining liabilities.

    If this plan of reorganization is accepted and becomes effective, what journal entries would Holmes Corporation record?

Develop Your Skills

RESEARCH CASE 1

Aberdeen Corporation is considering the possibility of filing a voluntary petition of bankruptcy because of its huge debt load. The company is publicly traded on a national stock exchange and, therefore, company officials are concerned about the role of the Securities and Exchange Commission in this legal action.

Required:

Go to the following Web site: http://www.sec.gov/investor/pubs/bankrupt.htm. List the information that the SEC provides in connection with the bankruptcy of a publicly held company.

RESEARCH CASE 2

An investment analyst has been investigating the long-term prospects of Hawaiian Airlines, Inc. Go to the Hawaiian Airlines Web site (www.hawaiianair.com) and click on "About Us." Then click on "Financial Reports." Finally, click on "2004 Financial Statements." Look over the entire set of financial statements. Focus primarily on Note 2 to the financial statements "Bankruptcy Filing, Liquidation, and Going Concern."

Required:

Write a memo to summarize the information found in this financial statement note and in the rest of the financial statements that could be helpful to the investment analyst.

ANALYSIS CASE 1

Go to the Web site of a company that has recently emerged from a Chapter 11 bankruptcy—for example, Dan River (www.danriver.com), Dow Corning (www.dowcorning.com), or Formica (www.formica.com). By looking at areas of the Web site such as "Investor Information" or "About Us," what information can you determine about the bankruptcy reorganization plan that was approved?

Then go to the Securities and Exchange Commission Web site (www.sec.gov) and enter the name of the same company in the filings search. What information is available from this source about the bankruptcy reorganization plan?

Finally, if available, go to an online index or obtain a hard copy index of *The Wall Street Journal*. Again, search for information that is available concerning this company's bankruptcy reorganization plan.

Required:

Based on these three searches:

1. What were the main provisions of the bankruptcy reorganization plan that brought the company out of Chapter 11?
2. Which of these three sources provided the best information?

ANALYSIS CASE 2

Go to the Web site of a company that is currently in bankruptcy reorganization such as Aloha Airlines (www.alohaairlines.com) or Winn-Dixie Stores (www.winndixie.com).

Required:

By looking at areas of the Web site such as "Investor Information" or "About Us," find what information the company is making available about its current financial difficulties. List the various operations of the company that are being affected.

COMMUNICATIONS CASE 1

If available, go to an online index or obtain a hard copy index of *The Wall Street Journal*. Look up a recent, well-known bankruptcy case such as Kaiser Aluminum, Congoleum, Kmart, or UAL. Search for articles that discuss the issues and problems that led this company to file for bankruptcy.

Required:

Write a short report on that company and the problems and mistakes that led to its insolvency and declaration of bankruptcy. If possible, indicate actions that the company could have taken to avoid its decline into bankruptcy.

COMMUNICATIONS CASE 2

Read the following articles as well as any other published pieces that describe the work of the accountant in bankruptcy cases:

"A New Chapter in Bankruptcy Reform," *Journal of Accountancy,* February 1999.

"The CPA's Role as Bankruptcy Examiner," *CPA Journal,* September 1991.

"Management Accounting—How a Workout Specialist Operates," *Journal of Accountancy,* January 1992.

"The Rewards of Insolvency," *The Practical Accountant,* August 1998.

"When Your Customer Goes Belly-Up," *Journal of Accountancy,* April 1999.

Required:

Write a report describing the services that an accountant can perform during a corporate bankruptcy. Include activities to be carried out prior to filing a petition and thereafter.

Chapter **Fourteen**

Partnerships: Formation and Operation

A reader of college accounting textbooks might well conclude that business activity is carried out exclusively by corporations. Because most large companies are legally incorporated, a vast majority of textbook references and illustrations concern corporate organizations. Contrary to the perception being relayed, partnerships (as well as sole proprietorships) make up a vital element of the business community. The Internal Revenue Service projected that in 2005, nearly 2.7 million partnership income tax returns would be filed (as compared to nearly 6.3 million corporation income tax returns).[1]

The partnership form is found in a wide range of business activities, from small local operations to worldwide enterprises. Examples found in the U.S. economy include these:

- Individual proprietors often join together in the formation of a partnership as a way to reduce expenses, expand services, and add increased expertise. As will be discussed, partnerships also provide important tax benefits.

- Partnerships are a common means by which friends and relatives can easily create and organize a business endeavor.

- Historically doctors, lawyers, and other professionals have formed partnerships because of legal prohibitions against the incorporation of their practices. Although most states now permit alternative forms for such organizations, operating as a partnership or sole proprietorship is still necessary in many areas.

Over the years, some partnerships have grown to enormous sizes. Connell Limited Partnership, for example, recycles and manufactures metal products; in 2004 it had revenues of $1 billion. The international accounting firm of PriceWaterhouseCoopers reported revenues of more than $15 billion.[2] In October 2004, Deloitte Touche Tohmatsu indicated operations in 148 countries[3] and KPMG International reported having more than 94,000 employees.[4]

---

[1] www.irs.gov.

[2] "Forbes Largest Private Companies," *Forbes,* 2004.

[3] www.deloitte.com.

[4] www.kpmg.com.

PARTNERSHIPS—ADVANTAGES AND DISADVANTAGES

The popularity of the partnership format is based on several advantages inherent to this type of organization. An analysis of these attributes explains why nearly 2.7 million enterprises in the United States are partnerships rather than corporations.

One of the most common motives is the ease of formation. Only an oral agreement is necessary to create a legally binding partnership. In contrast, depending on specific state laws, incorporation requires the filing of a formal application and the completion of various other forms and documents. Operators of small businesses may find the convenience and reduced cost involved in creating a partnership to be an especially appealing characteristic. As the American Bar Association noted:

> The principal advantage of partnerships is the ability to make virtually any arrangements defining their relationship to each other that the partners desire. There is no necessity, as there is in a corporation, to have the ownership interest in capital and profits proportionate to the investment made; and losses can be allocated on a different basis from profits. It is also generally much easier to achieve a desirable format for control of the business in a partnership than in a corporation, since the control of a corporation, which is based on ownership of voting stock, is much more difficult to alter.
>
> Partnerships are taxed on a conduit or flow-through basis under subchapter K of the Internal Revenue Code. This means that the partnership itself does not pay any taxes. Instead the net income and various deductions and tax credits from the partnership are passed through to the partners based on their respective percentage interest in the profits and losses of the partnership, and the partners include the income and deductions in their individual tax returns.[5]

Although a detailed investigation of taxation rules and regulations goes beyond the scope of this accounting textbook, a few aspects are quite relevant to the current discussion. One area of the law warrants particular attention: the method by which partnerships are taxed. Although an informational tax return must be filed on an annual basis, *the partnership itself pays no income taxes.* For taxation purposes, the government does not view a partnership as an entity apart from its owners.

Partnership revenue and expense items (as defined by the tax laws) must be assigned directly each year to the individual partners who pay the income taxes. Passing income balances through to the partners in this manner avoids double taxation of the profits that are earned by a business and then distributed to its owners. A corporation's income is taxed twice: when earned and again when conveyed as a dividend. A partnership's income is taxed only at the time that the business initially earned it.

As an illustration, assume that a business earns $100. After paying any income taxes, the remainder is immediately conveyed to its owners. An income tax rate of 30 percent is assumed for both individuals and corporations. Corporate dividends paid to owners, however, are taxed at a 15 percent rate.[6] As the following table shows, if this business is a partnership rather than a corporation, the owners are left with $21 more expendable income, which is 21 percent of the business income. Although significant in amount, this difference narrows as tax rates are lowered.

	Partnership	Corporation
Income before income taxes	$100.00	$100.00
Income taxes paid by business (30%)	–0–	(30.00)
Income distributed to owners	$100.00	$ 70.00
Income taxes paid by owners*	(30.00)	(10.50)
Expendable income	$ 70.00	$ 59.50

* 30% assumed rate on ordinary income.
  15% assumed rate on dividend income.

[5] American Bar Association, *Family Legal Guide,* 3rd ed. (New York: Random House Reference, 2004).

[6] The Jobs and Growth Tax Relief Reconciliation Act of 2003 cut the top tax rate on both dividend income and capital gains to 15 percent through 2008.

Historically, a second tax advantage has long been associated with partnerships. Because income is taxable to the partners as the business earns it, any operating losses can be used to reduce their personal taxable income directly. In contrast, a corporation is viewed as legally separate from its owners, so losses cannot be passed through to them. A corporation has the ability to carry back any net operating losses and reduce previously taxed income (usually for the two prior years) and carry forward remaining losses to decrease future taxable income (for up to 20 years). However, if a corporation is newly formed or has not been profitable, operating losses provide no immediate benefit to a corporation or its owners as losses do for a partnership.

The tax advantage of deducting partnership losses has been reduced somewhat in recent years by changes in the tax laws. Because of the chance to pass through losses and reduce personal taxes, partnerships were often structured as tax shelters to report immediate losses (and, hence, create tax deductions) with profits deferred into the future. Now, ownership of a partnership is labeled as a passive activity unless the partner materially participates in the actual business activities. For tax purposes, passive activity losses serve only to offset other passive activity profits. In most cases, these partnership losses can no longer be used to reduce earned income such as salaries. Thus, unless a taxpayer has significant passive activity income (from rents, for example), losses reported by a partnership create little or no tax advantage unless the partner materially participates in the actual business activity.

The partnership form of business also has certain significant disadvantages. Perhaps the most severe problem is the unlimited liability that each partner automatically incurs. Partnership law specifies that any partner can be held personally liable for *all* debts of the business. The potential risk is especially significant when coupled with the concept of *mutual agency.* This legal term refers to the right that each partner has to incur liabilities in the name of the partnership. Consequently, partners acting within the normal scope of the business have the power to obligate the company for any amount. If the partnership fails to pay these debts, creditors can seek satisfactory remuneration from any partner that they choose.

> Partners are jointly and severally liable for the firm's obligations. As an example, if a bank had made a $10 million loan to the partnership that it could not pay, and the bank obtained a judgment against the partnership, the bank could attempt to attach the assets of any particular partner in the firm. The bank could pick and choose the partners it wished to proceed against in order to satisfy the judgment. If a partner ended up paying more than his or her share, he or she would have a right to recover from the other partners.[7]

This problem is more than just a theoretical concern. As *The Wall Street Journal* noted,

> At least 10 partners of Laventhol & Horwath, a major accounting firm that collapsed two years ago, have filed for personal bankruptcy. They are trying to protect their savings and their homes because partners and principals of the now-defunct firm owe creditors $47.3 million.[8]

Such legal concepts as unlimited liability and mutual agency describe partnership characteristics that have been defined and interpreted over a number of years. To provide consistent application across state lines in regard to these terms as well as many other legal aspects of a partnership, the Uniform Partnership Act (UPA) was created. This act, which was first proposed in 1914 (and revised in 1994), now has been adopted by all states in some form. It establishes uniform standards in such areas as the nature of a partnership, the relationship of the partners to outside parties, and the dissolution of the partnership. For example, Section 6 of the act provide the most common legal definition of a partnership: "an association of two or more persons to carry on a business as co-owners for profit."

ALTERNATIVE LEGAL FORMS

Because of the possible liability, partnerships often experience difficulty in attracting large amounts of capital. Potential partners frequently prefer to avoid the risk that is a basic characteristic of a partnership. However, the tax benefits of avoiding double taxation still provide a

---

[7] An interview with Leslie D. Corwin, Esq., "What's a Partner to Do?" *The CPA Journal,* April 1991, p. 22.

[8] Lee Berton and Joann S. Lublin, "Partnership Structure Is Called in Question as Liability Risk Rises," *The Wall Street Journal,* June 10, 1992, p. A9.

strong pull toward the partnership form. Hence, in recent years, a number of alternative types of organizations have been developed. The availability of these legal forms depends on state laws as well as applicable tax laws. In each case, however, the purpose is to limit the owners' personal liability while providing the tax benefits of a partnership.[9]

Subchapter S Corporation

A Subchapter S Corporation (often referred to as an *S corporation*) is created as a corporation and, therefore, has all of the legal characteristics of that form.[10] According to the U.S. tax laws, if certain regulations are met, the corporation will be taxed in virtually the same way as a partnership. Thus, the Subchapter S corporation pays no income taxes although any income (and losses) pass directly through to the taxable income of the individual owners. This form avoids double taxation, and the owners do not face unlimited liability. To qualify, the business can have only one class of stock and is limited to 75 stockholders. All owners must be individuals, estates, certain tax-exempt entities, or certain types of trusts. The most significant problem associated with this business form is that its growth potential is limited because of the restriction on the number and type of owners.

Limited Partnership (LPs)

A limited partnership is a type of investment designed primarily for individuals who want the tax benefits of a partnership but who do not wish to work in a partnership or have unlimited liability. In such organizations, a number of limited partners invest money as owners but are not allowed to participate in the management of the company. These partners can still incur a loss on their investment, but the amount is restricted to what has been contributed. To protect the creditors of a limited partnership, one or more general partners must be designated to assume responsibility for all obligations created in the name of the business.

Buckeye Partners, L.P. (with annual revenues of more than $208 million), is an example of a limited partnership that trades on the New York Stock Exchange. Buckeye's December 31, 2004, balance sheet reported capital of $2.5 million for the company's general partners whereas the same account showed a total of $605.4 million for its limited partners.

Many limited partnerships were originally formed as tax shelters to create immediate losses (to reduce the taxable income of the partners) with profits spread out into the future. As mentioned earlier, changes in the tax laws to limit the deduction of passive activity losses have significantly reduced the number of limited partnerships being formed.

Limited Liability Partnerships (LLPs)

The limited liability partnership has most of the same characteristics of a general partnership except that it significantly reduces the partners' liability. Partners may lose their investment in the business and are also responsible for the contractual debts of the business. The advantage here is created in connection with any liability resulting from damages. In such cases, the partners are responsible for only their own acts or omissions plus the acts and omissions of individuals under their supervision. Thus, a partner in the Houston office of a public accounting firm would probably not be held liable for a poor audit performed by that firm's San Francisco office. Not surprisingly, limited liability partnerships have become very popular with professional service organizations that have multiple offices. In 1994, for example, all of the five largest accounting firms became LLPs.

Unfortunately, however, the limited liability partnership concept is relatively new and the degree of protection it provides has not been well established legally.

> Arthur Andersen LLP's 1,700 partners could be held personally liable for major chunks of the firm's debts, Enron Corp. creditors asserted in a bankruptcy-court filing Friday. Enron's official committee of unsecured creditors accused Andersen of trying to protect its partners by paying off the firm's ordinary business debts, for which partners are liable, it said. That practice will leave less money to pay malpractice claims, for which most partners cannot be held personally liable, the committee claimed. Enron's creditors have indicated they intend to press claims against Andersen stemming from its botched audit of Enron. Concern has been rampant among partners about whether they will ultimately face personal liability in connection with Enron. Andersen is incorporated in Illinois as a

---

[9] Many factors should be considered in choosing a specific legal form for an organization. The information shown here is merely an overview. For more information, consult a tax guide or a business law textbook.

[10] Unless a corporation qualifies as a Subchapter S corporation or some other legal variation, it is referred to as a *Subchapter C corporation*. Therefore, a vast majority of all businesses are C corporations.

limited-liability partnership, a structure designed to shield partners from firmwide liabilities. But the protection such structures offer has never been tested in a case as large as Andersen's.[11]

Limited Liability Companies (LLCs)

The limited liability company is a new type of organization in the United States although it has long been used in Europe and other areas of the world. It is classified as a partnership for tax purposes. However, depending on state laws, the owners risk only their own investments. In contrast to a Subchapter S corporation, the number of owners is not usually restricted so that growth is easier to accomplish.

PARTNERSHIP ACCOUNTING—CAPITAL ACCOUNTS

Despite legal distinctions, questions should be raised as to the need for an entirely separate study of partnership accounting:

• Does an association of two or more persons require accounting procedures significantly different from those of a corporation?
• Does proper accounting depend on the legal form of an organization?

The answers to these questions are both yes and no. Accounting procedures are normally standardized for assets, liabilities, revenues, and expenses regardless of the legal form of a business. *Partnership accounting, though, does exhibit unique aspects that warrant study, but they lie primarily in the handling of the partners' capital accounts.*

The stockholders' equity accounts of a corporation do not correspond directly with the capital balances found in a partnership's financial records. The various equity accounts reported by an incorporated enterprise display a greater range of information. This characteristic reflects the wide variety of equity transactions that can occur in a corporation as well as the influence of state and federal laws. Government regulation has had enormous effect on the accounting for corporate equity transactions in that extensive disclosure is required to protect stockholders and other outside parties such as potential investors.

To provide adequate information as well as to meet legal requirements, corporate accounting must provide details about numerous equity transactions and account balances. For example, the amount of a corporation's paid-in capital is shown separately from earned capital and other comprehensive income; the par value of each class of stock is disclosed; treasury stock, stock options, stock dividends, and other capital transactions are reported based on prescribed accounting principles.

In comparison, partnerships provide only a limited amount of equity disclosure primarily in the form of individual capital accounts that are accumulated for every partner or every class of partners. These balances measure each partner or group's interest in the book value of the net assets of the business. Thus, the equity section of a partnership balance sheet is composed solely of capital accounts that can be affected by many different events: contributions from partners as well as distributions to them, earnings, and any other equity transactions.

However, no differentiation is drawn in the reporting of a partnership between the various sources of ownership capital. Disclosing the composition of the partners' capital balances has not been judged necessary because partnerships have historically tended to be small with equity transactions that were rarely complex. Additionally, absentee ownership is not common, a factor that minimizes both the need for government regulation and outside interest in detailed information about the capital balances.

Articles of Partnership

Because the demand for information about capital balances is limited, accounting principles specific to partnerships are based primarily on traditional approaches that have evolved over the years rather than on official pronouncements. These procedures attempt to mirror the relationship between the partners and their business especially as defined by the partnership agreement. This legal covenant, which may be either oral or written, is often referred to as the

[11] Mitchell Pacelle, "Creditors Target Andersen's Partners," *The Wall Street Journal,* June 3, 2002, p. A3.

articles of partnership and forms the central governance for the operation of a partnership. The financial arrangements spelled out in this contract establish guidelines for the various capital transactions. Therefore, the articles of partnership, rather than either laws or official rules, provide much of the underlying basis for partnership accounting.

Because the articles of partnership are a negotiated agreement that the partners created, an unlimited number of variations can be encountered in practice. Partners' rights and responsibilities frequently differ from business to business. Consequently, firms often hire accountants in an advisory capacity to participate in creating this document to ensure the equitable treatment of all parties. Although the articles of partnership may contain a number of provisions, an explicit understanding should always be reached in regard to the following:

- Name and address of each partner.
- Business location.
- Description of the nature of the business.
- Rights and responsibilities of each partner.
- Initial contribution to be made by each partner and the method to be used for valuation.
- Specific method by which profits and losses are to be allocated.
- Periodic withdrawal of assets by each partner.
- Procedure for admitting new partners.
- Method for arbitrating partnership disputes.
- Life insurance provisions enabling remaining partners to acquire the interest of any deceased partner.
- Method for settling a partner's share in the business upon withdrawal, retirement, or death.[12]

Accounting for Capital Contributions

Several types of capital transactions occur in a partnership: allocation of profits and losses, retirement of a current partner, admission of a new partner, and so on. The initial transaction, however, is the contribution made by the original partners to begin the business. In the simplest situation, the partners invest only cash amounts. For example, assume that Carter and Green form a business to be operated as a partnership. Carter contributes $50,000 in cash and Green invests $20,000. The initial journal entry to record the creation of this partnership follows:

Cash	70,000	
Carter, Capital		50,000
Green, Capital		20,000
To record cash contributed to start new partnership.		

The assumption that only cash was invested avoids complications in this first illustration. Often, though, one or more of the partners transfers noncash assets such as inventory, land, equipment, or a building to the business. Although fair value is used to record these assets, a case could be developed for initially valuing any contributed asset at the partner's current book value. According to the concept of unlimited liability (as well as present tax laws), a partnership does not exist as an entity apart from its owners. A logical extension of the idea is that the investment of an asset is not a transaction occurring between two independent parties such as would warrant revaluation. This contention holds that the semblance of an arm's-length transaction is necessary to justify a change in the book value of any account.

Although retaining the recorded value for assets contributed to a partnership may seem reasonable, this method of valuation proves to be inequitable to any partner investing appreciated property. A $50,000 capital balance always results from a cash investment of that amount, but recording other assets depends entirely on the original book value.

[12] A complete discussion of the provisions to be included in a partnership agreement can be found in "Get It in Writing," *C A Magazine,* August 1996, and "The Importance of Partnership Agreements," *Journal of Accountancy,* January 1994.

Discussion **Question**

WHAT KIND OF BUSINESS IS THIS?

After graduating from college, Shelley Williams held several different jobs but found that she did not enjoy working for other people. Finally, she and Yvonne Hargrove, her college roommate, decided to start a business of their own. They rented a small building and opened a florist shop selling cut flowers such as roses and chrysanthemums that they bought from a local greenhouse.

Williams and Hargrove agreed orally to share profits and losses equally, although they also decided to take no money from the operation for at least four months. No other arrangements were made, but the business did reasonably well and, after the first four months had passed, each began to draw out $500 in cash every week.

At year's end, they took their financial records to a local accountant so that they could get their income tax returns completed. He informed them that they had been operating as a partnership and that they should draw up a formal articles of partnership agreement or consider incorporation or some other legal form of organization. They confessed that they had never really considered the issue and asked for his advice on the matter.

What advice should the accountant give to these clients?

For example, should a partner who contributes a building having a recorded value of $18,000 but a fair value of $50,000 be credited with only an $18,000 interest in the partnership? Since $50,000 in cash and $50,000 in appreciated property are equivalent contributions, a $32,000 difference in the partners' capital balances cannot be justified. To prevent such inequities, each item transferred to a partnership is initially recorded for external reporting purposes at current value.[13]

Requiring revaluation of contributed assets can, however, be advocated for reasons other than just the fair treatment of all partners. Despite some evidence to the contrary, a partnership can be viewed legitimately as an entity standing apart from its owners. As an example, a partnership maintains legal ownership of its assets and (depending on state law) can instigate lawsuits. For this reason, accounting practice traditionally has held that the contribution of assets (and liabilities) to a partnership is an exchange between two separately identifiable parties that should be recorded based on fair values.

The determination of an appropriate valuation for each capital balance is more than just an accounting exercise. Over the life of a partnership, these figures serve in a number of important capacities:

1. The totals in the individual capital accounts often influence the assignment of profits and losses to the partners.
2. The capital account balance is usually one factor in determining the final distribution that will be received by a partner at the time of withdrawal or retirement.
3. Ending capital balances indicate the allocation to be made of any assets that remain following the liquidation of a partnership.

To demonstrate, assume that Carter invests $50,000 in cash to begin the previously discussed partnership and Green contributes the following assets:

	Book Value to Green	Fair Value
Inventory	$ 9,000	$10,000
Land	14,000	11,000
Building	32,000	46,000
Totals	$55,000	$67,000

[13] For federal income tax purposes, the $18,000 book value is retained as the basis for this building, even after transfer to the partnership. Within the tax laws, no difference is seen between partners and their partnership so that no adjustment to fair value is warranted.

As an added factor, Green's building is encumbered by a $23,600 mortgage that the partnership has agreed to assume.

Green's net investment is equal to $43,400 ($67,000 less $23,600). The following journal entry records the formation of the partnership created by these contributions:

Cash	50,000	
Inventory	10,000	
Land	11,000	
Building	46,000	
Mortgage Payable		23,600
Carter, Capital		50,000
Green, Capital		43,400
To record properties contributed to start partnership. Assets and liabilities are recorded at fair value.		

We should make one additional point before leaving this illustration. Although Green has contributed inventory, land, and a building, this partner holds no further right to these individual assets; they now belong to the partnership. The $43,400 capital balance represents an ownership interest in the business as a whole but does not constitute a specific claim to any asset. Having transferred title to the partnership, Green has no more right to these assets than does Carter.

Intangible Contributions

In forming a partnership, the contributions made by one or more of the partners may go beyond assets and liabilities. A doctor, for example, can bring a particular line of expertise to a partnership, and a practicing dentist might have already developed an established clientele. These attributes, as well as many others, are frequently as valuable to a partnership as cash and fixed assets. *Hence, formal accounting recognition of such special contributions may be appropriately included as a provision of any partnership agreement.*

To illustrate, assume that James and Joyce plan to open an advertising agency and decide to organize the endeavor as a partnership. James contributes cash of $70,000, and Joyce invests only $10,000. Joyce, however, is an accomplished graphic artist, a skill that is considered especially valuable to this business. Therefore, in producing the articles of partnership, the partners agree to start the business with equal capital balances. Often such decisions result only after long, and sometimes heated, negotiations. Because the value assigned to an intangible contribution such as artistic talent is arbitrary at best, proper reporting depends on the ability of the partners to arrive at an equitable arrangement.

In recording this agreement, James and Joyce have two options available: (1) the bonus method and (2) the goodwill method. Each of these approaches achieves the desired result of establishing equal capital account balances. Recorded figures can vary significantly, however, depending on the procedure selected. Thus, the partners should reach an understanding prior to beginning business operations as to the method to be used. The accountant can help avoid conflicts by assisting the partners in evaluating the impact created by each of these two alternatives.

The Bonus Method The bonus method assumes that a specialization such as Joyce's artistic abilities does *not* constitute a recordable partnership asset with a measurable cost. Hence, this approach recognizes only the assets that are physically transferred to the business (such as cash, patents, inventory). Although these contributions determine total partnership capital, the establishment of specific capital balances is viewed as an independent process based solely on the agreement of the partners. Because the initial equity figures are the result of negotiation, they do not need to correspond directly with the individual investments.

James and Joyce have contributed a total of $80,000 in identifiable assets to their partnership and have decided on equal capital balances. According to the bonus method, this agreement is fulfilled simply by splitting the $80,000 capital evenly between the two partners. The following entry records the formation of this partnership under this assumption:

Cash	80,000	
James, Capital		40,000
Joyce, Capital		40,000
To record cash contributions with bonus to Joyce because of artistic abilities.		

Joyce received a capital bonus here of $30,000 (the $40,000 recorded capital balance in excess of the $10,000 cash contribution) from James in recognition of the artistic abilities she brought into the business.

The Goodwill Method   The goodwill method is based on the assumption that an implied value can be calculated mathematically and recorded for any intangible contribution made by a partner. In the present illustration, Joyce invested $60,000 less cash than James but receives an equal amount of capital according to the partnership agreement. Proponents of the goodwill method argue that Joyce's artistic talent has an apparent value of $60,000, a figure that should be included as part of this partner's capital investment. If not recorded, Joyce's primary contribution to the business is ignored completely within the accounting records.

Cash	80,000	
Goodwill	60,000	
James, Capital		70,000
Joyce, Capital		70,000
To record cash contributions with goodwill attributed to Joyce in recognition of artistic abilities.		

Comparison of Methods   Both of these approaches achieve the intent of the partnership agreement: to record equal capital balances despite a difference in the partners' cash contributions. The bonus method allocates the $80,000 invested capital according to the percentages designated by the partners, whereas the goodwill method capitalizes the implied value of Joyce's intangible contribution.

Although nothing prohibits the use of either technique, the recognition of goodwill poses definite theoretical problems. In previous discussions of both the equity method (Chapter 1) and purchase consolidations (Chapter 2), goodwill was recorded but only as a result of an acquisition made by the reporting entity. Consequently, this asset had a historical cost in the traditional accounting sense. Partnership goodwill has no such cost; the business recognizes an asset even though no funds have been spent.

The partnership of James and Joyce, for example, is able to record $60,000 in goodwill without any expenditure. Furthermore, the value attributed to this asset is based solely on a negotiated agreement between the partners; the $60,000 balance has no objectively verifiable basis. Thus, although partnership goodwill is sometimes encountered in actual practice, this "asset" should be viewed with a strong degree of professional skepticism.

Additional Capital Contributions and Withdrawals

Subsequent to the formation of a partnership, the owners may choose to contribute additional capital amounts during the life of the business. These investments can be made to stimulate expansion or to assist the business in overcoming working capital shortages or other problems. Regardless of the reason, the contribution is again recorded as an increment in the partner's capital account based on fair value. For example, in the previous illustration, assume that James decides to invest another $5,000 cash in the partnership to help finance the purchase of new office furnishings. The partner's capital account balance is immediately increased by this amount to reflect the transfer being made to the partnership.

The partners also may reverse this process by withdrawing assets from the business for their own personal use. For example, one partnership, Andersons, reported recently in its financial statements partner withdrawals of $1,759,072 for the year as well as increases in invested capital of $733,675. To protect the interests of the other partners, the amount and timing of such withdrawals should be clearly specified in the articles of partnership.

In many instances, the articles of partnership allow withdrawals on a regular periodic basis as a reward for ownership or as compensation for work done in the business. Often such distributions are recorded initially in a separate drawing account that is closed into the individual partner's capital account at year-end. Assume, for illustration purposes, that James and Joyce take out $1,200 and $1,500, respectively, from their business. The journal entry to record these payments is as follows:

James, Drawing	1,200	
Joyce, Drawing	1,500	
Cash		2,700
To record withdrawal of cash by partners.		

Larger amounts might also be withdrawn from a partnership on occasion. A partner may have a special need for money or just desire to reduce the basic investment that has been made in the business. Such transactions are usually sporadic occurrences and entail amounts significantly higher than the partner's periodic drawing. Prior approval by the other partners may be required by the articles of partnership.

Allocation of Income

At the end of each fiscal period, partnership revenues and expenses are closed out with the resulting net income or loss being reclassified to the partners' capital accounts. Because a separate capital balance is maintained for each partner, a method must be devised for this assignment of annual income. Because of the importance of the process, the procedure established by the partners should always be stipulated in the articles of partnership. If no arrangement has been specified, state partnership law normally holds that all partners receive an equal allocation of any income or loss earned by the business. If an agreement has been set forth specifying only the division of profits, any subsequent losses must be divided in that same manner.

An allocation pattern can be extremely important to the success of an organization because it can help emphasize and reward outstanding performance.

> The goal of a partner compensation plan is to inspire each principal's most profitable performance—and make a firm grow. When a CPA firm's success depends on partner contributions other than accounting expertise—such as bringing in business, developing a specialty or being a good manager—its compensation plan has to encourage those qualities, for both fairness and firm health.[14]

Actual procedures for allocating profits and losses can range from the simple to the elaborate.[15]

> Our system is as follows: a base draw to all partners, which grows over an eight-year period from 0.63x to a maximum of x, to which is added a 7 percent return on our accrual capital and our intangible capital. (Intangible capital is defined as the goodwill of the firm valued at 75 percent of gross revenues.) A separate pool of funds (about 20 percent of our compensation) is reserved for the performance pool. Each partner assesses how his or her goals helped firm goals for the year, reviews the other partners' assessment reports and then prepares an allocation schedule. Bonus pool shares are based on a group vote.[16]

Partnerships can avoid all complications by assigning net income on an equal basis among all partners. Other organizations attempt to devise plans that reward such factors as the expertise of

---

[14] Michael Hayes, "Pay for Performance," *Journal of Accountancy,* June 2002, p. 24.

[15] See, for example, "Selecting the Best Partner Compensation Method," *Journal of Accountancy,* December 1991, pp. 40–44; or Hayes, "Pay for Performance," pp. 24–28.

[16] Richard Kretz, "You Want to Minimize the Pain," *Journal of Accountancy,* June 2002, p. 28.

Discussion **Question**

HOW WILL THE PROFITS BE SPLIT?

James J. Dewars has been the sole owner of a small CPA firm for the past 20 years. Now 52 years old, Dewars is concerned about the continuation of his practice after he retires. He would like to begin taking more time off now although he wants to remain active in the firm for at least another 8 to 10 years. He has worked hard over the decades to build up the practice so that he presently makes a profit of $180,000 annually.

Lewis Huffman has been working for Dewars for the past four years. He now earns a salary of $68,000 per year. He is a very dedicated employee who generally works 44 to 60 hours per week. In the past, Dewars has been in charge of the larger, more profitable audit clients whereas Huffman, with less experience, worked with the smaller clients. Both Dewars and Huffman do some tax work although that segment of the business has never been emphasized.

Sally Scriba has been employed for the past seven years with another CPA firm as a tax specialist. She has no auditing experience but has a great reputation in tax planning and preparation. She currently earns an annual salary of $80,000.

Dewars, Huffman, and Scriba are negotiating the creation of a new CPA firm as a partnership. Dewars plans to reduce his time in this firm although he will continue to work with many of the clients that he has served for the past two decades. Huffman will begin to take over some of the major audit jobs. Scriba will start to develop an extensive tax practice for the firm.

Because of the changes in the firm, the three potential partners anticipate earning a total net income in the first year of operations of between $130,000 and $260,000. Thereafter, they hope that profits will increase at the rate of 10 to 20 percent annually for the next five years or so.

How should this new partnership allocate its future net income among these partners?

the individuals, number of years with the organization, or the amount of time that each works. Some agreements also consider the capital invested in the business as an element that should be recognized within the allocation process.

As an initial illustration, assume that Tinker, Evers, and Chance form a partnership by investing cash of $120,000, $90,000, and $75,000, respectively. The articles of partnership agreement specifies that Evers will be allotted 40 percent of all profits and losses because of previous business experience. Tinker and Chance are to divide the remaining 60 percent equally. This agreement also stipulates that each partner is allowed to withdraw $10,000 in cash annually from the business. The amount of this withdrawal does not directly depend on the method utilized for income allocation. *From an accounting perspective, the assignment of income and the setting of withdrawal limits are two separate decisions.*

At the end of the first year of operations, the partnership reports net income of $60,000. To reflect the changes made in the partners' capital balances, the closing process consists of the following two journal entries. The assumption is made here that each partner has taken the allowed amount of drawing during the year. In addition, for convenience, all revenues and expenses already have been closed into the Income Summary account.

Tinker, Capital	10,000	
Evers, Capital	10,000	
Chance, Capital	10,000	
Tinker, Drawing		10,000
Evers, Drawing		10,000
Chance, Drawing		10,000
To close out drawing accounts recording payments made to the three partners.		

Income Summary	60,000	
Tinker, Capital (30%)		18,000
Evers, Capital (40%)		24,000
Chance, Capital (30%)		18,000
To allocate net income based on provisions of partnership agreement.		

Statement of Partners' Capital

Because a partnership does not separately disclose a retained earnings balance, the statement of retained earnings usually reported by a corporation is replaced by a statement of partners' capital. The following financial statement is based on the data presented for the partnership of Tinker, Evers, and Chance. The changes made during the year in the individual capital accounts are outlined along with totals representing the partnership as a whole:

TINKER, EVERS, AND CHANCE
Statement of Partners' Capital
For Year Ending December 31, Year 1

	Tinker, Capital	Evers, Capital	Chance, Capital	Totals
Capital balances beginning of year	$120,000	$ 90,000	$ 75,000	$285,000
Allocation of net income	18,000	24,000	18,000	60,000
Drawings	(10,000)	(10,000)	(10,000)	(30,000)
Capital balances end of year	$128,000	$104,000	$ 83,000	$315,000

Alternative Allocation Techniques—Example 1

Assigning net income based on a ratio may be simple, but this approach is not necessarily equitable to all partners. For example, assume that Tinker does not participate in the operations of the partnership but is the contributor of the largest amount of capital. Evers and Chance both work full-time in the business, but Evers has considerably more experience in this line of work.

Under these circumstances, no single ratio is likely to reflect properly the various contributions made by each partner. Indeed, an unlimited number of alternative allocation plans could be devised in hope of achieving fair treatment for all parties. For example, because of the different levels of capital being invested, consideration should be given to including interest within the allocation process to reward the contributions. A compensation allowance is also a possibility, usually in an amount corresponding to the number of hours worked or the level of a partner's business expertise.

To demonstrate one possible option, assume that Tinker, Evers, and Chance begin their partnership based on the facts presented originally except that they arrive at a more detailed method of allocating profits and losses. After considerable negotiation, an articles of partnership agreement credits each partner annually for interest in an amount equal to 10 percent of that partner's beginning capital balance for the year. Evers and Chance also will be allotted $15,000 each as a compensation allowance in recognition of their participation in daily operations. Any remaining profit or loss will be split 4:3:3, with the largest share going to Evers because of the work experience that this partner brings to the business. As with any appropriate allocation, this pattern attempts to provide fair treatment for all three partners.

Under this arrangement, the $60,000 net income earned by the partnership in the first year of operation would be prorated as follows. The sequential alignment of the various provisions is irrelevant except that the ratio, which is used to assign the remaining profit or loss, must be calculated last.

	Tinker	Evers	Chance	Totals
Interest (10% of beginning capital)	$12,000	$ 9,000	$ 7,500	$28,500
Compensation allowance . . .	–0–	15,000	15,000	30,000
Remaining income:				
$ 60,000				
(28,500)				
(30,000)				
$ 1,500	450 (30%)	600 (40%)	450 (30%)	1,500
Totals	$12,450	$24,600	$22,950	$60,000

For the partnership of Tinker, Evers, and Chance, the allocations just calculated lead to the following year-end closing entry:

Income Summary	60,000	
Tinker, Capital		12,450
Evers, Capital		24,600
Chance, Capital		22,950
To allocate income for the year to the individual partner's capital accounts based on partnership agreement.		

Alternative Allocation Techniques—Example 2

As the preceding illustration indicates, the assignment process is no more than a series of mechanical steps reflecting the change in each partner's capital balance resulting from the provisions of the partnership agreement. The number of different allocation procedures that could be employed is limited solely by the partners' imagination. Although interest, compensation allowances, and various ratios are the predominant factors encountered in practice, other possibilities exist. Therefore, another approach to the allocation process is presented to further illustrate some of the variations that can be utilized. A two-person partnership is used here to simplify the computations.

Assume that Webber and Rice formed a partnership in 1993 to operate a bookstore. Webber contributed the initial capital, and Rice managed the business. With the assistance of their accountant, they wrote an articles of partnership agreement that contains the following provisions:

1. Each partner is allowed to draw $1,000 in cash from the business every month. Any withdrawal in excess of that figure will be accounted for as a direct reduction to the partner's capital balance.

2. Partnership profits and losses will be allocated each year according to the following plan:

    a. Each partner will earn 15 percent interest based on the monthly average capital balance for the year (calculated without regard for normal drawings or current income).

    b. As a reward for operating the business, Rice is to receive credit for a bonus equal to 20 percent of the year's net income. However, no bonus is earned if the partnership reports a net loss.

    c. The two partners will divide any remaining profit or loss equally.

Assume that Webber and Rice subsequently begin the year 2007 with capital balances of $150,000 and $30,000, respectively. On April 1 of that year, Webber invests an additional $8,000 cash in the business, and on July 1, Rice withdraws $6,000 in excess of the specified drawing allowance. Assume further that the partnership reports income of $30,000 for 2007.

Because the interest factor established in this allocation plan is based on a monthly average figure, the specific amount to be credited to each partner is determined by means of a preliminary calculation:

Webber—Interest Allocation

Beginning balance:	$150,000 × 3 months =	$ 450,000	
Balance, 4/1/07:	$158,000 × 9 months =	1,422,000	
		1,872,000	
		× ¹⁄₁₂	
Monthly average capital balance		156,000	
Interest rate		× 15%	
Interest credited to Webber		$ 23,400	

Rice—Interest Allocation

Beginning balance:	$30,000 × 6 months =	$180,000	
Balance, 7/1/07:	$24,000 × 6 months =	144,000	
		324,000	
		× ¹⁄₁₂	
Monthly average capital balance		27,000	
Interest rate		× 15%	
Interest credited to Rice		$ 4,050	

Following this initial computation, the actual assignment of income can proceed according to the provisions specified in the articles of partnership. The stipulations drawn up by Webber and Rice must be followed exactly, even though the business's $30,000 profit in 2007 is not sufficient to cover both the interest and the bonus. Income allocation is a mechanical process that should always be carried out as stated in the articles of partnership without regard to the specific level of income or loss.

Based on the plan that was created, Webber's capital increases by $21,675 during 2007 but Rice's account increases by only $8,325:

	Webber	Rice	Totals
Interest (above)	$23,400	$ 4,050	$27,450
Bonus (20% × $30,000)	–0–	6,000	6,000
Remaining income (loss):			
$ 30,000			
(27,450)			
(6,000)			
$ (3,450)	(1,725) (50%)	(1,725) (50%)	(3,450)
Totals	$21,675	$ 8,325	$30,000

ACCOUNTING FOR PARTNERSHIP DISSOLUTION

Many partnerships limit capital transactions almost exclusively to contributions, drawings, and profit and loss allocations. Normally, though, over any extended period, changes occur in the members who make up a partnership. Employees may be promoted into the partnership or new owners brought in from outside the organization to add capital or expertise to the business. Current partners eventually retire, die, or simply elect to leave the partnership. Large operations may even experience such changes on a routine basis. One international accounting firm has estimated that 50 to 70 partners leave the organization each year for a variety of reasons. That, apparently, is not an isolated situation; "major accounting firms have gotten rid of between 5 percent and 14 percent of their partners over the past 18 months."[17]

Regardless of the nature or the frequency of the event, any alteration in the specific individuals composing a partnership automatically leads to legal dissolution. In many instances,

[17] Berton and Lublin, "Partnership Structure," p. A9.

the breakup is merely a prerequisite to the formation of a new partnership. For example, if Abernethy and Chapman decide to allow Miller to become a partner in their business, the legally recognized partnership of Abernethy and Chapman has to be dissolved first. The business property as well as the right to future profits can then be conveyed to the newly formed partnership of Abernethy, Chapman, and Miller. The change is a legal change. Actual operations of the business would probably continue unimpeded by this alteration in ownership.

Conversely, should the partners so choose, dissolution can be a preliminary step in the termination and liquidation of the business. The death of a partner, lack of sufficient profits, or internal management differences can lead the partners to break up the partnership business. Under this circumstance, the partnership sells properties, pays debts, and distributes any remaining assets to the individual partners. Thus, in liquidations (which are analyzed in detail in the next chapter), both the partnership and the business cease to exist.

Dissolution—Admission of a New Partner

One of the most prevalent changes in the makeup of a partnership is the addition of a new partner. An employee may have worked for years to gain this opportunity, or a prospective partner might offer the new investment capital or business experience necessary for future business success. An individual can gain admittance to a partnership in one of two ways: (1) by purchasing an ownership interest from a current partner or (2) by contributing assets directly to the business.

In recording either type of transaction, the accountant has the option, once again, to retain the book value of all partnership assets and liabilities (as exemplified by the bonus method) or revalue these accounts to their present fair values (the goodwill method). The decision as to a theoretical preference between the bonus and goodwill methods hinges on one single question: *Should the dissolved partnership and the newly formed partnership be viewed as two separate reporting entities?*

If the new partnership is merely an extension of the old, no basis exists for restatement. The transfer of ownership is a change only in a legal sense and has no direct impact on business assets and liabilities. However, if the continuation of the business represents a legitimate transfer of property from one partnership to another, revaluation of all accounts and recognition of goodwill can be justified.

Because both approaches are encountered in practice, this textbook presents each. However, the concerns previously discussed in connection with partnership goodwill still exist: Recognition is not based on historical cost and no objective verification of the amount being capitalized can be made. One alternative revaluation approach that attempts to circumvent the problems involved with partnership goodwill has been devised. This hybrid method revalues all partnership assets and liabilities to fair value without making any corresponding recognition of goodwill.

Admission through Purchase of a Current Interest

As mentioned, one method of gaining admittance to a partnership is by the purchase of a current interest. One or more partners can choose to sell their portion of the business to an outside party. This type of transaction is most common in operations that rely primarily on monetary capital rather than on the business expertise of the partners.

In making a transfer of ownership, a partner can actually convey only three rights:

1. *The right of co-ownership in the business property.* This right justifies the partner's periodic drawings from the business as well as the distribution settlement paid at liquidation or at the time of a partner's withdrawal.
2. *The right to share in profits and losses as specified in the articles of partnership.*
3. *The right to participate in the management of the business.*

Unless restricted by the articles of partnership, every partner has the power to sell or assign the first two of these rights at any time. Their transfer poses no threat of financial harm to the remaining partners. In contrast, partnership law states that the right to participate in the management of the business can be conveyed only with the consent of all partners. This particular right is considered essential to the future earning power of the enterprise as well as the maintenance of business assets. Therefore, current partners are protected from the intrusion of parties who might be considered detrimental to the management of the company.

As an illustration, assume that Scott, Thompson, and York formed a partnership several years ago. Subsequently, York decides to leave the partnership and offers to sell his interest to Morgan. Although York may transfer the right of property ownership as well as the specified share of future profits and losses, the partnership does not automatically admit Morgan. York legally remains a partner until such time as both Scott and Thompson agree to allow Morgan to participate in the management of the business.

To demonstrate the accounting procedures applicable to the transfer of a partnership interest, assume that the following information is available relating to the partnership of Scott, Thompson, and York:

Partner	Capital Balance	Profit and Loss Ratio
Scott	$ 50,000	20%
Thompson	30,000	50
York	20,000	30
Total capital	$100,000	

As often happens, the relationship of the capital accounts to one another does not correspond with the partners' profit and loss ratio. Capital balances are historical cost figures. They result from contributions and withdrawals made throughout the life of the business as well as from the allocation of partnership income. Therefore, any correlation between a partner's recorded capital at a particular point in time and the profit and loss percentage would probably be coincidental. Scott, for example, has 50 percent of the current partnership capital ($50,000/$100,000) but is entitled to only a 20 percent allocation of income.

Instead of York selling his interest to Morgan, assume that each of these three partners elects to transfer a 20 percent interest to Morgan for a total payment of $30,000. According to the sales contract, *the money is to be paid directly to the owners.*

One approach to recording this transaction is that, because Morgan's purchase is carried out between the individual parties, the acquisition has no impact on the assets and liabilities the partnership holds. Because the business is not involved directly, the transfer of ownership requires a simple capital reclassification without any accompanying revaluation. Book value is retained. This approach is similar to the bonus method; only a legal change in ownership is occurring so that neither revaluation of assets or liabilities nor goodwill is appropriate.

Book Value Approach		
Scott, Capital (20% of capital balance)	10,000	
Thompson, Capital (20%)	6,000	
York, Capital (20%)	4,000	
Morgan, Capital (20% of total)		20,000
To reclassify capital to reflect Morgan's acquisition. Money is paid directly to partners.		

An alternative for recording this acquisition by Morgan relies on a different perspective of the new partner's admission. Legally, the partnership of Scott, Thompson, and York is transferring all assets and liabilities to the partnership of Scott, Thompson, York, and Morgan. Therefore, according to the logic underlying the goodwill method, a transaction is occurring between two separate reporting entities, an event that necessitates the complete revaluation of all assets and liabilities.

Because Morgan is paying $30,000 for a 20 percent interest in the partnership, the implied value of the business as a whole is $150,000 ($30,000/20%). However, the book value is only $100,000; thus, a $50,000 upward revaluation is indicated. This adjustment is reflected by restating specific partnership asset and liability accounts to fair value with any remaining balance being recorded as goodwill. After the implied value of the partnership is established, the reclassification of ownership can be recorded based on the new capital balances.

Goodwill (Revaluation) Approach		
Goodwill (or specific accounts)	50,000	
Scott, Capital (20% of goodwill)		10,000
Thompson, Capital (50%)		25,000
York, Capital (30%)		15,000
To recognize goodwill and revaluation of assets and liabilities based on value of business implied by size of Morgan's purchase price.		
Scott, Capital (20% of new capital balance)	12,000	
Thompson, Capital (20%)	11,000	
York, Capital (20%)	7,000	
Morgan, Capital (20% of new total)		30,000
To reclassify capital to reflect Morgan's acquisition. Money is paid directly to partners.		

As this entry indicates, the $50,000 revaluation is credited to the original partners based on the profit and loss ratio rather than on their percentages of capital. Recognition of goodwill (or an increase in the book value of specific accounts) indicates that unrecorded gains have accrued to the business during the previous years of operation. Therefore, the equitable treatment is to allocate this increment among the partners according to their profit and loss percentages.

Admission by a Contribution Made to the Partnership

Entrance into a partnership is not limited solely to the purchase of a current partner's interest. An outsider may be admitted to the ownership by contributing cash or other assets directly to the business rather than to the partners. For example, assume that King and Wilson maintain a partnership and presently report capital balances of $80,000 and $20,000, respectively. According to the articles of partnership, King is entitled to 60 percent of all profits and losses with the remaining 40 percent credited each year to Wilson. By agreement of the partners, Simpson is being allowed to enter the partnership for a payment of $20,000 *with this money going into the business.* Based on negotiations that preceded the acquisition, all parties have agreed that Simpson receives an initial 10 percent interest in partnership property.

Bonus Credited to Original Partners   The bonus (or no revaluation) method maintains the same recorded value for all partnership assets and liabilities despite Simpson's admittance. The capital balance for this new partner is simply set at the appropriate 10 percent level based on the book value of the partnership taken as a whole (after the payment is recorded). Because $20,000 is being invested, total reported capital increases to $120,000. Thus, Simpson's 10 percent interest is computed as $12,000. *The $8,000 difference between the amount contributed and this allotted capital balance is viewed as a bonus.* Because Simpson is willing to accept a capital balance that is less than the investment being made, this bonus is attributed to the original partners (again based on their profit and loss ratio). As a result of the nature of the transaction, no need exists to recognize goodwill or revalue any of the assets or liabilities.

Cash	20,000	
Simpson, Capital (10% of total capital)		12,000
King, Capital (60% of bonus)		4,800
Wilson, Capital (40% of bonus)		3,200
To record Simpson's entrance into partnership with $8,000 extra payment recorded as a bonus to the original partners.		

Goodwill Credited to Original Partners   The goodwill method views Simpson's payment as evidence that the partnership as a whole possesses an actual value of $200,000 ($20,000/10%). Because, even with the new partner's investment, only $120,000 in net assets is being reported, a valuation adjustment of $80,000 is implied.[18] Over the previous years, unrecorded gains have apparently accrued to the business. This $80,000 figure might reflect the need to revalue specific accounts such as inventory or equipment, although the entire amount, or some portion of it, may simply be recorded as goodwill.

Goodwill (or specific accounts)	80,000	
King, Capital (60% of goodwill)		48,000
Wilson, Capital (40%)		32,000
To recognize goodwill based on Simpson's purchase price.		
Cash	20,000	
Simpson, Capital		20,000
To record Simpson's admission into partnership.		

Comparison of Bonus Method and Goodwill Method   Completely different capital balances as well as asset and liability figures result from these two approaches. In both cases, however, the new partner is credited with the appropriate 10 percent of total partnership capital.

	Bonus Method	Goodwill Method
Assets less liabilities (as reported)	$100,000	$100,000
Simpson's contribution	20,000	20,000
Goodwill	–0–	80,000
Total	$120,000	$200,000
Simpson's capital	$ 12,000	$ 20,000

Because Simpson contributed an amount more than 10 percent of the resulting book value of the partnership, this business is perceived as being worth more than the recorded accounts presently indicate. Therefore, the bonus in the first instance and the goodwill in the second were both assumed as accruing to the two original partners. Such a presumption is not unusual in an established business, especially if profitable operations have developed over a number of years.

Hybrid Method of Recording Admission of New Partner   One other approach to the admission of Simpson can be devised. Assume that the assets and liabilities of the King and Wilson partnership have a book value of $100,000 as stated earlier. Also assume that a piece of land held by the business is actually worth $30,000 more than its currently recorded book value. Thus, the identifiable assets of the partnership are worth $130,000. Simpson pays $20,000 for a 10 percent interest.

In this approach, the identifiable assets (such as land) are revalued but no goodwill is recognized.

Land	30,000	
King, Capital (60% of revaluation)		18,000
Wilson, Capital (40%)		12,000
To record current fair value of land in preparation for admission of new partner.		

[18] Because the $20,000 is being put into the business in this example, total capital to be used in the goodwill computation has increased to $120,000. If, as in the previous illustration, payment had been made directly to the partners, the original capital of $100,000 is retained in determining goodwill.

The admission of Simpson and the payment of $20,000 bring the total capital balance to $150,000. Because Simpson is acquiring a 10 percent interest, a capital balance of $15,000 is recorded. The extra $5,000 payment ($20,000 − $15,000) is attributed as a bonus to the original partners. In this way, asset revaluation and a capital bonus are both used to align the accounts.

Cash	20,000	
Simpson, Capital (10% of total capital)		15,000
King, Capital (60% of bonus)		3,000
Wilson, Capital (40% of bonus)		2,000
To record entrance of Simpson into partnership and bonus assigned to original partners.		

Bonus or Goodwill Credited to New Partner   As previously discussed, Simpson also may be contributing some attribute other than tangible assets to this partnership. Therefore, the articles of partnership may be written to credit the new partner, rather than the original partners, with either a bonus or goodwill. Because of an excellent professional reputation, valuable business contacts, or myriad other possible factors, Simpson might be able to negotiate a beginning capital balance in excess of the $20,000 cash contribution. This same circumstance may also result if the business is desperate for new capital and is willing to offer favorable terms as an enticement to the potential partner.

To illustrate, assume that Simpson receives a 20 percent interest in the partnership (rather than the originally stated 10 percent) in exchange for the $20,000 cash investment. The specific rationale for the higher ownership percentage need not be identified.

The bonus method sets Simpson's initial capital at $24,000 (20 percent of the $120,000 book value). To achieve this balance, a capital bonus of $4,000 must be credited to Simpson and taken from the present partners:

Cash	20,000	
King, Capital (60% of bonus)	2,400	
Wilson, Capital (40% of bonus)	1,600	
Simpson, Capital		24,000
To record Simpson's entrance into partnership with reduced payment reported as a bonus from original partners.		

If goodwill rather than a bonus is attributed to the *entering partner,* a mathematical problem arises in determining the implicit value of the business as a whole. In the current illustration, Simpson paid $20,000 for a 20 percent interest. Therefore, the value of the company is calculated as only $100,000 ($20,000/20%), a figure that is less than the $120,000 in net assets being reported after the new contribution. Negative goodwill appears to exist. One possibility is that individual partnership assets are overvalued and require reduction. As an alternative, the cash contribution might not be an accurate representation of the new partner's investment. Simpson could be bringing an intangible contribution (goodwill) to the business along with the $20,000. This additional amount must be determined algebraically:

$$\text{Simpson's capital} = 20 \text{ percent of partnership capital}$$

Therefore

$$\$20,000 + \text{Goodwill} = 0.20\,(\$100,000 + \$20,000 + \text{Goodwill})$$
$$\$20,000 + \text{Goodwill} = \$20,000 + \$4,000 + 0.20\,\text{Goodwill}$$
$$0.80\,\text{Goodwill} = \$4,000$$
$$\text{Goodwill} = \$5,000$$

If the partners determine that Simpson is, indeed, making an intangible contribution (a particular skill, for example, or a loyal clientele), Simpson should be credited with a $25,000 capital investment: $20,000 cash and $5,000 goodwill. When added to the original $100,000 in net assets reported by the partnership, this contribution raises the total capital for the business to $125,000. As the articles of partnership specified, Simpson's interest now represents a 20 percent share of the partnership ($25,000/$125,000).

Recognizing $5,000 in goodwill has established the proper relationship between the new partner and the partnership. Therefore, the following journal entry should be recorded to reflect this transaction:

Cash	20,000	
Goodwill	5,000	
Simpson, Capital		25,000
To record Simpson's entrance into partnership with goodwill attributed to this new partner.		

Dissolution—Withdrawal of a Partner

Admission of a new partner is not the only method by which a partnership can undergo a change in composition. Over the life of the business, partners might leave the organization. Death or retirement can occur, or a partner may simply elect to withdraw from the partnership. The articles of partnership also can allow for the expulsion of a partner under certain conditions. Once again, any change in membership legally dissolves the partnership, although the business's operations usually continue uninterrupted under the ownership of the remaining partners.

Regardless of the reason for dissolution, some method of establishing an equitable settlement of the withdrawing partner's interest in the business is necessary. Often, the partner (or the partner's estate) may simply sell the interest to an outside party, with approval, or to one or more of the remaining partners. As an alternative, the business can distribute cash or other assets as a means of settling a partner's right of co-ownership. Consequently, many partnerships hold life insurance policies solely to provide adequate cash to liquidate a partner's interest upon death.

Whether death or some other reason caused the withdrawal, a final distribution will not necessarily equal the book value of the partner's capital account. A capital balance is only a recording of historical transactions and rarely represents the true value inherent in a business. Instead, payment is frequently based on the value of the partner's interest as ascertained by either negotiation or appraisal. Because the determination of a settlement can be derived in many ways, the articles of partnership should contain exact provisions regulating this procedure.

The withdrawal of an individual partner and the resulting distribution of partnership property can, as before, be accounted for by either the bonus (no revaluation) method or the goodwill (revaluation) method. Once again, a hybrid option is also available.

As in earlier illustrations, if a bonus is recorded, the amount can be attributed to either of the parties involved: the withdrawing partner or the remaining partners. Conversely, any revaluation of partnership property (as well as the establishment of a goodwill balance) is allocated among all partners to recognize possible unrecorded gains. The hybrid approach restates assets and liabilities to fair value but does not record goodwill. This last alternative reflects the legal change in ownership but avoids the theoretical problems associated with partnership goodwill.

Accounting for the Withdrawal of a Partner—Illustration

To demonstrate the various approaches that can be taken to account for a partner's withdrawal, assume that the partnership of Duncan, Smith, and Windsor has existed for a number of years.

At the present time, the partners have the following capital balances as well as the indicated profit and loss percentages:

Partner	Capital Balance	Profit and Loss Ratio
Duncan	$ 70,000	50%
Smith	20,000	30
Windsor	10,000	20
Total capital	$100,000	

Windsor decides to withdraw from the partnership, but Duncan and Smith plan to continue operating the business. As per the original partnership agreement, a final settlement distribution for any withdrawing partner is computed based on the following specified provisions:

1. An independent expert will appraise the business to determine its estimated fair value.
2. Any individual who leaves the partnership will receive cash or other assets equal to that partner's current capital balance after including an appropriate share of any adjustment indicated by the previous valuation. The allocation of unrecorded gains and losses is based on the normal profit and loss ratio.

Following Windsor's decision to withdraw from the partnership, its property is immediately appraised. Total fair value is estimated at $180,000, a figure $80,000 in excess of book value. According to this valuation, land held by the partnership is currently worth $50,000 more than its original cost. In addition, $30,000 in goodwill is attributed to the partnership based on the value of the business as a going concern. *Therefore, Windsor receives $26,000 on leaving the partnership: the original $10,000 capital balance plus a 20 percent share of this $80,000 increment.* The amount of payment is not in dispute, but the method of recording the withdrawal is in question.

Bonus Method Applied

If the partnership used the bonus method to record this transaction, the extra $16,000 paid to Windsor is simply assigned as a decrease in the remaining partners' capital accounts. Historically, Duncan and Smith have been credited with 50 percent and 30 percent of all profits and losses, respectively. This same relative ratio is used now to allocate the reduction between these two remaining partners on a ⅝ and ⅜ basis:

Bonus Method

Windsor, Capital (to remove account balance)	10,000	
Duncan, Capital (⅝ of excess distribution)	10,000	
Smith, Capital (⅜ of excess distribution)	6,000	
Cash		26,000
To record Windsor's withdrawal with $16,000 excess distribution taken from remaining partners.		

Goodwill Method Applied

This same transaction can also be accounted for by means of the goodwill (or revaluation) approach. The appraisal indicates that land is undervalued on the partnership's records by $50,000 and that goodwill of $30,000 has apparently accrued to the business over the years. The first of the following entries recognizes these valuations. This adjustment properly equates Windsor's capital balance with the $26,000 cash amount to be distributed. Windsor's equity balance is merely removed in the second entry at the time of payment.

Goodwill Method

Land	50,000	
Goodwill	30,000	
Duncan, Capital (50%)		40,000
Smith, Capital (30%)		24,000
Windsor, Capital (20%)		16,000
To recognize land value and goodwill as a preliminary step to Windsor's withdrawal.		
Windsor, Capital (to remove account balance)	26,000	
Cash		26,000
To distribute cash to Windsor in settlement of partnership interest.		

The implied value of a partnership as a whole cannot be determined directly from the amount distributed to a withdrawing partner. For example, paying Windsor $26,000 did not indicate that total capital should be $130,000 ($26,000/20%). This computation is appropriate only when (1) a new partner is admitted or (2) the percentage of capital is the same as the profit and loss ratio. Here, an outside valuation of the business indicated that the company was worth $80,000 more than book value. As a 20 percent owner, Windsor was entitled to $16,000 of that amount, raising the partner's capital account from $10,000 to $26,000, the amount of the final payment.

Hybrid Method Applied

As indicated previously, a hybrid approach also can be adopted to record a partner's withdrawal. It also recognizes asset and liability revaluations but ignores goodwill. A bonus must then be recorded to reconcile the partner's adjusted capital balance with the final distribution.

The following journal entry, for example, does not record goodwill. However, the book value of the land is increased by $50,000 in recognition of present worth. This adjustment increases Windsor's capital balance to $20,000, a figure that is still less than the $26,000 distribution. The $6,000 difference is recorded as a bonus taken from the remaining two partners according to their relative profit and loss ratio.

Hybrid Method

Land	50,000	
Duncan, Capital (50%)		25,000
Smith, Capital (30%)		15,000
Windsor, Capital (20%)		10,000
To adjust Land account to fair value as a preliminary step in Windsor's withdrawal.		
Windsor, Capital (to remove account balances)	20,000	
Duncan, Capital (⅝ of bonus)	3,750	
Smith, Capital (⅜ of bonus)	2,250	
Cash		26,000
To record final distribution to Windsor with $6,000 bonus taken from remaining partners.		

Summary

1. A partnership is defined as "an association of two or more persons to carry on a business as co-owners for profit." This form of business organization exists throughout the U.S. economy ranging in size from small, part-time operations to international enterprises. The partnership format is popular for many reasons, including the ease of creation and the avoidance of the double taxation that is inherent in corporate ownership. However, the unlimited liability incurred by each general partner normally restricts the growth potential of most partnerships. Thus, although the number of partnerships in the United States is large, the size of each tends to be small.

2. Over the years, a number of different types of organizations have been developed to take advantage of both the single taxation of partnerships and the limited liability afforded to corporate stockholders. Such legal forms include S corporations, limited partnerships, limited liability partnerships, and limited liability companies.

3. The unique elements of partnership accounting are found primarily in the capital accounts that are accumulated for each partner. The basis for recording these balances is the articles of partnership, a document that should be established as a prerequisite to the formation of any partnership. One of the principal provisions of this agreement is the initial investment to be made by each partner. Noncash contributions such as inventory or land are entered into the partnership's accounting records at fair value.

4. In forming a partnership, the partners' contributions need not be limited to tangible assets. A particular line of expertise possessed by a partner or an established clientele are attributes that can have a significant value to a partnership. Two methods of recording this type of investment are found in practice. The bonus method recognizes only identifiable assets. The capital accounts are then aligned to indicate the balances negotiated by the partners. According to the goodwill approach, all contributions (even those of a nebulous nature such as expertise) are valued and recorded, often as goodwill.

5. Another accounting issue to be resolved in forming a partnership is the allocation of annual net income. In closing out the revenue and expense accounts at the end of each period, some assignment must be made to the individual capital balances. Although an equal division can be used to allocate any profit or loss, partners frequently devise unique plans in an attempt to be equitable. Such factors as time worked, expertise, and invested capital should be considered in creating an allocation procedure.

6. Over time, changes occur in the makeup of a partnership because of death or retirement or because of the admission of new partners. Such changes dissolve the existing partnership, although the business frequently continues uninterrupted through a newly formed partnership. If, for example, a new partner is admitted by the acquisition of a present interest, the capital balances can simply be reclassified to reflect the change in ownership. As an alternative, the purchase price may be viewed as evidence of the underlying value of the organization as a whole. Based on this calculation, asset and liability balances are adjusted to fair value, and any residual goodwill is recognized.

7. Admission into an existing partnership also can be achieved by a direct capital contribution to the business. Because of negotiations between the parties, the amount invested will not always agree with the beginning capital balance attributed to the new partner. The bonus method resolves this conflict by simply reclassifying the various capital accounts to align the balances with specified totals and percentages. No revaluation is carried out under this approach. Conversely, according to the goodwill method, all asset and liability accounts are adjusted first to fair value. The price paid by the new partner is used to compute an implied value for the partnership, and any excess over fair value is recorded as goodwill.

8. The composition of a partnership also can undergo changes because of the death or retirement of a partner. Individuals may decide to withdraw. Such changes legally dissolve the partnership, although business operations frequently continue under the ownership of the remaining partners. In compensating the departing partner, the final asset distribution may differ from the ending capital balance. This disparity can, once again, be accounted for by means of the bonus method, which adjusts the remaining capital accounts to absorb the bonus being paid. The goodwill approach by which all assets and liabilities are restated to fair value with any goodwill being recognized also can be applied. Finally, a hybrid method revalues the assets and liabilities but ignores goodwill. Under this last approach, any amount paid to the departing partner in excess of the newly adjusted capital balance is accounted for by means of the bonus method.

Comprehensive Illustration

PROBLEM

(*Estimated Time: 30 to 55 Minutes*) Heyman and Mullins begin a partnership on January 1, 2007. Heyman invests $40,000 cash and inventory costing $15,000 but with a current appraised value of only $12,000. Mullins contributes a building with a $40,000 book value and a $48,000 fair value. The partnership also accepts responsibility for a $10,000 note payable owed in connection with this building.

The partners agree to begin operations with equal capital balances. The articles of partnership also provide that at the end of each year, profits and losses are allocated as follows:

1. For managing the business, Heyman is credited with a bonus of 10 percent of partnership income after subtracting the bonus. No bonus is accrued if the partnership records a loss.

2. Both partners are entitled to interest equal to 10 percent of the average monthly capital balance for the year without regard for the income or drawings of that year.

3. Any remaining profit or loss is divided 60 percent to Heyman and 40 percent to Mullins.

4. Each partner is allowed to withdraw $800 per month in cash from the business.

On October 1, 2007, Heyman invests an additional $12,000 cash in the business. For 2007, the partnership reports income of $33,000.

Lewis, an employee, is allowed to join the partnership on January 1, 2008. The new partner invests $66,000 directly into the business for a one-third interest in the partnership property. The revised partnership agreement still allows for both the bonus to Heyman and the 10 percent interest, but all remaining profits and losses are now split 40 percent each to Heyman and Lewis with the remaining 20 percent to Mullins. Lewis is also entitled to $800 per month in drawings.

Mullins chooses to withdraw from the partnership a few years later. After negotiations, all parties agree that Mullins should be paid a $90,000 settlement. The capital balances on that date were as follows:

Heyman, capital.	$88,000
Mullins, capital	78,000
Lewis, capital.	72,000

Required

a. Assuming that this partnership uses the bonus method exclusively, make all necessary journal entries. Entries for the monthly drawings of the partners are not required.

b. Assuming that this partnership uses the goodwill method exclusively, make all necessary journal entries. Again, entries for the monthly drawings are not required.

SOLUTION

a. **Bonus Method**

2007

Jan. 1 All contributed property is recorded at fair value. Under the bonus method, total capital is then divided as specified between the partners.

Cash	40,000	
Inventory	12,000	
Building	48,000	
Note Payable		10,000
Heyman, Capital (50%)		45,000
Mullins, Capital (50%)		45,000
To record initial contributions to partnership along with equal capital balances.		

Oct. 1

Cash	12,000	
Heyman, Capital		12,000
To record additional investment by partner.		

Dec. 31 Both the bonus assigned to Heyman and the interest accrual must be computed as preliminary steps in the income allocation process. Because the bonus is based on income after subtracting the bonus, the amount must be calculated algebraically:

$$\text{Bonus} = 0.10\ (\$33,000 - \text{Bonus})$$
$$\text{Bonus} = \$3,300 - 0.10\ \text{Bonus}$$
$$1.10\ \text{Bonus} = \$3,300$$
$$\text{Bonus} = \$3,000$$

According to the articles of partnership, the interest allocation is based on a monthly average figure. Mullins's capital balance of $45,000 did not change during the year; therefore

$4,500 (10 percent) is the appropriate interest accrual for that partner. However, because of the October 1, 2007, contribution, Heyman's interest must be determined as follows:

Beginning balance:	$45,000 × 9 months =	$405,000
New balance:	$57,000 × 3 months =	171,000
		576,000
		× ¹⁄₁₂
Monthly average—capital balance		48,000
Interest rate		× 10%
Interest credited to Heyman		$ 4,800

Following the bonus and interest computations, the $33,000 income earned by the business is allocated according to the previously specified arrangement:

	Heyman	Mullins	Totals
Bonus	$ 3,000	–0–	$ 3,000
Interest	4,800	$ 4,500	9,300
Remaining income:			
$33,000			
(3,000)			
(9,300)			
$20,700	12,420 (60%)	8,280 (40%)	20,700
Income allocation	$20,220	$12,780	$33,000

Thus, the partnership's closing entries for the year would be recorded as follows:

Heyman, Capital	9,600	
Mullins, Capital	9,600	
Heyman, Drawing		9,600
Mullins, Drawing		9,600
To close out $800 per month drawing accounts for the year.		
Income Summary	33,000	
Heyman, Capital		20,220
Mullins, Capital		12,780
To close out profit for year to capital accounts as computed above.		

At the end of this initial year of operation, the partners' capital accounts hold the following balances:

	Heyman	Mullins	Totals
Beginning balance	$45,000	$45,000	$ 90,000
Additional investment	12,000	–0–	12,000
Drawing	(9,600)	(9,600)	(19,200)
Net income (above)	20,220	12,780	33,000
Total capital	$67,620	$48,180	$115,800

2008

Jan. 1   Lewis contributed $66,000 to the business for a one-third interest in the partnership property. Combined with the $115,800 balance computed above, the partnership now has total capital of $181,800. Because no revaluation is recorded under the bonus approach, a one-third interest in the partnership equals $60,600 ($181,800 × ⅓). Lewis has invested $5,400 in excess of this amount, a balance viewed as a bonus accruing to the original partners:

Cash	66,000	
Lewis, Capital		60,600
Heyman, Capital (60% of bonus)		3,240
Mullins, Capital (40% of bonus)		2,160
To record Lewis's entrance into partnership with bonus to original partners.		

Several years later The final event in this illustration is Mullins's withdrawal from the partnership. Although this partner's capital balance reports only $78,000, the final distribution is set at $90,000. The extra $12,000 payment represents a bonus assigned to Mullins, an amount that decreases the capital of the remaining two partners. Because Heyman and Lewis have previously accrued equal 40 percent shares of all profits and losses, the reduction is split evenly between the two.

Mullins, Capital	78,000	
Heyman, Capital (½ of bonus payment)	6,000	
Lewis, Capital (½ of bonus payment)	6,000	
Cash		90,000

To record withdrawal of Mullins with bonus taken from remaining partners.

b. Goodwill Method

2007

Jan. 1 The fair value of Heyman's contribution is $52,000, whereas Mullins is investing only a net $38,000 (the value of the building less the accompanying debt). Because the capital accounts are initially to be equal, Mullins is presumed to be contributing goodwill of $14,000.

Cash	40,000	
Inventory	12,000	
Building	48,000	
Goodwill	14,000	
Note payable		10,000
Heyman, Capital		52,000
Mullins, Capital		52,000

Creation of partnership with goodwill attributed to Mullins.

Oct. 1

Cash	12,000	
Heyman, Capital		12,000

To record additional contribution by partner.

Dec. 31 Although Heyman's bonus is still $3,000 as derived in requirement (*a*), the interest accruals must be recalculated because the capital balances are different. Mullins's capital for the entire year was $52,000; thus, interest of $5,200 (10 percent) is appropriate. However, Heyman's balance changed during the year so that a monthly average must be determined as a basis for computing interest:

Beginning balance:	$52,000 × 9 months =	$468,000
New balance:	$64,000 × 3 months =	192,000
		660,000
		× ¹⁄₁₂
Monthly average—capital balance		55,000
Interest rate		× 10%
Interest credited to Heyman		$ 5,500

Consequently, the $33,000 partnership income is allocated as follows:

	Heyman	Mullins	Totals
Bonus (above)	$ 3,000	–0–	$ 3,000
Interest (above)	5,500	$ 5,200	10,700
Remaining income:			
$33,000			
(3,000)			
(10,300)			
$19,300	11,580 (60%)	7,720 (40%)	19,300
Income allocation	$20,080	$12,920	$33,000

The closing entries made under the goodwill approach would be as follows:

Heyman, Capital	9,600	
Mullins, Capital	9,600	
Heyman, Drawing		9,600
Mullins, Drawing		9,600
To close out drawing accounts for the year.		
Income Summary	33,000	
Heyman, Capital		20,080
Mullins, Capital		12,920
To assign profits per allocation determined above.		

After the closing process, the capital balances are composed of the following items:

	Heyman	Mullins	Totals
Beginning balance	$52,000	$52,000	$104,000
Additional investment	12,000	–0–	12,000
Drawing	(9,600)	(9,600)	(19,200)
Net income	20,080	12,920	33,000
Total capital	$74,480	$55,320	$129,800

2008

Jan. 1 Lewis's investment of $66,000 for a one-third interest in the partnership property implies that the business as a whole is worth $198,000 ($66,000 divided by ⅓). After adding Lewis's contribution to the present capital balance of $129,800, the business reports total net assets of only $195,800. Thus, a $2,200 increase in value ($198,000 − $195,800) is indicated and will be recognized at this time. Under the assumption that all partnership assets and liabilities are valued appropriately, this entire balance is attributed to goodwill.

Goodwill	2,200	
Heyman, Capital (60%)		1,320
Mullins, Capital (40%)		880
To recognize goodwill based on Lewis's acquisition price.		
Cash	66,000	
Lewis, Capital		66,000
To admit Lewis to the partnership.		

Several years later To conclude this illustration, Mullins's withdrawal must be recorded. This partner is to receive a distribution that is $12,000 more than the corresponding capital balance of $78,000. Because Mullins is entitled to a 20 percent share of profits and losses, the additional $12,000 payment indicates that the partnership as a whole is undervalued by $60,000 ($12,000/20%). Only in that circumstance would the extra payment to Mullins be justified. Therefore, once again, goodwill is recognized with the final distribution then being made.

Goodwill	60,000	
Heyman, Capital (40%)		24,000
Mullins, Capital (20%)		12,000
Lewis, Capital (40%)		24,000
Recognition of goodwill based on withdrawal amount paid to Mullins.		
Mullins, Capital	90,000	
Cash		90,000
To distribute money to partner.		

Questions

1. What are the advantages of operating a business as a partnership rather than as a corporation? What are the disadvantages?
2. How does partnership accounting differ from corporate accounting?
3. What information do the capital accounts found in partnership accounting convey?

4. Describe the differences between a Subchapter S corporation and a Subchapter C corporation.

5. A company is being created and the owners are trying to decide whether to form a general partnership, a limited liability partnership, or a limited liability company. What are the advantages and disadvantages of each of these legal forms?

6. What is an articles of partnership agreement, and what information should this document contain?

7. What valuation should be recorded for noncash assets transferred to a partnership by one of the partners?

8. If a partner is contributing attributes to a partnership such as an established clientele or a particular expertise, what two methods can record the contribution? Describe each method.

9. What is the purpose of a drawing account in a partnership's financial records?

10. At what point in the accounting process does the allocation of partnership income become significant?

11. What provisions can be used in a partnership agreement to establish an equitable allocation of income among all partners?

12. If no agreement exists in a partnership as to the allocation of income, what method is appropriate?

13. What is a partnership dissolution? Does dissolution automatically necessitate the cessation of business and the liquidation of partnership assets?

14. By what methods can a new partner gain admittance into a partnership?

15. When a partner sells an ownership interest in a partnership, what rights are conveyed to the new owner?

16. A new partner enters a partnership and goodwill is calculated and credited to the original partners. How is the specific amount of goodwill assigned to these partners?

17. Under what circumstance might goodwill be allocated to a new partner entering a partnership?

18. When a partner withdraws from a partnership, why is the final distribution often based on the appraised value of the business rather than on the book value of the capital account balance?

Problems

1. Which of the following is *not* a reason for the popularity of partnerships as a legal form for businesses?
   a. Partnerships need be formed only by an oral agreement.
   b. Partnerships can more easily generate significant amounts of capital.
   c. Partnerships avoid the double taxation of income that is found in corporations.
   d. In some cases, losses may be used to offset gains for tax purposes.

2. How does partnership accounting differ from corporate accounting?
   a. The matching principle is not considered appropriate for partnership accounting.
   b. Revenues are recognized at a different time by a partnership than is appropriate for a corporation.
   c. Individual capital accounts replace the contributed capital and retained earnings balances found in corporate accounting.
   d. Partnerships report all assets at fair value as of the latest balance sheet date.

3. Pat, Jean Lou, and Diane are partners with capital balances of $50,000, $30,000, and $20,000, respectively. These three partners share profits and losses equally. For an investment of $50,000 cash (being paid to the business), MaryAnn is to be admitted as a partner with a one-fourth interest in capital and profits. Based on this information, the amount of MaryAnn's investment can best be justified by which of the following?
   a. MaryAnn will receive a bonus from the other partners upon her admission to the partnership.
   b. Assets of the partnership were overvalued immediately prior to MaryAnn's investment.
   c. The book value of the partnership's net assets was less than the fair value immediately prior to MaryAnn's investment.
   d. MaryAnn is apparently bringing goodwill into the partnership, and her capital account will be credited for the appropriate amount.

4. A partnership has the following capital balances:

Albert (50% of gains and losses)	$ 80,000
Barrymore (20%)	60,000
Candroth (30%)	140,000

Danville is going to invest $70,000 into the business to acquire a 30 percent ownership interest. Goodwill is to be recorded. What will be Danville's beginning capital balance?

a. $70,000.

b. $90,000.

c. $105,000.

d. $120,000.

5. A partnership has the following capital balances:

Elgin (40% of gains and losses)	$100,000
Jethro (30%)	200,000
Foy (30%)	300,000

Oscar is going to pay a total of $200,000 to these three partners to acquire a 25 percent ownership interest from each. Goodwill is to be recorded. What will be Jethro's capital balance after the transaction?

a. $150,000.

b. $175,000.

c. $195,000.

d. $200,000.

6. The capital balance for Bolcar is $110,000 and for Neary is $40,000. These two partners share profits and losses 70 percent (Bolcar) and 30 percent (Neary). Kansas invests $50,000 in cash into the partnership for a 30 percent ownership. The bonus method will be used. What is Neary's capital balance after Kansas's investment?

a. $35,000.

b. $37,000.

c. $40,000.

d. $43,000.

7. Bishop has a capital balance of $120,000 in a local partnership, and Cotton has a $90,000 balance. These two partners share profits and losses by a ratio of 60 percent to Bishop and 40 percent to Cotton. Lovett invests $60,000 in cash in the partnership for a 20 percent ownership. The goodwill method will be used. What is Cotton's capital balance after this new investment?

a. $99,600.

b. $102,000.

c. $112,000.

d. $126,000.

8. The capital balance for Messalina is $210,000 and for Romulus is $140,000. These two partners share profits and losses 60 percent (Messalina) and 40 percent (Romulus). Claudius invests $100,000 in cash in the partnership for a 20 percent ownership. The bonus method will be used. What are the capital balances for Messalina, Romulus, and Claudius after this investment is recorded?

a. $216,000, $144,000, $90,000.

b. $218,000, $142,000, $88,000.

c. $222,000, $148,000, $80,000.

d. $240,000, $160,000, $100,000.

9. A partnership begins its first year with the following capital balances:

Arthur, Capital	$ 60,000
Baxter, Capital	80,000
Cartwright, Capital	100,000

The articles of partnership stipulate that profits and losses be assigned in the following manner:
- Each partner is allocated interest equal to 10 percent of the beginning capital balance.
- Baxter is allocated compensation of $20,000 per year.
- Any remaining profits and losses are allocated on a 3:3:4 basis, respectively.
- Each partner is allowed to withdraw up to $5,000 cash per year.

Assuming that the net income is $50,000 and that each partner withdraws the maximum amount allowed, what is the balance in Cartwright's capital account at the end of that year?

a. $105,800.

b. $106,200.

c. $106,900.

d. $107,400.

10. A partnership begins its first year of operations with the following capital balances:

Winston, Capital	$110,000
Durham, Capital	80,000
Salem, Capital	110,000

According to the articles of partnership, all profits will be assigned as follows:

- Winston will be awarded an annual salary of $20,000 with $10,000 assigned to Salem.
- The partners will be attributed interest equal to 10 percent of the capital balance as of the first day of the year.
- The remainder will be assigned on a 5:2:3 basis, respectively.
- Each partner is allowed to withdraw up to $10,000 per year.

Assume that the net loss for the first year of operations is $20,000 and that net income for the subsequent year is $40,000. Assume also that each partner withdraws the maximum amount from the business each period. What is the balance in Winston's capital account at the end of the second year?

a. $102,600.

b. $104,400.

c. $108,600.

d. $109,200.

11. A partnership has the following capital balances:

Allen, Capital	$60,000
Burns, Capital	30,000
Costello, Capital	90,000

Profits and losses are split as follows: Allen (20%), Burns (30%), and Costello (50%). Costello wants to leave the partnership and is paid $100,000 from the business based on provisions in the articles of partnership. If the partnership uses the bonus method, what is the balance of Burns's capital account after Costello withdraws?

a. $24,000.

b. $27,000.

c. $33,000.

d. $36,000.

12. As of the end of the year, the Cisco partnership has the following capital balances:

Montana, Capital	$130,000
Rice, Capital	110,000
Craig, Capital	80,000
Taylor, Capital	70,000

Profits and losses are split on a 3:3:2:2 basis, respectively. Craig decides to leave the partnership and is paid $90,000 from the business based on the original contractual agreement. If the goodwill method is to be applied, what is the balance of Montana's capital account after Craig withdraws?

a. $133,000.

b. $137,500.

c. $140,000.

d. $145,000.

Problems 13 and 14 are *independent* problems based on the following capital account balances:

William (40% of gains and losses)	$220,000
Jennings (40%)	160,000
Bryan (20%)	110,000

13. Darrow invests $270,000 in cash for a 30 percent ownership interest. The money goes to the original partners. Goodwill is to be recorded. How much goodwill should be recognized, and what is Darrow's beginning capital balance?

    a. $410,000 and $270,000.

    b. $140,000 and $270,000.

    c. $140,000 and $189,000.

    d. $410,000 and $189,000.

14. Darrow invests $250,000 in cash for a 30 percent ownership interest. The money goes to the business. No goodwill or other revaluation is to be recorded. After the transaction, what is Jennings's capital balance?

    a. $160,000.

    b. $168,000.

    c. $170,200.

    d. $171,200.

15. Lear is to become a partner in the WS partnership by paying $80,000 in cash to the business. At present, the capital balance for Hamlet is $70,000 and for MacBeth is $40,000. Hamlet and MacBeth share profits on a 7:3 basis. Lear is acquiring 40 percent of the new partnership.

    a. If the goodwill method is applied, what will the three capital balances be following the payment by Lear?

    b. If the bonus method is applied, what will the three capital balances be following the payment by Lear?

16. The AKS partnership has the following capital balances at the beginning of the current year:

Arond (40% of profits and losses)	$80,000
Kant (40%)	70,000
Selvin (20%)	60,000

    a. If Tronsty invests $60,000 in cash in the business for a 20 percent interest, what journal entry is recorded? Assume the bonus method is used.

    b. If Tronsty invests $50,000 in cash in the business for a 20 percent interest, what journal entry is recorded? Assume the bonus method is used.

    c. If Tronsty invests $55,000 in cash in the business for a 20 percent interest, what journal entry is recorded? Assume the goodwill method is used.

17. A partnership has the following account balances: Cash $50,000; Other Assets $600,000; Liabilities $240,000; Nixon, Capital (50% of profits and losses) $200,000; Hoover, Capital (20%) $120,000; and Polk, Capital (30%) $90,000. Each of the following questions should be viewed as an independent situation:

    a. Grant invests $80,000 in the partnership for an 18 percent capital interest. Goodwill is to be recognized. What are the capital accounts thereafter?

    b. Grant invests $100,000 in the partnership to get a 20 percent capital balance. Goodwill is not to be recorded. What are the capital accounts thereafter?

18. The C-P partnership has the following capital account balances on January 1, 2007:

Com, Capital	$150,000
Pack, Capital	110,000

    Com is allocated 60 percent of all profits and losses with the remaining 40 percent assigned to Pack after interest of 10 percent is given to each partner based on beginning capital balances.

    On January 2, 2007, Hal invests $76,000 cash for a 20 percent interest in the partnership. This transaction is recorded by the goodwill method. After this transaction, 10 percent interest is still to go to each partner. Profits and losses will then be split as follows: Com (50%), Pack (30%), and Hal (20%). In 2007, the partnership reports a net income of $36,000.

    a. Prepare the journal entry to record Hal's entrance into the partnership on January 2, 2007.

    b. Determine the allocation of income at the end of 2007.

19. The partnership agreement of Jones, King, and Lane provides for the annual allocation of the business's profit or loss in the following sequence:
    • Jones, the managing partner, receives a bonus equal to 20 percent of the business's profit.
    • Each partner receives 15 percent interest on average capital investment.
    • Any residual profit or loss is divided equally.

    The average capital investments for 2007 were as follows:

Jones	$100,000
King	200,000
Lane	300,000

    How much of the $90,000 partnership profit for 2007 should be assigned to each partner?

20. Purkerson, Smith, and Traynor have operated a bookstore for a number of years as a partnership. At the beginning of 2007, capital balances were as follows:

Purkerson	$60,000
Smith	40,000
Traynor	20,000

    Because of a cash shortage, Purkerson invests an additional $8,000 in the business on April 1, 2007.

    Each partner is allowed to withdraw $1,000 cash each month.

    The partners have used the same method of allocating profits and losses since the business's inception:
    • Each partner is given the following compensation allowance for work done in the business: Purkerson, $18,000; Smith, $25,000; and Traynor, $8,000.
    • Each partner is credited with interest equal to 10 percent of the average monthly capital balance for the year without regard for normal drawings.
    • Any remaining profit or loss is allocated 4:2:4 to Purkerson, Smith, and Traynor, respectively.

    The net income for 2007 is $23,600. Each partner withdraws the allotted amount each month. What are the ending capital balances for 2007?

21. On January 1, 2007, the dental partnership of Left, Center, and Right was formed when the partners contributed $20,000, $60,000, and $50,000, respectively. Over the next three years, the business reported net income and (loss) as follows:

2007	$(30,000)
2008	20,000
2009	40,000

    During this period, each partner withdrew cash of $10,000 per year. Right invested an additional $12,000 in cash on February 9, 2008.

    At the time that the partnership was created, the three partners agreed to allocate all profits and losses according to a specified plan written as follows:
    • Each partner is entitled to interest computed at the rate of 12 percent per year based on the individual capital balances at the beginning of that year.
    • Because of prior work experience, Left is entitled to an annual salary allowance of $12,000, and Center is credited with $8,000 per year.
    • Any remaining profit will be split as follows: Left, 20 percent; Center, 40 percent; and Right, 40 percent. If a loss remains, the balance will be allocated: Left, 30 percent; Center, 50 percent; and Right, 20 percent.

    Determine the ending capital balance for each partner as of the end of each of these three years.

22. The HELP partnership has the following capital balances as of December 31, 2008:

Lennon	$230,000
McCartney	190,000
Harrison	160,000
Starr	140,000
Total capital	$720,000

Answer each of the following *independent* questions:

a. Assume that the partners share profits and losses 3:3:2:2, respectively. Harrison retires and is paid $190,000 based on the terms of the original partnership agreement. If the goodwill method is used, what is the capital balance of the remaining three partners?

b. Assume that the partners share profits and losses 4:3:2:1, respectively. Lennon retires and is paid $280,000 based on the terms of the original partnership agreement. If the bonus method is used, what is the capital balance of the remaining three partners?

23. In the early part of 2008, the partners of Page, Childers, and Smith went to a local accountant seeking assistance. They had begun a new business in 2007 but had never previously used the services of an accountant.

Page and Childers began the partnership by contributing $80,000 and $30,000 in cash, respectively. Page was to work occasionally at the business, and Childers was to be employed full-time. They decided that year-end profits and losses should be assigned as follows:

- Each partner was to be allocated 10 percent interest computed on the beginning capital balances for the period.
- A compensation allowance of $5,000 was to go to Page with a $20,000 amount assigned to Childers.
- Any remaining income would be split on a 4:6 basis to Page and Childers, respectively.

In 2007, revenues totaled $90,000, and expenses were $64,000 (not including the compensation allowance assigned to the partners). Page withdrew cash of $8,000 during the year, and Childers took out $11,000. In addition, the business paid $5,000 for repairs made to Page's home and charged it to repair expense.

On January 1, 2008, the partnership sold a 20 percent interest to Smith for $43,000 cash. This money was contributed to the business with the bonus method used for accounting purposes.

Answer the following questions:

a. Why was the original profit and loss allocation, as just outlined, designed by the partners?

b. Why did the drawings for 2007 not agree with the compensation allowances provided for in the partnership agreement?

c. What journal entries should have been recorded by the partnership on December 31, 2007?

d. What journal entry should have been recorded by the partnership on January 1, 2008?

24. Following is the current balance sheet for a local partnership of doctors:

Cash and current		Liabilities	$ 40,000
assets	$ 30,000	A, capital	20,000
Land	180,000	B, capital	40,000
Building and		C, capital	90,000
equipment (net)	100,000	D, capital	120,000
Totals	$310,000	Totals	$310,000

The following questions represent *independent* situations:

a. E is going to invest enough money in this partnership to receive a 25 percent interest. No goodwill or bonus is to be recorded. How much should E invest?

b. E contributes $36,000 in cash to the business to receive a 10 percent interest in the partnership. Goodwill is to be recorded. Profits and losses have previously been split according to the following percentages: A, 30 percent; B, 10 percent; C, 40 percent; and D, 20 percent. After E makes this investment, what are the individual capital balances?

c. E contributes $42,000 in cash to the business to receive a 20 percent interest in the partnership. Goodwill is to be recorded. The four original partners share all profits and losses equally. After E makes this investment, what are the individual capital balances?

d. E contributes $55,000 in cash to the business to receive a 20 percent interest in the partnership. No goodwill or other asset revaluation is to be recorded. Profits and losses have previously been split according to the following percentages: A, 10 percent; B, 30 percent; C, 20 percent; and D, 40 percent. After E makes this investment, what are the individual capital balances?

e. C retires from the partnership and, as per the original partnership agreement, is to receive cash equal to 125 percent of her final capital balance. No goodwill or other asset revaluation is to be recognized. All partners share profits and losses equally. After the withdrawal, what are the individual capital balances of the remaining partners?

25. Boswell and Johnson form a partnership on May 1, 2007. Boswell contributes cash of $50,000; Johnson conveys title to the following properties to the partnership:

	Book Value	Fair Value
Land	$15,000	$28,000
Building and equipment	35,000	36,000

The partners agree to start their partnership with equal capital balances. No goodwill is to be recognized.

According to the articles of partnership written by the partners, profits and losses are allocated based on the following formula:
- Boswell receives a compensation allowance of $1,000 per month.
- All remaining profits and losses are split 60:40 to Johnson and Boswell, respectively.
- Annual cash drawings of $5,000 can be made by each partner beginning in 2008.

Net income of $11,000 is earned by the business during 2007.

Walpole is invited to join the partnership on January 1, 2008. Because of Walpole's business reputation and financial expertise, she is given a 40 percent interest for $54,000 cash. The bonus approach is used to record this investment, made directly to the business. The articles of partnership are amended to give Walpole a $2,000 compensation allowance per month and an annual cash drawing of $10,000. Remaining profits are now allocated:

Johnson	48%
Boswell	12
Walpole	40

All drawings are taken by the partners during 2008. At the end of that year, the partnership reports an earned net income of $28,000.

On January 1, 2009, Pope (previously a partnership employee) is admitted into the partnership. Each partner transfers 10 percent to Pope. Pope makes the following payments directly to the partners:

Johnson	$5,672
Boswell	7,880
Walpole	8,688

Once again, the articles of partnership must be amended to allow for the entrance of the new partner. This change entitles Pope to a compensation allowance of $800 per month and an annual drawing of $4,000. Profits and losses are now assigned as follows:

Johnson	40.5%
Boswell	13.5
Walpole	36.0
Pope	10.0

For the year of 2009, the partnership earned a profit of $46,000, and each partner withdrew the allowed amount of cash.

Determine the capital balances for the individual partners as of the end of each year: 2007 through 2009.

26. Gray, Stone, and Lawson open an accounting practice on January 1, 2007, in San Diego, California. The business is to be operated as a partnership. Gray and Stone will serve as the senior partners because of their years of experience. To establish the business, Gray, Stone, and Lawson contribute cash and other properties valued at $210,000, $180,000, and $90,000, respectively. An articles of partnership agreement is drawn up. It has the following stipulations:
- Personal drawings are allowed annually up to an amount equal to 10 percent of the beginning capital balance for the year.
- Profits and losses are allocated according to the following plan:
  (1) A salary allowance is credited to each partner in an amount equal to $8 per billable hour worked by that individual during the year.

(2) Interest is credited to the partners' capital accounts at the rate of 12 percent of the average monthly balance for the year (computed without regard for current income or drawings).

(3) An annual bonus is to be credited to Gray and Stone. Each bonus is to be 10 percent of net income after subtracting the bonus, the salary allowance, and the interest. Also included in the agreement is the provision that the bonus cannot be a negative amount.

(4) Any remaining partnership profit or loss is to be divided evenly among all partners.

Because of monetary problems encountered in getting the business started, Gray invests an additional $9,100 on May 1, 2007. On January 1, 2008, the partners allow Monet to buy into the partnership. Monet contributes cash directly to the business in an amount equal to a 25 percent interest in the book value of the partnership property subsequent to this contribution. The partnership agreement as to splitting profits and losses is not altered at the time of Monet's entrance into the firm; the general provisions continue to be applicable.

The billable hours for the partners during the first three years of operation are as follows:

	2007	2008	2009
Gray	1,710	1,800	1,880
Stone	1,440	1,500	1,620
Lawson	1,300	1,380	1,310
Monet	–0–	1,190	1,580

The partnership reports net income for 2007 through 2009 as follows:

2007	$ 65,000
2008	(20,400)
2009	152,800

Each partner withdraws the maximum allowable amount each year.

a. Determine the allocation of income for each of these three years (to the nearest dollar).

b. Prepare in appropriate form a statement of partners' capital for the year ending December 31, 2007.

27. A partnership of attorneys in the St. Louis, Missouri, area has the following balance sheet accounts as of January 1, 2008:

Assets	$320,000	Liabilities	$120,000
		Athos, capital	80,000
		Porthos, capital	70,000
		Aramis, capital	50,000

According to the articles of partnership, Athos is to receive an allocation of 50 percent of all partnership profits and losses while Porthos receives 30 percent and Aramis 20 percent. The book value of each asset and liability should be considered an accurate representation of fair value.

For each of the following *independent* situations, prepare the journal entry or entries to be recorded by the partnership. (Round to nearest dollar.)

a. Porthos, with permission of the other partners, decides to sell half of his partnership interest to D'Artagnan for $50,000 in cash. No asset revaluation or goodwill is to be recorded by the partnership.

b. All three of the present partners agree to sell 10 percent of each partnership interest to D'Artagnan for a total cash payment of $25,000. Each partner receives a negotiated portion of this amount. Goodwill is being recorded as a result of the transaction.

c. D'Artagnan is allowed to become a partner with a 10 percent ownership interest by contributing $30,000 in cash directly into the business. The bonus method is used to record this admission.

d. Use the same facts as in requirement (c) except that the entrance into the partnership is recorded by the goodwill method.

e. D'Artagnan is allowed to become a partner with a 10 percent ownership interest by contributing $12,222 in cash directly to the business. The goodwill method is used to record this transaction.

f. Aramis decides to retire and leave the partnership. An independent appraisal of the business and its assets indicates a current fair value of $280,000. Goodwill is to be recorded. Aramis will then be given the exact amount of cash that will close out his capital account.

28. Steve Reese is a well-known interior designer in Fort Worth, Texas. He wants to start his own business and convinces Rob O'Donnell, a local merchant, to contribute the capital to form a partnership. On January 1, 2007, O'Donnell invests a building worth $52,000 and equipment valued at $16,000 as well as $12,000 in cash. Although Reese makes no tangible contribution to the partnership, he will operate the business and be an equal partner in the beginning capital balances.

   To entice O'Donnell to join this partnership, Reese draws up the following profit and loss agreement:
   - O'Donnell will be credited annually with interest equal to 20 percent of the beginning capital balance for the year.
   - O'Donnell will also have added to his capital account 15 percent of partnership income each year (without regard for the preceding interest figure) or $4,000, whichever is larger. All remaining income is credited to Reese.
   - Neither partner is allowed to withdraw funds from the partnership during 2007. Thereafter, each can draw $5,000 annually or 20 percent of the beginning capital balance for the year, whichever is larger.

   The partnership reported a net loss of $10,000 during the first year of its operation. On January 1, 2008, Terri Dunn becomes a third partner in this business by contributing $15,000 cash to the partnership. Dunn receives a 20 percent share of the business's capital. The profit and loss agreement is altered as follows:
   - O'Donnell is still entitled to (1) interest on his beginning capital balance as well as (2) the share of partnership income just specified.
   - Any remaining profit or loss will be split on a 6:4 basis between Reese and Dunn, respectively.

   Partnership income for 2008 is reported as $44,000. Each partner withdraws the full amount that is allowed.

   On January 1, 2009, Dunn becomes ill and sells her interest in the partnership (with the consent of the other two partners) to Judy Postner. Postner pays $46,000 directly to Dunn. Net income for 2006 is $61,000 with the partners again taking their full drawing allowance.

   On January 1, 2010, Postner elects to withdraw from the business for personal reasons. The articles of partnership contain a provision stating that any partner may leave the partnership at any time and is entitled to receive cash in an amount equal to the recorded capital balance at that time plus 10 percent.

   a. Prepare journal entries to record the preceding transactions on the assumption that the bonus (or no revaluation) method is used. Drawings need not be recorded, although the balances should be included in the closing entries.

   b. Prepare journal entries to record the previous transactions on the assumption that the goodwill (or revaluation) method is used. Drawings need not be recorded, although the balances should be included in the closing entries.

   (Round all amounts off to the nearest dollar.)

Develop Your Skills

RESEARCH CASE 1

Jim Hammonds is a partner in a regional CPA firm that covers three states in the northwest section of the United States. The firm was organized as a limited liability partnership. A partner in an office in another state performed a client audit well below the level required by professional standards. As a result, stockholders and lenders of the audited company lost a significant amount of money and have filed suit against the CPA firm. Hammonds has never had any interaction with this particular client, but he is concerned by the potential loss that could result from this lawsuit.

Required:

Obtain a copy of the article "Partners at Risk" in the August 2002 issue of the *ABA Journal*. With that article as a basis, write an explanation of the possible liability that Hammonds may face.

RESEARCH CASE 2

Go to the Web site www.sec.gov where forms filed with the SEC are available. Look for a section entitled "Filings & Forms (EDGAR)," and click on "Search for Company Filings" within that section. On the next screen that appears, click on "Search Companies and Filings." On the next screen, enter the following company name: Buckeye Partners. A list of SEC filings made by that company will appear; scroll down to the first 10–K (annual report) filing that is available from Buckeye Partners. Click on that 10–K. This path will provide the latest financial information available for Buckeye Partners. Scroll through the statement information until the actual financial statements, followed by the notes, appear.

Required:

Review this set of financial statements as well as the accompanying notes. List information included for this partnership that would typically not appear in financial statements produced for a corporation.

ANALYSIS CASE

Brenda Wilson, Elizabeth Higgins, and Helen Poncelet form a partnership as a first step in creating a business. Wilson invests most of the capital but does not plan to be actively involved in the day-to-day operations. Higgins has had some experience and is expected to do a majority of the daily work. Poncelet has been in this line of business for some time and has many connections. Therefore, she will devote a majority of her time to getting new clients.

Required:

Read the article "Pay for Performance" in the June 2002 issue of the *Journal of Accountancy*. Write a memo to these three partners suggesting at least two different ways in which the profits of the partnership can be allocated each year in order to be fair to all parties.

COMMUNICATION CASE 1

Heidi Birmingham and James T. Roberts have decided to create a business. They have financing available and have a well-developed business plan. However, they have not yet decided which type of legal business structure would be best for them.

Required:

Write a report for these two individuals outlining the types of situations in which the corporate form of legal structure would be the best choice.

COMMUNICATION CASE 2

Use the information in Communication Case 1.

Required:

Write a report for these two individuals outlining the types of situations in which the partnership form of legal structure would be the best choice.

EXCEL CASE

The Red and Blue partnership has been created to operate a law firm. The partners have been attempting to devise a fair system to allocate profits and losses. Red plans to work more billable hours each year than Blue. However, Blue has more experience and can charge a higher hourly rate. Red expects to invest more money in the business than Blue.

Required:

Build a spreadsheet that can be used to allocate profits and losses to these two partners each year. The spreadsheet should be constructed so that the following variables can be entered:

Net income for the year.

Number of billable hours for each partner.

Hourly rate for each partner.

Capital investment by each partner.

Interest rate on capital investment.

Profit and loss ratio.

Use this spreadsheet to determine the allocation if partnership net income for the current year is $200,000, the number of billable hours is 2,000 for Red and 1,500 for Blue, the hourly rate for Red is $20 and for Blue is $30, and investment by Red is $80,000 and by Blue is $50,000. Interest on capital will be accrued each year at 10 percent of the beginning balance. Any remaining income amount will be split 50–50.

Use the spreadsheet a second time but make these changes: Blue reports 1,700 billable hours, Red invests $100,000, and interest will be recognized at a 12 percent annual rate. How do these three changes impact the allocation of the $200,000?

Chapter **Fifteen**

Partnerships: Termination and Liquidation

Questions to Consider

- Under what conditions would a partnership be liquidated?

- What information should an accountant report to reflect the liquidation of a partnership?

- In a partnership liquidation, what happens if one or more partners report a deficit capital balance?

- How are any remaining assets distributed if a partnership or one of its partners becomes insolvent?

- What are *safe capital balances,* and how are they determined?

- How does an accountant determine which partners receive cash during a partnership liquidation?

Partnerships can be rather frail organizations. Termination of business activities followed by the liquidation of partnership property can take place for a variety of reasons, both legal and personal.

> I'm spending a great deal of time helping physician clients patch up partnership disputes and pull together. That is until I run up against a group where personalities, philosophies, or work styles are truly irreconcilable. In these cases, the best solution is a split. . . . Once the doctors know they want to split, they can meet to discuss their problems. While these sessions are often stormy, in the end the doctors usually find themselves agreeing for once. Their consensus? They'll each benefit more from going their separate ways than enduring a situation that's not working. Still, there's no denying that severing any partnership is emotionally wrenching.[1]

Although a business organized as a partnership can exist indefinitely through periodic changes within the ownership, the actual cessation of operations is not an uncommon occurrence. "Sooner or later, all partnerships end, whether a partner dies, moves to Hawaii, or gets into a different line of business."[2] The partners simply may be incompatible and choose to cease operations. The same choice could be reached if profit figures fail to equal projected levels. "In the best of times, partnerships are fragile."[3]

The death of a partner is an event that dissolves a partnership and frequently leads to the termination of business operations. Rather than continuing under a new partnership arrangement, the remaining owners could discover that liquidation is necessary to settle the claims of the deceased partner's estate. A similar action could be required if one or more partners elect to change careers or retire. Under that circumstance, liquidation is often the most convenient method for winding up the financial affairs of the business.

As a final possibility, bankruptcy can legally force a partnership into selling its noncash assets. Laventhol & Horwath, the seventh largest public accounting firm in the United States at the time, filed for bankruptcy protection after the firm came under intense financial pressure from numerous lawsuits. "Laventhol said that at least 100 lawsuits are pending in state and federal courts. Bankruptcy court protection 'is absolutely

---

[1] Leif C. Beck, "When a Group Is Better Off Splitting Up," *Medical Economics,* March 5, 1984, p. 183.

[2] Camilla Cornell, "Breaking Up (with a Business Partner) Is Hard To Do," *Profit,* November 2004, p. 69.

[3] Sue Shellenbarger, "Cutting Losses When Partners Face a Breakup," *The Wall Street Journal,* May 21, 1991, p. B1.

necessary in order to protect the debtor and its creditors from the devastating results a destructive race for assets will cause' the firm said."[4]

The bankruptcy of Laventhol & Horwath was not an isolated incident.

> Law firms are going out of business at a steady clip, and a few major accounting firms have collapsed in recent years. "At least a dozen [major law] firms have failed in the past three or four years," figures Bradford W. Hildebrandt, chairman of a legal consulting firm in Somerville, N.J. "In the next year or two, there could be another half-dozen."[5]

TERMINATION AND LIQUIDATION—PROTECTING THE INTERESTS OF ALL PARTIES

As the chapter on bankruptcy discussed, accounting for the termination and liquidation of a business can prove to be a delicate task. Losses are commonly incurred. For example, "Former partners in Keck, Mahin and Cate have pledged to pay slightly over $3 million to general unsecured creditors to settle the bankrupt firm's debts . . . this figure represents about 36 percent of the money owed."[6] Here, both the partners and the debtors suffered heavy losses.

Other partnerships have experienced a similar fate.

> In 1990, prior to the advent of limited-liability partnerships, the accounting firm of Laventhol & Horwath filed for Chapter 11 bankruptcy-court protection, in part due to lawsuits over questionable accounting. The firm's assets were insufficient to cover the claims of creditors and litigants. Under a plan negotiated with the firm's creditors, the 360 partners and former partners who had spent time at the firm since 1984 were required to dig into their own pockets to share a $46 million liability. Under a formula hammered out by partner Jacob Brandzel, now an executive at American Express Co. in Chicago, they were obligated to contribute between about $5,000 and $450,000, depending on factors including seniority. Managers were levied a 5 percent to 10 percent surcharge on top. Everyone was given 10 years to pay.[7]

Consequently, throughout any liquidation, both creditors and owners demand continuous accounting information that enables them to monitor and assess their financial risks. In generating these data for a partnership, the accountant must record the following:

- The conversion of partnership assets into cash.
- The allocation of the resulting gains and losses.
- The payment of liabilities and expenses.
- Any remaining unpaid debts to be settled or the distribution of any remaining assets to the partners based on their final capital balances.

Beyond the goal of merely reporting these transactions, the accountant must work to ensure the equitable treatment of all parties involved in the liquidation. The accounting records, for example, serve as the basis for allocating available assets to creditors as well as to the individual partners. If assets are limited, the accountant also may have to make recommendations as to the appropriate method for distributing any remaining funds. Protecting the interests of partnership creditors is an especially significant duty because the Uniform Partnership Act specifies that they have first priority to the assets held by the business at the time of dissolution. The accountant's desire for an equitable settlement is enhanced, no doubt, in that any party to a liquidation who is not treated fairly can seek legal recovery from the responsible party.

---

[4] Peter Pae, "Laventhol Bankruptcy Filing Indicates Liabilities May Be as Much as $2 Billion," *The Wall Street Journal,* November 23, 1990, p. A4.

[5] Lee Berton and Joann S. Lublin, "Partnership Structure Is Called in Question as Liability Risk Rises," *The Wall Street Journal,* June 10, 1992, p. A9.

[6] *Chicago Daily Law Bulletin*, August 13, 1999, p. 3.

[7] Mitchell Pacelle and Ianthe Jeanne Dugan, "Partners Forever? Within Andersen, Personal Liability May Bring Ruin," *The Wall Street Journal*, April 2, 2002, p. C1.

Not only the creditors but also the partners themselves have a great interest in the financial data produced during the period of liquidation. They must be concerned, as indicated above, by the possibility of incurring substantial monetary losses. The potential for loss is especially significant because of the unlimited liability to which the partners are exposed.

Even the new legal formats that have been developed do not necessarily provide safety. "Because it is unclear how much protection the LLP structure will provide Andersen partners, partnership and bankruptcy lawyers are expected to be following the matter closely. 'As far as I know, there has never been a litigation test of the extent of the LLP shield, and there have been very few LLP cases about liability at all,' said Larry Ribstein, a law professor at George Mason University."[8]

As long as a partnership can meet all of its obligations, a partner's risk is normally no more than that of a corporate stockholder. However, should the partnership become insolvent, each partner faces the possibility of having to satisfy *all* remaining obligations personally. Although any partner suffering more than a proportionate share of these losses can seek legal retribution from the remaining owners, this process is not always an effective remedy. The other partners may themselves be insolvent, or anticipated legal costs might discourage the damaged party from seeking recovery. Therefore, each partner usually has a keen interest in monitoring the progress of a liquidation as it transpires.

Termination and Liquidation Procedures Illustrated

The procedures involved in terminating and liquidating a partnership are basically mechanical. Partnership assets are converted into cash that is then used to pay business obligations as well as liquidation expenses. *Any remaining assets are distributed to the individual partners based on their final capital balances.* Because no other ledger accounts exist, the partnership's books are permanently closed. If each partner has a capital balance large enough to absorb all liquidation losses, the accountant should experience little difficulty in recording this series of transactions.

To illustrate the typical process, assume that Morgan and Houseman have been operating an art gallery as a partnership for a number of years. On May 1, 2007, the partners decide to terminate business activities, liquidate all noncash assets, and dissolve their partnership. Morgan and Houseman allocate all profits and losses on a 6:4 basis, respectively. Although they give no specific explanation for this action, any number of reasons could exist. The partners, for example, could have come to a disagreement so that they no longer believe they can work together. Another possibility is that business profits could have been inadequate to warrant the continuing investment of their time and capital.

Following is a balance sheet for the partnership of Morgan and Houseman as of the termination date. The revenue, expense, and drawing accounts have been closed as a preliminary step in terminating the business. A separate reporting of the gains and losses that occur during the final winding-down process will subsequently be made.

MORGAN AND HOUSEMAN
Balance Sheet
May 1, 2007

Assets		Liabilities and Capital	
Cash	$ 45,000	Liabilities	$ 32,000
Accounts receivable	12,000	Morgan, capital	50,000
Inventory	22,000	Houseman, capital	38,000
Land, building, and equipment (net)	41,000		
Total assets	$120,000	Total liabilities and capital	$120,000

[8] Ibid.

We assume here that the liquidation of Morgan and Houseman proceeds in an orderly fashion through the following events:

2007

June 1	The inventory is sold at auction for $15,000.
July 15	Of the total accounts receivable, the partnership collected $9,000 and wrote off the remainder as bad debts.
Aug. 20	The fixed assets are sold for a total of $29,000.
Aug. 25	All partnership liabilities are paid.
Sept. 10	A total of $3,000 in liquidation expenses is paid to cover costs such as accounting and legal fees as well as the commissions incurred in disposing of partnership property.
Oct. 15	All remaining cash is distributed to the owners based on their final capital account balances.

Accordingly, the partnership of Morgan and Houseman incurred a number of losses in liquidating its property. Such losses are almost anticipated because the need for immediate sale usually holds a high priority in a liquidation. Furthermore, a portion of the assets used by any business, such as its equipment and buildings, could have a utility that is strictly limited to a particular type of operation. If the property is not easily adaptable, disposal at any reasonable price often proves to be a problem.

To record the liquidation of Morgan and Houseman, the following journal entries would be made. Rather than report specific income and expense balances, gains and losses are traditionally recorded directly to the partners' capital accounts. Because operations have ceased, determination of a separate net income figure for this period would provide little informational value. *Instead, a primary concern of the parties involved in any liquidation is the continuing changes in each partner's capital balance.*

6/1/07	Cash	15,000	
	Morgan, Capital (60% of loss)	4,200	
	Houseman, Capital (40% of loss)	2,800	
	Inventory		22,000
	To record sale of partnership inventory at a $7,000 loss.		
7/15/07	Cash	9,000	
	Morgan, Capital	1,800	
	Houseman, Capital	1,200	
	Accounts Receivable		12,000
	To record collection of accounts receivable with write-off of remaining $3,000 in accounts as bad debts.		
8/20/07	Cash	29,000	
	Morgan, Capital	7,200	
	Houseman, Capital	4,800	
	Land, Building, and Equipment (net)		41,000
	To record sale of fixed assets and allocation of $12,000 loss.		
8/25/07	Liabilities	32,000	
	Cash		32,000
	To record payment made to settle the liabilities of the partnership.		
9/10/07	Morgan, Capital	1,800	
	Houseman, Capital	1,200	
	Cash		3,000
	To record payment of liquidation expenses with the amounts recorded as direct reductions to the partners' capital accounts.		

After liquidating the partnership assets and paying off all obligations, the cash that remains can be divided between Morgan and Houseman personally. The following schedule is utilized to determine the partners' ending capital account balances and, thus, the appropriate distribution for this final payment:

Cash and Capital Account Balances

	Cash	Morgan, Capital	Houseman, Capital
Beginning balances*	$ 45,000	$50,000	$38,000
Sold inventory	15,000	(4,200)	(2,800)
Collected accounts receivable	9,000	(1,800)	(1,200)
Sold fixed assets	29,000	(7,200)	(4,800)
Paid liabilities	(32,000)	–0–	–0–
Paid liquidation expenses	(3,000)	(1,800)	(1,200)
Final totals	$ 63,000	$35,000	$28,000

*Because of the presence of other assets as well as liabilities, the beginning balances in Cash and in the capital accounts are not equal.

After the ending capital balances have been calculated, the remaining cash can be distributed to the partners to close out the financial records of the partnership:

10/15/07	Morgan, Capital	35,000	
	Houseman, Capital	28,000	
	Cash		63,000
	To record distribution of cash to partners in accordance with final capital balances.		

Schedule of Liquidation

Liquidation can take a considerable length of time to complete. Because the various parties involved seek continually updated financial information, the accountant should produce frequent reports summarizing the transactions as they occur. Consequently, a statement (often referred to as the *schedule of liquidation*) can be prepared at periodic intervals to disclose

- Transactions to date.
- Property still being held by the partnership.
- Liabilities remaining to be paid.
- Current cash and capital balances.

Although the preceding Morgan and Houseman example has been condensed into a few events occurring during a relatively brief period of time, partnership liquidations usually require numerous transactions that transpire over months and, perhaps, even years. By receiving frequent schedules of liquidation, both the creditors and the partners are able to stay apprised of the results of this lengthy process.

Exhibit 15.1 presents the final schedule of liquidation for the partnership of Morgan and Houseman. The accountant should have distributed previous statements at each important juncture of this liquidation to meet the informational needs of the parties involved. The example produced here demonstrates the stair-step approach incorporated in preparing a schedule of liquidation. The effects of each transaction (or group of transactions) are outlined in a horizontal fashion so that current account balances as well as all prior transactions are evident. This structuring also facilitates the preparation of future statements: A new layer summarizing recent events can simply be added at the bottom each time that a new schedule is to be produced.

EXHIBIT 15.1

MORGAN AND HOUSEMAN
Schedule of Partnership Liquidation
Final Balances

	Cash	Noncash Assets	Liabilities	Morgan, Capital (60%)	Houseman, Capital (40%)
Beginning balances, 5/1/07	$ 45,000	$ 75,000	$ 32,000	$ 50,000	$ 38,000
Sold inventory, 6/1/07	15,000	(22,000)		(4,200)	(2,800)
Updated balances	60,000	53,000	32,000	45,800	35,200
Collected receivables, 7/15/07	9,000	(12,000)		(1,800)	(1,200)
Updated balances	69,000	41,000	32,000	44,000	34,000
Sold fixed assets, 8/20/07	29,000	(41,000)		(7,200)	(4,800)
Updated balances	98,000	–0–	32,000	36,800	29,200
Paid liabilities, 8/25/07	(32,000)		(32,000)		
Updated balances	66,000	–0–	–0–	36,800	29,200
Paid liquidation expenses, 9/10/07	(3,000)			(1,800)	(1,200)
Updated balances	63,000	–0–	–0–	35,000	28,000
Distributed remaining cash, 10/15/07	(63,000)			(35,000)	(28,000)
Closing balances	–0–	–0–	–0–	–0–	–0–

Deficit Capital Balance—Contribution by Partner

In Exhibit 15.1, the liquidation process ended with both partners continuing to report positive capital balances. Thus, Morgan and Houseman were both able to share in the $63,000 cash that remained. Unfortunately, such an outcome is not always assured. At the end of a liquidation, one or more partners could have a negative capital account, or the partnership could be unable to generate even enough cash to satisfy all of the claims of its creditors. Such deficits are most likely to occur when the partnership is already insolvent at the start of the liquidation or when the disposal of noncash assets results in material losses. Under these circumstances, the accounting procedures to be applied depend on legal regulations as well as the individual actions of the partners.

To illustrate, assume that the partnership of Holland, Dozier, and Ross was dissolved at the beginning of the current year. Business activities were terminated and all noncash assets were subsequently converted into cash. During the liquidation process, the partnership incurred a number of large losses that have been allocated to the partners' capital accounts on a 4:4:2 basis, respectively. A portion of the resulting cash is then used to pay all partnership liabilities and liquidation expenses.

Following these transactions, assume that only the following four account balances remain open within the partnership's records:

Cash	$20,000	Holland, Capital	$(6,000)
		Dozier, Capital	15,000
		Ross, Capital	11,000
		Total	$20,000

Holland is now reporting a negative capital balance of $6,000; the assigned share of partnership losses has exceeded this partner's net contribution. In such cases, the Uniform Partnership Act (Section 18[a]) stipulates that the partner "must contribute toward the losses, whether of capital or otherwise, sustained by the partnership according to his share in the profits." Therefore, Holland legally is required to convey an additional $6,000 to the partnership at this time to eliminate the deficit balance. This contribution raises the cash balance to $26,000, which allows a complete distribution to be made to Dozier ($15,000) and Ross ($11,000) in line with their capital accounts. The journal entry for this final payment closes out the partnership records:

Cash	6,000	
Holland, Capital		6,000
To record contribution made by Holland to extinguish negative capital balance.		
Dozier, Capital	15,000	
Ross, Capital	11,000	
Cash		26,000
To record distribution of remaining cash to partners in accordance with their ending capital balances.		

Deficit Capital Balance—Loss to Remaining Partners

Unfortunately, an alternative scenario can easily be conceived for the previous partnership liquidation. Although Holland's capital account shows a $6,000 deficit balance, this partner could resist any attempt to force an additional investment, especially because the business is in the process of being terminated. The possibility of such recalcitrance is enhanced if the individual is having personal financial difficulties. Thus, the remaining partners may eventually have to resort to formal litigation to gain Holland's contribution. Until that legal action is concluded, the partnership records remain open although inactive.

Distribution of Safe Payments

While awaiting the final resolution of this matter, no compelling reason exists for the partnership to continue holding $20,000 in cash. These funds will eventually be paid to Dozier and Ross regardless of any action that Holland takes. An immediate transfer should be made to these two partners to allow them the use of their money. However, because Dozier has a $15,000 capital account balance and Ross currently reports $11,000, a complete distribution is not possible. A method must be devised, therefore, to allow for a fair allocation of the available $20,000.

    To ensure the equitable treatment of all parties, this initial distribution is based on the assumption that the $6,000 capital deficit will prove to be a total loss to the partnership. Holland may, for example, be completely insolvent so that no additional payment will ever be forthcoming. By making this conservative presumption, the accountant is able to calculate the lowest possible amounts (or *safe balances*) that Dozier and Ross must retain in their capital accounts to be able to absorb all future losses.

    Should Holland's $6,000 deficit (or any portion of it) prove uncollectible, the loss will be written off against the capital accounts of Dozier and Ross. Allocation of this amount is based on the relative profit and loss ratio specified in the articles of partnership. According to the information provided, Dozier and Ross are credited with 40 percent and 20 percent of all partnership income, respectively. This 40:20 ratio equates to a 2:1 relationship (or $\frac{2}{3}$:$\frac{1}{3}$) between the two. Thus, if no part of the $6,000 deficit balance is ever recovered from Holland, $4,000 (two-thirds) of the loss will be assigned to Dozier and $2,000 (one-third) to Ross:

Allocation of Potential $6,000 Loss

Dozier . . . . $\frac{2}{3}$ of $(6,000) = $(4,000)
Ross . . . . $\frac{1}{3}$ of $(6,000) = $(2,000)

These amounts represent the maximum potential reductions that the two remaining partners could still incur. Depending on Holland's actions, Dozier could be forced to absorb an additional

$4,000 loss, and Ross's capital account could decrease by as much as $2,000. These balances must therefore remain in the respective capital accounts until the issue is resolved. Hence, Dozier is entitled to receive $11,000 in cash at the present time; this distribution reduces that partner's capital account from $15,000 to the minimum $4,000 level. Likewise, a $9,000 payment to Ross decreases the $11,000 capital balance to the $2,000 limit. These $11,000 and $9,000 amounts represent safe payments that can be distributed to the partners without fear of new deficits being created in the future.

Dozier, Capital	11,000	
Ross, Capital	9,000	
Cash		20,000
To record distribution of cash to Dozier and Ross based on safe capital balances, using the assumption that Holland will not contribute further to the partnership.		

After this $20,000 cash distribution, only a few other events can possibly occur during the remaining life of the partnership. Holland, either voluntarily or through legal persuasion, may contribute the entire $6,000 needed to eradicate the capital deficit. In that situation, the money should be immediately turned over to Dozier ($4,000) and Ross ($2,000) based on their remaining capital balances. The partnership records are effectively closed by this final distribution.

A second possibility is that Dozier and Ross could be unable to recover any part of the deficit from Holland. These two remaining partners must then absorb the $6,000 loss themselves. Because adequate safe capital balances have been maintained, recording a complete default by Holland serves to close out the partnership books.

Dozier, Capital (⅔ of loss)	4,000	
Ross, Capital (⅓ of loss)	2,000	
Holland, Capital		6,000
To record allocation of deficit capital balance of insolvent partner.		

Deficit Is Partly Collectible

One other ending to this partnership liquidation is conceivable. The partnership could recover a portion of the $6,000 from Holland, but the remainder could prove to be uncollectible. This partner could become bankrupt, or the other partners could simply give up trying to collect. The partners could also negotiate this settlement to avoid protracted legal actions.

To illustrate, assume that Holland manages to contribute $3,600 to the partnership but subsequently files for relief under the provisions of the bankruptcy laws. In a later legal arrangement, $1,000 additional cash goes to the partnership, but the final $1,400 will never be collected. This series of events creates the following effects within the liquidation process:

1. The $3,600 contribution is distributed to Dozier and Ross based on a new computation of their safe capital balances.
2. The $1,400 default is charged against the two positive capital balances in accordance with the relative profit and loss ratio.
3. The final $1,000 contribution is then paid to Dozier and Ross in amounts equal to their ending capital accounts, a transaction that closes the partnership's financial records.

The distribution of the first $3,600 depends on a recalculation of the minimum capital balances that Dozier and Ross must maintain to absorb all potential losses. Each of these computations is necessary because of a basic realization: Holland's remaining deficit balance

($2,400 at this time) could prove to be a total loss. This approach guarantees that the other two partners will continue to report sufficient capital until the liquidation is ultimately resolved.

	Current Capital	Allocation of Potential Loss	Safe Capital Payments
Dozier	$4,000	⅔ of $(2,400) = $(1,600)	$2,400
Ross	2,000	⅓ of $(2,400) = $ (800)	1,200

Thus, the $3,600 in cash that is now available is distributed immediately to Dozier and Ross based on their safe balances:

Cash	3,600	
Holland, Capital		3,600
Dozier, Capital	2,400	
Ross, Capital	1,200	
Cash		3,600
To record capital contribution by Holland and subsequent distribution of funds to Dozier and Ross based on safe capital balances.		

After recording this $3,600 contribution from Holland and the subsequent disbursement, the capital accounts for the partnership stay open, registering the following individual balances:

Holland, Capital (deficit)	$(2,400)
Dozier, Capital (safe balance)	1,600
Ross, Capital (safe balance)	800

These accounts continue to remain on the partnership books until the final resolution of Holland's obligation.

In this illustration, the $1,000 legal settlement and the remaining $1,400 loss ultimately allow the parties to close out the records:

Cash	1,000	
Dozier, Capital (⅔ of loss)	933	
Ross, Capital (⅓ of loss)	467	
Holland, Capital		2,400
To record final $1,000 cash settlement of Holland's interest and resulting $1,400 loss.		
Dozier, Capital	667	
Ross, Capital	333	
Cash		1,000
To record distribution of final cash balance based upon remaining capital account totals.		

Marshaling of Assets

In the previous example, one partner (Holland) became insolvent during the liquidation process. Personal bankruptcy is not uncommon and raises questions as to the legal right that damaged partners have to proceed against an insolvent partner. *More specifically, is a deficit capital balance the legal equivalent of any other personal liability? Do partners who must absorb additional losses have the same rights against their partners as other creditors?*

Addressing this issue, the Uniform Partnership Act (Section 40[i]) stipulates the following:

Where a partner has become bankrupt or his estate is insolvent the claims against his separate property shall rank in the following order:

(I) Those owing to separate creditors,

(II) Those owing to partnership creditors,

(III) Those owing to partners by way of contribution.

This ranking of the claims against an individual partner is normally referred to as the *marshaling of assets* and allows for an orderly distribution of property in bankruptcy cases. It clearly shows that partners rank last in collecting from a bankrupt partner.

To demonstrate the effects created by this legal doctrine, assume that Stone is a partner in a business that is undergoing final liquidation. The partnership is insolvent: All assets have been expended, but liabilities of $15,000 still remain. Stone is also personally insolvent. The assets that Stone currently holds cannot satisfy all obligations:

Personal assets	$50,000
Personal liabilities	40,000
Deficit capital balance—partnership	19,000

Under these circumstances, the ranking established by the Uniform Partnership Act becomes extremely important. Stone holds $50,000 in assets. However, because these assets are limited, recovery by the various parties depends on the pattern of distribution. According to the marshaling of assets doctrine, Stone's own creditors have first priority. After these claims have been satisfied, the $10,000 in remaining assets should be used to remunerate any partnership creditors who have sought recovery directly from Stone.

As indicated, partnership debts are $15,000, and its creditors can seek to collect from Stone (or any other general partner). Only then, after personal creditors as well as partnership creditors have been paid, can the other partners claim the residual portion of Stone's assets. Obviously, because of Stone's financial condition, the chances are not good that these partners will be able to recover all or even a significant portion of the $19,000 deficit capital balance. By ranking last on this priority list, partners are forced to accept whatever assets remain.

To help analyze and understand the possible effects created by the marshaling of assets concept, we consider a variety of other scenarios. Assume, as an alternative to the previous example, that Stone failed to have sufficient property to satisfy even personal creditors: Stone holds $50,000 in assets but $80,000 in personal liabilities. Because of the volume of these debts, neither the partnership creditors nor the other partners will be able to recoup any money from this partner. All personal assets must be used to pay Stone's own obligations. Even with preferential treatment, the personal creditors still face a $30,000 shortfall because of the limited amount of available assets. This potential loss raises another legal question: Can Stone's personal creditors seek recovery of the $30,000 remaining debt directly from the partnership?

In response to this question, the marshaling of assets doctrine specifies that personal creditors can, indeed, claim a partner's share of partnership assets. However, recovery of all, or even a portion, of the $30,000 is possible only by meeting two specific criteria:

1. Payment of all partnership debts is assured.
2. The insolvent partner has a positive capital balance.

Even if both of these conditions are met, personal creditors have no right to receive more than the total of that partner's capital balance nor more than the amount of the debt.

This priority ranking of claims provides legal guidance in insolvency cases. Three additional examples follow to present a more complete demonstration of the marshaling of assets principle. Each presents the legal and accounting responses to a specific partnership liquidation problem. In the first two illustrations, one or more of the partners is personally insolvent. The third analyzes the marshaling of assets in connection with an insolvent partnership.

Insolvency—Example 1

The following balance sheet has been produced for the Able, Baker, Cannon, and Duke partnership. Profit and loss allocation percentages are also included.

Cash	$ 30,000	Liabilities	$ 80,000
Noncash assets	150,000	Able, capital (40%)	15,000
		Baker, capital (30%)	40,000
		Cannon, capital (20%)	30,000
		Duke, capital (10%)	15,000
Total assets	$180,000	Total liabilities and capital	$180,000

Baker is insolvent, and personal creditors have filed a $30,000 claim against this partner's share of partnership property. The litigation has forced the partnership to begin liquidation to settle Baker's interest. As shown in the balance sheet, the partnership has $30,000 in cash and Baker has a capital balance of $40,000.

Assume in this example that the partnership sells its noncash assets (with a book value of $150,000) for $100,000 and then pays its liabilities ($80,000). These two actions increase the cash balance by $20,000 to a $50,000 figure. No other assets or liabilities exist. The adjusted capital accounts for each partner follow. Other than Baker, all partners are personally solvent.

	Able, Capital	Baker, Capital	Cannon, Capital	Duke, Capital
Beginning balances	$15,000	$40,000	$30,000	$15,000
$50,000 loss on liquidation of assets	(20,000) (40%)	(15,000) (30%)	(10,000) (20%)	(5,000) (10%)
Capital balances	$ (5,000)	$25,000	$20,000	$10,000

An additional $5,000 contribution should be forthcoming from Able to eradicate the single negative capital balance. After this contribution has been made, this investment raises the partnership's cash to $55,000 and permits a final distribution to Cannon ($20,000), Duke ($10,000), and *Baker's creditors* ($25,000). The liquidation losses have reduced Baker's capital account below the $30,000 level; therefore, this partner's personal creditors will be unable to recover the entire amount of their claims. Despite the remaining $5,000 debt, they have no further legal recourse here; no right of recovery exists against the other partners once the capital account has been depleted.

Baker will receive nothing from this liquidation settlement because the personal obligations have not been completely satisfied. In contrast, if the final capital balance had been in excess of $30,000, Baker would have been entitled to any residual amount after extinguishing all personal liabilities.

Insolvency—Example 2

The following balance sheet for the partnership of Morris, Newton, Olsen, and Prince also indicates the applicable profit and loss percentages. Both Morris and Prince are personally insolvent. Morris's creditors have brought an $8,000 claim against the partnership's assets, and Prince's creditors are seeking $15,000. These claims have forced the partnership to terminate operations so that the business property can be liquidated. The question as to which partner is entitled to any cash balance that remains is again raised.

Cash	$ 10,000	Liabilities	$ 70,000
Noncash assets	140,000	Morris, capital (40%)	15,000
		Newton, capital (20%)	10,000
		Olsen, capital (20%)	23,000
		Prince, capital (20%)	32,000
Total assets	$150,000	Total liabilities and capital	$150,000

Assume that the partnership sells the noncash assets for a total of $80,000, creating a $60,000 loss, and pays all its liabilities. The partnership's accounting system records these two events as follows:

Cash	80,000	
Morris, Capital (40% of loss)	24,000	
Newton, Capital (20% of loss)	12,000	
Olsen, Capital (20% of loss)	12,000	
Prince, Capital (20% of loss)	12,000	
Noncash Assets (or specific accounts)		140,000
To record sale of noncash assets and allocation of resulting $60,000 loss.		
Liabilities	70,000	
Cash		70,000
To record extinguishment of partnership obligations.		

Because of these two transactions, the partnership's cash has increased from $10,000 to $20,000.

After the allocation of this loss, the capital accounts for Morris and Newton report deficit balances of $9,000 ($15,000 − $24,000) and $2,000 ($10,000 − $12,000), respectively. Although Newton is solvent and would be expected to compensate the partnership, Morris's personal financial condition does not allow for any further contribution. Therefore, Newton, Olsen, and Prince must absorb Morris's $9,000 deficit. Because these three partners have historically shared profits evenly (20:20:20), they continue to do so in recording this additional capital loss:

Newton, Capital (⅓ of loss)	3,000	
Olsen, Capital (⅓ of loss)	3,000	
Prince, Capital (⅓ of loss)	3,000	
Morris, Capital		9,000
To record write-off of deficit capital balance of insolvent partner.		

This last allocation increases Newton's deficit to a $5,000 balance ($2,000 + $3,000), an amount that the partner should now contribute in accordance with partnership law:

Cash	5,000	
Newton, Capital		5,000
To record contribution from solvent partner necessitated by negative capital balance.		

Following this series of transactions, only the cash balance (now $25,000) and Olsen's and Prince's capital accounts remain open within the partnership records:

	Cash	Morris, Capital	Newton, Capital	Olsen, Capital	Prince, Capital
Beginning balances	$10,000	$15,000	$10,000	$23,000	$32,000
Sold assets	80,000	(24,000)	(12,000)	(12,000)	(12,000)
Paid liabilities	(70,000)	–0–	–0–	–0–	–0–
Default by Morris	–0–	9,000	(3,000)	(3,000)	(3,000)
Contribution by Newton	5,000	–0–	5,000	–0–	–0–
Current balances	$25,000	–0–	–0–	$ 8,000	$17,000

Although $8,000 of the partnership's remaining cash goes directly to Olsen, the $17,000 attributed to Prince is first subjected to the claims of the partner's personal creditors. Because of their claims, $15,000 of this amount must be used to satisfy these obligations, with only the final $2,000 being paid to Prince.

Insolvency—Example 3

The two previous illustrations analyzed liquidations in which one or more of the partners has been personally insolvent. Another possibility is that the partnership itself meets this same fate. In an active partnership, insolvency can occur if losses, partner drawings, or litigation deplete the working capital of the operation. A bankruptcy petition could follow if the partnership cannot meet its debts as they come due. Liquidation of business assets could be necessary unless the partnership can generate additional capital quickly. Even a financially sound partnership can become insolvent if it incurs material losses during a voluntary liquidation.

To serve as a basis for examining the accounting and legal ramifications of an insolvent partnership, assume that the law firm of Keller, Lewis, Monroe, and Norris is in the final stages of liquidation. The firm has sold all noncash assets and has used available cash to pay a portion of the business's liabilities. After these transactions, the following account balances remain open within the partnership's records. The four partners in this endeavor share profits and losses equally.

Liabilities	$ 20,000
Keller, capital	(30,000)
Lewis, capital	(5,000)
Monroe, capital	5,000
Norris, capital	10,000

Note: Parentheses indicate deficit.

This partnership is insolvent; it continues to owe creditors $20,000, even after liquidation and distribution of all assets. However, additional money should be forthcoming from two of the partners. Because of their deficit capital accounts, Keller and Lewis are legally required to contribute an additional $30,000 and $5,000, respectively, to the business. With these newly available funds, the partnership will be able to pay all $20,000 of its remaining liabilities as well as make cash distributions to Monroe ($5,000) and Norris ($10,000) in accordance with their capital account balances. This final payment would close the partnership books.

Once again, the possibility exists that one or more of the partners who are reporting a negative capital balance will not step forward to make any further investment. Assume, for example, that Keller is personally insolvent and cannot contribute, whereas Lewis simply refuses to supply additional funds in hope of avoiding the obligation. *At this point, the remaining creditors can instigate legal recovery proceedings against any or all of the partners regardless of their capital balances.* Any action, however, against the insolvent partner could prove to be a futile effort because of the marshaling of assets principle.

Predicting the exact outcome of litigation is rarely possible. Thus, we assume here that Norris is forced to contribute $20,000 cash to settle the remaining liabilities. The following journal entries would then be required for this partnership:

Cash	20,000	
Norris, Capital		20,000
Liabilities	20,000	
Cash		20,000
To record capital contribution by Norris made to pay remaining partnership creditors.		

After all liabilities have been extinguished, the partners who still maintain positive capital accounts can demand remuneration from any partner with a negative balance. Despite this legal obligation, the chances of a significant recovery from the insolvent Keller, especially

WHAT HAPPENS IF A PARTNER BECOMES INSOLVENT?

In 1995, three dentists—Ben Rogers, Judy Wilkinson, and Henry Walker—formed a partnership to open a practice in Toledo, Ohio. The partnership's primary purpose was to reduce expenses by sharing building and equipment costs, supplies, and the services of a clerical staff. Each contributed $70,000 in cash and, with the help of a bank loan, constructed a building and acquired furniture, fixtures, and equipment. Because the partners maintained their own separate clients, annual net income has been allocated as follows: Each partner receives the specific amount of revenues that he or she generated during the period less one-third of all expenses. From the beginning, the partners did not anticipate expansion of the practice; consequently, they could withdraw cash each year up to 90 percent of their share of income for the period.

The partnership had been profitable for a number of years. Over the years, Rogers has used much of his income to speculate in real estate in the Toledo area. By 2007, he was spending less time with the dental practice so that he could concentrate on his investments. Unfortunately, a number of these deals proved to be bad decisions and he incurred significant losses. On November 8, 2007, while Rogers was out of town, his personal creditors filed a $97,000 claim against the partnership assets. Unbeknownst to Wilkinson and Walker, Rogers had become insolvent.

Wilkinson and Walker hurriedly met to discuss the problem because Rogers could not be located. Rogers's capital account was currently at $105,000, but the partnership had only $27,000 in cash and liquid assets. The partners knew that Rogers's equipment had been used for a number of years and could be sold for relatively little. In contrast, the building had appreciated in value, and the claim could be satisfied by selling the property. However, this action would have a tremendously adverse impact on the dental practice of the remaining two partners.

What alternatives are available to Wilkinson and Walker, and what are the advantages and disadvantages of each?

under the marshaling of assets doctrine, is not likely. Thus, the partners could choose to write off this deficit as a step toward closing the partnership's financial records. Legal recovery proceedings can still continue against Keller regardless of the accounting treatment. As equal partners, Lewis, Monroe, and Norris absorb the $30,000 loss evenly.

Lewis, Capital (⅓ of loss)	10,000	
Monroe, Capital (⅓ of loss)	10,000	
Norris, Capital (⅓ of loss)	10,000	
Keller, Capital		30,000
To record write-off of deficit capital balance of insolvent partner.		

The partners' capital accounts now have the following balances:

	Keller, Capital	Lewis, Capital	Monroe, Capital	Norris, Capital
Beginning balances	$(30,000)	$ (5,000)	$ 5,000	$10,000
Capital contribution	–0–	–0–	–0–	20,000
Write-off of deficit balance	30,000	(10,000)	(10,000)	(10,000)
Current balances	–0–	$(15,000)	$(5,000)	$20,000

Both Lewis and Monroe now have a legal obligation to reimburse the partnership to offset their deficit capital balances. Upon their payment of $15,000 and $5,000, respectively, the entire $20,000 will be distributed to Norris (the only partner with a positive balance), and the partnership's books will be closed. Should either Lewis or Monroe fail to make the appropriate contribution, the additional loss must be allocated between the two remaining partners.

Preliminary Distribution of Partnership Assets

In all of the illustrations analyzed in this chapter, distributions were made to the partners only after all assets were sold and all liabilities paid. As previously mentioned, a liquidation can take an extended time to complete. During this lengthy process, the partnership need not retain any assets that will eventually be disbursed to the partners. If the business is safely solvent, waiting until all affairs have been settled before transferring property to the owners is not warranted. The partners should be allowed to use their own funds at the earliest possible time.

The objective in making any type of preliminary distribution is to ensure that the partnership maintains enough capital to absorb all future losses. Any capital in excess of this maximum requirement is a safe balance, an amount that can be immediately conveyed to the partner. To determine safe capital balances at any time, the accountant simply assumes that all subsequent events will result in maximum losses: No cash will be received in liquidating remaining noncash assets and each partner is personally insolvent. Any positive capital balance that would remain even after the inclusion of all potential losses can be paid to the partner without delay. Although the assumption that no further funds will be generated could be unrealistic, it does ensure that negative capital balances are not created by premature payments being made to any of the partners.

Preliminary Distribution Illustrated

To demonstrate the computation of safe capital distributions, assume that a liquidating partnership reports the following balance sheet:

Cash	$60,000	Liabilities		$40,000
Noncash assets	140,000	Mason, loan		20,000
		Mason, capital (50%)		60,000
		Lee, capital (30%)		30,000
		Dixon, capital (20%)		50,000
Total assets	$200,000	Total liabilities and capital		$200,000

Assume also that the partners estimate that $6,000 will be the maximum expense incurred in carrying out this liquidation. Consequently, the partnership needs only $46,000 to meet all obligations: $40,000 to satisfy partnership liabilities and $6,000 for these final expenses. Because the partnership holds $60,000 in cash, it can transfer the extra $14,000 to the partners immediately without fear of injuring any participants in the liquidation. However, the appropriate allocation of this money is not readily apparent; safe capital balances must be computed to guide the actual distribution.

Before the allocation of this $14,000 is demonstrated, we examine the appropriate handling of a partner's loan balance. According to the balance sheet, Mason has conveyed $20,000 to the business at some point in the past, an amount that was considered a loan rather than additional capital. Perhaps the partnership was in desperate need of funds and Mason was willing to contribute only if the contribution was structured as a loan. Regardless of the reason, the question as to the status of this account remains: Is the $20,000 to be viewed as a liability to the partner or as a capital balance? The answer becomes especially significant during the liquidation process because available funds often are limited. In this regard, the Uniform Partnership Act (UPA) (Section 40[b]) stipulates that loans to partners rank behind obligations to outside creditors in order of payment but ahead of the partners' capital balances.

Although this legal provision indicates that the debt to Mason must be repaid entirely before any distribution of capital can be made to the other partners, actual accounting practice takes a different view. "In preparing predistribution schedules, accountants typically offset partners' loans with the partners' capital accounts and then distribute funds accordingly."[9]

---

[9] Robert E. Whitis and Jeffrey R. Pittman, "Inconsistencies between Accounting Practices and Statutory Law in Partnership Liquidations," *Accounting Educators' Journal,* Fall 1996, p. 99.

In other words, the loan is merged in with the partner's capital account balance at the beginning of liquidation. Thus, accounting practice and the UPA seem to differ on the handling of a loan from a partner.

To illustrate the potential problem with this conflict, assume that a partnership has $20,000 in cash left after liquidation. Partner A has a positive capital balance of $20,000 whereas Partner B has a negative capital balance of $20,000. In addition, Partner B has previously loaned the partnership $20,000. If Partner B is insolvent, a distribution problem arises.[10] If the provisions of the UPA are followed literally, the $20,000 cash should be given to Partner B (probably to the creditors of Partner B) to repay the loan. Because Partner B is insolvent, no more assets can be expected from this individual. Thus, Partner A would have to absorb the entire $20,000 deficit capital balance and will get no portion of the $20,000 in cash that the business holds.

However, despite the UPA, common practice appears to be that the loan from Partner B will be used to offset that partner's negative capital balance. Using that approach, Partner B is left with a zero capital balance so that the entire $20,000 goes to Partner A; neither Partner B nor the creditors of Partner B get anything. Thus, when a loan comes from a partner who later becomes insolvent and reports a negative capital balance, the handling of the loan becomes significant. Unfortunately, further legal guidance does not exist at this time because "no reported state or federal opinion has directly ruled on the right of offset of potential capital deficits."[11]

To follow common practice, this textbook accounts for a loan from a partner in liquidation as if the balance were a component of the partner's capital. By this offset, the accountant can reduce the amount accumulated as a negative capital balance for any insolvent partner. Any such loan can be transferred into the corresponding capital account at the start of the liquidation process. Similarly, any loans due from a partner should be shown as a reduction in the appropriate capital balance.

Proposed Schedule of Liquidation

Returning to the current illustration, the accountant needs to determine an equitable distribution for the $14,000 cash presently available. To structure this computation, a proposed schedule of liquidation is developed *based on the underlying assumption that all future events will result in total losses.* Exhibit 15.2 presents this statement for the Mason, Lee, and Dixon partnership. To expedite coverage, the $20,000 loan has already been transferred into Mason's capital account. Thus, regardless of whether this partner arrives at a deficit or a safe capital balance, the loan figure already has been included.

Production of Exhibit 15.2 forecasts complete losses ($140,000) in connection with the disposition of all noncash assets and anticipates liquidation expenses at maximum amounts ($6,000). Following the projected payment of liabilities, any partner reporting a negative capital account is assumed to be personally insolvent. These potential deficit balances are written off and the losses are assigned to the remaining solvent partners based on their relative profit and loss ratio. Lee, with a negative $13,800, is eliminated first. This allocation creates a deficit of $2,857 for Mason, an amount that Dixon alone must absorb. After this series of maximum losses has been simulated, any positive capital balance that still remains is considered safe; a cash distribution of that amount can be made to the specific partners.

Exhibit 15.2 indicates that only Dixon has a large enough capital balance at the present time to absorb all possible future losses. Thus, the entire $14,000 can be distributed to this partner with no fear that the capital account will ever report a deficit. Based on current practice, Mason, despite having made a $20,000 loan to the partnership, is entitled to no part of this initial distribution. The loan is of insufficient size to prevent potential deficits from occurring in Mason's capital account.

---

[10] The same problem should not exist if the partner is solvent. The partner is legally required to contribute enough funds to delete any capital deficit. Thus, in this case, Partner B would be entitled to the $20,000 loan repayment but then must contribute $20,000 because of the negative capital balance. That cash amount would go to Partner A because of that partner's positive capital balance.

[11] Whitis and Pittman, "Inconsistencies between Accounting Practices," p. 93.

EXHIBIT 15.2

				Mason, Capital (50%)	Lee, Capital (30%)	Dixon, Capital (20%)
MASON, LEE, AND DIXON						
Proposed Schedule of Liquidation—Initial Safe Capital Balances						
	Cash	Noncash Assets	Liabilities			
Beginning balances	$ 60,000	$140,000	$40,000	$80,000	$ 30,000	$ 50,000
Maximum loss on noncash assets	–0–	(140,000)	–0–	(70,000)	(42,000)	(28,000)
Maximum liquidation expenses	(6,000)	–0–	–0–	(3,000)	(1,800)	(1,200)
Payment of liabilities	(40,000)	–0–	(40,000)	–0–	–0–	–0–
Potential balances	14,000	–0–	–0–	7,000	(13,800)	20,800
Assume Lee to be insolvent	–0–	–0–	–0–	(9,857) (5⁄7)	13,800	(3,943) (2⁄7)
Potential balances	14,000	–0–	–0–	(2,857)	–0–	16,857
Assume Mason to be insolvent	–0–	–0–	–0–	2,857	–0–	(2,857)
Safe balances	$ 14,000	–0–	–0–	–0–	–0–	$ 14,000

One series of computations found in this proposed schedule of liquidation merits additional attention. The simulated losses initially create a $13,800 negative balance in Lee's capital account while the other two partners continue to report positive figures. Mason and Dixon must then absorb Lee's projected deficit according to their relative profit and loss percentages. Previously, Mason was allocated 50 percent of net income with 20 percent recorded to Dixon. These figures equate to a $^{50}/_{70}{:}^{20}/_{70}$, or a $^5/_7{:}^2/_7$ ratio. Based on this realigned relationship, the $13,800 potential deficit is allocated between Mason ($^5/_7$, or $9,857) and Dixon ($^2/_7$, or $3,943), reducing Mason's own capital account to a negative balance as shown in Exhibit 15.2.

Continuing with the assumption that maximum losses occur in all cases, Mason's $2,857 deficit is accounted for as if that partner were also personally insolvent. Therefore, the entire negative balance is assigned to Dixon, the only partner still retaining a positive capital account. Because all potential losses have been recognized at this point, the remaining $14,000 capital is a safe balance that should be paid to Dixon. Even after the money is distributed, Dixon's capital account will still be large enough to absorb all future losses.

Liquidation in Installments

In practice, maximum liquidation losses are not likely to occur to any business. Thus, at various points during this process, additional cash amounts can become available as partnership property is sold. If the assets are disposed of in a piecemeal fashion, cash can actually flow into the company on a regular basis for an extended period of time. As needed, updated safe capital schedules must be developed to dictate the recipients of newly available funds. Because numerous capital distributions could be required, this process is often referred to as a *liquidation made in installments.*

To illustrate, assume that the partnership of Mason, Lee, and Dixon actually undergoes the following events in connection with its liquidation:

- As the proposed schedule of liquidation in Exhibit 15.2 indicates, Dixon receives $14,000 in cash as a preliminary capital distribution.
- Noncash assets with a book value of $50,000 are sold for $20,000.
- All $40,000 in liabilities are settled.
- Liquidation expenses of $2,000 are paid; the partners now believe that only a maximum of $3,000 more will be expended in this manner. The original estimation of $6,000 was apparently too high.

As a result of these transactions, the partnership has an additional $21,000 in cash now available to distribute to the partners: $20,000 received from the sale of noncash assets and

EXHIBIT 15.3 Liquidation for Installments

<table>
<tr><td colspan="7" align="center">MASON, LEE, AND DIXON
Proposed Schedule of Liquidation—Subsequent Safe Capital Balances</td></tr>
<tr><th></th><th>Cash</th><th>Noncash Assets</th><th>Liabilities</th><th>Mason, Capital (50%)</th><th>Lee, Capital (30%)</th><th>Dixon, Capital (20%)</th></tr>
<tr><td>Beginning balances ....</td><td>$ 60,000</td><td>$140,000</td><td>$ 40,000</td><td>$ 80,000</td><td>$ 30,000</td><td>$ 50,000</td></tr>
<tr><td>Capital distribution—safe balances ....</td><td>(14,000)</td><td>–0–</td><td>–0–</td><td>–0–</td><td>–0–</td><td>(14,000)</td></tr>
<tr><td>Disposal of noncash assets ....</td><td>20,000</td><td>(50,000)</td><td>–0–</td><td>(15,000)</td><td>(9,000)</td><td>(6,000)</td></tr>
<tr><td>Liabilities paid ....</td><td>(40,000)</td><td>–0–</td><td>(40,000)</td><td>–0–</td><td>–0–</td><td>–0–</td></tr>
<tr><td>Liquidation expenses ....</td><td>(2,000)</td><td>–0–</td><td>–0–</td><td>(1,000)</td><td>(600)</td><td>(400)</td></tr>
<tr><td>Current balances ....</td><td>24,000</td><td>90,000</td><td>–0–</td><td>64,000</td><td>20,400</td><td>29,600</td></tr>
<tr><td>Maximum loss on remaining noncash assets ....</td><td>–0–</td><td>(90,000)</td><td>–0–</td><td>(45,000)</td><td>(27,000)</td><td>(18,000)</td></tr>
<tr><td>Maximum liquidation expenses ....</td><td>(3,000)</td><td>–0–</td><td>–0–</td><td>(1,500)</td><td>(900)</td><td>(600)</td></tr>
<tr><td>Potential balances ....</td><td>21,000</td><td>–0–</td><td>–0–</td><td>17,500</td><td>(7,500)</td><td>11,000</td></tr>
<tr><td>Assume Lee to be insolvent ....</td><td>–0–</td><td>–0–</td><td>–0–</td><td>(5,357) (⅝)</td><td>7,500</td><td>(2,143) (⅜)</td></tr>
<tr><td>Safe balances—current ....</td><td>$ 21,000</td><td>–0–</td><td>–0–</td><td>$ 12,143</td><td>–0–</td><td>$ 8,857</td></tr>
</table>

another $1,000 because of the reduced estimation of liquidation expenses. Once again, the accountant must assume maximum future losses as a means of determining the appropriate distribution of these funds. The accountant produces a second proposed schedule of liquidation (Exhibit 15.3), indicating that $12,143 of this amount should go to Mason with the remaining $8,857 to Dixon. To facilitate a better visual understanding, actual transactions are recorded first on this schedule, followed by the assumed losses. *A dotted line separates the real from the potential occurrences.*

Predistribution Plan

The liquidation of a partnership can require numerous transactions occurring over a lengthy period of time. The continual production of proposed schedules of liquidation could become a burdensome chore. The previous illustration already has required two separate statements, and the partnership still possesses $90,000 in noncash assets awaiting conversion. *Therefore, at the start of a liquidation, most accountants produce a single predistribution plan to serve as a guideline for all future payments.* Thereafter, whenever cash becomes available, this plan indicates the appropriate recipient(s) without the necessity of drawing up ever-changing proposed schedules of liquidation.

A predistribution plan is developed by simulating a series of losses, each of which is just large enough to eliminate, one at a time, all of the partners' claims to partnership property. This approach recognizes that the individual capital accounts exhibit differing degrees of sensitivity to losses. Capital accounts possess varying balances and could be charged with losses at different rates. Consequently, a predistribution plan is based on calculating the losses (the "maximum loss allowable") that would eliminate each of these capital balances in a sequential pattern. This series of absorbed losses then forms the basis for the predistribution plan.

To demonstrate the creation of a predistribution plan, assume that the following partnership is to be liquidated:

Cash	–0–	Liabilities	$100,000
Noncash assets	$221,000	Rubens, capital (50%)	30,000
		Smith, capital (20%)	40,000
		Trice, capital (30%)	51,000
Total assets	$221,000	Total liabilities and capital	$221,000

The partnership capital reported by this organization totals $121,000. However, the individual balances for the partners range from $30,000 to $51,000, and profits and losses are assigned according to three different percentages. Thus, differing losses would reduce each partner's current capital balance to zero. *As a prerequisite to developing a predistribution plan, the sensitivity to losses exhibited by each of these capital accounts must be measured:*

Partner	Capital Balance/ Loss Allocation	Maximum Loss That Can Be Absorbed
Rubens	$30,000/50%	$60,000 ✔
Smith	40,000/20	200,000
Trice	51,000/30	170,000

According to this initial computation, Rubens is the partner in the most vulnerable position at the present time. Based on a 50 percent share of income, a loss of only $60,000 would reduce this partner's capital account to a zero balance. If the partnership does incur a loss of this amount, Rubens can no longer hope to recover any funds from the liquidation process. Thus, the following schedule simulates the potential effects of this loss (referred to as a *Step 1 loss*):

	Rubens, Capital	Smith, Capital	Trice, Capital
Beginning balances	$ 30,000	$ 40,000	$ 51,000
Assumed $60,000 loss	(30,000) (50%)	(12,000) (20%)	(18,000) (30%)
Step 1 balances	–0–	$ 28,000	$ 33,000

As previously discussed, the predistribution plan is based on describing the series of losses that would eliminate each partner's capital in turn and, thus, all claims to cash. In the previous Step 1 schedule, the $60,000 loss did reduce Rubens's capital account to zero. Assuming, as a precautionary step, that Rubens is personally insolvent, all further losses would have to be allocated between Smith and Trice. Because these two partners have previously shared partnership profits and losses on a 20 percent and 30 percent basis, a 20/50:30/50 (or 40%:60%) relationship exists between them. Therefore, these realigned percentages must now be utilized in calculating a *Step 2 loss,* the amount just large enough to exclude another of the remaining partners from sharing in any future cash distributions:

Partner	Capital Balance/ Loss Allocation	Maximum Loss That Can Be Absorbed
Smith	$28,000/40%	$70,000
Trice	33,000/60	55,000 ✔

Because Rubens's capital balance already has been eliminated, Trice is now in the most vulnerable position: Only a $55,000 Step 2 loss is required to reduce this partner's capital account to a zero balance.

	Rubens, Capital	Smith, Capital	Trice, Capital
Beginning balances	$ 30,000	$ 40,000	$ 51,000
Assumed $60,000 loss	(30,000) (50%)	(12,000) (20%)	(18,000) (30%)
Step 1 balances	–0–	$ 28,000	$ 33,000
Assumed $55,000 loss	–0–	(22,000) (40%)	(33,000) (60%)
Step 2 balances	–0–	$ 6,000	–0–

According to this second schedule, a total loss of $115,000 ($60,000 from Step 1 plus $55,000 from Step 2) leaves capital of only $6,000, a balance attributed entirely to Smith. At this final point in the simulation, an additional loss of this amount also ends Smith's right to receive any funds from the liquidation process. Having the sole positive capital account remaining, this partner would have to absorb the entire amount of the final loss.

	Rubens, Capital	Smith, Capital	Trice, Capital
Beginning balances	$ 30,000	$ 40,000	$ 51,000
Assumed $60,000 loss	(30,000) (50%)	(12,000) (20%)	(18,000) (30%)
Step 1 balances	–0–	$ 28,000	$ 33,000
Assumed $55,000 loss	–0–	(22,000) (40%)	(33,000) (60%)
Step 2 balances	–0–	6,000	–0–
Assumed $6,000 loss	–0–	(6,000) (100%)	–0–
Final balances	–0–	–0–	–0–

Once this series of simulated losses has reduced each partner's capital account to zero, a predistribution plan for the liquidation can be devised. *This procedure requires working backward through the preceding final schedule to determine the effects that will result if the assumed losses do not occur.* Without these losses, cash becomes available for the partners; therefore, a direct relationship exists between the volume of losses and the distribution pattern. For example, Smith will entirely absorb the last $6,000 loss. Should that loss fail to materialize, Smith is left with a positive safe capital balance of this amount. Thus, as cash becomes available, the first $6,000 received (in excess of partnership obligations and anticipated liquidation expenses) should be distributed solely to Smith.

In a similar manner, the preceding $55,000 Step 2 loss was divided between Smith and Trice on a 4:6 basis. Again, if such losses do not occur, these balances need not be retained to protect the partnership against capital deficits. Therefore, after Smith has received the initial $6,000, any additional cash that becomes available (up to $55,000) will be split between Smith (40 percent) and Trice (60 percent). For example, if the partnership holds exactly $61,000 in cash in excess of liabilities and possible liquidation expenses, the following distribution should be made:

	Rubens	Smith	Trice
First $6,000	–0–	$ 6,000	–0–
Next $55,000	–0–	22,000 (40%)	$33,000 (60%)
Cash distribution . . .	–0–	$28,000	$33,000

The predistribution plan can be completed by including the Step 1 loss, an amount that was to be absorbed by the partners on a 5:2:3 basis. Thus, all money that becomes available to the partners after the initial $61,000 is to be distributed according to the original profit and loss ratio. At this point in the liquidation, enough cash would have been generated to ensure that each partner has a safe capital balance: No possibility exists that a future deficit can occur. Any additional increases in the projected capital balances will be allocated by the 5:2:3 allocation pattern. *For this reason, once all partners begin to receive a portion of the cash disbursements, any remaining funds are divided based on the original profit and loss percentages.*

To inform all parties of the pattern by which available cash will be disbursed, the predistribution plan should be formally prepared in a schedule format prior to beginning liquidation. Following is the predistribution plan for the partnership of Rubens, Smith, and Trice. To complete this illustration, liquidation expenses of $12,000 have been estimated. Because these expenses have the same effect on the capital accounts as losses, they do not change the sequential pattern by which assets eventually will be distributed.

RUBENS, SMITH, AND TRICE
Predistribution Plan

Available Cash		Recipient
First	$112,000	Creditors ($100,000) and liquidation expenses (estimated at $12,000)
Next	6,000	Smith
Next	55,000	Smith (40%) and Trice (60%)
All further cash balances		Rubens (50%), Smith (20%), and Trice (30%)

Summary

1. Although a partnership can exist indefinitely through the periodic admission of new partners, termination of business activities and liquidation of property can take place for a number of reasons. A partner's death or retirement and the insolvency of a partner or even the partnership itself can trigger this process. Because of the risk that the partnership will incur large losses during liquidation, all parties usually seek frequent and timely information describing ongoing developments. The accountant is expected to furnish these data while also working to ensure the equitable treatment of all parties.

2. The liquidation process entails (*a*) converting partnership property into cash, (*b*) paying off liabilities and liquidation expenses, and (*c*) conveying any remaining property to the partners based on their final capital balances. As a means of reporting these transactions, a schedule of liquidation should be produced at periodic intervals. This statement discloses all recent transactions, the assets and liabilities still being held, and the current capital balances. Distribution of this schedule on a regular basis allows the various parties involved in the liquidation to monitor the progress being made.

3. During a liquidation, negative capital balances can arise for one or more of the partners, especially if the partnership incurs material losses in disposing of its property. In such cases, the specific partner or partners should contribute enough additional assets to eliminate their deficits. If payment is slow in coming, the partners who have safe capital balances can immediately divide any cash still held by the partnership. A *safe balance* is the amount of capital that would remain even if maximum future losses occur: Noncash assets are lost in total and all partners with deficits fail to fulfill their legal obligations. In making these computations, the remaining partners absorb negative capital balances based on their relative profit and loss ratio.

4. To enable an orderly and fair distribution during liquidation, the Uniform Partnership Act establishes a priority listing for all claims, a ranking referred to as the *marshaling of assets*. This principle states that partners with positive capital balances can recover losses from a partner reporting a deficit but only after ensuring adequate protection for the creditors of that individual and those of the partnership. The UPA also specifies that a partner's personal creditors can seek recovery of losses from the partnership to the extent of that partner's capital balance after protection of partnership creditors has been assured.

5. Completion of the actual liquidation of a partnership can take an extended period. Often, cash is generated during the early stages of this process in excess of the amount needed to cover liabilities and liquidation expenses. The accountant should propose a fair and immediate distribution of these available funds. A proposed schedule of liquidation can be created as a guide for such cash distributions. This statement is based on a *simulated* series of transactions: sale of all noncash assets, payment of liquidation expenses, and so on. At every point, maximum losses are assumed: Noncash assets have no resale value, liquidation expenses are set at the maximum level, and all partners are personally insolvent. Any safe capital balance remaining after incurring such losses represents a distribution that can be made at the present time. Even after this payment, the capital account will still be large enough to absorb all potential losses.

6. The liquidation of a partnership can require numerous transactions over a lengthy time period. Thus, the accountant could discover that the continual production of proposed schedules of liquidation becomes a burdensome chore. For this reason, the accountant usually produces a single predistribution plan at the start of the liquidation process. This plan serves as a definitive guideline for all payments to be made to the partners. To create this plan, the accountant simulates a series of losses with each loss, in turn, exactly eliminating the capital balance of a partner. After these assumed losses have reduced all capital accounts to zero, the accountant devises the predistribution plan by working backward through the series. In effect, the accountant is measuring the cash that will become available if such losses do not occur.

Comprehensive Illustration

PROBLEM

(Estimated Time: 30 to 40 Minutes) For the past several years, the partnership of Andrews, Caso, Quinn, and Sheridan has operated a local department store. Based on the provisions of the original articles of partnership, all profits and losses have been allocated on a 4:3:2:1 ratio, respectively. Recently, both Caso and Quinn have undergone personal financial problems, and as a result, these two individuals are now insolvent. Caso's creditors have filed a $20,000 claim against the partnership's assets, and $22,000 is being sought to repay Quinn's personal debts. To satisfy these legal obligations, the partnership property must liquidate. The partners estimate that they will incur $12,000 in expenses in disposing of all noncash assets.

At the time that active operations cease and the liquidation begins, the following balance sheet is produced for this partnership. All measurement accounts have been closed out to arrive at the current capital balances.

Cash	$ 20,000	Liabilities		$140,000
Noncash assets	280,000	Caso, loan		10,000
		Andrews, capital (40%)		76,000
		Caso, capital (30%)		14,000
		Quinn, capital (20%)		51,000
		Sheridan, capital (10%)		9,000
Total assets	$300,000	Total liabilities and capital		$300,000

During the lengthy liquidation process, the following transactions take place:

* Sale of noncash assets with a book value of $190,000 for $140,000 cash.
* Payment of $14,000 liquidation expenses. No further expenses are expected.
* Distribution of safe capital balances to the partners.
* Payment of all business liabilities.
* Sale of the remaining noncash assets for $10,000.
* Determination of deficit capital balances for any insolvent partners as uncollectible.
* Receipt of appropriate cash contributions from any solvent partner who is reporting a negative capital balance.
* Distribution of final cash.

Required:

a. Using the information available prior to the start of the liquidation process, develop a predistribution plan for this partnership.

b. Prepare journal entries to record the actual liquidation transactions.

SOLUTION

a. This partnership begins the liquidation process with capital amounting to $160,000. This total includes the $10,000 loan from Caso because the partnership must retain the liability as a possible offset against any eventual deficit capital balance. Therefore, the predistribution plan is based on the assumption that $160,000 in losses will be incurred, entirely eliminating all partnership capital. As discussed in this chapter, these simulated losses are arranged in a series so that each capital account is sequentially reduced to a zero balance.

At the start of the liquidation, Caso's capital position is the most vulnerable.

Partner	Capital Balance/ Loss Allocation	Maximum Loss That Can Be Absorbed
Andrews	$76,000/40%	$190,000
Caso	24,000/30	80,000 ✔
Quinn	51,000/20	255,000
Sheridan	9,000/10	90,000

As this schedule indicates, an $80,000 loss would eradicate both Caso's $14,000 capital balance and the $10,000 loan. Therefore, to start the development of a predistribution plan, this loss is assumed to have occurred.

	Andrews, Capital	Caso, Loan and Capital	Quinn, Capital	Sheridan, Capital
Beginning balances	$ 76,000	$ 24,000	$ 51,000	$ 9,000
Assumed $80,000 loss	(32,000) (40%)	(24,000) (30%)	(16,000) (20%)	(8,000) (10%)
Step 1 balances	$ 44,000	–0–	$ 35,000	$ 1,000

With Caso's capital account eliminated, further losses are to be split among the remaining partners in the ratio of 4:2:1 (or 4/7:2/7:1/7). Because only an additional $7,000 loss (the preceding $1,000 capital divided by 1/7) is now needed to reduce Sheridan's account to zero, this partner is in the second most vulnerable position.

	Andrews	Caso	Quinn	Sheridan
Step 1 balances (above)	$44,000	–0–	$35,000	$ 1,000
Assumed $7,000 loss	(4,000) (4/7)	–0–	(2,000) (2/7)	(1,000) (1/7)
Step 2 balances	$40,000	–0–	$33,000	–0–

Following these two simulated losses, only Andrews and Quinn continue to report positive capital balances. Thus, they divide any additional losses on a 4:2 basis, or 66⅔%:33⅓%. Based on these realigned percentages, Andrews's position has become the more vulnerable. An additional loss of $60,000 ($40,000/66⅔%) reduces this partner's remaining capital to zero whereas a $99,000 loss ($33,000/33⅓%) is required to eliminate Quinn's balance.

	Andrews	Caso	Quinn	Sheridan
Step 2 balances (above)	$ 40,000	–0–	$33,000	–0–
Assumed $60,000 loss	(40,000) (66⅔%)	–0–	(20,000) (33⅓%)	–0–
Step 3 balances	–0–	–0–	$13,000	–0–

The final $13,000 capital balance belongs to Quinn; an additional loss of this amount is necessary to remove the last element of partnership capital.

Based on the results of this series of simulated losses, the accountant can create a predistribution plan. However, the $140,000 in liabilities owed by the partnership still retains first priority to any available cash. Additionally, $12,000 must be held to cover the anticipated liquidation expenses.

ANDREWS, CASO, QUINN, AND SHERIDAN
Predistribution Plan

Available Cash		Recipient
First	$152,000	Creditors and anticipated liquidation expenses
Next	13,000	Quinn
Next	60,000	Andrews (66⅔%) and Quinn (33⅓%)
Next	7,000	Andrews (4/7), Quinn (2/7), and Sheridan (1/7)
All further cash		Andrews (40%), Caso (30%), Quinn (20%), and Sheridan (10%)

Because of their insolvency, initial payments to Caso ($20,000) and Quinn ($22,000) will actually go to their personal creditors.

b. Journal entries for the liquidation:

Caso, Loan	10,000	
Caso, Capital		10,000
To record offset of loan against capital balance in anticipation of liquidation.		
Cash	140,000	
Andrews, Capital (40% of loss)	20,000	
Caso, Capital (30% of loss)	15,000	
Quinn, Capital (20% of loss)	10,000	
Sheridan, Capital (10% of loss)	5,000	
Noncash Assets		190,000
To record sale of noncash assets and allocation of $50,000 loss.		
Andrews, Capital (40%)	5,600	
Caso, Capital (30%)	4,200	
Quinn, Capital (20%)	2,800	
Sheridan, Capital (10%)	1,400	
Cash		14,000
To record payment of liquidation expenses.		

- The partnership now holds $146,000 in cash, $6,000 more than is needed to satisfy all liabilities and estimated expenses. According to the predistribution plan drawn up in requirement (*a*), this entire amount can be safely distributed to Quinn (or to Quinn's creditors).

Quinn, Capital	6,000	
Cash		6,000
To record distribution of available cash based on safe capital balance.		
Liabilities	140,000	
Cash		140,000
To record extinguishment of all partnership debts.		
Cash	10,000	
Andrews, Capital (40% of loss)	32,000	
Caso, Capital (30% of loss)	24,000	
Quinn, Capital (20% of loss)	16,000	
Sheridan, Capital (10% of loss)	8,000	
Noncash Assets		90,000
To record sale of remaining noncash assets and allocation of $80,000 loss.		

- At this point in the liquidation, only the cash and the capital accounts remain open on the partnership books.

	Cash	Andrews, Capital	Caso, Capital	Quinn, Capital	Sheridan, Capital
Beginning balances	$ 20,000	$ 76,000	$ 14,000	$ 51,000	$ 9,000
Loan offset	–0–	–0–	10,000	–0–	–0–
Sale of noncash assets	140,000	(20,000)	(15,000)	(10,000)	(5,000)
Liquidation expenses	(14,000)	(5,600)	(4,200)	(2,800)	(1,400)
Cash distribution	(6,000)	–0–	–0–	(6,000)	–0–
Payment of liabilities	(140,000)	–0–	–0–	–0–	–0–
Sale of noncash assets	10,000	(32,000)	(24,000)	(16,000)	(8,000)
Current balances	$ 10,000	$ 18,400	$ (19,200)	$ 16,200	$(5,400)

Because Caso is personally insolvent, the $19,200 deficit balance will not be repaid, and the remaining three partners must absorb it on a 4:2:1 basis.

Andrews, Capital (⁴/₇ of loss)	10,971	
Quinn, Capital (²/₇ of loss)	5,486	
Sheridan, Capital (¹/₇ of loss)	2,743	
Caso, Capital		19,200

To record write-off of deficit capital balance of insolvent partner.

- This last allocation decreases Sheridan's capital account to an $8,143 negative total. Because this partner is personally solvent, that amount should be contributed to the partnership in accordance with regulations of the Uniform Partnership Act.

Cash	8,143	
Sheridan, Capital		8,143

To record contribution made to eliminate deficit capital balance.

- Sheridan's contribution brings the final cash total for the partnership to $18,143. This amount is distributed to the two partners who continue to maintain positive capital balances: Andrews and Quinn (or Quinn's creditors).

	Andrews, Capital	Quinn, Capital
Balances above	$18,400	$16,200
Caso deficit	(10,971)	(5,486)
Final balances	$ 7,429	$10,714

Andrews, Capital	7,429	
Quinn, Capital	10,714	
Cash		18,143

To record distribution of remaining cash according to final capital balances.

Questions

1. What is the difference between the dissolution of a partnership and the liquidation of partnership property?
2. Why would the members of a partnership elect to terminate business operations and liquidate all noncash assets?
3. Why are liquidation gains and losses usually recorded as direct adjustments to the partners' capital accounts?
4. After liquidating all property and paying partnership obligations, what is the basis for allocating remaining cash among the partners?
5. What is the purpose of a schedule of liquidation? What information does this statement convey to its readers?
6. According to the Uniform Partnership Act, what events should occur if a partner incurs a negative capital balance during the liquidation process?
7. How are safe capital balances computed when preliminary distributions of cash are to be made during a partnership liquidation?
8. What is the purpose of the marshaling of assets doctrine? What does this doctrine specifically state?
9. A partner is personally insolvent. Can this partner's creditors claim partnership assets?

10. How do loans from partners affect the distribution of assets in a partnership liquidation? What alternatives can affect the handling of such loans?

11. What is the purpose of a proposed schedule of liquidation, and how is it developed?

12. How is a predistribution plan created for a partnership liquidation?

Problems

1. If a partnership is liquidated, how is the final allocation of business assets made to the partners?
    a. Equally.
    b. According to the profit and loss ratio.
    c. According to the final capital account balances.
    d. According to the initial investment made by each of the partners.

2. Which of the following statements is true concerning the accounting for a partnership going through liquidation?
    a. Gains and losses are reported directly as increases and decreases in the appropriate capital account.
    b. A separate income statement is created to measure only the profit or loss generated during liquidation.
    c. Because gains and losses rarely occur during liquidation, no special accounting treatment is warranted.
    d. Within a liquidation, all gains and losses are divided equally among the partners.

3. During a liquidation, if a partner's capital account balance drops below zero, what *should* happen?
    a. The other partners file a legal suit against the partner with the deficit balance.
    b. The partner with the highest capital balance contributes sufficient assets to eliminate the deficit.
    c. The deficit balance is removed from the accounting records with only the remaining partners sharing in future gains and losses.
    d. The partner with a deficit contributes enough assets to offset the deficit balance.

4. What is the marshaling of assets?
    a. A list of all partnership assets prepared when a formal accounting is to be made.
    b. A ranking of claims to be paid when a partner has become insolvent.
    c. The method by which a retiring partner's share of partnership is determined.
    d. The gathering of partnership assets just prior to the commencement of the liquidation process.

5. A local partnership is in the process of liquidating and is currently reporting the following capital balances:

Angela, capital (50% share of all profits and losses)	$ 19,000
Woodrow, capital (30%)	18,000
Cassidy, capital (20%)	(12,000)

    Cassidy has indicated that a forthcoming contribution will cover the $12,000 deficit. However, the two remaining partners have asked to receive the $25,000 in cash that is presently available. How much of this money should each of the partners be given?
    a. Angela, $13,000; Woodrow, $12,000.
    b. Angela, $11,500; Woodrow, $13,500.
    c. Angela, $12,000; Woodrow, $13,000.
    d. Angela, $12,500; Woodrow, $12,500.

6. A local partnership is considering possible liquidation because one of the partners (Bell) is insolvent. Capital balances at the current time are as follows. Profits and losses are divided on a 4:3:2:1 basis, respectively.

Bell, capital	$50,000
Hardy, capital	56,000
Dennard, capital	14,000
Suddath, capital	80,000

Bell's creditors have filed a $21,000 claim against the partnership's assets. The partnership currently holds assets reported at $300,000 and liabilities of $100,000. If the assets can be sold for $190,000, what is the minimum amount that Bell's creditors would receive?

a. –0–.

b. $2,000.

c. $2,800.

d. $6,000.

7. What is a predistribution plan?

a. A guideline for the cash distributions to partners during a liquidation.

b. A list of the procedures to be performed during a liquidation.

c. A determination of the final cash distribution to the partners on the settlement date.

d. A detailed list of the transactions that will transpire in the reorganization of a partnership.

8. A partnership has the following balance sheet just before final liquidation is to begin:

Cash	$ 26,000	Liabilities	$ 50,000
Inventory	31,000	Art, capital (40% of profits and losses)	18,000
Other assets	62,000	Raymond, capital (30%)	25,000
		Darby, capital (30%)	26,000
Total	$119,000	Total	$119,000

Liquidation expenses are estimated to be $12,000. The other assets are sold for $40,000. What distribution can be made to the partners?

a. –0– to Art, $1,500 to Raymond, $2,500 to Darby.

b. $1,333 to Art, $1,333 to Raymond, $1,334 to Darby.

c. –0– to Art, $1,200 to Raymond, $2,800 to Darby.

d. $600 to Art, $1,200 to Raymond, $2,200 to Darby.

9. A partnership has the following capital balances: A (20% of profits and losses) = $100,000; B (30% of profits and losses) = $120,000; C (50% of profits and losses) = $180,000. If the partnership is to be liquidated and $30,000 becomes immediately available, who gets that money?

a. $6,000 to A, $9,000 to B, $15,000 to C.

b. $22,000 to A, $3,000 to B, $5,000 to C.

c. $22,000 to A, $8,000 to B, –0– to C.

d. $24,000 to A, $6,000 to B, –0– to C.

10. A partnership is currently holding $400,000 in assets and $234,000 in liabilities. The partnership is to be liquidated, and $20,000 is the best estimation of the expenses that will be incurred during this process. The four partners share profits and losses as shown. Capital balances at the start of the liquidation are as follows:

Kevin, capital (40%)	$59,000
Michael, capital (30%)	39,000
Brendan, capital (10%)	34,000
Jonathan, capital (20%)	34,000

The partners realize that Brendan will be the first partner to start receiving cash. How much cash will Brendan receive before any of the other partners collect any cash?

a. $12,250.

b. $14,750.

c. $17,000.

d. $19,500.

11. Carney, Pierce, Menton, and Hoehn are partners who share profits and losses on a 4:3:2:1 basis, respectively. They are presently beginning to liquidate the business. At the start of this process, capital balances are as follows:

Carney, capital $60,000
Pierce, capital 27,000
Menton, capital 43,000
Hoehn, capital 20,000

Which of the following statements is true?

a. The first available $2,000 will go to Hoehn.

b. Carney will be the last partner to receive any available cash.

c. The first available $3,000 will go to Menton.

d. Carney will collect a portion of any available cash before Hoehn receives money.

12. A partnership has gone through liquidation and now reports the following account balances:

Cash $16,000
Loan from Jones 3,000
Wayman, capital . . . . (2,000) (deficit)
Jones, capital . . . . (5,000) (deficit)
Fuller, capital 13,000
Rogers, capital 7,000

Profits and losses are allocated on the following basis: Wayman, 30 percent; Jones, 20 percent; Fuller, 30 percent; and Rogers, 20 percent. Which of the following events should occur now?

a. Jones should receive $3,000 cash because of the loan balance.

b. Fuller should receive $11,800 and Rogers $4,200.

c. Fuller should receive $10,600 and Rogers $5,400.

d. Jones should receive $3,000, Fuller $8,800, and Rogers $4,200.

13. A partnership has the following account balances: Cash, $70,000; Other Assets, $540,000; Liabilities, $260,000; Nixon (50% of profits and losses), $170,000; Cleveland (30%), $110,000; Pierce (20%), $70,000. The company liquidates, and $8,000 becomes available to the partners. Who gets the $8,000?

14. A local partnership has only two assets (cash of $10,000 and land with a cost of $35,000). All liabilities have been paid and the following capital balances are currently being recorded. The partners share profits and losses as follows. All partners are insolvent.

Brown, capital (40%) $25,000
Fish, capital (30%) 15,000
Stone, capital (30%) 5,000

a. If the land is sold for $25,000, how much cash does each partner receive in a final settlement?

b. If the land is sold for $15,000, how much cash does each partner receive in a final settlement?

c. If the land is sold for $5,000, how much cash does each partner receive in a final settlement?

15. A local dental partnership has been liquidated and the final capital balances are as follows:

Atkinson, capital (40% of all profits and losses) . . . . $ 60,000
Kaporale, capital (30%) 20,000
Dennsmore, capital (20%) . . . . (30,000)
Rasputin, capital (10%) . . . . (50,000)

If Rasputin contributes additional cash of $20,000 to the partnership, what should happen to that money?

16. A partnership currently holds three assets: cash, $10,000; land, $35,000; and a building, $50,000. The partners anticipate that expenses required to liquidate their partnership will amount to $5,000. Capital balances are as follows:

Ace, capital $25,000
Ball, capital 28,000
Eaton, capital 20,000
Lake, capital 22,000

The partners share profits and losses as follows: Ace (30%), Ball (30%), Eaton (20%), and Lake (20%). If a preliminary distribution of cash is to be made, how much will each of these partners receive?

17. The following condensed balance sheet is for the partnership of Hardwick, Saunders, and Ferris, who share profits and losses in the ratio of 4:3:3, respectively:

Cash	$ 90,000	Accounts payable	$210,000
Other assets	820,000	Ferris, loan	40,000
Hardwick, loan	30,000	Hardwick, capital	300,000
		Saunders, capital	200,000
		Ferris, capital	190,000
Total assets	$940,000	Total liabilities and capital	$940,000

The partners decide to liquidate the partnership. Forty percent of the other assets are sold for $200,000. Prepare a proposed schedule of liquidation.

18. The following condensed balance sheet is for the partnership of Miller, Tyson, and Watson, who share profits and losses in the ratio of 6:2:2, respectively:

Cash	$ 40,000	Liabilities	$ 70,000
Other assets	140,000	Miller, capital	50,000
		Tyson, capital	50,000
		Watson, capital	10,000
Total assets	$180,000	Total liabilities and capital	$180,000

For how much money must the other assets be sold so that each partner receives some amount of cash in a liquidation?

19. A partnership's balance sheet is as follows:

Cash	$ 60,000	Liabilities	$ 50,000
Noncash assets	120,000	Babb, capital	60,000
		Whitaker, capital	20,000
		Edwards, capital	50,000
Total assets	$180,000	Total liabilities and capital	$180,000

Babb, Whitaker, and Edwards share profits and losses in the ratio of 4:2:4, respectively. This business is to be terminated, and the partners estimate that $8,000 in liquidation expenses will be incurred. How should the $2,000 in safe cash that is presently held be disbursed?

20. A partnership has liquidated all assets but still reports the following account balances:

Loan from White	$ 6,000
Black, capital	3,000
White, capital	(9,000) (deficit)
Green, capital	(3,000) (deficit)
Brown, capital	15,000
Blue, capital	(12,000) (deficit)

The partners split profits and losses as follows: Black, 30 percent; White, 30 percent; Green, 10 percent; Brown, 20 percent; and Blue, 10 percent.

Assuming that all partners are personally insolvent except for Green and Brown, how much cash must Green now contribute to this partnership?

21. The following balance sheet is for a local partnership in which the partners have become very unhappy with each other.

Cash	$ 40,000	Liabilities	$ 30,000
Land	130,000	Adams, capital	80,000
Building	120,000	Baker, capital	30,000
		Carvil, capital	60,000
		Dobbs, capital	90,000
Total assets	$290,000	Total liabilities and capital	$290,000

To avoid more conflict, they have decided to cease operations and sell all assets. Using this information, answer the following questions. Each question should be viewed as an *independent* situation related to the partnership's liquidation.

 a. The $10,000 cash that exceeds the partnership liabilities is to be disbursed immediately. If profits and losses are allocated to Adams, Baker, Carvil, and Dobbs on a 2:3:3:2 basis, respectively, how will the $10,000 be divided?

 b. The $10,000 cash that exceeds the partnership liabilities is to be disbursed immediately. If profits and losses are allocated on a 2:2:3:3 basis, respectively, how will the $10,000 be divided?

 c. The building is immediately sold for $70,000 to give total cash of $110,000. The liabilities are then paid, leaving a cash balance of $80,000. This cash is to be distributed to the partners. How much of this money will each partner receive if profits and losses are allocated to Adams, Baker, Carvil, and Dobbs on a 1:3:3:3 basis, respectively?

 d. Assume that profits and losses are allocated to Adams, Baker, Carvil, and Dobbs on a 1:3:4:2 basis, respectively. How much money must the firm receive from selling the land and building to ensure that Carvil receives a portion?

22. The partnership of Larson, Norris, Spencer, and Harrison has decided to terminate operations and liquidate all business property. During this process, the partners expect to incur $8,000 in liquidation expenses. All partners are currently solvent.

 The balance sheet reported by this partnership at the time that the liquidation commenced follows. The percentages indicate the allocation of profits and losses to each of the four partners.

Cash	$ 28,250	Liabilities	$ 47,000
Accounts receivable	44,000	Larson, capital (20%)	15,000
Inventory	39,000	Norris, capital (30%)	60,000
Land and buildings	23,000	Spencer, capital (20%)	75,000
Equipment	104,000	Harrison, capital (30%)	41,250
Total assets	$238,250	Total liabilities and capital	$238,250

 Based on the information that has been provided, prepare a predistribution plan for the liquidation of this partnership.

23. The following partnership is being liquidated beginning on July 13, 2007:

Cash	$ 36,000	Liabilities	$50,000
Noncash assets	174,000	Able, loan	10,000
		Able, capital (20%)	40,000
		Moon, capital (30%)	60,000
		Yerkl, capital (50%)	50,000

 a. Liquidation expenses are estimated to be $12,000. Prepare a predistribution schedule to guide the distribution of cash.

 b. Assume that assets costing $28,000 are sold for $40,000. How is the available cash to be divided?

24. A local partnership is to be liquidated. Commissions and other liquidation expenses are expected to total $19,000. The business's balance sheet prior to the commencement of liquidation is as follows:

Cash	$ 27,000	Liabilities	$ 40,000
Noncash assets	254,000	Simpson, capital (20%)	18,000
		Hart, capital (40%)	40,000
		Bobb, capital (20%)	48,000
		Reidl, capital (20%)	135,000
Total assets	$281,000	Total liabilities and capital	$281,000

Prepare a predistribution schedule for this partnership.

25. The following information concerns two different partnerships. These problems should be viewed as independent situations.

Part A

The partnership of Ross, Milburn, and Thomas has the following account balances:

Cash	$ 36,000	Liabilities	$17,000
Noncash assets	100,000	Ross, capital	69,000
		Milburn, capital	(8,000) (deficit)
		Thomas, capital	58,000

This partnership is in the process of being liquidated. Ross and Milburn are each entitled to 40 percent of all profits and losses with the remaining 20 percent to Thomas.

a. What is the maximum amount that Milburn might have to contribute to this partnership because of the deficit capital balance?

b. How should the $19,000 cash that is presently available in excess of liabilities be distributed?

c. If the noncash assets are sold for a total of $41,000, what is the minimum amount of cash that Thomas could receive?

Part B

The partnership of Sampson, Klingon, Carton, and Romulan is being liquidated. It currently holds cash of $9,000 but no other assets. Liabilities amount to $24,000. The capital balances are as follows:

Sampson	$ 9,000
Klingon	(17,000)
Carton	5,000
Romulan	(12,000)

Profits and losses are allocated on the following basis: Sampson, 40 percent, Klingon, 20 percent, Carton, 30 percent, and Romulan, 10 percent.

a. If both Klingon and Romulan are personally insolvent, how much money must Carton contribute to this partnership?

b. If only Romulan is personally insolvent, how much money must Klingon contribute? How will these funds be disbursed?

c. If only Klingon is personally insolvent, how much money should Sampson receive from the liquidation?

26. March, April, and May have been in partnership for a number of years. The partners allocate all profits and losses on a 2:3:1 basis, respectively. Recently, each partner has become personally insolvent and, thus, the partners have decided to liquidate the business in hope of remedying their personal financial problems. As of September 1, 2007, the partnership's balance sheet is as follows:

Cash	$ 11,000	Liabilities	$ 61,000
Accounts receivable	84,000	March, capital	25,000
Inventory	74,000	April, capital	75,000
Land, building, and			
equipment (net)	38,000	May, capital	46,000
Total assets	$207,000	Total liabilities and capital	$207,000

Prepare journal entries for the following transactions:

a. Sold all inventory for $56,000 cash.

b. Paid $7,500 in liquidation expenses.

c. Paid $40,000 of the partnership's liabilities.

d. Collected $45,000 of the accounts receivable.

e. Distributed safe cash balances; the partners anticipate no further liquidation expenses.

f. Sold remaining accounts receivable for 30 percent of face value.

g. Sold land, building, and equipment for $17,000.

h. Paid all remaining liabilities of the partnership.

i. Distributed cash held by the business to the partners.

27. The partnership of W, X, Y, and Z has the following balance sheet:

Cash	$ 30,000	Liabilities	$42,000
Other assets	220,000	W, capital (50% of profits and losses)	60,000
		X, capital (30%)	78,000
		Y, capital (10%)	40,000
		Z, capital (10%)	30,000

Z is personally insolvent, and one of his creditors is considering suing the partnership for the $5,000 that is currently due. The creditor realizes that liquidation could result from this litigation and does not wish to force such an extreme action unless the creditor is reasonably sure of getting the money that is due. If the partnership sells the other assets, how much money must it receive to ensure that $5,000 would be available from Z's portion of the business? Liquidation expenses are expected to be $15,000.

28. On January 1, 2007, the partners of Van, Bakel, and Cox (who share profits and losses in the ratio of 5:3:2, respectively) decide to liquidate their partnership. The trial balance at this date is as follows:

	Debit	Credit
Cash	$ 18,000	
Accounts receivable	66,000	
Inventory	52,000	
Machinery and equipment, net	189,000	
Van, loan	30,000	
Accounts payable		$ 53,000
Bakel, loan		20,000
Van, capital		118,000
Bakel, capital		90,000
Cox, capital		74,000
Totals	$355,000	$355,000

The partners plan a program of piecemeal conversion of the business's assets to minimize liquidation losses. All available cash, less an amount retained to provide for future expenses, is to be distributed to the partners at the end of each month. A summary of the liquidation transactions follows:

2007

January   Collected $51,000 of the accounts receivable; the balance is deemed uncollectible.

Received $38,000 for the entire inventory.

Paid $2,000 in liquidation expenses.

Paid $50,000 to the outside creditors after offsetting a $3,000 credit memorandum received by the partnership on January 11, 2007.

Retained $10,000 cash in the business at the end of January to cover any unrecorded liabilities and anticipated expenses. The remainder is distributed to the partners.

February   Paid $3,000 in liquidation expenses.

Retained $6,000 cash in the business at the end of the month to cover unrecorded liabilities and anticipated expenses.

March   Received $146,000 on the sale of all machinery and equipment.

Paid $5,000 in final liquidation expenses.

Retained no cash in the business.

Prepare a schedule to compute the safe installment payments made to the partners at the end of each of these three months.

29. Following is a series of *independent cases*. In each situation, indicate the cash distribution to be made at the end of the liquidation process. *Unless otherwise stated, assume that all solvent partners will reimburse the partnership for their deficit capital balances.*

Part A

The Simon, Haynes, and Jackson partnership presently reports the following accounts. Jackson is personally insolvent and can contribute only an additional $3,000 to the partnership. Simon is also insolvent and has no available funds.

Cash	$ 30,000
Liabilities	22,000
Haynes, loan	10,000
Simon, capital (40%)	16,000
Haynes, capital (20%)	(6,000)
Jackson, capital (40%)	(12,000)

Part B

Hough, Luck, and Cummings operate a local accounting firm as a partnership. After working together for several years, they have decided to liquidate the partnership's property. The partners have prepared the following balance sheet:

Cash	$ 20,000		Liabilities	$ 40,000
Hough, loan	8,000		Luck, loan	10,000
Noncash assets	162,000		Hough, capital (50%)	90,000
			Luck, capital (40%)	30,000
			Cummings, capital (10%)	20,000
Total assets	$190,000		Total liabilities and capital	$190,000

The firm sells the noncash assets for $80,000; it will use $21,000 of this amount to pay liquidation expenses. All three of these partners are personally insolvent.

Part C

Use the same information as in Part B, but assume that the profits and losses are split 2:4:4 to Hough, Luck, and Cummings, respectively, and that liquidation expenses are only $6,000.

Part D

Following the liquidation of all noncash assets, the partnership of Redmond, Ledbetter, Watson, and Sandridge has the following account balances:

Liabilities	$ 28,000
Redmond, loan	5,000
Redmond, capital (20%)	(21,000)
Ledbetter, capital (10%)	(30,000)
Watson, capital (30%)	3,000
Sandridge, capital (40%)	15,000

Redmond is personally insolvent.

30. The partnership of Frick, Wilson, and Clarke has elected to cease all operations and liquidate its business property. A balance sheet drawn up at this time shows the following account balances:

Cash	$ 48,000		Liabilities	$ 35,000
Noncash assets	177,000		Frick, capital (60%)	101,000
			Wilson, capital (20%)	28,000
			Clarke, capital (20%)	61,000
Total assets	$225,000		Total liabilities and capital	$225,000

The following transactions occur in liquidating this business:
- Distributed safe capital balances immediately to the partners. Liquidation expenses of $9,000 are estimated as a basis for this computation.
- Sold noncash assets with a book value of $80,000 for $48,000.
- Paid all liabilities.
- Distributed safe capital balances again.
- Sold remaining noncash assets for $44,000.
- Paid liquidation expenses of $7,000.
- Distributed remaining cash to the partners and closed the financial records of the business permanently.

Produce a final schedule of liquidation for this partnership.

31. **Part A**

The partnership of Wingler, Norris, Rodgers, and Guthrie was formed several years ago as a local architectural firm. Several partners have recently undergone personal financial problems and have decided to terminate operations and liquidate the business. The following balance sheet is drawn up as a guideline for this process:

Cash	$ 15,000	Liabilities		$ 74,000
Accounts receivable	82,000	Rodgers, loan		35,000
Inventory	101,000	Wingler, capital (30%)		120,000
Land	85,000	Norris, capital (10%)		88,000
Building and		Rodgers, capital (20%)		74,000
equipment (net)	168,000	Guthrie, capital (40%)		60,000
Total assets	$451,000	Total liabilities and capital		$451,000

When the liquidation commenced, expenses of $16,000 were anticipated as being necessary to dispose of all property.

Prepare a predistribution plan for this partnership.

Part B

The following transactions transpire during the liquidation of the Wingler, Norris, Rodgers, and Guthrie partnership:
- Collected 80 percent of the total accounts receivable with the rest judged to be uncollectible.
- Sold the land, building, and equipment for $150,000.
- Made safe capital distributions.
- Learned that Guthrie, who has become personally insolvent, will make no further contributions.
- Paid all liabilities.
- Sold all inventory for $71,000.
- Made safe capital distributions again.
- Paid liquidation expenses of $11,000.
- Made final cash disbursements to the partners based on the assumption that all partners other than Guthrie are personally solvent.

Prepare journal entries to record these liquidation transactions.

Develop Your Skills

RESEARCH CASE

A client of the CPA firm of Harston and Mendez is a medical practice of seven local doctors. One doctor has been sued for several million dollars as the result of a recent operation. Because of what appears to be this doctor's very poor judgment, a patient died. Although that doctor was solely involved with the patient in question, the lawsuit names the entire practice as a defendant. Originally, four of these doctors formed this business as a general partnership. However, five years ago, the partners converted the business to a limited liability partnership based on the laws of the state in which they operate.

Read the following articles as well as any other published information that is available on partner and partnership liability:

"Partners Forever, Within Andersen, Personal Liability May Bring Ruin," *The Wall Street Journal,* April 2, 2002, p. C1.

"Collapse: Speed of Andersen's Demise Amazing," *Milwaukee Journal Sentinel,* June 16, 2002, p. D1.

Required:

Based on the facts presented in this case, answer these questions:

1. What liability do the other six partners in this medical practice have in connection with this lawsuit?
2. What factors will be important in determining the exact liability (if any) of these six doctors?

ANALYSIS CASE

Go to the Web site http://www.napico.com and click on "Partnership Financial Information—Click Here." Then click on "2004 Annual Reports" to access the annual report for National Tax Credit Investors II (NTCI II).

Read the financial statements contained in the 2004 annual report and the accompanying notes, especially any that discuss the partnership form of organization.

Assume that an investor is considering investing in this partnership and has downloaded this report for study and analysis.

Required:

1. What differences are there between NTCI II's financial statements and those of an incorporated entity?
2. Assume that this potential investor is not aware of the potential implications of owning a partnership rather than a corporation. What information is available in these statements to advise this individual of the unique characteristics of this legal business form?

COMMUNICATION CASE 1

Read the following as well as any other published articles on the bankruptcy of the partnership of Laventhol & Horwath:

"Laventhol Says It Plans to File for Chapter 11," *The Wall Street Journal,* November 20, 1990, p. A3.

"Laventhol Partners Face Long Process That Could End in Personal Bankruptcy," *The Wall Street Journal,* November 20, 1990, p. B5.

"Laventhol Bankruptcy Filing Indicates Liabilities May Be as Much as $2 Billion," *The Wall Street Journal,* November 23, 1990. p. A4.

Required:

Write a report describing the potential liabilities that the members of a partnership could incur.

COMMUNICATION CASE 2

Read the following as well as any other published articles on the breakup of a partnership:

"Partnerships: If There's a Beginning . . . There's an End," *National Public Accountant,* April 1992.
"Reconcilable Differences," *Inc.,* April 1991.
"Cutting Losses When Partners Face a Breakup," *The Wall Street Journal,* May 21, 1991, p. B1.

Required:

Write a report describing various situations that can lead to the dissolution of a partnership.

EXCEL CASE

The partnership of Wilson, Cho, and Arrington has the following account information:

Partner	Capital Balance	Share of Profits and Losses
Wilson	$200,000	40%
Cho	180,000	20
Arrington	110,000	40

This partnership will be liquidated, and the partners are scheduled to receive cash equal to any ending positive capital balance. If a negative capital balance results, the partner is expected to contribute that amount.

Assume that losses of $50,000 occur during the liquidation followed later by additional and final losses of $100,000.

Required:

1. Create a spreadsheet to determine the capital balances that remain for each of the three partners after these two losses are incurred.
2. Modify this spreadsheet so that it can be used for different capital balances, different allocation patterns, and different liquidation gains and losses.

Chapter Sixteen

Accounting for State and Local Governments (Part 1)

Questions to Consider

- Who uses the financial data produced by state and local government units, and why is such a wide variety of informational needs encountered?

- What is fund accounting, and why do state and local governments utilize it?

- Why is financial accountability considered so important in a government? In what ways is financial accountability established in the accounting system?

- How do government-wide financial statements differ from fund-based financial statements and why are two sets of financial statements necessary?

- What measurement focus and basis of accounting do the various financial statements produced for a state or local government utilize?

- When does a government recognize revenues, expenses, and expenditures?

To even a seasoned veteran of accounting and its reported information, the financial statements produced for a state or local government can appear to resemble something created in a complex foreign language.

- The 2003 financial statements for Bismarck, North Dakota, report other financing sources and uses for its governmental funds that include $17.0 million of operating transfers-in and $13.8 million of operating transfers-out.

- The 2004 balance sheet for Portland, Maine, discloses a $4.3 million fund balance reserved for encumbrances.

- The 2004 financial statements for Phoenix, Arizona, are 259 pages of data including the dollar amounts of expenditures made in connection with public safety, community enrichment, and debt service.

- In 2004, Greensboro, North Carolina, reported (as do almost all such governments) two complete and distinct sets of financial statements. One disclosed that the city's Governmental Activities owed more than $239 million in liabilities whereas the second set indicated that, at the same point in time, the city's Governmental Funds had only $46 million in liabilities.

- For 2004, Nashville and Davidson County, Tennessee, reported that the public library system created a net financial burden of $24 million for the citizens.

Merely a quick perusal of such information points to fundamental differences with the type of reporting that most people associate with the financial statements of for-profit businesses. The purpose of this chapter and the next is to (1) introduce the principles and practices that underlie state and local government accounting and (2) explain the logic behind their application.

One or more underlying causes must be responsible for the uniqueness of the financial statements of state and local governments. These chapters are designed not only to demonstrate routine reporting procedures but also to explain the evolution that has taken place to lead state and local governments to produce financial statements that are markedly different in many places from those of a for-profit business.

INTRODUCTION TO THE ACCOUNTING FOR STATE AND LOCAL GOVERNMENTS

In the United States, literally thousands of state and local government reporting entities touch the lives of the citizenry on a daily basis. In addition to the federal and 50 state governments, there are 87,849 local governments. Of these, 38,971 are general purpose local governments—3,034 county governments and 35,937 subcounty governments, including 19,431 municipal governments and 16,506 township governments. The remainder, which comprise more than one-half of the total, are special purpose local governments, including 13,522 school district governments and 35,356 special district governments.[1] Income and sales taxes are collected, property taxes are assessed, schools are operated, fire departments are maintained, garbage is collected, and roads are paved. Actions of one or more governments affect every individual.

Accounting for such governments is not merely a matching of expenses with revenues so that net income can be determined. The changing of the tax rates and the allocation of limited resources among such worthy causes as education, police, welfare, and the environment create heated debates throughout the nation. To keep the public informed so that proper decisions can be made, government reporting has historically identified the methods used to generate financial resources and what use is made of them, which activities are financed and which are not.

Indeed, this approach is appropriate for the short-term decisions necessitated by gathering and utilizing financial resources to carry out public policy. For the longer term, though, information to reflect the overall financial stability of the government is also needed. Hence, in 1999, the Governmental Accounting Standards Board (GASB) adopted *Statement 34,* "Basic Financial Statements—and Management's Discussion and Analysis—for State and Local Governments." This authoritative standard mandated for state and local governments the most unusual task of preparing not one but two complete and distinct sets of financial statements. The perceived necessity of this dual reporting system demonstrates the difficulty that governments have faced in satisfying a wide array of user needs. For the student of government accounting, nothing is more vital than recognizing that these governments now produce two sets of statements, each with their own unique principles and objectives.

Statement 34 is probably the most significant step that has transpired over the decades in the evolution of the generally accepted accounting principles used by state and local governments. The American Institute of Certified Public Accountants (AICPA) and the National Council on Governmental Accounting (NCGA) made significant strides during earlier decades in establishing sound accounting principles.[2] In June 1984, the Governmental Accounting Standards Board (GASB) became the public-sector counterpart of the Financial Accounting Standards Board. The GASB holds the primary responsibility in the United States for setting authoritative accounting standards for state and local government units.[3] In the same manner as the Financial Accounting Standards Board, the GASB is an independent body functioning under the oversight of the Financial Accounting Foundation. Thus, a formal mechanism is in place to guide the development of governmental accounting.

[1] U.S. Department of Commerce, Bureau of the Census, 2002 Census of Governments, GC02-1(P) (Washington, DC: U.S. Government Printing Office), p. 1.

[2] The NCGA was a quasi-independent agency of the Government Finance Officers Association. The NCGA held authority for state and local government accounting from 1973 through 1984. The National Committee on Municipal Accounting had this responsibility from 1934 until 1941, and the National Committee on Governmental Accounting established government accounting principles from 1949 through 1954 and again from 1967 until 1973. During several periods, no group held primary responsibility for the development of governmental accounting. For an overview of the work of the GASB, see Terry K. Patton and Robert J. Freeman, "Government Accounting Standards Come of Age: Highlights of the First 20 Years," *Government Finance Review,* April 2005.

[3] In 1990, the Director of the Office of Management and Budget, the Secretary of the Treasury, and the Comptroller General created the Federal Accounting Standards Advisory Board (FASAB). FASAB recommends accounting principles and standards for the U.S. federal government and its agencies to use.

Governmental Accounting—User Needs

The unique aspects of any system of accounting should be a direct result of the perceived needs of financial statement users. Identification of these informational requirements is, therefore, a logical first step in the study of the accounting principles applied to state and local governments. Specific procedures utilized in the reporting process can be understood best as an outgrowth of these needs.

Often, though, user expectations are complex and even contradictory, especially for governmental entities. The taxpayer, the government employee, the bondholder, and the public official may each be seeking distinctly different types of financial information about a governmental unit.

> My own reflection on the subject leads me to the conviction that appropriate and adequate accounting for state and local governmental units involves a far more complex set of interrelationships, to be reported to a more diverse set of users with a greater variety of interests and needs, than exists in business accounting and reporting.[4]

In its *Concepts Statement No. 1,* "Objectives of Financial Reporting," the GASB recognized this same problem by identifying three groups of primary users of external state and local governmental financial reports: the citizenry, legislative and oversight bodies, and creditors and investors. It then described the needs and interests of each of these groups.

> **Citizenry**—Want to evaluate the likelihood of tax or service fee increases, to determine the sources and uses of resources, to forecast revenues in order to influence spending decisions, to ensure that resources were used in accordance with appropriations, to assess financial condition, and to compare budgeted to actual results.
> **Legislative and oversight bodies**—Want to assess the overall financial condition when developing budgets and program recommendations, to monitor operating results to assure compliance with mandates, to determine the reasonableness of fees and the need for tax changes, and to ascertain the ability to finance new programs and capital needs.
> **Investors and creditors**—Want to know the amount of available and likely future financial resources, to measure the debt position and the ability to service that debt, and to review operating results and cash flow data.[5]

Thus, the quest for fair governmental reporting encounters a significant obstacle: User needs are so broad that no one set of financial statements or accounting principles can possibly satisfy all expectations. How can voters, bondholders, city officials, and the other users of the financial statements provided by state and local governments receive the information that they need for decision-making purposes?

Historically, and still today, many hold that public awareness should always be the number one goal of such statements. "The most important users of financial reports are citizens acting through their elected representatives."[6] The question, though, has been constantly debated in connection with state and local government accounting: How can statements for citizens also be sufficient for the needs of creditors and investors?

Two Sets of Financial Statements

Eventually, the desire to create statements that could satisfy such broad demands for information led the GASB in *Statement 34* to require the production of two distinct sets of statements:

> **Fund-based financial statements** have been designed "to show restrictions on the planned use of resources or to measure, *in the short term,* the revenues and expenditures arising from certain activities."[7]
> **Government-wide financial statements** will have a longer-term focus because they will report "*all* revenues and *all* costs of providing services each year, not just those received or paid in the current year or soon after year-end."[8]

---

[4] Robert K. Mautz, "Financial Reporting: Should Government Emulate Business?" *Journal of Accountancy,* August 1981, p. 53.

[5] *GASB Concepts Statement No. 1,* "Objectives of Financial Reporting," May 1987, para. 33–37.

[6] Jeffrey L. Esser, "Standard Setting—How Much Is Enough?" *Government Finance Review,* April 2005, p. 3.

[7] *Governmental Accounting Standards Board Statement No. 34,* "Basic Financial Statements—and Management's Discussion and Analysis—for State and Local Governments," June 1999, preface p. 1.

[8] Ibid., p. 2.

Fund-based financial statements focus on specific activities and the amount of financial resources given to those activities as well as the use made of those resources. These fund-based statements help citizens assess the government's fiscal accountability in raising and utilizing resources. For example, fund-based financial statements should tell the amount spent this year on such services as public safety, education, health and sanitation, and the construction of a new road. The primary measurement focus in these statements, at least for the public service activities, is on the flow and amount of current financial resources, while the timing of recognition in most cases is a system known as *modified accrual accounting*. Modified accrual accounting recognizes (1) revenues when resulting current financial resources are measurable and available to be used and (2) expenditures when they cause a reduction in current financial resources.

In contrast, government-wide financial statements report a government's activities and financial position as a whole. These statements provide a method of assessing operational accountability, the ability of the government to meet its operating objectives. This approach helps users make long-term evaluations of the financial decisions and stability of the government by allowing them to

- Determine whether the government's overall financial position improved or deteriorated.
- Evaluate whether the government's current-year revenues were sufficient to pay for current-year services.
- See the cost of providing services to its citizenry.
- See how the government finances its programs—through user fees and other program revenues versus general tax revenues.
- Understand the extent to which the government has invested in capital assets, including roads, bridges, and other infrastructure assets.[9]

To achieve these goals, the government-wide financial statements' measurement focus is on all economic resources (not just current financial resources such as cash and receivables), and these statements utilize accrual accounting much like any for-profit entity. They report all assets and liabilities and recognize all revenues and expenses in a way that is comparable to business-type accounting. In announcing the change to *GASB Statement 34,* the city manager of Sacramento, California, explained that the purpose of new government-wide financial statements is to provide readers a broad overview of the city in a manner similar to private-sector business financial statements.

Financial Reporting and Accountability

Despite the variety of users and the dual set of statements, one aspect of governmental reporting has remained constant over the years: the goal of making the government accountable to the public. Because of the essential role of democracy within U.S. society, governmental accounting principles have attempted to provide a vehicle for evaluating governmental actions. Citizens should be aware of the means that officials use to raise money and allocate scarce resources. Voters must evaluate the wisdom, as well as the honesty, of the members of government. Most voters are also taxpayers, thus they naturally exhibit special interest in the results obtained from their involuntary contributions, such as taxes. *Because elected and appointed officials hold authority over the public's money, governmental reporting has traditionally stressed this stewardship responsibility.*

> Accountability is the cornerstone of all financial reporting in government. . . . Accountability requires governments to answer to the citizenry—to justify the raising of public resources and the purposes for which they are used. Governmental accountability is based on the belief that the citizenry has a "right to know," a right to receive openly declared facts that may lead to public debate by the citizens and their elected representatives.[10]

For this reason, accounting emphasis has traditionally been directed toward measuring and identifying the resources generated and expended by each of a government's diverse activities. *GASB Statement 34* clarified and expanded the notion of accountability to encompass both

[9] Ibid., p. 3.
[10] *GASB Concepts Statement No. 1,* para. 56.

fiscal accountability (in the fund-based statements) and operational accountability (in the government-wide financial statements). This pronouncement is not an attempt to overturn the traditional reporting philosophy. Instead, *GASB Statement 34* actually seeks to refine the reporting of individual government activities and then go beyond that to provide information about the government as a whole—hence the need for two sets of financial statements.

At least in connection with public service activities, such as the police department and public library, the fund-based financial statements answer three questions:

- How did the government generate its current financial resources?
- Where did those financial resources go?
- What amount of those financial resources is presently held?

The term *current financial resources* normally encompasses monetary assets available for officials to spend to meet the government's needs. Thus, when measuring current financial resources, a government is primarily monitoring its cash, investments, and receivables. To stress accountability, the traditional government accounting system has focused almost exclusively on these financial resources as well as current claims against them. For this reason, little reporting emphasis has been historically placed on accounts such as Buildings, Equipment, and Long-Term Debts that have no direct impact on current financial resources.

Obviously, stressing accountability in the use of current financial resources is an approach that by itself cannot meet all user needs; thus, many conventional reporting objectives have long been ignored. Not surprisingly, investors and creditors have frequently been sharp critics of governmental accounting. "When cities get into financial trouble, few citizens know about it until the day the interest can't be met or the teachers paid. . . . Had the books been kept like any decent corporation's that could never have happened."[11]

Consequently, *GASB Statement 34* has mandated the inclusion of government-wide financial statements to provide an additional dimension for government reporting. These statements do not focus solely on current financial resources but seek to report all assets at the disposal of government officials as well as all liabilities that must eventually be paid. Likewise, all revenues and expenses are recognized according to accrual accounting to provide a completely different level of financial information.

With two sets of financial statements available, each user (whether citizen or investor) can select the information viewed as being most relevant. Of course, not everyone believes that additional information is always helpful. "One of the tougher challenges of the current information age is sorting out the information most relevant for decision making from the vast amounts of data generated by today's state-of-the-art information systems. Financial reports cannot simply keep growing in size indefinitely to encompass every new type of information that becomes available."[12]

Reporting Diverse Governmental Activities—Fund Accounting

In gathering financial information for most state and local governments, the accountant faces the challenge of reporting a diverse array of activities. Accountability and control become special concerns for governments that operate through a multitude of relatively independent departments and functions. Consequently, for internal purposes, the accounting for each government activity is maintained in separate quasi-independent bookkeeping systems referred to as *funds*. Hence, the accounting process accumulates data to describe the financial results of every activity (library, school system, fire department, road construction, and the like). The internal information gathered has then traditionally served as the foundation for fund-based financial statements. An underlying assumption of government accounting has long been that most statement users prefer to see information segregated by function to assess each activity individually.

Because no common profit motive exists to tie all of these various functions and services together, consolidated balances have historically been omitted. Combining operating results from the city zoo, fire department, water system, print shop, and the like would provide figures of

---

[11] Richard Greene, "You Can't Fight City Hall—If You Can't Understand It," *Forbes,* March 3, 1980, p. 92.

[12] Esser, "Standard Setting," p. 3.

questionable utility if accountability and control over the usage of current financial resources are the primary goals. The purpose of reporting was to show the individual activities, not the government as a whole.

GASB Statement 34 does not affect the use of fund accounting for internal recording and control purposes. It did require modifications in the method by which these records were presented in fund-based financial statements, but such changes were not the major thrust of that standard. Instead, the pronouncement focused on the creation of a second set of statements, the government-wide financial statements.

Consequently, the use of separate funds by a state or local government still serves as the basic foundation for internal reporting. Although a single list of identifiable functions is not possible, the following frequently are included:

Public safety	Judicial system
Highway maintenance	Debt repayment
Sanitation	Bridge construction
Health	Water and sewer system
Welfare	Municipal swimming pool
Culture and recreation	Data processing center
Education	Endowment funds
Parks	Employee pensions

The actual number of funds in use depends on the extent of services the government offers and the grouping of related activities. For example, separate funds may be set up to account for a high school and its athletic programs, or these activities may be combined into a single fund.

> The general rule is to establish the minimum number of separate funds consistent with legal specifications and operational requirements. . . . Using too many funds causes inflexibility and undue complexity . . . and is best avoided in the interest of efficient and economical financial administration.[13]

Fund Accounting Classifications

For internal recordkeeping, all funds (whether for the police department, the municipal golf course, or some other activity) can be categorized into one of three distinct groups. This classification system allows for a clearer reporting of the government's various activities. Furthermore, having three separate groups allows for different accounting principles to be applied to different activities. The three are as follows:

- *Governmental funds*—include all funds that account for activities that a government carries out primarily to provide services to citizens and that are financed primarily through taxes. A police or fire department should be reported within the governmental funds.
- *Proprietary funds*—account for a government's ongoing organizations and activities similar to those operated by for-profit organizations. This fund type normally encompasses operations that assess a user charge so that determining operating income or cost recovery is important. A toll road would be reported within the proprietary funds.
- *Fiduciary funds*—account for monies held by the government in a trustee capacity. Such assets must be held for others and cannot be used by the government for its own programs. Assets held for a pension plan of government employees would be reported within the fiduciary funds.

Governmental Funds

In most state or municipal accounting systems, the governmental funds tend to dominate because a service orientation usually prevails. The internal accounting system maintains individual funds for every distinct service function: public safety, libraries, construction of a town hall, and so on. Each of these governmental funds accumulates and expends current financial resources to achieve one or more desired public goals.

---

[13] GASB Cod. Sec. 1100.108.

To provide better reported information and control, the governmental funds are subdivided into five categories: the General Fund, Special Revenue Funds, Capital Projects Funds, Debt Service Fund, and Permanent Funds. This classification system allows specific accounting guidelines to be directed toward each fund type while providing an overall structure for financial reporting purposes.

The General Fund   The GASB's definition of the General Fund appears to be somewhat understated: "to account for all financial resources except those required to be accounted for in another fund."[14] This description seems to imply that the General Fund records only miscellaneous revenues and expenditures when, in actuality, it accounts for many of a government's most important services. Whereas the other governmental funds report specific events or projects, the General Fund records a broad range of ongoing activities. For example, the 2004 financial statements for the City of Baltimore, Maryland, disclose 11 major areas of current expenditures within its General Fund: general government, public safety and regulations, conservation of health, social services, education, public library, recreation and culture, highways and streets, sanitation and waste removal, public service, and economic development. Expenditures reported for these categories of the General Fund made up more than 55 percent of the total for all of the city's governmental funds for the year ended June 30, 2004.

Special Revenue Funds   Special Revenue Funds account for assets that have been legally restricted as to expenditure. Because of donor restrictions or legislative mandates, these financial resources must be spent in a specified fashion. Saint Paul, Minnesota, for example, reported approximately $77 million of revenues within 40 Special Revenue Funds during the 2003 fiscal year. Sources as diverse as cable television franchising fees, rent received from the use of Municipal Stadium, administration fees for charitable gambling, money received from recycling programs, and parking meter fees generated this money. The Special Revenue Funds category accounts for these monies because *legal restrictions had been attached to the revenue to require that expenditure be limited to specific purposes.* As an example, Saint Paul's city council specified that any revenue derived from the public library must be used only for library purposes. Thus, the accounting system monitors any financial resources received from this source by including them in the Special Revenue Funds.

Capital Projects Funds   As the title implies, this fund type accounts for costs incurred in acquiring or constructing major government facilities such as bridges, high schools, roads, or municipal office complexes. Funding for these projects normally comes from grants or the sale of bonds or is transferred from general revenues. The actual asset being obtained is not recorded here, but the money to finance the purchase or construction is recorded. For example, the Lexington-Fayette Urban County Government in Kentucky reported as of June 30, 2004, that it was holding more than $14 million in financial resources in its Capital Projects Funds to be used in projects such as acquisition or construction in connection with a cultural center, road projects, a golf course, and equipment leasing.

Debt Service Funds   These funds record financial resources accumulated to pay long-term liabilities and interest as they come due.[15] However, this fund type does not account for a government's long-term debt. Rather, Debt Service Funds monitor the monetary balances currently available to satisfy long-term liabilities and make the eventual payment. Thus, on June 30, 2003, the city of Birmingham, Alabama, reported nearly $60 million of cash and investments in its debt service funds, money being held to pay long-term debt and interest. For the year then ended, this fund made more than $12 million in principal payments and $15 million in interest payments.

Permanent Funds   The Permanent Funds category accounts for assets contributed to the government by an external donor with the stipulation that the principal cannot be spent but any income can be used within the government, often for a designated purpose. As an example, the City of Dallas, Texas, reported holding nearly $8 million as of September 30, 2003, that had come almost entirely from private donations whose income was designated to maintain four different parks. Such gifts are frequently referred to as *endowments*.

---

[14] GASB Cod. Sec. 1300.104.

[15] Some state and local governments choose to maintain assets for debt service within the General Fund rather than in a separate category. This approach is acceptable, especially if the amounts are relatively small.

Proprietary Funds

The Proprietary Funds category accounts for government activities, such as a bus system or subway line, that assess a user charge. Such services resemble those found in the business world. To facilitate financial reporting, the proprietary funds are broken down into two major divisions:

Enterprise Funds Any government operation that is open to the public and financed, at least in part, by user charges may be classified as an Enterprise Fund. A municipality, for example, may generate revenues from the use of a public swimming pool, golf course, airport, water and sewage service, and the like. As an illustration, the City of Charlotte, North Carolina, reports the operation of its airport as an Enterprise Fund.

The number of Enterprise Funds has increased rather dramatically over recent years as governments have attempted to expand services without raising taxes. This situation requires those citizens utilizing a particular service to shoulder a higher percentage of its costs. "Enterprise funds have become an attractive alternative revenue source for local governments to recover all or part of the cost of goods or services from those directly benefiting from them."[16]

Enterprise Fund activities that assess direct fees from customers resemble business activities. Not surprisingly, even in the fund-based financial statements, the accounting process very much parallels that found in for-profit reporting. These funds use accrual basis accounting with a focus on economic, not just current financial, resources.

A question arises, though, as to how much revenue an activity must generate before it is viewed as an Enterprise Fund. For example, if a city wants to promote mass transit and charges only a nickel to ride on its bus line, should that activity be viewed as part of an Enterprise Fund (a business-type activity) or within the General Fund (a governmental activity)?

According to *GASB Statement 34,* any activity that charges a user fee to the public may be classified as an Enterprise Fund. However, this designation is *required* if the activity meets any one of the following criteria so that the amount of revenue is viewed as significant:

- The activity generates net revenues that provide the sole security for the debts of the activity.
- Laws or regulations require recovering the activity's costs (including depreciation and debt service) through fees or charges.
- Fees and charges are set at prices intended to recover costs including depreciation and debt service.

Internal Service Funds This second proprietary fund type accounts for any operation that provides services to another department or agency within the government on a cost-reimbursement basis. As with Enterprise Funds, Internal Service Funds charge fees but perform the service for the primary benefit of the government rather than for outside users. Also, in the same manner as Enterprise Funds, Internal Service Funds are accounted for similarly to a for-profit operation in the private sector.

The City of Lincoln, Nebraska, lists seven operations in its 2004 financial statements that are accounted for as separate internal service funds:

Information services fund—to account for the cost of operating a central data processing facility.

Engineering revolving fund—to account for the cost of operating a central engineering pool.

Insurance revolving fund—to account for the cost of providing several types of self-insurance programs.

Fleet services fund—to account for the operations of a centralized maintenance facility for city equipment.

Police garage fund—to account for the operation of a maintenance facility for police and other government vehicles.

Communication services fund—to account for the costs of providing graphic arts and telecommunications services.

Copy services fund—to account for the cost of providing copy services.

---

[16] Jeffrey Molinari and Charlie Tyer, "Local Government Enterprise Fund Activity: Trends and Implications," *Public Administration Quarterly,* Fall 2003, p. 369.

Fiduciary Funds

The final classification, fiduciary funds, accounts for assets held in a trustee capacity for external parties so that the money cannot be used to support the government's own programs. Like proprietary funds, all fiduciary funds use the economic resources measurement focus and accrual accounting for the timing of revenues and expenses. Because these assets are not to be used for the government, fiduciary funds are not included in government-wide financial statements but do have separate statements presented within the fund-based financial statements.

Four distinct types of fiduciary funds can exist:

Investment Trust Funds   The first fund type accounts for the outside portion of investment pools when the reporting government has accepted funds from other governments to have more money to invest and, it is hoped, earn a higher return for both parties.

Private-Purpose Trust Funds   The second fund type accounts for any monies held in a trustee capacity when principal and interest are for the benefit of external parties outside the government such as individuals, private organizations, or other governments.

Pension Trust Funds   The third type accounts for an employee retirement system. Because of the need to provide adequate benefits for government workers, this fund type can become quite large. The City of Baltimore, for example, reported assets of more than $3.7 billion in its pension trust fund at the end of 2004.

Agency Funds   The fourth type records any resources a government holds as an agent for individuals, private organizations, or other government units. For example, one government occasionally collects taxes and tolls on behalf of another. To ensure safety and control, the Agency Fund separately maintains this money until it is transferred to the proper authority.

Coverage of Fund Accounting Procedures

The formal classification system just described is extremely useful in understanding the financial reporting of a state or local government.

- *What is being measured:* With the current financial resources measurement focus, statements measure resources that can be spent in the near future and any claims on them. The typical assets reported are cash, receivables, and investments. The liabilities reported are debts now owed that will be paid quickly enough to require the use of the current financial resources reported as assets.

  With an economic resources measurement focus, statements report all assets and all liabilities regardless of whether they are current or long-term.
- *Timing of recognition:* Modified accrual accounting recognizes revenues when they are measurable and available. *Available* typically means that current financial resources will be received quickly enough to be used to pay for current period expenditures. The determination of what is meant by "quickly enough" is up to the reporting government. The 2003 financial statements for the City of Norfolk, Virginia, disclose "the City generally considers revenues to be available if they are collected within 60 days of the end of the fiscal year." For that reason, a 2003 revenue that was expected to be collected within the first 60 days of 2004 is still recognized in 2003. However, the financial statements for Raleigh, North Carolina, show a slightly different accounting decision: The city considers all revenues to be available if they are collected within 90 days after year-end, except for property taxes.[17] The number of days can vary widely by government.

  In contrast, accrual accounting recognizes revenues when the earning process is substantially completed and the amount to be received is subject to a reasonable estimation. Accrual accounting recognizes expenses by matching them, in most cases, in the time period of the revenues they helped to generate.

Because of the variety of funds and the alternatives for measurement and timing, the appropriate reporting can best be visualized by setting up a matrix:

---

[17] Under modified accrual accounting, a 60-day period is mandated for the recognition of property taxes.

	Fund-Based Financial Statements	Government-Wide Financial Statements
Governmental funds	Use the current financial resources measurement focus and modified accrual accounting for the timing of revenue and expenditure recognition.	Use the economic resources measurement focus and accrual accounting for the timing of revenue and expense recognition.
Proprietary funds	Use the economic resources measurement focus and accrual accounting for the timing of revenue and expense recognition.	Use the economic resources measurement focus and accrual accounting for the timing of revenue and expense recognition.
Fiduciary funds	Use the economic resources measurement focus and accrual accounting for the timing of revenue and expense recognition.	Funds are not included.

Students of state and local government accounting find that truly significant reporting issues are most prevalent as a result of the differences between the guidelines for the governmental funds within the fund-based financial statements and the government-wide financial statements. In contrast, reporting for the proprietary funds is similar between the two sets of statements. Both the proprietary funds and the fiduciary funds utilize the economic resources measurement focus and accrual accounting so that their reporting resembles that of for-profit businesses. Not surprisingly, therefore, the remaining coverage here focuses on reporting the governmental funds and the differences seen in recording almost every transaction in the two sets of statements.

OVERVIEW OF STATE AND LOCAL GOVERNMENT FINANCIAL STATEMENTS

Although a complete analysis of the financial statements of a state or local government is presented in the subsequent chapter, an overview of four basic financial statements is helpful here to illustrate how certain events are reported. These examples are not complete but simply demonstrate the presentation of various accounts.

Government-Wide Financial Statements

Only two financial statements make up the government-wide financial statements: *the statement of net assets* and *the statement of activities.* These statements separate the reporting into governmental activities (all governmental funds and most Internal Service Funds) and business-type activities (all Enterprise Funds and any remaining Internal Service Funds).[18] As mentioned earlier, these government-wide financial statements do not report the assets of any fiduciary funds, which are shown only in separate fund-based financial statements.

Exhibit 16.1 shows the basic outline of a statement of net assets. Under the economic resources measurement focus used in the government-wide financial statements, all assets and liabilities are reported. The final section of this statement, the net assets category, indicates (1) the amount of capital assets reported less related debt, (2) restrictions on any net assets, and (3) the total amount of unrestricted net assets. For example, in Exhibit 16.1, Governmental Activities has $80 of completely unrestricted net assets to use and Business-Type Activities has $30 of unrestricted net assets.

The statement of activities in Exhibit 16.2 provides details about revenues and expenses, once again separated into governmental activities and business-type activities. The statement shows

---

[18] Government-wide financial statements report Internal Service Funds with the governmental funds in the governmental activities if their primary purpose is to serve the governmental funds. Conversely, Internal Service Funds are grouped with the Enterprise Funds as business-type activities if they mainly exist to assist one or more Enterprise Funds. For example, a print shop (an Internal Service Fund) should be reported within the governmental activities if its work is primarily for the benefit of the public library (a governmental fund). However, if its work is for a bus line (an Enterprise Fund), the print shop is classified within the business-type activities.

EXHIBIT 16.1
Statement of Net Assets—
Government-Wide
Financial Statements

	Governmental Activities	Business-Type Activities	Total
Assets			
Cash	$ 100	$ 130	$ 230
Investments	900	40	940
Receivables	600	400	1,000
Internal amounts due	50	(50)	–0–
Supplies and materials	30	40	70
Capital assets (net of depreciation)	2,950	2,750	5,700
Total assets	$4,630	$3,310	$7,940
Liabilities			
Accounts payable	$ 750	$ 230	$ 980
Noncurrent liabilities			
Due within one year	400	180	580
Due in more than one year	1,800	700	2,500
Total liabilities	$2,950	$1,110	$4,060
Net Assets			
Invested in capital assets, net of related debt	$1,410	$2,110	$3,520
Restricted for:			
Capital projects	50	–0–	50
Debt service	140	60	200
Unrestricted	80	30	110
Total net assets	$1,680	$2,200	$3,880

EXHIBIT 16.2   Statement of Activities—Government-Wide Financial Statements

			Net (Expense) Revenue		
Function	Expenses	Program Revenues	Governmental Activities	Business-Type Activities	Total
Governmental activities					
General government	$ 3,200	$ 1,400	$ (1,800)	n/a	$ (1,800)
Public safety	9,700	880	(8,820)	n/a	(8,820)
Public works	2,600	600	(2,000)	n/a	(2,000)
Education	8,400	300	(8,100)	n/a	(8,100)
Total governmental activities	$23,900	$ 3,180	$(20,720)	n/a	$(20,720)
Business-type activities					
Water	$ 3,600	$ 4,030	n/a	$ 430	$ 430
Sewer	4,920	5,610	n/a	690	690
Airport	2,300	3,120	n/a	820	820
Total business-type activities	$10,820	$12,760	n/a	$1,940	$ 1,940
Total government	$34,720	$15,940	$(20,720)	$1,940	$(18,780)
General revenues:					
Property taxes			$ 20,400	–0–	$ 20,400
Investment earnings			420	70	490
Transfers			600	(600)	–0–
Total general revenues and transfers			$ 21,420	$ (530)	$ 20,890
Change in net assets			$ 700	$1,410	$ 2,110
Beginning net assets			980	790	1,770
Ending net assets			$ 1,680	$2,200	$ 3,880

EXHIBIT 16.3 Balance Sheet—Governmental
Funds Fund-Based Financial Statements

	General Fund	Library Program	Other Governmental Funds	Total Governmental Funds
Assets				
Cash	$ 40	$ 10	$ 50	$ 100
Investments	580	120	200	900
Receivables	120	200	210	530
Supplies and materials	10	10	10	30
Total assets	$750	$340	$470	$1,560
Liabilities				
Accounts payable	$230	$170	$110	$ 510
Notes payable—current	300	–0–	100	400
Total liabilities	$530	$170	$210	$ 910
Fund Balances				
Reserved for:				
Supplies	$ 10	$ 10	$ 10	$ 30
Encumbrances	120	30	40	190
Debt service	–0–	–0–	110	110
Unreserved:				
General fund	90	–0–	–0–	90
Special revenue fund	–0–	130	20	150
Capital projects fund	–0–	–0–	80	80
Total fund balances	$220	$170	$260	$ 650
Total liabilities and fund balances	$750	$340	$470	$1,560

direct expenses and program revenues for each function. Program revenues are fines, fees, grants, and the like that the specific activity generates. Thus, the net revenues or net expenses are determined horizontally for each function as a way of indicating each financial burden or financial benefit. Here, for example, the public safety category has a net cost to the government of $8,820. The total of these amounts is summed vertically to show the total cost of operating the government, an amount that is offset by general revenues such as property taxes and sales taxes.

Fund-Based Financial Statements

A state or local government produces a number of fund-based financial statements. However, at this introductory stage, we present only two fundamental statements that parallel the two government-wide statements just shown. First, Exhibit 16.3 shows *a balance sheet* for the governmental funds and then Exhibit 16.4 is *a statement of revenues, expenditures, and changes in fund balances* produced for the same governmental funds. Note that the figures here will not be the same as those presented for the governmental activities in the government-wide statement of net assets (Exhibit 16.1) and statement of activities (Exhibit 16.2), primarily for three reasons:

1. Government-wide statements report most internal service funds within the governmental activities. However, fund-based statements report all internal service funds as proprietary funds, not as governmental funds. Thus, funds are grouped differently.

2. Governmental activities use the economic resources measurement focus whereas the governmental funds, in the fund-based statements, use the current financial resources measurement focus. Therefore, different assets and liabilities are being reported.

3. Governmental activities use accrual accounting in government-wide statements; governmental funds use modified accrual accounting in creating fund-based financial statements. The timing of recognition is different.

Because of these differences, reconciliations between the governmental totals presented in Exhibits 16.1 and 16.3 and between Exhibits 16.2 and 16.4 should be reported. Those reconciliations are discussed in the following chapter.

EXHIBIT 16.4   **Statement of Revenues, Expenditures, and Other Changes in Fund Balances—Governmental Funds**
Fund-Based Financial Statements

	General Fund	Library Program	Other Governmental Funds	Total Governmental Funds
Revenues				
Property taxes	$17,200	$ 900	$ 2,300	$20,400
Investment earnings	100	200	180	480
Program revenues	500	100	2,500	3,100
Total revenues	$17,800	$1,200	$ 4,980	$23,980
Expenditures				
Current:				
General government	$ 3,400	–0–	$ 100	$ 3,500
Public safety	5,100	–0–	400	5,500
Education	6,700	800	–0–	7,500
Debt service:				
Principal	–0–	–0–	1,000	1,000
Interest	–0–	–0–	600	600
Capital outlay	1,100	300	3,300	4,700
Total expenditures	$16,300	$1,100	$ 5,400	$22,800
Excess (deficiency) of revenues over expenditures	$ 1,500	$ 100	$ (420)	$ 1,180
Other Financing Sources (Uses)				
Bond proceeds	–0–	–0–	$ 1,000	$ 1,000
Transfers in	–0–	$ 20	580	600
Transfers out	$ (1,300)	–0–	$(1,000)	(2,300)
Total other financing sources and uses	$ (1,300)	$ 20	$ 580	$ (700)
Change in fund balances	$ 200	$ 120	$ 160	$ 480
Fund balances—beginning	20	50	100	170
Fund balances—ending	$ 220	$ 170	$ 260	$ 650

Two accounts should be noted specifically on these statements because they reflect the size of the activity or organization. On the government-wide financial statements, the Net Assets balance is a measure of total assets less total liabilities. On the fund-based statements for the governmental funds, a fund balance amount is reported. Again, this amount reflects the assets minus the liabilities, but these assets are current financial resources, and the liabilities are limited to claims that will be paid from those resources. Each separate fund will report its own fund balance to indicate the amount of resources being held.

In looking at both of the fund-based financial statements being presented, note that the General Fund and every other individual fund that qualifies as major requires a separate column. The assumption here is that the Library Fund (probably one of this government's Special Revenue Funds) is the only individual fund outside the General Fund that is considered to be major. All other funds are then grouped together. Identification of a "major" fund becomes quite important for disclosure purposes. It is defined as follows:

> The reporting government's main operating fund (the general fund or its equivalent) should always be reported as a major fund. Other individual governmental and enterprise funds should be reported in separate columns as major funds based on these criteria:
>
> *a.* Total assets, liabilities, revenues, or expenditures/expenses of that individual governmental or enterprise fund are at least 10 percent of the corresponding total (assets, liabilities, and so forth) for all funds of that category or type (that is, total governmental or total enterprise funds), *and*

  b. Total assets, liabilities, revenues, or expenditures/expenses of the individual governmental fund or enterprise fund are at least 5 percent of the corresponding total for all governmental and enterprise funds combined.

  In addition to funds that meet the major fund criteria, any other governmental or enterprise fund that the government's officials believe is particularly important to financial statement users (for example, because of public interest or consistency) may be reported as a major fund.[19]

ACCOUNTING FOR GOVERNMENTAL FUNDS

As indicated, the remainder of this chapter presents many of the unique aspects of the accounting process utilized within the governmental funds: the General Fund, Special Revenue Funds, Capital Projects Funds, Debt Service Funds, and Permanent Funds. Because of the dual nature of the reporting required by *GASB Statement 34,* much of this accounting must be demonstrated twice, once for fund-based financial statements and then for the government-wide financial statements.

Much discussion has occurred as to whether governments will keep two separate sets of financial records or merely one set that must be adjusted significantly at the end of the year to create the second set of financial statements. Initially, keeping one set of books for the fund-based statements probably is easiest. The resulting figures can then be adjusted at year-end to create the government-wide statements. However, over time, as software programs and computer systems become more sophisticated, many governments will probably find simply keeping two sets of books more convenient. Being able to analyze complex transactions completely as they happen seems to be advantageous, and maintaining two sets of records reduces what otherwise could be a massive amount of work at the end of each year.

For that reason, this textbook examines transactions from both fund-based and government-wide perspectives at the same time. Looking at these events in two different ways seems to be an easier mental process than learning one method now and later attempting to convert that entire set of reported data into the second method. Thus, for each example, students should be especially careful to note whether the fund-based financial statements for the governmental funds are being affected (so that current financial resources are being measured based on modified accrual accounting) or government-wide statements for the governmental activities are being reported (following the economic resources measurement basis and accrual accounting).

The Importance of Budgets and the Recording of Budgetary Entries

"Financing is an important part of the governmental environment, particularly for governmental type activities. For those activities, the budget is the primary method of directing and controlling the financial process."[20] In a chronological sense, the first significant accounting procedure encountered in a state or locality is the recording of budgetary entries. To enhance accountability, government officials normally are required to adopt an annual budget for each separate activity to anticipate the inflow of financial resources and establish approved expenditure levels. The budget serves several important purposes:

1. *Expresses public policy.* If, for example, more money is budgeted for child care and less for the environment, the citizens are made aware of the decision to allocate limited government resources in this manner.
2. *Serves as an expression of financial intent for the upcoming fiscal year.* The budget presents the financial plan for the government for the period.
3. *Provides control because it establishes spending limitations.*
4. *Offers a means of evaluating performance* by allowing a comparison of actual results with the levels found in the budget.

[19] *GASB Statement 34,* para. 76.
[20] *GASB Statement 11,* para. 9.

The GASB even states that "many believe the budget is the most significant financial document produced by a government unit."[21]

Once a budget has been produced and enacted into law, formal accounting recognition is frequently required as a means of enhancing the benefits just described. In this way, the public has the opportunity to learn the amount of financial resources that should be received and expended. Reporting revenue projections and complying with spending limitations are considered essential for government accountability. Furthermore, many governments must legally have balanced budgets. Therefore, approved budget figures are entered into the accounting records formally at the start of each fiscal year. Citizens can then make comparisons between actual and budgeted figures at any interim point during the period.

In recognition of the importance of the information conveyed by budget figures, each government must report comparisons between the original budget, the final budget, and the actual figures for the period as required supplemental information presented after the notes to its financial statements. As an alternative, the information can be shown as a separate statement within the government's fund-based financial statements. This budget information must be disclosed for the General Fund and each major fund within the Special Revenue Funds.

As an illustration of the budgetary reporting process, assume that a city enacts a motel excise tax that it will use to promote tourism and conventions. Because the funding is legally restricted for this specified purpose, the city must establish a separate Special Revenue Fund. Assume also that for the 2007 fiscal year, the tax is estimated to generate $490,000 in revenues. Based on this projection, the city council authorizes the expenditure of $400,000 (referred to as an *appropriation*) for programs during the current year. Of this amount, $200,000 is designated for salaries, $30,000 for utilities, $80,000 for advertising, and $90,000 for supplies. The $90,000 difference between the anticipated revenue inflow and this appropriation is a budgeted surplus accumulated by the government for future use or in case the levy tax proves to be too small.

To highlight the council's action, the accounting records of this fund include the following journal entry. Although this information is not required to be presented in the fund-based statements, we include it for ease of labeling. Even if it is reported separately as required supplemental information, the recording would be made internally with the other fund-based information.

Special Revenue Fund—Tourism and Convention Promotions		
Estimated Revenues—Tax Levy	490,000	
Appropriations—Salaries		200,000
Appropriations—Utilities		30,000
Appropriations—Advertising		80,000
Appropriations—Supplies		90,000
Budgetary Fund Balance		90,000
To record annual budget for tourism and convention promotions.		

This entry indicates the source of the funding (the tax levy) and the approved amount of expenditures. The Budgetary Fund Balance account indicates the presence of an anticipated surplus (or, in some cases, a shortage) projected for the period. Here, the size of the fund is expected to increase by $90,000 during the year.

Each of these figures remains in the records of this Special Revenue Fund for the entire year to allow for planning, disclosure, and control. Citizens can see how much is to be spent for each program and the source of funding.

Use of budgetary entries is also a method by which readers can learn of *interperiod equity.* This concept reflects whether spending and revenues are in alignment for a period or whether money must be borrowed to fund current expenditures, debt that future citizens will pay back. If a government projects revenues as $10 million but budgets expenditures at $11 million, the extra million must be financed in some manner, usually by debt to be

[21] *GASB Concepts Statement No. 1,* para. 19.

repaid in the future. The benefits of the additional expenditures are enjoyed today, but citizens of a later time period must bear the cost.

The original budget is not always the final appropriations budget for the year. For example, more or less money may become available than had been anticipated and government officials may vote to change the appropriations. Assume, to illustrate, that officials in charge of tourism for this city appeal during the year for an additional $50,000 to create a special advertising campaign. If properly approved, the original budgetary entry must be adjusted:

Fund-Based Financial Statements

Special Revenue Fund—Tourism and Convention Promotions		
Budgetary Fund Balance	50,000	
Appropriations—Advertising		50,000
To record additional appropriation for advertising.		

Assume that the city actually received $488,000 during the year and spent $437,000 as follows:

Salaries	$196,000
Utilities	29,000
Advertising	125,000
Supplies	87,000

This information should be disclosed as follows. The Variance column is recommended but not required:

TOURISM AND CONVENTION PROMOTIONS
Year Ended December 31, 2007
Budget Comparison Schedule

	Budgeted Amounts		Actual Amounts	Variance with Final Budget—
	Original	Final	(budgetary basis)	Positive (negative)
Resources (inflows):				
Tax levy	$490,000	$490,000	$488,000	$ (2,000)
Charges to appropriations (outflows):				
Salaries	$200,000	$200,000	$196,000	$ 4,000
Utilities	30,000	30,000	29,000	1,000
Advertising	80,000	130,000	125,000	5,000
Supplies	90,000	90,000	87,000	3,000
Total charges	$400,000	$450,000	$437,000	$13,000
Change in fund balance	$ 90,000	$ 40,000	$ 51,000	$11,000

Budgetary reporting is normally optional except for the General Fund and Special Revenue Funds because contractual arrangements or other legal agreements more often set resource inflows and outflows in other funds so that such entries do not enhance financial control.

Encumbrances

One additional budgetary procedure that plays a central role in this system is the recording of financial commitments referred to as *encumbrances. In diametric contrast to for-profit accounting, purchase commitments and contracts are recorded in the governmental funds prior to becoming legal liabilities.* This recording of encumbrances simply provides an efficient method for keeping up with financial commitments so that a fund will not overspend its appropriated amount. Encumbrance accounting is appropriate in any governmental fund. At any point during the fiscal year, information on both expended and committed funds is available.

To illustrate, assume that a city's police department orders $18,000 in equipment. As an ongoing service activity, the police department is accounted for within the General Fund. Because only an order has been made but no transaction has occurred, no entry is recorded at this point for the government-wide financial statements that tend to resemble for-profit accounting. However, this amount of the government's financial resources has been committed even though no formal liability will exist until the equipment is received. To control against spending more than has been appropriated, an encumbrance is actually recorded any time one of the governmental funds makes a purchase order, contract, or other formal commitment.

Fund-Based Financial Statements

General Fund—Police Department		
Encumbrances Control	18,000	
Fund Balance—Reserved for Encumbrances		18,000
To record an order placed for equipment.		

The Encumbrances account records the commitment that has been incurred, and the Fund Balance—Reserved account is an equity-type balance indicating the amount of the city's resources required to fulfill future obligations.

The use of a control account here simply indicates that the government's accounting system was created with a subsidiary ledger that maintains more detailed information on this $18,000 amount. Without a subsidiary ledger, the debit entry here would have been made to Encumbrances—Equipment or a similar account.

When the police department receives the equipment, a legal liability replaces the commitment. Hence, the encumbrance is removed from the accounting records and an expenditures account is recognized. Often, because of sales taxes, freight costs, or other price adjustments, the actual invoice total differs from the estimated figure recorded when the order was processed. For this reason, the expenditure will not necessarily agree with the corresponding encumbrance. Assume, for illustration purposes, that an invoice for $18,160 accompanies the equipment received.

Fund-Based Financial Statements

General Fund		
Fund Balance—Reserved for Encumbrances	18,000	
Encumbrances Control		18,000
To remove encumbrance for equipment that has now been received.		
Expenditures—Equipment	18,160	
Vouchers Payable		18,160
To record the receipt of equipment and the accompanying liability.		

In producing government-wide financial statements, the only entry created by this ordering and receiving of equipment is an increase in the specific asset and the related liability when legal title is conveyed.

Over the years, a number of different reporting techniques have been created to reflect the impact of commitments that were not fulfilled prior to the end of the year. For example, such commitments may simply lapse and await the government's new action in the subsequent year. These encumbrances are reversed from the records because no current reporting is necessary.

Other governments may plan, or be legally required, to satisfy such commitments even though the concluding event occurs in a later period. In recent years, most governments seem to prefer the following approach to report the impact of such encumbrances in the current year:

- At the end of the initial year, officials reverse the entry that established the encumbrance to eliminate it. In this way, no financial effect is reported because no transaction actually occurred during the period.
- On the balance sheet for the governmental fund that made the commitment, a portion of the Fund Balance figure is separated to indicate that this amount of current financial resources will be needed in the future to meet the requirements of the commitment.

For example, assume a city has $800,000 in current financial resources (cash, receivables, and investments) and $700,000 in claims to those current financial resources so that its fund balance is $100,000. Assume that $18,000 in equipment has been ordered but not received at year's end. However, the city must meet the commitment when it receives the equipment. Using the approach just described, the only acknowledgment of the commitment is shown in the Fund Balance section of the balance sheet:

Fund Balance		
Reserved for Encumbrances	$18,000	
Unreserved, Unrestricted	82,000	$100,000

The fund balance is still $100,000, but the reader sees that $18,000 will be needed to cover a commitment made in this year that will be finalized in the subsequent period.

Recognition of Expenditures for Operations and Capital Additions

Although budgetary and encumbrance entries are unique, their impact on the accounting process is somewhat limited because they do not directly affect a fund's financial results for the period. Conversely, the method by which a state or locality records the receipt and disbursement of assets can significantly alter results of the reported data. For example, because a primary emphasis in the governmental funds is on measuring changes in current financial resources, *neither expenses nor capital assets are recorded in the fund-based financial statements.* Probably no larger distinction exists between the fund-based statements and the government-wide statements.

As shown earlier, governmental funds use an Expenditures account in the fund-based statements. This term is used to explain outflows or other reductions in current financial resources caused by the acquisition of a good or service (or some other utility). The actual use of resources is recorded as an expenditure whether it is for rent, a fire truck, salaries, or a computer. The statement of revenues, expenditures, and other changes in fund balances shows that this method of recording allows the reader to see the utilization of an activity's current financial resources. Spending $1,000 for electricity for the past three months is an expenditure of a fund's current financial resources in exactly the same way that buying a $70,000 ambulance is:

Fund-Based Financial Statements

Expenditures—Electricity	1,000	
Vouchers (or Accounts) Payable		1,000
To record charges covering the past three months.		
Expenditures—Ambulance	70,000	
Vouchers (or Accounts) Payable		70,000
To record acquisition of new ambulance.		

Within the governmental funds, the timing of the recognition of expenditures (and revenues) follows the *modified accrual basis* of accounting. For expenditures, modified accrual accounting requires recognizing a claim against current financial resources when it is created. If a claim is established in one period to be settled in the second period using year-end current financial resources, the expenditure and liability are recorded in the initial year. As discussed earlier, the maximum length of time for payment to occur—often 60 days into the subsequent period—should be disclosed. Thus, if equipment is received 15 days before the end of the year but payment will not be made until 75 days later, the recording is still made in the first year.

The recording of expenditures rather than expenses and capital assets is one of the most distinctive characteristics of traditional governmental accounting. Thus, a for-profit business enterprise that purchases a building or a machine capitalizes all related costs and then recognizes depreciation expense during each year of the asset's useful life. This depreciation is a factor in the computation of the organization's annual net income.

In contrast, in its fund-based statements, a governmental fund records both cash expenses and the entire cost of all buildings, machines, and other capital assets as expenditures. No income figure is calculated for these funds; thus, the computation and recording of subsequent depreciation is not relevant to the reporting process and is omitted entirely.

For the government-wide financial statement, all economic resources are being measured. Consequently, the previous two journal entries would be changed as follows:

Government-Wide Financial Statements

Utilities Expense	1,000	
Voucher (or Accounts) Payable		1,000
To record electricity charges for the past three months.		
Ambulance	70,000	
Voucher (or Accounts) Payable		70,000
To record acquisition of new ambulance.		

Capital Assets and Fund-Based Financial Statements

One interesting result of measuring and reporting only expenditures within the fund-based statements of the governmental funds is that virtually no assets are reported other than current financial resources such as cash, receivables, and investments. All capital assets have been recorded as expenditures at the time of purchase and then closed out at the end of the fiscal period. Note that the statement in Exhibit 16.3 shows no buildings, schools, computers, trucks, or other equipment as assets.

With the creation of government-wide financial statements, a record of all capital assets is available in the statement of net assets (see Exhibit 16.1). Thus, recording only expenditures in the fund-based financial statements does not leave a gap in the information being presented. Previously, a separate account group had been maintained for such assets (and for the long-term liabilities of the governmental funds). These two account groups (the General Fixed Assets account group and the General Long-Term Debt account group) were no more than a listing of the individual accounts whose balances were not otherwise recorded or presented by the traditional accounting model. *Statement 34* eliminated the need for these two account groups because government-wide statements now report fixed assets and long-term liabilities.

In the initial production of government-wide financial statements, officials simply took the cost of fixed assets found in the General Fixed Assets account group (or fair value for donated items) to determine the initial asset balances to be reported. One problem, though, has been the initial reporting of "infrastructure" assets including roads, sidewalks, bridges, and the like that are normally stationary and can be preserved for a significant period of time. A bridge, for example, might last for more than 100 years. Traditionally, the recording of such infrastructure assets within the General Fixed Assets account group was optional. To save time and energy, many governments simply did not record these assets after the initial expenditure was recorded. Thus, in creating the first set of government-wide financial statements, records were often unavailable for some or all of the infrastructure assets that have been bought or constructed over the years.

Because of the problem of establishing initial balances for infrastructure assets, the GASB made an exception in reporting for government-wide financial statements. After adopting *Statement 34*, a government must capitalize new infrastructure assets bought or built. However, an additional four years beyond the date when *Statement 34* became effective was

Discussion **Question**

IS IT AN ASSET OR A LIABILITY?

In the August 1989 issue of the *Journal of Accountancy,* R.K. Mautz discussed the unique reporting needs of governments and not-for-profit organizations (such as charities) in "Not-For-Profit Financial Reporting: Another View." As an illustration of their accounting problems, Mautz examined the method by which a city should record a newly constructed high school building. Conventional business wisdom would say that such a property represents an asset of the government. Thus, the cost should be capitalized and then depreciated over an estimated useful life. However, in paragraph 26 of FASB *Concepts Statements No. 6,* an essential characteristic of an asset is "a probable future benefit . . . to contribute directly or indirectly to future cash inflows."

Mautz reasoned that the school building cannot be considered an asset because it provides no net contribution to cash inflows. In truth, a high school requires the government to make significant cash outflows for maintenance, repairs, utilities, salaries, and the like. Public educational facilities (as well as many of the other properties of a government such as a fire station or municipal building) are acquired with the understanding that net cash outflows will result.

Consequently, Mautz considered whether the construction of a high school is not actually the incurrence of a liability because the government is taking on an obligation that will necessitate future cash payments. This idea also is rejected, once again based on the guidance of *Concepts Statement No. 6* (para. 36), because the cash outflow is not required at a "specified or determinable date, on occurrence of a specified event, or on demand."

Is a high school building an asset or is it a liability? If it is neither, how should the cost be recorded? Prior to adoption of *GASB Statement 34,* how would a government have reported a high school building? After adoption of *Statement 34,* how would a government report a high school building? Which of these two approaches provides the best portrayal of the decision to acquire or construct this building? Can a government be accounted for in the same manner as a for-profit enterprise?

---

allowed to establish the capitalization of previous infrastructure assets. In this manner, government officials were given extra time to arrive at cost figures for miles of highways, curbing, sidewalks, and the like. The GASB suggested methods by which these costs could be approximated for reporting purposes. For example, current costs for such projects could be determined and then adjusted for inflation and usage since the assets were originally obtained. However, an important limitation was placed on the need for such complex calculations. This type of historical estimation and reporting is required only for major general infrastructure assets acquired or significantly improved since June 30, 1980. Thus, *Statement 34* does not require a cost approximation for a sidewalk built in 1928.

As mentioned previously, fund-based financial statements do not recognize depreciation expense in connection with governmental funds for two reasons:

1. These funds reflect expenditures rather than expenses, and the entire cost of the asset was reported as an expenditure at the time of the original claim against current financial resources. Thus, the impact of the acquisition was recorded when obtained so that reporting a depreciation expense account would reflect the impact twice: once when acquired and once when depreciated.

2. These funds traditionally do not record expenses. Reporting depreciation expense (rather than an expenditure) is not consistent with measuring the change in current financial resources.

However, the government-wide financial statements list assets rather than expenditures, and therefore depreciation is appropriate. Consequently, on these financial statements, depreciation on all long-lived assets with finite lives should be calculated and reported each period.

Supplies and Prepaid Items

In gathering information for government-wide financial statements, the acquisition of supplies and prepaid costs such as rent or insurance is not particularly complicated. An asset is recorded at the time of acquisition and then subsequently reclassified to an expense account as the asset's utility is consumed. However, in reporting the governmental funds in the fund-based financial statements, appropriate handling is not so clear. Such assets are neither current financial resources that can be expended nor capital assets with long lives to be reported immediately as expenditures. Thus, neither method of recording utilized for these fund-based statements seems to apply exactly.

Traditionally, supplies and prepaid items have been recorded as expenditures at the point in time that a claim to current financial resources is created. No asset is recorded initially because neither supplies nor prepaid items (such as rent or insurance) can be expended. For disclosure purposes, though, materials or prepayments that remain at year's end have been entered into the accounting records as assets prior to production of financial statements. This adjustment is created by utilizing a balance with a title such as Fund Balance Reserved for Inventory of Supplies (or Prepaid Items). This account indicates that the fund is holding additional assets and this specific amount is not available for future spending.

This traditional approach, referred to as the *purchases method,* is based on the modified accrual method of accounting. The expenditure is recorded when the claim to current financial resources is first incurred. However, many governments choose to report supplies and prepaid expenses using an alternative, the *consumption method.*

The consumption method parallels the process utilized in creating the government-wide financial statements. Any supplies or prepayments are recorded as assets when acquired. Subsequently, as the items are consumed by usage or over time, the cost is reclassified into an expenditures account. Therefore, under this approach, the expenditure is matched with the period of specific usage. Because this asset cannot be spent for government programs or other needs, a portion of the Fund Balance account should be reclassified as Reserved for Inventory of Supplies as is shown in the balance sheet in Exhibit 16.3.

As an illustration, assume that $20,000 in supplies is purchased by a municipality for various General Fund activities. During the remainder of the period, $18,000 of this amount is used so that only $2,000 remains at year's end. These events could be recorded through either of the following sets of entries:

Fund-Based Financial Statements

Purchases Method

Expenditures—Supplies	20,000	
Vouchers Payable		20,000
To record purchase of supplies for various ongoing activities.		
Inventory of Supplies	2,000	
Fund Balance—Reserved for Inventory of Supplies		2,000
To record supplies remaining at year's end.		

Consumption Method

Inventory of Supplies	20,000	
Vouchers Payable		20,000
To record purchase of supplies for various ongoing activities.		
Expenditures—Control	18,000	
Inventory of Supplies		18,000
To record consumption of supplies during period. Because a $2,000 asset that cannot be spent remains, an equal portion of the Fund Balance should be reclassified as Reserved for Inventory of Supplies.		

Recognition of Revenues—Overview

The recognition of revenues has always posed a problem for state and local government units. For most revenues, such as property taxes, income taxes, and grants, no earning process exists as in a for-profit business. Neither property taxes, income taxes, nor many other sources of government fund are "earned." Taxes, fines, and the like are assessed or imposed on the citizens to support the government's operations.

In December 1998, the GASB released *Statement Number 33,* "Accounting and Financial Reporting for Nonexchange Transactions," to provide a comprehensive system for recognizing many of the revenues specifically applicable to state and local government units. This statement did not apply to true revenues such as interest or rents for which an earning process does exist. Instead, the GASB concentrated on "nonexchange transactions," a classification that encompasses most taxes, fines, grants, and the like because the government does not have to provide a direct and equal benefit for the amount received.

> In a nonexchange transaction, a government (including the federal government, as a provider) either gives value (benefit) to another party without directly receiving equal value in exchange or receives value (benefit) from another party without directly giving equal value in exchange.[22]

For organizational purposes, the GASB classified all such nonexchange transactions into four distinct classifications, each with its own rules as to proper recognition:

- *Derived tax revenues.* Income taxes and sales taxes are the best example of this type of revenue. In a derived tax revenue transaction, a tax assessment is imposed when an underlying exchange takes place. A sale occurs, for example, and a tax is imposed, or income is earned and an income tax is assessed.

- *Imposed nonexchange revenues.* Property taxes and fines and penalties are viewed as imposed nonexchange revenues because the government mandates an assessment, but no underlying transaction exists. For example, real estate or other property is owned and a property tax is levied each period. The government is taxing ownership, not a specific transaction.

- *Government-mandated nonexchange transactions.* This category is used for monies such as grants conveyed from one government to another to help cover the costs of required programs. As an example, if a state specifies that a city must create a homeless shelter and then provides a grant of $400,000 to help defray the cost, the city should record that money using these prescribed rules because the state has mandated the utilization of the money to meet the law. City officials have no choice; the state government has required the shelter to be constructed and is providing part or all of the funding.

- *Voluntary nonexchange transactions.* In this final classification, money has been conveyed willingly to the state or local government by an individual, another government, or an organization, usually for a particular purpose. For example, assume that a state grants a city $300,000 to help improve reading programs in its schools. Unless the state has mandated an improvement in these reading programs, this grant would be accounted for as a voluntary nonexchange transaction. The decision has been made that the use of the money will provide an important benefit, but no state government requirement led to the conveyance.

Derived Tax Revenues Such as Income Taxes and Sales Taxes

Accounting for derived tax revenues is relatively straightforward. These revenues are normally recognized in government-wide financial statements when the underlying transaction occurs. Thus, when a taxpayer earns income, the government should record the income tax revenue. Likewise, when a sale is made, the government should recognize the resulting sales tax revenue.

Assume, for example, that sales within a government amount to $10 million for the current year and a sales tax of 4 percent is assessed. In the period in which the sales are made, the following entry is required. The amounts should be reported net of any estimated refunds or uncollectible balances.

---

[22] *GASB Statement 33,* "Accounting and Financial Reporting for Nonexchange Transactions," December 1998, para. 7.

Government-Wide Financial Statements

Receivable—Sales Taxes	400,000	
Revenue—Sales Taxes		400,000
To recognize amount of sales tax that will be collected in connection with sales for the current period.		

For fund-based financial statements, the preceding rules also apply except for one additional requirement that the resources must be available before the revenue can be recognized. That is, the amounts must be received during the year or soon enough thereafter to satisfy claims to current financial resources. In that way, the essence of modified accrual accounting is still being utilized at the fund level of reporting. As mentioned previously, except in connection with the reporting of property taxes, the government selects (and must disclose) the length of time that serves as the boundary for financial resources to be viewed as available.

A separate issue is raised if government officials have specified that the resources received must be used in a certain way. For example, in the preceding entry, assume that the city government has stated that 25 percent of this tax must be used for park beautification. Thus, $100,000 must be spent in this designated fashion. Such restrictions are disclosed in the financial statements by reclassifying an appropriate amount of the fund balance or net assets to disclose the intended usage. Revenue recognition is not altered:

> Purpose restrictions do not affect the timing of recognition for any class of nonexchange transactions. Rather, recipients of resources with purpose restrictions should report resulting net assets (or equity or fund balance, as appropriate) as restricted until the resources are used for the specified purpose or for as long as the provider requires the resources to be maintained intact (for example, endowment principal.)[23]

Consequently, in the statement of net assets for the government-wide financial statements (as shown in Exhibit 16.1), a $100,000 amount should be reclassified in the net assets section as restricted for park beautification. A similar treatment is proper for the balance sheet created according to the fund-based financial statements (as shown in Exhibit 16.3) except that the amount is shown as a separate fund balance restricted for park beautification.

Imposed Nonexchange Revenues Such as Property Taxes and Fines

Accounting for imposed nonexchange revenues is a bit more complicated than for derived tax revenues because no underlying transaction exists to guide the timing of the revenue recognition. Interestingly, the GASB set up separate rules for recognizing the asset and the related revenue. A receivable is to be recorded when the government first has an enforceable legal claim as defined in that particular jurisdiction (or when cash is received if a prepayment is made). For the revenue side of the transaction, recognition should be made in the time period when the resulting resources are required to be used or in the first period in which use is permitted.

For example, assume that officials of the City of Alban need to generate property tax revenues of at least $500,000 to finance budgeted government spending for Year 2. On October 1, Year 1, property tax assessments for a total of $530,000 are mailed to the citizens. Assume that according to applicable state law, the city has no enforceable claim until January 1, Year 2 (often called the *lien date*). However, to encourage early payment, the city gives a 5 percent discount on any payment received by December 31, Year 1.

No entry is recorded on October 1, Year 1. Although the assessments have been delivered, no enforceable legal claim yet exists, and the proceeds from the tax cannot be used until Year 2. However, assume that $30,000 of the assessments is collected from citizens during the first three months. After reduction for the 5 percent discount, the collection would be $28,500.

---

[23] Ibid., para. 14.

Government-Wide Financial Statements

Year 1		
Cash	28,500	
Deferred Property Tax Revenues		28,500
To record collection of property tax prior to the start of the levy year.		

Assume that city officials expect to collect 96 percent of the $500,000 remaining assessments, or $480,000. At the beginning of Year 2, both this receivable and the related revenue can be recognized. The receivable is reported because there is an enforceable claim and the revenue is reported because Year 2 is the year in which the money is required to be used. Note that the revenue is reduced directly by the estimate of taxes deemed uncollectible. In addition, the previously collected amount should be recognized in Year 2 as revenue because this is the period for which use is allowed.

January 1, Year 2		
Property Tax Receivable	500,000	
Allowance for Uncollectible Taxes		20,000
Revenues—Property Taxes		480,000
To recognize property tax assessment for Year 2.		
Deferred Property Tax Revenues	28,500	
Revenues—Property Taxes		28,500
To recognize property tax proceeds for Year 2 collected during Year 1.		

This recording would be the same for the fund-based financial statements unless the current financial resources were not viewed as being available. Because property taxes are such a significant source of revenue for many governments, a specific 60-day period has been standardized here rather than allowing the government to choose the period.

To illustrate, we reexamine the recording of the $480,000 revenue. Assume that historical records indicate that $400,000 of that amount will be collected during Year 2, another $50,000 will be collected in the first 60 days of Year 3, and the final $30,000 will be collected beyond 60 days into Year 3. This last $30,000 is not viewed as being available for expenditure in Year 2 so that revenue recognition is not appropriate until Year 3. Only $450,000 of the resources are expected to be available for Year 2 expenditures. For the fund-based statements, this entry must be adjusted to conform to modified accrual accounting. Again, revenues are recorded net of estimated uncollectible taxes.

Fund-Based Financial Statements

January 1, Year 2		
Property Tax Receivable	500,000	
Allowance for Uncollectible Taxes		20,000
Revenues—Property Taxes		450,000
Deferred Property Tax Revenues		30,000
To record amount of property taxes measurable and available for Year 2 expenditures.		

Government-Mandated Nonexchange Transactions and Voluntary Nonexchange Transactions

Although these two sources of revenues are identified separately, the timing of accounting recognition is the same so that they are logically discussed together. The government recognizes these grants and other revenue sources when all eligibility requirements have been met. Until eligibility has been established, the existence of some degree of uncertainty precludes recognition. Thus, revenue reporting occurs at the time of eligibility even if the money was actually received earlier.

GASB Statement 33 divides all eligibility requirements into four general classifications. All applicable requirements must be met before revenues can be recorded for either government-mandated nonexchange transactions or voluntary nonexchange transactions.

1. *Required characteristics of the recipients.* In many programs, the unit receiving funds is provided with standards that must be met in advance. For example, assume that a state grant has been awarded to a city to help teach all kindergarten children in its school system to read. However, as part of this program, state law has been changed to mandate that all kindergarten teachers must become properly certified. Consequently, the state will not convey the grant to the city until all kindergarten teachers have met this standard. The city must conform to state law first. Because of this eligibility requirement, revenue recognition should be delayed until all teachers have become certified.

2. *Time requirements.* Programs can specify when money is to be used. To illustrate, assume that in April, a state provides a grant to a city to buy milk for each child during the subsequent school year starting in September. The grant should be recognized as revenue in the period of use or in the period when the use of the funds is first permitted.

3. *Reimbursement.* Many grants and other forms of support are designed to reimburse a government for amounts spent appropriately. These arrangements are often called *expenditure-driven programs.* For example, assume that a state informs a locality that it will reimburse the city government for money paid to provide milk to schoolchildren who could not otherwise afford it. In such cases, proper spending is the eligibility requirement, and the city recognizes no revenue until it spends the money for milk. Thus, the expense should equal the amount of revenue recognized.

4. *Contingencies.* In voluntary nonexchange transactions (but not in government-mandated nonexchange transactions), revenue may be withheld until a specified action has been taken. A grant might be given to buy park equipment, for example, but only after an appropriate piece of land has been acquired for the park. Until the lot is obtained, a contingency exists, and the revenue should not be recognized.

Issuance of Bonds

Although not a revenue, the issuance of bonds serves as a major source of funding for many state and local governments. In 2001, the total of all long-term debt outstanding for state and local governments amounted to the almost unbelievable balance of $1.38 trillion.[24] Proceeds from these debt issuances are used for many purposes, including general financing and a wide variety of construction projects. As of December 31, 2003, the City of Seattle, Washington, had approximately $3.350 billion of long-term debts outstanding. Of that amount, $842 million had been issued by governmental activities and $2.508 billion by business-type activities.

Because the proceeds of a bond issuance must be repaid, the government recognizes no revenues under either method of financial reporting. In the government-wide financial statements, the reporting is quite easy: Both the cash and the debt are increased to reflect the issuance. Conversely, in the fund-based financial statements, recording is not so simple because cash is received but the debt is not a claim on current financial resources. Thus, from that perspective, the inflow of current financial resources does not create a revenue or a debt that can be reported.

Assume, for example, that the Town of Ruark sells $5 million in general obligation bonds to finance the construction of a new school building. Because of the intended use of this money, the town designated a Capital Projects Fund to receive the cash. To emphasize that this inflow of money is not derived from a revenue, Ruark utilizes a special designation, *Other Financing Sources.* Note in Exhibit 16.4 the placement of Other Financing Sources (Uses) at the bottom of the statement of revenues, expenditures, and other changes in fund balance to identify

[24] U.S. Federal Reserve, *Federal Reserve Statistical Release,* "Flow of Funds Account of the United States" (Washington, D.C.: Federal Reserve, June 6, 2002), Table D-3, p. 8.

changes in the amount of current financial resources created through transactions other than revenues and expenditures.

Thus, the following journal entry is needed to reflect the sale of these bonds:

Fund-Based Financial Statements

Capital Projects Funds—School Building		
Cash	5,000,000	
Other Financing Sources—Bond Proceeds		5,000,000
To record issuance of bonds to finance construction project.		

Although an inflow of cash into this fund has taken place, no revenue has been generated. However, in the same manner as a revenue, the Other Financing Sources is a measurement account that is closed out at the end of the year. As the preceding entry shows, the $5 million liability is completely omitted from the Capital Projects Funds. Because the governmental funds stress accountability for the inflows and outflows of current financial resources, recognition of long-term debts in fund-based accounting has traditionally been considered inappropriate. For example, the balance sheet in Exhibit 16.3 shows no long-term liabilities at all for the governmental funds but only claims to current financial resources. Any user of the financial statements who wants to see the amount of the government's long-term debts can simply examine the statement of net assets in the government-wide financial statements (see Exhibit 16.1).

Payment of Long-Term Liabilities

The payment of long-term liabilities again demonstrates the huge differences between the government-wide financial statements and the fund-based financial statements. For the government-wide financial statements, payment of principal and interest is the same as payment by a for-profit organization. Conversely, for the fund-based statements, an expenditure account is recognized for the debt and for the related interest (often in a Debt Service Fund).

Assume as an illustration that a government has a $500,000 bond payment coming due in October with three months of interest that amounts to $10,000. This example assumes that cash had been set aside previously in the Debt Service Fund to satisfy this payment. The needed entries follow:

Fund-Based Financial Statements

Debt Service Funds		
Expenditure—Bond Principal	500,000	
Expenditure—Interest	10,000	
Cash		510,000
To record payment of bond and related interest.		

Government-Wide Financial Statements

Bond Payable	500,000	
Interest Expense	10,000	
Cash		510,000
To record payment of bond and related interest.		

Tax Anticipation Notes

One type of formal debt is recorded in the same manner for government-wide and fund-based financial statements. State and local governments often issue short-term debts to provide financing until revenue sources have been collected. For example, if property tax payments are expected at a particular point in time, the government could need to borrow money for operations until that date. These short-term liabilities are often referred to as *tax anticipation notes* because they are being issued until a sufficient amount of taxes can be collected. As short-term liabilities, these debts are a claim on current financial resources. Thus, for the fund-based financial statements, the issuance is not recorded as an other financing source but as a liability in the same manner as the government-wide financial statements. Amounts paid for interest, though, would be recorded as an expenditure in producing fund-based statements and as an expense on the government-wide financial statements.

To illustrate, assume that a city borrows $300,000 on a 60-day note on January 1 and agrees to pay back $305,000 on March 1. The city will repay the debt with receipts from property taxes. For both sets of financial statements, the following entry is made on January 1:

Cash	300,000	
Tax Anticipation Note Payable		300,000
To record issuance of short-term debt to be repaid using money collected from property taxes.		

At repayment, however, two different entries are required because the fund-based statement measures current financial resources while the government-wide statement measures all economic resources:

Fund-Based Financial Statements

Tax Anticipation Note Payable	300,000	
Expenditure—Interest	5,000	
Cash		305,000
To record payment of short-term debt and interest for two months.		

Government-Wide Financial Statements

Tax Anticipation Note Payable	300,000	
Interest Expense	5,000	
Cash		305,000
To record payment of short-term debt and interest for two months.		

Special Assessments

Governments occasionally provide improvements or services that directly benefit a particular property and assess the costs (in whole or part) to the owner. In many cases, the owners actually petition the government to initiate such projects because of the enhancement of property values. Paving streets, laying water and sewage lines, and constructing curbs and sidewalks are typical examples. To finance the work, the government usually issues debt and places a lien on the property being improved to ensure reimbursement.

Government-wide financial statements handle the debt and subsequent construction as a for-profit enterprise would. The asset is recorded at cost and taxes are assessed and collected. These receipts are then used to settle the debt. For example, assume that a sidewalk is to be added to a neighborhood by a city at a cost of $20,000. A bond of this amount is to be sold to finance the construction with repayment eventually to be made using funds collected from the owners of the property benefited. Total interest to be paid is $2,000. The assessment to the owners is set at $22,000 to cover all costs.

Government-Wide Financial Statements

Cash	20,000	
Bond Payable—Special Assessment		20,000
To record debt issued to finance sidewalk construction.		
Infrastructure Asset—Sidewalk	20,000	
Cash		20,000
To record payment to contractor for the cost of building new sidewalk.		
Taxes Receivable—Special Assessment	22,000	
Revenue—Special Assessment		22,000
To record citizens' charges for special assessment project.		
Cash	22,000	
Taxes Receivable—Special Assessment		22,000
To record collection of money from assessment of citizens for sidewalk construction.		
Bond Payable—Special Assessment	20,000	
Interest Expense	2,000	
Cash		22,000
To record payment of debt on special assessment bond.		

In the fund-based financial statements, this same series of transactions has a completely different appearance. Neither the infrastructure nor the long-term debt would be recorded because the current financial resources measurement basis is being used.

Fund-Based Financial Statements

Capital Projects Fund—Special Assessment Project		
Cash	20,000	
Other Financing Sources—Bond Proceeds		20,000
To record issuance of bonds to finance sidewalk construction with payment to be made from a special assessment levy.		
Expenditures—Special Assessment	20,000	
Cash		20,000
To record payment to contractor for the cost of constructing sidewalk.		

Debt Service Fund—Special Assessment Project		
Tax Receivable—Special Assessment	22,000	
Revenue—Special Assessment		22,000
To record assessment that will be used to pay bond principal and related interest incurred after construction.		
Cash	22,000	
Tax Receivable—Special Assessment		22,000
To record collection of assessment paid by citizens to extinguish bond and interest incurred in construction of sidewalk.		
Expenditure—Special Assessment Bond	20,000	
Expenditure—Interest	2,000	
Cash		22,000
To record payment of bonds payable and interest incurred in construction of sidewalk.		

One other aspect of special assessment projects should be mentioned. In some cases, the government may facilitate a project but accept no legal obligation for it. The government's role will be limited to conveying funds from one party to another although the government assumes no liability (either primary or secondary) for the debt. Normally, the money goes from citizens to the government and then directly to the contractors. If the government has no liability for defaults, overruns, or other related problems, recording the special assessment assets, liabilities, revenues, expenses, other financing sources, and expenditures is not really relevant to the government's resources. In that situation, all transactions are recorded in an agency fund as increases and decreases in cash, amount due from citizens, and amount due to contractors. No reportable impact appears within the government-wide or the fund-based financial statements (except for the Agency Fund).

Interfund Transactions

Interfund transactions are commonly used within government units as a way to direct sufficient resources to all activities and functions. Monetary transfers made from the General Fund are especially prevalent because general tax revenues are initially accumulated in this fund. For example, the General Fund for Baltimore, Maryland, indicated in the fund-based financial statements for the year ending June 30, 2004, that approximately $67 million had been transferred out to other funds while $31 million had been transferred in from other funds.

However, the government-wide financial statements do not report many such transfers because they frequently occur solely within the governmental activities or solely within the business-type activities. A transfer from the General Fund to the Debt Service Fund would be reported in both funds on fund-based financial statements but would create no net impact in the government-wide financial statements because they are both classified as governmental activities.

Thus, for government-wide financial reporting, the following distinctions are drawn for transfers:

- *Intra-activity transactions* are those that occur between governmental funds (so that net totals reported for governmental activities are not affected) or between enterprise funds (totals reported for business-type activities are not affected). Transfers between governmental funds and most Internal Service Funds are also included in this classification because, as discussed previously, Internal Service Funds are usually reported as governmental activities in government-wide statements despite being proprietary funds. Government-wide financial statements do not report intra-activity transactions because they create no overall change in either the governmental or the business-type activities.

- *Interactivity transactions* occur between governmental funds and enterprise funds. They impact the totals reported for both governmental activities and business-type activities. Government-wide financial statements do report interactivity transactions. In Exhibit 16.1, for example, internal amounts due are reported within the asset section of the statement of net assets and then are eliminated to arrive at overall government totals. Likewise, in Exhibit 16.2, transfers between the two activity classifications appear at the very bottom of the general revenues section. Again, individual totals are shown and then are offset so that no total amount is reported.

Consequently, in discussing interfund transactions, the reporting for government-wide statements is appropriate only when an interactivity transaction is involved.

Interfund Transfers

The most common interfund transactions are transfers within the governmental funds to ensure adequate financing of budgeted expenditures. A city council could vote to transfer $800,000 from the General Fund to the Capital Projects Funds to cover a portion of the cost of a new school building. This scenario involves recording the following entries:

Fund-Based Financial Statements

General Fund		
Other Financing Uses—Transfers Out—Capital Projects Fund	800,000	
Due to Capital Projects Fund		800,000
To record authorization transfer for school construction.		

Capital Projects Funds

Due from General Fund	800,000	
Other Financing Sources—Transfers In—General Fund		800,000
To record transfer to be received for school construction.		

The *Other Financing Uses/Sources* designations are appropriate here; financial resources are being moved into and out of these funds although neither revenues nor expenditures have been earned or incurred. As Exhibit 16.4 shows, these balances are eventually reported by each fund in the statement of revenues, expenditures, and other changes in fund balances. Each figure is shown but is not offset in any way. Both accounts are then closed out at the end of the current year. The *Due to/Due from* accounts are the equivalent of interfund payable and receivable balances, and each account is reported within the proper fund on its balance sheet.

Because this is an intra-activity transaction, none of the above entries is made within the government-wide financial statements. Financial resources are simply being shifted around within the governmental activities.

Not all monetary transfers are for normal operating purposes; nonrecurring or nonroutine transfers may also take place. For example, money might be transferred from the General Fund to create or expand an enterprise fund such as a subway system. Assume that a city sets aside $1 million of unrestricted money to help permanently finance a new subway system that will be open to the public. For convenience here, the transaction is recorded as if the cash is transferred immediately so that no type of receivable or payable is necessary:

Fund-Based Financial Statements

General Fund

Other Financing Uses—Transfers Out—Subway System	1,000,000	
Cash		1,000,000
To record transfer to help finance subway system.		

Enterprise Fund

Cash	1,000,000	
Capital Contributions		1,000,000
To record receipt of transfer from unrestricted funds.		

Because this transfer is an interactivity transaction (between governmental activities and business-type activities), a similar entry is made for the government-wide financial statements. This transfer reduces the assets of the governmental activities but increases the assets in the business-type activities:

Government-Wide Financial Statements

Governmental Activities

Transfers Out—Subway System	1,000,000	
Cash		1,000,000
To record transfer to help finance subway system.		

Business-Type Activities

Cash	1,000,000	
Transfers In—General Fund		1,000,000
To record receipt of transfer from unrestricted funds.		

Internal Exchange Transactions

Some transfers made within a government are actually the same as revenues and expenditures. For example, a city's payment to its own print shop (or any other Internal Service Fund or Enterprise Fund) for services or materials is the equivalent of a transaction with an outside party. To avoid confusion in reporting, such transfers are recorded as revenues and expenditures or expenses as if the transaction had occurred with an unrelated party. No differentiation is made; these are not treated as transfers designed to shift resources.

The fund-based financial statements record all such internal exchange transactions. However, because Internal Service Funds are usually reported as governmental activities in the government-wide statements, any such exchanges between governmental funds and one of these internal service funds has no net impact on overall figures being reported and should be omitted.

To illustrate, assume that a government pays its print shop (an internal service fund) $8,000 for work done for the fire department. In addition, the government pays another $1,000 to a toll road operated as an enterprise fund to allow government vehicles to ride on the highway without having to make individual payments. Both of these internal exchange transactions are made for services being rendered:

Fund-Based Financial Statements

General Fund		
Expenditures—Printing	8,000	
Expenditures—Toll Road Privileges	1,000	
Cash		9,000
To record payment for printing supplies for fire department and for use of toll road.		

Internal Service Fund—Print Shop		
Cash	8,000	
Revenues		8,000
To record collection of money paid by the fire department for printing supplies.		

Enterprise Fund—Toll Road		
Cash	1,000	
Revenues		1,000
To record money collected from government for vehicular use of toll roads.		

The $8,000 transaction with the print shop would not be reflected on government-wide financial statements if this internal service fund is classified within the governmental activities. If it is classified in this way, the transfer is the equivalent of an intra-activity transaction. However, the $1,000 payment made by the fire department (a governmental activity) to the enterprise fund (a business-type activity) is the same as an interactivity transfer and is reported as an internal exchange transaction.

Government-Wide Financial Statements

Governmental Activities		
Expenses—Toll Road Privileges	1,000	
Cash		1,000
To record payment for use of toll road by government's vehicles.		

Business-Type Activities
Cash 1,000
    Revenues   1,000
    To record money collected from government for vehicular use of toll roads.

Summary

1. Government accounting was radically altered in 1999 when the Governmental Accounting Standards Board issued *Statement 34,* "Basic Financial Statements—and Management's Discussion and Analysis—for State and Local Governments." This pronouncement made numerous changes in traditional government accounting procedures and added a second set of financial statements to reflect government-wide activities.

2. The readers of government financial statements have a wide variety of informational needs. No one set of financial statements seems capable of meeting all user needs, a factor that influenced the GASB's actions in its *Statement 34.* Accountability of government officials and control over public spending have always been essential elements of government accounting. The GASB attempted to keep those priorities in place but to broaden the scope of the financial statements being produced.

3. A state or local government unit produces fund-based financial statements utilizing fund accounting. In this system, activities are classified into three broad categories (governmental, proprietary, and fiduciary). Governmental funds account for service activities; proprietary funds account for activities for which a user charge is assessed; and fiduciary funds account for assets that the government holds for an external party.

4. Governmental funds have several fund types: the General Fund, Special Revenue Funds, Capital Projects Funds, Debt Service Funds, and Permanent Funds. Proprietary funds are made up of Enterprise Funds and Internal Service Funds. Fiduciary Funds encompass Pension Trust Funds, Investment Trust Funds, Private-Purpose Trust Funds, and Agency Funds.

5. Government-wide financial statements present a statement of net assets and a statement of activities that are separated into governmental activities (the governmental funds and usually the Internal Service Funds) and business-type activities (Enterprise Funds and occasionally an Internal Service Fund). These statements measure all economic resources whose timing of recognition is guided by accrual accounting.

6. Fund-based financial statements include a number of financial statements. This chapter focused on the balance sheet and the statement of revenues, expenditures, and other changes in fund balances for the governmental funds. These statements must show the General Fund and any other major fund separately. These statements measure current financial resources whose timing of recognition is guided by modified accrual accounting.

7. To aid in control over financial resources, most governmental funds record their approved budgets each year. This initial budget as well as any final amended budget and actual figures for the period are then reported as required supplemental information to the financial statements or as a separate statement within the fund-based financial statements.

8. Commitments for purchase orders and contracts are actually recorded in the individual governmental funds by recognizing encumbrances. These balances are recorded when the commitment is made and removed when an actual claim to current financial resources replaces them to help government officials avoid spending more than the amounts properly appropriated.

9. The fund-based financial statements recognize expenditures for capital outlay, long-term debt payment, and expense-type costs when a claim to current financial resources comes into existence. Government-wide financial statements capitalize capital outlay, reduce liabilities for debt payments, and record expenses in expense accounts.

10. Revenue recognition for nonexchange transactions such as sales taxes and property taxes is based on a classification system. Recognition depends on whether the revenue is a derived tax revenue, imposed nonexchange revenue, government-mandated nonexchange transaction, or voluntary nonexchange transaction.

11. The issuance of long-term bonds is recorded as an "other financing source" by the governmental funds but as a long-term liability both by the proprietary funds and the government-wide financial statements.

12. Transfers between funds are normally reported as an "other financing source" and "other financing use" within the fund-based financial statements. The government-wide statements do not report such transactions unless they create an impact in overall governmental activities and business-type activities. For internal exchange transactions in which payment is being made for a good or service, the fund-based statements recognize a revenue and an expenditure. The government-wide financial statements normally do not reflect such transfers unless they occur between an enterprise fund and a governmental fund. In that case, both a revenue and an expense are increased.

Comprehensive Illustration

PROBLEM

(Estimated Time: 50 Minutes). The Town of Drexel has the following financial transactions. The government has formally adopted *GASB Statement 34*.

1. The town council adopts an annual budget for the General Fund estimating general revenues of $1.7 million, approved expenditures of $1.5 million, and approved transfers out of $120,000.
2. The town levies property taxes of $1.3 million. It expects to collect all but 3 percent of these taxes during the year.
3. The town orders two new police cars at an approximate cost of $150,000.
4. A transfer of $50,000 is made from the General Fund to the Debt Service Fund.
5. The town pays a bond payable of $40,000 and $10,000 of interest using money previously set aside.
6. Drexel issues a $2 million bond at face value to acquire a building to convert into a high school.
7. The two police cars are received with an invoice price of $152,000. The voucher has been approved for this amount but not yet been paid.
8. The town acquires the building for the high school for $2 million in cash and immediately begins renovating it.
9. Depreciation on the new police cars is computed as $30,000 for the period.
10. The town borrows $100,000 on a 30-day tax anticipation note.
11. Drexel begins a special assessment curbing project. The government sells $80,000 in bonds at face value to finance this project. The town has pledged to guarantee the debt if the assessments collected do not pay it all.
12. A contractor completes the curbing project and is paid $80,000.
13. The town assesses citizens $85,000 for the complete curbing project.
14. The town collects the special assessments of $85,000 in full and repays the debt plus $5,000 in interest.
15. The town receives a $10,000 cash grant to beautify a park. The grant must be used to reimburse specific costs that the town incurs.
16. The town spends $4,000 to beautify the park.

Required:

a. Prepare journal entries for the town based on the production of fund-based financial statements.
b. Prepare journal entries in anticipation of preparing government-wide financial statements.

SOLUTION

a. **Fund-Based Financial Statements**

1.   **General Fund**

Estimated Revenues Control	1,700,000	
Appropriations Control		1,500,000
Estimated Other Financing Uses Control		120,000
Budgetary Fund Balance		80,000

2.   **General Fund**

Property Tax Receivable	1,300,000	
Allowance for Uncollectible Taxes		39,000
Revenues—Property Taxes		1,261,000

3. **General Fund**

Encumbrances Control	150,000	
Fund Balance—Reserved for Encumbrances		150,000

4. **General Fund**

Other Financing Uses—Transfers Out	50,000	
Cash		50,000

Debt Service Funds

Cash	50,000	
Other Financing Sources—Transfers In		50,000

5. **Debt Service Funds**

Expenditures—Principal	40,000	
Expenditures—Interest	10,000	
Cash		50,000

6. **Capital Projects Funds**

Cash	2,000,000	
Other Financing Sources—Bond Proceeds		2,000,000

7. **General Fund**

Fund Balance—Reserved for Encumbrances	150,000	
Encumbrances Control		150,000
Expenditures Control	152,000	
Vouchers Payable		152,000

8. **Capital Projects Funds**

Expenditures—Building	2,000,000	
Cash		2,000,000

9. No entry is recorded. Expenditures rather than expenses are recorded by the governmental funds.

10. **General Fund**

Cash	100,000	
Tax Anticipation Note Payable		100,000

11. **Capital Projects Funds**

Cash	80,000	
Other Financing Sources—Special Assessments Note		80,000

12. **Capital Projects Funds**

Expenditures—Curbing	80,000	
Cash		80,000

13. **Debt Service Funds**

Taxes Receivable—Special Assessment	85,000	
Revenues—Special Assessment		85,000

14.   **Debt Service Funds**

Cash	85,000	
Taxes Receivable—Special Assessment		85,000
Expenditures—Principal	80,000	
Expenditures—Interest	5,000	
Cash		85,000

15.   **Special Revenue Funds**

Cash	10,000	
Deferred Revenues		10,000

16.   **Special Revenue Funds**

Expenditures—Park Beautification	4,000	
Cash		4,000
Deferred Revenues	4,000	
Revenues—Grants		4,000

b. *Government-Wide Financial Statements*

1. Budgetary entries are not reported within the government-wide financial statements. They are recorded in the individual funds and are then shown as required supplementary information.

2.   **Governmental Activities**

Property Tax Receivable	1,300,000	
Allowance for Uncollectible Taxes		39,000
Revenues—Property Taxes		1,261,000

3. Commitments are not reported in the government-wide financial statements.

4. This transfer was within the governmental funds and, therefore, had no net effect on the governmental activities. No journal entry is needed.

5.   **Governmental Activities**

Bonds Payable	40,000	
Interest Expense	10,000	
Cash		50,000

6.   **Governmental Activities**

Cash	2,000,000	
Bonds Payable		2,000,000

7.   **Governmental Activities**

Police Cars (or Vehicles)	152,000	
Vouchers Payable		152,000

8.   **Governmental Activities**

Building	2,000,000	
Cash		2,000,000

9. | | **Governmental Activities** | |
|---|---|---|
| Depreciation Expense | 30,000 | |
| Accumulated Depreciation | | 30,000 |

10. | | **Governmental Activities** | |
|---|---|---|
| Cash | 100,000 | |
| Tax Anticipation Note Payable | | 100,000 |

11. | | **Governmental Activities** | |
|---|---|---|
| Cash | 80,000 | |
| Special Assessment Notes Payable | | 80,000 |

12. | | **Governmental Activities** | |
|---|---|---|
| Infrastructure Assets—Curbing | 80,000 | |
| Cash | | 80,000 |

13. | | **Governmental Activities** | |
|---|---|---|
| Taxes Receivable—Special Assessment | 85,000 | |
| Revenues—Special Assessment | | 85,000 |

14. | | **Governmental Activities** | |
|---|---|---|
| Cash | 85,000 | |
| Taxes Receivable—Special Assessment | | 85,000 |
| Special Assessment Notes Payable | 80,000 | |
| Interest Expense | 5,000 | |
| Cash | | 85,000 |

15. | | **Governmental Activities** | |
|---|---|---|
| Cash | 10,000 | |
| Deferred Revenues | | 10,000 |

16. | | **Governmental Activities** | |
|---|---|---|
| Expenses—Park Beautification | 4,000 | |
| Cash | | 4,000 |
| Deferred Revenues | 4,000 | |
| Revenues—Grants | | 4,000 |

Questions

1. How have users' needs impacted the development of accounting principles for state and local government units?
2. Why have accountability and control been so important in the traditional accounting for state and local government units?
3. In general, how has *GASB Statement 34* impacted the financial reporting of state and local governments?
4. What are the basic financial statements that a state or local government now produces?
5. What measurement focus is used in fund-based financial statements, and what system is applied to determine the timing of revenue and expenditure recognition?

6. What measurement focus is used in government-wide financial statements, and what system is applied to determine the timing of revenue and expense recognition?

7. What accounts are included in current financial resources?

8. In applying the current financial resources measurement focus, when are liabilities recognized?

9. What are the three classifications of funds? What funds are included in each of these three?

10. What are the five fund types within the governmental funds? What types of events does each of these report?

11. What are the two fund types within the proprietary funds? What types of events does each report?

12. What are the four fund types within the fiduciary funds? What types of events does each report?

13. What are the two major divisions reported in government-wide financial statements? What funds are *not* reported in these financial statements?

14. Fund-based financial statements have separate columns for each activity. Which activities are reported in this manner?

15. Why are budgetary entries recorded in the individual funds of a state or local government?

16. How are budget results shown in the financial reporting of a state or local government?

17. When is an encumbrance recorded? What happens to this balance? How are encumbrances reported in government-wide financial statements?

18. An encumbrance is still outstanding at the end of the fiscal year. The government anticipates that it will honor this encumbrance in the next year. How does the government report this encumbrance?

19. What costs cause a governmental fund to report an expenditure?

20. At what point in time does a governmental fund report an expenditure?

21. How do governmental funds report capital outlay? How do government-wide financial statements report capital expenditures?

22. What are the two different ways that supplies and prepaid items can be recorded on fund-based financial statements?

23. What are the four classifications of nonexchange revenues that a state or local government can recognize? In each case, when does it recognize revenues normally?

24. When is a receivable recognized for property tax assessments? When is the revenue recognized?

25. How is the issuance of a long-term bond reported on fund-based financial statements? How is the issuance of a long-term bond reported on government-wide financial statements?

26. What is a special assessment project? How are special assessment projects reported?

27. How are interfund transfers reported in fund-based financial statements?

28. In government-wide financial statements, how do an intra-activity transaction and an interactivity transaction differ? How is each reported?

29. What is an internal exchange transaction, and how is it reported?

Problems

1. Which of the following is *not* a governmental fund?
   a. Special Revenue Fund.
   b. Internal Service Fund.
   c. Capital Projects Fund.
   d. Debt Service Fund.

2. What is the purpose of a Special Revenue Fund?
   a. To account for revenues legally restricted as to expenditure.
   b. To account for ongoing activities.
   c. To account for gifts when only subsequently earned income can be expended.
   d. To account for the cost of long-lived assets bought with designated funds.

3. What is the purpose of Enterprise Funds?
   a. To account for operations that provide services to other departments within a government.
   b. To account for asset transfers.
   c. To account for ongoing activities such as the police and fire departments.
   d. To account for operations financed in whole or in part by outside user charges.

4. Which of the following statements is true?

   a. There are three different types of proprietary funds.

   b. There are three different types of fiduciary funds.

   c. There are five different types of fiduciary funds.

   d. There are five different types of governmental funds.

5. A government expects to receive revenues of $400,000 but has approved expenditures of $430,000. The anticipated shortage will have an impact on which of the following terms?

   a. Interperiod equity.

   b. Modified accrual accounting.

   c. Consumption accounting.

   d. Account groups.

6. A citizen of the City of Townsend gives it a gift of $22,000 in investments. The citizen requires that the investments be held but any resulting income must be used to help maintain the city's cemetery. In which fund should this asset be reported?

   a. Special Revenue Funds.

   b. Capital Projects Funds.

   c. Permanent Funds.

   d. General Fund.

7. Which of the following statements is correct for the governmental funds?

   a. Fund-based financial statements measure economic resources.

   b. Government-wide financial statements measure only current financial resources.

   c. Fund-based financial statements measure both economic resources and current financial resources.

   d. Government-wide financial statements measure economic resources.

8. Which of the following statements is correct for the governmental funds?

   a. Fund-based financial statements measure revenues and expenditures based on modified accrual accounting.

   b. Government-wide financial statements measure revenues and expenses based on modified accrual accounting.

   c. Fund-based financial statements measure revenues and expenses based on accrual accounting.

   d. Government-wide financial statements measure revenues and expenditures based on accrual accounting.

9. During the current year, a government buys land for $80,000. Which of the following is *not* true?

   a. The land could be reported as an asset by the business-type activities in the government-wide financial statements.

   b. The land could be reported as an asset by the governmental activities in the government-wide financial statements.

   c. The land could be reported as an asset by the proprietary funds in the fund-based financial statements.

   d. The land could be reported as an asset by the governmental funds in the fund-based financial statements.

10. Which of the following statements is true concerning the recording of a budget?

   a. At the beginning of the year, debit Appropriations.

   b. A debit to the Budgetary Fund Balance account indicates an expected surplus.

   c. At the beginning of the year, debit Estimated Revenues.

   d. At the end of the year, credit Appropriations.

11. The General Fund pays rent for two months. Which of the following is *not* correct?

   a. Rent expense should be reported in the government-wide financial statements.

   b. Rent expense should be reported in the General Fund.

   c. An expenditure should be reported in the fund-based financial statements.

   d. If one month of rent is in the first year with the other month in the next year, either the purchases method or the consumption method can be used in fund-based statements.

12. A purchase order for $3,000 is recorded in the General Fund for the purchase of a new computer. The computer is received at an actual cost of $3,020. Which of the following is correct?

    a. Machinery is increased in the General Fund by $3,020.

    b. An encumbrance account is reduced by $3,020.

    c. An expenditure is increased by $3,020.

    d. An expenditure is recorded for the additional $20.

13. At the end of the current year, a government reports a fund balance reserved for encumbrances of $9,000. What information is being conveyed?

    a. A donor has given the government $9,000 that must be used in a specified fashion.

    b. The government has made $9,000 in commitments in one year that will be honored in the subsequent year.

    c. Encumbrances exceeded expenditures by $9,000 during the current year.

    d. The government spent $9,000 less than was appropriated.

14. A government buys equipment for its police department at a cost of $54,000. Which of the following is *not* true?

    a. Equipment will increase by $54,000 in the government-wide financial statements.

    b. Depreciation in connection with this equipment will be reported in the fund-based financial statements.

    c. The equipment will not appear within the reported assets in the fund-based financial statements.

    d. An expenditure for $54,000 will be reported in the fund-based financial statements.

15. A city acquires supplies for its fire department and uses the consumption method of accounting. Which of the following statements is true for the fund-based statements?

    a. An expenditures account was debited at the time of receipt.

    b. An expense is recorded as the supplies are consumed.

    c. An inventory account is debited at the time of the acquisition.

    d. The supplies are recorded within the General Fixed Assets Account Group.

16. An income tax is an example of which of the following?

    a. Derived tax revenue.

    b. Imposed nonexchange revenue.

    c. Government-mandated nonexchange revenue.

    d. Voluntary nonexchange transaction.

17. The state government passes a law requiring localities to upgrade their water treatment facilities. The state then awards a grant of $500,000 to the Town of Midlothian to help pay for this cost. What type of revenue is this grant?

    a. Derived tax revenue.

    b. Imposed nonexchange revenue.

    c. Government-mandated nonexchange revenue.

    d. Voluntary nonexchange transaction.

18. The state awards a grant of $50,000 to the Town of Glenville. The state will pay the grant money to the town as a reimbursement for money spent on road repair. At the time of the grant, the state pays $8,000 in advance. During the first year of this program, the town spent $14,000 and applied for reimbursement. What amount of revenue should be recognized?

    a. $–0–.

    b. $8,000.

    c. $14,000.

    d. $50,000.

19. A city issues a 60-day tax anticipation note to fund operations. What recording should it make?

    a. The liability should be reported in the government-wide financial statements; an other financing source should be shown in the fund-based financial statements.

    b. A liability should be reported in the government-wide financial statements and in the fund-based financial statements.

   c. An other financing source should be shown in the government-wide financial statements and in the fund-based financial statements.

   d. An other financing source should be shown in the government-wide financial statements; a liability is reported in the fund-based financial statements.

20. A city issues five-year bonds payable to finance construction of a new school. What recording should be made?

   a. Report the liability in the government-wide financial statements; show an other financing source in the fund-based financial statements.

   b. Report a liability in the government-wide financial statements and in the fund-based financial statements.

   c. Show an other financing source in the government-wide financial statements and in the fund-based financial statements.

   d. Show an other financing source in the government-wide financial statements; report a liability in the fund-based financial statements.

21. A $110,000 payment is made on a long-term liability. Of this amount, $10,000 represents interest. Which of the following is *not* true?

   a. Reduce liabilities by $100,000 in the government-wide financial statements.

   b. Record a $110,000 expenditure in the fund-based financial statements.

   c. Reduce liabilities by $100,000 in the fund-based financial statements.

   d. Recognize $10,000 interest expense in the government-wide financial statements.

22. A city constructs a special assessment project (a sidewalk) for which it is secondarily liable. The city issues bonds of $90,000. It authorizes another $10,000 that is transferred out of the General Fund. The sidewalk is built for $100,000. The citizens are billed for $90,000. They pay this amount and the debt is paid off. Where is the $100,000 expenditure for construction recorded?

   a. It is not recorded by the city.

   b. It is recorded in the Agency Fund.

   c. It is recorded in the General Fund.

   d. It is recorded in the Capital Projects Fund.

23. A city constructs curbing in a new neighborhood and finances it as a special assessment. Under what condition should this activity be recorded in the Agency Fund?

   a. Never; the work is reported in the Capital Projects Funds.

   b. Only if the city is secondarily liable for any debt incurred to finance construction costs.

   c. Only if the city is in no way liable for the costs of the construction.

   d. In all cases.

24. Which of the following is an example of an interactivity transaction?

   a. Money is transferred from the General Fund to the Debt Service Fund.

   b. Money is transferred from the Capital Projects Fund to the General Fund.

   c. Money is transferred from the Special Revenue Fund to the Debt Service Fund.

   d. Money is transferred from the General Fund to the Enterprise Fund.

25. Cash of $60,000 is transferred from the General Fund to the Debt Service Fund. What is reported on the government-wide financial statements?

   a. No reporting is made.

   b. Other Financing Sources increase by $60,000; Other Financing Uses increase by $60,000.

   c. Revenues increase by $60,000; Expenditures increase by $60,000.

   d. Revenues increase by $60,000; Expenses increase by $60,000.

26. Cash of $60,000 is transferred from the General Fund to the Debt Service Fund. What is reported on the fund-based financial statements?

   a. No reporting is made.

   b. Other Financing Sources increase by $60,000; Other Financing Uses increase by $60,000.

   c. Revenues increase by $60,000; Expenditures increase by $60,000.

   d. Revenues increase by $60,000; Expenses increase by $60,000.

27. Cash of $20,000 is transferred from the General Fund to the Enterprise Fund to pay for work that was done. What is reported on the government-wide financial statements?

    a. No reporting is made.

    b. Other Financing Sources increase by $20,000; Other Financing Uses increase by $20,000.

    c. Revenues increase by $20,000; Expenditures increase by $20,000.

    d. Revenues increase by $20,000; Expenses increase by $20,000.

28. Cash of $20,000 is transferred from the General Fund to the Enterprise Fund to pay for work that was done. What is reported on the fund-based financial statements?

    a. No reporting is made.

    b. Other Financing Sources increase by $20,000; Other Financing Uses increase by $20,000.

    c. Revenues increase by $20,000; Expenditures increase by $20,000.

    d. Revenues increase by $20,000; Expenses increase by $20,000.

29. The board of commissioners of the City of Hartmoore adopted a General Fund budget for the year ending June 30, 2007, which included revenues of $1,000,000, bond proceeds of $400,000, appropriations of $900,000, and operating transfers out of $300,000. If this budget is formally integrated into the accounting records, what journal entry is required at the beginning of the year? What later entry is required?

30. A city orders a new computer for its General Fund at an anticipated cost of $88,000. Its actual cost when received is $89,400. Payment is subsequently made. Give all required journal entries for fund-based and government-wide financial statements. What information do the government-wide financial statements present? What information do the fund-based financial statements present?

31. Cash of $90,000 is transferred from a city's General Fund to start construction on a police station. The city issues a bond at its $1.8 million face value. The police station is built for $1.89 million. Prepare all necessary journal entries for these transactions for fund-based and government-wide financial statements. Assume that the city does not record the commitment. What information do the government-wide financial statements present? What information do the fund-based financial statements present?

32. A local government incurs the following transactions during the current fiscal period. Prepare journal entries without dollar amounts, first for fund-based financial statements and then for government-wide financial statements.

    a. The budget for the police department, ambulance service, and other ongoing activities is passed. Funding is from property taxes, transfers, and bond proceeds. All monetary outflows will be for expenses and fixed assets. A deficit is projected.

    b. A bond is issued at face value to fund the construction of a new municipal building.

    c. A computer is ordered for the tax department.

    d. The computer is received.

    e. The invoice for the computer is paid.

    f. The city council agrees to transfer money from the General Fund as partial payment for a special assessments project but has not done so. The city will be secondarily liable for any money borrowed for this work.

    g. The city council creates a motor pool to service all government vehicles. Money is transferred from the General Fund to permanently finance this facility.

    h. Property taxes are levied. Although officials believe that most of these taxes should be collected during the current period, a small percentage is estimated to be uncollectible.

    i. The city collects grant money from the state that must be spent as a supplement to the salaries of the police force. No entry has been recorded.

    j. A portion of the grant money in (i) is properly spent.

33. Prepare journal entries for the City of Pudding's governmental funds to record the following transactions, first for fund-based financial statements and then for government-wide financial statements.

    a. A new truck for the sanitation department was ordered at a cost of $94,000.

    b. The city print shop did $1,200 worth of work for the school system (but has not yet been paid).

    c. An $11 million bond was issued to build a new road.

    d. Cash of $140,000 is transferred from the General Fund to provide permanent financing for a municipal swimming pool that will be viewed as an Enterprise Fund.

e. The truck ordered in (*a*) is received at an actual cost of $96,000. Payment is not made at this time.

f. Cash of $32,000 is transferred from the General Fund to the Capital Projects Fund.

g. A state grant of $30,000 is received that must be spent to promote recycling.

h. The first $5,000 of the state grant received in (*g*) is appropriately expended.

34. Prepare journal entries for a local government to record the following transactions, first for fund-based financial statements and then for government-wide financial statements.

a. The government sells $900,000 in bonds at face value to finance construction of a warehouse.

b. A $1.1 million contract is signed for construction of the warehouse.

c. A $130,000 transfer of unrestricted funds was made for the eventual payment of the debt in (*a*).

d. Equipment for the fire department is received with a cost of $12,000. When it was ordered, an anticipated cost of $11,800 had been recorded.

e. Supplies to be used in the schools are bought for $2,000 cash. The consumption method is used.

f. A state grant of $90,000 is awarded to supplement police salaries. The money will be paid to re-imburse the government after the supplements have been paid to the police officers.

g. Property tax assessments are mailed to citizens of the government. The total assessment is $600,000, although officials anticipate that 4 percent will never be collected. There is an enforceable legal claim for this money and the government can use it immediately.

35. The following trial balances are for the governmental funds of the City of Copeland prepared from the current accounting records:

General Fund

	Debit	Credit
Cash	$ 19,000	
Taxes Receivable	202,000	
Allowance for Uncollectible Taxes		$ 2,000
Vouchers Payable		24,000
Due to Debt Service Fund		10,000
Deferred Revenues		16,000
Fund Balance—Reserved for Encumbrances		9,000
Fund Balance—Unreserved, Undesignated		103,000
Revenues Control		176,000
Expenditures Control	110,000	
Encumbrances Control	9,000	
Estimated Revenues Control	190,000	
Appropriations Control		171,000
Budgetary Fund Balance		19,000
Totals	$530,000	$530,000

Debt Service Fund

	Debit	Credit
Cash	$ 8,000	
Investments	51,000	
Taxes Receivable	11,000	
Due from General Fund	10,000	
Fund Balance—Designated for Debt Service		$ 45,000
Revenues Control		20,000
Other Financing Sources—Operating Transfers In		90,000
Expenditures Control	75,000	
Totals	$155,000	$155,000

(continued)

Capital Projects Fund

	Debit	Credit
Cash	$ 70,000	
Special Assessments Receivable	90,000	
Contracts Payable		$ 50,000
Deferred Revenues		90,000
Fund Balance—Reserved for Encumbrances		16,000
Fund Balance—Unreserved, Undesignated		–0–
Other Financing Sources		150,000
Expenditures Control	130,000	
Encumbrances	16,000	
Estimated Other Financing Sources	150,000	
Appropriations		150,000
Totals	$456,000	$456,000

Special Revenue Fund

	Debit	Credit
Cash	$ 14,000	
Taxes Receivable	41,000	
Inventory of Supplies	4,000	
Vouchers Payable		$ 25,000
Deferred Revenues		3,000
Fund Balance—Reserved for Inventory of Supplies		4,000
Fund Balance—Reserved for Encumbrances		3,000
Fund Balance—Unreserved, Undesignated		19,000
Revenues Control		56,000
Expenditures Control	48,000	
Encumbrances	3,000	
Estimated Revenues	75,000	
Appropriations		60,000
Budgetary Fund Balance		15,000
Totals	$185,000	$185,000

Based on the information presented for each of these governmental funds, answer the following questions:

a. How much more money can the General Fund expend or commit during the remainder of the current year?

b. Why does the Capital Projects Fund have no construction or capital asset accounts?

c. What does the $150,000 Appropriations balance found in the Capital Projects Fund represent?

d. Several funds have balances for Encumbrances and Fund Balance—Reserved for Encumbrances. How will these amounts be accounted for at the end of the fiscal year?

e. Why does the Fund Balance—Unreserved, Undesignated account in the Capital Projects Fund have a zero balance?

f. What are possible explanations for the $150,000 Other Financing Sources balance found in the Capital Projects Fund?

g. What does the $75,000 balance in the Expenditures Control account of the Debt Service Fund represent?

h. What is the purpose of the Special Assessments Receivable found in the Capital Projects Fund?

i. In the Special Revenue Fund, what is the purpose of the Fund Balance—Reserved for Inventory of Supplies account?

j. Why does the Debt Service Fund not have budgetary account balances?

36. Following are descriptions of transactions and other financial events for the City of Tetris for the year ending December 2007. Not all transactions have been included here. Only the General Fund formally records a budget. No encumbrances were carried over from 2006.

Paid salary for police officers	$ 21,000
Received government grant to pay ambulance drivers	40,000
Estimated revenues	232,000
Received invoices for rent on equipment used by fire department during last four months of the year	3,000
Paid for newly constructed city hall	1,044,000
Made commitment to acquire new ambulance	111,000
Received cash from bonds sold for construction purposes	300,000
Placed order for new sanitation truck	154,000
Paid salary to ambulance drivers—money derived from state government grant given for that purpose	24,000
Paid for supplies for school system	16,000
Made transfer from General Fund to eventually pay off a long-term debt	33,000
Received but did not pay for new ambulance	120,000
Levied property tax receivables for 2007. City anticipates that 95 percent will be collected during the year and 5 percent will be bad	200,000
Acquired and paid for new school bus	40,000
Received cash from business taxes and parking meters (not previously accrued)	14,000
Made appropriations	225,000

The following questions are *independent* although each is based on the preceding information. Assume that the government is preparing information for its fund-based financial statements.

a. What is the balance in the Budgetary Fund Balance account for the budget for the year? Is it a debit or credit?

b. Assume that 60 percent of the school supplies are used during the year so that 40 percent remain. If the consumption method is being applied, how is this recorded?

c. The sanitation truck that was ordered was not received before the end of the year. The commitment will be honored in the subsequent year when the truck arrives. What reporting is made at the end of 2007?

d. Assume that the ambulance was received on December 31, 2007. Provide all necessary journal entries on that date.

e. Give all journal entries that should have been made when the $33,000 transfer was made to eventually pay off a long-term debt.

f. What amount of revenue would be recognized for the period? Explain the composition of this total.

g. What are the total expenditures? Explain the makeup of this total. Include (*b*) here.

h. What journal entry or entries were prepared when the bonds were issued?

37. Chesterfield County incurred the following transactions. Prepare the entries first for fund-based financial statements and then for government-wide financial statements.

a. A budget is passed for all ongoing activities. Revenue is anticipated to be $834,000 with approved spending of $540,000 and operating transfers out of $242,000.

b. A contract is signed with a construction company to build a new central office building for the government at a cost of $8 million. A budget for this project has previously been recorded.

c. Bonds are sold for $8 million (face value) to finance construction of the new office building.

d. The new building is completed. An invoice for $8 million is received and paid.

e. Previously unrestricted cash of $1 million is set aside to begin paying the bonds issued in (*c*).

f. A portion of the bonds comes due and $1 million is paid. Of this total, $100,000 represents interest. The interest had not been previously accrued.

g. Citizens' property tax levies are assessed. Total billing for this tax is $800,000. On this date, the assessment is a legally enforceable claim according to the laws of this state. The money to be received is designated for the current period and 90 percent is assumed to be collectible in this period with receipt of an additional 6 percent during subsequent periods but in time to be available to pay current period claims. The remainder is expected to be uncollectible.

h. Cash of $120,000 is received from a toll road. This money is restricted for highway maintenance.

i. The county received investments valued at $300,000 as a donation from a grateful citizen. Income from these investments must be used to beautify local parks.

38. The following trial balance is taken from the General Fund of the City of Jennings for the year ending December 31, 2007. Prepare a condensed statement of revenues, expenditures, and other changes in fund balance and also prepare a condensed balance sheet.

	Debit	Credit
Accounts Payable		$ 90,000
Cash	$ 30,000	
Contracts Payable		90,000
Deferred Revenues		40,000
Due from Capital Projects Funds	60,000	
Due to Debt Service Funds		40,000
Expenditures	510,000	
Fund Balance—Unreserved, Undesignated		170,000
Investments	410,000	
Revenues		740,000
Other Financing Sources—Bond Proceeds		300,000
Other Financing Sources—Transfers In		50,000
Other Financing Uses—Transfers Out	470,000	
Taxes Receivable	220,000	
Vouchers Payable		180,000
Totals	$1,700,000	$1,700,000

39. A city has only one activity, its school system. The school system is accounted for within the General Fund. For convenience, assume that, at the start of 2007, the school system and the city have no assets. During the year, the city assessed $400,000 in property taxes. Of this amount, it collected $320,000 during the year, received $50,000 within a few weeks after the end of the year, and expected the remainder to be collected about six months later. The city makes the following payments during 2007: salary expense, $100,000; rent expense, $70,000; equipment (received on January 1 with a five-year life and no salvage value), $50,000; land, $30,000; and maintenance expense, $20,000. In addition, on the last day of the year, the city purchased a $200,000 building by signing a long-term liability. The building has a 20-year life and no salvage value, and the liability accrues interest at a 10 percent annual rate. The city also buys two computers on the last day of the year for $4,000 each. One will be paid for in 30 days and the other in 90 days. The computers should last for four years and have no salvage value. During the year, the school system charged students $3,000 for school fees and collected the entire amount. Any depreciation is recorded using the straight-line method.

    a. Produce a statement of net assets and a statement of activities for this city's government-wide financial statements.

    b. Produce a balance sheet and a statement of revenues, expenditures, and changes in fund balance for the fund-based financial statements. Assume that *available* is defined by the city as anything to be received within 60 days.

40. The following transactions relate to the General Fund of the city of Lost Angel for the year ending December 31, 2007. Prepare a statement of revenues, expenditures, and other changes in fund balance for the General Fund for the period to be included in the fund-based financial statements. Assume the fund balance at the beginning of the year was $180,000. Assume also that the purchases method is applied to the supplies and that receipt within 60 days is used as the definition of available resources.

    a. Collected property tax revenue of $700,000. A remaining assessment of $100,000 will be collected in the subsequent period. Half of that amount should be collected within 30 days, and the remainder will be received in about five months after the end of the year.

    b. Spent $200,000 on two new police cars with 10-year lives. A price of $207,000 had been anticipated when the cars were ordered. The city calculates all depreciation using the straight-line method with no salvage value. The half-year convention is used.

    c. Transferred $90,000 to a debt service fund.

    d. Issued a long-term bond for $200,000 on July 1. Interest at a 10 percent annual rate will be paid each year starting on June 30, 2008.

    e. Ordered a new computer with a five-year life for $40,000.

    f. Paid salaries of $30,000. Another $10,000 will be owed at the end of the year but will not be paid for 30 days.

 g. Received the new computer but at a cost of $41,000; payment to be made in 45 days.

 h. Bought supplies for $10,000 in cash.

 i. Used $8,000 of the supplies in (*h*).

41. Use the transactions in Problem 40 but prepare a statement of net assets for the government-wide financial statements. Assume that the General Fund had $180,000 in cash on the first day of the year and no other assets or liabilities.

42. Government officials of the City of Jones expect to receive General Fund revenues of $400,000 in 2007 but approve spending only $380,000. Later in the year, as they receive more information, they increase the revenue projection to $420,000. Officials approve the spending of an additional $15,000. For each of the following, indicate whether the statement is true or false and, if false, explain why.

 a. In recording this budget, appropriations should be credited initially for $380,000.

 b. The city must disclose this budgetary data within the required supplemental information section reported after the notes to the financial statements.

 c. When reporting budgetary information for the year, three figures should be reported: amended budget, initial budget, and actual figures.

 d. In making the budgetary entry, a debit must be made to some type of Fund Balance account to indicate the projected surplus.

 e. The reporting of the budget is reflected in the government-wide financial statements.

43. On December 1, 2007, a state government awards a city government a grant of $1 million to be used specifically to provide hot lunches for all schoolchildren. No money is received until June 1, 2008. For each of the following, indicate whether the statement is true or false and, if false, explain why.

 a. Because the government received no money until June 1, 2008, no amount of revenue can be recognized in 2007 on the government-wide financial statements.

 b. If this grant has no eligibility requirements and the money is properly spent in September 2008 for the hot lunches, the revenue should be recognized in September.

 c. Because the money came from the state government and because the government specified the use, this is a government-mandated nonexchange transaction.

 d. If the government had received the money on December 1, 2007, but eligibility requirements had not been met yet, a deferred revenue of $1 million would have been recognized on the government-wide financial statements.

 e. The rules for recognition of this revenue were created by *GASB Statement 34*.

44. Indicate (i) how each of the following transactions impacts the fund balance of the General Fund for fund-based financial statements and (ii) what the impact is on the net asset balance of the governmental funds for government-wide financial statements.

 a. Issue a five-year bond for $6 million to finance general operations.

 b. Pay cash of $149,000 for a truck to be used by the police department.

 c. The fire department pays $17,000 to a government motor pool that services the vehicles of only the police and fire departments.

 d. Levy property taxes of $75,000 for the current year that will not be collected until four months into the subsequent year.

 e. Receive a grant for $7,000 that must be returned unless the money is spent according to the stipulations of the conveyance.

 f. Sales of $20 million are made during the current year. The government charges a 5 percent sales tax. Half of this amount is to be collected 10 days after the end of the year with the remainder to be collected 10 weeks after the end of the year. "Available" has been defined by this government as 75 days.

 g. A computer is ordered for the school system at an anticipated cost of $23,000.

 h. A cash transfer of $18,000 is approved from the General Fund to a Capital Projects Fund.

45. Fund A transfers $20,000 to Fund B. For each of the following, indicate whether the statement is true or false and, if false, explain why.

 a. If Fund A is the General Fund and Fund B is an Enterprise Fund, nothing will be shown for this transfer on the statement of activities within the government-wide financial statements.

 b. If Fund A is the General Fund and Fund B is a Debt Service Fund, nothing will be shown for this transfer on the statement of activities within the government-wide financial statements.

c. If Fund A is the General Fund and Fund B is an Enterprise Fund, a $20,000 reduction will be reported on the statement of revenues, expenditures, and other changes for the governmental funds within the fund-based financial statements.

d. If Fund A is the General Fund and Fund B is a Special Revenue Fund (which is not considered a major fund), no changes will be shown on the statement of revenues, expenditures, and other changes within the fund-based financial statements.

e. If Fund A is the General Fund and Fund B is an Internal Service Fund and this is for work done, the General Fund will report an expense of $20,000 within the fund-based financial statements.

Use the following information for Problems 46–52:

Assume that the City of Coyote has already produced its financial statements for December 31, 2007, and the year then ended. The city's General Fund was only for education and parks. Its Capital Projects Funds worked with each of these functions at times. The city also had established an Enterprise Fund to account for its art museum.

On the government-wide financial statements, the following figures were indicated:

- Education reported net expenses of $600,000.
- Parks reported net expenses of $100,000.
- Art museum reported net revenues of $50,000.
- General government revenues for the year were $800,000 with an overall increase in the city's net assets of $150,000.

The fund-based financial statements indicated the following for the entire year:

- The General Fund reported a $30,000 increase in its fund balance.
- The Capital Projects Fund reported a $40,000 increase in its fund balance.
- The Enterprise Fund reported a $60,000 increase in its net assets.

The CPA firm of Abernethy and Chapman has been asked to review several transactions that occurred during 2007 and indicate how to correct any erroneous reporting and the impact of each error. View each situation as *independent*.

46. During 2007, the City of Coyote contracted to build a sidewalk costing $10,000 as a special assessments project for which it collected $10,000 from affected citizens. The government had no obligation in connection with this project. Both a $10,000 revenue and a $10,000 expenditure were recorded in the Capital Projects Fund. In preparing government-wide financial statements, an asset and a general revenue were recorded for $10,000.

   a. In the general information, the Capital Projects Fund reported an increase in its fund balance of $40,000. What was the correct overall change in the Capital Projects Fund's balance during 2007?

   b. In the general information, a $150,000 overall increase in the city's net assets was found on the government-wide financial statements. What was the correct overall change in the city's net assets on the government-wide financial statements?

47. On December 30, 2007, the City of Coyote borrowed $20,000 for the General Fund on a 60-day note. In that fund, both Cash and Other Financing Sources were recorded. In the general information, a $30,000 overall increase was reported in the General Fund balance. What was the correct change in the General Fund's balance for 2007?

48. An art display set up for the community was recorded within the General Fund and generated revenues of $9,000 but had expenditures of $45,000 ($15,000 in expenses and $30,000 to buy land for the display). The CPA firm has determined that this program should have been recorded as an Enterprise Fund activity because it was offered in association with the art museum.

   a. What was the correct change in the General Fund's balance for 2007?

   b. What was the correct overall change in the city's net assets on the government-wide financial statements?

   c. What was the correct change in the net assets of the Enterprise Fund on the fund-based financial statements?

49. The City of Coyote mailed property tax bills for 2008 to its citizens during August 2007. Payments could be made early to receive a discount. The levy becomes legally enforceable on February 15, 2008. All money received must be spent during 2008 or later. The total assessment is $300,000; 40 percent of that amount, less a 10 percent discount, is collected in 2007. The city expects to

receive all of the remaining money during 2008 with no discount. During 2007, the government increased cash as well as a revenue for the same amount. No change was made in creating the government-wide financial statements.

    a. What was the correct overall change in the city's net assets as shown on the government-wide financial statements?

    b. What was the correct change for 2007 in the fund balance reported in the General Fund?

50. The City of Coyote mailed property tax bills for 2008 to its citizens during August 2007. Payments could be made early to receive a discount. The levy becomes legally enforceable on February 15, 2008. All money received must be spent during 2008 or later. The total assessment is $300,000, and 40 percent of that amount is collected in 2007 less a 10 percent discount. The city expects to receive all the rest of the money during 2008 with no discount. During 2007, the government increased cash and a revenue for the amount received. In addition, a receivable account and a deferred revenue account for $180,000 were recognized.

    a. In the general information, an overall increase in the city's net assets of $150,000 was found on the government-wide financial statements. What was the correct overall change in the city's net assets as reported on the government-wide financial statements?

    b. In the general information, an overall increase of $30,000 was reported in the General Fund balance. What was the correct change during 2007 in the General Fund's balance?

51. In 2007, the City of Coyote received a $320,000 cash grant from the state to stop air pollution. Assume that although a special revenue fund could have been set up, the money remained in the General Fund. Cash was received immediately but had to be returned if the city had not lowered air pollution by 25 percent by 2010. On December 31, 2007, Coyote spent $210,000 of this money for a large machine to help begin to reduce pollution. The machine is expected to last for five years and was recorded as an expenditure in the General Fund and as an asset on the government-wide financial statements where it was depreciated based on the straight-line method and the half-year convention. Because the money had been received, all $320,000 was recorded as a revenue on both the fund-based and the government-wide financial statements.

    a. What was the correct change for 2007 in the General Fund's balance?

    b. What was the correct overall change in the net assets reported on the government-wide financial statements?

52. During 2007, the City of Coyote's General Fund received $10,000, which was recorded as a general revenue when it was actually a program revenue earned by its park program.

    a. What was the correct overall change for 2007 in the net assets reported on the government-wide financial statements?

    b. In the general information, the parks reported net expenses for the period of $100,000. What was the correct amount of net expenses reported by the parks?

Develop Your Skills

RESEARCH CASE 1

The City of Hampshore is currently preparing financial statements for the past fiscal year. The city manager is concerned because the city encountered some unusual transactions during the current fiscal period and is unsure as to their handling.

Required:

Use a copy of *GASB Statement 34* to answer each of the following questions.

1. For government accounting, what is the definition of *extraordinary item?*
2. For government accounting, what is the definition of *special item?*
3. On government-wide financial statements, how should extraordinary items and special items be reported?

RESEARCH CASE 2

The City of Danmark is preparing financial statements. Officials are currently working on the statement of activities within the government-wide financial statements. A question has arisen as to whether a particular revenue should be identified on government-wide statements as a program revenue or a general revenue.

Required:

Use a copy of *GASB Statement 34* to answer each of the following questions.

1. How is a program revenue defined?
2. What are common examples of program revenues?
3. How is a general revenue defined?
4. What are common examples of general revenues?

ANALYSIS CASE 1

Search the Internet for the official Web site of one or more state or local governments. After reviewing this Web site, determine whether the latest comprehensive annual financial report (CAFR) is available on the site. For example, the most recent comprehensive annual financial report for the City of Sacramento can be found at www.cityofsacramento.org/cafr/. Use the financial statements that you find to answer the following questions.

Required:

1. How does the audit opinion given to this city by its independent auditors differ from the opinion rendered on the financial statements for a for-profit business?
2. A reconciliation should be presented to explain the difference between the net changes in fund balances for the governmental funds (fund-based financial statements) and the change in net assets for the governmental activities (government-wide financial statements). What were several of the largest reasons for the difference?
3. What were the city's largest sources of general revenues?
4. What was the total amount of expenditures recorded by the General Fund during the period? How were those expenditures classified?
5. What assets are reported for the General Fund?
6. Review the notes to the financial statements and then determine the number of days the government uses to define the end-of-year financial resources that are viewed as currently available.
7. Did the size of the General Fund balance increase or decrease during the most recent year and by how much?

ANALYSIS CASE 2

Go to the Web site www.gasb.org and click on "What's New?" Scroll down to the topic "Exposure Drafts." Review any exposure drafts currently being considered by the GASB.

Required:

Identify the major impacts that the proposed changes would create in government accounting.

COMMUNICATION CASE 1

Go to the Web site www.gasb.org and click on "Site Map." Find the GASB Mission Statement.

Required:

Write a memo on the changes created by *GASB Statement 34* and how those changes reconcile with the GASB's mission.

COMMUNICATION CASE 2

Obtain a copy of *GASB Statement 34*. Read paragraphs 239 through 277.

Required:

Write a report describing alternatives that the GASB considered when it created *Statement 34*. Indicate the alternative that you would have viewed as most appropriate, and describe why the GASB did not choose it.

COMMUNICATION CASE 3

Search the Internet for the official Web site of one or more state or local governments. After reviewing this Web site, determine whether the latest comprehensive annual financial report (CAFR) is available on the site. For example, the most recent comprehensive annual financial report for the City of Minneapolis can be found at www.ci.minneapolis.mn.us/financial-reports/cafr2004/. Read the Management's Discussion and Analysis (MD&A) that should be located near the beginning of the annual report.

Required:

Write a memo to explain four or five of the most interesting pieces of information that the Management's Discussion and Analysis provides.

EXCEL CASE

The City of Bainland has been undergoing financial difficulties because of a decrease in its tax base caused by corporations leaving the area. On January 1, 2007, the city has a fund balance of $400,000 in its governmental funds. In 2006, the city had revenues of $1.4 million and expenditures of $1.48 million. The city's treasurer has forecast that, unless something is done, revenues will decrease at 2 percent per year while expenditures will increase at 3 percent per year.

Required:

1. Create a spreadsheet to predict what year the government will have a zero fund balance.
2. One proposal is that the city slash its expenditures by laying off government workers. That action will lead to a 3 percent decrease in expenditures each year rather than a 3 percent increase. However, because of the unemployment, the city will receive less tax revenue. Thus, instead of a 2 percent decrease in revenues, the city expects a 5 percent decrease per year. Adapt the spreadsheet created in requirement (1) to predict what year the government will have a zero fund balance if this option is taken.
3. Another proposal is to increase spending to draw new businesses to the area. This action will lead to a 7 percent increase in expenditures every year, but revenues are expected to rise by 4 percent per year. Adapt the spreadsheet created in requirement (1) to predict what year the government will have a zero fund balance under this option.

Chapter **Seventeen**

Accounting for State and Local Governments (Part 2)

Questions to Consider

- How does the accounting for capital leases utilized for fund-based financial statements differ from the procedures used in producing government-wide financial statements?

- What liability does a government have for closure and cleanup costs of a solid waste landfill, and how are these costs reported?

- How does a state or local government record artworks or historical treasures that it buys or obtains through donation?

- What is meant by using the modified approach in connection with the depreciation of infrastructure assets?

- What is included in the management's discussion and analysis (MD&A), and why is it required of state and local governments?

- What is a component unit, and how does a state or local government report it?

- How does governmental accounting apply to public colleges and universities?

The previous chapter of this book introduced the unique aspects of financial reporting applicable to state and local governments. That chapter analyzed fund accounting, encumbrances, expenditures, revenue recognition, the issuance of bonds, and the like in light of both traditional government accounting procedures and the massive changes brought about by the creation of government-wide financial statements. That initial coverage of these statements was designed to present the basic essentials underlying the accounting required of these government entities, especially the differences caused by the dual nature of financial reporting that leads to the preparation of both fund-based financial statements and government-wide financial statements.

The current chapter carries this analysis further, first by delving into more complex financial situations. Many state and local government units are quite large and face transactions as complicated as any a for-profit business encounters. This chapter examines issues such as solid waste landfills, donated artworks, and the depreciation of infrastructure assets to broaden the scope of understanding of state and local government accounting.

Second, this chapter discusses the overall financial reporting model. Within this coverage, we examine the actual composition of a government. Because of the wide variety of agencies and other activities that can operate in connection with a government, necessary inclusion within the financial statements is not as easy to specify as it is in a for-profit business where ownership of more than 50 percent of the voting stock is the primary criterion.

CAPITAL LEASES

The notes to the 2003 financial statements of the City of Birmingham, Alabama, describe specific capital leases as follows:

> The City leases certain street and sanitation equipment, fire equipment, and telecommunications equipment. All of the lease agreements qualify as capital leases for accounting purposes and, therefore, have been recorded at the present value of their future minimum lease payments as of the inception date. All of the leased equipment has been capitalized as governmental activity assets.

Likewise, the City of Greensboro, North Carolina, notes in 2004 that the

> City has entered into lease-purchase and other financing agreements for certain equipment, land and infrastructure that bear interest at fixed rates from 2.6% to 6.7% and redevelopment projects that bear interest at an approximate rate of 1.5%. Interest and principal are payable monthly and quarterly through 2022. Principal and interest requirements will be provided by an appropriation in the year in which they become due.

Obviously, state and local governments (in the same manner as a for-profit business) sometimes lease the use of property rather than purchasing it directly. Leasing can provide lower interest rates or reduce the risk of obsolescence and damage. Leasing is simply a way that many organizations (for-profit or governmental) can acquire needed equipment, machinery, buildings, or other assets.

For reporting purposes, such leases must be recorded as either capital leases or operating leases. The initial issue is to separate one type from another. In that regard, the GASB has accepted the criteria applied in FASB *SFAS 13,* "Accounting for Leases," as the method of differentiation. *SFAS 13* established the following four criteria; a lease that meets any one of these is held to be a *capital lease:*

1. The lease transfers ownership of the property to the lessee by the end of the lease term.
2. The lease contains an option to purchase the leased property at a bargain price.
3. The lease term is equal to or more than 75 percent of the estimated economic life of the leased property.
4. The present value of rental or other minimum lease payments equals or exceeds 90 percent of the fair value of the leased property.

Thus, for example, assume that a city leases a truck that has a 10-year life and a fair value of $50,000. In each of these four sample situations, the city is required to account for the property as a capital lease:

- The lease is for six years, but the city automatically receives title to the truck at the end of that term (so that criterion 1 is met).
- The lease is for five years, but the city can buy the truck for $3,000 at the end of that time, an amount that is viewed as significantly less than the expected fair value at that point in time (so that criterion 2 is met).
- The lease is for eight years, after which the truck will be returned to the lessor (so that criterion 3 is met).
- The lease is for seven years, but the present value of minimum lease payments is more than $45,000, or 90 percent of the fair value (so that criterion 4 is met). In this last example, the lessee is viewed as paying the equivalent of the purchase price to obtain the use of the asset.

Government-Wide Financial Statements

In reporting property obtained by capital lease, accounting for the government-wide financial statements is the same as for a for-profit enterprise. The government-wide financial statements report both an asset and a liability, initially at the present value of the minimum lease payments, in the same manner as they would a debt-financed acquisition. Assume, for example, that a police department signs an 8-year lease for a truck with a 10-year life. Because this meets the third criterion, this transaction must be recorded as a capital lease. Assume also that the lease calls for annual payments of $10,000 per year with the first payment made at the signing of the lease and that a 10 percent interest rate is appropriate for the city.

The present value of the minimum lease payments applying a 10 percent interest rate to an annuity due for eight years is $58,680 (rounded). The city makes the following entries to be reported within the governmental activities because the lease relates to the police department. However, the same reporting is appropriate within the business-type activities if an enterprise fund had been involved. As indicated in the previous chapter, no accounting distinction is made for the two types of activities.

Government-Wide Financial Statements

Truck—Capital Lease	58,680	
Capital Lease Obligation		58,680
To record capital lease.		
Capital Lease Obligation	10,000	
Cash		10,000
To record first payment on leased truck.		

Assuming that the straight-line method is being used, the city should recognize depreciation expense of $7,335 ($58,680/8 years) at the end of this first year. However, if the title to the asset will be transferred to the city or if a bargain purchase option exists, the full 10-year life should be used for depreciation purposes because the lessee (the city) will expect to get full use of the asset.

At the end of the first year, when the city makes the next payment, part of that $10,000 will be attributed to interest with the remainder viewed as a reduction in the liability principal. Because the obligation has been reduced to $48,680 and the interest rate is 10 percent, the interest recorded for the first year will be $4,868. The remaining $5,132 ($10,000 less $4,868) decreases the debt to $43,548.

Government-Wide Financial Statements

Interest Expense	4,868	
Capital Lease Obligation	5,132	
Cash		10,000
To record payment on capital lease at end of first year.		

Fund-Based Financial Statements

Assume that the same lease is being recorded in the fund-based financial statements for the governmental funds. If a proprietary fund is involved, the handling is the same as in the preceding situation. A difference appears only for the governmental funds.

Assume the same lease as the previous one is being recorded to produce fund-based financial statements. Using the same eight-year lease in connection with the truck requiring payments of $10,000 per year, an amount with a present value of $58,680, the General Fund (or whichever governmental fund was gaining use of the asset) records the following entry:

Fund-Based Financial Statements

General Fund		
Expenditures—Leased Asset	58,680	
Other Financing Sources—Capital Lease		58,680
To record signing of an eight-year lease for a truck that meets the requirements of a capital lease.		
Expenditures—Lease Principal	10,000	
Cash		10,000
To record first payment on leased truck.		

Note that the General Fund reports neither the capital asset nor the long-term liability because such balances are not reported in the fund-based statements. At the end of this initial year, when the next payment is made, $4,868 (10 percent of the obligation after the first payment) is considered interest; the rest reduces the principal.

Fund-Based Financial Statements

General Fund		
Expenditures—Interest	4,868	
Expenditures—Lease Principal	5,132	
Cash		10,000
To record payment at the end of first year on leased truck recorded as a capital lease.		

At first glance, the fund-based journal entries appear to be double counting the expenditures, once when the asset is obtained and again when periodic payments are made. This approach, though, can be justified. The government had an option; it could have either leased the asset or borrowed money and bought the asset. Because the overall result is the same in both cases, the reporting should not create different pictures. The preceding two entries seek to mirror the presentation that would have resulted in fund-based statements if the city had followed an alternative strategy for acquiring the asset: (1) borrowed money on a long-term liability, (2) used the money to acquire the asset, and (3) subsequently paid the long-term liability and interest. If the city had used this borrow-and-buy approach, the recording would have been as follows in the fund-based statements:

1. To reflect the borrowing, the city would have reported an other financing source because the money received did not come from a revenue.
2. At the time of the asset's acquisition, the city would have shown an expenditure in keeping with the goal of presenting the changes in current financial resources.
3. For the same reason, the subsequent payment of debt and interest would have led to a second recording of expenditures.

Consequently, if the city had borrowed money and bought the asset, one "other financing source" and two separate "expenditures" would have resulted. The preceding journal entries created for the capital lease are structured to arrive at that same impact.

The radical differences between fund-based financial statements and government-wide financial statements are, once again, quite striking. At the end of this first year, the resulting figures in the two statements are not comparable in any way:

	Fund-Based Financial Statements	**Government-Wide Financial Statements**
Asset	Not applicable	$58,680
Accumulated depreciation	Not applicable	7,335
Liability	Not applicable	43,548
Expenditures:		
Asset acquisition	$58,680	Not applicable
Debt principal	5,132	Not applicable
Interest	4,868	Not applicable
Other financing sources	58,680	Not applicable
Depreciation expense	Not applicable	7,335
Interest expense	Not applicable	4,868

SOLID WASTE LANDFILL

The following information is disclosed in the notes to the financial statements of the City of Greensboro, North Carolina, as of June 30, 2004:

> The City owns and operates a regional landfill site located in the northeast portion of the City. State and federal laws require the City to place a final cover on its White Street landfill site and to perform certain maintenance and monitoring functions at the site for thirty years after closure. The City reports a portion of these closure and postclosure care costs as an operating expense in each period based on landfill capacity used as of each June 30. The $10,503,616 reported as landfill closure and postclosure care liability at June 30, 2004, is based on the use of 100% of the estimated capacity of Phase II and Phase III, Cell 1. Phase III, Cell 2, is estimated at 75.3% filled.
>
> These amounts are based on what it would cost to perform all closure and postclosure care in the current year. Actual cost may be higher due to inflation, changes in technology, or changes in regulations. At June 30, 2004, the City had expended $3,876,035 to complete closure for the White Street facility, Phase II. The balance of closure costs, estimated at $6,156,000 for Phase III, Cells 1 and 2, will be funded over the remaining life of the landfill.

A great many governments operate solid waste landfills to provide a place for citizens and local companies to dispose of trash and other forms of garbage and refuse. Governments frequently report landfill operations within the enterprise funds because many of these facilities require a user fee. However, some landfills are open to the public for free, and therefore reporting within the General Fund is more appropriate.

Regardless of the type of fund utilized, solid waste landfills can be sources of huge liabilities for governments. The U.S. Environmental Protection Agency has strict rules on closure requirements as well as groundwater monitoring and other postclosure activities. Satisfying such requirements can be quite costly. Thus, the operation of a landfill almost always necessitates large payments to ensure that the facility is properly closed and then monitored and maintained for an extended period. Theoretically, the accounting question has always been how to report closure costs while the landfill is still in operation.

To illustrate, assume that a city opens a landfill in Year 1 that is expected to take 10 years to fill. As part of the recording process each year, the city must estimate the current costs required to close the landfill. Such costs include the amount to be paid to cover the area and for all postclosure maintenance. The city uses current rather than future costs as a better measure of the current obligation but then must adjust such amounts each period for inflation as well as technology and regulation changes.

Assume, for this example, that the current cost for closure is estimated at $1 million and for postclosure maintenance at $400,000. Assume that during Year 1, the city makes an initial payment of $30,000 toward the closure costs. At the end of this first year, the city engineers estimate that 16 percent of the space has been filled.

Government-Wide Financial Statements

Regardless of whether the city reports this solid waste landfill as a governmental activity (within the General Fund) or as a business-type activity (within an enterprise fund), it must recognize it in the government-wide statements based on accrual accounting and the economic resources measurement basis. Because the government anticipates total costs of $1.4 million and the landfill is 16 percent filled, $224,000 should be accrued in this first year ($1.4 million $\times$ 16%):

Government-Wide Financial Statements: Year 1

Expense—Landfill Closure	224,000	
Landfill Closure Liability		224,000
To recognize the Year 1 portion of total costs for eventual closure of landfill.		

The city made an initial payment during the year. This payment simply reduces the liability being reported:

Landfill Closure Liability	30,000	
Cash		30,000
To record first payment of costs necessitated by eventual closure of the landfill.		

To extend this example, assume that the landfill is judged to be 27 percent filled at the end of Year 2 and the city makes another $30,000 payment. However, because of inflation and newly anticipated changes in technology, the city now believes that current closure costs would total $1.1 million with postclosure costs amounting to $500,000.

Using this new and revised information, the city should recognize that it has estimated total costs to date of $432,000 by the end of Year 2 ($1.6 million × 27%). Because it already recorded $224,000 in Year 1, it now accrues an additional $208,000 in Year 2 ($432,000 − $224,000):

Government-Wide Financial Statements: Year 2

Expense—Landfill Closure	208,000	
Landfill Closure Liability		208,000
To recognize Year 2 portion of costs for eventual closure of landfill.		
Landfill Closure Liability	30,000	
Cash		30,000
To record second payment of costs necessitated by eventual closure of the landfill.		

Consequently, in the Year 2 government-wide financial statements, the city reports this:

Expense—Landfill closure	$208,000
Landfill closure liability	
($224,000 + $208,000 − $30,000 − $30,000)	372,000

Fund-Based Financial Statements

If the city is recording a solid waste landfill as an enterprise fund, the reporting will be the same in the fund-based financial statements as just shown. All economic resources are again being measured based on accrual accounting.

However, if the landfill is recorded in the General Fund, the city reports only the change in current financial resources. Despite the huge eventual liability, the reduction in current financial resources has been limited to the annual payment of $30,000. Thus, the only entry required each year in this example for the fund-based financial statements is as follows:

Fund-Based Financial Statements: Year 1 and Year 2

General Fund		
Expenditures—Closure Costs	30,000	
Cash		30,000
To record annual payment toward the eventual closure costs of the city's solid waste landfill.		

COMPENSATED ABSENCES

State and local governments have numerous employees: police officers, schoolteachers, maintenance workers, and the like. As of June 30, 2004, the City of Baltimore, Maryland, reported having 15,385 employees.[1] In the same manner as the employees of a for-profit organization,

[1] Statistical information listed at the end of the comprehensive annual financial report provides a wide array of information about the reporting government. For example, in 2004, Baltimore had 2,000 miles of streets, 39 fire stations, 3,100 miles of sanitary sewer lines, 22 libraries (containing 2.7 million volumes), and 2 ice rinks.

government employees earn vacation days, sick leave days, and holidays, collectively known as *compensated absences,* that can amount to a significant amount of money. For example, at June 30, 2004, the City of Baltimore reported a debt of more than $90 million for such compensated absences. This obligation was explained in part through footnote disclosure: "Employees earn one day of sick leave for each completed month of service, and there is no limitation on the number of sick leave days that can be accumulated."

Accounting for such liabilities is much the same as was demonstrated for capital leases and solid waste landfills. In the government-wide financial statements, the city accrues the expense as incurred. Conversely, for the governmental funds producing fund-based financial statements, only actual payments and claims to current financial resources are included. For example, assume that a city reaches the end of Year 1 and owes its General Fund employees $40,000 because of compensated absences to be taken in the future for vacation days, holidays, and sick leave that have been earned. However, only $5,000 of these absences is expected early enough in Year 2 to require current financial resources. Perhaps a number of employees are scheduled to take their vacations in the first two months of the subsequent period.

Consequently, a $40,000 liability exists at the end of Year 1 but only $5,000 of that amount will be a claim on the government's current financial resources:

Government-Wide Financial Statements: Year 1

Expenses—Compensated Absences	40,000	
Liability—Compensated Absences		40,000
To accrue amount owed at the end of Year 1 to employees for vacations, sick leave, and holidays.		

Reporting made for the governmental funds in the fund-based financial statements reflects the changes in current financial resources. As the following entry shows, only the $5,000 that will be paid early in the next year is included. The remainder of the debt is not reported because it is not a claim to current financial resources. Again, however, if the employees work in an area reported as an enterprise fund, the accounting is the same as in the government-wide statements.

Fund-Based Financial Statements: Year 1

General Fund		
Expenditures—Compensated Absences	5,000	
Liability—Compensated Absences		5,000
To accrue amount of compensated absences that will be taken early in Year 2 so that it requires the use of Year 1 financial resources.		

WORKS OF ART AND HISTORICAL TREASURES

As discussed in the following chapter, private not-for-profit organizations have long debated the proper reporting of artworks and other museum pieces they buy or receive by gift. Governmental accounting occasionally faces the same issue. How should a government report works of art, museum artifacts, and other historical treasures in its financial statements?

Assume, for example, that a city maintains a small museum in the basement of its main office building. The museum was created to display documents, maps, and paintings that depict the history of the city and the surrounding area. The city government bought several of these items, but local citizens donated a number of them. Many of these purchased and donated pieces are quite valuable.

GASB Statement 34 is clear on the handling of the items acquired for this city museum. Paragraph 27 states that, except in certain specified cases, "governments should capitalize works of art, historical treasures, and similar assets at their historical cost or fair value at date of donation." Thus, the government-wide statement of net assets should report an antique map bought for $5,000 as an asset at that cost. In the same manner, a similar map received as a gift is also recorded as a $5,000 asset.

If the city bought the map for cash, the appropriate journal entry is

Government-Wide Financial Statements

Museum Piece—Map	5,000	
Cash		5,000
To record acquisition of map for the city's museum.		

Because the city paid cash for the map, a decrease occurs in current financial resources so that an entry is also needed in the fund-based financial statements if the museum is accounted for within the General Fund. However, if the museum has a user charge and is reported in an enterprise fund, the preceding entry is replicated in accounting for this proprietary fund:

Fund-Based Financial Statements

General Fund		
Expenditure—Museum Piece	5,000	
Cash		5,000
To record acquisition of map for the city's museum, an activity which is being reported within the General Fund.		

Conversely, if this map had been donated to the city, capitalization of the asset for government-wide financial statements should still be reported based on its fair value at the date of the gift. The gift is viewed as a voluntary nonexchange transaction so that a revenue is properly recognized when all eligibility requirements have been met.

The following entry is appropriate if all eligibility requirements have been met, but, if not, the credit should be a deferred revenue. No parallel entry is made in the fund-based financial statements for the governmental funds because no change occurs in the amount of available current financial resources.

Government-Wide Financial Statements

Museum Piece—Map	5,000	
Revenue—Donation		5,000
To record gift of map for the city's museum.		

A theoretical problem arises in the recognition of this asset for government-wide financial reporting regardless of whether it was purchased or obtained by gift. Unless a user charge is assessed, a map displayed for the public to see does not generate cash flows or any other direct economic benefit. Therefore, does the map actually qualify as an asset to be reported?

In *Statement 34,* the GASB "encouraged" the capitalization of all such artworks and historical treasures. However, if the following three criteria are met, recording such an item as an asset is optional:

1. Held for public exhibition, education, or research in furtherance of public service rather than financial gain.
2. Protected, kept unencumbered, cared for, and preserved.
3. Subject to an organizational policy that requires the proceeds from sales of collection items to be used to acquire other items for collections.[2]

---

[2] *GASB Statement No. 34,* "Basic Financial Statements—and Management's Discussion and Analysis—for State and Local Governments," June 1999, para. 27.

If all of these guidelines are met, the artwork or historical treasure does have value, but it will not provide any direct economic benefit to the government. Thus, an asset does not have to be reported. Instead, in the entries previously shown for the government-wide statements, an expense rather than an asset can be shown regardless of whether the item was obtained by purchase or gift. The GASB's handling of this issue closely parallels rules established previously by the FASB in its *SFAS 116,* "Accounting for Contributions Received and Contributions Made," utilized by private not-for-profit organizations. However, as the next chapter will show, the optional handling does differ.

If a work of art or other historical treasure is capitalized by a government, an additional theoretical question arises, this time about depreciation. Does the map on display in the museum actually depreciate in value over time? In connection with this type of asset, *GASB Statement 34* requires depreciation only if the asset is "exhaustible"—that is, if its utility will be used up by display, education, or research. Depreciation is not necessary however, if the work of art or historical treasure is viewed as being inexhaustible. For example, a bronze statue could well be viewed as an inexhaustible asset according to these guidelines so that depreciation would be allowed but not required.

INFRASTRUCTURE ASSETS AND DEPRECIATION

Paragraph 19 of *GASB Statement 34* defines infrastructure assets as "long-lived capital assets that normally are stationary in nature and normally can be preserved for a significantly greater number of years than most capital assets." Examples include roads, bridges, tunnels, lighting systems, curbing, and sidewalks. As the previous chapter discussed, recording infrastructure items as assets was an optional practice prior to the issuance of *GASB Statement 34.* However, this pronouncement mandates that new infrastructure costs be recorded as assets on the government-wide statement of net assets. For the governmental funds, these same costs are recorded as expenditures in the fund-based statements because acquisition and construction create a reduction in current financial resources.

Beyond simply recording new infrastructure items as assets, a state or local government also has to capitalize many infrastructure assets previously acquired. A major road system constructed in 1988, for example, must be shown as an asset in the government-wide statements. Because cost figures for these earlier acquisitions and constructions may not be readily available, estimations are allowed. In addition, because approximating the cost of all previously acquired infrastructure items would be virtually impossible, this capitalization requirement is limited to major assets that (1) were acquired in fiscal years ending after June 30, 1980, or that (2) had major renovations, restorations, or improvements since that date.

For this reason, notes to the 2003 financial statements for the City of Cleveland, Ohio, disclosed "the historical cost of infrastructure assets (retroactive to 1980) is included as part of the governmental capital assets. Thus, the depreciated value of construction costs for the roadway network including streets, sidewalks, curbs and gutters, guard rails, traffic lights, signals, parking meters and the bridge network is reported in the government-wide statement of net assets."

As discussed previously, depreciation is now required for all capital assets appearing in the government-wide financial statements except for land as well as artworks and historical treasures that are deemed to be inexhaustible. A similar issue was debated in connection with infrastructure items: Is depreciation appropriate for this type of asset? For example, construction of the Brooklyn Bridge was finished in 1883 at a cost of about $15 million. That particular piece of infrastructure has been operating for more than 120 years and, with proper maintenance, might well be able to continue to carry traffic for another 120 years. Much the same can be said of some roads, sidewalks, and the like built today. With appropriate repair and maintenance care, such assets could have lives that are almost indefinite. What life should New York City use to depreciate the initial cost incurred in constructing a street such as Fifth Avenue?

Not surprisingly, governments tend to depreciate some of their infrastructure assets over extended periods. The City of Bismarck, North Dakota, uses lives that range from 20 to 100 years whereas the City of Cleveland, Ohio, depreciates these assets over periods from 5 to 50 years.

However, *GASB Statement 34* provides an alternative to depreciating the cost of eligible infrastructure assets such as the Brooklyn Bridge or Fifth Avenue. This method, known as the *modified approach,* eliminates the need for depreciation for qualifying infrastructure. If specified guidelines are met, the government can choose to expense all maintenance costs each year in lieu of recording depreciation. Additions and improvements still must be capitalized, but the cost of maintaining the infrastructure in proper working condition is expensed. Thus, if it uses this method, New York City can directly expense the amount it spends on repair and other maintenance of Fifth Avenue so that depreciation of the street's capitalized cost is not recorded.

Use of the modified approach requires the government to accumulate information about particular infrastructure assets within either a network or a subsystem of a network. For example, all roads could be deemed a network while state roads, rural roads, and interstate highways might make up three subsystems of that network.

- For these eligible assets, the government must establish a minimum acceptable condition level for the network or subsystem of the network and then maintain documentation that this minimum level is being met.
- The government must have an asset management system in place to monitor the particular network or subsystem of a network in question. This system should assess the ongoing condition of the eligible assets to ensure that they are, indeed, able to operate at the predetermined level.

GASB Statement 34 provides an example of the type of disclosure necessary to explain the use of the modified approach:

> The City manages its streets using the XYZ pavement management system. The City's policy is to maintain 85 percent of its streets at a pavement condition index of at least 70 (on a 100-point scale) and no more than 10 percent of its streets at a pavement condition index below 50. The most recent assessment found that the City's streets were within the prescribed parameters with 87 percent having a pavement condition index of 70 or better and only 2 percent of the streets having a pavement condition index below 50.[3]

The modified approach does provide a method by which governments can avoid depreciating infrastructure assets such as the Brooklyn Bridge that potentially have an almost unlimited life. The issue is, How many governments will go to the trouble of creating the standards and documentation required by this approach simply to avoid recording depreciation expense? "I am beginning to see more enterprise funds, especially airports, select the modified approach. However, to date, I have not encountered too many general government entities that have considered using it."[4]

MANAGEMENT'S DISCUSSION AND ANALYSIS

As an earlier chapter of this textbook on the Securities and Exchange Commission described, the SEC has long advocated inclusion of a verbal explanation of a for-profit company's operations and financial position to accompany its financial statements. This memorandum, known generally as the *management's discussion and analysis* (MD&A), provides a wealth of vital information for the reader of the financial statements. Thus, in evaluating such for-profit organizations, outside decision makers are quite used to having a "plain English" explanation of the figures and other critical information disclosed within the statements. For example, the 2004 financial statements of the General Electric Company contained a Management's Discussion and Analysis of Financial Condition and Results of Operation that covered approximately 31 pages. Consequently, this section provides a stockholder, creditor, potential investor, or other interested party with extensive details to describe and supplement the facts and figures presented within the company's financial statements.

---

[3] Ibid., p. 181.
[4] E-mail from John Reagan III, partner, KPMG, Washington, D.C., June 5, 2005.

One of the most important changes created by *GASB Statement 34* was the requirement that state and local governments provide a similar MD&A. This authoritative pronouncement actually divides the general purpose external financial statements of a state or local government into three distinct sections:

1. Management's discussion and analysis.
2. Financial statements:
   a. Government-wide financial statements.
   b. Fund-based financial statements.
   c. Notes to the financial statements.
3. Required supplementary information (other than the MD&A). For example, this final section, as the previous chapter mentioned, now shows a comparison of budgetary figures to actual figures although a separate statement within the fund-based financial statements can also be used.

The GASB explains its justification for requiring officials to provide readers of the government's financial statements with an MD&A:

> The basic financial statements should be preceded by MD&A, which is required supplementary information (RSI). MD&A should provide an objective and easily readable analysis of the government's financial activities based on currently known facts, decisions, or conditions. The financial managers of governments are knowledgeable about the transactions, events, and conditions that are reflected in the government's financial report and of the fiscal policies that govern its operations. MD&A provides financial managers with the opportunity to present both a short- and a long-term analysis of the government's activities. MD&A should discuss current-year results in comparison with the prior year, with emphasis on the current year. This fact-based analysis should discuss the positive and negative aspects of the comparison with the prior year. The use of charts, graphs, and tables is encouraged to enhance the understandability of the information.[5]

As an illustration, the 2004 financial statements for the City of Greensboro, North Carolina, begin with a Management's Discussion and Analysis of approximately 20 pages that present information such as this:

> The assets of the City of Greensboro exceeded its liabilities at the close of the fiscal year by $715.2 million (net assets). The City's net assets increased by $9.5 million (1.3%) compared to FY 2003. The governmental net assets increased slightly by $1.7 million (.5%) due to our continuing to provide basic services at higher costs with slowing revenue growth. The business-type net assets increased by $7.8 million (2.3%) primarily due to changes in the City's rate structures and capital contributions to outside agencies.

The general purpose external financial statements outlined previously are presented to the public as part of a comprehensive annual financial report (often referred to as a *CAFR*). The CAFR always includes other extensive information about the reporting government. For example, the 2003 CAFR for the City of Saint Paul, Minnesota, with total revenues of about $435 million, was 234 pages long. In comparison, the 2003 annual report for the Schering-Plough Corporation, with more than $8.3 billion in revenues, was only 50 pages.

GASB Statement 34 stipulates that the CAFR of a state or local government include three broad sections:

1. *Introductory section*—includes a letter of transmittal from appropriate government officials, an organization chart, and a list of principal officers.
2. *Financial section*—presents the general purpose external financial statement and reproduces the auditor's report. The government also usually prepares additional supplementary information such as combining statements to present financial information for funds that do not qualify as major.
3. *Statistical section*—presents a wide range of data about the government.

---

[5] *GASB Statement No. 34,* para. 8 and 9.

THE PRIMARY GOVERNMENT AND COMPONENT UNITS

Primary Government

The primary government serves as the nucleus and focus of the financial reporting entity as defined by GAAP. All state governments and general-purpose local governments automatically should be treated as primary governments.[6]

According to governmental accounting, a reporting entity must produce a comprehensive annual financial report. Each reporting entity starts with a primary government such as a town, city, county, or state. This primary government then must include all funds, activities, organizations, agencies, offices, and departments that are not legally separate from it.

However, states and localities often encounter a unique problem: determining whether certain activities should be presented with the primary government as part of the reporting entity. Except in rare cases, a business enterprise such as IBM or Ford Motor Company simply consolidates all corporations over which it has control. A state or locality, however, can interact with numerous departments, agencies, boards, institutes, commissions, and the like. Should all of these functions be included as either governmental activities or business-type activities within the government's CAFR? If not, what reporting is appropriate?

The almost unlimited number of activities that can be related in some way to a government raises problems for officials attempting to outline the parameters of the entity being reported. Separate organizations such as turnpike commissions, port authorities, public housing boards, and downtown development commissions have become commonplace in recent years. The government created many of these but they remain legally separate from it. Such entities are designed to focus attention on specific issues or problems and can offer better efficiency because of their corporate-style structure.

As an example, in the notes to the financial statements in its 2004 CAFR, the City of Boston, Massachusetts, lists several organizations related to the government but whose financial information had *not* been included with that of the city:

- Boston Housing Authority.
- Boston Industrial Development Financing Authority.
- Boston Water and Sewer Commission.

Conversely, the City of Atlanta, Georgia, at December 31, 2003, indicated several activities that were legally separate from the city government but were still presented within that city's financial information. These activities included

- Atlanta Empowerment Zone Corporation.
- Atlanta Development Authority.
- Atlanta Clean City Commission Fund.

Clearly, these two examples indicate that activities related to a government can be included with or excluded from the information produced by the primary government. Some method of standardization is needed.

Because of the extremely wide variety of possible activities, determining which functions actually comprise a state or locality is not always an easy task. According to paragraphs 2 and 8 of *GASB Statement 14,* "The Financial Reporting Entity," the major criterion for inclusion in a government's comprehensive annual financial report is financial accountability:

Financial reporting based on accountability should enable the financial statement reader to focus on the body of organizations that are related by a common thread of accountability to the constituent citizenry. . . . Elected officials are accountable to those citizens for their public policy decisions, regardless of whether these decisions are carried out directly by the elected officials through the operations of the primary government or *by their designees through the operations of specially created organizations* (emphasis added).

[6] Stephen J. Gauthier, *Governmental Accounting, Auditing, and Financial Reporting—Using the GASB 34 Model* (Chicago: Government Finance Officers Association, 2005), p. 58.

Component Units

Some activities can be legally separate from a primary government but still be so closely connected that their omission from the statements of the primary government cannot be justified. Because of the relationship, the elected officials of the primary government are still financially accountable for these separate organizations known as *component units*. That is why the City of Atlanta, in the previous discussion, included the Atlanta Empowerment Zone Corporation and the other activities in its CAFR; they were viewed as component units.

Despite being legally separate, component units are included within the financial statements of the primary government to indicate that the connection is viewed as close enough to warrant inclusion. Thus, identification of such activities can be quite important. Two sets of criteria have been established. If either set of criteria is met, the activity in question is a component unit to be reported within the CAFR of the primary government. The parameters of the reporting entity have been expanded to include both the primary government and any component units.

Criterion 1

The separate organization is viewed as a component unit if it fiscally depends on the primary organization regardless of the extent of other relationships. As defined, *fiscal dependency* means that the organization cannot do one or more of the following without approval of the primary government: adopt its own budget, levy taxes or set rates, or issue bonded debt.

Criterion 2

First, the officials of the primary government must appoint a voting majority of the governing board of the separate organization. Second, either the primary government must be able to impose its will on the board of the separate organization or the separate organization must provide a financial benefit or impose a financial burden on the primary government.

For example, a state (the primary government) might establish a commission to oversee off-track betting as a separate entity. However, if the state appoints a voting majority of the board membership and the financial benefits from revenues generated by the commission accrue to the state, the commission is considered a component unit of the state for reporting purposes.

Three aspects of the second criterion should be explained to allow for proper application.

Voting Majority of the Governing Board   The authority to elect a voting majority must be substantive. If, for example, the primary government simply confirms the choices that other parties make, financial accountability is not created. In the same way, financial accountability does not result when the primary government selects the governing board from only a limited slate of candidates (such as picking three individuals from an approved list of five). Thus, the primary government must have the actual responsibility of appointing a voting majority of the board before the organization qualifies as a component unit.

Imposition of the Primary Government's Will on the Governing Board   Such power is indicated if the government can significantly influence the programs, projects, activities, or level of services the organization provides. This degree of influence is present if the primary government can remove an appointed board member at will, modify or approve budgets, override decisions of the board, modify or approve rate or fee changes, and hire or dismiss the individuals responsible for day-to-day operations.

Financial Benefit or Financial Burden on the Primary Government   A financial connection exists between the organization and the primary government if the government is entitled to the organization's resources, the government is legally obligated to finance any deficits or provide support, or the government is responsible for the organization's debts.

Reporting Component Units

Component units normally are reported in one of two ways. Many component units are discretely presented at the far right side of the government-wide statements. For example, the 2004 CAFR for the City of Dallas, Texas, shows that the primary government had total revenues of more than $1.4 billion and its discretely presented component units just to the right

Discussion **Question**

IS IT PART OF THE COUNTY?

Harland County is in a financially distressed portion of Missouri. In hopes of enticing business to this area, the state legislature appropriated $3 million to start an industrial development commission. The federal government provided an additional $1 million. The state appointed 15 individuals to a board to oversee the operations of this commission, and county officials named 5 members. The commission began operations by raising funds from local citizens and businesses. It received $700,000 in donations and pledges. The county provided clerical assistance and allowed the commission to use one floor of the county office building for its headquarters. The county government must approve the commission's budget.

During the current period, the commission spent $2.4 million. It achieved notable success as several large manufacturing companies have recently begun to explore the possibility of opening plants in the county.

Harland County is presently beginning the production of its own comprehensive annual financial report. Should it include the revenues, expenditures, assets, expenses, and liabilities of the industrial development commission? Is it part of the county's primary government, a component unit, or a related organization?

Is the industrial development commission a component unit of the State of Missouri? How should its activities be presented in the state's comprehensive annual financial report?

of the primary government had revenues of $219 million. These activities are explained in the notes to the city's financial statements:

> The following legally separate entities are reported as discretely presented component units of the City because the City appoints a voting majority of the boards, approves budgets, and maintains the ability to impose its will on the entities.
>
> - Housing Finance Corporation—organized to issue tax-exempt mortgage revenue bonds to encourage low- to moderate-income citizens' opportunities for single-family residential home ownership.
> - Housing Acquisition and Development Corporation—organized solely and exclusively for the public purpose of providing safe, affordable housing facilities for low- and moderate-income persons.

As an alternative placement, a primary government can include certain component units as if they were part of the government (a process referred to as *blending*). Although the organization is legally separate, it is so intertwined with the primary government that inclusion is necessary to appropriately present the financial information. In discussing the accounting for the Housing and Redevelopment Authority of the City of Saint Paul, the notes to the 2003 financial statements explain that the "following component unit has been presented as a blended component unit because the component unit's governing body is substantively the same as the governing body of the City."

One other aspect of the reporting process should be noted: the possible existence of related organizations. In such cases, the primary government is accountable because it appoints a voting majority of the governing board. However, financial accountability does not exist. Fiscal dependency as defined earlier is not present, and the primary government cannot impose its will on the board or gather financial benefits or burdens from the relationship. Without financial accountability, the organization does not qualify as a component unit to be included in the government's financial reporting. Instead, the primary government must disclose the nature of the relationship. That is the rationale for the disclosure by the City of Boston mentioned earlier in connection with the Boston Housing Authority, the Boston Industrial Development Financing Authority, and the Boston Water and Sewer Commission. Apparently, none of these qualified as a component unit of the city and, therefore, were mentioned only in the notes as related organizations.

Special Purpose Governments

Cities, counties, states, and the like are known as general purpose governments. They provide a wide range of services such as police protection, road repair, and sanitation. They are primary governments, each within its own reporting entity. However, activities that qualify as special purpose governments are also viewed as primary governments for separate reporting purposes.

Thousands of special purpose governments exist throughout the country; they carry out only a single function for the public or a limited number of functions. For example, the 2003 financial statements for the Seattle Popular Monorail Authority state that "financial statement presentation follows accounting principles defined for special-purpose governments." As such, even though it is not a government in the traditional sense, this Authority must follow the accounting and reporting pronouncements of the GASB.

When considering a single activity, such as a monorail authority, independent school system, or water control board, the question arises as to whether it is (1) part of a larger government such as a city or county, (2) a not-for-profit organization, or (3) a special purpose government that produces its own financial statements according to governmental accounting principles.

Any activity or function is deemed a special purpose government if it meets the following three criteria. For example, a school system that satisfies all three is reported as a special purpose government that produces its own financial statements. However, if the school system fails to meet any one of these, its financial condition and operations are likely to be maintained within the General Fund or Special Revenue Funds of a city or county government. To be a special purpose government, the activity or function must

1. Have a separately elected governing body.
2. Be legally independent, which it can demonstrate by having corporate powers such as the right to sue and be sued in its own name as well as the right to buy, sell, and lease property in its own name.
3. Be fiscally independent of other state and local governments.

The term *fiscally independent* used here requires clarification. An activity is normally considered to be fiscally independent if its leadership can determine the activity's budget without having to seek the approval of an outside party, levy taxes or set rates without having to seek outside approval, and issue bonded debt without outside approval.

Thus, the comprehensive annual financial report for the Charlotte-Mecklenburg County, North Carolina, Board of Education shows total expenses for the year ended June 30, 2004, of more than $919 million for this special purpose government. A note to these statements explains why the Board represents a primary government separate from the local general purpose government:

> The Charlotte-Mecklenburg Board of Education (Board) is a separate legal government with responsibility and control over all activities related to public school education in Mecklenburg County, North Carolina. The members of the Board are elected by the public and have decision-making authority. Although the County levies all taxes, the Board determines how the school system will spend the funds generated for schools. The County cannot modify the school system's budget, nor is the County entitled to share in any surpluses or required to finance any deficits of the school system. For these reasons, the Board is not fiscally dependent on the County and therefore is recognized as a primary government.

GOVERNMENT-WIDE AND FUND-BASED FINANCIAL STATEMENTS ILLUSTRATED

At the core of a governmental reporting entity's comprehensive annual financial report are the general purpose financial statements. As described throughout these two chapters, these statements are made up of government-wide financial statements and fund-based financial statements. Government-wide statements present financial information for both governmental activities and business-type activities. These statements measure economic resources and utilize accrual accounting.

The fund-based statements separately present the governmental funds, the proprietary funds, and the fiduciary funds. At the fund level, the measurement focus and the method of accounting depend on the fund in question. For governmental funds, the current financial resources measurement focus is used with modified accrual accounting. However, both proprietary funds and fiduciary funds use accrual accounting to measure economic resources.

The previous chapter briefly outlined four of these statements to introduce the initial coverage. However, now that a deeper understanding of government accounting has been established, you can study these same statements as well as several other fund-based statements in more detail. Having an appreciation for the end result of the accounting process helps to show how the diverse elements of government accounting fit together into a complete reporting package.[7]

Statement of Net Assets—Government-Wide Financial Statements

Exhibit 17.1 presents the June 30, 2004, statement of net assets for the City of Sacramento, California. As a government-wide financial statement, it is designed to report the economic resources of the government as a whole (except for the fiduciary funds, which are not included because those assets must be used for a purpose outside the primary government).

Several aspects of this example of the statement of net assets should be noted specifically:

- All assets including capital assets are reported because the measurement focus is the economic resources controlled by the government. Long-term liabilities are presented for the same reason.

- Capital assets other than land, land improvements, inexhaustible artworks, and construction in progress are reported net of accumulated depreciation because depreciation is required on the government-wide statements. Newly acquired infrastructure assets are included within the capital assets. The remaining historical cost basis of previously acquired infrastructure, if major and acquired or renovated since 1980, has been estimated and capitalized. Infrastructure depreciation is omitted if the modified approach is used.

- The primary government is divided into governmental activities and business-type activities. Governmental funds are found in the governmental activities whereas enterprise funds comprise most, if not all, of the business-type activities. Even though recorded within the proprietary funds, internal service funds are normally included within the governmental activities because those services are rendered primarily to benefit activities within the governmental funds. However, if a particular internal service fund predominantly serves an enterprise fund, that internal service fund should be included as a business-type activity.

- The internal balances shown in the asset section come from interactivity receivables and payables between the governmental activities and the business-type activities. The internal balances reported on this statement offset each other (except for a small $563,000 balance that may well be owed to one of the fiduciary funds) so that no impact affects the total for the primary government.

- Investments are reported at fair value rather than historical cost.

- Discretely presented component units are grouped and shown to the far right side of the statement so that the reported amounts do not affect the primary government figures. However, if any blended component units exist, those balances are included, as appropriate, within either the governmental activities or the business-type activities as if they were individual funds. According to the notes to the City of Sacramento's financial statements, there were three discretely presented component units including the Sacramento Regional Arts Facilities Financing Authority as well as three blended component units such as the Sacramento Housing and Redevelopment Agency.

- Because this is a statement of net assets, the format is not structured to stress that assets are equal to liabilities plus equities as is found in a typical balance sheet. Rather, the assets ($3.77 billion for the primary government) less liabilities of $1.42 billion indicated net assets of $2.35 billion.

---

[7] The examples presented here illustrate the government-wide financial statements and the fund-based financial statements for both governmental funds and proprietary funds. Because they are more specialized, we omit the fund-based statements for the fiduciary funds. However, those other statements can be found at www.cityofsacramento.org/cafr/.

EXHIBIT 17.1   Government-Wide Financial Statements

CITY OF SACRAMENTO
Statement of Net Assets
June 30, 2004
(in thousands)

	Primary Government			
	Governmental Activities	Business-Type Activities	Total	Component Units
Assets				
Cash and investments	$ 585,982	$ 147,416	$ 733,398	$ 229
Receivables, net	271,995	55,233	327,228	6,592
Internal balances	42,491	(43,054)	(563)	—
Inventories	1,024	1,978	3,002	93
Prepaid items	395	69	464	131
Restricted cash and investments	86,787	41,049	127,836	19,152
Deferred charges	6,728	6,190	12,918	3,855
Land and other capital assets not being depreciated	395,157	349,272	744,429	4,954
Other capital assets, net of depreciation	951,941	864,885	1,816,826	74,168
Total assets	2,342,500	1,423,038	3,765,538	119,174
Liabilities				
Securities lending obligations	73,330	28,433	101,763	—
Payables	73,503	21,599	95,102	8,303
Deferred revenue	21,210	1,449	22,659	6
Long-term liabilities:				
Due within one year	56,906	15,984	72,890	320
Due in more than one year	669,774	455,575	1,125,349	114,890
Total liabilities	894,723	523,040	1,417,763	123,519
Net Assets				
Invested in capital assets, net of related debt	1,135,271	782,620	1,917,891	(10,449)
Restricted for:				
Capital projects	110,794	—	110,794	—
Debt service	11,508	—	11,508	3,493
Housing and redevelopment	273,473	3,421	276,894	—
Trust and endowments:				
Expendable	4,962	—	4,962	—
Nonexpendable	1,927	—	1,927	—
Other	21,394	—	21,394	881
Unrestricted (deficit)	(111,552)	113,957	2,405	1,730
Total net assets	$1,447,777	$ 899,998	$2,347,775	$ (4,345)

- As the final section shows, several amounts within the Net Assets have been restricted for capital projects, debt service, and the like. Restrictions are shown in this manner only if usage of the assets has been restricted either by creditors, grantors, or other external party, or because of laws passed through constitutional provisions or enabling legislation.
- Although not restricted, the amount of net assets tied up in capital assets less any related debt is reported as a separate figure within the Net Assets section.

Statement of Activities—Government-Wide Financial Statements

The statement of activities is one of the most important governmental financial statements because of the wide array of information that it presents. As the statement for the City of

Sacramento, California, in Exhibit 17.2 shows, the same general classification system of governmental activities, business-type activities, and component units used in Exhibit 17.1 provides the basis for reporting revenues and expenses. However, the format is much more complex and requires close analysis.

- Operating expenses are presented in the first column. They are not classified according to individual causes such as salaries, rent, depreciation, or insurance. Instead, all expenses are shown by function, which is more relevant to readers: general government, police, fire, public works, and the like. As paragraph 41 of *GASB Statement 14* states, "as a minimum, governments should report direct expenses for each function. Direct expenses are those that are specifically associated with a service, program, or department and, thus, are clearly identifiable to a particular function."

- Interest expense on general long-term debt is normally an indirect expense because it benefits many government operations. However, because of its size, informational value, and difficulty of allocation, this expense frequently is shown as in Exhibit 17.2 as a separate "function."

- After operating and indirect expenses have been determined for each function (governmental activities, business-type activities, and component units), related program revenues are reported in the next three columns. Program revenues are those revenues derived from the function itself or from outsiders seeking to reduce the government's cost. As Exhibit 17.2 shows, program revenues are classified as

  1. *Charges for services.* For example, a monthly charge is normally assessed for water service; therefore, the first business-type activity shows more than $45.9 million in program revenues. Most government functions generate some small amount of monetary charges such as parking meter revenues, fines for speeding tickets, concessions at parks, and the like.
  2. *Operating grants and contributions.* This column reports amounts received from grants and similar sources that were designated for some type of operating purpose. For example, $25.9 million in operating grants and contributions is shown for housing and development.
  3. *Capital grants and contributions.* This column shows grants and similar sources when the resources were designated for capital asset additions.

- After expenses have been assigned to each function and related program revenues, a net (expense) or revenue figure can be determined for each function. This net figure provides a measure of the cost of the various operations of the government. As explained in paragraph 38 of *GASB Statement 14,* "an objective of using the net (expense) revenue format is to report the relative financial burden of each of the reporting government's functions on its taxpayers." For example, in Exhibit 17.2, the City of Sacramento shows that the police department had more than $106 million in operating expenses but generated program revenues of only $17 million from charges for services and operating grants and contributions. Thus, as disclosed on this statement, the taxpayers of that city had to bear the financial burden for police protection of more than $89 million. That cost should be important information to any citizen reading these statements. In contrast, the water system reported operating and indirect expenses of $48 million, but its charges, grants, and contributions totaled $56 million. Thus, this business-type activity generated net revenues of $8 million that served as a benefit for the government during this period.

- Net expenses and revenues can be determined in total for each category of the government. In this example, all governmental activities combined to report net expenses of more than $145 million while the business-type activities generated net revenues of approximately $4 million. The two component units reported net expenses of almost $6 million.

- Again, the internal service funds have been combined with the governmental activities (or with the business-type activities if that is more appropriate). The revenues and expenses should be assigned to the appropriate functions. For example, the cost of work done by an internal service fund created to assist the work of economic development should be assigned to that function.

EXHIBIT 17.2 Government-Wide Financial Statements

CITY OF SACRAMENTO
Statement of Activities
For the Fiscal Year Ended June 30, 2004
(in thousands)

Functions/Programs	Operating Expenses	Indirect Expenses Allocation	Program Revenues: Charges for Services	Operating Grants and Contributions	Capital Grants and Contributions	Net (Expense) Revenue — Primary Government: Governmental Activities	Business-Type Activities	Total	Component Units
Primary government:									
Governmental activities:									
General government	$ 34,058	$(7,319)	$ 4,766	$ —	$ 596	$ (21,377)		$ (21,377)	
Police	106,676	—	3,126	14,459	—	(89,091)		(89,091)	
Fire	57,799	—	5,022	1,374	—	(51,403)		(51,403)	
Public works	110,458	(2,045)	39,942	8,899	184,337	124,765		124,765	
Economic development	4,283	—	212	—	1,372	(2,699)		(2,699)	
Convention, culture, and leisure	6,823	—	4,526	703	62	(1,532)		(1,532)	
Parks and recreation	41,486	—	4,193	8,256	13,838	(15,199)		(15,199)	
Planning and building	18,780	—	17,600	250	—	(930)		(930)	
Neighborhood services	6,883	—	2,755	—	—	(4,128)		(4,128)	
Housing and redevelopment	46,774	—	1,389	25,880	3,706	(15,799)		(15,799)	
Library	8,185	—	376	—	—	(8,185)		(8,185)	
Nondepartmental	32,725	(252)	376	—	1,044	(31,053)		(31,053)	
Interest on long-term debt	29,306	—	—	—	—	(29,306)		(29,306)	
Total governmental activities	504,236	(9,616)	83,907	59,821	204,955	(145,937)		(145,937)	
Business-type activities:									
Water	45,163	2,680	45,994	—	9,925		$ 8,076	8,076	
Sewer	11,927	807	15,304	—	504		3,074	3,074	
Storm drainage	25,208	1,802	30,086	—	8,163		11,239	11,239	
Solid waste	33,174	2,928	38,423	836	—		3,157	3,157	
Community center	18,029	281	5,843	—	—		(12,467)	(12,467)	
Parking	13,016	564	16,210	—	—		2,630	2,630	
Advanced life support	7,823	—	11,035	—	—		3,212	3,212	
Golf	6,502	344	6,329	—	—		(517)	(517)	
Child development	4,492	—	4,361	573	—		442	442	

continued from page 774

	Expenses	Charges for Services	Operating Grants and Contributions	Capital Grants and Contributions	Governmental Activities	Business-type Activities	Total	Component Units
Marina	1,446	210	—	—		55	55	
Housing and redevelopment	123,892	—	10,899	98,173		(14,820)	(14,820)	
Total business-type activities	290,872	9,616	186,195	99,592		18,592	4,081	4,081
Total primary government	$794,908	$—	$270,102	$159,403		$223,547	$(141,856)	
Component units:								
Sacramento Hotel Corporation	$35,061	$29,910	$—	$—				$(5,151)
Sacramento Regional Arts Facilities Financing Authority	770	—	—	—				(770)
Total component units	$35,831	$29,910	$—	$—				$(5,921)

	Governmental Activities	Business-type Activities	Total	Component Units
Change in net assets:				
Net (expense) revenue	$(145,937)	$ 4,081	$ (141,856)	$(5,921)
General revenues:				
Taxes:				
Property taxes	63,877	—	63,877	—
Redevelopment tax increment	35,314	—	35,314	—
Utility user taxes	52,538	—	52,538	—
Other taxes	25,984	13,436	39,420	—
Sales taxes shared state revenue	61,822	—	61,822	—
State of California in-lieu	27,179	—	27,179	—
Grants and other intergovernmental revenue not restricted to specific programs	4,137	—	4,137	—
Investment earnings	18,290	2,437	20,727	578
Contributions to permanent fund	124	—	124	—
Miscellaneous	6,966	676	7,642	—
Transfers	(25,546)	25,546	—	—
Total general revenues and transfers	270,685	42,095	312,780	578
Change in net assets	124,748	46,176	170,924	(5,343)
Net assets, beginning of year	1,322,947	853,947	2,176,894	998
Prior period adjustments	82	(125)	(43)	—
Net assets, beginning of year, as restated	1,323,029	853,822	2,176,851	998
Net assets, end of year	$1,447,777	$899,998	$2,347,775	$(4,345)

EXHIBIT 17.3 Fund-Based Financial Statements

CITY OF SACRAMENTO
Balance Sheet
Governmental Funds
June 30, 2004 (in thousands)

	General Fund	SHRA Capital Projects Fund	SHRA Special Revenue Fund	1997 Lease Revenue Bond Fund	Transportation and Development Fund	Other Governmental Funds	Total Governmental Funds
Assets							
Cash and investments held by City	$155,284	$129,549	$29,222	$ —	$72,465	$166,805	$553,325
Cash and investments held by fiscal agent	—	—	—	$110	—	1,163	1,273
Receivables, net:							
Taxes	18,645	—	1,856	—	—	7,630	28,131
Accounts	14,389	166	939	—	541	9,839	25,874
Loans	1,823	46,729	45,918	72,710	—	1,864	169,044
Intergovernmental	—	1,444	2,876	—	6,617	21,837	32,774
Interest	595	—	—	957	109	691	2,352
Due from other funds	—	16,777	2,095	—	—	212	19,084
Inventories	233	—	—	—	—	8	241
Prepaid items	381	—	—	—	14	—	395
Restricted assets:							
Cash and investments held by City	—	1,953	2,446	—	—	71,977	76,376
Cash and investments held by fiscal agent	—	—	—	—	—	9,903	9,903
Advances to other funds	400	7,825	11,187	1,295	—	3,113	23,820
Totals assets	$191,750	$204,443	$96,539	$75,072	$79,746	$295,042	$942,592
Liabilities and Fund Balances:							
Securities lending obligations	$ 34,134	$ —	$ —	$ —	$ 6,268	$ 30,390	$ 70,792
Accounts payable	22,106	1,501	8,798	—	1,660	16,450	50,515
Due to other funds	—	1,177	364	—	5,547	13,921	21,009
Matured bonds and interest payable	—	—	—	—	—	542	542

continued from page 776

Deposits	171	267	961	—	861	6,726	8,986
Deferred revenue	11,025	672	63,340	73,667	7,251	37,691	193,646
Advances from other funds	836	1,008	1,257	—	—	3,892	6,993
Total liabilities	68,272	4,625	74,720	73,667	21,587	109,612	352,483
Fund Balances:							
Reserved:							
For noncurrent assets	1,200	54,453	7,427	1,295	—	4,977	69,352
For encumbrances	12,410	14,706	375	—	6,510	49,020	83,021
For debt service	—	1,957	2,285	—	—	19,243	23,485
For housing/redevelopment	—	87	1,323	—	—	—	1,410
For trust obligations	—	—	—	—	—	1,927	1,927
Unreserved:							
Designated for economic uncertainty	29,150	—	—	—	—	—	29,150
Designated for capital projects	20,143	123,766	—	—	24,381	—	168,290
Designated for future PERS costs	20,300	—	—	—	—	—	20,300
Designated for disaster recovery	4,000	—	—	—	—	—	4,000
Designated for grant match	2,200	—	—	—	—	—	2,200
Designated for subsequent years' expenditures	22,829	—	—	110	4,471	—	27,410
Undesignated	11,246	4,849	10,409	—	22,797	—	49,301
Unreserved, reported in:							
Special revenue funds	—	—	—	—	—	14,913	14,913
Debt service funds	—	—	—	—	—	6,448	6,448
Capital projects funds	—	—	—	—	—	86,196	86,196
Permanent funds	—	—	—	—	—	2,706	2,706
Total fund balances	123,478	199,818	21,819	1,405	58,159	185,430	590,109
Total liabilities and fund balances	$191,750	$204,443	$96,539	$75,072	$79,746	$295,042	$942,592

- General revenues are reported at the bottom of the statement as additions to either the governmental activities, business-type activities, or component units. All taxes are general revenues because they do not reflect a charge for services; they are obtained from the population as a whole. In addition, such transactions as unrestricted grants and investment income fall under this same category.

- Transfers of $25,546,000 during the year between governmental activities and business-type activities are also shown under the general revenues, but they are offset, so they create no impact on the total that the primary government reports.

Balance Sheet—Governmental Funds—Fund-Based Statements

Switching now to the fund-based financial statements, Exhibit 17.3 presents a balance sheet for the governmental funds recorded by the City of Sacramento. This statement measures only current financial resources and uses modified accrual accounting for timing purposes. No proprietary funds, component units, or fiduciary funds are included; the statement reflects just the governmental funds. Several parts of this statement should be noted:

- A separate column must be shown for the General Fund and any other major fund monitored within the governmental funds. The city has identified four funds as major including both the Capital Projects Fund and the Special Revenue Fund associated with the Sacramento Housing and Redevelopment Agency (SHRA). The government can classify any fund as major if officials believe it is particularly important to statement users. However, as mentioned in the previous chapter, a fund is considered major and must be reported separately if it meets two criteria:

  1. Total assets, liabilities, revenues, or expenses/expenditures of the fund are at least 10 percent of the corresponding total for all such funds.

  2. Total assets, liabilities, revenues, or expenses/expenditures of the fund are at least 5 percent of the corresponding total for all governmental funds and enterprise funds combined.

  All funds that are not considered to be major are combined and reported as "Other Governmental Funds."

- This balance sheet reports no capital assets or long-term debts because only current financial resources are being measured.

- Totals for the governmental funds appear in the final column. However, internal balances such as "due from other funds" (a receivable) and "due to other funds" (a liability) have not been offset. Thus, the governmental totals are just mathematical summations, not consolidated balances.

- In the Fund Balances section of this balance sheet, both "reserved" and "designated" amounts are shown. The word *reserved* indicates that some portion of the assets being reported (such as inventory) cannot be spent or has been separated for legal reasons. In contrast, designated figures disclose tentative plans that are subject to change in the future.

- The total Fund Balances figure for the governmental funds of $590.1 million is significantly different from the $1,447.8 million in total net assets reported for governmental activities as a whole in the statement of net assets (Exhibit 17.1). To help understand that large discrepancy, a reconciliation is included along with the balance sheet (titled Reconciliation of the Balance Sheet to the Statement of Net Assets—Governmental Funds). Because of space considerations, the reconciliation reported by the City of Sacramento has not been included in these examples, but can be found at www.cityofsacramento.org/cafr/. According to this reconciliation, the four largest items that formed the link between the governmental activities of the government-wide financial statements and the governmental funds of the fund-based financial statements follow:

  1. More than $1.2 billion of capital assets reported by the governmental activities on the government-wide financial statements were omitted on the comparable fund-based financial statement.

  2. Revenues of $170 million had not been recognized in the fund-based statements because the financial resources were not viewed as being available in the current period.

3. Long-term liabilities of approximately $655 million were reported only on the government-wide financial statements because they did not represent claims to current financial resources.

4. Internal service funds with net assets of $44 million were included in the governmental activities although, for fund-based financial statements, they were classified as proprietary funds.

Statement of Revenues, Expenditures, and Changes in Fund Balances—Governmental Funds—Fund-Based Statements

Exhibit 17.4 shows a statement of revenues, expenditures, and changes in fund balances for the governmental funds. Once again, the General Fund is detailed in a separate column along with each of the major funds previously identified in the balance sheet in Exhibit 17.3. All remaining nonmajor funds are then accumulated and shown together.

In examining Exhibit 17.4, note each of the following:

- Revenues are not separately identified as either program revenues or general revenues as was the case in Exhibit 17.2. For that reason, no net revenue or expense figure is determined for each of the functions such as general government or public safety.

- Because the current financial resources measurement focus is being utilized, expenditures rather than expenses are being reported. For example, Capital Outlay is presented here but would not have been appropriate on the statement of activities. In the same way, Debt Service—Principal is reported on the statement in Exhibit 17.4 as an expenditure.

- Because the modified accrual method of accounting is used for timing purposes, reported amounts will be different than previously shown. For example, total expenditures for interest and fiscal charges are listed on Exhibit 17.4 as $34,945,000 whereas interest on long-term debt disclosed in Exhibit 17.2 is $29,306,000. The difference results because the first figure measures expenditures during the period using modified accrual accounting and the second figure is the amount of expense recognized according to accrual accounting.

- This statement presents other financing sources and uses to reflect the issuance of long-term debt, the sale of property, and transfers made between the funds. Because the fund-based statements are designed to present individual fund activities rather than government-wide figures, no elimination of the transfers is made.

- A reconciliation should be shown between the ending change in governmental fund balances (an increase of $76,332,000) in Exhibit 17.4 and the ending change in net assets for governmental activities in Exhibit 17.2 (an increase of $124,748,000). Because of space considerations, that reconciliation is not presented here although it would be required in the general purpose external financial statements. For the City of Sacramento, the major differences shown on this reconciliation involved the acquisition of capital assets, the recording of depreciation, the recording of revenues that did not provide current financial resources, the issuance of long-term debt, and the repayment of long-term debt.

Statement of Net Assets—Proprietary Funds—Fund-Based Statements

The assets and liabilities of the proprietary funds of the City of Sacramento, as found in the fund-based financial statements, are presented in Exhibit 17.5. This statement shows information about six individual enterprise funds separately, with a single total column for all other enterprise funds. In addition, it presents a column to provide a total for all of these business-type activities. In this way, specific information is available for the water fund, sewer fund, storm drainage fund, solid waste fund, community center fund, and SHRA enterprise fund as well as the total for all enterprise funds.

In examining Exhibit 17.5, a considerable amount of other significant information should be noted:

- This statement also combines and exhibits the internal service funds because they are proprietary funds. However, government-wide financial statements usually report these same internal service funds as part of the governmental activities.

EXHIBIT 17.4 Fund-Based Financial Statements

CITY OF SACRAMENTO
Statement of Revenues, Expenditures, and Changes in Fund Balances
Governmental Funds
For the Fiscal Year Ended June 30, 2004 (in thousands)

	General Fund	SHRA Capital Projects Fund	SHRA Special Revenue Fund	1997 Lease Revenue Bond Fund	Transportation and Development Fund	Other Governmental Funds	Total Governmental Funds
Revenues:							
Taxes	$207,860	—	$7,160	—	$ 5,876	$28,154	$249,050
Intergovernmental	32,488	$6,268	21,593	—	30,992	45,893	137,234
Charges for services	38,850	—	1,389	—	4,407	580	45,226
Fines, forfeits, and penalties	5,795	—	—	—	1,428	—	7,223
Interest, rents, and concessions	2,199	1,818	2,111	$ 585	1,094	6,191	13,998
Community service fees	—	—	—	—	269	45,667	45,936
Assessment levies	—	—	—	—	—	17,387	17,387
Contributions from property owners	—	—	—	5,448	—	49,488	54,936
Donations	—	—	—	—	—	215	215
Miscellaneous	546	891	1,546	—	93	22	3,098
Total revenues	287,738	8,977	33,799	6,033	44,159	193,597	574,303
Expenditures:							
Current:							
General government	24,006	—	—	—	—	497	24,503
Police	95,293	—	—	—	13	9,783	105,089
Fire	55,649	—	—	—	—	1,337	56,986
Public works	14,700	—	—	—	16,051	17,715	48,466
Utilities	274	—	—	—	—	—	274
Economic development	2,361	—	—	—	—	—	2,361
Convention, culture, and leisure	3,617	—	—	—	—	1,212	4,829

continued from page 780

Parks and recreation	19,715	—	—	—	—	17,452	37,167
Planning and building	16,808	—	—	—	502	250	17,560
Neighborhood services	6,883	—	—	—	—	—	6,883
Library	7,636	—	—	—	—	—	7,636
Housing and redevelopment	—	17,086	30,145	—	—	—	47,231
Nondepartmental	21,462	—	—	—	57	4,817	26,336
Capital outlay	13,305	7,832	3,373	—	29,426	102,156	156,092
Debt service:							
Principal	171	1,008	2,113	395	—	34,207	37,894
Interest and fiscal charges	147	1,691	2,038	5,053	—	26,016	34,945
Total expenditures	282,027	27,617	37,669	5,448	46,049	215,442	614,252
Excess (deficiency) of revenues over (under) expenditures	5,711	(18,640)	(3,870)	585	(1,890)	(21,845)	(39,949)
Other financing sources (uses):							
Transfers in	29,046	15,351	3,774	—	4,289	38,492	90,952
Transfer out	(26,501)	(6,578)	(3,662)	—	(1,676)	(76,160)	(114,577)
Issuance of long-term debt	1,363	48,135	1,720	—	—	86,218	137,436
Discount on long-term debt	—	(616)	—	—	—	(629)	(1,245)
Proceeds from sale of property	—	167	6,260	—	—	6,427	6,427
Payment to refunded bond escrow	—	—	(686)	—	—	(2,026)	(2,712)
Total other financing sources (uses)	3,908	56,459	7,406	585	2,613	45,895	116,281
Net change in fund balances	9,619	37,819	3,536	585	723	24,050	76,332
Fund balances, beginning of year	113,859	161,999	18,811	820	57,436	161,380	514,305
Prior period adjustments	—	—	(528)	—	—	—	(528)
Fund balances, beginning of year, as restated	113,859	161,999	18,283	820	57,436	161,380	513,777
Fund balances, end of year	$123,478	$199,818	$21,819	$1,405	$58,159	$185,430	$590,109

EXHIBIT 17.5 Fund-Based Financial Statements

CITY OF SACRAMENTO
Statement of Net Assets
Proprietary Funds
June 30, 2004
(in thousands)

	Business-Type Activities—Enterprise Funds								Governmental Activities—Internal Service Funds
	Water Fund	Sewer Fund	Storm Drainage Fund	Solid Waste Fund	Community Center Fund	SHRA Enterprise Fund	Other Enterprise Funds	Total	
Assets									
Current assets:									
Cash and investments held by City	$ 53,516	$ 14,432	$ 32,784	—	$ 4,371	$ 4,673	$ 35,493	$ 145,269	$ 31,268
Cash and investments held by fiscal agent	—	—	130	—	514	—	271	915	116
Receivables, net:									
Taxes	—	—	—	—	1,877	—	—	1,877	—
Accounts	5,928	5,075	4,817	6,856	443	472	2,676	26,267	171
Loans	502	101	302	—	—	—	—	905	—
Intergovernmental	302	264	209	398	—	12,987	—	14,160	52
Interest	319	72	191	—	114	—	101	797	44
Due from other funds	—	—	—	—	—	409	—	409	16,122
Inventories	1,435	79	202	—	—	262	—	1,978	783
Prepaid items	—	—	—	43	2	24	—	69	95
Total current assets	62,002	20,023	38,635	7,297	7,321	18,827	38,541	192,646	48,651
Noncurrent assets:									
Restricted assets:									
Cash and investments held by City	18,505	289	868	4,321	—	1,771	2,203	27,957	508
Cash and investments held by fiscal agent	—	—	765	—	9,804	—	2,523	13,092	—
Investments	—	—	1,232	—	—	—	—	1,232	—
Advances to other funds	—	—	—	—	—	1,000	200	1,200	15,697
Loans receivable	3,256	1,943	5,830	—	56	142	—	11,227	11,618
Deferred charges	2,832	—	70	646	1,928	—	714	6,190	67
Capital assets:									
Land	644	1,137	8,059	1,133	21,739	16,486	12,570	61,768	979
Buildings and improvements	26,718	14,906	7,995	31,191	109,981	240,966	82,841	514,598	6,250
Machinery and equipment	4,404	1,905	9,815	720	2,646	4,506	3,011	27,007	3,563
Vehicles	274	487	599	817	—	—	—	2,177	87,680
Transmission and distribution system	260,045	89,928	262,192	—	—	—	3,622	615,787	—
Construction in progress	187,845	15,456	72,854	2,198	69	2,415	6,667	287,504	1,175

continued from page 782

Less: accumulated depreciation	(51,665)	(294,684)	(30,074)	(64,184)	(32,946)	(7,230)	(49,915)	(30,626)	(79,709)
Total noncurrent assets	75,872	1,275,055	84,277	203,102	113,277	33,796	320,364	95,425	424,814
Total assets	124,523	1,467,701	122,818	221,929	120,598	41,093	358,999	115,448	486,816
Liabilities									
Current liabilities:									
Securities lending obligations	2,538	28,433	4,283	—	—	—	6,764	2,865	14,521
Accounts payable and accrued expenses	6,508	17,015	2,797	669	995	1,704	1,472	3,632	5,746
Accrued compensated absences	1,674	370	67	—	22	61	85	31	104
Due to other funds	—	15,011	91	13,426	—	1,494	—	—	838
Interest payable	21	3,378	648	—	1,167	124	471	130	—
Liability for landfill closure	—	760	—	—	—	760	—	—	—
Deposits	—	1,205	89	1,116	—	—	—	—	—
Deferred revenue	505	1,449	332	128	821	167	1	—	—
Accrued claims	19,346	—	—	—	—	—	—	—	—
Revenue and other bonds payable, net, current portion	236	9,252	1,245	—	4,194	503	240	—	3,070
Certificates of participation payable, net, current portion	—	28	—	—	28	—	—	—	—
Notes payable, current portion	—	5,575	184	3,050	—	—	1,756	585	—
Total current liabilities	30,828	82,476	9,736	18,389	7,227	4,813	10,789	7,243	24,279
Noncurrent liabilities:									
Accrued compensated absences	2,180	6,801	1,045	—	505	1,072	1,663	582	1,934
Advances from other funds	2,295	29,652	6,103	15,011	8,538	—	—	—	—
Accrued claims	40,150	15,189	—	—	—	—	—	—	—
Liability for landfill closure	—	—	—	—	—	15,189	—	—	—
Revenue and other bonds payable, net	5,281	371,834	51,933	—	93,325	25,987	8,222	—	192,367
Certificates of participation payable, net	—	15	—	—	15	—	—	—	—
Notes payable	—	61,736	6,687	10,119	—	—	33,697	11,233	—
Total noncurrent liabilities	49,906	485,227	65,768	25,130	102,383	42,248	43,582	11,815	194,301
Total liabilities	80,734	567,703	75,504	43,519	109,610	47,061	54,371	19,058	218,580
Net Assets									
Invested in capital assets, net of related debt	42,437	782,620	19,188	172,110	12,564	5,926	268,846	81,534	222,452
Restricted for:									
Housing and redevelopment	508	3,421	—	3,421	—	—	—	—	—
Nonrestricted (deficit)	844	113,957	28,126	2,879	(1,576)	(11,894)	35,782	14,856	45,784
Total net assets (deficit)	$43,789	$899,998	$47,314	$178,410	$10,988	$(5,968)	$304,628	$96,390	$268,236

- Because the proprietary funds utilize accrual accounting to measure economic resources, the totals for the business-type activities in Exhibit 17.5 agree in most ways with the total figures in Exhibit 17.1. The amount of detail, however, is more extensive in the fund-based financial statements. For example, the statement in Exhibit 17.1 uses only two accounts to describe capital assets whereas Exhibit 17.5 uses seven accounts.

- The Internal Balance amounts (interactivity receivables and payables) of $43,054,000, which were reported in Exhibit 17.1 within the Assets section so that they could be offset, are reported in Exhibit 17.5 separately in the Assets section as Due from Other Funds and Advances to Other Funds and in the liabilities section as Due to Other Funds and Advances from Other Funds. However, none of these four figures is eliminated; all four are reported in the Total column. That is the reason that the total assets and the total liabilities reported in Exhibit 17.1 for the business-type activities differ from the reported figures shown in Exhibit 17.5 for the enterprise funds.

- Restricted cash and investments of more than $41 million are listed under Noncurrent assets. An external source or specific laws must have designated the use of this money in some manner.

Statement of Revenues, Expenses, and Changes in Fund Net Assets—Proprietary Funds—Fund-Based Statements

Just as the statement of net assets in Exhibit 17.5 provides individual information about specific enterprise funds (and the total for the internal service funds), the statement of revenues, expenses, and changes in fund net assets in Exhibit 17.6 gives the revenues and expenses for those same funds. In Exhibit 17.2, operating and indirect expenses of the water fund totaled $47,843,000. Exhibit 17.6 delineates this amount more completely within several categories: employee services, $14,970,000; services and supplies, $15,310,000; depreciation, $7,155,000; interest expense, $10,307,000; and amortization of deferred charges, $101,000. Because this statement reflects all changes in the activity's net assets, it also reports both capital contributions and transfers.

Statement of Cash Flows—Proprietary Funds—Fund-Based Statements

One of the most interesting of the fund-based financial statements is the statement of cash flows for the proprietary funds (see Exhibit 17.7). Because the proprietary funds operate in a manner similar to for-profit businesses, information about cash flows is considered as vital as it is for Intel and Coca-Cola. In addition, this information is not already available within the government-wide financial statements.

As compared to a for-profit business, the statement of cash flows shown here for the proprietary funds has four sections rather than just three:

1. Cash flows from operating activities.
2. Cash flows from noncapital financing activities.
3. Cash flows from capital and related financing activities.
4. Cash flows from investing activities.

- The presentation of cash flows from operating activities is very similar to that prepared by a for-profit business. However, the direct method of reporting operating activities is required. In for-profit accounting, the direct method is recommended but not mandatory; thus, the indirect method is frequently encountered. It is not allowed in governmental accounting.

- Cash flows from noncapital financing activities should include (1) proceeds and payments on debt *not* attributable to the acquisition or construction of capital assets and (2) grants and subsidies *not* restricted for capital purposes or operating activities.

- Cash flows from capital and related financing activities focus on the amounts spent on capital assets and the source of that funding. Exhibit 17.7 shows typical examples: proceeds from issuance of debt, capital contributions (from the governmental funds), acquisition and construction of capital assets, principal payments on capital debt, and the like.

- Cash flows from investing activities disclose amounts paid and received from investments.

REPORTING PUBLIC COLLEGES AND UNIVERSITIES

At times in the past, public colleges and universities such as The Ohio State University and the University of Kansas have been in a somewhat awkward position in terms of financial accounting. Private schools including Harvard, Duke, and Stanford follow the pronouncements of the FASB, especially those created for private not-for-profit organizations. FASB statements issued on contributions and the form of financial statements have provided a significant amount of official guidance for the financial information that these private institutions report. As will be discussed extensively in the following chapter, the reporting standards developed for not-for-profit organizations have progressed greatly over the last few years.

In contrast, the GASB has retained primary authority over the reporting of public colleges and universities. Much of the GASB's work, however, has been directed at improving the accounting standards utilized by state and local government units. Consequently, until recently the evolution of financial statements for public schools has lagged behind that for other types of reporting.

For decades the question of whether the financial statements of public colleges and universities should be any different from those of private schools has been the subject of much theoretical discussion. Generally, the operations of public colleges differ in at least two important ways from private schools: First, the state or other governments directly provide a significant amount of funding (at least for qualifying students), lessening the reliance on tuition charges. For example, information provided with the 2004 financial statements of Utah State University disclosed state appropriations of more than $146 million and federal grants and contracts of approximately $143 million during the year in comparison to revenues of only $56 million from tuition and fees (after scholarship allowances).

Second, because of the ability to generate money each year from the government, public schools often raise and accumulate a smaller amount of endowment funds than private schools. Private schools usually try to build a large endowment to ensure financial security; this is not always necessary at a public school backed by the state or another government. That is one of the main reasons that at June 30, 2004, Princeton University held investments with a fair value of nearly $10.5 billion, an amount almost beyond the comprehension of officials at most public colleges.

The question of whether these and other differences warrant unique financial statements for public colleges and universities should be raised. In many ways, public and private schools are very much alike: They both educate students, charge tuition and other fees, conduct scholarly research, maintain libraries and sports teams, operate cafeterias and museums, and the like. What measurement basis should be applied and what should be the form of the financial statements to reflect the financial activity and position of a public college or university? These questions are especially relevant because of the frustration about the utilization of such statements: "The Board has found that few resource providers—especially citizens and legislators—or others with an interest in the financial activities of public colleges and universities read the institutions' external financial reports."[8]

Four alternatives have been suggested for the proper construction of the financial statements that public colleges and universities should prepare and distribute:

1. Simply adopt the FASB's requirements for private not-for-profit organizations so that all colleges and universities (public and private) prepare comparable financial statements. As the

---

[8] *GASB Statement 35,* "Basic Financial Statements—and Management's Discussion and Analysis—for Public Colleges and Universities—An Amendment of *GASB Statement 34,*" para. 25.

EXHIBIT 17.6 Fund-Based Financial Statements

CITY OF SACRAMENTO
Statement of Revenues, Expenses, and Changes in Fund Net Assets
Proprietary Funds
For the Fiscal Year Ended June 30, 2004
(in thousands)

	Business-Type Activities—Enterprise Funds								Governmental Activities—Internal Service Funds
	Water Fund	Sewer Fund	Storm Drainage Fund	Solid Waste Fund	Community Center Fund	SHRA Enterprise Fund	Other Enterprise Funds	Total	
Operating revenues:									
Charges for services:									
User fees and charges	$ 44,178	$14,312	$ 29,936	$37,336	$ 1,948	$ 276	$36,965	$164,951	$53,572
Rents and concessions		—	—	56	3,790	9,792	2,485	16,123	—
Charge to Regional Sanitation District for operating and maintaining treatment plant		962						962	
Miscellaneous	1,791	26	109	1,020	105	1,458	196	4,705	710
Total operating revenues	45,969	15,300	30,045	38,412	5,843	11,526	39,646	186,741	54,282
Operating expenses:									
Employee services	14,970	5,522	13,782	12,230	4,695	10,555	15,479	77,233	12,281
Services and supplies	15,310	4,142	3,717	21,192	4,371	24,130	12,655	85,517	17,840
Housing assistance payments						82,176		82,176	—
Depreciation	7,155	2,755	7,977	1,149	2,541	6,099	2,442	30,118	8,984
Insurance premiums									1,923
Claims expense									22,858
Total operating expenses	37,435	12,419	25,476	34,571	11,607	122,960	30,576	275,044	63,886
Operating income (loss)	8,534	2,881	4,569	3,841	(5,764)	(111,434)	9,070	(88,303)	(9,604)

786

continued from page 786

Nonoperating revenues (expenses):

Interest and investment revenue	576	150	408	89	514	150	550	2,437	1,337
Transient occupancy taxes	—	—	—	—	13,436	—	—	13,436	—
Revenue from other agencies	—	—	—	836	—	98,173	573	99,582	—
Interest expense	(10,307)	(315)	(1,530)	(1,506)	(6,571)	(932)	(3,786)	(24,947)	(264)
Amortization of deferred charges	(101)	—	(4)	(25)	(132)	—	(35)	(297)	(2)
Gain or (loss) on disposition of fixed assets	25	4	41	11	—	49	—	130	195
Total nonoperating revenues (expenses)	(9,807)	(161)	(1,085)	(595)	7,247	97,440	(2,698)	90,341	1,266
Income (loss) before contributions and transfers	(1,273)	2,720	3,484	3,246	1,483	(13,994)	6,372	2,038	(8,338)
Capital contributions	9,925	504	8,163	—	—	7,674	—	26,266	1,589
Transfers in	3,207	215	29,683	—	1,344	2,971	306	37,726	5,753
Transfers out	(4,554)	(1,556)	(3,269)	(4,082)	(1,479)	(2,535)	(2,379)	(19,854)	—
Changes in net assets	7,305	1,883	38,061	(836)	1,348	(5,884)	4,299	46,176	(996)
Total net assets (deficit), beginning of year	260,931	94,507	266,567	(5,132)	9,640	184,419	43,015	853,947	44,785
Prior period adjustments	—	—	—	—	—	(125)	—	(125)	—
Total net assets, beginning of year, as restated	260,931	94,507	266,567	(5,132)	9,640	184,294	43,015	853,822	44,785
Total net assets (deficit), end of year	$268,236	$96,390	$304,628	$(5,968)	$10,988	$178,410	$47,314	$899,998	$43,789

EXHIBIT 17.7 Fund-Based Financial Statements

CITY OF SACRAMENTO
Statement of Cash Flows
Proprietary Funds
For the Fiscal Year Ended June 30, 2004
(in thousands)

	Business-Type Activities—Enterprise Funds								Governmental Activities—Internal Service Funds
	Water Fund	Sewer Fund	Storm Drainage Fund	Solid Waste Fund	Community Center Fund	SHRA Enterprise Fund	Other Enterprise Funds	Total	
Cash flows from operating activities:									
Receipts from customers and users	$ 45,897	$15,526	$ 30,164	$ 38,264	$ 5,907	$ 11,926	$39,752	$187,436	$ 82,242
Receipts from interfund services provided	—	—	—	—	—	—	—	—	—
Payments to suppliers	(22,212)	(3,897)	(3,836)	(21,969)	(4,295)	(21,463)	(12,382)	(90,054)	(46,030)
Payments to employees	(14,757)	(5,397)	(13,422)	(12,152)	(4,596)	(13,236)	(15,372)	(78,932)	(12,420)
Housing assistance payments on behalf of tenants	—	—	—	—	—	(82,176)	—	(82,176)	—
Claims paid	—	—	—	—	—	—	—	—	(16,987)
Net cash provided by (used for) operating activities	8,928	6,232	12,906	4,143	(2,984)	(104,949)	11,998	(63,726)	6,805
Cash flows from noncapital financing activities:									
Transient occupancy taxes	—	—	—	—	13,551	—	—	13,551	—
Revenue from other agencies	—	—	—	836	—	85,643	573	87,052	16
Transfers in from other funds	—	—	—	—	1,344	2,971	306	4,621	4,289
Transfers out to other funds	(4,554)	(1,556)	(3,269)	(4,082)	(1,479)	(2,535)	(2,379)	(19,854)	—
Increase in due to other funds	—	—	—	—	—	18,766	24	18,790	(8)
Increase in due from other funds	—	—	—	—	—	—	—	—	(2,717)
Decrease in due to other funds	—	—	—	604	—	—	—	604	—
Decrease in due from other funds	—	—	—	—	—	161	—	161	—
Increase in advances to other funds	—	—	—	—	—	—	—	—	(815)
Increase in advances from other funds	—	—	—	—	304	—	482	786	584
Decrease in advances to other funds	—	—	—	—	—	—	—	—	93
Decrease in advances from other funds	—	—	—	—	—	—	(51)	(51)	—
Issuance of notes receivable	—	—	—	—	—	—	—	—	(1)
Net cash provided by (used for) noncapital financing activities	(4,554)	(1,556)	(3,269)	(2,642)	13,720	105,006	(1,045)	105,660	1,441

continued from page 788

Cash flows from capital and related financing activities:									
Proceeds from issuance of debt	—	—	—	—	—	6,000	—	6,000	—
Acquisition and construction of capital assets	(60,556)	(4,309)	(40,403)	(1,808)	(67)	(4,886)	(1,580)	(113,609)	(7,430)
Proceeds from sale of capital assets	26	6	51	20	—	12	—	115	684
Principal payments on capital debt	(3,030)	(577)	(2,068)	(485)	(4,895)	(47)	(1,685)	(12,787)	(220)
Interest payments on capital debt	(10,109)	(282)	(1,332)	(1,500)	(5,729)	(251)	(3,529)	(22,732)	(247)
Transfers in from other funds	3,207	215	29,683	—	—	—	—	33,105	1,464
Capital contributions	7,706	492	—	—	—	4	—	8,202	361
Net cash provided by (used for) capital and related financing activities	(62,756)	(4,455)	(14,069)	(3,773)	(10,691)	832	(6,794)	(101,706)	(5,388)
Cash flows from investing activities:									
Proceeds from sale of investments	—	—	308	—	—	—	—	308	—
Collection of interest	2,307	7	809	89	651	143	737	4,743	1,270
Net unrealized investments gains (losses)	(1,353)	143	(376)	—	(138)	—	(197)	(1,921)	(1,510)
Loans advanced	—	—	—	—	—	—	—	—	—
Loan repayments	472	98	295	—	3	37	—	905	—
Change in securities lending obligation	(13,007)	132	(524)	—	—	—	539	(12,860)	2,538
Net cash provided by (used for) investing activities	(11,581)	380	512	89	516	180	1,079	(8,825)	2,298
Net increase (decrease) in cash and cash equivalents	(69,963)	601	(3,920)	(2,183)	561	1,069	5,238	(68,597)	5,156
Cash and cash equivalents, beginning of year	141,984	14,120	38,467	6,504	14,128	5,375	35,252	255,830	26,736
Cash and cash equivalents, end of year	$ 72,021	$14,721	$ 34,547	$ 4,321	$ 14,689	$ 6,444	$40,490	$187,233	$ 31,892

next chapter discusses, the private reporting model is now relatively well developed. This suggestion presents some potential problems, however, because the FASB, a group that has not had to deal with the intricacies found in governmental entities, could misunderstand the unique aspects of public schools. It might simply ignore the unique reporting needs associated with public schools. In addition, the loss of authority to the FASB could weaken the GASB somewhat. Politically, reducing the power of this board might not be pleasing to organizations that provide much of the GASB's support and financing.

2. Continue to use the traditional model that focused on fund-based statements and the wide variety of funds that such schools maintain. However, private not-for-profit organizations and governments (at least in part) have abandoned the reporting of individual funds so that continuing to rely on this approach for a public school seems to be outdated.

3. Create an entirely new set of financial statements designed specifically to meet the unique needs of a public college or university. If the FASB's pronouncements are not to be followed, the fundamental differences between the two types of schools must be quite significant. If those differences can be identified, new statements could be developed to satisfy the informational needs of users and mirror the events and transactions of these public institutions. Unfortunately, however, the creation of a new set of financial statements would require an enormous amount of work by the GASB. Would the benefit gained from tailor-made financial statements outweigh the cost of producing new standards for reporting by public schools?

4. Adopt the same reporting model that has been created for state and local governments in *GASB Statement 34.* Because a large amount of funding comes directly from governments based on oversight by the appropriate legislative body, the same financial statements utilized by a city or county could be applied.

In *GASB Statement 35,* "Basic Financial Statements—and Management's Discussion and Analysis—for Public Colleges and Universities," issued in November 1999, this fourth option was officially selected. According to paragraph 25, "the objective of this Statement is to amend *Statement 34* to include public colleges and universities in the financial reporting model established by that Statement." This authoritative pronouncement creates a formal reporting model for public colleges and universities such as the University of Florida and Michigan State University.

However, a review of public college and university financial statements on the Internet shows that few prepare both government-wide and fund-based financial statements as established by *GASB Statement 34.* The reason is that many such schools can logically be viewed as rather large enterprise funds: They have a user charge (tuition and fees), and they are open to the public. As this chapter and the previous one have discussed, the accounting for Enterprise Funds as proprietary funds is very similar between government-wide statements and fund-based statements. Both statements report all economic resources and use accrual accounting.

Thus, having two sets of almost identical statements was viewed by the GASB as not necessary in such cases. For this reason, most public schools are allowed to prepare a single set of statements but still use the reporting model created by *GASB Statement 34.* Consequently, a note to the financial statements for Middle Tennessee State University for June 30, 2004, and the year then ending provides a common rationale for the method by which the statements are structured:

> For financial statement purposes, the university is considered a special-purpose government engaged *only in business-type activities.* Accordingly, the financial statements have been prepared using the economic resources measurement focus and the accrual basis of accounting. Revenues are recorded when earned, and expenses are recorded when a liability is incurred, regardless of the timing of related cash flows. Grants and similar items are recognized as revenue as soon as all eligibility requirements imposed by the provider have been met. [Emphasis added.]

Exhibit 17.8 presents the financial statements for June 30, 2003, and the year then ended for James Madison University for illustration purposes. Note that these statements are quite similar to the fund-based financial statements presented in this chapter for the proprietary funds of the City of Sacramento, California (Exhibits 17.5, 17.6, and 17.7).

EXHIBIT 17.8

JAMES MADISON UNIVERSITY
Statement of Net Assets
As of June 30, 2003

	2003	
	James Madison University	Component Unit
Assets		
Current assets:		
Cash and cash equivalents (Note 2)	$ 49,170,617	$ 944,126
Short-term investments (Note 2)	4,177,619	—
Accounts receivable (net of allowance for doubtful accounts of $396,330) (Note 3)	3,961,352	65,487
Contributions receivable (net of allowance for doubtful contributions of $32,505)	—	1,839,924
Due from the Commonwealth (Note 7)	6,320,472	—
Prepaid expenses	3,723,104	2,166
Inventory	754,572	2,646
Notes receivable (net of allowance for doubtful accounts of $39,356)	466,951	—
Total current assets	68,574,687	2,854,349
Noncurrent assets:		
Restricted cash and cash equivalents (Note 2)	462,575	—
Endowment investments (Note 2)	190,989	17,701,871
Other long-term investments (Note 2)	3,873,300	14,987,053
Contributions receivable (net of allowance for doubtful contributions of $87,531)	—	4,289,019
Notes receivable (net of allowance for doubtful accounts of $193,455)	2,176,348	—
Capital assets, net: (Note 4)		
Nondepreciable	25,000,115	800,056
Depreciable	254,797,506	900,309
Other assets	—	12,786
Total noncurrent assets	286,500,833	38,691,094
Total assets	355,075,520	41,545,443
Liabilities		
Current liabilities:		
Accounts payable and accrued expenses (Note 5)	18,621,401	250,344
Deferred revenue	4,073,498	—
Obligations under securities lending	3,084,721	—
Deposits held in custody for others	2,743,677	—
Long-term liabilities—current portion (Note 6)	7,825,050	74,934
Advance from the Treasurer of Virginia	59,000	—
Total current liabilities	36,407,347	325,278
Noncurrent liabilities (Note 6)	82,724,220	2,222,235
Total liabilities	119,131,567	2,547,513

(continued)

EXHIBIT 17.8
(*continued*)

	2003	
	James Madison University	**Component Unit**
Net Assets		
Invested in capital assets, net of related debt.	203,488,453	1,408,115
Restricted for:		
Nonexpendable:		
Scholarships and fellowships	259,507	13,612,427
Research and public service	—	323,051
Other	—	4,560,344
Expendable:		
Scholarships and fellowships	37,514	1,060,075
Research and public service	2,509,238	1,422,491
Debt service	7,647	782,285
Capital projects	4,391,809	7,634,527
Loans	357,516	—
Other	—	5,649,830
Unrestricted	24,892,269	2,544,785
Total net assets	$235,943,953	$38,997,930

JAMES MADISON UNIVERSITY
Statement of Revenues, Expenses, and Changes in Net Assets
For the Year Ended June 30, 2003

	2003	
	James Madison University	**Component Unit**
Operating revenues:		
Student tuition and fees (net of scholarship allowances of $3,851,901)	$ 59,152,970	—
Gifts and contributions	—	$6,043,470
Federal grants and contracts	13,657,335	—
State grants and contracts	7,775,928	—
Nongovernmental grants and contracts	2,593,115	—
Auxiliary enterprises (net of scholarship allowances of $4,500,656) (Note 9)	85,188,974	—
Other operating revenues	849,889	63,808
Total operating revenues	169,218,211	6,107,548
Operating expenses (Note 10):		
Instruction	72,384,226	272,222
Research	4,509,392	10,383
Public service	10,141,666	84,604
Academic support	17,347,854	230,042
Student services	6,804,003	31,124
Institutional support	10,837,539	816,433
Operation and maintenance—plant	13,533,167	148,252
Depreciation	15,067,069	46,790
Student aid	3,554,177	1,126,890
Auxiliary activities (Note 9)	64,884,111	560,337
Total operating expenses	219,063,204	3,327,077
Operating gain (loss)	(49,844,993)	2,780,471
Nonoperating revenues (expenses):		
State appropriations (Note 11)	61,963,431	—

(*continued*)

EXHIBIT 17.8
(*continued*)

	2003	
	James Madison University	Component Unit
Gifts	582,470	—
Investment income (net of investment expense of $61,942 for the University and $227,724 for the Foundation)	1,758,325	447,942
Interest on capital asset—related debt.	(3,706,570)	(54,441)
Loss on disposal of plant assets	(543,691)	—
Payment to the Commonwealth	(1,231,830)	—
Net nonoperating revenues (expenses)	58,822,135	393,501
Income (loss) before other revenues, expenses, gains, or losses	8,977,142	3,173,972
Capital appropriations	8,502,938	—
Capital gifts	3,917,981	—
Additions to permanent endowments	—	972,131
Net other revenues	12,420,919	972,131
Increase (decrease) in net assets	21,398,061	4,146,103
Net assets—beginning of year	214,545,892	34,851,827
Net assets—end of year	$235,943,953	$38,997,930

JAMES MADISON UNIVERSITY
Statement of Cash Flows
For the Year Ended June 30, 2003

	2003
Cash flows from operating activities:	
Student tuition and fees	$ 58,882,476
Grants and contracts	23,718,830
Auxiliary enterprises	85,555,411
Other receipts	721,255
Payments to employees	(100,430,282)
Payments for fringe benefits	(25,402,925)
Payments for services and supplies	(55,733,211)
Payments for utilities	(8,995,936)
Payments for scholarships and fellowships	(3,515,736)
Payments for noncapitalized plant improvements and equipment	(9,034,742)
Loans issued to students	(563,770)
Collections of loans from students	628,804
Net cash used by operating activities	(34,169,826)
Cash flows from noncapital financing activities:	
State appropriations	61,805,997
Payment to the Commonwealth	(1,231,830)
Gifts and grants for other than capital purposes	582,470
Loans issued to students and employees	(46,086)
Collections of loans from students and employees	17,417
Agency receipts	8,304,389
Agency payments	(8,372,139)
Net cash provided by noncapital financing activities	61,060,218
Cash flows from capital financing activities:	
Proceeds from investments	2,032,782
Proceeds from capital debt	6,636,573
Capital appropriations	3,857,659
Capital gifts	3,055,727

(*continued*)

EXHIBIT 17.8
(*concluded*)

	2003
Proceeds from sale of capital assets	15,680
Purchase of capital assets	(26,998,972)
Principal paid on capital debt, leases, and installments	(6,778,061)
Interest paid on capital debt, leases, and installments	(3,893,436)
Net cash used by capital financing activities	(22,072,048)
Cash flows from investing activities:	
Interest on investments	266,887
Interest on cash management pools	1,538,866
Net cash provided by investing activities	1,805,753
Net increase in cash	6,624,097
Cash and cash equivalents—beginning of the year	43,009,095
Cash and cash equivalents—end of the year	$ 49,633,192

Summary

1. As with businesses, state and local governments can obtain assets through lease arrangements. Government accounting applies the same criteria for identifying a capital lease as a for-profit organization. Government-wide financial statements report both the resulting asset and liability initially at the present value of the minimum lease payments. This asset is depreciated over the time that the government uses it. Interest expense on the reported liability is recognized each period. Fund-based financial statements recognize an expenditure and an other financing source at present value when the contract is initiated. They also recognize subsequent payments on the debt and interest as expenditures.

2. Solid waste landfills create large potential debts for a government because of closure and postclosure costs. Government-wide statements accrue this liability each period based on the latest cost estimations and the portion of the property that has been filled. Fund-based financial statements report no expenditures until a claim to current financial resources is made.

3. Government employees often have the right to future compensated absences because of holidays, vacations, sick leave, and the like. Government-wide statements must estimate and report the debt for these absences as the employees earn them. Fund-based statements do not recognize a liability until current financial resources are expected to be used.

4. A state or local government that obtains a work of art or historical treasure normally must record it as a capital asset on the government-wide financial statements. However, if specified guidelines are met, an expense can replace recognition of the asset. A state or local government that receives a work of art or historical treasure through donation must still recognize revenue according to the rules established for voluntary nonexchange transactions. In contrast, the fund-based financial statements report no capital assets.

5. Depreciation must be recorded each period for works of art and historical treasures that are capitalized unless they are viewed as inexhaustible.

6. Infrastructure assets must be capitalized and depreciated on the government-wide financial statements. However, depreciation is not recorded if the modified approach is applied. Under this method, if a system is created to ensure that a network of infrastructure is maintained yearly at a predetermined condition, the cost of this care is expensed in lieu of recording depreciation.

7. A state or local government must include a Management's Discussion and Analysis (MD&A) as part of its general purpose external financial reporting. This MD&A provides a verbal explanation of the government's operations and financial position.

8. A primary government must produce a comprehensive annual financial report (CAFR). Both state and local governments as well as any special purpose government that meets certain provisions are viewed as primary governments. A component unit is any function that is legally separate from the primary government but for which financial accountability still exists. In the government-wide statements, component units can be discretely presented to the right of the primary government or can be blended within the actual funds of the primary government.

9. A statement of net assets and a statement of activities are prepared as government-wide financial statements based on the economic resources measurement focus and accrual accounting. These statements separate governmental activities from business-type activities. Internal service funds are usually included within the governmental activities. The statement of activities reports expenses by function along with

related program revenues to determine the net expenses or revenues resulting from each function. The government then shows general revenues as its way of covering the net expenses of the various functions.

10. Fund-based financial statements report the governmental funds by showing separately the General Fund and any other major fund. The statements reporting the governmental funds are based on measuring current financial resources using modified accrual accounting. Additional statements are presented for proprietary funds and fiduciary funds.

11. The financial statements prepared by public colleges and universities must now follow the same guidelines as those created in *GASB Statement 34* for state and local government units. Those statements differ from statements produced by private schools that follow FASB guidelines. Most of these public schools view themselves as a special purpose government engaged only in business-type activities, so these schools need only fund-based statements for a proprietary fund.

Comprehensive Illustration

PROBLEM

(Estimated Time: 40 minutes) The following is a series of transactions for a city. Indicate how the city should report each transaction on the government-wide financial statements and then on the fund-based financial statements. Assume the city has a policy that resources are considered available if they will be received within 60 days. Incurred liabilities are assumed to be claims to current resources if they will be paid within 60 days.

1. Borrowed money by issuing a 20-year bond for $3 million, its face value. This money is to be used to construct a highway around the city.

2. Transferred cash of $100,000 from the General Fund to the debt service funds to make the first payment of principal and interest on the bond in (1).

3. Paid the cash in (2) on the bond. Of this total, $70,000 represents interest; the remainder reduces the principal of the bond payable.

4. Completed construction of the highway and paid the entire $3 million.

5. The highway is expected to last for 30 years. However, the government qualifies to use the modified approach, which it has adopted for this system. A $35,000 cost is incurred during the year to maintain the highway at an appropriate, predetermined condition. Of this amount, paid $29,000 immediately but will not pay the other $6,000 until the sixth month of the subsequent year.

6. Received donated lights for the new highway from a local business. The lights are valued at $200,000 and should last for 20 years. The modified approach is not used for this network of infrastructure, but straight-line depreciation is applied using the half-year convention.

7. Leased a truck to maintain the new highway. The lease qualifies as a capital lease. The present value of the minimum payments is $70,000. Depreciation for this year is $10,000 and interest is $6,000. A single payment of $11,000 in cash is made.

8. Recorded cash revenues of $2 million from the local subway system and salary expense payments of $300,000 to its employees.

9. Opened a solid waste landfill at the beginning of the year that will take 20 years to fill. This year an estimated 4 percent of the capacity was filled. The city anticipates total closure and postclosure costs of $2 million although no costs have been incurred to date.

SOLUTION

1. *Government-wide financial statements.* On the statement of net assets, under the Governmental Activities column, both Cash and Noncurrent Liabilities increase by $3 million.

   Fund-based financial statements. The Cash balance increases on the balance sheet whereas Other Financing Sources increases on the statement of revenues, expenditures, and changes in fund balances. These amounts will be shown in the Other Governmental Funds column unless this particular capital projects fund is judged to be major so that a separate column is presented.

2. *Government-wide financial statements.* No recording of this transfer is shown because the amount was an intra-activity transaction entirely carried out within the governmental activities.

   Fund-based financial statements. The Cash balance for the General Fund on the balance sheet will go down while the cash listed for other governmental funds (or debt service fund) increases. On the statement of revenues, expenditures, and other changes in fund balances, the General Fund shows an Other Financing Use whereas the other governmental funds report an Other Financing Source. These balances will not be offset.

3. *Government-wide financial statements.* On the statement of net assets, Cash for the governmental activities decreases by $100,000 and the Noncurrent Liabilities drop by $30,000 because of the principal payment. The statement of activities should report $70,000 in interest expense as a governmental activity.

   Fund-based financial statements. First, Cash decreases by $100,000 on the balance sheet under the Other Governmental Funds (or Debt Service Fund) column. Second, on the statement of revenues, expenditures, and changes in fund balances, a $30,000 principal expenditure is reported with a $70,000 interest expenditure. These amounts are shown within the other governmental funds (or debt service fund) under debt service.

4. *Government-wide financial statements.* Under the governmental activities listed on the statement of net assets, Cash decreases by the $3 million amount and Capital Assets increases by the same amount. All new infrastructure costs must be capitalized.

   Fund-based financial statements. On the balance sheet, cash reported for other governmental funds decreases. Again, if this particular capital projects fund qualifies as major, the effects are shown in a separate column rather than in the Other column. The statement of revenues, expenditures, and changes in fund balances reports a $3 million expenditure as a capital outlay.

5. *Government-wide financial statements.* The statement of net assets reports a $29,000 decrease in Cash under governmental activities and a $6,000 increase in a current liability. The statement of activities includes the $35,000 expense within an appropriate function such as public works. Because the modified approach is being applied, the maintenance expense is recognized instead of depreciation expense.

   Fund-based financial statements. Because the $6,000 liability will not require the use of current financial resources (it will not be paid within 60 days), it is not recorded at this time at the fund level. Thus, the balance sheet reports only a $29,000 drop in cash, probably under the General Fund. A $29,000 expenditure is recorded on the statement of revenues, expenditures, and changes in fund balances for public works.

6. *Government-wide financial statements.* The lights do not qualify as works of art or historical treasures and must therefore be reported as capital assets on the statement of net assets at the $200,000 value. Based on a 20-year life and the half-year convention, $5,000 in accumulated depreciation must be recognized to reduce the reported net asset to $195,000. For the statement of activities, a $200,000 revenue is appropriate unless eligibility requirements for the donation have not yet been fulfilled. This revenue should be shown as a program revenue (Capital Grants and Contributions) to offset the expenses reported for public works. Depreciation of $5,000 should also be included as an expense for public works ($200,000/20 years × 0.5 year).

   Fund-based financial statements. No reporting is required because current financial resources were not affected.

7. *Government-wide financial statements.* On the statement of net assets, report both the leased truck and the lease liability under the governmental activities, at $70,000. Then $10,000 in accumulated depreciation reduces the truck's book value. The liability is reduced by $5,000, the amount of the $11,000 payment less $6,000 attributed to interest. Next, the statement of activities reports interest of $6,000 and depreciation of $10,000 as expenses directly related to the public works function.

   Fund-based financial statements. The balance sheet, probably under the General Fund, reports an $11,000 reduction in cash. The statement of revenues, expenditures, and changes in fund balances records a $70,000 expenditure as a capital outlay and recognizes an Other Financing Source of the same amount. Finally, it should show another $11,000 in expenditures: $6,000 as interest and $5,000 for debt reduction.

8. *Government-wide financial statements.* Cash on the statement of net assets increases under the business-type activities by $1.7 million. The statement of activities reports expenses for the subway system as $300,000 while the related program revenues for charges for services rendered increases by $2 million so that the net revenue resulting from this business-type activity is shown as $1.7 million.

   Fund-based financial statements. The statement of net assets for the proprietary funds (see Exhibit 17.5) should include a separate column for the subway system, assuming that it is a major fund. Cash in this column increases by $1.7 million. Likewise, the statement of revenues, expenses, and changes in fund net assets for the proprietary funds (see Exhibit 17.6) reports operating revenues of $2 million for the subway system. In addition, the list of operating expenses should include personnel services of $300,000. The statement of cash flows (see Exhibit 17.7) also reports both the inflow and outflow of cash under Cash Flows from Operating Activities.

9. *Government-wide financial statements.* Because the landfill is 4 percent filled and this is its first year, that portion of the overall $2 million ($80,000) cost must be recognized to date. The statement of net assets shows this amount as a noncurrent liability. The balance could be presented as either a governmental activity or a business-type activity, depending on the internal classification of the landfill. Likewise, the statement of activities reports the same $80,000 expense figure.

Fund-based financial statements. This liability does not require the use of current financial resources and would not be reported if the landfill is considered a governmental fund. However, if the landfill is viewed as an enterprise fund, the separate statements prepared for the proprietary funds would show both the $80,000 expense and liability (see Exhibits 17.5 and 17.6).

Questions

1. What criteria does a state or local government apply to determine whether to capitalize a lease?

2. On January 1, 2007, a city signs a capital lease for new equipment for the police department. How does it report this transaction on the government-wide financial statements? On the fund-based financial statements?

3. On December 31, 2007, the city in Question 2 makes its first annual lease payment. How does it report the payment on the government-wide financial statements? On the fund-based financial statements?

4. Why does the operation of a solid waste landfill create reporting concerns for a local government?

5. A landfill is scheduled to be filled to capacity over a 10-year period. However, at the end of the first year of operations, the landfill is only 7 percent filled. How much liability for closure and post-closure costs should be recognized on the government-wide financial statements? How much liability should be recognized on the fund-based financial statements assuming that the landfill is recorded in an enterprise fund? How much liability should be recognized on the fund-based financial statements assuming that the landfill is recorded in the General Fund?

6. A city operates a solid waste landfill. This facility is 11 percent filled after the first year of operation and 24 percent filled after the second year. How much expense should be recognized on the government-wide financial statements in the second year for closure costs? Assuming the landfill is reported in the General Fund, how much of an expenditure should be recognized in the second year on the fund-based financial statements?

7. A teacher working for the City of Lights earns vacation pay of $2,000 during 2007. However, the vacation will not be taken until the end of 2008. In the government-wide financial statements for 2007, how is this compensated absence reported? How is this compensated absence reported in the fund-based financial statements for 2007?

8. In Question 7, assume the teacher takes the vacation late in 2008 and is paid the entire $2,000. What journal entry is reported on each of the two types of financial statements?

9. The City of Salem is given a painting by Picasso to display in its city hall. Under what condition will the city *not* report this painting as a capital asset on its government-wide financial statements? If it does report the painting as a capital asset, must the city report depreciation?

10. In Question 9, assume that the city does not report the painting on the government-wide financial statements as a capital asset. Must the city report a revenue for the gift?

11. Under what condition is the modified approach applied?

12. What impact does the use of the modified approach have on reporting within the government-wide financial statements?

13. What does the Management's Discussion and Analysis (MD&A) normally include? Where does a state or local government present this information?

14. What does a comprehensive annual financial report (known as the CAFR) include?

15. A primary government can be either a general purpose government or a special purpose government. What is the difference in these two? How does an activity qualify as a special purpose government?

16. The Willingham Museum qualifies as a component unit of the City of Willingham. How does an activity or function qualify to be a component unit of a primary government?

17. What is the difference between a blended component unit and a discretely presented component unit?

18. What are the two government-wide financial statements? What does each normally present?

19. What are the two fund-based financial statements for governmental funds? What does each normally present?

20. What is the difference in program revenues and general revenues? Why is that distinction important?

21. Why does a government determine the net expenses or revenues for each of the functions within its statement of activities?

22. How are internal service funds reported on government-wide financial statements?

23. How are fiduciary funds reported on government-wide financial statements?

24. What are some of the major differences that exist between private colleges and universities and public colleges and universities?

25. What is the most common form for the financial statements of public colleges and universities?

Problems

1. A city government has obtained an asset through a capital lease. Which of the following is true for the government-wide financial statements?
   a. The accounting parallels that used in for-profit accounting.
   b. The city must report an other financing source.
   c. The city must report an expenditure.
   d. Recognition of depreciation is optional.

2. A city government has a six-year capital lease for property being used within the General Fund. Minimum lease payments total $70,000 starting next year but have a current present value of $49,000. What is the total amount of expenditures to be recognized on the fund-based financial statements over the six-year period?
   a. –0–.
   b. $49,000.
   c. $70,000.
   d. $119,000.

3. A city government has a six-year capital lease for property being used within the General Fund. Minimum lease payments total $70,000 starting next year but have a current present value of $49,000. What is the total amount of other financing sources to be recognized on the fund-based financial statements over the six-year period?
   a. –0–.
   b. $49,000.
   c. $70,000.
   d. $119,000.

4. A city government has a nine-year capital lease for property being used within the General Fund. The lease was signed on January 1, 2007. Minimum lease payments total $90,000 starting at the end of the first year but have a current present value of $69,000. Annual payments are $10,000, and the interest rate being applied is 10 percent. When the first payment is made on December 31, 2007, which of the following recordings is made?

	Government-Wide Statements	Fund-Based Statements
a.	Interest Expense $0	Interest Expense $0
b.	Interest Expense $6,900	Expenditures $6,900
c.	Expenditures $10,000	Expenditures $10,000
d.	Interest Expense $6,900	Expenditures $10,000

5. A city government has a nine-year capital lease for property being used within the General Fund. The lease was signed on January 1, 2007. Minimum lease payments total $90,000 starting at the end of the first year but have a current present value of $69,000. Annual payments are $10,000, and the interest rate being applied is 10 percent. What liability is reported on the fund-based financial statements as of December 31, 2007, after the first payment has been made?
   a. –0–.
   b. $59,000.
   c. $65,900.
   d. $80,000.

6. A city creates a solid waste landfill. Every person or company that uses the landfill is assessed a charge based on the amount of materials contributed. In which of the following will the landfill probably be recorded?
   a. General Fund.
   b. Special revenues funds.

  c. Internal service funds.

  d. Enterprise funds.

Use the following information for Problems 7, 8, and 9:

A city starts a solid waste landfill that it expects to fill to capacity evenly over a 10-year period. At the end of the first year, it is 8 percent filled. At the end of the second year, it is 19 percent filled. Closure and postclosure costs are estimated at $1 million. None of this amount will be paid until the landfill has reached its capacity.

 7. Which of the following is true for the Year 2 government-wide financial statements?

  a. Both expense and liability will be zero.

  b. Both expense and liability will be $110,000.

  c. Expense will be $110,000 and liability will be $190,000.

  d. Expense will be $100,000 and liability will be $200,000.

 8. If this landfill is judged to be a proprietary fund, what liability will be reported at the end of the second year on fund-based financial statements?

  a. –0–.

  b. $110,000.

  c. $190,000.

  d. $200,000.

 9. If this landfill is judged to be a governmental fund, what liability will be reported at the end of the second year on fund-based financial statements?

  a. –0–.

  b. $110,000.

  c. $190,000.

  d. $200,000.

Use the following information for Problems 10 and 11:

The employees of the City of Jones earn vacation time that totals $1,000 per week during the year. Of this amount, $12,000 is actually taken in Year 1 and the remainder is taken in Year 2.

 10. What liability should the city report on government-wide financial statements at the end of Year 1?

  a. It depends on whether the employees work at governmental activities or business-type activities.

  b. –0–.

  c. $40,000.

  d. $52,000.

 11. What amount of liability should the city recognize on fund-based financial statements at December 31, Year 1? *Assume that all remaining vacations will be taken in July.*

  a. It depends on whether the employees work at governmental activities or business-type activities.

  b. –0–.

  c. $40,000.

  d. $52,000.

 12. The City of Wilson receives a large piece of sculpture valued at $240,000 as a gift to be placed in front of the municipal building. Which of the following is true for reporting the gift on the government-wide financial statements?

  a. A capital asset of $240,000 must be reported.

  b. No capital asset will be reported.

  c. If conditions are met, recording the sculpture as a capital asset is optional.

  d. The sculpture will be recorded but only for the amount paid by the city.

 13. In Problem 12, which of the following statements is true about reporting a revenue?

  a. A revenue will be reported.

  b. Revenue is reported but only if the asset is reported.

  c. If the asset is not capitalized, no revenue should be recognized.

  d. As a gift, no revenue would ever be reported.

14. In Problem 12, assume that the city reports the work as a capital asset. Which of the following is true?

   a. Depreciation is not recorded because the city has no cost.

   b. Depreciation is not required if the asset is held to be inexhaustible.

   c. Depreciation must be recognized because the asset is capitalized.

   d. Because the property was received as a gift, recognition of depreciation is optional.

15. A city builds sidewalks throughout its various neighborhoods at a cost of $200,000. Which of the following is *not* true?

   a. Because the sidewalks qualify as infrastructure, the asset is viewed in the same way as land so that no depreciation is recorded.

   b. Depreciation is required unless the modified approach is utilized.

   c. The modified approach recognizes maintenance expense in lieu of depreciation expense for qualifying infrastructure assets.

   d. The modified approach is allowed only if the city maintains the network of sidewalks at least at a predetermined condition.

16. Which of the following is true about use of the modified approach?

   a. It can be applied to all capital assets of a state or local government.

   b. It is used to adjust depreciation expense either up or down based on conditions for the period.

   c. It is required for infrastructure assets.

   d. For qualified assets, it eliminates the recording of depreciation.

17. Which of the following is true about the Management's Discussion and Analysis (MD&A)?

   a. It is an optional addition to the comprehensive annual financial report, but the GASB encourages its inclusion.

   b. It adds a verbal explanation for the numbers and trends presented in the financial statements.

   c. It appears at the very end of a government's comprehensive annual financial report.

   d. It replaces a portion of the fund-based financial statements traditionally presented by a state or local government.

18. Which of the following is *not* necessary for a special purpose local government to be viewed as a primary government for reporting purposes?

   a. It must have a separately elected governing body.

   b. It must have specifically defined geographic boundaries.

   c. It must be fiscally independent.

   d. It must have corporate powers to prove that it is legally independent.

19. An accountant is trying to determine whether the school system of the City of Abraham is fiscally independent. Which of the following is *not* a requirement for being deemed fiscally independent?

   a. Holding property in its own name.

   b. Issuing bonded debt without outside approval.

   c. Passing its own budget without outside approval.

   d. Setting taxes or rates without outside approval.

20. An employment agency for the handicapped works closely with the City of Hanover. The employment agency is legally separate from the city but still depends on it for financial support. How should Hanover report the employment agency in its comprehensive annual financial report?

   a. Not at all because the agency is legally separate.

   b. As a part of the General Fund.

   c. As a component unit.

   d. As a related organization.

21. The Edison County Art Museum is legally separate from the City of Edison. Which of the following is true?

   a. If the art museum qualifies as a special purpose local government, it cannot be a component unit for the city.

   b. If the art museum qualifies as a component unit for the city, it can be a special purpose local government.

c. If the art museum does not qualify as a component unit for the city, it cannot be a special purpose local government.

d. If the art museum qualifies as a special purpose local government, it can still be a component unit for the city.

22. For component units, what is the difference in discrete presentation and blending?

   a. A blended component unit is shown to the left of the statements; a discretely presented component unit is shown to the right.

   b. A blended component unit is shown at the bottom of the statements; a discretely presented component unit is shown within the statements like a fund.

   c. A blended component unit is shown within the statements like a fund; a discretely presented component unit is shown to the right.

   d. A blended component unit is shown to the right of the statements; a discretely presented component unit is shown in completely separate statements.

23. A government reports that its public safety function had expenses of $900,000 last year and program revenues of $200,000 so that its net expenses were $700,000. On which financial statement is this information presented?

   a. Statement of activities.

   b. Statement of cash flows.

   c. Statement of revenues and expenditures.

   d. Statement of net assets.

24. Government-wide financial statements make a distinction between program revenues and general revenues. How is that difference shown?

   a. Program revenues are offset against the expenses of a specific function; general revenues are assigned to governmental activities and business-type activities in general.

   b. General revenues are shown at the top of the statement of revenues and expenditures; program revenues are shown at the bottom.

   c. General revenues are labeled as operating revenues; program revenues are shown as miscellaneous income.

   d. General revenues are broken down by type; program revenues are reported as a single figure for the government.

25. Which of the following is true about the statement of cash flows for the proprietary funds of a state or local government?

   a. The indirect method of reporting cash flows from operating activities is allowed although the direct method is recommended.

   b. The structure of the statement is virtually identical to that of a for-profit business.

   c. The statement is divided into four separate sections of cash flows.

   d. Amounts spent on capital assets are reported in a separate section from amounts raised to finance those capital assets.

26. Which of the following is most likely to be true about the financial reporting of a public college or university?

   a. It resembles the financial reporting of private colleges and universities.

   b. It will continue to use its own unique style of financial reporting.

   c. It resembles the financial reporting made by a proprietary fund within the fund-based financial statements for a state or local government.

   d. It will soon be reported using a financial statement format unique to the needs of public colleges and universities that the GASB is scheduled to create.

27. On January 1, 2007, a city government leased the following pieces of equipment. Each lease qualifies as a capital lease. Initial payments are on December 31, 2007. An interest rate of 10 percent is viewed as appropriate. No bargain purchase options exist.

Fund	Annual Payments	Total Payments	Present Value of Total Payments
General (5-year life)	$8,000	$40,000	$33,350
Enterprise (6-year life)	6,000	36,000	28,750

    a. On government-wide financial statements for December 31, 2007, and the year then ended, what balances should be reported?

    b. On fund-based financial statements for December 31, 2007, and the year then ended, what balances should be reported?

28. On January 1, 2007, a city government leased the following pieces of equipment. Each lease qualifies as a capital lease. Initial payments are on December 31, 2007. An interest rate of 12 percent is viewed as appropriate. No bargain purchase options exist.

Fund	Annual Payments	Total Payments	Present Value of Total Payments
General (10-year life)	$3,000	$30,000	$19,000
Enterprise (4-year life)	9,000	36,000	30,600

    a. Prepare journal entries for the year of 2007 for both of these leases for government-wide financial statements.

    b. Prepare journal entries for the year of 2007 for both of these leases for fund-based financial statements.

29. On January 1, 2007, the City of Verga leased a large truck for five years and made the initial annual payment of $22,000 immediately. The present value of these payments based on an 8 percent interest rate is assumed to be $87,800. The truck has an expected useful life of five years.

    a. Assuming that the city's fire department will use the truck, what journal entries should be made for 2007 and 2008 on the government-wide financial statements?

    b. Assuming that city's fire department will use the the truck, what journal entries should be made for 2007 and 2008 on the fund-based financial statements?

    c. Assuming that the airport (an enterprise fund) operated by the city will use the truck, what journal entries should be made for 2007 and 2008 on the fund-based financial statements?

30. On January 1, 2007, the City of Hastings created a solid waste landfill that it expects to reach capacity gradually over the next 20 years. If the landfill were to be closed at the current time, closure costs would be approximately $1.2 million plus an additional $700,000 for postclosure work. Of these totals, the city must pay $50,000 on December 31 of each year for preliminary closure work. At the end of 2007, the landfill reached 3 percent of capacity. At the end of 2008, the landfill reached 9 percent of capacity. Also, at the end of 2008, a reassessment is made; total closure costs are determined to be $1.4 million rather than $1.2 million.

    a. Assuming that the landfill is viewed as an enterprise fund, what journal entries are made in 2007 and 2008 on the government-wide financial statements?

    b. Assuming that the landfill is viewed as a general fund, what journal entries are made in 2007 and 2008 on the government-wide financial statements?

    c. Assuming that the landfill is viewed as an enterprise fund, what journal entries are made in 2007 and 2008 on fund-based financial statements?

    d. Assuming that the landfill is viewed as a general fund, what journal entries are made in 2007 and 2008 on fund-based financial statements?

31. The City of Lawrence opens a solid waste landfill in 2007 that is at 54 percent of capacity on December 31, 2007. The city had initially anticipated closure costs of $2 million but later that year decided that closure costs would actually be $2.4 million. None of these costs will be incurred until 2014 when the landfill is scheduled to be closed.

    a. What will appear on the government-wide financial statements for this landfill for the year ended December 31, 2007?

    b. Assuming that the landfill is recorded within the General Fund, what will appear on the fund-based financial statements for this landfill for the year ended December 31, 2007?

32. Mary T. Lincoln works for the City of Columbus. She volunteered to work over the 2007 Christmas break so that she could earn a short vacation during the first week of January 2008. She earns three vacation days and will be paid $400 per day. She takes her vacation in January and is paid for those days.

    a. Prepare the journal entries on the government-wide financial statements for 2007 and 2008 because of these events.

  b. Assume that Lincoln works in an activity reported within the General Fund. Prepare journal entries for the fund-based financial statements for 2007 and 2008 because of these events.

  c. Assume that Lincoln works in an activity reported within the General Fund but that she does not plan to take her three vacation days until near the end of 2008. What journal entries should be made for the fund-based financial statements in 2007 and 2008?

33. On January 1, 2007, a rich citizen of the Town of Ristoni donates a painting valued at $300,000 to be displayed to the public in a government building. Although this painting meets the three criteria to qualify as an artwork, town officials choose to record the painting as an asset. There are no eligibility requirements for the gift. The asset is judged to be inexhaustible so that depreciation will not be reported.

  a. For the year ended December 31, 2007, what will be reported on government-wide financial statements in connection with this gift?

  b. How does the answer to question (*a*) change if the government decided to depreciate this asset over a 10-year period using straight-line depreciation?

  c. How does the answer to question (*a*) change if the government decided not to capitalize the asset?

34. On January 1, 2007, a city pays $60,000 for a work of art that will be put on display in the local library. The city will take appropriate measures to protect and preserve the piece. However, if the work is ever sold, the money received will go into unrestricted funds. The work is viewed as inexhaustible, but the city has opted to depreciate this cost over 20 years (using the straight-line method).

  a. How will this work be reported on the government-wide financial statements for the year ended December 31, 2007?

  b. How will this work be reported in the fund-based financial statements for the year ended December 31, 2007?

35. A city government adds street lights within its boundaries at a total cost of $100,000. The lights should burn for at least 10 years but can last significantly longer if maintained properly. The city sets up a system to monitor these lights with the goal that 97 percent will be working at any one time. During the year, the city spends $6,300 to clean and repair the lights so that they are working according to the specified conditions. However, it spends another $9,000 to construct lights for several new streets in the city.

  Describe the various ways these costs could be reported on government-wide statements.

36. The City of Francois, Texas, has begun the process of producing its comprehensive annual financial report (CAFR). Several organizations that operate within the city are related in some way to the primary government. The city's accountant is attempting to determine how these organizations should be included in the reporting process.

  a. What is the major criterion for inclusion in a government's CAFR?

  b. How does an activity or function qualify as a special purpose government?

  c. How is the legal separation of a special purpose government evaluated?

  d. How is the fiscal independence of a special purpose government evaluated?

  e. What is a component unit, and how is it normally reported on government-wide financial statements?

  f. How does a primary government prove that it can impose its will on a component unit?

  g. What does the blending of a component unit mean?

  h. What is a related organization, and how does a primary government report it?

37. The County of Maxnell decides to create a sanitation department and offer its services to the public for a fee. As a result, county officials plan to account for this activity within the enterprise funds. Make journal entries for this operation for the following 2007 transactions as well as necessary adjusting entries at the end of the year. Assume that the information is being gathered for fund-based financial statements. Only entries for the sanitation department are required here:

  January 1—Received unrestricted funds of $90,000 as a transfer from the General Fund as permanent financing.

  February 1—Borrowed an additional $130,000 from a local bank at a 12 percent annual interest rate.

March 1—Ordered a truck at an expected cost of $108,000.

April 1—Received the truck and made full payment. The actual cost amounted to $110,000. The truck has a 10-year life and no salvage value. Straight-line depreciation is to be used.

May 1—Received a $20,000 cash grant from the state to help supplement the pay of the sanitation workers. The money must be used for that purpose.

June 1—Rented a garage for the truck at a cost of $1,000 per month and paid 12 months of rent in advance.

July 1—Charged citizens $13,000 for services. Of this amount, $11,000 has been collected.

August 1—Made a $10,000 cash payment on the 12 percent note of February 1. This payment covers both interest and principal.

September 1—Paid salaries of $18,000 using the grant received on May 1.

October 1—Paid truck maintenance costs of $1,000.

November 1—Paid additional salaries of $10,000, first using the rest of the grant money received May 1.

December 31—Sent invoices totaling $19,000 to customers for services over the past six months. Collected $3,000 cash immediately.

38. The following information pertains to the City of Williamson for 2007, its first year of legal existence. For convenience, assume that all transactions are for the General Fund, which carries out three separate functions: general government, public safety, and health and sanitation.

Receipts:	
Property taxes	$320,000
Franchise taxes	42,000
Charges for general government services	5,000
Charges for public safety services	3,000
Charges for health and sanitation services	42,000
Issued long-term note payable	200,000
Receivables at end of year:	
Property taxes (90 percent estimated to be collected)	90,000
Payments:	
Salary:	
General government	66,000
Public safety	39,000
Health and sanitation	22,000
Rent:	
General government	11,000
Public safety	18,000
Health and sanitation	3,000
Maintenance:	
General government	21,000
Public safety	5,000
Health and sanitation	9,000
Insurance:	
General government	8,000
Public safety ($2,000 still prepaid at end of year)	11,000
Health and sanitation	12,000
Interest on debt	16,000
Principal payment on debt	4,000
Building	120,000
Equipment	80,000
Supplies (20 percent still held) (public safety)	15,000
Investments	90,000
Ordered but not received:	
Equipment	12,000
Due in one month at end of year:	
Salaries:	
General government	4,000
Public safety	7,000
Health and sanitation	8,000

Compensated absences for general government workers at the end of the year total $13,000. These amounts will not be taken until late in the year 2008.

The city received a piece of art this year valued at $14,000 that it is using for general government purposes. There are no eligibility requirements. The city chose not to capitalize this property.

The general government uses the building acquired and is depreciating it over 10 years using the straight-line method with no salvage value. The city uses the equipment for health and sanitation and depreciates it using the straight-line method over five years with no salvage value.

The investments are valued at $103,000 at the end of the year.

a. Prepare a statement of activities and a statement of net assets for governmental activities for December 31, 2007, and the year then ended.

b. Prepare a statement of revenues, expenditures, and other changes in fund balances and a balance sheet for the General Fund as of December 31, 2007, and the year then ended. Assume that the city applies the consumption method.

39. The City of Bernard starts the year of 2007 with the following unrestricted amounts in its General Fund: cash of $20,000 and investments of $70,000. In addition, it holds a building bought on January 1, 2006, for general government purposes for $300,000 and related long-term debt of $240,000. The building is being depreciated on the straight-line method over 10 years. The interest rate is 10 percent. The General Fund carries out four separate functions: general government, public safety, public works, and health and sanitation. Other information includes the following:

Receipts:
Property taxes	$510,000
Sales taxes	99,000
Dividend income	20,000
Charges for general government services	15,000
Charges for public safety services	8,000
Charges for public works	4,000
Charges for health and sanitation services	31,000
Charges for landfill	8,000
Grant to be used for salaries for health workers (no eligibility requirements)	25,000
Issued long-term note payable	200,000
Sold above investments	84,000

Receivables at end of year:
Property taxes ($10,000 is expected to be uncollectible)	130,000

Payments:
Salary:
General government	90,000
Public safety	94,000
Public works	69,000
Health and sanitation (all from grant)	22,000

Utilities:
General government	9,000
Public safety	16,000
Public works	13,000
Health and sanitation	4,000

Insurance:
General government	25,000
Public safety	12,000
Public works (all prepaid as of the end of the year)	6,000
Health and sanitation	4,000

Miscellaneous:
General government	12,000
Public safety	10,000
Public works	9,000
Health and sanitation	7,000
Interest on previous debt	24,000
Principal payment on previous debt	10,000

(continued)

Interest on new debt	18,000
Building (public works)	210,000
Equipment (public safety)	90,000
Public works supplies (30 percent still held)	20,000
Investments	111,000

Ordered but not received:
Equipment	24,000
Supplies	7,000

Due at end of year:
Salaries:
General government	14,000
Public safety	17,000
Public works	5,000

The city leased a truck on the last day of the year. The first payment will be at the end of the next year. Total payments will amount to $90,000 but have a present value of $64,000.

The city started a landfill this year that it is recording within its General Fund. It is included as a public works function. Closure costs today would be $260,000 although the landfill is not expected to be filled for nine more years. The city has incurred no costs to date although the landfill is now 15 percent filled.

The new building is being depreciated over 20 years using the straight-line method and no salvage value, whereas depreciation of the equipment is similar except that its life is only 10 years. Assume the city records a full year depreciation in the year of acquisition.

The investments are valued at $116,000 at the end of the year.

a. Prepare a statement of activities and a statement of net assets for governmental activities for December 31, 2007, and the year then ended.

b. Prepare a statement of revenues, expenditures, and changes in fund balances and a balance sheet for the General Fund as of December 31, 2007, and the year then ended. Assume that the purchases method is being applied.

40. The City of Pfeiffer starts the year of 2007 with the General Fund and an enterprise fund. The General Fund has two activities: education and parks/recreation. For convenience, assume that the General Fund holds $123,000 cash and a new school building costing $1 million. The city utilizes straight-line depreciation. The building has a 20-year life and no salvage value. The enterprise fund has $62,000 cash and a new $600,000 civic auditorium with a 30-year life and no salvage value. The enterprise fund monitors just one activity, the rental of the civic auditorium for entertainment and other cultural affairs.

The following transactions for the city take place during 2007. Assume that the city's fiscal year ends on December 31.

a. Decides to build a municipal park and transfers $70,000 into a capital projects fund and immediately expends $20,000 for a piece of land.

b. Borrows $110,000 cash on a long-term bond for use in creating the new municipal park.

c. Assesses property taxes on the first day of the year. The assessment, which is immediately enforceable, totals $600,000. Of this amount, $510,000 will be collected during 2007 and another $50,000 is expected in the first month of 2008. The remainder is expected about halfway through 2008.

d. Constructs a building on the park in (*b*) for $80,000 cash for playing basketball and other sports. It is put into service on July 1 and should last 10 years with no salvage value.

e. Builds a sidewalk around the new park for $10,000 cash and puts it into service on July 1. It should last for 10 years, but the city plans to keep it up to a predetermined quality level so that it will last almost indefinitely.

f. Opens the park and charges an entrance fee of only a token amount so that it records the park, therefore, in the General Fund. Collections during this first year total $8,000.

g. Buys a new parking deck for $200,000, paying $20,000 cash and signing a long-term note for the rest. The parking deck, which is to go into operation on July 1, is across the street from the city auditorium and is considered part of that activity. It has a 20-year life and no salvage value.

h. Receives a $100,000 cash grant for the city school system that must be spent for school lunches for the poor. Appropriate spending of these funds is viewed as an eligibility requirement of this grant. During the current year, $37,000 of the amount received was properly spent.

i. Charges students in the school system a total fee of $6,000 for books and the like. Of this amount, 90 percent is collected during 2007 with the remainder expected to be collected in the first few weeks of 2008.

j. Buys school supplies for $22,000 cash and uses $17,000 of them. The General Fund uses the purchases method.

k. Receives a painting by a local artist to be displayed in the local school. It qualifies as a work of art, and officials have chosen not to capitalize it. The painting has a value of $80,000. It is viewed as inexhaustible.

l. Transfers $20,000 cash from the General Fund to the Enterprise Fund as a capital contribution.

m. Orders a school bus for $99,000.

n. Receives the school bus and pays an actual cost of $102,000. The bus is put into operation on October 1 and should last for five years with no salvage value.

o. Pays salaries of $240,000 to schoolteachers. In addition, owes and will pay $30,000 during the first two weeks of 2008. Vacations worth $23,000 have also been earned but will not be taken until July 2008.

p. Pays salaries of $42,000 to city auditorium workers. In addition, owes and will pay $3,000 in the first two weeks of 2008. Vacations worth $5,000 have also been earned but will not be taken until July 2008.

q. Charges customers $130,000 for the rental of the city auditorium. Of this balance, collected $110,000 in cash and will collect the remainder in April 2008.

r. Pays $9,000 maintenance charges for the building and sidewalk in (*d*) and (*e*).

s. Pays $14,000 on the bond in (*b*) on the last day of 2007: $5,000 principal and $9,000 interest.

t. Accrues interest of $13,000 on the note in (*g*) as of the end of 2007, an amount that it will pay in June 2008.

u. Assumes that a museum that operates within the city is a component unit that will be discretely presented. The museum reports to city officials that it had $42,000 of direct expenses this past year and $50,000 revenues from admission charges. The only assets that it had at the end of the year were cash of $24,000, building (net of depreciation) of $300,000, and a long-term liability of $210,000.

Prepare the 2007 government-wide financial statements for this city. Assume the use of modified approach.

41. Use the information in Problem 40 to prepare the 2007 fund-based financial statements for the governmental funds and the proprietary funds. A statement of cash flows is not required. Assume that "available" is defined as within 60 days and that all funds are major. The General Fund is used for debt repayment.

42. For each of the following, indicate whether the statement is true or false and include a brief explanation for your answer.

a. A pension trust fund appears in the government-wide financial statements but not in the fund-based financial statements.

b. Permanent funds are included as one of the governmental funds.

c. A fire department placed orders of $20,000 for equipment. The equipment is received at a cost of $20,800. In compliance with requirements for fund-based financial statements, an encumbrance of $20,000 was recorded when the order was placed, and an expenditure of $20,800 was recorded when the order was received.

d. The government reported a landfill as an enterprise fund. At the end of Year 1, the government estimated that the landfill will cost $800,000 to clean up when it is eventually full. Currently, it is 12 percent filled. At the end of Year 2, the estimation was changed to $860,000 when it was 20 percent filled. No payments are due for several years. Fund-based financial statements for Year 2 should report a $76,000 expense.

e. A city reports a landfill in the General Fund. At the end of Year 1, the government anticipated the landfill will cost $900,000 to clean up when it is full and reported that it was 11 percent filled. At the end of Year 2, the estimates were changed to $850,000 and 20 percent filled. No payments are due for several years. Government-wide financial statements for Year 2 should report a $71,000 expense.

f. A lease for a computer (that has a six-year life) is signed on January 1, Year 1, with six annual payments of $10,000. The computer is to be used by the police department. The first payment is to be made immediately. The present value of the $60,000 in cash flows is $39,000 based on a 10 percent rate. Fund-based financial statements for Year 1 should report total expenditures of $10,000.

g. An agency fund has neither revenues nor expenditures but reports expenses.

h. A lease for a computer (that has a six-year life) is signed on January 1, Year 1, with six annual payments of $10,000. The computer is to be used by the police department. The first payment is to be made immediately. The present value of the $60,000 in cash flows is $39,000 based on a 10 percent rate. Government-wide financial statements for Year 1 should report expenses of $9,400.

For Problems 43 through 48, use the following introductory information:
The City of Wolfe has issued its financial statements for Year 4 (assume that the city uses a calendar year). The city maintains the General Fund made up of (1) education and (2) parks. The city also utilizes capital projects funds for construction projects and an enterprise fund to account for its art museum. It also has one discretely presented component unit.

The government-wide financial statements indicated the following Year 4 totals:

Education had net expenses of $710,000.
Parks had net expenses of $130,000.
Art museum had net revenues of $80,000.
General revenues were $900,000; the overall increase in net assets was $140,000.

The fund-based financial statements issued for Year 4 indicated the following:

The General Fund had an increase of $30,000 in its fund balance.
The Capital Projects Fund had an increase of $40,000 in its fund balance.
The Enterprise Fund had an increase of $60,000 in its net assets.

Wolfe defines "available" as current financial resources to be paid or collected within 60 days.

43. On the first day of Year 4, the city receives a painting as a gift that qualifies as a work of art. It has a 30-year life, is worth $15,000, and is being displayed at one of the parks. The accountant accidentally capitalized and depreciated it although officials had wanted to use the allowed alternative. Respond to the following:

a. According to the information provided, the General Fund reported an increase of $30,000 in its fund balance. If city officials had used proper alternatives in this reporting, what would have been the correct change in the fund balance for the General Fund for the year?

b. According to the information provided, the parks reported net expenses of $130,000. If city officials had used proper alternatives in this reporting, what was the correct net expense for parks for the year?

c. Assume the same information except that the art was given to the art museum but not recorded at all. What should have been the overall change in net assets for Year 4 on government-wide financial statements, assuming that officials still preferred the allowed alternative?

44. On January 1, Year 4, the government leased a police car for five years at $20,000 per year with the first payment being made on December 31, Year 4. This is a capitalized lease. Assume that, at a reasonable interest rate of 10 percent, the present value of a five-year annuity due is $62,000. In the government-wide financial statements, the government recorded an increase in expense for $20,000 and a reduction in cash for $20,000 as its only entry. In the fund-based financial statements, the government increased Expenditures by $20,000 and reduced Cash for $20,000 as its only entry.

a. According to the information provided, the overall increase in net assets reported was $140,000. What was the correct overall change in the net assets in the government-wide financial statements?

b. According to the information provided, the General Fund reported an increase of $30,000 in its fund balance. What was the correct change in the fund balance for the General Fund?

45. Assume that the one component unit had program revenues of $30,000 and expenses of $42,000 and spent $10,000 for land during Year 4. However, it should have been handled as a blended component unit, not as a discretely presented component unit. According to the information provided, the overall increase in net assets reported was $140,000. What was the correct overall change in the net assets in the government-wide financial statements?

46. At the end of Year 4, the city owed teachers $60,000 in vacation pay that had not been recorded. The assumption is that these vacations will be taken evenly over the next year.

a. What is the correct change in the fund balance of the General Fund for the year?

b. What is the correct overall change in the net assets in the government-wide financial statements?

47. The city has a landfill that has been recorded within its parks. The landfill generated program revenues of $4,000 in Year 4 and cash expenses of $15,000. It also paid $3,000 cash for a piece of land.

These transactions were recorded as would have been anticipated, but no other recording was made this year. The city assumes that it will have to pay $200,000 to clean up the landfill when it is closed in several years. The landfill was 18 percent filled at the end of Year 3 and is 26 percent filled at the end of Year 4. No payments will be necessary for several more years. For convenience, assume that the entries in all previous years were correctly handled regardless of the situation.

    a. The city believes that the landfill was included correctly in all previous years as one of its Enterprise Funds. According to the information provided, the overall increase in net assets reported was $140,000. What is the correct overall change in the net assets in the government-wide financial statements?

    b. The city believes that the landfill was included correctly in all previous years in one of the Enterprise Funds. According to the information provided, the Enterprise Fund reported an increase in its net assets of $60,000. What is the correct change in the net assets of the Enterprise Fund in the fund-based financial statements?

    c. The city believes that the landfill was included correctly in all previous years within the General Fund. What is the correct change in the fund balance of the General Fund?

48. The City of Wolfe bought a $20,000 machine with a five-year life and no salvage value for its school system. It was capitalized but no other entries were ever made. The machine was monitored using the modified approach.

    a. What was the correct overall change in the net assets in the government-wide financial statements?

    b. What was the total of correct net expenses for education in the government-wide statements?

49. A police department leases a car on July 1, Year 1, with five annual payments of $20,000 each. It immediately makes the first payment, and the present value of the annuity due is $78,000 based on an assumed rate of 10 percent. The car has a five-year life. Assume that this is a capitalized lease. Indicate whether each of the following *independent* statements is true or false and briefly explain each answer.

    a. The fund-based financial statements will show a total liability of $3,900 at the end of Year 1.

    b. The government-wide financial statements will show a total liability of $58,000 at the end of Year 1.

    c. The government-wide financial statements will show total interest expense of $2,900 in Year 1.

    d. The fund-based financial statements will show total expenditures of $20,000 in Year 1.

    e. The government-wide financial statements will show a net leased asset of $70,200 at the end of Year 1.

    f. If this were an ordinary annuity so that the first payment was made in Year 2, no expenditure would be reported in the fund-based financial statements in Year 1.

    g. If the car had an eight-year life, this contract could not be a capitalized lease.

    h. Over the entire life of the car, the amount of expense recognized in the government-wide financial statements will be the same as the amount of expenditures recognized in the fund-based financial statements.

50. A city has a solid waste landfill that was filled 12 percent in Year 1 and 26 percent in Year 2. During those periods, the government expected that total closure costs would be $2 million. As a result, it paid $50,000 to an environmental company on July 1 of each of these two years. Such payments will continue for several years to come. Indicate whether each of the following *independent* statements is true or false and briefly explain each answer.

    a. The government-wide financial statements will show a $230,000 expense in Year 2 but only if reported in an enterprise fund.

    b. The fund-based financial statements will show a $50,000 liability in Year 2 if this landfill is reported in the General Fund.

    c. The fund-based financial statements will show a $50,000 liability at the end of Year 2 if this landfill is reported in an enterprise fund.

    d. If this landfill is reported in an enterprise fund, the government-wide financial statements and the fund-based financial statements will basically have the same reporting.

    e. The government-wide financial statements will show a $420,000 liability at the end of Year 2.

    f. Over the entire life of the landfill, the amount of expense recognized in the government-wide financial statements will be the same as the amount of expenditures recognized in the fund-based financial statements.

51. Use the same information as in Problem 50 except that, by the end of Year 3, the landfill is 40 percent filled. The city realizes that the total closure costs will be $3 million. Indicate whether each of the following *independent* statements is true or false and briefly explain each answer.

  a. If the city had known the costs were going to be $3 million from the beginning, the reporting on the fund-based financial statements would have been different in the past years if the landfill had been reported in an enterprise fund.

  b. If the landfill is monitored in the General Fund, a liability will be reported for the governmental activities in the government-wide financial statements at the end of Year 3.

  c. A $680,000 expense should be recognized in Year 3 in the government-wide financial statements.

  d. Because the closure costs reflect a future flow of cash, any liability reported in the government-wide financial statements must be reported at present value.

52. A city receives a copy of its original charter from the year 1799 as a gift from a citizen. The document will be put under glass and displayed in the city hall for all to see. The fair value is estimated at $10,000. Indicate whether each of the following *independent* statements is true or false and briefly explain each answer.

  a. If the city government does not have a policy for handling any proceeds if it ever sells the document, the city will have to report a $10,000 asset within its government-wide financial statements.

  b. Assume that this gift qualifies for optional handling and that the city chooses to report it as an asset. For the government-wide financial statements, depreciation is required.

  c. Assume this gift qualifies for optional handling and the document is deemed to be exhaustible. The city must report an immediate expense of $10,000 in the government-wide financial statements.

  d. Assume that this gift qualifies for optional handling. The city must make a decision as to whether to recognize a revenue of $10,000 in the government-wide financial statements.

  e. Assume that this gift qualifies for optional handling. The city can choose to report the gift in the statement of net activities for the government-wide financial statements in a way so that there is no overall net effect.

53. A city starts a public library that has separate incorporation and gets some of its money from the state and some from private donations. Indicate whether each of the following *independent* statements is true or false and briefly explain each answer.

  a. If the city appoints 7 of the 10 directors, it must report the library as a component unit.

  b. If the library is a component unit and its financial results are shown as part of the governmental activities of the city, it is known as a *blended component unit.*

  c. If the library appoints its own board but the city must approve its budget, the library must be reported as a blended component unit.

  d. The choice of whether a component unit is blended or reported discretely is up to the city's discretion.

Develop Your Skills

RESEARCH CASE 1

The City of Abernethy has adopted the requirements of *GASB Statement 34,* "Basic Financial Statements—and Management's Discussion and Analysis—for State and Local Governments" in its financial reporting. The city's accountant has now shifted attention to the reporting of infrastructure items that were acquired or constructed prior to adoption of this pronouncement. The city has three large bridges built in the later part of the 1980s that were not capitalized at the time. The accountant is interested in receiving suggestions as to how to determine a valid amount to report for these bridges.

Required:

Use a copy of *GASB Statement 34* as the basis for writing a report to this accountant to indicate various ways to make this calculation. Use examples if that will help illustrate the process.

RESEARCH CASE 2

In the November 2001 issue of *The Journal of Accountancy,* the article "How to Implement *GASB Statement No. 34*" presented financial statements created according to *GASB Statement 34* for the City of Alexandria, Virginia. Obtain a copy of that article.

Required:

1. Identify the component units included in these statements.
2. Determine whether these component units are discretely presented or blended.
3. Using a copy of *GASB Statement 34,* discuss the possible reasons that each of these activities or functions was judged to be a component unit.

ANALYSIS CASE 1

Go to the Web site www.cityofsacramento.org/cafr/2000.htm. Find the 2000 financial statements for the City of Sacramento that were produced prior to adoption of *GASB Statement 34.* This textbook chapter presented the 2004 financial statements for the same city *after* implementation of *GASB Statement 34.* Compare the form and informational content of the 2000 statements to those prepared for 2004.

Required:

Prepare the following two lists with adequate explanation:

1. Three aspects of the 2004 financial statements that seem to be superior to the 2000 financial statements.
2. Three aspects of the 2000 financial statements that seem to be superior to the 2004 financial statements.

ANALYSIS CASE 2

Go to Web site www.portlandonline.com/index.cfm?c=36692 and find the 2004 comprehensive annual financial report for the City of Portland, Oregon. This document was prepared using *GASB Statement 34.* One of the most important changes created by this standard is the requirement for inclusion of a Management's Discussion and Analysis. Read this section of the report.

Required:

Write a report indicating the types of information found in this government's MD&A that would not have previously been available in the financial statements.

COMMUNICATION CASE 1

Read the following articles and any other papers that are available on setting governmental accounting standards:

"25 Years of State and Local Governmental Financial Reporting—An Accounting Standards Perspective," *The Government Accountants Journal,* Fall 1992.

"The Governmental Accounting Standards Board: Factors Influencing Its Operation and Initial Technical Agenda," *The Government Accountants Journal,* Spring 2000.

"Governmental Accounting Standards Come of Age: Highlights from the First 20 Years," *Government Finance Review,* April 2005.

Required:

Write a short paper discussing the changes in governmental accounting that have occurred in the past few decades.

COMMUNICATION CASE 2

The City of Larissa recently opened a solid waste landfill to serve the area's citizens and businesses. The city's accountant has gone to city officials for guidance as to whether to record the landfill within the General Fund or as a separate Enterprise Fund. Officials have asked for guidance on how to make that decision and how the answer will impact the government's financial reporting.

Required:

Write a memo to the government officials describing the factors that should influence the decision as to the fund in which to report the landfill. Describe the impact that this decision will have on the city's future comprehensive annual financial reports.

EXCEL CASE

The City of Loveland has adopted *GASB Statement 34*. Now city officials are attempting to determine reported values for major infrastructure assets that it had obtained prior to the implementation of the statement. The chief concern is determining a value for the city's hundreds of miles of roads that were built at various times over the past 20 years. Each road is assumed to last for 50 years (depreciation is 2 percent per year).

As of December 31, 2007, city engineers believe that one mile of new road would cost $2.3 million. For convenience, each road is assumed to have been acquired as of January 1 of the year in which it was put into operation. Officials have done some investigation and believe that the cost of a mile of road has increased by 8 percent each year over the past 20 years.

Required:

Build a spreadsheet to determine what value should now be reported for each mile of road depending on the year it was put in operation. For example, what reported value should be disclosed in the government-wide financial statements for 10 miles of roads put into operation on January 1, 2000?

Please visit the text Web site for the online CPA Simulation: mhhe.com/hoyle8e

The City of Clarksville (Clarksville) is incorporated and has a December 31 year-end. The budget is approved by the City Council (Council) annually. For internal reporting purposes, Clarksville uses the modified accrual basis of accounting to record its General Fund transactions. For external reporting purposes, Clarksville prepares a comprehensive annual financial report that includes both government-wide and fund-based financial statements.

The city has a policy that any amounts to be received within 60 days are viewed as currently being available.

At the beginning of Year One, the Council authorized the construction of a new recreation center. The estimated cost of the recreation center is $25 million. Clarksville plans to finance the construction by (1) combining bond proceeds with a state grant and (2) a transfer from the general fund.

Topics to be covered in simulation:

- Transfers.
- Infrastructure and modified approach.
- Statement of cash flows.
- Property taxes.
- Budgetary entries.
- Nonexchange transactions.
- Revenue and expenditure recognition.
- Encumbrances.

Chapter **Eighteen**

Accounting and Reporting for Private Not-for-Profit Organizations

Questions to Consider

- Individuals, foundations, and businesses contribute large amounts of resources to not-for-profit organizations, such as charities and colleges and universities. What financial information do these contributors want regarding these not-for-profit organizations?

- What is the form of financial statements for a not-for-profit organization?

- How should a not-for-profit organization account for any restricted gifts that it receives?

- How can a contributor to a charity determine how contributed resources are used?

- How should a not-for-profit organization recognize pledges of support?

- Should a not-for-profit organization record donations of services?

America loves nonprofits. They represent what is best about the country: generosity, compassion, vision, and the eternal optimism that we can resolve our most serious problems. Unlike the for-profit sector that employs most Americans, nonprofits have a higher calling, a more noble purpose. Each week millions of people volunteer their time to nonprofits, reading to the blind, raising money for the Cancer Society, mentoring adolescents from troubled backgrounds, or doing countless other good deeds. Nonprofits show loving kindness to the most vulnerable and the most wretched in society.[1]

Not-for-profit organizations operate literally throughout the world. Many are well known for their ongoing work to achieve one or more stated objectives such as the cure for a particular disease, the eradication of hunger and poverty, or the cleanup of the environment. However, the title of *not-for-profit organization* does not have to be limited to groups with such noble goals; a wide array of entities such as civic organizations, political parties, trade associations, and fraternal organizations also are often formed as not-for-profit organizations. In fact, in 1998, more than 1.6 million not-for-profit organizations existed in the United States alone.[2]

The general characteristics that help to define a not-for-profit organization follow:

1. They receive significant amounts of contributed resources from providers who do not expect a commensurate return.
2. They have an operating purpose that is something other than providing goods and services for a profit.
3. They do not have ownership interests like those of a for-profit business enterprise.

Some not-for-profit organizations are viewed as governmental because they receive tax revenues or are controlled by a government. A state-operated hospital, for example, or

[1] Jeffrey M. Berry with David F. Arons, *A Voice for Nonprofits* (Washington, DC: Brookings Institution Press, 2003), p. 1.

[2] *The New Nonprofit Almanac & Desk Reference* (Washington, DC: Independent Sector and the Urban Institute, 2002), p. 3-5.

a public university are both governmental not-for-profit organizations. Most not-for-profit organizations, however, are nongovernmental (or private). The American Cancer Society and Mothers Against Drunk Driving are just two examples of not-for-profit organizations that do not qualify as governmental.

The amount of giving to not-for-profit organizations each year is staggering. "Estimated charitable giving reached $248.52 billion for 2004, a new record for philanthropic giving in the United States, the Giving USA Foundation announced today."[3] This generosity comes from a wide sector:

Individuals	$187.92 billion
Foundations	28.80 billion
Bequests	19.80 billion
Corporations	12.00 billion[4]

The recipients of these contributions are not-for-profit organizations representing an assortment of missions:

Religious	$ 88.30 billion
Education	33.84 billion
Foundations	24.00 billion
Unallocated giving	21.36 billion
Health	20.89 billion
Human services	19.17 billion
Arts, culture, and humanities	13.99 billion
Public society benefit	12.96 billion
Environmental/animals	7.61 billion
International affairs	5.34 billion[5]

FINANCIAL REPORTING

With so much money at stake, the interest in a not-for-profit organization's adequate and fair presentation of financial information is not surprising. Individuals, foundations, and corporations (especially current and potential contributors) are interested in knowing how financially stable the organizations are and how they spend the monies that they receive. Future gifts or grants are often based, at least in part, on the organization's ability to convince donors that it is using its resources wisely to accomplish stated goals. Financial statements are vital to this objective because they report both the resources generated and the spending decisions that have been made.

As the previous two chapters discussed, the Governmental Accounting Standards Board (GASB) has the authority to establish accounting standards for state and local governments and any organization that these governments control, such as governmental not-for-profit organizations. In contrast, the Financial Accounting Standards Board (FASB) sets accounting standards for for-profit business organizations and private not-for-profit organizations.

The current chapter presents the appropriate accounting for private not-for-profit organizations. However, an occasional comparison with the statements discussed at the end of Chapter 17 for a public college or university can be helpful in visualizing the differences that have evolved in the two sets of standards.

Prior to 1993, private not-for-profit organizations utilized a wide variety of financial reporting practices. Statements often varied significantly, depending on the specific type of organization. In that year, the FASB standardized much of the reporting to be made by private

---

[3] AAFRC Foundation Press Release, "Charitable Giving Rises 5 Percent to Nearly $250 Billion in 2004," www.aafrc.org.

[4] AAFRC Trust for Philanthropy Web site, www.aafrc.org.

[5] Ibid.

not-for-profit organizations with the issuance of two official standards. FASB *Statement (SFAS) No. 116,* "Accounting for Contributions Received and Contributions Made," established guidelines for determining when and how donations should be recognized and reported. FASB *Statement No. 117,* "Financial Statements of Not-for-Profit Organizations," specified the required financial statements and their format for these organizations.[6]

Several basic goals form the framework for the FASB's standards for private not-for-profit organizations, including these:

1. The financial statements should focus on the entity as a whole.
2. Reporting requirements for private not-for-profit organizations should be similar to those for business entities unless critical differences in the information needs of financial statement users exist.

The first of these goals is important because it asserts that the organization's financial statements should not center around the individual funds that many not-for-profit organizations use for internal recordkeeping. Historically, the reporting of not-for-profit organizations was patterned after traditional government accounting with a heavy emphasis on separate fund types. The FASB eliminated this approach to focus on the operations and financial position of the entire entity.

The second goal is significant because it allows the use of many of the same accrual basis techniques used by for-profit business entities in recording and reporting most transactions. Consequently, existing FASB standards for capital leases, pensions, contingent liabilities, and many other issues do not have to be rewritten for private not-for-profit organizations.

Financial Statements for Private Not-for-Profit Organizations

Although private not-for-profit organizations have much in common with for-profit business entities, the FASB identified three critical differences. First, the contributions that private not-for-profit organizations receive create transactions that have no counterparts in commercial accounting. Second, these contributions often have donor-imposed restrictions as to their use for a specified purpose or not until a specified time. Third, no single indicator can describe performance as effectively as net income does for commercial entities; thus, other indicators are necessary.

These differences suggest the need for a somewhat different set of financial statements for not-for-profit organizations. As a result, FASB *SFAS 117,* "Financial Statements of Not-for-Profit Organizations," requires that three financial statements be prepared and reported:

1. The *statement of financial position* reports the assets, liabilities, and net assets of private not-for-profits. The final category, net assets, replaces owners' equity or fund balance. The amount of net assets the organization holds must be classified as unrestricted, temporarily restricted, or permanently restricted. Disclosing these three categories is fundamental to the reporting of these organizations.
2. The *statement of activities and changes in net assets* reports revenues, expenses, gains, and losses for the period. Revenues and expenses are determined using the accrual basis of accounting, including depreciation of fixed assets. The statement presents the *change in each category of net assets* for the period.
3. The *statement of cash flows* uses the standard FASB classifications of cash flows from operations, investing activities, and financing activities. Cash flows from operating activities may be prepared on either the direct or indirect basis. Because this statement follows the traditional format for a business, it will not be discussed in this coverage.

In addition to these statements, voluntary health and welfare organizations are required to prepare a *statement of functional expenses* (see Exhibit 18.3 later in the chapter). Voluntary health and welfare organizations are entities that promote humanitarian activities, such as public health clinics, homeless shelters, the cure of disease, and the like. These organizations

---

[6] The American Institute of Certified Public Accountants (AICPA) issues an annual audit and accounting guide, *Not-for-Profit Organizations,* to provide additional guidance in preparing and auditing the financial statements issued by these organizations.

EXHIBIT 18.1

CHRISTIAN CHILDREN'S FUND, INC.
Consolidated Statement of Financial Position
As of June 30, 2004

Assets	2004
Cash and cash equivalents	$ 4,367,523
Investments, at fair value	26,665,751
Accounts receivable, net and other assets	7,504,907
Intangible pension asset	2,651,309
Land, buildings, and equipment, net	16,609,605
Total assets	$57,799,095
Liabilities and net assets	
Liabilities:	
Accounts payable and accrued expenses	$13,827,883
Accrued benefit liability	2,433,002
Debt	350,476
Total liabilities	16,611,361
Net assets:	
Unrestricted	7,996,434
Temporarily restricted	27,908,447
Permanently restricted	5,282,853
Total net assets	41,187,734
Total liabilities and net assets	$57,799,095

could receive some revenues from their activities but rely heavily on support from gifts from individuals, foundations, government grants, United Way allocations, and similar sources to support their work. These not-for-profit organizations are different from most private universities or hospitals that generate a considerable amount of revenue from services rendered. Normally, voluntary health and welfare organizations rely much more on donations, so the wise utilization of these resources is of special importance. The statement of functional expenses provides a detailed schedule of expenses by function (such as various programs and administrative activities) and by object (salaries, supplies, depreciation, etc.).

Statement of Financial Position

Exhibit 18.1 presents the statement of financial position for Christian Children's Fund, Inc. The asset and liability sections resemble those of business enterprises. Unlike business enterprises, individuals and organizations provide resources to not-for-profit organizations without the expectation of earning a return on their investment. As a result, the concept of owners' equity does not apply. In the place of paid-in-capital and retained earnings, the final section of the statement presents the amount of net assets, which is the excess of the organization's assets over liabilities.

Net assets are presented in three categories: unrestricted, temporarily restricted, and permanently restricted. Restrictions must be imposed by donors from outside the organization before an asset is classified as restricted. Board-designated or internally restricted assets continue to be classified as unrestricted for financial statement purposes.

Temporarily restricted assets are restricted for a particular purpose or for use in a future time period. For example, a private college could receive a grant for medical research. The amounts received from the grant are reported as being temporarily restricted for that particular use. Alternatively, the college could receive a grant supporting education programs over the next three years. The amounts received or promised for future periods also are viewed as temporarily restricted. Temporarily restricted assets represent resources that are expected to be released from restriction based on performance of some act or the passage of time. The statement of financial position published for Christian Children's Fund discloses that outside donors had restricted $27,908,447 of its net assets as of June 30, 2004, for a particular purpose or until a specific point in time. Likewise, the statement of financial position for the University of Notre Dame as of June 30, 2004, indicates temporarily restricted net assets of more than $1.18 billion.

In contrast, permanently restricted assets are those that are expected to remain restricted for as long as the organization exists, although some or all of the income is available for general or specified use. A note to the 2004 financial statements of Yale University explains its permanently restricted net asset total as "net assets that are subject to explicit donor-imposed stipulations that they be maintained permanently by the University. Generally, the donors of these assets permit the University to use the returns on the related investments over time for general or specific purposes." In the same manner, a footnote to the financial statements of the Christian Children's Fund indicates that "permanently restricted net assets were $5,282,853 and $5,056,032 at June 30, 2004 and 2003, respectively. The principal of these net assets must be invested in perpetuity; however, the income is expendable to support subsidy for children and other restricted program activities."

Statement of Activities and Changes in Net Assets

Exhibit 18.2 presents the statement of activities and changes in net assets for Christian Children's Fund. Note the format adopted here: A separate column is used for each of the three categories of net assets: unrestricted, temporarily restricted, and permanently restricted. The bottom line agrees with the net asset balances presented on the statement of financial position. Measured on the accrual basis, recognition of revenues and expenses follows the same timing standards applicable to business enterprises.

Recognition of Pledges

As stated earlier, a unique feature of not-for-profit organizations is that many receive a significant portion of their resources from contributions. One main purpose of the statement of activities is to provide a clear picture of those donations and whether the gifts were unrestricted, temporarily restricted, or permanently restricted. As in Exhibit 18.2, public support (sponsorships, contributions, and grants) is reported separately from revenues such as investment income for which an earning process exists. For the year ending June 30, 2004, Christian Children's Fund reports that it received $31 million of public support that was unrestricted, $128 million that was temporarily restricted, and $226,821 that was permanently restricted.

Many not-for-profit organizations seek pledges of support that will be followed up by actual giving. A question has always existed as to whether such pledges represent receivables that should be reported as assets. As this chapter discusses later, private not-for-profit organizations do recognize unconditional promises to give as both a receivable and a contribution revenue in the period promised. For example, as of June 30, 2004, Wake Forest University reported contributions receivable (net) of nearly $48 million. In an accompanying footnote, the school explained that "contributions, including unconditional promises to give, are recognized as revenues in the period received. Conditional promises to give are not recognized until they become unconditional, that is, when the conditions on which they depend are substantially met."

Expenses and Release of Temporarily Restricted Net Assets

All expenses are reported in a statement of activities (as in Exhibit 18.2) solely within the Unrestricted Net Assets column. In that way, this first column can be viewed as a reflection of current operations for the not-for-profit organization. For Christian Children's Fund, total unrestricted public support and revenues totaled $160.3 million while all of the organization's expenses were $158.6 million. The $1.7 million increase in unrestricted net assets is one possible measure of operating efficiency.

Recording all expenses within the unrestricted net assets causes a problem, however, in that some expenses are incurred in connection with temporarily restricted net assets. A gift, for example, could be made specifically to support the salary of the organization's employees. If the contribution is reported as temporarily restricted, how can the eventual salary expense be reflected as unrestricted? Mechanically, that does not match.

EXHIBIT 18.2

CHRISTIAN CHILDREN'S FUND, INC.
Consolidated Statement of Activities and Changes in Net Assets
For the Year Ended June 30, 2004

	Unrestricted	Temporarily Restricted	Permanently Restricted	Total 2004
Public Support:				
Sponsorships:				
U.S. sponsors	—	$ 80,719,482	—	$ 80,719,482
International sponsors	—	26,830,607	—	26,830,607
Special gifts from sponsors for children	—	13,705,046	—	13,705,046
Total sponsorships	—	121,255,135	—	121,255,135
Contributions:				
General contributions	$ 9,165,380	7,188,721	$ 224,811	16,578,912
Major gifts and bequests	4,155,246	149,807	2,010	4,307,063
Gifts in kind	325,825	—	—	325,825
Total contributions	13,646,451	7,338,528	226,821	21,211,800
Grants:				
Grants and contracts	17,481,276	—	—	17,481,276
Total public support	31,127,727	128,593,663	226,821	159,948,211
Revenue:				
Investment and currency transactions	90,161	—	—	90,161
Service fees and other	1,944,226	—	—	1,944,226
Total revenue	2,034,387	—	—	2,034,387
Net assets released from restrictions:				
Satisfaction of program and time restrictions	127,142,850	(127,142,850)	—	—
Total public support and revenue	160,304,964	1,450,813	226,821	161,982,598
Expenses:				
Program:				
Basic education	43,779,530	—	—	43,779,530
Health and sanitation	30,197,636	—	—	30,197,636
Nutrition	20,097,619	—	—	20,097,619
Early childhood development	14,708,385	—	—	14,708,385
Micro enterprise	13,530,690	—	—	13,530,690
Emergencies	5,696,459	—	—	5,696,459
Total program	128,010,319	—	—	128,010,319
Supporting services:				
Fund-raising	17,938,754	—	—	17,938,754
Management and general	12,655,166	—	—	12,655,166
Total supporting services	30,593,920	—	—	30,593,920
Total expenses from operations	158,604,239	—	—	158,604,239
Change in net assets from operations	1,700,725	1,450,813	226,821	3,378,359
Nonoperating revenue (expenses):				
Realized gain on investments	663,120	—	—	663,120
Unrealized gain on investments	2,824,029	—	—	2,824,029
Total nonoperating revenues	3,487,149	—	—	3,487,149
Change in net assets	5,187,874	1,450,813	226,821	6,865,508
Net assets at beginning of year	3,154,236	26,457,634	5,056,032	34,667,902
Minimum pension liability adjustment	(345,676)	—	—	(345,676)
Net assets at end of year	$ 7,996,434	$ 27,908,447	$5,282,853	$ 41,187,734

In such cases, the expense is still reflected as a reduction in unrestricted net assets. To the extent that any of these expenses meet stipulations established by external donors, net assets are viewed as being released from temporary restriction. As in Exhibit 18.2, this reclassification is reflected in the statement of activities by a line at the bottom of the Public Support and Revenue section. Christian Children's Fund shows more than $127 million being reclassified as "net assets released from restrictions."

Thus, that amount of temporarily restricted net assets was no longer restricted because of one or more of the following:

1. Appropriately expended for an expense as designated by the donor.
2. Appropriately expended for an asset as designated by the donor.
3. A donor restriction based on time was satisfied.

To illustrate, assume that in Year 1 a private not-for-profit organization receives three cash gifts of $10,000 each. The donor has specified that the first gift is for employee salaries, the second gift is for the purchase of equipment, and the third gift must be held until Year 2 before being expended. In Year 1, the statement of activities would show all three gifts as increases in Temporarily Restricted Net Assets.

Assume that this example is extended into Year 2 when the first two gifts are properly spent and the time restriction on the third gift is satisfied. For the first gift, cash is decreased and a salary expense is recorded in the Unrestricted Net Asset column. In addition, $10,000 is reclassified on the statement of activities from the Temporarily Restricted column to the Unrestricted column in the same manner as the $127 million in Exhibit 18.2. For the second gift, equipment (an asset) is increased and cash is decreased, but the same reclassification is made to indicate that the restriction has been met. A $10,000 reclassification must also be made for the third gift even though it has not been spent because it was restricted only as to time. The statement of activities would show a total of $30,000 as Net Assets Released from Restriction as an increase in the unrestricted net assets with an equal decrease in temporarily restricted net assets.

An alternative for handling the equipment bought with the restricted gift exists. A time restriction can be specified by the donor or assumed by the organization for the use of the asset. For example, the decision might be made to hold the equipment for its entire expected life or for a specific number of years. In that case, no immediate reclassification is made from temporarily restricted net assets to unrestricted net assets. Instead, a gradual reclassification equal to the depreciation of the asset is made each year.

Detailed information about the expenses incurred by a not-for-profit organization is considered important to contributors. One primary concern of contributors is the extent to which the not-for-profit is using the resources provided to fulfill the organizational mission. For this reason, expenses are presented in two broad categories: *program services* and *supporting services.* Program services are the organization's activities relating to its social services, research, or other objectives. Within this category, organizations may report several programs or only one. Christian Children's Fund reports six program categories: basic education, health and sanitation, nutrition, early childhood development, micro enterprise, and emergencies. Supporting service costs consist of administrative costs (management and general costs) and fund-raising expenses. These latter activities generally are not regarded as directly related to one of the organization's stated missions. Analysts frequently use the ratio of program service expenses to total expenses as one way to evaluate not-for-profits. The Better Business Bureau has suggested that ratio values of less than 60 percent are not desirable. Christian Children's Fund reports a ratio of 80.7 percent ($128.010 million/$158.604 million) for the year ended June 30, 2004.

Below the Expenses and Supporting Services sections, Christian Children's Fund reports "Nonoperating Revenue (Expenses)." FASB *SFAS 124,* "Accounting for Certain Investments Held by Not-for-Profit Organizations," requires that investments in equity securities with readily determinable market values and all debt investments be reported at fair value.[7] A not-for-profit

---

[7] The system of classifying marketable securities into portfolios such as trading securities and available-for-sale securities that business entities must utilize does not apply to private not-for-profit organizations.

entity reports the resulting unrealized gains and losses in the statement of activities. These entities report gains and losses on investments, along with dividend and interest income, as increases or decreases in unrestricted net assets unless the donor explicitly restricted this income or a law extends a donor's restrictions to it. Christian Children's Fund separately reports these gains and losses in a nonoperating section. Here, the organization shows a realized gain on the sale of investments of $663,120, along with an unrealized gain on adjusting investments to fair value of $2,824,029.

Statement of Functional Expenses

Exhibit 18.3 presents the statement of functional expenses for the Christian Children's Fund. As indicated previously, the statement of functional expenses is required only of voluntary health and welfare organizations although it is allowed for all private not-for-profit organizations.

Because contributors are concerned with how their gifts are used, this statement provides a detailed analysis of expenses by both function and object. The columns represent functions and include the six identified programs and the supporting services of management and general as well as fund-raising. These are the same categories reported on the statement of activities, and column totals agree with operating expenses reported on that statement. The rows list expenses according to their nature—for example, subsidy for children, travel, supplies, and professional services.

As a result of the scrutiny placed on the amount that a not-for-profit organization spends on fund-raising, the allocation of costs is quite important. Until a few years ago, joint costs expended for fund-raising appeals that also contained educational literature were routinely divided between fund-raising and program services. Thus, most direct mail appeals for contributions were accompanied by informational pamphlets and the like so that some portion of the cost of the mailing could be reflected as a program service expense such as educating the public.

To improve reporting in this area, the American Institute of Certified Public Accountants issued its *Statement of Position (SOP) 98–2,* "Accounting for Costs of Activities of Not-for-Profit Organizations and State and Local Governmental Entities That Include Fund-Raising." A full description of *SOP 98–2* is beyond the scope of this textbook; however, a portion of the costs of such fund-raising campaigns can still be assigned to program service costs but only if they meet several identified criteria.[8] The literature that is mailed or otherwise distributed must include a specific call for action that would have been the same even without the fund-raising appeal. This appeal cannot be directed purely at potential contributors, and the requested action must be specific and help accomplish the entity's overall mission. If all of these criteria are met, some or all of the costs associated with this call for action should be reported under program services rather than fund-raising.

For this reason, the June 30, 2004, financial statements of the American Heart Association, Inc., included the following note:

> In 2004 and 2003, the Association conducted joint cost activities that included a fund-raising appeal. Those activities primarily included direct mail campaigns and special events. The costs of conducting those activities were as follows:

	2004	2003
Fund-raising	$30,205,250	$26,732,438
Public health education	50,256,229	45,126,703
Professional education and training	2,477,516	133,101
Community services	416,006	81,923
Management and general	2,409,572	2,050,454
Total joint costs	$85,764,573	$74,124,619

> The Association allocates joint costs using the physical units methodology.

Evolution of Standard-Setting Authority

Hospitals as well as colleges and universities can function as private not-for-profit organizations, as part of a government, or as for-profit businesses. A municipal hospital, for example, may be

---

[8] For more information on *SOP 98–2,* see "How to Report a Joint Activity," *Journal of Accountancy,* August 1998.

EXHIBIT 18.3

CHRISTIAN CHILDREN'S FUND, INC.
Consolidated Statement of Functional Expenses
Year Ended June 30, 2004

	Program Services				
	Basic Education	Health and Sanitation	Nutrition	Early Childhood Development	Micro Enterprise
Subsidy for children	$28,244,409	$19,482,036	$12,966,001	$9,489,131	$8,729,340
Program grants	7,653,994	5,279,465	3,513,675	2,571,473	2,365,576
Supplies.	260,339	179,574	119,513	87,465	80,462
Occupancy.	291,022	200,737	133,598	97,773	89,944
Professional services.	162,317	111,961	74,514	54,533	50,166
Contract services	788,928	544,176	362,169	265,052	243,830
Travel.	682,117	470,501	313,136	229,167	210,818
Conferences and meetings.	561,718	387,454	257,864	188,717	173,607
Automobile and truck expense	162,239	111,907	74,478	54,507	50,142
Advertising and public education	31,859	21,976	14,626	10,704	9,847
Equipment purchases and rentals.	143,397	98,910	65,828	48,176	44,319
Telephone and cables.	211,585	145,944	97,131	71,085	65,393
Postage and freight	154,755	106,744	71,042	51,992	47,829
Staff training	187,072	129,036	85,878	62,849	57,817
Miscellaneous expenses	251,334	173,361	115,378	84,439	77,678
Total expenses before personnel costs and other expenses	39,787,085	27,443,782	18,264,831	13,367,063	12,296,768
Salaries	2,845,055	1,962,423	1,306,063	955,839	879,305
Employee benefits	554,838	382,708	254,706	186,406	171,480
Payroll taxes.	223,669	154,279	102,678	75,145	69,128
Total personnel costs	3,623,562	2,499,410	1,663,447	1,217,390	1,119,913
Interest	13,926	9,606	6,393	4,679	4,304
Depreciation	354,957	244,838	162,948	119,253	109,705
Total other expenses	368,883	254,444	169,341	123,932	114,009
Total expenses from operations	$43,779,530	$30,197,636	$20,097,619	$14,708,385	$13,530,690

in direct competition with either a private not-for-profit hospital or a for-profit hospital. After the creation of the Governmental Accounting Standards Board (GASB) in 1984, questions of standard setting for governmental not-for-profit organizations and private not-for-profit organizations began to be raised:

• Should two sets of accounting principles or just one be developed?
• If just one set of principles was to be applied to all not-for-profit organizations, which body should create these principles?

A crisis eventually arose in connection with the recording of depreciation expense by not-for-profit organizations that led to a solution as to the division of authority for standard setting.

Prior to 1987, not-for-profit organizations, especially colleges and universities, had been permitted but not required to report depreciation expense. Not surprisingly, because of the impact on current balances (and the work necessary to compute the amounts), few institutions chose to include annual depreciation figures voluntarily. In discussing depreciation, the argument was frequently made that profitability is not a goal of these organizations so that the calculation and recording of this expense is inappropriate. Some college officials also contended

| Emergencies | Total Program Services | Supporting Services | | | Program and Supporting Services |
		Fund-Raising	Management and General	Total Supporting Services	2004
$3,675,077	$ 82,585,994	—	—	—	$ 82,585,994
995,914	22,380,097	—	—	—	22,380,097
33,875	761,228	$ 81,826	$ 610,812	$ 692,638	1,453,866
37,867	850,941	5,418	422,176	427,594	1,278,535
21,120	474,611	373,529	489,261	862,790	1,337,401
102,653	2,306,808	1,262,695	1,535,713	2,798,408	5,105,216
88,755	1,994,494	308,470	172,222	480,692	2,475,186
73,089	1,642,449	34,902	58,569	93,471	1,735,920
21,110	474,383	2,426	1,680	4,106	478,489
4,145	93,157	13,212,992	—	13,212,992	13,306,149
18,658	419,288	14,330	338,356	352,686	771,974
27,531	618,669	18,404	106,171	124,575	743,244
20,136	452,498	107,664	942,681	1,050,345	1,502,843
24,341	546,993	30,393	20,808	51,201	598,194
32,703	734,893	283,501	1,213,040	1,496,541	2,231,434
5,176,974	116,336,503	15,736,550	5,911,489	21,648,039	137,984,542
370,190	8,318,875	1,821,551	4,155,308	5,976,859	14,295,734
72,194	1,622,332	253,584	1,390,106	1,643,690	3,266,022
29,103	654,002	125,184	302,056	427,240	1,081,242
471,487	10,595,209	2,200,319	5,847,470	8,047,789	18,642,998
1,812	40,720	—	9,138	9,138	49,858
46,186	1,037,887	1,885	887,069	888,954	1,926,841
47,998	1,078,607	1,885	896,207	898,092	1,976,699
$5,696,459	$128,010,319	$17,938,754	$12,655,166	$30,593,920	$158,604,239

that fund-raising campaigns (rather than operations) commonly financed new acquisitions so that ensuring the availability of adequate resources through the recognition of depreciation was not considered necessary.

However, in August 1987, the FASB issued *SFAS 93,* "Recognition of Depreciation by Not-for-Profit Organizations." This pronouncement required all not-for-profit organizations (other than state and local governments) to recognize depreciation. The rule pertained to both purchased assets and properties acquired by donation. It was aimed at colleges and universities, religious institutions, and other not-for-profit organizations. The FASB justified this action by stating in paragraph 20,

> Using up assets acquired involves a cost to the organization because the economic benefits (or service potential) used up are no longer available to the organization. That is as true for assets acquired without cost as it is for assets acquired at a cost.

At that time, several types of public not-for-profit organizations (governmental colleges and universities, public benefit corporations and authorities, public employee retirement systems, governmental utilities, and governmental hospitals and other health care providers) had been directed to follow GASB pronouncements. However, according to the rules of the day, if the accounting treatment of a transaction or event was not explicitly specified by a GASB pronouncement, applicable FASB pronouncements had to be utilized.

Consequently, in January 1988, the GASB countered with a pronouncement of its own, *Statement 8,* "Applicability of FASB Statement No. 93, *Recognition of Depreciation by Not-for-Profit Organizations* (*SFAS No. 93*), to Certain State and Local Governmental Entities." This standard exempted public colleges and universities (as well as the other governmental not-for-profit institutions) from recording depreciation. According to paragraph 4,

> Some governmental entities that engage in activities similar to private, not-for-profit organizations covered by *FASB Statement 93* follow governmental fund accounting and reporting principles. Those governmental entities follow GASB standards for depreciation and are therefore not affected by *FASB Statement 93.*

Until that time, the FASB had focused on accounting for for-profit businesses and the GASB had concentrated on state and local governments. The lines of authority over not-for-profit organizations had not been subjected to intense scrutiny. Suddenly, colleges and other not-for-profits found themselves being guided by two different authoritative bodies. Public schools, such as The Ohio State University and The University of Texas, were to follow GASB so that recording depreciation was voluntary. In contrast, private institutions such as Harvard University and Duke University came under the auspices of the FASB and had to report depreciation expense.

A power struggle quickly resulted with the reporting organizations caught in the middle. "I see the two groups as somewhat entrenched in their positions," said Carl Hanes, the vice president for administration at the State University of New York at Stony Brook. "I see it as a real mess. We have two credible, professional organizations with different voices, and the imposition of their views on the different types of institutions could generate financial information that's not comparable."[9]

Officials reacted with dismay at the dual set of rules that had been established. Debates arose as to whether depreciation was truly applicable to not-for-profit organizations. Many administrators (but certainly not all) seemed to prefer the traditional view that the cost of generating depreciation data would outweigh any possible benefits:

> Depreciating the university's 160 buildings and equipment worth over $1 billion could cost us up to $200,000 for new computer software to do the figuring each year," estimates William J. Hogan, comptroller of the University of Chicago, a private institution. "It really isn't worth it."[10]

versus

> Depreciation accounting not only ought to be adopted, but it should be adopted in the operating statement and funded by mandatory transfer to the plant funds. Only in this way will financial statements show the true impact and cost of depreciation, providing users of such statements with more accurate information.[11]

Just before *SFAS 93* was scheduled to take effect, the FASB postponed the effective date to allow time for a compromise to be developed. The Financial Accounting Foundation (FAF), which oversees and funds both the FASB and the GASB, stepped in to help mediate a solution to the territorial argument. Numerous compromises were proposed. On October 30, 1989, the FAF voted to give the FASB jurisdiction over both governmental and private not-for-profit organizations. Thus, only one set of accounting standards would apply to all such entities.

However, that ruling only escalated the controversy. Ten different government groups immediately threatened to stop supporting the GASB unless all public entities (such as state universities)

[9] John B. Thomas, "Higher Education Is the Victim in FASB–GASB Dispute," *Business Officer,* January 1988, p. 20.

[10] Lee Berton, "Several Private Colleges May Ignore New Accounting Rule on Depreciation," *The Wall Street Journal,* February 4, 1988.

[11] Phillip Jones, Sr., Clarence Jung, Jr., and Herbert Peterson, "Why Not Depreciate and Why Not in Operations?" *Business Officer,* April 1989, p. 33.

remained under its jurisdiction.[12] Faced with a problem having no end in sight, the FAF reversed itself and gave the GASB authority over governmental not-for-profit organizations.

Following that final assignment of authority in 1989, the differences in financial reporting for private and governmental not-for-profit organizations continued to become more numerous. Consequently, the financial statements produced by these two groups of organizations in the 1990s could hardly be considered comparable.

Accounting for public colleges and universities, however, became standardized in November 1999 when the GASB issued its *Statement 35,* "Basic Financial Statements—and Management's Discussion and Analysis—for Public Colleges and Universities—An Amendment to GASB *Statement 34,*" which applied the reporting standards (including depreciation) established by GASB *Statement 34* to public schools. As noted previously, many governmental schools have decided that they are solely proprietary funds so that only fund-based statements are needed. Thus, this pronouncement narrowed many of the distinctions between the two reporting models but not all. Apparently, the need for precise comparability between these public and private organizations is not viewed as essential.

The GAAP Hierarchy

At some point in the development of accounting standards, the relationship between governmental not-for-profit organizations and FASB pronouncements almost had to be redefined. Even after its authority was reinstated, the GASB could not stop its ongoing work, every time FASB issued a new statement, to evaluate whether the standard should be voided for governmental not-for-profit organizations. The AICPA Auditing Standards Board crafted a resolution in its *Statement on Auditing Standards 69,* "The Meaning of 'Presents Fairly in Conformity with Generally Accepted Accounting Principles' in the Independent Auditor's Report," issued in 1991. This standard created a hierarchy for determining whether an accounting treatment should be judged as being in compliance with generally accepted accounting principles (GAAP). Accounting pronouncements and other potential guidelines for both nongovernmental entities as well as state and local governments[13] are grouped into levels. The higher levels are more authoritative than the lower ones.

The GAAP hierarchy placed GASB statements and interpretations at the highest level for state and local governments. This same ranking is appropriate for AICPA and FASB pronouncements *but only if they are made applicable to state and local governments by a GASB statement or interpretation.* Thus, even though a GASB statement may not provide specific guidance in a particular area of financial reporting, FASB statements no longer become automatically appropriate for governmental not-for-profit organizations. Instead, the GASB can study and evaluate each new pronouncement and act if it believes that the guidelines should be followed.

For state and local governments, the GAAP hierarchy is structured as follows with the sources listed at higher levels having the most authority:

Level 1: Governmental Accounting Standards Board (GASB) statements and interpretations, plus AICPA and Financial Accounting Standards Board (FASB) pronouncements if made applicable to state and local governments by a GASB statement or interpretation.

Level 2: GASB technical bulletins, and the following pronouncements if specifically made applicable to state and local governments by the GASB: AICPA industry audit and accounting guides and AICPA statements of position.

Level 3: AICPA Accounting Standards Executive Committee practice bulletins if specifically made applicable to state and local governmental entities and cleared by the GASB. Also, consensus positions of a group of accountants organized by the GASB that attempts to reach consensus positions on accounting issues applicable to state and local governmental entities.

---

[12] See, for more information, "The Great GASB," *Forbes,* December 11, 1989, p. 60.

[13] The Auditing Standards Board has also created a separate hierarchy for the reporting of the federal government in its *Statement on Auditing Standards No. 91,* "Federal GAAP Hierarchy."

Level 4: Implementation guides (Q&As) published by the GASB, as well as industry practices widely recognized and prevalent.

Other Sources: Other accounting literature, including GASB concepts statements and AICPA and FASB pronouncements when not specifically made applicable to state and local governmental entities.

However, as the following news release specified, the GAAP hierarchy for nongovernmental entities is apparently in a period of transition:

> In connection with its effort to improve the quality of financial accounting standards and the standard-setting process, the Financial Accounting Standards Board (FASB) has published an Exposure Draft, *The Hierarchy of Generally Accepted Accounting Principles.* The GAAP hierarchy, which currently resides in American Institute of Certified Public Accountants Statement on Auditing Standards No. 69, *The Meaning of Present Fairly in Conformity with Generally Accepted Accounting Principles (SAS 69),* ranks the relative authority of accounting principles issued from multiple standard setters. Recently, the Securities and Exchange Commission reaffirmed the FASB as the designated private-sector standard setter for public companies, and the FASB has implemented procedures to narrow the types of accounting principles that it issues. Further, the FASB's codification and retrieval project will integrate existing U.S. GAAP into a single authoritative retrievable source, thereby creating a single authoritative codification of GAAP. This proposed Statement, in connection with those developments and efforts, represents a necessary step toward achieving the ultimate vision for simplification of standard setting: one process and one form of guidance.
>
> The Exposure Draft carries forward the GAAP hierarchy as set forth in *SAS 69,* subject to certain modifications that are not expected to result in a change in current practice. In commenting on the Exposure Draft, FASB Chairman Robert Herz stated, "The proposed statement is an important first step toward improving the GAAP hierarchy. Several other FASB projects, such as the codification and retrieval project, aim to simplify standards and the standard-setting process. This proposed statement facilitates those future improvements."[14]

This proposed change establishes the FASB's authority over the GAAP hierarchy for nongovernmental entities rather than creating significant changes. Although predictions about the outcome of any FASB exposure draft are laced with uncertainty, here is the expected hierarchy that would be created by this exposure draft. The sources of accounting principles that are generally accepted would be categorized in descending order of authority as follows:

1. AICPA Accounting Research Bulletins and Accounting Principles Board Opinions that are not superseded by action of the FASB, FASB Statements of Financial Accounting Standards and Interpretations, FASB *Statement 133* Implementation Issues, and FASB Staff Positions.
2. FASB Technical Bulletins and, if cleared by the FASB, AICPA Industry Audit and Accounting Guides and Statements of Position.
3. AICPA Accounting Standards Executive Committee Practice Bulletins that have been cleared by the FASB and consensus positions of the FASB Emerging Issues Task Force (EITF).
4. Implementation guides (Q&As) published by the FASB staff, AICPA accounting interpretations, and practices that are widely recognized and prevalent either generally or in the industry.

If these sources do not cover the issue in question, other accounting literature should be consulted including, for example, FASB concepts statements; AICPA issues papers; International Financial Reporting Standards (IFRSs) of the International Accounting Standards Board (IASB); pronouncements of other professional associations or regulatory agencies; Technical Information Service Inquiries and Replies included in AICPA Technical Practice Aids; and accounting textbooks, handbooks, and articles.

---

[14] Financial Accounting Standards Board News Release, "FASB Issues Proposal on the GAAP Hierarchy," April 28, 2005.

ACCOUNTING FOR CONTRIBUTIONS

Contributions are obviously a major source of support for many private not-for-profits. FASB *SFAS 116* defines contributions as unconditional transfers of cash or other resources to an entity in a voluntary nonreciprocal transaction. According to *SFAS 116,* contributions are recognized as revenue in the period received at their fair value.

Conditional promises to give are not recognized as revenue until the conditions are met. Conditions, however, differ from restrictions. Conditional promises require some future action on the part of the not-for-profit organization before the asset can be transferred. Restricted contributions specify how the contributions are expected to be used and are recognized as increases in either temporarily restricted net assets or permanently restricted net assets when the promise is received.

Thus, a $1,000 pledge to be paid in eight months that is restricted for the purchase of library books is recorded as follows because it is not conditional. However, a $9,000 pledge to be made if a famous biology professor could be hired is not recorded until that person is hired. In the second case, the conditions have not yet been met.

Pledge Receivable	1,000	
Temporarily Restricted Net Assets—Contributions		1,000
Unconditional pledge of gift made to organization to buy library books.		

Because contribution revenue is recognized at fair value, the estimated uncollectible portion of pledged amounts should be deducted from contribution revenue and an allowance account established to present the receivable at its expected net realizable value. Furthermore, promises that are not expected to be collected within one year are discounted to present value using an appropriate interest rate, such as the organization's incremental borrowing rate or the rate of return on its investment portfolio.

For example, as of June 30, 2004, Georgetown University reported contributions receivable of nearly $98 million, approximately $34 million of which were not expected to be received for more than one year. The balance being reported was reduced by (1) $5.6 million to arrive at the present value of the expected cash flows and (2) an allowance for doubtful accounts of nearly $27.7 million. Thus, this school reported a net receivable balance of $64.6 million as a result of its unconditional pledges. A note to the financial statements indicated that the discount rate for determining present value had varied from 3.49 percent to 6.42 percent during 2003 and 2004.

Cash is not the only type of support that not-for-profits receive. Many organizations receive donations of materials intended either to be used by the charity itself (such as vehicles, office furniture, and computers) or to be distributed to needy groups or individuals (food, clothing, and toys). Organizations such as the Salvation Army and Goodwill Industries use these types of donations to provide a central resource essential to the charity's ongoing operations.

Because donated supplies and other materials provide resources for the organization, it should report these contributions as support unless the organization cannot use or sell them. Although a value is sometimes apparent (for example, if a new vehicle is given), donations such as used clothing, furniture, and toys can be difficult to assess. In such cases, the use of estimates and averages is allowed provided that they reasonably approximate the results of detailed measurements.

Assume as an illustration that a local voluntary health and welfare organization begins a drive to gather furniture and clothing for needy families living in the area. It receives the following items:

Bed	$200 fair value
Tables and chairs	130 fair value
New clothing	500 fair value
Used clothing	75 estimated resale value
Total	$905

ARE TWO SETS OF GAAP REALLY NEEDED FOR COLLEGES AND UNIVERSITIES?

As this and the previous chapter discussed, governmental colleges and universities must follow GASB standards. For that reason, these schools have been directed to use the same reporting model that state and local governments follow, although such schools frequently view themselves as consisting solely of business-type activities so that they need only fund-based statements.

Private not-for-profit colleges and universities adhere to FASB requirements and prepare financial statements as illustrated in this chapter. GAAP for public schools comes from the GASB; for private schools, it comes from the FASB.

Readers of college and university financial statements may want to compare the data presented by various institutions. The use of this information is especially important to potential donors who are attempting to evaluate each school's efficiency and effectiveness in utilizing the funding that it receives.

Does the division between the financial reporting appropriate for public colleges and universities and that utilized by private colleges and universities serve these users well? Are these two types of schools so different that they require two different sets of generally accepted accounting principles created by two different official bodies? Should one set of GAAP apply to all schools? Should only one group be in charge of developing GAAP for colleges and universities?

In addition, one patron donates $32,000 in marketable securities to the charity with the stipulation that it hold the investments in perpetuity and use all income to support local needy families.

Assuming that the charity distributed the furniture and clothing almost immediately after it received them, the not-for-profit organization records the following journal entries:

Inventory of Donated Material	905	
Unrestricted Net Assets—Contributions		905
To record gifts made to organization to be distributed to needy individuals.		
Community Service Expenses—Assistance to Needy	905	
Inventory of Donated Materials		905
To record distribution of furniture and clothing to needy individuals.		
Investments in Marketable Securities	32,000	
Permanently Restricted Net Assets—Contributions		32,000
To record donation of investments to be held by the organization forever with all income to be used to aid needy families in the local area.		

In connection with the donation of marketable securities as recorded here, the organization will record income, when it is eventually earned, as an increase in temporarily restricted net assets. That particular money must be used for the purpose designated by the donor. So it is temporarily restricted until the purpose is met, and then it will be released from restriction to unrestricted net assets.

Donations of Works of Art and Historical Treasures

In 1990, the FASB issued an exposure draft that would have required the recipient to record all contributions, including works of art and museum pieces, as assets with a corresponding increase in revenues. Rarely has an accounting proposal created such adverse public reaction. The FASB was deluged with more than 1,000 letters, virtually all in opposition. The argument against recognizing additions to collections is that works of art and the like do not provide the same types of benefits as contributions of cash or investments. Items held for research or public exhibit create little or no direct increase in cash flows. In fact, most such items will actually require continual outflows of cash for insurance, maintenance, and the like. Thus, they are not assets in the traditional sense. Opponents of the exposure draft argued that recognizing donations as revenues would mislead potential donors who were evaluating the organization's operating results.

The opposition apparently influenced the FASB because *SFAS 116* exempted gifts of works of art, historical treasures, and similar assets. Recognition of these contributions is *not* required if they are (1) added to a collection for public exhibition, education, or research; (2) protected and preserved; and (3) sold, at which time any proceeds generated will be used to acquire other collection items. For this reason, a note to Georgetown University's 2004 financial statements explains that the school has elected not to capitalize the cost or value of its collection of works of art, historical treasures, and similar assets. However, a note to Princeton University's financial statements for the year ended June 30, 2001, shows a different approach: "Art objects acquired subsequent to June 30, 1973, are recorded at cost or fair value at the date of gift."

A very subtle difference between private not-for-profit accounting and that utilized for state and local government units is evident here. The criteria for qualifying as a work of art or historical treasure is basically the same. However, the choice here is between recording the revenue and the asset versus no reporting. Governments do not have the same choice. A government must record the contributed revenue (if received by donation). It then has the choice of recording either an asset or an expense when the item in question is a work of art or historical treasure.

Capitalizing art works or historical treasures as assets again raises the issue of depreciation. Private not-for-profit organizations are not required to record depreciation on such assets if the assets' lives are viewed as extraordinarily long. The assumption must be that the organization has the technological and financial ability to preserve an item and that the item's value is such that the organization has committed to preserve it.

Holding Contributions for Others

Some not-for-profit organizations, such as the United Way, raise donations that will be distributed to other designated charities, or they accept gifts that must be conveyed to other specified beneficiaries. A community group might solicit donations by allowing the donor to identify the charity to be benefited. Such conveyances raise questions as to the appropriate recording for the donor, the initial recipient, and the specified beneficiary. For example, assume that Donor A gives $10,000 in cash to Charity M that it must then convey to Beneficiary Z. This contribution raises several reporting questions:

• Does Donor A always record an expense when it conveys the cash to the charity, or must there be an actual transfer to the eventual beneficiary before it records an expense?
• Does Charity M report a contribution revenue of $10,000 or only a liability to Z?
• At what point should Beneficiary Z recognize a contribution revenue in connection with this gift?

For a conveyance of this type of gift, the donor normally records an expense when it conveys the property to the not-for-profit organization (Charity M) because it has relinquished control over the asset. In this case, Donor A makes the following entry:

Donor A

Expense—Charitable Contribution	10,000	
Cash		10,000

However, if the donor retains the right to redirect the use of the gift or if the donation can be revoked, Donor A continues to hold power over the asset and should not record an expense until it conveys the item. Until that time, Donor A makes the following entry instead of the previous one:

Donor A

Refundable Advance to Charity M	10,000	
Cash		10,000

The not-for-profit organization usually records a liability to the beneficiary for such gifts (rather than a contribution revenue). The money is simply passing through the not-for-profit organization and is not creating any direct benefit. Thus, for this example, the charity will most likely make the following journal entry for the money received:

Charity M		
Cash	10,000	
Liability to Beneficiary Z		10,000

However, if the donor retains the right to revoke or redirect the gift, the charity will not be certain as to whether the money will actually go to the named beneficiary. Thus, if the donor retains such rights, the charity's preceding entry is changed to the following:

Charity M		
Cash	10,000	
Refundable Advance from Donor A		10,000

In this type of arrangement, the charitable organization records only a contribution revenue and a contribution expense in one situation. If the donor has not retained the right to revoke or redirect the gift and has given the charity variance powers that allow it to change the beneficiary, the charity controls the asset and should record the following entry rather than either of the previous two entries. Subsequently, the charity records an expense when the $10,000 goes to the beneficiary.

Charity M		
Cash	10,000	
Temporarily Restricted Net Assets—Contributions		10,000

The beneficiary of such a gift eventually must record its own contribution revenue. In these cases, if the donor has retained the right to revoke or redirect the gift or if the charitable organization is given variance powers to change the beneficiary, the named beneficiary makes no entry until it receives the gift. Too much uncertainty exists until then. The beneficiary really has no power to control the property's movement until it possesses the property. However, if the donor has not kept the right to revoke or redirect the gift and the charity has not received variance powers, the beneficiary should record the donation as soon as the donor makes the gift to the not-for-profit organization:

Beneficiary Z		
Contribution Receivable	10,000	
Contribution Revenue		10,000

If Beneficiary Z is a not-for-profit organization, this final entry also needs to indicate whether the donation was unrestricted, temporarily restricted, or permanently restricted.

Contributed Services

Donated services are an especially significant means of support for many not-for-profits. The number of volunteers working in some organizations can reach into the thousands. Charities rely heavily on these individuals to fill administrative positions and to serve in fund-raising and program activities. For example, for the year ended June 30, 2004, the American Heart

Association recognized more than $31.5 million in contributed services. The notes to its financial statements indicate that these donations included research program services, public health education, professional education, community service, management and general administration, and fund-raising.

Not-for profits recognize contributed services as revenue but only if the service (1) creates or enhances a nonfinancial asset or (2) requires a specialized skill possessed by the contributor that would typically need to be purchased if not donated. Examples of the first type include donated labor by carpenters, electricians, and masons. If these services enhanced nonfinancial assets, the organization would recognize the fair value of the services received as an increase in both fixed assets and contribution revenue. Examples of the second type of donation include contributed legal or accounting services that are recognized as both an expense and a revenue when contributed.

The organization does not recognize contributed services (such as volunteer servers at a soup kitchen) as revenue if they fail to meet these criteria. This is not because the services have no value but because of the difficulty in measuring their fair value. For example, the American Heart Association's financial statements explain,

> The Association receives services from a large number of volunteers who give significant amounts of their time to the Association's programs, fund-raising campaigns, and management. No amounts have been reflected for these types of donated services as they do not meet the criteria outlined.

To illustrate, assume that a certified public accountant provides accounting services that would have cost a local charity $2,000 if they were not donated. Assume also that a carpenter donated materials ($4,000) and labor ($3,500) to construct an addition to the charity's facilities. The not-for-profit organization records the following journal entries:

General and Administrative Expenses—Accounting Services	2,000	
Unrestricted Net Assets—Contributed Services		2,000
To record contribution of professional services.		
Buildings and Improvements	7,500	
Unrestricted Net Assets—Contributed Services		3,500
Unrestricted Net Assets—Contributed Materials		4,000
To record contribution of professional services and materials.		

As with virtually all official rules, this standard cannot cover every possible scenario. For example, assume that a children's hospital has never performed heart surgery and has no plan to do so in the future. However, a local heart surgeon donates $500,000 worth of services to the hospital to allow it to perform a number of heart operations on local children who are without insurance coverage. Should the hospital recognize the donation of this specialized skill in the financial statements even though the hospital would not have otherwise purchased it? The precise wording of the rule implies that the answer is no, but the spirit of the pronouncement (to record donations of real value) seems to indicate yes as the proper answer. Situations such as this require a very careful reading of the standard and all available background information during the preparation of the financial statements. Official rules never eliminate the need for the accountant to use professional judgment.

Exchange Transactions

Exchange transactions are reciprocal transfers when both parties give and receive something of value. Many not-for-profit organizations have regular charges. The local YMCA might have monthly membership dues, and Christian Children's Fund has monthly sponsorship fees. The reminders that arrive in the mail each month look very similar, but should the accounting for both be the same? Membership dues and the like are frequently considered reciprocal transfers; the member typically receives benefits in the form of newsletters, journals, and use of organization facilities and services. Because these transactions do not meet the definition of a contribution, they follow normal accrual basis accounting and are recognized as revenue when earned. However, if the paying person derives no benefits from the monthly charges, the conveyance is viewed as a contribution. In some situations, the value of the benefits to be derived is less than the amount paid. Logically, the not-for-profit organization should report the excess amount as a contribution.

Recording membership dues as either earned revenue or contributed revenue causes no net effect on the financial statements but does shift the way in which the organization appears to gain support. For example, assume that a not-for-profit organization receives $5,000 in dues from its membership. These members receive a journal and several other benefits valued at $3,600. The organization reports the receipt of this money as follows:

Cash	5,000	
Unrestricted Net Assets—Revenue from Dues		3,600
Unrestricted Net Assets—Contributions		1,400
To record receipt of membership dues where members receive benefits valued at $3,600.		

TRANSACTIONS ILLUSTRATED

The following transactions demonstrate some typical journal entries for a private not-for-profit organization. Because FASB *SFAS 117* focuses on the entity as a whole, the organization does not need to record transactions in separate funds. However, many not-for-profits choose to use a fund format for internal management purposes and frequently design their general ledger using separate funds. FASB *SFAS 117* permits reporting by funds as supplemental information, provided that all interfund transactions have been eliminated.

Assume, for example, that Shenandoah Seminary, a private college, began the year 2007 with unrestricted net assets of $1,250,000 and a permanently restricted endowment of $700,000. During 2007 the seminary received the following contributions from alumni and friends:

Unrestricted pledges due within 12 months $130,000
Cash contributions to the endowment 50,000

Because the seminary should collect the pledges within 12 months, it need not compute or record present value. The seminary estimated that it will collect 85 percent of these unrestricted pledges and made the following entry:

1. Cash	50,000	
Pledges Receivable	130,000	
Allowance for Uncollectible Pledges ($130,000 × 15%)		19,500
Unrestricted Net Assets—Contributions		110,500
Permanently Restricted Net Assets—Contributions		50,000
To record contributions received.		

Before the end of the fiscal period, the seminary collected $100,000 of the amount pledged and wrote off $5,000 of the pledges as this journal entry reflects:

2. Cash	100,000	
Allowance for Uncollectible Pledges	5,000	
Pledges Receivable		105,000
To record pledges collected and written off.		

The seminary later receives a $20,000 cash gift that the outside donor has restricted to provide support for a series of lectures by visiting scholars. In addition, the seminary charges its students $800,000 in tuition and other fees. Assume, however, that the seminary awards $200,000 in scholarships and other financial assistance.

Because of the high costs involved in obtaining a college education, many schools award a significant amount of financial aid to their students. At one time, schools reported such scholarships and other financial assistance as operating expenses separately from revenue. Now, however, to provide a more accurate picture of the impact that scholarships and financial assistance have on tuition, schools report the two figures together and then net them.

Consequently, for illustration purposes, a comparison of tuition and fees to scholarships and other assistance can be easily made for private colleges and universities:

School	Student Tuition and Fees	Scholarships and Other Assistance	Net Amount/Percentage
Notre Dame	$295.4 million	$100.3 million	$195.1 million (66.0%)
Wake Forest	159.0 million	47.0 million	112.0 million (70.4)
Colgate	77.4 million	24.3 million	53.1 million (68.6)
Georgetown	364.3 million	61.6 million	302.7 million (83.1)
Vanderbilt	317.1 million	112.3 million	204.8 million (64.6)

Thus, students at these schools paid an average of 64.6 to 83.1 percent of the tuition and fees that their schools charged.

The journal entries for the restricted gift and for the tuition charges and scholarships follow:

3. Cash	20,000	
Temporarily Restricted Net Assets—Contributions		20,000
Gift restricted for use in a lecture series.		
Tuition Receivable	800,000	
Unrestricted Net Assets—Tuition Revenue		800,000
Tuition charged for the current period.		
Financial Aid	200,000	
Tuition Receivable		200,000
To record financial aid awards for the current year.		

Assume further that the seminary in this illustration incurred liabilities of $640,000 ($575,000 for operating expenses broken down as the following entry shows and $65,000 for equipment). Of this total, it paid $625,000 before year-end:

4. Instructional Expenses	265,000	
Student Services Expenses	120,000	
Maintenance Expense	75,000	
Administrative Expenses	115,000	
Accounts Payable		575,000
To record expenses for the year.		
5. Equipment	65,000	
Accounts Payable		65,000
To record purchases of equipment.		
6. Accounts Payable	625,000	
Cash		625,000
To record partial payment of outstanding accounts payable.		

Depreciation on buildings and equipment amounted to $135,000 for the year, as shown in the following journal entry:

7. Depreciation Expense—Instruction	80,000
Depreciation Expense—Student Services	20,000
Depreciation Expense—Administration	35,000
Accumulated Depreciation, Buildings, and Equipment	135,000
To record depreciation on fixed assets.	

Reporting Transactions on Statement of Activities

The year-end reporting must reflect the changes within the three categories of net assets. In preparing the statement of activities, private not-for-profits must report any temporarily restricted resources that have been released from restriction because the nonprofit performed some activity or the passage of time occurred. Assume here that the instructional expenses shown in entry (4) include $15,500 of expenses relating to the series of lectures by visiting scholars. The following table summarizes changes in unrestricted, temporarily restricted, and permanently restricted net assets for the year:

	Calculation of Change in Net Assets		
Journal Entry	Unrestricted Net Assets	Temporarily Restricted Net Assets	Permanently Restricted Net Assets
1	$ 110,500		$50,000
3	800,000	$ 20,000	
	(200,000)		
4	(575,000)		
7	(135,000)		
Net assets released from restriction	15,500	(15,500)	
Increase (decrease) in net assets	$ 16,000	$ 4,500	$50,000

Because all expenses are reflected as a decrease in unrestricted net assets, the $15,500 release of the temporarily restricted net assets is added to unrestricted net assets so that the increase and the expense appear in the same column. The preceding table does not reflect journal entries 2, 5, and 6 because they did not create a change in the seminary's net assets.

ACCOUNTING FOR HEALTH CARE ORGANIZATIONS

Each type of not-for-profit organization tends to retain some unique elements of financial reporting that have evolved over the years. Voluntary health and welfare organizations, for example, must report a statement of functional expenses. Probably the most distinctive version of not-for-profit accounting belongs to health care organizations. From a quantitative perspective, the providers of health care services have created many thousands of institutions in operation throughout the United States; virtually every city and town has hospitals, nursing homes, and medical clinics. The large number of enterprises is not surprising; health care expenditures now make up more than 15 percent of the gross national product in this country.[15] Because of society's focus on health care, a wide array of organizations including for-profit endeavors, governmental operations, and not-for-profit entities have emerged.

One major factor influencing the financial reporting of health care organizations is the presence of third-party payors such as insurance companies, Medicare, and Medicaid. These organizations, rather than the individual patient, pay all or some of the cost of medical services the patient receives. Because of the significant monetary amounts involved, third-party payors

[15] Earl R. Wilson, Susan C. Kattelus, and Leon E. Hay, *Accounting for Governmental and Nonprofit Entities,* 12th ed. (Burr Ridge, IL: McGraw-Hill/Irwin, 2001), p. 770.

have historically sought reliable financial data, especially concerning the sources of revenue and the costs of patient care.

Accounting for Patient Service Revenues

The largest source of health care revenues normally is patient services. For example, the Lucile Packard Children's Hospital of the Stanford Medical Center reported in 2004 that $380 million of its total revenue of $426 million came from net patient service revenue. These amounts include fees for surgery, nursing services, medicine, laboratory work, X rays, blood, housing, food, and so forth.

Reductions in Patient Service Revenues

For a variety of reasons, health care entities (especially hospitals) often receive much less in total payment than the amount they would normally charge for specific patient services. Bad debts and other fee reductions can be significant. However, to provide complete financial data about their operations, these organizations initially record revenues at standard rates. Then they report each of the various reductions incurred in a specified manner to best reflect these activities. For example, a note to the 2004 financial statements for Duke University explains that the Duke University Health System

> has agreements with third-party payors that provide for payments to DUHS at amounts different from its established rates. Payment arrangements include prospectively determined rates per discharge, reimbursed costs, discounted charges, per diem payments, and capitation. Net patient service revenue is reported at the estimated net realizable amounts from patients, third-party payors, and others for services rendered.

Assume, as an illustration, that patient charges for the current month at a local hospital total $750,000. Of this amount, $170,000 is due from patients, and the remaining $580,000 was billed to third-party payors: Medicare, Medicaid, and various insurance companies. Regardless of expected receipts, the hospital should record these revenues through the following journal entry:

Accounts Receivable—Third-Party Payors	580,000	
Accounts Receivable—Patients	170,000	
Patient Service Revenues		750,000
To record accrual of patient charges for current month.		

This hospital initially reports the entire $750,000 as patient service revenue although complete collection is doubtful. This approach is considered the best method of allowing the health care organization to monitor activities during the period.

To continue this example, assume that the hospital estimates that $20,000 of the patient receivables will be uncollectible. Furthermore, not-for-profit hospitals and other similar entities often make no serious attempt to collect amounts that indigent patients owe. In many cases, these facilities were originally created to serve the poor. Assume, therefore, that $18,000 of the accounts receivable will never be collected because several patients earn incomes at or below the poverty level. Thus, to mirror these anticipated revenue reductions, the hospital records two additional entries.

As the following shows, the handling of the two reductions is not the same. The bad debts create an expense as in a for-profit business, but the revenue and receivable for the charity care are removed entirely so that no financial reporting is shown. If the work was performed with no intention to seek collection, no basis exists for recognizing either a receivable or a revenue.

Bad Debt Expense	20,000	
Allowance for Uncollectible and Reduced Accounts		20,000
To record estimation of receivables that will prove to be uncollectible.		
Patient Service Revenues	18,000	
Accounts Receivable—Patients		18,000
To remove accounts that will not be collected because patients' earned income is at the poverty level.		

IS THIS REALLY AN ASSET?

Mercy Hospital is located near Springfield, Missouri. A religious organization created the not-for-profit hospital more than 70 years ago to meet the needs of area residents who could not otherwise afford adequate health care. Although the hospital is open to the public in general, its primary mission has always been to provide medical services for the poor.

On December 23, 2007, a gentleman told the hospital's chief administrative officer the following story: "My mother has been in your hospital since October 30. The doctors have just told me that she will soon be well and can go home. I cannot tell you how relieved I am. The doctors, the nurses, and your entire staff have been just wonderful; my mother could not have gotten better care. She owes her life to your hospital.

"I am from Idaho. Now that my mother is on the road to recovery, I must return immediately to my business. I am in the process of attempting to sell an enormous tract of land in Idaho. When this acreage is sold, I will receive $15 million in cash. Because of the services that Mercy Hospital has provided for my mother, I want to donate $5 million of this money." The gentlemen proceeded to write this promise on a piece of stationery that he dated and signed.

Obviously, all of the hospital's officials were overwhelmed by the gentleman's generosity. This $5 million gift was 50 times larger than the largest gift ever received. However, the controller was a bit concerned about preparing the financial statements for 2007. "I have a lot of problems with recording this type of donation as an asset. At present, we are having serious cash flow problems; but if we show $5 million in this manner, our normal donors are going to think we have become rich and don't need their support."

What problems are involved in accounting for the $5 million pledge? How should Mercy Hospital report the amount?

Contractual Agreements with Third-Party Payors

The adjustments in the preceding entries reflect amounts that the entity will not collect from patients. Such organizations make an additional reduction in connection with receivables due from third-party payors. Organizations such as insurance companies and Medicare often establish contractual arrangements with health care providers stipulating that they will pay set rates for specific services. The entity agrees, in effect, to accept as *payment in full* an amount that the third-party payor computes as reasonable (based normally on the average cost within the locality in which the service was rendered). Thus, although a health care entity charges a patient $3,000, for example, it might collect only $2,700 (or some other total) from a third-party payor if the lower figure is determined to be an appropriate cost. The entity must write off the remaining $300, which is commonly referred to as a *contractual adjustment*.

Because of the current cost of health care, contractual adjustments can be huge. For example, Duke University's 2004 financial statements indicate that the receivable balances shown by Duke University Health Services "are reported net of allowances for contractual adjustments and uncollectible accounts of $306,142,000."

An alternative method of determining the amount to be paid is known as a *prospective payment plan.* Under this system, reimbursement is based not on the cost of the health services being provided but on the diagnosis of the patient's illness or injury. Thus, if a patient has a broken leg, for example, the health care entity would be entitled to a set reimbursement regardless of the actual expense incurred. Such plans were developed in an attempt to encourage a reduction in medical costs because the facility collects no additional amount if a patient remains in a hospital longer than necessary or receives more expensive treatment.

Thus, the health care entity should estimate and recognize these reductions in the same period that it earns the patient service revenue. In the example just presented, the hospital probably does not anticipate collecting the entire $580,000 billed to third-party payors. Assume, for illustration purposes, that this hospital projects that it will receive only $420,000 of the $580,000 charge. To establish a proper value for the hospital's revenues, the entity must record another $160,000 adjustment:

Contractual Adjustments	160,000	
Allowance for Uncollectible and Reduced Accounts		160,000
To recognize estimated reduction in patient billings because of contractual arrangements made with third-party payors.		

As indicated earlier, the AICPA audit and accounting guide requires that entities show bad debts as expenses rather than as reductions to patient service revenues. Furthermore, revenues and related charity care deductions are not recorded at all if the health care entity has no intention of collecting. Finally, contractual adjustments reduce patient service revenues but do not appear explicitly on the financial statements. Rather, patient service revenues are shown on the statement of activities as a net figure after removing all such reductions. Because the entity has little chance of collecting the entire balance, reporting total revenues could mislead readers.

Summary

1. FASB *SFAS 117* established reporting requirements for private not-for-profit organizations. The intent was to provide financial statement users, including contributors, an overall view of the organization's financial position and results of operations.

2. The required financial statements for not-for-profit organizations include the statement of financial position, statement of cash flows, and statement of activity and changes in net assets. Voluntary health and welfare organizations also are required to issue statements of functional expenses.

3. The statements must distinguish among assets, liabilities, revenues, and expenses that are permanently restricted, temporarily restricted, and unrestricted. Such restrictions are donor imposed. Temporarily restricted assets are expected to be released from restriction due to the passage of time or the not-for-profit's performance of some act. That release causes an increase in unrestricted net assets and a decrease in temporarily restricted net assets. Permanently restricted net assets are expected to be restricted for as long as the organization exists.

4. Not-for-profit organizations should report expenses as reductions in unrestricted net assets by their functional classification such as major classes of program services and supporting services. Program services are goods or services provided to beneficiaries or customers that fulfill the organization's purpose or mission. Supporting services are general administration and fund-raising.

5. Because of a conflict over the recording of depreciation expense, a GAAP hierarchy was created to identify the applicability of GASB and FASB pronouncements and other authoritative sources to businesses and nonbusiness entities.

6. FASB *SFAS 116* establishes accounting and reporting requirements for contributions. Contributions are unconditional transfers of cash or other resources to an entity in a voluntary nonreciprocal transaction.

7. Not-for-profit organizations recognize contributions, including unconditional written or oral promises to give, as revenues or support in the period received at fair value.

8. Not-for-profit organizations recognize contributed services as revenues if they either create or enhance nonfinancial assets or require a specialized skill (for example, accountant, architect, nurse) and would have to be purchased if not provided by donation.

9. Not-for-profit organizations can sometimes receive donations that must be given to a different beneficiary. While such organizations hold the gift, they normally record it as an asset with an accompanying liability. However, if the organization is given variance powers to change the beneficiary, the not-for-profit records a revenue rather than a liability.

10. Health care organizations frequently receive less than the full amount of patient charges. These entities show contractual adjustments with third-party payors as deductions from revenue in reporting *net patient service revenue*. These entities estimate bad debts and report them as expenses. Charity care charges are not recorded as revenue.

Comprehensive Illustration

PROBLEM

(Estimated time: 30 to 45 minutes) Augusta Regional Hospital is a private not-for-profit hospital offering medical care to a variety of patients, including some with no ability to pay for the services received. In addition, the hospital sponsors a consortium on childhood diseases with the financial support of a private foundation. The hospital holds an endowment, the principal of which must be maintained but whose earnings are available to provide charity care. During 2007, the hospital has the financial transactions listed here.

Required:

a. Prepare the journal entries for each of the following transactions.

1. The hospital rendered $950,000 in services to patients, of which it charged $700,000 to third-party payors. The administration estimated that only $800,000 would be collected. Of the $150,000 difference, $85,000 represented estimated contractual allowances with insurance and Medicare providers, $20,000 is charity care, and $45,000 is estimated bad debts.
2. A local business donated linens with a $3,000 fair value.
3. Cafeteria sales to nonpatients and gift shop receipts totaled $76,000.
4. The hospital incurred expenses of $12,000 in connection with the childhood disease consortium. Funding for this consortium had been received as a restricted donation in 2006.
5. The hospital received unrestricted, unconditional pledges of $12,500. The administration expected to collect only 80 percent of them. In addition, it received securities with a fair value of $8,000 that the donor designated for the endowment.
6. A computer consultant donated services to upgrade several of the hospital's computer systems. The value of these services was $3,000 and would have been acquired if not donated.
7. The hospital incurred the following liabilities:

   $102,000 for purchase of supplies
   $699,000 for salaries
   $50,000 for purchase of equipment

8. End-of-year adjustment included supplies expense of $99,000 and depreciation expense of $72,000.

b. Prepare a schedule showing the change in unrestricted, temporarily restricted, and permanently restricted net assets.

SOLUTION

a. 1.

Accounts Receivable—Patients	250,000	
Accounts Receivable—Third-Party Payors	700,000	
Patient Service Revenues (Unrestricted)		950,000
To accrue billings for the current period.		
Contractual Adjustments	85,000	
Allowance for Contractual Adjustment		85,000
To recognize estimated amounts not expected to be collected from third-party payors.		
Patient Service Revenues (Unrestricted)	20,000	
Accounts Receivable—Patients		20,000
To remove the amount for charity care for which no expectation to collect exists.		
Bad Debt Expense	45,000	
Allowance for Uncollectible Accounts		45,000
To recognize estimated amounts not expected to be collected from patients.		

2.

Inventory of Supplies	3,000	
Unrestricted Net Assets—Contribution of Materials		3,000
To recognize fair value of donated items.		

3.

Cash	76,000	
Unrestricted Net Assets—Revenues—Cafeteria and Shops		76,000

To record cafeteria and gift shop revenue.

4.

Consortium Expenses	12,000	
Cash		12,000

To record expenses in connection with the childhood disease consortium.

5.

Pledges Receivable	12,500	
Investments	8,000	
Allowance for Uncollectible Pledges		2,500
Unrestricted Net Assets—Contributions		10,000
Permanently Restricted Net Assets—Contributions		8,000

To record pledges and investments received at estimated fair value.

6.

Expenses for Professional Services	3,000	
Unrestricted Net Assets—Contributed Services		3,000

To record donated services.

7.

Supplies Inventory	102,000	
Equipment	50,000	
Accounts Payable		152,000

To record goods received.

Salaries Expense	699,000	
Accrued Salaries Payable		699,000

To record salaries payable.

8.

Supplies Expense	99,000	
Supplies Inventory		99,000

To record supplies expense for the period.

Depreciation Expense	72,000	
Accumulated Depreciation		72,000

To record depreciation expense for the period.

b.

Calculation of Change in Net Assets			
Journal Entry	Unrestricted Net Assets	Temporarily Restricted Net Assets	Permanently Restricted Net Assets
1	$950,000		
	(85,000)		
	(20,000)		
	(45,000)		
2	3,000		
3	76,000		
4	(12,000)		
5	10,000		$8,000
6	(3,000)		
	3,000		
7	(699,000)		
8	(99,000)		
	(72,000)		
Net assets released from restriction—childhood disease consortium	12,000	$(12,000)	
Increase (decrease) in net assets	$ 19,000	$(12,000)	$8,000

Questions

1. Which organization is responsible for issuing reporting standards for private not-for-profit colleges and universities?
2. What information do financial statement users want to know about a not-for-profit organization?
3. What financial statements are required for private not-for-profit colleges and universities?
4. What are temporarily restricted assets?
5. What are permanently restricted assets?
6. What two general types of expenses do private not-for-profit organizations report?
7. What ratio is frequently used to assess the efficiency of not-for-profit organizations?
8. Why is a statement of functional expenses prepared for a voluntary health and welfare organization?
9. What controversy did the debate over whether not-for-profit organizations should record depreciation expense create? How was this issue resolved?
10. What is the GAAP hierarchy? What purpose does it serve? Why was it developed?
11. If a donor gives a charity a gift that the charity must convey to a separate beneficiary, what is the normal method of reporting for each party?
12. If a donor gives a charity a gift that the charity must convey to a separate beneficiary, what is the method of reporting for each party if the donor retains the right to revoke or redirect use of the gift?
13. If a donor gives a charity a gift that the charity must convey to a separate beneficiary, what is the method of reporting for each party if the charity receives variance powers enabling it to change the identity of the beneficiary?
14. When does a not-for-profit organization record donated services?
15. A private not-for-profit organization sends out a direct mail solicitation for donations. However, the organization also includes other information with the mailing. Under what conditions can the organization report part of the cost of this mailing as a program service cost rather than as a fund-raising cost?
16. A private not-for-profit organization receives numerous pledges of financial support to be conveyed at various times over the next few years. Under what condition should it recognize these pledges as receivables and contribution revenues? At what amount should it report these pledges?
17. What is the difference between an unconditional promise to give and an intention to give?
18. When should membership dues be considered revenue rather than contributions?

19. What is a third-party payor, and how does the presence of such payors affect the financial accounting of a health care organization?

20. What is a contractual adjustment? How does a health care organization account for a contractual adjustment?

Problems

1. A hospital has the following account balances:

Revenue from newsstand	$ 50,000
Amounts charged to patients	800,000
Interest income	30,000
Salary expense—nurses	100,000
Bad debts	10,000
Undesignated gifts	80,000
Contractual adjustments	110,000

What is the hospital's net patient service revenue?

a. $880,000.

b. $800,000.

c. $690,000.

d. $680,000.

2. A large not-for-profit organization's statement of activities should report the net change for net assets that are

	Unrestricted	Permanently Restricted
a.	Yes	Yes
b.	Yes	No
c.	No	No
d.	No	Yes

3. Which of the following statements is true?

    I. Private not-for-profit universities must report depreciation expense.

    II. Public universities must report depreciation expense.

a. Neither I nor II is true.

b. Both I and II are true.

c. Only I is true.

d. Only II is true.

4. A private not-for-profit organization receives three donations:

    One gift of $70,000 is unrestricted.

    One gift of $90,000 is restricted to pay the salary of the organization's workers.

    One gift of $120,000 is restricted forever with the income to be used to provide food for needy families.

Which of the following statements is not true?

a. Temporarily restricted net assets have increased by $90,000.

b. Permanently restricted net assets have increased by $210,000.

c. When the donated money is spent for salaries, unrestricted net assets increase and decrease by the same amount.

d. When the donated money is spent for salaries, temporarily restricted net assets decrease.

5. A donor gives Charity 1 $50,000 in cash that it must convey to Charity 2. However, the donor can revoke the gift at any time prior to its conveyance to Charity 2. Which of the following statements is true?

a. Charity 1 should report a contribution revenue.

b. The donor continues to report an asset even after it is given to Charity 1.

c. As soon as the gift is made to Charity 1, Charity 2 should recognize a contribution revenue.

d. As soon as the gift is made to Charity 1, Charity 2 should recognize an asset.

6. A private not-for-profit university charges its students tuition of $1 million. However, financial aid grants total $220,000. In addition, the school receives a $100,000 grant restricted for faculty salaries. Of this amount, it spent $30,000 appropriately this year. On the statement of activities, the school reports three categories: (1) revenues and support, (2) net assets reclassified, and (3) expenses. Which of the following is *not* true?

   a. Unrestricted net assets should show an increase of $30,000 for net assets reclassified.

   b. In the unrestricted net assets, the revenues and support should total $1 million.

   c. Unrestricted net assets should recognize expenses of $30,000.

   d. Unrestricted net assets shows the $220,000 as a direct reduction to the tuition revenue balance.

7. A private not-for-profit organization has the following activities performed by volunteers for no charge. In which case should it report *no* amount of contribution?

   a. A carpenter builds a porch on the back of one building so that patients can sit outside.

   b. An accountant does the organization's financial reporting.

   c. A local librarian comes each day to read to the patients.

   d. A computer expert repairs the organization's computer.

8. A private not-for-profit organization spends $100,000 to send out a mailing. The mailing solicits donations and provides educational and other information about the charity. Which of the following is true?

   a. No part of the $100,000 can be reported as a program service expense.

   b. Some part of the $100,000 must be reported as a program service expense.

   c. No authoritative guidance exists, so the organization can allocate the cost as it believes best.

   d. Under certain specified circumstances, the organization should allocate a portion of the $100,000 to program service expenses.

9. FASB *SFAS 117,* "Financial Statements of Not-for-Profit Organizations," focuses on

   a. Basic information for the organization as a whole.

   b. Standardization of fund information reported.

   c. Inherent differences of not-for-profit organizations that impact reporting presentations.

   d. Distinctions between current fund and noncurrent fund presentations.

10. On December 30, 2007, Leigh Museum, a not-for-profit organization, received a $7,000,000 donation of Day Co. shares with donor-stipulated requirements as follows:

    The museum is to sell shares valued at $5,000,000 and use the proceeds to erect a public viewing building.

    The museum is to retain shares valued at $2,000,000 and use the dividends to support current operations.

    As a consequence of its receipt of the Day shares, how much should Leigh report as temporarily restricted net assets on its 2007 statement of financial position?

    a. –0–.

    b. $2,000,000.

    c. $5,000,000.

    d. $7,000,000.

11. The Jones family lost its home in a fire. On December 25, 2007, a philanthropist sent money to the Amer Benevolent Society, a not-for-profit organization, to purchase furniture for the Jones family. During January 2008, Amer purchased furniture for the Jones family. How should Amer report the receipt of the money in its 2007 financial statements?

    a. As an unrestricted contribution.

    b. As a temporarily restricted contribution.

    c. As a permanently restricted contribution.

    d. As a liability.

12. Pel Museum is a private not-for-profit organization. If it received a contribution of historical artifacts, it need not recognize the contribution if the artifacts are to be sold and it will use the proceeds to

    a. Support general museum activities.

    b. Acquire other items for collections.

    c. Repair existing collections.

    d. Purchase buildings to house collections.

13. What is the significance of the GAAP hierarchy?

    a. It tells which accounting body has more overall authority.

    b. When two sources of accounting guidance are in conflict, it identifies the one that has priority.

    c. It describes the development of new accounting principles.

    d. It lists the various FASB and GASB statements.

14. A not-for-profit organization receives two gifts. One is $80,000 and is restricted for use in paying salaries of teachers who teach children to read. The other is $110,000, which is restricted for the purchase of playground equipment. The organization spends both amounts properly at the end of this year. No depreciation is recorded this period, and the organization has elected to view the equipment as having a time restriction. On the statement of activities, what is reported for unrestricted net assets?

    a. An increase of $80,000 and a decrease of $80,000.

    b. An increase of $190,000 and a decrease of $190,000.

    c. An increase of $190,000 and a decrease of $80,000.

    d. An increase of $80,000 and no decrease.

15. In the accounting for health care providers, what are third-party payors?

    a. Doctors who reduce fees for indigent patients.

    b. Charities that supply medicines to hospitals and other health care providers.

    c. Friends and relatives who pay the medical costs of a patient.

    d. Insurance companies and other groups that pay a significant portion of the medical fees in the United States.

16. Mercy for America, a private not-for-profit health care facility located in Durham, North Carolina, charged a patient $8,600 for services. This amount was actually billed to a third-party payor. The third-party payor submitted a check for $7,900 with a note stating that "the reasonable amount is paid in full per contract." Which of the following statements is true?

    a. The patient is responsible for paying the remaining $700.

    b. The health care facility will rebill the third-party payor for the remaining $700.

    c. The health care facility recorded the $700 as a contractual adjustment that it will not collect.

    d. The third-party payor retained the $700 and will convey it to the health care facility at the start of the next fiscal period.

17. What is a contractual adjustment?

    a. An increase in a patient's charges caused by revisions in the billing process utilized by a health care entity.

    b. A year-end journal entry to recognize all of a health care entity's remaining receivables.

    c. A reduction in patient service revenues caused by agreements with third-party payors that allows them to pay a health care entity based on their determination of reasonable costs.

    d. The results of a cost allocation system that allows a health care entity to determine a patient's cost by department.

18. A not-for-profit hospital provides its patients with services that would normally be charged at $1 million. However, it estimates a $200,000 reduction because of contractual adjustments. It expects another $100,000 reduction because of bad debts. Finally, the hospital does not expect to collect $400,000 because this amount is deemed to be charity care. Which of the following is correct?

    a. Patient service revenues = $1 million; net patient service revenues = $300,000.

    b. Patient service revenues = $1 million; net patient service revenues = $400,000.

    c. Patient service revenues = $600,000; net patient service revenues = $300,000.

    d. Patient service revenues = $600,000, net patient service revenues = $400,000.

19. A local citizen gives a not-for-profit organization a cash donation that is restricted for research activities. The money should be recorded in
    a. Unrestricted Net Assets.
    b. Temporarily Restricted Net Assets.
    c. Permanently Restricted Net Assets.
    d. Deferred Revenue.

20. Theresa Johnson does volunteer work for a local not-for-profit organization as a community service. She replaces without charge an administrator who would have otherwise been paid $31,000. Which of the following statements is true?
    a. The organization should recognize a restricted gain of $31,000.
    b. The organization should recognize public support of $31,000 as an increase in unrestricted net assets.
    c. The organization should recognize a reduction in expenses of $31,000.
    d. The organization should make no entry.

21. In 2007, Wells Hospital received an unrestricted bequest of common stock with a fair value of $50,000. The testator paid $20,000 for the stock in 2000. Wells should record the bequest to
    a. Increase temporarily restricted net assets by $50,000.
    b. Increase temporarily restricted net assets by $20,000.
    c. Increase unrestricted net assets by $50,000.
    d. Increase unrestricted net assets by $20,000.

22. An organization of high school seniors performs volunteer services for patients at a nearby nursing home. These are services that the nursing home would not otherwise provide, such as wheeling patients in the park and reading to them. At the minimum wage rate, these services would amount to $21,320, but their actual value is estimated to be $27,400. In the nursing home's statement of revenues and expenses, what amount should be reported as public support?
    a. $27,400.
    b. $21,320.
    c. $6,080.
    d. –0–.

23. A voluntary health and welfare organization receives a gift of new furniture having a fair value of $2,100. The group then gives the furniture to needy families following a flood. How should the organization record receipt and distribution of this donation?
    a. No entry should be made.
    b. Record public support of $2,100 and community assistance expense of $2,100.
    c. Recognize revenue of $2,100.
    d. Recognize revenue of $2,100 and community expenditures of $2,100.

24. George H. Ruth takes a leave of absence from his job to work full-time for a voluntary health and welfare organization for six months. Ruth fills the position of finance director, a position that normally pays $88,000 per year. Ruth accepts no remuneration for his work. How should these donated services be recorded?
    a. As public support of $44,000 and an expense of $44,000.
    b. As public support of $44,000.
    c. As an expense of $44,000.
    d. They should not be recorded.

25. A voluntary health and welfare organization produces a statement of functional expenses. What is the purpose of this statement?
    a. Separates current unrestricted and current restricted funds.
    b. Separates program service expenses from supporting service expenses.
    c. Separates cash expenses from noncash expenses.
    d. Separates fixed expenses from variable expenses.

26. A voluntary health and welfare organization has the following expenditures:

Research to cure disease	$60,000
Fund-raising costs	70,000
Work to help disabled	40,000
Administrative salaries	90,000

How should the organization report these items?

a. Program service expenses of $100,000 and supporting service expenses of $160,000.

b. Program service expenses of $160,000 and supporting service expenses of $100,000.

c. Program service expenses of $170,000 and supporting service expenses of $90,000.

d. Program service expenses of $190,000 and supporting service expenses of $70,000.

27. A voluntary health and welfare organization sends a mailing to all of its members including those who have donated in the past and others who have not donated. The mailing, which cost $22,000, asks for monetary contributions to help achieve the organization's mission. In addition, 80 percent of the material included in the mailing is educational in nature, providing data about the organization's goals. Which of the following is true?

a. Some part of the $22,000 should be reported as a program service cost because of the educational materials included.

b. No part of the $22,000 should be reported as a program service cost because there is no specific call to action.

c. No part of the $22,000 should be reported as a program service cost because the mailing was sent to both previous donors and individuals who have not made donations.

d. Some part of the $22,000 should be reported as a program service cost because more than 50 percent of the material was educational in nature.

28. A voluntary health and welfare organization receives $32,000 in cash from solicitations made in the local community. The organization receives an additional $1,500 from members in payment of annual dues. Members are assumed to receive benefits roughly equal in value to the amount of dues paid. How should this money be recorded?

a. Revenues of $33,500.

b. Public support of $33,500.

c. Public support of $32,000 and a $1,500 increase in the fund balance.

d. Public support of $32,000 and revenue of $1,500.

29. During the year ended December 31, 2007, Anderson Hospital (operated by a not-for-profit organization) received and incurred the following:

Fair value of donated medicines	$ 54,000
Fair value of donated services (replaced salaried workers)	38,000
Fair value of additional donated services (did not replace salaried workers)	11,000
Interest income on board-designated funds	23,000
Regular charges to patients	176,000
Charity care	210,000
Bad debts	66,000

How should this hospital report each of these items?

30. The following questions concern the appropriate accounting for a not-for-profit health care entity. Write complete answers for each question.

a. What is a third-party payor, and how have third-party payors affected the development of accounting principles for health care entities?

b. What is a contractual adjustment, and how does a health care entity record this figure?

c. How does a not-for-profit health care entity account for donated materials and services?

31. Under Lennon Hospital's rate structure, it earned patient service revenue of $9 million for the year ended December 31, 2007. However, Lennon did not expect to collect this entire amount because it deemed $1.4 million to be charity care and estimated contractual adjustments to be $800,000.

During 2007, Lennon purchased medical supplies from Harrison Medical Supply Company at a cost of $4,000. Harrison notified Lennon that it was donating the supplies to the hospital.

At the end of 2007, Lennon had board-designated assets consisting of cash of $60,000 and investments of $800,000.

How much should Lennon record as patient service revenue and how much as net patient service revenue? How should Lennon record the donation of the supplies? How are the board-designated assets shown on the balance sheet?

32. Wilson Center is a voluntary health and welfare organization. During 2007, it received unrestricted pledges of $600,000, 60 percent of which were payable in 2007, with the remainder payable in 2008 (for use in 2008). Officials estimate that 15 percent of all pledges will be uncollectible.

    a. How much should Wilson Center report as contribution revenue for 2007?

    b. In addition, a local social worker, earning $9 per hour working for the state government, contributed 600 hours of time to Wilson Center at no charge. Except for these donated services, an additional staff person would have been hired by the organization. How should Wilson Center record the contributed service?

33. A private not-for-profit organization is working to create a cure for a deadly disease. The organization starts the year with cash of $700,000. Of this amount, unrestricted net assets total $400,000, temporarily restricted net assets total $200,000, and permanently restricted net assets total $100,000. Within the temporarily restricted net assets, the organization must use 80 percent for equipment and the rest for salaries. No implied time restriction has been designated for the equipment when purchased. For the permanently restricted net assets, 70 percent of resulting income must be used to cover the purchase of advertising for fund-raising purposes and the rest is unrestricted.

    During the year 2007, the organization has the following transactions:

    · Received unrestricted cash gifts of $210,000.
    · Paid salaries of $80,000 with $20,000 of that amount coming from restricted funds. Of the total salaries, 40 percent is for administrative personnel and the remainder is evenly divided between individuals working on research to cure the designated disease and individuals employed for fund-raising purposes.
    · Bought equipment for $300,000 with a long-term note signed for $250,000 and restricted funds used for the remainder. Of this equipment, 80 percent is used in research, 10 percent is used in administration, and the remainder is used for fund-raising.
    · Collected membership dues of $30,000. The members receive a reasonable amount of value in exchange for these dues including a monthly newsletter describing research activities.
    · Received $10,000 from a donor that must be conveyed to another organization doing work on a related disease.
    · Received investment income of $13,000 generated by the permanently restricted net assets. The donor has stipulated that 70 percent of the income is to be used for advertising, and the remainder may be used at the organization's discretion.
    · Paid advertising of $2,000.
    · Received an unrestricted pledge of $100,000 that will be collected in three years. The organization expects to collect the entire amount. The pledge has a present value of $78,000 and related interest (additional contribution revenue) of $3,000 in the year.
    · Computed depreciation on the equipment acquired as $20,000.
    · Spent $93,000 on research supplies that it utilized during the year.
    · Owed salaries of $5,000 at the end of the year. Half of this amount is for individuals doing fund-raising and half for individuals doing research.
    · Received a donated painting that qualifies as a museum piece. It has a value of $800,000. Officials do not want to record this gift if possible.

    a. Prepare a statement of activities for this organization for this year.

    b. Prepare a statement of financial position for this organization for this year.

34. A local private not-for-profit health care entity incurred the following transactions during 2007. Record each of these transactions in appropriate journal entry form. Prepare a schedule calculating the change in unrestricted, permanently restricted, and temporarily restricted net assets.

    a. The governing board of the organization announced that $160,000 in previously unrestricted cash will be used in the future for the acquisition of equipment. The funds are invested until the purchase eventually occurs.

    b. Received a donation of $80,000 with the stipulation that all income derived from this money be used to supplement nursing salaries.

c. Expended $25,000 for medicines. It received the money the previous year as a restricted gift for this purpose.

d. Charged patients $600,000, 80 percent of which is expected to be covered by third-party payors.

e. Calculated depreciation expense of $38,000.

f. Received interest income of $15,000 on the investments the board acquired in transaction (*a*).

g. Estimated that $20,000 of current accounts receivable from patients will not be collected and amounts owed by third-party payors will be reduced by $30,000 because of contractual adjustments.

h. Consumed the medicines acquired in (*c*).

i. Sold the investments acquired in (*a*) for $172,000. All restricted cash and $25,000 that had been previously given to the organization (with the stipulation that the money be used to acquire plant assets) are spent for new equipment.

j. Received pledges for $126,000 in unrestricted donations. Of the pledges, 10 percent are paid immediately with 90 percent to be received and used in future years. Officials estimate that $9,000 of this money will never be collected. Present value of the receivable is $98,000.

35. The University of Danville is a private not-for-profit university that starts the current year with $700,000 in net assets: $400,000 unrestricted, $200,000 temporarily restricted, and $100,000 permanently restricted. The transactions listed occur during the year.

   Make journal entries for the following transactions. Then determine the end-of-year balances for unrestricted net assets, temporarily restricted net assets, and permanently restricted net assets by creating a statement of activities.

a. Charged students $1.2 million in tuition

b. Received a donation of investments that had cost the owner $100,000 but was worth $300,000 at the time of the gift. According to the gift's terms, the university must hold the investments forever but can spend the dividends for any purpose. Any gains/losses on changes in the value of these securities must be held forever and cannot be spent.

c. Received a cash donation of $700,000 that must be used for laboratory equipment.

d. Gave scholarships in the amount of $100,000 to students.

e. Paid salary expenses of $310,000 in cash.

f. Learned that a tenured faculty member is contributing his services in teaching and will not accept his $80,000 salary.

g. Spent $200,000 of the money in (*c*) on laboratory equipment (no time restriction is assumed on this equipment).

h. Learned that at the end of the year, the investments in (*b*) are worth $330,000.

i. Received dividends of $9,000 cash on the investments in (*b*).

j. Computed depreciation expense as $32,000.

k. The school's board of trustees decides to set aside $100,000 of previously unrestricted cash for the future purchase of library books.

l. Received an unconditional promise of $10,000, which the school fully expects to collect in three years although its present value is only $7,000. The school assumes that the money cannot be used until the school receives it.

m. Received an art object as a gift that is worth $70,000 and that qualifies as a work of art. The school prefers not to record this gift.

n. Paid utilities and other general expenses of $212,000.

o. Received free services from alumni who come to campus each week and put books on the shelves in the library. Over the course of the year, the school would have paid $103,000 to have this work done.

36. The following questions concern the accounting principles and procedures applicable to a private not-for-profit organization. Write answers to each of these questions.

a. What is the difference between revenue and public support?

b. What is the significance of the statement of functional expenses?

c. What accounting process does it use in connection with donated materials?

d. What is the difference in the two types of restricted net assets found in the financial records of a private not-for-profit organization?

e. Under what conditions should the organization record donated services?

    f. What controversy arose as to the handling of costs associated with direct mail and other solicitations for money that also contain educational materials?

    g. A not-for-profit organization receives a painting. Under what conditions would this painting be judged as a work of art? If it meets the criteria for a work of art, how is the financial reporting of the organization affected?

37. The College of Central North (a private school) has the following events and transactions:

    a. On January 1, Year 1, the board of trustees voted to restrict $1.9 million of previously unrestricted investments to construct a new football stadium at some future time.

    b. On April 1, Year 1, Dr. Johnson gives the school $4 million in investments that is to be held forever, but all subsequent cash income is to be used to help pay for construction (and, later, maintenance) of the football stadium.

    c. On December 31, Year 1, the investments in (*b*) generate $500,000 in cash interest revenue. In addition, the investments went up in value by $44,000.

    d. On January 1, Year 2, the school builds a football stadium with the restricted $2.4 million in funds. Cash is paid. The stadium has a 20-year life and no salvage value.

    e. On January 2, Year 2, Dr. Johnson buys a lifetime seat on the 50-yard line of the stadium for $30,000 in cash when this seat's fair value is actually $12,000.

    f. On January 3, Year 2, Dr. Johnson provides medical services to the school for free. These services have a $14,000 value and require a specialized skill that the school needed and would have bought otherwise.

    g. On January 4, Year 2, Dr. Johnson donated a painting to be displayed in the school library. It is appraised at a value of $30,000.

Unless otherwise noted, assume that the school does not have a policy that assumes a time restriction on assets bought with restricted funds.

    For each of the following independent situations, indicate whether the statement is true or false and briefly state the reason for your answer.

  (1) On January 1, Year 1, unrestricted net assets reported by the school will be reduced.

  (2) As of December 31, Year 1, temporarily restricted net assets will have increased by $500,000 during the year.

  (3) On December 31, Year 1, permanently restricted net assets went up by $44,000.

  (4) On January 1, Year 2, unrestricted net assets increased $500,000.

  (5) Unless a time restriction is placed on the use of the football stadium, depreciation expense will not be recorded in Year 2.

  (6) If a time restriction is placed on the use of the football stadium, depreciation expense will not be recorded in Year 2.

  (7) For reporting purposes, unrestricted net assets increased by $30,000 on January 2, Year 2.

  (8) For reporting purposes, contribution revenues increased by $18,000 on January 2, Year 2.

  (9) On January 3, Year 2, unrestricted net assets were reported as going both up and down.

 (10) On January 3, Year 2, unrestricted net assets might be reported as going both up and down.

 (11) On January 3, Year 2, unrestricted net assets will go down and might go up.

 (12) On January 4, Year 2, a contribution revenue of $30,000 must be reported.

 (13) On January 4, Year 2, a contribution revenue of $30,000 must not be reported.

38. You are preparing a statement of activities for the University of Richland, a private not-for-profit organization. The following questions should be viewed as independent of each other.

Part 1

During the current year, a donor gives $400,000 in cash to the school stipulating that it must hold this money forever. However, any investment income earned on this money must be used for faculty salaries. During the current year, the investment earned $31,000 and, of that amount, the school has expended $22,000 appropriately to date. As a result of these events, what was the overall change in each of the following for the current year?

    a. Unrestricted net assets.

    b. Temporarily restricted net assets.

    c. Permanently restricted net assets.

Part 2

A donor gives a large machine to the school on January 1 of the current year. It has a value of $200,000, no salvage value, and a 10-year life. The donor requires that the school keep the machine and use it for all 10 years, and the school agrees. It cannot sell or retire the machine in the interim. As a result of these events, what was the overall change in each of the following for the current year?

a. Unrestricted net assets.

b. Temporarily restricted net assets.

c. Operating expenses.

Part 3

Several years ago, a donor gave the school $400,000 in cash to help fund its financial aid program. This year, the school charged $2 million in tuition but granted $700,000 in financial aid. Collections to date from the students have totaled $1.1 million. The donor's gift has offset $300,000 of the financial aid. As a result of these events, what was the overall change in each of the following for the current year?

a. Unrestricted net assets.

b. Operating expenses.

c. Temporarily restricted net assets.

39. The Watson Foundation, a not-for-profit organization, starts the year with cash of $100,000, pledges receivable (net) of $200,000, investments of $300,000, and land, buildings, and equipment of $200,000. In addition, its unrestricted net assets were $400,000, temporarily restricted net assets were $100,000, and permanently restricted net assets were $300,000. Of the temporarily restricted net assets, 50 percent must be used for a new building; the remainder is restricted for salaries. No implied time restriction was designated for the building when it was purchased. For the permanently restricted net assets, all income is unrestricted.

During the year of 2007, the organization has the following transactions:

- Computed interest of $20,000 on the pledge receivable.
- Received cash of $100,000 on the pledges and wrote off another $4,000 as uncollectible.
- Received unrestricted cash gifts of $180,000.
- Paid salaries of $90,000 with $15,000 of that amount coming from restricted funds.
- Received a cash gift of $12,000 that the organization must convey to another not-for-profit organization. However, Watson has the right to give the money to a different organization if it so chooses.
- Bought a building for $500,000 by signing a long-term note for $450,000 and using restricted funds for the remainder.
- Collected membership dues of $30,000. Individuals receive substantial benefits from the memberships.
- Received income of $30,000 generated by the permanently restricted net assets.
- Paid rent of $12,000, advertising of $15,000, and utilities of $16,000.
- Received an unrestricted pledge of $200,000; it will be collected in five years. The organization expects to collect the entire amount. Present value is $149,000. It then recognized interest of $6,000 for the year.
- Computed depreciation as $40,000.
- Paid $15,000 in interest on the note signed to acquire the building.

a. Prepare a statement of activities for this organization for this year.

b. Prepare a statement of financial position for this organization for this year.

The following information relates to Problems 40 through 45:

For a number of years, a private not-for-profit organization has been preparing financial statements that do not necessarily follow generally accepted accounting principles. At the end of the most recent year (Year 2), those financial statements show total assets of $900,000, total liabilities of $100,000, total unrestricted net assets of $400,000, total temporarily restricted net assets of $300,000, and total permanently restricted net assets of $100,000. In addition, total expenses for the year were $500,000 (shown in unrestricted net assets).

40. Assume that this organization is a private college that charged students $600,000 but then provided $140,000 in financial aid. The $600,000 was reported as a revenue; the $140,000 was shown as an expense. Both amounts were included in the unrestricted net assets.

a. What was the correct amount of unrestricted net assets at the end of the year?

b. What was the correct amount of expenses for the year?

41. During Year 1, the organization received a gift of $80,000. The donor specified that this money be invested in government bonds with the interest to be used to pay the salaries of the organization's employees. The gift was recorded as an increase in permanently restricted net assets. It earned interest income of $5,000 during Year 1 and $7,000 during Year 2. The organization reported this interest on the statement of activities as an increase in unrestricted net assets. In both cases, the money was immediately expended for salaries, amounts that were recorded as expenses within unrestricted net assets. No other entries were made in connection with these funds.

    a. What was the correct amount of unrestricted net assets at the end of Year 2?

    b. What was the correct amount of expenses in unrestricted net assets for Year 2?

    c. What was the correct amount of temporarily restricted net assets at the end of Year 2?

42. At the beginning of Year 1, the organization received $50,000 in cash as a gift with the stipulation that the money be used to buy a bus for its use. It made the appropriate entry at that time. On the first day of Year 2, the organization spent the $50,000 for the bus, an asset that will last for 10 years and will have no salvage value. Because the money came from an outside donor, the organization decided that a time restriction should be assumed for 10 years on the bus. In Year 2, it reported $5,000 as depreciation expense in unrestricted net assets. In addition, the organization made a $50,000 reduction in permanently restricted net assets along with a $50,000 increase in unrestricted net assets.

    a. What was the correct amount of unrestricted net assets at the end of Year 2?

    b. What was the correct amount of expenses for Year 2?

    c. What was the correct amount of temporarily restricted net assets at the end of Year 2?

43. Assume that the organization is a charity that charges its "members" monthly dues totaling $100,000 per year (in both Year 1 and Year 2). However, the members get nothing for their dues. The organization has consistently recorded this amount as an increase in Cash along with an increase in revenues within the unrestricted net assets.

    What was the correct amount of unrestricted net assets at the end of Year 2?

44. On January 1, Year 2, several supporters of the organization spent their own money to construct a garage for its vehicles that is worth $70,000. It should last for 10 years and will have no salvage value although no time restriction was assumed. The organization increased its contributions within the unrestricted net assets for $70,000 and increased its expenses within unrestricted net assets for $70,000.

    a. What was the correct amount of unrestricted net assets at the end of Year 2?

    b. What was the correct amount of total assets at the end of Year 2?

    c. What was the correct amount of expenses for Year 2?

45. On December 25 of Year 2, the organization received a $40,000 cash gift. The donor specified that the organization hold the money for four months. If at the end of four months, the donor still wished to do so, the money was to be given to the local Kidney Fund (a separate not-for-profit organization). However, during these four months, the donor could use the money for any other purpose. The reporting organization recorded the money as an increase in Cash and in contributions within its unrestricted net assets.

    a. What was the correct amount of unrestricted net assets at the end of Year 2?

    b. What was the correct amount of total assets at the end of Year 2?

Develop Your Skills

RESEARCH CASE

The law firm of Hackney and Walton has decided to start supporting a worthy charity. The partners want to select an organization that makes good use of its resources to meet its stated mission.

Go to the Web site www.give.org. Then click on "Charity Reports," and a list of hundreds of not-for-profit organizations will appear. Select two or more of these charities and read the information available on this Web site.

Required:

Write a report to the partners of Hackney and Walton recommending which of these charities they should support. Give adequate justification for this recommendation.

ANALYSIS CASE 1

Go to the Web site of a private not-for-profit organization such as Christian Children's Fund (www.christianchildrensfund.org), the American Heart Association (www.americanheart.org), or Goodwill Industries (www.goodwill.org). Find the latest annual report for the charity, which usually can be found by clicking on a button such as "About Our Charity" and then clicking on "Annual Report."

Required:

After examining this annual report, answer the following questions about the not-for-profit organization:

1. How many different program services were listed? Name each.
2. What percentage of total expenses went to supporting services?
3. Were any contributed services recognized and, if so, for how much?
4. What dollar amount was spent on fund-raising?
5. What was the year-end total for unrestricted net assets, temporarily restricted net assets, and unrestricted net assets?
6. What amount of net assets was reclassified from temporarily restricted to unrestricted net assets this past year because the external restriction had been satisfied?

ANALYSIS CASE 2

Go to the Web site of a private not-for-profit college or university such as Duke (www.duke.edu), Vanderbilt (www.vanderbilt.edu), Notre Dame (www.nd.edu), or Georgetown (www.georgetown.edu) and locate the latest set of financial statements for the institution.

Required:

Use this report to answer the following questions:

1. What was the percentage of financial aid to total student tuition and fees?
2. Did the school report any pledges receivable and, if so, for how much?
3. Looking at the school's expenses, what was the total amount spent on educating the students versus what was spent on research during the period?
4. What was the total amount donated to the school during the previous year?
5. What was the total amount of temporarily restricted net assets and permanently restricted net assets?
6. What was the unrealized gain or loss on the school's investments (caused by changes in fair value) and the realized gain or loss (caused by sales of these investments)?
7. Compare the amount earned in tuition and student fees to the amount of education expenses incurred by the school to determine whether it generated a profit or a loss this past year on educating its students.

COMMUNICATION CASE

At the Web site ksghome.harvard.edu/~ekeatin/finassess.pdf, locate the paper titled "How to Assess Nonprofit Financial Performance."

Required:

This paper opens with this sentence: "The fundamental reason for nonprofit financial performance assessment is to determine how well an organization is fulfilling its mission." Write a short memo describing some of the information the authors provide as to the types of financial evaluations that can be made to determine whether a not-for-profit organization is indeed fulfilling its mission.

Please visit the text Web site for the online CPA Simulation: mhhe.com/hoyle8e

Situation: Jones University starts the current year with net assets of $1.5 million: $800,000 in unrestricted net assets, $500,000 in temporarily restricted net assets, and $200,000 in permanently restricted net assets. Unless otherwise stated, assume that Jones University is a private not-for-profit organization.

Topics to be covered in simulation:

- Pledges.
- Public versus private colleges and universities.
- Contributions—restricted.
- Contributions—unrestricted.
- Contributions—works of art.
- Contributions—services.
- Financial aid.
- Membership dues.

Chapter **Nineteen**

Accounting for Estates and Trusts

Over the next decade or so, some $10 trillion is going to pass from one generation to another. It is a sum equal to the recent value of all the companies listed on the stock exchange.[1]

Individuals labor throughout their lives in part to accumulate property that they eventually can convey for the benefit of spouses, children, relatives, friends, charities, and the like. After amassing such funds, humans usually seek to achieve two goals:

- To minimize the amount of these assets that must be surrendered to the government.
- To ensure that the ultimate disposition of all property is consistent with the person's own wishes.

Questions to Consider

- If a person dies without having written a valid will (intestate), how are the estate's assets managed and distributed?

- If the assets an estate holds are insufficient to satisfy all claims against the estate, as well as all devises and bequests made by the decedent, what distributions are made?

- Will the federal estate tax actually be eliminated?

- How can an individual or a couple limit the federal estate taxes that must be paid to maximize the amount of assets being conveyed to beneficiaries?

- In accounting for an estate or trust, why is the distinction between principal and income considered to be especially significant?

- What are the most common types of trust funds?

- What is each type of trust designed to accomplish?

Therefore, accountants (as well as attorneys and financial planners) often assist individuals who are developing estate plans or creating trust funds to accomplish these goals. At a later date, the accountant may serve in the actual administration of the estate or trust. In either estate or trust planning, the person's intentions must be spelled out in clear detail so that no misunderstanding arises. All available techniques also should be considered to limit the impact of taxes. To carry out these varied responsibilities properly, it is of paramount importance that the person doing so have a knowledge of the legal and reporting aspects of estates and trusts.

Although many of the complex legal rules and regulations in these areas are beyond the scope of an accounting textbook, an overview of both estates and trusts can introduce the issues that members of the accounting profession frequently encounter.

ACCOUNTING FOR AN ESTATE

While none of us want to contemplate our death, or that of our spouse, we all need an estate plan. If you need motivation to reach this decision, remember that every dollar you keep from the folks in Washington goes to someone you like a heck of a lot better—such as your kids, your younger sister, or your alma mater.[2]

---

[1] Gregory Bresiger, "Prudence Redefined," *Financial Planning,* October 1, 1999, p. 165.
[2] Ellen P. Gunn, "How to Leave the Tax Man Nothing," *Fortune,* March 18, 1996, p. 94.

The term *estate* simply refers to the property owned by an individual. However, in this chapter, an estate is more specifically defined as a separate legal entity holding title to the assets of a deceased person. *Thus, estate accounting refers to the recording and reporting of financial events from the time of a person's death until the ultimate distribution of all property the estate holds.* To ensure that this disposition is as intended and to avoid disputes, each individual should prepare a *will,* "a legal declaration of a person's wishes as to the disposition of his or her property after death."[3] If an individual dies *testate* (having written a valid will), this document serves as the blueprint for settling the estate, disbursing all remaining assets, and appointing fiduciaries to accomplish these tasks.

When a person dies *intestate* (without a legal will), state laws control the administration of the decedent's estate. Although these legal rules vary from state to state, they normally correspond with the most common patterns of distribution. When inheritance laws rather than a will apply, real property is conveyed based on the *laws of descent* whereas personal property transfers are made according to the *laws of distribution.*

Each individual state establishes laws governing wills and estates known as *probate laws. The National Conference of Commissioners on Uniform State Laws* developed the Uniform Probate Code in hope of creating consistent treatment in this area. To date, almost half of the states have officially adopted the Uniform Probate Code. In many of the other states, the rules and regulations applied are somewhat similar to those of the Uniform Probate Code. In practice, however, an accountant must become familiar with the specific laws of the state having jurisdiction over the estate of the specific decedent.

Administration of the Estate

Regardless of the locale, probate laws generally are designed to achieve three goals:

1. Gather and preserve all of the decedent's property.
2. Carry out an orderly and fair settlement of all debts.
3. Discover and implement the decedent's intent for the remaining property held at death.

This process usually begins by filing a will with the probate court or indicating that no will has been discovered. If a will is presented, the probate court must rule on the document's validity. A will must meet specific legal requirements to be accepted. These requirements may vary from state to state. For example, would the following signed and dated statement constitute a valid will?

"I want my children to have my money."

Because the writer is dead, the intention of this statement cannot be verified. Was this an idle wish made without thought, or did the decedent truly intend for this one sentence to constitute a will conveying all money to these specified individuals upon death? Did the decedent mean for all noncash assets to be liquidated with the proceeds being split among the children? Or did the writer strictly mean that just the cash on hand at the time of death should be transferred to these individuals? Obviously, in some cases, the validity (and the intention) of a will are not easily proven.

If deemed to be both authentic and valid, a will is admitted to probate, and the decedent's specific intentions will be carried to conclusion. All of the decedent's property must be located, debts paid, and distributions appropriately conveyed. Whether a will is present or not, an estate administrator must be chosen to serve in a stewardship capacity. This individual serves in a fiduciary position and is responsible for (1) satisfying all applicable laws and (2) making certain that the decedent's wishes are achieved (if known and if possible).

If a specific person is named in the will to hold this position, the individual is referred to as the *executor* (*executrix* if female; this text will generically use the term *executor*) *of the estate.* If the will does not designate an executor or if the named person is unwilling or unable to serve in this capacity (or if the decedent dies without a will), the courts must select a representative.

---

[3] *The Random House Dictionary of the English Language,* 2nd ed. (New York: Random House, 1987), p. 2175.

A court-appointed individual is known legally as the *administrator* (female: *administratrix*) *of the estate.* An executor/administrator is not forced to serve in this role for free; that person is legally entitled to reasonable compensation for all services rendered.[4]

The executor is normally responsible for fulfilling several tasks:

- Taking possession of all of the decedent's assets and completing an inventory of this property.
- Discovering all claims against the decedent and settling these obligations.
- Filing estate income tax returns, federal estate tax returns, and state inheritance or estate tax returns.
- Distributing property according to the provisions of the will (according to state laws if a valid will is not available) or according to court order if necessary.
- Making a full accounting to the probate court to demonstrate that the executor has properly fulfilled the fiduciary responsibility.

Property Included in the Estate

The basis for all estate accounting is the property the decedent held at death. These assets are used to settle claims and pay taxes. Any property that remains is distributed according to the decedent's will (or applicable state intestacy laws). For reporting purposes, all items are shown at fair value; the historical cost paid by the deceased individual is no longer relevant. Fair value is especially important because the sale of some or all properties may be required to obtain enough cash to satisfy claims against the estate. If valuation problems arise, hiring an appraiser could become necessary.

Normally, an estate includes assets such as these:

- Cash.
- Investments in stocks and bonds.
- Interest accrued to the date of death.
- Dividends declared prior to death.
- Investments in businesses.
- Unpaid wages.
- Accrued rents and royalties.
- Valuables such as paintings and jewelry.

At the time of death, the decedent legally owned a certain amount of assets. The executor is merely trying to locate and value each item belonging to the estate as of that date.

Some state laws specify that real property such as land and buildings (and possibly certain types of personal property) be conveyed directly to the beneficiary or co-owner at the time of death. Therefore, in these states, the inventory of the estate property that the executor develops for probate purposes does not include these assets. However, such items must still be listed in the filing of estate and inheritance tax returns because a legal transfer has occurred.

Discovery of Claims against the Decedent

An adequate opportunity should be given to the decedent's creditors to allow them to file claims against the estate. Usually, a public notice must be printed in an appropriate newspaper once a week for three weeks.[5] In many states, all claims must be presented within four months of the first of these notices. The executor must verify the validity of these claims and place them in order of priority. If insufficient funds are available, this ordering becomes quite important in establishing which parties receive payment. Consequently, claims in category 4 of the following list, most of which are paid before a beneficiary receives any assets, have the greatest chance of going unpaid.

---

[4] To avoid using convoluted terminology, the term *executor* is generally used throughout this textbook to indicate both executors and administrators.

[5] Although many states require three weeks, *Ind. Code* §29-1-7-7(b) requires publication of notice for only two consecutive weeks. The CPA must understand the particular state's requirement(s) because this is a typical statutory variance from state to state.

Order of Priority

1. Expenses of administering the estate. Without this preferential treatment, the appointment of an acceptable executor and the hiring of lawyers, accountants, and/or appraisers could become a difficult task in estates with limited funds.
2. Funeral expenses and the medical expenses of any last illness.
3. Debts and taxes given preference under federal and state laws.
4. All other claims.

Protection for Remaining Family Members

As indicated, a number of states have adopted the Uniform Probate Code. However, other states have passed a wide variety of individual probate laws that differ in many distinct ways. Thus, no absolute rules about probate laws can be listed. Normally, they provide some amount of protection for a surviving spouse and/or the decedent's minor and dependent children. Small monetary allowances are conveyed to these parties prior to the payment of legal claims. For example, a *homestead allowance* is provided to a surviving spouse[6] and/or minor and dependent children. Even an estate heavily in debt would furnish some amount of financial relief for the members of the decedent's immediate family.

In addition, these same individuals frequently receive a small *family allowance* during a limited period of time while the estate is being administered. Family members are also entitled to a limited amount of exempt property such as automobiles, furniture, and jewelry. All other property is included in the estate to pay claims and be distributed according to the decedent's will or state inheritance laws.

Estate Distributions

If a will has been located and probated, property remaining after all claims are settled is conveyed according to that document's specifications.[7] A gift of real property such as land or a building is referred to as a *devise;* a gift of personal property such as stocks or furniture is a *legacy* or a *bequest*. A devise is frequently specific: "I leave three acres of land in Henrico County to my son," or "I leave the apartment building on Monument Avenue to my niece." Unless the estate is unable to pay all claims, a devise is simply conveyed to the intended party. However, if claims cannot be otherwise satisfied, the executor could be forced to sell or otherwise encumber the property despite the will's intention.

In contrast, a legacy may take one of several forms. The identification of the type of legacy becomes especially important if the estate has insufficient resources to meet the specifications of the will.

A *specific legacy* is a gift of personal property that is directly identified. "I leave my collection of pocket watches to my son" is an example of a specific legacy because the property is named.

A *demonstrative legacy* is a cash gift made from a particular source. The statement "I leave $10,000 from my savings account in the First National Bank to my sister" is a demonstrative legacy because the source is identified. If the savings account does not hold $10,000 at the time of death, the beneficiary will receive the amount available. In addition, the decedent may specify alternative sources if sufficient funds are not available. Ultimately, any shortfall usually is considered a general legacy.

A *general legacy* is a cash gift whose source is undesignated. "I leave $8,000 in cash to my nephew" is a gift viewed as a general legacy.

A *residual legacy* is a gift of any remaining estate property. Thus, it is assets left after all claims, taxes, and other distributions are conveyed according to the residual provisions of the will. "The balance of my estate is to be divided evenly between my brother and the University of Notre Dame" is an example of a residual legacy.

---

[6] Many states provide a $25,000 protective allowance for a surviving spouse. See *Ind. Code* §29-1-4-1.

[7] An exception, however, is that property legally held in joint tenancy with one or more individuals will pass to the surviving joint tenants at death and not be subject to the provisions of a will or intestate distribution.

An obvious problem arises if an estate does not hold enough funds to satisfy all legacies the will specified. The necessary reduction of the various gifts is referred to as the *process of abatement.* For illustration purposes, assume that a will lists the following provisions:

I leave 1,000 shares of AT&T to my brother (a specific legacy).

I leave my savings account of $20,000 to my sister (a demonstrative legacy).

I leave $40,000 cash to my son (a general legacy).

I leave all remaining property to my daughter (a residual legacy).

Example 1

Assume that after paying all claims, the estate holds the shares of AT&T stock, the $20,000 savings account, and $46,000 in other cash. The first three parties (the brother, sister, and son) get the specific assets stated in the will, and the residual legacy (to the daughter) would be the $6,000 cash balance left after the $40,000 general legacy is paid.

Example 2

Assume that after paying all claims, the estate holds the shares of AT&T stock, the savings account, and only $35,000 in other cash. The first two individuals (the brother and sister) get the specified assets, but the son can claim only the remaining $35,000 cash rather than the promised $40,000. Based on the process of abatement, the daughter receives nothing; no amount is left after the other legacies have been distributed.

Example 3

Assume that after paying all claims, the estate holds the shares of AT&T stock, but the savings account has a balance of only $12,000 rather than the promised $20,000. Other cash held by the estate totals $51,000. The stock is distributed to the brother, but the sister gets just the $12,000 cash in the savings account. In most states, the remaining $8,000 is treated as a general legacy. Consequently, the sister gets the additional $8,000 in this manner and the son receives the specified $40,000. The daughter is then left with only the $3,000 in cash that remains.

Example 4

Assume that the decedent sold the shares of AT&T stock before death and that after paying all claims, the savings account holds $22,000. Other cash amounts to $30,000. The brother receives nothing from the estate because the specific legacy did not exist at death.[8] The sister collects the promised $20,000 from the savings account, and the remaining $2,000 is added to the general legacy. Therefore, the son receives a total of $32,000 from the two cash sources. Because the general legacy was not fulfilled, no remainder exists as a residual legacy; thus, the daughter collects nothing from the estate.

Insufficient Funds

The debts and expenses of the administration are paid first in settling an estate. If the estate has insufficient available resources to satisfy these claims, the process of abatement is again utilized. Each of the following categories is exhausted completely to pay all debts and expenses before money is taken from the next category:

Residual legacies.

General legacies.

Demonstrative legacies.

Specific legacies and devises.

---

[8] The legal term *ademption* refers to a situation in which a specific bequest or devise fails because the property is not available for distribution. As a different possibility, a bequest or devise is said to lapse if the beneficiary cannot be located or dies before the decedent. This property then becomes part of the residual estate.

Estate and Inheritance Taxes

Taxes incurred after death can be quite costly. For example, Helen Walton received $5.1 billion in stock at the death of her husband Sam Walton (founder of Wal-Mart Stores). At this value, these shares could eventually cost her heirs as much as *$2.8 billion* in taxes at her death: $2.2 billion to the U.S. government and $640 million to the State of Arkansas.[9]

Historically, estate taxes have been used as a method for redistributing wealth and raising revenues. According to the Internal Revenue Service in 2003, estate taxes raised $20.9 billion in net revenue.[10] This total amounted to 1.1 percent of all tax money generated by the federal government in that year.

The budget surpluses that appeared in the latter part of the 1990s began to cast doubts on the continued need for a federal estate tax. Many arguments can be made both for this tax (to some there is a perceived limit to the amount that a beneficiary should receive without work or effort) and against it (income that has been taxed once when earned should not be taxed again when the resulting assets are conveyed at death).

In 1999 (and again in 2000), the U.S. Congress voted a phased-in repeal of the estate tax, a measure that then President Bill Clinton vetoed as being too costly. However, in 2001, Congress passed the Economic Growth and Tax Relief Reconciliation Act of 2001, which included provisions to gradually reduce and then abolish this tax by 2010. President George W. Bush signed the measure into law.

Estate planning, however, is still very difficult because the estate tax is scheduled to reappear in 2011 unless Congress moves to make the repeal permanent in the interim. "Because fewer than 60 senators voted for the tax bill on May 26, 2001 (58 for to 33 against), the Byrd rule applies. The net effect of that rule is that, unless Congress votes to permanently extend the estate tax repeal, it applies only in year 2010."[11] Without being able to anticipate the exact laws that will apply at the date of a future death, estate planning becomes uncertain at best. Unless the repeal is extended, the financial impact of dying on January 1, 2011, rather than on December 31, 2010, could be catastrophic for a large estate.

Furthermore, the large budget deficits that began to appear early in the 21st century brought the entire Economic Growth and Tax Relief Reconciliation Act back into the political debate. Some argued that the implementation of its wide-ranging provisions should be made permanent or even escalated to stimulate the economy. Others suggested the benefits should be deferred or repealed completely to help increase tax revenues and reduce budget deficits. Whether the estate tax is permanently abolished or reappears in 2011 is almost impossible to predict. As one observer wrote early in 2002, "There will be two presidential elections and four congressional elections by 2011. No one can predict accurately the future political climate."[12]

The ongoing debate over the eventual abolition of this tax will have a major impact on estate planning. Prior to passage of this legislation, the tax was as high as 55 percent, with an added 5 percent surcharge on large estates. Consequently, most individuals who were subject to the tax were willing to spend significant amounts to reduce the eventual burden. However, for the next few years, during the phase-out period, estates of a substantial size will still be subject to a federal estate tax although at a lower rate. Estate planning will undoubtedly continue as an important issue at least during this period.

The new law has no impact on the payment of state inheritance taxes.[13] In the past, the federal government allowed a limited credit for such taxes assessed by the state. Within certain parameters, amounts paid to a state could be used to reduce assessments that were due to the

[9] Warren Midgett, "Mrs. Walton's Options," *Forbes,* October 19, 1992, pp. 22–23.

[10] Center for the Study of Taxation, http://www.center4studytax.com/html/faq.html.

[11] William M. Vandenburgh and Philip J. Harmelink, "The Uncertainty of Death and Taxes," *Journal of Accountancy*, October 2001, p. 99. Under the Byrd rule, the Senate may not consider extraneous matters as part of a reconciliation bill, resolution, or conference report, unless a Senate majority of 60 senators vote to waive the rule.

[12] Paul J. Piergallini, "Going, Going, Gone?" *Journal of Accountancy*, March 2002, p. 29.

[13] Coverage of the many and varied state inheritance and estate tax laws is beyond the scope of this textbook. An overview is provided by Paul J. Lochray, "How to Minimize State Death Tax Liabilities," *Journal of Financial Planning,* July 1990, pp. 120–23.

federal government. For 2002 through 2004, however, this credit was reduced significantly and then changed to a deduction (a decrease in the size of the estate).

Federal Estate Taxes

The federal estate tax is an excise tax assessed on the right to convey property. The computation begins by determining the fair value of all property held at death. Therefore, even if real property is transferred immediately to the beneficiary and is not subject to probate, the value must still be included for federal estate tax purposes.[14] In establishing fair value, the executor may choose an alternate valuation date if that decision will reduce the amount of estate taxes to be paid. This date is six months after death (or the date of disposition for any property disposed of within six months after death). Thus, the federal estate tax process starts by determining all asset values at death or this alternate date. Note that a piecemeal valuation cannot be made; one of these dates must be used for all properties.

Several items then reduce the gross estate figure to arrive at the taxable value of the estate:

- Funeral expenses.
- Estate administration expenses.
- Liabilities.
- Casualties and thefts during the administration of estate.
- Charitable bequests.
- Marital deduction for property conveyed to spouse.
- State inheritance taxes.

Individuals are allowed to deduct a specified amount from the value of the estate in arriving at the federal estate tax. The new tax legislation has escalated the portion of an estate that is exempted. Any remaining amount is taxed at graduated rates based on the year of death.

Date of Death	Estate Tax Exemption at Death	Highest Estate Tax Rate
2005	$1.5 million	47%
2006	2 million	46
2007	2 million	45
2008	2 million	45
2009	3.5 million	45
2010	Tax is repealed	N/A
2011	Estate tax returns unless repealed permanently in the interim	

In the past, individuals have often sought to decrease the size of their estates to reduce estate taxes by making gifts during their lifetimes. Annual gifts of $11,000 per person (an amount that is indexed to change with inflation) can be made tax free to an unlimited number of donees. The gift tax has not been eliminated by the new tax legislation, but a $1 million lifetime tax-free exclusion has now been established over and above the $11,000 exclusion per person per year. Furthermore, instead of having a separate tax rate schedule as in the past, the maximum gift tax rate eventually will be the same as the maximum individual income tax rate.

What is the impact of all these changes?

> The death of the estate tax is at best premature, and any planner thinking of abandoning an estate planning practice is missing a large opportunity. In fact, the estate planning provisions within the Economic Growth and Tax Relief Reconciliation Act of 2001 should be a boon for most planners, not a death toll.[15]

[14] Life insurance policies with named beneficiaries are also included in the value of the estate as long as the decedent had the right to change the beneficiary. This rule often results in decedents of modest means having taxable estates.

[15] Thomas J. Brzezenski, "New Era for Estate Planning," *Financial Planning*, July 1, 2001.

Federal Estate Taxes—Example 1   The determination of the taxable estate is obviously an important step in calculating estate taxes. Assume for illustration purposes that a person dies holding assets valued at $4 million and has total debts of $400,000 at death. Funeral expenses cost $20,000, and estate administration expenses amount to $10,000. This person's will left $300,000 to charitable organizations, and the remaining $3,270,000 (after debts and expenses) goes to the surviving spouse.[16] Under this set of circumstances, no taxable estate exists:

Gross estate (fair value)		$ 4,000,000
Funeral expenses	$ 20,000	
Administration expenses	10,000	
Debts	400,000	
Charity bequests	300,000	
Marital deduction	3,270,000	(4,000,000)
Taxable estate		–0–
Estate tax		–0–

Federal Estate Taxes—Example 2   Because of the current exemptions, a limited amount of estate property ($1.5 million in 2005 and $2.0 million in 2006 and 2007) can be conveyed tax free to a beneficiary other than a spouse. The ability to shelter this amount of assets from tax has an important impact on estate planning. For example, in the preceding case, if the couple has already identified the recipient of the estate at the eventual death of the second spouse (their children, for example), a conveyance of the tax-free exclusion amount at the time of the first death is usually advantageous. The second estate will then be smaller for subsequent taxation purposes. Frequently, individuals establish a trust fund for this purpose as a means of protecting their money and ensuring its proper distribution.

To illustrate, assume that the first spouse died in 2005. Assume also that the will that is written is identical to the example preceding except that only $1,770,000 is conveyed to the surviving spouse and the remaining $1.5 million is placed in a trust fund for the couple's children (a nondeductible amount for estate tax purposes). The estate tax return must now be adjusted to appear as follows:

Gross estate		$ 4,000,000
Funeral expenses	$ 20,000	
Administration expenses	10,000	
Debts	400,000	
Charity bequests	300,000	
Marital deduction	1,770,000	(2,500,000)
Taxable estate (conveyed to trust) . . .		$ 1,500,000
Estate tax on $1,500,000 value in 2005		$ 448,300
Tax-free amount (first $1,500,000) . .		(448,300)
Taxes to be paid		–0–

Again, the estate pays no taxes, but only $1,770,000 is added to the surviving spouse's taxable estate rather than $3,270,000 as in the previous example. Thus, an eventual decrease in the couple's *total* estate taxes of $448,300 has been established.

However, this strategy may not work for couples unless the title to their assets is properly designated. This illustrates a situation in which the success of estate planning can hinge on a proper understanding of how the laws function.

The trick is to divide the first $1.2 million[17] of your assets between you so that you and your spouse have separate estates that can each receive the tax credit. The standard individual credit is

[16] Although not applicable in this case, surviving spouses have the right in many states to denounce the provisions of a will and take an established percentage (normally one-third) of the decedent's estate. Such laws protect surviving spouses from being disinherited.

[17] The exemption amount has now increased because of changes in the tax laws. In 2005, the trick was to divide the first $3.0 million in this manner.

$192,800, essentially the tax that would be due on an estate of $600,000. If everything is jointly owned, you'd get that deduction only once because the tax man considers jointly held assets to constitute a single estate that isn't taxed until the second death.[18]

Legally, if a couple holds property as joint tenants or tenants by the entirety, the property passes automatically to the survivor at the death of the other party. Thus, if all property were held in one of these ways, the decedent would have no estate and would not be able to experience the benefit of the tax-free amount. However, if property is held by the couple as tenants in common, the portion the decedent owned is included in that person's estate and, up to the set limit, can be conveyed tax free to a nonspouse beneficiary.

Other Approaches to Reducing Estate Taxes One technique previously used by families with large fortunes to reduce estate taxes was to transfer assets to grandchildren and even great-grandchildren. This manner reduced the number of separate conveyances (each of which would have been subject to taxation at the top rate) from parent to child to grandchild. However, the government effectively eliminated the appeal of this option several years ago by establishing a generation-skipping transfer tax. Under this law, after an exemption, a flat tax was assessed on transfers by gift, bequest, or trust distribution to individuals two or more generations younger than the donors or decedents. (However, the exemption was unlimited for a transfer to a grandchild when the grandchild's parent was deceased and she was a lineal descendent of the transferor.)

More recently, with its passage of the Economic Growth and Tax Relief Reconciliation Act of 2001, Congress has begun to phase out the generation-skipping transfer tax. Without an estate tax, no justification exists for a generation-skipping tax. The exemptions and the highest tax rates will follow the same changes shown earlier for the federal estate tax so that complete repeal will occur in 2010. Of course, in the interim, individuals can also take advantage of the $1 million lifetime exemption for gifts as well as the annual $11,000 per donee gift tax exclusion.

State Inheritance Taxes

States assess inheritance taxes on the right to receive property, with the levy and all other regulations varying, as discussed earlier, based on state laws. However, the specifications of the will determine the actual impact on the individual beneficiaries. Many wills dictate that all inheritance tax payments are to be made from any residual cash amounts that the estate holds. Consequently, individuals receiving residual legacies are forced to bear the entire burden of this tax.

If the will makes no provisions for state inheritance taxes (or if the decedent dies intestate), the amounts conveyed to each party must be reduced proportionately based on the fair value received. Thus, the recipient of land valued at $200,000 would have to contribute twice as much for inheritance taxes as a beneficiary collecting cash of $100,000. Decreasing a cash legacy to cover the cost of inheritance taxes creates little problem for the executor. However, a direct reduction of an estate asset such as land, buildings, or corporate stocks might be virtually impossible. Normally, the beneficiary in such cases is required to pay enough cash to satisfy the applicable inheritance tax. Often, the estate planning process establishes life insurance policies to provide cash for such payments.

Estate and Trust Income Taxes

Although all estates require time to be settled, the period can become quite lengthy if complex matters arise. From the date of death until ultimate resolution, the estate is viewed legally as a taxable entity and must file and pay income taxes to the federal government if gross income is $600 or more. The return is due by the 15th day of the fourth month following the close of the estate's taxable year. The calendar year or any other fiscal year may be chosen as the taxable year. In 2003, nearly 3.7 million estate and trust income tax returns were filed with the Internal Revenue Service.[19]

---

[18] Gunn, "How to Leave the Tax Man Nothing," p. 94.

[19] Internal Revenue Service Web site www.irs.gov/pub/lirs-soi/o3dbo3nr.xls.

Applicable income tax rules for estates and trusts are generally the same as for individual taxpayers. Therefore, dividend, rental, interest, and other income earned by an estate in the period following death is taxable to the estate unless the income is of a type that is specifically nontaxable (such as municipal bond interest).

A $600 personal exemption is provided as a decrease to the taxable balance. In addition, a reduction is allowed for (1) any taxable income donated to charity and (2) any taxable income for the year distributed to a beneficiary. In 2005, federal tax rates were 15 percent on the first $2,000 of taxable income per year with various rates levied on any excess income earned up to $9,750. At a taxable income level more than $9,750, a 35 percent rate is incurred.

As an illustration, assume that in 2005 an estate earns net rental income of $30,000 and dividend income of $8,000. The dividend income is distributed immediately to a beneficiary and is taxable income for that individual, and $6,000 of the rental income is given to charity. Estate income taxes for the year would be computed as follows:

Rental income	$30,000
Dividend income	8,000
Total revenue	$38,000
Personal exemption	(600)
Gift to charity	(6,000)
Distributed to beneficiary	(8,000)
Taxable income	$23,400

Income tax:	
15% of first $2,000	$ 300.00
25% of next $2,700 ($4,700 − $2,000)	675.00
28% of next $2,450 ($7,150 − $4,700)	686.00
33% of next $2,600 ($9,750 − $7,150)	858.00
35% of next $13,650 ($23,400 − $9,750)	4,777.50
	$7,296.50[20]

The Distinction between Income and Principal

In many estates, the executor faces the problem of differentiating between income and principal transactions. For example, a will might state "all income earned on my estate for five years after death is to go to my sister, with the estate then being conveyed to my children." The recipient of the income is known as an *income beneficiary* whereas the party who ultimately receives the principal (also known as the *corpus*) is called a *remainderman.* As the fiduciary for the estate, the executor must ensure that all parties are treated fairly. Thus, if amounts are distributed incorrectly, the court can hold the executor legally liable.

The definitional difference between principal and income appears to pose little problem. The estate principal encompasses all of the decedent's assets at death; income is the earnings on these assets after death. However, many transactions are not easily categorized as either principal or income. As examples, consider these:

- Are funeral expenses charged to principal or income?
- Is the executor's fee charged to principal or income?
- Are dividends that are declared before death but received after death viewed as principal or income?
- If stocks are sold for a gain, is this gain viewed as income or an increase in principal?
- Are repairs to rental property considered a reduction of principal or of income?

---

[20] As fiduciary entities, estates and trusts are taxed at the same income tax rates. Note that their top rate of 35 percent becomes applicable at a taxable income level of only $9,750. In comparison, for 2005, this same top income tax rate of 35 percent is not assessed for a single taxpayer, head of household, or joint return until taxable income reaches $326,450. Historically, fiduciary entities have had lower income tax rates so that taxpayers would move income-producing property into trusts to lower the taxes to be paid. As mentioned, Congress has changed the rate schedules so that it is now advantageous to keep income-producing property out of trusts and estates.

Clearly, the distinction between principal and income is not always obvious. For this reason, in writing a will, an individual may choose to spell out the procedure by which principal and income are to be calculated. If defined in this manner, the executor merely has to follow these instructions.

In many cases, the decedent will have provided no guidance as to the method by which transactions are to be classified. The executor must apply state laws to determine these two figures. Many states have adopted the Revised Uniform Principal and Income Act as a standard for this purpose. However, some states have created their own distinct laws, and still others have adopted modified versions of the Revised Uniform Principal and Income Act. Generally accepted accounting principles are not applicable; the distinction between principal and income is defined solely by the decedent's intentions or by state laws.

Although differences exist because of unique state laws or the provisions of a will, the following transactions are normally viewed as adjustments (either increases or decreases) to the *principal of the estate:*

- Life insurance proceeds if the estate is named as the beneficiary.
- Dividends declared prior to death and any other income earned prior to death.
- Liquidating dividends even if declared after death.
- Debts incurred prior to death.
- Gains and losses on the sale of corporate securities or rental property.
- Major repairs (improvements) to rental property.
- Investment commissions and other costs.
- Funeral expenses.
- Homestead and family allowances.

The *income of the estate* includes all revenues and expenses recognized after the date of death. Within this calculation, the following items are included as reductions to income:

- Recurring taxes such as real and personal property taxes.
- Ordinary repair expenses.
- Water and other utility expenses.
- Insurance expenses.
- Other ordinary expenses necessary for the management and preservation of the estate.

Several costs such as the executor's fee, court costs, and attorneys' and accountants' charges must be apportioned between principal and interest in some fair manner.

Recording the Transactions of an Estate

The accounting process that the executor of an estate uses is quite unique. *Because the probate court has given this individual responsibility over the assets of the estate, the accounting system is designed to demonstrate the proper management and distribution of these properties.* Thus, several features of estate accounting should be noted:

- All estate assets are recorded at fair value to indicate the amount and extent of the executor's accountability. Any assets subsequently discovered are disclosed separately so that these adjustments to the original estate value can be noted when reporting to the probate court. The ultimate disposition of all properties must be recorded to provide evidence that the executor's fiduciary responsibility has been fulfilled.
- Debts, taxes, or other obligations are recorded only at the date of payment. In effect, the system is designed to monitor the disposition of assets. Thus, claims are relevant to the accounting process only at the time that the assets are disbursed. Likewise, distributions of legacies are not entered into the records until actually conveyed. As mentioned earlier, devises of real property are often transferred at death so that no accounting is necessary.
- Because of the importance of separately identifying income and principal transactions in many estates, the accounting system must always note whether income or principal is being affected. Quite frequently, the executor maintains two cash balances to assist in this process.

To illustrate, assume that James T. Wilson dies on April 1, 2006. The following valid will has been discovered:

I name Bob King as executor of my estate.

I leave my house, furnishings, and artwork to my aunt, Ann Wilson.

I leave my investments in stocks to my uncle, Jack E. Wilson.

I leave my automobile and personal effects to my grandmother, Nancy Wilson.

I leave $38,000 in cash to my brother, Brian Wilson.

I leave any income earned on my estate to my niece, Karen Wilson.

All remaining property is to be placed in trust for my children.

The executor must (1) perform a search to discover all estate assets and (2) allow an adequate opportunity for every possible claim to be filed. The assets should be recorded immediately at fair value with the creation of the Estate Principal account. This total represents the amount of assets for which the executor is initially accountable. The following journal entry establishes the values for the assets owned by James T. Wilson at his death that have been found to date:

Cash—Principal	11,000	
Interest Receivable on Bonds	3,000	
Dividends Receivable on Stocks	4,000	
Life Insurance—Payable to Estate	40,000	
Residence	90,000	
Household Furnishings and Artwork	24,000	
Automobile	4,000	
Personal Effects	2,000	
Investment in Bonds	240,000	
Investment in Stocks	50,000	
Estate Principal		468,000

Following is a list of subsequent transactions incurred by this estate with each appropriate journal entry. Because estate income is to be conveyed to one party (Karen Wilson) but the remaining principal is to be placed in trust, careful distinction between these two elements is necessary.

Transaction 1

The executor paid funeral expenses of $4,000.

Funeral and Administrative Expenses	4,000	
Cash—Principal		4,000

Transaction 2

The life insurance policy payable to the estate (shown in the initial entry) is collected.

Cash—Principal	40,000	
Life Insurance—Payable to Estate		40,000

Transaction 3

The title to 4.0 acres of land is discovered in a safe deposit box. This asset was not included in the original inventory of estate property. An appraiser sets the value of the land at $22,000.

Land	22,000	
Assets Subsequently Discovered		22,000

Transaction 4

The executor receives claims totaling $24,000 for debts the decedent incurred prior to death. This amount includes medical expenses covering the decedent's last illness ($11,000), property taxes ($4,000), utilities ($1,000), personal income taxes ($5,000), and other miscellaneous expenses ($3,000). The executor pays all of these claims.

Debts of the Decedent	24,000	
Cash—Principal		24,000

Transaction 5

Interest of $8,000 is collected on the bonds held by the estate. Of this amount, $3,000 was earned prior to the decedent's death and was included as a receivable in the initial recording of the estate assets.

Cash—Principal	3,000	
Cash—Income	5,000	
Interest Receivable on Bonds		3,000
Estate Income		5,000

Transaction 6

Dividends of $6,000 are collected from the stocks held by the estate. Of this amount, $4,000 was declared prior to the decedent's death and was included as a receivable in the initial recording of the estate assets.

Cash—Principal	4,000	
Cash—Income	2,000	
Dividends Receivable on Stocks		4,000
Estate Income		2,000

Transaction 7

The executor now has a problem. The Cash—Principal balance is currently $30,000:

Beginning balance	$ 11,000
Funeral expenses	(4,000)
Life insurance	40,000
Payment of debts	(24,000)
Interest income	3,000
Dividends	4,000
Current balance	$ 30,000

However, the decedent bequeathed his brother, Brian Wilson, $38,000 in cash. This general legacy cannot be fulfilled without selling some property. Most assets have been promised as specific legacies and cannot, therefore, be used to satisfy a general legacy. Two assets, though, are residual: the investment in bonds and the land that was discovered. The executor must sell enough of these properties to generate the remaining funding needed for the $38,000 conveyance. In this illustration, assume that the executor chooses to dispose of

Discussion **Question**

IS THIS REALLY AN ASSET?

Robert Sweingart died during December 2005 at the age of 101. Sweingart had outlived many of his relatives, including the person named in his will as executor of his estate. Thus, the probate court selected the decedent's nephew Timothy J. Lee as administrator. Lee promptly began his duties including reading the will and taking an inventory of Sweingart's properties. Although the will had been written in 1972, Lee could see that most of the provisions would be easy to follow. Sweingart had made a number of specific and demonstrative legacies that could simply be conveyed to the beneficiaries. The will also included a $20,000 general legacy to a local church with a residual legacy to a well-known charity. Unfortunately, after all other legacies were distributed, the estate would have only about $14,000 cash.

One item in the will concerned the administrator. Sweingart had made the following specific legacy: "I leave my collection of my grandfather's letters which are priceless to me, to my cousin, William." Lee discovered the letters in a wall safe in Sweingart's home. About 40 letters existed, all in excellent condition. They were written by Sweingart's grandfather during the Civil War and described in vivid detail the Second Battle of Bull Run and the Battle of Gettysburg. Unfortunately, Lee could find no trace of a cousin named William. He apparently had died or vanished during the period since the will was written.

Lee took the letters to two different antique dealers. One stated, "A museum that maintains a Civil War collection would love to have these. They do a wonderful job of explaining history. But a museum would not pay for them. They have no real value since many letters written during this period still exist. I would recommend donating them to a museum."

The second dealer took a different position: "I think if you can find individuals who specialize in collecting Civil War memorabilia they might be willing to pay a handsome price especially if these letters help to fill out their collections. A lot of people in this country are fascinated by the Civil War. The number seems to grow each day. The letters are in great condition. It would take some investigation on your part but they could be worth a small fortune."

Lee now has to prepare an inventory of his uncle's property for probate purposes. How should he report these letters? What should Lee do next with the letters?

the land and negotiates a price of $24,000. Because a principal asset is being sold, the extra $2,000 received above the recorded value is considered an adjustment to principal rather than an increase in income.

Cash—Principal	24,000	
Land		22,000
Gain on Realization		2,000

Transaction 8

Fees of $1,000 charged for administering the affairs of the estate are paid. Of this amount, we assume that $200 is considered to be applicable to estate income.

Funeral and Administrative Expenses	800	
Expenses—Income	200	
Cash—Principal		800
Cash—Income		200

Transaction 9

On October 13, 2006, the house, furnishings, and artwork are given to the decedent's aunt (Ann); the stocks are transferred to the uncle (Jack); and the grandmother (Nancy) receives the decedent's automobile and personal effects.

Legacy—Ann Wilson (residence, furnishings, and artwork)	114,000	
Legacy—Jack E. Wilson (stocks)	50,000	
Legacy—Nancy Wilson (automobile and personal effects)	6,000	
Residence		90,000
Household Furnishings and Artwork		24,000
Investment in Stocks		50,000
Automobile		4,000
Personal Effects		2,000

Charge and Discharge Statement

As necessary, the executor files periodic reports with the probate court to disclose the progress being made in settling the estate. This report is referred to as a *charge and discharge statement.* If income and principal must be accounted for separately, the statement is prepared in two parts. For both principal and income, the statement should indicate the following:

1. The assets under the executor's control.
2. Disbursements made to date.
3. Any property still remaining.

Thus, the executor of James T. Wilson's estate can produce Exhibit 19.1 immediately after Transaction 9. (Transaction numbers are included in parentheses for clarification purposes.)

At this point in the illustration, only three transactions remain: distribution of the $38,000 cash to the decedent's brother, conveyance of the $6,800 cash generated as income since death to the niece, and establishment of the trust fund with the remaining principal. The trust fund will receive the $240,000 in bonds and the $15,200 in cash that is left in principal ($53,200 total less $38,000 paid to the brother).

Legacy—Brian Wilson	38,000	
Cash—Principal		38,000
Distribution to Income Beneficiary—Karen Wilson	6,800	
Cash—Income		6,800
Principal Assets Transferred to Trustee	255,200	
Cash—Principal		15,200
Investment in Bonds		240,000

The executor would then prepare a final charge and discharge statement and then closing entries to signal the conclusion of the estate as a reporting entity.

ACCOUNTING FOR A TRUST

A trust is created by the conveyance of assets to a fiduciary (or trustee) who manages the assets and ultimately disposes of them to one or more beneficiaries. The trustee may be an individual or an organization such as a bank or other financial institution. Over the years, trust funds have become quite popular in this country for a number of reasons. Often they are established to reduce the size of a person's taxable estate and, thus, the amount of estate taxes that must eventually be paid. As one financial adviser has stated, "Who needs to

EXHIBIT 19.1   Executor's Charge and Discharge Statement

ESTATE OF JAMES T. WILSON
Charge and Discharge Statement
April 1, 2006–October 13, 2006
Bob King, Executor

As to Principal

I charge myself with:

Assets per original inventory		$468,000
Assets subsequently discovered: land (Trans. 3)		22,000
Gain on sale of land (Trans. 7)		2,000
Total charges		$492,000

I credit myself with:

Debts of decedent (Trans. 4):

Medical expenses	$ 11,000		
Property taxes	4,000		
Utilities	1,000		
Personal income taxes	5,000		
Others	3,000	$ 24,000	
Funeral and administrative expenses (Trans. 1 and 8)		4,800	

Legacies distributed (Trans. 9):

Ann Wilson (house, furnishings, and artwork)	114,000		
Jack E. Wilson (stocks)	50,000		
Nancy Wilson (automobile and personal effects)	6,000	170,000	
Total credits			198,800
Estate principal			$293,200 ←

Estate principal:

Cash		$ 53,200
Investment in bonds		240,000
Estate principal		$293,200 ←

As to Income

I charge myself with:

Interest income (Trans. 5)		$ 5,000
Dividend income (Trans. 6)		2,000
Total charges		7,000

I credit myself with:

Administrative expenses charged to income (Trans. 8)		200
Balance as to income		$ 6,800 ←

Balance as to income:

Cash		$ 6,800 ←

---

establish a trust? You do, and so does your spouse. There may be several good reasons, but start with this: If you don't set up trusts, your heirs may pay hundreds of thousands of dollars in unnecessary estate taxes."[21]

Estate taxes are not the only reason for establishing a trust. People form trust funds to protect assets and ensure that the eventual use of these assets is as intended. Trusts can also result from the provisions of a will, specified by the decedent as a means of guiding the distribution of estate property. In legal terms, an *inter vivos trust* is one started by a living individual, whereas a *testamentary trust* is created by a will.

---

[21] Jeff Burger, "Which Trust Is Best for Your Family?" *Medical Economics,* August 1, 1988, p. 141.

Frequently, the *trustor* (the person who funds the trust) will believe that a chosen trustee is simply better suited to manage complicated investments than is the beneficiary. A young child, for example, is not capable of directing the use of a large sum of money. The trustor may have the same opinion of an individual who possesses little business expertise. Likewise, the creation of a trust for the benefit of a person with a mental or severe physical handicap might be considered a wise decision.

During recent years, one specific type of trust, a *revocable living trust,* has become especially popular and controversial. The trustor usually manages the fund and receives most, if not all, of the income until death. After that time, future income and possibly principal payments are made to one or more previously named beneficiaries. Because the trust is revocable, the trustor can change these beneficiaries or other terms of the fund at any time.

> You want to leave knowing your loved ones have the best financial breaks possible. That's why the idea of a revocable living trust may sound so promising. During your lifetime, you turn over all assets to a trust. But you act as your own trustee, so you determine how the assets will be managed and distributed. Then, happy in the knowledge that you can change the trust at any time, you have the joy of knowing you're setting up a financial plan for your life and after death.[22]

Revocable living trusts offer several significant advantages that appeal to certain individuals. First, this type of trust avoids the delay and expense of probate. At the trustor's death, the trust continues and makes future payments as defined in the trust agreement. In some states, this advantage can be quite important, but in others the cost of establishing the trust may be more expensive than the potential probate costs.

Second, conveyance of assets through a trust can be made without publicity whereas a will is a public document. Thus, anyone who values privacy may want to consider the revocable living trust. The entertainer Bing Crosby, for example, set up such a trust so that no outsider would know how his estate was distributed.[23]

Although the number of other types of trusts is quite large,[24] several of the more common include these:

- *Credit shelter trust* (also known as a *bypass trust* or *family trust*). A credit shelter trust is designed for couples. Each spouse agrees to transfer at death an amount of up to the tax-free exclusion ($2.0 million in 2006) to a trust fund for the benefit of the other. Thus, the income that these funds generate goes to the surviving spouse, but at the time of this second individual's subsequent death, the principal is conveyed to a different beneficiary. As discussed in the previous section, this arrangement can be used to reduce the estate of the surviving spouse and, therefore, the amount of estate taxes paid by the couple.

  > If your estate is large enough to be threatened by the federal estate tax, you can incorporate provisions to soften the blow. This year [2003], federal law permits each person to leave $1 million in assets tax-free—in addition to the unlimited amount that can go to a surviving spouse. But leaving everything to a spouse can be a costly mistake if it inflates the survivor's estate to the level at which it may be hit by the tax. To avoid this, couples should make sure each owns enough individually to take advantage of the $1 million tax-free allowance, even if it means splitting jointly owned assets. Then, both husband and wife could include in their wills a trust (called a bypass or credit shelter trust) to hold $1 million, from which the survivor would get all the income and possibly some principal during his or her lifetime, with the balance going to the children upon the spouse's death. That $1 million would go to the kids tax-free, rather than being included—and possibly taxed—in the surviving spouse's estate. (Even if the drive to make repeal of the estate tax permanent succeeds, it will still be with us through 2010.)[25]

- *Qualified terminable interest property trust* (known as a *QTIP trust*). Individuals frequently create a QTIP trust to serve as a credit shelter trust. They convey property to the trust and

[22] Estelle Jackson, "Living Trust May Sound Promising," *Richmond Times—Dispatch,* October 13, 1991, p. C1.

[23] Ibid., p. C5.

[24] The cost of establishing and maintaining trusts can be significant. Therefore, use of these trusts may be limited to taxpayers of substantial means.

[25] Josephine Rossi, "Your Will Be Done," *Kiplinger's Personal Finance,* January 2003.

specify that the income, and possibly a portion of the principal, be paid to the surviving spouse (or other beneficiary). At a specified time, the trust conveys the remainder to a designated party. Such trusts are popular because they provide the spouse a steady income but the trustee can guard the principal and then convey it at a later date to the individual's children or other designated parties. However, no trust exists without some potential problems: "During the spouse's lifetime, no one else—not even the children—can benefit from the QTIP trust. However, this can mean years of potential conflict as the children wait for their inheritance. To minimize this potential problem, it often makes sense to set up another trust for the benefit of the children. This is particularly so if a new spouse (stepparent) is close in age to your children."[26]

- *Charitable remainder trust.* All income is paid to one or more beneficiaries identified by the trustor. After a period of time (or at the death of the beneficiaries), the principal is given to a stated charity. Thus, the trustor is guaranteeing a steady income to the intended parties while still making a gift to a charitable organization. These trusts are especially popular if a taxpayer holds property that has appreciated greatly (such as real estate or stocks) that is to be liquidated. By conveying it to the trust prior to liquidation, the sale is viewed as that of the charity and is, hence, nontaxable. Thus, tax on the gain is avoided and significantly more money remains available to generate future income for the beneficiaries (possibly the original donor). "This trust lets you leave assets to your favored charity, get a tax break, but retain income for life."[27]

- *Charitable lead trust.* This trust is the reverse of a charitable remainder trust. Income from the trust fund goes to benefit a charity for a specified time with the remaining principal then going to a different beneficiary. For example, a charity might receive the income from trust assets until the donor's children reach their 21st birthdays. "Jacqueline Kennedy Onassis used this technique and ended up sheltering roughly 90 percent of the trust assets from estate taxes. Setup and operating costs, however, preclude the use of this type of trust unless the assets involved are substantial. As such this is a vehicle for the very wealthy, allowing them to keep an asset in the family but greatly reducing the cost of passing it on."[28]

- *Grantor retained annuity trusts* (known as *GRATs*). The trustor maintains the right to collect fixed payments from the trust fund while giving the principal to a beneficiary after a stated time or at the trustor's death. For example, the trustor might retain the right to receive an amount equal to 7 percent of the initial investment annually with any remaining balance of the trust fund to go to his or her children at death. Because the beneficiary will not receive the residual amount for years, a current value is computed for gift tax purposes. Depending on (1) the length of time before final distribution to the beneficiary, (2) the assumed rate of income, and (3) the amounts to be distributed periodically to the trustor, this value is often quite small so that the gift tax is reduced or eliminated entirely. However, GRATs can have certain risks. "When setting up a GRAT, remember that the annuity you establish at its outset could drain the trust if the expected growth doesn't materialize. Then you will have paid taxes and legal costs . . . and will have left little to your heirs. Equally important, the grantor must outlive the trust. If you die before the GRAT ends, the assets will revert to your estate."[29]

- *Minor's Section 2503(c) trust.* Established for a minor, this trust fund usually is designed to receive a tax-free gift of up to $11,000 each year ($22,000 if the transfer is made by a couple). Over a period of time, especially if enough beneficiaries are available, this trust can remove a significant amount of assets from a person's estate. The change in the gift tax laws and the gradual repeal of the estate tax will impact this type of trust.

- *Spendthrift trust.* This trust is established so that the beneficiary cannot transfer or assign any unreceived payments. The purpose of such trusts is to prevent the beneficiary from squandering the assets the trust fund is holding or the beneficiary's creditors from reaching the assets.

[26] Philip Maynard, "A QTIP Protects the Family," *CreativeLiving Magazine,* Autumn 2001.
[27] Lynn Asinof, "Estate-Planning Techniques for the Rich," *The Wall Street Journal,* January 11, 1995, p. C1.
[28] Ibid., p. C15.
[29] Pam Black, "A GRAT Can Be Great for Saving Your Kids a Bundle," *BusinessWeek,* March 1, 1999, p. 116.

- *Irrevocable life insurance trust.* With this trust, the donor contributes money to buy life insurance on the donor. If a couple is creating the trust, usually the life insurance policy is designed to pay the proceeds only after the second spouse dies. The proceeds are not part of the estate and the beneficiary can use the cash to pay estate and inheritance taxes.
- *Qualified personal resident trust (QPRT).* The donor gives his or her home to the trust but the donor retains the right to live in the house for a period of time rent free. This removes what is often an individual's most valuable asset from the estate. This type of trust has characteristics similar to a GRAT.

> The term of the trust can be as short or as long as desired. The longer the term the lower the value of the gift. If the grantor dies before the term of the trust expires, however, the property will revert back to the estate of the deceased and be subject to estate taxes at its current value. Therefore, a term should be picked that the grantor believes he or she will outlive for the benefits of the QPRT to be effective.[30]

As these examples indicate, many trust funds generate income for one or more beneficiaries (known as *life tenants* if the income is to be conveyed until the person dies). At death or the end of a specified period, the remaining principal is transferred to a different beneficiary (a *remainderman*). Therefore, as with estates, differentiating between principal and income is ultimately important in accounting for trust funds. This distinction is especially significant because trusts frequently exist for decades and can control and generate enormous amounts of assets.

The reporting function is also important because of the trustee's legal responsibilities. This fiduciary is charged with the wise use of all funds and may be sued by the beneficiaries if actions are considered to be unnecessarily risky or in contradiction to the terms of the trust arrangement. To avoid potential legal problems, the trustee is normally called on to exercise reasonable and prudent care in managing the assets of the fund.

Record-Keeping for a Trust Fund

Trust accounting is quite similar to the procedures demonstrated previously for an estate. However, because many different types of trusts can be created and an extended time period might be involved, the accounting process may become more complex than that for an estate. As an example, an apartment house or a significant portion of a business could be placed in a trust for 20 years or longer. Thus, the possible range of transactions to be recorded becomes quite broad. In such cases, the fiduciary might choose to establish two separate sets of accounts, one for principal and one for income. As an alternative, the fiduciary could utilize a single set of records with the individual accounts identified as to income or principal.

In the same manner as an estate, the trust agreement should specify the distinction between transactions to be recorded as income and those to be recorded as principal. If the agreement is silent or if a transaction that is not covered by the agreement is incurred, state laws apply to delineate the accounting. Generally accepted accounting principles usually are not considered appropriate. For example, trusts utilize the cash method rather than accrual accounting in recording most transactions. Although a definitive set of rules is not possible, the following list indicates the typical division of principal and income transactions:

Adjustments to the Trust's Principal

Investment costs and commissions.

Income taxes on gains added to the principal.

Costs of preparing property for rent or sale.

Extraordinary repairs (improvements).

Adjustments to the Trust's Income

Rent expense.

Lease cancellation fees.

Interest expense.

---

[30] Michael Mingione, "Trust Your House," *The CPA Journal,* September 1996, p. 40.

Insurance expense.

Income taxes on trust income.

Property taxes.

Trustee fees and the cost of periodic reporting must be allocated between trust income and principal. This allocation is often based on the value of assets within each (principal/income) category.

Accounting for the Activities of a Trust

An *inter vivos* trust reports on an annual basis (or perhaps more frequently) to all income and principal beneficiaries. However, testamentary trusts come under the jurisdiction of the courts so that additional reporting regularly becomes necessary. Normally, a statement resembling the charge and discharge statement of an estate is adequate for these purposes. Two accounts, Trust Principal and Trust Income, monitor changes that occur. For a testamentary trust, the opening principal balance is the fair value used by the executor for estate tax purposes.

To illustrate, assume that the following events occur in connection with the creation of a charitable remainder trust. The will of Samuel Statler created a trust with the income earned each year to go to his niece for 10 years and the principal then conveyed to a local university (the charity).

1. Cash of $80,000 and stocks (that originally cost $39,000 but are now worth $47,000) are transferred from the estate to the First National Bank of Michigan because this organization has agreed to serve as trustee for these funds.
2. The trustee invested cash of $76,000 in bonds paying 11 percent annual cash interest.
3. Dividends of $6,000 on the stocks are collected, and interest of $7,000 is received on the bonds. No receivables had been included in the estate for these amounts.
4. At the end of the year, an additional $3,000 in interest is due on the bonds.
5. As trustee, the bank charges $2,000 for services rendered for the year. Statler's will provided that such fees should be allocated equally between principal and income.
6. The niece is paid the appropriate amount of money from the trust fund.

As the trustee, the bank should record these transactions as follows:

1. Cash—Principal	80,000	
Investment in Stocks	47,000	
Trust Principal		127,000
To record trust assets at the fair value figure used for estate tax purposes.		
2. Investment in Bonds	76,000	
Cash—Principal		76,000
To record acquisition of bonds using cash in trust fund.		
3. Cash—Income	13,000	
Trust—Income		13,000
To record dividends and interest collected.		
4. No entry is recorded. These earnings cannot be paid to the income beneficiary until collected so that accrual provides no benefit. Therefore, the trustee uses a cash basis system rather than accrual accounting.		
5. Expenses—Income	1,000	
Expenses—Principal	1,000	
Cash—Income		1,000
Cash—Principal		1,000
To allocate the trustee's fees evenly between principal and income.		
6. Equity in Income: Beneficiary	12,000	
Cash—Income		12,000
To record yearly payment made to income beneficiary. Amount is computed as the total of the dividends and interest of $13,000 less expenses of $1,000.		

Summary

1. An estate is the legal entity that holds title to a decedent's property until a final settlement and distribution can be made. State laws, known as *probate laws,* govern this process. These laws become particularly significant if the decedent has died intestate (without a will).

2. A decedent's will should name an executor to oversee the estate. If it does not, the probate court selects an administrator. The executor or administrator takes possession of all properties, settles valid claims, files tax returns, pays taxes due, and distributes any remaining assets according to the provisions of the decedent's will or state inheritance laws. The executor must issue a public notice so that all creditors have adequate opportunity to file a claim against the estate. Prior to paying these claims, a homestead allowance and a family allowance are provided to the members of the decedent's immediate family. Claims are then ranked in order of priority to indicate the payment schedule if existing funds prove to be insufficient. For example, administrative expenses and funeral expenses are at the top of this priority listing.

3. *Devises* are gifts of real property; *legacies* (or *bequests*) are gifts of personal property. Legacies can be classified legally as specific, demonstrative, general, or residual, depending on the type of property and the identity of the source. If insufficient funds are available to fulfill all legacies, the process of abatement is applied to determine the loss allocations. After residual legacies are reduced to zero, general legacies are decreased if necessary. Demonstrative legacies are reduced next, followed by specific legacies.

4. Federal estate taxes are assessed on the value of estate property. Reductions in the total value of an estate are allowed for funeral and administrative expenses as well as for liabilities, charitable gifts, and all property conveyed to a spouse. If made permanent, the Economic Growth and Tax Relief Reconciliation Act of 2001 will eventually lead to the complete elimination of the federal estate tax but not until the year 2010. In the interim period, a tax-free exemption amount is allowed that grows from $2.0 million in 2006 to $3.5 million in 2009. The same gradual elimination is made to the generation-skipping tax. Gift taxes will remain, but individuals now will be allowed a $1 million lifetime exclusion.

5. The distinction between income and principal for both estates and trusts is frequently an important issue. Income may be assigned to one party with the principal eventually going to a different beneficiary. Such arrangements are especially common in trust funds such as charitable remainder trusts. The decedent (for an estate) or the trustor (for a trust) should have identified the method of classification to be used for complicated transactions. If no guidance is provided, state laws apply. For example, major repairs and investment costs usually are considered reductions in principal, whereas expenses such as property taxes and ordinary repairs are charged to income. The bookkeeping procedures for estates and trusts are designed to separate and then reflect the transactions affecting principal and income.

6. To provide evidence of proper handling of an estate or trust, the fiduciary produces a charge and discharge statement. This statement reports the assets over which the individual has been given responsibility. The statement also indicates all disbursements of assets and the property remaining at the current time. Separate reports are prepared for income and principal.

Comprehensive Illustration

PROBLEM

(Estimated Time: 45 Minutes)

Part A

Upon her death, Marie Peterson's will contained the following provisions:

1. I leave my home, personal effects, and stock investments to my husband, Erik.
2. I leave my savings account at State Bank, up to a total of $20,000, to my oldest son, Zach.
3. I leave $5,000 to my niece, Nikki.
4. I leave all remaining assets, including my valuable coin collection, to be placed in trust and managed by Kevin Leahy, if he is willing and able to do so. If not, then I request that a financial institution be engaged to manage such assets. The income from these assets shall be utilized for the benefit of my husband, Erik. At his death, the principal of this trust shall be distributed to St. Patrick's Church, Elkhorn, Wisconsin.
5. In the event that it is necessary for a custodian or guardian to be appointed for any of my children, I request that Mary Breese be appointed in this capacity.
6. I appoint my sister Jodie to manage my estate.

Jodie has now paid all taxes and other claims, and the following assets remain. The assets and their fair value(s) follow:

Home	$400,000
Personal effects	100,000
Stock investments	50,000
Bond investments	75,000
State Bank savings account	10,000
Cash	60,000
Coin collection	Disposed of prior to death

Required:

a. Identify the following:

    (1) Testatrix.

    (2) Trustor.

    (3) Life tenant.

    (4) Remainderman.

    (5) Beneficiaries.

    (6) Devise.

    (7) General legacy.

    (8) Demonstrative legacy.

    (9) Trustee.

    (10) Executrix.

b. Address the following questions:

    (1) Is this trust an *inter vivos* trust or a testamentary trust?

    (2) What specific type of trust has been created?

    (3) How will Marie Peterson's assets be distributed?

Part B

Upon his death on July 4, 2006, Brian Ulvog's will contained the following provisions:

1. I leave my home and personal effects to my wife, Linny.

2. I leave $20,000 cash to my son, Jake.

3. I leave all my investments to Marquette University.

4. I leave all income earned on my investments prior to distribution to Marquette University.

5. I leave the remainder of my estate to Jamie O'Brien.

6. I appoint Jodie Reichel to be the executrix of my estate.

The executrix, Jodie Reichel, prepares an inventory and identifies the assets. Each asset's fair value, as determined by a qualified appraiser, follows:

Cash	$400,000
Home	500,000
Personal effects	75,000
Stock investments	50,000
Bond investments	70,000
Rental building	200,000
Coin collection	90,000
Dividends receivable	1,000
Interest receivable	2,000
Rent receivable	4,000

The executrix paid the following claims against the estate:

Funeral expenses	$ 20,000
Appraisal expenses	15,000
Executor fees	25,000
Medical expenses	10,000
Debts	125,000

The estate received the following cash payments:

Dividends	$ 2,000
Interest	3,000
Rent	7,000
Sale of coin collection	92,000

Assume that today is December 31, 2006, and that the executrix has completed the distributions to Linny and Jake.

Required:

Prepare a charge and discharge statement for Brian's estate.

SOLUTIONS

Part A

a. (1) The testatrix, a female dying with a valid will, is Marie Peterson.

(2) The trustor is also Marie Peterson, the person creating the trust.

(3) The life tenant is Erik, the person possessing an interest in assets, or their income, during a measuring life.

(4) The remainderman is St. Patrick's Church, the legal person receiving the *remainder* of assets after the life tenant's interest terminates.

(5) The beneficiaries include all persons receiving *benefits* from the testatrix via her testamentary documents: Erik, Zach, Nikki, and St. Patrick's Church.

(6) The devise includes Ms. Peterson's home, which the executrix will transfer to her husband, Erik.

(7) The general legacy, the transfer not originating from a designated fund, includes the transfer of $5,000 to Nikki.

(8) The demonstrative legacy, the testamentary transfer derived from a specific source, includes Zach's interest in his mother's savings account.

(9) The trustee, Kevin Leahy, is the person or entity managing trust assets for the benefit of the trust beneficiaries. If Kevin is unable or unwilling to serve as the trustee, then a court may appoint a financial institution as an alternate or successor trustee.

(10) The executrix is Jodie, the female handling the testatrix's estate.

b. (1) Since she created the trust through the provisions of her will, Marie Peterson's trust is a *testamentary trust*.

(2) Marie Peterson's trust is an example of a *charitable remainder trust*. This type of trust provides earnings for a specific period of time to a specific income beneficiary, the life tenant. After the specific time, the remainder is transferred to a charitable organization.

(3) Jodie, the executrix, should distribute the estate assets as follows:

- Erik—Home ($400,000); personal effects ($100,000); and stock investments ($50,000).

- Zach—State Bank Savings Account ($10,000). Note that since the account is not large enough to satisfy the upper limit of this demonstrative legacy, Zach will not receive the maximum amount specified by his mother.

- Nikki—Cash ($5,000).

- Trustee—Bond Investments ($75,000); and Balance of Cash ($55,000).

Part B

ESTATE OF BRIAN ULVOG
Charge and Discharge Statement
July 4, 2006–December 31, 2006
Jodie Reichel, Executrix

As to Principal

I charge myself with:

Assets per original inventory		$1,392,000
Gain on sale of coin collection		2,000
Total charges		1,394,000

I credit myself with:

Decedent's debts:

Medical expenses	$ 10,000	
Other debts	125,000	$135,000
Funeral and administrative expenses (20,000 + 15,000 + 25,000)		60,000

Devises and legacies distributed:

Linny (home and personal effects)	575,000	
Jake	20,000	595,000
Total credits		790,000
Estate principal		604,000

Estate principal:

Cash	284,000
Investments:	
Stocks	50,000
Bonds	70,000
Rental building	200,000
Estate principal	604,000

Cash balance analysis:

Beginning cash	400,000
Sale of coin collection	92,000
Collection of interest	2,000
Collection of dividend	1,000
Collection of rent	4,000
Payment of funeral expense	(20,000)
Payment of appraisal expense	(15,000)
Payment of executor fees	(25,000)
Payment of medical expenses	(10,000)
Payment of other debts	(125,000)
Legacy distribution to Jake	(20,000)
Cash balance	$ 284,000

As to Income

I charge myself with:

Dividend income (gross less receivable amount at date of death)	1,000
Interest income (gross less receivable amount at date of death)	1,000
Rent income (gross less receivable amount at date of death)	3,000
Balance as to income	$ 5,000

Balance as to income

Cash	$ 5,000

Questions

1. Distinguish between *testate* and *intestate*.
2. If a person dies without leaving a valid will, how is the distribution of property regulated?
3. What are probate laws?
4. What are the objectives of probate laws?
5. What are the responsibilities of the executor of an estate?
6. At what value are the assets within an estate reported?
7. If an asset of an estate has no readily ascertainable fair value, how should it be presented/valued on the charge/discharge statement?
8. How does an executor discover the claims against an estate?
9. What claims against an estate have priority?
10. What are homestead and family allowances?
11. What are the differences among a devise, a legacy, and a bequest?
12. Describe the four types of legacies, and give examples of each.
13. What is the purpose of the process of abatement? How does the executor of an estate utilize this process?
14. How is the federal estate tax computed?
15. What was the impact of the Economic Growth and Tax Relief Reconciliation Act of 2001 on the conveyance of property?
16. What is a taxable gift?
17. Why is the establishment of a credit shelter trust fund considered a good estate planning technique?
18. What deductions are allowed in computing estate income taxes?
19. Other than financial considerations, why should individuals consider preparing a valid will?
20. In accounting for an estate or trust, how is the distinction between principal and income determined?
21. What transactions are normally viewed as changes in the principal of an estate? What transactions are normally viewed as changes in the income of an estate?
22. What is the alternate date for valuing the assets of an estate? When should this alternate date be used?
23. In the initial accounting for an estate, why does the executor record only the assets?
24. What is the purpose of the charge and discharge statement that the executor of an estate issues?
25. What is a trust fund?
26. Why have trust funds become especially popular in recent years?
27. What is an *inter vivos* trust?
28. What is a testamentary trust?
29. What are QTIP trusts, GRATs, and charitable remainder trusts?
30. Why is the distinction between principal and income so important in accounting for most trusts?

Problems

1. Which of the following is *not* a true statement?
   a. *Testate* refers to a person having a valid will.
   b. The laws of descent convey personal property if an individual dies without a valid will.
   c. *Intestate* refers to a person having no valid will.
   d. A specific legacy is a gift of personal property that is specifically identified.

2. Why might real estate be omitted from an inventory of estate property?
   a. Real estate is subject to a separate inheritance tax.
   b. State laws prohibit real property from being conveyed by an estate.
   c. State laws require a separate listing of all real estate.
   d. In some states, depending on the ownership, real estate is considered to be conveyed directly to a beneficiary at the time of death.

3. What is the purpose of the laws of distribution?
   a. To guide the distribution of personal property when an individual dies without a will.
   b. To verify the legality of a will, especially an oral will.
   c. To guide the distribution of real property when an individual dies without a will.
   d. To outline the functions of the executor of an estate.

4. A deceased individual owned a bond. Which of the following is included in the estate principal?
   a. All interest collected prior to distributing the bonds to a beneficiary is considered part of the estate principal.
   b. Only the first cash payment after death is included in the estate principal.
   c. Interest that was not collected prior to death is excluded from the estate principal.
   d. Interest earned prior to death is considered part of the estate principal even if received after death.

5. Which of the following is *not* a goal of probate laws?
   a. To gather and preserve all of the decedent's property.
   b. To ensure that each individual produces a valid will.
   c. To discover the decedent's intent for property held at death and then to follow those wishes.
   d. To carry out an orderly and fair settlement of all debts and distribution of property.

6. How are claims against a decedent's estate discovered by an executor?
   a. Public notice must be printed in an appropriate newspaper to alert all possible claimants.
   b. The executor waits for nine months until all possible bills have been received.
   c. The executor directly contacts all companies that the decedent did business with.
   d. Claims the estate is to pay are limited to all of the bills received but not paid prior to the date of death.

7. Why are claims against an estate put into an order of priority?
   a. To help the executor determine the due date for each claim.
   b. To determine which claims are to be paid if funds are insufficient to pay all claims.
   c. To assist in determining which specific assets are to be used to satisfy these claims.
   d. To list the claims in order of age so that the oldest can be paid first.

8. Which of the following claims against an estate does not have priority?
   a. Funeral expenses because the amounts incurred are usually at the discretion of family members.
   b. Medical expenses associated with the decedent's last illness.
   c. The costs of administering the estate.
   d. Unpaid rent on the decedent's home if not paid for the three months immediately prior to death.

9. How does a devise differ from a legacy?
   a. A devise is a gift of money and a legacy is a nonmonetary gift.
   b. A devise is a gift to an individual and a legacy is a gift to a charity or other organization.
   c. A devise is a gift of real property and a legacy is a gift of personal property.
   d. A devise is a gift made prior to death and a legacy is a gift made at death.

10. What is the homestead allowance?
    a. A reduction of $20,000 in estate assets prior to computing the amount of federal estate taxes.
    b. The amount of property conveyed in a will to a surviving spouse.
    c. An allotment of cash from an estate to a surviving spouse and/or minor and dependent children before any claims are paid.
    d. A decrease in the value of property on which state inheritance taxes are assessed. The reduction is equal to the value of property conveyed to a surviving spouse.

11. Which of the following is a specific legacy?
    a. The gift of all remaining estate property to a charity.
    b. The gift of $44,000 cash from a specified source.
    c. The gift of $44,000 cash.
    d. The gift of 1,000 shares of stock in IBM.

12. A will has the following statement: "I leave $20,000 cash from my savings account in the Central Fidelity Bank to my sister, Angela." This gift is an example of
    a. A residual legacy.
    b. A general legacy.

     c. A demonstrative legacy.

     d. A specific legacy.

13. What is the objective of the process of abatement?

     a. To give legal structure to the reductions that must be made if an estate has insufficient assets to satisfy all legacies.

     b. To ensure that all property distributions take place in a timely manner.

     c. To provide adequate compensation for the estate executor and any appraisers or other experts that must be hired.

     d. To ensure that all legacies are distributed to the appropriate party as specified by the decedent's will or state laws.

14. For estate tax purposes, what date is used for valuation purposes?

     a. Property is always valued at the date of death.

     b. Property is always valued at the date of distribution.

     c. Property is valued at the date of death unless the alternate date, which is the date of distribution or six months after death, whichever comes first, is selected.

     d. Property is valued at the date of death although a reduction is allowed if the value declines within one year of death.

15. Which of the following is true concerning the Economic Growth and Tax Relief Reconciliation Act of 2001?

     a. This tax law leads to the immediate elimination of the federal estate tax.

     b. This tax law leads to the immediate elimination of the federal gift tax.

     c. This tax law provides for a $2.0 million tax-free exemption for estates created in 2006.

     d. This tax law leads to the immediate elimination of the generation-skipping tax.

16. In computing federal estate taxes, deductions from the value of the estate are allowed for all of the following except

     a. Charitable bequests.

     b. Losses on the disposal of investments.

     c. Funeral expenses.

     d. Debts of the decedent.

17. The following individuals died in 2006. The estate of John Lexington has a taxable value of $1,590,000. The estate of Dorothy Alexander has a taxable value of $1.9 million. The estate of Scotty Fitzgerald has a taxable value of $2.6 million. None of these individuals made any taxable gifts during their lifetimes. Which of the following statements is true?

     a. Only Fitzgerald's estate will have to pay federal estate taxes.

     b. All three of the estates will have to pay federal estate taxes.

     c. None of these estates is large enough to necessitate the payment of estate taxes.

     d. Only the estates of Alexander and Fitzgerald are large enough to necessitate the payment of estate taxes.

18. Sally Anne Williams dies on January 1, 2006. All of her property is conveyed to several relatives on April 1, 2006. For federal estate tax purposes, the executor chooses the alternate valuation date. On what date is the value of the property determined?

     a. January 1, 2006.

     b. April 1, 2006.

     c. July 1, 2006.

     d. December 31, 2006.

19. M. Wilson Waltman died on January 1, 2006. All of his property is conveyed to beneficiaries on October 1, 2006. For federal estate tax purposes, the executor chooses the alternate valuation date. On what date is the value of the property determined?

     a. January 1, 2006.

     b. July 1, 2006.

     c. October 1, 2006.

     d. December 31, 2006.

20. Which of the following is *not* true concerning gift taxes?

    a. Gift taxes will not be abolished but a lifetime exclusion of $1 million is created.

    b. The Economic Growth and Tax Relief Reconciliation Act of 2001 will eventually eliminate the federal gift tax.

    c. Historically, gift taxes and estate taxes have been linked through a unified transfer credit.

    d. Gift taxes are different from generation-skipping taxes.

21. A couple has written a will that leaves part of their money to a trust fund. The income from this trust will benefit the surviving spouse until death, with the principal then going to their children. Why was the trust fund created?

    a. To reduce the estate of the surviving spouse and, thus, decrease the total amount of estate taxes to be paid by the couple.

    b. To make certain that the surviving spouse is protected from lawsuits filed by the children of the couple.

    c. To give the surviving spouse discretion over the ultimate use of these funds.

    d. Trust funds generate more income than other investments so that the earning potential of the money is maximized.

22. The executor of an estate is filing an income tax return for the current period. Revenues of $12,000 have been earned. Which of the following is not a deduction allowed in computing taxable income?

    a. Income distributed to a beneficiary.

    b. Funeral expenses.

    c. A personal exemption.

    d. Charitable donations.

23. What is a remainderman?

    a. A beneficiary that receives the principal left in an estate or trust after a specified time.

    b. The beneficiary of the decedent's life insurance policy.

    c. An executor or administrator after an estate has been completely settled.

    d. If a legacy is given to a group of people, the remainderman is the last of the individuals to die.

24. In an estate, which of the following is charged to income rather than to principal?

    a. Funeral expenses.

    b. Investment costs.

    c. Property taxes.

    d. Losses on the sale of investments.

25. In recording the transactions of an estate, when are liabilities recorded?

    a. When incurred.

    b. At the date of death.

    c. When the executor takes responsibility for the estate.

    d. When paid.

26. What is the difference between an *inter vivos* trust and a testamentary trust?

    a. A testamentary trust conveys money to a charity; an *inter vivos* trust conveys money to individuals.

    b. A testamentary trust is created by a will; an *inter vivos* trust is created by a living individual.

    c. A testamentary trust conveys income to one party and the principal to another; an *inter vivos* trust conveys all monies to the same party.

    d. A testamentary trust ceases after a specified period of time; an *inter vivos* trust is assumed to be permanent.

27. Which of the following is a charitable lead trust?

    a. The income of the trust fund goes to an individual until death at which time the principal is conveyed to a charitable organization.

    b. Charitable gifts are placed into the trust until a certain dollar amount is achieved and is then transferred to a specified charitable organization.

    c. The income of a trust fund goes to a charitable organization for a specified time with the principal then being conveyed to a different beneficiary.

    d. A charity conveys money to a trust that generates income for the charity's use in its various projects.

28. The estate of Nancy Hanks reports the following information:

Value of estate assets	$1,400,000
Conveyed to spouse	700,000
Conveyed to children	100,000
Conveyed to charities	420,000
Funeral expenses	50,000
Administrative expenses	20,000
Debts	110,000

What is the taxable estate value?

    a. $70,000.

    b. $100,000.

    c. $180,000.

    d. $420,000.

29. An estate has the following income:

Rental income	$5,000
Interest income	3,000
Dividend income	1,000

The interest income was immediately conveyed to the appropriate beneficiary. The dividends were given to charity as per the decedent's will. What is the taxable income of the estate?

    a. $4,400.

    b. $5,000.

    c. $8,000.

    d. $8,400.

30. Define each of the following terms:

    a. Will.

    b. Estate.

    c. Intestate.

    d. Probate laws.

    e. Trust.

    f. Inter vivos trust.

    g. Charitable remainder trust.

    h. Remainderman.

    i. Executor.

    j. Homestead allowance.

31. Answer each of the following questions:

    a. What are the objectives of probate laws?

    b. What tasks does the executor of an estate perform?

    c. What assets are normally included as estate properties?

    d. What claims have priority to the distributions made by an estate?

32. The will of Josh O'Brien has the following stipulations:

    Antique collection goes to Ilsa Lunn.

    All money in the First Savings Bank goes to Richard Blaine.

    Cash of $9,000 goes to Nelson Tucker.

    All remaining assets are put into a trust fund with the income going to Lucy Van Jones. At her death, the principal is to be conveyed to Howard Amadeus.

Identify the following:

a. Remainderman.

b. Trustor.

c. Demonstrative legacy.

d. General legacy.

e. Specific legacy.

f. Life tenant.

g. Testator.

33. Marie Hardy's will has the following provisions:

  "I leave the cash balance deposited in the First National Bank (up to a total of $50,000) to Jack Abrams. I leave $18,000 cash to Suzanne Benton. I leave 1,000 shares of Coca-Cola Company stock to Cindy Cheng. I leave my house to Dennis Davis. I leave all of my other assets and properties to Wilbur N. Ed."

  a. Assume that the estate has the following assets: $41,000 cash in the First National Bank, $16,000 cash in the New Hampshire Savings and Loan, 800 shares of Coca-Cola stock, 1,100 shares of Xerox stock, a house, and other property valued at $13,000. What distributions will be made from this estate?

  b. Assume that the estate has the following assets: $55,000 cash in the First National Bank, $6,000 cash in the New Hampshire Savings and Loan, 1,200 shares of Coca-Cola stock, 600 shares of Xerox stock, and other property valued at $22,000. What distributions will be made from this estate?

34. Zac Peterson's estate reports the following information:

Value of estate assets	$2,300,000
Conveyed to spouse	1,000,000
Conveyed to children	230,000
Conveyed to trust fund for benefit of spouse	500,000
Conveyed to charities	260,000
Funeral expenses	23,000
Administrative expenses	41,000
Debts	246,000

What is the taxable estate value?

35. Donna Stober's estate has the following assets (all figures approximate fair value):

Investments in stocks and bonds	$1,400,000
House	700,000
Cash	70,000
Investment land	60,000
Automobiles (three)	51,000
Other assets	100,000

  The house, cash, and other assets are left to the decedent's spouse. The investment land is contributed to a charitable organization. The automobiles are to be given to the decedent's brother. The investments in stocks and bonds are to be put into a trust fund. The income generated by this trust will go to the decedent's spouse annually until all of the couple's children have reached the age of 25. At that time, the trust will be divided evenly among the children.

  The following amounts are paid prior to distribution and settlement of the estate: funeral expenses of $20,000 and estate administration expenses of $10,000.

  a. What value is to be reported as the taxable estate for federal estate tax purposes?

  b. How does the year in which an individual dies affect the estate tax computation? For example, what is the impact of dying on December 30, 2008, versus January 2, 2009?

36. During 2005, an estate generates income of $20,000:

Rental income	$9,000
Interest income	6,000
Dividend income	5,000

The interest income is conveyed immediately to the beneficiary stated in the decedent's will. Dividends of $1,200 are given to the decedent's church.

What amount of federal income tax must be paid by this estate?

37. The executor of Rose Shield's estate listed the following properties (at fair value):

Cash	$300,000
Life insurance receivable	200,000
Investments in stocks and bonds	100,000
Rental property	90,000
Personal property	130,000

a. Prepare journal entries to record the property held by Ms. Shield's estate and then each of the following transactions that occur in the months following the decedent's death:

(1) Claims of $80,000 are made against the estate for various debts incurred before the decedent's death.

(2) Interest of $12,000 is received from bonds held by the estate. Of this amount, $5,000 had been earned prior to death.

(3) Ordinary repairs costing $6,000 are made to the rental property.

(4) All debts ($80,000) are paid.

(5) Stocks recorded in the estate at $16,000 are sold for $19,000 cash.

(6) Rental income of $14,000 is collected. Of this amount, $2,000 had been earned prior to the decedent's death.

(7) Cash of $6,000 is distributed to Jim Arness, an income beneficiary.

(8) The proceeds from the life insurance policy are collected and the money is immediately distributed to Amanda Blake as specified in the decedent's will.

(9) Funeral expenses of $10,000 are paid.

b. Prepare in proper form a charge and discharge statement.

38. The executor of Gina Purcell's estate has recorded the following information:

Assets discovered at death (at fair value):

Cash	$600,000
Life insurance receivable	200,000
Investments:	
Walt Disney Company	11,000
Polaroid Corporation	27,000
Ford Motor Company	34,000
Dell Computer Corporation	32,000
Rental property	300,000

Cash outflows:

Funeral expenses	$ 21,000
Executor fees	12,000
Ordinary repairs of rental property	2,000
Debts	81,000
Distribution of income to income beneficiary	4,000
Distribution to charitable remainder trust	300,000

Cash inflows:

Sale of Polaroid stock	$ 30,000
Rental income ($4,000 earned prior to death)	11,000
Dividend income ($2,000 declared prior to death)	12,000
Life insurance proceeds	200,000

Debts of $17,000 still remain to be paid. The Dell shares have been conveyed to the appropriate beneficiary. Assume that Ms. Purcell's will stated that all executor fees are to be paid from principal.

Prepare an interim charge and discharge statement for this estate.

39. Jerry Tasch's will has the following provisions:
    - $150,000 in cash goes to Thomas Thorne.
    - All shares of Coca-Cola go to Cindy Phillips.
    - Residence goes to Kevin Simmons.
    - All other estate assets are to be liquidated with the resulting cash going to the First Church of Freedom, Missouri.

    Prepare journal entries for the following transactions:

    a. Discovered the following assets (at fair value):

Cash	$ 80,000
Interest receivable	6,000
Life insurance policy	300,000
Residence	200,000
Shares of Coca-Cola Company	50,000
Shares of Polaroid Corporation	110,000
Shares of Ford	140,000

    b. Collected interest of $7,000.
    c. Paid funeral expenses of $20,000.
    d. Discovered debts of $40,000.
    e. Located an additional savings account of $12,000.
    f. Conveyed title to the residence to Kevin Simmons.
    g. Collected life insurance policy.
    h. Discovered additional debts of $60,000. Paid debts totaling $100,000.
    i. Conveyed cash of $150,000 to appropriate beneficiary.
    j. Sold the shares of Polaroid for $112,000.
    k. Paid administrative expenses of $10,000.

40. After the death of Lennie Pope, his will was read. It contained the following provisions:
    - $110,000 in cash goes to decedent's brother, Ned Pope.
    - Residence and other personal property go to his sister, Sue Pope.
    - Proceeds from the sale of Ford stock go to uncle, Harwood Pope.
    - $300,000 goes into a charitable remainder trust.
    - All other estate assets are to be liquidated with the cash going to Victoria Jones.

    a. Prepare journal entries for the following transactions that subsequently occur:

    (1) Discovered the following assets (at fair value):

Cash	$ 19,000
Certificates of deposit	90,000
Dividends receivable	3,000
Life insurance policy	450,000
Residence and personal effects	470,000
Shares of Ford Motor Company	72,000
Shares of Xerox Corporation	97,000

    (2) Collected life insurance policy.
    (3) Collected dividends of $4,000.
    (4) Discovered debts of $71,000.
    (5) Conveyed title to the residence to Sue Pope along with the decedent's personal effects.
    (6) Discovered title to land valued at $15,000.
    (7) Discovered additional debts of $37,000. Paid all of the debts totaling $108,000.
    (8) Paid funeral expenses of $31,000.
    (9) Conveyed cash of $110,000 to Ned Pope.
    (10) Sold the shares of Ford for $81,000.
    (11) Paid administrative expenses of $16,000.
    (12) Made the appropriate payment to Harwood Pope.

    b. Prepare a charge and discharge statement.

41. James Albemarle creates a trust fund at the beginning of 2006. The income from this fund will go to his son Edward. When Edward reaches the age of 25, the principal of the fund will be conveyed to United Charities of Cleveland. Mr. Albemarle specifies that 75 percent of trustee fees are to be paid from principal. Terry Jones, CPA, is the trustee.

    Prepare all necessary journal entries for the trust to record the following transactions:

    a. James Albemarle transferred cash of $300,000, stocks worth $200,000, and rental property valued at $150,000 to the trustee of this fund.

    b. Immediately invested cash of $260,000 in bonds issued by the U.S. government. Commissions of $3,000 are paid on this transaction.

    c. Incurred permanent repairs of $7,000 so that the property can be rented. Payment is made immediately.

    d. Received dividends of $4,000. Of this amount, $1,000 had been declared prior to the creation of the trust fund.

    e. Paid insurance expense of $2,000 on the rental property.

    f. Received rental income of $8,000.

    g. Paid $4,000 from the trust for trustee services rendered.

    h. Conveyed cash of $5,000 to Edward Albemarle.

42. Henry O'Donnell created an *inter vivos* trust fund. He owns a large department store in Higgins, Utah. He also owns a tract of land adjacent to the store used as an extra parking lot when the store is having a sale or during the Christmas season. O'Donnell expects the land to appreciate in value and eventually be sold for an office complex or additional stores.

    O'Donnell places this land into a charitable lead trust, which will hold the land for 10 years until O'Donnell's son is 21. At that time, title will transfer to the son. The store will pay rent to use the land during the interim. The income generated each year from this usage will be given to a local church. The land is currently valued at $320,000.

    During the first year of this arrangement, the trustee records the following cash transactions:

Cash inflows:	
Rental income	$60,000
Cash outflows:	
Insurance	$ 4,000
Property taxes	6,000
Paving (considered an extraordinary repair)	4,000
Maintenance	8,000
Distribution to income beneficiary	30,000

    Prepare all journal entries for this trust fund including the entry to create the trust.

Develop Your Skills

RESEARCH CASE 1

CPA skills

The CPA firm of Simon, Winslow, and Tate has been approached by a client who is interested in information about the possibility of establishing a minor's Section 2503(c) trust.

Go to the Web site www.finaid.org and then link to http://www.nysscpa.org/sound_advice/money_6.30.03.htm. Do a search to find information about this type of trust fund.

Required:

Based on the results of this search, write a memo for the client outlining the requirements, design, advantages, and disadvantages of a minor's Section 2503(c) trust so the client can make an informed decision.

RESEARCH CASE 2

A staff employee for the CPA firm of O'Brien, Leahy, and Sweeney is currently preparing Form 1041 as an income tax return for an estate. The staff employee knows that the estate is allowed a deduction for income distributions to beneficiaries up to the amount of the estate's distributable net income (DNI) for the period. However, the employee is not certain how to compute the exact amount of this deduction.

Go to the Web site www.irs.gov. Under Forms and Publications, do a search for "Instruction 1041" to get the instruction information for estate and trust income taxes published by the IRS.

Required:

Read the information provided, and write a memo to the employee explaining (in general terms) how to calculate this deduction.

RESEARCH CASE 3

A client, Beth Voga, asks for advice. She tells you that her grandmother, a widowed resident of Montana, has no will. She asks whether any portion of her grandmother's estate will pass to her (Beth's) cousins, whom her grandmother despises.

Required:

Use an Internet search engine to locate the Montana version of the Uniform Probate Code. Then briefly advise Ms. Voga, answering her specific question. Also advise her on the necessity of a will for her grandmother.

ANALYSIS CASE 1

Use an Internet search engine to locate an explanation of the benefits of a grantor retained annuity trust. If you are unable to locate relevant resources, try linking to http://www.mcguirewoods.com/news-resources/publications/taxation/GRAT.doc.

Required:

Write a memo describing the circumstances that would make this type of trust most advantageous.

ANALYSIS CASE 2

A law firm is preparing to file a federal estate tax return (Form 706). The executor of the estate has elected to use the alternate valuation date. The partner in charge of filing this return is not certain about all of the ramifications of having chosen to use this alternate date.

Go to the Web site www.irs.gov. Under Forms and Publications, do a search for "Instruction 706" to get the instruction information published by the IRS for federal estate taxes.

Required:

Read the information provided, and write a memo to the partner outlining the information the IRS provides as to the significance of the alternate valuation date.

Index

A

A. H. Robins, 592n
Abatement process, 857
Abbott Laboratories, 441–442
Accounting clusters, 531–532
Accounting firms. *See* Public accounting firms
Accounting Principles Board (APB)
  Accounting Interpretation No. 1, 20
  Opinions, 70
    No. 16, 63, 69
    No. 18, 3, 4, 8–9, 11, 20, 22
    No. 20, 387
    No. 26, 267
    No. 28, 383–384, 389–390
    No. 29, 541
    No. 30, 10, 184n
Accounting Research Bulletin (ARB) *No. 51,* 3, 36, 39, 40–41,
    180, 183, 211, 260, 325
Accounting Standards Board (ASB), 549
Accounting Standards Committee (ASC), 548–549
Accrual accounting, 714
  for foreign currency transactions, 416
  modified, 709, 723–724
Acquisition method for consolidations, 53–58
  illustrations of, 54–58
Adelphia Communications, 572, 591
Ademption, 857n
Administrator of the estate, 855
Advanced Micro Devices, Inc., 576
AEG, 554
Affiliated groups, income taxes and, 334
Afterman, Allan B., 530n
Agency funds, 714
AICPA. *See* American Institute of Certified Public Accountants
    (AICPA)
AIMR (Association for Investment Management and Research),
    Financial Reporting in the 1990s and Beyond of, 367
Alliant Food Service, Inc., 95
Altria Group, Inc., 364
American Cancer Society, 815
American Express Co., 671
American Heart Association, 830–831
American Institute of Certified Public Accountants
    (AICPA), 707
  Accounting Trends & Techniques of, 368
  Auditing Standards Board *Statements on Auditing Standards*
    No. 69, 825, 826
    No. 91, 825n
  code of conduct of, 572
  on not-for-profit accounting, 825, 826
  Not-for-Profit Organizations of, 816n
  Statement of Position 90–7, 607–608, 609–610
  Statement of Position 98–2, 821

Ameritech Corporation, 13
Amoco, 490
Amortizations
  consolidated statement of cash flows and, 281
  in equity method of accounting for investments,
    15–17
Anheuser-Busch Companies, Inc., 379
APB. *See* Accounting Principles Board (APB)
Appropriations, 720
ARB (Accounting Research Bulletin) *No. 51,* 3, 36, 39, 40–41,
    180, 183, 211, 260, 325
ARCO (Atlantic Richfield Company), 289
Arnold, Jerry L., 479n
Arons, David F., 814n
Art, works of
  donations of, to not-for-profit organizations,
    828–829
  government accounting and, 762–764
Arthur Andersen LLP, 635–636
Articles of partnership, 636–637
ASB (Accounting Standards Board), 549
ASB (Auditing Standards Board), 573
ASC (Accounting Standards Committee), 548–549
Asinof, Lynn, 870n
Assets
  capital, fund-based financial statements and, 724–725
  depreciable, intercompany transfer of, 231–235
    deferral of unrealized gains and, 232
    downstream, using equity method, 234–235
    effect on noncontrolling interest valuation, 235
    illustration of, 232–234
  foreign currency denominated, foreign currency options to
    hedge, 428–433
  infrastructure, 764–765
  intangible, consolidations subsequent to acquisition and, 94,
    115–116
  marshaling of, 678–684
  net. *See also specific financial statements*
    temporarily restricted, in not-for-profit accounting, 818,
    820–821
  partnership, preliminary distribution of, 684–687
Asset test, for determining reportable operating segments,
    371, 373
Asset transactions, consolidated financial statements. *See*
    Intercompany transactions
Association for Investment Management and Research
    (AIMR), *Financial Reporting in the 1990s and
    Beyond* of, 367
Atlanta, Georgia, City of, 768
Atlantic Richfield Company (ARCO), 289
AT&T, 59
AT&T Broadband, 36, 59, 181
ATT Wireless, 38
Auditing Standards Board (ASB), 573

B

BADC (Business Accounting Deliberation Council), 555
Baja Fresh, 116
Balance sheet
    current rate method for translation of, 484–485
    foreign currency transactions and, 415–417
    fund-based, 776–777, 778–779
    during reorganization, 608–609
Balance sheet exposure, 472
    hedging, 491–492
Baltimore, Maryland, City of, 761–762
Bank of America, 36
Bank One, 36
Bankruptcy, 590–614
    Bankruptcy Reform Act of 1978 and, 592–596
    Chapter 7 (liquidation), 600–604
        reorganization versus, 595–596
        statement of realization and liquidation and, 602–604
        trustee's role in, 601–602
    Chapter 11 (reorganization), 604–613
        financial reporting during, 607–609
        financial reporting for companies emerging from,
            609–610
        fresh start accounting and, 609–613
        liquidation versus, 595–596
        plan for, 605–607
    classification of creditors and, 593–595
    involuntary, 592–593
    statement of financial affairs and, 596–600
    voluntary, 592–593
Bankruptcy Reform Act of 1978, 592–596
BASF, 530, 553
Bayless, Robert, 379
Beck, Leif C., 670n
Benston, George J., 21n, 583n
Bequests, 856
Beresford, Dennis R., 533–534
Berry, Jeffrey M., 814n
Berton, Lee, 634n, 645, 671n, 824n
Birds Eye, Inc., 315
Birmingham, Alabama, 757
Bismarck, North Dakota, City of, 764
Black, Pam, 870n
Black-Scholes option pricing formula, 413
Block, Sandra, 582n
Blue sky laws, 579
Blumenthal, Robin Goldwyn, 575n
Boeing Company, 364
Bond issuance, 730–732
Bonhiver, Homer A., 592n, 600n
Bonuses
    to new partner, 650–651
    to original partners, 648
Bonus method
    for intangible contributions to partnerships, 639–640,
        649
    for withdrawal of partner, 652
Book value
    investment cost exceeding, 13–17
    of subsidiary stock

Book value—Cont.
    of subsidiary stock—Cont.
        changes in, stock transactions and, 288–290
        establishing, 184–185
Book value method, for consolidations, 125
Borrowing, foreign currency, 442–443
Boston, Massachusetts, City of, 767, 769
Bourque, Donald D., 613n
Brady, Thomas, 70n
Brandzel, Jacob, 671
Brau und Brunnen AG, 551
Brayshaw, R. E., 548n
Bresiger, Gregory, 853n
Briggs & Stratton Corporation, 382
British-American accounting model, 531–532
Brooks, Jermyn Paul, 528n
Brunswick Corporation, 120–121
Brzezenski, Thomas J., 859n
Buckeye Partners, L.P., 635
Budgets, in governmental accounting, 719–721
Burger, Jeff, 868n
Burton, Thomas M., 606n
Bush, George W., 568, 858
Bushee, Brian J., 583n
Business Accounting Deliberation Council (BADC), 555
Business combination. See Consolidated financial statements;
        Consolidations
Bypass trusts, 869

C

Cadbury Schweppes, 524
Cafe Express, 116
CAFRs (comprehensive annual financial reports), 766
Call options, for purchase of foreign currency, 412, 413
Canada, accounting model in, 532
Capital additions, expenditures for, recognition of,
        723–727
Capital assets, fund-based financial statements and,
        724–725
Capital balance, deficit, termination and liquidation of
        partnerships and, 675–678
Capital contributions to partnerships, 637–640
    additional, after formation of partnership, 640–641
    dissolution of partnership by, 648–651
Capital leases, government accounting and, 757–759
    fund-based financial statements and, 758–759
    government-wide financial statements and, 757–758
Capital projects funds, 712
Cash flow exposure, 420
Cash flow hedges, 420–421, 423–425
    fair value hedges versus, 420–421
    options designated as, 429–431
Caterpillar, Inc., 367
Catlett, George R., 4n
CCE (Coca-Cola Enterprises Inc.), 17, 19
Celeron Corporation, 63
Celtel International BV, 469
Cemex SA, 469
Chandler Act (1938), 592

Chapter 7 bankruptcy, 600–604
    reorganization versus, 595–596
    statement of realization and liquidation and, 602–604
    trustee's role in, 601–602
Chapter 11 bankruptcy, 604–613
    financial reporting during, 607–609
    financial reporting for companies emerging from, 609–610
    fresh start accounting and, 609–613
    liquidation versus, 595–596
    plan for, 605–607
Charge and discharge statement, 867, 868
Charitable land trusts, 870
Charitable remainder trusts, 870
Charlotte-Mecklenburg County, North Carolina Board of
    Education, 770
Chesapeake Corporation, 124, 125
Chewco, 260n
China Eastern Airlines Corporation, 545, 546
Christian Children's Fund, 818, 819, 820, 821, 831
Cingular Wireless, 11, 38
Cirrus Logic, Inc., 409
Cisco Systems, Inc., 35
Citrix Systems, 57n
Claims, against decedent, discovery of, 855–856
Cleveland, Ohio, City of, 764
Clinton, Bill, 858
CNBC, 314
Coca-Cola Amatil Ltd., 530
Coca-Cola Company, 3, 17, 19, 21, 379, 442, 469,
    529–530, 784
Coca-Cola Enterprises Inc. (CCE), 17, 19
Coca-Cola Italia SRL, 530
Cochrane, James L., 530n
Code law, 528
Colgate-Palmolive Company, 366
Collateral, 593
Colleges and universities
    private, 827, 828, 829
    public, 785, 790–794
Collins, Stephen H., 530n, 536n
Comcast Corporation, 36, 181
Commercial code
    Japanese, 554–555
    U.S., 528
Common law, 528
Companies acts, 528
Compaq, 282n
Compensated absences, 761–762
Component units, government accounting and, 768–769
Comprehensive annual financial reports (CAFRs), 766
Conglomerates, 37
Connecting affiliations, 323–324
Connell Limited Partnership, 632
Conseco Inc., 591
Consolidated earnings per share, 284–287
Consolidated financial statements, 35, 203
    intercompany asset transactions and. *See* Intercompany
        transactions
    parent company concept and, 172
Consolidated statement of cash flows, 280–284
    acquisition year cash flow adjustments and, 281–282

Consolidated statement of cash flows—*Cont.*
    amortizations and, 281
    intercompany transactions and, 281
    noncontrolling interest and, 280–281
Consolidations, 35–71, 314–344
    acquisition method for, 53–58
        illustrations of, 54–58
    control and, 40–42
    economic unit concept and, 157–160, 173–176
        sales of subsidiary stock and, 186
        step acquisitions and, 180–181
    effects created by passage of time and, 93–94
    examples of, 37–39
    of foreign subsidiaries, 494–497
    income tax accounting for, 333–343
        affiliated groups and, 334
        assigning income tax expense and, 336–337
        deferred income taxes and, 334–335
        illustration of consolidated tax returns and, 335–336
        operating loss carryforwards and, 342–343
        separate tax returns and, 337–341
        temporary differences generated by business combinations
          and, 341–342
    indirect subsidiary control and, 314–323
        connecting affiliations and, 323–324
    intercompany debt transactions and. *See* Intercompany
        transactions, debt
    involving noncontrolling interest, 156–164
        economic unit concept and, 157–160, 173–176
        intercompany inventory transfers and, 217–218
        parent company concept and, 157, 161–164, 166–173
        proportionate consolidation concept and, 157, 160–161
        subsequent to acquisition, 166–176
        valuation theories and, 164–166
    mid-year acquisitions and, revenue and expense reporting for,
        181–183
    mutual ownership and, 324–325
        conventional approach to, 326–327, 329–332
        illustration of, 327–333
        treasury stock approach to, 325–326, 327–329
    parent company concept and, 157, 161–164, 166–173
        step acquisitions and, 177–179
    pooling of interests method for. *See* Pooling of interests
        method for consolidations
    process of, 39–40
        with indirect control, 317–323
    proportionate consolidation concept and, 157, 160–161
    purchase method for, 43, 44–53
        related costs of business combinations and, 48–49
        when dissolution takes place, 44–48
        when separate incorporation is maintained, 49–53
    purchase price allocations and, 59–62
        intangibles and, 59
        purchased in-process research and development
          and, 59–62
    reasons for, 36–37
    statutory, 40
    step acquisitions and, 176–181
        economic unit concept and, 180–181
        parent company concept and, 177–179
        retroactive treatment caused by, 179–180

Consolidations—*Cont.*
  subsequent to acquisition, 93–127
    contingent consideration and, 120–123
    cost method for, 110–112
    equity method for, 96–106
    goodwill and, 94, 116–120
    intangible assets and, 94, 115–116
    investment accounting by acquiring company and, 94–96
    involving noncontrolling interest, 166–176
    partial equity method for, 106–115
    pooling of interests method for, 125–127
    push-down accounting and, 123–125
  subsidiary stock and. *See* Subsidiary stock
  of variable interest entities, 260–266
    procedures for, 264–266
  variable interest entities and. *See* Variable interest
    entities (VIEs)
Consolidation worksheet, 496–497
Consultative Committee of Accountancy Bodies, 554–557
Consumption method, for capital assets and prepaid
    items, 726
Continental accounting model, 531–532
Continental Airlines Corporation, 613
Contingent consideration, consolidations subsequent to
    acquisition and, 120–123
Contractual agreements, with third-party payors, 836–837
Contributed services, 830–831
Contributions
  capital, to partnerships
    additional, after formation of partnership, 640–641
    to partnerships, 637–640
  to not-for-profit organizations, 827–832
    holding for others, 829–830
    recognition of, 818
    of services, 830–831
    of works of art and historical treasures, 828–829
Control, consolidation and, 40–42. *See also* Consolidations,
    involving noncontrolling interest
  indirect subsidiary control and, 314–324
    connecting affiliations and, 323–324
Convenience translations, 555
Conventional approach, to mutual ownership, 326–327, 329–332
Cornell, Camilla, 670n
Corporate accounting scandals, 568, 571–584
  EDGAR and, 582–584
  filings with SEC and, 577–582
  public Company Accounting Oversight Board and,
    572–573
  registration of public accounting firms and, 573–577
Corpus, 862
Corr, Paul J., 613n
Corwin, Leslie D., 634n
Cost method
  for consolidations subsequent to acquisition, 110–112
  parent company concept and, 172–173
Cost of goods sold, in interim reports, 384–385
Costs not directly matched with revenues, in interim reports,
    385–386
Cram downs, 607
Cramer, J. M., 548n
Creditors, classification of, 593–595

Credit shelter trusts, 869
Crestliner, Inc., 120
Currency
  functional, 479–480
  reporting, 479
Currency balances, nonlocal, 489
Currency options, foreign, 417
Current exchange rate, 470, 472
Current rate method for financial statement translation, 473,
    483–485
  cost of goods sold under, 476
  fixed assets, depreciation, and accumulated depreciation
    under, 477
  gain or loss on sale of an asset and, 477
  lower-of-cost-or-market rule and, 476
Customers, enterprisewide disclosures about, 381–383

D

Daimler-Benz AG, 554
Daimler-Chrysler, 537n
Dallas, Texas, 768–769
Davidson, Sidney, 70
Davis, Michael, 70n
Debtor in possession, 605
Debts
  fully secured, 593
  intercompany transactions involving. *See* Intercompany
    transactions, debt
  partially secured, 593
Debt service funds, 712
Decision making, equity method and, 20–21
Deferral approach, for foreign currency transactions, 416
Deficiency letters, 579
Deficit capital balance, termination and liquidation of
    partnerships and, 675–678
Dell Computer Corporation, 13
Deloitte Touche Tohmatsu, 632
Demonstrative legacies, 856
Depreciable asset transfers, intercompany, 231–235
  deferral of unrealized gains and, 232
  downstream, using equity method, 234–235
  effect on noncontrolling interest valuation, 235
  illustration of, 232–234
Derivatives, 418–419
  accounting for changes in fair value of, 419
  determining fair value of, 418–419
  fundamental requirement of *SFAS 133 and 138* and, 418
Derived tax revenues, in governmental accounting, 727–728
Devises, 856
Digital, 282n
Direct quotes, 412
Disclosures
  financial statement translation and, 492–494
  IFRSs and GAAP compared with regard to, 545
  SEC requirements for, 575–576
Discount, foreign currency selling at, 412
Dissolution of partnerships, 645–653
  by admission of new partner, 646–651
  by withdrawal of partner, 651–653

Donaldson, William H., 540, 571
Donations. *See also* Contributions, to not-for-profit
    organizations
    of works of art and historical treasures, to not-for-profit
      organizations, 828–829
Doost, Roger K., 551n
Doupnik, Timothy S., 490n, 532n
Dow Corning Corp., 606
Downstream sales
    alternative approaches for, 240–241
    of inventory, intercompany, 220, 221, 224
    of land, intercompany, 231
Drexel Burnham Lambert Group Inc., 601
Dugan, Ianthe Jeanne, 671n
Duke, Paul, Jr., 581n
Duke University, 836
Duke University Medical System, 835
DuPont, 282n
DVFA (German Association of Financial Analysts), 551

E

E. I. du Pont de Nemours and Company, 380, 383, 428, 530
Earehart, Allen, 95
Earnings per share (EPS), consolidated, 284–287
Ebbers, Bernard, 572
Economic Growth and Tax Relief Reconciliation Act of 2001,
    858, 859, 861
Economic unit concept, consolidations and, 157–160, 173–176
    sales of subsidiary stock and, 186
    step acquisitions and, 180–181
EDGAR, 582–584
Electrolux, 530
Emshwiller, John, 583n
Encumbrances, 721–723
Endowments, 712
Enron Corporation, 3, 214, 260, 568, 571–572, 591, 635–636
Enterprise funds, 713
Enterprise Products Partners L. P., 579
EPS (earnings per share), consolidated, 284–287
Equity method, 1–22
    for acquisitions made during current year, 96–98
    changes to, reporting, 8–10
    for consolidations subsequent to acquisition, 95, 96–106
    for corporate equity securities, 1–3
    criteria for using, 4–6
    criticisms of, 21–22
    decision making and, 20–21
    for determination of balance in Investment account, 495–496
    downstream depreciable intercompany asset transfers and,
      234–235
    elimination of unrealized gains in inventory and, 17–22
    excess of investment cost over book value acquired
      and, 13–17
    investee income from sources other than continuing
      operations and, 10–11
    investee losses and, 11–12
    partial
      for consolidations subsequent to acquisition, 95, 106–115
      parent company concept and, 173

Equity method—*Cont.*
    reporting procedures for, 6–8
    sale of equity investments and, 12–13
Esser, Jeffrey L., 708n, 710n
Estates, 853–867
    administration of, 854–855
    charge and discharge statement and, 867, 868
    defined, 854
    discovery of claims against decedent and,
      855–856
    distinction between income and principal and,
      862–863
    distributions and, 856–857
    estate and inheritance taxes and, 858–862
    property included in, 855
    protection for remaining family members and, 856
    recording transactions of, 863–867
Euro, 442
European Central Bank, 410
European Monetary System (euro), 410
European Union, harmonization and, 534–535
Evans, Thomas G., 490n, 551n
Exchange rate mechanisms, 410
Exchange transactions, not-for-profit organizations and,
    831–832
Executor of the estate, 854
Expenditures, for operations and capital additions, recognition
    of, 723–727
Expenses
    not directly matched with revenues, in interim reports,
      385–386
    in not-for-profit accounting, 818, 820–821
Extraordinary items, in interim reports, 386
Exxon, 490

F

FAF (Financial Accounting Federation), 824
Fair value exposure, 419–420
Fair value hedges, 420, 421, 425–428
    cash flow hedges versus, 420–421
    of firm commitments
      forward contracts as, 434–435
      options as, 436–437
    options designated as, 431–432
Fair-value method, 2
Family trusts, 869
FASB. *See* Financial Accounting Standards Board (FASB)
FASB 140, 261n
Father-son-grandson relationships, 314
FedEx, 36
Fiduciary funds, 711, 714, 715
Financial Accounting Federation (FAF), 824
Financial Accounting Standards Board (FASB), 707
    Concept Statement No. 7, 122, 263n
    convergence with IASB, 540–542
    Discussion Memorandum *An Analysis of Issues*
      Related to Consolidation Policy and Procedures,
      162n, 176n
    Emerging Issues Task Force *Issue 96-16,* 5

Financial Accounting Standards Board (FASB)—*Cont.*
  Exposure Drafts
    Accounting Changes and Error Corrections—a replacement
      of APB Opinion No. 20 and FASB Statement
      No. 3, 541
    Accounting for Financial Instruments with Characteristics
      of Liabilities, Equity, or Both, 156, 289
    Business Combinations, 36, 43, 53–54, 62, 120, 121,
      122–123, 156, 157, 162
    Business Combinations and Intangible Assets, 59
    Consolidated Financial Statements, Including Accounting
      and Reporting of Noncontrolling Interests in Sub-
      sidiaries, 36, 53, 156, 157, 162, 181n, 211n, 264n,
      289–290, 325
    Consolidated Financial Statements: Policy and
      Procedures, 218
    "Earnings per Share—An Amendment of FASB Statement
      No. 128," 541
    Fair Value Measurements, 43n
  future of, 573
  Interpretations
    No. 4, 60
    No. 18, 387
    No. 35, 5
    No. 46R, 3, 5, 36, 41–42, 258–266
  on not-for-profit accounting, 815, 826
  on pooling of interests method, 70–71
  SEC overruling of, 576–577
  Statements of Financial Accounting Standards
    No. 1, 478
    No. 2, 60
    No. 3, 383–384, 387
    No. 6, 162, 725
    No. 8, 478, 824
    No. 13, 757
    No. 14, 365–368, 379, 380, 381, 383
    No. 16, 10
    No. 19, 576–577
    No. 52, 414–415, 416–417, 478–480
    No. 57, 20
    No. 93, 823, 824
    No. 94, 39
    No. 105, 474n
    No. 109, 335n, 335–343
    No. 115, 2, 3
    No. 116, 764, 816, 827
    No. 117, 816, 832
    No. 123, 537n, 541
    No. 128, 284
    No. 131, 118, 369–370, 372, 374, 375–376, 379, 381,
      383, 390
    No. 133, 418, 419, 420, 429, 438
    No. 138, 418, 419
    No. 141, 36, 39, 43, 47n, 48, 54, 58, 59–62, 64n, 115, 116,
      118, 120–122, 264
    No. 142, 15, 115, 116, 118, 120
    No. 151, 541
    No. 154, 387–388
Financial Corp. of America, 591
Financial Reporting Releases (FRRs), 575
Financial Reporting Review Panel (FRRP), 549

Financial statements. *See also specific statements*
  for companies emerging from reorganization, 609–610
  consolidation of, 203
  fund-based. *See* Fund-based financial statements
  government-wide. *See* Government-wide financial
    statements
  for not-for-profit organizations, 816–818
  during reorganization, 607–609
Financial statement translation, 469–498
  balance sheet exposure and, 472
  comparison of methods for, 490–491
  consolidation of foreign subsidiary and, 494–497
  current rate method for, 473, 483–485
  disclosures related to, 492–494
  exchange rates used in, 470–472
  hedging balance sheet exposure and, 491–492
  illustration of process, 481–483
  retained earnings and, 474–475
  temporal method for, 473–474, 475, 486, 487–489
    complicating aspects of, 476–477
    cost of goods sold under, 476
    fixed assets, depreciation, and accumulated depreciation
      under, 476–477
    gain or loss on sale of an asset and, 477
    lower-of-cost-or-market rule and, 476
  translation adjustments and, 472
    disposition of, 477–478
  U.S. rules for, 478–481
Financing sources, international accounting diversity
    and, 529
The FINOVA Group Inc., 591
Fioriti, Andrew, 70n
First Executive Corp., 591
FleetBoston Financial, 36
Ford Motor Company, 37, 211, 213, 274
Foreign Corrupt Practices Act of 1977, 568
Foreign currency borrowing, 442–443
Foreign currency denominated assets, foreign currency options
    to hedge, 428–433
Foreign currency denominated transactions, hedges of,
    438–441
  forward contract cash flow hedge of forecasted transaction
    and, 438–439
  option designated as cash flow hedge of forecasted transaction
    and, 439–441
Foreign currency financial statement translation. *See* Financial
    statement translation
Foreign currency firm commitments, 417
  unrecognized, hedges of, 433–437
Foreign currency forward contacts, 417
Foreign currency loans, 443
Foreign currency options, 412–413, 417
  designated as cash flow hedges, 429–431
  designated as fair value hedges, 431–432
Foreign currency transactions, 413–417
  accounting alternatives for, 414–415
  balance sheet date before date of payment and,
    415–417
Foreign exchange markets, 410–413
Foreign exchange rates, 410–413
  exchange rate mechanisms and, 410

Foreign exchange rates—*Cont.*
  option contracts and, 412–413
  spot and forward, 412
  used in financial statement translation, 470–472
Foreign exchange risk, hedging of. *See* Hedging foreign
    exchange risk
Foreign subsidiaries, consolidation of, 494–497
Form 8–K, 581
Form 10–K, 580–581
Form 10–Q, 581
Forward contracts
  as fair value hedge of firm commitment, 434–435
  foreign currency, 417
    cash flow versus fair value hedges and, 428
    designated as cash flow hedges, 423–425
    designated as fair value hedges, 425–428
    to hedge foreign currency denominated assets, 421–428
    as hedge of forecasted foreign currency denominated
      transactions, 438–439
Forward rates, 412
Foss, Brad, 572n
Freeman, Catherine M., 124n
Freeman, Robert J., 707n
Fresh start accounting, 609–613
Frito-Lay, 35
FRRP (Financial Reporting Review Panel), 549
FRRs (Financial Reporting Releases), 575
Fully secured debts, 593
Functional currency, 479–480
Fund accounting, 710–711, 719–729
  classifications for, 711–715
  derived tax revenues and, 727–728
  encumbrances and, 721–723
  importance of budgets and recording of budgetary entries
    and, 719–721
  imposed nonexchange revenues and, 728–729
  measurement and, 714–715
  recognition of expenditures and, 723–726
  recognition of revenues and, 726–727
  timing of recognition and, 714–715
Fund-based financial statements, 708, 709, 717–719, 721,
    770–790
  bond issuance and, 731, 732
  capital assets and, 724–725
  capital leases and, 758–759
  compensated absences and, 762
  encumbrances and, 722–723
  historical treasures and, 763
  imposed nonexchange revenues and, 729
  interfund transactions and, 734–735, 736
  recognition of expenditures for operations and capital
    additions and, 723–724, 726
  solid waste landfill and, 761
  special assessments and, 733–734
  statement of activities, 776–777, 778–779
  statement of cash flows—proprietary funds, 784–785,
    788–789
  statement of net assets—proprietary funds, 779,
    782–784
  statement of revenues, expenditures, and changes in fund
    balances—governmental funds, 779, 780–781

Fund-based financial statements—*Cont.*
  statement of revenues, expenditures, and changes in fund net
    assets—proprietary funds, 784, 786–787
  works of art and, 763

G

GAAP (generally accepted accounting principles)
  hierarchy of, 825–827
  IFRSs compared with, 542–548
  SEC's authority over, 574–575
Gains
  retirement, intercompany debt transactions and, 270–271
  on sale of an asset, 477
  unrealized. *See* Unrealized gains
Garber, Joseph R., 582n
Garden Ridge, 606
GASB. *See* Governmental Accounting Standards Board (GASB)
Gauthier, Stephen J., 767n
General Electric Company (GE), 40, 57n, 93, 265, 314, 765
General Foods, 315
General fund, 712
General legacies, 856
Generally accepted accounting principles (GAAP)
  hierarchy of, 825–827
  IFRSs compared with, 542–548
  SEC's authority over, 574–575
Geographic areas, enterprisewide disclosures about,
    379–381, 382
Georgetown University, 827, 829
Gerber Products Company, 287
German Association of Financial Analysts (DVFA), 551
Germany
  accounting profession and financial statement preparation
    in, 549–554
  legal system in, 528
Gernon, Helen, 531n
Gibraltar Financial Corp., 591
Gillette Company, 36, 37, 38, 492
Giving USA Foundation, 815
Global Crossing Ltd., 568, 591
Goeltz, Richard Karl, 534
Golden Books Entertainment, 609
Goldschmid, Harvey, 577
Goll, Al, 604n
Goodman, James A., 596n
Goodwill
  consolidations subsequent to acquisition and, 94,
    116–120
  credited to original partners, 649
  deferred income taxes and, 335
  to new partner, 650–651
  testing for impairment, 116–117
Goodwill method
  for intangible contributions to partnerships, 640, 649
  for withdrawal of partner, 652–653
Goodyear Tire & Rubber Company, 63
Gorton, Donald, 577n
Government accounting, 706–738, 756–795
  capital leases and, 757–759

Government accounting—*Cont.*
  capital leases and—*Cont.*
    fund-based financial statements and, 758–759
    government-wide financial statements and,
      757–758
  compensated absences and, 761–762
  component units and, 768–769
  financial reporting and accountability and, 709–710
  fund accounting and. *See* Fund accounting
  fund-based financial statements and. *See* Fund-based
    financial statements
  government-wide financial statements and. *See* Government-
    wide financial statements
  historical treasures and, 762–764
  infrastructure assets and depreciation and, 764–765
  management's discussion and analysis and, 765–766
  nonexchange transactions and, 729–737
    bond issuance and, 730–732
    interfund transactions and, 734–737
    special assignments and, 732–734
  primary government and, 767
  solid waste landfill and, 760–761
    fund-based financial statements and, 761
    government-wide financial statements and, 760–761
  special purpose governments and, 769–770
  user needs and, 708
  works of art and, 762–764
Governmental Accounting Standards Board (GASB), 815
  not-for-profit accounting and, 825
  Statements
    No. 1, 708, 720n
    No. 11, 719n
    No. 14, 767, 773
    No. 33, 727, 730
    No. 34, 707, 709, 710, 711, 713, 719, 724–725, 762–763,
      764, 765, 766, 825
    No. 35, 785n, 825
Governmental funds, 711–712, 715
Government-wide financial statements, 708, 709, 715–717,
    770–790
  bond issuance and, 731, 732
  capital leases and, 757–758
  compensated absences and, 762
  historical treasures and, 763–764
  interfund transactions and, 735, 736–737
  nonexchange revenues and, 729
  prepaid items and, 725–726
  recognition of expenditures for operations and capital
    additions and, 724
  solid waste landfill and, 760–761
  special assessments and, 733
  statement of activities, 772–775, 778
  works of art and, 763–764
Grantor retained annuity trusts (GRATs), 870
GRATs (grantor retained annuity trusts), 870
Gray, Sidney J., 379n, 548n
Greene, Richard, 710n
Greensboro, North Carolina, 757, 760, 766
Grupo Coral, S. A., 287
Guidant, 36
Gunn, Ellen P., 853n, 861n

H

Halvorson, Newman T., 9n
Hanes, Carl, 824
Harhan, Timothy M., 124n, 125n
Harland County, Missouri, 769
Harmelink, Philip J., 858n
Harmonization
  international, of financial reporting, 533–535
    arguments against, 533–534
    arguments for, 533
  major efforts at, 534–535
Hartgraves, A., 21n
Hasbro, Inc., 367
Hay, Leon E., 834n
Hayes, Michael, 641n
Hedging balance sheet exposure, 491–492
Hedging foreign exchange risk, 417–442
  derivatives for, 418–419
  documentation of, 420
  effectiveness of, 420
  of forecasted foreign currency firm commitments,
    438–441
  foreign currency denominated assess and liabilities and,
    420–421
  foreign currency options for, 428–433
  forward contacts for, 421–428
  nature of hedged risk and, 419–420
  of unrecognized foreign currency firm commitments,
    433–437
  use of hedging instruments and, 441–442
Heins, John, 490n
Hertz Rental, 37
Herz, Robert, 826
Hewlett-Packard Company, 366, 409
Highly inflationary economies, financial statement restatement
    and, 480–481
Hildebrandt, Bradford W., 671
Historical exchange rate, 470, 472
Historical treasures
  donations of, 828–829
  government accounting and, 762–764
Hogan, William J., 824
Holder, William W., 479n
Homestead allowance, 856
Horngren, Charles, 4n, 70
Hortons Canada, 116
Hortons U.S., 116
Hybrid method
  for admission of new partner, 649–650
  for withdrawal of partner, 653

I

IASB (International Accounting Standards Board), 536–540
  FASB convergence with, 540–542
IASC (International Accounting Standards Committee), 535
IASs. *See* International Accounting Standards (IASs)
IBM (International Business Machines Corporation),
    380–381, 383

IFRSs (international financial reporting standards), 536–540
  GAAP compared with, 542–548
Impairment, testing goodwill for, 116–117
Income, of partnerships, allocation of, 641–645
Income beneficiary, 862
Income statement
  during reorganization, 607–608, 609
  temporal method for restatement of, 486, 487, 488
Income taxes
  of consolidations. *See* Consolidations, income tax
    accounting for
  in interim reports, 386–387
Indefinite life, 115
Independent float, 410
Indirect quotes, 412
Indirect subsidiary control, 314–323
  connecting affiliations and, 323–324
Inflation, international accounting diversity and, 529
Inflationary economies, financial statement restatement and,
    480–481
Infrastructure assets and depreciation, 764–765
Inheritance taxes, 858–862
In-process research and development (IPR&D), 59–62
Inside parties, 568
Insider Trading and Securities Fraud Enforcement Act of 1988,
    568
Insider Trading Sanctions Act of 1984, 568
Inspections, of registered public accounting firms, 574
Installments, partnership liquidation in, 686–687
Institute of Chartered Accountants, 548–549
Intangibles
  consolidations subsequent to acquisition and, 94,
    115–116
  contributions to partnerships, 639–640
  purchase price allocation and, 59
Intel Corporation, 118, 784
Intercompany dividends, deferred income taxes and, 335
Intercompany transactions, 211–236
  alternative approaches for, 240–241
  debt, 266–273
    acquisition of affiliate's debt from an outside party
      and, 267
    assignment of retirement gain or loss and, 270–271
    effects on consolidation process, 269
    individual financial records and, 267–269, 270
    subsequent to year of acquisition, 271–273
  depreciable asset transfers, 231–235
    deferral of unrealized gains and, 232
    downstream, using equity method, 234–235
    effect on noncontrolling interest valuation, 235
    illustration of, 232–234
  inventory, 212–235
    alternative investment methods and, 225–229
    illustration of, 219–225
    Sales and Purchases accounts and, 212–213
    unrealized gains and, 213–218
  land, 229–231
    effect on noncontrolling interest valuation, 231
    eliminating unrealized gains and, 230–231
Interest, current, dissolution of partnership by purchase of,
    646–648

Interfund transactions, 734–737
Interim reporting, 383–390
  change in accounting principle for, 387–389
  costs and expenses not directly matched with revenues and,
    385–386
  extraordinary items and, 386
  income taxes and, 386–387
  inventory and cost of goods sold and, 384–385
  minimum disclosures in, 389–390
  revenues and, 384
  seasonal items and, 389
  segment information in, 390
Internal service funds, 713
International accounting, 524–558. *See also* Foreign *entries*
  accounting clusters and, 531–532
  accounting profession and financial statement preparation
    and, 548–557
  differences between IFRSs and U.S. GAAP and, 542,
    543–548
  evidence of accounting diversity and, 525–527
  FASB–IASB convergence and, 540–542
  harmonization of financial reporting and, 533–534
  IASB and, 536–540
  IASC and, 535
  IOSCO and, 536
  magnitude of accounting diversity and, 525–527
  problems caused by accounting diversity and, 529–531
  reasons for accounting diversity and, 528–529
International Accounting Standards (IASs)
  No. 2, 544
  No. 14, 545
  No. 16, 545
  No. 19, 542
  No. 23, 544–545
  No. 38, 544
International Accounting Standards Board (IASB),
    536–540
  FASB convergence with, 540–542
International Accounting Standards Committee (IASC), 535
International Business Machines Corporation (IBM),
    380–381, 383
International financial reporting standards (IFRSs),
    536–540
  GAAP compared with, 542–548
International Organization of Securities Commissions
    (IOSCO), 536
International Paper Company, 5
Interperiod equity, 720
Inter vivos trusts, 868, 872
Intestate, defined, 854
Inventory
  downstream sales of, 17–18
  intercompany transactions involving, 212–235
    alternative investment methods and, 225–229
    illustration of, 219–225
    Sales and Purchases accounts and, 212–213
    unrealized gains and, 213–218
  in interim reports, 384–385
  unrealized gains and
    elimination of, 17–22
    intercompany transactions involving, 213–218

Inventory—*Cont.*
   upstream sales of, 19–20
Investment Advisers Act of 1940, 568
Investment Company Act of 1940, 568
Investments, equity method for. *See* Equity method
Investment trust funds, 714
Involuntary bankruptcy, 592–593
IOSCO (International Organization of Securities
      Commissions), 536
IPR&D (in-process research and development), 59–62
Irrevocable life insurance trusts, 871
Ivey, Mark, 605n

J

Jack Eckerd Corporation, 605
Jackson, Estelle, 869n
James River Corporation, 124
Japan, accounting profession and financial statement preparation
      in, 554–557
Japanese Institute of Certified Public Accountants (JICPA),
      555
JB Hunt Transport Services, 1, 3
Jereski, Laura, 582n, 608n
JICPA (Japanese Institute of Certified Public Accountants),
      555
Johns Manville, 613
Johnson, L. Todd, 116
Johnson & Johnson, 36
Jones, Phillip, Sr., 824n
J.P. Morgan Chase, 36
Jung, Clarence, Jr., 824n

K

Kattelus, Susan C., 834n
Keck, Mahin and Cate, 671
Kinko's, 36
Kmart Corp., 36, 591
Kmart Holdings, 610
Kohlberg Kravis Roberts & Company, 274
KPMG, 259n
KPMG International, 632
Kraft Foods, 364
Krantz, Matt, 604n
Kretz, Richard, 641n

L

L. L. Knickerbocker Co., 593
Labaton, Stephen, 571n, 582n
Land transfers, intercompany, 229–231
   effect on noncontrolling interest valuation, 231
   eliminating unrealized gains and, 230–231
Lavelle, Louis, 573n
Laventhol & Horwath, 634, 670–671
Lay, Kenneth, 571–572

Leases, capital, government accounting and, 757–759
   fund-based financial statements and, 758–759
   government-wide financial statements and, 757–758
Lee, Geoffrey Alan, 548n
Leech, Noyes E., 583n
Legacies, 856
Legal systems, international accounting diversity and, 528
Letters of comments, 579
Leuz, Christian, 583n
Liabilities
   long-term, payment of, 731
   priority of, bankruptcy and, 594
Life tenants, 871
LIFO liquidation, 384–385
Ligon, Karen M., 551n
Limited liability companies (LLCs), 636
Limited liability partnerships (LLPs), 635–636
Limited partnerships (LPs), 635
Liquidation
   chapter 7, 600–604
      reorganization versus, 595–596
      statement of realization and liquidation and, 602–604
      trustee's role in, 601–602
   LIFO, 384–385
   of partnerships. *See* Partnerships, termination and
         liquidation of
LLCs (limited liability companies), 636
LLPs (limited liability partnerships), 635–636
LMJ1, 260n
Loans, foreign currency, 443
Lochray, Paul J., 858n
Lockheed Martin Corporation, 367, 409
Log-Me-On.com, 61
Long-term liabilities, payment of, 731
Losses
   equity method for, 11–12
   operating, business combinations and, 342–343
   to remaining partners, termination and liquidation of
         partnerships and, 676–678
   retirement, intercompany debt transactions and, 270–271
   on sale of an asset, 477
Lowe Boats, Inc., 120
Lower-of-cost-or-market rule, 385
Lowe's Companies, Inc., 379
LPs (limited partnerships), 635
Lublin, Joann S., 634n, 645n, 671n
Lucile Packard Children's Hospital, 835
Lund Boat Company, 120
Lund Boats Canada, Inc., 120

M

Mamis, Robert A., 596n
Management approach for segment reporting, 369–370
Management's discussion and analysis (MD&A), government
      accounting and, 765–766
Manville Corporation, 592n, 606
Marriott International, Inc., 176–177
Marshaling of assets, 678–684
Mautz, Robert K., 708n, 725

Maxwell House Coffee Company, 315

Maynard, Philip, 870n

McCreevy, Charlie, 540

McDonald's Corporation, 368, 379

McNamee, Mike, 573n

MCorp., 591

MD&A (management's discussion and analysis), government accounting and, 765–766

Measurement, IFRSs and GAAP compared with regard to, 544–545

Medicaid, 834, 835

Medicare, 834, 835, 836

Meek, Gary, 528n, 531n

Merck & Co., Inc., 155–156

Mergers. *See also* Consolidations
statutory, 40

Mertin, Dietz, 528n

Messenger Service Stolica S.A., 469

Metromedia Company, 606

MGM Grand, Inc., 43

Microsoft, 3, 39

Midgett, Warren, 858n

Miller, Richard I., 572n, 574n

Mills Corporation, 5

Mingione, Michael, 871n

Minority interest, 156

Minor's Section 2503(c) trusts, 870

Mirage Resorts, Inc., 43

Mirant Corporation, 591

Mitchell, Cynthia F., 606n

Mixed Economy accounting model, 531

Mobil, 490

Mobile Telecommunications Co., 469

Modified accrual accounting, 709, 723–724

Modified approach, for infrastructure assets, 765

Molinari, Jeffrey, 713n

Moran, Mark, 568n

Moratorium, on specific accounting practices, issued by SEC, 576

Morris, Thomas R., 605n

Moskowitz, Daniel B., 605n

Mothers Against Drunk Driving, 815

MSNBC, 3

Mueller, Gerhard G., 531n

Multon Company, 469

Mundheim, Robert H., 583n

Mutual agency, 634

Mutual ownership, 324–325
conventional approach to, 326–327, 329–332
illustration of, 327–333
treasury stock approach to, 325–326, 327–329

N

National Broadcasting Company (NBC), 3, 40, 93

National Council on Governmental Accounting (NCGA), 707

NBC (National Broadcasting Company), 3, 40, 93

NBC Universal, Inc., 93, 314

NCGA (National Council on Governmental Accounting), 707

Negative translation adjustments, 472

Net assets, temporarily restricted, in not-for-profit accounting, 818, 820–821

Netherlands, accounting model in, 532

New Asia Fund, 530

Nextel Communications, Inc., 36, 37, 38

Nichols, Nancy B., 379n

Nike, 379

Nippon Light Metal Company, Ltd., 555, 556

Nobes, Chris W., 531

Noise Cancellation Technologies, Inc., 12

Noncontrolling interest, 156. *See also* Consolidations, involving noncontrolling interest

Nonexchange revenues, in governmental accounting, 727–729

Nonlocal currency balances, 489

Norfolk, Virginia, 714

Not-for-profit organizations. *See* Private not-for-profit organizations

Novartis AG, 547

O

Occidental, 490

Off-balance sheet structures. *See* Variable interest entities (VIEs)

Ohio State University, 785

Operating loss carryforwards, business combinations and, 342–343

Operations, expenditures for, recognition of, 723–727

Option contracts
as fair value hedge of firm commitment, 436–437
for foreign currency, 412–413
foreign currency, as hedge of forecasted foreign currency denominated transactions, 439–441

Oracle, 36, 39

Order for relief, 593

Orey, Michael, 594n

Orion Pictures, 606

Oscar Mayer Foods Corporation, 315

Owens-Illinois, Inc., 274

P

Pacelle, Mitchell, 636n, 671n

Pacific Gas and Electric Co., 591

Pae, Peter, 671n

Parent company, 35

Parent company concept, consolidations and, 157, 161–164, 166–173
step acquisitions and, 177–179

Parker, Robert A., 364n

Partial equity method
for consolidations subsequent to acquisition, 95, 106–115
parent company concept and, 173

Partially secured debts, 593

Partnerships, 632–654
additional capital contributions and withdrawals from, 640–641
advantages and disadvantages of, 633–636

Partnerships—*Cont.*
  articles of, 636–637
  capital contributions to, 637–640
  dissolution of, 645–653
    by admission of new partner, 646–651
    by withdrawal of partner, 651–653
  income of, allocation of, 641–645
  limited, 635
  limited liability, 635–636
  termination and liquidation of, 670–690
    with deficit capital balance, 675–678
    illustration of procedures for, 672–674
    liquidation in installments and, 686–687
    marshaling of assets and, 678–684
    predistribution plan and, 687–690
    preliminary distribution of partnership assets and,
      684–687
    schedule of liquidation and, 674, 675, 685–686
Pashkoff, Paul H., 572n, 574n
Paterson, Ron, 527n
Patient service revenues, 835–837
Patton, Terry K., 707n
Pearson, John K., 592n, 593n
Pegging of currencies, 410
Pension trust funds, 714
Penski Truck Leasing Company, 265
PeopleSoft, 36
PepsiCo, Inc., 35
Pepsi-Cola Company, 35
Percentage allocation method, for allocating income tax expense,
      336, 338
Periar, Vivian, 527n
Permanent funds, 712
Peterson, Herbert, 824n
Petrone, Kimberly R., 116
Philip Morris Corporation, 315, 364
Philips, 524
Picker, Ida, 491n
Piergallini, Paul J., 858n
Pittman, Jeffrey R., 684n, 685n
Political factors, international accounting diversity and, 529
Pooling of interests method for consolidations, 62–71
  continuity of ownership and, 62–64
  controversy about, 69–71
  criteria for, 76–77
  subsequent to acquisition, 125–127
  when dissolution takes place, 64–66
  when separate incorporation is maintained, 66–69
Positive translation adjustments, 472
Predistribution plan, for partnership liquidation, 687–690
Preferred stock, subsidiary, 274–280
  FASB *Business Consolidations* Exposure Draft and, 280
  viewed as debt instrument, 274–277
  viewed as equity interest, 277–280
Premium, foreign currency selling at, 412, 413
Prepaid items, government-wide financial statements and,
      725–726
Presentation, IFRSs and GAAP compared with regard
      to, 545
Previts, Gary John, 568n
PriceWaterhouseCoopers, 632

Primary government, 767
Princeton University, 829
Private not-for-profit organizations, 814–837
  contributions to, 827–832
    exchange transactions and, 831–832
    holding for others, 829–830
    of services, 830–831
    of works of art and historical treasures, 828–829
  expenses and release of temporarily restricted net assets and,
      818, 820–821
  financial reporting by, 825–826
  financial statements for, 816–818
  GAAP hierarchy and, 825–826
  health care organizations, 834–837
    patient service revenues and, 835–837
  illustration of transactions involving, 832–834
  standard-setting authority and, 821–825
Private-purpose trust funds, 714
Probate laws, 854
Procter & Gamble, 36, 37, 38
Products, enterprisewide disclosures about, 379
Profit or loss test, for determining reportable operating
      segments, 371, 372–373
Proportionate consolidation concept, consolidations and, 157,
      160–161
Proprietary funds, 711, 713, 715
Prospective payment plans, 836
Prospectus, 578, 579
Proxy statements, 581–582
Public accounting firms
  auditor independence and, 574
  disclosure requirements and, 575–576
  inspections of, 574
  moratorium on specific accounting practices and, 576
  overruling of FASB and, 576–577
  registration of, 573–577
  SEC authority over GAAP and, 574–575
Public Accounting Oversight Board, 574
Public colleges and universities, 785, 790–794
Public Company Accounting Oversight Board, 572–573
Public Utility Holding Company Act of 1935, 568
Purchased in-process research and development (IPR&D),
      59–62
Purchase method for consolidations, 43, 44–53
  related costs of business combinations and, 48–49
  when dissolution takes place, 44–48
  when separate incorporation is maintained, 49–53
Purchase price allocations, consolidations and, 59–62
  intangibles and, 59
  purchased in-process research and development
      and, 59–62
Purchases account, intercompany inventory transactions and,
      212–213
Purchases method, for capital assets and prepaid
      items, 726
Push-down accounting, consolidations subsequent to acquisition
      and, 123–125
  external reporting and, 123–124
  internal reporting and, 124–125
Put options, for sale of foreign currency, 412
Pyramids, 314

Q

QTIP (qualified terminable interest property) trusts, 869–870
Qualified personal resident trusts (QPRTs), 871

R

Radebaugh, Lee H., 548n
Raleigh, North Carolina, 714
RCA Corporation, 93
R&D (research and development), in-process, 59–62
Reagan, John, III, 765n
Realized income, computation of, with indirect control, 315–317
Recognition
    of contributions, 818
    of expenditures for operations and capital additions, 723–727
    IFRSs and GAAP compared with regard to, 542, 544
    of revenues, in governmental accounting, 726–727
Reconciliation, IFRSs and GAAP compared with regard to, 545–548
Registrants, 568
Registration statements, 577, 578
Regulation S–K, 568, 571, 575, 578, 580
Regulation S–X, 568, 574–575, 578, 580
Remainderman, 862, 871
Reorganization, chapter 11, 604–613
    financial reporting during, 607–609
    financial reporting for companies emerging from, 609–610
    fresh start accounting and, 609–613
    liquidation versus, 595–596
    plan for, 605–607
Reporting currency, 479
Reporting units, 46n
    assigning values to, 117–120
Research and development (R&D), in-process, 59–62
Residual legacies, 856
Retained earnings, translation of, 474–475
Revco D. S., Inc., 605
Revenue Reconciliation Act of 1993, 335
Revenues
    in interim reports, 384
    nonexchange, in governmental accounting, 727–728
    patient service, 835–837
    tax, derived, in governmental accounting, 727–728
Revenue test, for determining reportable operating segments, 370, 371–372
Revocable living trusts, 869
Reynolds Metals Corporation, 95
Ribstein, Larry, 672
Rigas, John J., 572
Risk, foreign exchange. *See* Hedging foreign exchange risk
Rite Aid Corporation, 605
Ritz-Carlton Hotel Company LLC, 176–177
RJR Nabisco, 48n
RMC Group Plc, 469
Robbins, John, 604n
Rolfe, Robert J., 551n
Roman law, 528
Rosenfield, Paul, 604n
Rossi, Josephine, 869n

S

SABs (Staff Accounting Bulletins), 575
    No. 54, 124
    No. 73, 124
    No. 101, 575
Sacramento, California, 709, 771–772, 773, 778
Saint Paul, Minnesota, 769
Sales
    downstream
        alternative approaches for, 240–241
        of inventory, intercompany, 220, 221, 224
        of land, intercompany, 231
    of equity investment, equity method for, 12–13
    of inventory
        downstream, 17–18, 220, 221, 224
        upstream, 19–20, 222–224
    upstream
        alternative approaches for, 240–241
        of inventory, intercompany, 222–224
        of land, intercompany, 231
Sales account, intercompany inventory transactions and, 212–213
Salter, Stephen B., 532n
Salwen, Kevin G., 575n, 581n
Samuels, J. M., 548n
SAP, 39
Sara Lee Corporation, 183
Sarbanes-Oxley Act of 2002, 568, 572, 574, 577
Saudagaran, Sharokh M., 528n
Schedule of liquidation, 674, 675, 685–686
Scitex Corporation, 5
S corporations, 635
Seagram's, 534
Sears Roebuck, 36
Seckler, Günter, 549
Section 197 property, 335
Securities Act of 1933, 568, 569, 570
Securities and Exchange Commission (SEC), 566–584
    authority over GAAP, 574–575
    corporate accounting scandals and. *See* Corporate accounting scandals
    Division of Corporation Finance of, 579
    EDGAR system of, 582–584
    filings with, 577–582
    Financial Reporting Releases of, 575
    full and fair disclosure and, 569–571
    purpose of federal securities laws and, 568–569
    registration of public accounting firms with, 573–577
    requirements of, 568
    Staff Accounting Bulletins, 575
        No. 54, 124
        No. 73, 124
        No. 101, 575
Securities Exchange Act of 1934, 568, 570, 571
Securities Investor Protection Act of 1970, 568
Segment reporting, 365–383
    determining reportable operating segments and, 370–371
    enterprisewide disclosures and, 379–383
    examples of operating segment disclosures and, 378, 379

Segment reporting—*Cont.*
  information to be disclosed by operating segment and, 375–377
  management approach for, 369–370
  reconciliation of segment revenues to consolidated revenues, 376–377
  SFAS 14 and, 365–368
  SFAS 131 and, 369–370, 374, 375, 376
  testing procedures for, illustration of, 371–374
  usefulness of, 367–370
Seidman, J. S., 70
Selz, Michael, 604n
Separate return method, for allocating income tax expense, 337, 339
Services
  contributed, 830–831
  enterprisewide disclosures about, 379
  patient service revenues and, 835–837
Shapiro, James E., 530n
Shelf registration, 579
Shellenbarger, Sue, 670n
Single-line consolidation, 95
Sinopec, 530
Sirower, Mark, 37
Skousen, K. Fred, 577n, 579n, 582n
Solid waste landfill, 761
South American accounting model, 531
Special assessments, 732–734
Special purpose entities (SPEs), 3, 41, 214. *See also* Variable interest entities (VIEs)
Special purpose governments, 769–770
Special revenue funds, 712
Specific legacies, 856
Spendthrift trusts, 870
SPEs (special purpose entities), 3, 41, 214. *See also* Variable interest entities (VIEs)
Spot rate, 412
  exceeding strike price, 432–433
Sprint Corporation, 36, 37, 38
Staff Accounting Bulletins (SABs), 575
  No. 54, 124
  No. 73, 124
  No. 101, 575
Standard costing, 385
Standards, for not-for-profit accounting, 821–825
Stanford Medical Center, 835
Statement of activities, 715–717
  fund-based, 776–777, 778–779
  government-wide, 772–775, 778
Statement of activities and changes in net assets, for not-for-profit organizations, 816, 818, 819
Statement of cash flows
  consolidated. *See* Consolidated statement of cash flows
  current rate method for translation of, 485, 486
  for not-for-profit organizations, 816
  temporal method for restatement of, 489
Statement of cash flows—proprietary funds, fund-based, 784–785, 788–789
Statement of financial affairs, 596–600

Statement of financial position, for not-for-profit organizations, 816, 817–818
Statement of functional expense, for not-for-profit accounting, 821, 822–823
Statement of net assets, 715–717
  government-wide, 771–772
Statement of net assets—proprietary funds, fund-based, 779, 782–784
Statement of realization and liquidation, 602–604
Statement of revenues, expenditures, and changes in fund balances—governmental funds, fund-based, 779, 780–781
Statement of revenues, expenditures, and changes in fund net assets—proprietary funds, fund-based, 784, 786–787
State University of New York at Stony Brook, 824
Statutory consolidations, 40
Statutory mergers, 40
Step acquisitions, 176–181
Stern, Gabriella, 605n
Stock
  consolidated earnings per share and, 284–287
  subsidiary. *See* Subsidiary stock
Stock, Howard, 577n
Stockholders, financial reporting to, SEC's impact on, 571
Street, Donna L., 379n
Strike price, 412–413
  spot rate exceeding, 432–433
Subchapter S corporations, 635
Subsidiaries, 35. *See also* Consolidations
Subsidiary stock
  preferred, 274–280
    FASB *Business Consolidations* Exposure Draft and, 280
    viewed as debt instrument, 274–277
    viewed as equity interest, 277–280
  sales of, 183–186
    accounting for shares that remain and, 185–186
    cost-flow assumptions and, 185
    economic unit concept and, 186
    establishment of investment book value and, 184–185
  transactions involving, 287–293
    changes in subsidiary book value and, 288–290
    illustration of, 290–293
SunTrust Banks, 57n
Supplies, government-wide financial statements and, 725–726
Sweden, accounting model in, 532
Symantec Corporation, 36, 37, 38–39

T

T. Rowe Price, 530
Tax anticipation notes, 731–732
Taxes
  estate and inheritance, 858–862

Taxes—*Cont.*
  income
    of consolidations. *See* Consolidations, income tax
      accounting for
    in interim reports, 386–387
  international accounting diversity and, 528–529
Tax revenues, derived, in governmental accounting,
  727–728
Taylor, Martin E., 551n
Tele Danmark, 13
Temporal method for financial statement translation, 473–474,
  475
  complicating aspects of, 476–477
  cost of goods sold under, 476
  fixed assets, depreciation, and accumulated depreciation
    under, 476–477
  gain or loss on sale of an asset and, 477
  lower-of-cost-or-market rule and, 476
Termination of partnerships. *See* Partnerships, termination and
  liquidation of
Testamentary trusts, 868
Texaco Inc., 490, 591, 592n
Third-party payors, contractual agreements with, 836–837
Thomas, John B., 824n
Tobin, Jean E., 530n
Tomczak, Joe, 95
Toys R Us, Inc., 367
Transplace, Inc. (TPI), 1
Treasury stock approach, to mutual ownership, 325–326,
  327–329
Trial balance, foreign subsidiary, translation of, 494–495
Tropicana Products, 35
Trump Hotels & Casino Resorts, 607
Trustees, bankruptcy and, 601
Trust Indenture Act of 1939, 568
Trustors, 869
Trusts, 867–872
  accounting for activities of, 872
  record-keeping for, 871–872
Turner, Lynn, 62
Tyco, 568
Tyer, Charlie, 713n

U

UAL Corp., 591
Uniform Partnership Act (UPA), 634
Uniform Probate Code, 854, 856
United Kingdom
  accounting model in, 532
  accounting profession and financial statement preparation
    in, 548–549, 550
  legal system in, 528
United Parcel Service (UPS), 469
United States, accounting model in, 532
Universities
  private, 818
  public, 785, 790–794
University of Kansas, 785

Unocal, 490
Unrealized gains
  deferred income taxes and, 335
  on depreciable asset transfers, deferral of, 232
  intercompany inventory transactions and, 213–218
    effect on noncontrolling interest valuation,
      217–218
    in year following transfer, 215–217
    in year of transfer, 213–215
  inventory
    elimination of, 17–22
    equity method for elimination of, 17–22
    intercompany transactions involving, 213–218
  on land transfers, eliminating, 230–231
UPA (Uniform Partnership Act), 634
UPS (United Parcel Service), 469
Upstream sales
  alternative approaches for, 240–241
  of inventory, intercompany, 222–224
  of land, intercompany, 231
US Airways Group, Inc., 609

V

Vandenburgh, William M., 858n
Variable interest entities (VIEs), 258–266
  consolidation of, 260–264
    procedures for, 264–266
  description of, 259–260
  FIN 46R disclosure requirements for, 258–266
Variable interests, 5
Variable purpose entities, 41
Veritas Software Corporation, 36, 37, 38–39
Verizon Wireless, 38
VIEs (variable interest entities), 258–266
  consolidation of, 260–264
    procedures for, 264–266
  description of, 259–260
  FIN 46R disclosure requirements for, 258–266
Voluntary bankruptcy, 592–593

W

Wake Forest University, 818
Wal-Mart Stores, Inc., 367, 379, 858
Walt Disney Company, 5, 261–262
Walters, Ralph E., 530
Walton, Helen, 858
Walton, Sam, 858
Wandycz, Katarzyna, 365n
Wechsler, Dana, 365n
Weir, James, 490
Wendy's Canada, 116
Wendy's U. S., 116
Whitis, Robert E., 684n, 685n
Wills, 854
Wilson, Allister, 527n
Wilson, Earl R., 834n

Wilson Foods Corporation, 613
Withdrawal of partner, dissolution of partnership by, 651–653
Withdrawals, after formation of partnership, 640–641
Woolf, Emilie, 549n
Works of art
   donations of, to not-for-profit organizations, 828–829
   government accounting and, 762–764
WorldCom Inc., 568, 572, 591, 596
Wraparound filing, 580
Wyeth, 379

Y

Yahoo!, 61
Yale University, 818
YMCA, 831
Young, Shawn, 591n, 594n

Z

Zecher, J. Richard, 583n
Zeff, Stephen A., 575n